Readings in the Philosophy

of the Social Sciences

Readings in the Philosophy

of the Social Sciences

EDITED BY *May Brodbeck*

UNIVERSITY OF MINNESOTA

The Macmillan Company | Collier-Macmillan Limited, London

Fourth Printing, 1969

Library of Congress catalog card number: 67-15533

THE MACMILLAN COMPANY
COLLIER-MACMILLAN CANADA, LTD., TORONTO, ONTARIO

Printed in the United States of America

PREFACE

The operative words in the title of this volume are *philosophy* and *sciences*. With respect to the first, this means that the book concerns the most general and fundamental questions about the nature of our knowledge of man and society. With respect to the second, this means that social inquiry is "accepted" as a scientific endeavor, more or less in the spirit in which a famous lady was admonished to accept the universe. However, by virtue of asking the fundamental questions, philosophy is also critical. The problems raised by the possibility of a science of man are therefore subject to close examination.

The social sciences have become a conspicuous and important part of the intellectual scene. The intriguing facts they uncover about the patterns of individual and group behavior enter into our common consciousness of the social environment and the way we talk about it. One thinking social animal attempts to describe, explain, and predict the conduct of others. How are the concepts he uses related to the behavior he observes? What are the bases for reliable description and explanation of human affairs? What special difficulties confront the social scientist and how are these to be met? What are the limits, potentialities, and implications of a science of man? Such questions, cutting across the varying technical problems of each specialty, are recognizably philosophical and call for logical analysis of the structure of our knowledge of men as individuals and members of groups.

Fortunately, many of our best philosophers of science have recognized that the problems of knowledge and explanation in the social sciences merit careful analysis in their own right. Also fortunate is the fact that many social scientists have been sensitive to the need for philosophical clarity about their enterprise. The selections in this book are by philosophers who have taken the social sciences seriously and by social scientists who have taken philosophical reflection seriously; they provide a broad basis for critical discussion and clarification of the special philosophical problems of the social sciences.

The eight topics that divide this book are by no means closed compartments, nor is the order I have chosen the only desirable one. Many of the papers necessarily overlap and supplement those in other sections. In particular, the paper by W. G. Runciman in Section Six and that by Margaret MacDonald in Section Eight both contain material bearing on the discussions of values and of ideology in Section Two. David B. Truman's paper in Section Six and the papers by Paul Lazarsfeld and Kenneth Arrow in Section Seven are all relevant to the analysis of group concepts in Section Four. Occasional cross-references have been added by the editor, but the reader is urged to consult the detailed index as a guide to the many different discussions of particular subjects throughout the book. Section Six contains no paper specifically devoted to theory construction in psychology because the issue is treated in detail in the articles by I. E. Farber and Jerry A. Fodor in Section Three.

Considerations of logical order and degree of difficulty guided the sequence of topics. The issues, discussed in Section Four, concerning holism versus individualism with respect to group concepts follow naturally the discussion of social action and purposive behavior. However, because of the close connection between the problems of reduction and explanation, one obvious alternative to my arrangement would be to interchange the order of Sections Four and Five. Doubtless many instructors will find other arrangements within and among sections more congenial to their mode of approach. My considerations for placing the topic of freedom at the end were partly systematic and partly strategic. On the one hand, discussion of this sensitive issue benefits from being based upon the clarifications resulting from the preceding analyses. On the other hand, the end of term puts a natural close to an otherwise interminable, perhaps in more ways than one, discussion.

Thanks are due to many friends in philosophy and the social sciences for calling my attention to valuable papers, included either in the text or in the bibliography, that I might otherwise have missed. The University of Minnesota granted me a leave from teaching duties for the Fall quarter of 1967 that greatly facilitated the work of writing the introductions. I am grateful to The Macmillan Company's editor, Mr. John D. Moore, for suggesting this volume to me and for the gentle persistence with which he guided me to completion of the undertaking. Mr. Ronald C. Harris, production editor, has been extremely helpful with all the many details of this large and technically difficult task.

M. B.

CONTENTS

vii

Four   SOCIAL FACTS, SOCIAL LAWS, AND REDUCTION

Five   EXPLANATION, PREDICTION, AND
         IMPERFECT KNOWLEDGE

Six   THEORY CONSTRUCTION

Seven   MODELS AND MEASUREMENT

Eight   FREEDOM, DETERMINISM, AND MORALITY

GENERAL INTRODUCTION

Thou shalt not sit
With statisticians nor commit
A social science.

W . H . A U D E N

That social science is at best irrelevant, at worst inimical, to the proper study of man is widely and fervently believed—and not only by poets. In an age of the ubiquitous survey, the impertinent test, and heavily financed social scientists in high places, only the most insensitive or defensive will not be amused by Auden's sally. Truly witty, he insinuates a wicked half-truth. Counting and measuring *are* sometimes substitutes for thought. Social scientists, like other specialists, are not always conspicuously at ease with our literary tradition. Too often the notion of "culture" has only an anthropological resonance. No doubt. Yet this is not the whole story.

Two centuries have passed since the vision of a science of man first fired the imaginations of the great social critics of the Enlightenment. Seeing man as part of the natural order, they envisaged a science of man and society, modeled on Newton's explanation of heaven and earth, by whose application the potentialities of man could be realized to form a more just and humane social order. Doubtless their vision was clouded. Most tragically it was vitiated by an overestimation of human rationality and a too optimistic faith that knowledge would always serve the common good. Yet in essence the vision has withstood all challenges. The possibility of a social science in principle as perfect as physics remains the unexamined premise of the vast majority of present-day social scientists.

It is part of the function of this volume to subject that premise and its implications to examination, for the philosophy of science seeks to examine certain fundamental ideas and principles which the working scientist himself takes for granted. If we grant the premise that the social disciplines are (or more realistically, *can be*) sciences, then the philosophical problems of social science are those of all science: What are the criteria for "good" concepts? What is the nature of a scientific law and theory? How are laws and theories related to the evidence for them? What is the difference between an adequate scientific explanation and a specious one? What kind of knowledge must we have to make justified and not merely plausible predictions about

1

the future? That the answers to these and related questions are essentially the same, whether we are studying the stars or mice or men, is a vindication of that eighteenth-century vision.

THE RESISTANCE AGAINST SOCIAL SCIENCE

The study of man, his nature and destiny, was for centuries the province of poets, philosophers, and men of letters. These, skilled in the resources of language, conveyed—frequently with subtlety and power—insights drawn from their personal experience and reflection. Very early a line was drawn between them—the humanists, on the one hand, and the men of laboratories, experiments, and quantification—the scientists, on the other. Despite the division of labor between the humanist's study of man and the scientist's study of matter, the line soon became a barricade. By its fruits science gained affluence, power, prestige—and resentment. Not surprisingly the resentment deepened when the methods of science were extended to the humanist's ancient preserve, the study of man and society. The extension has always been bitterly resented; the opposition has never been wholly allayed, cropping up from time to time with renewed fervor.

In part the opposition is merely a tedious jurisdictional dispute, backed more by malice and irrelevant sniping at unfulfilled promise than by rational argument. About such disputes little can be said beyond emphasizing that, for any civilization worth having, the task of bearing, preserving, and perpetuating the literary tradition is not only honorable and essential in itself, but complementary to a scientific study of man. We may well agree that science isn't everything and that the questions only science can answer are not the only questions worth asking. We may also agree that as yet social science only barely deserves the name of science and that those who seek to earn this name all too often ignore, at the peril of a new barbarism, the fruits of our literary culture and tradition. Yet scientific truth and the standards necessary to attain it still remain one thing and literature and philosophy are other things. More perplexing than the literary resistance is the hostility expressed by some who are nominally within social science itself.

Indeed, there are clearly two factions within the social disciplines. One of them exuberantly embraces the scientific ideal; the other exalts its own intuitive understanding as being superior in logic and in principle to scientific explanation of the ways of man. Insofar as the division falls between those who count and measure what is not worth counting or measuring and those who speak shrewdly though imprecisely about more interesting matters, the issue is one of strategy rather than of logic or principle. Whatever is accessible to insight and intuitive understanding is also, in principle, accessible to scientific explanation. Until they are so explained, insights however shrewd remain precarious as knowledge. Less name calling and more cooperation is wanted. Imaginative "cloud hoppers" can provide hypotheses whose testing and extension will raise more cautious "clodhoppers" to broader, more fruitful realms. Such merging of talents and techniques, ideally coexisting in the same person, is more sensible than continuing a bootless cold war in which, after all, the protagonists on both sides profess a common goal—increased knowledge of man and society.

Traditional vested interests and differences in temperament are not the only sources of opposition to social science. There is also a strong general cultural resistance, bred of the suspicion not (or at least not consistently) that social science is impossible, but that it may become all too successful. The foundations of our own self-image, our beliefs about human destiny, and our confident moral appraisals, rest on what we believe or may yet learn about man and his relation to the natural environment. Some of the pillars of the old foundations were first shaken by Copernicus; others were then rudely shattered by Darwin. And we have not lacked for more recent and still ruder blows to our self-esteem, no matter how resolutely the Rational Animal, including many a social scientist, averts his eyes from those lower depths. Perhaps we could bear having our character impugned if it were not also in danger of being manipulated. We feel threatened by "engineers of the soul"; we fear, indeed, that they are already upon us. Men are no longer so sanguine that the truth will make them free. Scientific understanding of the behavior of matter has meant control of the material world. Does knowledge of man imply control of man? Some fear that it does, but even if they are right, it is a *non sequitur* to argue that knowledge, because fearful, must be impossible. But, then, does "control" mean the same when applied to floods and diseases as when applied to the conduct of men? Raising the question, we approach our task. What does it mean to explain and to understand something scientifically? How is such explanation related to prediction and control? Does social science explain differently from other science, or does it merely explain in the same way different sorts of things?

In this book, treatment of these and related questions is consigned to the reading selections and the separate introductions for each section. But here, as a background and perspective for those discussions, I shall sketch certain basic ideas of scientific method, particularly ones concerning the criteria for concept formation and the nature of scientific laws and theories. Concepts provide the vocabulary in which the scientist can talk about the world. By means of laws and theories he explains what he describes.

SCIENTIFIC CONCEPTS AND DEFINITION

Some features of the world *stand out*, almost begging for names. Concepts of clouds, thunder, table, dog, wealth, hunger, color, shape, and the like, name differentiated slices of reality that impinge willy-nilly on all of us. The terms of commonsense name these obtrusive daily experiences. Other features of the world have to be *cut out*, as it were. They are discerned only by a more subtle and devious examination of nature, man, and society than is made in everyday life. These more covert aspects of experience are named by the concepts of science. Terms like *mass* and *momentum, IQ* and *primary group, anomie* and *repression* name attributes that do not stand out as do *love* and *hunger, green, round,* and *huge.* By occurring in laws and theories, the features that must be cut out explain those that merely stand out. Much of everyday language consists of names for features of experience that either cannot be further defined, such as the names for colors, or that for all practical purposes need not be defined, like *cat* and *eating,* because they are generally unambiguous. But even in everyday language many terms occur that must be defined before we know how they are being used. One who has never seen a gnu must have the term explained to him. We explain it by citing the attributes by which we can tell a gnu when we see one.

Merely by looking at a surface we can tell whether it is white or by looking at an animal whether it is a gnu. We cannot so simply tell the mass of an object or the IQ of a child. Yet a body has mass as well as color; a child has IQ as well as blond hair. What is *momentum* or *bureaucracy* or *hysteria?* The question in each case is not, "What does the concept 'really' mean?" For it means what we say it does. The question is one of words and is answered in the same way. The technical terms of science, referring to features that we do not directly experience, must always be defined. Their characteristic abstractness lies in the fact that they cannot be defined simply by citing a cluster of directly observable attributes. No single observation, but a complex pattern of observations is typically required to determine whether the more abstract features are present or absent.

To characterize a social institution as, say, a "bureaucracy," we must observe how people in a specified kind of situation behave toward each other. Similarly, terms referring to personality traits, attitudes, and capacities must be defined in terms of patterns of behavior exhibited under certain conditions. At any given moment a submissive woman need not be submitting, an authoritarian person giving orders, or a malleable piece of iron being bent. In order to tell whether a statement that an individual has any of these properties is true or false, scientific terms are defined, not in isolation as in a dictionary, but by statement of the observable conditions under which a sentence containing the term is true or false. Such definitions are called definitions in use, for they state the meaning of a term as it is used in a sentence. For instance, to an economist "X behaves rationally" means by definition, "*If* X is presented with several alternatives, *then* he orders his preferences among them in a certain consistent way."

Typically, the definitions of abstract scientific terms have the form of such conditional or if-then sentences. The antecedent or "if" clause specifies how and in what circumstances the observations are to be made. The consequent or "then" clause specifies the behavior under these conditions that will count as an instance of the concept being defined. A political scientist may characterize a conservative as one who gives a certain pattern of responses to a battery of questions. The questions constitute the antecedent conditions. The pattern of responses constitutes the observations that will make the sentence "X is a conservative" true. The entire conditional sentence, stating a connection between antecedent and consequent conditions, defines the concept. For if a different battery of questions were administered, we would not expect the same pattern of responses. Similarly, behavior characterized as "aggressive" in one set of circumstances might not be so considered under different circumstances. Such complex and conditional definitions, like all others, are statements about the use of words, stating how one term may be eliminated by substituting others. We keep exchanging one word for another until we reach a point where we can tell unambiguously whether or not we have an instance of the concept. The considerations that determine which conditions and consequent observations shall be included in a definition are part and parcel of the problem of how to find good or worth-while concepts. Before turning to that issue, it will help to make a few further comments about the social scientist's technical vocabulary.

Man the social animal is also man the talking animal—perhaps he is one by virtue of being the other; it does not matter for our purposes. What does matter is that what people say (and what and how they mean by what they say) is part of the social scientist's subject matter. To speak about it, to describe and explain it, he uses a different language. The scientist's language, therefore, is *in principle* not that of common speech. This funda-mental fact affects our appreciation of the characteristics of reliable, objective knowledge and, more generally, of the nature of scientific explana-tion. Here comment will be made only on the not infrequent complaint that definition deprives science of the rich halo of meanings surrounding terms in ordinary use. Far from being a weakness, this is as it should be. A concept means what its definition says it means. If it does not say this clearly so that we know when we do or when we do not have an instance of it, then the concept may be criticized legitimately as being inadequately defined. To criticize a concept on the ground that its definition is not "really" what the concept means makes sense only if the definition is proffered as an explica-tion of how a term is already being used. In that case we are given not a definition—which is always stipulative—but a report, which may be true or false. If such reports explicate the concepts that certain interesting social theorists have already employed, however imprecisely, then they may be very useful. They may suggest a more precise vocabulary for speaking about the same interesting things. The explication then becomes a new stipulation. It will thenceforth mean only what it is said to mean.

This meaning need not include all or even any of the meanings various people associate with the concept. Generally, in fact, it will include *some* of these associations because the scientist has picked this particular term and not some other from common sense. But it is unlikely to include all of them and need not include any. The scientist may draw upon the halo surround-ing terms which also have a commonsense use for *hunches* about laws, but if he wants objective knowledge of behavior, he cannot carry over the vagueness of ordinary use into his technical vocabulary. The concept of IQ, for instance, is by now a classic target for this kind of misplaced criticism. It does not, so the complaint goes, measure intelligence in the commonsense use of that term. Of course it does not, but the criticism is irrelevant. If IQ is a good concept, it is so not because of any consonance with common sense, but because we can measure it with fair reliability and because we know, with moderately high probability, its connection with other attributes and kinds of behavior. Some of these other things, like general information, success in school, professional achievement, and social adjustment, are part of the meanings commonly associated with "intelligence." But this merely shows that when choosing the ordinary word for their particular concept, the scientists made some rather successful hypotheses about laws connecting performance on certain kinds of tests with some components of the common-sense notion of intelligence. Because certain of its concepts, like *force* and *energy*, are also in common sense, physics once had to endure similarly irrelevant criticism. By now the technical terms of social science remain the only target.

SIGNIFICANT CONCEPTS AND LAWS

All scientific concepts, whether they concern things, persons, or groups of persons, must ultimately be defined in terms of observable characters. All good concepts are adequately defined, but not all adequately defined concepts are good ones. Definition is important, but it is by no means the only important thing about a worthwhile concept. Something else is needed before we call a concept good. Definition is only a necessary first step to science's main business, which is, of course, the discovery of truths about the world. Truths state facts, either individual, like "Smith is bald," or general, like "Dogs are carnivorous." The truth of either is ascertained by observation. Statements of fact, either individual or general, are about things. Definitions are merely about words. Statements of fact convey knowledge about the world; definitions are wholly innocent of any such intent. Even so, it would be misleading to say that science is interested in discovering facts and, therefore, the more facts the better. For, though any knowledge is surely better than none, not everything is equally worth knowing. When is a fact trivial and when is it significant? The answer to this question reveals what else, besides adequate definition, is needed for a good concept.

Bathtub or, less archaically, television-set counting is a much abused occupation. After all, of what significance is it that 90 per cent of the families in a certain city own television sets, 85 per cent own cars, and 60 per cent live in their own homes? Useful information, perhaps, for manufacturers or contractors interested in marketing potentialities, but hardly a contribution to knowledge. For that matter, of what use is it to know the proportion of people who vote Republican, the amount of money stashed away in savings accounts, the increase in church membership, the decline in capital goods production, a certain mother's alleged preference for sons over daughters, Johnny's IQ, or Mary's fatal predilection for married men? Apart from gossip, gratified moral sentiments, or winning of bets, what use are all these facts? In and of itself, no statement of individual fact is scientifically interesting. An individual fact, as distinguished from a generalization, refers to the existence of a particular thing, characteristic, event, or kind of event, like Johnny's IQ, Smith's baldness, or the size of the Republican vote. To state a fact, then, is to state that a concept has an instance or a number of instances. "Smith is bald" says that the concept *baldness* has an instance and that this instance is the man we call Smith. Such individual facts are significant only insofar as they are connected with other facts.

Connections among individual facts are *general* facts. Thus, an organism's being a dog is connected with its being a meat eater. Or, to say the same thing differently, all instances of the concept *dog* are also instances of *meat eater*. The connection is stated by the generalization "All dogs are carnivorous" or "If anything is a dog, then it is carnivorous." The generalization or universal statement "If there is a rise in wages, then prices increase" states a connection between instances of wage increases and of price increases. The connection is that whenever there is the one, there is also the other. Only "instances" that are in this manner connected with other "instances" are significant. These generalizations or universal statements connecting individual facts are also called laws. The fact that Johnny's IQ is 110 is significant only if we know a law connecting this fact with some other fact, such as his doing well in school. To find such connections among individual facts is the purpose of counting and measuring, whether one is counting heads or electrons. Counting is sterile only when it is not guided by the attempt to arrive at a scientific law relating what is being counted to something else.

Laws express regularities. Just as a concept names what is the same in different individuals—that is, a character they all exemplify—so a law describes another constancy, namely, one instance of a concept always being connected with an instance of another, as thunder always follows lightning. A generalization is such by virtue of its form, stating that *all* things having a certain character also have another, or *whenever* we have the first then we also have the second. This form does not depend upon how we come to assert it, whether it is by the inductive process of generalizing from a finite number of observations, by a hunch, or by a dream. No matter how we happen to hit upon it, a generalization always asserts more than what either has been or can be actually observed, and it may, therefore, turn out to be false. We do not, and in principle cannot, test all of a law's instances. Because of this fragility inherent in all generalizations, laws are also called hypotheses. Science is concerned with testing such hypotheses, no matter how these may have been reached initially, about connections among facts. Science looks for laws, because without them neither explanation nor prediction is possible. We shall discuss this in more detail later, but a few comments now will help. From the fact that Johnny's IQ is 110 nothing at all follows. It is only from this fact, about Johnny, in conjunction with the law connecting IQ with school achievement that we can make a prediction about his future school behavior. Conversely, the law permits us to explain his success by means of his IQ. Without laws or generalizations, no explanation is possible. The mere accumulation of individual facts brings no explanation; hence, neither understanding nor control. Facts are trivial then only when we do not know their connection with other facts, that is, when we know no laws or generalizations about them.

Concepts are not statements; they are names or labels. They cannot therefore be said to be either true or false. Yet there are differences among concepts. Just as a fact may be true but not worth knowing, so a concept may be adequately defined but not worth having. For instance, the concept *cephalic index* can be quite adequately defined in terms of the ratio of the width of a person's head to its length, with the method of measurement precisely stated. Yet, for the psychologist at least, a person's cephalic index is an uninteresting fact. It is not interesting because a person's cephalic index has no connection, as far as we know, with any of his behavior. There are, in other words, no laws connecting it with behavioral concepts. It is, therefore, not a useful concept. Because *cephalic index* does not enter into laws, the concept is useless for predicting or explaining behavior. It lacks "meaning" in the sense of *significance*. Consider, on the contrary, that if the folklore generalization about redheads being quick-tempered were true, then the concept *red-haired* would be significant because the alleged "law" permits us to make certain predictions about red-headed people. Less frivolously, the concept of, say, *frustration* is significant because we know certain laws that enable us to predict the consequences of frustration. We know that under certain circumstances it leads to aggression.

The reason for a fact being trivial or not worth knowing is, thus, the same as that for a concept not being worth having. Nor, upon reflection, is this surprising, because to assert an individual fact is to assert that a concept has an instance. A law states that two or more kinds of individual facts are invariably connected, that is, whenever there is an instance of one (or more) concept(s), then there are also instances of (one, or more) others. A concept is significant only if it enters into laws. It is significant, in other words, only if we know something about its referent, know how it is connected with other things. And to know that, in turn, is to know what effects it has, when it occurs, or how it changes. This is why adequate definition is not a sufficient condition for a good concept. Is a certain concept "good" or not? The question is ambiguous. Does it ask whether the concept is adequately defined or whether it is significant?

These are clearly two questions, not one, and each must be answered separately. *A good concept has both meaning and significance.* To say the same thing differently, a good concept has a reliably identifiable referent (meaning) about which we know one or more laws (significance). The more laws into which a concept enters, the more significant it is, because the more we then know about how it is connected with other things. If we know, for instance, not only that college education is connected with income, but also how it affects social status, success in marriage, and political and religious attitudes, then the concept is more significant than if we know only one of these things. It is a more fruitful variable because, given any instance of it—namely, a college-educated person—the generalizations permit us to say several other things about him.

Laws, not concepts, are discovered. A concept, after all, is just a name. And names are bestowed not found. A concept is introduced into language when certain kinds of phenomena are selected for attention. The scientist names not, like Adam, for the sake of naming, but only when he has a hunch about a connection between what he names and something else. If his hunch is right, then he has discovered not a concept, but a law. Concepts are not sentences. Only sentences, either of individual fact or generalizations, state that something is or is not the case. Therefore, only sentences are either true or false. Concepts are either well or ill defined, significant or useless, good or bad, but they are not true or false. To look for a good concept is to look for a law. There is no recipe or prescription for finding laws, or, therefore, for finding significant concepts. Scientific method is not a set of rules for discovery, but a certain way of formulating concepts, confirming hypotheses, and constructing theories. We can state the principles of proper concept formation. We can state the nature of proper scientific evidence for the truth of a hypothesis. But we cannot give any recipes for selecting the concepts and finding the hypotheses to which the method of science is then applied. The scientist in any area needs a firm and broad grasp of already established knowledge and techniques. This he can be taught. The rest is imagination and ingenuity—with these he must be born.

EXPLANATION, PREDICTION, AND THEORIES

As I mentioned briefly before, the scientist looks for laws or connections among facts in order to explain and to predict phenomena. Speaking loosely, we may "explain" the fact that Jones makes more money than Smith by pointing to Jones' superior education. But a man from Mars or anyone else may well wonder why we cite Jones' education rather than, say, his height. Speaking more strictly, we then expand our explanation. To cite a cause as explanation of an event is, implicitly at least, to cite an instance of a law. Jones' education rather than his height is relevant to his income because we know a law or generalization connecting education with income, but no such law connects height with income. This law and the fact about Jones' education together give a *reason,* in a strict logical sense, for Jones' superior income, because they are the premises of a deductive argument from which that fact may be derived. The conclusion may be deduced from the premises because the premises logically imply the conclusion. And the premises logically imply the conclusion because the corresponding conditional "If the premises are true, then the conclusion is true" is a tautology. It is a tautology, or logical truth, because the conclusion merely makes explicit what is already implicit in the premises. The fact to be explained, therefore, *must* be true if the explaining premises are true. That is why explanation is always deductive, no matter how covertly. For, otherwise, the statements that purport to do the explaining will fail to explain why what happened did happen instead of something else. Either the explanation is deductive or else it does not justify what it is said to explain.

Prediction has the same logical form as explanation. In predicting something as yet unknown, we deductively infer it from particular facts and laws that are already known. This deductive tautological connection among statements also shows why observations confirm or refute hypotheses. If a prediction inferred from a set of premises turns out to be true, then the generalization is further confirmed. If it turns out to be false, then we know that either the generalization or the individual fact used in making the prediction *must* be false. Because we are less likely to be mistaken about individual facts, in most cases the failure of a prediction means that the generalization is thereby refuted.

It makes no difference whether the premises are statistical or deterministic, as nonstatistical generalizations are called. If they are deterministic, we may predict an individual event; if they are statistical, only statements about classes of events may be either explained or predicted. Because explanation is always of statements by means of other statements, concepts alone have no explanatory or predictive power. Only sentences, never concepts, can serve as either premises or conclusion of a deduction. The notion of an "explanatory concept" is simply a confused way of speaking about significant concepts, those about which we know laws permitting explanation and prediction. (For a contrasting view, see the article by William Dray in Section Five.)

An explanation of an individual fact always includes at least one law or generalization among its premises. This law may in turn be explained by deducing it from other laws. The connection between education and income, for instance, may be explained by deducing it from generalizations connecting, say, education with social mobility and social mobility, in turn, with income. Although all three laws are empirical generalizations which may turn out to be false, the *connection among them* is such that *if* the last two are true, then the law to be explained *must* be true. A theory is such a deductively connected set of laws. It thus has the logical form of an explanation. Some explanations (those that explain statements of individual facts) contain both laws and statements of individual facts as premises. In a theory all the statements, both explained and explaining, are generalizations. Those that do the explaining are called the axioms of the theory. The laws that are explained are the theorems of the theory. The axioms are such only by virtue of their place in a theory. Neither self-evident nor otherwise privileged, they are empirical laws whose truth is, temporarily at least, taken for granted in order to see what other empirical assertions—the theorems—must be true if they are. An axiom in one theory may be a theorem in another. Thus, what is an axiom in Galileo's theory about the free fall of bodies on earth is a theorem in the Newtonian theory of gravitation which explains Galileo's laws. The Newtonian axiom is in turn explained, in conjunction with other statements, by Einstein's theory. Explanation is always relative to a set of premises that logically imply what is to be explained. We stop explaining when we do not know any more. There is no logically "ultimate" explanation.

The features singled out by the technical terms of science must be connected to other things in such a way as to explain the facts of experience. Laws and theories containing the technical terms of physics explain, for instance, why the sun is hot, glue is sticky, or a missile follows a certain path. Theoretical physics is relevant because, via chains of definitions and deductive connections among its laws, it ultimately speaks in the language of common sense about ordinary material objects and what observably happens to them. That indeed is how we know what it is talking about and whether what it says is true or false. The social scientist also looks for features of our individual and social life that escape common observation. The laws about these features must explain why men think, feel, and act as they do. Otherwise, they are not the laws we want to know, and the concepts they contain, no matter how precisely defined, are not worth having. Because meaningful behavior is part of our everyday experience, our common language has a rich vocabulary for it. But our everyday terms for human actions, such as *fixing* and *playing,* have an essential reference to thoughts, purposes, emotions, and the like. Yet we do not observe other people's states of mind. The social scientist is thus faced with special problems in concept formation and explanation which do not affect the physical scientist. These problems and their ramifications are discussed in the writings that follow.

One ⋆ THE NATURE

OF HUMAN ACTION

INTRODUCTION

Men and inanimate things alike are said to *do* things. An acid corrodes metals. A man tills the soil; he does so intentionally. And one man may help another because he believes that he ought to. In contrast, inanimate things do not act intentionally or from a sense of obligation. People often act in accordance with social conventions and moral standards. Animals and inanimate things act only in accordance with natural laws.

Some things a man does not really *do* at all; they just happen to him. For inanimate things, this is a distinction without a difference. Not so for man. Accident, disease, circumstance, luck—the things that "happen" to a man are those that affect him independently of his own desires, decisions, and purposes. Action, understood as meaningful behavior, is only part of a broader category. *Behavior* in its broadest use comprehends any change or tendency to change in things, living or nonliving. An eyeblink is behavior; a wink is *meaningful* behavior. As Weber points out, no sharp line can be drawn empirically between meaningful action and "merely reactive" behavior. We cannot always be sure whether a man's behavior is intentional or not, for the causes, from within and from without, of a specific act are frequently complex and even more frequently obscure. Yet the distinction remains, and meaningful behavior is the province of social science.

The opening essay by Max Weber is richly relevant to many issues discussed throughout this volume. Primarily, however, it sets the stage by characterizing the subject matter and the task of social science. Its theme is human action; its task, the causal explanation of such action, individual or social. Though all agree about the subject matter, many disagree about the task. Does the difference between men and nonhuman things entail a further difference between the study of men and the study of things?

The nineteenth-century German Romanticists believed that the answer was decidedly "yes." Accordingly, they drew a sharp distinction between *Geisteswissenschaften,* the study of spirit—or, less grandiloquently, the human sciences—on the one hand, and *Naturwissenschaften* or the natural sciences, on the other. *Wissenschaft* is a broad term akin to the English *discipline*. Only *Naturwissenschaften* were held to be sciences in the strict sense, that is, disciplines that seek to explain objectively observed phenomena by means of general laws. They maintained that the actions of men, as essentially involving thought and purpose, could not be understood by merely observing manifest behavior. Nor, because each man is a unique individual, did they consider human action to be subject to the causal uniformities governing the behavior of matter. The methods and goals of natural science were therefore deemed inappropriate to the study of man and society. Such study was held, instead, to be an irremediably subjective and noncausal inquiry.

The German Romanticists insisted—and many scholars today still insist —that the investigator, as a fellow actor in the human drama, can surmount the limits imposed by the external methods of natural science. At his disposal is the faculty of *Verstehen* or *understanding*. By *understanding* we empathically grasp the minds of others and, thereby, the subjective meaning of their outer behavior. To those who saw the course of history as itself a directed, purposive process, *understanding* also conveyed insight into its goals and into the "objective meaning" of human actions as contributing —willy-nilly and unknown to the individual—to the march of history. For those advocates of *Verstehen* who reject the notion of "objective" historical meanings, *understanding* amounts to interpreting the overt behavior of others in the light of our own inner experiences.

Ordinary material objects, such as trees, tables, and the human body, are called objective phenomena because they exist independently of our perception of them and are publicly observable. By contrast, we cannot inspect the minds of others as we can inspect their bodies. We are each directly aware only of our own feelings, dreams, thoughts, and memories. Mental states are therefore called subjective phenomena. How, then, do we know the thoughts and purposes of others? We can only know them, according to the proponents of *Verstehen,* by an imaginative projection of our own states of mind. When we behave in certain ways, we know directly our own motives and we attribute these to others when we see them behaving in similar ways. Our knowledge about the meaningful behavior of others is held to be based solely on this inner self-examination and therefore to be subjective knowledge.

In the second selection, Ernest Nagel exposes to searching critical examination various aspects of the doctrine that our knowledge of the meaningful behavior of others must be radically subjective. He points out the limits of *Verstehen,* or empathy, as a source of knowledge and discusses how ordinary observation can provide objective knowledge of human action. *Behaviorism,* as a methodological program for attaining objective knowledge of man, is distinguished from certain substantive doctrines that are often confused with it. He thus brings to light certain mistaken assumptions and misconceptions about that program and its possibilities.

A bias against a science of man naturally must be "justified." Recently that animus has been rationalized by the view that explanation by motives is allegedly incompatible with explanation by causes. Motives, intentions, and the like, it is contended, are just not the kind of things that can be causes. Accordingly, the explanation of human action by means of motives cannot be the kind of causal explanation that concerns science. One implausible consequence of this doctrine is that if a man intends to buy a house and does so, then his intentions and motives were not part of the cause of his action. Against this position, Davidson's primary concern is to defend the commonsense view that explanation by motives is a species of causal explanation rather than incompatible with it. He considers the relation between justifying an action and causally explaining it and argues that a reason can justify an action only if it is also a cause of that action.

The plausibility of many objections to a science of man rests upon the conflation of various meanings of *meaning* and of *understanding. Concept* is also notoriously ambiguous, as it sometimes stands for a word and sometimes for a thought. My paper unpacks several different uses of these key terms and also tries to show how and why the possibility of an objective account of human action is entirely compatible with the obvious distinction between states of mind and bodily states.

Max Weber's essay provides an explication of *Verstehen* from one born and bred in the tradition and ambience of *verstehende* social science. Unlike its romantic proponents, however, he also firmly embraced the ideal of an empirical science of man and society. The cultural ambience had complex strands, and Weber's thought reflects its complexity. If a cult extolling feeling over reason flourished, so did the natural sciences. Nor were the ideals of the Enlightenment as yet wholly submerged in Germany. Weber, sociology's greatest genius, skillfully and profoundly chose the sense and rejected the nonsense in both traditions. He conceives *Verstehen* as supplementing, rather than replacing, empirical observational methods. Interpretive understanding indeed plays a dual role for Weber in our knowledge of man.

It is, first, a source of hypotheses about the occurrence and explanation of human actions. Literally, we see physical objects in space. Seeing a man's hand with an axe in it coming down on a log, we interpret what we see as purposive woodcutting. There is interpretation, because inference is involved. Because the inference is usually unconscious, Weber calls such perceptions direct observational understanding. A bit of manifest behavior is identified as an action, rather than an involuntary or haphazard movement, by describing it in terms that incorporate its "subjective meaning" or purpose. Our everyday terms for human actions, like *reaching, handwashing, fishing,* or *voting,* refer to a complex of inner and outer events. Meaningful behavior manifests mind. The meaning is "subjective," for Weber, only in the sense that it is attributed to an individual person. Imputations of motive are empirically testable and, for knowledge, must be so tested.

We may misinterpret overt behavior; perhaps the man was swinging the axe in anger or was even having a fit. We *meaningfully explain overt behavior* by characterizing it as an action. But to understand that someone is cutting wood is not yet to understand why he is doing so. We *meaningfully explain the action,* in turn, by making explicit inferences about its motives and its relation to certain assumed goals. By placing it in this broader context, we achieve "explanatory understanding" of the action. The explanation is inadequate, Weber maintains, if it is not psychologically plausible. But no matter how plausible, it is not explanatory *knowledge* until we have found empirical generalizations by virtue of which the imputed motives are shown, with high probability, to be the actual causes of the action. Only such verified generalizations permit *scientific explanation of meaningful behavior.* Thus, according to Weber, social science does not explain differently from other sciences. It explains in the same way different sorts of things—namely, meaningful human action.

Though *Verstehen* is a heuristic device for arriving at causal hypotheses, it is not merely that for Weber. To ensure the relevance of social science is the second function of interpretive understanding. Uniformities that make no reference to human motives, beliefs, or social conventions are "incomprehensible," for they are not about meaningful actions. Meteorological or physiological generalizations, for instance, are relevant to social science only insofar as they are connected to human goals and attitudes. In other words, we cannot talk about man by changing the subject. Weber's real concern here is for the autonomy of social science. The issue, part of the so-called problem of reduction, is discussed directly in Section Four. But in the context of *Verstehen,* a few comments are in order.

Weber is not maintaining the extreme view (indeed he explicitly denies) that all meaningful behavior must also be psychologically understandable. But his discussion is blurred and not altogether consistent. The blur is evident in his two characterizations of *action.* He initially defines action as behavior to which the individual attaches subjective meaning—that is, as motivated behavior. He then also refers to it as behavior that is subjectively understandable by the investigator. But these, he also sees, are not the same thing nor are they necessarily coextensive. Behavior might be motivated by goals and values which we can neither empathize with nor "rationally" assess as means toward further ends. Was Hitler following a path appropriate to his goals, however unspeakable, when he murdered several million persons who otherwise could have served as soldiers in the German army? It is hard to know how to begin to answer the question, nor is it evident that an answer would be theoretically useful or even interesting historical information. The requirement of "understanding" unduly restricts the kinds of questions we may raise about the causes of social events, though to be sure it did not inhibit Weber's own impressive sociological investigations. More pertinently, action belongs to the individual and must be characterized in terms of his motives, conscious or not, and his circumstances, social and physical. Weber's irresolution about whether "subjective understanding" is a necessary criterion for meaningful action reflects his concern that man and society be explained in their own terms. One may reasonably doubt, however, that "subjective understanding" is really indispensable for ensuring that we do not heedlessly turn our attention from men to molecules.

In any case, Weber also emphasizes the importance of "nonunderstandable" uniformities to explain the conditions and circumstances of action.

Davidson comments shrewdly about the relation between individual causal imputations and the general laws from which they might be inferred. It is interesting to compare these comments with Weber's remarks about "non-understandable" uniformities. To both discussions might be added a further reflection about the laws of some future recognizably sociopsychological, nonphysiological, theory. Assume that from this theory we could derive specific causal imputations of motives for individual and social behavior. That is, it would explain ordinary actions. The laws of this theory, however, might well contain terms for patterns of behavior and social structure so complex and abstract that, unlike the actions that they explain, these patterns are not themselves "understandable." To explain, however, is neither to identify nor to explain away. Possibly this is the retrievable core of truth in the dubious doctrine of *Verstehen*.

[1] The Interpretive Understanding of Social Action

MAX WEBER

Prefatory Note

An introductory discussion of concepts can hardly be dispensed with, in spite of the fact that it is unavoidably abstract and hence gives the impression of remoteness from reality. Its method, however, makes no claim to any kind of novelty. On the contrary it attempts only to formulate what all empirical sociology really means when it deals with the same problems, in what it is hoped is a more convenient and somewhat more exact terminology, even though on that account it may seem pedantic. This is true even where terms are used which are apparently new or unfamiliar. As compared to the author's essay in *Logos*,[1] the terminology has been simplified as far as possible and hence considerably changed in order to render it more easily understandable. Unfortunately the most precise formulation cannot always be reconciled with a form which can readily be popularized. In such cases the latter aim has had to be sacrificed.

On the concept of 'understanding'[2] compare the *Allgemeine Pscho-*

[1] Vol. iv (1913, pp. 253 ff.); reprinted in *Gesammelte Aufsätze zur Wissenschaftslehre*, pp. 403–450.

[2] The German term is *Verstehen*. As Weber uses it this is a technical term with a distinctly narrower meaning than either the German or the English in everyday usage. Its primary reference in this work is to the observation and theoretical interpretation of the subjective 'states of mind' of actors. But it also extends to the grasp of the meaning of logical and other systems of symbols, a meaning which is usually thought of as in some sense 'intended' by a mind or intelligent being of some sort. The most important point about this concept seems to the editor to be the fact that in so far as phenomena are 'understood' in this technical sense, the relevant facts are stated and analysed within a certain frame of reference, that of 'action.' For present purposes the most important feature of this frame of reference is its use of 'subjective categories.' The essential thing is the operational applicability of such categories, not the common sense empirical question of whether the actor is conscious of the meanings imputed to him or in the ordinary sense 'intended' a given course of action. For a further discussion of these problems, see Talcott Parsons, *The Structure of Social Action*, especially chaps. ii and xix.

pathologie of Karl Jaspers, also a few observations by Heinrich Rickert in the second edition of the *Grenzen der Naturwissenschaftlichen Begriffsbildung* and particularly some of Simmel's discussions in the *Probleme der Geschichtsphilosophie*. For certain methodological considerations the reader may here be referred, as often before in the author's writings, to the procedure of Friedrich Gottl in his work *Die Herrschaft des Wortes*. This book, to be sure, is written in a somewhat difficult style and its argument does not appear everywhere to have been thoroughly thought through. As regards content, reference may be made especially to the fine work of Ferdinand Tönnies, *Gemeinschaft und Gesellschaft,* and also to the gravely misleading book of Rudolph Stammler, *Wirtschaft und Recht,* which may be compared with my criticism in the *Archiv für Sozialwissenschaft* (vol. xxiv, 1907). This critical essay contains many of the fundamental ideas of the following exposition. The present work departs from Simmel's method (in the *Soziologie* and the *Philosophie des Geldes*) in drawing a sharp distinction between subjectively intended and objectively valid 'meanings'; two different things which Simmel not only fails to distinguish but often deliberately treats as belonging together.

The Definitions of Sociology and of Social Action

Sociology (in the sense in which this highly ambiguous word is used here) is a science which attempts the interpretive understanding of social action in order thereby to arrive at a causal explanation of its course and effects. In 'action' is included all human behavior when and in so far as the acting individual attaches a subjective meaning to it. Action in this sense may be either overt or purely inward or subjective; it may consist of positive intervention in a situation, or of deliberately refraining from such intervention or passively acquiescing in the situation. Action is social in so far as, by virtue of the subjective meaning attached to it by the acting individual (or individuals), it takes account of the behavior of others and is thereby oriented in its course.[3]

It has not seemed advisable to attempt a rigorous use of a single English term whenever Weber employs *Verstehen*. 'Understanding' has been most commonly used. Other expressions such as 'subjectively understandable,' 'interpretation in subjective terms,' 'comprehension,' etc., have been used from time to time as the context seemed to demand.— Talcott Parsons, editor.

[3] In this series of definitions Weber employs several important terms which need discussion. In addition to *Verstehen*, which has already been commented upon, there are four important ones: *Deuten, Sinn, Handeln,* and *Verhalten. Deuten* has generally been translated as 'interpret.' As used by Weber in this context it refers to the interpretation of subjective states of mind and the meanings which can be imputed as intended by an actor. Any other meaning of the word 'interpretation' is irrelevant to Weber's discussion. The term *Sinn* has generally been translated as 'meaning'; and its variations, particularly the corresponding adjectives, *sinnhaft, sinnvoll, sinnfremd,* have been dealt with by appropriately modifying the term meaning. The reference here again is always to features of

THE METHODOLOGICAL FOUNDATIONS OF SOCIOLOGY [4]

1. 'Meaning' may be of two kinds. The term may refer first to the actual existing meaning in the given concrete case of a particular actor, or to the average or approximate meaning attributable to a given plurality of actors; or secondly to the theoretically conceived *pure type* [5] of subjective meaning attributed to the hypothetical actor or actors in a given type of action. In no case does it refer to an objectively 'correct' meaning or one which is 'true' in some metaphysical sense. It is this which distinguishes the empirical sciences of action, such as sociology and history, from the dogmatic disciplines in that area, such as jurisprudence, logic, ethics, and esthetics, which seek to ascertain the 'true' and 'valid' meanings associated with the objects of their investigation.

2. The line between meaningful action and merely reactive behavior to which no subjective meaning is attached, cannot be sharply drawn empirically. A very considerable part of all sociologically relevant behavior, especially purely traditional behavior, is marginal between the two. In the

---

the content of subjective states of mind or of symbolic systems which are ultimately referable to such states of mind.

The terms *Handeln* and *Verhalten* are directly related. *Verhalten* is the broader term referring to any mode of behaviour of human individuals, regardless of the frame of reference in terms of which it is analysed. 'Behaviour' has seemed to be the most appropriate English equivalent. *Handeln*, on the other hand, refers to the concrete phenomenon of human behaviour only in so far as it is capable of 'understanding,' in Weber's technical sense, in terms of subjective categories. The most appropriate English equivalent has seemed to be 'action.' This corresponds to the editor's usage in *The Structure of Social Action* and would seem to be fairly well established. 'Conduct' is also closely similar and has sometimes been used. *Deuten, Verstehen,* and *Sinn* are thus applicable to human behaviour only in so far as it constitutes action or conduct in this specific sense.—T.P.

4 Weber's text is organized in a somewhat unusual manner. He lays down certain fundamental definitions and then proceeds to comment upon them. The definitions themselves are in the original printed in large type, the subsidiary comments in smaller type. For the purposes of this translation it has not seemed best to make a distinction in type form, but the reader should be aware that the numbered paragraphs which follow a definition or group of them are in the nature of comments, rather than the continuous development of a general line of argument. This fact accounts for what is sometimes a relatively fragmentary character of the development and for the abrupt transition from one subject to another. Weber apparently did not intend this material to be 'read' in the ordinary sense, but rather to serve as a reference work for the clarification and systematization of theoretical concepts and their implications. While the comments under most of the definitions are relatively brief, under the definitions of Sociology and of Social Action, Weber wrote what is essentially a methodological essay. This makes sec. I out of proportion to the other sections of this and the following chapters. It has, however, seemed best to retain Weber's own plan for the subdivision of the material.—T.P.

5 Weber means by 'pure type' what he himself generally called and what has come to be known in the literature about his methodology as the 'ideal type.' The reader may be referred for general orientation to Weber's own Essay (to which he himself refers below), "Objectivity in Social Science"; [the section on ideal types is reprinted in this volume, pp. 496-507] to two works of Dr. Alexander von Schelting, 'Die logische Theorie der historischen Kulturwissenschaften von Max Weber' (*Archiv fuer Sozialwissenscraft,* vol. xlix), and *Max Webers Wissenschaftslehre;* and to the editor's *Structure of Social Action,* chap. xvi. A somewhat different interpretation is given in Theodore Abel, *Systematic Sociology in Germany,* chap. iv.—T.P.

case of many psychophysical processes, meaningful, i.e. subjectively understandable, action is not to be found at all; in others it is discernible only by the expert psychologist. Many mystical experiences which cannot be adequately communicated in words are, for a person who is not susceptible to such experiences, not fully understandable. At the same time the ability to imagine one's self performing a similar action is not a necessary prerequisite to understanding; 'one need not have been Caesar in order to understand Caesar.' For the verifiable accuracy [6] of interpretation of the meaning of a phenomenon, it is a great help to be able to put one's self imaginatively in the place of the actor and thus sympathetically to participate in his experiences, but this is not an essential condition of meaningful interpretation. Understandable and nonunderstandable components of a process are often intermingled and bound up together.

3. All interpretation of meaning, like all scientific observation, strives for clarity and verifiable accuracy of insight and comprehension (*Evidenz*). The basis for certainty in understanding can be either rational, which can be further subdivided into logical and mathematical, or it can be of an emotionally empathic or artistically appreciative quality. In the sphere of action things are rationally evident chiefly when we attain a completely clear intellectual grasp of the action-elements in their intended context of meaning. Empathic or appreciative accuracy is attained when, through sympathetic participation, we can adequately grasp the emotional context in which the action took place. The highest degree of rational understanding is attained in cases involving the meanings of logically or mathematically related propositions; their meaning may be immediately and unambiguously intelligible. We have a perfectly clear understanding of what it means when somebody employs the proposition $2 \times 2 = 4$ or the Pythagorean theorem in reasoning or argument, or when someone correctly carries out a logical train of reasoning according to our accepted modes of thinking. In the same way we also understand what a person is doing when he tries to achieve certain ends by choosing appropriate means on the basis of the facts of the situation as experience has accustomed us to interpret them. Such an interpretation of this type of rationally purposeful action possesses, for the

---

[6] This is an imperfect rendering of the German term *Evidenz*, for which, unfortunately, there is no good English equivalent. It has hence been rendered in a number of different ways, varying with the particular context in which it occurs. The primary meaning refers to the basis on which a scientist or thinker becomes satisfied of the certainty or acceptability of a proposition. As Weber himself points out, there are two primary aspects of this. On the one hand a conclusion can be 'seen' to follow from given premises by virtue of logical, mathematical, or possibly other modes of meaningful relation. In this sense one 'sees' the solution of an arithmetical problem or the correctness of the proof of a geometrical theorem. The other aspect is concerned with empirical observation. If an act of observation is competently performed, in a similar sense one 'sees' the truth of the relevant descriptive proposition. The term *Evidenz* does not refer to the process of observing, but to the quality of its result, by virtue of which the observer feels justified in affirming a given statement. Hence 'certainty' has seemed a suitable translation in some contexts, 'clarity' in others, 'accuracy' in still others. The term 'intuition' is not usable because it refers to the process rather than to the result.—T.P.

understanding of the choice of means, the highest degree of verifiable certainty. With a lower degree of certainty, which is, however, adequate for most purposes of explanation, we are able to understand errors, including confusion of problems of the sort that we ourselves are liable to, or the origin of which we can detect by sympathetic self-analysis.

On the other hand, many ultimate ends or values toward which experience shows that human action may be oriented, often cannot be understood completely, though sometimes we are able to grasp them intellectually. The more radically they differ from our own ultimate values, however, the more difficult it is for us to make them understandable by imaginatively participating in them. Depending upon the circumstances of the particular case we must be content either with a purely intellectual understanding of such values or when even that fails, sometimes we must simply accept them as given data. Then we can try to understand the action motivated by them on the basis of whatever opportunities for approximate emotional and intellectual interpretation seem to be available at different points in its course. These difficulties apply, for instance, for people not susceptible to the relevant values, to many unusual acts of religious and charitable zeal; also certain kinds of extreme rationalistic fanaticism of the type involved in some forms of the ideology of the 'rights of man' are in a similar position for people who radically repudiate such points of view.

The more we ourselves are susceptible to them the more readily can we imaginatively participate in such emotional reactions as anxiety, anger, ambition, envy, jealousy, love, enthusiasm, pride, vengefulness, loyalty, devotion, and appetites of all sorts, and thereby understand the irrational conduct which grows out of them. Such conduct is 'irrational,' that is, from the point of view of the rational pursuit of a given end. Even when such emotions are found in a degree of intensity of which the observer himself is completely incapable, he can still have a significant degree of emotional understanding of their meaning and can interpret intellectually their influence on the course of action and the selection of means.

For the purposes of a typological scientific analysis it is convenient to treat all irrational, affectually determined elements of behavior as factors of deviation from a conceptually pure type of rational action. For example a panic on the stock exchange can be most conveniently analysed by attempting to determine first what the course of action would have been if it had not been influenced by irrational affects; it is then possible to introduce the irrational components as accounting for the observed deviations from this hypothetical course. Similarly, in analysing a political or military campaign it is convenient to determine in the first place what would have been a rational course, given the ends of the participants and adequate knowledge of all the circumstances. Only in this way is it possible to assess the causal significance of irrational factors as accounting for the deviations from this type. The construction of a purely rational course of action in such cases serves the sociologist as a type ('ideal type') which has the merit of clear understandability and lack of ambiguity. By comparison with this it is possible to understand the ways in which actual action is influenced by irrational factors of all sorts, such as affects [7] and errors, in that they account for the deviation from the line of conduct which would be expected on the hypothesis that the action were purely rational.

Only in this respect and for these reasons of methodological convenience, is the method of sociology 'rationalistic.' It is naturally not legitimate to interpret this procedure as involving a 'rationalistic bias' of sociology, but only as a methodological device. It certainly does not involve a belief in the actual predominance of rational elements in human life, for on the question of how far this predominance does or does not exist, nothing whatever has been said. That there is, however, a danger of rationalistic interpretations where they are out of place naturally cannot be denied. All experience unfortunately confirms the existence of this danger.

4. In all the sciences of human action, account must be taken of processes and phenomena which are devoid of subjective meaning,[8] in the role of stimuli, results, favoring or hindering circumstances. To be devoid of meaning is not identical with being lifeless or non-human; every artifact, such as for example a machine, can be understood only in terms of the meaning which its production and use have had or will have for human action; a meaning which may derive from a relation to exceedingly various purposes. Without reference to this meaning such an object remains wholly unintelligible.[9] That which is intelligible or understandable about it is thus its relation to human action in the role either of means or of end; a relation of which the actor or actors can be said to have been aware and to which their action has been oriented. Only in terms of such categories is it possible to 'understand' objects of this kind.[9a] On the other hand processes or conditions, whether they are animate or inanimate, human or non-human, are in the present sense devoid of meaning in so far as they cannot be related to an intended purpose. That is to say they are devoid of meaning if they cannot be related to action in the role of means or ends but constitute only the stimulus, the favoring or hindering circumstances.[10] It may be that the

---

[7] A term now much used in psychological literature, especially that of Psychoanalysis. It is roughly equivalent to 'emotion' but more precise.—T.P.

[8] The German term is *sinnfremd*. This should not be translated by 'meaningless,' but interpreted in the technical context of Weber's use of *Verstehen* and *Sinndeutung*. The essential criterion is the impossibility of placing the object in question in a complex of relations on the meaningful level.—T.P.

[9] *Unverstehbar*.

[9a] [For treatment of this 'meaning' in contemporary psychology see Farber, pp. 166–67.—Ed.]

[10] Surely this passage states too narrow a conception of the scope of meaningful interpretation. It is certainly not *only* in terms such as those of the rational means-end schema, that it is possible to make action understandable in terms of subjective categories. This probably can actually be called a source of rationalistic bias in Weber's work. In practice he does not adhere at all rigorously to this methodological position. For certain possibilities in this broader field, see Talcott Parsons' *Structure of Social Action*, chaps. vi and xi. —T.P.

incursion of the Dollart at the beginning of the twelfth century [11] had historical significance as a stimulus to the beginning of certain migrations of considerable importance. Human mortality, indeed the organic life cycle generally from the helplessness of infancy to that of old age, is naturally of the very greatest sociological importance through the various ways in which human action has been oriented to these facts. To still another category of facts devoid of meaning belong certain psychic or psychophysical phenomena such as fatigue, habituation, memory, etc.; also certain typical states of euphoria under some conditions of ascetic mortification; finally, typical variations in the reactions of individuals according to reaction-time, precision, and other modes. But in the last analysis the same principle applies to these as to other phenomena which are devoid of meaning. Both the actor and the sociologist must accept them as data to be taken into account.

It is altogether possible that future research may be able to discover non-understandable uniformities underlying what has appeared to be specifically meaningful action, though little has been accomplished in this direction thus far. Thus, for example, differences in hereditary biological constitution, as of 'races,' would have to be treated by sociology as given data in the same way as the physiological facts of the need of nutrition or the effect of senescence on action. This would be the case if, and in so far as, we had statistically conclusive proof of their influence on sociologically relevant behavior. The recognition of the causal significance of such factors would naturally not in the least alter the specific task of sociological analysis or of that of the other sciences of action, which is the interpretation of action in terms of its subjective meaning. The effect would be only to introduce certain nonunderstandable data of the same order as others which, it has been noted above, are already present, into the complex of subjectively understandable motivation at certain points. Thus it may come to be known that there are typical relations between the frequency of certain types of teleological orientation of action or of the degree of certain kinds of rationality and the cephalic index or skin colour or any other biologically inherited characteristic.

5. *Understanding* may be of two kinds: the first is the direct observational understanding [12] of the subjective meaning of a given act as such, including verbal utterances. We thus understand by direct observation, in this sense,

---

[11] A gulf of the North Sea which broke through the Netherlands coast, flooding an area.—T.P.

[12] Weber here uses the term *aktuelles Verstehen*, which he contrasts with *erklärendes Verstehen*. The latter he also refers to as *motivationsmaessig*. 'Aktuell' in this context has been translated as 'observational.' It is clear from Weber's discussion that the primary criterion is the possibility of deriving the meaning of an act or symbolic expression from immediate observation without reference to any broader context. In *erklärendes Verstehen*, on the other hand, the particular act must be placed in a broader context of meaning involving facts which cannot be derived from immediate observation of a particular act or expression.—T.P.

the meaning of the proposition $2 \times 2 = 4$ when we hear or read it. This is a case of the direct rational understanding of ideas. We also understand an outbreak of anger as manifested by facial expression, exclamations or irrational movements. This is direct observational understanding of irrational emotional reactions. We can understand in a similar observational way the action of a woodcutter or of somebody who reaches for the knob to shut a door or who aims a gun at an animal. This is rational observational understanding of actions.

Understanding may, however, be of another sort, namely explanatory understanding. Thus we understand in terms of *motive* the meaning an actor attaches to the proposition twice two equals four, when he states it or writes it down, in that we understand what makes him do this at precisely this moment and in these circumstances. Understanding in this sense is attained if we know that he is engaged in balancing a ledger or in making a scientific demonstration, or is engaged in some other task of which this particular act would be an appropriate part. This is rational understanding of motivation, which consists in placing the act in an intelligible and more inclusive context of meaning.[13] Thus we understand the chopping of wood or aiming of a gun in terms of motive in addition to direct observation if we know that the woodchopper is working for a wage or is chopping a supply of firewood for his own use or possibly is doing it for recreation. But he might also be 'working off' a fit of rage, an irrational case. Similarly we understand the motive of a person aiming a gun if we know that he has been commanded to shoot as a member of a firing squad, that he is fighting against an enemy, or that he is doing it for revenge. The last is affectually determined and thus in a certain sense irrational. Finally we have a motivational understanding of the outburst of anger if we know that it has been provoked by jealousy, injured pride, or an insult. The last examples are all affectually determined and hence derived from irrational motives. In all the above cases the particular act has been placed in an understandable sequence of motivation, the understanding of which can be treated as an explanation of the actual course of behavior. Thus for a science which is concerned with the subjective meaning of action, explanation requires a grasp of the complex of meaning in which an actual course of understandable action thus interpreted belongs.[14] In all such cases, even where the processes are largely affectual,

13 The German term is *Sinnzusammenhang*. It refers to a plurality of elements which form a coherent whole on the level of meaning. There are several possible modes of meaningful relation between such elements, such as logical consistency, the esthetic harmony of a style, or the appropriateness of means to an end. In any case, however, a *Sinnzusammenhang* must be distinguished from a system of elements which are causally interdependent. There seems to be no single English term or phrase which is always adequate. According to variations in the context, 'context of meaning,' 'complex of meaning,' and sometimes 'meaningful system' have been employed.—T.P.

14 On the significance of this type of explanation for causal relationship. See para. 6, pp. 27–29 below in the present section.

the subjective meaning of the action, including that also of the relevant meaning complexes, will be called the 'intended' meaning.[15] This involves a departure from ordinary usage, which speaks of intention in this sense only in the case of rationally purposive action.

6. In all these cases understanding involves the interpretive grasp of the meaning present in one of the following contexts: (a) as in the historical approach, the actually intended meaning for concrete individual action; or (b) as in cases of sociological mass phenomena the average of, or an approximation to, the actually intended meaning; or (c) the meaning appropriate to a scientifically formulated pure type (an ideal type) of a common phenomenon. The concepts and 'laws' of pure economic theory are examples of this kind of ideal type. They state what course a given type of human action would take if it were strictly rational, unaffected by errors or emotional factors and if, furthermore, it were completely and unequivocally directed to a single end, the maximization of economic advantage. In reality, action takes exactly this course only in unusual cases, as sometimes on the stock exchange; and even then there is usually only an approximation to the ideal type.[16]

Every interpretation attempts to attain clarity and certainty, but no matter how clear an interpretation as such appears to be from the point of view of meaning, it cannot on this account alone claim to be the causally valid interpretation. On this level it must remain only a peculiarly plausible hypothesis. In the first place the 'conscious motives' may well, even to the actor himself, conceal the various 'motives' and 'repressions' which constitute the real driving force of his action. Thus in such cases even subjectively honest self-analysis has only a relative value. Then it is the task of the sociologist to be aware of this motivational situation and to describe and analyse it, even though it has not actually been concretely part of the conscious 'intention' of the actor; possibly not at all, at least not fully. This is a borderline case of the interpretation of meaning. Secondly, processes of action which seem to an observer to be the same or similar may fit into exceedingly various complexes of motive in the case of the actual actor. Then even though the situations appear superficially to be very similar we must

[15] The German is *gemeinter Sinn*. Weber departs from ordinary usage not only in broadening the meaning of this conception. As he states at the end of the present methodological discussion, he does not restrict the use of this concept to cases where a clear self-conscious awareness of such meaning can be reasonably attributed to every individual actor. Essentially, what Weber is doing is to formulate an operational concept. The question is not whether in a sense obvious to the ordinary person such an intended meaning 'really exists,' but whether the concept is capable of providing a logical framework within which scientifically important observations can be made. The test of validity of the observations is not whether their object is immediately clear to common sense, but whether the results of these technical observations can be satisfactorily organized and related to those of others in a systematic body of knowledge.—T.P.

[16] The scientific functions of such construction have been discussed in the author's article in the *Archiv für Sozialwissenschaft*, vol. xix, pp. 64 ff. [Reprinted in this volume, pp. 496–507.]

actually understand them or interpret them as very different, perhaps, in terms of meaning, directly opposed.[17] Third, the actors in any given situation are often subject to opposing and conflicting impulses, all of which we are able to understand. In a large number of cases we know from experience it is not possible to arrive at even an approximate estimate of the relative strength of conflicting motives and very often we cannot be certain of our interpretation. Only the actual outcome of the conflict gives a solid basis of judgment.

More generally, verification of subjective interpretation by comparison with the concrete course of events is, as in the case of all hypotheses, indispensable. Unfortunately this type of verification is feasible with relative accuracy only in the few very special cases susceptible of psychological experimentation. The approach to a satisfactory degree of accuracy is exceedingly various, even in the limited number of cases of mass phenomena which can be statistically described and unambiguously interpreted. For the rest there remains only the possibility of comparing the largest possible number of historical or contemporary processes which, while otherwise similar, differ in the one decisive point of their relation to the particular motive or factor the role of which is being investigated. This is a fundamental task of comparative sociology. Often, unfortunately, there is available only the dangerous and uncertain procedure of the 'imaginary experiment' which consists in thinking away certain elements of a chain of motivation and working out the course of action which would then probably ensue, thus arriving at a causal judgment.[18]

For example, the generalization called Gresham's Law is a rationally clear interpretation of human action under certain conditions and under the assumption that it will follow a purely rational course. How far any actual course of action corresponds to this can be verified only by the available statistical evidence for the actual disappearance of under-valued monetary units from circulation. In this case our information serves to demonstrate a high degree of accuracy. The facts of experience were known before the generalization, which was formulated afterwards; but without this successful interpretation our need for causal understanding would evidently be left unsatisfied. On the other hand, without the demonstration that what can here be assumed to be a theoretically adequate interpretation also is in some degree relevant to an actual course of action, a 'law,' no matter how fully demonstrated theoretically, would be worthless for the understanding of action in the real world. In this case the correspondence between the theo-

---

17 Simmel, in his *Probleme der Geschichtsphilosophie*, gives a number of examples.

18 The above passage is an exceedingly compact statement of Weber's theory of the logical conditions of proof of casual relationship. He developed this most fully in his essay "Objectivity in Social Science," op. cit. It is also discussed in certain of the other essays which have been collected in the volume, *Gesammelte Aufsätze zur Wissenschaftslehre*. The best and fullest secondary discussion is to be found in Von Schelting's book, *Max Webers Wissenschaftslehre*. There is a briefer discussion in chap. xvi of Talcott Parsons' *Structure of Social Action*.—T.P.

retical interpretation of motivation and its empirical verification is entirely satisfactory and the cases are numerous enough so that verification can be considered established. But to take another example, Eduard Meyer has advanced an ingenious theory of the causal significance of the battles of Marathon, Salamis, and Platea for the development of the cultural peculiarities of Greek, and hence, more generally, Western, civilization.[19] This is derived from a meaningful interpretation of certain symptomatic facts having to do with the attitudes of the Greek oracles and prophets towards the Persians. It can only be directly verified by reference to the examples of the conduct of the Persians in cases where they were victorious, as in Jerusalem, Egypt, and Asia Minor, and even this verification must necessarily remain unsatisfactory in certain respects. The striking rational plausibility of the hypothesis must here necessarily be relied on as a support. In very many cases of historical interpretation which seem highly plausible, however, there is not even a possibility of the order of verification which was feasible in this case. Where this is true the interpretation must necessarily remain a hypothesis.

7. A motive is a complex of subjective meaning which seems to the actor himself or to the observer an adequate ground for the conduct in question. We apply the term 'adequacy on the level of meaning' [20] to the subjective interpretation of a coherent course of conduct when and in so far as, according to our habitual modes of thought and feeling, its component parts taken in their mutual relation are recognized to constitute a 'typical' complex of meaning. It is more common to say 'correct.' The interpretation of a sequence of events will on the other hand be called *causally* adequate in so far as, according to established generalizations from experience, there is a probability that it will always actually occur in the same way. An example of adequacy on the level of meaning in this sense is what is, according to our current norms of calculation or thinking, the correct solution of an arithmetical problem. On the other hand, a causally adequate interpretation of the same phenomenon would concern the statistical probability that, according to verified generalizations from experience, there would be a correct or an erroneous solution of the same problem. This also refers to currently accepted norms but includes taking account of typical errors or of typical confusions. Thus causal explanation depends on being able to determine that there is a probability, which in the rare ideal case can be numerically

[19] See Eduard Meyer, *Geschichte des Altertums*, Stuttgart, 1901, vol. iii, pp. 420, 444 ff.
    [20] The expression *sinnhafte Adäquanz* is one of the most difficult of Weber's technical terms to translate. In most places the cumbrous phrase 'adequacy on the level of meaning' has had to be employed. It should be clear from the progress of the discussion that what Weber refers to is a satisfying level of knowledge for the particular purposes of the subjective state of mind of the actor or actors. He is, however, careful to point out that *causal* adequacy involves in addition to this a satisfactory correspondence between the results of observations from the subjective point of view and from the objective; that is, observations of the overt course of action which can be described without reference to the state of mind of the actor. For a discussion of the methodological problem involved here, see *Structure of Social Action*, chaps. ii and v.—T.P.

stated, but is always in some sense calculable, that a given observable event (overt or subjective) will be followed or accompanied by another event.

A correct causal interpretation of a concrete course of action is arrived at when the overt action and the motives have both been correctly apprehended and at the same time their relation has become meaningfully comprehensible. A correct causal interpretation of typical action means that the process which is claimed to be typical is shown to be both adequately grasped on the level of meaning and at the same time the interpretation is to some degree casually adequate. If adequacy in respect to meaning is lacking, then no matter how high the degree of uniformity and how precisely its probability can be numerically determined, it is still an incomprehensible statistical probability, whether dealing with overt or subjective processes. On the other hand, even the most perfect adequacy on the level of meaning has causal significance from a sociological point of view only in so far as there is some kind of proof for the existence of a probability [21] that action in fact normally takes the course which has been held to be meaningful. For this there must be some degree of determinable frequency of approximation to an average or a pure type.

Statistical uniformities constitute understandable types of action in the sense of this discussion, and thus constitute 'sociological generalizations,' only when they can be regarded as manifestations of the understandable subjective meaning of a course of social action. Conversely, formulations of a rational course of subjectively understandable action constitute sociological types of empirical process only when they can be empirically observed with a significant degree of approximation. It is unfortunately by no means the case that the actual likelihood of the occurrence of a given course of overt action is always directly proportional to the clarity of subjective interpretation. There are statistics of processes devoid of meaning such as death rates, phenomena of fatigue, the production rate of machines, the amount of rainfall, in exactly the same sense as there are statistics of meaningful phenomena. But only when the phenomena are meaningful is it convenient to speak of sociological statistics. Examples are such cases as crime rates, occupational distributions, price statistics, and statistics of crop acreage. Naturally there are many cases where both components are involved, as in crop statistics.

8. Processes and uniformities which it has here seemed convenient not to designate as (in the present case) sociological phenomena or uniformi-

---

21 This is the first occurrence in Weber's text of the term *Chance* which he uses very frequently. It is here translated by 'probability,' because he uses it as interchangeable with *Wahrscheinlichkeit*. As the term 'probability' is used in a technical mathematical and statistical sense, however, it implies the possibility of numerical statement. In most of the cases where Weber uses *Chance* this is out of the question. It is, however, possible to speak in terms of higher and lower degrees of probability. To avoid confusion with the technical mathematical concept, the term 'likelihood' will often be used in the translation. It is by means of this concept that Weber, in a highly ingenious way, has bridged the gap between the interpretation of meaning and the inevitably more complex facts of overt action.—T.P.

ties because they are not 'understandable,' are naturally not on that account any the less important. This is true even for sociology in the present sense which restricts it to subjectively understandable phenomena—a usage which there is no intention of attempting to impose on anyone else. Such phenomena, however important, are simply treated by a different method from the others; they become conditions, stimuli, furthering or hindering circumstances of action.

9. Action in the sense of a subjectively understandable orientation of behaviour exists only as the behaviour of one or more *individual* human beings. For other cognitive purposes it may be convenient or necessary to consider the individual, for instance, as a collection of cells, as a complex of biochemical reactions, or to conceive his 'psychic' life as made up of a variety of different elements, however these may be defined. Undoubtedly such procedures yield valuable knowledge of causal relationships. But the behaviour of these elements, as expressed in such uniformities, is not subjectively understandable. This is true even of psychic elements because the more precisely they are formulated from a point of view of natural science, the less they are accessible to subjective understanding. This is never the road to interpretation in terms of subjective meaning. On the contrary, both for sociology in the present sense, and for history, the object of cognition is the subjective meaning-complex of action. The behaviour of physiological entities such as cells, or of any sort of psychic elements may at least in principle be observed and an attempt made to derive uniformities from such observations. It is further possible to attempt, with their help, to obtain a causal explanation of individual phenomena, that is, to subsume them under uniformities. But the subjective understanding of action takes the same account of this type of fact and uniformity as of any others not capable of subjective interpretation. This is true, for example, of physical, astronomical, geological, meteorological, geographical, botanical, zoological, and anatomical facts and of such facts as those aspects of psychopathology which are devoid of subjective meaning or the facts of the natural conditions of technological processes.

For still other cognitive purposes as, for instance, juristic, or for practical ends, it may on the other hand be convenient or even indispensable to treat social collectivities, such as states, associations, business corporations, foundations, as if they were individual persons. Thus they may be treated as the subjects of rights and duties or as the performers of legally significant actions. But for the subjective interpretation of action in sociological work these collectivities must be treated as *solely* the resultants and modes of organization of the particular acts of individual persons, since these alone can be treated as agents in a course of subjectively understandable action. Nevertheless, the sociologist cannot for his purposes afford to ignore these collective concepts derived from other disciplines. For the subjective interpretation of action has at least two important relations to these concepts. In the first place it is often necessary to employ very similar collective concepts, indeed often using the same terms, in order to obtain an understandable terminology. Thus both in legal terminology and in everyday speech the term 'state' is used both for the legal concept of the state and for the phenomena of social action to which its legal rules are relevant. For sociological purposes, however, the phenomenon 'the state' does not consist necessarily or even primarily of the elements which are relevant to legal analysis; and for sociological purposes there is no such thing as a collective personality which 'acts.' When reference is made in a sociological context to a 'state,' a 'nation,' a 'corporation,' a 'family,' or an 'army corps,' or to similar collectivities, what is meant is, on the contrary, *only* a certain kind of development of actual or possible social actions of individual persons. Both because of its precision and because it is established in general usage the juristic concept is taken over, but is used in an entirely different meaning.[21a]

Secondly, the subjective interpretation of action must take account of a fundamentally important fact. These concepts of collective entities which are found both in common sense and in juristic and other technical forms of thought, have a meaning in the minds of individual persons, partly as of something actually existing, partly as something with normative authority. This is true not only of judges and officials, but of ordinary private individuals as well. Actors thus in part orient their action to them, and in this role such ideas have a powerful, often a decisive, causal influence on the course of action of real individuals. This is above all true where the ideas concern a recognized positive or negative normative pattern.[22] Thus, for instance, one of the important aspects of the 'existence' of a modern state, precisely as a complex of social interaction of individual persons, consists in the fact that the action of various individuals is oriented to the belief that it exists or should exist, thus that its acts and laws are valid in the legal sense. . . . Though extremely pedantic and cumbersome it would be possible, if purposes of sociological terminology alone were involved, to eliminate such terms entirely, and substitute newly-coined words. This would be possible even though the word 'state' is used ordinarily not only to designate the legal concept but also the real process of action. But in the above important connexion, at least, this would naturally be impossible.

Thirdly, it is the method of the so-called 'organic' school of sociology [23] to attempt to understand social interaction by using as a point of departure the 'whole' within which the individual acts. His action and behaviour are then interpreted somewhat in the way that a physiologist would treat the role of an organ of the body in the 'economy' of the organism, that

---

21a [The papers in Section Four of this volume contain detailed discussions of collective concepts. See also the Introduction for that section.—Ed.]

22 By a negative normative pattern, Weber means one which prohibits certain possible modes of action.—T.P.

23 A classical example is Schäffle's brilliant work, *Bau und Leben des sozialen Körpers*.

is from the point of view of the survival of the latter.[24] How far in other disciplines this type of functional analysis of the relation of 'parts' to a 'whole' can be regarded as definitive, cannot be discussed here; but it is well known that the bio-chemical and bio-physical modes of analysis of the organism are on principle opposed to stopping there. For purposes of sociological analysis two things can be said. First this functional frame of reference is convenient for purposes of practical illustration and for provisional orientation. In these respects it is not only useful but indispensable. But at the same time if its cognitive value is overestimated and its concepts illegitimately 'reified,' [25] it can be highly dangerous. Secondly, in certain circumstances this is the only available way of determining just what processes of social action it is important to understand in order to explain a given phenomenon.[26] But this is only the beginning of sociological analysis as here understood. In the case of social collectivities, precisely as distinguished from organisms, we are in a position to go beyond merely demonstrating functional relationships and uniformities. We can accomplish something which is never attainable in the natural sciences, namely the subjective understanding of the action of the component individuals. The natural sciences on the other hand cannot do this, being limited to the formulation of causal uniformities in objects and events and the explanation of individual facts by applying them. We do not 'understand' the behaviour of cells, but can only observe the relevant functional relationships and generalize on the basis of these observations. This additional achievement of explanation by interpretive understanding, as distinguished from external observation, is of course attained only at a price—the more hypothetical and fragmentary character of its results. Nevertheless, subjective understanding is the specific characteristic of sociological knowledge.

[24] One of the most illuminating treatments of physiological problems from such a functional point of view, which is readily understandable to the layman, is W. B. Cannon: *The Wisdom of the Body*, second edition, 1938. The point of reference on this physiological level is not primarily survival value to the species in the sense of the Darwinian theory of evolution, but rather the maintenance of the individual organism as a 'going concern' in carrying through its typical life cycle. What is the life cycle, is to the physiologist essentially a matter of empirical observation.—T.P.

[25] The term 'reification' as used by Professor Morris Cohen in his book, *Reason and Nature*, seems to fit Weber's meaning exactly. A concept or system of concepts, which critical analysis can show to be abstract, is 'reified' when it is used naively as though it provided an adequate total description of the concrete phenomenon in question. The fallacy of 'reification' is virtually another name for what Professor Whitehead has called 'the fallacy of misplaced concreteness.' See his *Science and the Modern World*.—T.P.

[26] Compare the famous dictum of a well-known physiologist: 'sec. 10. The spleen. Of the spleen, gentlemen, we know nothing. So much for the spleen.' Actually, of course, he 'knew' a good deal about the spleen—its position, size, shape, etc.; but he could say nothing about its function, and it was his inability to do this that he called 'ignorance.'

[2] The Subjective Nature of Social Subject Matter

ERNEST NAGEL

The subject matter of the social sciences is frequently identified as purposive human action, directed to attaining various ends or "values," whether with conscious intent, by force of acquired habit, or because of unwitting involvement. A somewhat more restrictive characterization limits that subject matter to the responses men make to the actions of other men, in the light of expectations and "evaluations" concerning how these others will respond in turn.[1] On either delimitation of that subject matter, its study is commonly said to presuppose familiarity with the motives and other psychological matters that constitute the springs of purposive human behavior, as well as with the aims and values whose attainment is the explicit or implicit goal of such behavior.

According to many writers, however, motives, dispositions, intended goals, and values are not matters open to sensory inspection, and can be neither made familiar nor identified by way of an exclusive use of procedures that are suitable for exploring the publicly observable subject matters of the "purely behavioral" (or natural) sciences. On the contrary, these are matters with which we can become conversant solely from our "subjective experience." Moreover, the distinctions that are relevant to social science subject matter (whether they are employed to characterize inanimate objects, as in the case of terms such as 'tool' and 'sentence,' or to designate types of human behavior, as in the case of terms such as 'crime' and 'punishment') cannot be defined except by reference to "mental attitudes" and cannot be understood except by those who have had the subjective experience of possessing such attitudes. To say that an object is a tool, for example, is allegedly to say that it is *expected* to produce certain effects by those who so characterize that

From *The Structure of Science* by Ernest Nagel, © 1961, by Harcourt, Brace & World, Inc., New York, and by Routledge & Kegan Paul Ltd., London, pp. 473–485, and reprinted with permission of the publishers.

1 Max Weber, *The Theory of Social and Economic Organization*, New York, 1947, p. 118. On the more restrictive definition, a farmer tilling the soil merely to provide food for himself is not engaged in social activity. His behavior is social only if he evaluates plans to satisfy his own wants by reference to the assumed wants of other men.

object. Accordingly, the various "things" that may need to be mentioned in explaining purposive action must be construed in terms of what the human actors *themselves believe* about those things, rather than in terms of what can be discovered about the things by way of the objective methods of the natural sciences. As one proponent of this claim states the case, "A medicine or a cosmetic, e.g., for the purposes of social study, are not what cures an ailment or improves a person's looks, but what people think will have that effect." And he goes on to say that, when the social sciences explain human behavior by invoking men's knowledge of laws of nature, "what is relevant in the study of society is not whether these laws of nature are true in any objective sense, but solely whether they are believed and acted upon by the people." [2]

In short, the categories of description and explanation in the social sciences are held to be radically "subjective," so that these disciplines are forced to rely on "nonobjective" techniques of inquiry. The social scientist must therefore "interpret" the materials of his study by imaginatively identifying himself with the actors in social processes, viewing the situations they face as the actors themselves view them, and constructing "models of motivation" in which springs of action and commitments to various values are imputed to these human agents. The social scientist is able to do these things, only because he is himself an active agent in social processes, and can therefore understand in the light of his own "subjective" experiences the "internal meanings" of social actions. A purely "objective" or "behavioristic" social science is in consequence held to be a vain hope; for to exclude on principle every vestige of subjective, motivational interpretation from the study of human affairs is in effect to eliminate from such study the consideration of every genuine social fact.[3]

This account of social science subject matter raises many issues, but only the following three will receive attention in the present context: (1) Are the distinctions required for exploring that subject matter exclusively "subjective?" (2) Is a "behavioristic" account of social phenomena inadequate? and (3) Do imputations of "subjective" states to human agents fall outside the scope of the logical canons employed in inquiries into "objective" properties?

1. It is beyond dispute that human behavior is frequently purposive; and it is likewise beyond question that when such behavior is described or explained, whether by social scientists or by laymen, various kinds of "subjective" (or psychological) states are commonly assumed to underlie

2 F. A. Hayek, *The Counter-Revolution of Science*, Glencoe, Ill., 1952, p. 30.

3 R. M. MacIver, *Social Causation*, New York, 1942, Chap. 14; Max Weber, *op. cit.*, Chap. 1, esp. Sec. 1; [Reprinted as the first selection in this volume.] Charles H. Cooley, *Sociological Theory and Social Research*, New York, 1930, pp. 290–308; Ludwig von Mises, *Theory and History*, New Haven, Conn., 1957, Chap. 11; Peter Winch, *The Idea of a Social Science*, London, 1958, esp. Chap. 2.

its manifestations. Nevertheless, as is evident from the biological sciences, many aspects of goal-directed activities can frequently be investigated without requiring the postulation of such states. But what is more to the point, even when the behaviors studied by the social sciences are indisputably directed toward some consciously entertained ends, the social sciences do not confine themselves to using only distinctions that refer to psychological states exclusively; nor is it clear, moreover, why these disciplines should place such restrictions upon themselves. For example, in order to account for the adoption of certain rules of conduct by a given community, it may be relevant to inquire into the ways in which members of the community cultivate the soil, construct shelters, or preserve food for future use; and the overt behaviors these individuals exhibit in pursuing these tasks cannot be described in purely "subjective" terms.

Furthermore, even though purposive action is sometimes partly explained with the help of assumptions concerning dispositions, intentions, or beliefs of the actors, other assumptions concerning matters with which the actors are altogether unfamiliar may also contribute to the explanation of their action. Thus, as the passage quoted above makes clear, if we wish to account for the behavior of men who believe in the medicinal properties of a given substance, it is obviously important to distinguish between the question whether that belief has any influence upon the conduct of the believers, and the question whether the substance does in fact have the assumed medicinal properties. On the other hand, there appear to be excellent reasons for rejecting the conclusion, alleged to follow from this distinction, that in explaining purposive behavior the social scientist must use no information available to himself but not available to those manifesting the behavior.[4] For example, southern cotton planters in the United States before the Civil War were certainly unacquainted with the laws of modern soil chemistry, and mistakenly believed that the use of animal manure would preserve indefinitely the fertility of the cotton plantations. Nevertheless, a social scientist's familiarity with those laws can help explain why, under that treatment, the soil upon which cotton was grown gradually deteriorated, and why in consequence there was an increasing need for virgin land to raise cotton if the normal cotton crop was not to decrease. It is certainly not evident why such explanations should be ruled out from the social sciences. But if they are not ruled out, and since they patently involve notions not referring to the "subjective" states of purposive agents, it does become evident that the categories of description and explanation in those sciences are not exclusively "subjective" ones.

----

4 "Any knowledge which we may happen to possess about the true nature of the material thing [i.e., the alleged medicine], but which the people whose actions we want to explain do not possess, is as little relevant to the explanation of their actions as our private disbelief in the efficacy of a magic charm will help us to understand the behavior of the savage who believes in it."—F. A. Hayek, op. cit., p. 30.

2. The standpoint in social science known as "behaviorism" is an adaptation of the program of research first adopted by many psychologists in the second decade of this century. That program was the expression of a widespread revolt against the vagueness and general unreliability of psychological data obtained by introspective analyses of mental states, and its proponents took as their immediate model for psychological inquiry the procedures employed by students of animal behavior. In its initial formulation, behaviorism recommended the wholesale rejection of introspection as a technique of psychological study, and its announced aim was to investigate human behavior in the manner of inquiries into chemical processes or into the behavior of animals, without any appeal or reference to the contents of consciousness. Moreover, some of its advocates advanced distinctive views on substantive psychological issues (for example, on the "conditioning" mechanisms involved in learning or in literary creation), though the simpleminded "mechanistic" theories they adopted were not entailed by their rejection of introspection. It is worth passing notice, however, that even exponents of this radical form of behaviorism did not *deny the existence* of conscious mental states; and their rejection of introspection, in favor of the study of overt behavior, was controlled primarily by a *methodological* concern to base psychology upon publicly observable data.[5]

But in any event, behaviorism has undergone important transformation since its initial formulation, and there are perhaps no psychologists (or for that matter, social scientists) currently calling themselves "behaviorists" who subscribe to the earlier version's unqualified condemnation of introspection. On the contrary, professed behaviorists today generally accept introspective *reports* by experimental subjects, not as statements *about* private psychic states of the subjects, but as observable verbal *responses* the subjects make under given conditions; and accordingly, introspective reports are included among the objective data upon which psychological generalizations are to be founded. Furthermore, contemporary behaviorists operating within this more liberal methodological framework have been investigating many (frequently nonoverlapping) areas of human behavior, both individual (e.g., perceptual discrimination, learning, or problem solving) and social (e.g., communication, group decisions, or group cohesiveness); and they have proposed a number of special mechanisms to account for these various phenomena—mechanisms that for the most part differ among themselves and also differ substantially from the simple mechanisms associated with earlier expounders of the behavioristic standpoint. However, none of these more recently suggested mechanisms is known to be adequate for explaining the entire range of human conduct, so that behaviorism (like most "schools" of contemporary psychology) continues to be a diversified program of research which stresses certain methodological considerations, rather than a

[5] Cf. J. B. Watson, "Psychology as the Behaviorist Views It," *Psychological Review*, Vol. 20 (1913), pp. 158–77, and the same author's *Behaviorism*, New York, 1930.

school committed to some particular, minutely articulated substantive theory. A similar state of affairs exists at present among social scientists who either profess to be behaviorists or manifest sympathies for a behavioristic approach. In consequence, the term "behaviorism" does not have a precise doctrinal connotation; and students of human conduct who designate themselves as behaviorists do so chiefly because of their adherence to a methodology that places a premium on objective (or intersubjectively observable) data.[6]

In the light of this situation, however, it is not easy to assess the claim that a "behavioristic" approach to the study of social phenomena is self-defeating, because it is usually not clear what is the intended target of the criticism. Much of the criticism is certainly directed against what is a caricature of that approach. Thus, when it is asserted that a consistent behaviorist cannot properly talk of "the reactions of people to what our senses tell us are similar objects" (such as red circles), but only of "the reactions to stimuli which are identical in a strictly physical sense" (i.e., of the effects of light waves of a given frequency on a particular part of the retina of the human eye),[7] or when it is said that a behaviorist does not recognize the difference between purely reflex action (such as a knee jerk) and purposive behavior (such as is manifested in the building of a railroad),[8] the attack is in each case leveled against a straw man, created on the model of a biophysicist debauched by dubious epistemology, and not against a position held by any existing behaviorists. To be sure, behaviorists have sometimes shown themselves to be grossly insensitive to important features of human experience; and they have also often proposed explanations of psychological and social processes that turned out to be far too crude to deal adequately with the actual complexities of human conduct. But behaviorists do not have a monopoly in either type of failing; and as has been already indicated, acceptance of behaviorism as a methodological approach in no way necessitates the acceptance of any particular substantive theory.

An assumption underlying much criticism of behaviorism is that a consistent behavorist must deny the very existence of "subjective" or "private" mental states; and it is therefore pertinent to discuss this contention briefly. In the first place, probably everyone recognizes the distinction between, say, a directly felt pain and the overtly behavioral manifestations of being in pain (such as groans or muscular spasms). In any event, anyone who rejects such distinctions as invalid is controverting facts too well established to be

---

6 Cf. Kenneth W. Spence, "The Postulates of 'Behaviorism,'" *Psychological Review*, Vol. 55 (1948), pp. 67–78; Gardiner Murphy, *Historical Introduction to Modern Psychology*, New York, 1951, Chaps. 18 and 19; *The Science of Man in the World Crisis* (ed. by Ralph Linton), New York, 1945, esp. the chapters by Clyde Kluckhohn and William H. Kelly, "The Concept of Culture," Melville J. Herskovits, "The Processes of Cultural Change," and George P. Murdock, "The Common Denominator of Culture"; and Paul F. Lazarsfeld, "Problems in Methodology," in *Sociology Today* (ed. by Robert K. Merton, Leonard Broom, and Leonard S. Cottrell, Jr.), New York, 1959.

7 F. H. Hayek, *op. cit.*, p. 45.

8 Ludwig von Mises, *op. cit.*, p. 246.

open to significant doubt. But in the second place, a behaviorist to be consistent is compelled neither to renounce such familiar distinctions nor to abandon the central postulates of his methodological position. For he need not be a "reductive materialist," for whom the term 'pain' (or other admittedly "subjective" terms) is *synonymous* with some expression containing only terms belonging unmistakably to the languages of physics, physiology, or general logic. On the contrary, he will be well advised to reject this reductive thesis, since it confounds facts established in physics or physiology with the quite different types of facts established in logical inquiries into relations of meaning—so that it commits the error commonly made in another context when, for example, the meaning of the word 'red' (as used both currently as well as long before the advent of the electromagnetic theory of light, to designate a visible color) is identified with the meaning of, say, 'electromagnetic vibrations with wave lengths of approximately 7100 angstrom units.' [9] A behaviorist who does reject this mistaken thesis can therefore readily acknowledge that men are capable of having emotions, images, ideas, or plans; that these psychic states are "private" to the individual in whose body they occur, in the sense that this individual alone can *directly* experience their occurrence, because of the privileged relation his body has to those states; and that consequently a man can in general attest to being in some psychic state without having to examine first the publicly observable state of his own body (e.g., his own facial expression or his own utterances), although other men can ascertain whether he is in that psychic state only on the basis of such examination.[10]

However, the behaviorist also assumes that psychic states occur only in bodies having certain types of organization; that such states are "adjectival" or "adverbial" of those bodies, rather that substantive agents (or "entities") inhabiting the bodies; that the occurrence of a psychic state in a body is always accompanied by certain overt and publicly observable behaviors (frequently on a "molar" or macroscopic level) of that body; that such overt behaviors (including verbal responses) constitute a sufficient basis for grounding conclusions about the entire range of human experience; and that observation of such overt behavior is not only the sole source of information anyone has concerning other men's experiences and actions, but also provides

[9] Cf. the discussion of this issue in Chapter 11, *The Structure of Science* by Ernest Nagel.

[10] Just how much confirming evidence for a statement is needed to warrant its acceptance is a difficult problem for which there is no general solution. There are undoubtedly many cases in which a minimum of confirming evidence suffices, so that additional evidence is sometimes regarded as gratuitous. Introspective statements frequently fall into this class, although not all of them are of this sort, since they may indeed be false and are sometimes accepted as true only when elaborate controls are instituted. However, introspective statements are not unique in being accepted on the basis of a bare minimum of supporting evidence. Thus, a chemist who observes that a piece of blue litmus paper turns red when it is immersed in a liquid may assert that the paper has indeed turned red and that the liquid is an acid. Moreover, he may regard it a waste of time to look for further evidence to support these claims, even though additional evidence could be found for his statements.

generally more reliable data for conclusions even about an individual's own character and capacities than is supplied by introspective analyses of psychic states. Accordingly, a behaviorist can maintain without inconsistency that there are indeed such things as private psychic states, and also that the controlled study of overt behavior is nevertheless the only sound procedure for achieving reliable knowledge concerning individual and social action.

Moreover, although some contemporary behaviorists believe a science of man can be developed which employs only distinctions "definable" in terms of molar human behavior, there is nothing in the methodological orientation of behaviorism to preclude even such behaviorists from adopting psychological theories postulating various kinds of mechanisms that are not open to direct public observation. Many such behaviorists do in fact subscribe to theories of this type. There are, to be sure, some behaviorists who, without denying the *existence* of psychic states, seek to develop theories all of whose terms refer exclusively to states and processes (whether molar or molecular) that are either physical, chemical, or physiological. Behaviorists in this category are therefore hostile to psychological theories purporting to *explain* overt human behavior by reference to various "mentalistic" occurrences —for example, theories invoking "subjective" intentions or ends-in-view to account for men's overt behaviors. However, behaviorism of this variety is clearly a program of theoretical and experimental research, comparable to the program of mechanists in biology, which hopes to achieve a comprehensive system of explanation for human behavior through the "reduction" of psychology to other sciences. The objectives of the program have certainly not been attained, and perhaps never will be. But provided that the program does not dismiss well-attested forms of human conduct as in some sense "unreal"—and there is no reason inherent to the program why it should—it cannot be ruled out on a priori grounds as illegitimate or as intrinsically absurd.

It is therefore difficult to escape the conclusion that behaviorism as a methodological orientation (as distinct from behaviorism as some particular substantive theory of human behavior) is not inherently inadequate to the study of purposive human action, and that in consequence the repeated claims asserting the essential inappropriateness of a behavioristic approach to the subject matter of the social sciences rest on no firm foundations.

3. But however this may be, let us assume that the distinctive aim of the social sciences is to "understand" social phenomena in terms of "meaningful" categories, so that the social scientist seeks to explain such phenomena by imputing various "subjective" states to human agents participating in social processes. The crucial question that thus remains to be examined is whether such imputations involve the use of logical canons which are different from those employed in connection with the imputation of "objective" traits to things in other areas of inquiry.

It will be helpful in discussing this issue to have before us some examples of "meaningful" explanations of human actions. Let us begin with a simple one, in which the writer stresses the essential difference

between a paper flying before the wind and a man flying from a pursuing crowd. The paper knows no fear and the wind no hate, but without fear and hate the man would not fly nor the crowd pursue. If we try to reduce fear to its bodily concomitants we merely substitute the concomitants for the reality expressed as fear. We denude the world of meanings for the sake of a theory, itself a false meaning which deprives us of all the rest. We can interpret experience only on the level of experience.[11]

A more complex illustration is supplied by a historian, who maintains that

We reject the theory that the intellectual movement of the 18th century was the sole cause of the French Revolution because we know that there participated in that upheaval large masses of peasants and workers, illiterate masses lacking any knowledge of philosophical or political doctrines; and by analogy with our own personal experience we hold that, were we illiterate and ignorant, and were we to revolt against the society in which we live, the cause of our revolutionary activities should be traced not to ideological impulses but to other causes—for instance, to our economic ills. On the other hand, we hold that among the causes of the French Revolution should be numbered the philosophical and political doctrines developed in France during the half century preceding the Revolution, because we have noticed that the cultivated classes continually invoked such doctrines while they were destroying the old regime; and again the analogy with our personal experience leads us to think that none of us when taking part in a revolutionary movement would publicly profess philosophical and political doctrine which did not really form an ingredient in our beliefs. All the reasonings of the historian and the social scientist can be reduced to this common denominator of analogy with our inward experience, whereas the [natural] scientist lacks the help of this analogy.[12]

But the example that has come to serve as the classical model for "meaningful" explanations of social phenomena is Max Weber's carefully worked out account of modern capitalism, in which he attributes the development of this type of economic enterprise at least in part to the spread of the religious beliefs and the precepts of practical conduct associated with ascetic forms of Protestantism.[13] Weber's discussion is too detailed to permit brief summary. However, the structure of his argument (and of other "meaningful" explanations) can be represented by the following abstract schema. Suppose a social phenomenon E (e.g., the development of modern capitalistic enterprise) is found to occur under a complex set of social conditions C (e.g., widespread membership in certain religious groups, such as those professing Calvinistic Protestantism), where some of the individuals participating in C generally also participate in E.[14] But individuals who participate in E are assumed to

[11] R. M. MacIver, *Society*, New York, 1931, p. 530.
[12] Gaetano Salvemini, *The Historian and Scientist*, Cambridge, Mass., 1939, p. 71.
[13] Max Weber, *The Protestant Ethic and the Spirit of Capitalism*, London, 1930.
[14] Weber tried to show that E did not occur in the absence of C. But this point is not directly relevant to the specific issue under discussion.

be committed to certain values (or to be in certain "subjective" states) V_E (e.g., they prize honesty, orderliness, and abstemious labor); and individuals who participate in C are assumed to be in the subjective state V_C (e.g., they believe in the sacredness of a worldly calling). However, V_C and V_E are also alleged to be "meaningfully" related, in view of the motivational patterns we find in our own personal experiences—for example, by reflecting on how our own emotions, values, beliefs, and actions hang together, we come to recognize an intimate connection between believing that one's vocation in life is consecrated by divine ordinance, and believing that one's life should not be marked by indolence or self-indulgence. Accordingly, by imputing subjective states to the agents engaged in E and C, we can "understand" why it is that E occurs under conditions C, not simply as a mere conjuncture or succession of phenomena, but as manifestations of subjective states whose interrelations are familiar to us from a consideration of our own affective and cognitive states.

These examples make it clear that such "meaningful" explanations invariably employ two types of assumptions which are of particular relevance to the present discussion: an assumption, singular in form, characterizing specified individuals as being in certain psychological states at indicated times (e.g., the assumption, in the first quotation above, that members of the crowd hated the man they were pursuing); and an assumption, general in form, stating the ways such states are related to one another as well as to certain overt behaviors (e.g., the assumption in the second quotation that men participating in revolutionary movements do not publicly profess a political doctrine unless they believe in it). However, neither of such assumptions is self-certifying, and evidence is required for each of them if the explanation of which they are parts is to be more than an exercise in uncontrolled imagination. Competent evidence for assumptions about the attitudes and actions of other men is often difficult to obtain; but it is certainly not obtained merely by introspecting one's own sentiments or by examining one's own beliefs as to how such sentiments are likely to be manifested in overt action—as responsible advocates of "interpretative" explanations have themselves often emphasized (e.g., with vigor and illumination by Max Weber). We may identify ourselves in imagination with a trader in wheat, and conjecture what course of conduct we would adopt were we confronted with some problem requiring decisive action in a fluctuating market for that commodity. But conjecture is not fact. The sentiments or envisioned plans we may impute to the trader either may not coincide with those he actually possesses, or even if they should so coincide may eventuate in conduct on his part quite different from the course of action we had imagined would be the "reasonable" one to adopt under the assumed circumstances. The history of anthropology amply testifies to the blunders that can be committed when categories appropriate for describing familiar social processes are extrapolated without further scrutiny to the study of strange cultures. Nor is the frequent claim well founded that relations of dependence between psychological processes with which we have personal experience, or between such processes and the overt actions in which they may be manifested, can be comprehended with a clearer "insight" into the reasons for their being what they are than can any relations of dependence between nonpsychological events and processes. Do we really understand more fully and with greater warranted certainty why an insult tends to produce anger, than why a rainbow is produced when the sun's rays strike raindrops at a certain angle?

Moreover, it is by no means obvious that a social scientist cannot account for men's actions unless he has experienced in his own person the psychic states he imputes to them or unless he can successfully recreate such states in imagination. Must a psychiatrist be at least partly demented if he is to be competent for studying the mentally ill? Is a historian incapable of explaining the careers and social changes effected by men like Hitler unless he can recapture in imagination the frenzied hatreds that may have animated such an individual? Are mild-tempered and emotionally stable social scientists unable to understand the causes and consequences of mass hysteria, institutionalized sexual orgy, or manifestations of pathological lusts for power? The factual evidence certainly lends no support to these and similar suppositions. Indeed, *discoursive* knowledge—i.e., knowledge statable in *propositional form*, about "common-sense" affairs as well as about the material explored by the specialized procedures of the natural and social sciences—is not a matter of *having* sensations, images, or feelings, whether vivid or faint; and it consists neither in identifying oneself in some ineffable manner with the objects of knowledge, nor in reproducing in some form of direct experience the subject matter of knowledge. On the other hand, discoursive knowledge is a *symbolic* representation of only certain selected phases of some subject matter; it is the product of a process that deliberately aims at formulating relations between traits of a subject matter, so that one set of traits mentioned in the formulations can be taken as a reliable sign of other traits mentioned; and it involves as a necessary condition for its being warranted, the possibility of verifying these formulations through controlled sensory observation by anyone prepared to make the effort to verify them.

In consequence, we *know* that a man fleeing from a pursuing crowd that is animated by hatred toward him is in a state of fear, without our having experienced such violent fears and hatred or without imaginatively recreating such emotions in ourselves—just as we can *know* that the temperature of a piece of wire is rising because the velocities of its constituent molecules are increasing, without having to imagine what it is like to be a rapidly moving molecule. In both instances "internal states" that are not directly observable are imputed to the objects mentioned in explanation of their behaviors. Accordingly, if we can rightly claim to *know* that the individuals do possess the states imputed to them and that possession of such states tends to produce the specified forms of behavior, we can do so only on the basis of evidence obtained by observation of "objective" occurrences—in one case, by observation of overt human behavior (including men's verbal responses), in the other case, by observation of purely physical changes. To be sure, there are important differences between the specific characters of the states imputed in the two cases: in the case of the human actors the states are psychological or "subjective," and the social scientist making the imputation may indeed have first-hand personal experience of them, but in the case of the wire and other inanimate objects they are not. Nevertheless, despite these differences, the crucial point is that the logical canons employed by responsible social scientists in assessing the objective evidence for the imputation of psychological states do not appear to differ essentially (though they may often be applied less rigorously) from the canons employed for analogous purposes by responsible students in other areas of inquiry.

In sum, the fact that the social scientist, unlike the student of inanimate nature, is able to project himself by sympathetic imagination into the phenomena he is attempting to understand, is pertinent to questions concerning the *origins* of his explanatory hypotheses but not to questions concerning their validity. His ability to enter into relations of empathy with the human actors in some social process may indeed be heuristically important in his efforts to *invent* suitable hypotheses which will explain the process. Nevertheless, his empathic identification with those individuals does not, by itself, constitute *knowledge*. The fact that he achieves such identification does not annul the need for objective evidence, assessed in accordance with logical principles that are common to all controlled inquiries, to support his imputation of subjective states to those human agents.[15]

[3] Actions, Reasons, and Causes

DONALD DAVIDSON

What is the relation between a reason and an action when the reason explains the action by giving the agent's reason for doing what he did? We

Reprinted from *The Journal of Philosophy*, LX, No. 23 (November 7, 1963), pp. 685–700 with permission of the author and the editors.

15 The heuristic function of such imaginary identification is discussed by Theodore Abel, "The Operation Called *Verstehen*," *American Journal of Sociology*, Vol. 54 (1948), pp. 211–18. [Reprinted in Herbert Feigl and May Brodbeck, eds., *Readings in the Philosophy of Science*, Appleton-Century-Crofts, New York, 1953, pp. 677–687.]

may call such explanations *rationalizations,* and say that the reason *rationalizes* the action.

In this paper I want to defend the ancient—and commonsense—position that rationalization is a species of ordinary causal explanation. The defense no doubt requires some redeployment, but not more or less complete abandonment of the position, as urged by many recent writers.[1]

– I –

A reason rationalizes an action only if it leads us to see something the agent saw, or thought he saw, in his action—some feature, consequence, or aspect of the action the agent wanted, desired, prized, held dear, thought dutiful, beneficial, obligatory, or agreeable. We cannot explain why someone did what he did simply by saying the particular action appealed to him; we must indicate what it was about the action that appealed. Whenever someone does something for a reason, therefore, he can be characterized as (*a*) having some sort of pro attitude toward actions of a certain kind, and (*b*) believing (or knowing, perceiving, noticing, remembering) that his action is of that kind. Under (*a*) are to be included desires, wantings, urges, promptings, and a great variety of moral views, aesthetic principles, economic prejudices, social conventions, and public and private goals and values in so far as these can be interpreted as attitudes of an agent directed toward actions of a certain kind. The word 'attitude' does yeoman service here, for it must cover not only permanent character traits that show themselves in a lifetime of behavior, like love of children or a taste for loud company, but also the most passing fancy that prompts a unique action, like a sudden desire to touch a woman's elbow. In general, pro attitudes must not be taken for convictions, however temporary, that every action of a certain kind ought to be performed, is worth performing, or is, all things considered, desirable. On the contrary, a man may all his life have a yen, say, to drink a can of paint, without ever, at the moment he yields, believing it would be worth doing.

Giving the reason why an agent did something is often a matter of naming the pro attitude (*a*) or the related belief (*b*) or both; let me call this pair the *primary reason* why the agent performed the action. Now it is possible to reformulate the claim that rationalizations are causal explanations, and give structure to the argument as well, by stating two theses about primary reasons:

[1] Some examples: G. E. M. Anscombe, *Intention,* Oxford, 1959; Stuart Hampshire, *Thought and Action,* London, 1959; H. L. A. Hart and A. M. Honoré, *Causation in the Law,* Oxford, 1959; William Dray, *Laws and Explanation in History,* Oxford, 1957; and most of the books in the series edited by R. F. Holland, *Studies in Philosophical Psychology,* including Anthony Kenny, *Action, Emotion and Will,* London, 1963, and A. I. Melden, *Free Action,* London, 1961. Page references in parentheses will all be to these works.

1. For us to understand how a reason of any kind rationalizes an action it is necessary and sufficient that we see, at least in essential outline, how to construct a primary reason.
2. The primary reason for an action is its cause.

I shall argue for these points in turn.

–II–

I flip the switch, turn on the light, and illuminate the room. Unbeknownst to me I also alert a prowler to the fact that I am home. Here I do not do four things, but only one, of which four descriptions have been given.[2] I flipped the switch because I wanted to turn on the light, and by saying I wanted to turn on the light I explain (give my reason for, rationalize) the flipping. But I do not, by giving this reason, rationalize my alerting of the prowler nor my illuminating of the room. Since reasons may rationalize what someone does when it is described in one way and not when it is described in another, we cannot treat what was done simply as a term in sentences like 'My reason for flipping the switch was that I wanted to turn on the light'; otherwise we would be forced to conclude, from the fact that flipping the switch was identical with alerting the prowler, that my reason for alerting the prowler was that I wanted to turn on the light. Let us mark this quasi-intensional [3] character of action descriptions in rationalizations by stating a bit more precisely a necessary condition for primary reasons:

C1. R is a primary reason why an agent performed the action A under the description d only if R consists of a pro attitude of the agent toward

2 We would not call my unintentional alerting of the prowler an action, but it should not be inferred from this that alerting the prowler is therefore something different from flipping the switch, say just its consequence. Actions, performances, and events not involving intention are alike in that they are often referred to or defined partly in terms of some terminal stage, outcome, or consequence.

The word 'action' does not very often occur in ordinary speech, and when it does it is usually reserved for fairly portentous occasions. I follow a useful philosophical practice in calling anything an agent does intentionally an action, including intentional omissions. What is really needed is some suitably generic term to bridge the following gap: suppose 'A' is a description of an action, 'B' is a description of something done voluntarily, though not intentionally, and 'C' is a description of something done involuntarily and unintentionally; finally, suppose $A = B = C$. Then A, B, and C are the same—what? 'Action,' 'event,' 'thing done,' each have, at least in some contexts, a strange ring when coupled with the wrong sort of description. Only the question "Why did you (he) do A?" has the true generality required. Obviously, the problem is greatly aggravated if we assume, as Melden does (*Free Action*, 85), that an action ("raising one's arm") can be identical with a bodily movement ("one's arm going up").

3 "Quasi-intensional" because, besides its intensional aspect, the description of the action must also refer in rationalizations; otherwise it could be true that an action was done for a certain reason and yet the action not have been performed. Compare 'the author of *Waverly*' in 'George IV knew the author of *Waverly* wrote *Waverly*.'

actions with a certain property, and a belief of the agent that A under the description d, has that property.

How can my wanting to turn on the light be (part of) a primary reason, since it appears to lack the required element of generality? We may be taken in by the verbal parallel between 'I turned on the light' and 'I wanted to turn on the light.' The first clearly refers to a particular event, so we conclude that the second has this same event as its object. Of course it is obvious that the event of my turning on the light can't be referred to in the same way by both sentences, since the existence of the event is required by the truth of 'I turned on the light' but not by the truth of 'I wanted to turn on the light.' If the reference were the same in both cases, the second sentence would entail the first; but in fact the sentences are logically independent. What is less obvious, at least until we attend to it, is that the event whose occurrence makes 'I turned on the light' true cannot be called the object, however intensional, of 'I wanted to turn on the light.' If I turned on the light, then I must have done it at a precise moment, in a particular way— every detail is fixed. But it makes no sense to demand that my want be directed at an action performed at any one moment or done in some unique manner. Any one of an indefinitely large number of actions would satisfy the want, and can be considered equally eligible as its object. Wants and desires often are trained on physical objects. However, 'I want that gold watch in the window' is not a primary reason, and explains why I went into the store only because it suggests a primary reason—for example, that I wanted to buy the watch.

Because 'I wanted to turn on the light' and 'I turned on the light' are logically independent, the first can be used to give a reason why the second is true. Such a reason gives minimal information: it implies that the action was intentional, and wanting tends to exclude some other pro attitudes, such as a sense of duty or obligation. But the exclusion depends very much on the action and the context of explanation. Wanting seems pallid beside lusting, but it would be odd to deny that someone who lusted after a woman or a cup of coffee wanted her or it. It is not unnatural, in fact, to treat wanting as a genus including all pro attitudes as species. When we do this and when we know some action is intentional, it is empty to add that the agent wanted to do it. In such cases, it is easy to answer the question 'Why did you do it?' with 'For no reason,' meaning not that there is no reason but that there is no *further* reason, no reason that cannot be inferred from the fact that the action was done intentionally; no reason, in other words, besides wanting to do it. This last point is not essential to the present argument, but it is of interest because it defends the possibility of defining an intentional action as one done for a reason.

A primary reason consists of a belief and an attitude, but it is generally otiose to mention both. If you tell me you are easing the jib because you think that will stop the main from backing, I don't need to be told that you want to stop the main from backing; and if you say you are biting your thumb at me because you want to insult me, there is no point in adding that you think that by biting your thumb at me you will insult me. Similarly, many explanations of actions in terms of reasons that are not primary do not require mention of the primary reason to complete the story. If I say I am pulling weeds because I want a beautiful lawn, it would be fatuous to eke out the account with 'And so I see something desirable in any action that does, or has a good chance of, making the lawn beautiful.' Why insist that there is any *step,* logical or psychological, in the transfer of desire from an end that is not an action to the actions one conceives as means? It serves the argument as well that the desired end explains the action only if what are believed by the agent to be means are desired.

Fortunately, it is not necessary to classify and analyze the many varieties of emotions, sentiments, moods, motives, passions, and hungers whose mention may answer the question 'Why did you do it?' in order to see how, when such mention rationalizes the action, a primary reason is involved. Claustrophobia gives a man's reason for leaving a cocktail party because we know people want to avoid, escape from, be safe from, put distance between themselves and, what they fear. Jealousy is the motive in a poisoning because, among other things, the poisoner believes his action will harm his rival, remove the cause of his agony, or redress an injustice, and these are the sorts of things a jealous man wants to do. When we learn a man cheated his son out of greed, we do not necessarily know what the primary reason was, but we know there was one, and its general nature. Ryle analyzes 'he boasted from vanity' into "he boasted on meeting the stranger and his doing so satisfies the lawlike proposition that whenever he finds a chance of securing the admiration and envy of others, he does whatever he thinks will produce this admiration and envy" (*The Concept of Mind,* 89). This analysis is often, and perhaps justly, criticized on the ground that a man may boast from vanity just once. But if Ryle's boaster did what he did from vanity, then something entailed by Ryle's analysis is true: the boaster wanted to secure the admiration and envy of others, and he believed that his action would produce this admiration and envy; true or false, Ryle's analysis does not dispense with primary reasons, but depends upon them.

To know a primary reason why someone acted as he did is to know an intention with which the action was done. If I turn left at the fork because I want to get to Katmandu, my intention in turning left is to get to Katmandu. But to know the intention is not necessarily to know the primary reason in full detail. If James goes to church with the intention of pleasing his mother, then he must have some pro attitude toward pleasing his mother, but it needs more information to tell whether his reason is that he enjoys pleasing his mother, or thinks it right, his duty, or an obligation. The expression 'the intention with which James went to church' has the outward form of a description, but in fact it is syncategorematic and cannot be taken to refer to an entity, state, disposition, or event. Its function in context is to generate new descriptions of actions in terms of their reasons; thus 'James went to church with the intention of pleasing his mother' yields a new, and fuller, description of the action described in 'James went to church.' Essentially the same process goes on when I answer the question 'Why are you bobbing around that way?' with 'I'm knitting, weaving, exercising, sculling, cuddling, training fleas.'

Straight description of an intended result often explains an action better than stating that the result was intended or desired. 'It will soothe your nerves' explains why I pour you a shot as efficiently as 'I want to do something to soothe your nerves,' since the first in the context of explanation implies the second; but the first does better, because, if it is true, the facts will justify my choice of action. Because justifying and explaining an action so often go hand in hand, we frequently indicate the primary reason for an action by making a claim which, if true, would also verify, vindicate, or support the relevant belief or attitude of the agent. 'I knew I ought to return it,' 'The paper said it was going to snow,' 'You stepped on *my* toes,' all, in appropriate reason-giving contexts, perform this familiar dual function.

The justifying role of a reason, given this interpretation, depends upon the explanatory role, but the converse does not hold. Your stepping on my toes neither explains nor justifies my stepping on your toes unless I believe you stepped on my toes, but the belief alone, true or false, explains my action.

–III–

In the light of a primary reason, an action is revealed as coherent with certain traits, long- or short-termed, characteristic or not, of the agent, and the agent is shown in his role of Rational Animal. Corresponding to the belief and attitude of a primary reason for an action, we can always construct (with a little ingenuity) the premises of a syllogism from which it follows that the action has some (as Miss Anscombe calls it) "desirability characteristic." [4] Thus there is a certain irreducible—though somewhat anemic—sense in which every rationalization justifies: from the agent's point of view there was, when he acted, something to be said for the action.

Noting that nonteleological causal explanations do not display the element of justification provided by reasons, some philosophers have concluded

[4] Miss Anscombe denies that the practical syllogism is deductive. This she does partly because she thinks of the practical syllogism, as Aristotle does, as corresponding to a piece of practical reasoning (whereas for me it is only part of the analysis of the concept of a reason with which someone acted), and therefore she is bound, again following Aristotle, to think of the conclusion of a practical syllogism as corresponding to a judgment, not merely that the action has a desirable characteristic, but that the action is desirable (reasonable, worth doing, etc.).

that the concept of cause that applies elsewhere cannot apply to the relation between reasons and actions, and that the pattern of justification provides, in the case of reasons, the required explanation. But suppose we grant that reasons alone justify in explaining actions; it does not follow that the explanation is not also—and necessarily—causal. Indeed our first condition for primary reasons (C1) is designed to help set rationalizations apart from other sorts of explanation. If rationalization is, as I want to argue, a species of causal explanation, then justification, in the sense given by C1, is at least one differentiating property. How about the other claim: that justifying is a kind of explaining, so that the ordinary notion of cause need not be brought in? Here it is necessary to decide what is being included under justification. Perhaps it means only what is given by C1: that the agent has certain beliefs and attitudes in the light of which the action is reasonable. But then something essential has certainly been left out, for a person can have a reason for an action, and perform the action, and yet this reason not be the reason why he did it. Central to the relation between a reason and an action it explains is the idea that the agent performed the action *because* he had the reason. Of course, we can include this idea too in justification; but then the notion of justification becomes as dark as the notion of reason until we can account for the force of that 'because'.

When we ask why someone acted as he did, we want to be provided with an interpretation. His behavior seems strange, alien, outré, pointless, out of character, disconnected; or perhaps we cannot even recognize an action in it. When we learn his reason, we have an interpretation, a new description of what he did which fits it into a familiar picture. The picture certainly includes some of the agent's beliefs and attitudes; perhaps also goals, ends, principles, general character traits, virtues or vices. Beyond this, the redescription of an action afforded by a reason may place the action in a wider social, economic, linguistic, or evaluative context. To learn, through learning the reason, that the agent conceived his action as a lie, a repayment of a debt, an insult, the fulfillment of an avuncular obligation, or a knight's gambit is to grasp the point of the action in its setting of rules, practices, conventions, and expectations.

Remarks like these, inspired by the later Wittgenstein, have been elaborated with subtlety and insight by a number of philosophers. And there is no denying that this is true: when we explain an action, by giving the reason, we do redescribe the action; redescribing the action gives the action a place in a pattern, and in this way the action is explained. Here it is tempting to draw two conclusions that do not follow. First, we can't infer, from the fact that giving reasons merely redescribes the action and that causes are separate from effects, that therefore reasons are not causes. Reasons, being beliefs and attitudes, are certainly not identical with actions; but, more important, events are often redescribed in terms of their causes. (Suppose someone was injured. We could redescribe this event "in terms of a cause" by saying he was burned.) Second, it is an error to think that, because placing the action in a larger pattern explains it, therefore we now understand the sort of explanation involved. Talk of patterns and contexts does not answer the question of how reasons explain actions, since the relevant pattern or context contains both reason and action. One way we can explain an event is by placing it in the context of its cause; cause and effect form the sort of pattern that explains the effect, in a sense of 'explain' that we understand as well as any. If reason and action illustrate a different pattern of explanation, that pattern must be identified.

Let me urge the point in connection with an example of Melden's. A man driving an automobile raises his arm in order to signal. His intention, to signal, explains his action, raising his arm, by redescribing it as signaling. What is the pattern that explains the action? Is it the familiar pattern of an action done for a reason? Then it does indeed explain the action, but only because it assumes the relation of reason and action that we want to analyze. Or is the pattern rather this: the man is driving, he is approaching a turn; he knows he ought to signal; he knows how to signal, by raising his arm. And now, in this context, he raises his arm. Perhaps, as Melden suggests, if all this happens, he does signal. And the explanation would then be this: if, under these conditions, a man raises his arm, then he signals. The difficulty is, of course, that this explanation does not touch the question of why he raised his arm. He had a reason to raise his arm, but this has not been shown to be the reason why he did it. If the description 'signaling' explains his action by giving his reason, then the signaling must be intentional; but, on the account just given, it may not be.

If, as Melden claims, causal explanations are "wholly irrelevant to the understanding we seek" of human actions (184) then we are without an analysis of the 'because' in 'He did it because . . . ,' where we go on to name a reason. Hampshire remarks, of the relation between reasons and action, "In philosophy one ought surely to find this . . . connection altogether mysterious" (166). Hampshire rejects Aristotle's attempt to solve the mystery by introducing the concept of wanting as a causal factor, on the grounds that the resulting theory is too clear and definite to fit all cases and that "There is still no compelling ground for insisting that the word 'want' *must* enter into every full statement of reasons for acting" (168). I agree that the concept of wanting is too narrow, but I have argued that, at least in a vast number of typical cases, some pro attitude must be assumed to be present if a statement of an agent's reasons in acting is to be intelligible. Hampshire does not see how Aristotle's scheme can be appraised as true or false, "for it is not clear what could be the basis of assessment, or what kind of evidence could be decisive" (167). Failing a satisfactory alternative, the best argument for a scheme like Aristotle's is that it alone promises to give an account of the "mysterious connection" between reasons and actions.

–IV–

In order to turn the first 'and' to 'because' in 'He exercised *and* he wanted to reduce and thought exercise would do it', we must, as the basic move,[5] augment condition C1 with:

C2. A primary reason for an action is its cause.

The considerations in favor of C2 are by now, I hope, obvious; in the remainder of this paper I wish to defend C2 against various lines of attack and, in the process, to clarify the notion of causal explanation involved.

A. The first line of attack is this. Primary reasons consist of attitudes and beliefs, which are states or dispositions, not events; therefore they cannot be causes.

It is easy to reply that states, dispositions, and conditions are frequently named as the causes of events: the bridge collapsed because of a structural defect; the plane crashed on takeoff because the air temperature was abnormally high; the plate broke because it had a crack. This reply does not, however, meet a closely related point. Mention of a causal condition for an event gives a cause only on the assumption that there was also a preceding event. But what is the preceding event that causes an action?

In many cases it is not difficult at all to find events very closely associated with the primary reason. States and dispositions are not events, but the onslaught of a state or disposition is. A desire to hurt your feelings may spring up at the moment you anger me; I may start wanting to eat a melon just when I see one; and beliefs may begin at the moment we notice, perceive, learn, or remember something. Those who have argued that there are no mental events to qualify as causes of actions have often missed the obvious because they have insisted that a mental event be observed or noticed (rather than an observing or a noticing) or that it be like a stab, a qualm, a prick or a quiver, a mysterious prod of conscience or act of the will. Melden, in discussing the driver who signals a turn by raising his arm, challenges those who want to explain actions causally to identify "an event which is common and peculiar to all such cases" (87), perhaps a motive or an intention, anyway "some particular feeling or experience" (95). But of course there is a mental event; at some moment the driver noticed (or thought he noticed) his turn coming up, and that is the moment he signaled. During any continuing activity, like driving, or elaborate performance, like swimming the Hellespont, there are more or less fixed purposes, standards, desires, and habits that give direction and form to the entire enterprise, and there is the continuing input of information about

---

[5] I say "as the basic move" to cancel the suggestion that C1 and C2 are jointly *sufficient* to define the relation of reasons to the actions they explain. I believe C2 can be strengthened to make C1 and C2 sufficient as well as necessary conditions, but here I am concerned only with the claim that both are, as they stand, necessary.

what we are doing, about changes in the environment, in terms of which we regulate and adjust our actions. To dignify a driver's awareness that his turn has come by calling it an experience, much less a feeling, is no doubt exaggerated, but whether it deserves a name or not, it had better be the reason why he raises his arm. In this case, and typically, there may not be anything we would call a motive, but if we mention such a general purpose as wanting to get to one's destination safely, it is clear that the motive is not an event. The intention with which the driver raises his arm is also not an event, for it is no thing at all, neither event, attitude, disposition, nor object. Finally, Melden asks the causal theorist to find an event that is common and peculiar to all cases where a man intentionally raises his arm, and this, it must be admitted, cannot be produced. But then neither can a common and unique cause of bridge failures, plane crashes, or plate breakings be produced.

The signaling driver can answer the question 'Why did you raise your arm when you did?', and from the answer we learn the event that caused the action. But can an actor always answer such a question? Sometimes the answer will mention a mental event that does not give a reason: 'Finally I made up my mind.' However, there also seem to be cases of intentional action where we cannot explain at all why we acted when we did. In such cases, explanation in terms of primary reasons parallels the explanation of the collapse of the bridge from a structural defect: we are ignorant of the event or sequence of events that led up to (caused) the collapse, but we are sure there was such an event or sequence of events.

B. According to Melden, a cause must be "logically distinct from the alleged effect" (52); but a reason for an action is not logically distinct from the action; therefore, reasons are not causes of actions.[6]

One possible form of this argument has already been suggested. Since a reason makes an action intelligible by redescribing it, we do not have two events, but only one under different descriptions. Causal relations, however, demand distinct events.

Someone might be tempted into the mistake of thinking that my flipping of the switch caused my turning on of the light (in fact it caused the light to go on). But it does not follow that it is a mistake to take 'My reason for flipping the switch was that I wanted to turn on the light' as entailing, in part, 'I flipped the switch, and this action is further describable as having been caused by my wanting to turn on the light.' To describe an event in terms of its cause is not to identify the event with its cause, nor does explanation by redescription exclude causal explanation.

The example serves also to refute the claim that we cannot describe the action without using words that link it to the alleged cause. Here the action

---

[6] This argument can be found, in one or more versions, in Kenny, Hampshire, and Melden, as well as in P. Winch, *The Idea of a Social Science*, London, 1958, and R. S. Peters, *The Concept of Motivation*, London, 1958. In one of its forms, the argument was of course inspired by Ryle's treatment of motives in *The Concept of Mind*.

is to be explained under the description: 'my flipping the switch,' and the alleged cause is 'my wanting to turn on the light.' What possible logical relation is supposed to hold between these phrases? It seems more plausible to urge a logical link between 'my turning on the light' and 'my wanting to turn on the light,' but even here the link turned out, on inspection, to be grammatical rather than logical.

In any case there is something very odd in the idea that causal relations are empirical rather than logical. What can this mean? Surely not that every true causal statement is empirical. For suppose 'A caused B' is true. Then the cause of $B = A$; so substituting, we have 'The cause of B caused B,' which is analytic. The truth of a causal statement depends on *what* events are described; its status as analytic or synthetic depends on *how* the events are described. Still, it may be maintained that a reason rationalizes an action only when the descriptions are appropriately fixed, and the appropriate descriptions are not logically independent.

Suppose that to say a man wanted to turn on the light *meant* that he would perform any action he believed would accomplish his end. Then the statement of his primary reason for flipping the switch would entail that he flipped the switch—"straightway he acts," as Aristotle says. In this case there would certainly be a logical connection between reason and action, the same sort of connection as that between 'It's water-soluble and was placed in water' and 'It dissolved.' Since the implication runs from description of cause to description of effect but not conversely, naming the cause still gives information. And, though the point is often overlooked, 'Placing it in water caused it to dissolve' does not entail 'It's water-soluble'; so the latter has additional explanatory force. Nevertheless, the explanation would be far more interesting if, in place of solubility, with its obvious definitional connection with the event to be explained, we could refer to some property, say a particular crystalline structure, whose connection with dissolution in water was known only through experiment. Now it is clear why primary reasons like desires and wants do not explain actions in the relatively trivial way solubility explains dissolvings. Solubility, we are assuming, is a pure disposition property: it is defined in terms of a single test. But desires cannot be defined in terms of the actions they may rationalize, even though the relation between desire and action is not simply empirical; there are other, equally essential criteria for desires—their expression in feelings and in actions that they do not rationalize, for example. The person who has a desire (or want or belief) does not normally need criteria at all—he generally knows, even in the absence of any clues available to others, what he wants, desires, and believes. These logical features of primary reasons show that it is not just lack of ingenuity that keeps us from defining them as dispositions to act for these reasons.

C. According to Hume, "we may define a cause to be an object, followed by another, and where all the objects similar to the first are followed by objects similar to the second." But, Hart and Honoré claim, "The statement that one person did something because, for example, another threatened him, carries no implication or covert assertion that if the circumstances were repeated the same action would follow" (52). Hart and Honoré allow that Hume is right in saying that ordinary singular causal statements imply generalizations, but wrong for this very reason in supposing that motives and desires are ordinary causes of actions. In brief, laws are involved essentially in ordinary causal explanations, but not in rationalizations.

It is common to try to meet this argument by suggesting that we do have rough laws connecting reasons and actions, and these can, in theory, be improved. True, threatened people do not always respond in the same way; but we may distinguish between threats and also between agents, in terms of their beliefs and attitudes.

The suggestion is delusive, however, because generalizations connecting reasons and actions are not—and cannot be sharpened into—the kind of law on the basis of which accurate predictions can reliably be made. If we reflect on the way in which reasons determine choice, decision, and behavior, it is easy to see why this is so. What emerges, in the *ex post facto* atmosphere of explanation and justification, as *the* reason frequently was, to the agent at the time of action, one consideration among many, *a* reason. Any serious theory for predicting action on the basis of reasons must find a way of evaluating the relative force of various desires and beliefs in the matrix of decision; it cannot take as its starting point the refinement of what is to be expected from a single desire. The practical syllogism exhausts its role in displaying an action as falling under one reason; so it cannot be subtilized into a reconstruction of practical reasoning, which involves the weighing of competing reasons. The practical syllogism provides a model neither for a predictive science of action nor for a normative account of evaluative reasoning.

Ignorance of competent predictive laws does not inhibit valid causal explanations, or few causal explanations could be made. I am certain the window broke because it was struck by a rock—I saw it all happen; but I am not (is anyone?) in command of laws on the basis of which I can predict what blows will break which windows. A generalization like 'Windows are fragile, and fragile things tend to break when struck hard enough, other conditions being right' is not a predictive law in the rough—the predictive law, if we had it, would be quantitative and would use very different concepts. The generalization, like our generalizations about behavior, serves a different function: it provides evidence for the existence of a causal law covering the case at hand.

We are usually far more certain of a singular causal connection than we are of any causal law governing the case; does this show that Hume was wrong in claiming that singular causal statements entail laws? Not necessarily, for Hume's claim, as quoted above, is ambiguous. It may mean that '*A* caused *B*' entails some particular law involving the predicates used in the descriptions '*A*' and '*B*,' or it may mean that '*A* caused *B*' entails that there exists a causal law instantiated by some true descriptions of *A* and *B*.[7] Obviously, both versions of Hume's doctrine give a sense to the claim that singular causal statements entail laws, and both sustain the view that causal explanations "involve laws." But the second version is far weaker, in that no particular law is entailed by a singular causal claim, and a singular causal claim can be defended, if it needs defense, without defending any law. Only the second version of Hume's doctrine can be made to fit with most causal explanations; it suits rationalizations equally well.

The most primitive explanation of an event gives its cause; more elaborate explanations may tell more of the story, or defend the singular causal claim by producing a relevant law or by giving reasons for believing such exists. But it is an error to think no explanation has been given until a law has been produced. Linked with these errors is the idea that singular causal statements necessarily indicate, by the concepts they employ, the concepts that will occur in the entailed law. Suppose a hurricane, which is reported on page 5 of Tuesday's *Times*, causes a catastrophe, which is reported on page 13 of Wednesday's *Tribune*. Then the event reported on page 5 of Tuesday's *Times* caused the event reported on page 13 of Wednesday's *Tribune*. Should we look for a law relating events of these *kinds*? It is only slightly less ridiculous to look for a law relating hurricanes and catastrophes. The laws needed to predict the catastrophe with precision would, of course, have no use for concepts like hurricane and catastrophe. The trouble with predicting the weather is that the descriptions under which events interest us—'a cool, cloudy day with rain in the afternoon'—have only remote connections with the concepts employed by the more precise known laws.

The laws whose existence is required if reasons are causes of actions do not, we may be sure, deal in the concepts in which rationalizations must deal. If the causes of a class of events (actions) fall in a certain class (reasons) and there is a law to back each singular causal statement, it does not follow that there is any law connecting events classified as reasons with events classified as actions—the classifications may even be neurological, chemical, or physical.

D. It is said that the kind of knowledge one has of one's own reasons in acting is not compatible with the existence of a causal relation between reasons and actions: a person knows his own intentions in acting infallibly, without induction or observation, and no ordinary causal relation can be known in this way. No doubt our knowledge of our own intentions in acting will show many of the oddities peculiar to first-person knowledge of one's

---

7 We could roughly characterize the analysis of singular casual statements hinted at here as follows: '*A* caused *B*' is true if and only if there are descriptions of *A* and *B* such that the sentence obtained by putting these descriptions for '*A*' and '*B*' in '*A* caused *B*' follows from a true casual law. This analysis is saved from triviality by the fact that not all true generalizations are causal laws; causal laws are distinguished (though of course this is no analysis) by the fact that they are inductively confirmed by their instances and by the fact that they support counterfactual and subjunctive singular causal statements.

own pains, beliefs, desires, and so on; the only question is whether these oddities prove that reasons do not cause, in any ordinary sense at least, the actions that they rationalize.

You may easily be wrong about the truth of a statement of the form 'I am poisoning Charles because I want to save him pain,' because you may be wrong about whether you are poisoning Charles—you may yourself be drinking the poisoned cup by mistake. But it also seems that you may err about your reasons, particularly when you have two reasons for an action, one of which pleases you and one which does not. For example, you do want to save Charles pain; you also want him out of the way. You may be wrong about which motive made you do it.

The fact that you may be wrong does not show that in general it makes sense to ask you how you know what your reasons were or to ask for your evidence. Though you may, on rare occasions, accept public or private evidence as showing you are wrong about your reasons, you usually have no evidence and make no observations. Then your knowledge of your own reasons for your actions is not generally inductive, for where there is induction, there is evidence. Does this show the knowledge is not causal? I cannot see that it does.

Causal laws differ from true but nonlawlike generalizations in that their instances confirm them; induction is, therefore, certainly a good way to learn the truth of a law. It does not follow that it is the only way to learn the truth of a law. In any case, in order to know that a singular causal statement is true, it is not necessary to know the truth of a law; it is necessary only to know that some law covering the events at hand exist. And it is far from evident that induction, and induction alone, yields the knowledge that a causal law satisfying certain conditions exists. Or, to put it differently, one case is often enough, as Hume admitted, to persuade us that a law exists, and this amounts to saying that we are persuaded, without direct inductive evidence, that a causal relation exists.[8]

E. Finally I should like to say something about a certain uneasiness some philosophers feel in speaking of causes of actions at all. Melden, for example, says that actions are often identical with bodily movements, and that bodily movements have causes; yet he denies that the causes are causes of the actions. This is, I think, a contradiction. He is led to it by the following sort of consideration: "It is futile to attempt to explain conduct through the causal efficacy of desire—*all* that can explain is further happenings, not actions performed by agents. The agent confronting the causal nexus in which such happenings occur is a helpless victim of all that occurs in and to him" (128, 129). Unless I am mistaken, this argument, if it were valid, would show that actions cannot have causes at all. I shall not point out the obvious difficulties in removing actions from the realm of causality entirely. But

---

[8] My thinking on the subject of this section, as on most of the topics discussed in this paper, has been greatly influenced by years of talk with Professor Daniel Bennett, now of Brandeis University.

perhaps it is worth trying to uncover the source of the trouble. Why on earth should a cause turn an action into a mere happening and a person into a helpless victim? Is it because we tend to assume, at least in the arena of action, that a cause demands a causer, agency an agent? So we press the question; if my action is caused, what caused it? If I did, then there is the absurdity of infinite regress; if I did not, I am a victim. But of course the alternatives are not exhaustive. Some causes have no agents. Primary among these are those states and changes of state in persons which, because they are reasons as well as causes, make persons voluntary agents.

[4] Meaning and Action

MAY BRODBECK

"What is left over if I subtract the fact that my arm goes up from the fact that I raise my arm?" ([9], p. 161, §621) One may interpret Wittgenstein's question to concern the nature of human action. Recently, that question has been given a certain answer from which a moral has been drawn regarding the nature of our knowledge and understanding of man. Briefly, the something "left over" that distinguishes a mere bodily movement from an action is, according to the answer, the *meaning* of that movement. The moral drawn is that the meaningful constituents of an action make it logically impossible to explain human actions causally, in the sense in which we can causally explain physical events like bodily movements. Though the answer itself requires considerable unpacking, it is, I believe, essentially correct. But once that necessary analysis is made, the moral drawn, I shall try to show, is a *non sequitur*.

An action, as I shall use that term, is any bit of behavior whose complete description, that is, an account of *what* is occurring, requires mention, in addition to manifest behavior, either of such things as the person's motives, intentions and thoughts or of such things as moral, legal, or conventional standards or rules. Strictly speaking, an explicit mention of standards is redundant, since they essentially involve thoughts or purposes. However, since these standards need not be in the mind of the person acting in accordance with a rule, as well as for other reasons that will appear as the argument unfolds, it may help to mention standards separately.

Reprinted, with minor revisions, from *Philosophy of Science*, **30**, 1963, 309–324, with permission of the editor.

The discussions stimulated by Wittgenstein's question have revived one side of an old controversy embodied in the question, "Can there be a science of man and society?" The side now revived opposes the affirmative answer of those who stress an essential identity in method between the physical sciences and the study of man. The latter reason (in part) along the following lines. Other people's mental states, their thoughts, feelings, wishes, and hopes, are not directly accessible to public inspection. Nor can we test the everyday inferences we make to them, from what we do observe, in the same way that we can independently test, for instance, the inference from an observed change in color of a piece of litmus paper to a liquid's acidity. Though we frequently may be right in our everyday inferences to other people's mental states from their behavior, all we have to go on is what people choose to tell us or their observable behavior. Since there is no way of independently testing for the occurrence of these criteria and what they are criteria for, the proponents of a science of man eschew all talk about mental states. They maintain that nevertheless a complete description and causal explanation of human actions can be given *in principle* by means of terms that, like those of physical science, have reference only to objectively observable properties of material objects. The material objects of their concern are of course people's bodies, the characters, among others, are the observable behaviors of these bodies under certain conditions and in certain environments. The mentalistic terms characterizing actions, like 'purpose' and 'thought,' are, on this account, all eliminable by definitions using only nonmentalistic terms. On this view, the social scientist is a spectator of the human scene, noting its observable features and the connections among them. He seeks regularities in human behavior, just as the physicist looks for them in inanimate behavior. His assertions being based upon observation are also refutable by it. Like those of natural science, they are at best contingent, empirical truths. This view, within psychology, is of course known as behaviorism. For a broader notion to encompass all social areas, as well as to avoid certain connotations of that term, I shall call the doctrine "objectivism."

Revived now is the negative side of the controversy, namely, the insistence upon an intrinsic difference between the study of man and of things. The objectivist program is held to be hopelessly misguided, not merely because it is practically unfeasible but because it is radically mistaken. By the spectator methods, all that the objectivist can learn are, on this view, the external, overt features of actions. Their internal aspects, the motives, intentions, and reflections, by which overt behavior is understood as meaningful human action elude him entirely. To understand a human action is to know its motive. Motive explanations, however, are neither a species of causal explanations nor are they replaceable by such explanations. Social concepts, like money or voting, cannot be adequately described in "neutral" nonmentalistic terms or understood by objectivist methods. We observe only manifest behavior, like a hand going up or pulling a lever, not the internal meaning of an action, like hand-raising or voting. This meaning lies in the logical connections the action has with the complex of desires, intentions, choices, reasons, conventions and moral rules that are all inextricably involved together in social life. As participants in a community, we have learned to use these concepts. Understanding the language, we understand the meaning of other people's overt acts by analyzing the concepts appropriately applied to the situation, tracing their logical connections with the other mentalistic concepts. A matter of conceptual analysis, our understanding and knowledge of man is therefore *a priori* and necessary rather than, as with the natural sciences, *a posteriori* and contingent. The empirical science of man envisaged by the objectivist is thus *in principle,* that is, conceptually or logically, impossible.[1]

Since belief in the essential ineliminability of mentalistic terms is central to the current rejection of "objectivism," I shall call this position "mentalism." Possibly there is some incongruity in attributing "mentalism" to some among these critics who deny, or appear to deny, that terms ever have a reference to private mental states. But the mentalistic label seems to be justifiable not only historically, but also systematically, by the emphasis on the unelimnability of the mentalistic terms. The incongruity, if any, is, I suggest, not of my making.

First of all, I wish to explain some notions which, though now controversial, are nevertheless indispensable to clarity about the issues at stake.

Concepts Versus Terms: Four Meanings of 'Meaning'

The word 'concept' is ambiguous. In one usage, 'concept' is applied to those classes of words, either sounds or marks, that are used to refer to characters of things, either properties or relations. I shall call them terms. 'White' and *'blanco'* are two different words, but only one term. 'Concept' also has a mentalistic use, as applied to the content of a thought. I shall use 'concept' in this way for, generally, the content of any mental act, whether it be thinking, perceiving, believing, hoping, or intending. (A mental act is not, of course, an action, though they are intimately connected.) The *thought* of something's being green, of a unicorn in the garden, or of rain tomorrow, are all, in this usage, concepts. Terms may be used to refer either to concepts, that is, to someone's thought of something, or to nonmentalistic things and their characters. When, in any context, we know the character or characters that a term is being used to refer to, the term has a reference or, as I shall call it, meaning $_1$. When, within natural science, the reference of a term, say, 'pressure,' is known to be lawfully connected to other things, as the pressure of a gas is connected with its volume and temperature, then the term is also significant or "meaningful" or has what I shall call meaning $_2$.

---

1 Extended statements of the position here outlined are to be found in [8] and [7]. I shall be concerned in this paper primarily, though not solely, with their formulations.

The meaning $_1$ of a term is a matter of convention; its meaning $_2$, if any, is a matter of fact. Only these two uses of 'meaning' are appropriately applied to scientific terms. They do not, however, exhaust the uses of 'meaning.'

Though concepts or mental states are the reference of some terms, they do not themselves refer to anything, any more than (nonlinguistic) physical states refer to anything. Yet, thoughts do "mean" other things, in a way in which nonmental or physical events do not "mean" anything. It is characteristic of mental acts generally, and of mental acts alone, that they "mean" or are directed toward something else. The thought or concept of a castle or of rain tomorrow is about a kind of material thing or event. What the thought "means" is, by a dead teleological metaphor, called its intention. Obviously, one need not adopt the metaphysics of an active Self to recognize that thoughts are about something. 'Meaning' is ambiguous even in this particular context. Sometimes the thought itself is called the "meaning," for it is that which means or intends. When used in this way, a "meaning" is what I am calling a concept. Sometimes, what the thought intends or means is called the "meaning." In this use, a meaning is often something nonmental, though, of course, we often also think about thoughts, our own and others.' I shall here use 'intentional meaning' so that intentional meaning or, briefly, meaning $_3$ is what a mental act intends, means, or is about. To have a thought or to think about something is one fact; what this thought intends or means $_3$ is a different, usually nonmental, fact.

Terms refer, concepts intend. The term 'green' means $_1$ the color green, because we have chosen to use the term in this way. Meaning $_1$ or reference is a complex natural or descriptive relation between language users, language, and the world. A set of marks or sounds does not intrinsically refer to anything. On the other hand, it is intrinsic to mental concepts that they mean or intend something else, either in the present, past, or future. Intentionality or meaning $_3$ is characteristic of thoughts, not something we bestow upon them. However, the meaning $_3$ relation between a thought and its intention is neither a natural relation, like taller or being to the left of, nor a causal relation. The reasons it is neither are fairly obvious. For there to be a descriptive relation, both terms of that relation must exist. But we can think what is false or imagine something that does not exist. Moreover, thinking about something does not, in any relevant sense, causally affect the thing thought about. Meaning $_3$, the relation between a thought and its intention, is, in a specificable sense, a logical relation.[2]

Still another difference between concepts and terms is crucial. Two terms may refer to or mean $_1$ the same thing. Two concepts never intend or mean $_3$ the same thing. The expressions 'the square of three' and 'the sum of 7 and 2' both may be used to refer to the same thing, namely, nine. But the concept or thought-of-three-square does not intentionally mean the same as the thought-of-the-sum-of-7-and-2. We may express thoughts in various ways,

[2] For details, see [1], [2], and [3].

by action or speech, but to describe them we need language. The linguistic expression describing the thought is the text of that thought. Two different linguistic events may express the same facts, but are the texts of two different thoughts. The sentence, S_1, "There are seven plus two buttons in the box" referentially means the same as the sentence, S_2, "There are three-square buttons in the box," but they are the texts of two different thoughts, for the thought-that-S_1 does not intentionally mean the same as the thought-that-S_2, since one may firmly believe the former and doubt the latter. Though the *term* 'nine,' means$_1$ the same as the *term* 'the square of three,' the *concept* of nine does not intentionally mean$_3$ the same as the *concept* of the square of three. Even when two different expressions refer to the same thing, the concepts of which they are the texts do not have the same (intentional) meaning$_3$. Generally, in mental contexts, like Mary knows, believes, or remembers that-S, replacing the text of S with another expression having the same referential meaning need not preserve the truth of the whole statement. In fact, no two different concepts ever mean$_3$ the same, for they are different just because they have different intentional meanings. Intentional meaning of concepts is unique, while referential meaning of terms is not.

OUR KNOWLEDGE OF OTHER MINDS

To think that it might snow tomorrow and to think about putting snow-tires on the car are different thoughts, nor is either the same as actually performing that task or having a disposition to do so. Thinking about some-thing, say, castles in Spain, is, like the dreary rain that may evoke the thought, a particular occurrence at a particular time. Generally such mental episodes are not *identical* with any behavior or dispositions to behave that, as we significantly say, manifest them. Moreover, bodily states manifest mental ones, not tautologically, as bending "manifests" flexibility, but con-tingently, as exploding manifests chemical composition. Our everyday state-ments about minds, our own and others, are categorical. The mentalistic terms they contain have reference to states of mind that, unlike bodily states, cannot be inspected publicly. Since mentalistic terms do not either referentially or intentionally mean the same as nonmentalistic terms, they cannot be replaced "without residue" by such terms. All this I take to be common sense, that is, something we all know from our own experience. I take it also to be a commonsensical core of the mentalistic thesis, whether or not its proponents would agree with my way of putting it.

Though we cannot observe another man's conscious states, we certainly often can tell what other people are thinking or feeling. We can do so be-cause, whether voluntarily or involuntarily, we evince our mental states by overt physical features, including behavior, or by dispositions to exhibit such features under certain conditions. Privacy, in other words, does not entail ignorance about other people's mental states, merely that we know them differently from the way we know our own. Yet, though these are minds and bodies, there are no interacting minds. This is a piece of scientific common sense, that is, something scientists believe on the basis of their extended experience. This belief has two components. First, that there are no disembodied minds or, more precisely, whenever there is a mental state, there is always a corresponding bodily state, either neurological, physiological, behavioral, or some combination of these. The connection between mental states and such bodily states is correlational. That is how we can tell, by inference, what other people are thinking. Secondly, mental events parallel but do not interact with physical events. In other words, despite the correlation between mind and body, no mental state causally affects any material state and conversely. In a phrase, the view is that the physical world, including men's bodies, is causally closed with respect to minds. Unpacked, the phrase means that the laws used to explain and to predict physical phenomena need mention nothing nonphysical, in the broad sense of 'physical' which includes not only the terms of physics, but also overt behavior, utterances, physiological, and environmental characters that are describable in nonmentalistic terms. To deny that minds and bodies interact is to assert that the laws permitting us scientifically to explain human behavior need not mention anything mental. Parallelism and the belief in physical determinism form the basis for the objectivist belief that a *complete* account of human activities can be given in nonmentalistic terms.

Some philosophical problems arise because certain sets of facts, taken together, are perplexing. In the present instance, the commonsense fact, upon which the mentalists rightly insist, that mind and intelligence make a difference in the world seems to conflict with the denial of causal interaction between mind and body. Yet this denial is justified by what we know from the natural sciences. This is what makes it a piece of scientific common sense. To deny it outright is to tilt quixotically at wind mills. The contemporary mentalist does not deny it outright. Instead, he denies its relevance, by asserting that scientific, that is, causal explanation and description are "inappropriate" to the explanation and description of human activities. He accepts physical determinism for physical events, agrees and even insists that both cause and effect must be physical, but, denying that human actions can be completely described in physical terms, denies that causal attribution can legitimately be made to actions. Bodies and minds neither interact nor don't interact. Rather, there is a sort of parallelism between mind and body, reflected by two different realms of discourse or "conceptual systems"—one for the mental, the other for the physical. Within each realm of discourse, different sorts of explanation are appropriate. We *understand* man by mentalistic explanation, for instance, by motives; we understand body by physical explanation, that is, by causes. The attempt to replace the former by the latter is a "conceptual" error, *a priori* doomed to failure.

Even granting such a "conceptual" parallelism, an action, like signalling or buying a house, is an event taking place at a particular time. Actions are as much facts in the world as earthquakes or any natural phenomenon in which mind does not play a role. A world with actions is different from one without them. Questions about actions, therefore, cannot *merely* be linguistic, for the conceptual systems in which action-terms occur, if they are to be of any relevance, must be about actual occurrences, in exactly the same sense as conceptual systems of physics are not speculative fancies but about physical occurrences. Two kinds of questions, in particular, that may be asked regarding any event cannot arbitrarily be ruled out on linguistic grounds alone. For one, one may ask whether action-events have causes, for there is nothing in the meaning of 'cause,' as that term is normally used in science, to make this question in any sense "ungrammatical." The denial of interactionism does not follow from the meaning of 'cause,' but from facts and laws of the kind I mentioned. It could be false, but it is not linguistic nonsense. Moreover, since actions are events, one may also legitimately ask how we know when statements about them are true or false. The answer given, as I mentioned earlier, is that all such statements are "conceptually," hence *a priori*, true. The *prima facie* rationalism of this answer to questions about matters of fact may, with some justice, lead one to suspect that something has gone radically wrong. Later, I shall try to locate what has gone wrong.

On the positive side, there is at least one sense in which the mentalists are certainly right in asserting that talk about actions or, for that matter, motives cannot have the same "meaning" as talk about behavior or, for that matter, causes. For such statements have, at the very least, different intentional meanings.[3] The objectivist must show how, eschewing mentalistic terms, he can account for this difference in (intentional) meaning $_3$. And, since actions are events, he must also show how parallelism allows him to account adequately for the presence and efficacy of mind in the world. I shall first suggest how, within his framework, the objectivist can in principle accomplish this first goal and, then, by considering certain mentalistic objections, show how he can in principle also accomplish the second.

To every mental event there corresponds one or, more likely, several material events. What occurs when Jones sees a tree? There are the mental act of seeing, certain states of his body and, presumably, a tree in his immediate environment. When Jones says, "I see a tree," he describes directly his mental state. The objectivist scientist cannot do this, since the mentalistic term is not part of his vocabulary. This does not mean that Jones describes the situation for him. Jones' utterance is just part of the

---

3 It follows that in mental-act contexts the terms 'cause' and 'motive' are not interchangeable. If Jones wants to know the motive for Smith's action, he need not also want to know its cause, even if cause and motive are one. The terms express different thoughts and, in this psychological sense, are "conceptually" distinct. But this difference in intentional meaning does not imply that motives and causes are themselves "logically" distinct.

total situation that the scientist must describe in his own language. In his language, which is in principle different from that of his subject, he introduces an inseparable complex term 'seeing-a-tree,' which contains neither 'seeing' nor, for that matter, 'tree.' This term is defined dispositionally by means of terms referring to those physical states of the person (including his verbal behavior if asked what he sees) that accompany Jones' state of consciousness when he sees a tree. Although *Jones'* term 'see' refers to a conscious state and the *scientist's* complex term 'sees-a-tree' refers to behavioral and environmental items, the latter term will be truly applicable to Jones if and only if Jones is in fact at that time seeing a tree. He knows this commonsensically, so to speak, not as a scientist. He knows it from self-examination when he applies the defined term to himself, or from what Jones tells him, though again, what Jones tells him is *data,* not description.

The investigator may of course make mistakes. But his mistakes will reveal themselves by failure of the predictions that he makes from his description. He will predict something different from Jones sees-a-tree, than from Jones sees-a-tiger. If Jones turns and runs, he may conclude that either he was wrong in applying his complex terms to Jones, or else he was wrong in defining 'seeing-a-tree' in the way he did. "Wrong" in the only way a definition can be wrong, namely, that it does not provide a significant term, that is, one that figures in confirmable laws. On the other hand, he might still be right. Jones might have a neurotic fear of trees. In that case, he has failed to take account of other operative factors. If he is right and, in principle, there is always a right physical description corresponding to the mental event, then we may speak of the former as an indirect reference to the latter. Analogously, the physicist indirectly refers to the perceptual color red when he speaks of "the color with the longest wave length." Seen in this way, objectivism is merely a way of talking about minds. By capturing its reflection in the material world, the behavior scientist can indirectly speak about mind. What then is the reflection of intentional meaning?

Meaning $_1$ (reference) and meaning $_2$ (significance) are applicable to the technical terms of science. Terms and expressions have meaning for persons. When the scientist investigates this "meaning," then 'meaning' becomes one of his technical terms, call it psychological meaning or meaning $_4$. Meaning $_4$ is thus a term within science, which must itself be given meaning $_1$.[4] Certain physical patterns have meaning $_4$ for an individual. Depending upon the circumstances and manner in which it is uttered, the sound 'fire' for instance may mean $_4$ to Jones either danger or warmth. Which it means $_4$, we determine by the bodily states, behavioral and physiological, that hearing the word elicits in Jones. Generally, 'meaning $_4$' refers to, or means $_1$, certain other things, verbal or nonverbal, that a person does upon hearing sounds or seeing certain marks. Jones' awareness of the referential use, if any, of the expression he hears is an essential part of the situation to which he reacts.

---

[4] Meaning$_4$ and meaning$_2$ may both be called 'contextual meaning'; but meaning$_2$, like meaning$_1$, is *applicable to* scientific terms, including meaning$_4$.

But an expression need not have (referential) meaning $_1$, in order for it to have (psychological) meaning $_4$ for someone. 'The Lord is my shepherd' has no meaning $_1$, but it has meaning $_4$. People use it, utter it, and behave upon hearing or uttering it in certain ways. Similarly with many expressions of religion, poetry, exclamations, commands, and so forth. Being used on certain occasions, they have meaning $_4$.

As with 'seeing,' so with 'meaning.' The psychologist's technical term occurs in a hyphenated expression, say, 'S-means-P-to-Jones,' defined in terms of a certain dispositional relation holding between, first, the sounds S and Jones, he hears them, and, secondly, certain later stages of Jones' body. Just as neither 'see' nor 'tree' occurs in 'seeing-a-tree,' so neither 'S' nor 'means' occurs in 'S-means-P-to-Jones.' To put it differently, since S is a pattern of sounds and P a pattern of bodily states, verbal responses, and overt behavior, no substitution can occur in the hyphenated expression.[5] Therefore, from the fact that two expressions, two patterns of sounds, may both be used to refer to the same states of affairs, it does not follow that they both mean $_4$ the same to Jones. The intentional uniqueness of concepts is reflected by their having different linguistic texts. The observable responses to two different expressions may be different. (Psychological) meaning $_4$ depends, in other words, not only upon *what* is being asserted, but also upon the linguistic form in which it is asserted. This uniqueness of meaning $_4$, objectively defined, of linguistic expressions—experimentally established, by the way—reflects the uniqueness of (intentional) meaning $_3$ of thought or concepts. The shadow, if not the substance, of intentionality can thus be captured by the objectivist.

Before considering certain objections to this optimistic objectivist tale, it will be helpful to sort out some uses of 'understand.' I shall indicate the various uses by subscripts. The contexts in which these subscript-terms occur will explicate their uses.

Five Kinds of "Understanding"

I can understand $_1$ English but not Finnish. To understand a language is to know how to use certain classes of sounds or marks to express and to convey to others our thoughts, attitudes, queries, wishes, and, among other things, information about the world. To accomplish this, I must know the conditions for applying certain expressions and not others. What is involved in understanding $_1$ varies with the kind of expression. Some I understand $_1$ only in context when they are combined with other terms. Clearly, we could not use or understand $_1$ a language if all of its terms were understood only in context by means of other terms. Armed only with a wholly Finnish dictionary, I could not understand $_1$ Finnish. Some expressions,

5 See also Grossmann, [5].

therefore, I understand $_1$ only if I know what conditions of myself, the world, or other people they are being used to express, that is, only if I know their (referential) meaning $_1$.

I do not understand $_2$ what it meant to have been a member of the Italian Resistance. Nor do I understand $_2$ what it means to lose an only son. This sense of 'understanding' has nothing to do with language, for of course I understand $_1$ what it is that I am said not to understand $_2$. I do not understand $_2$ these things because I have not had the special feelings, emotions, or attitudes that are aroused only by having undergone certain experiences or participated in certain kinds of events. Toward those who have my empathy is limited in a way it is not limited toward people with toothaches. For I understand $_2$ what it is to have a toothache. Understanding $_2$ is a mixture of knowing meaning $_1$ and meaning $_2$. I must know to what unique feelings, of pain or of grief, the terms are being used to refer, or, as in the case of being a member of the Italian Resistance, I must know what feelings were *associated with* those underground activities referred to by the term.

I do understand $_3$ what it meant to be a member of the Resistance, just as I understand $_3$ what a golden mountain would be like. The unique phenomenological experience that is the resultant of fear, patriotism, courage, hatred of tyranny, all acting jointly, I do not understand $_2$. But, because I understand $_1$ the meaning $_1$ of the phrase 'being a member of the Italian Resistance' and because I *also* understand $_2$ the meaning of fear, patriotism, and so on, I can understand $_3$ what it meant to be a member of the Resistance. In this sense too, since I have suffered the loss of loved ones, I can understand $_3$ what it means to have lost an only son, though I have never had a son. By understanding $_3$ one may empathize with the bereaved mother, though less completely than one who understands $_2$, that is, one who has also lost a son.

I understand $_4$ why Tom Jones left school; he wanted to make a lot of money quickly. If we know the motives and purposes of people's actions, then we understand $_4$ why people did what they did. Here we must distinguish between understanding $_1$ the action-term, that is, knowing to what the term is referring, and knowing the motive for the action. The purposes, duties, and so on, mentioned in the description of the action will, of course, be different from the purpose for which the action is performed. I shall return to this distinction presently. For the moment, let it stand that understanding $_4$ consists in knowing motives. This may mean knowing what an action itself is or in knowing motives for it.

I understand $_5$ that increased costs of production mean an increase in selling price. The pious man understands $_5$ that regular church attendance means salvation in afterlife. The wife understood $_5$ that her husband's silence meant disapproval. The farmer understands $_5$ that a fiery red sunset means rain the next day. Generally, we understand $_5$ a kind of thing, event, or behavior when we know or believe that there are some *other* things, events, and so on, with which it is in some way associated. In other words, we understand $_5$ the meaning of something when it does not stand isolated, so to speak, before our minds. The "meaning" that we thus understand or attribute to events is what I called significance or meaning $_2$. If we do not know the meaning $_2$ of an event, then we do not understand $_5$ the phenomenon referred to by the term expressing the occurrence. Again, I can understand $_1$ what I do not understand $_5$. Obviously, this significance or meaning $_2$ need not reflect any true connections among things. Yet, true or false, imaginary or superstitious, all of these occurrences of 'understand $_5$' are the same use, for they imply that one kind of thing is believed to be connected with something else. Understanding $_5$ thus comprehends tested generalizations of science that give their terms significance, as well as the connections, whether from common experience or fancy, that people believe certain things have with others. When these associations of one thing with another actually do reflect empirical lawful connections, then understanding $_5$ coincides with scientific explanation. There are of course other uses of 'explain.' [6]

Criticisms of a Science of Man

I turn now to criticisms of the objectivist program. The mentalist claims that "understanding of society cannot be observational and experimental" ([8], p. 110) because, first of all, the investigator must understand the language of the people he studies. One learns a language by sharing a mode of life. The investigator, therefore, cannot stand in the observor-observed relation to his subject matter. Moreover, the natural scientist uses external criteria to decide when two events are of the same kind. But that two actions sharing no overt features are of the "same kind" must be decided by the participant, not the spectator. The method by which we understand others is accordingly subjective, not objective. Logically, therefore, there cannot be generalizations about man and society, as there are about stones and stars. What is involved in the idea, for instance, of prayer is a *religious* not a sociological question. An idea cannot be torn out of context, for it gets its meaning from the role it plays in the system. Men's actions are intelligible when we understand their motives and the rules in accordance with which they act. But appeals to standards and to motives "rule out" appeals to causes. Mechanical, causal explanations of human actions are therefore logically inappropriate.[7] Using the distinctions drawn among the various uses of 'meaning' and of 'understanding,' I should like to examine these claims.

Does the fact that the investigator must understand $_1$ the language of the people he studies vitiate the objectivist thesis? By a fairly elaborate conditioning process, a child learns, say, to call a small, furry, meowing animal

---

[6] See also [4].

[7] Cf. [7], pp. 4, 12, *et pass.* and [8], pp. 78, 82, *et pass.* With respect to the ineliminability of mentalistic terms and the claim that motives cannot be causes, see also [6].

a cat, not a dog. He also learns to say "He was . . ." not "He were . . . ." Pointing, obviously, is not the only method used in teaching a language. Nor can we teach the (referential) meaning $_1$ of mentalistic terms, like 'headache' and 'sorrow,' by pointing. These are learned by means of their public accompaniments. It is truistic that learning a language is "rooted in a social context." Far from vitiating the objectivist thesis, the truism is a fundamental part of it. Yet undoubtedly there is a difficulty. An almost infinite number of sound patterns can be used to express the same terms. Moreover, only slight oral or typographical changes create huge differences in behavior. As the old "telegram-argument," frequently adduced by the idealists, insisted, there is an enormous difference between a telegram from a friend that says "Our son was killed" and one that reads "Your son was killed." The difference in (referential) meaning $_1$ and consequently in the reactions they arouse (meaning $_4$) is hugely disproportionate to the slight typographical differences between the marks on paper. A man presumably also reacts differently when he hears the words "I love you" than upon hearing "I love him." The considerable physical difference between 'you' and 'him' suggests how, *in principle,* the investigator could dispense with knowing a common language. And the argument on both sides is one of principle or "logic" only.

Still, the enormous difficulty of correlating slight differences in physical cues with huge differences in behavior are obvious. In *practice,* these difficulties may well be insuperable. In practice, therefore, except when he is actually studying (psychological) meaning $_4$, the investigator simply assumes that he and the subject understand $_1$ the same language. It is not hard to tell, in purely objective ways, whether or not a person understands $_1$ what is being said to him. People behave very differently if they understand $_1$ what is being said than if they do not. If two people understand $_1$ the same language, presumably because they have both learned it in the same social context, then they can communicate with each other. There is nothing inherently subjective about the success or failure of this communication. Once we know from a prior and different investigation that a language is understood $_1$, its users may be observed. The fact that the scientist *learns* the language as a participant in the social process does not imply that he can never, so to speak, stop being a participant. To think that it does is to fall victim to the genetic fallacy. The mentalist confuses how we come to understand $_1$ a statement of, say, a belief with using that understanding $_1$, once learned, to observe that an individual has a certain belief or, at least, says he has.

Most probably, in practice subject and scientist must, as we say, speak the same language. But our saying this leads to a second confusion, namely, between the scientist's language and that which he shares with the subject. For, as I mentioned earlier, in another sense they do not "speak the same language." The language that the scientist uses to *describe* what he learns about his subject is in principle not the same language that he may use to *communicate* with him. What Jones says (and what the investigator says to him in Jones' language) is part of what is going on, which the investigator describes in his own language. In other words, everything that Jones says occurs only within quotation marks in the investigator's language. The subject's use of, say, the term 'prayer' in certain ways and under specifiable conditions is an interesting and important, because meaningful $_2$ or lawfully significant, part of the investigator's *data*. If the latter *uses* that term to describe what is going on, its "meaning" in any and all senses of 'meaning' will not be the same as the subject's term.

The subject's *concept* of prayer will of course have an (intentional) meaning $_3$ for him that it will not have for a nonreligious person and need not have for the investigator. Only in this sense of 'meaning,' is it even plausible to say that only the religious man can "make sense" of religion. The sociologist may understand $_5$ religion without also understanding $_2$ it. For the participant, 'attending church services regularly' means $_{3,\,4}$ salvation in afterlife. For the observor-scientist, the same behavior means $_2$ something quite different, namely, certain other actions of the person and perhaps certain effects upon the community. A sociologist may call two patterns of behavior in different cultures 'baptism,' or two other patterns 'marriage,' even though the Christian "would not agree" they were the same ([8], p. 108), not merely because they happen to have certain overt features in common, nor yet "arbitrarily," but because they are believed to be similarly connected to other aspects of behavior and society. To the economist, automobiles and human labor are both commodities, not because he is insensitive to human dignity, but because they have similar properties in relation to other things, such as supply and demand. In sum, the use of a common language for purposes of communication is not in itself "incompatible," as alleged, with the external observor-observed point of view.[8]

Actions, Artifacts, and Patterns of Behavior

To what are we referring when we use such terms as 'a smile,' 'a salute,' or 'money'? A salute, surely, had better be something observable. A smile is, according to Webster, a brightening of the eyes and upward curving of the corners of the mouth. Yet, a salute is more than a position of the hand. And to describe "writhing in pain" or "signing a contract" is indeed more than to give a description "in purely mechanical terms, using a set of space-time coordinates" ([8], p. 73 and [7], p. 13). "Money" is more than pieces of metal, paper, or beads. But is the "something more" of actions and artifacts only describable in nonphysical terms? *One* reason for thinking so is an invidious use of 'physical' in the narrow sense of that term. Such items as muscle-twitches, glandular secretions, shape and size are, on this usage, the only "physical" properties. But a pattern of overt behavior is also some-

---

[8] See also the remarks by Ernest Nagel, pp. 106–107 of this volume.

thing physical, since it is certainly nonmental. A *second* reason for the belief that terms referring to actions and artifacts must mean ₁ something "nonphysical" or "something more" than overt behavior is a mistaken notion of observable reference. On this usage, only manifest or "occurrent" characters are observable. But flexibility is no less observable than bent. Our everyday statements about actions are, as I mentioned before, mentalistic and categorical. But the scientific terms corresponding to these mentalistic ones, like 'seeing-green' or 'meaning-p,' are all dispositional. Dispositional characters merely require more complex observations than do manifest ones; they are no less observable.

Actions, in one way or another, involve a reference to thought or purposes. An objectivist definition of 'purpose,' corresponding to the mental state, can be constructed. The difference between just "walking down the street" and doing so "in order to mail a letter" is not in what is presently observed, but a way of speaking about something else which we expect to occur later bringing this action to a close. Or, as with 'looking for' something, it may be a way of speaking about some past event which led to the present behavior or, possibly, some combination of things in the past and future. All this makes 'purpose' a more complex term than 'tall,' but not on that account "nonphysical." Generally, a *pattern* of behavior observed in the past or to be observed in the future toward things and other people is the "something more" than present or manifest characters that is meant ₁ by defined terms referring to actions.

Social artifacts, like money, tools, and weapons, are defined by the behavior of people with respect to inanimate, material objects. In and of itself, a scarlet letter or a yellow arm-badge is no different in "meaning" from an iron cross or a purple heart. As material objects they are all equally "meaningless." What gives them (referential) meaning ₁ as rewards or punishments is, of course, the behavior of people toward them. A cathedral is not just a pile of stones, not even just a pile of stones arranged in a certain pattern. 'Cathedral' (referentially) means ₁ a physical structure of a certain kind *and* certain ways people behave towards it, like entering it at certain intervals and performing certain activities, which *the people,* not the investigator, describe as worshipping. For the rest, the "meaning" of 'cathedral' is either the associations that people have to it, meaning ₄ (reflecting intentional meaning ₃), or else its meaning ₂, that is, its connections with other aspects of the culture, such as the kind of economy or other behaviors, like being charitable. Such connections among kinds of behavior are observable. The investigator's own past experience, aided perhaps by a class of judges, may be drawn upon to determine tentatively the identifying characteristics of, say, "friendly" behavior. But this usable past is not part of the criteria by which he now identifies the action. The belief that it is and thus requires "participation," confuses the origins of a classification with what that category now refers to.

MEANING AND CONTEXT

Not *all* of the past and future behaviors that are connected with, say, 'friendly,' but not with 'hostile' actions, are part of the (referential) meaning $_1$ of the terms, only enough of them to distinguish friendly from hostile actions. How else could we assent to the proposition that a man may smile and smile, yet be a villain? It is true, even tautologically true, that "an idea gets its sense from the role it plays in a system" only if "meaning" is construed intentionally, as meaning $_3$ (reflected by the psychologist's meaning $_4$), or, for scientific terms, as significance or meaning $_2$. If I understand $_1$ another person's language, I don't necessarily also know all the "meaning" that his terms carry for him. From understanding $_1$ alone, we do not *ipso facto* learn everything that any user of that language might associate with terms. This must be discovered. Nor need I know everything about a system of religious beliefs in order to know the meaning $_1$ of 'baptism,' any more than I need to know everything about an economic system in order to know the meaning $_1$ of 'money.' Neither to understand $_1$ a language nor to know the meaning $_1$ of its referential terms, need I know how everything is connected with everything else. I understand $_1$ the meaning $_1$ of 'sell' and of 'price,' both terms with complex definitions, without also understanding $_5$ the connection between, say, selling price and cost price. Nor is the way they vary together merely a "conceptual" matter. Learning to use the word 'cost' does not entail learning all the laws of economics, any more than learning to use the word 'marriage' tells me all about marriage. Of course, to have "genuine understanding," if that means understanding $_2$, then one must *be* married. But "genuine understanding" may also mean knowing connections among things. And a bachelor sociologist's understanding $_5$ of this meaning $_2$, that is, the connections the institution of marriage has with, say, property-distribution, education, job-stability, and so on, may well exceed that of the most-often married person. Nor can he discover these things by analyzing the concept of marriage. The most one can thus discover, besides the legal definition of the term, is the (psychological) meaning $_4$ it has for certain people, the gratifications and responsibilities they associate with it. For the meaning $_2$ or significance of marriage he will have to grub among the facts.

A pervasive fusion of the various meanings of 'meaning' and of 'understanding,' lends a specious plausibility to the insistence upon the "total context" in order to grasp "meaning" and have "genuine understanding." What a term is used to refer to (meaning $_1$) is confused, on the one hand, with the psychological associations (meanings $_{3,4}$) we have to it and, on the other, with the lawful connections (meaning $_2$) the object of reference has with other things. An uncritical use of 'concept,' blurs the distinction between our thought of something, "our idea of it," and the characteristics referred to by a term which is the text of that thought. Thoughts or concepts are sometimes also called "meanings." By spinning out these "meanings," we are said to "understand" human and social concepts, man and society. If we unpack the various uses of 'meaning' and of 'understanding,' it is clear that at best such "conceptual analysis" can tell us what things (some) people think go together, not how things are actually connected.

The difference between the action of raising my arm and the movement of my arm going up is that the former is done intentionally or for a purpose. The purpose need not be conscious; an action may be performed habitually, as reaching for a cigarette, or spontaneously, as jumping to dodge a car. In other words, there need not be any mental act present when performing an action. Automatic signalling for a left turn is also an action. However, a complete description of *what* was done, of the (referential) meaning $_1$ of 'signalling,' requires mention of motives or purposes that are *part* of the action. Nor need these purposes be those of the person performing the action. Many of our actions require reference to a standard for complete description. To describe what is happening when a man tips his hat to a woman acquaintance requires a set of statements that mention, besides the regularity of his behavior, the presence in society of certain standards or norms. Norms don't exist by themselves; they ultimately involve mental acts. They may be explicated as, say, certain definite and durable expectations that people in a society have about each other's behavior. 'Expectation,' in turn, can be defined by certain dispositions, such as the imposition of penalties if certain behavior does not occur. The new recruit's salute is not yet habitual, but may well become so. What makes it "rule-governed," while the habit of chain-smoking is not, is the recruit's membership in a hierarchically-structured institution in which such behavior is "expected." Regularity of behavior under certain circumstances characterizes both "rule-governed" and merely habitual behavior. The "something more" in the former is the different way in which these regularities were acquired.

The two expressions 'raising an arm' and 'arm going up' differ in "meaning" in all four senses of 'meaning,' referentially, intentionally, psychologically, and in significance. In this sense, and so far as it goes, the mentalist's answer to Wittgenstein's question is correct. There is certainly difference in "meaning." The relevant differences, however, can be objectively construed without appealing to any vitiating participant "inside knowledge." In this respect, there is nothing about such terms marking them as "logically" different from those of natural science.

Behind the rejection of so-called "mechanical" explanation seems to lie the notion that any explanation that does not use mentalistic terms in their mentalistic sense is "mechanical," that is, is about movements in space, not about intelligent, purposive behavior. Partly, we have again the narrow use of 'physical,' so that only the terms of physics and chemistry are physical or nonmental. But the definition of an action as a set of behavioral dispositions, bodily states, and environmental circumstances surely does not mention merely "movements." Nor, as I have suggested schematically in discussing 'purpose,' is there any reason to believe that an objectivist account cannot be given of "intelligent" behavior, that is, the ability to vary behavior relative to a goal, under changing circumstances. Man of course "understands his situation," while a dog does not. This use of 'understanding' can be objectively construed by means of dispositional and occurrent factors present in and operating on the man but not the dog; for instance, his past learning of certain rules (standards and regularities) or his present awareness of them.[9]

Motives and Causes

To be sure, explanation by causes is only one use of 'explain.' Citing a motive also explains, as does giving a detailed description, as when we explain, say, the structure of feudalism ([4]). These different uses of 'explain,' among others, also have their corresponding senses of 'understand.' They are not mutually incompatible. Which is "appropriate" depends upon what the person wants to know. Sometimes motives are causes, sometimes not. Buying a house is an action whose complete description in "neutral" or nonmentalistic terms would be quite complicated, requiring mention among other things of certain legal statutes. But an answer to why Jones bought a house might well state a motive, namely, a desire for privacy. This motive is hardly part of the (referential) meaning $_1$ of 'buying a house.' It is, though, part of its meaning $_2$, that is, living in one's own house is a way of getting privacy. Here a motive is also a cause. Doubtless other (concurrent) causes are also operative. At other times, to cite a motive is not to give a cause but to tell *what* is happening, as when explaining what a signal or salute *is*. A reference to standards and motives will occur in the descriptions of these actions. But explaining *what* an action is and explaining *why* it occurred are two different things. Each may require mention of motives, though, of course, not *the same* ones. Jumping out a window is one action, of which the desire for death might be a cause. On the other hand, we would not say that a man committed suicide because he wanted to kill himself, since this wish is part of the (referential) meaning $_1$ of suicide.

Over-attention to cases of the latter kind perhaps is the source of a basic error that unfortunately pervades Melden's temperate and frequently illuminating book. He argues that a motive can never be a cause since, on good Humean principles, the cause must be logically distinct from the effect. He interprets this to imply that a description of the cause must not contain "any reference" to the effect. But 'wanting-to-do-X' mentions 'doing-X' and, generally, a description of a desire requires reference to the object desired.

[9] For more detailed discussions of how psychologists distinguish between meaningful behavior and mere movements, see I. E. Farber, pp. 165–67 and J. A. Fodor, pp. 228–330 in this volume.

Hence, Melden concludes, they are not logically independent and motives cannot be causes for actions ([6], pp. 53, 114, 128). But there is no logical *implication* between wanting-to-do-X and actually doing X. The thought-of-snow-tomorrow means $_3$ or intends snow tomorrow, but it does not logically entail that it will snow tomorrow. No more does the thought-of-doing-X logically entail doing-X. An adequate analysis of the nature of mental acts and how they are related to their intentions is indispensable. Although the relation of meaning $_3$ between a thought and its intention is a logical one, the (occurrence of) thought itself no more entails its intention than, analogously, the logical relation 'or' permits the deduction of 'q' from 'p or q.' A thought, after all, can mean $_3$ what does not and never will exist. *The mental act of wanting-to-do-X is one fact. Doing-X is quite another and distinct fact. The former might on some occasions cause the latter.*

In some contexts standards and motives are causes; in some other contexts, they describe the action. Those enchanted by "rule-governed" behavior now tell us again and again that unless something is done in accordance with a rule, it is not really an action. This restriction has the odd consequence that a man may act purposively and yet not be doing anything. A married man making advances to a choir boy is not really doing anything, but instead has something "happening" to him ([7], p. 10). I see no warrant either in common usage or in common sense for this restrictive use of 'action,' based, at least in part, on a bad pun on "what is done" or "not done." Even granting the dubious doctrine that we only ask for a man's motives when he deviates from the "done" thing, we want the motives for his action, that is, for his purposive behavior, not for something, like a brick falling on his head, that merely happened to him. People are often punished for doing the "not done" thing, which is hardly reasonable if, like the brick, it just "happened" to them. Freud indeed taught us how narrow is the line between what a man does and what happens to him. But it was, alas, the extent of what happens to us, not that of what we do, which he restricted.

The distinction between the what and the why of actions is also relevant to the notion that causal explanations are only appropriate to our "deviations from norms" ([7], p. 10)—(which, not quite incidentally, also may be instances of rational, purposive behavior). Partly, this view seems to stem from the fact that when we reply to a why-question by stating a norm, we often are explaining what is occurring, that being all the person wants to know. By definition, such an answer could not be given for "deviant" behavior. Even more fundamental is a pervasive equivocation between different uses of 'rule,' once as a descriptive regularity and once as a prescriptive standard or norm. We do indeed consider that an insane man, incapable of judging between alternative courses of action, thus deviating from descriptively regular or normal human behavior, has things "happen" to him that a normal man "does." A man who deviates from a prescriptive norm, however, is not necessarily insane. He may be the only sane one among us.

Three Senses of "Same Fact"

On this possibly frivolous note, I conclude that the objectivist program emerges unscathed from the barrage of criticisms recently directed against it. Yet, some uneasiness about the objectivist thesis remains to be allayed. When all is is said and done, is the objectivist talking about the "same facts" as we describe in everyday mentalistic language? *Can* talk about causes replace, without residue, talk about motives? Can the scientist's non-interactionist account be made to accord with our commonsense (and clinical) belief that mind and body do affect each other? As a final therapeutic step, it may pay to be explicit by distinguishing three uses of the phrase "same fact" that are relevant to this discussion.

1) Two statements may describe different states of affairs, yet be such that one of them is true (false) if and only if the other is also true (false). Such (synthetically) extensional equivalences may be said to express the same $_1$ fact. In particular, if to any given statement about a person's motives or other mental states, there is another containing only physiological, behavioral, and environmental terms that is extensionally equivalent to the first, then they express the same $_1$ fact. They do not mean the same either intentionally or referentially. The scientist's description, containing no terms referring to conscious states, thus "leaves out" minds. Talk about overt behavior and other physical items does not replace "without residue" talk about motives. On the other hand, since they express the same $_1$ fact, whenever the objectivist description is true of anyone, a corresponding mentalistic account will also be true.

2) We can strengthen, beyond mere extensional equivalence, the use of "same fact." The term 'red,' for instance, directly refers to a color. Light waves cause but are not colors. However, the descriptive phrase 'the color with the longest wave length' is a way of indirectly referring to the color red. 'The color of this book is red' and 'The color of this book is the color with the longest wave length' express the same $_2$ fact. Similarly, a mentalistic term, like 'thinking-about-Italy$_m$' directly describes a state of consciousness, while its objectivist parallel 'thinking-about-Italy $_0$' indirectly refers to this state. Generally, two different statements express the same $_2$ fact, if the terms in which they differ are related to each other as direct and indirect descriptions or ways of referring. Since corresponding mentalistic and objectivist statements in this twofold way express the same $_{1, 2}$ facts, their "sameness" is stronger than the mere extensional equivalence of, say, 'Roses are red' and 'Sugar is sweet.'

We say that mental anguish, for instance, anxiety, causes ulcers or that a bodily wound causes pain. Our common language is interactionist through and through. Extensional equivalence and direct *versus* indirect reference permit us to fit scientific parallelism with this piece of interactionist commonsense. On the objectivist account, a mental state can affect the body only through its corresponding physical state. But the objectivist term 'anxiety $_0$' is an indirect description of the mentalistic 'anxiety $_m$.' They may thus each be used to express the same $_2$ fact. In particular, if it is true that anxiety $_0$ causes ulcers, we may also truly say that anxiety $_m$ causes ulcers. The two causal attributions, the everyday interactionist one and that of the objectivist, are extensionally equivalent and express the same $_1$ fact. Since they also express the same $_2$ fact, there is more than mere extensional equivalence. We can thus make sense both of our commonsense interactionism as well as of its scientific denial. This is as it should be for, as we know, philosophy leaves everything as it is.

3) The statement-form 'P or Q' is logically equivalent to "not both not-P and not-Q." By virtue of this tautology, 'Either Jones has a daughter or he has a son' expresses the same $_3$ fact as 'It is not the case that Jones has neither a daughter nor a son.' Generally, two statements may be said to express the same $_3$ fact, if they are logically, that is, tautologically equivalent, or, to say the same thing differently, if the statement of their equivalence is analytic. Statements containing terms directly referring to mental states are not *tautologically* equivalent to statements containing their corresponding indirectly-referring objectivist terms. They do not therefore express the same $_3$ facts. However, most if not all action and other social terms must be explicated, that is, given "real definitions" of their (referential) meaning $_1$, whether in everyday speech or in science. Given such explications of usage, the terms, like 'owning property' or even 'behaving according to a standard,' serve as abbreviatory expressions for the more complex ones. Statements containing the abbreviatory terms are then analytically equivalent to statements containing, in their place, the longer explicating expressions. They thus express the same $_3$ fact. But even in such cases, the two expressions, the short and the long ones, would not have the same (intentional or associational) meanings $_{3,\,4}$. Two expressions that are "logically" different in a use of 'logical' that encompasses and conflates several different ways that an expression can mean may yet be logically the same in a different and precise sense of 'logical.'

The crucial terms in this controversy are 'meaning' and 'understanding.' Often in philosophical controversy, once several uses of certain crucial terms have been distinguished, little remains to argue about. Doubtless this happy outcome is too much to hope for now, though I hope that some contribution has at least been made to clarity about the issues at stake. I hazard the diagnosis that a vast irresolution about the status of mind lies at the root of the revived attempt to resolve empirical matters of fact "logically" or "conceptually." Unwilling to grant ontological status to mind, what properly belongs to mind, our thoughts or concepts, is projected on to the world. This is the road, not trodden for the first time, that leads to anthropomorphic rationalism.

REFERENCES

1. BERGMANN, GUSTAV, *Meaning and Existence* (Wisconsin, 1959), pp. 3–38, 106–14.
2. BERGMANN, GUSTAV, "Acts," in *Logic and Reality* (Wisconsin, 1964), pp. 3–44.
3. BERGMANN, GUSTAV, "Purpose, Function, Scientific Explanation," *Acta Sociologica*, 5 (1962), pp. 225–238. [Reprinted in this volume, pp. 211–23]
4. BRODBECK, MAY, "Explanation, Prediction, and 'Imperfect' Knowledge," *Minnesota Studies in the Philosophy of Science*, vol. III. H. Feigl & G. Maxwell, eds., Univer. of Minnesota Press (Minneapolis, 1962), pp. 231–272. [Reprinted in this volume, pp. 363–398]
5. GROSSMANN, R., "Propositional Attitudes," *Philosophical Quarterly*, *10* (1960), pp. 301–12.
6. MELDEN, A. I., *Free Action* (London, 1961).
7. PETERS, R. S., *The Concept of Motivation* (London, 1958).
8. WINCH, P., *The Idea of a Social Science* (London, 1958).
9. WITTGENSTEIN, L., *Philosophical Investigations* (Oxford, 1953).

Two ★ VALUES

AND SOCIAL SCIENCE

INTRODUCTION

The subjective-objective dichotomy is troublesome, for its terms are used in more than one way. On one use, conscious states—emotions, sensations, acts of imagining, perceiving, desiring, and the like—are subjective events, and our inner awareness of them is subjective knowledge. Things external to the mind, on the other hand—material objects and overt bodily behavior —are objective, and observation provides objective knowledge of them. In the last section the terms were used in this way as we examined the question of how we know about other people's states of mind.

In another use, the subjective-objective dichotomy distinguishes biased from unbiased judgments. Accordingly, an objective report, whatever its content—whether of motives (our own or others), a social occurrence, or the results of a laboratory experiment—is one in which the reporter's feelings, wishes, or values do not, consciously or unconsciously, distort his description of the situation. If they do, then his account is subjective; it is a biased representation of the facts that also misrepresents them or, at least, evaluates rather than merely describes them. Is it possible to give descriptions and explanations of social events that are unaffected by bias? That issue and its ramifications are discussed in this section.

The physical scientist, studying inanimate objects which do not choose their behavior, does not pass moral judgment on the facts he uncovers. He does not blame or praise the atom—not even the hydrogen atom—for acting as it does, though he may, of course, make such judgments about the purposes to which this knowledge is put. The social scientists, on the other hand, studying human behavior, most of it in situations where choice between alternatives is possible, very likely has moral convictions about the behavior he observes. He not only observes, he may also praise or condemn. Can his description of behavior be separated from the moral judgment he passes on it? Sociological relativists believe that this separation cannot be made. They hold that statements about human affairs are relative to our values in such a way that they cannot properly be characterized as factually true or false. Max Weber and Karl Mannheim, whose position is more extreme than Weber's, have been influential exponents of this doctrine. Others, represented here by Ernest Nagel and Gustav Bergmann, vigorously reject it as philosophically untenable.

Weber's argument is complex and its import is easily misunderstood and exaggerated. His *obiter dictum,* "There is no absolutely objective scientific analysis of culture," placed in the context of his thought and mode of expression, is not quite as sweeping as it appears. Values, he believes, intrude into even the most austere attempts at objectivity at two points in our investigations. First, they determine the subject matter we select for study, and, secondly, they influence our judgment about the cause of a specific event. By virtue of these evaluative choices, we endow certain situations and not others with "significance." Because their significance thus depends upon our interests, they cannot be value-free. We shall return presently to his views about causality. What can be said about the argument from the selection of subject matter? Now, it may very well be the case that, for example, the interests of a physicist are channeled into nuclear physics rather than, say, optics by the government's need and financial support. Values, both social and personal, thus play a role in the selection of problems. But they do not necessarily play a role in their solution, as Nagel points out. The laws discovered about the structure of the nucleus do not say anything about values; nor are they, in any meaningful sense of the word, relative to anything. They are either true or false, no matter what the causes leading to their discovery. Is social science different in principle?

An ambiguity in the term *significant* may lead one to think that social science is different. A characteristic or kind or event—physical or social— is significant or meaningful if it enters into laws, that is, if we know something about its causes and effects. Such events therefore will, on what we may call theoretical grounds, be *worth knowing.* But individual and social actions are also significant in the different sense that we judge them to be *worth doing* (or not doing). That is, we take a moral stance toward the behavior. Social actions are significant in both the moral and theoretical senses of the term. But we must first know what an action is, that is, what is occurring, before we can either judge it morally or find its connections with other things. We may indeed have to know these connections before we can morally appraise it, because the consequences of an action affect our moral judgment of it. But what the action is, the consequences that it has, and the moral judgment that we pass on it in the light of these consequences are all different things. We cannot disagree about the value or significance —in either its moral or theoretical senses—of a certain kind of conduct unless that behavior is identifiable independently of our evaluations.

The undeniable fact that our values may determine the problems we select for study is only one among several reasons that have been cited to justify the view that bias cannot be eliminated from social science. In the selection by Ernest Nagel, he subjects this and several other arguments to careful analysis. The claim of these arguments to demonstrate the impossibility of a value-free social science dissolves under his close scrutiny.

Nagel concludes his analysis with a discussion of Mannheim's historical relativism. Mannheim's ideas are a development of Marx's notion of *ide-*

ology. This is the doctrine that, except for the "privileged" proletariat (or, rather, its self-conscious avant-garde), men do not possess truth, but merely systems of belief (ideologies) that reflect and support the interests of their economic class. Mannheim "transcends" Marx by rejecting the privileged status of the proletariat. Marx is superseded not by granting truth to others, but by denying it to all. Our social perspective systematically distorts all beliefs about human affairs. By pooling their biases the intellectuals may arrive at a new "relational" view of the world, but no group or individual has access to the truth. All systems of belief are ideologies. The investigator must therefore renounce the illusory search for truth and turn instead to the "sociology of knowledge." This Mannheim conceives as the study of the social basis of ideologies or systems of false belief.

"Sociology of knowledge," as Mannheim speaks of it, is clearly a misnomer for the sociology of *belief.* For knowledge is the body of true belief; we cannot *know* that which is not true. Nor can we characterize a belief as false, unless we know what would make it true. In order to know, as we do, that perception sometimes deceives us, we must also know what is really there. If we cannot know this, then it makes no sense to speak either, as psychologists do, about the causes for sense deception or, with the sociologists, about the causes for social distortion of belief. Just as we cannot say that something is a lie unless we know the truth, so *deception* and *distortion* have no meaning unless we know what is being misperceived or distorted. If social factors are among the causes of false belief, they are also among the causes of the grasp of truth. Why some social milieus promote distortion and others further the search for truth is a fine and fascinating question. But we cannot answer it without *nonsocial* criteria for distinguishing truth from falsehood.

Bergmann's paper presents a philosophical critique of Mannheim's doctrine and a new analysis of the concept of ideology. As Mannheim used the term, *ideology* covered everything without distinction, and therefore nothing. Probably its most common use today is for any system of value beliefs—especially political values—as distinguished from beliefs about fact. The term retains, however, its derogatory connotations. Its use thereby intimates, however subtly, that all judgments of value are discreditable and should be shunned—as if value judgment had become outmoded in a cold world of fact. Forcefully insisting upon the indispensability of values, Bergmann utilizes the notion of a rationale for the body of beliefs that motivate our actions. A rationale is typically a mixture of factual beliefs, value judgments, and a third category which is neither the one nor the other, but consists instead of value judgments masquerading as facts. He reserves the term *ideology* for these values in disguise. The power of a value judgment to win our assent and influence behavior increases greatly if it appears in the guise of a statement of fact. We recognize the insidious mechanism of effective propaganda. He discusses several illuminating examples from intellectual history of unwitting ideological thought. Patent errors of logic and of fact, otherwise inexplicable, are seen as the effect of unacknowledged values. In consequence, these thinkers produce theories that covertly plead a cause. They are scientific ideologies which their authors, in all good faith, propound as objective scientific theories.

Weber's belief that our values determine what we select as the cause of a cultural event requires further comment. It is his deepest reason for denying that we can have "absolutely objective" knowledge of human affairs. Weber makes clear that by *culture* and *cultural reality* he means a concrete, individual case—a particular bureaucracy or a particular financial transaction. Objectivity deserts us when we explain such individual events or configurations rather than in our knowledge of general laws. This view depends upon his conception of the relation between individual causal imputations and general social laws and also upon his conception of the aim of social science. His ideas about causality, though unperspicuously expressed, are very perspicacious. However, they do not in fact imply that objectivity is beyond our reach. The notion that the goal of social science is to explain the "unique," concrete event surely misplaces the emphasis of any science. Why my car broke down interests the garage mechanic, but not the physicist. The cause of a rise in the price of milk is not of direct concern to the economist, nor do either the theoretical psychologist or the sociologist seek to explain Teddy's delinquency. This is the job of the psychotherapist and the social worker. The scientist seeks general truths or laws and is interested in the particular occurrence only as an instance of a type.

The romantics extolled the unique, concrete, and inexhaustible over the general, abstract, and limited. But no concrete event—this sunset, that flash of lightning, this generous act, that war—is wholly unique; otherwise we could not refer to it at all. We can use language only because there is a sameness and constancy among all the difference and change in the world. Besides the sameness of characteristics, by virtue of which two sunsets, say, are both sunsets, there is also a constancy amidst the changing flux that we express by general laws. Thunder, for instance, always follows lightning. Although the romanticism of his time resonates in Weber's language, he did not of course share the romantic's irrational notion that reality is ineffable, to be lived and felt rather than described and thought about. Nor did he deny the objectivity of our *general* knowledge. We use general laws in order to explain causally individual events. But there is frequently, perhaps always, a gap between theory and application. Values, according to Weber, fill this gap. When, therefore, we impute causes to individual events, this imputation cannot be value free.

An event has many causes; which cause we select for mention depends upon our values; the ascription of a cause to an event cannot therefore be wholly objective. This is Weber's argument. To see why he made it and to assess its merit, three different cases involving the selection of causes will be discussed briefly.

First, assume that we know the general laws about all the necessary and sufficient conditions for the occurrence of a specific event that we wish to explain. Suppose that a sealed tank containing certain liquids explodes. Among the determining factors for this event are the materials of which the tank was made, the build-up of pressure, the rise in temperature, certain chemical reactions, and so on. Clearly, which among these we select as *the* cause depends upon our interest. Temporal priority, manipulability, control, and the ascription of moral responsibility are some of the factors that determine which condition we select. We may mention that feature we can do something about (for instance, the type of container), or how this situation differed from others where an explosion did not occur (for instance, the presence of a spark). Either of these, as well as others, may be mentioned as the cause, and all can be right, just as the physician who mentions the victim's loss of blood as the cause of death is not disagreeing with the detective who mentions a murderer's weapon or motives. In this respect social and physical events are in the same boat. Though the cause selected as "significant" depends upon our interests and values, clearly whether or not it is *in fact* a cause does not depend upon them.

The second case is more realistic for social science. We may have some generalizations which are of quite broad scope but which do not alone give the necessary and sufficient conditions for a specific event. Our most comprehensive laws are also the most abstract, for their terms refer to complex patterns of behavior that cannot be observed directly. Far from being the most "devoid of content," as Weber asserts, in an important sense these laws are much richer than laws of lesser scope. A law such as Newton's that can explain the motion of the planets, the fall of an apple, the path of a bullet, and the movement of the tides obviously has more "content" than a law that can explain only one of these. Similarly, sociological laws about patterns of behavior that are common to many different types of institutions (such as bureaucracies) have greater scope and therefore content than laws about less general structures (such as trade unions).

When we seek the causes of specific events, however, the more comprehensive laws will not alone enable us to answer them. We may, for instance, know a generalization about the behavior of business corporations in certain circumstances. They will merge with smaller companies, diversify their products, and so on. But suppose we want to explain why a particular automobile company bought out a firm making radios. Our general law does not state the necessary and sufficient conditions for this occurrence. We have to show that the behavior of this company is an instance of the concepts mentioned in the law. Nor is that all we need to know. The general law need not explain why they chose radios instead of bicycles, or why they bought this radio company here rather than another there. To select the cause of this firm's buying that one, we have to know a great many more facts about each firm. When we do decide on the causes of this particular action, we assume that there is some generalization covering that behavior in these special circumstances. We have to conjecture a lawful connection among these more specific kinds of events that, together with the more comprehensive laws at hand, will explain this particular firm's behavior. These conjectures are inferences that we make on the basis of past experience and other knowledge. We evaluate the probable causal efficacy of some features over others. The truth of these evaluations, which must be tested empirically, does not depend upon our values.

The third case is unique to social science, for it concerns the desire for a "rational" explanation of action, that is, an explanation in terms of motives and reasons. We know an abundance of statistical correlations about the behavior of certain kinds of social groups. By the nature of such generalizations, they do not tell us anything about the behavior of any particular member of that group. We cannot predict how any individual will behave, and more to the point for our purpose, even if we know that a particular person has exhibited the behavior mentioned in the correlation, we do not thereby know the cause of his action. Suppose, for instance, that bankers usually vote Republican and we know that Brown, a banker, voted Republican. We cannot say that his being a banker was the cause of the way he voted. Causal laws permit the prior prediction of behavior, and we could not have predicted how he voted from the merely statistical correlation. However, even if the law were universal and stated that such behavior invariably occurs, though we could predict it, we might still be reluctant to accept Brown's occupation as the cause of his behavior. Being a banker is not *in itself* a motive or reason for voting one way rather than another. Precisely because people's motives and reasons are so various, we only have statistical correlations about persons characterized by their membership in a social group.

It is a mistake to expect to universalize all such statistical correlations. The prospect is not only appalling, it is happily also most unlikely. People are not all that conformist. We expect instead to find more basic laws about people's motives, needs, beliefs, and circumstances that will explain the statistical regularities. When we can do this, we will know not only why most bankers vote Republican, but also why some do not. When we do know the motives, beliefs, and expectations that cause behavior, then we find it intelligible. But there is nothing "irrational" about explaining a person's action by means of his occupation, social status, habits, or, for that matter, his blood pressure. It merely does not tell us what we in everyday life frequently want to know—namely, those causes by virtue of which we ascribe moral responsibility. These causes are usually motives and reasons, but they need not be. If a man acts thoughtlessly or merely from habit, we may also judge him harshly for that. Which of all the causes of his action we select for mention depends upon those we consider to be morally relevant. But these moral considerations do not affect whether or not the cause mentioned actually is a cause. Nor do they affect the fact that, in addition to conscious motives and reasons, there are also other complex social and psychological causes of human conduct which interest the social scientist.

In general, there are two kinds of decisions about causality that we may have to make. Confusion arises from not distinguishing them. First, we may not know the causes of an event and we may have to choose among many possibilities. We make a judgment, which does not depend upon our values, of *causal* significance. Second, we do already know the causes, or some of them, and our interest centers on choosing those that are relevant to ascribing responsibility. We make a judgment, which does depend upon our values, of *moral* significance.

A completely adequate analysis of all the logical problems involved in imputing causes to particular events or actions requires further discussion of the relation of social laws to the behavior of individuals (Section Four), of the characteristic imperfection of our social knowledge (Section Five), and of Weber's views about ideal types and their role in theories (Section Six). The philosophical problems of the social sciences interlock, and questions about causal imputation are at the center of a closely knit web.

[5] "Objectivity" in Social Science

MAX WEBER

There is no absolutely "objective" scientific analysis of culture—or put perhaps more narrowly but certainly not essentially differently for our purposes—of "social phenomena" independent of special and "one-sided" viewpoints according to which—expressly or tacitly, consciously or unconsciously—they are selected, analyzed and organized for expository purposes. The reasons for this lie in the character of the cognitive goal of all research in social science which seeks to transcend the purely *formal* treatment of the legal or conventional norms regulating social life.

The type of social science in which we are interested is an *empirical science* of concrete *reality* (*Wirklichkeitswissenschaft*). Our aim is the understanding of the characteristic uniqueness of the reality in which we move. We wish to understand on the one hand the relationships and the cultural significance of individual events in their contemporary manifestations and on the other the causes of their being historically *so* and not *otherwise*. Now, as soon as we attempt to reflect about the way in which life confronts us in immediate concrete situations, it presents an infinite multiplicity of successively and coexistently emerging and disappearing events, both "within" and "outside" ourselves. The absolute infinitude of this multiplicity is seen to remain undiminished even when our attention is focused on a single "object," for instance, a concrete act of exchange, as soon as we seriously attempt an exhaustive description of *all* the individual components of this "individual phenomena," to say nothing of explaining it causally. All the analysis of infinite reality which the finite human mind can conduct rests on the tacit assumption that only a finite portion of this reality constitutes the object of scientific investigation, and that only it is "important" in the sense of being "worthy of being known." But what are the criteria by which this segment is selected? It has often been thought that the decisive criterion in the cultural sciences, too, was in the last analysis, the "regular" recurrence of certain causal relationships. The "laws" which we are able to perceive in the infinitely manifold stream of events must— according to this conception—contain the scientifically "essential" aspect of reality. As soon as we have shown some causal relationship to be a "law," i.e., if we have shown it to be universally valid by means of comprehensive historical induction or have made it immediately and tangibly plausible according to our subjective experience, a great number of similar cases order themselves under the formula thus attained. Those elements in each individual event which are left unaccounted for by the selection of their elements subsumable under the "law" are considered as scientifically unintegrated residues which will be taken care of in the further perfection of the system of "laws." Alternatively they will be viewed as "accidental" and therefore scientifically unimportant *because* they do not fit into the structure of the "law"; in other words, they are not typical of the event and hence can only be the objects of "idle curiosity." Accordingly, even among the followers of the Historical School we continually find the attitude which declares that the ideal which all the sciences, including the cultural sciences, serve and towards which they should strive even in the remote future is a system of propositions from which reality can be "deduced." As is well known, a leading natural scientist believed that he could designate the (factually unattainable) ideal goal of such a treatment of cultural reality as a sort of *"astronomical"* knowledge.

Let us not, for our part, spare ourselves the trouble of examining these matters more closely—however often they have already been discussed. The first thing that impresses one is that the "astronomical" knowledge which was referred to is not a system of laws at all. On the contrary, the laws which it presupposes have been taken from other disciplines like mechanics. But it too concerns itself with the question of the *individual* consequence which the working of these laws in an unique *configuration* produces, since it is these individual configurations which are *significant* for us. Every individual constellation which it "explains" or predicts is causally explicable only as the consequence of another equally individual constellation which has preceded it. As far back as we may go into the grey mist of the far-off past, the reality to which the laws apply always remains equally *individual,* equally *undeducible* from laws. A cosmic "primeval state" which had no individual character or less individual character than the cosmic reality of the present would naturally be a meaningless notion. But is there not some trace of similar ideas in our field in those propositions sometimes derived from natural law and sometimes verified by the observation of "primitives," concerning an economic-social "primeval state" free from historical "accidents," and characterized by phenomena such as "primitive agrarian communism," sexual "promiscuity," etc., from which individual historical development emerges by a sort of fall from grace into concreteness?

The social-scientific interest has its point of departure, of course, in the *real,* i.e., concrete, individually-structured configuration of our cultural life in its universal relationships which are themselves no less individually-structured, and in its development out of other social cultural conditions, which themselves are obviously likewise individually structured. It is clear here that the situation which we illustrated by reference to astronomy as a limiting case (which is regularly drawn on by logicians for the same purpose) appears in a more accentuated form. Whereas in astronomy, the heavenly bodies are of interest to us only in their *quantitative* and exact aspects, the *qualitative* aspect of phenomena concerns us in the social sciences. To this should be added that in the social sciences we are concerned with psychological and intellectual (*geistig*) phenomena the empathic understanding of which is naturally a problem of a specifically different type from those which the schemes of the exact natural sciences in general can or seek to solve. Despite that, this distinction in itself is not a distinction in principle, as it seems at first glance. Aside from pure mechanics, even the exact natural sciences do not proceed without qualitative categories. Furthermore, in our own field we encounter the idea (which is obviously distorted) that at least the phenomena characteristic of a money-economy—which are basic to our culture—are quantifiable and on that account subject to formulation as "laws." Finally it depends on the breadth or narrowness of one's definition of "law" as to whether one will also include regularities which because they are not quantifiable are not subject to numerical analysis. Especially insofar as the influence of psychological and intellectual (*gestige*) factors is concerned, it does not in any case exclude the establishment of *rules* governing rational conduct. Above all, the point of view still persists which claims that the task of psychology is to play a role comparable to mathematics for the *Geisteswissenschaften* in the sense that it analyzes the complicated phenomena of social life into their psychic conditions and effects, reduces them to their most elementary possible psychic factors and then analyzes their functional interdependences. Thereby, a sort of "chemistry" if not "mechanics" of the psychic foundations of social life would be created. Whether such investigations can produce valuable and—what is something else—useful results for the cultural sciences, we cannot decide here. But this would be irrelevant to the question as to whether the aim of social-economic knowledge in our sense, i.e., knowledge of *reality* with respect to its cultural *significance* and its causal relationships can be attained through the quest for recurrent sequences. Let us assume that we have succeeded by means of psychology or otherwise in analyzing all the observed and imaginable relationships of social phenomena into some ultimate elementary "factors," that we have made an exhaustive analysis and classification of them and then formulated rigorously exact laws covering their behavior.—What would be the significance of these results for our knowledge of the *historically* given culture or any individual phase thereof, such as capitalism, in its development and cultural significance? As an analytical tool, it would be as useful as a textbook of organic chemical combinations would be for our knowledge of the biogenetic aspect of the animal and plant world. In each case, certainly an important and useful preliminary step would have been taken. In neither case can concrete reality be deduced from "laws" and "factors." This is not because some higher mysterious powers reside in living phenomena (such as "dominants," "entelechies," or whatever they might be called). This, however, is a problem in its own right. The real reason is that the analysis of reality is concerned with the *configuration* into which those (hypothetical!) "factors" are arranged to form a cultural phenomenon which is historically significant to us. Furthermore, if we wish to "explain" this individual configuration "causally" we must invoke other equally individual configurations on the basis of which we will explain it with the aid of those (hypothetical!) "laws."

The determination of those (hypothetical) "laws" and "factors" would in any case only be the first of the many operations which would lead us to the desired type of knowledge. The analysis of the historically given individual configuration of those "factors" and their *significant* concrete interaction, conditioned by their historical context and especially the *rendering intelligible* of the basis and type of this significance would be the next task to be achieved. This task must be achieved, it is true, by the utilization of the preliminary analysis but it is nonetheless an entirely new and *distinct* task. The tracing as far into the past as possible of the individual features of these historically evolved configurations which are *contemporaneously* significant, and their historical explanations by antecedent and equally individual configurations would be the third task. Finally the prediction of possible future constellations would be a conceivable fourth task.

For all these purposes, clear concepts and the knowledge of those (hypothetical) "laws" are obviously of great value as heuristic means—but only as such. Indeed they are quite indispensable for this purpose. But even in this function their limitations become evident at a decisive point. In stating this, we arrive at the decisive feature of the method of the cultural sciences. We have designated as "cultural sciences" those disciplines which analyze the phenomena of life in terms of their cultural significance. The *significance* of a configuration of cultural phenomena and the basis of this significance cannot however be derived and rendered intelligible by a system of analytical laws (*Gesetzesbegriffen*), however perfect it may be, since the significance of cultural events presupposes a *value-orientation* towards these events. The concept of culture is a *value-concept*. Empirical reality becomes "culture" to us because and insofar as we relate it to value ideas. It includes those segments and only those segments of reality which have become significant to us because of this value-relevance. Only a small portion of existing concrete reality is colored by our value-conditioned interest and it alone is significant to us. It is significant because it reveals relationships which are important to us due to their connection with our values. Only because and to the extent that this is the case is it worthwhile for us to know it in its individual features. We cannot discover, however, what is meaningful to us by means of a "presuppositionless" investigation of empirical data. Rather perception of its meaningfulness to us is the presupposition of its becoming an *object* of investigation. Meaningfulness naturally does not coincide with laws as such, and the more general the law the less the coincidence. For the specific meaning which a phenomenon has for us is naturally *not* to be found in those relationships which it shares with many other phenomena.

The focus of attention on reality under the guidance of values which lend it significance and the selection and ordering of the phenomena which are thus affected in the light of their cultural significance is entirely different from the analysis of reality in terms of laws and general concepts. Neither of these two types of the analysis of reality has any necessary logical relationship with the other. They can coincide in individual instances but it would be most disastrous if their occasional coincidence caused us to think that they were not distinct *in principle*. The *cultural significance* of a phenomenon, e.g., the significance of exchange in a money economy, can be the fact that it exists on a mass scale as a fundamental component of modern culture. But the historical fact that it plays this role must be causally explained in order to render its cultural significance understandable. The analysis of the *general* aspects of exchange and the technique of the market is a—highly important and indispensable—*preliminary task*. For not only does this type of analysis leave unanswered the question as to how exchange historically acquired its fundamental significance in the modern world; but above all else, the fact with which we are primarily concerned, namely, the *cultural significance* of the money-economy, for the sake of which we are interested in the description of exchange technique and for the sake of which alone a science exists which deals with that technique—is not derivable from any "law." The *generic features* of exchange, purchase, etc., interest the jurist—but we are concerned with the analysis of the *cultural significance* of the concrete *historical* fact that today exchange exists on a mass scale. When we require an explanation, when we wish to understand what distinguishes the social-economic aspects of our culture for instance from that of antiquity in which exchange showed precisely the same generic traits as it does today and when we raise the question as to where the significance of "money economy" lies, logical principles of quite heterogeneous derivation enter into the investigation. We will apply those concepts with which we are provided by the investigation of the general features of economic mass phenomena—indeed, insofar as they are relevant to the meaningful aspects of our culture, we shall use them as *means* of exposition. The *goal* of our investigation is not reached through the exposition of those laws and concepts, precise as it may be. The question as to what should be the object of universal conceptualization cannot be decided "presuppositionlessly" but only with reference to the *significance* which certain segments of that infinite multiplicity which we call "commerce" have for culture. We seek knowledge of an historical phenomenon, meaning by historical: significant in its individuality (*Eigenart*). And the decisive element in this is that only through the presupposition that a finite part alone of the infinite variety of phenomenon is significant, does the knowledge of an individual phenomenon become meaningful. Even with the widest imaginable knowledge of "laws," we are helpless in the face of the question: how is the *causal explana-*

tion of an *individual* fact possible—since a *description* of even the smallest slice of reality can never be exhaustive? The number and type of causes which have influenced any given event are always infinite and there is nothing in the things themselves to set some of them apart as alone meriting attention. A chaos of "existential judgments" about countless individual events would be the only result of a serious attempt to analyze reality "without presuppositions." And even this result is only seemingly possible, since every single perception discloses on closer examination an infinite number of constituent perceptions which can never be exhaustively expressed in a judgment. Order is brought into this chaos only on the condition that in every case only a *part* of concrete reality is interesting and *significant* to us, because only it is related to the *cultural values* with which we approach reality. Only certain sides of the infinitely complex concrete phenomenon, namely those to which we attribute a general *cultural significance*—are therefore worthwhile knowing. They alone are objects of causal explanation. And even this causal explanation evinces the same character; an *exhaustive* causal investigation of any concrete phenomenon in its full reality is not only practically impossible—it is simply nonsense. We select only those causes to which are to be imputed in the individual case, the "essential" feature of an event. Where the *individuality* of a phenomenon is concerned, the question of causality is not a question of *laws* but of concrete causal *relationships;* it is not a question of the subsumption of the event under some general rubric as a representative case but of its imputation as a consequence of some constellation. It is in brief a *question of imputation.* Wherever the causal explanation of a "cultural" phenomenon—an "historical individual" [1] is under consideration, the knowledge of causal *laws* is not the *end* of the investigation but only a *means.* It facilitates and renders possible the causal imputation to their concrete causes of those components of the phenomenon the individuality of which is culturally significant. So far and only so far as it achieves this, is it valuable for our knowledge of concrete relationships. And the more "general," i.e., the more abstract the laws, the less they can contribute to the causal imputation of *individual* phenomenon and, more indirectly, to the understanding of the significance of cultural events.

What is the consequence of all this?

Naturally, it does not imply that the knowledge of *universal* propositions, the construction of abstract concepts, the knowledge of regularities and the attempt to formulate *"laws"* have no scientific justification in the cultural sciences. Quite the contrary, if the causal knowledge of the historians consists of the imputation of concrete effects to concrete causes, a *valid* imputation of any individual effect without the application of *"nomological" knowledge*—i.e., the knowledge of recurrent causal sequences—would in general be impossible. Whether a single individual component of a rela-

---

1 We will use the term which is already occasionally used in the methodology of our discipline and which is now becoming widespread in a more precise formulation in logic.

tionship is, in a concrete case, to be assigned causal responsibility for an effect, the causal explanation of which is at issue, can in doubtful cases be determined only by estimating the effects which we *generally* expect from it and from the other components of the same complex which are relevant to the explanation. In other words, the *"adequate"* effects of the causal elements involved must be considered in arriving at any such conclusion. The extent to which the historian (in the widest sense of the word) can perform this imputation in a reasonably certain manner with his imagination sharpened by personal experience and trained in analytic methods and the extent to which he must have recourse to the aid of special disciplines which make it possible, varies with the individual case. Everywhere, however, and hence also in the sphere of complicated economic processes, the more certain and the more comprehensive our general knowledge the greater is the *certainty* of imputation. This proposition is not in the least affected by the fact that even in the case of all so-called "economic laws" without exception, we are concerned here not with "laws" in the narrower exact natural science sense, but with *adequate* causal relationships expressed in rules and with the application of the category of "objective possibility." The establishment of such regularities is not the *end* but rather the *means* of knowledge. It is entirely a question of expediency, to be settled separately for each individual case, whether a regularly recurrent causal relationship of everyday experience should be formulated into a "law." Laws are important and valuable in the exact natural sciences, in the measure that those sciences are *universally valid*. For the knowledge of historical phenomena in their concreteness, the most general laws, because they are most devoid of content are also the least valuable. The more comprehensive the validity,—or scope—of a term, the more it leads us away from the richness of reality since in order to include the common elements of the largest possible number of phenomena, it must necessarily be as abstract as possible and hence *devoid* of content. In the cultural sciences, the knowledge of the universal or general is never valuable in itself.

The conclusion which follows from the above is that an "objective" analysis of cultural events, which proceeds according to the thesis that the ideal of science is the reduction of empirical reality to "laws," is meaningless. It is not meaningless, as is often maintained, because cultural or psychic events for instance are "objectively" less governed by laws. It is meaningless for a number of other reasons. Firstly, because the knowledge of social laws is not knowledge of social reality but is rather one of the various aids used by our minds for attaining this end; secondly, because knowledge of *cultural* events is inconceivable except on a basis of the *significance* which the concrete constellations of reality have for us in certain *individual* concrete situations. In *which* sense and in *which* situations this is the case is not revealed to us by any law; it is decided according to the *value-ideas* in the light of which we view "culture" in each individual case. "Culture" is a finite segment of the meaningless infinity of the world process, a segment on which *human beings* confer meaning and significance. This is true even for the human being who views a *particular* culture as a mortal enemy and who seeks to "return to nature." He can attain this point of view only after viewing the culture in which he lives from the standpoint of his values, and finding it "too soft." This is the purely logical-formal fact which is involved when we speak of the logically necessary rootedness of all historical entities (*historische Individuen*) in "evaluative ideas." The transcendental presupposition of every *cultural science* lies not in our finding a certain culture or any "culture" in general to be *valuable* but rather in the fact that we are *cultural beings,* endowed with the capacity and the will to take a deliberate attitude towards the world and to lend it *significance.* Whatever this significance may be, it will lead us to judge certain phenomena of human existence in its light and to respond to them as being (positively or negatively) meaningful. Whatever may be the content of this attitude— these phenomena have cultural significance for us and on this significance alone rests its scientific interest. Thus when we speak here of the conditioning of cultural knowledge through *evaluative* ideas (*Wertideen*) (following the terminology of modern logic), it is done in the hope that we will not be subject to crude misunderstandings such as the opinion that cultural significance should be attributed only to *valuable* phenomena. Prostitution is a *cultural* phenomenon just as much as religion or money. All three are cultural phenomena *only* because and *only* insofar as their existence and the form which they historically assume touch directly or indirectly on our cultural *interests* and arouse our striving for knowledge concerning problems brought into focus by the evaluative ideas which give *significance* to the fragment of reality analyzed by those concepts.

All knowledge of cultural reality, as may be seen, is always knowledge from *particular points of view.* When we require from the historian and social research worker as an elementary presupposition that they distinguish the important from the trivial and that he should have the necessary "point of view" for this distinction, we mean that they must understand how to relate the events of the real world consciously or unconsciously to universal "cultural values" and to select out those relationships which are significant for us. If the notion that those standpoints can be derived from the "facts themselves" continually recurs, it is due to the naive self-deception of the specialist who is unaware that it is due to the evaluative ideas with which he unconsciously approaches his subject matter, that he has selected from an absolute infinity a tiny portion with the study of which he *concerns* himself. In connection with this selection of individual special "aspects" of the event which always and everywhere occurs, consciously or unconsciously, there also occurs that element of cultural-scientific work which is referred to by the often-heard assertion that the "personal" element of a scientific work is what is really valuable in it, and that personality must be expressed in every work if its existence is to be justified. To be sure, without the investigator's evaluative ideas, there would be no principle of selection of subject-matter and no meaningful knowledge of the concrete reality. Just as without the investigator's conviction regarding the significance of particular cultural facts, every attempt to analyze concrete reality is absolutely meaningless, so the direction of his personal belief, the refraction of values in the prism of his mind, gives direction to his work. And the values to which the scientific genius relates the object of his inquiry may determine, i.e., decide the "conception" of a whole epoch, not only concerning what is regarded as "valuable" but also concerning what is significant or insignificant, "important" or "unimportant" in the phenomena.

Accordingly, cultural science in our sense involves "subjective" presuppositions insofar as it concerns itself only with those components of reality which have some relationship, however indirect, to events to which we attach cultural *significance*. Nonetheless, it is entirely *causal* knowledge exactly in the same sense as the knowledge of significant concrete (*individueller*) natural events which have a qualitative character. Among the many confusions which the overreaching tendency of a formal-juristic outlook has brought about in the cultural sciences, there has recently appeared the attempt to "refute" the "materialistic conception of history" by a series of clever but fallacious arguments which state that since all economic life must take place in legally or conventionally *regulated forms,* all economic "development" must take the form of striving for the creation of new *legal* forms. Hence, it is said to be intelligible only through ethical maxims and is on this account essentially different from every type of "natural" development. Accordingly the knowledge of economic development is said to be "teleological" in character. Without wishing to discuss the meaning of the ambiguous term "development," or the logically no less ambiguous term "teleology" in the social sciences, it should be stated that such knowledge need not be "teleological" in the sense assumed by this point of view. The cultural significance of normatively regulated legal *relations* and even norms themselves can undergo fundamental revolutionary changes even under conditions of the formal identity of the prevailing legal norms. Indeed, if one wishes to lose one's self for a moment in phantasies about the future, one might theoretically imagine, let us say, the "socialization of the means of production" unaccompanied by any conscious "striving" towards this result, and without even the disappearance or addition of a single paragraph of our legal code; the statistical frequency of certain legally regulated relationships might be changed fundamentally, and in many cases, even disappear entirely; a great number of legal norms might become *practically* meaningless and their whole cultural significance changed beyond identification. *De lege ferenda* discussions may be justifiably disregarded by the "materialistic conception of history" since its central proposition is the indeed inevitable change in the *significance* of legal institutions. Those who view the painstaking labor of causally understanding historical reality as of secondary importance can disregard it, but it is impossible to supplant it by any type of "teleology." From our viewpoint, "purpose" is the conception of an *effect* which becomes a *cause* of an action. Since we take into account every cause which produces or can produce a significant effect, we also consider this one. Its specific significance consists only in the fact that we not only *observe* human conduct but can and desire to understand it.

Undoubtedly, all evaluative ideas are "subjective." Between the "historical" interest in a family chronicle and that in the development of the greatest conceivable cultural phenomena which were and are common to a nation or to mankind over long epochs, there exists an infinite gradation of "significance" arranged into an order which differs for each of us. And they are, naturally, historically variable in accordance with the character of the culture and the ideas which rule men's minds. But it obviously does not follow from this that research in the cultural sciences can only have results which are "subjective" in the sense that they are *valid* for one person and not for others. Only the degree to which they interest different persons varies. In other words, the choice of the object of investigation and the extent or depth to which this investigation attempts to penetrate into the infinite causal web, are determined by the evaluative ideas which dominate the investigator and his age. In the *method* of investigation, the guiding "point of view" is of great importance for the *construction* of the conceptual scheme which will be used in the investigation. In the mode of their *use,* however, the investigator is obviously bound by the norms of our thought just as much here as elsewhere. For scientific truth is precisely what is *valid* for all who *seek* the truth.

However, there emerges from this the meaninglessness of the idea which prevails occasionally even among historians, namely, that the goal of the cultural sciences, however far it may be from realization, is to construct a closed system of concepts, in which reality is synthesized in some sort of *permanently* and *universally* valid classification and from which it can again be deduced. The stream of immeasurable events flows unendingly towards eternity. The cultural problems which move men form themselves ever anew and in different colors, and the boundaries of that area in the infinite stream of concrete events which acquires meaning and significance for us, i.e., which becomes an "historical individual," are constantly subject to change. The intellectual contexts from which it is viewed and scientifically analyzed shift. The points of departure of the cultural sciences remain changeable throughout the limitless future as long as a Chinese ossification of intellectual life does not render mankind incapable of setting new questions to the eternally inexhaustible flow of life. A systematic science of culture, even only in the sense of a definitive, objectively valid, systematic fixation of the problems which it should treat, would be senseless in itself. Such an attempt could only produce a collection of numerous, specifically particularized, heterogeneous and disparate viewpoints in the light of which reality becomes "culture" through being significant in its unique character. . . .

Returning to our special case,[2] it may be asserted without the possibility of a doubt that as soon as one seeks to derive concrete directives from practical political (particularly economic and social-political) evaluations, (1) the indispensable means, and (2) the inevitable repercussions, and (3) the thus conditioned competition of numerous possible evaluations in their *practical* consequences, are all that an *empirical* discipline can demonstrate with the means at its disposal. Philosophical disciplines can go further and lay bare the "meaning" of evaluations, i.e., their ultimate meaningful structure and their meaningful consequences, in other words, they can indicate their "place" within the totality of all the possible "ultimate" evaluations and delimit their spheres of meaningful validity. Even such simple questions as the extent to which an end should sanction unavoidable means, or the extent to which undesired repercussions should be taken into consideration, or how conflicts between several concretely conflicting ends are to be arbitrated, are entirely matters of choice or compromise. There is no (rational or empirical) scientific procedure of any kind whatsoever which can provide us with a decision here. The social sciences, which are strictly empirical sciences, are the least fitted to presume to save the individual the difficulty of making a choice, and they should therefore not create the impression that they can do so.

Finally it should be explicitly noted that the recognition of the existence of this situation is, as far as our disciplines are concerned, completely independent of the attitude one takes toward the very brief remarks made above regarding the theory of value. For there is, in general, no logically tenable standpoint from which it could be denied except a hierarchical ordering of values unequivocally prescribed by *ecclesiastical* dogmas. I need not consider whether there really are persons who assert that such problems as (a) does a concrete event occur thus and so or otherwise, or (b) why do the concrete events in question occur thus and so and not otherwise, or (c) does a given event ordinarily succeed another one according to a certain law and with what degree of probability—are not basically different from the problems: (a^1) what should one do in a concrete situation, or (b^2) from which standpoints may those situations be satisfactory or unsatisfactory, or (c^3) whether they are—whatever their form—generally formulatable propositions (axioms) to which these standpoints can be reduced. There are many who insist further that there is no logical disjunction between such enquiries as, (a) in which direction will a concrete situation (or generally, a situation of a certain type) develop and with what greater degree of probability in which particular direction than in any other and (b) a problem which investigates whether one *should* attempt to influence the development of a certain situation in a given direction—regardless of whether it be the

[2] The concluding pages of this selection are reprinted from pp. 18–22, Max Weber, *Methodology of the Social Sciences*. [A valuable adaptation of the points Weber makes in this section is to be found in the article by W. G. Runciman, pp. 561–571 of this volume—Ed.]

one in which it would also move if left alone, or the opposite direction or one which is different from either. There are those who assert that (a) the problem as to which attitudes towards any given problem specified persons or an unspecified number of persons under specified conditions will probably or even certainly take and (b) the problem as to whether the attitude which emerged in the situation referred to above is *right*—are in no way different from one another. The proponents of such views will resist any statement to the effect that the problems in the above-cited juxtapositions do not have even the slightest connection with one another and that they really are "to be separated from one another." These persons will insist furthermore that their position is not in contradiction with the requirements of scientific thinking. Such an attitude is by no means the same as that of an author who conceding the absolute heterogeneity of both types of problems, nevertheless, in one and the same book, on one and the same page, indeed in a principal and subordinate clause of one and the same sentence, makes statements bearing on each of the two heterogeneous problems referred to above. Such a procedure is strictly a matter of choice. All that can be demanded of him is that he does not unwitingly (or just to be clever) deceive his readers concerning the absolute heterogeneity of the problems. Personally I am of the opinion that nothing is too "pedantic" if it is useful for the avoidance of confusions.

Thus, the discussion of value-judgments can have only the following functions:

a) The elaboration and explication of the ultimate, internally "consistent" value-axioms, from which the divergent attitudes are derived. People are often in error, not only about their opponent's evaluations, but also about their own. This procedure is essentially an operation which begins with concrete particular evaluations and analyzes their meanings and then moves to the more general level of irreducible evaluations. It does not use the techniques of an empirical discipline and it produces no new knowledge of facts. Its "validity" is similar to that of logic.

b) The deduction of "implications" (for those accepting certain value-judgments) which follow from certain irreducible value-axioms, when the practical evaluation of factual situations is based on these axioms alone. This deduction depends on one hand, on logic, and on the other, on empirical observations for the completest possible casuistic analyses of all such empirical situations as are in principle subject to practical evaluation.

c) The determination of the factual consequences which the realization of a certain practical evaluation must have: (1) in consequence of being bound to certain indispensable means, (2) in consequence of the inevitability of certain, not directly desired repercussions. These purely empirical observations may lead us to the conclusion that (a) it is absolutely impossible to realize the object of the preference, even in a remotely approximate way, because no means of carrying it out can be discovered; (b) the more or less considerable improbability of its complete or even approximate realization, either for the same reason or because of the probable appearance of undesired repercussions which might directly or indirectly render the realization undesirable, (c) the necessity of taking into account such means or such repercussions as the proponent of the practical postulate in question did not consider, so that his evaluation of end, means, and repercussions becomes a new problem for him. Finally: (*d*) the uncovering of new axioms (and the postulates to be drawn from them) which the proponent of a practical postulate did not take into consideration. Since he was unaware of those axioms, he did not formulate an attitude towards them although the execution of his own postulate conflicts with the others either (1) in principle or (2) as a result of the practical consequences, (i.e., logically or actually). In (1) it is a matter in further discussion of problems of type (*a*); in (2), of type (*c*).

Far from being meaningless, value-discussions of this type can be of the greatest utility as long as their potentialities are correctly understood.

The utility of a discussion of practical evaluations at the right place and in the correct sense is, however, by no means exhausted with such direct "results." When correctly conducted, it can be extremely valuable for empirical research in the sense that it provides it with problems for investigation.

The problems of the empirical disciplines are, of course, to be solved "non-evaluatively." They are not problems of evaluation. But the problems of the social sciences are selected by the value-relevance of the phenomena treated. Concerning the significance of the expression "relevance to values" I refer to my earlier writings and above all to the works of Heinrich Rickert and will forbear to enter upon that question here. It should only be recalled that the expression "relevance to values" refers simply to the philosophical interpretation of that specifically scientific "interest" which determines the selection of a given subject-matter and the problems of an empirical analysis.

[6] The Value-Oriented Bias of Social Inquiry

ERNEST NAGEL

We turn, finally, to the difficulties said to confront the social sciences because the social values to which students of social phenomena are committed not only color the contents of their findings but also control their assessment of the evidence on which they base their conclusions. Since social scientists generally differ in their value commitments, the "value neutrality" that seems to be so pervasive in the natural sciences is therefore often held to be impossible in social inquiry. In the judgment of many thinkers, it is accordingly absurd to expect the social sciences to exhibit the unanimity so common among natural scientists concerning what are the established facts and satisfactory explanations for them. Let us examine some of the reasons that have been advanced for these contentions. It will be convenient to distinguish four groups of such reasons, so that our discussion will deal in turn with the alleged role of value judgments in (1) the selection of problems, (2) the determination of the contents of conclusions, (3) the identification of fact, and (4) the assessment of evidence.

1. The reasons perhaps most frequently cited make much of the fact that the things a social scientist selects for study are determined by his conception of what are the socially important values. According to one influential view, for example, the student of human affairs deals only with materials to which he attributes "cultural significance," so that a "value orientation" is inherent in his choice of material for investigation. Thus, although Max Weber was a vigorous proponent of a "value-free" social science—i.e., he maintained that social scientists must appreciate (or "understand") the values involved in the actions or institutions they are discussing but that it is not their business as objective scientists to approve or disapprove either those values or those actions and institutions—he nevertheless argued that

From *The Structure of Science* by Ernest Nagel, © 1961, by Harcourt, Brace & World, Inc., New York, and by Routledge & Kegan Paul Ltd., London, pp. 485–502, and reprinted with permission of the publishers.

The concept of culture is a *value-concept*. Empirical reality becomes "culture" to us because and insofar as we relate it to value ideas. It includes those segments and only those segments of reality which have become significant to us because of this value-relevance. Only a small portion of existing concrete reality is colored by our value-conditioned interest and it alone is significant to us. It is significant because it reveals relationships which are important to us due to their connection with our values. Only because and to the extent that this is the case is it worthwhile for us to know it in its individual features. We cannot discover, however, what is meaningful to us by means of a "presuppositionless" investigation of empirical data. Rather perception of its meaningfulness to us is the presupposition of its becoming an *object* of investigation.[1]

It is well-nigh truistic to say that students of human affairs, like students in any other area of inquiry, do not investigate everything, but direct their attention to certain selected portions of the inexhaustible content of concrete reality. Moreover, let us accept the claim, if only for the sake of the argument, that a social scientist addresses himself exclusively to matters which he believes are important because of their assumed relevance to his cultural values.[2] It is not clear, however, why the fact that an investigator selects the materials he studies in the light of problems which interest him and which seem to him to bear on matters he regards as important, is of greater moment for the logic of social inquiry than it is for the logic of any other branch of inquiry. For example, a social scientist may believe that a free economic market embodies a cardinal human value, and he may produce evidence to show that certain kinds of human activities are indispensable to the perpetuation of a free market. If he is concerned with processes which maintain this type of economy rather than some other type, how is this fact more pertinent to the question whether he has adequately evaluated the evidence for his conclusion, than is the bearing upon the analogous question of the fact that a physiologist may be concerned with processes which maintain a constant internal temperature in the human body rather than with something else? The things a social scientist *selects for study* with a view to determining the conditions or consequences of their existence may indeed be dependent on the indisputable fact that he is a "cultural being." But similarly, were we not human beings though still capable of conducting scientific inquiry, we might conceivably have an interest neither in the conditions that maintain a free market, nor in the processes involved in the homeostasis of the internal temperature in human bodies, nor for that matter in the mechanisms that regulate the height of tides, the succession of seasons, or the motions of the planets.

In short, there is no difference between any of the sciences with respect to the fact that the interests of the scientist determine what he selects for

---

[1] Max Weber, *The Methodology of the Social Sciences*, The Free Press, New York, 1949, p. 76. [Reprinted in this volume, p. 88.]

[2] This question receives some attention below in the discussion of the fourth difficulty.

investigation. But this fact, by itself, represents no obstacle to the successful pursuit of objectively controlled inquiry in any branch of study.

2. A more substantial reason commonly given for the value-oriented character of social inquiry is that, since the social scientist is himself affected by considerations of right and wrong, his own notions of what constitutes a satisfactory social order and his own standards of personal and social justice do enter, in point of fact, into his analyses of social phenomena. For example, according to one version of this argument, anthropologists must frequently judge whether the means adopted by some society achieves the intended aim (e.g., whether a religious ritual does produce the increased fertility for the sake of which the ritual is performed); and in many cases the adequacy of the means must be judged by admittedly "relative" standards, i.e., in terms of the ends sought or the standards employed by that society, rather than in terms of the anthropologist's own criteria. Nevertheless, so the argument proceeds, there are also situations in which

we must apply absolute standards of adequacy, that is evaluate the end-results of behavior in terms of purposes we believe in or postulate. This occurs, first, when we speak of the satisfaction of psycho-physical 'needs' offered by any culture; secondly, when we assess the bearing of social facts upon survival; and thirdly, when we pronounce upon social integration and stability. In each case our statements imply judgments as to the worth-whileness of actions, as to 'good' or 'bad' cultural solutions of the problems of life, and as to 'normal' and 'abnormal' states of affairs. These are basic judgments which we cannot do without in social enquiry and which clearly do not express a purely personal philosophy of the enquirer or values arbitrarily assumed. Rather do they grow out of the history of human thought, from which the anthropologist can seclude himself as little as can anyone else. Yet as the history of human thought has led not to one philosophy but to several, so the value attitudes implicit in our ways of thinking will differ and sometimes conflict.[3]

It has often been noted, moreover, that the study of social phenomena receives much of its impetus from a strong moral and reforming zeal, so that many ostensibly "objective" analyses in the social sciences are in fact disguised recommendations of social policy. As one typical but moderately expressed statement of the point puts it, a social scientist

cannot wholly detach the unifying social structure that, as a scientist's theory, guides his detailed investigations of human behavior, from the unifying structure which, as a citizen's ideal, he thinks ought to prevail in human affairs and hopes may sometimes be more fully realized. His social theory is thus essentially a program of

---

[3] S. F. Nadel, *The Foundations of Social Anthropology*, The Free Press, New York, 1951, pp. 53–54. The claim is sometimes also made that the exclusion of value judgments from social science is undesirable as well as impossible. "We cannot disregard all questions of what is socially desirable without missing the significance of many social facts; for since the relation of means to ends is a special form of that between parts and wholes, the contemplation of social ends enables us to see the relations of whole groups of facts to each other and to larger systems of which they are parts."—Morris R. Cohen, *Reason and Nature*, New York, 1931, p. 343.

action along two lines which are kept in some measure of harmony with each other by that theory—action in assimilating social facts for purposes of systematic understanding, and action aiming at progressively molding the social pattern, so far as he can influence it, into what he thinks it ought to be.[4]

It is surely beyond serious dispute that social scientists do in fact often import their own values into their analyses of social phenomena. It is also undoubtedly true that even thinkers who believe human affairs can be studied with the ethical neutrality characterizing modern inquiries into geometrical or physical relations, and who often pride themselves on the absence of value judgments from their own analyses of social phenomena, do in fact sometimes make such judgments in their social inquiries.[5] Nor is it less evident that students of human affairs often hold conflicting values; that their disagreements on value questions are often the source of disagreements concerning ostensibly factual issues; and that, even if value predications are assumed to be inherently capable of proof or disproof by objective evidence, at least some of the differences between social scientists involving value judgments are not in fact resolved by the procedures of controlled inquiry.

In any event, it is not easy in most areas of inquiry to prevent our likes, aversions, hopes, and fears from coloring our conclusions. It has taken centuries of effort to develop habits and techniques of investigation which help safeguard inquiries in the natural sciences against the intrusion of irrelevant personal factors; and even in these disciplines the protection those procedures give is neither infallible nor complete. The problem is undoubtedly more acute in the study of human affairs, and the difficulties it creates for achieving reliable knowledge in the social sciences must be admitted.

However, the problem is intelligible only on the assumption that there is a relatively clear distinction between factual and value judgments, and that however difficult it may sometimes be to decide whether a given statement has a purely factual content, it is in principle possible to do so. Thus, the claim that social scientists are pursuing the twofold program mentioned in the above quotation makes sense, only if it is possible to distinguish between, on the one hand, contributions to theoretical understanding (whose factual validity presumably does not depend on the social ideal to which a social scientist may subscribe), and on the other hand contributions to the dissemination or realization of some social ideal (which may not be accepted by all social scientists). Accordingly, the undeniable difficulties that stand in the way of obtaining reliable knowledge of human affairs because of the fact that social scientists differ in their value orientations are practical difficulties. The difficulties are not necessarily insuperable, for since by hypothesis it is not impossible to distinguish between fact and value, steps

4 Edwin A. Burtt, *Right Thinking*, New York, 1946, p. 522.
5 For a documented account, see Gunnar Myrdal, *Value in Social Theory*, London, 1958, pp. 134–52.

can be taken to identify a value bias when it occurs, and to minimize if not to eliminate completely its perturbing effects.

One such countermeasure frequently recommended is that social scientists abandon the pretense that they are free from all bias, and that instead they state their value assumptions as explicitly and fully as they can.[6] The recommendation does not assume that social scientists will come to agree on their social ideals once these ideals are explicitly postulated, or that disagreements over values can be settled by scientific inquiry. Its point is that the question of how a given ideal is to be realized, or the question whether a certain institutional arrangement is an effective way of achieving the ideal, is on the face of it not a value question, but a factual problem— to be resolved by the objective methods of scientific inquiry—concerning the adequacy of proposed means for attaining stipulated ends. Thus, economists may permanently disagree on the desirability of a society in which its members have a guaranteed security against economic want, since the disagreement may have its source in inarbitrable preference for different social values. But when sufficient evidence is made available by economic inquiry, economists do presumably agree on the factual proposition that, *if* such a society is to be achieved, then a purely competitive economic system will not suffice.

Although the recommendation that social scientists make fully explicit their value commitments is undoubtedly salutary, and can produce excellent fruit, it verges on being a counsel of perfection. For the most part we are unaware of many assumptions that enter into our analyses and actions, so that despite resolute efforts to make our preconceptions explicit some decisive ones may not even occur to us. But in any event, the difficulties generated for scientific inquiry by unconscious bias and tacit value orientations are rarely overcome by devout resolutions to eliminate bias. They are usually overcome, often only gradually, through the self-corrective mechanisms of science as a social enterprise. For modern science encourages the invention, the mutual exchange, and the free but responsible criticisms of ideas; it welcomes competition in the quest for knowledge between independent investigators, even when their intellectual orientations are different; and it progressively diminishes the effects of bias by retaining only those proposed conclusions of its inquiries that survive critical examination by an indefinitely large community of students, whatever be their value preferences or doctrinal commitments. It would be absurd to claim that this institutionalized mechanism for sifting warranted beliefs has operated or is likely to operate in social inquiry as effectively as it has in the natural sciences. But it would be no less absurd to conclude that reliable knowledge of human affairs is unattainable merely because social inquiry is frequently value-oriented.

---

6 See, e.g., S. F. Nadel, *op. cit.*, p. 54; also Gunnar Myrdal, *op. cit.*, p. 120, as well as his *Political Element in the Development of Economic Theory*, Cambridge, Mass., 1954, esp. Chap. 8.

3. There is a more sophisticated argument for the view that the social sciences cannot be value-free. It maintains that the distinction between fact and value assumed in the preceding discussion is untenable when purposive human behavior is being analyzed, since in this context value judgments enter inextricably into what appear to be "purely descriptive" (or factual) statements. Accordingly, those who subscribe to this thesis claim that an ethically neutral social science is in principle impossible, and not simply that it is difficult to attain. For if fact and value are indeed so fused that they cannot even be distinguished, value judgments cannot be eliminated from the social sciences unless all predications are also eliminated from them, and therefore unless these sciences completely disappear.

For example, it has been argued that the student of human affairs must distinguish between valuable and undesirable forms of social activity, on pain of failing in his "plain duty" to present social phenomena truthfully and faithfully:

Would one not laugh out of court a man who claimed to have written a sociology of art but who actually had written a sociology of trash? The sociologist of religion must distinguish between phenomena which have a religious character and phenomena which are a-religious. To be able to do this, he must understand what religion is. . . . Such understanding enables and forces him to distinguish between genuine and spurious religion, between higher and lower religions; these religions are higher in which the specifically religious motivations are effective to a higher degree. . . . The sociologist of religion cannot help noting the difference between those who try to gain it by a change of heart. Can he see this difference without seeing at the same time the difference between a mercenary and nonmercenary attitude? . . . The prohibition against value-judgments in social science would lead to the consequence that we are permitted to give a strictly factual description of the overt acts that can be observed in concentration camps, and perhaps an equally factual analysis of the motivations of the actors concerned: we would not be permitted to speak of cruelty. Every reader of such a description who is not completely stupid would, of course, see that the actions described are cruel. The factual description would, in truth, be a bitter satire. What claimed to be a straightforward report would be an unusually circumlocutory report. . . . Can one say anything relevant on public opinion polls . . . without realizing the fact that many answers to the questionnaires are given by unintelligent, uninformed, deceitful, and irrational people, and that not a few questions are formulated by people of the same caliber—can one say anything relevant about public opinion polls without committing one value-judgment after another? [7]

Moreover, the assumption implicit in the recommendation discussed above for achieving ethical neutrality is often rejected as hopelessly naive

[7] Leo Strauss, "The Social Science of Max Weber," *Measure*, Vol. 2 (1951), pp. 211–14. For a discussion of this issue as it bears upon problems in the philosophy of law, see Lon Fuller, "Human Purpose and Natural Law," *Natural Law Forum*, Vol. 3 (1958), pp. 68–76; Ernest Nagel, "On the Fusion of Fact and Value: A Reply to Professor Fuller," *op. cit.*, pp. 77–82; Lon L. Fuller, " A Rejoinder to Professor Nagel," *op. cit.*, pp. 83–104; Ernest Nagel, "Fact, Value, and Human Purpose," *Natural Law Forum*, Vol. 4 (1959), pp. 26–43.

—that is the assumption, it will be recalled, that relations of means to ends can be established without commitments to these ends, so that the conclusions of social inquiry concerning such relations are objective statements which make *conditional* rather than categorical assertions about values. This assumption is said by its critics to rest on the supposition that men attach value only to the ends they seek, and not to the means for realizing their aims. However, the supposition is alleged to be grossly mistaken. For the character of the means one employs to secure some goal affects the nature of the total outcome; and the choice men make between alternative means for obtaining a given end depends on the values they ascribe to those alternatives. In consequence, commitments to specific valuations are said to be involved even in what appear to be purely factual statements about means-ends relations.[8]

We shall not attempt a detailed assessment of this complex argument, for a discussion of the numerous issues it raises would take us far afield. However, three claims made in the course of the argument will be admitted without further comment as indisputably correct: that a large number of characterizations sometimes assumed to be purely factual descriptions of social phenomena do indeed formulate a type of value judgment; that it is often difficult, and in any case usually inconvenient in practice, to distinguish between the purely factual and the "evaluative" contents of many terms employed in the social sciences; and that values are commonly attached to means and not only to ends. However, these admissions do not entail the conclusion that, in a manner unique to the study of purposive human behavior, fact and value are fused beyond the possibility of distinguishing between them. On the contrary, as we shall try to show, the claim that there is such a fusion and that a value-free social science is therefore inherently absurd, confounds two quite different senses of the term "value judgment": the sense in which a value judgment expresses *approval or disapproval* either of some moral (or social) ideal, or of some action (or institution) because of a commitment to such an ideal; and the sense in which a value judgment expresses *an estimate* of the degree to which some commonly recognized (and more or less clearly defined) type of action, object, or institution is embodied in a given instance.

It will be helpful to illustrate these two senses of "value judgment" first with an example from biology. Animals with blood streams sometimes exhibit the condition known as "anemia." An anemic animal has a reduced number of red blood corpuscles, so that, among other things, it is less able to maintain a constant internal temperature than are members of its species with a "normal" supply of such blood cells. However, although the meaning of the term "anemia" can be made quite clear, it is not in fact defined with complete precision; for example, the notion of a "normal" number of red corpuscles that enters into the definition of the term is itself

8 Cf. Gunnar Myrdal, *Value in Social Theory*, London, 1958, pp. xxii, 211–13.

somewhat vague, since this number varies with the individual members of a species as well as with the state of a given individual at different times (such as its age or the altitude of its habitat). But in any case, to decide whether a given animal is anemic an investigator must judge whether the available evidence *warrants* the conclusion that the specimen is anemic.[9] He may perhaps think of anemia as being of several distinct kinds (as is done in actual medical practice), or he may think of anemia as a condition that is realizable with greater or lesser completeness (just as certain plane curves are sometimes described as better or worse approximations to a circle as defined in geometry); and, depending on which of these conceptions he adopts, he may decide either that his specimen has a certain kind of anemia or that it is anemic only to a certain degree. When the investigator reaches a conclusion, he can therefore be said to be making a "value judgment," in the sense that he has in mind some standardized type of physiological condition designated as "anemia" and that he *assesses* what he knows about his specimen with the measure provided by this assumed standard. For the sake of easy reference, let us call such evaluations of the evidence, which conclude that a given characteristic is in some degree present (or absent) in a given instance, "characterizing value judgments."

On the other hand, the student may also make a quite different sort of value judgment, which asserts that, since an anemic animal has diminished powers of maintaining itself, anemia is an undesirable condition. Moreover, he may apply this general judgment to a particular case, and so come to deplore the fact that a given animal is anemic. Let us label such evaluations, which conclude that some envisaged or actual state of affairs is worthy of approval or disapproval, "appraising value judgments." [10] It is clear, however, that an investigator making a characterizing value judgment is not thereby logically bound to affirm or deny a corresponding appraising evaluation. It is no less evident that he cannot consistently make an appraising value judgment about a given instance (e.g., that it is undesirable for a given animal to continue being anemic), unless he can affirm a characterizing judgment about that instance independently of the appraising one (e.g., that the animal is anemic). Accordingly, although characterizing judgments are necessarily entailed by many appraising judgments, making appraising judgments is not a necessary condition for making characterizing ones.

---

[9] The evidence is usually a count of red cells in a sample from the animal's blood. However, it should be noted that "The red cell count gives only an estimate of the *number of cells per unit quantity of blood,*" and does not indicate whether the body's total supply of red cells is increased or diminished.—Charles H. Best and Norman B. Taylor, *The Physiological Basis of Medical Practice,* 6th ed., Baltimore, 1955, pp. 11, 17.

[10] It is irrelevant to the present discussion what view is adopted concerning the ground upon which such judgments supposedly rest—whether those grounds are simply arbitrary preferences, alleged intuitions of "objective" values, categorical moral imperatives, or anything else that has been proposed in the history of value theory. For the distinction made in the text is independent of any particular assumption about the foundations of appraising value judgments, "ultimate" or otherwise.

Let us now apply these distinctions to some of the contentions advanced in the argument quoted above. Consider first the claim that the sociologist of religion must recognize the difference between mercenary and nonmercenary attitudes, and that in consequence he is inevitably committing himself to certain values. It is certainly beyond dispute that these attitudes are commonly distinguished; and it can also be granted that a sociologist of religion needs to understand the difference between them. But the sociologist's obligation is in this respect quite like that of the student of animal physiology, who must also acquaint himself with certain distinctions —even though the physiologist's distinction between, say, anemic and non-anemic may be less familiar to the ordinary layman and is in any case much more precise than is the distinction between mercenary and nonmercenary attitudes. Indeed, because of the vagueness of these latter terms, the scrupulous sociologist may find it extremely difficult to decide whether or not the attitude of some community toward its acknowledged gods is to be characterized as mercenary; and if he should finally decide, he may base his conclusion on some inarticulated "total impression" of that community's manifest behavior, without being able to state exactly the detailed grounds for his decision. But however this may be, the sociologist who claims that a certain attitude manifested by a given religious group is mercenary, just as the physiologist who claims that a certain individual is anemic, is making what is primarily a characterizing value judgment. In making these judgments, neither the sociologist nor the physiologist is necessarily committing himself to any values other than the values of scientific probity; and in this respect, therefore, there appears to be no difference between social and biological (or for that matter, physical) inquiry.

On the other hand, it would be absurd to deny that in characterizing various actions as mercenary, cruel, or deceitful, sociologists are frequently (although perhaps not always wittingly) asserting appraising as well as characterizing value judgments. Terms like 'mercenary,' 'cruel,' or 'deceitful' as commonly used have a widely recognized pejorative overtone. Accordingly, anyone who employs such terms to characterize human behavior can normally be assumed to be stating his disapprobation of that behavior (or his approbation, should he use terms like 'nonmercenary,' 'kindly,' or 'truthful'), and not simply characterizing it.

However, although many (but certainly not all) ostensibly characterizing statements asserted by social scientists undoubtedly express commitments to various (not always compatible) values, a number of "purely descriptive" terms as used by natural scientists in certain contexts sometimes also have an unmistakably appraising value connotation. Thus, the claim that a social scientist is making appraising value judgments when he characterizes respondents to questionnaires as uninformed, deceitful, or irrational can be matched by the equally sound claim that a physicist is also making such judgments when he describes a particular chronometer as inaccurate, a pump as inefficient, or a supporting platform as unstable. Like the social scientist in this example, the physicist is characterizing certain objects in his field of research; but, also like the social scientist, he is in addition expressing his disapproval of the characteristics he is ascribing to those objects.

Nevertheless—and this is the main burden of the present discussion—there are no good reasons for thinking that it is inherently impossible to *distinguish* between the characterizing and the appraising judgments implicit in many statements, whether the statements are asserted by students of human affairs or by natural scientists. To be sure, it is not always easy to make the distinction formally explicit in the social sciences—in part because much of the language employed in them is very vague, in part because appraising judgments that may be implicit in a statement tend to be overlooked by us when they are judgments to which we are actually committed though without being aware of our commitments. Nor is it always useful or convenient to perform this task. For many statements implicitly containing both characterizing and appraising evaluations are sometimes sufficiently clear without being reformulated in the manner required by the task; and the reformulations would frequently be too unwieldy for effective communication between members of a large and unequally prepared group of students. But these are essentially practical rather than theoretical problems. The difficulties they raise provide no compelling reasons for the claim that an ethically neutral social science is inherently impossible.

Nor is there any force in the argument that, since values are commonly attached to means and not only to ends, statements about means-ends relations are not value-free. Let us test the argument with a simple example. Suppose that a man with an urgent need for a car but without sufficient funds to buy one can achieve his aim by borrowing a sum either from a commercial bank or from friends who waive payment of any interest. Suppose further that he dislikes becoming beholden to his friends for financial favors, and prefers the impersonality of a commercial loan. Accordingly, the comparative values this individual places upon the alternative means available to him for realizing his aim obviously control the choice he makes between them. Now the *total* outcome that would result from his adoption of one of the alternatives is admittedly different from the *total* outcome that would result from his adoption of the other alternative. Nevertheless, irrespective of the values he may attach to these alternative means, each of them would achieve a result—namely, his purchase of the needed car—that is common to both the total outcomes. In consequence, the validity of the statement that he could buy the car by borrowing money from a bank, as well as of the statement that he could realize this aim by borrowing from friends, is unaffected by the valuations placed upon the means, so that neither statement involves any special appraising evaluations. In short, the statements about means-ends relations are value-free.

4. There remains for consideration the claim that a value-free social science is impossible, because value commitments enter into the very

assessment of evidence by social scientists, and not simply into the content of the conclusions they advance. This version of the claim itself has a large number of variant forms, but we shall examine only three of them.

The least radical form of the claim maintains that the conceptions held by a social scientist of what constitute cogent evidence or sound intellectual workmanship are the products of his education and his place in society, and are affected by the social values transmitted by this training and associated with this social position; accordingly, the values to which the social scientist is thereby committed determine which statements he *accepts* as well-grounded conclusions about human affairs. In this form, the claim is a *factual* thesis, and must be supported by detailed empirical evidence concerning the influences exerted by a man's moral and social values upon what he is ready to acknowledge as sound social analysis. In many instances such evidence is indeed available; and differences between social scientists in respect to what they accept as credible can sometimes be attributed to the influence of national, religious, economic, and other kinds of bias. However, this variant of the claim excludes neither the possibility of recognizing assessments of evidence that are prejudiced by special value commitments, nor the possibility of correcting for such prejudice. It therefore raises no issue that has not already been discussed when we examined the second reason for the alleged value-oriented character of social inquiry [pages 100–102 in this volume].

Another but different form of the claim is based on recent work in theoretical statistics dealing with the assessment of evidence for so-called "statistical hypotheses"—hypotheses concerning the probabilities of random events, such as the hypothesis that the probability of a male human birth is one-half. The central idea relevant to the present question that underlies these developments can be sketched in terms of an example. Suppose that, before a fresh batch of medicine is put on sale, tests are performed on experimental animals for its possible toxic effects because of impurities that have not been eliminated in its manufacture, for example, by introducing small quantities of the drug into the diet of one hundred guinea pigs. If no more than a few of the animals show serious after-effects, the medicine is to be regarded as safe, and will be marketed; but if a contrary result is obtained the drug will be destroyed. Suppose now that three of the animals do in fact become gravely ill. Is this outcome significant (i.e., does it indicate that the drug has toxic effects), or is it perhaps an "accident" that happened because of some peculiarity in the affected animals? To answer the question, the experimenter must *decide* on the basis of the evidence between the hypothesis H_1: the drug is toxic, and the hypothesis H_2: the drug is not toxic. But how is he to decide, if he aims to be "reasonable" rather than arbitrary? Current statistical theory offers him a rule for making a reasonable decision, and bases the rule on the following analysis.

Whatever decision the experimenter may make, he runs the risk of committing either one of two types of errors: he may reject a hypothesis though in fact it is true (i.e., despite the fact that H_1 is actually true, he mistakenly decides against it in the light of the evidence available to him); or he may accept a hypothesis though in fact it is false. His decision would therefore be eminently reasonable, were it based on a rule guaranteeing that no decision ever made in accordance with the rule would commit either type of error. Unhappily, there are no rules of this sort. The next suggestion is to find a rule such that, when decisions are made in accordance with it, the relative frequency of each type of error is quite small. But unfortunately, the risks of committing each type of error are not independent; for example, it is in general logically impossible to find a rule so that decisions based on it will commit each type of error with a relative frequency not greater than one in a thousand. In consequence, before a reasonable rule can be proposed, the experimenter must compare the relative importance to himself of the two types of error, and state what risk he is willing to take of committing the type of error he judges to be the more important one. Thus, were he to reject H_1 though it is true (i.e., were he to commit an error of the first type), all the medicine under consideration would be put on sale, and the lives of those using it would be endangered; on the other hand, were he to commit an error of the second type with respect to H_1, the entire batch of medicine would be scrapped, and the manufacturer would incur a financial loss. However, the preservation of human life may be of greater moment to the experimenter than financial gain; and he may perhaps stipulate that he is unwilling to base his decision on a rule for which the risk of committing an error of the first type is greater than one such error in a hundred decisions. If this is assumed, statistical theory can specify a rule satisfying the experimenter's requirement, though how this is done, and how the risk of committing an error of the second type is calculated, are technical questions of no concern to us. The main point to be noted in this analysis is that the rule presupposes certain appraising judgments of value. In short, if this result is generalized, statistical theory appears to support the thesis that value commitments enter decisively into the rules for assessing evidence for statistical hypotheses.[11]

However, the theoretical analysis upon which this thesis rests does not entail the conclusion that the rules actually employed in every social inquiry for assessing evidence necessarily involve some *special* commitments, i.e., commitments such as those mentioned in the above example, as distinct from those generally implicit in science as an enterprise aiming to achieve reliable knowledge. Indeed, the above example illustrating the reasoning in current statistical theory can be misleading, insofar as it suggests that alternative decisions between statistical hypothesis must invariably lead to

[11] The above example is borrowed from the discussion in J. Neymann, *First Course in Probability and Statistics*, New York, 1950, Chap. 5, where an elementary technical account of recent developments in statistical theory is presented. For a nontechnical account, see Irwin D. J. Bross, *Design for Decision*, New York, 1953, also R. B. Braithwaite, *Scientific Explanation*, Cambridge, Eng., 1953, Chap. 7.

alternative actions having immediate practical consequences upon which different special values are placed. For example, a theoretical physicist may have to decide between two statistical hypotheses concerning the probability of certain energy exchanges in atoms; and a theoretical sociologist may similarly have to choose between two statistical hypotheses concerning the relative frequency of childless marriages under certain social arrangements. But neither of these men may have any *special* values at stake associated with the alternatives between which he must decide, other than the values, to which he is committed as a member of a scientific community, to conduct his inquiries with probity and responsibility. Accordingly, the question whether any special value commitments enter into assessments of evidence in either the natural or social sciences is not settled one way or the other by theoretical statistics; and the question can be answered only by examining actual inquiries in the various scientific disciplines.

Moreover, nothing in the reasoning of theoretical statistics depends on what particular subject matter is under discussion when a decision between alternative statistical hypotheses is to be made. For the reasoning is entirely general; and reference to some special subject matter becomes relevant only when a definite numerical value is to be assigned to the risk some investigator is prepared to take of making an erroneous decision concerning a given hypothesis. Accordingly, if current statistical theory is used to support the claim that value commitments enter into the assessment of evidence for statistical hypotheses in social inquiry, statistical theory can be used with equal justification to support analogous claims for all other inquiries as well. In short, the claim we have been discussing establishes no difficulty that supposedly occurs in the search for reliable knowledge in the study of human affairs which is not also encountered in the natural sciences.

A third form of this claim is the most radical of all. It differs from the first variant mentioned above in maintaining that there is a necessary *logical* connection, and not merely a contingent or causal one, between the "social perspective" of a student of human affairs and his standards of competent social inquiry, and in consequence the influence of the special values to which he is committed because of his own social involvements is not eliminable. This version of the claim is implicit in Hegel's account of the "dialectical" nature of human history and is integral to much Marxist as well as non-Marxist philosophy that stresses the "historically relative" character of social thought. In any event, it is commonly based on the assumption that, since social institutions and their cultural products are constantly changing, the intellectual apparatus required for understanding them must also change; and every idea employed for this purpose is therefore adequate only for some particular stage in the development of human affairs. Accordingly, neither the substantive concepts adopted for classifying and interpreting social phenomena, nor the logical canons used for estimating the worth of such concepts, have a "timeless validity"; there is no analysis of social phenomena which is not the expression of some special social standpoint, or which does not reflect the interests and values dominant in some sector of the human scene at a certain stage of its history. In consequence, although a sound distinction can be made in the natural sciences between the origin of a man's views and their factual validity, such a distinction allegedly cannot be made in social inquiry; and prominent exponents of "historical relativism" have therefore challenged the universal adequacy of the thesis that "the genesis of a proposition is under all circumstances irrelevant to its truth." As one influential proponent of this position puts the matter,

The historical and social genesis of an idea would only be irrelevant to its ultimate validity if the temporal and social conditions of its emergence had no effect on its content and form. If this were the case, any two periods in the history of human knowledge would only be distinguished from one another by the fact that in the earlier period certain things were still unknown and certain errors still existed which, through later knowledge were completely corrected. This simple relationship between an earlier incomplete and a later complete period of knowledge may to a large extent be appropriate for the exact sciences. . . . For the history of the cultural sciences, however, the earlier stages are not quite so simply superseded by the later stages, and it is not so easily demonstrable that early errors have subsequently been corrected. Every epoch has its fundamentally new approach and its characteristic point of view, and consequently sees the "same" object from a new perspective. . . . The very principles, in the light of which knowledge is to be criticized, are themselves found to be socially and historically conditioned. Hence their application appears to be limited to given historical periods and the particular types of knowledge then prevalent.[12]

Historical research into the influence of society upon the beliefs men hold is of undoubted importance for understanding the complex nature of the scientific enterprise; and the sociology of knowledge—as such investigations have come to be called—has produced many clarifying contributions to such an understanding. However, these admittedly valuable services of the sociology of knowledge do not establish the radical claim we have been stating. In the first place, there is no competent evidence to show that the principles employed in social inquiry for assessing the intellectual products are *necessarily* determined by the social perspective of the inquirer. On the contrary, the "facts" usually cited in support of this contention establish at best only a contingent causal relation between a man's social commitments and his canons of cognitive validity. For example, the once fashionable view that the "mentality" or logical operations of primitive societies differ from those typical in Western civilization—a

---

[12] Karl Mannheim, *Ideology and Utopia*, New York, 1959, pp. 271, 288, 292. The essay from which the above excerpts are quoted was first published in 1931, and Mannheim subsequently modified some of the views expressed in it. However, he reaffirmed the thesis stated in the quoted passages as late as 1946, the year before his death. See his letter to Kurt H. Wolff, dated April 15, 1946, quoted in the latter's "Sociology of Knowledge and Sociological Theory," in *Symposium on Sociological Theory* (ed. by Llewellyn Gross), Evanston, Ill., 1959, p. 571.

discrepancy that was attributed to differences in the institutions of the societies under comparison—is now generally recognized to be erroneous, because it seriously misinterprets the intellectual processes of primitive peoples. Moreover, even extreme exponents of the sociology of knowledge admit that most conclusions asserted in mathematics and natural science are neutral to differences in social perspective of those asserting them, so that the genesis of these propositions is irrelevant to their validity. Why cannot propositions about human affairs exhibit a similar neutrality, at least in some cases? Sociologists of knowledge do not appear to doubt that the truth of the statement that two horses can in general pull a heavier load than can either horse alone, is logically independent of the social status of the individual who happens to affirm the statement. But they have not made clear just what are the inescapable considerations that allegedly make such independence inherently impossible for the analogous statement about human behavior, that two laborers can in general dig a ditch of given dimensions more quickly than can either laborer working alone.

In the second place, the claim faces a serious and frequently noted dialectical difficulty—that proponents of the claim have succeeded in meeting only by abandoning the substance of the claim. For let us ask what is the cognitive status of the thesis that a social perspective enters essentially into the content as well as the validation of every assertion about human affairs. Is this thesis meaningful and valid only for those who maintain it and who thus subscribe to certain values because of their distinctive social commitments? If so, no one with a different social perspective can properly understand it; its acceptance as valid is strictly limited to those who can do so, and social scientists who subscribe to a different set of social values ought therefore dismiss it as empty talk. Or is the thesis singularly exempt from the class of assertions to which it applies, so that its meaning and truth are not inherently related to the social perspectives of those who assert it? If so, it is not evident why the thesis is so exempt; but in any case, the thesis is then a conclusion of inquiry into human affairs that is presumably "objectively valid" in the usual sense of this phrase—and, if there is one such conclusion, it is not clear why there cannot be others as well.

To meet this difficulty, and to escape the self-defeating skeptical relativism to which the thesis is thus shown to lead, the thesis is sometimes interpreted to say that, though "absolutely objective" knowledge of human affairs is unattainable, a "relational" form of objectivity called "relationism" can nevertheless be achieved. On this interpretation, a social scientist can discover just what his social perspective is; and if he then formulates the conclusions of his inquiries "relationally," so as to indicate that his findings conform to the canons of validity implicit in his prespective, his conclusions will have achieved a "relational" objectivity. Social scientists sharing the same perspective can be expected to agree in their answers to a given problem when the canons of validity characteristic of their common perspective are correctly applied. On the other hand, students of social phenomena who operate within different but incongruous social perspectives can also achieve objectivity, if in no other way than by a "relational" formulation of what must otherwise be incompatible results obtained in their several inquiries. However, they can also achieve it in "a more roundabout fashion," by undertaking "to find a formula for translating the results of one into those of the other and to discover a common denominator for these varying perspectivistic insights." [13]

But it is difficult to see in what way "relational objectivity" differs from "objectivity" without the qualifying adjective and in the customary sense of the word. For example, a physicist who terminates an investigation with the conclusion that the velocity of light in water has a certain numerical value when measured in terms of a stated system of units, by a stated procedure, and under stated experimental conditions, is formulating his conclusion in a manner that is "relational" in the sense intended; and his conclusion is marked by "objectivity," presumably because it mentions the "relational" factors upon which the assigned numerical value of the velocity depends. However, it is fairly standard practice in the natural sciences to formulate certain types of conclusions in this fashion. Accordingly, the proposal that the social sciences formulate their findings in an analogous manner carries with it the admission that it is not in principle impossible for these disciplines to establish conclusions having the objectivity of conclusions reached in other domains of inquiry. Moreover, if the difficulty we are considering is to be resolved by the suggested translation formulas for rendering the "common denominators" of conclusions stemming from divergent social perspectives, those formulas cannot in turn be "situationally determined" in the sense of this phrase under discussion. For if those formulas were so determined, the same difficulty would crop up anew in connection with them. On the other hand, a search for such formulas is a phase in the search for invariant relations in a subject matter, so that formulations of these relations are valid irrespective of the particular perspective one may select from some class of perspectives on that subject matter. In consequence, in acknowledging that the search for such invariants in the social sciences is not inherently bound to fail, proponents of the claim we have been considering abandon what at the outset was its most radical thesis.

In brief, the various reasons we have been examining for the intrinsic impossibility of securing objective (i.e., value-free and unbiased) conclusions in the social sciences do not establish what they purport to establish, even though in some instances they direct attention to undoubtedly important practical difficulties frequently encountered in these disciplines.

[13] Karl Mannheim, *op. cit.*, pp. 300–01.

[7] Ideology and the Sociology of Knowledge

KARL MANNHEIM

Definition of Concepts

In order to understand the present situation of thought, it is necessary to start with the problems of "ideology." For most people, the term "ideology" is closely bound up with Marxism, and their reactions to the term are largely determined by the association. It is therefore first necessary to state that although Marxism contributed a great deal to the original statement of the problem, both the word and its meaning go farther back in history than Marxism, and ever since its time new meanings of the word have emerged, which have taken shape independently of it.

There is no better introduction to the problem than the analysis of the meaning of the term "ideology": firstly we have to disentangle all the different shades of meaning which are blended here into a pseudo-unity, and a more precise statement of the variations in the meanings of the concept, as it is used to-day, will prepare the way for its sociological and historical analysis. Such an analysis will show that in general there are two distinct and separable meanings of the term "ideology"—the particular and the total.

The particular conception of ideology is implied when the term denotes that we are sceptical of the ideas and representations advanced by our opponent. They are regarded as more or less conscious disguises of the real nature of a situation, the true recognition of which would not be in accord with his interests. These distortions range all the way from conscious lies to half-conscious and unwitting disguises; from calculated attempts to dupe others to self-deception. This conception of ideology, which has only gradually become differentiated from the commonsense notion of the lie is particular in several senses. Its particularity becomes evident when it is contrasted with the more inclusive total conception of ideology. Here we refer to the ideology of an age or of a concrete historico-social group, e.g.

From *Ideology and Utopia* by Karl Mannheim, 1936. Reprinted by permission of Harcourt, Brace & World, Inc. and Routledge & Kegan Paul Ltd.

of a class, when we are concerned with the characteristics and composition of the total structure of the mind of this epoch or of this group.

The common as well as the distinctive elements of the two concepts are readily evident. The common element in these two conceptions seems to consist in the fact that neither relies solely on what is actually said by the opponent in order to reach an understanding of his real meaning and intention.[1] Both fall back on the subject, whether individual or group, proceeding to an understanding of what is said by the indirect method of analysing the social conditions of the individual or his group. The ideas expressed by the subject are thus regarded as functions of his existence. This means that opinions, statements, propositions, and systems of ideas are not taken at their face value but are interpreted in the light of the life-situation of the one who expresses them. It signifies further that the specific character and life-situation of the subject influence his opinions, perceptions, and interpretations.

Both these conceptions of ideology, accordingly, make these so-called "ideas" a function of him who holds them, and of his position in his social milieu. Although they have something in common, there are also significant differences between them. Of the latter we mention merely the most important:—

(*a*) Whereas the particular conception of ideology designates only a part of the opponent's assertions as ideologies—and this only with reference to their content, the total conception calls into question the opponent's total *Weltanschauung* (including his conceptual apparatus), and attempts to understand these concepts as an outgrowth of the collective life of which he partakes.

(*b*) The particular conception of "ideology" makes its analysis of ideas on a purely psychological level. If it is claimed for instance that an adversary is lying, or that he is concealing or distorting a given factual situation, it is still nevertheless assumed that both parties share common criteria of validity—it is still assumed that it is possible to refute lies and eradicate sources of error by referring to accepted criteria of objective validity common to both parties. The suspicion that one's opponent is the victim of an ideology does not go so far as to exclude him from discussion on the basis of a common theoretical frame of reference. The case is different with the total conception of ideology. When we attribute to one historical epoch one intellectual world and to ourselves another one, or if a certain historically determined social stratum thinks in categories other than our own, we refer not to the isolated cases of thought-content, but to fundamentally divergent

---

[1] If the interpretation relies solely upon that which is actually said we shall speak of an "immanent interpretation": if it transcends these data, implying thereby an analysis of the subject's life-situation, we shall speak of a "transcendental interpretation." A typology of these various forms of interpretation is to be found in the author's "Ideologische und soziologische Interpretation der geistigen Gebilde," *Jahrbuck für Soziologie*, vol. ii (Karlsruhe, 1926), p. 424 ff.

thought-systems and to widely differing modes of experience and interpretation. We touch upon the theoretical or noological level whenever we
consider not merely the content but also the form, and even the conceptual
framework of a mode of thought as a function of the life situation of a
thinker. "The economic categories are only the theoretical expressions, the
abstractions, of the social relations of production. . . . The same men who
establish social relations conformably with their material productivity,
produce also the principles, the ideas, the categories, conformably with
their social relations." (Karl Marx, *The Poverty of Philosophy*, being a translation of *Misère de la Philosophie*, with a preface by Frederick Engels,
translated by H. Quelch, Chicago, 1910, p. 119). These are the two ways of
analysing statements as functions of their social background; the first
operates only on the psychological, the second on the noological level.

(*c*) Corresponding to this difference, the particular conception of ideology
operates primarily with a psychology of interests, while the total conception
uses a more formal functional analysis, without any reference to motivations,
confining itself to an objective description of the structural differences in
minds operating in different social settings. The former assumes that this or
that interest is the cause of a given lie or deception. The latter presupposes
simply that there is a correspondence between a given social situation and a
given perspective, point of view, or apperception mass. In this case, while an
analysis of constellations of interests may often be necessary it is not to
establish causal connections but to characterize the total situation. Thus
interested psychology tends to be displaced by an analysis of the correspondence between the situation to be known and the forms of knowledge.

Since the particular conception never actually departs from the psychological level, the point of reference in such analyses is always the individual.
This is the case even when we are dealing with groups, since all psychic
phenomena must finally be reduced to the minds of individuals. The term
"group ideology" occurs frequently, to be sure, in popular speech. Group
existence in this sense can only mean that a group of persons, either in their
immediate reactions to the same situation or as a result of direct psychic
interaction, react similarly. Accordingly, conditioned by the same social
situation, they are subject to the same illusions. If we confine our observations to the mental processes which take place in the individual and regard
him as the only possible bearer of ideologies, we shall never grasp in its
totality the structure of the intellectual world belonging to a social group
in a given historical situation. Although this mental world as a whole could
never come into existence without the experiences and productive responses
of the different individuals, its inner structure is not to be found in a mere
integration of these individual experiences. The individual members of the
working-class, for instance, do not experience *all* the elements of an outlook
which could be called the proletarian *Weltanschauung*. Every individual
participates only in certain fragments of this thought-system, the totality

of which is not in the least a mere sum of these fragmentary individual experiences. As a totality the thought-system is integrated systematically, and is no mere casual jumble of fragmentary experiences of discrete members of the group. Thus it follows that the individual can only be considered as the bearer of an ideology as long as we deal with that conception of ideology which, by definition, is directed more to detached contents than to the whole structure of thought, uncovering false ways of thought and exposing lies. As soon as the total conception of ideology is used, we attempt to reconstruct the whole outlook of a social group, and neither the concrete individuals nor the abstract sum of them can legitimately be considered as bearers of this ideological thought-system as a whole. The aim of the analysis on this level is the reconstruction of the systematic theoretical basis underlying the single judgments of the individual. Analyses of ideologies in the particular sense, making the content of individual thought largely dependent on the interests of the subject, can never achieve this basic reconstruction of the whole outlook of a social group. They can at best reveal the collective psychological aspects of ideology, or lead to some development of mass psychology, dealing either with the different behavior of the individual in the crowd, or with the results of the mass integration of the physic experiences of many individuals. And although the collective-psychological aspect may very often approach the problems of the total ideological analysis, it does not answer its questions exactly. It is one thing to know how far my attitudes and judgments are influenced and altered by the co-existence of other human beings, but it is another thing to know what are the theoretical implications of my mode of thought which are identical with those of my fellow members of the group or social stratum.

We content ourselves here merely with stating the issue without attempting a thorough-going analysis of the difficult methodological problems which it raises. . . .

From the Particular to the Total Conception of Ideology

What were the steps in the history of ideas that prepared the way for the total conception of ideology? Certainly it did not merely arise out of the attitude of mistrust which gradually gave rise to the particular conception of ideology. More fundamental steps had to be taken before the numerous tendencies of thought moving in the same general direction could be synthesized into the total conception of ideology. Philosophy played a part in the process, but not philosophy in the narrow sense (as it is usually conceived) as a discipline divorced from the actual context of living. Its role was rather that of the ultimate and fundamental interpreter of the flux in the contemporary world. This cosmos in flux is in its turn to be viewed as a series of conflicts arising out of the nature of the mind and its responses to the continually changing structure of the world. We shall indicate here only the principal stages in the emergence of the total conception of ideology on the noological and ontological levels.

The first significant step in this direction consisted in the development of a philosophy of consciousness. The thesis that consciousness is a unity consisting of coherent elements sets a problem of investigation which, especially in Germany, has been the basis of monumental attempts at analysis. The philosophy of consciousness has put in place of an infinitely variegated and confused world an organization of experience the unity of which is guaranteed by the unity of the perceiving subject. This does not imply that the subject merely reflects the structural pattern of the external world, but rather that, in the course of his experience with the world, he spontaneously evolves the principles of organization that enable him to understand it. After the objective ontological unity of the world had been demolished, the attempt was made to substitute for it a unity imposed by the perceiving subject. In the place of the medieval-Christian objective and ontological unity of the world, there emerged the subjective unity of the absolute subject of the Enlightenment—"consciousness in itself."

Henceforth the world as "world" exists only with reference to the knowing mind, and the mental activity of the subject determines the form in which the world appears. This constitutes in fact the embryonic total conception of ideology, though it is, as yet, devoid of its historical and sociological implications.

At this stage, the world is conceived as a structural unity, and no longer as a plurality of disparate events as it seemed to be in the intermediate period when the breakdown of the objective order seemed to bring chaos. It is related in its entirety to a subject, but in this case the subject is not a concrete individual. It is rather a fictitious "consciousness in itself." In this view, which is particularly pronounced in Kant, the noological level is sharply differentiated from the psychological one. This is the first stage in the dissolution of an ontological dogmatism which regarded the "world" as existing independently of us, in a fixed and definitive form.

The second stage in the development of the total conception of ideology is attained when the total but super-temporal notion of ideology is seen in historical perspective. This is mainly the accomplishment of Hegel and the Historical school. The latter, and Hegel to an even greater degree, start from the assumption that the world is a unity and is conceivable only with reference to a knowing subject. And now at this point, what is for us a decisive new element is added to the conception—namely, that this unity is in a process of continual historical transformation and tends to a constant restoration of its equilibrium on still higher levels. During the Enlightenment the subject, as carrier of the unity of consciousness, was viewed as a wholly abstract, super-temporal, and super-social entity: "consciousness in itself." During this period the *Volksgeist,* "folk spirit," comes to represent the historically differentiated elements of consciousness, which are integrated by Hegel into the "world spirit." It is evident that the increasing concreteness of this type of philosophy results from the more immediate concerns with the ideas arising from social interaction and the incorporation of historical-political currents of thought into the domain of philosophy. Thenceforth, however, the experiences of everyday life are no longer accepted at face value, but are thought through in all their implications and are traced back to their presuppositions. It should be noted, however, that the historically changing nature of mind was discovered not so much by philosophy as by the penetration of political insight into the everyday life of the time.

The reaction following upon the unhistorical thought of the period of the French Revolution revitalized and gave new impetus to the historical perspective. In the last analysis, the transition from the general, abstract, world-unifying subject ("consciousness in itself") to the more concrete subject (the nationally differentiated "folk spirit") was not so much a philosophical achievement as it was the expression of a transformation in the manner of reacting to the world in all realms of experience. This change may be traced to the revolution in popular sentiment during and after the Napoleonic Wars when the feeling of nationality was actually born. The fact that more remote antecedents may be found for both the historical perspective and the *Volksgeist* does not detract from the validity of this observation.[2]

The final and most important step in the creation of the total conception of ideology likewise arose out of the historical-social process. When "class" took the place of "folk" or nation as the bearer of the historically evolving consciousness, the same theoretical tradition, to which we have already referred, absorbed the realization which meanwhile had grown up through the social process, namely—that the structure of society and its corresponding intellectual forms vary with the relations between social classes.

Just as at an earlier time, the historically differentiated "folk spirit" took the place of "consciousness as such," so now the concept of *Volksgeist*, which is still too inclusive, is replaced by the concept of class consciousness, or more correctly class ideology. Thus the development of these ideas follows a two-fold trend—on the one hand, there is a synthesizing and integrating process through which the concept of consciousness comes to furnish a unitary center in an infinitely variable world; and on the other, there is a constant attempt to make more pliable and flexible the unitary conception which has been too rigidly and too schematically formulated in the course of the synthesizing process.

---

[2] For future reference, we state here that the sociology of knowledge, unlike the orthodox history of ideas, does not aim at tracing ideas back to all their remote historical prototypes. For if one is bent on tracing similar *motifs* in thought to their ultimate origins, it is always possible to find "precursors" for every idea. There is nothing which has been said, which has not been said before (*Nullum est iam dictum, quod non sit dictum prius*). The proper theme of our study is to observe how and in what form intellectual life at a given historical moment is related to the existing social and political forces. Cf. my study, "Das konservative Denken." [Translated as "Conservative Thought" and reprinted in Karl Mannheim, *Essays on Sociology and Social Psychology*, ed. Paul Kecskemeti, 1953.—Ed.]

The result of this dual tendency is that instead of a fictional unity of a timeless, unchanging "consciousness as such" (which was never actually demonstrable) we get a conception which varies in accordance with historic periods, nations, and social classes. In the course of this transition, we continue to cling to the unity of consciousness, but this unity is now dynamic and in constant process of becoming. This accounts for the fact that despite the surrender of the static conception of consciousness, the growing body of material discovered by historical research does not remain an incoherent and discontinuous mass of discrete events. This latest conception of consciousness provides a more adequate perspective for the comprehension of historical reality.

Two consequences flow from this conception of consciousness: first we clearly perceive that human affairs cannot be understood by an isolation of their elements. Every fact and event in an historical period is only explicable in terms of meaning, and meaning in its turn always refers to another meaning. Thus the conception of the unity and interdependence of meaning in a period always underlies the interpretation of that period. Secondly, this interdependent system of meanings varies both in all its parts and in its totality from one historical period to another. Thus the re-interpretation of that continuous and coherent change in meaning becomes the main concern of our modern historical sciences. Although Hegel has probably done more than anyone else in emphasizing the need for integrating the various elements of meaning in a given historical experience, he proceeded in a speculative manner, while we have arrived at a stage of development where we are able to translate this constructive notion, given us by the philosophers, into empirical research.

What is significant for us is that although we separated them in our analysis, the two currents which led to the particular and total conceptions of ideology, respectively, and which have approximately the same historical origin, now begin to approach one another more closely. The particular conception of ideology merges with the total. This becomes apparent to the observer in the following manner: previously, one's adversary, as the representative of a certain political-social position, was accused of conscious or unconscious falsification. Now, however, the critique is more thoroughgoing in that, having discredited the total structure of his consciousness, we consider him no longer capable of thinking correctly. This simple observation means, in the light of a structural analysis of thought, that in earlier attempts to discover the sources of error, distortion was uncovered only on the psychological plane by pointing out the personal roots of intellectual bias. The annihilation is now more thoroughgoing since the attack is made on the noological level and the validity of the adversary's theories is undermined by showing that they are merely a function of the generally prevailing social situation. Herewith a new and perhaps the most decisive stage in the history of modes of thought has been reached. It is difficult, however, to deal with this development without first analysing some of its fundamental implications. The total conception of ideology raises a problem which has frequently been adumbrated before, but which now for the first time acquires broader significance, namely the problem of how such a thing as the "false consciousness" (*falsches Bewusstsein*)—the problem of the totally distorted mind which falsifies everything which comes within its range—could ever have arisen. It is the awareness that our total outlook as distinguished from its details may be distorted, which lends to the total conception of ideology a special significance and relevance for the understanding of our social life. Out of this recognition grows the profound disquietude which we feel in our present intellectual situation, but out of it grows also whatever in it is fruitful and stimulating. . . .

The Transition from the Theory of Ideology to the Sociology of Knowledge

As long as one does not call his own position into question but regards it as absolute, while interpreting his opponents' ideas as a mere function of the social positions they occupy, the decisive step forward has not yet been taken. It is true, of course, that in such a case the total conception of ideology is being used, since one is interested in analysing the structure of the mind of one's opponent in its totality, and is not merely singling out a few isolated propositions. But since, in such an instance, one is interested merely in a sociological analysis of the opponent's ideas, one never gets beyond a highly restricted, or what I should like to call a special, formulation of the theory. In contrast to this special formulation, the general [3] form of the total conception of ideology is being used by the analyst when he has the courage to subject not just the adversary's point of view but all points of view, including his own, to the ideological analysis.

At the present stage of our understanding it is hardly possible to avoid this general formulation of the total conception of ideology, according to which the thought of all parties in all epochs is of an ideological character. There is scarcely a single intellectual position, and Marxism furnishes no exception to this rule, which has not changed through history and which even in the present does not appear in many forms. Marxism, too, has taken on many diverse appearances. It should not be too difficult for a Marxist to recognize their social basis.

With the emergence of the general formulation of the total conception of ideology, the simple theory of ideology develops into the sociology of know-

---

[3] We add here another distinction to our earlier one of "particular and total," namely that of "special and general." While the first distinction concerns the question as to whether single isolated ideas or the entire mind is to be seen as ideological, and whether the social situation conditions merely the psychological manifestations of concepts, or whether it even penetrates to the noological meanings, in the distinction of special *versus* general, the decisive question is whether the thought of all groups (including our own) or only that of our adversaries is recognized as socially determined.

ledge. What was once the intellectual armament [4] of a party is transformed into a method of research in social and intellectual history generally. To begin with, a given social group discovers the "situational determination" (*Seinsgebundenheit*) of its opponents' ideas. Subsequently the recognition of this fact is elaborated into an all-inclusive principle according to which the thought of every group is seen as arising out of its life conditions.[5] Thus, it becomes the task of the sociological history of thought to analyse without regard for party biases all the factors in the actually existing social situation which may influence thought. This sociologically oriented history of ideas is destined to provide modern men with a revised view of the whole historical process.

It is clear, then, that in this connection the conception of ideology takes on a new meaning. Out of this meaning two alternative approaches to ideological investigation arise. The first is to confine oneself to showing everywhere the interrelationships between the intellectual point of view held and the social position occupied. This involves the renunciation of every intention to expose or unmask those views with which one is in disagreement.

In attempting to expose the views of another, one is forced to make one's own view appear infallible and absolute, which is a procedure altogether to be avoided if one is making a specifically non-evaluating investigation. The second possible approach is nevertheless to combine such a non-evaluative analysis with a definite epistemology. Viewed from the angle of this second approach there are two separate and distinct solutions to the problem of what constitutes reliable knowledge—the one solution may be termed *relationism,* and the other *relativism.*

Relativism is a product of the modern historical-sociological procedure which is based on the recognition that all historical thinking is bound up with the concrete position in life of the thinker (*Standortsgebundenheit des Denkers*). But relativism combines this historical-sociological insight with an older theory of knowledge which was as yet unaware of the interplay between conditions of existence and modes of thought, and which modelled its knowledge after static prototypes such as might be exemplified by the proposition $2 \times 2 = 4$. This older type of thought, which regarded such examples as the model of all thought, was necessarily led to the rejection of all those forms of knowledge which were dependent upon the subjective standpoint and the social situation of the knower, and which were, hence, merely "relative." Relativism, then, owes its existence to the discrepancy between this newly-won insight into the actual processes of thought and a theory of knowledge which had not yet taken account of this new insight.

If we wish to emancipate ourselves from this relativism we must seek to understand with the aid of the sociology of knowledge that it is not epis-

[4] Cf. the Marxist expression "To forge the intellectual weapons of the proletariat."
[5] By the term "situational determination of knowledge" I am seeking to differentiate the propagandistic from the scientific sociological content of the ideological concept.

temology in any absolute sense but rather a certain historically transitory type of epistemology which is in conflict with the type of thought oriented to the social situation. Actually, epistemology is as intimately enmeshed in the social process as is the totality of our thinking, and it will make progress to the extent that it can master the complications arising out of the changing structure of thought.

A modern theory of knowledge which takes account of the relational as distinct from the merely relative character of all historical knowledge must start with the assumption that there are spheres of thought in which it is impossible to conceive of absolute truth existing independently of the values and position of the subject and unrelated to the social context. Even a god could not formulate a proposition on historical subjects like $2 \times 2 = 4$, for what is intelligible in history can be formulated only with reference to problems and conceptual constructions which themselves arise in the flux of historical experience.

[8] Ideology [1]

GUSTAV BERGMANN

Many philosophies have come and gone within the span of historical memory; the very conception of the nature and function of philosophy has changed in the course of Western civilization. Yet it is fair to say that, whenever a philosopher addressed himself to a problem, he considered it his privilege and his duty to penetrate to the heart of the matter. Wherever he starts, he will, if he is a philosopher, soon arrive at those rather few fundamental questions which, once firmly grasped, help us to understand, though not necessarily to answer, all others. In this respect nothing has changed and nothing, I hope, ever will. One important change that did occur during the last half-century or so is, therefore, a change in method only. A rather large group of recent and contemporary philosophers insists that what they bring to their task—that perennial task of recognizing and clarifying the basic

Reprinted from *Ethics,* **LXI** (April, 1951), 205–18, by permission of the University of Chicago Press.

[1] This is, with very minor alterations, the text of an address delivered in the spring of 1950 at the University of Illinois before an audience of social scientists. I have tried to preserve as much of the livelier and less formal tone of the spoken word as was possible and seemed proper.

issues—is not any special knowledge—philosophical knowledge on a par, as it were, with zoölogical or geographical or economic knowledge—but merely a special technique, the technique of *logical analysis*. Quite appropriately, these philosophers are known by the name of "logical analysts." What logical analysis is, is more easily shown by a concrete demonstration than by an abstract explanation. I shall present such a demonstration by attempting a logical analysis of the notion of ideology.

But there is also a sense in which I shall not speak as a technical philosopher. This requires a word or two to put myself at peace with my conscience and, if that is not hoping for too much, with my philosophical friends. These friends will notice that on this occasion I shall use the language of representative realism, though technically I am not a realist. Again, in ethics I shall sometimes sound as if I belonged to the garden variety of relativists, though I do hold that some ethical predicates are not reducible in the sense in which technical relativists must insist that they are. The reason for this, aside from the obvious demands of expository economy, is that I appreciate the common-sense core of both representative realism and ethical relativism. But, of course, I do recognize the assertions that go by these names for what they are, the nontechnical expression of (scientific) common sense; and, unlike the technical realists and relativists, I do not mistake them for what they are not, the solution of the epistemological puzzles which they pose but cannot answer. Only, these puzzles are one thing; the puzzlement sometimes caused by the concepts and problems of science, including the social sciences, is another thing. To dispel the latter, one does not need to dissolve the former. Again, I shall not undertake to prove that this is so; I merely hope to demonstrate it for the example of ideology.

If I were to play the analytical game strictly, I would now have to start by considering the several ways in which we, laymen and social scientists, use the term ideology and to proceed from there dialectically, by raising questions, until we arrive at the fundamental issues involved. To save time I shall begin by stating and explaining what I believe to be the basic issue, not only for ideology but, to be quite blunt, for all social science. I refer, not surprisingly, to the dichotomy of *fact* and *value*.

Assume that, recently standing before a certain canvas, I exclaimed, "This is Van Gogh's 'Berceuse.'" What happened was that I had a percept which, as one ordinarily says, is a state of mind, a conscious content or *mental* object; and that my having had this percept was the ground for my then saying, truly, that there was in front of me what we ordinarily call a *physical* object, namely, the painted canvas known as Van Gogh's "Berceuse." Similarly, when I see a tree with seared leaves and broken limbs, there are, on the one hand, the leaves and the limbs and, on the other, my percepts of them. These two sorts of things stand, as it were, in the relation of original and picture to each other. (This is the common-sense core of representative realism.) Assume, next, that, having said, "This is Van Gogh's 'Berceuse,'"

I add, "This is beautiful." Or consider the case when, witnessing a certain action, say that of a friend courageously speaking his mind, I say, "This is good." How shall we describe these situations? We need not doubt—indeed, we would be very foolish to doubt—that in these two cases, that of an aesthetic and of an ethical judgment respectively, there is in the speaker a state of mind or an aspect of his state of mind which is the ground of his judging "This is beautiful" or "This is good" in exactly the same sense in which his percept or an aspect of it is the ground for his saying about a tree, not about his percept of it, "This is green." What is doubtful is, rather, whether there is something not in his mind but, as philosophers sometimes say, "out there," in the canvas or in the act, that corresponds to these experiences in exactly the same sense in which the color of a tree corresponds to an aspect of the percept of a tree. The answer to this question is, to me quite patently, negative. (This is the common-sense core of ethical relativism.)

If we call such statements as, "This is a tree" or "This is Van Gogh's 'Berceuse'" statements of fact and, on the other hand, such statements as "The 'Berceuse' is beautiful" or "This action is good" value judgments, then the difference between these two kinds of statement can be put as follows: A statement of fact says something about the object or objects it mentions; and, depending only on the properties of these objects, it is either true or false. A value judgment is misunderstood if it is taken to ascribe a property to the object, act, or situation it mentions in the same sense in which a statement of fact is such an ascription; it is, therefore, literally neither true nor false. What it involves and misleadingly states as the property of an object, act, or situation alone is the fact that this object, act, or situation causes in the one who makes the judgment a certain state of mind, say, for instance, of positive aesthetic appreciation or of moral approval.

To prevent misunderstanding, I shall next point out the comprehensiveness, in at least two directions, of the category of fact which I have thus set aside. First, a statement of fact is not necessarily so simple as "This is a tree." Galileo's law of falling bodies is also a statement of fact, and so is a whole theory couched in highly abstract terms, as, for instance, the modern theory of the structure of matter. I shall, of course, not tarry for a detailed justification of such wholesale lumping together. Yet I hope it is not implausible. For, all subtleties apart, statements of laws, of theories, and the so-called "abstract" terms are in one sense merely tools we use to speak of and predict individual, immediately observable facts. Second, let me remind you that when I discussed value judgments I spoke of the fact of somebody being in a certain state of mind, whether this be a state of seeing green or, perhaps, of morally approving a certain course of action. That somebody is in a certain state of mind, then, is a fact. Call it, if you please, a "psychological fact." It follows that, while value judgments are not statements of fact, it is a statement of fact to say that a certain person makes a value judgment or, to put it quite unambiguously, it is a fact that a person now has the kind of experience which he may or may not verbalize as a value judgment.

But I notice that if I do not wish to be misunderstood when I speak in this common-sense manner about psychological facts, I must make one more digression. We cannot literally look into other people's minds. The difficulties and arguments to which this has led, both in philosophy and in the science of psychology, are notorious. The upshot of them, for all we need to care here, is this: All we know and, even more important, everything there is to be known about people's mental states can in principle be known from observing their bodies and their overt behavior, including, of course, their speech. (This is the common-sense core of behaviorism.) Also, a person's mental states are nothing but certain parts or aspects of his bodily states, including his nervous system, seen, as it were, from within. (This is the common-sense core of the so-called "double-aspect" theory of mind. What goes for representative realism and ethical relativism goes for this "theory" as well. One gets hopelessly entangled if one mistakes it for the dissolution of the puzzles and absurdities which it yields under a little dialectical probing.) But since I am not at the moment concerned with these subtleties, I shall feel free to speak about people's minds in general, and about their values, ideals, and motives in particular, without further epistemological pedantry and without emphasizing apologetically again and again how little we actually know about people's minds if we apply those high standards on which the behaviorists so admirably insist in their heroic efforts to build a science of behavior that is both reliable and worth while. Such reliability is, after all, a matter of degree. Nor would it be wise to abstain from dealing as well as we can with matters that are both interesting and important to us merely because we cannot do better, as long as we pursue these difficult studies within the right frame of reference. Such a frame has, indeed, emerged from, or at least is implicit in, what I have said so far. Let me say explicitly, then, that the idea of an exhaustive and comprehensive science of behavior offers in principle no difficulties whatsoever. Like physical science, behavior science with its various branches—psychology, sociology, economics, and so on—deals with facts and with facts only. Like physical science, it tries to organize its facts by means of laws and theories which are of the same logical nature as those of physical science. Unlike physical science, it concerns itself with people's motives, values, and ideals and with those facts—institutional, historical, and so on—of which such psychological facts are important ingredients. But this does not mean either that behavior science makes value judgments or that the truth of its findings is in principle dependent upon value judgments.

Behavior science, since it is a science, tries to find laws. Laws, roughly speaking, predict what will happen if an object of a specified kind finds itself in a specified environment. To arrive at a just idea about the kind of law we seek in behavior science, let us take a glance at the white rat, that great totem animal and martyr of American psychology, which some of our friends chase so tirelessly through their mazes. For, however one may judge its eventual usefulness, experimental animal psychology is undoubtedly the simplest and at the moment the most successful piece of behavior science. Thus we are wise, I believe, if we turn to it for logical discipline. A historical analogy should make this plausible. The mechanics of rigid bodies to the extent that it was known to Newton is, to be sure, not the whole of physics. Yet this elementary fragment of physics may still be used to advantage if one wishes to explain the logic of the whole; how powerful a stimulus it has been historically for the first explicit formulations of this logic is a matter of record. Take, then, a white rat and put it in a maze in which food can be obtained if the right path is followed. What factors enter into the prediction that the animal will or will not, as the case may be, go down this path? Or, to say the same thing differently, what in addition to the characteristics of the environment are the causes that determine the animal's behavior? For to look for laws is, of course, the same as to look for causes. Very roughly and very schematically, there are two groups of such factors. The animal will go down the right path (1) if it is hungry or, as one also says, is motivated or has a need, and (2) if it "knows" the maze. As it must be if we are to have a genuine law, i.e., a generalization that allows for prediction, both these factors or groups of factors—let us call them "state variables," since they characterize the momentary state of the organism—can be ascertained in advance; the first one, e.g., by measuring the animal's blood sugar, the second from information concerning its past history. It is also worth our while to notice the difference in the role of these two groups of factors, the animal's needs and its knowledge. If it is not at the moment instigated by a need, the animal will not, even though it has the knowledge, go down the path that leads to food. If, on the other hand, it has the need without as yet having the knowledge, it will exhibit the kind of behavior, known as "learning," that will eventually lead to the selection of the right path and thus to the temporary satisfaction of the need and, simultaneously to the (as a rule more permanent) acquisition of the relevant knowledge.

These, then, are the three groups of causal factors that must in principle be represented in all laws of behavior science: the environmental conditions, on the one hand, and, on the other, the two kinds of state variables, the individual's needs and his knowledge. There is, in addition, a further group of variables, biologically determined and known as "individual differences." For our purposes it will suffice to mention them. This general schema, it seems obvious, applies to man, as an individual and in his society, as well as to the white rat. But there are, of course, also important differences or, as I had better say, complications. These I shall now briefly discuss, in three steps, by explicating one after the other the following three statements: Man is a propositional animal. Man is an ethical animal. Man is an ideological animal.

The first of these complications, which is at the root of the others, is involved in the full meaning of the verb "to know." When we say the rat knew at the end of which path food was to be had, we do not mean all that is meant by saying, for instance, that I knew how to get into this room in time to deliver this lecture. Both of us, the rat and I, do, when the need arises and under a certain range of conditions, which in my case is rather wider than in the rat's, display the appropriate behavior. In this respect there is no difference. The difference is that I, unlike the rat, have, upon this as upon other such occasions, a certain mental state, which is best called "verbal" whether or not I explicitly verbalize it either to myself or to others. If so verbalized or tagged, as it were, this kind of state variable takes the form of a proposition or of a series of propositions. This is what I mean by calling us "propositional animals." But by calling us so I wish to imply more than that we are afforded the luxury of some sort of inner light by which we can watch ourselves act where the dumb creature merely acts. The presence or absence and the kind of propositional states make a difference, or, as some like to say, a dynamic difference, in that, all other things being equal, the course of our behavior still depends on them. In other words, our propositional states are themselves among the causal factors that determine our behavior. Also, some propositional states represent, and some, to put it quite bluntly, are, needs. To avoid at this point the colloquial ambiguity of "knowing" that appears in such phrases as "We know what we need," permit me to introduce some new terms. Let me from now on call the system of a person's actual and potential propositional states his "rationale," and let me also discard the clumsy phrase "propositional state" in favor of "proposition." We can say, then, that bits of skill are not the only things that can become parts of a person's rationale; the same may happen with his needs. These latter propositions we call "motives" or, somewhat redundantly, "conscious motives." This clarification of terms which we often use quite loosely and, I fear, quite carelessly helps one to grasp firmly the peculiar dynamic significance of our rationale. For we know well—the psychoanalysts, but not they alone, have brought this home to us—that there are very important differences between the behavior of two persons who find themselves under exactly the same circumstances and who are, for the sake of the argument, assumed to be in all other respects alike, if the one is, as one ordinarily says, aware of his needs while the other acts automatically or, perhaps, under a different motive.

It will not take quite so long to explain the remaining two formulas: man is an ethical animal; man is an ideological animal. To begin with the first, it is safe to say that every man's rationale contains certain propositions which combine in themselves two characters: they are value judgments, and they play the role of very powerful motives. In the form in which they actually occur in consciousness, they are known by various names; we call them a man's standards, his ideals, the rules of conduct he tries to follow, or his moral code. More often than not they are what we mean when we speak of a man's philosophy, for only technical philosophers reserve this name for their more recondite pursuits. To deny the power of these motives, the influence they exercise upon our actions, is like denying that water flows downhill. In this sense man does not live by bread alone and has, indeed, a higher nature. But to insist that man is thus, quite uniquely, an ethical animal does not commit one to deny that these peculiar motives and the influence they have on our actions are as ineluctably causally determined and therefore in principle as predictable as, say, our tissue needs. It could even be, as the psychoanalysts and, again, not they alone, tell us, that the rise of our higher motives can be genetically traced to these very tissue needs. Whether or not this is so is, relatively speaking, a matter of scientific detail. Whatever the answer to these intriguing causal questions may be, the sway of ethical motives among men is universal. To take pride, for instance, in rejecting the standards that prevail in one's society is, as we use the term, itself a standard. Nor does it make any difference whether such a private or minority standard is, as one ordinarily says, one of cynical opportunism or, perhaps, one of self-sacrificing reformist zeal.

As we survey man's history, we cannot, I believe, escape the following conclusion. *The motive power of a value judgment is often greatly increased when it appears within the rationale of those who hold it not under its proper logical flag as a value judgment but in the disguise of a statement of fact.* A statement of this kind, that is, a value judgment disguised as, or mistaken for, a statement of fact, I shall call an "ideological statement." A rationale or an important part of a rationale that contains in logically crucial places ideological statements I shall call an "ideology." And, finally, I call man an "ideological animal" because, at least up to this point in his history, his rationales were more often than not ideologies and because, whether we like it or not, the motive power of his standards is, at least sometimes, greatly increased if they take the form of an ideology. Take just one obvious example, the doctrine of natural law which inspires our classical constitutional documents. It is, I believe, open to serious doubt whether the effect on the people would have been the same had the text read "These we hold to be self-evident value judgments" instead of the clarion call "These truths we hold to be self-evident." What goes for the people goes also, I believe, for most of the founding fathers and perhaps even for a man of the intellectual pre-eminence of Thomas Jefferson.

Having defined my terms, which always takes the philosopher a long time, I can now turn to the problems that have been raised in connection with "ideology" and "ideological." But it seems proper that I first mention the name of the late Karl Mannheim, who started these terms on the present, second phase of their career in the social sciences. (A first brief popularity they owed to their inventors, those *idéologues* who were the last flower of the great eighteenth century and whom, therefore, Stendhal admired and Napoleon so heartily disliked.) The experts will easily recognize where I follow Mannheim as well as where I deviate and, by implication, criticize. So I shall not, as a rule, bother either to give or to claim credit beyond this general acknowledgment. Perhaps this is not the worst way to do justice to both the stimulation and the confusion that may be traced back to this vigorous writer.

Systems of ideas as they are actually held by people and social groups, or, as Mannheim would say, ideas existentially considered, are facts. As such, we know they are potent causes. But what is a cause is of necessity also an effect. In other words, rationales themselves are causally determined; accordingly, it is the business of social science to discover their causes as well as their effects. Students devoting themselves to this task hope to build a scientific foundation for those variegated and interesting pursuits that have long flowered in our civilization and which are now, somewhat self-consciously, known as the sociology of knowledge and the history of ideas. More important than any such names is one point that must be kept clearly in mind. What a person knows and believes is in principle predictable from the two classical factors, his needs and his environment, his environment being essentially his society. This goes for the factual part of a rationale as well, and for its truths as well as for its errors. In other words, we must in principle be prepared to explain why a person knows what he knows truly as well as why he errs when he errs, as Ptolemy erred when he propounded the factual falsehood known as the geocentric system. In fact, these two things cannot be separated from each other any more than one can separate the recognition and diagnosis of disease from the physiology of the healthy organism. Again, if a rationale happens to be an ideology, the fact that this is so, the particular form the ideology takes, and the kind of defective logic involved are, on the one hand, all causally determined and, on the other, amenable to explanation. Nor do we need to know many such laws or explanations—it may, in fact, be doubted whether we know any that are really satisfactory —in order to realize that it makes a difference whether a proposition that was actually held is a factual truth, a factual falsehood, an ideological statement or, perhaps, a complex mixture and, in the case of an inferential belief, by what "logic" it has been "established." This leads to some questions which, I suspect, have been uppermost in your mind for quite some time. So let me ask them myself. How can I be sure, in the light of what I have just said, that my own rationale is not an ideology? How, in particular, can I be sure that the distinction between fact and value, on which everything I have said and shall say rests, is not itself an ideological distinction? Who shall guard the guardians? Now, in one sense, which is a human and practical sense, I myself would insist that there is not much of which I am certain. In fact, I am so impressed with this that I have come to think the analysis of this very confused and difficult idea of certainty is one of the more important tasks of systematic philosophizing, just as the tracing of its vicissitudes is, in my opinion, one of the challenges in the history of philosophical ideas. But if this is once understood, it must be admitted that the questions I just raised deserve an answer. Permit me to approach them by means of a historical analogy which, as will soon transpire, is more than just an analogy.

"Sociological subjectivity" is, perhaps, a suggestive name for our puzzle. At any rate, I shall call it so, since the older puzzle, of which I shall make use in my analogy, is known as the problem of "epistemological subjectivity." During the seventeenth century physics, physiology, and the psychology of perception reached a stage in which one could, in a careless and misleading language, argue like this. What a person sees, hears, or smells is not the "real" object but his own percepts or, perhaps, his brain states; hence the possibility of perceptual error or even of systematic delusions produced in his subjects by a scientist who is familiar with the laws of physics, physiology, and perception. But then, one may pursue, how does this scientist himself achieve anything but a "subjective" picture of the real object or, to put it as radically as possible, how does he know that there is any real object at all? The history of philosophy from Descartes to Kant and J. S. Mill is in a sense the history of all variations on this theme. The decisive turn, also known as the "positivistic turn," occurred when it was recognized a generation ago that the original questions (How do we know that there is a real or objective world? Assuming there is one, how could we ever know what it is like?) are not good questions but, in a certain technical sense which I cannot stop to explain, mere verbalisms, and that, therefore, if we accept them uncritically, we enter a dialectical squirrel cage that has indeed no issue. The task of epistemological analysis is, therefore, not the impossible one of answering these questions in their original intent but that of doing whatever can and needs to be done about them by means of logical analysis. If this is done, then we see that we know perfectly well what we mean when we speak, in the ordinary nonphilosophical sense, of truth and falsehood, of physical objects, percepts, and illusions. And not only do we know this in general, we know also in each case how to apply these terms, using, as we do and must, the methods of science. These methods are, to be sure, subject to doubt and error; but these are merely doubt and error in the ordinary self-correcting sense, not in that sterile "philosophical" sense which commits us to the squirrel cage. The structural similarity between the problem of epistemological and sociological subjectivity is, I trust, by now obvious. There is also a historical similarity. As the one has been created by the development of physics and physiology, so the other has been precipitated by the rise of the social sciences.

Like the problem of epistemological subjectivity, though for different reasons, the problem of sociological subjectivity is, I submit, a pseudo-problem. There appears to be a problem only as long as one fails to distinguish between value judgments and statements of fact, treating some of the former like statements of perceptual error or, more significantly, like systematic delusions due to one's social circumstances. If one does this, then the notorious subjectivity of our value judgments may mislead him into believing, as Mannheim does, that the discovery of their causal dependence has reopened the epistemological question. In contradistinction to this I and, I believe, most analytical philosophers would insist that the distinction between fact

and value, which explains this notorious subjectivity, is as clear and unproblematic as those between a physical object, a percept, and an illusion.
Moreover—and this is the crucial point—all these distinctions are matters
of logical, not of sociological, analysis, just as they are systematically prior
to and independent of all sociological considerations. Who denies this
must, if he is to be consistent, also maintain that Locke, who in a quite
obvious sense called green a simple idea, has since been proved wrong by
the scientists' discovery of the very "complex" physical and physiological
events on which the perception of a "simple" hue causally depends. And,
obviously, whoever maintains this confuses two very different sorts of things.

Mannheim, as I have hinted, did not and, as we shall presently see, could
not within his own rationale accept this dissolution of the alleged puzzle
of sociological subjectivity. But he had at least the courage of his convictions,
for which we may admire him. As some of the classical philosophers, accepting their predicament, with quixotic heroism denied the existence of the
physical universe, so Mannheim accepts his and, greatly impressed as he
is with the conflict among the partly ideological structures that passed and
still pass for science, denies in principle the possibility of an objective social
science. Or, to say the same thing by means of the familiar terms as I use
them and he, naturally, doesn't, he insists that every rationale is an ideology.
This formulation has the merit of revealing, in a pattern only too familiar
to the historian of philosophy, the intrinsic difficulty of a position like
Mannheim's. If this proposition that every rationale is an ideology is itself
objectively true, how can he know it? If it is not, why should we pay any
attention to it? And what, in particular, is the value of a social science thus
construed? To this last question Mannheim gives, in his famous theory
of the "free intelligentsia," an answer that is surprising and, besides, of some
logical interest. Social scientists who, as members of the intelligentsia, circulate rather freely among the various social groups are, he suggests, by this
very fact as well as by their own group interest led to collect and compare
all kinds of ideologies. From these they construct, very roughly speaking, a
new composite ideology which, by virtue of being such a composite (and
often compromise), finds acceptance and achieves progress. To expose the
weakness of this argument, one merely needs to ask: Progress toward what?
Permit me a comparison. If I show you a snapshot of a person you do not
happen to know, it is hardly fair to ask whether you think it a good likeness. The question remains unfair, no matter how many portraits of this
person I show you—snapshots, water colors, oil paintings, or even a montage
(composite or synthesis) of all of them. As it is meant, the argument is therefore without force. A subjectivist cannot in this manner define progress and,
in particular, approximation toward an objective truth whose very existence
he in principle denies. But one may insist on this and yet think that as a
sociological *aperçu* about the way certain groups function Mannheim's
so-called theory of the free intelligentsia is, perhaps, a brilliant insight. I,
for one, believe that it is. Let us further note, for later reference, that it

assigns to the social scientist qua scientist a rather spectacular part in the social drama.

Such internal difficulties indicate what I am indeed prepared to maintain: like many other logically similar approaches, Mannheim's original doctrine of ideology is itself an ideological structure. And it is of logical interest that within a rationale of the type I have proposed one can at least consistently maintain that this rationale itself is not an ideology. But consistency as such is no criterion of truth, so this remark adds nothing to what I have so far attempted, namely, to demonstrate that the other side errs. Crude and sketchy as it is, this primary and central part of my case must be left to speak for itself, by its logic and by what it adduces to be the case (facts). Yet it should help us to grasp the total dialectic of the situation if we realize that such demonstration, no matter how complete, is not the only sort of thing that can be done. I should also be able to explain causally why the other side errs and why that which is happily my own beholds the truth without ideological distortion. But, to be sure, what is needed is a sociological explanation. To say simply that the one side is brighter than the other would not only be most ungracious; it would not be true. Personal ingenuity, or so at least I sincerely believe, is, by and large, quite evenly distributed among the several sides of the great controversies which together constitute the intellectual history of our civilization.

For the idea of the desired explanation we can amusingly draw upon another brilliant *aperçu* by Mannheim. For he takes pains to explain why my side, those who believe in objective (factual) truths and in the possibility of an objective nonideological social science, have come to hold their views. He suggests that the objectivist rationale is a survival from earlier times when the functions of the intelligentsia were exercised by an essentially conservative priestly caste that claimed privileged access to eternal verities, verities that stood immutably above the "ideological" strife of the day and thus secured to their professional beholders a similar enviable exemption. Primarily interested as I am in what I just called the "total dialectic" of the situation, I wish to point out that I could without any intellectual embarrassment accept this explanation or, more accurately, this *aperçu*. For I do believe that there are causes that make some of us see the truth, just as other causes make others fall into error. So, if sociological factors enter, as they probably do, though they are very likely not the whole story, why couldn't it be as Mannheim suggests? This is, after all, merely a matter of detail—I would say scientific detail if we were not, all of us, limited to *aperçus* rather than to scientifically trustworthy explanations. Even so, I am inclined to think that Mannheim's explanation is a little lopsided; so I shall make my next point by using a part of his idea to propose an alternative that deals simultaneously with both sides. Let me, then, remind you of the two classical factors, needs and knowledge. As for needs, I believe both objectivists and subjectivists, like all other intellectuals, provide, incidentally and for the most part unconsciously, an argument to bolster the social status of the intelligentsia.[2] In this respect there is no difference between them. The difference is that the objectivist temper craves the spectator safety as well as the intellectual and emotional delights of the neutral expert and critic, while the subjectivist rationalizes his desire for social leadership. (You remember what stellar role Mannheim assigned to the social scientist as a social leader.) Knowledge, in cases like this, means primarily intellectual ambience and tradition. In this respect, there is again a difference. Objectivism takes its inspiration from the natural sciences and the empiricist philosophies of the last century. Subjectivism stands in the tradition of Hegelian idealism, which is history-centered, could not accept the "positivistic" distinction between fact and value, and even denies that there is any such thing as objective self-contained truth in the sense in which all nonidealistic philosophers, realist and positivist alike, insist that there is such truth. Mannheim as an individual certainly stems from Hegel; so, by the way, does Dewey, who in many respects holds structurally very similar views.

In nonacademic discourse "ideology" and "ideological" are nowadays almost terms of abuse. This is why I feel I should stress again that value judgments as such are not ideological. Nor is there anything wrong with them because they are not logically the same sort of thing as statements of fact, including those of science. We could not for one moment live without making value judgments, and who, even if we could, would want to? But if one is so overimpressed with science that he deprecates all value judgments as ideological simply because they are not scientific, he will perhaps also reject as futile that reflective, critical, and, in an obvious sense, highly rational discourse about values without which life is not worth living. Unfortunately, such a person does not cease to make value judgments; he merely tends to make them unreflectively. One danger of this attitude is greatest in our rulers and those who assist them or wish to assist them as experts. They may think that they still act as scientists when, in fact, they act as policy-makers. This, as we all know to our sorrow, is the soil in which callousness and fanaticism thrive. Loathe as I do that smooth-faced "well-adjusted" new barbarism, I regret one implication of the way I defined my terms. (But then, no terminology is perfect.) If I am to be consistent, I must call ideology every rationale, no matter how explicit and articulate on the fact-value issue and other fundamental questions, that assimilates facts and values to each other in a way in which the tradition in which I stand insists that this cannot be done. Clearly, this is a special case, and the application to it of what is popularly almost a derogatory term is rather unfortunate. So let me set it aside by speaking about such systems of thought as "philosophical ideologies."

2 For an elaboration of this idea cf. W. P. Metzger, "Ideology and the Intellectual: A Study of Thorstein Veblen," *Philosophy of Science*, XVI (1949), 125–33.

Most systems of social thought and of what passed or still passes for social science are not philosophical ideologies. This sort of literature is, by and large, not concerned with the basic philosophical issues and, therefore, even though sometimes inspired by and congenial to a technical philosophy, in the technical sense philosophically naïve. But such systems often show another interesting feature that one may well call ideological, in a somewhat extended sense of the term, which I shall indicate by speaking of "scientific ideologies." What I have in mind is this. We sometimes find in the scientific and methodological discussions of writers whom we otherwise greatly admire passages which are so obviously either factually false or logically inadequate that we cannot help wondering how they passed the censorship of their authors' self-criticism. In themselves these passages are not necessarily ideological. What marks them is either fallacious logic or statements of fact and theory extremely implausible on the evidence that was available to the author. These trouble spots, I submit, these lows where the argument drops, as it were, beneath its own level, are more often than not the results of motivational pressure. More specifically, while these bits of rationale are not literally either value judgments or ideological statements, they yet assert facts or, rather, alleged facts and logical connections or, rather, alleged logical connections which the author, if he has or had consciously attended to the matter, has or would have thought congenial to his values. Permit me again an illustration. Imagine a small boy very fond of fruit who is told that he may take as many apples as he wishes from a certain basket, provided only he leaves four. The basket contains six apples; the boy reasons hastily "$6 - 3 = 4$" and takes three apples! "$6 - 3 = 4$" is not an ideological statement but, to use Pareto's term, a logico-empirical falsehood. I don't think we shall be very wrong if we attribute, at least in part, this error in arithmetic to motivational pressures of the kind that operate in scientific ideologies. Only, the worth-while and historically important cases are not always quite so transparent as the little boy. A few examples should be of interest.

As my first case I take an opinion of J. S. Mill, a thinker whom I greatly admire; but uncritical hero worship is pagan and, I am convinced, one of the great sources of evil. Mill insists that "human beings in society have no properties but those which are derived from and may be resolved into the laws of the nature of individual man." Put as we would put it today and also as conservatively as possible, this means that the laws governing the behavior of (individuals in) large groups can be deductively derived from the laws that govern their behavior in isolation or in very small groups, just as all geometrical theorems can be derived from the axioms of geometry. The point at issue is thus, as we would say, the methodological relation between psychology and sociology. This, as you know, is still an issue. Now for analysis. The assertion that sociology is in this sense reducible to psychology is indubitably of a factual nature. As to its truth, I incline to believe on the basis of the evidence now available that it may well be true, though one can never be too sure about such a sweeping prognosis concerning the future results of science. This, however, is not the point. The point is that Mill mistakenly offered his thesis not as a factual prognosis but as a logical truth, i.e., as the result of a purely logical analysis of the subject matters of the two disciplines. The value involved is, I submit, Mill's commitment to the dignity of the individual and to the pre-eminence of individual ethics over social expediency and the so-called *raisons d'état*. The verbal bridge, as it were, leads from individual to individualism.

My second case is a rather notorious argument Herbert Spencer made against poor relief, purporting to show that such public charity was bound to produce evils even greater than those it was designed to prevent. The gist of the argument is that such measures are unnatural in that they futilely attempt to interfere with inexorable laws of nature, namely, those of a free-market economy. The factual error involved is nowadays, after the rise of institutional economics, obvious. On the other hand, it is only fair to say that, for all we know, overreliance on the economic bounty of an unlimited welfare state could well produce social phenomena which some of us would agree with Spencer in considering most undesirable. But again, this is not the point. What concerns me is the stupendous logical blunder. Spencer says, in effect: Do not interfere with the laws of nature. As if anybody conceivably could! It is logically like exhorting water not to flow uphill. On the other hand, in what sense do we interfere with the law that it does, in fact, flow downhill when, say, we pump it up? Do we not, rather, utilize this law, in conjunction with others, to produce by proper arrangement a desired result? (These other laws correspond, of course, to the noneconomic dynamisms that operate in every institutional structure.) The motive behind this particular piece of scientific ideology is, I suggest, Spencer's fierce noncomformist devotion to freedom of the individual from all interference by the state, including even benevolent interference.

As my third case I take one part of the argument the classical marginalists made for the distribution of the social product among the several so-called factors of production, land, capital, and labor, in proportion to their marginal productivity. Very roughly, this part of the argument runs as follows. The proposed distribution is at least just, in that each factor receives what it has actually produced, i.e., what it has, in the sense of "cause" that occurs in science, caused to exist. As for the appeal to justice, it is either a frank value judgment or manifestly ideological. For justice in its relevant root meaning is a value. Accordingly, my concern is with the other part of the thesis, the part which says that in this manner each factor receives what it has actually produced. The fallacy is, very simply, that all factors are necessary conditions for the existence of the product; and if A, B, C, D, etc., are all necessary to produce the effect X, then it makes no sense, either empirically or logically, to ask for which quantitative part of X each of the several joined causes is responsible.

My fourth and last case deals not with an individual writer or school but with a general difficulty caused by our relative ignorance in the area of the social sciences. We know today that the volume of a given quantity of a gas depends in a certain manner, which is expressed by a certain formula, on its pressure, its temperature and, within certain limits on nothing else. Within these limits, pressure and temperature are a complete set of relevant factors or, as one also says, variables. Boylé in the seventeenth century knew only of the dependence on pressure and proposed for it a formula that yields correct predictions only as long as the temperature happens to remain constant. His formula is, therefore, literally false, though historically it was quite an achievement and though it does hold under certain conditions which we know but which the formula itself does not mention. The import of this (rather oversimplified) illustration is, I trust, obvious. In the social sciences we not only often do not know the laws (formulas), we do not even know a complete set of relevant variables. (In fact, one is not likely to discover the former without discovering the latter.) In such situations many Boyles may arise, each with his partial truth which is, literally, a falsehood. If this is so, as I believe it to be, then the laws proposed and even the variables entering them may well be determined, at least in part and either consciously or unconsciously, by the values of the author. Practically this is, I believe, one of the most important mechanisms by which scientific ideologies establish themselves as social science, sometimes dangerously and with disastrous consequences, as in the case of Marxism, which—let us be just—brought home to us the relevance of the economic variables as it had never been brought home to us before. Burdensome as this phenomenon is in practice, logically it is merely a by-product of our ignorance. It is not, as, for instance, Max Weber thought, an objection in principle against the possibility of a nonideological social science.

I have come to the end of this string of comments which, if I am not too mistaken, amount to a logical analysis of the notion of ideology or at least to the outline of such an analysis. In conclusion, I should like to say a few words about two questions of a very different sort. *Is an ideology-free society possible?* More precisely, can a society recognize its values for what they are, without any ideological support and yet with reasonable stability remain committed to them? This is clearly a matter of factual prognosis, not of logical anaylsls. Our ignorance being what it is, the most honest answer is, in my opinion, that we do not know. The positive answer appeals more to the radical-optimistic temper, the negative one goes by and large more readily with a conservative-pessimistic outlook. Each side can point to some evidence; each side tries to make its case from what we believe we know about human nature. The evidence is, naturally, inconclusive; though surely the historical record as well as the soul-shaking experiences of our troubled present should keep anybody's optimism from growing too sanguine. Nevertheless, the arguments on both sides are more often than not themselves ideological. So my first question, which is one of fact, remains open and I turn to the second. *Is an ideology-free society desirable?* To answer this question is to make a value judgment. Now, naturally, one cannot prove values, but you remember I insisted that one can reason about them. I would say, then, that by the standards of classical nineteenth-century liberalism, which, freed from some historical dross, happen to be my own, the ideal of an ideology-free society is a consummation devoutly to be desired, if for no other reason than the humanity, the intelligence, and the courage it takes to bear life without the support of ideological illusion. To me such a world is the only one worth living in and therefore, if necessary, worth dying for. Perhaps we shall be called upon to die; I have no easy optimism to dispense. But then, again, we may increase our chances if we can learn to stand by our values without clutching at an ideology.

Three ⋆ PURPOSE

AND FUNCTION

INTRODUCTION

Men have their own purposes and may also, as in their daily jobs, serve the purposes of others. Serving a purpose, their actions also have a function. Tools and machines, having no purposes of their own, only have functions. With respect to artifacts, *purpose* and *function* are roughly interchangeable. We may speak of the purpose or the function of a saw, meaning in either case the human purpose that it serves. Although we can sometimes interchange the terms with respect to human actions, this is by no means always the case. A man's act may have a function, for others or even for himself, which is different from his purpose in doing it. Though the context permits a lot of leeway, generally we speak of a function when the end served is not consciously intended by whoever or whatever is a means to that end. The function, but not the purpose, of the heart is to circulate the blood. The function of marriage is quite different from the purposes for which people marry. People do not marry in order, say, to promote social stability.

A man behaves purposefully when he does things that he believes will bring him to a certain goal. When natural processes or social institutions are interpreted as analogously "goal directed," the locutions *in order to* or *for the sake of* may be applied to them. The heart beats in order to circulate the blood; the family exists for the sake of social stability. Although such locutions for nonintentional "goals" are commonly used, it is by no means clear exactly what they mean or how and what they explain. A natural process or a social institution generally has many different consequences. Which of these is its "function"? Just how much and what kind of information is supplied by "functional explanation"?

A less obvious but similar question may be raised about purposive explanation. Even over a brief span of time, a man performs many intentional actions that are irrelevant to a certain goal. How do we decide which of these actions are directed toward that goal? There may be many different ways to realize a given purpose. Why does a man choose one path rather than another? If a "purposive explanation" merely states the purpose of an action, this may not be very enlightening. The purposive explanation in turn has to be explained. Why did the agent have these purposes, and why did he try to realize them in just this way? The question asks for the causes and effects of purposes. This suggests that the explanation of purposive behavior may not be a purposive explanation, and the explanation of a function may not be a functional explanation. The papers in this section provide analyses of the concepts of purpose and function and of the logical structure of explanations utilizing these concepts.

The opening selection by I. E. Farber concerns the study of personality in behavioral terms. This paper has been presented first because, in order to deal adequately with this delicate and even inflammatory issue, Farber undertakes a broad survey of the methodological assumptions concerning science and scientific method which divide behavior scientists from their critics. His lucid sketch of these basic ideas provides a valuable background for all further discussion. Farber is a psychologist whose primary research interest has been to extend the basic laws of behavior theory to complex, motivated behavior. Such behavior is highly variable from individual to individual and constitutes what we call a man's personality. Traditionally, general theoretical psychology was concerned with those features of behavior that are relatively independent of individual differences. The use of a general theory of behavior to account for the particular characteristics of individuals has suffered a barrage of hostile criticism. In his sweeping and often pungent review of these objections, Farber clarifies many misunderstandings about the science of man in general and about behavior theory in particular.

Many social scientists, and not they alone, are pained by the terms *stimulus* and *response*. The use of these terms evokes the image of the knee jerk and the eye blink. Automatically it is assumed that theories couched in that language treat all behavior on the model of simple reflexes. Farber emphasizes that a convenient terminology for classifying events ("variables") occurring in the laws of behavior is not a theory about what these events are and the connections among them. Originally, a stimulus was an environmental event presumed to be a cause of overt behavior, the response. But environmental events are not the only causes of behavior. Hunger, for instance, is also a stimulus. And simple bits of behavior are not the only responses to a situation. Anxiety is also a response. The implication of Farber's discussion is clear: As the science of psychology passed from seeking isolated empirical correlations to constructing explanatory theories, the language of stimulus-and-response became a language for speaking about the cause-and-effect components of behavior, *whatever these causes and effects might be*. The notion of stimulus-and-response is the notion of cause-and-effect applied to individual behavior.

By discussing the concept of a "mediating process," Farber reveals the great distance between actual behavior theory and its caricature as a "muscle-twitch" or reflex psychology, a psychology, in effect, without psychology. The so-called intervening variables name the emotional states, motives, habits, needs, attitudes, and purposes that intervene or mediate between overt behavior and the immediate situation. They are defined independently of the behavior they explain as complex patterns of dispositions to act in certain ways which are not discernible by the naked eye. They incorporate such items as the person's past learning, his family background, his needs, and beliefs, and specified relations among such conditions and dispositions. These "mediating processes" vary from person to person and explain why different people behave differently in similar situations.

Mediating processes are also part of the criteria used to identify classes of responses as the same or different. They explain why an overt act may be characterized as aggressive when performed by one person but not by another, or even if performed by the same person under different circumstances. A response does not consist merely of the movements of a person's body. Two different sorts of overt behavior may be characterized as the same kind of action or response. Given Brown's inner states and the environment in which he is placed, a remark he makes to Jones may be as much an act of aggression as his striking him. Both acts may count as aggressive responses if they are similarly related to Brown's needs, beliefs, intentions, and to the external situation. They are functionally equivalent by virtue of being lawfully related in the same way to Brown's inner states and his environment. Which overt act occurs depends upon what these inner states and environmental conditions are. Clearly, a certain remark might not be aggressive if Brown had different beliefs about what would offend Jones, or if the remark were uttered by someone else to another person.

The notion of *meaning* is a ubiquitous source of confusion and misunderstanding. In the present context, Farber points out that the behavior theorist does not neglect the fact that people respond not merely to a physical stimulus but to its symbolic meaning. A flag or a set of sounds that we call a word have no meaning as physical objects. They have meaning *for* someone. The meaning of a physical object, conceptualized as an intervening variable, is part of someone's response to that object. This inner response, in turn, acts as a further stimulus which causes overt behavior. If he hears the word *fire* he runs; if he sees a flag, he salutes. The meaning within and the physical event without both play a causal role in behavior. Both, therefore, must be mentioned.

Fodor also discusses certain misconceptions about psychological theory, particularly those that have been prevalent among philosophers. He disposes of the odd and, for a period, oddly popular view that psychological explanation can only be given of man's aberrant behavior, his slips of the tongue, and other deviations from the "normal." Like Farber, but explicitly in those terms, he also shows how psychologists distinguish mere bodily movements from meaningful actions. However, he and Farber give very different accounts of the nature of psychological explanation. Farber's "mediating processes," conceived as complex behavioral dispositions, are couched in wholly nonphysiological terms. That is why his view is called a behavior theory. It explains behavior in behavioral (and environmental) terms. Fodor's "internal states," on the other hand, are conceived as hypothetical, physiological entities. To understand his position requires some preparation.

Man is made of flesh and blood. His particular constitution may account not only for how he resembles but for how he differs from other animals. That our thoughts, emotions, and overt behavior have corresponding physiological states is beyond reasonable doubt. When a man is embarrassed, feels pain, or wishes upon a star, something happens in his central nervous system. The mind affects the body and, conversely, the body affects the mind. The organic processes inside the skin are one thing; our meaningful behavior is another. If by knowing the former we could infer the latter, then psychology would be *reduced* to physiology. Two things are necessary for such reduction.

First, we must know the neurophysiological laws of the organic processes. Because these laws do not mention behavior or psychological states, from them alone we could neither predict nor explain behavior. Therefore, second, we must also know the empirical laws connecting each psychological state at a given time (such as a motive or an action) with its corresponding physiological event at the same time. These are called cross-sectional laws. [See Index.] If we knew *both* these things, then the laws of psychological theory would be derivable from those of neurophysiology, in conjunction with the laws connecting physiological states to behavior. This is what it means to say that psychology would be reduced to physiology. If this were accomplished, then each psychological concept could at some time and for some purposes be dispensed with. If, for instance, we knew the state of a man's brain at a certain time, then from the physiological and cross-sectional laws we could predict his subsequent behavior without having to mention the motive, say, that was a mediating cause. But at *no* time, if we wish to talk about what people are doing or thinking, could we dispense with all such terms together. If psychological concepts were never used, we should have only the physics and physiology of human nature, not its psychology.

In fact we do not now know the physiological states corresponding to our psychological states. Doubtless the connections are extremely complicated. One may of course speculate about them. Psychologists disagree about the value of such speculation as a program of research. Some, of whom Farber is representative, believe that it is more fruitful to stay with behavior theory and a behaviorial explanation of behavior. Some others, particularly in recent years, prefer to look for the "underlying" physiological causes. Fodor, a philosopher who has turned to substantive psychological research, opts for the physiological way. Substantively that is neither here nor there, nor is his paper concerned with substantive matters. But it is in the light of this preference that the intriguing picture he gives of psychological explanation is to be understood.

Fodor conceives psychological explanation to be a two-phase process, one "functional," the other causal. These phases correspond to the difference between saying what something *does,* on the one hand, and the explanation of *how* it does it, on the other. When a device is called a can opener, we refer to it by its function. That is what it does; doing that, it serves a purpose. It can have that function as a consequence of its structure and the laws of physics. When we explain how the can opener works, we give the mechanism of the process, that is, the causal laws that account for its being able to open cans. Analogously, according to Fodor, the internal physiological states have a function. This function is to bring about certain behavior. In the first-stage psychological explanation, these physiological states are referred to by their functions. We describe these functions by using such terms as *memory, attitude,* and *belief.* These "functions" account for the overt behavior. A second-stage psychological explanation explains how the physiological states can have this function by stating the electrochemical laws by which they work. Because we do not in fact know the physiological causes of behavior, we can merely speculate about what physiological states and laws would be compatible with our first-stage functional explanations. We thus produce physiological models, or speculative theories, about the underlying physiological mechanisms. Fodor's two-stage picture of psychological explanation—one functional, the other causal—subtly raises many interesting logical and conceptual problems. An adequate appraisal of his proposal requires, among other things, a closer analysis of the concept of function. The papers by Hempel and Bergmann provide such analyses.

A man behaving purposefully adapts his behavior in various ways so as to achieve that end. Biological phenomena may also be conceived as being "goal directed." However, biologists generally agree that purposive or teleological locutions, such as *in order to,* can be eliminated from a complete, causal explanation of vital processes. A causal explanation tells us how the physiological variables interact to produce certain effects. One effect, for instance, is to maintain a certain state, such as constant body temperature, without which the organism sickens and dies.

In biology we can unambiguously characterize the equilibrium states by virtue of which certain "goals," such as health and life, are maintained. These can be shown to be the effect of physiological laws. Statements about the functions that an organ serves are replaced or supplemented by a causal explanation of how these functions are achieved. What, however, are the equilibrium conditions and desired consequences that enable us to specify the function of a social custom or an institution? Do all customs and institutions serve a function? We know when a man is dying. How do we specify a dysfunction in society? Despite these obvious perplexities, functional explanation is very common in social science. It has indeed been maintained that functional explanations are the only kind adequate to an explanation of social phenomena. Hempel, drawing upon this considerable literature, analyzes in detail the various functional explanations that have been proposed by sociologists and anthropologists. He discusses the comparison of society with self-regulating biological systems and with servomechanisms. The relations between functional analyses and deductive and inductive explanations are examined and Hempel concludes with various suggestions about the uses and limitations of the functionalist approach.

Bergmann compares various uses of *purpose* and of *function* and discusses certain connections, often unrecognized, among them. Some extended uses of these terms can be scientifically suggestive, but others create confusion. He explains the general conditions for the existence of an equilibrium state and an appropriate use of the term function. Bergmann gives reasons for asserting that as we increase our knowledge of man, the less scientific use we have for the concepts of purpose and function.

[9] Personality and Behavioral Science

I. E. FARBER

Almost half a century ago, Watson (1919) had, among other things, this to say about personality:

> Let us mean by the term personality an individual's total assets (actual and potential) and liabilities (actual and potential) on the reaction side. By assets we mean first the total mass of organized habits; the socialized and regulated instincts; the socialized and tempered emotions; and the combinations and interrelations among these; and secondly, high coefficients both of plasticity (capability of new habit formation or altering of old) and of retention (readiness of implanted habits to function after disuse). Looked at in another way, assets are that part of the individual's equipment which make for his adjustment and balance in his present environment and for readjustment if the environment changes.
>
> By liabilities we mean similarly that part of the individual's equipment which does not work in the present environment and the potential or possible factors which would prevent his rising to meet a changed environment (p. 397).

And, again:

> During the whole process of human development from infancy to old age, . . . there goes on not only the process of acquisition of habit and the modification of hereditary reaction but also and equally important that of the elimination of reaction systems which work only up to a certain age. Old situations give way to new and as the situation changes old ways of reacting should be cast off and new ones formed (p. 415).

In my opinion the point of view expressed in these passages is neither tendentious nor antiquated. Among other things, it emphasizes the importance of two aspects of the study of personality: personality as product or structure, the state at any given moment of the ceaseless stream of processes and activities that constitute behavior; and personality as process, change, development. Personality can be fully understood in its cross-sectional aspects only if we know the nature of the events and circumstances of which

First published under the title "A Framework for the Study of Personality as a Behavioral Science," *Personality and Personality Change*, P. Worchel and D. Byrne, eds., John Wiley & Sons, Inc., New York, 1964, pp. 3–37; reprinted with permission of the publishers. [References are listed at the end of the article.]

it is the result, and in its developmental aspects, only if we know the particular behaviors or processes that are modified.

But this view does more than assert the importance of specifying the nature both of reaction systems and their modulators. It treats the probability or degree of susceptibility of the various systems to change in particular ways and degrees under given conditions as fundamental descriptive characteristics of personality. Insofar as personality is described in these terms, it may be unnecessary and even misleading to distinguish between the concept of personality and that of personality change.

The foregoing portrayal of personality differs from others, of course, as other current approaches differ among themselves, in respect to the conceptualizations of the systems or processes that are subject to change, and of the dimensions whereby change may be described. At the same time, divested of metaphysical implications and of commitment to any particular hypotheses concerning the determinants of behavior, this formulation appears quite consonant with a good many others frequently characterized as "dynamic," in at least one sense of this much-abused term. With this salute to good company, one may classify it a little more definitely, because of its evident concern with behavior and the learning process, as a behavior- or learning-theoretical view. Though I should be comfortable with these designations, the label "behavioral science" or "behavioral approach" may be preferred by those who consider the adjective "theoretical" gratuitous. None of these terms is altogether unobjectionable, but insofar as they refer to attempts at systematic formulations of the determinants of the acquisition, maintenance, and elimination of particular kinds of behavior or behavior tendencies, they will serve to identify the perspective of the present paper.

Theories of Behavior Versus Theories of Personality

Whether any behavior system or theory can be at once comprehensive enough and detailed enough to encompass the mysteries of personality and personality change is still an open question. One reason why some psychologists are skeptical is that such formulations do not seem to refer at all to a special class of concepts or phenomena called "personality," but rather to behavior in general, or to predispositions inferred from behavior in general. I believe this observation to be quite accurate. Behavior theorists ordinarily do not distinguish between the task of explaining or predicting personality and that of explaining or predicting behavior. To be sure, in discussing personality they are likely to stress certain processes or concepts such as learning and motivation, but this is characteristic of their general approach to psychology. In their typical view, the study of personality is essentially coterminous with the study of behavior.

I must confess to a certain puzzlement concerning some other views of personality, especially in regard to the distinctions between those behaviors or processes that are supposed to comprise or reflect personality and those that are not. Statements such as "Personality is what a man really is" are simply not helpful, since any kind of behavior or hypothetical variable that might reasonably be used to account for behavior, e.g., habit, libido, press, or positive self-regard, seems equally realistic. Nor does the following amplification seem more satisfying: "Personality is the dynamic organization within the individual of those psychophysical systems that determine his unique adjustments to his environment" (Allport, 1937, p. 48). Except for the term "unique," which is better calculated to reassure people than enlighten them (cf. Eysenck, 1952; Meehl, 1954), this statement does not appear to exclude from consideration any aspect of behavior or a single variable of which behavior in general may be considered a function. Indeed, at the risk of offending both sides, one might point out that the two definitions, the one by Watson and the other by Allport, seem more remarkable for their similarities than their differences.

Still, discussions of personality do not, as a rule, cover every aspect of behavior, though some, even of a non-behavioral sort (e.g., Murphy, 1947), come close. Most frequently, as Hall and Lindzey (1957) observe in their excellent text, they concentrate on motivational variables, i.e., those used to account for the apparently purposive, striving, goal-directed aspects of behavior. Thus, performance on an intelligence test may not be regarded as an index of personality unless there is reason to suppose it is affected by such variables as boredom, achievement needs, anxiety, or hostility toward the tester. Since any kind of behavior, including that involved in taking an intelligence test, running the hundred-yard dash, or whatever, might conceivably be affected by such variables, there seems no clear basis for excluding any kind of behavior from consideration.

I would maintain, therefore, that any relatively comprehensive theory of behavior, especially if it includes variables of a motivational sort, qualifies as a theory of personality. The relative adequacy of the various behavioral approaches in accounting for the complexities of human behavior is, of course, another question.

Presuppositions and Assumptions

If behavior theories are, at least in principle, like theories of personality in their emphasis on the variety and interdependence of variables influencing behavior, particularly those of a motivational sort, how do they differ from personality theories? Or, to put the question differently, since behavior theories show great diversity, and especially, perhaps, in regard to their treatment of motivation (Brown, 1961), what do they have in common that distinguishes them from other kinds of theories?

The answers to these questions are not easily formulated and, to the extent that they seem easy, are likely to be banal and superficial. They lie, I believe, not in any considerable agreement concerning substantive or systematic issues, such as what variables determine what behaviors under what conditions, but rather in certain characteristic views concerning the nature of science and scientific method and their place in psychology. The agreements among behavioral scientists and their disagreements with other formulations lie mainly in the area of metatheory, i.e., their methodological assumptions, or orienting attitudes, if you will.

I must confess to some uneasiness about my competence to treat these issues. They are enormously complicated, and seem to engender disagreement even among highly trained philosophers of science. Fortunately, many of them have been ably discussed elsewhere in the context of general psychological theorizing (e.g., Bergmann, 1943, 1951, 1953, 1956; Bergmann and Spence, 1941; Spence, 1944, 1948, 1956, 1957), so what follows presumes to do little more than to point, without technical elaboration, to some of the presuppositions of behavioral scientists that, in my opinion, underlie their approach to the study of personality. To some, particularly to experimental psychologists, the explicit statement of some of these assumptions and beliefs may appear gratuitous. But they are not by any means taken for granted by all personality theorists, perhaps, as Hall and Lindzey (1957) suggest, because "the stiffening brush of positivism has spread much more lightly over the personality psychologist than over the experimental psychologist" (p. 7).

LAWFULNESS, FREEDOM, AND THE ANALYSIS OF MENTAL CONTENTS

The basic assumption of behavioral scientists is that behavior is a function of its antecedents. These antecedents are natural events in the natural world, and the laws relating behavior to its antecedents can be discovered in the manner of other natural sciences, by the observation and analysis of empirical events. These laws of behavior are, at least in principle, susceptible of discovery. Not all will, as a matter of fact, be known at any given time, since they are exceedingly complex, and new information tends to uncover new complexities. But this is merely a recognition of pragmatic difficulties. It does not make a virtue of obscurantism nor elevate ignorance of ultimate causes to the status of a scientific principle. Once the laws of behavior, or enough of them, are known, the behavior can be predicted. And if the determinants, or enough of them, are manipulable, the behavior can be controlled.

One might suppose that these assumptions, which involve little more than the denial of transcendental or supernatural causation, would be accepted as a matter of course, but, in fact, they seem to arouse intense dissatisfaction. One reason is that, for some, lawfulness implies fatalism, and a second is that, for some (usually the same people), lawfulness implies coercion.

These objections are not usually among those voiced by psychologists, and can be quickly disposed of. In the fatalistic view, certain consequences are inevitable regardless of the antecedent conditions. The antecedents may change, but the consequence does not. This, of course, is exactly the opposite of a deterministic view, which considers consequences to be a function of their antecedents, i.e., if the antecedents change, the consequences change. In the one view, behavior is lawful; in the other, it is unlawful.

The notion of scientific laws as mandatory or coercive results from confusing scientific laws with judicial or legislative laws. If one does not obey a judicial law, one is punished; but if one does not obey a scientific law, the law is inaccurate and must be modified. Scientific laws do not make anything happen. They are merely statements of what does happen under certain conditions. Natural phenomena do not depend on scientific laws. Rather, the converse is true—the statement of the law depends on the nature of the observed phenomena.

Although psychologists do not usually object to determinism on the foregoing grounds, many join the humanists in the protest, on related grounds, that it relegates man to the level of a robot, a senseless and purposeless machine reacting to every fortuitous change in the external and internal environment. Instead, they insist, men actively select the environmental changes to which they respond, and actively decide what responses they shall make.

This position certainly has a strong emotional appeal, as evidenced by the storm of protest raised against both Watson and Freud, in part because of their insistence on a thorough-going determinism. Most people not only do not want to believe they are mere robots; they do not actually feel that they are. Whether there is any autism in this self-perception may be a moot question. Practically, anyone who regards himself as a machine is likely to be subjected to therapeutic treatments aimed at modifying this view. Certainly, normal phenomenological experience runs counter to the notion that people are helpless victims of inexorable circumstances. Rogers (see Murray et al., 1961) has recently affirmed both his acceptance of this position and his conviction of its untenability: "I prefer to live with what seems to me to be a genuine paradox, . . . that in our pursuit of science, we are fools if we do not assume that everything that occurs is a portion of a cause-and-effect sequence, and that nothing occurs outside of that. But I also feel that if we adopt that point of view in our living as human beings, in our confrontation with life, then that is death" (p. 575).

It seems to me this statement epitomizes a rather widespread attitude, that the rules of the scientific game are all very well on the home grounds—in the laboratory, in dealing with insentient objects—but ought not be applied to the study of real persons in the real world. By contrast, behavioral scientists insist on attempting to apply these rules under all conditions, even in the face of the complexities of human personality.

It is important, at this point, to distinguish between the contention on phenomenological grounds that behavior is unlawful, and the possible role of an analysis of mental events in constructing psychological concepts. To the best of my knowledge, no one these days denies the existence of mental events.

Watson did on occasion, but in Bergmann's perspicuous phrase, "Watson's particular mistake was that in order to establish that there are no interacting minds, which is true, he thought it necessary to assert that *there are no minds,* which is not only false but silly" (1965, p. 266). To follow Bergmann's analysis, no one doubts that there are such things as mental concepts, awarenesses, cognitive states, percepts, etc. However, to any statement containing such terms it is possible, at least in principle, to coordinate another ". . . which mentions only behavioral, physiological, and environmental items, such that they are either both true or both false. Otherwise one would have to maintain that we can, literally and not metaphorically speaking, directly observe other people's states of mind" (p. 270). Thus, mental events exist, and in a commonsense way we know what we mean when we refer to them, but it is unnecessary to appeal to them in a thorough-going account of behavior.

So far as I understand this view, it does not preclude the possibility that some kinds of systematic analyses of mental contents, i.e., the contents of observable indexes or reports of mental states, may serve a useful purpose in the discovery of behavioral laws. It is undoubtedly true that psychologists' preoccupation with such analyses has declined since the heyday of Structural Psychology. But I doubt whether this occurred, as Koch (1959) has recently implied, because of the pernicious influence of behavioristic epistemology. It occurred, I believe, because the particular contents emerging from the structuralists' analyses were simply inadequate to the ordering of the kinds of psychological phenomena in which most psychologists had become interested. It may be time, as McClelland (1955) and Koch (1959) maintain, for psychologists generally to recognize that other kinds of experiential analyses *can* be useful to psychological science. One might offer a slight demurral to Koch's (1959) conclusion that current theoretical formulations show a *trend* in this direction, on the grounds that many of the authors cited were never persuaded that significant psychological laws could be discovered by any method other than the analysis of mental contents. But this would be somewhat irrelevant. So long as such analyses are concerned with the formulation of psychological laws, including those relating experiential data to behavior, they do not oppose, but rather support a deterministic view of behavior. [See the papers by Berlin, Raab, and Nowell-Smith in Section Eight of this volume for further discussion of freedom and determinism—Ed.]

It is a curious fact that the claims of phenomenological experience apparently still lead some psychologists, who are otherwise at a polar extreme from Watson, to his own mistaken conclusion that admission of the existence of private experience is prejudicial to the notion of lawfulness. An examination of both the methodological positions (cf. Skinner, 1953, p. 257 ff.) and the research strategies of those within the behavioral camp reveals no reluctance to use introspective reports or any other observable indexes that might be coordinated to mental events. Indeed, insofar as the concepts of mediating processes relates to such events, they have been used for a long while (vid.

Goss, 1961). And their current utilization within the framework of behavior theory in investigations of such problems as stimulus equivalence and distinctiveness (e.g., Spiker, 1962), concept formation (e.g., Kendler and Kendler, 1962), and human operant conditioning (e.g., Farber, 1963), speaks for itself. It is true that these formulations frequently refer to language, but as the Kendlers (1962) carefully point out, it is neither necessary nor desirable to identify mediational events with any particular process. It is only necessary to demonstrate that such concepts are useful elements in the understanding and prediction of behavior.

CAUSATION, FINALISM, AND EXPLANATORY FICTIONS

The preoccupation of personality theorists with motivation, the apparently purposive, striving, goal-directed aspects of behavior referred to earlier, has sometimes led to the adoption of a finalistic or teleological view of behavior. The biological counterpart of this view has been aptly summarized by Simpson (1950):

The distinctive finalist belief is that of progression toward a goal or end. The end is not reached, the finalist believes, because of what goes before, but what goes before is but a means for reaching the end. The end, although later in time, is, then, the cause and the preceding course of history is the effect. The history of life is thus to be viewed as purposeful, and (it almost goes without saying) finalists usually consider man as the essential feature of that purpose (pp. 126–127).

The degree of conviction with which this belief has been held by some theorists is indicated in the following quotation from Adler's (1930) chapter in the *Psychologies of 1930:*

Individual Psychology insists absolutely on the indispensability of finalism for the understanding of all psychological phenomena. Causes, powers, instincts, impulses, and the like cannot serve as explanatory principles. The final goal alone can explain man's behavior (p. 400).

To the typical non-scientist man-in-the-street this view seems not only reasonable but self-evident. Asked why an acorn planted in the ground grows as it does, he is likely to reply, "So that it can become an oak tree." Or, if he has had the benefit of a liberal education, asked why people sleep, he may answer, "To restore homeostasis." Even psychologists who know better fall into the habit of explaining one kind of behavior or another by referring to the goals to be attained.

Quite apart from the reversal of the order of materialistic cause and effect, such explanations tend to account for either too little or too much. They account for too little when the expected goal is not reached. Not all acorns become oak trees. Some rot and others are eaten by hogs. People and animals who have suffered injury to the anterior portion of the hypothalamus may be unable to sleep. And people all too frequently fail to achieve goals or achieve them by the most diverse means. Such explanations are too comprehensive when they are used to account for every conceivable kind of eventuality. To explain all behavior in terms of "adjustment" or "satisfaction of the pleasure drive," for instance, explains nothing, since one must still account for the different kinds of behavior.

I must confess to the belief that some constructions of the concept of self-actualization, which in one form or another appears to have wide currency in personality theories, suffer from this defect. Rogers, for instance, assigns to human beings only a single motive, the actualizing tendency. "This is the inherent tendency of the organism to develop all its capacities in ways which serve to maintain or enhance the organism" (1959, p. 196). It includes the concepts of tension reduction, growth motivation, differentiation of organs and functions, enhancement through reproduction, autonomy, and indeed, so far as I can tell, almost any predisposition one can think of that results in the expanded effectiveness of the organism. This seems equivalent to saying that organisms tend under all conditions to do those things that are "good" for them, in a vague sense of the word "good." Unfortunately, even if one adopts this optimistic view of man, one still does not know what a given individual will do, or why one individual differs from another. To know this, one would have to identify the particular factors, whether hereditary or environmental, that occasion different behaviors. This is not to say that the postulated correlates of the actualizing tendency, e.g., originality, creativity, and spontaneity, are fictitious or unimportant. On the contrary, precisely because they are important, a behavior science ought to be adequate to their prediction and explanation. And this can be done, not by defining them as the culminating aspects of a universal *élan vital,* but by discovering their particular determinants. In the present view, if we knew the independently defined variables of which such behaviors or behavior characteristics are a function, we would dispense with such overarching concepts as self-actualization.

It is interesting to contemplate the number of concepts that might be dispensed with in psychology, if we only knew more about the determinants of given kinds of behavior. For instance, behavior theorists, like everyone else, occasionally talk about the phenomenon of "choosing." It is notable, however, that the term "choice" usually refers to nothing more than the descriptive fact that an organism behaves in one way rather than another. Suppose we know that a person has repeatedly heard a tone just before receiving an air puff on the cornea of his eye. If we then note that he blinks when the tone is presented, we add nothing to our explanation by saying he chose to blink. Similarly, when after prolonged food deprivation, a person identifies an ambiguous picture as a steak rather than something else, it is trivial to say this is because he decided to say "steak." Since the evidence of the decision is the behavior itself, attributing the behavior under these circumstances to choice is exactly as useful as attributing it to demons. Note should be made of the qualification, "under these circumstances." If the definition of choice is made independently of the behavior it is supposed to explain, this concept may, of course, be useful.

In general, the frequency of appeals to such explanatory fictions is an index of our ignorance of the antecedents of the phenomenon under consideration. All too often, the sole evidence for the supposed cause is the very behavior it is supposed to explain. Thus, as Skinner (1961, p. 535) has observed, it is useless to say that forms of life that have survived did so because they had survival value, if all we know is that they survived. And it is useless to argue that people adjust to their environment because of some special capacities such as intelligence, if these are defined in terms of their adjustive value. Similarly:

> When we say that a man eats *because* he is hungry, smokes a great deal *because* he has the tobacco habit, fights *because* of the instinct of pugnacity, behaves brilliantly *because* of his intelligence, or plays the piano well *because* of his musical ability, we seem to be referring to causes. But on analysis these phrases prove to be merely redundant descriptions (Skinner, 1953, p. 31).

THE CONTROL OF BEHAVIOR

It was stated earlier that, if the determinants of behavior were known, and if enough of them were susceptible to manipulation, then it would be possible to control behavior. It was also noted that this proposition arouses the most intense annoyance and anxiety in many people, including psychologists, who for good reasons, abhor the idea of a totalitarian technocracy (Bergmann, 1956). In its superficial aspects, one can rather readily understand why the concepts of "control" and "despotism" are sometimes equated. If behavior can indeed be controlled by manipulating its determinants, then individuals with the requisite knowledge could and very possibly would exercise this control. In this light, any deterministic view of behavior may be suspect. For instance, psychoanalytic theory, which on other grounds does not perhaps qualify as a behavioral approach, has, because of its thoroughgoing determinism, also been accused of sinister and exploitative advocations.

The reaction against the proposition that behavior is susceptible of manipulation tends to take two different and rather contradictory forms. At one extreme, it emerges as a flat denial—the use of the Freudian term is not unintentional—that behavior, particularly implicit behavior, is controllable or even predictable. According to this view, the deterministic thesis, as applied to human behavior, is simply false. At the other extreme, it consists of the condemnation and proscription of attempts to discover the laws of behavior. According to the latter view, behavior is not only lawful and predictable, but the laws are already well-known and the techniques for their effective application all-too-readily available. Couched in less extreme terms, the two arguments, oddly enough, frequently appear in a single context, without recognition of their inconsistency.

Some aspects of the first objection concerning the essential unpredictability of behavior have already been referred to. Beliefs to the contrary rest on philosophical assumptions not subject to empirical proof or disproof. It might be commented, not altogether frivolously, that anyone who sincerely believes *as a matter of principle* that behavior is unlawful and unpredictable ought to complain about the expenditure of his tax dollar for such things as schools and mental hospitals, since they are established on the supposition that at least some behaviors are somewhat amenable to control.

The second reaction, that the laws of behavior are well-known, and are even now being applied in one or another program of exploitation, is, despite allegations from the best-seller list, unwarranted by the facts. The facts are that, at present, much human behavior is unpredictable because its laws, though discoverable, are as yet largely unknown. This is not exactly news to informed individuals, and affords psychologists scant basis for self-congratulation. It may conceivably comfort those who regard the acquisition and application of psychological knowledge as a threat to human welfare, including, paradoxically, some psychologists who appear to see in the advancement of behavioral science only the grim prospect of 1984. As Skinner (1955) observes:

Such predictions of the havoc to be wreaked by the application of science to human affairs are usually made with surprising confidence. They not only show a faith in the orderliness of human behavior: they presuppose an established body of knowledge with the help of which it can positively be asserted that the changes which scientists propose to make will have quite specific results—albeit not the results they foresee (p. 61).

The essential ingredient in such views is a distrust of science. Those who bemoan our lack of knowledge concerning the factors governing intersocietal and interpersonal relations are frequently the same people who condemn the use of those procedures best calculated to achieve that knowledge—the methods of science. If these forebodings were taken seriously, we should have to conclude that even if we knew how to make our educational system more effective, even if we knew what kinds of conditions in our homes would increase the probabilities of our children's becoming responsible and useful citizens, we nevertheless ought to refuse to establish such conditions on the grounds that this would constitute undesirable control; even if we knew how to allay those suspicions and change those motives or cognitive structures of individuals, the consequences of which threaten our country with racial upheaval or the world with nuclear disaster, we ought not act because this would violate men's freedom.

Surely, few persons would care to push the argument for the inviolability of human freedom so far. Nevertheless, the issue is not a simple one, and will certainly not be resolved here. I merely wish to point to the illogicality of an automatic rejection of any plan calculated on the basis of scientific knowledge to modify the behavior of individuals or societies.

On the one hand, we must recognize that different societies and different individuals have different goals. What is desirable or reinforcing for one may be frustrating and punishing for another. We are only too liable to the delusion that our own goals are the only reasonable ones. Thus, when I try to change a person's behavior or attitudes, I am appealing to his better judgment; when you try to do so, you are using propaganda; and when "they" do so, they are brainwashing. To complicate matters further, this multiplicity of motives and goals extends to the intrapersonal sphere. The behavior that is instrumental to the satisfaction of one motive may frustrate the satisfaction of another.

On the other hand, our respect for the rights of others to their particular goals and the instrumental acts whereby they are achieved should not lead us to the romantic delusion that these are spontaneous products of unfettered choice. No one escapes control by the physical environment short of death; and no one escapes control by his social environment short of complete isolation. Almost the entire period of childhood is given over to the acquisition of new behaviors, goals, and motives, under the guidance of parents, family, and teachers. Be it wise or unwise, deliberate, impulsive, or unconscious, such guidance inevitably has its effects. It is difficult, in fact, to think of any kind of social interaction that has absolutely no effect on behavior. That the effects are unintentional or unwanted does not negate them. There is some feeling among those who read popular discussions of persuasive techniques that frank and open appeals to frank and open motives such as hunger and thirst may be tolerable; but disguised and subtle appeals to disguised and possibly disreputable motives such as sex or dominance are illegitimate. This reaction probably results from the belief that behavior related to the first class of motives is more liable to self-control and less liable to control by others. This is extremely doubtful. But, in any event, those who would proscribe the use of such techniques on the grounds that they constitute unwarranted control are usually not nearly so concerned with the ethical implications of their own proposal to control the attitudes and behavior of others. The plain fact is, the obdurate refusal to arrange circumstances for influencing others, on ethical or moral grounds, may simply serve as a mask for indecision and irresponsibility. Furthermore, such refusal ignores the evident fact that we influence others in unintended and unplanned ways.

Even non-directive psychotherapists adopt their procedures on the assumption that they have certain behavioral consequences. If refusing to say or do something produces given effects, this constitutes control no less than does active intervention. Which of these kinds of antecedents is more closely related to the desired behaviors is an empirical matter, not to be decided on a priori philosophical grounds. Advocates of a non-interventionist approach to psychology know this, of course, since they frequently refer to empirical evidence indicating that their procedures are more effective than some others.

It seems to me there is much more agreement concerning the kind of world most of us want and the kinds of people we should like to have in it than one would suppose from the interminable arguments about such matters. The disagreements among social scientists or, for that matter, between social scientists and humanists, relate not so much to goals as to the means by which they can best be achieved. For example, in a recent symposium (Murray et al., 1961), Rogers suggests that an alternative to control is the release of potentialities and capacities, leading to ". . . behavior that is more variable, more spontaneous, more creative, and hence in its specifics, more unpredictable" (p. 575). Surely no one would question the desirability of such behavior. We might question whether the optimal conditions for creativity and spontaneity are those of laissez-faire or accident. And we might question whether such conditions do, as a matter of fact, constitute an alternative to control, since some sorts of controls by parents, teachers, and many other individuals and institutions are inevitable. Whether such fortuitous controls are likely to encourage or stifle creativity needs to be investigated, not taken for granted.

There may be some who would deny the desirability of such empirical investigations, presumably on the principle that ignorance is bliss. But if as a result of investigations such as those Rogers himself has inspired, there were good reason to suppose that certain conditions have a greater likelihood than others of eliciting behavior upon whose worth almost all can agree, then I doubt that one could reasonably argue against the deliberate institution of such conditions on the grounds of ethical propriety. We are mainly ignorant about the controls that now exist, so we can only be sure they are man-made and far from perfect. It seems inconceivable and, indeed, a contradiction in terms to suppose that controls based on scientific knowledge would be worse. Unfortunately, influential writers, including some psychologists in the field of personality, seem otherwise persuaded.

PREDICTION VERSUS UNDERSTANDING

It is possible that we have been setting up a straw man, since relatively few individuals in our time would condemn the pursuit and application of empirical knowledge, though not many years ago a congressional committee investigating the social sciences heard such complaints. However this may be, there are certainly differences of opinion concerning the criteria whereby knowledge may be verified. In one aspect, they relate to the foregoing discussion of prediction and control. Thus, Maslow, in the aforementioned symposium (Murray et al., 1961), suggests that the testing of scientific hypotheses in terms of prediction and control implies an "overactive and interfering conception of science" (p. 572). He prefers a conception whose "key characteristics are receptivity to knowledge . . . , understanding as the main goal of science, rather than prediction and control . . . , the freer use of intuition, empathy, and identification with the object of study, a greater stress on experiential knowledge, a less pragmatic attitude" (p. 572).

This statement addresses two somewhat independent problems which may be easily confused. The one has to do with techniques or modes of acquiring knowledge; the other with procedures for verifying knowledge.

In respect to the first, one may note that we frequently do not know the circumstances that yield useful hunches concerning the determinants of behavior in specific instances. The context of discovery, to use Reichenbach's (1938) excellent term, is uncertain. This is so, not because the determinants of useful hunches are in principle unknowable, but because we are as yet relatively ignorant about them. We do know that many hunches, including those asseverated by psychologists, turn out to be mistaken. Citing the conclusion of one investigator, that non-psychologists appear to be able to judge others more accurately than do clinical psychologists, Allport suggests that the present training of psychologists merely ". . . leads them to a *knowledge about,* rather than an *acquaintance with,* human nature in its concrete manifestations" (1961, p. 543). This may be so, and we may be training our students badly. This should not be surprising, since psychologists, like other educators, know less than they should about the conditions of effective training for various purposes. Though I very much doubt that psychological training generally impairs one's ability to judge others, it is unquestionably true that others can do a better job than psychologists of predicting behavior under some circumstances.

Sometimes the reasons for this are perfectly evident. On occasion, my neighbor, who is a dentist, can predict the behavior of my dog—understands its personality, if by that one means its behavioral tendencies—much better than I, because, for good reasons, it spends its time around his garden bed and garbage cans. On the other hand, I can occasionally predict the condition of my children's teeth better than he, because I am in a better position to control their predilection for sweets. In these instances, as in all others, successful prediction depends on the amount and kind of information available. Psychologists, including personality theorists, simply do not predict behavior in general. They can only say, given such and such conditions, a given behavior should ensue. As Dollard and Miller (1950) nicely point out in respect to the cultural determinants of behavior, they may not always be in a position to know just what these conditions may be in specific instances.

In this regard, we may frequently be impressed with the perceptiveness of politicians, salesmen, and animal trainers. Many of the more highly educated in our society are even more likely to be impressed with the insights of novelists, poets, biographers, and the great religious and social essayists who have written so well and wisely about the nature and condition of man. We should certainly not disparage such insights as these persons may have. Psychologists have no monopoly of access to the cues that may serve as the basis for successful prediction and evaluation of behavior.

But this recognition of the variety of sources of possible knowledge, that is, the diverse contexts of discovery, should not blind us to the second problem, the necessity for verifying knowledge. The context of justification (Reichenbach, 1938) has its own ineluctable requirements. The accuracy of statements by those whose writings appear to embody the wisdom of the ages must, like those by dentists and psychologists, be evaluated in the light of their predictive value.

The deficiencies of speculative wisdom, as of intuition and empathic understanding generally, lie not in their inaccuracy. They may be quite accurate. Their fault is that they give no adequate basis for knowing whether or not they are accurate. As Campbell (1959) has observed, the speculative wisdom of the ages has often proposed contradictory resolutions of the same problem. The insights of classical wisdom, in contrast to scientific knowledge, are notoriously equivocal and non-cumulative. The reason is that science insists that insights and hypotheses be tested and sets up a machinery for this purpose, whereas classical wisdom is content with the mere experience of certitude. Even the putative wisdom of Allport's commonsensical homespun philosopher must be tested, else we should never know when he is truly being wise and when, like the rest of us, he is merely a victim of undisciplined conviction.

ON THE SIGNIFICANCE OF PSYCHOLOGICAL CONCEPTS

One may accept the view that personality and its changes are lawful, that their antecedents are discoverable by the methods of natural science, that statements concerning the relations between personality variables and their antecedents must be verified by predictive test, and that once known, information concerning such laws ought to be used for the benefit of individuals and society. Granting all this, one may still regard the whole enterprise, in its present stages, at least, as a fantastic network of trivialities. We need, desperately, to solve the social and political problems of our times; meanwhile, the behavioral scientist busies himself with the variables determining a rat's speed of running down a straight alley, the rate of bar-pressing in a Skinner box, and eyeblinks. And perhaps, judging from the disagreements concerning even such simple matters, busying themselves none too successfully, at that.

The justification for such interests may not be readily apparent to those concerned with the threat of thermonuclear warfare, or, as in the case of many personality theorists, to those concerned with the problems of mental illness, education, or group productivity. If behavioral science can do no more, many people believe, the whole sorry business really ought to be abandoned.

It would be foolish to suppose that behavioral science promises solution of our social and personal problems in the foreseeable future. Many behavioral scientists would regard any proposal that their activities be justified on this ground as impertinent and insulting. But they are even more likely to point out that preoccupation with such problems, even by those most vitally concerned with them, is not necessarily the best guarantee nor even a very good guarantee of their solution. Science differs from speculative wisdom in its cumulative nature. Each advance rests on the broad structure of what is already known, and without that substructure further advance is often impossible. As Campbell (1959) has noted, "Science has solved important problems, but this final achievement should not obscure the modesty and caution of the initial steps." Nor are the initial steps usually oriented toward those problems to whose solution they may lead. We may be quite sure that in 1912, when Rutherford was measuring the deflection of alpha particles by gold foil, he was not thinking of a hydrogen bomb. Yet, according to historians of physics (Condon, 1955), this work led directly to the nuclear atom model which was the basis for all subsequent work in physics.

Spence (1956) has pointed to two major deterrents to the establishment of a scientific body of psychological knowledge:

The first of these . . . is reflected in . . . the tendency to criticize theoretical concepts in this field as being too elementaristic, too mechanistic, and as failing to portray the real essence or true nature of man's behavior. In particular, these critics have complained about the artificiality of the objective types of concepts such as offered by the behavioristic psychologist (p. 20).

The second factor is the tendency to evaluate the significance of psychological concepts and research in terms of the degree to which they are applicable to some immediate practical or technological problem rather than the extent to which they enter into or contribute toward the development of a body of lawful relations . . . (p. 21).

The notion that behavioral scientists pursue what is precise at the expense of what is important appears to be one of those insights so highly regarded by admirers of speculative wisdom. I, for one, doubt whether the principles thus far derived by behavior theoretical approaches are demonstrably less useful for the understanding of complex social problems than those deriving from other approaches. But more importantly, the view that precision implies triviality mistakes the nature of scientific laws and theories.

A concept is trivial only if it is isolated, i.e., does not enter into a system of interlocking laws. Stated otherwise, a concept may be considered significant only insofar as it enters into such a nomological network (Cronbach and Meehl, 1955). In physics, for instance, the test of the accuracy of theories of very great power may depend on the precise measurement of phenomena that would in themselves be quite inconsequential. Certainly, precision does not guarantee significance. On the other hand, concepts having any great degree of imprecision are unlikely to have a useful function in the development of a systematic body of lawful relations. Such concepts, no matter how profound or compelling they may appear, are truly trivial. An important part of the history of physical and even behavioral science deals with the abandonment of just such meretricious concepts.

The work of behavioral science, or any science, may seem rather pedestrian, not suited to men of grand vision and extravagant expression. But it does not seem beside the mark to note that some three thousand years of the application of the speculative wisdom of the best minds of the ages have failed to illuminate very much the problems of behavior (cf. Campbell, 1959). As Spence (1956) puts it:

> The science-oriented psychologist merely asks that he be given the same opportunity to develop a scientific account of his phenomena that his colleagues in the physical and biological fields have had. If there are aspects of human behavior for which such an account cannot ever be developed, there are not, so far as I know, any means of finding this out without a try (pp. 20–21).

Sources of Information Concerning the Determinants of Behavior

We know, of course, that the variables influencing behavior are many, and their interactions extremely complex. For this reason, if one wants to know whether a given kind of behavior is some function of one, or, at most, a restricted set of these variables, one must either construct or find situations such that the effects of the one variable or the particular set of variables may be isolated. This can be done by eliminating the other relevant variables, holding them constant, or in some way measuring their effects.

This does not imply the expectation that in other combinations the variable(s) under consideration will invariably affect behavior in ways clearly evident from their relatively isolated effect on behavior. It merely presupposes that the study of the effects of restricted sets of variables on the behavior of relatively simple organisms may lead to useful hypotheses concerning their effects in more complex combinations and in more complex organisms. This method of science is usually necessary because "it is seldom possible to proceed directly to complex cases. We begin with the simple and build up to the complex, step by step" (Skinner, 1953, p. 204).

Now, nothing is more certain than the fact that relations found in such simple instances will sometimes, perhaps usually, fail to hold in more complex instances. No one would deny that changes in the combinations of variables may affect behavior. But unless one has fairly precise notions about the conditions under which a given kind of behavior occurs, it seems exceedingly unlikely that one can decide with any certainty what particular aspects of different or more complex conditions are responsible for a change in that behavior.

GENERALIZING FROM THE LABORATORY TO REAL LIFE

Those who argue that the observation of behavior under the artificial and highly controlled conditions of the laboratory has no predictive value for behavior under "real life" conditions sometimes appear to fail to understand the necessity for doing more than simply pointing to the change.

What we wish to know is the nature of the variables of which that change is a function. In any event, there is universal agreement on one point: before one generalizes from observations of behavior in the laboratory to real-life situations, one had better consider very carefully the differences between the laboratory conditions and those in real life.

In the light of this recognition of the necessity for considering the variables involved, it is puzzling why anyone who objects to generalizations from laboratory findings should consider it safe to generalize from behavior in one complex, uncontrolled situation to behavior in another. Obviously, circumstances change from one uncontrolled situation to another. When one does not know what variables have changed, generalizations from one real-life situation to another are at least as uncertain as those from controlled situtions to real-life situations. An added disadvantage lies in the relatively greater difficulty of disentangling the particular variables that have changed. This is not easy, whether one deals with either controlled or uncontrolled conditions, but under any circumstances the lack of control or information concerning the effects of specific variables can hardly be regarded as a positive aid to understanding and prediction.

GENERALIZING FROM ANIMALS TO PEOPLE

In view of the well-known differences between rats, which are non-social and non-verbal, and human beings, who are exceedingly social and verbal, it is not surprising to find a good deal of skepticism concerning the applicability of rat laws to human behavior. Occasionally, there is an autistic element in such criticisms. Some people consider it degrading to be compared with rats, just as some consider it insulting to be compared with infants, as in psychoanalytic theory. But most criticisms of this sort are based on the objective fact that rats and people differ in many and possibly crucial respects. Koch (1956) has expressed in eloquent detail his disbelief in the probability of generating the essential laws of human behavior from rat data. He points out that one may not even be able to generate decent laws concerning rats by observing rats, especially if they inhabit different laboratories.

In regard to the latter observation, that one cannot generalize from rats to rats without risk, one can only agree that animal experimenters ought perhaps to describe their experimental conditions more adequately, or to try harder to discover those conditions whose variation is responsible for the reported inconsistencies. I do not believe animal psychologists are generally regarded as unusually deficient in their specification of the variables they know about or in their zeal to discover the ones they do not know about. But perhaps they ought to be doing a more careful job. It is important to note that this calls for more analytic precision, not less.

In regard to the former observation, that one cannot generalize from rats to human beings, it seems fair to repeat that frequently one also cannot generalize from human beings to human beings. Koch (1956) for instance, in describing his own "B states," i.e., his experiences while deeply engrossed in work, maintains that despite the importance of such states, despite their exemplification of behavior in its most organized, energized, and motivated form, current psychological theories are inadequate to the recognition of such states, let alone their explanation. "Subtle and organized descriptive phenomenologies of B states are badly needed by science—but not from individuals whose B-state products are 'creative' only by extravagant metaphor" (p. 68). Whatever one thinks of this pronouncement, it is certain that B-states cannot be observed in rats, and unlikely that they could be even partially accounted for in terms of principles based on rat behavior. But, as Koch himself suggests in the foregoing quotations, it would be rash to suppose that all human beings share these experiences. And in view of the restriction imposed, even among those who might have such experiences, very few could claim the privilege of attempting to communicate them. This is not to say that B-states do not exist, nor that they are unimportant. It does suggest the uncertainties of attemping to generalize from what may be discovered about Koch's B-states to the experiential states of people whose phenomenological descriptions may be limited to a phrase such as "Man, it's the most!" There is a grave risk in generalizing from both rats and human beings when important variables differ.

Despite these cautionary notes, I think it possible to point to some instances of successful generalizations from animal as well as other human behavior, i.e., to hypotheses that have turned out to be fruitful. Instead, I should like to tell of an "Aha!" experience I recently had while listening to Frank A. Logan describe some of his animal experiments at Yale, in which delay of reward was balanced against amount of reward in simple choice situations. The experimental results showed that, within limits, rats will choose a longer delay, if the reward is large enough, in preference to shorter delays with lesser rewards. Probably because of obtuseness, it had never before occurred to me in quite the same way that the morality of human beings in giving up the pleasures of this world for the sake of eternal salvation may have something in common with the morality of rats in giving up an immediate reinforcement for the sake of a bigger piece of Purina dog chow. Now, this is undoubtedly a specious analogy at best. It ignores the many disanalogies in the two instances, and may be utterly foolish. But until this has been demonstrated, it suggests some, not by any means all, of the variables of which even such sublime sentiments may be a function. Of course, it goes without saying that no matter how intriguing this notion may appear in the context of discovery, it must make its scientific way in the context of justification.

The distaste of some psychologists for animal studies frequently extends to conditioning studies as well, in part because the conditioned reflex appears characteristic of subhuman or subnormal behavior. Again, we might attempt to show how the laws of conditioning have been used as a basis for predicting some relatively complex human activities, such as verbal learning. Instead, we can point to a curious inconsistency in our treatments of such concepts. According to the earlier Gestalt psychologists, insight, or perception of relations, is also a primitive process, altogether characteristic of animals. Yet we seldom hear the argument that this concept is, therefore, useless for the understanding of human behavior. Unfortunately, judgments of what is scientifically useful are all-too-frequently confounded with judgments of what is good or bad. Thus, the successful efforts of Communists to modify beliefs and actions are likely to be attributed to the use of Pavlovian conditioning techniques, which work only if men are reduced to the level of witless automatons (cf. Farber, Harlow, and West, 1957); our own successful efforts, on the other hand, are likely to be attributed to methods engaging the higher mental processes. It seems just possible, does it not, that many of the same determinants may be operative in both instances?

Proponents of a behavioral approach are likely to answer this question affirmatively because, for the most part, they distrust the doctrines of emergentism. While the variables influencing animal behavior are certainly different and less complex than those influencing human behavior, most behavioral scientists, nevertheless, prefer to look for continuity in the explanatory principles involved. Similarly, they look for continuity between the laws of child and adult behavior, between social and non-social behavior, and between normal and abnormal behavior. Whether this sort of search is useful may be open to question. At this stage of the game there appears to be no way of deciding this to everyone's satisfaction.

GENERAL LAWS AND THE INDIVIDUAL CASE

The foregoing discussion has dwelt on two apparently contradictory principles. The one stresses the necessity for caution in generalizing from one circumstance to another, in the face of inevitable changes in the variables represented. The second holds to the optimistic belief that generalization is frequently possible, even in the face of changes in some of the variables affecting behavior. Behavioral scientists, like others, differ in their relative emphases on these two principles, depending in part on the relative strengths of their empiricist or theoretical predilections; but they are likely to agree that the question whether one can successfully predict from one context to another can be answered only by empirical test.

Some personality theorists, however, appear to consider this a methodological rather than an empirical issue. They may deny, for instance, even the possibility of applying general laws to the prediction of individual behavior. Since, they argue, the variables influencing a given individual's behavior are not exactly duplicated for any other person, and since these variables interact in complicated ways, it is simply not possible to predict anything about one person from laws based on the observation of others. Since each individual is unique, the only legitimate predictions concerning any given person must be based on what is known about that person. Curiously enough, this reasoning is ordinarily not extended to the intraindividual case. If it were, we would have to deny the possibility of predicting an individual's behavior even on the basis of what is known about that person, since the variables influencing his behavior at one time can never be exactly duplicated at any other time. At the very least, the ordinal positions of the two occasions differ.

Most behavioral scientists believe that general laws can be reasonably and usefully applied to individuals (Eysenck, 1952; Meehl, 1954). At the same time, they can readily agree that predictions about a given individual will frequently be more precise if they are based on the observation of his own past behavior. Perhaps the main reason for this is that many of the important determinants of his past behavior are likely to persist as determinants of his future behavior. Individuals carry such determinants around with them, so to speak, in the form of their inherited and learned predispositions. Nevertheless, if there is reason to suppose that present conditions are quite different from those in the individual's past, predictions are likely to be more successful if they are based on the behavior of others for whom we know these conditions have obtained. It is gratuitous to say so, but this merely means it may be more useful, in predicting the effects of aging on a given person, to look at old people than at that person at age two; or it may be more useful, in predicting the effects of a certain drug on a person's behavior, to observe other people drunk than that person sober. Of course, the more nearly alike the reference group and the individual in question, the more accurate the prediction. This simply means that the probability of successful prediction from one instance to another is some positive function of the communality of their behavioral determinants (cf. Meehl, 1954).

We should note that this formulation of the issue does not dispose of the empirical question whether general laws can at present be usefully applied to a particular individual in any given instance. The hard job of ascertaining just what the important variables are in any given context, and when a change in one variable changes the significance of another, must still be done. We may hypothesize to our hearts' content about such matters. But we should not mistake the hypothesis, no matter how firmly held, for empirical proof.

Personality Variables and Behavioral Laws

The preceding section has barely touched on the exceedingly complicated problem of general versus individual prediction. One aspect of this problem relates to the interaction between situational or environmental variables and individual differences variables. Early in this discussion it was stated that behavioral scientists ordinarily find no clear-cut basis for distinguishing between the study of personality and the study of behavior in general.

What view does this imply concerning the role of individual differences, especially those customarily classified under the heading of personality? According to many personality theorists, the existence of individual differences constitutes the most significant datum of psychology, yet the general psychologist persists in regarding them as mere annoyances, sources of error variance, to be eliminated or disregarded.

It is a matter of historical fact that, traditionally, experimental psychologists have been primarily interested in variables whose main effects or interactions are more or less independent of the kinds of subconditions known as individual differences. They have never denied the existence or even the importance of individual differences. After all, the classical Structuralists did not restrict their investigations to normal, adult, human observers because they supposed the observations would be unaffected by such variables as psychopathology, age, or species membership. They simply were not interested in the interactive effects of such variables. Many experimental psychologists still are not very interested in these kinds of variables, though this picture has been changing somewhat.

Many personality theorists, on the other hand, are frequently interested only in the kinds of variables that do interact with individual differences. They, in turn, do not usually deny that there may be important situational variables whose main effects override individual differences of one sort or another, but they are simply not so interested in them. We may find intransigents in both camps who absolutely deny the importance of any kinds of variables except the ones they happen to be interested in, but such persons are fortunately not numerous.

ENVIRONMENTAL EVENTS, INTERVENING VARIABLES, AND THE INDIVIDUAL

Psychologists who deplore the traditional emphasis by experimental psychologists on manipulable environmental variables, to the denigration, as they suppose, of the role of the behaving organism, frequently state their position in a characteristic way, by pointing to the necessity for considering not only the external event, but also its meaning to the individual, or how the individual perceives it.

In a commonsensical way, there is no doubt they are correct. If a physicalistically defined stimulus is presented to an organism, our estimate of the probability of a given response is always contingent on certain assumptions, usually implicit, concerning some characteristics of that organism, e.g., adequate sensory and motor equipment, a relatively intact nervous system, and so on. Woodworth's well-known suggestion that the S-R formula ought to be modified to read "S-O-R" was designed to take account of such contributions by the organism to its own behavior, though he undoubtedly intended the "O" to include more than physiological structures and processes.

Behavioral scientists differ, as we have noted, in their estimates of the usefulness of attributing to organisms such hypothetical, non-observable characteristics as habits, intentions, cognitions, etc. Though all would agree with Skinner that one must beware of the dangers of hypostatization and reification, many are convinced that empiricism is quite compatible with the use of abstract concepts and theories. The construction of intervening variables, for instance, represents one sort of attempt by behavior theorists to delineate the kinds of organismic characteristics that might be useful in accounting for behavior (cf. Spence, 1952). Thus, intervening variables are inferred characteristics of organisms, calculated, among other things, to explain why different individuals, or the same individual at different times, may sometimes behave differently under the same environmental conditions, and sometimes similarly under different enviromental conditions. This portrayal may remind some of Allport's definition of a trait as a "neuropsychic system . . . with the capacity to render many stimuli functionally equivalent, and to initiate and guide consistent (equivalent) forms of . . . behavior" (1937, p. 295). According to a behavioral view, of course, the usefulness of the concept of a trait, as of that of any other intervening variable, is not assured by the simple expedient of tacking on a reference to unspecified neuropsychic events.

In light of the foregoing analysis, it might be startling, but not altogether beside the mark, to maintain that a theory such as Hull's is the exemplar of personality theories, on the assumption that some of his intervening variables, or some of the constants defining their growth or decline, differ from person to person in a relatively consistent way. One may not like the particular intervening variables Hull has proposed, because they may not appear to bridge the gap between stimulus and response in a satisfactory manner, or because there is reason to suppose that different characteristics or classifications of characteristics would do a better job. It is apparent to everyone, including those who have been influenced by Hull, that more precise and comprehensive conceptualizations are needed to account for behavior. It is simply suggested that the construction of such systems will, as a matter of course, increase our understanding of the individual.

In brief, whatever their particular nature and interrelations, the states and processes conceptualized as intervening variables are indisputably the properties of the individuals from whose behavior they are inferred. Of course, abstract properties do not literally occupy a place in space, but this does not imply that such concepts as drive level, self-regard, or cathexes are not attributes of "real" flesh-and-blood people (cf. Bergmann, 1953).

Despite this happy unanimity of concern for the nature of the behaving organism, it does not necessarily follow that stimuli ought to be *defined* in terms of their meaning to the organism. Rather, the meaning itself must be accounted for in terms of objective factors in the past and present states of the organism and its environment (cf. Bergmann, 1943). From a behavioral standpoint, meanings are certainly important, and conceptualized as mediating processes, play a prominent role in current theoretical formulations. Thus, it is useful, in a variety of situations, to suppose that external events elicit some sort of implicit response whose stimulus components in one way or another modify the overt response to the external event. Familiar examples of such mediating processes are the fractional anticipatory goal response (r_g-s_g), emotional states (r_e-s_e), and anticipatory frustration (r_F-s_F) discussed by such theorists as Spence (e.g., 1956) and Amsel (e.g., 1962).

Another sort of mediating mechanism is the one discussed by Kendler and Kendler (1962), among others, representing a symbolic response to external cues. This implicit response and its accompanying stimulus components can be used to explain a wide variety of phenomena, including, as we have noted, stimulus equivalence and distinctiveness. Since the hypothetical implicit stimulus may serve to explain why ostensibly different environmental events may elicit the same response, and apparently similar environmental events may lead to different responses, one may be tempted to regard the "real" stimulus as consisting of both the external event *and* its accompanying mediator, or even to consider the external event inconsequential, the only relevant factor being the nature of the mediational process, i.e., the "meaning" of the external event. I must leave the question of what can reasonably be meant by "reality" to those more competent to discuss the philosophical issues, but it seems to me that if one insists that stimuli be defined in terms of one sort of inferred process, i.e., symbolic mediation, one could with equal justification insist that they be defined in terms of any or all the others, e.g., motives, expectancies, inhibitory states, and so on. This sort of equating of observable events with inferred events, i.e., intervening variables, seems a dubious basis for clarifying theoretical problems.

Although I believe it necessary to distinguish between stimuli as observables and inferred characteristics of the organism as non-observables, it seems reasonable to consider behavior as the invariable function of both. If we think the stimulus is unimportant, we might try substituting a very different stimulus, to see whether the response does not change; and if we think the organism is unimportant, let us substitute a bag of potatoes in place of the usual psychological subject (Bergmann, 1951).

To say that every response is a function of both stimulus conditions and the organism is to say it is not possible to attribute any behavior exclusively to either the one or the other. There is something puzzling, for instance, about the supposition that the effects of length of a word list or the degree of similarity of the items in the list are attributable to extraorganismic factors, whereas the arousal of disgust by the same items is due to an intraorganismic factor. Why should variations in motivation or inhibitory tendency due to massing of practice be considered the result of extraorganismic variables exclusively, but variations in the same states due to anticipation of failure because of the same antecedents be considered the result of intraorganismic variables exclusively?

A case in point is Gill's (1959) recent classification of ego-functions, including perception, thought, memory, and concept formation as intrapsychic, but interpersonal and social factors as extraorganismic. We wonder how interpersonal and social factors are to have any effect on the organism independently of the processes of perception, thought, and memory. Perhaps all that is meant in this instance is that environmental events and hypothetical organismic processes or states can, and ought to be, independently defined. If so, this and similar formulations are in good accord with the behavior theoretical view that stimuli ought not be defined in terms of "what they mean" to the individual.

A consideration of the historical roots of the widespread tendency to classify behaviors according to inner or outer determinants would take us far afield. It may be of interest, however, to observe that one historical basis for this dichotomy appears to be the conventional distinction between associative and non-associative determinants of behavior. In the old days of classical associationism, ideas were endowed with their own adhesive qualities. They came together, stuck, or were separated in accordance with certain principles; but though their locus was presumably somewhere inside the organism, the power of association resided, not in the organism, but rather, in some sense, in the ideas themselves. Some psychologists may suppose that behavior theorists, particularly since they typically use an S-R terminology, still conceive of the association between environmental events and behavior according to this old associationistic formula. It must be admitted that they often speak as though associative strength is a characteristic of stimuli. But this is merely a verbal shorthand, perhaps an unfortunate one, if it is so liable to misunderstanding. Let it be noted that it is the organism, not the stimulus impinging on his receptors that does the associating. The term $_sH_R$ refers to an intraorganismic process, just as much as do the terms relating to motivation or emotion.

After all this, it may be salutary to recall the reservations held by behavioral scientists, in common with Skinner, respecting explanations of behavior in terms of inferred characteristics of the organism. Such inferences must be made on the basis of observations that are independent of the particular instance of behavior the characteristic is supposed to explain. There is no use saying a person runs away because he is afraid, if the fear is inferred wholly from his running away. If we observe that a given person habitually behaves in an inconsiderate, selfish, and malicious way, whereas in the same situations another habitually behaves in a kind and considerate way, it may be useful to characterize these behaviors, or for that matter, the persons, as respectively "mean" and "generous." But saying that these people behave in their respective ways *because* the one is mean and the other generous is to appeal to the kind of empty explanatory fiction Skinner and many others warn against. When we know the objective conditions under which a given behavior or behavioral characteristic occurs, we can explain any relevant behavior in terms of those conditions. We need not appeal to some hypothetical characteristic to which they supposedly give rise. This caveat applies as well to intervening variables. If they do no more than account for the particular behavior from which they are adduced, they are fatuitous.

Traditionally, the kinds of objective conditions to which behavior theorists have given most attention have been temporally antecedent events, i.e., they have relied more on historical than on ahistorical laws. This does not imply that anyone supposes that the variables affecting behavior can be anything but contemporaneous. Events in the past history of organisms can influence current behavior only insofar as they are represented in their current traces. Anyone who thinks otherwise believes in ghosts. Historical laws are used, *faute de mieux,* in the absence either of satisfactory measures of these traces that are independent of the observable behaviors they occasion, or of techniques for manipulating them directly.

This strategy involves no basic theoretical issue. Thus, behavioral scientists fully appreciate the current advances in our understanding of the physiological processes and anatomical structures mediating behavior, recognizing that this knowledge is indispensible to the bridging of the gap between past events and current behavior. From their view, the import of the breakthrough in physiological psychology lies precisely in its departure from the dismal tradition of inferring physiological processes solely on the basis of the behaviors they are intended to explain. It is the definitional independence of the variables in a law that is important, not their reference to historical rather than ahistorical events. [On historical laws, see last section of Bergmann, Selection 23.—Ed.]

RESPONSE-DEFINED CONCEPTS

Behavioral scientists differ, as we have indicated, in their evaluation of the usefulness of attempts to explain behavior in terms of hypothetical states or processes of the organism. And they are particularly skeptical when the inferred characteristics are defined in terms of behavior rather than environmental conditions. Even apart from the dangers referred to, the difficulties in attempting to decide on the basis of behavior alone whether variations in a given performance are more probably due to variations in one class of hypothetical determinants than another are formidable (vid., Brown and Farber, 1951). Everyone, so far as I know, takes it for granted that every kind of behavior is multiply determined, and that the determinants may interact. To use an obvious example, at any given moment two people may perform in the same way because one has high drive and low habit strength and the other high habit strength and weak drive. It is not easy to devise techniques that permit the disentangling of these different strands.

A related difficulty to which experimentalists are likely to point is the fact that many behavioral measures may be intrinsically interrelated. For instance, to use only one of innumerable possible examples, it is known that the correlation between Manifest Anxiety Scale scores and those on the psychasthenia (*Pt*) scale of the MMPI is about $+.70$ to $+.80$ for college sophomores, even after the common items are removed. *Pt* scores are sometimes considered a measure of emotional expressiveness, as contrasted with repressiveness. The correlation of the MAS scores with the *K*-Scale of the MMPI is frequently found to be about $-.70$. *K* is supposedly a measure of defensiveness. And Edwards (1957) reports a correlation of $-.84$ between the MAS and his Social Desirability Scale, which is supposed to measure strength of desire to make a good impression. In the face of these impressive relations, how can one say whether the MAS measures drive level, emotional expressiveness, lack of defensiveness, or disinterest in making a good impression, or any, or all of these? And what about all the other tests, present and future, whose relations with the MAS, though not yet computed, will undoubtedly reach comparable orders of magnitude? What, then, does the test measure?

In one sense, this is a trivial question, and requires but a trivial answer, though, unfortunately, one that constructors and users of tests sometimes fail to see, namely, that giving tests different names does not guarantee that they reflect different characteristics, and giving them the same names does not necessarily mean they reflect the same determinants. If all these highly interrelated measures are related to all other kinds of behaviors in the same way, they measure the same thing, regardless of their labels.

Occasionally, however, this confusion among the characteristics inferred from behavior is not merely nominal. For instance, height and weight are highly correlated in the general population, yet no one supposes they are merely different names for the same thing. What if defensiveness and desire to make a favorable impression are independent, but nevertheless empirically related in a given population? How, then, could we decide whether they reflect different organismic states or processes? Or better, if the one measure is related to some other mode of behavior, which hypothetical variable is responsible for the relation?

These are not trivial questions, and their answers are not easily come by. One kind of answer is simply the observation that there is never any guarantee in science against the inaccurate identification of determinants. And this holds as well for experimental variables, i.e., those that are directly manipulable, as for differential variables, whose values must be selected wherever and whenever they occur. Suppose, for instance, the number of food responses in a free association test or, for that matter, speed of running in a straight alley, is shown to be a function of length of food deprivation. How do we know these results are not due to variations in blood-sugar level, or changes in bodily weight, or any number of other variables associated with food deprivation? As Miller (1959) points out, in attempting to specify behavioral antecedents "It is possible to proceed down the scale to an almost infinite number of possible empirical independent variables; even the most detailed operational description of procedure involves assumptions about the general applicability of the terms used. It is impossible for a theorist to be completely certain in advance whether or not these assumptions are justifiable. It is equally impossible for a person who believes himself to be a pure empiricist to avoid such assumptions" (p. 215).

It is usually possible, given skill and patience, to tease out ever-finer specifications of the variables entering into behavioral laws. So too with response-defined variables; by careful selection of cases, statistical correction, or the elimination of errors of measurement, we can frequently decide which of several variables, even though they be highly correlated, determine the form of the relation under consideration. If it turns out, as it frequently does, that a given behavior is a joint function of several response variables, the circumstance is one quite familiar to experimentalists. For instance, no one is unduly disturbed by the finding that the probability of drinking is a function of both dryness of the mucous membranes and general water deficit. The additional fact that these two variables are themselves frequently related under many conditions is a complication, to be sure, but not an insuperable one.

All we can reasonably ask in regard to either experimental or differential variables is that they be specified as precisely as possible. We should then be prepared to discover, soon enough, that more precise and detailed specifications are necessary.

The Nature and Function of Theories

Thus far, relatively little of our discussion has been directly concerned with the nature or role of theory in psychology, at least as this term is typically used by personality theorists. It has been mainly concerned, instead, with some fundamental propositions: that behavior is lawful; its antecedents are discoverable by naturalistic methods; guesses as to the antecedents of behavior are best verified by the method of prediction; the laws relating behavior to its antecedents are initially most easily discovered by observing simple behavior in simple situations; at least some of the variables and laws identified in simple situations are likely to be useful, in interaction with new factors, in explaining more complex behavior in more complex situations; it may sometimes be useful to infer or guess at certain characteristics or properties of organisms that might account for variations in behavior under ostensibly similar environmental conditions; and, finally, these hypothetical properties, whether defined in terms of behavioral antecedents or some aspects of behavior itself, might reasonably be considered as personality variables. Clearly, only the last two points bear very closely on the question of theory.

BEHAVIOR THEORIES AND S-R LANGUAGE

It will be recalled that this entire discussion started with the question: "What do behavioral approaches to personality have in common, and how do they differ from other views?" A partial answer, with some elaborations and digressions, has been given in terms of the foregoing propositions. What they come to, in a word, is an emphasis on the formulation of empirical laws and the analysis of the variables comprising them. As we have noted, the assumption that it is the business of behavioral science to explicate the relations between objectively defined environmental and behavioral events is in itself no theory, but rather a metatheoretical or pretheoretical preference. Those who adopt this approach, especially if they have an interest in the phenomena of learning, are likely to use the terms "S" and "R" to refer, respectively, to the environmental and behavioral events, and the familiar formula "S-R" to indicate a relation between these two classes of variables. In addition, those who use this terminology are perhaps more than others committed to the view that complex behavior can be understood, at least in part, in terms of concepts and relations adumbrated in the observation of simpler sorts of behavior. Not all theorists, not even all behavior theorists, entirely share the belief that S-R concepts are adequate to this task (cf. Koch, 1959). Kendler and Kendler (1962) have commented on one reason for such misgivings:

> Much of the objection to S-R language stems from the apparent discrepancy between active, flowing behavior and the inert, static, single S-R association. Using S-R language does not mean complex behavior *actually* consists of S-R connections. After analyzing the concept of light, Toulmin (1953) concludes: "We do not *find* light atomized into individual rays: we *represent* it as consisting of such rays" (p. 29). Applying the same idea to the concept of the S-R association: "We do not *find* behavior atomized into individual S-R associations: we *represent* it as consisting of such S-R associations." The concept of S-R association, therefore, must be judged not in terms of its ability to provide a clear image of behavior, but rather in its capacity to represent the facts of behavior (p. 3).

Although S-R formulations share a certain strategy, as the foregoing quotation indicates, the notion of S-R is not a theory either, but rather a pretheoretical model. Thus, its adoption does not imply a single level or kind of conceptualization of either "stimulus" or "response" (Brown, 1961; Miller, 1959). It does not imply that S-R laws are the only ones of importance in psychology (Spence, 1948). It does not imply any particular stand with respect to the necessity or desirability of introducing hypothetical constructs in accounting for behavior. And it certainly does not imply any substantial agreement concerning either the specific observable variables or hypothetical variables of which particular responses or response classes are a function. In brief, "S-R" is simply a type of terminology employed by some empirically-minded psychologists, including some who are also theoretically inclined.

What, then, is meant by a "behavioral theory?" In physics, the term "theory" refers to a system of interrelations among highly abstract concepts which serves to organize a very large number of laws that were previously unrelated (Spence, 1956, 1957). Comprehensive theories, i.e., those serving to organize a considerable number of laws, depend on the state of knowledge in a given area. If many empirical relations are known, then the theories may unify a large area. In psychology, at least according to the view of behavior theorists such as Spence, the development of a body of empirical laws is still in its early stages, so the possible unifying power of theory is relatively small.

This rather modest conception of theory is a far cry from the grandiose conceptualizations of some personality theorists. One reason for this is the insistence that every term in the system, no matter how abstract, be referable in some way to observable events. This requirement, sometimes referred to, not altogether correctly, as that of "operational definition," simply states the necessity for indicating more or less unambiguously the nature of the circumstances under which the term is to be used. Furthermore, these circumstances ought to be of a sort concerning which there is a high degree of intersubjective agreement. Theories that achieve apparent comprehensiveness by the use of concepts that have no clear-cut referents of this sort may have a certain suggestive value in the context of discovery, but in the context of justification their ambiguity precludes any rigorous test of their purported relations. It is apparently possible, however, for behavior theorists to take somewhat different stands in respect to the methodological implications of this requirement, as the recent discussions of the notion of construct validity amply demonstrate (e.g., Bechtoldt, 1959; Campbell, 1960; Cronbach and Meehl, 1955).

THE ECONOMIC FUNCTION OF THEORIES

Theories, even of such limited scope as those now existing in psychology, seem to serve two functions, the one economic and the other integrative. The economic function appears to have been the one emphasized by Tolman (1936) when he introduced the concept of the "intervening variable." He noted that the function relating any kind of behavior to its many determinants is likely to be exceedingly complex, and also, that these functions differ for different sets of antecedent conditions and for different kinds of behaviors. Therefore, he proposed that certain hypothetical notions be introduced to decrease the number of statements necessary to indicate all these relations. Feigl (1945), observing that the concept "electric current" has precisely this status of an intervening variable between numerous causal conditions and numerous effects has clearly indicated the nature of this stratagem:

If there are m causal conditions and n possible effects we would need mn statements in order to formulate all possible observable relations. If, however, we introduce our auxiliary concepts the number of statements required shrinks to $m + n$. For large numbers m and n the conceptual economy is accordingly quite considerable (p. 257).

Miller (1959) has recently suggested how one might design experiments to test the hypothesis that various kinds of behavioral indexes in various experimental contexts might actually be accounted for in terms of a single construct of this sort.

There is some reason to believe that the economic function of such theorizing is served in part by Skinner's procedure of classifying antecedents of various kinds under the same rubric, e.g., "motivation," because they bear the same kinds of functional relations to a given aspect of behavior. As he says of the concept of "drive":

> The term is simply a convenient way of referring to the effects of deprivation and satiation and of other operations which alter the probability of behavior in more or less the same way. It is convenient because it enables us to deal with many cases at once. There are many ways of changing the probability that an organism will eat; at the same time, a single kind of deprivation strengthens many kinds of behavior. The concept of hunger as a drive brings these various relations together in a single term (1953, p. 144).

Thus, despite his renunciation of theory, Skinner's procedure, and even its rationale, appears to bear a certain resemblance to those followed by self-acknowledged behavior theorists. Perhaps, as Miller (1959) has suggested, Skinner has not been too impressed with the theoretical significance of this procedure, because he tends to deal with only one index of behavior, rate of bar-pressing. Obviously, even if the number of m causal variables is very large, if the number n of response variables is only one, mn will always be less than $m + n$. Consequently, no simplification can ensue from the use of intervening variables.

THE INTEGRATIVE FUNCTION OF THEORIES

The second function of a theoretical structure is to integrate various empirical laws within a given domain, by linking the constructs used to account for one set of laws with those used to account for other sets. In this way, one may establish a "network of connected concepts" (Feigl, 1945). In a theoretical structure detailed enough to include statements of relations among several hypothetical variables, the deductive consequences of the supposition that an empirical variable is related to one or another of these intervening variables may be quite far-reaching, and in some cases may lead to unexpected conclusions.

Since such abstract statements about the merits of theory are rather unconvincing, we might consider an example of such guessed-at interrelations and their empirical implications, even at the risk of getting finally to some substantive issues. This example is from the theoretical structure formulated by Hull and Spence—only because it is the one I am most familiar with. There is no implication that different formulations would not yield equally pertinent instances.

Consider the consequences of the supposition that a given variable Y is related to general drive level (D). If it is further assumed that the strength of responses is some function of habit strength (H) multiplied by drive level ($R = H \times D$), one can make a rather large number of predictions concerning the effects on behavior of variations in Y. For instance, increases in the value of Y should lead to the following consequences: improved performance in situations in which the strongest habit is correct, but poorer performance when the strongest habit is incorrect; greater responsiveness to generalized stimuli, but better discrimination between the training and generalized stimuli when presented simultaneously; steepened slopes of psychophysical functions relating to sensory thresholds, but no change in the absolute threshold. All these, and a substantial number of other consequences may be deduced from the Hull-Spence theory, on the hypothesis that Y is a drive factor (e.g., Brown, 1961; Spence, 1956). These consequences depend, of course, on the assumed relations between empirical variables and intervening variables as well as those among the intervening variables.

In the case of any particular varible Y, of course, the predicted consequences may not appear. In this eventuality, one must conclude either that Y is not a drive variable, or some of the assumptions relating drive to other constructs and to behavior are incorrect, or both. The point is, unless one has a theory in which these relations are made explicit, there would be no reason even to look for these possible effects on behavior.

In an earlier section, note was taken of the wide variety of tests that have yielded scores highly correlated with those on the Manifest Anxiety Scale. A few years ago, Davids (1955) asked a question that has probably occurred to many psychologists: in view of these high relations between MAS scores and those on other, well-established instruments, some of which may be even more valid measures of anxiety, why has there been so much emphasis on the MAS? In my opinion, the answer is obvious: because of the supposition that these scores might be related to one of the intervening variables in the Hull-Spence theory and, consequently, to variations in all the kinds of behaviors theoretically affected by this variable. In other words, the popularity of the MAS resulted, not necessarily from any intrinsic value of the test itself, and certainly not from its title, which is in some respects misleading, but from its presumptive relation to constructs within a comparatively highly integrated theory.

Since, as Spence (1958) has stated, the primary function of the sort of theoretical scheme he employs ". . . is to provide for the unification of what, without the theory, would be a multiplicity of isolated or unconnected facts and laws" (p. 140), assigning any variable to a place in the theory permits the deduction of a variety of behaviors which would otherwise not be suspected. For example, it is quite probable that MAS scores represent, in part, the strength of the desire to make a good impression (Edwards, 1957). But I wonder whether anyone seriously believes that this conceptualization would have led to studies of eyelid conditioning, or psychophysical functions, or the steepness of stimulus generalization gradients, or paired-associates learning, or for that matter Davids' own investigation of productivity in a word association test (Davids and Eriksen, 1955).

It may be of some interest to note that many of the predictions based on the assumption that the MAS measures drive level have been borne out; in other instances, the predictions have met with but indifferent success. Indeed, if the Hull-Spence theory is correct, then some of these findings demonstrate that the MAS also measures characteristics other than D. Since no one, to the best of my knowledge, ever doubted this (Farber, 1954, 1955), these demonstrations are not too surprising. Whether the evidence indicates that it measures D at all is perhaps still a moot question. Indeed, in a larger context, it may be questioned whether it is necessary or useful for theoretical purposes to posit a non-associative concept of D at all (e.g., Brown, 1961; Estes, 1958; Postman, 1953).

These questions are of the utmost importance. Nevertheless, in considering the metatheoretical nature and functions of theory, they are in a sense quite irrelevant. If the MAS does not measure D, perhaps some other indexes, such as certain kinds of autonomic or cortical activity will do so. Perhaps no kind of behavior indexes will prove useful for this purpose. Perhaps the kinds of behavioral phenomena accounted for in terms of the Hull-Spence theoretical formulation will be better integrated within new theoretical systems, which may not contain the construct of drive level at all. Theories are not sacrosanct. They are formulated for only one purpose—to account for the behavioral data. If they fail to do so, they must be modified or discarded.

I believe a number of behavior theories have proved useful in providing a basis for predicting behavioral phenomena of interest even to those who consider such approaches too simplistic to account for the complexities of personality. Miller's studies of fear and conflict, Skinner's studies of operant conditioning, and the extension of both to the area of psychotherapy are cases in point. New theories are being constructed and older ones revised, the better to incorporate and account for new findings. It is in the very nature of behavior theoretical formulations that they be modified on the basis of empirical facts. Since the empirical facts of psychology include those relating to individual differences, one may anticipate that as behavior theories become more precise and more comprehensive they will encompass more and more phenomena now referred to under the rubric of "personality." I, for one, look forward to the day, which I do not expect to see myself, when personality theories are regarded as historical curiosities.

REFERENCES

ADLER, A. Individual psychology. In C. Murchison (Ed.), *Psychologies of 1930*. Worcester, Mass.: Clark University Press, 1930, pp. 395–405.

ALLPORT, G. W. *Personality*. New York: Holt, Rinehart & Winston, Inc., 1937.

ALLPORT, G. W. *Pattern and growth in personality*. New York: Holt, Rinehart & Winston, Inc., 1961.

AMSEL, A. Frustrative nonreward in partial reinforcement and discrimination learning: Some recent history and a theoretical extension. *Psychol. Rev.*, 1962, **69,** 306–328.

BECHTOLDT, H. P. Construct validity: a critique. *Amer. Psychologist*, 1959, **14,** 619–629.

BERGMANN, G. Psychoanalysis and experimental psychology: A review from the standpoint of scientific empiricism. *Mind*, 1943, **52,** 122–140.

———. The logic of psychological concepts. *Phil. Sci.*, 1951, **18,** 93–110.

———. Theoretical psychology. In C. P. Stone (Ed.), *Ann. Rev. Psychol.*, Vol. 4. Stanford, Calif.: Annual Reviews, 1953, pp. 435–458.

———. The contribution of John B. Watson. *Psychol. Rev.*, 1956, **63,** 265–276.

BERGMANN, G. AND SPENCE, K. W. Operationism and theory in psychology. *Psychol. Rev.*, 1941, **48,** 1–14.

BROWN, J. S. *The motivation of behavior*. New York: McGraw-Hill Book Company, Inc., 1961.

BROWN, J. S. AND FARBER, I. E. Emotions conceptualized as intervening variables—with suggestions toward a theory of frustration. *Psychol. Bull.*, 1951, **48,** 465–495.

CAMPBELL, D. T. Lectures in Social Psychology: unpublished manuscript. 1959.

———. Recommendations for APA test standards regarding construct, trait, or discriminant validity. *Amer. Psychologist*, 1960, **15,** 546–553.

CONDON, E. V. Physics. In J. R. Newman (Ed.), *What is science?* New York: Simon & Schuster, Inc., 1955, pp. 102–149.

CRONBACH, L. J., AND MEEHL, P. E. Construct validity in psychological tests. *Psychol. Bull.*, 1955, **52,** 281–302.

DAVIDS, A. Relations among several objective measures of anxiety under different conditions of motivation. *J. consult. Psychol.*, 1955, **19,** 275–279.

DAVIDS, A., AND ERIKSEN, C. W. The relation of manifest anxiety to association productivity and intellectual attainment. *J. consult. Psychol.*, 1955, **19,** 219–222.

DOLLARD, J., AND MILLER, N. E. *Personality and psychotherapy*. New York: McGraw-Hill Book Company, Inc., 1950.

EDWARDS, A. L. *The social desirability variable in personality assessment and research*. New York: Holt, Rinehart, & Winston, Inc., 1957.

ESTES, W. K. Stimulus-response theory of drive. In M. R. Jones (Ed.), *Nebraska symposium on motivation*. Lincoln, Neb.: University of Nebraska Press, 1958, pp. 35–69.

EYSENCK, H. J. *The scientific study of personality*. London: Routledge & Kegan Paul, 1952.

FARBER, I. E. Anxiety as a drive state. In M. R. Jones (Ed.). *Nebraska symposium on motivation*. Lincoln, Neb.: University of Nebraska Press, 1954, pp. 1–46.

———. The role of motivation in verbal learning and performance. *Psychol. Bull.*, 1955, **52,** 311–327.

———. The things people say to themselves. *Amer. Psychologist*, 1963, **18,** 185–197.

FARBER, I. E., HARLOW, H. F., AND WEST, L. J. Brainwashing, conditioning, and *DDD* (debility, dependency, and dread). *Sociometry*, 1957, **20,** 271–285.

FEIGL, H. Operationism and scientific method. *Psychol. Rev.*, 1945, **52,** 250–259.

GILL, M. The present state of psychoanalytic theory. *J. abnorm. soc. Psychol.,* 1959, **58,** 1–8.

GOSS, A. E. Early behaviorism and verbal mediating responses. *Amer. Psychologist,* 1961, **16,** 285–298.

HALL, C. S., AND LINDZEY, G. *Theories of personality.* New York: John Wiley & Sons, Inc., 1957.

KENDLER, H. H., AND KENDLER, TRACY S. Vertical and horizontal processes in problem solving. *Psychol. Rev.,* 1962, **69,** 1–16.

KOCH, S. Behavior as "intrinsically" regulated: work notes towards a pre-theory of phenomena called "motivational." In M. R. Jones (Ed.), *Nebraska symposium on motivation.* Lincoln, Neb.: University of Nebraska Press, 1956, pp. 42–86.

———. Epilogue. In S. Koch (Ed.), *Psychology: A study of a science.* Vol 3. *Formulations of the person and the social context.* New York: McGraw-Hill Book Company, Inc., 1959, pp. 729–788.

MCCLELLAND, D. C. The psychology of mental content reconsidered. *Psychol. Rev.,* 1955, **62,** 297–302.

MEEHL, P. E. *Clinical vs. statistical prediction.* Minneapolis: University of Minnesota Press, 1954.

MILLER, N. E. Liberalization of basic S-R concepts: Extensions to conflict behavior, motivation, and social learning. In S. Koch (Ed.), *Psychology: A study of a science.* Vol. 2. *General systematic formulations, learning, and special processes.* New York: McGraw-Hill Book Company, Inc., 1959, pp. 196–292.

MURPHY, G. *Personality.* New York: Harper & Row, Publishers, Inc., 1947.

MURRAY, H. A., SKINNER, B. F., MASLOW, A. H., ROGERS, L. R., FRANK, L. K., RAPOPORT, A., AND HOFFMAN, H. Cultural evolution as viewed by Psychologists. *Daedalus,* 1961, **90,** 570–586.

POSTMAN, L. Comments on papers by Professors Brown and Harlow. In *Current theory and research in motivation: a symposium.* Lincoln, Neb.: University of Nebraska Press, 1953, pp. 55–58.

ROGERS, C. R. A theory of therapy, personality, and interpersonal relationships, as developed in the client-centered framework. In S. Koch (Ed.), *Psychology: A study of a science.* Vol. 3. *Formulations of the person and the social context.* New York: McGraw-Hill Book Company, Inc., 1959.

SIMPSON, G. G. *The meaning of evolution.* New Haven: Yale University Press, 1950.

SKINNER, B. F. *Science and human behavior.* New York: The Macmillan Company, 1953.

———. The design of cultures. *Daedalus,* 1961, **90,** 534–546.

———. Freedom and the control of men. *Amer. Scholar,* 1955–56, **25,** 47–65.

SPENCE, K. W. The nature of theory construction in contemporary psychology. *Psychol. Rev.,* 1944. **51,** 47–68.

———. The postulates and methods of behaviorism. *Psychol. Rev.,* 1948, **55,** 67–78.

———. Clark Leonard Hull: 1884–1952. *Amer. J. Psychol.* 1952, **65,** 639–646.

———. *Behavior theory and conditioning.* New Haven: Yale University Press, 1956.

———. The empirical basis and theoretical structure of psychology. *Philos. Sci.,* 1957, **24,** 97–108.

————. A theory of emotionally based drive (D) and its relation to preformance in simple learning situations. *Amer. Psychologist*, 1958, **13**, 131–141.

SPIKER, C. C. Verbal factors in the discrimination learning of children. *Child Develpm. Monogr.*, 1962, **28**, 53–71.

TOLMAN, E. C. Operational behaviorism and current trends in psychology. *Proc. 25th Anniv. Celebration Inaug. Grad. Stud.* Los Angeles: University of Southern California, 1936, pp. 89–103.

TOULMIN, S. *The philosophy of science.* London: Hutchinson University Library, 1953.

WATSON, J. B. *Psychology from the standpoint of a behaviorist.* Philadelphia: J. B. Lippincott Company, 1919.

[10] The Logic of Functional Analysis

CARL G. HEMPEL

1. Introduction

Empirical science, in all its major branches, seeks not only to *describe* the phenomena in the world of our experience, but also to *explain* or *understand* them. While this is widely recognized, it is often held, however, that there exist fundamental differences between the explanatory *methods* appropriate to the different fields of empirical science. In the physical sciences, according to this view, all explanation is achieved ultimately by reference to causal or correlational antecedents; whereas in psychology and the social and historical disciplines—and, according to some, even in biology—the establishment of causal or correlational connections, while desirable and important, is not sufficient. Proper understanding of the phenomena studied in these fields is held to require other types of explanation.

One of the explanatory methods that have been developed for this purpose is that of functional analysis, which has found extensive use in biology, psychology, sociology, and anthropology. This procedure raises problems of considerable interest for the comparative methodology of empirical science.

The present essay is an attempt to clarify some of these problems; its object is to examine the logical structure of functional analysis and its explanatory and predictive significance by means of a confrontation with the principal characteristics of the explanatory procedures used in the physical sciences. We begin therefore with a brief examination of the latter.

2. Nomological Explanation: Deductive and Inductive

In a beaker filled to the brim with water at room temperature, there floats a chunk of ice which partly extends above the surface. As the ice gradually melts, one might expect the water in the beaker to overflow. Actually the water level remains unchanged. How is this to be explained? The key to an answer is provided by Archimedes' principle, according to which a solid body floating in a liquid displaces a volume of liquid which has the same weight as the body itself. Hence the chunk of ice has the same weight as the volume of water its submerged portion displaces. Since melting does not affect the weights involved, the water into which the ice turns has the same weight as the ice itself, and hence, the same weight as the water initially displaced by the submerged portion of the ice. Having the same weight, it also has the same volume as the displaced water; hence the melting ice yields a volume of water that suffices exactly to fill the space initially occupied by the submerged part of the ice. Therefore, the water level remains unchanged.

This account (which deliberately disregards certain effects of small magnitude) is an example of an argument intended to explain a given event. Like any explanatory argument, it falls into two parts, which will be called the *explanans* and the *explanandum*.[1] The latter is the statement, or set of statements, describing the phenomenon to be explained; the former is the statement, or set of statements, adduced to provide an explanation. In our illustration, the explanandum states that at the end of the process, the beaker contains only water, with its surface at the same level as at the beginning. To explain this, the explanans adduces, first of all, certain laws of physics; among them, Archimedes' principle; laws to the effect that at

---

1 These terms are given preference over the more familiar words 'explicans' and 'explicandum,' in order to reserve the latter for use in the context of philosophical explication in the technical sense proposed by R. Carnap; see, for example, his *Logical Foundations of Probability* (Chicago: University of Chicago Press, 1950), secs. 1–3. The terms 'explanans' and 'explanandum' were introduced, for this reason, in an earlier article: Carl G. Hempel and P. Oppenheim, "Studies in the Logic of Explanation," *Philosophy of Science*, 15 (1948), pp. 135–75 (reprinted in C. G. Hempel, *Aspects of Scientific Explanation*, The Free Press, New York). While that article does not deal explicitly with inductive explanation, its first four sections contain various further considerations on deductive explanation that are relevant to the present study. For a careful critical examination of some points of detail discussed in the earlier article, such as especially the relation between explanation and prediction, see the essay by I. Scheffler, "Explanation, Prediction, and Abstraction," *The British Journal for the Philosophy of Science*, 7 (1957), pp. 293–309, which also contains some interesting comments bearing on functional analysis.

temperatures above 0°C. and atmospheric pressure, a body of ice turns into a body of water having the same weight; and the law that, at any fixed temperature and pressure, amounts of water that are equal in weight are also equal in volume.

In addition to these laws, the explanans contains a second group of statements; these describe certain particular circumstances which, in the experiment, precede the outcome to be explained; such as the facts that at the beginning, there is a chunk of ice floating in a beaker filled with water; that the water is at room temperature; and that the beaker is surrounded by air at the same temperature and remains undisturbed until the end of the experiment.

The explanatory import of the whole argument lies in showing that the outcome described in the explanandum was to be expected in view of the antecedent circumstances and the general laws listed in the explanans. More precisely, the explanation may be construed as an argument in which the explanandum is deduced from the explanans. Our example then illustrates what we will call explanation by deductive subsumption under general laws, or briefly, *deductive-nomological explanation*. The general form of such an explanation is given by the following schema:

$$\left.\begin{array}{l} L_1, L_2, \ldots, L_m \\ \\ C_1, C_2, \ldots, C_n \end{array}\right\} \text{Explanans} \tag{2.1}$$

$$\overline{}$$

$$E \qquad \text{Explanandum}$$

Here, $L_1, L_2, \ldots, L_m$ are general laws and $C_1, C_2, \ldots, C_n$ are statements of particular fact; the horizontal line separating the conclusion E from the premises indicates that the former follows logically from the latter.

In our example, the phenomenon to be explained is a particular event that takes place at a certain place and time. But the method of deductive subsumption under general laws lends itself also to the explanation of what might be called "general facts" or uniformities, such as those expressed by laws of nature. For example, the question why Galileo's law holds for physical bodies falling freely near the earth's surface can be answered by showing that the law refers to a special case of accelerated motion under gravitational attraction, and that it can be deduced from the general laws for such motion (namely, Newton's laws of motion and of gravitation) by applying these to the special case where two bodies are involved, one of them the earth and the other the falling object, and where the distance between their centers of gravity equals the length of the earth's radius. Thus, an explanation of the regularities expressed by Galileo's law can be achieved by deducing the latter from the Newtonian laws and from statements specifying the mass and the radius of the earth; the latter two yield the value of the constant acceleration of free fall near the earth.

It might be helpful to mention one further illustration of the role of deductive-nomological explanation in accounting for particular facts as well as for general uniformities or laws. The occurrence of a rainbow on a given occasion can be deductively explained by reference to (1) certain particular determining conditions, such as the presence of raindrops in the air, sunlight falling on these drops, the observer facing away from the sun, etc., and (2) certain general laws, especially those of optical reflection, refraction, and dispersion. The fact that these laws hold can be explained in turn by deduction from the more comprehensive principles of, say, the electromagnetic theory of light.

Thus, the method of deductive-nomological explanation accounts for a particular event by subsuming it under general laws in the manner represented by the schema (2.1); and it can similarly serve to explain the fact that a given law holds by showing that the latter is subsumable, in the same fashion, under more comprehensive laws or theoretical principles. In fact, one of the main objectives of a theory (such as, say, the electromagnetic theory of light) is precisely to provide a set of principles—often expressed in terms of "hypothetical," not directly observable, entities (such as electric and magnetic field vectors)—which will deductively account for a group of antecedently established "empirical generalizations" (such as the laws of rectilinear propagation, reflection, and refraction of light). Frequently, a theoretical explanation will show that the empirical generalizations hold only approximately. For example, the application of Newtonian theory to free fall near the earth yields a law that is like Galileo's except that the acceleration of the fall is seen not to be strictly constant, but to vary slightly with geographical location, altitude above sea level, and certain other factors.

The general laws or theoretical principles that serve to account for empirical generalizations may in turn be deductively subsumable under even more comprehensive principles; for example, Newton's theory of gravitation can be subsumed, as an approximation, under that of the general theory of relativity. Obviously, this explanatory hierarchy has to end at some point. Thus, at any time in the development of empirical science, there will be certain facts which, at that time, are not explainable; these include the most comprehensive general laws and theoretical principles then known and, of course, many empirical generalizations and particular facts for which no explanatory principles are available at the time. But this does not imply that certain facts are intrinsically unexplainable and thus must remain unexplained forever: any particular fact as yet unexplainable, and any general principle, however comprehensive, may subsequently be found to be explainable by subsumption under even more inclusive principles.

Causal explanation is a special type of deductive nomological explanation; for a certain event or set of events can be said to have caused a specified "effect" only if there are general laws connecting the former with the latter in such a way that, given a description of the antecedent events, the occurrence of the effect can be deduced with the help of the laws. For example, the explanation of the lengthening of a given iron bar as having been caused by an increase in its temperature amounts to an argument of the form (2.1) whose explanans includes (*a*) statements specifying the initial length of the bar and indicating that the bar is made of iron and that its temperature was raised, (*b*) a law pertaining to the increase in the length of any iron bar with rising temperature.[2]

Not every deductive-nomological explanation is a causal explanation, however. For example, the regularities expressed by Newton's laws of motion and of gravitation cannot properly be said to *cause* the free fall of bodies near the earth's surface to satisfy Galileo's laws.

Now we must consider another type of explanation, which again accounts for a given phenomenon by reference to general laws, but in a manner which does not fit the deductive pattern (2.1). When little Henry catches the mumps, this might be explained by pointing out that he contracted the disease from a friend with whom he played for several hours just a day before the latter was confined with a severe case of mumps. The particular antecedent factors here invoked are Henry's exposure and, let us assume, the fact that Henry had not had the mumps before. But to connect these with the event to be explained, we cannot adduce a general law to the effect that under the conditions just mentioned, the exposed person invariably contracts the mumps: what can be asserted is only that the disease will be transmitted with high statistical probability. Again, when a neurotic trait in an adult is psychoanalytically explained by reference to critical childhood experiences, the argument explicitly or implicitly claims that the case at hand is but an exemplification of certain general laws governing the development of neuroses. But surely, whatever specific laws of this kind might be adduced at present can purport, at the very best, to express probabilistic trends rather than deterministic uniformities: they may be construed as *laws of statistical form,* or briefly as *statistical laws,* to the effect that, given the childhood experiences in question—plus, presumably, certain particular environmental conditions in later life—there is such and such a statistical probability that a specified kind of neurosis will develop. Such statistical laws differ in form from strictly universal laws of the kind mentioned in our earlier examples of explanatory arguments. In the simplest case, a *law of strictly universal form,* or briefly, a *universal law,* is a statement to the effect that in *all* cases satisfying certain antecedent conditions *A* (e.g., heating of a gas under constant pressure), an event of a specified kind *B* (e.g., an

---

[2] An explanation by means of laws which are causal in the technical sense of theoretical physics also has the form (2.1) of a deductive-nomological explanation. In this case, the laws invoked must meet certain conditions as to mathematical form, and $C_1, C_2, \ldots, C_n$ express so-called boundary conditions. For a fuller account of the concepts of causal law and of causality as understood in theoretical physics, see, for example, H. Margenau, *The Nature of Physical Reality* (New York: McGraw-Hill Book Company, Inc., 1950), Chapter 19; or Ph. Frank, *Philosophy of Science* (Englewood Cliffs, N.J.: Prentice-Hall, Inc., 1957), Chapters 11, 12.

increase in the volume of the gas) will occur; whereas a law of statistical form asserts that the probability for conditions A to be accompanied by an event of kind B has some specific value p.

Explanatory arguments which, in the manner just illustrated, account for a phenomenon by reference to statistical laws are not of the strictly deductive type (2.1). For example, the explanans consisting of information about Henry's exposure to the mumps and of a statistical law about the transmission of this disease does not logically imply the conclusion that Henry catches the mumps; it does not make that conclusion necessary, but, as we might say, more or less probable, depending upon the probability specified by the statistical laws. An argument of this kind, then, accounts for a phenomenon by showing that its occurrence is highly probable in view of certain particular facts and statistical laws specified in the explanans. An account of this type will be called an *explanation by inductive subsumption under statistical laws,* or briefly, an *inductive explanation.*

Closer analysis shows that inductive explanation differs from its deductive counterpart in several important respects; [3] but for the purposes of the following discussion, our sketchy account of explanation by statistical laws will suffice.

The two types of explanation we have distinguished will both be said to be varieties of *nomological explanation;* for either of them accounts for a given phenomenon by "subsuming it under laws," i.e., by showing that its occurrence could have been inferred—either deductively or with a high probability—by applying certain laws of universal or of statistical form to specified antecedent circumstances. Thus, a nomological explanation shows that we might in fact have *predicted* the phenomenon at hand, either deductively or with a high probability, if, at an earlier time, we had taken cognizance of the facts stated in the explanans.

But the predictive power of a nomological explanation goes much farther than this: precisely because its explanans contains general laws, it permits predictions concerning occurrences other than that referred to in the explanandum. In fact, such predictions provide a means of testing the empirical soundness of the explanans. For example, the laws invoked in a deductive explanation of the form (2.1) imply that the kind of event described in E will recur whenever and wherever circumstances of the kind described by $C_1, C_2, \ldots , C_n$ are realized; e.g., when the experiment with ice floating in water is repeated, the outcome will be the same. In addition, the laws will yield predictions as to what is going to happen under certain specifiable conditions which differ from those mentioned in $C_1, C_2, \ldots , C_n$.

3 For details, see C. G. Hempel, *Aspects of Scientific Explanation, op. cit.,* pp. 376–412. Some stimulating comments on explanation by means of statistical laws will be found in S. E. Gluck, "Do Statistical Laws Have Explanatory Efficacy?" *Philosophy of Science,* 22 (1955), 34–38. For a much fuller analysis of the logic of statistical inference, see R. B. Braithwaite, *Scientific Explanation* (Cambridge: Cambridge University Press, 1953), chapters V, VI, VII. For a study of the logic of inductive inference in general, Carnap's *Logical Foundations of Probability, op. cit.,* is of great importance.

For example, the laws invoked in our illustration also yield the prediction that if a chunk of ice were floating in a beaker filled to the brim with concentrated brine, which has a greater specific gravity than water, some of the liquid would overflow as the ice was melting. Again, the Newtonian laws of motion and of gravitation, which may be used to explain various aspects of planetary motion, have predictive consequences for a variety of totally different phenomena, such as free fall near the earth, the motion of a pendulum, the tides, and many others.

This kind of account of further phenomena which is made possible by a nomological explanation is not limited to future events; it may refer to the past as well. For example, given certain information about the present locations and velocities of the celestial bodies involved, the principles of Newtonian mechanics and optics yield not only predictions about future solar and lunar eclipses, but also "postdictions," or "retrodictions," about past ones. Analogously, the statistical laws of radioactive decay, which can function in various kinds of predictions, also lend themselves to retrodictive use; for example, in the dating, by means of the radiocarbon method, of a bow or an ax handle found in an archaeological site.

A proposed explanation is scientifically acceptable only if its explanans is capable of empirical test, i.e., roughly speaking, if it is possible to infer from it certain statements whose truth can be checked by means of suitable observational or experimental procedures. The predictive and postdictive implications of the laws invoked in a nomological explanation clearly afford an opportunity for empirical tests; the more extensive and varied the set of implications that have been borne out by empirical investigation, the better established will be the explanatory principles in question.

3. The Basic Pattern of Functional Analysis

Historically speaking, functional analysis is a modification of teleological explanation, i.e., of explanation not by reference to causes which "bring about" the event in question, but by reference to ends which determine its course. Intuitively, it seems quite plausible that a teleological approach might be required for an adequate understanding of purposive and other goal-directed behavior; and teleological explanation has always had its advocates in this context. The trouble with the idea is that in its more traditional forms, it fails to meet the minimum scientific requirement of empirical testability. The neovitalistic idea of entelechy or of vital force is a case in point. It is meant to provide an explanation for various characteristically biological phenomena, such as regeneration and regulation, which according to neovitalism cannot be explained by physical and chemical laws alone. Entelechies are conceived as goal-directed nonphysical agents which affect the course of physiological events in such a way as to restore an organism to a more or less normal state after a disturbance has occurred.

However, this conception is stated in essentially metaphorical terms: no testable set of statements is provided (i) to specify the circumstances in which an entelechy will supervene as an agent directing the course of events otherwise governed by physical and chemical laws, and (ii) to indicate precisely what observable effects the action of an entelechy will have in such a case. And since neovitalism thus fails to state general laws as to when and how entelechies act, it cannot explain any biological phenomena; it can give us no grounds to expect a given phenomenon, no reasons to say: "Now we see that the phenomenon had to occur." It yields neither predictions nor retrodictions: the attribution of a biological phenomenon to the supervention of an entelechy has no testable implications at all. This theoretical defect can be thrown into relief by contrasting the idea of entelechy with that of a magnetic field generated by an electric current, which may be invoked to explain the deflection of a magnetic needle. A magnetic field is not directly observable any more than an entelechy; but the concept is governed by strictly specifiable laws concerning the strength and direction, at any point, of the magnetic field produced by a current flowing through a given wire, and by other laws determining the effect of such a field upon a magnetic needle in the magnetic field on the earth. And it is these laws which, by their predictive and retrodictive import, confer explanatory power upon the concept of magnetic field. Teleological accounts referring to entelechies are thus seen to be pseudo-explanations. Functional analysis, as will be seen, though often formulated in teleological terms, need not appeal to such problematic entities and has a definitely empirical core.

The kind of phenomenon that a functional analysis [4] is invoked to explain is typically some recurrent activity or some behavior pattern in an individual or a group, such as a physiological mechanism, a neurotic trait, a culture pattern or a social institution. And the principal objective of the analysis is to exhibit the contribution which the behavior pattern makes to the preservation or the development of the individual or the group in which it occurs. Thus, functional analysis seeks to understand a behavior pattern or a sociocultural institution by determining the role it plays in keeping the given system in proper working order or maintaining it as a going concern.

By way of a simple and schematized illustration, consider first the statement:

(3.1) The heartbeat in vertebrates has the function of circulating blood through the organism.

---

[4] For the account of functional analysis presented in this section, I have obtained much stimulation and information from the illuminating essay "Manifest and Latent Functions" in R. K. Merton's book, *Social Theory and Social Structure* (New York: The Free Press; revised and enlarged edition, 1957), 19–84. Each of the passages from this work which is referred to in the present essay may also be found in the first edition (1949), on a page with approximately the same number.

Before examining the possibilities of its explanatory use, we should ask ourselves: What does the statement *mean*? What is being asserted by this attribution of function? It might be held that all the information conveyed by a sentence such as (3.1) can be expressed just as well by substituting the word "effect" for the word "function." But this construal would oblige us to assent also to the statement:

(3.2) The heartbeat has the function of producing heart sounds; for the heartbeat has that effect.

Yet a proponent of functional analysis would refuse to assert (3.2), on the ground that heart sounds are an effect of the heartbeat which is of no importance to the functioning of the organism; whereas the circulation of the blood effects the transportation of nutriment to, and the removal of waste from, various parts of the organism—a process that is indispensable if the organism is to remain in proper working order, and indeed if it is to stay alive. Thus understood, the import of the functional statement (3.1) might be summarized as follows:

(3.3) The heartbeat has the effect of circulating the blood, and this ensures the satisfaction of certain conditions (supply of nutriment and removal of waste) which are necessary for the proper working of the organism.

We should notice next that the heart will perform the function here attributed to it only if certain conditions are met by the organism and by its environment. For example, circulation will fail if there is a rupture of the aorta; the blood can carry oxygen only if the environment affords an adequate supply of oxygen and the lungs are in proper condition; it will remove certain kinds of waste only if the kidneys are reasonably healthy; and so forth. Most of the conditions that would have to be specified here are usually left unmentioned, partly no doubt because they are assumed to be satisfied as a matter of course in situations in which the organism normally finds itself. But in part, the omission reflects lack of relevant knowledge, for an explicit specification of the relevant conditions would require a theory in which (*a*) the possible states of organisms and of their environments could be characterized by the values of certain physicochemical or perhaps biological "variables of state," and in which (*b*) the fundamental theoretical principles would permit the determination of that range of internal and external conditions within which the pulsations of the heart would perform the function referred to above.[5] At present, a general theory of this kind, or even one that could deal in this fashion with some particular class of organisms, is unavailable, of course.

[5] For a fuller statement and further development of this point, see the essay "A Formalization of Functionalism" in E. Nagel, *Logic Without Metaphysics* (New York: The Free Press, 1957), 247–83. Part I of that study offers a detailed analysis of Merton's essay mentioned in Note 4.

Also, a full restatement of (3.1) in the manner of (3.3) calls for criteria of what constitutes "proper working," "normal functioning," and the like, of the organism at hand; for the function of a given trait is here construed in terms of its causal relevance to the satisfaction of certain necessary conditions of proper working or survival of the organism. Here again, the requisite criteria are often left unspecified—an aspect of functional analysis whose serious implications will be considered later (in section 5).

The considerations here outlined suggest the following schematic characterization of a functional analysis:

(3.4) *Basic pattern of a functional analysis:* The object of the analysis is some "item" i, which is a relatively persistent trait or disposition (e.g., the beating of the heart) occurring in a system s (e.g., the body of a living vertebrate); and the analysis aims to show that s is in a state, or internal condition, c_i and in an environment representing certain external conditions c_e such that under conditions c_i and c_e (jointly to be referred to as c) the trait i has effects which satisfy some "need" or "functional requirement" of s, i.e., a condition n which is necessary for the system's remaining in adequate, or effective, or proper, working order.

Let us briefly consider some examples of this type of analysis in psychology and in sociological and anthropological studies. In psychology, it is especially psychoanalysis which shows a strong functional orientation. One clear instance is Freud's functional characterization of the role of symptom formation. In *The Problem of Anxiety,* Freud expresses himself as favoring a conception according to which "all symptom formation would be brought about solely in order to avoid anxiety; the symptoms bind the psychic energy which otherwise would be discharged as anxiety." [6] In support of this view, Freud points out that if an agoraphobic who has usually been accompanied when going out is left alone in the street, he will suffer an attack of anxiety, as will the compulsion neurotic, who, having touched something, is prevented from washing his hands. "It is clear, therefore, that the stipulation of being accompanied and the compulsion to wash has as their purpose, and also their result, the averting of an outbreak of anxiety." [7] In this account, which is put in strongly teleological terms, the system s is the individual under consideration; i is agoraphobic or compulsive behavior pattern; n the binding of anxiety, which is necessary to avert a serious psychological crisis that would make it impossible for the individual to function adequately.

In anthropology and sociology the object of functional analysis is, in Merton's words, "a *standardized* (i.e., patterned and repetitive) item, such as social roles, institutional patterns, social processes, cultural pattern, culturally patterned emotions, social norms, group organizations, social struc-

---

[6] S. Freud, *The Problem of Anxiety* (Transl. by H. A. Bunker. New York: Psychoanalytic Quarterly Press, and W. W. Norton & Company, Inc., 1936), p. 111.
[7] *Ibid.,* p. 112.

ture, devices for social control, *etc.*" [8] Here, as in psychology and biology, the function, i.e., the stabilizing or adjusting effect, of the item under study may be one not consciously sought (and indeed, it might not even be consciously recognized) by the agents; in this case, Merton speaks of *latent* functions—in contradistinction to *manifest* functions, i.e., those stabilizing objective effects which are intended by participants in the system.[9] Thus, e.g., the rain-making ceremonials of the Hopi fail to achieve their manifest meteorological objective, but they "may fulfill the latent function of reinforcing the group identity by providing a periodic occasion on which the scattered members of a group assemble to engage in a common activity." [10]

Radcliffe-Brown's functional analysis of the totemic rites of certain Australian tribes illustrates the same point:

> To discover the social function of the totemic rites we have to consider the whole body of cosmological ideas of which each rite is a partial expression. I believe that it is possible to show that the social structure of an Australian tribe is connected in a very special way with these cosmological ideas and that the maintenance of its continuity depends on keeping them alive, by their regular expression in myth and rite.
>
> Thus, any satisfactory study of the totemic rites of Australia must be based not simply on the consideration of their ostensible purpose . . . , but on the discovery of their meaning and of their social function.[11]

Malinowski attributes important latent functions to religion and to magic: he argues that religious faith establishes and enhances mental attitudes such as reverence for tradition, harmony with environment, and confidence and courage in critical situations and at the prospect of death—attitudes which, embodied and maintained by cult and ceremonial, have "an immense biological value." He points out that magic, by providing man with certain ready-made rituals, techniques, and beliefs, enables him "to maintain his poise and his mental integrity in fits of anger, in the throes of hate, of unrequited love, of despair and anxiety. The function of magic is to ritualize man's optimism, to enhance his faith in the victory of hope over fear." [12]

---

[8] Merton, *op. cit.*, p. 50 (Author's italics).

[9] *Ibid.*, p. 51. Merton defines manifest functions as those which are both intended and recognized, and latent functions as those which are neither intended nor recognized. But this characterization allows for functions which are neither manifest nor latent; e.g., those which are recognized though not intended. It would seem to be more in keeping with Merton's intentions, therefore, to base the distinction simply on whether or not the stabilizing effect of the given item was deliberately sought.

[10] *Ibid.*, pp. 64–65.

[11] A. R. Radcliffe-Brown, *Structure and Function in Primitive Society* (London: Cohen and West Ltd., 1952), 145.

[12] B. Malinowski, *Magic, Science and Religion, and Other Essays* (Garden City, N.Y.: Doubleday Anchor Books, 1954), p. 90. For an illuminating comparison of Malinowski's views on the functions of magic and religion with those advanced by Radcliffe-Brown, see G. C. Homans, *The Human Group* (New York: Harcourt, Brace & World, Inc., 1950), 321 ff. (Note also Homan's general comments on "the functional theory," *ibid.*, pp. 268–72.) This issue and other aspects of functional analysis in anthropology are critically examined in the following article, which confronts some specific applications of the method with programmatic declarations by its proponents: Leon J. Goldstein, "The Logic of Explanation in Malinowskian Anthropology," *Philosophy of Science*, **24** (1957), 156–66.

There will soon be occasion to add to the preceding examples from psychoanalysis and anthropology some instances of functional analysis in sociology. To illustrate the general character of the procedure, however, the cases mentioned so far will suffice: they all exhibit the basic pattern outlined in (3.4). From our examination of the form of functional analysis we now turn to an appraisal of its significance as a mode of explanation.

4. The Explanatory Import of Functional Analysis

Functional analysis is widely considered as achieving an *explanation* of the "items" whose functions it studies. Malinowski, for example, says of the functional analysis of culture that it "aims at the explanations of anthropological facts at all levels of development by their function . . ." [13] and he adds, in the same context: "To explain any item of culture, material or moral, means to indicate its functional place within an institution, . . ." [14] At another place, Malinowski speaks of the "functional explanation of art, recreation, and public ceremonials." [15]

Radcliffe-Brown, too, considers functional analysis as an explanatory method, though not as the only one suited for the social sciences: "Similarly one 'explanation' of a social system will be its history, where we know it— the detailed account of how it came to be what it is and where it is. Another 'explanation' of the same system is obtained by showing (as the functionalists attempt to do) that is it a special exemplification of laws of social physiology or social functioning. The two kinds of explanation do not conflict, but supplement one another." [16]

Apart from illustrating the attribution of explanatory import to functional analysis, this passage is of interest because it stresses that a functional analysis has to rely on general laws. This is shown also in our schematic characterization (3.4): the statements that i, in the specified setting c, has effects that satisfy n, and that n is a necessary condition for the proper functioning of the system, both involve general laws. For a statement of causal connection this is well known; and the assertion that a condition n constitutes a functional prerequisite for a state of some specified kind (such as proper functioning) is tantamount to the statement of a law to the effect that whenever condition n fails to be satisfied, the state in question fails to occur. Thus, explanation by functional analysis requires reference to laws. [17]

---

13 B. Malinowski, "Anthropology," *Encyclopaedia Britannica*, First Supplementary volume (London and New York: The Encyclopaedia Britannica, Inc., 1926), 132.

14 *Ibid.*, p. 139.

15 B. Malinowski, *A Scientific Theory of Culture, and Other Essays* (Chapel Hill: University of North Carolina Press, 1944), 174.

16 Radcliffe-Brown, *op. cit.*, p. 186. For an analysis of the idea of historic-genetic explanation, referred to in this passage, see section 7 of the essay "Aspects of Scientific Explanation," in C. G. Hempel, *op. cit.*, pp. 447–453.

17 Malinowski, at one place in his writings, endorses a pronouncement which might appear to be at variance with this conclusion: "Description cannot be separated from ex-

What explanatory import may properly be claimed for functional analysis? Suppose, then, that we are interested in explaining the occurrence of a trait i in a system s (at a certain time t), and that the following functional analysis is offered:

(4.1)

    (a) At t, s functions adequately in a setting of kind c (characterized by specific internal and external conditions)

    (b) s functions adequately in a setting of kind c only if a certain necessary condition, n, is satisfied

    (c) If trait i were present in s then, as an effect, condition n would be satisfied

    (d) (Hence), at t, trait i is present in s

For the moment, let us leave aside the question as to what precisely is meant by statements of the types (a) and (b), and especially by the phrase "s functions adequately"; these matters will be examined in section 5. Right now, we will concern ourselves only with the *logic* of the argument; i.e., we will ask whether (d) formally follows from (a), (b), (c), just as in a deductive-nomological explanation the explanandum follows from the explanans. The answer is obviously in the negative, for, to put it pedantically, the argument (4.1) involves the fallacy of affirming the consequent in regard to premise (c). More explicitly, the statement (d) could be validly inferred if (c) asserted that *only* the presence of trait i could effect satisfaction of condition n. As it is, we can infer merely that condition n must be satisfied in some way or other at time t; for otherwise by reason of (b), the system s could not be functioning adequately in its setting, in contradiction to what (a) asserts. But it might well be that the occurrence of any one of a number of alternative items would suffice no less than the occurrence of i to satisfy requirement n, in which case the account provided by the premises of (4.1) simply fails to explain why the trait i rather than one of its alternatives is present in s at t.

---

planation, since in the words of a great physicist, 'explanation in nothing but condensed description.' " (Malinowski, "Anthropology," *op. cit.*, p. 132.) He seems to be referring here to the views of Ernst Mach or of Pierre Duhem, who took a similar position on this point. Mach conceived the basic objective of science as the brief and economic description of recurrent phenomena and considered laws as a highly efficient way of compressing, as it were, the description of an infinitude of potential particular occurrences into a simple and compact formula. But, thus understood, the statement approvingly quoted by Malinowski is, of course, entirely compatible with our point about the relevance of laws for functional explanation.

Besides, a law can be called a description only in a Pickwickian sense. For even so simple a generalization as "All vertebrates have hearts" does not describe any particular individual, such as Rin-Tin-Tin, as being a vertebrate and having a heart; rather, it asserts of Rin-Tin-Tin and of any other object, whether vertebrate or not—that *if* it is a vertebrate *then* it has a heart. Thus, the generalization has the import of an indefinite set of conditional statements about particular objects. In addition, a law might be said to imply statements about "potential events" which never actually take place. The gas law, for example, implies that if a given body of gas were to be heated under constant pressure at time t, its volume would increase. But if in fact the gas is not heated at t this statement can hardly be said to be a description of any particular event.

As has just been noted, this objection would not apply if premise (c) could be replaced by the statement that requirement n can be met *only* by the presence of trait i. And indeed, some instances of functional analysis seem to include the claim that the specific item under analysis is, in this sense, functionally indispensable for the satisfaction of n. For example, Malinowski makes this claim for magic when he asserts that "magic fulfills an indispensable function within culture. It satisfies a definite need which cannot be satisfied by any other factors of primitive civilization," and again when he says about magic that "without its power and guidance early man could not have mastered his practical difficulties as he has done, nor could man have advanced to the higher stages of culture. Hence the universal occurrence of magic in primitive societies and its enormous sway. Hence we do find magic an invariable adjunct of all important activities." [18]

However, the assumption of functional indispensability for a given item is highly questionable on empirical grounds: in all concrete cases of application, there do seem to exist alternatives. For example, the binding of anxiety in a given subject might be effected by an alternative symptom, as the experience of psychiatrists seems to confirm. Similarly, the function of the rain dance might be subserved by some other group ceremonial. And interestingly, Malinowski himself, in another context, invokes "the principle of limited possibilities, first laid down by Goldenweiser. Given a definite cultural need, the means of its satisfaction are small in number, and therefore the cultural arrangement which comes into being in response to the need is determined within narrow limits." [19] This principle obviously involves at least a moderate liberalization of the conception that every cultural item is functionally indispensable. But even so, it may still be too restrictive. At any rate, sociologists such as Parsons and Merton have assumed the existence of "functional equivalents" for certain cultural items; and Merton, in his general analysis of functionalism, has insisted that the conception of the functional indispensability of cultural items be replaced explicitly by the assumption of "functional alternatives, or functional equivalents, or functional substitutes." [20] This idea, incidentally, has an interesting parallel in the "principle of multiple solutions" for adaptational problems in evolution. This principle, which has been emphasized by functionally oriented biologists, states that for a given functional problem (such as that of perception of light) there are usually a variety of possible solutions, and many

18 Malinowski, "Anthropology," ~~b~~. *cit.*, p. 136; and *Magic, Science and Religion, and Other Essays, op. cit.*, p. 90. (Note the explanatory claim implicit in the use of the word "hence.")

19 B. Malinowski, "Culture," *Encyclopedia of the Social Sciences*, IV (New York: The Macmillan Company, 1931), 626.

20 Merton, *op. cit.*, p. 34. Cf. also T. Parsons, *Essays in Sociological Theory, Pure and Applied* (New York: The Free Press, 1949), 58. For an interesting attempt to establish the existence of functional alternatives in a specific case, see R. D. Schwartz, "Functional alternatives to inequality," *American Sociological Review*, **20** (1955), 424–30.

of these are actually used by different—and often closely related—groups of organisms.[21]

It should be noted here that, in any case of functional analysis, the question whether there are functional equivalents to a given item i has a definite meaning only if the internal and external conditions c in (4.1) are clearly specified. Otherwise, any proposed alternative to i, say i', could be denied the status of a functional equivalent on the ground that, being different from i, the item i' would have certain effects on the internal state and the environment of s which would not be brought about by i; and that therefore, if i' rather than i were realized, s would not be functioning in the same internal and external situation. Suppose, for example, that the system of magic of a given primitive group were replaced by an extension of its rational technology plus some modification of its religion, and that the group were to continue as a going concern. Would this establish the existence of a functional equivalent to the original system of magic? A negative answer might be defended on the ground that as a result of adopting the modified pattern, the group had changed so strongly in regard to some of its basic characteristics (i.e., its internal state, as characterized by c_i, had been so strongly modified) that it was not the original kind of primitive group any more; and that there simply was no functional equivalent to magic which would leave all the "essential" features of the group unimpaired. Consistent use of this type of argument would safeguard the postulate of the functional indispensability of every cultural item against any conceivable empirical disconfirmation—but at the cost of turning it from an empirical hypothesis into a covert definitional truth.

That unilluminating procedure certainly must be eschewed. But what can a functional analysis in the general manner of (4.1) establish if the possibility of functional equivalents of i is not thus ruled out by definitional fiat? [22] Let I be the class of all those items which are empirically sufficient for n under the circumstances indicated in (4.1), so that an item j will be included in I just in case its realization in system s under conditions of kind c would be empirically sufficient to ensure the satisfaction of requirement n. (The qualification 'empirically' is to indicate that the satisfaction of n by j must be a matter of empirical fact and not just of pure logic. This proviso excludes from I trivial items, such as n itself.) The class I will then be a class of functional equivalents in the sense mentioned above. Let us now replace premise (c) in (4.1) by the following statement:

(c') I is the class of all empirically sufficient conditions for the fulfillment of requirement n in the context determined by system s in setting c.

[21] See G. G. Simpson, *The Meaning of Evolution* (New Haven: Yale University Press, 1949), 164 ff., **190**, 342–43; and G. G. Simpson, C. S. Pittendrigh, L. H. Tiffany, *Life* (New York: Harcourt, Brace & World, Inc., 1957), 437.

[22] (Added in 1964.) The balance of this section has been revised to remedy a flaw in the original version, called to my attention by Professor John R. Gregg.

What the premises (*a*), (*b*), and (*c′*) enable us to infer is then at best this:

(4.2) Some one of the items included in class I is present in system s at time t

But this conclusion offers no grounds for expecting the occurrence of any particular item from I rather than of one of its functional equivalents. And strictly, even the weak conclusion (4.2) is warranted only on the further premise that the class I is not empty, i.e., that there is at least one item whose occurrence would, by law, ensure satisfaction of n.

Thus, functional analysis surely does not account in the manner of a deductive argument for the presence of the particular item i that it is meant to explain. Perhaps, then, it could more adequately be construed as an inductive argument which exhibits the occurrence of i as highly probable under the circumstances described in the premises? Might it not be possible, for example, to add to the premises of (4.1) a further statement to the effect that the functional prerequisite n can be met only by i and by a few specifiable functional alternatives? And might not these premises make the presence of i highly probable? This course is hardly promising, for in most, if not all, concrete cases it would be impossible to specify with any precision the range of alternative behavior patterns, institutions, customs, or the like that would suffice to meet a given functional prerequisite or need. And even if that range could be characterized, there is no satisfactory method in sight for dividing it into some finite number of cases and assigning a probability to each of these.

Suppose, for example, that Malinowski's general view of the function of magic is correct: how are we to determine, when trying to explain the system of magic of a given group, all the different systems of magic and alternative cultural patterns which would satisfy the same functional requirements for the group as does the actually existing system of magic? And how are we to ascribe probabilities of occurrence to each of these potential functional equivalents? Clearly, there is no satisfactory way of answering these questions, and practitioners of functional analysis do not claim to achieve their explanation in this extremely problematic fashion.

Nor is it any help to construe the general laws implicit in the statements (*b*) and (*c*) in (4.1) as statistical rather than strictly universal in form, i.e., as expressing connections that are very probable, but do not hold universally; for the premises thus obtained again would not preclude functional alternatives of i (each of which would make satisfaction of n highly probable), and thus the basic difficulty would remain: the premises taken jointly could still not be said to make the presence just of i highly probable.

In sum then, the information typically provided by a functional analysis of an item i affords neither deductively nor inductively adequate grounds for expecting i rather than one of its alternatives. The impression that a functional analysis does provide such grounds, and thus explains the occurrence of i, is no doubt at least partly due to the benefit of hindsight: when we seek to explain an item *i*, we presumably know already that *i* has occurred.

As was noted a moment ago, however, functional analysis might be construed as a deductive explanation with a very weak explanandum, thus:

(4.3)

    (*a*) At time *t*, system *s* functions adequately in a setting of kind *c*

    (*b*) *s* functions adequately in a setting of kind *c* only if requirement *n* is satisfied

    (*c′*) *I* is the class of empirically sufficient conditions for *n*, in the context determined by *s* and *c*; and *I* is not empty

    (*d′*) Some one of the items included in *I* is present in *s* at *t*

This kind of inference is rather trivial, however, except when we have additional knowledge about the items contained in class *I*. Suppose for example that at time *t*, a certain dog (system *s*) is in good health in a "normal" kind of setting *c* which precludes the use of such devices as artificial hearts, lungs, and kidneys. Suppose further that in a setting of kind *c*, the dog can be in good health only if his blood circulates properly (condition *n*). Then schema (4.3) leads in effect only to the conclusion that in some way or other, the blood is being kept circulating properly in the dog at *t*—hardly a very illuminating result. If however, we have additional knowledge of the ways in which the blood may be kept circulating under the circumstances and if we know, for example, that the only feature that would ensure proper circulation (the only item in class *I*) is a properly working heart, then we may draw the much more specific conclusion that at *t* the dog has a properly working heart. But if we make explicit the further knowledge here used by expressing it as an additional premise, then our argument can be restated in the form (4.1), except that premise (*c*) has been replaced by the statement that *i* is the *only* trait by which *n* can be satisfied in setting *c*; and, as was pointed out above, the conclusion (*d*) of (4.1) does follow in this case.

In general, however, additional knowledge of the kind here referred to is not available, and the explanatory import of functional analysis is then limited to the precarious role schematized in (4.3).

5. The Predictive Import of Functional Analysis

We noted earlier the predictive significance of nomological explanation; now we will ask whether functional analysis can be put to predictive use.

First of all, the preceding discussion shows that the information which is typically provided by a functional analysis yields at best premises of the forms (*a*), (*b*), (*c*) in (4.1); and these afford no adequate basis for the deductive or inductive prediction of a sentence of the form (*d*) in (4.1). Thus, functional analysis no more enables us to predict than it enables us to explain the occurrence of a particular one of the items by which a given functional requirement can be met.

Second, even the much less ambitious explanatory schema (4.3) cannot readily be put to predictive use; for the derivation of the weak conclusion (*e*) relies on the premise (*a*); and if we wish to infer (*e*) with respect to some future time *t*, that premise is not available, for we do not know whether *s* will or will not be functioning adequately at that time. For example, consider a person developing increasingly severe anxieties, and suppose that a necessary condition for his adequate functioning is that his anxiety be bound by neurotic symptoms, or be overcome by other means. Can we predict that one or another of the modes of "adjustment" in the class *I* thus roughly characterized will actually come to pass? Clearly not, for we do not know whether the person in question will in fact continue to function adequately or will suffer some more or less serious breakdown, perhaps to the point of self-destruction.

It is of interest to note here that a somewhat similar limitation exists also for the predictive use of nomological explanations, even in the most advanced branches of science. For example, if we are to predict, by means of the laws of classical mechanics, the state in which a given mechanical system will be at a specified future time *t*, it does not suffice to know the state of the system at some earlier time t_0, say the present; we also need information about the boundary conditions during the time interval from t_0 to *t*, i.e., about the external influences affecting the system during that time. Similarly, the "prediction," in our first example, that the water level in the beaker will remain unchanged as the ice melts assumes that the temperature of the surrounding air will remain constant, let us say, and that there will be no disturbing influences such as an earthquake or a person upsetting the beaker. Again when we predict for an object dropped from the top of the Empire State Building that it will strike the ground about eight seconds later, we assume that during the period of its fall, the object is acted upon by no forces other than the gravitational attraction of the earth. In a full and explicit formulation then, nomological predictions such as these would have to include among their premises statements specifying the boundary conditions obtaining from t_0 up to the time *t* to which the prediction refers. This shows that even the laws and theories of the physical sciences do not actually enable us to predict certain aspects of the future exclusively on the basis of certain aspects of the present: the prediction also requires certain assumptions about the future. But in many cases of nomological prediction, there are good inductive grounds, available at t_0, for the assumption that during the time interval in question the system under study will be practically "closed," i.e., not subject to significant outside interference (this case is illustrated, for example, by the prediction of eclipses) or that the boundary conditions will be of a specified kind—a situation illustrated by predictions of events occurring under experimentally controlled conditions.

The predictive use of (4.3) likewise requires a premise concerning the future, namely (*a*); but there is often considerable uncertainty as to whether (*a*) will in fact prove to be true. Furthermore, if in a particular instance there should be good inductive grounds for considering (*a*) as true, the forecast yielded by (4.3) is still rather weak; for the argument then leads from the inductively warranted assumption that the system will be properly functioning at *t* to the "prediction" that a certain condition *n*, which is empirically necessary for such functioning, will be satisfied at *t* in some way or other.

The need to include assumptions about the future among the premises of predictive arguments can be avoided, in nomological predictions as well as in those based on functional analysis, if we are satisfied with predictive conclusions which are not categorical, but only conditional, or hypothetical, in character. For example, (4.3) may be replaced by the following argument, in which premise (*a*) is avoided at the price of conditionalizing the conclusion:

(5.1)

    (*b*) System *s* functions adequately in a setting of kind *c* only if condition *n* is satisfied

    (*c*′) *I* is the class of empirically sufficient conditions for *n* in the context determined by *s* and *c*; and *I* is not empty

    (*d*″) If *s* functions adequately in a setting of kind *c* at time *t*, then some one of the items in class *I* is present in *s* at *t*

This possibility deserves mention because it seems that at least some of the claims made by advocates of functional analysis may be construed as asserting no more than that functional analysis permits such conditional predictions. This may be the intent, for example, of Malinowski's claim: "If such [a functional] analysis discloses to us that, taking an individual culture as a coherent whole, we can state a number of general determinants to which it has to conform, we shall be able to produce a number of predictive statements as guides for field-research, as yardsticks for comparative treatment, and as common measures in the process of cultural adaptation and change." [23] The statements specifying the determinants in question would presumably take the form of premises of type (*b*); and the "predictive statements" would then be hypothetical.

Many of the predictions and generalizations made in the context of functional analysis, however, do not have this conditional form. They proceed from a statement of a functional prerequisite or need to the categorical assertion of the occurrence of some trait, institution, or other item presumably sufficient to meet the requirement in question. Consider, for example, Sait's functional explanation of the emergence of the political boss: "Leadership is necessary; and *since* it does not develop readily within the constitutional framework, the boss provides it in a crude and irresponsible form from the outside." [24] Or take Merton's characterization of one function of the political machine: referring to various specific ways in which the

23 Malinowski, *A Scientific Theory of Culture, and Other Essays, op. cit.,* p. 38.

24 E. M. Sait, "Machine, Political," *Encyclopedia of the Social Sciences,* IX (New York: The Macmillan Company, 1933), p. 659. (Italics supplied.)

political machine can serve the interests of business, he concludes, "These 'needs' of business, as presently constituted, are not adequately provided for by conventional and culturally approved social structures; *consequently*, the extra-legal but more-or-less efficient organization of the political machine comes to provide these services." [25] Each of these arguments, which are rather typical of the functionalist approach, is an inference from the existence of a certain functional prerequisite to the categorical assertion that the prerequisite will be satisfied in some way. What is the basis of the inferential claims suggested by the words, 'since' and 'consequently' in the passages just quoted? When we say that *since* the ice cube was put into warm water it melted; or that the current was turned on, and *consequently*, the ammeter in the circuit responded, these inferences can be explicated and justified by reference to certain general laws of which the particular cases at hand are simply special instances; and the logic of the inferences can be exhibited by putting them into the form of the schema (2.1). Similarly, each of the two functionalist arguments under consideration clearly seems to presuppose a general principle to the effect that, within certain limits of tolerance or adaptability, a system of the kind under analysis will—either invariably or with high probability—satisfy, by developing appropriate traits, the various functional requirements (necessary conditions for its continued adequate operation) that may arise from changes in its internal state or in its environment. Any assertion of this kind, no matter whether of strictly universal or of statistical form, will be called a (*general*) *hypothesis of self-regulation*.

Unless functional analyses of the kind just illustrated are construed as implicitly proposing or invoking suitable hypotheses of self-regulation, it remains quite unclear what connections the expressions 'since,' 'consequently,' and others of the same character are meant to indicate, and how the existence of those connections in a given case is to be objectively established.

Conversely, if a precise hypothesis of self-regulation for systems of a specified kind is set forth, then it becomes possible to explain, and to predict categorically, the satisfaction of certain functional requirements simply on the basis of information concerning antecedent needs; and the hypothesis can then be objectively tested by an empirical check of its predictions. Take, for example, the statement that if a hydra is cut into several pieces, most of these will grow into complete hydras again. This statement may be considered as a hypothesis concerning a specific kind of self-regulation in a particular kind of biological system. It can clearly be used for explanatory and predictive purposes, and indeed the success of the predictions it yields confirms it to a high degree.

We see, then, that whenever functional analysis is to serve as a basis for categorical prediction or for generalizations of the type quoted from Sait

25 Merton, *op. cit.*, p. 76. (Italics supplied.)

and from Merton, it is of crucial importance to establish appropriate hypotheses of self-regulation in an objectively testable form.

The functionalist literature does contain some explicitly formulated generalizations of the kind here referred to. Merton, for example, after citing the passage from Sait quoted above, comments thus: "Put in more generalized terms, *the functional deficiencies of the official structure generate an alternative (unofficial) structure to fulfill existing needs somewhat more effectively.*" [26] This statement seems clearly intended to make explicit a hypothesis of self-regulation that might be said to underlie Sait's specific analysis and to provide the rationale for his 'since.' Another hypothesis of this kind is suggested by Radcliffe-Brown: 'it may be that we should say that . . . a society that is thrown into a condition of functional disunity or inconsistency . . . will not die, except in such comparatively rare instances as an Australian tribe overwhelmed by the white man's destructive force, but will continue to struggle toward . . . some kind of social health. . . ." [27]

But, as was briefly suggested above, a formulation proposed as a hypothesis of self-regulation can serve as a basis for explanation or prediction only if it is sufficiently definite to permit objective empirical test. And indeed many of the leading representatives of functional analysis have expressed their concern to develop hypothesis and theories which meet this rquirement. Malinowski, for example, in his essay significantly entitled "A Scientific Theory of Culture," insists that "each scientific theory must start from and lead to observation. It must be inductive and it must be verifiable by experience. In other words, it must refer to human experiences which can be defined, which are public, that is, accessible to any and every observer, and which are recurrent, hence fraught with inductive generalizations, that is, predictive." [28] Similarly, Murray and Kluckhohn have this to say about the basic objective of their functionally oriented theory, and indeed about any scientific "formulation," of personality: "the general purposes of formulation are three: (1) to *explain* past and present events; (2) to *predict* future events (the conditions being specified); and (3) to serve, if required, as a basis for the selection of effective measures of *control.*" [29]

Unfortunately, however, the formulations offered in the context of concrete functional analyses quite often fall short of these general standards. Among the various ways in which those conditions may be violated, two call for special consideration because of their pervasiveness and central importance in functional analysis. They will be referred to as (i) *inadequate specification of scope,* and (ii) *nonempirical use of functionalist key terms* (such as 'need,' 'functional requirement,' 'adaptation,' and others). We will

[26] Merton, *op. cit.*, p. 73. (Author's italics.)

[27] Radcliffe-Brown, *op. cit.*, p. 183.

[28] Malinowski, *A Scientific Theory of Culture, and Other Essays, op. cit.*, p. 67.

[29] Henry A. Murray and Clyde Kluckhohn, "Outline of a Conception of Personality," in Clyde Kluckhohn and Henry A. Murray, eds., *Personality in Nature, Society, and Culture* (New York: Alfred A. Knopf, Inc., 1950), pp. 3–32; quotation from p. 7; authors' italics.

consider these two defects in turn: the former in the balance of the present section, the latter in the next.

Inadequate specification of scope consists in failure to indicate clearly the kind of system to which the hypothesis refers, or the range of situations (the limits of tolerance) within which those systems are claimed to develop traits that will satisfy their functional requirements. Merton's formulation, for example, does not specify the class of social systems and of situations to which the proposed generalization is meant to apply; as it stands, therefore, it cannot be put to an empirical test or to any predictive use.

The generalization tentatively set forth by Radcliffe-Brown has a similar shortcoming. Ostensibly, it refers to any society whatever, but the conditions under which social survival is claimed to occur are qualified by a highly indefinite "except" clause, which precludes the possibility of any reasonably clear-cut test. The clause might even be used to protect the proposed generalization against any conceivable disconfirmation: If a particular social group should "die," this very fact might be held to show that the disruptive forces were as overwhelming as in the case of the Australian tribe mentioned by Radcliffe-Brown. Systematic use of this methodological strategy would, of course, turn the hypothesis into a covert tautology. This would ensure its truth, but at the price of depriving it of empirical content: thus construed, the hypothesis can yield no explanation or prediction whatever.

A similar comment is applicable to the following pronouncement by Malinowski, in which we italicize the dubious qualifying clause: "When we consider any culture *which is not on the point of breaking down or completely disrupted, but which is a normal going concern,* we find that need and response are directly related and tuned up to each other." [30]

To be sure, Radcliffe-Brown's and Malinowski's formulations do not *have to* be construed as covert tautologies, and their authors no doubt intended them as empirical assertions; but, in this case, the vagueness of the qualifying clauses still deprives them of the status of definite empirical hypothesis that might be used for explanation or prediction.

6. The Empirical Import of Functionalist Terms and Hypotheses

A second flaw that may vitiate the scientific role of a proposed hypothesis of self-regulation consists in using key terms of functional analysis, such as 'need' and 'adequate (proper) functioning' [31] in a nonempirical manner, i.e.,

---

30 Malinowski, *A Scientific Theory of Culture, and Other Essays, op. cit.,* p. 94.

31 In accordance with a practice followed widely in contemporary logic, we will understand by terms certain kinds of words or other linguistic expressions, and we will say that a term expresses or signifies a concept. For example, we will say that the term 'need' signifies the concept of need. As this illustration shows, we refer to, or mention, a linguistic expression by using a name for it which is formed by simply enclosing the expression in single quotes.

without giving them a clear "operational definition," or more generally, without specifying objective criteria of application for them.[32] If functionalist terms are used in this manner, then the sentences containing them have no clear empirical meaning; they lead to no specific predictions and thus cannot be put to an objective test; nor, of course, can they be used for explanatory purposes.

A consideration of this point is all the more important here because the functionalist key terms occur not only in hypotheses of self-regulation, but also in functionalist sentences of various other kinds, such as those of the types (*a*), (*b*), and (*d''*) in (4.1), (4.3), and (5.1). Nonempirical use of functionalist terms may, therefore, bar sentences of these various kinds from the status of scientific hypotheses. We turn now to some examples.

Consider first the terms 'functional prerequisite' and 'need,' which are used as more or less synonymous in the functionalist literature, and which serve to define the term 'function' itself. "Embedded in every functional analysis is some conception, tacit or expressed, of the functional requirements of the system under observation,"[33] and indeed, "a definition [of function] is provided by showing that human institutions, as well as partial activities within these, are related to primary, that is, biological, or derived, that is, cultural needs. Function means, therefore, always the satisfaction of a need. . . ."[34]

How is this concept of need defined? Malinowski gives an explicit answer: "By need, then, I understand the system of conditions in the human organism, in the cultural setting, and in the relation of both to the natural environment, which are sufficient and necessary for the survival of group and organism."[35] This definition sounds clear, and straightforward; yet it is not even quite in accord with Malinowski's own use of the concept of need. For he distinguishes, very plausibly, a considerable number of different needs, which fall into two major groups: primary biological needs and derivative cultural ones; the latter include "technological, economic, legal, and even magical, religious, or ethical"[36] needs. But if every single one of these needs did actually represent not only a necessary condition of survival but also a sufficient one, then clearly the satisfaction of just one need would suffice to ensure survival, and the other needs could not constitute necessary conditions of survival at all. It seems reasonable to assume, therefore, that what Malinowski intended was to construe the needs of a group as a

---

[32] A general discussion of the nature and significance of "operational" criteria of application for the terms used in empirical science, and references to further literature on the subject, may be found in C. G. Hempel, *Fundamentals of Concept Formation in Empirical Science* (University of Chicago Press, 1952), sections 5–8; and in the symposium papers on the present state of operationalism by G. Bergmann, P. W. Bridgman, A. Grunbaum, C. G. Hempel, R. B. Lindsay, H. Margenau, and R. J. Seeger, which form chapter II of Philipp G. Frank, ed., *The Validation of Scientific Theories* (Boston: The Beacon Press, 1956).

[33] Merton, *op. cit.*, p. 52.

[34] Malinowski, *A Scientific Theory of Culture, and other Essays*, *op. cit.*, p. 159.

[35] Malinowski, *ibid.*, p. 90.

[36] Malinowski, *ibid.*, p. 172; see also *ibid.*, pp. 91 ff.

set of conditions which are individually necessary and jointly sufficient for its survival.[37]

However, this correction of a minor logical flaw does not remedy a more serious defect of Malinowski's definition, which lies in the deceptive appearance of clarity of the phrase "survival of group and organism." In reference to a biological organism, the term 'survival' has a fairly clear meaning, though even here, there is need for further clarification. For when we speak of biological needs or requirements—e.g., the minimum daily requirements, for human adults, of various vitamins and minerals—we construe these, not as conditions of just the barest survival but as conditions of persistence in, or return to, a "normal," or "healthy" state, or to a state in which the system is a "properly functioning whole." For the sake of objective testability of functionalist hypotheses, it is essential, therefore, that definitions of needs or functional prerequisites be supplemented by reasonably clear and objectively applicable criteria of what is to be considered a healthy state or a normal working order of the systems under consideration; and that the vague and sweeping notion of survival then be construed in the relativized sense of survival in a healthy state as specified. Otherwise, there is definite danger that different investigators will use the concept of functional prerequisite—and hence also that of function—in different ways, and with valuational overtones corresponding to their diverse conceptions of what are the most "essential" characteristics of "genuine" survival for a system of the kind under consideration.

Functional analyses in psychology, sociology, and anthropology are even more urgently in need of objective empirical criteria of the kind here referred to; for the characterization of needs as necessary conditions of psychological or emotional survival for an individual, or of survival of a group is so vague as to permit, and indeed invite, quite diverse subjective interpretations.

Some authors characterize the concept of functional prerequisite or the concept of function without making use of the term 'survival' with its misleading appearance of clarity. Merton, for example, states: *"Functions* are those observed consequences which make for the adaptation or adjustment of a given system; and *dysfunctions,* those observed consequences which lessen the adaptation or adjustment of the system."[38] And Radcliffe-Brown characterizes the function of an item as its contribution to the maintenance of a certain kind of unity of a social system, "which we may speak of as a

---

[37] In some of his statements Malinowski discards, by implication, even the notion of function as satisfaction of a condition that is at least *necessary* for the survival of group or organism. For example, in the essay containing the two passages just quoted in the text, Malinowski comments as follows on the function of some complex cultural achievements: "Take the airplane, the submarine, or the steam engine. Obviously, man does not need to fly, nor yet to keep company with fishes, and move about within a medium for which he is neither anatomically adjusted nor physiologically prepared. In defining, therefore, the function of any of those contrivances, we can not predicate the true course of their appearance in any terms of metaphysical necessity." (*Ibid.*, pp. 118–19.)

[38] Merton, *op. cit.*, p. 51. (Author's italics.)

functional unity. We may define it as a condition in which all parts of the social system work together with a sufficient degree of harmony or internal consistency, i.e., without producing persistent conflicts which can neither be resolved nor regulated." [39] But like the definitions in terms of survival, these alternative characterizations, though suggestive, are far from giving clear empirical meanings to the key terms of functional analysis. The concepts of adjustment and adaptation, for example, require specification of some standard; otherwise, they have no definite meaning and are in danger of being used tautologically or else subjectively, with valuational overtones.

Tautological use could be based on construing *any* response of a given system as an adjustment, in which case it becomes a trivial truth that any system will adjust itself to any set of circumstances. Some instances of functional analysis seem to come dangerously close to this procedure, as is illustrated by the following assertion: "Thus we are provided with an explanation of suicide and of numerous other apparently antibiological effects as so many forms of relief from intolerable suffering. Suicide does not have *adaptive* (survival) value but it does have *adjustive* value for the organism. Suicide is *functional* because it abolishes painful tension." [40]

Or consider Merton's formulation of one of the assumptions of functional analysis: ". . . when *the net balance of the aggregate of consequences* of an existing social structure is clearly dysfunctional, there develops a strong and insistent pressure for change." [41] In the absence of clear empirical criteria of adaptation and thus of dysfunction, it is possible to treat this formulation as a covert tautology and thus to render it immune to empirical disconfirmation. Merton is quite aware of such danger: in another context he remarks that the notion of functional requirements of a given system "remains one of the cloudiest and empirically most debatable concepts in functional theory. As utilized by sociologists, the concept of functional requirement tends to be tautological or *ex post facto.*" [42] Similar warnings against tautological use and against *ad hoc* generalizations about functional prerequisites have been voiced by other writers, such as Malinowski [43] and Parsons.[44]

In the absence of empirical criteria of adjustment or adaptation, there is also the danger of each investigator's projecting into those concepts (and thus also into the concept of function) his own ethical standards of what would constitute a "proper" or "good" adjustment of a given system—a danger which has been pointed out very clearly by Levy.[45] This procedure

[39] Radcliffe-Brown, *op. cit.,* p. 181.
[40] Murray and Kluckhohn, *op. cit.,* p. 15 (Author's italics.)
[41] Merton, *op. cit.,* p. 40.
[42] Merton, *op. cit.,* p. 52.
[43] See, for example, Malinowski, *A Scientific Theory of Culture, and Other Essays, op. cit.,* pp. 169–70; but also compare this with pp. 118–19 of the same work.
[44] See, for example, T. Parsons, *The Social System* (New York: The Free Press, 1951), 29, n. 4.
[45] Marion J. Levy, Jr., *The Structure of Society* (Princeton: Princeton University Press, 1952), 76 ff.

would obviously deprive functionalist hypotheses of the status of precise objectively testable scientific assertions. And, as Merton notes, "If theory is to be productive, it must be sufficiently *precise* to be *determinate*. Precision is an integral element of the criterion of *testability*." [46]

It is essential, then, for functional analysis as a scientific procedure that its key concepts be explicitly construed as relative to some standard of survival or adjustment. This standard has to be specified for each functional analysis, and it will usually vary from case to case. In the functional study of a given system *s*, the standard would be indicated by specifying a certain class or range *R* of possible states of *s*, with the understanding that *s* is to be considered as "surviving in proper working order," or as "adjusting properly under changing conditions" just in case *s* remains in, or upon disturbance returns to, some state within the range *R*. A need, or functional requirement, of system *s* relative to *R* is then a necessary condition for the system's remaining in, or returning to, a state in *R*; and the function, relative to *R*, of an item *i* in *s* consists in *i*'s effecting the satisfaction of some such functional requirement.

In the field of biology, Sommerhoff's analysis of adaptation, appropriateness, and related concepts, is an excellent illustration of a formal study in which the relativization of the central functionalist concepts is entirely explicit.[47] The need of such relativization is made clear also by Nagel, who points out that "the claim that a given change is functional or dysfunctional must be understood as being relative to a specified G (or sets of G's)," [48] where the G's are traits whose preservation serves as the defining standard of adjustment or survival. In sociology, Levy's analysis of the structure of society [49] clearly construes the functionalist key concepts as relative in the sense just outlined.

Only if the key concepts of functional analysis are thus relativized can hypotheses involving them have the status of determinate and objectively testable assumptions or assertions; only then can those hypotheses enter significantly into arguments such as those schematized in (4.1), (4.3), and (5.1).

But although such relativization may give definite empirical content to the functionalist hypotheses that serve as premises or conclusions in those arguments, it leaves the explanatory and predictive import of the latter as limited as we found it in sections 4 and 5; for our verdict on the logical force

[46] R. K. Merton, "The Bearing of Sociological Theory on Empirical Research" in Merton, *Social Theory and Social Structure, op. cit.,* pp. 85–101; quotation from 98. (Author's italics) [Reprinted in this volume as Selection 2.6.]

[47] See G. Sommerhoff, *Analytical Biology* (New York: Oxford University Press, Inc., 1950).

[48] Nagel, "A Formalization of Functionalism," *op. cit.,* p. 269. See also the concluding paragraph of the same essay (pp. 282–83).

[49] Levy speaks of eufunction and dysfunction of a unit (i.e., a system) and characterizes these concepts as relative to "the unit as defined." He points out that relativization is necessary "because it is to the definition of the unit that one must turn to determine whether or not 'adaptation or adjustment' making for the persistence or lack of persistence of the unit is taking place." (Levy, *ibid.,* pp. 77–78).

of those arguments depended solely on their formal structure and not on the meaning of their premises and conclusions.

It remains true, therefore, even for a properly relativized version of functional analysis, that its explanatory force is rather limited; in particular, it does not provide an explanation of why a particular item *i* rather than some functional equivalent of it occurs in system *s*. And the predictive significance of functional analysis is practically nil—except in those cases where suitable hypotheses of self-regulation can be established. Such a hypothesis would be to the effect that within a specified range *C* of circumstances, a given system *s* (or: any system of a certain kind *S*, of which *s* is an instance) is self-regulating relative to a specified range *R* of states; i.e., that after a disturbance which moves *s* into a state outside *R*, but which does not shift the internal and external circumstances of *s* out of the specified range *C*, the system *s* will return to a state in *R*. A system satisfying a hypothesis of this kind might be called *self-regulating with respect to R*.

Biological systems offer many illustrations of such self-regulation. For example, we mentioned earlier the regenerative ability of a hydra. Consider the case, then, where a more or less large segment of the animal is removed and the rest grows into a complete hydra again. The class *R* here consists of those states in which the hydra is complete; the characterization of range *C* would have to include (i) a specification of the temperature and the chemical composition of the water in which a hydra will perform its regenerative feat (clearly, this will not be just one unique composition, but a class of different ones: the concentrations of various salts, for example, will each be allowed to take some value within a specified, and perhaps narrow, range; the same will hold of the temperature of the water); and (ii) a statement as to the kind and size of segment that may be removed without preventing regeneration.

It will no doubt be one of the most important tasks of functional analysis in psychology and the social sciences to ascertain to what extent such phenomena of self-regulation can be found, and can be represented by corresponding laws.

7. Functional Analysis and Teleology

Whatever specific laws might be discovered by research along these lines, the kind of explanation and prediction made possible by them does not differ in its logical character from that of the physical sciences.

It is true that hypotheses of self-regulation, which would be the results of successful functionalist research, appear to have a teleological character since they assert that within specified conditions systems of some particular kind will tend toward a state within the class *R*, which thus assumes the appearance of a final cause determining the behavior of the system.

But, first of all, it would be simply untenable to say of a system *s* which is self-regulating with respect to *R* that the future event of its return to (a state in) R is a "final cause" which determines its present behavior. For even if s is self-regulating with respect to R and if it has been shifted into a state outside R, the future event of its return to R may never come about: in the process of its return toward R, s may be exposed to further disturbances, which may fall outside the permissible range C and lead to the destruction of s. For example, in a hydra that has just had a tentacle removed, certain regenerative processes will promptly set in; but these cannot be explained teleologically by reference to a final cause consisting in the future event of the hydra being complete again. For that event may never actually come about since in the process of regeneration, and before its completion, the hydra may suffer new, and irreparably severe, damage, and may die. Thus, what accounts for the present changes of a self-regulating system s is not the "future event" of s being in R, but rather the *present disposition* of s to return to R; and it is this disposition that is expressed by the hypothesis of self-regulation governing the system s.

Whatever teleological character may be attributed to a functionalist explanation or prediction invoking (properly relativized) hypotheses of self-regulation lies merely in the circumstance that such hypotheses assert a tendency of certain systems to maintain, or return to, a certain kind of *state*. But such laws attributing, as it were, a characteristic goal-directed behavior to systems of specified kinds are by no means alien to physics and chemistry. On the contrary, it is these latter fields which provide the most adequately understood instances of self-regulating systems and corresponding laws. For example, a liquid in a vessel will return to a state of equilibrium, with its surface horizontal, after a mechanical disturbance; an elastic band, after being stretched (within certain limits), will return to its original shape when it is released. Various systems controlled by negative feedback devices, such as a steam engine whose speed is regulated by a governor, or a homing torpedo, or a plane guided by an automatic pilot, show, within specifiable limits, regulation with respect to some particular class of states.

In all of these cases, the laws of self-regulation exhibited by the systems in question are capable of explanation by subsumption under general laws of a more obviously causal form. But this is not even essential, for the laws of self-regulation themselves are causal in the broad sense of asserting that for systems of a specified kind, any one of a class of different "initial states" (any one of the permissible states of disturbance) will lead to the same kind of final state. Indeed as our earlier formulations show, functionalist hypotheses, including those of self-regulation, can be expressed without the use of any teleological phraseology at all.[50]

[50] For illuminating discussions of further issues concerning "teleological explanation," especially with respect to self-regulating systems, see R. B. Braithwaite, *Scientific Explanation* (Cambridge: Cambridge University Press, 1953), chapter X; and E. Nagel, "Teleological Explanation and Teleological Systems" in S. Ratner, ed., *Vision and Action: Essays in Honor of Horace Kallen on His Seventieth Birthday* (New Brunswick, N.J.: Rutgers University Press, 1953); reprinted in H. Feigl and M. Brodbeck, eds., *Readings in the Philosophy of Science* (New York: Appleton-Century-Crofts, Inc., 1953).

There are, then, no systematic grounds for attributing to functional analysis a character *sui generis* not found in the hypotheses and theories of the natural sciences and in the explanations and predictions based on them. Yet, psychologically, the idea of function often remains closely associated with that of purpose, and some functionalist writing has no doubt encouraged this association, by using a phraseology which attributes to the self-regulatory behavior of a given system practically the character of a purposeful action. For example, Freud, speaking of the relation of neurotic symptoms to anxiety, uses strongly teleological language when he says that "the symptoms are created in order to remove or rescue the ego from the situation of danger"; [51] the quotations given in section 3 provide further illustrations. Some instructive examples of sociological and anthropological writings which confound the concepts of function and purpose are listed by Merton, who is very explicit and emphatic in rejecting this practice.[52]

It seems likely that precisely this psychological association of the concept of function with that of purpose, though systematically unwarranted, accounts to a large extent for the appeal and the apparent plausibility of functional analysis as a mode of explanation; for it seems to enable us to "understand" self-regulatory phenomena of all kinds in terms of purposes or motives, in much the same way in which we "understand" our own purposive behavior and that of others. Now, explanation by reference to motives, objectives, or the like may be perfectly legitimate in the case of purposive behavior and its effects. An explanation of this kind would be causal in character, listing among the causal antecedents of the given action, or of its outcome, certain purposes or motives on the part of the agent, as well as his beliefs as to the best means available to him for attaining his objectives. This kind of information about purposes and beliefs might even serve as a starting point in explaining a self-regulatory feature in a human artifact. For example, in an attempt to account for the presence of the governor in a steam engine, it may be quite reasonable to refer to the purpose its inventor intended it to serve, to his beliefs concerning matters of physics, and to the technological facilities available to him. Such an account, it should be noted, might conceivably give a probabilistic explanation for the presence of the governor, but it would not explain why it functioned as a speed-regulating safety device: to explain this latter fact, we would have to refer to the construction of the machine and to the laws of physics, not to the intentions and beliefs of the designer. (An explanation by reference to motives and beliefs can be given as well for certain items which do not, in fact, function as intended; e.g., some superstitious practices, unsuccessful flying machines, ineffective economic policies, etc.) Furthermore—and this is the crucial point in our context—for most of the self-regulatory phenomena that come within the purview of functional analysis, the attribution of purposes is an illegitimate transfer of the concept of purpose from its

51 Freud, *op. cit.*, p. 112.
52 Merton, "Manifest and Latent Functions," *op. cit.*, pp. 23–25, 60 ff.

domain of significant applicability to a much wider domain, where it is devoid of objective empirical import. In the context of purposive behavior of individuals or groups, there are various methods of testing whether the assumed motives or purposes are indeed present in a given situation; interviewing the agents in question might be one rather direct way, and there are various alternative "operational" procedures of a more indirect character. Hence, explanatory hypotheses in terms of purposes are here capable of reasonably objective test. But such empirical criteria are lacking in other cases of self-regulating systems, and the attribution of purposes to them has therefore no scientific meaning. Yet, it tends to encourage the illusion that a profound understanding is achieved, that we gain insight into the nature of these processes by likening them to a type of behavior with which we are thoroughly familiar from daily experience. Consider, for example, the law of "adaptation to an obvious end" set forth by the sociologist L. Gumplowicz with the claim that it holds both in the natural and the social domains. For the latter, it asserts that "every social growth, every social entity, serves a definite end, however much its worth and morality may be questioned. For the universal law of adaptation signifies simply that no expenditure of effort, no change of condition, is purposeless on any domain of phenomena. Hence, the inherent reasonableness of all social facts and conditions must be conceded." [53] There is a strong suggestion here that the alleged law enables us to understand social dynamics in close analogy to purposive behavior aimed at the achievement of some end. Yet that law is completely devoid of empirical meaning since no empirical interpretation has been given to such key terms as 'end,' 'purposeless,' and 'inherent reasonableness' for the contexts to which it is applied. The "law" asserts nothing whatever, therefore, and cannot possibly explain any social (or other) phenomena.

Gumplowicz's book antedates the writings of Malinowski and other leading functionalists by several decades, and certainly these more recent writers have been more cautious and sophisticated in stating their ideas. Yet, there are certain quite central assertions in the newer functionalist literature which are definitely reminiscent of Gumplowicz's formulation in that they suggest an understanding of functional phenomena in the image of deliberate purposive behavior or of systems working in accordance with a preconceived design. The following statements might illustrate this point: "[Culture] is a system of objects, activities, and attitudes in which every part exists as a means to an end," [54] and "The functional view of culture insists therefore upon the principle that in every type of civilization, every custom, material object, idea and belief fulfills some vital function, has some task to accomplish, represents an indispensable part within a working

53 L. Gumplowicz, *The Outlines of Sociology;* translated by F. W. Moore (Philadelphia: American Academy of Political and Social Science, 1899), pp. 79–80.

54 Malinowski, *A Scientific Theory of Culture, and Other Essays, op. cit.,* p. 150.

whole." [55] These statements express what Merton, in a critical discussion, calls the postulate of universal functionalism.[56] Merton qualifies this postulate as premature; [57] the discussion presented in the previous section shows that, in the absence of a clear empirical interpretation of the functionalist key terms, it is even less than that, namely, empirically vacuous. Yet formulations of this kind may evoke a sense of insight and understanding by likening sociocultural developments to purposive behavior and in this sense reducing them to phenomena with which we feel thoroughly familiar. But scientific explanation and understanding are not simply a reduction to the familiar: otherwise, science would not seek to explain familiar phenomena at all; besides, the most significant advances in our scientific understanding of the world are often achieved by means of new theories which, like quantum theory, assume some quite unfamiliar kinds of objects or processes which cannot be directly observed, and which sometimes are endowed with strange and even seemingly paradoxical characteristics. A class of phenomena has been scientifically understood to the extent that they can be fitted into a testable, and adequately confirmed, theory or a system of laws; and the merits of functional analysis will eventually have to be judged by its ability to lead to this kind of understanding.

8. The Heuristic Role of Functional Analysis

The preceding considerations suggest that what is often called "functionalism" is best viewed, not as a body of doctrine or theory advancing tremendously general principles such as the principle of universal functionalism, but rather as a program for research guided by certain heuristic maxims or "working hypotheses." The idea of universal functionalism, for example, which becomes untenable when formulated as a sweeping empirical law or theoretical principle, might more profitably be construed as expressing a directive for inquiry, namely to search for specific self-regulatory aspects of social and other systems and to examine the ways in which various traits of a system might contribute to its particular mode of self-regulation. (A similar construal as heuristic maxims for empirical research might be put upon the "general axioms of functionalism" suggested by Malinowski, and considered by him as demonstrated by all the pertinent empirical evidence.[58])

In biology, for example, the contribution of the functionalist approach does not consist in the sweeping assertion that all traits of any organism satisfy some need and thus serve some function; in this generality, the claim

---

[55] Malinowski, "Anthropology," *op. cit.,* p. 133.
[56] Merton, "Manifest and Latent Functions," *op. cit.,* pp. 30 ff.
[57] *Ibid.,* p. 31.
[58] Malinowski, *A Scientific Theory of Culture, and Other Essays, op. cit.,* p. 150.

is apt to be either meaningless or covertly tautologous or empirically false (depending on whether the concept of need is given no clear empirical interpretation at all, or is handled in a tautologizing fashion, or is given a specific empirical interpretation). Instead, functional studies in biology have been aimed at showing, for example, how in different species, specific homeostatic and regenerative processes contribute to the maintenance and development of the living organism; and they have gone on (i) to examine more and more precisely the nature and limits of those processes (this amounts basically to establishing various specific empirical hypotheses or laws of self-regulation), and (ii) to explore the underlying physiological or physicochemical mechanisms, and the laws governing them, in an effort to achieve a more thorough theoretical understanding of the phenomena at hand.[59] Similar trends exist in the study of functional aspects of psychological processes, including, for example, symptom formation in neurosis.[60]

Functional analysis in psychology and in the social sciences no less than in biology may thus be conceived, at least ideally, as a program of inquiry aimed at determining the respects and the degrees in which various systems are self-regulating in the sense here indicated. This conception is clearly reflected in Nagel's essay, "A Formalization of Functionalism," [61] which develops an analytic scheme inspired by, and similar to, Sommerhoff's formal analysis of self-regulation in biology [62] and uses it to exhibit and clarify the structure of functional analysis, especially in sociology and anthropology.

The functionalist mode of approach has proved illuminating, suggestive, and fruitful in many contexts. If the advantages it has to offer are to be reaped in full, it seems desirable and indeed necessary to pursue the investigation of specific functional relationships to the point where they can be expressed in terms of reasonably precise and objectively testable hypotheses. At least initially, these hypotheses will likely be of quite limited scope. But this would simply parallel the present situation in biology, where the kinds of self-regulation, and the uniformities they exhibit, vary from species to species. Eventually, such "empirical generalizations" of limited scope might provide a basis for a more general theory of self-regulating systems. To what extent these objectives can be reached cannot be decided in *a priori* fashion by logical analysis or philosophical reflection: the answer has to be found by intensive and rigorous scientific research.

[59] An account of this kind of approach to homeostatic processes in the human body will be found in Walter B. Cannon, *The Wisdom of the Body* (New York: W. W. Norton & Company, Inc.; revised edition 1939).

[60] See, for example, J. Dollard and N. E. Miller, *Personality and Psychotherapy* (New York: McGraw-Hill Book Company, Inc., 1950), chapter XI, "How Symptoms Are Learned," and note particularly pp. 165–66.

[61] Nagel, "A Formalization of Functionalism," *op. cit.* See also the more general discussion of functional analysis included in Nagel's paper, "Concept and Theory Formation in the Social Sciences," in *Science, Language, and Human Rights;* American Philosophical Association, Eastern Division, Volume 1 (Philadelphia: University of Pennsylvania Press, 1952), pp. 43–64. Reprinted in J. L. Jarrett and S. M. McMurrin, eds., *Contemporary Philosophy* (New York: Holt, Rinehart & Winston, Inc., 1954).

[62] Sommerhoff, *op. cit.*

[11] Purpose, Function, Scientific Explanation *

GUSTAV BERGMANN

Speaking nonscientifically about certain states of affairs, or facts, or situations, we often use the two words 'purpose' and 'function.' Call these facts the critical facts. Call the two words, 'function' and 'purpose,' the two critical words. The problems I wish to talk about all arise in connection with three questions. *First.* Can the scientist, speaking scientifically, do justice to the critical facts? *Second.* Assuming that he can, must he in speaking about them himself use the two critical words? *Third.* Assuming that he need not use them, may he use them?

The difference between the second and the third question hangs by the difference between must and may. Must he use them? May he use them? To appreciate it one has to appreciate that when we speak scientifically we are more self-conscious, more critical about our vocabulary than when we don't. Some words the scientist accepts as basic or unproblematic. Philosophers, when speaking about this situation in science, say that the scientist accepts those words as undefined. Any other word he admits into this vocabulary only if its use has in certain ways been tied to or hooked up with the use of the basic ones. The most obvious way of such tying or hooking is definition. In scientific discourse the distinction between these two kinds of words, undefined or basic and defined, is clear-cut. The idea of the distinction applies to all kinds of discourse. Let us see what it does for us in the case of 'purpose.'

We all speak nonscientifically about states of mind, our own and others'. Call this kind of talk mental discourse. In mental discourse the word 'purpose' is indispensable. That is not to say that we must use just this word. We may instead speak of our goals, of what we want, what we intend, and so on. We may, as one now says, use any of a whole family of words. By choosing either this or that we are able to express many subtle differences. But the logic of any of these several words is sufficiently similar to that of any other

Reprinted with permission from *Acta Sociologica*, 5, 1962, 225–238.

* This is the text of a lecture delivered before the sociological seminar at the University of Lund, during tenure of a visiting professorship in the Swedish universities.

to make it safe for us to ignore those subtle differences. What matters to us is merely that in mental discourse at least one member of that family is indispensable. It suits my purposes best to cast 'purpose' in the role of this one indispensable word. That makes states of mind one kind of critical facts. Call them *mental facts* and return to the three questions. With respect to 'purpose,' we can now sharpen the second as follows: Can the scientist do justice to mental facts without himself using 'purpose' as a basic word? Or, equivalently: Can the scientist do justice to mental facts without himself engaging in mental discourse? We cannot go on without first unpacking a certain phrase. What does it mean to do justice to a fact, or to a certain kind or class of facts? Science describes and explains facts. Our question thus becomes two. Can the scientist describe mental facts without himself using 'purpose' as a basic word? Can the scientist explain mental facts without himself using 'purpose' as a basic word?

Call mental discourse the direct description of mental fact. In mental discourse 'purpose' is basic. It follows immediately that the scientist cannot describe all mental facts directly unless he may use 'purpose' as a basic word. That, though, is only one half of the story. The other half starts with a certain hypothesis, the so-called parallelistic hypothesis. If we only knew enough, by way of fact and law, of what according to this hypothesis is there to be known, then we could from the description of the state of a man's body at any given moment infer the description of the state of his mind at that moment. The laws which permit this inference are among the basic laws of nature. Suppose that the hypothesis is true. Suppose also that a scientist knows enough to infer from the present state of Mr. Smith's body that Mr. Smith now has the purpose of getting married. If he so chooses our scientist can then propose the following definition for the phrase 'having the purpose of getting married':

'X has the purpose of getting married' means by definition
'the body of X is in that and that state.'

Notice that he does not define the word 'purpose' but, rather, certain phrases containing it, such as 'having the purpose of getting married,' 'having the purpose of getting rich,' and so on. The result is no less striking. The string of words 'Smith has the purpose of getting married' can now be read in two ways. Or, to say the same thing differently, it may be taken to stand for two sentences. One describes a mental state directly. In it the word 'purpose' is basic. The other describes a bodily state directly. In it the phrase containing the word 'purpose' is defined. Moreover, the two sentences are either both true or both false. In this sense the sentence with the defined phrase may be said to describe the mental state indirectly. Three comments should help to clarify this idea.

First. Mental states cannot be described indirectly unless two conditions are fulfilled. For one, the parallelistic hypothesis must be true. For another, we must know enough of what according to the hypothesis is there to be known, or, as one says, can be known in principle. All the evidence favors the parallelistic hypothesis. None, if properly analysed, is against it. Under the circumstances, the reasonable thing to do is to accept the hypothesis as part of one's frame of reference. Virtually all scientists accept it, either explicitly or implicitly; many philosophers, including myself, except it quite explicitly. So I shall take it for granted that *in principle* mental facts can be described indirectly without the use of 'purpose' as a basic term. The opposite of 'in principle,' as here used, is 'in practice.' That brings us to the second condition. We do at present not know enough. For some elementary situations we probably do possess the indirect descriptions. For all others we have as yet at best definition sketches or logical schemata. Practically, therefore, much of what is now being said about mental facts in the behavior sciences is mental discourse. Nor is there anything wrong with that as long as we are as sober and as cautious as we can and as the principle may well inspire us to be. Some of the so-called behaviorists have caused much unnecessary irritation and confusion by making the principle, which is more than reasonable, into a pretext for criticisms or restrictions, which are not at all reasonable, of our practice.

Second. In the definitions and definitional schemata we now possess, behavior plays a much larger role than the facts of physiology. Speaking of definitions in terms of bodily states rather than in terms of both bodily states and behavior or behavior alone, I did not mean to criticize this practice. Far from so. I merely wanted to call attention to a certain blur in the present use of 'behavior.' Suppose I see a dog moving in the same direction as a hare, the dog behind the hare. Describing the situation as I just did, I describe it in terms of bodily behavior. If, however, I describe it by saying that the dog pursues the hare without being able to define 'pursue' in terms of bodily states and behavior, then I use 'pursue' as it is used in mental discourse. Nor of course will it do to define 'pursue' as meaning 'moving behind the other *in order* to kill.' For behind the two little words 'in order' lurks the basic use of 'purpose.' What holds for pursuing holds equally for all so-called language behavior.

The *third* and last comment brings us back to the last of the three original questions: May the scientist use the critical words? Of course he may use them, as defined words, in the indirect description of the critical facts. Nor does it make any difference in principle if in practice he uses them, as at present he must, in describing the critical facts without being able to eliminate them by means of definitions. More precisely, it makes no difference in principle as long as one accepts the parallelistic frame of reference.

That much for 'purpose' in connection with scientific description. Concerning explanation, the question was: Can the scientist explain mental facts without himself using 'purpose' as a basic word? As it stands, the question is not very clear. To reword it so that it becomes clear, we must first turn our attention to the nature of scientific explanation. It reveals itself most clearly in the case of process knowledge. The earliest instance of such knowledge is Newtonian astronomy.

To possess process knowledge is to know (1) the conditions of closure, (2) a complete set of relevant variables, and (3) the process law. A system is closed if and only if nothing outside of it affects what goes on inside. The pertinent generalization of the idea is that of controlled boundary conditions. Newton's assumption that, for his purposes, the solar system is closed, was borne out by the success of his predictions. The values of the masses, positions, and velocities of the bodies in the system at any given moment, being a complete set of relevant variables, determine what is called the state of the system at this moment. From a state of the system (i.e., the values of all relevant variables at time t_1) any later or earlier state (i.e., the values of all relevant variables at time t_2) can be computed. The formula or formulae that permit the computation are the process law. If the state computed is the later state one speaks of prediction. With one exception, who can predict can explain, and conversely. The exception is the case of cross-section laws, such as those of geometry or the fundamental laws connecting mind and body. In this case no temporal element is involved. The values computed, or, in the nonquantified case, the features inferred and those from which they are inferred are simultaneous. Hence the name, cross-section law. With this obvious exception, to be able to predict a fact, to be able to explain it, and to know its causes are one and the same thing.

Among the features of process explanation two stand out. In principle, the value of *any* variable in the later state depends on, or, in the quite unproblematic mathematical sense of 'function,' is a function of the values of *all* variables of the earlier state. Or, as one says, the variables of the system interact. To have process knowledge is to know all there is to be known about their interaction. This is the *interaction feature* of process explanation. The later state, as a whole and in all details, depends on the earlier state, as a whole and in all details, and on nothing else. Or, as one says, the later state is completely determined by the earlier. This is the *mechanistic* feature of process.

Process knowledge is the ideal in the sense of being the ultimate goal of all science. Call such knowledge complete, any piece or body of knowledge that falls short of it, incomplete. The knowledge that water if heated boils is incomplete. The complete knowledge of which it is a very small part is thermodynamics. Yet, as far as it goes, there is nothing wrong with this small piece of incomplete knowledge. In general, to say of any body of information or of the present state of a science that it is incomplete is not in any sense an adverse criticism but merely a methodological diagnosis. That should prevent any misunderstanding.

Whether or not the ideal has been reached, will be reached, or ever can be reached, it has provided us with the only clear idea we have of the nature of science, or, what amounts to the same, of scientific explanation.

It is a consequence of this idea that from the process laws of an area all the incomplete laws in the area can be deduced. From the process laws of thermodynamics, for instance, the law that water if heated boils can be deduced. In fact, one can do much better. As one says, very confusingly, incomplete laws typically have exceptions. Or, a bit less confusingly, they do not state the conditions under which they hold, this for the very good reason that we do not know them. Equally typically, incomplete laws fail to cover some relevant features; in our illustration, the temperature at which the water boils, how long it takes until it begins to boil, what these two features depend on, and so on. From the process law, on the other hand, all the relevant features of, as well as the necessary and sufficient conditions for, water boiling if heated can be deduced. Let me express this idea by saying that what we mean by scientific knowledge or explanation is what, if there were process knowledge in the area, would be a part of it. Or, as one also says, all scientific explanation is *causal*.

"There is in principle no process knowledge of human behavior, either individual or in groups." Call this the negative thesis. Notice once more the phrase "in principle." The issue is not what actually has been attained or practically can be attained, but, rather, of the kind called philosophical. The negative thesis always has been and still is very influential. It has taken many different forms and has been much argued about, in each of these forms, both for and against. In the Scandinavian and Anglo-Saxon countries it lies underneath much of the current discussion about the methodology of the behavior sciences. On the Continent it now appears as a plea, always impassioned, often pathetic, sometimes moving, for human freedom. The arguments for the negative thesis, though they too take many different forms, are all variations of one master argument. So one may, as I now shall, refute the thesis by showing that one of the premisses of the master argument is false.

(1) Human purposes are effective; i.e., what will happen in the future depends in part on present human purposes. (2) In a process the future depends only on (is completely determined by) the present. (3) Human purposes essentially involve the future. These are the three premisses of the master argument; the negative thesis is its conclusion. (1) and (2) are true. That present mental states in general and present human purposes in particular are among the causes of some future facts I take to be a truism. (1) merely asserts this truism. Even so, it may be worth pointing out that the causal effectiveness of mental states is perfectly compatible with the parallelistic hypothesis. The hypothesis merely means that in any complete set of relevant variables the descriptions of corresponding bodily and mental states can be substituted for each other. (2) merely states the mechanistic (causal) feature of process. The false premiss is (3). The mistake hides behind the vagueness of 'involves.' A state of mind is a fact that intends another fact. The two facts need not be and often are not simultaneous. A present state of mind which is a purposing intends a future fact which may

or may not come to pass. If it is a remembering it intends a past state of affairs that may or may not have been. In either case, as in all others, the connection between the two facts, the mental state and its intention, is purely logical. A present mental state, whether it be a purposing, a remembering, a perceiving, or what have you, is thus as completely and as unproblematically a present fact as that it is now raining. Nor of course does it make any difference for this argument whether we describe the critical fact directly or indirectly. That shows that the refutation of the negative thesis does not depend on the parallelistic hypothesis. It is only a refutation in principle, of course. But, then, the issue itself is one of principle. Thus no other refutation is either needed or possible.

Human purposes are facts among facts, causes among causes, effects among effects. In the behavior sciences they are naturally among the most important causes and effects. In this sense, purpose does enter into scientific explanations. On the other hand, the connections scientific explanation seeks to establish among facts are all causal. The connection between a mental fact of the kind called a purposing and the fact which is its intention is not causal! This is so irrespective of whether the intended fact itself is or is not mental and, of course, irrespective of whether mental facts are described directly or indirectly. In this sense, purpose does not enter in scientific explanation.

Let us take stock. I promised to talk about purpose, function, and scientific explanation. 'Function' hasn't even been used so far (except once, in the unproblematic mathematical sense). 'Purpose' has so far been used in one sense only. It always meant a conscious human purpose. That was deliberate of course. For this is the only clear and unproblematic use of the word. In mental discourse it (or one of its near synonyms) is even basic. All other uses, in science or elsewhere, are either metaphorical or must be defined. Some of these uses we shall presently examine. But it will pay if we first attend to 'function.'

'Function' has quite a few uses, some of them shading into each other. It will suffice to clarify two. One I shall call problematic, the other unproblematic. In one of these two uses, to "have a certain function" means to serve a certain purpose. A fact, a feature, an arrangement "serves a purpose" if, unless it were there, the purpose could not be achieved, or not achieved as easily, or not in a certain way, and so on. There is no need for even trying to exhaust the details and variants covered by "and so on." What serves a purpose often would not exist had it not been caused to exist by the one whose purpose it serves. The logic of "causing," subtle and complex as it is, is but a part of the logic of scientific explanation. So we need not tarry. If the purpose of which I spoke is a conscious human purpose, then, as far as we are concerned, this use of 'function' in which to have a function means to serve a purpose, is unproblematic. If 'purpose' is used differently, then the problems of this use of 'function' are those of the different uses of 'purpose.' Since the latter are problematic, I call this the problematic use of 'function,' even though, in spite of its name, we shall not need to return to it. It will suffice to clarify the problematic uses of 'purpose.' The other use of 'function,' the one I call unproblematic, does, in spite of its name, require some clarification. But it can be completely clarified by attending to the interaction feature of inorganic processes, astronomical, chemical, electrical, and so on. Such processes differ from socio-psychological ones in containing no conscious human purposes; and they differ from biological processes in containing nothing to invite any of the other uses of 'purpose.' In our context, that makes "unproblematic" a rather suitable designation for a use of 'function' that can be completely clarified by attending to inorganic processes.

To know a process law is to know all there is to be known about interaction among its variables. Consider two systems, A and B, whose initial states agree in some relevant variables, disagree in some others. Nothing essential will be lost if we assume that they disagree in only one. Let the value of this one variable be a in A, b in B. The use of a quantified illustration is, as always, merely a convenience, not a limitation. $a = O$, $b \neq O$, for instance, is a very convenient stand-in for the absence or presence of an unquantified feature. The two courses of events, in A and B, respectively, will differ. E.g., in A a certain chemical reaction will take place, in B it won't. Or, in A an equilibrium of a certain kind will eventually be reached, in B it won't. In B an equilibrium of another kind is eventually reached. Or perhaps none is reached. There is no point in multiplying examples. But there is, I think, some point in clarifying this broad use of 'equilibrium.' For the word as well as the idea play a very large role, not only in the social but also in the biological sciences, in connection with the two uses of 'function.'

Equilibrium in *all* respects simply means no change in any of the relevant variables. Clearly, that is the uninteresting limiting case, not only of equilibrium but of process. The interesting case, equilibrium in *some* respects, means no change (or only little change, or slow change) in *these* respects, throughout the process. That does not mean that some relevant variable or variables do not change throughout the process. In some special case it may mean that. In general, it means that some function, in the unproblematic mathematical sense of the word, of the changing relevant variables remains unchanged throughout the process. In the solar system, for instance, the positions of the planets change from moment to moment. So do the orbits, if only because the sun moves, from revolution to revolution. But they are and remain (approximate) ellipses around the sun. In this respect, the system is in equilibrium. This use of 'equilibrium,' I repeat, is broad, so broad indeed that it covers the case of so-called trends. (What remains unchanged in a trend is a rate of change, or the fact that such a rate is positive, and so on.) But a little reflection will show that the broad use covers all the cases in which scientists speak of equilibrium. So I conclude the digression by pointing out that while one who knows the process law can compute the necessary and sufficient conditions for *all* possible equilibria, to know *some* equilibrium conditions is merely imperfect knowledge.

Assume now that $a = O$, $b \neq O$, and that a certain chemical reaction takes place in B but not in A. If you fail to be impressed by the pertinence of the example, you may in your own mind replace the chemical reaction by one of those equilibria that interest social scientists, if only you will permit me, for the reasons I gave, to stick with the inorganic example. One who knows or believes that he knows something about the relevant interactions may describe the situation by saying, in speaking about A, that, if the factor had been present, the reaction would have taken place; or, in speaking about B, that, if the factor had been absent, the reaction would not have taken place. Instead of saying that, he may and in fact often will say, in speaking about B, that it is the function of the factor's presence to bring about the reaction, or, in speaking about A, that it is the function of its absence to prevent the reaction. This is an example of the second use of 'function.' It shows that what one says in so using the word can be said just as well without using it at all, by means of one or several sentences of the form: If something *were* this-and-this instead of that-and-that, another thing *would* be such-and-such instead of so-and-so. The logic of 'were-would' is subtle indeed, but it is all a part of the logic of 'cause,' which in our context is unproblematic. That is why I called the second use unproblematic.

I interrupt once more, this time not for a useful digression but in order to prevent harmful misunderstanding. I distinguished two meanings of 'function,' making them as clear and distinct as the context requires; called one problematic, the other unproblematic, for reasons I have stated as fully as the context requires. To do this is one thing. It is quite another thing, and a very silly thing indeed, to believe that whenever scientists use the word they use it clearly and distinctly with one of these two meanings. Of course they don't. Otherwise the word wouldn't get them into the kind of trouble in which they turn to the philosophical analyst. The point is, rather, that each such trouble can be cured by revealing the use or uses of the word which caused it as an unclear mixture of the two clear ones. As for 'function,' so for 'functionalism.' There has been around the turn of the century in psychology and there is now in sociology a good deal of talk about functionalism. To separate sense from nonsense in this talk, the distinction between the two meanings of 'function' always helps, often suffices. I want to conclude with some comments on the current discussion. Thus, since one meaning of 'function' depends on that of 'purpose,' we must first examine the derivative use of 'purpose.'

These uses are of three kinds. Experimental psychologists do not use 'purpose'; but they do call certain sequences of animal behavior "purposive." Psychoanalysts and, under their influence, all clinical psychologists speak of "unconscious" purposes. Students of society speak of the purposes of groups. Discussing these three uses, in this order, I shall often use 'function.' That will always be the unproblematic use. E.g., a certain response has the function to avoid electric shock will mean no more nor less than that if the animal had not made the response, it would have received an electric shock. A certain institution, say, the law, having a certain function, say, to settle a certain kind of dispute without violence, will mean no more nor less than that if the law didn't exist, these disputes would produce violence. The second example shows that I use 'group' so broadly that it covers what more commonly are called institutions. This use, I submit, is not only defensible; it is also enlightening. But I cannot take the time to defend it.

Animals respond to stimuli. The function of the response is either to attain or to maintain certain biological equilibria. Responses are either learned or unlearned. The behavior sequences called purposive are those that are learned. The facts are by now very familiar. As the error curve drops the animal learns how to get food. And so on. The similarity of such behavior with that a person would display if it were his purpose to obtain what the animal obtains is obvious, at least within limits which are equally obvious. But experimental psychologists do not ascribe (conscious) purposes to animals. Hence, they must tell us how to recognize the sequences they call purposive. That is, they must define the term. The dropping error curve is a plausible ingredient of the definition. That gives at least the idea, and the idea suffices for the two points I want to make. *First.* 'Purposive,' so defined, is a very broad *descriptive term,* covering many different subkinds of behavior, acquired or not acquired and subsequently displayed or not displayed, depending on the state the animal is in when the stimulus is presented, on antecedent conditions, and on individual differences within the species. The italicized phrase is redundant. All terms are descriptive. Science describes, and in describing often finds it convenient to define, in order to explain. To find explanations and to discover laws is one and the same thing. As explanation of animal behavior proceeds, the less likely are the laws to contain the broad term, mentioning instead the various subkinds, their conditions, and so on. To put it paradoxically, the more one comes to know about purposive behavior, the less will he be interested in the definition of 'purposive.' The *second* point merely spells out the idea that all scientific explanation is causal (mechanistic). To state the function of a response is one thing; to explain it is another thing. Its explanation never mentions the state of affairs it brings about. Or, as one says, all explanation is in terms of mechanisms. Experimental psychologists by now understand both points very well. Around the turn of the century there was some confusion about "functionalism." Its remote source was philosophical Darwinism; the proximate source was John Dewey.

In principle, prediction and scientific explanation are but the two sides of one coin. One who can always predict knows all the laws, and conversely. Practically, when it comes to human behavior, we are often still better at prediction than at scientific explanation. Or, rather, some of us are, some times. That is the phenomenon of empathy on the one hand, the as yet precarious achievement of clinical psychology as a science on the other. To deny the phenomenon of empathy is foolish. To deny that in principle it can be scientifically explained is just as foolish. 'Intuition' and 'understanding' are also used in the context. With 'understanding,' the idea may be expressed as follows. To deny the psychological phenomenon of understanding is merely foolish. But it is equally foolish, in psychology as elsewhere, to hypostatize it into a category coordinate to scientific explanation.

If a man develops a hysterical paralysis he will not be drafted for military service. The functional connection is rather obvious. Freud has enlarged our horizon by calling attention to many kinds of human behavior to which no one had ever paid attention before, some of them rather inconspicuous, some of their functions anything but obvious. Using 'empirical' and 'theoretical' loosely, one may call this the empirical side of his epochal contribution. Men of course do have (conscious) purposes. To say about the patient in the example that he has behaved as if he had had the (conscious) purpose of avoiding the draft is therefore intelligible, even though it is not very accurate. It is intelligible because a man may deliberately maim himself in order to avoid the draft. It is not very accurate because one cannot of course deliberately produce a hysterical paralysis. Literally, 'unconscious purpose' is a contradiction in terms. Hence the phrase must be defined. To define it so that whenever a piece of behavior has a certain function the corresponding unconscious purpose is ascribed to the one who displays it, is neither very useful nor very subtle. Nor, as we just saw, is it very accurate. Freud's theoretical subtlety consists in conceiving of human motivation and personality as a whole system of purposes, some conscious, some unconscious, thus *making an "enlarged" personality accessible to our empathy and, eventually, to scientific explanation.* Think of the so-called instances, Id, Ego, and Superego. Or return to our patient who, after he fell ill, was nursed by his mother. Was it his unconscious purpose to avoid the draft or to be nursed by his mother? Or did he have both purposes? The example shows what is meant by the italicized phrase. It also shows that an adequate definition of 'unconscious purpose' would be very difficult indeed. Fortunately, the situation is again dialectical, exactly as in the case of the experimentalist's 'purposive.' There is no need to explain the dialectic again. To put it paradoxically, as before, the more one comes to know about unconscious purposes, the less will he be interested in defining 'unconscious purpose.'

In the social area the crucial idioms mention the purposes of groups. Under the influence of Hegelian idealism, many did and some perhaps still do take them literally. Such nonsense we can dismiss without further ado, turn instead to two nonliteral uses, one heuristic, the other systematic.

Groups, not being people, are not accessible to empathy. Yet they consist of people who are. Thus groups might become accessible if one could find a way of coordinating to each group a representative person, i.e., a person such that by understanding it empathetically one could successfully predict the behavior of the group. This is the heuristic use. Surely you recognize Max Weber's ideal type. Its difficulties and limitations are not hard to discover. By what rules are we to select the representative persons? To ask the question is to ask for a definition. That makes the situation once more dialectical, in the same way as before. An adequate definition will not come forth unless we shall, in a scientific way, know so much about the social process that we shall no longer be interested in ideal types, particularly as long as, supposing that we could define them, the predictions based on them would be empathetic rather than scientific.

Before examining the systematic use of 'purpose' in the social disciplines, it will be well if I try to forestall a misunderstanding to which the two labels, 'heuristic' and 'systematic,' could easily give rise. I do not mean to belittle the achievements of such men as Weber, Simmel, and Mannheim. To reject insights as suggestive as some of theirs as long as one has nothing better to put in their place is merely pedantic. The philosopher of science need not and should not be a pedant. Rather, he ought to spread clarity or, at least, prevent confusion by calling things by their right names. The right name of Weber's method is heuristic. Nor does that, in another sense of the term, deny the "methodological" merit it had in its time and place. It did help to combat all kinds of foolish ideas typically propounded by those who insist on literally ascribing purposes to groups. It did call attention to the importance of psychological mechanisms in the eventual explanation of social processes. These are two very major "methodological" merits.

Scientists want their results to be as reliable as they can make them. The desire may and does find expression in the methodological idea, or ideal, of limiting in various ways the words admitted as basic (undefined). Broadly speaking, we observe (a) physical objects; we observe (b) other minds; and we observe (c) groups. Less broadly, there is a difference. We can observe physical objects (a) in a sense in which we cannot observe other minds (b); we can observe other minds in a sense in which we cannot observe groups (c). These differences are often brought out by insisting that the words a scientist may admit as basic must refer to what is "observable" and then giving rather special meanings to 'observe.' Thus one may insist that we "observe" (a) but not (b) or (c); or, alternatively, that while we can observe (a) and (b), we cannot observe (c). The difference between (a) on the one hand and (b) and (c) on the other was indeed an important intellectual motive for the attempt to describe mental states indirectly.

Sociologists are, and I think ought to be, sensitive to the difference between (c) on the one hand and (a) and (b) on the other. In a sense, that is, we do not observe groups. I, for one, have never seen "the law" punish an offender. I have only seen a judge pronounce sentence, a jailer leading the sentenced man to jail, and so on. The methodological ideal, therefore, is to define all the words on the group level (c) in terms of the other two levels, (a) and (b). We do possess some such definitions, e.g., in economics. For some other terms we have only definition sketches. For still others we cannot, or cannot as yet, do even that well. One must not allow one's methodological ideas and ideals to cripple his practice. On that I have insisted often enough.

On the other hand, given the difference in "directness" of observation and the differences in reliability that go with it, attempts to define all group terms cannot be dismissed as mere pedantry.

If we could devise adequate definitions of other group terms, we probably could also devise one for the phrase 'the purpose of a group.' If we had such a definition we could use the phrase systematically, not merely heuristically. But the situation is again dialectical. To understand its dialectic one merely has to remember what was said about the subtle and the unsubtle definition of 'unconscious purpose.' To define the purpose of a group or institution as that of this or that member, of this or that functionary, and so on, would be most unsubtle indeed. On the other hand, is there really any one who believes that if we knew as much, by way of mechanisms, as would be necessary to come up with really subtle definitions of group terms, we would still derive much benefit from this particular group notion, the purpose of a group, however subtly we may then be able to define it? So I suggest once more that the more one comes to know about the purposes of groups, the less will he be interested in defining 'purpose of a group.'

I conclude with some comments on the current emphasis on "functionalism" or "functional analysis" in sociology. The emphasis is on the dynamic, the longitudinal; the corresponding dissatisfaction, with the "merely" static, the cross-sectional; away from equilibrium conditions, towards laws of change. Inseparable from this urge toward process knowledge, there is the emphasis on interaction. All this is sound, of course, at least in principle. A doctrinaire may overvalue a "functional" generality because of its form, even though it is rather obvious, or vague, or unreliable, at the expense of a "mere" correlation which is more substantial. That, though, is nothing specific. There are doctrinaires everywhere. And the tendency to overestimate what can be achieved by a methodological commitment seems characteristic of all the young disciplines.

"One cannot understand an institution without understanding its function." To understand the formula, recall the empirical aspect of Freud's contribution. He enlarged our horizon by discovering a large number of surprising were-would connections. One may reasonably hope that the new emphasis will lead to the discovery of some such connections. To this extent the formula is sound. Its danger is twofold. One may be tempted to blur the distinction between description and explanation. And one may forget that the were-would connections so discovered, even if reliable, are not yet themselves the process knowledge which remains the ultimate goal.

"Acorns tend to grow into oaks," even though an estimable piece of knowledge, is yet typically incomplete. Some acorns are devoured by pigs; some others rot on barren ground; for the survivors much still depends on soil, sun, water, and wind. That a group under certain conditions tends toward certain kinds of equilibria is a piece of knowledge of the same kind, worth while as long as one does not know more and yet typically incomplete. To the extent the new emphasis encourages the search for such knowledge it is sound. To discern a tendency, however dimly, provided only it is there, is better than not to discern it at all. On the other hand, it would be dangerous to overestimate such discoveries. For they are merely steps on the way toward the discovery of the mechanisms "behind" the tendency.

Human purposes are facts among facts. In any other sense, purpose has no place in science. Those who demur are the teleologists. While I avoided the word, deliberately of course, I have not, I trust, left any doubt about the thing. To the extent one thinks teleologically, he does not think scientifically. The orthodoxy nowadays in the sciences of man and society is to denounce teleological thinking. Yet the propensity toward it is deeply ingrained. Thus the heart does not always know what the mouth professes. Those who without knowing it are teleologists at heart may well find some aid and comfort in the new vocabulary. If that should ever become a danger, then I would rather do without the vocabulary. For what is sound in the ideas which it is now used to express is, as we saw, anything but new and can very well be expressed without it.

[12] Functional Explanation in Psychology [1]

JERRY A. FODOR

In this paper I will try to say what a psychological explanation is. This project should be distinguished from others to which it is indirectly related. Thus, I shall not be trying to settle the mind-body problem, nor shall I examine the alleged incompatibility between freedom of choice and the existence of psychological laws. What I shall have to say will be relevant to those problems only in this respect: Philosophers who have argued that

Originally published under the title "Explanations in Psychology," *Philosophy in America,* Max Black, ed., Ithaca, N.Y. and London, 1965. Used by permission of Cornell University Press and George Allen & Unwin Ltd.

[1] This paper has been influenced by several discussions of psychological explanation, and not least by those with which it explicitly takes issue. I wish to acknowledge a particular indebtedness to J. A. Deutsch, *The Structural Basis of Behaviour,* Chicago, 1960, and Hilary Putnam, "Minds and Machines," in Sidney Hook (ed.) *Dimensions of Mind,* New York, 1960.

psychology could (or could not) account for consciousness or for choice have sometimes supported their arguments by reference to features psychological explanations are alleged to have: that they employ causal laws, that they are concerned only with motions, that they are concerned only with aberrant behaviour, that they consist solely in the delineation of stimulus-response connections, and so on. In so far as philosophical claims have been based upon such analyses of psychological explanation, what I have to say should be relevant to assessing those claims. Moreover, there is at least one philosophical issue to which this paper is directly relevant. It is sometimes said that the programme implicit in the doctrine of the unity of science cannot be carried through unless it is possible to reduce the concepts employed in psychology to neurological concepts. We shall see that, though such reduction is not possible in principle, this fact is nevertheless compatible with the unity of science.

In so far as psychology affords explanations of behaviour, saying what a psychological explanation is involves saying what it is to explain behaviour.[2] However, not all explanations of behaviour are psychological explanations. You bought the chocolate one and I want to know why. Well, because you prefer chocolate, because vanilla was more expensive, because chocolate keeps better, because you were asked to buy chocolate, because you felt like it. Any or all of these may do as explanations, for any or all of them may be what I want to know. None of them, however, is a psychological explanation. To say what a psychological explanation is involves distinguishing psychological explanations from such explanations as those.

'But surely what you propose to do would be a waste of effort? Psychological explanations are what psychology texts supply. If you want to know what a psychological explanation is, go and look.' Psychologists do not always agree about what sort of thing a psychological explanation is or about what sort of things are psychological explanations. Such disagreements are important because they affect the course of research and the constraints that psychological theories are required to meet. Lashley showed that the presence of conductive metal strips in the cortex of a chimpanzee did not materially interfere with shape recognition and hence that the 'fields' some gestalt theorists had supposed must function in visual perception could not involve macroscopic variation of the electrical potential of the chimpanzee's brain.[3]

---

2 Throughout this paper I shall follow the current psychological practice of using 'behaviour' in a much more general way than ordinary language would appear to warrant. It is, perhaps, not an accident that ordinary language often fails to supply words sufficiently general to describe the subject-matter of a special science (Cf. the use of 'matter' and 'energy' in physics); among the insights a science may achieve is the discovery that phenomena that appear dissimilar to uninstructed intuition are susceptible of similar explanations and thus ought to fall within the domain of a single discipline. The fact that we must invent a term like 'matter' to say what physics is about is related to the fact that it is not *obvious* (for example) that the laws determining the trajectory of missiles also account for the orbit of the moon.

3 Cf. Lashley, K. S., K. L. Chow and J. Semmes, 'An Examination of the Electrical Field Theory of Cerebral Integration,' *Psychological Review*, Vol. 58, 1951, pp. 123–136.

What, then, must we say about field theories of perception? That depends in part upon what we say about the status of theoretical constructs in psychological explanations, and, in particular, upon whether we hold such constructs admissible even when their identification with neurological states or processes seems unlikely or impossible. What is involved is a question about the constraints theories in psychology ought to be required to meet, hence a question about what a psychological explanation is.

'Psychological explanations are what psychology texts supply. If you want to know what a psychological explanation is, go and look.' An account of psychological explanation on which *no* psychological theory turned out to be an explanation would be *ipso facto* unacceptable. One must start by assuming some clear cases if one is to start at all. But we need not suppose even the clear cases immaculate. It will be no surprise if it turns out that the best available psychological theories could be improved by simplification, by integration with theories in related disciplines, and so on. One reason for wanting to characterize psychological explanation is that an acceptable account would afford a basis for the criticism and improvement of theories psychologists propose.

We want an account of psychological explanation that shows what makes the clear cases clear. One might say we are trying to discover the criteria psychologists use to assess the adequacy of psychological explanations, except that this formulation is misleading in two ways. First, it fails to do justice to the extent to which an account of psychological explanation may require reconstruction: the criteria psychologists use may, on some occasions or to some extent, be inconsistent, or unreasonable, or too weak, or too strong, and in such cases we would wish to substitute criteria that are consistent, and reasonable and just strong enough. Secondly, we must not confuse the task of saying what a psychological explanation is with that of saying how psychologists use the verb 'explain.' The former investigation is not linguistic in any of the usual senses of that term, nor do I suppose that the account of psychological explanation I will propose is analytically true by virtue of the meaning of 'explain.' That is, I reject the view that the metatheory of a science must consist solely of analytic statements. On the contrary, it may well be characteristic of psychological explanations that they presuppose the truth of some such empirical assumptions as: that all behaviour is directed towards drive reduction, or that it is under the control of the central nervous system, or that it tends towards the achievement of a state of equilibrium, or whatever. If this is the case, then such assumptions will be built into our characterization of psychological explanation: to explain behaviour will involve showing how it affects reduction of drive, how it is controlled by the central nervous system, or how it tends towards the establishment of an equilibrium.

Philosophers have often remarked that consonance with very general propositions about the world sometimes achieves the status of a necessary condition upon explanations in the sciences. But the conclusion they have drawn is only that such propositions serve as implicit definitions of key terms and are thus effectively analytic despite their empirical appearance. If, however, this entails that we could never have grounds for abandoning such propositions, it would appear to be false.

I want to claim that not only psychological theories, but also the meta-theory of psychology may, in the relevant sense, be subject to empirical disconfirmation. To show that learning can occur without reward is to show both that some behaviour is *not* directed towards the reduction of drive and that an account of psychological explanation according to which explaining learned behaviour invariably consists in showing how it affects drive reduction is an inadequate account.

This view may seem simply paradoxical. 'If consonance with the proposition *P* is a necessary condition placed upon the acceptability of psychological theories by some metatheory, then surely no disconfirmation of *P* is possible since, *ex hypothesis,* no theory incompatible with *P* is acceptable.' What that argument overlooks is that major revolutions in scientific thought often affect not only our beliefs as to what explanations are true, but also our notions about what constitutes an explanation. Thus, it may be true both that our notion of a satisfactory explanation includes consonance with some very general empirical assumptions and that such assumptions could be abandoned in face of overwhelmingly persuasive counter-explanations of a previously unanticipated type.

I want to say what a psychological explanation of behaviour is, for I hold that behaviour is susceptible of psychological explanation. Some philosophers deny this. They maintain either that psychological explanation is concerned soley with *aberrant* behaviour or that psychological explanation is not concerned with behaviour at all, but only with motions. We shall have to examine these views. An account of psychological theories is required to say what psychological theories are about.

In the *Concept of Mind,* Gilbert Ryle writes: [4]

The classification and diagnosis of exhibitions of our mental impotences require specialized research methods. The explanation of the exhibitions of our mental competences often requires nothing but ordinary good sense, or it may require the specialized methods of economists, scholars, strategists and examiners. But their explanations are not cheques drawn on the accounts of some yet more fundamental diagnoses. So not all, or even most, causal explanations of human actions and reactions are to be ranked as psychological.

It is clear that Ryle has been careful not to burn his bridges. He says only that explaining mental competences *often* requires nothing but good sense. This might equally be said of 'impotences' and lapses, for 'his attention wandered,' 'it slipped his mind,' 'he was tired,' 'he didn't think what he was doing,' etc. may all be satisfactory explanations. If, however, Ryle holds that psychological explanations can be given only in cases of failure to per-

---

4 Ryle, G., *The Concept of Mind*, New York, 1949, p. 326.

form, or in cases where the performance somehow runs contrary to expectations, then Ryle is simply wrong.

That normal functioning often needs to be accounted for is clear enough in cases other than behaviour. To explain how an internal combustion engine works is to account for its normal performance; the account will not include an explanation of backfires, misfires, and overheating. Backfires and misfires can be explained, but explaining them is not part of explaining how an internal combustion engine works. And backfires and misfires are certainly not *all* that can be explained. Engineering schools offer courses in the theory of the internal combustion engine, not in the theory of backfires and misfires.

If the situation is less obvious in the case of behaviour, that is because, of the variety of types of explanation we can give to account for what someone did, the one we want for practical purposes is rarely couched in terms of underlying psychological mechanisms. Analogously, if the insurance agent wants an explanation of the fire, we do not offer him physics. Yet presumably a physical explanation could be given and would be appropriate on certain occasions. Roughly: the appropriateness of an explanation is determined not by the phenomena it seeks to account for but by the question it seeks to answer.

It is clear from myriad examples that psychological explanations of normal behaviour can be (and often are) given and accepted. Thus, consider:

1. Freud explained that the occurrence of dreams is a mechanism for dealing with stimuli which would otherwise interrupt sleep.[5]
2. An explanation of the perceptual constancies accounts for our ability to see true colour even under adverse lighting conditions.[6]
3. Broadbent explained our ability to follow two conversations at once by reference to a hypothetical system of filters and stores.[7]
4. Skinner explained learned perceptual distinctions by reference to histories of reinforcement.[8]

It is irrelevant whether the explanations instanced in 1–4 are in fact correct accounts of the phenomena with which they are concerned. I am interested only in the point that what each purports to explain is either a 'competence' or a bit of perfectly normal human behaviour. It is a sufficient argument against Ryle's account of psychological explanation that it renders such explanations as 1–4 logically inappropriate. If a certain view of explanation entails that most of psychology will have to be abandoned without hope of replacement, that shows something is wrong with the view, not that something is wrong with psychology.

It appears that neither an appeal to explanations of phenomena other

[5] Cf. e.g. Freud, S., *General Introduction to Psychoanalysis*, New York, 1920.
[6] Cf. Teuber, H.-L., 'Perception,' *Handbook of Physiology*, Vol. 3, Washington, 1960.
[7] Cf. Broadbent, D. E. *Perception and Communication*, New York, 1958.
[8] Cf. Skinner, B. F. *The Behaviour of Organisms*, New York, 1938.

than behaviour nor an appeal to the received practices of psychologists uncovers support for the claim that psychological explanations must be limited
to accounting for aberrations. On the contrary, the psychologist's concern
with aberrant phenomena is often motivated primarily by the belief that
they represent the automatic consequence of the application to atypical
situations of the principles governing normal behaviour. What Teuber
has said about the motivation for studying illusions applies, *mutatis
mutandis,* to areas of psychology other than perception: '. . . to speak of
illusions as special cases—curiosa of perception, as it were—is tendentious
. . . the explanation for perceptual illusions will be sought among the
general laws of perception. Once these laws are known, the illusions themselves will be understood.' [9]

In so far as psychology is concerned to explain behaviour at all, it is concerned to explain normal behaviour *inter alia.* But philosophers have sometimes argued that psychological explanations are not (that is, cannot be)
explanations of behaviour. In an article entitled 'Behaviour,' Hamlyn
writes: [10]

No mechanism of any sort can do more than account for movements, reactions, and
the like. It may, of course, be the case that a particular movement or series of
movements may exemplify a kind of behaviour; it may be classifiable as such, and
capable of such an interpretation. It is this possibility which permits us on any
particular occasion to describe both the movements and the behaviour, though to do
these things will by no means be to do the same thing. Thus, no mechanism can be
given which will account for behaviour *per se* however much we may feel that the
behaviour will have been accounted for incidentally in providing a mechanism
for the movements which constitute behaviour on a particular occasion. At other
times, however, the movements involved may be different, though we may still
describe the behaviour in the same way.

Unlike Ryle's, this view of psychological explanation is found among psychologists. Thus, to choose an example at random, Tinbergen [11] characterizes the domain of the behaviour sciences as '. . . the total *movements*
made by the intact animal.'

There are two sorts of reasons for holding that psychology is concerned
to explain movements in the sense in which movements are contrasted with
behaviour. First, one may be impressed, as Hamlyn is, with the fact that
why-questions about behaviour are appropriately answered by citing reasons
rather than causes. Hence, it is argued, if psychology is a causal science, its
explanations cannot be explanations of behaviour. Second, one may be
impressed, as psychologists often are, by the need to eliminate from the
'observation base' of the science (i.e. from the vocabulary in which its predictions are couched) any term whose application requires interpretation of the

9 Teuber, *op. cit.,* p. 1601.

10 Hamlyn, D. W. 'Behaviour,' reprinted in Chappell, V. C. (ed.) *The Philosophy of
Mind,* Englewood Cliffs, N.J., 1962, p. 65.

11 Tinbergen, N. *The Study of Instinct,* Oxford 1951, p. 2. Emphasis mine.

phenomena. It must be possible to determine by purely observational procedures whether a prediction of the theory has been verified, since to use
theoretical constructs in describing the phenomena upon which the confirmation of the theory depends is held to be circular. 'To describe behaviour
requires interpretation of movements according to certain standards . . .' [12]
Hence, it is only by limiting the theory to accounting for motions that we
can assure ourselves that its explanations and predictions will be susceptible
of purely objective verification.

It is notable that this position is open to a *reductio ad absurdum* argument
similar to that to which Ryle's succumbed. That is, if we were literally to
proscribe the psychological explanation of behaviour, it would turn out
that not even learning theory is properly part of psychology, since *not even
so basic a psychological notion as that of a response can be characterized in
terms of movements alone.*[13] In laboratory situations, an organism is said
to have mastered a response when it regularly produces any of an indefinite
number of types of functionally equivalent motions under the appropriate
stimulus conditions. That some reasonable notion of functional equivalence
can be specified is essential, since we cannot in general require that two
motions manifesting the same response be identical either in their observable properties or in their physiological basis. Thus, a rat has 'got' the
bar pressing response if and only if it habitually presses the bar upon food
deprivation. Whether it presses with its left or right front paw or with three
or six grams of pressure is, or may be, irrelevant. Training is to some previously determined criterion of homogeneity of performance, which is to say
that we permit variation among the *motions* belonging to a response so long
as each of the variants is functionally equivalent to each of the others: *viz.*
so long as each of the motions is correctly related to the bar, to the general
stimulus situation, and to the history of the organism.

Not only does the requirement that psychology concern itself with
motions alone prohibit the employment of such basic notions as 'response,'
it also prohibits the construction of a reasonable criterion of identity for
motions themselves. An otherwise indistinguishable pair of motions may
be produced by quite different physiological mechanisms and hence be
the outcome of quite different psychological processes. In order to take
account of this fact, it may very often be necessary to determine identity and
difference of motions by identity and difference of the muscular contractions that produce them [14] and, in case the same muscular contractions are
sometimes under the control of different central processes, we may finally
have to determine identity and difference of motions by identity and difference of hypothetical underlying causal mechanisms at the neural level.[15]

[12] Hamlyn, *op. cit.*, pp. 63–64.

[13] Cf. Chomsky, N. 'Review of Skinner's *Verbal Behaviour*,' *Language*, Vol. 3, No. 1,
1959.

[14] This is, in fact, what Tinbergen does in the volume cited above.

[15] For an interesting example, cf. Luria, A. R., *Speech and the Development of Mental
Processes in the Child*, London 1959.

In short, the requirement that we characterize the events upon which the confirmation of a theory depends *only* in terms of their immediately observable properties may render the systematic explanation of those events impossible. Among the goals of theory construction is that of providing a conceptual framework for the coherent description of the phenomena with which the theory is concerned. That is, it is one of the achievements of a satisfactory theory that it provides a way of determining identity and difference of the confirming events such that, *on that determination,* the occurrence of those events is rendered susceptible of explanation. The view that such determinations can in principle be made on the basis of purely observable features of behaviour is so far from being obviously true as to make its adoption as a methodological rule extremely ill-advised. In the present case, it is by no means clear that a science of the motions of organisms is possible: that is, it is unclear that anything systematic could be said about the motions of an organism unless we permitted ourselves to identify motions not solely on the basis of their immediately observable properties, but also by their relation to such hypothetical states as drives, needs, goals, muscle contractions, neurological firings, and so on. To put it somewhat differently, among the facts which drive us to theory construction in psychology is the existence in nonverbal behaviour of the counterparts of ambiguity and synonymy. Just as, in linguistics, not every utterance of the phonemic sequence 'bank' is an utterance of the same word, so in psychology, not every occurrence of a given movement or muscular contraction is an instance of the same behaviour. Conversely, in linguistics two phonemically distinct utterances ('bachelor,' 'unmarried man') may be equivalent in significant respects. So, in psychology, two quite different patterns of motions (swimming to the right and running to the right in a T-maze) may be instances of the same behaviour: a fact we notice when we discover that an organism trained to produce one will, under appropriate circumstances, produce the other without further training. The consequences of such facts are identical in both sciences. If we are to capture the relevant generalizations, identity and difference of the events with which the science is concerned must often be determined by reference to properties other than those that are directly observable. In particular, in both sciences we attempt to construct theories containing levels sufficiently abstract to enable us to mark the respects in which events whose observable properties are identical may nevertheless be functionally distinct and the respects in which events whose observable properties are distinct may nevertheless be functionally identical.[16]

But it may still be said that the explanation of behaviour requires reasons while causal explanations provide not reasons but causes. There is, I think, something to this argument: explanations of behaviour are very often given

[16] Cf. Chomsky, N., *Syntactic Structures,* The Hague 1957; J. J. Katz and J. A. Fodor, 'The Structure of a Semantic Theory,' *Language,* Vol. 39, No. 2, June 1963.

by appealing to motives, utilities, strategies, goals, needs, desires, and so on.[17] It seems clear that such explanations will not be forthcoming from a causal science where this is understood to be a science which affords explanations *only* by appealing to causal chains and causal laws.[18] I shall argue that psychology is not a causal science in *that* sense. At any event, at the present stage there is no need to suppose that, because some explanations of behaviour are not causal, psychology must be limited to saying '. . . that in certain circumstances people behave in certain ways . . .' [19] or that we should '. . . content ourselves with the programme of accounting for behaviour in terms of the capacities or dispositions from which it is derivable,' [20] an undertaking which, as Hamlyn rightly remarks, 'is not a scientific programme, but one which may be carried out by anyone with sufficient experience of human affairs.' [21] Rather, the argument shows that we need to understand how a science can afford explanations and predictions of events in terms which do not refer solely to the causes of those events.

Psychology is the systematic attempt to explain and predict the behaviour of organisms. It is assumed that at any instant behaviour is the joint product of two sorts of factors:

1. Stimuli currently impinging upon the sensory receptors of the organism.
2. Internal states of the organism.

The relative contribution of each of these factors to the determination of behaviour probably varies greatly for behaviour of different kinds. While knowledge of local stimulus conditions contributes greatly to accurate prediction of certain kinds of instinctive behaviour and certain kinds of conditioned behaviour, in the case of verbal behaviour knowledge of the stimulus situation often affords very little grounds for predicting what the organism will do.

I shall argue that psychological explanation is essentially a two-phase process, the first phase of which is the development of a theory of the internal states of the organism such that (*a*) the terms of the theory which do not refer to behaviour are functionally characterized and (*b*) the theory is capable of adequately predicting the behaviour of the organism given

[17] Which need not blind us to the fact that causal explanations of behaviour are sometimes precisely what the situation requires. 'It was the liquor he drank that made him behave so badly.'

[18] The notion of a causal explanation is not itself so clear that it is evident precisely what is being asserted or denied when it is claimed that psychology is or is not a causal science. I shall follow Hamlyn in adopting the most restricted interpretation of this notion. In particular, I shall use 'causal explanation' and 'mechanistic explanation' as roughly interchangeable. To deny that psychological explanations are causal in this sense is not, of course, to deny that they may be causal in some broader sense.

[19] Hamlyn, *op. cit.*, p. 66
[20] *Ibid.*
[21] *Ibid.*

knowledge of the current stimulus situation. Each of these conditions must be discussed at length.

Quite aside from any physiological considerations, it is possible to say a number of things about the kinds of internal states organisms must be supposed to have if characteristic features of their behaviour are to be accounted for. For example: the behaviour of an organism in a specified stimulus situation is very often partly determined by the previous stimulations it has encountered. Much of the most careful work in recent psychology has been devoted to exhibiting the differences between naive and sophisticated behaviour and to determining which patterns of stimulation are conducive to the development of sophistication. But though it is obvious that organisms of identical genetic endowment often differ profoundly in their response to novel stimulations depending on features of their individual life histories, it is not obvious how this fact should be accounted for. The problem becomes apparent when we notice that the degree to which, and the conditions under which, prior stimulations determine current behaviour differ markedly from species to species: discriminations difficult for the octopus to learn are easy for the rat, imprinting is known in birds but not in monkeys, operant conditioning is easier with fish than with planaria, verbal learning occurs only in man. The susceptibility of behaviour to alteration by experience would thus appear to vary from species to species.[22]

If we are to account for the alteration of behaviour as a result of prior stimulation, we must assume that some at least of the internal states that determine the way an organism responds to current stimulation are themselves the product of its previous experiences. Since the laws governing the formation of such states may be supposed to differ from species to species, it becomes understandable that the same history of stimulation produces very different behaviour in organisms of sufficiently different biological types. Conversely, if genetically identical organisms have such internal states in common only in case their life histories have been similar in relevant respects, then we expect relevantly dissimilar life histories to produce differences in behaviour. Finally, the assumption that some such experientially induced states are inherently unstable and tend to decay in a lawful fashion provides for the possibility of explaining such characteristic features of long term memory as stereotyping, elimination of detail, tendency towards 'good form,' etc.[23]

It goes without saying that the laws which presumably determine the careers of such internal states (and, in particular, the laws which determine under what stimulus conditions they arise and how they contribute to the production of behaviour) are arrived at indirectly. The internal states of the organism are assumed to have those properties required to account for

22 Cf. Thorpe, W. H. *Learning and Instinct in Animals,* London 1956.
23 Cf. e.g. Bartlett, F. C. *Remembering,* New York 1932, for a discussion of characteristic features of the decay of memories.

the observed features of its behaviour. This is a sort of reasoning that is perfectly ordinary in sciences other than psychology. Radio telescopy shows the star to be very active, light telescopy shows it to be very dim. Perhaps we are dealing with a bright star very far away. The function of the theory is, *inter alia,* to save the appearances.

The sense in which terms referring to internal states are functionally characterized in theories developed in the first phase of psychological explanation may now be made clear. Phase one psychological theories characterize the internal states of organisms only in respect of the way they function in the production of behaviour. In effect, the organism is thought of as a device for producing certain behaviour given certain sensory stimulations. A phase one psychological explanation attempts to determine the internal states through which such a device must pass if it is to produce the behaviour the organism produces on the occasions when the organism produces it. Since, at this stage, the properties of these states are determined by appeal to the assumption that they have whatever features are required to account for the organism's behavioural repertoire, it follows that what a phase one theory tells us about such states is what role they play in the production of behaviour. It follows too that the evidence to be adduced in favour of the claim that such states exist is just that assuming they do is the simplest way of accounting for the behavioural capacities the organism is known to have.

It should be noticed that explanations afforded by phase one theories are *not* causal explanations, although a fully elaborated phase one theory claims to be able to predict behaviour given sufficient information about current sensory stimulations. Phase one explanations purport to account for behaviour in terms of internal states, but they give no information whatever about the mechanisms underlying these states. That is, theory construction proceeds in terms of such functionally characterized notions as memories, motives, needs, drives, desires, strategies, beliefs, etc. with no reference to the physiological structures which may, in some sense, correspond to these concepts. Now, if I say 'He left abruptly upon remembering a prior engagement' I am giving an explanation in terms of an internal event postulated in order to account for behaviour (including, perhaps, behaviour which consists in his telling me why he left). Moreover, it is an explanation which, *ceteris paribus,* might have been adequate for the prediction of behaviour since I might have known that *if* he had been reminded of his engagement he would certainly have left. Yet, it is not a causal explanation in the sense in which that term is usually used. That is, it is not at all like a reflex-arc explanation of a knee-jerk response or an explanation of the trajectory of a billiard ball; no causal laws are invoked, nor is any notion of a causal chain at issue.

We thus arrive at the following view of phase one psychological explanations. Organisms are observed to produce certain types of behaviour either spontaneously or as the consequence of certain types of stimulation. A phase one psychological theory attempts to account for these observations by reference to hypothetical internal states which, together with the relevant stimulation, are supposed to produce the observed behaviour. The regularity of the observed behaviour is thus explained and rules provided which enable us to predict what the organism will do in any of indefinitely many novel situations. Phase one explanations are arrived at indirectly in that we attribute to the organism whatever internal states are required to account for its behavioural repertoire. The characterization of these states is thus purely functional since we know about them only what role they play in the production of behaviour.

A characteristic feature of phase one explanations is that they are compatible with indefinitely many hypotheses about the physiology of the organism. We have seen that phase one explanations are *not* causal explanations precisely because they make no claims about the mechanisms underlying internal states. In a phase one explanation, we picture the organism as proceeding through a series of internal states that terminate in the production of observable behaviour. But we make no attempt to say what these states are states of: what internal mechanisms correspond to the functionally defined states we have invoked. Now, the set of mechanisms capable of realizing a series of such functionally defined states is indefinitely large. Only our ingenuity limits the number of mechanisms we could devise which, upon exposure to the relevant stimulations, would go through a sequence of internal states each functionally equivalent to a corresponding state of an organism and would then produce behaviour indistinguishable in relevant respects from the behaviour of the organism.

We may say that each mechanism capable of realizing the series of states a phase one theory attributes to an organism is a *model* of the theory. And we may now see why phase one explanations are inadequate accounts of behaviour. For, in the first phase of psychological explanation, we say no more of an organism than that it is one of an indefinitely large number of possible models of a theory. Which such model the organism is is something a phase one explanation does not determine.

Many psychologists would claim that this last question is not properly within the domain of their science. J. A. Deutsch, for example, has argued persuasively that the production of adequate phase one theories exhausts the psychologist's professional responsibilities.

For instance, to attempt to guess at the particular change which occurs in the central nervous system during learning in the framework of a theory purporting to explain behaviour is not only unnecessary but also purely speculative. That some type of change occurs may be inferred from the behaviour of an animal. What this type of change is cannot be arrived at, nor is it very important for the psychologist to know. This can be shown by taking the example of an insightful learning machine. . . . To be told that the semipermanent change in the machine which occurs when it learns is due to a uniselector arm coming to rest does not help us to understand the behavioural properties of the machine. Nor can it be checked by performing experiments on the behaviour of the machine. For the change could equally well be due to a self-holding relay, a dekatron selector, or any type of gadget known to technology capable of being turned from one steady state into another. In the same way, to speculate about terminal end boutons in the way that Hebb does or about changes of synaptic resistance seems to be trying to answer a question irrelevant, strictly speaking, to the psychological theorist. What behaviour would one of these assumptions explain which the others would not? [24]

Border disputes tend to be philosophical in the sense of that term in which it is synonymous with 'uninteresting.' But more is at issue here than whether the determination of the physical representation of a phase one theory in the nervous system of an organism is the duty of the psychologist or the neurologist or both.

It must be remembered that the talk of a first and second phase of psychological explanation cannot be understood as expressing a chronological relation between types of psychological theories. It is offered as a reconstruction of psychological explanation, not as a history of the development of psychology. In historical fact, what happens is that research directed towards a functional account of behaviour is simultaneous with research directed towards determining the nature of the mechanisms whose functional characteristics phase one theories specify. This fact has two fairly important consequences. First, information about the mechanisms underlying behaviour may sometimes lead to hypotheses that are most naturally stated in functional terms and tested in terms of behaviour. The history of psychological research on memory is filled with experiments originally inspired by speculations about the neurology of the memory trace, just as the history of perception theory is filled with experiments inspired by speculations about the character of the neural events triggered by a stimulus array. Secondly, and more important, it seems reasonable to maintain that any phase one theory that is incompatible with known facts of neurology must be, *ipso facto*, unacceptable. To put it slightly differently, it is sufficient to disconfirm a functional account of the behaviour of an organism to show that its nervous system is incapable of assuming states manifesting the functional characteristics that account requires. To accept this principle is, of course, to build into our characterization of psychological explanation a blatantly empirical assumption about the causation of behaviour: namely that the nervous system does, in fact, constitute a model of some phase one theory. This may be an incorrect view of the relation between neural and molar events (we had anticipated the possibility that the metatheory of psychology might itself prove susceptible of empirical discomfirmation). But,

[24] Deutsch, *op. cit.* p. 12.

if it is correct, it provides an extremely important constraint upon phase one theories. Moreover, it provides motive for precisely the sort of neurological speculations about which Deutsch professes suspicion. If consonance with neurological fact is a condition upon the adequacy of phase one theories, it is clearly good strategy for the psychologist to construct such theories in awareness of the best estimates of what the neurological facts are likely to be.

It should be noticed that the view of the relation between psychological and neurological theories espoused here is to be distinguished from all varieties of reductionism. On this view neurological structures are models of certain functionally characterized relations. A neurological theory thus provides an account of the mechanics of systems whose functional characteristics are given by phase one theories. But to attempt to reduce a functional account to a mechanistic account would be patently absurd; the relation between functional analysis and mechanistic analysis is not at all like the relation between macroanalysis and microanalysis, though the two have sometimes been confused.

In microanalysis one asks: 'What does X consist of?' and the answer has the form of a specification of the microstructure of Xs. Thus: 'What does water consist of?' 'Two molecules of hydrogen linked with one molecule of oxygen.' 'What does lightning consist of?' 'A stream of electrons.' And so on. In functional analysis, one asks about a part of a mechanism what role it plays in the activities characteristic of the mechanism as a whole: 'What does the camshaft do?' 'It opens the valves, permitting the entry into the cylinder of fuel which will be detonated to drive the piston.' Successful microanalysis is thus often contingent upon the development of more powerful instruments of observation or more precise methods of dissection. Successful functional analysis, on the other hand, requires an appreciation of the sorts of activities characteristic of a mechanism and of the contribution of the functioning of each part to the economy of the whole.

Explanation in psychology consists of a functional analysis and a mechanistic analysis: a phase one theory and a determination of which model of the theory the nervous system of the organism represents. Neither aspect of the explanation is dispensable. In particular, a neurological account without the corresponding phase one account would amount to no more than a description of a series of biochemical and electrical interactions. It would fail to describe the role of these interactions in the production of behaviour.[25] To put it succinctly, a complete psychological explanation requires more than an account of what the neurological circuitry is; it requires also an account of what such circuitry does. This second sort of account is

[25] I want to make it clear that I do *not* deny that accounts of functional relations may play an important role within neurology. There is, of course, nothing wrong with saying that the firing of a certain neuron inhibits the firing of some other. My point is rather that, *vis-à-vis* explanations of behaviour, neurological theories specify mechanisms and psychological theories do not.

given in terms of the familiar constructs of psychology: drives, motives, strategies, and so forth.

Notice that explanations outside psychology often have this same double aspect: functional analysis plus mechanistic analysis. We say 'The camshaft functions to lift the valves at the proper time by displacing the tappets.' That is, we say what the camshaft does and we say how it does it. Neither account is adequate without the other.

Psychologists and philosophers who have complained that it is possible to trace an input from afferent to central to efferent neurological systems without once encountering motives, strategies, drives, needs, hopes, and so forth have thus been right in one sense but wrong in another, just as one would be if one argued that a complete causal account of the operation of an internal combustion engine never encounters such a thing as a valve lifter. In each case, the confusion occurs when a term properly figuring in functional accounts of mechanisms is confronted with terms that properly appear in causal accounts. From a functional point of view, a camshaft is a valve lifter. But a mechanistic account of the operations of internal combustion engines does not seek to replace the concept of a valve lifter with the concept of a camshaft, nor does it seek to reduce the former to the latter. What it does do is explain how the valves get lifted, what mechanical transactions are involved when the camshaft lifts the valves.

There is no sense to the question 'What does a valve opener consist of?' where this is understood as a request for a microanalysis. Functions do not have parts; valve openers are not made of rods, springs and atoms in the sense that camshafts are.[26] There is a sensible question: 'How are the valves opened in this (sort of) engine?' This question invites a mechanistic account, and in such an account the term 'camshaft' may appear. Analogously, there is a sensible question: 'What is the mechanism of drive reduction in this (sort of) organism?' This question invites a neurological account, and in such accounts the term 'circuit' may appear.

Drives, motives, strategies, etc. are internal states postulated in attempts to account for behaviour in phase one theories. In completed psychological explanations they serve to characterize the functional aspects of neurological mechanisms. That is, they function in accounts of the relation between the operation of such mechanisms and the molar behaviour of organisms. But drives, motives and strategies are not themselves neurological mechanisms nor do they have a microanalysis in terms of neurological mechanisms. The remark 'A drive is not a neurological state' has the same logical status

---

[26] To add to the confusion, however, it may be observed that some *mechanisms* are designated by their function. This is why in one sense it does and in another sense it does not make sense to ask: 'What is a can opener made of?' Again, it is because 'mousetrap' is ambiguous between function and mechanism that it makes sense to talk of building a better one. Analogously, it is customary to designate *neurological* structures in terms of their supposed *psychological* functions: hence, the 'speech centre,' the 'association cortex,' etc.

as the remark 'A valve lifter is not a camshaft.' That is, it expresses a necessary truth.

If the position just presented is correct, it would appear that much of the discussion of theoretical identification [27] that has arisen in attempting to determine the relation between neurological and psychological concepts must in fact be irrelevant to that problem. It need not be denied that, in general, no *a priori* determination can be made of the cases in which considerations of economy or elegance may require scientists to identify states or events, previously held to be distinct. Nor need it be denied that, far from being arbitrary decisions, such identifications often have the status of major scientific discoveries. Above all, there is no reason to suppose an adequate view of language would require us to hold that such identifications invariably involve changes of meaning. But, important though these insights are for a proper understanding of scientific explanation, on the present view they do not apply to the relation between neurological and psychological theories; since psychological terms are understood to be names for functions, psychological states are not available for microanalysis and theoretical revision could identify them only with other functions, not with mechanisms.

[27] Cf. Place, U. T. 'Is Consciousness a Brain Process,' reprinted in Chappell, *op. cit.*, Smart, J. J. C. 'Sensations and Brain Processes,' reprinted in Chappell, *op. cit.*; and Putnam, *op. cit.*

Four ★ SOCIAL FACTS,

SOCIAL LAWS, AND REDUCTION

INTRODUCTION

"The achievements of Roosevelt, Churchill, Gandhi, Hitler, Stalin, and Mussolini are not matters of speculation but solid fact. Certainly they were swept along by forces far beyond their control, but they did manipulate and to a certain extent direct these forces and their effectiveness in this regard made them memorable." These sentiments, expressed by a book reviewer in a national magazine, seem unexceptionable, even trite. The review continues, "Had none of these men existed would the world today have been appreciably different? The author gives enough evidence of thinking so to bring upon himself the wrath of the determinists." Clearly, there are some who would take exception. The reviewer, however, seems unaware that it is not only the "more frantic" antagonists of the Great Man theory of history who might object to the passage. What, some others might ask, are these "forces" that supposedly are beyond the control of individuals and that they can direct only "to a certain extent"? Society is made up of men, and human passions, goals, and decisions, not impersonal forces, determine what happens. Yet the reviewer has a point.

It seems obvious, on the one hand, that certain unique individuals affected, for good or for evil, the course of history. It seems equally obvious, on the other hand, that they could make their mark only by virtue of their ability to seize the day. They reacted to a world that imposed itself on them, as it does on all men, and that circumscribed their course of action. All the papers in this section are, in one way or another, germane to the issues dramatically posed by the quoted passage. The problem is to give an analysis of the relation between individual action and social events that will adequately account for how they impinge on one another. Clearly, an adequate analysis must be consonant with the logical criteria for admissible scientific concepts, and it seems sensible to add that it should at least not conflict with the body of reasonably well-established factual knowledge.

A social fact is a fact expressed by a sentence containing terms that are used collectively for human groups and institutions. Groups have charac-

teristics that individuals do not. No man alone is an army or a family. Statements about the family, crowds, the Inquisition, the economic system, wars,
elections, the law, and the moral customs of a community all express social
facts. No one denies that there are such facts. The issue concerns not their
existence, but the proper analysis of the collective terms used to talk about
them. If an angry crowd burns down a library, is the angry crowd an unanalyzable entity or is it "reducible" to the feelings and behavior of many
individual persons in the presence of each other? If someone acts as an organ
of the State, what is "the State" whose function he serves? Are collective
terms definable in terms of individual behavior, or is there some unity to
which they refer? If there is something more, how do we identify it and
what is its relation to individual behavior? These are requests for a *description* of social events, properties, or entities that will enable us to know what
we are talking about when we use collective terms.

A second issue concerns the *explanation* of social facts. To explain a social
fact is to find a law or generalization about it. Are there social laws, that is,
laws containing *only* collective or institutional terms? Such laws express a
connection between, say, family structure and the religious institutions of a
society. Again, probably no one seriously doubts that many social generalizations can be found. The controversial issue is whether we can have a
comprehensive social theory, that is, a set of laws containing only collective
terms that would permit the complete explanation and prediction of all and
any social occurrences. If a comprehensive theory of the social process is
possible, then the Great Man theory of history is false, for no particular,
unique individual need be mentioned in the social laws. In other words, "social determinism" would be true because all changes in the social process
would be explainable in social terms alone. But social determinism can take
two different forms which shall be called "hard" and "soft" determinism. Before distinguishing these, it will be well to comment on three notions whose
ambiguities confound discussion.

First, there are different kinds of explanation. The resulting controversy
is discussed in Section Five. Right now we need only one distinction. We
explain *what* something is by mentioning its identifying features. We describe it. An analysis of a collective term thus *describes* the entity or event
to which it refers. But it does not explain *why* the described event occurs,
that is, how it is lawfully connected to other events, either individual or
social. Description and explanation of social occurrences are two distinct
things. If inflation is explained as being caused by full employment, this
generalization is different from the mere analysis of the collective terms it
contains. Similarly, if John married because he was going to be drafted,
being draftable into the Army is a social fact which is among the causes
of John's social behavior. The analysis of the social facts involved is another
question. In particular, one may agree that social events are frequently
causes and effects, but deny that they are unanalyzable unities, collective
individuals, or wholes. The view that all collective terms are analyzable
as referring to complex patterns of behavior, beliefs, and attitudes of various
people in certain situations is called *individualism*. Its denial is *holism*.

That leads to the second difficulty. The individualistic analysis of group
concepts in terms of patterns of individual behavior is sometimes referred

to as "psychological explanation." If it is an analysis, however, then it is not in the relevant sense just mentioned an explanation, but a description. And it is "psychological" only in the sense that it refers to individual persons acting together. The term *mob*, for instance, may be defined as a group of people behaving in a certain way. By this individualistic analysis, a mob isn't terrorizing a community. Many persons, who are animated by certain feelings and desires, are together conducting themselves in a certain way. Similarly, the Inquisition didn't do anything. Rather, one Lopez lit a fire at the feet of one Pablo from certain motives in a certain situation. On the opposite, holistic view, the mob and the Inquisition are collective entities whose characteristics are not specifiable in terms of individual ways of acting, thinking, or feeling. This is Durkheim's view.

An archaic notion of psychology frequently, though not invariably, reinforces whatever other reasons people may have for espousing holism. Psychological features are then interpreted to be those inherited and constitutional factors that all races and conditions of men have in common. Such factors can hardly explain institutional and cultural differences among peoples. To divide the issue as it must be divided: We could not *describe* a collective event in such narrowly psychological terms alone, nor could we *explain* its occurrence by such causes alone. But to say that group terms are definable is not to say that they are "really" psychological terms. The social group, defined as a set of persons having certain roles in relation to each other, remains the unit of description and of explanation. Thus defined, it is an individualistic notion, but not thereby psychological in any narrow and restricted sense.

Finally, the various meanings of *determinism* inevitably contribute to the muddle. If the existence of the draft was a cause of John's decision, at long last, to marry, that social fact "determined" his behavior. Clearly, it did not compel or coerce him into marrying. Yet another source of Durkheim's holism is what he calls the "external coercive power" of social facts. According to him we do not even choose our style of house or clothing. These are "imposed on us" from without. The vehicles of this coercion are group minds and collective drives. How, then, do we distinguish the coercive power of custom from the quite different coercive power of the legal order? The legal order is a set of rules or norms prescribing our behavior. These rules provide for sanctions to be imposed by a designated authority for the opposite behavior. There is all the difference in the world between, say, my political behavior being caused by the external family circumstances into which I was born and it being caused by the external threat of imprisonment. The threat backed by officially sanctioned force coerces me, but my family need not do so. Only in a police state which provided rules with sanctions for every detail of human action would all social facts have "coercive power." By the same token, there may well be laws about the effects of institutions on each other or on individuals, without any force being applied to anyone. The so-called forces "impelling" the behavior of, say, Churchill were all the events leading up to and including the Second World War. These were the conditions in which he acted and among the causes of the choices that he made. But they did not force him to become Prime Minister or to heighten public morale during the Battle of Britain.

If someone else had been in his place, would the outcome have been different? Social determinists, of either the hard or the soft variety, must answer "no." Yet there is an important difference between them. Hardline social determinism is the view that sociological laws, that is, laws mentioning only collectivities and their properties, can completely explain and predict social events without any reference to the behavior of individuals. Social concepts are holistically construed, and society or culture has its own laws to which individual choices, be they of heroes or of plain men, contribute little or nothing. Durkheim's holism commits him to this view. Soft social determinists, on the other hand, agree that there are comprehensive social laws, but maintain that patterns of individual acts and attitudes are the elements of the social facts occurring in these laws. The behavior of individuals therefore does make a difference, but not in such a way as to rule out a comprehensive social theory. Soft social determinism is attractive to the social scientist who wants no truck with unique, undefinable group properties and "forces." If true, it would imply the existence of a set of social laws—laws containing only group or institutional terms—that completely explain all social occurrences. Would such a comprehensive and individualistic, non-holistic, social theory permit us to say that Churchill's actions made a difference? It is interesting to see why it would not.

There may be laws linking the occurrence of specific personality types with social phenomena. Such a law might, for instance, assert that given a man like Churchill and the social situation of England in 1940, one kind of consequence rather than another would follow. England fought rather than let Hitler take over Europe. It might not have done so if a man like Churchill had not been there. Soft determinism accepts the methodological assumption that every social concept is definable in terms of individuals interacting with one another. Presumably, we could therefore just add this "personality-type" variable to our definition of the social event. (Addis suggests this in his paper.) However, we would no longer have a purely social law and, therefore, we would not have a comprehensive *social* theory. We would have a mixed psychosociological law which covertly contained the personality element in the definition of the collective term.

Precisely because the definitions of group concepts in terms of patterns of individuals are not of this sort they are sociological rather than psychological terms. They do not mention unique personalities or personality types, but interchangeable *roles*. They are nonetheless individualistic. For a role is a position occupied by a person in a group relative to other persons in that group. It carries with it certain expected regularities of behavior toward others in the group and by them toward the person in the role. As defined by their roles, any two heads of state are interchangeable. If social laws were sufficient, then it would not matter that Churchill was Prime Minister and Hitler the Fuehrer. If group behavior is only determined by the roles of its members and the environment, then specific personalities or even personality types need not be mentioned in laws about the social process. But if these personality variables make a difference, then no theory of the social process that omitted them could be complete. Soft social determinism denies that specific personality variables are necessary. In contrast to hard determinism, individual choices do make a difference, but all choices are, so to speak, equal in the social process. Against this, one may suggest that even in a perfect democracy the choices of some men are, in George Orwell's immortal words, more equal than others. By virtue of the kind of men they are, they exert a different and greater influence on events than would the actions of others in their position.

This is not to deny, of course, that many laws about social phenomena can doubtless be discovered that need not mention individual personalities. It does deny, however, the likelihood of a comprehensive sociological theory, that is, a theory couched only in collective terms that could completely explain and predict all social events. Part of the problem of causal imputation is to decide when the social fact and when the individual personality was the decisive factor. Doubtless, they interact. As Addis says, when discussing the doctrine of "total social interaction," probably everything that occurs at a given time makes some difference to what occurs at another time. Mac-Iver points out that the question is not whether the individual makes a difference, but how much. He distinguishes "levels" of explanation in terms of the units involved. Whether a given human act has distinguishable consequences depends upon the size of the social unit and the time span we want to explain. An act that has distinguishable causal consequences for the family over a short period of time need not have them for a civilization over a long period of time.

The issues raised here are usually discussed under the rubric "the problem of reduction." In the introduction to Section Three, the reduction of psychology to physiology was explained as the deduction, via certain connecting links, of the laws of psychology from the laws of physiology. All the papers in this section bear on the problem of the connection between *sociology*, as shorthand for all the areas that employ collective concepts, and psychology or the science of individual behavior. It becomes evident that the term *reduction* may be applied to two different sorts of things. It is used for the analysis or definition of group concepts in terms of individual behavior. In this respect a writer may be either individualistic or holistic. It is also used for the deduction of the laws of sociology from the laws of psychology. In this respect a writer may be either reductionist or nonreductionist. Different combinations of these two views are represented by the various authors.

Durkheim, as we saw, is a holist. His unanalyzable collective properties are instances of what Brodbeck refers to as "descriptive emergents." Durkheim is also an antireductionist for he holds that social laws are unpredictable from laws about individuals. This view is called explanatory emergence. The laws of a complex system may be different from, or novel with respect to, the laws of its parts. This is novelty of laws through complexity. It does not imply explanatory emergence, as the laws of the complex may be derivable from composition laws, that is, laws about how the elements of the complex combine. Or laws may be novel because of different initial conditions, as the laws of a capitalist economy may be different from the laws of a socialist one. This does not imply explanatory emergence either, because the two sets of laws may both be derivable as approximations or special cases of more general economic laws.

Holists with respect to concepts tend to be antireductionist with respect to laws. Logically, however, the two views need not go together because a holist could hold that the unanalyzable properties of groups are connected by empirical laws to the behavior of individuals in groups. As Brodbeck points out (p. 301), descriptive emergence does not imply explanatory emergence. In any event, whether or not all holists are in fact also anti-reductionist, not all antireductionists are holists. Gellner disavows concept holism ("history is about chaps") and acknowledges, therefore, that group properties are analyzable in individualistic terms. But he is also a non-reductionist ("its explanations are not in terms of chaps"). Stated less opaquely, he holds that there are group laws whose terms refer to complexes of individual behavior, but these laws are not derivable from laws about the behavior of individuals. Like Durkheim, therefore, he is an explanatory emergentist. Maintaining that "the proper study of mankind is groups and institutions," he also quite clearly accepts the possibility of a comprehensive social theory. In contrast to Durkheim, however, his is a soft rather than a hard determinism, because he construes social concepts individualistically.

Watkins, partly reacting to some criticisms of his views by Gellner, distinguishes methodological individualism from sociological holism and discusses some limitations and misunderstandings of individualism. He directs his fire especially at holist and historicist explanations of individual beliefs and behavior in terms of impersonal social "forces." He contrasts such "sinister" explanations of large-scale phenomena with their "innocent" explanation as the unintended consequences of individual characteristics. His views are individualistic with respect to social terms and reductionist with respect to social laws. Addis, investigating the role of individual choice in Marx's philosophy of history, provides a clear analytical review of many of the key issues in the holist-individualist controversy and its connection with the problem of reduction.

[13] Social Facts

EMILE DURKHEIM

Before inquiring into the method suited to the study of social facts, it is important to know which facts are commonly called "social." This information is all the more necessary since the designation "social" is used with little precision. It is currently employed for practically all phenomena generally diffused within society, however small their social interest. But on that basis, there are, as it were, no human events that may not be called social. Each individual drinks, sleeps, eats, reasons; and it is to society's interest that these functions be exercised in an orderly manner. If, then, all these facts are counted as "social" facts, sociology would have no subject matter exclusively its own, and its domain would be confused with that of biology and psychology.

But in reality there is in every society a certain group of phenomena which may be differentiated from those studied by the other natural sciences. When I fulfil my obligations as brother, husband, or citizen, when I execute my contracts, I perform duties which are defined, externally to myself and my acts, in law and in custom. Even if they conform to my own sentiments and I feel their reality subjectively, such reality is still objective, for I did not create them; I merely inherited them through my education. How many times it happens, moreover, that we are ignorant of the details of the obligations incumbent upon us, and that in order to acquaint ourselves with them we must consult the law and its authorized interpreters! Similarly, the church-member finds the beliefs and practices of his religious life ready-made at birth; their existence prior to his own implies their existence outside of himself. The system of signs I use to express my thought, the system of currency I employ to pay my debts, the instruments of credit I utilize in my commercial relations, the practices followed in my profession, etc., function independently of my own use of them. And these statements can be repeated for each member of society. Here, then, are ways of acting, thinking, and feeling that present the noteworthy property of existing outside the individual consciousness.

These types of conduct or thought are not only external to the individual but are, moreover, endowed with coercive power, by virtue of which they impose themselves upon him, independent of his individual will. Of course, when I fully consent and conform to them, this constraint is felt only slightly, if at all, and is therefore unnecessary. But it is, nonetheless, an intrinsic characteristic of these facts, the proof thereof being that it asserts itself as soon as I attempt to resist it. If I attempt to violate the law, it reacts against me so as to prevent my act before its accomplishment, or to nullify my violation by restoring the damage, if it is accomplished and reparable, or to make me expiate it if it cannot be compensated for otherwise.

In the case of purely moral maxims, the public conscience exercises a check on every act which offends it by means of the surveillance it exercises over the conduct of citizens, and the appropriate penalties at its disposal. In many cases the constraint is less violent, but nevertheless it always exists. If I do not submit to the conventions of society, if in my dress I do not conform to the customs observed in my country and in my class, the ridicule I provoke, the social isolation in which I am kept, produce, although in an attenuated form, the same effects as a punishment in the strict sense of the word. The constraint is nonetheless efficacious for being indirect. I am not obliged to speak French with my fellow-countrymen nor to use the legal currency, but I cannot possibly do otherwise. If I tried to escape this necessity, my attempt would fail miserably. As an industrialist, I am free to apply the technical methods of former centuries; but by doing so, I should invite certain ruin. Even when I free myself from these rules and violate them successfully, I am always compelled to struggle with them. When finally overcome, they make their constraining power sufficiently felt by the resistance they offer. The enterprises of all innovators, including successful ones, come up against resistance of this kind.

Here, then, is a category of facts with very distinctive characteristics: it consists of ways of acting, thinking, and feeling, external to the individual, and endowed with a power of coercion, by reason of which they control him. These ways of thinking could not be confused with biological phenomena, since they consist of representations and of actions; nor with psychological phenomena, which exist only in the individual consciousness and through it. They constitute, thus, a new variety of phenomena; and it is to them exclusively that the term "social" ought to be applied. And this term fits them quite well, for it is clear that, since their source is not in the individual, their substratum can be no other than society, either the political society as a whole or some one of the partial groups it includes, such as religious denominations, political, literary, and occupational associations, etc. On the other hand, this term "social" applies to them exclusively, for it has a distinct meaning only if it designates exclusively the phenomena which are not included in any of the categories of facts that have already been established and classified. These ways of thinking and acting therefore constitute the proper domain of sociology. It is true that, when we define them with this word "constraint," we risk shocking the zealous partisans of absolute individualism. For those who profess the complete autonomy of the individual, man's dignity is diminished whenever he is made to feel that he is not completely self-determinant. It is generally accepted today, however, that most of our ideas and our tendencies are not developed by ourselves but come to us from without. How can they become a part of us except by imposing themselves upon us? This is the whole meaning of our definition. And it is generally accepted, moreover, that social constraint is not necessarily incompatible with the individual personality.[1]

Since the examples that we have just cited (legal and moral regulations, religious faith, financial systems, etc.) all consist of established beliefs and practices, one might be led to believe that social facts exist only where there is some social organization. But there are other facts without such crystallized form which have the same objectivity and the same ascendancy over the individual. These are called "social currents." Thus the great movements of enthusiasm, indignation, and pity in a crowd do not originate in any one of the particular individual consciousnesses. They come to each one of us from without and can carry us away in spite of ourselves. Of course, it may happen that, in abandoning myself to them unreservedly, I do not feel the pressure they exert upon me. But it is revealed as soon as I try to resist them. Let an individual attempt to oppose one of these collective manifestations, and the emotions that he denies will turn against him. Now, if this power of external coercion asserts itself so clearly in cases of resistance, it must exist also in the first-mentioned cases, although we are unconscious of it. We are then victims of the illusion of having ourselves created that which actually forced itself from without. If the complacency with which we permit ourselves to be carried along conceals the pressure undergone, nevertheless it does not abolish it. Thus, air is no less heavy because we do not detect its weight. So, even if we ourselves have spontaneously contributed to the production of the common emotion, the impression we have received differs markedly from that which we would have experienced if we had been alone. Also, once the crowd has dispersed, that is, once these social influences have ceased to act upon us and we are alone again, the emotions which have passed through the mind appear strange to us, and we no longer recognize them as ours. We realize that these feelings have been impressed upon us to a much greater extent than they were created by us. It may even happen that they horrify us, so much were they contrary to our nature. Thus, a group of individuals, most of whom are perfectly inoffensive, may, when gathered in a crowd, be drawn into acts of atrocity. And what we say of these transitory outbursts applies similarly to those more permanent currents of opinion on religious, political, literary, or artistic matters which are constantly being formed around us, whether in society as a whole or in more limited circles.

To confirm this definition of the social fact by a characteristic illustration from common experience, one need only observe the manner in which chil-

---

[1] We do not intend to imply, however, that all constraint is normal. We shall return to this point later.

dren are brought up. Considering the facts as they are and as they have always been, it becomes immediately evident that all education is a continuous effort to impose on the child ways of seeing, feeling, and acting which he could not have arrived at spontaneously. From the very first hours of his life, we compel him to eat, drink, and sleep at regular hours; we constrain him to cleanliness, calmness, and obedience; later we exert pressure upon him in order that he may learn proper consideration for others, respect for customs and conventions, the need for work, etc. If, in time, this constraint ceases to be felt, it is because it gradually gives rise to habits and to internal tendencies that render constraint unnecessary; but nevertheless it is not abolished, for it is still the source from which these habits were derived. It is true that, according to Spencer, a rational education ought to reject such methods, allowing the child to act in complete liberty; but as this pedagogic theory has never been applied by any known people, it must be accepted only as an expression of personal opinion, not as a fact which can contradict the aforementioned observations. What makes these facts particularly instructive is that the aim of education is, precisely, the socialization of the human being; the process of education, therefore, gives us in a nutshell the historical fashion in which the social being is constituted. This unremitting pressure to which the child is subjected is the very pressure of the social milieu which tends to fashion him in its own image, and of which parents and teachers are merely the representatives and intermediaries.

It follows that sociological phenomena cannot be defined by their universality. A thought which we find in every individual consciousness, a movement repeated by all individuals, is not thereby a social fact. If sociologists have been satisfied with defining them by this characteristic, it is because they confused them with what one might call their reincarnation in the individual. It is, however, the collective aspects of the beliefs, tendencies, and practices of a group that characterize truly social phenomena. As for the forms that the collective states assume when refracted in the individual, these are things of another sort. This duality is clearly demonstrated by the fact that these two orders of phenomena are frequently found dissociated from one another. Indeed, certain of these social manners of acting and thinking acquire, by reason of their repetition, a certain rigidity which on its own account crystallizes them, so to speak, and isolates them from the particular events which reflect them. They thus acquire a body, a tangible form, and constitute a reality in their own right, quite distinct from the individual facts which produce it. Collective habits are inherent not only in the successive acts which they determine but, by a privilege of which we find no example in the biological realm, they are given permanent expression in a formula which is repeated from mouth to mouth, transmitted by education, and fixed even in writing. Such is the origin and nature of legal and moral rules, popular aphorisms and proverbs, articles of faith wherein religious or political groups condense their beliefs, standards of taste established by literary schools, etc. None of these can be found entirely reproduced in the applications made of them by individuals, since they can exist even without being actually applied.

No doubt, this dissociation does not always manifest itself with equal distinctness, but its obvious existence in the important and numerous cases just cited is sufficient to prove that the social fact is a thing distinct from its individual manifestations. Moreover, even when this dissociation is not immediately apparent, it may often be disclosed by certain devices of method. Such dissociation is indispensable if one wishes to separate social facts from their alloys in order to observe them in a state of purity. Currents of opinion, with an intensity varying according to the time and place, impel certain groups either to more marriages, for example, or to more suicides, or to a higher or lower birthrate, etc. These currents are plainly social facts. At first sight they seem inseparable from the forms they take in individual cases. But statistics furnish us with the means of isolating them. They are, in fact, represented with considerable exactness by the rates of births, marriages, and suicides, that is, by the number obtained by dividing the average annual total of marriages, births, suicides, by the number of persons whose ages lie within the range in which marriages, births, and suicides occur.[2] Since each of these figures contains all the individual cases indiscriminately, the individual circumstances which may have had a share in the production of the phenomenon are neutralized and, consequently, do not contribute to its determination. The average, then, expresses a certain state of the group mind (*l'âme collective*).

Such are social phenomena, when disentangled from all foreign matter. As for their individual manifestations, these are indeed, to a certain extent, social, since they partly reproduce a social model. Each of them also depends, and to a large extent, on the organopsychological constitution of the individual and on the particular circumstances in which he is placed. Thus they are not sociological phenomena in the strict sense of the word. They belong to two realms at once; one could call them sociopsychological. They interest the sociologist without constituting the immediate subject matter of sociology. There exist in the interior of organisms similar phenomena, compound in their nature, which form in their turn the subject matter of the "hybrid sciences," such as physiological chemistry, for example.

The objection may be raised that a phenomenon is collective only if it is common to all members of society, or at least to most of them—in other words, if it is truly general. This may be true; but it is general because it is collective (that is, more or less obligatory), and certainly not collective because general. It is a group condition repeated in the individual because imposed on him. It is to be found in each part because it exists in the whole, rather than in the whole because it exists in the parts. This becomes conspicuously evident in those beliefs and practices which are transmitted to us ready-made by previous generations; we receive and adopt them because, being both collective and ancient, they are invested with a particular author-

---

[2] Suicides do not occur at every age, and they take place with varying intensity at the different ages in which they occur.

ity that education has taught us to recognize and respect. It is, of course, true that a vast portion of our social culture is transmitted to us in this way; but even when the social fact is due in part to our direct collaboration, its nature is not different. A collective emotion which bursts forth suddenly and violently in a crowd does not express merely what all the individual sentiments had in common; it is something entirely different, as we have shown. It results from their being together, a product of the actions and reactions which take place between individual consciousness; and if each individual consciousness echoes the collective sentiment, it is by virtue of the special energy resident in its collective origin. If all hearts beat in unison, this is not the result of a spontaneous and pre-established harmony but rather because an identical force propels them in the same direction. Each is carried along by all.

We thus arrive at the point where we can formulate and delimit in a precise way the domain of sociology. It comprises only a limited group of phenomena. A social fact is to be recognized by the power of external coercion which it exercises or is capable of exercising over individuals, and the presence of this power may be recognized in its turn either by the existence of some specific sanction or by the resistance offered against every individual effort that tends to violate it. One can, however, define it also by its diffusion within the group, provided that, in conformity with our previous remarks, one takes care to add as a second and essential characteristic that its own existence is independent of the individual forms it assumes in its diffusion. This last criterion is perhaps, in certain cases, easier to apply than the preceding one. In fact, the constraint is easy to ascertain when it expresses itself externally by some direct reaction of society, as is the case in law, morals, beliefs, customs, and even fashions. But when it is only indirect, like the constraint which an economic organization exercises, it cannot always be so easily detected. Generality combined with externality may, then, be easier to establish. Moreover, this second definition is but another form of the first; for if a mode of behavior whose existence is external to individual consciousnesses becomes general, this can only be brought about by its being imposed upon them.[3]

---

[3] It will be seen how this definition of the social fact diverges from that which forms the basis of the ingenious system of M. Tarde. First of all, we wish to state that our researches have nowhere led us to observe that preponderant influence in the genesis of collective facts which M. Tarde attributes to imitation. Moreover, from the preceding definition, which is not a theory but simply a résumé of the immediate data of observation, it seems indeed to follow, not only that imitation does not always express the essential and characteristic features of the social fact, but even that it never expresses them. No doubt, every social fact is imitated; it has, as we have just shown, a tendency to become general, but that is because it is social, i.e., obligatory. Its power of expansion is not the cause but the consequence of its sociological character. If, further, only social facts produced this consequence, imitation could perhaps serve, if not to explain them, at least to define them. But an individual condition which produces a whole series of effects remains individual nevertheless. Moreover, one may ask whether the word "imitation" is indeed fitted to designate an effect due to a coercive influence. Thus, by this single expression, very different phenomena, which ought to be distinguished, are confused.

But these several phenomena present the same characteristic by which we defined the others. These "ways of existing" are imposed on the individual precisely in the same fashion as the "ways of acting" of which we have spoken. Indeed, when we wish to know how a society is divided politically, of what these divisions themselves are composed, and how complete is the fusion existing between them, we shall not achieve our purpose by physical inspection and by geographical observations; for these phenomena are social, even when they have some basis in physical nature. It is only by a study of public law that a comprehension of this organization is possible, for it is this law that determines the organization, as it equally determines our domestic and civil relations. This political organization is, then, no less obligatory than the social facts mentioned above. If the population crowds into our cities instead of scattering into the country, this is due to a trend of public opinion, a collective drive that imposes this concentration upon the individuals. We can no more choose the style of our houses than of our clothing—at least, both are equally obligatory. The channels of communication prescribe the direction of internal migrations and commerce, etc., and even their extent. Consequently, at the very most, it should be necessary to add to the list of phenomena which we have enumerated as presenting the distinctive criterion of a social fact only one additional category, "ways of existing"; and, as this enumeration was not meant to be rigorously exhaustive, the addition would not be absolutely necessary.

Such an addition is perhaps not necessary, for these "ways of existing" are only crystallized "ways of acting." The political structure of a society is merely the way in which its component segments have become accustomed to live with one another. If their relations are traditionally intimate, the segments tend to fuse with one another, or, in the contrary case, to retain their identity. The type of habitation imposed upon us is merely the way in which our contemporaries and our ancestors have been accustomed to construct their houses. The methods of communication are merely the channels which the regular currents of commerce and migrations have dug, by flowing in the same direction. To be sure, if the phenomena of a structural character alone presented this permanence, one might believe that they constituted a distinct species. A legal regulation is an arrangement no less permanent than a type of architecture, and yet the regulation is a "physiological" fact. A simple moral maxim is assuredly somewhat more malleable, but it is much more rigid than a simple professional custom or a fashion. There is thus a whole series of degrees without a break in continuity between the facts of the most articulated structure and those free currents of social life which are not yet definitely molded. The differences between them are, therefore, only differences in the degree of consolidation they present. Both are simply life, more or less crystallized. No doubt, it may be of some advantage to reserve the term "morphological" for those social facts which concern the social substratum, but only on condition of not overlooking the fact that they are of the same nature as the others. Our definition will then include the whole relevant range of facts if we say: *A social fact is every way of acting, fixed or not, capable of exercising on the individual an external constraint;* or again, *every way of acting which is general throughout a given society, while at the same time existing in its own right independent of its individual manifestations.*[4]

. . . Social phenomena are things and ought to be treated as things. To demonstrate this proposition, it is unnecessary to philosophize on their nature and to discuss the analogies they present with the phenomena of lower realms of existence. It is sufficient to note that they are the unique data of the sociologist. All that is given, all that is subject to observation, has thereby the character of a thing. To treat phenomena as things is to treat them as data, and these constitute the point of departure of science. Now, social phenomena present this character incontestably. What is given is not the idea that men form of value, for that is inaccessible, but only the values established in the course of economic relations; not conceptions of the moral ideal, but the totality of rules which actually determine conduct; not the idea of utility or wealth, but all the details of economic organization. Even assuming the possibility that social life is merely the development of certain ideas, these ideas are nevertheless not immediately given. They cannot be perceived or known directly, but only through the phenomenal reality expressing them. We do not know a priori whether ideas form the basis of the diverse currents of social life, nor what they are. Only after having traced these currents back to their sources shall we know whence they issue.

We must, therefore, consider social phenomena in themselves as distinct from the consciously formed representations of them in the mind; we must study them objectively as external things, for it is this character that they present to us. If this exteriority should prove to be only apparent, the advance of science will bring the disillusionment and we shall see our conception of social phenomena change, as it were, from the objective to the subjective. But in any case, the solution cannot be anticipated; and even if we finally arrive at the result that social phenomena do not possess all the intrinsic characteristics of the thing, we ought at first to treat them as if they had. This rule is applicable, then, to all social reality without exception. Even phenomena which give the strongest impression of being arbitrary arrangements ought to be thus considered. *The voluntary character of a practice or an institution should never be assumed beforehand.* Moreover, if we may introduce our personal observation, it has always been our experience that, when this procedure is followed, facts most arbitrary in

---

4 This close connection between life and structure, organ and function, may be easily proved in sociology because between these two extreme terms there exists a whole series of immediately observable intermediate stages which show the bond between them. Biology is not in the same favorable position. But we may well believe that the inductions on this subject made by sociology are applicable to biology and that, in organisms as well as in societies, only differences in degree exist between these two orders of facts.

appearance will come to present, after more attentive observation, qualities of consistency and regularity that are symptomatic of their objectivity.

The foregoing statements concerning the distinctive characteristics of the social fact give us sufficient assurance about the nature of this objectivity to prove that it is not illusory. Indeed, the most important characteristic of a "thing" is the impossibility of its modification by a simple effort of the will. Not that the thing is refractory to all modification, but a mere act of the will is insufficient to produce a change in it; it requires a more or less strenuous effort due to the resistance which it offers, and, moreover, the effort is not always successful. We have already seen that social facts have this characteristic. Far from being a product of the will, they determine it from without; they are like molds in which our actions are inevitably shaped. This necessity is often inescapable. But even when we triumph over it, the opposition encountered signifies clearly to us the presence of something not depending upon ourselves. Thus, in considering social phenomena as things, we merely adjust our conceptions in conformity to their nature.

Clearly, the reform needed in sociology is at all points identical with that which has transformed psychology in the last thirty years. Just as Comte and Spencer declare that social facts are facts of nature, without, however, treating them as things, so the different empirical schools had long recognized the natural character of psychological phenomena, but continued to apply to them a purely ideological method. In fact, the empiricists, not less than their adversaries, proceeded exclusively by introspection. Now, the facts obtained thereby are too few in number, too fleeting and plastic, to be able to control and to correct the corresponding ideas fixed in us by habit. If they are not subjected to some other check, nothing counterbalances them; consequently, they take the place of facts and become the subject matter of science. Thus, neither Locke nor Condillac studied psychological phenomena objectively. They did not study sensation in itself but their particular idea of it. Therefore, although in certain respects they prepared the way for scientific psychology, its actual origin is to be dated much later, when it had finally been established that states of consciousness can and ought to be considered from without, and not from the point of view of the consciousness experiencing them. Such is the great revolution accomplished in this branch of studies. All the specific procedures and all the new methods by which this science has been enriched are only diverse means of realizing more completely this fundamental idea. It remains for sociology to make this same advance, to pass from the subjective stage, which it has still scarcely outgrown, to the objective.

Fortunately, this transformation is less difficult to effect here than in psychology. Indeed, psychological facts are naturally given as conscious states of the individual, from whom they do not seem to be even separable. Internal by definition, it seems that they can be treated as external only by doing violence to their nature. Not only is an effort of abstraction necessary, but in addition a whole series of procedures and artifices in order to hold them continuously within this point of view. Social facts, on the contrary, qualify far more naturally and immediately as things. Law is embodied in codes; the currents of daily life are recorded in statistical figures and historical monuments; fashions are preserved in costumes; and taste in works of art. By their very nature they tend toward an independent existence outside the individual consciousnesses, which they dominate. In order to disclose their character as things, it is unnecessary to manipulate them ingeniously. From this point of view, sociology has a significant advantage over psychology, an advantage not hitherto perceived, and one which should hasten its development. Its facts are perhaps more difficult to interpret because more complex, but they are more easily arrived at. Psychology, on the contrary, has difficulties not only in the manipulation of its facts but also in rendering them explicit. Consequently, we believe that, once this principle of sociological method is generally recognized and practiced, sociology will progress with a rapidity difficult to forecast from its present tardiness of development and will even overtake psychology, whose present relative advantage is due solely to historical priority.[5]

  [5] It is true that the greater complexity of social facts makes the science more difficult. But, in compensation, precisely because sociology is the latest comer, it is in a position to profit by the progress made in the sciences concerned with lower stages of existence and to learn from them. This utilization of previous experiments will certainly accelerate its development.

[14] Holism Versus Individualism

ERNEST GELLNER

   The problem of explanation in history is also the problem of the nature of sociology. The views adopted in this field are held to have profound moral and political implications. We have recently often been reminded of this. The simplest argument connecting a premiss about the nature of historical explanation with political or ethical consequences runs as follows: if rigid, unchangeable, and wide-ranging generalisations are attainable with regard to historical processes, then an outlook which presupposes individual responsibility is basically misguided. Having pointed out this implication, philoso-

Originally published under the title "Explanations in History," in the *Proceedings of the Aristotelian Society*, Supplementary Vol. 30, 1956, pp. 157–176 and reprinted with kind permission of the author and the Editor of the Aristotelian Society.

phers hostile to the conclusion then devote themselves to undermining the premiss. They may do so either by pointing out that the required historical laws have not been found, or by arguing that they could not be.

I shall not directly concern myself with this matter of the existence or possibility of historical *laws,* but attempt to isolate the issues which arise here that can be stated without at any rate explicit reference to the law-like nature of history. I shall concern myself with the kind of concept or term characteristically employed when we talk of history or of societies. Notoriously the grammatical subject of sentences written or uttered by social scientists is often not a man, or enumerated or characterized men, but groups, institutions, "cultures," etc. The proper study of mankind is human groups and institutions.

Thus the alleged argument leading to the elimination of individual autonomy and responsibility may be stated without at least explicit and obvious presupposition of the attainment of causal generalizations in history. Those concerned with defending humanity against historicist or other mythologies —I shall call these defenders "Individualists"—notice this fact. This gives rise to an attempt to "eliminate" so-called "holistic" concepts, or rather to show that these are in principle eliminable. That such an elimination should be possible seems strongly suggested by the fact that, after all, groups consist of people, and institutions are what people do, etc. A state cannot exist without citizens, nor a legal system without judges, litigants, etc. The worst obstacle such elimination could encounter, it seems, would be complexity.[1]

The matter, however, is not so simple. Arguments have been put forward to the effect that the elimination is in principle impossible.[2] Moreover, it is a weighty fact that at least some explanations in social sciences would in practice not be stated or be at all easily statable in individualist terms.[3]

To each side in this dispute, its own position appears very nearly self-evident, and the opponents' position something that can be *said,* but not

---

[1] There is one foreseeable objection to both my arguments and those I criticize, namely, that a "naming" theory of meaning underlies both the approaches contemplated. For instance, Mr. R. Wollheim in his review of Mr. Weldon's "Vocabulary of Politics" in *Mind,* 1955, makes a point of this kind in a similar context. Now this type of currently fashionable general appeal to the heterogeneity of meaning does not seem to me to cut much ice; perhaps because the "naming theory" of meaning has not been adequately exorcized from my mind, but perhaps for better reasons. These might be along the following lines: not all reductions are impossible, but on the contrary some are both possible and salutary. The general acceptance of the great variety of ways in which words have meaning does indeed leave us with the baby, but also with much undesirable bath water. It does not by itself give us any insight into how various concepts are used. We gain that, amongst other ways, by trying to reduce some concepts to others. For instance, the Individualist is quite right in insisting that a rising marriage rate is not the kind of thing which could be the cause of an individual marriage. It only records the fact that more such marriages occur. At the same time when reductions fail, the fact that they do and the reasons they do, give us some understanding of the nature of the unreduced concepts.

[2] *Cf.* Maurice Mandelbaum, "Societal Facts" in *The British Journal of Sociology,* 1955. [Reprinted in *Theories of History,* P. Gardiner, ed., The Free Press, New York, 1959, pp. 476–488.—Ed.]

[3] Cf. M. Ginsberg, "The Individual and Society" in *The Diversity of Morals,* 1956.

seriously practised. To the Individualist, his own position appears so true that it barely needs the confirmation of actually carried out eliminations, whilst he gleefully points out that in practice the holist can and does only approach his institutions, etc., through what concrete people do, which seems to the Individualist a practical demonstration and implicit confession of the absurdity of holism. By contrast (and with neat symmetry) the holist sees in the fact that the individualist continues to talk in holistic terms a practical demonstration of the unworkability of individualism, and he certainly does not consider the fact that he can only approach groups and institutions through the doings of individuals to be something which he had implicitly denied and which could count against him. Both sides find comfort in the actual practice of the opponent.

One should add here that the possibility of political implications cuts both ways. Individualists who attempt to save us, in the name of logic and liberty, from misconstruing our situation, are not wholly free at all times from the suspicion that a little propaganda for *laissez faire* is being hitched on to those very general issues.[4]

What is at issue is the ontological status of the entities referred to by the holistic terms. As the notion of ontological status is not as clear as it might be, I shall at some stages shift provisionally to something which is as important to the reductionist and which to him is an index of existence—namely, causation. He does not wish to allow that the Whole could ever be a cause, and to insist that explanations which make it appear that it is can be translated into others. That which is a mere construct cannot causally affect that which "really exists"; this is, I suspect, the feeling of the Individualist, the reductionist. This in conjunction with the truism that a whole is made up of its parts, that nothing can happen to a whole without something happening to either some at least of its parts or to their mutual relations,—leads him to the misleading conclusion that explanation in history and in social studies must ultimately be in terms of individual dispositions. The holistic counter-argument works in reverse; if something (*a*) is a causal factor (*b*) cannot be reduced, then in some sense it "really and independently exists."

When we face a problem of "reduction" in philosophy we are often confronted with a dilemma; on the one hand forceful formal arguments tend to show that a reduction must be possible, on the other hand all attempted reductions fail or are incomplete, and features can be found which suggest

---

4 As Ginsberg says: 'Similarly those who refuse to accept methodological individualism . . . are not committed . . . to a totalitarian view of political action. They are well aware . . . of the dangers of concentrated power. But they deny that the only choice open to us is between a spontaneous competitive order on one hand, and a system of all-pervading control on the other. It is odd that those who attack what they call scientism should feel able to predict with certainty that any form of socialism must necessarily lead to cultural and political totalitarianism . . . In any event, "logicism" is no improvement on "scientism".' *Op. cit.* pp. 161–162.

or prove that they cannot succeed or be complete. For instance, phenomenalism is supported not by the plausibility or success of actual reductions but by the force of the arguments to the effect that there must be a reduction, whilst at the same time the interesting arguments against it as cogently indicate that phenomenalist translation can never be completed.

The situation is similar with regard to the present problem. I consider, for instance, one particular, rather ambitious attempt to demonstrate that a reduction must be possible.

"All social phenomena are, directly or indirectly, human creations. A lump of matter may exist which no one has perceived but not a price which no one has charged, or a disciplinary code to which no one refers, or a tool which no one would dream of using. From this truism I infer the methodological principle . . . that the social scientist can continue searching for explanations of a social phenomenon until he has reduced it to psychological terms."

The conclusion reached in the end is:

"Individualistic ideal types of explanatory power are constructed by first discerning the form of typical . . . dispositions, and then by demonstration how these lead to certain principles of social behaviour." [5]

As the argument also maintains that "individualistic ideal types" are alone possible, what the conclusion amounts to is something like this: to explain a social or historical situation is to deduce it from what the individuals involved in it are disposed to do.

This contention can be broken up into two claims; that an explanation specifies *individual* dispositions, and that it specifies individual *dispositions*. In other words: (1) Statements about things other than individuals are excluded from a final explanation; (2) Statements which are not about dispositions are similarly excluded. By "disposition" here is meant something "intelligible," a conceivable reaction of human beings to circumstances; not necessarily one we share, still less necessarily one we can "introspect"; but still something opposed to what we would call "dead" physical causation where "anything could cause anything."

Having broken up the requirements of reduction into two parts, we get four possibilities, of which three are excluded. Let us consider these excluded ones in turn.

(1) Holistic subject plus intelligible disposition. This is equivalent to a "group mind" theory. I take it no one is advocating this seriously.

---

[5] J. W. N. Watkins, "Ideal Types and Historical Explanation" in *The British Journal for the Philosophy of Science*, vol. iii, no. 9, 1952. [Reprinted in *Readings in the Philosophy of Science*, H. Feigl and M. Brodbeck, eds., Appleton-Century-Crofts, Inc., New York, 1953, pp. 723–743.—Ed.] See also Discussion of this paper by the same author in the following issue of the same *Journal*.

When in this paper I say "Individualism" I mean "methodological individualism," roughly along the lines outlined in these two articles.

(2) Holistic subject without *intelligible* dispositions—*i.e.* attributions of regularity or pattern to wholes, without any suggestion that these patterns express conscious or purposive reactions.

(3) Individualistic subjects without *intelligible* dispositions.

Let it be said that events explicable along the lines of alternative (3) can be excluded from history or sociology only by an inconvenient and arbitrary fiat. The destruction of Pompeii or the Black Death are historical events. It is true that the *reaction* of survivors to these "blindly causal" events calls for explanation not in terms of "dead" causation but possibly in terms of aims, dispositions, expectations, convictions. So be it; but the very fact that semi-deliberate and blindly causal events are so often and intimately fused in life brings out the inconvenience of excluding one kind.

Consider now exclusion of kind (2). When an historian speaks of the maintenance or growth of an institution, or a linguist about phonetic change, or an anthropologist about the maintenance of a system of kinship structure, they do not in fact always or often mention individual dispositions. The question is, *could* they?

The first step towards such a translation is easy. "The monarchy is strong" can be translated into a disposition of subjects to have a certain set of attitudes to the monarch. Note: not necessarily all subjects or all the time, but a sufficient number of them sufficiently often, and above all at crucial times. Neither "sufficient number" nor "sufficiently often" nor "crucial times" can be defined with precision, nor ultimately without referring back to the holist term "monarchy." The same applies to the "set of attitudes."

By and large, institutions and social structures and climates of opinion are not the results of what people want and believe, but of what they take for granted. Let us allow the reductionist to class tacit acceptance amongst dispositions, though I suspect we shall find the same circularity here as occurs above. Such translations would, however, be clumsy, nebulous, long and vague, where the original statement about an institution or feature of the social scene was clear, brief and intelligible.

If, however, we grant that "in principle" this translation is possible, it in no way follows that these tacit and irregularly diffused dispositions are in turn explicable in terms of familiar, intelligible human responses. The existence of a diffused monarchical disposition was inferred logically from the truth of "The monarchy is strong"; the dependence of the latter on the former, if it obtains at all, does so in virtue of logic or the truism that an institution is what people do. The dependence of the perhaps validly inferred disposition on a piece of intuitively obvious psychology would be a causal matter, and there are no reasons in logic or fact for supposing it to hold. On the contrary, in as far as such a procedure seems to assume the possibility of isolating more elementary dispositions "as they are prior to their manifestations in a social context," formal doubts may be raised concerning the realisability of such a programme.

There are two specific points, possibly inconclusive by themselves but worth noting, which influence the holist at this stage.

First, very small differences in individual conduct distributed irregularly over a large population, may have important consequences for the society at large without being detectable individually. The argument in favour of "social facts" is historically connected with the presence of statistical regularities where none can be found at the molecular, individual level. The statistical regularity can be explained in terms of features of the social situation as a whole, but in practice it is seldom possible to trace the nexus in individual cases. To insist that it is always "in principle" possible is to prejudge the issue under discussion. Moreover, something like a Principle of Indeterminacy may very well operate here, for the amount of disturbance involved in observing the individual case may very often be much larger than the small difference which accounts for the statistical result and may, so to speak, "drown it."

Secondly, individuals do have holistic concepts and often act in terms of them. For instance, a number of reviewers of the recently published Memoirs of Général de Gaulle have commented on the fact that de Gaulle's actions were inspired by his *idea* of France—which may perhaps have had little relation to actual Frenchmen. When the holistic ideas of many individuals are co-ordinated and reinforced by public behaviour and physical objects—by ceremonials, rituals, symbols, public buildings, etc.—it is difficult for the social scientist, though he observes the scene from the outside, not to use the holistic concept. It is quite true that the fact that X acts and thinks in terms of an holistic idea—*e.g.* he treats the totem as if it were his tribe, and the tribe as if it were more than the tribesmen—is itself a fact about an individual. On the other hand, though the holistic term as used by the observer may be eliminable, as used by the participant it is not. Are we to say that a logical impeccable explanation of a social situation is committed to crediting its subjects with nonsensical thought? Perhaps we are. On the other hand, the fact that holistic terms are ineliminable from the thought of participants may well be a clue to their ineliminability from that of observers.

It is perhaps unnecessary at this stage to insist on the fact that very little is gained by having individual dispositions as the bedrock of a historical or social explanation. Their "intelligibility" is either familiarity, or, as often, springs from the fact that dispositional terms come in clusters each of which is a more or less exhaustive crude taxonomy: such as, perhaps, for instance: "Knowing — believing — considering — tacitly accepting — disregarding," or "wanting — being indifferent to — not wanting." If with the help of such terms we characterize someone's conduct, on the analogy of the parallelogram of forces, do we thereby really approach the actual causal sequences?

It is true that this kind of diagnosis fits fairly well in the case of one social science, namely, economics. This, however, is presumably due to the fact that this science restricts itself to behaviour with regard to which aims and relevant convictions and explanations are reasonably avowable and specifiable; to some extent it may be said that economic theory applies to people who have been taught to act in accordance with it. Also, the words most frequently used by economists happen to be *ceteris paribus*. Moreover, whilst an economist may explain a man's behaviour in a market situation, it takes a non-economist to explain how he ever comes to be economically rational. If, for instance, one comes to explain that in terms of the mundane application of a religious notion of "vocation," is that transition an "intelligible disposition"? Yes, in the sense that I see, roughly, what happens, know that it could happen to me, and if I believe it to be a regular occurrence may use it to explain particular incidents. But by those criteria any disposition can become "intelligible." [6]

The real oddity of the reductionist case is that it seems to preclude *a priori* the possibility of human dispositions being the dependent variable in an historical explanation—when in fact they often or always are—and secondly to preclude the possibility of causes, in the sense of initial conditions, being a complex fact which is not desirable in terms of the characteristics of its constituent parts alone—which in turn seems often to be the case.

Let it be added that in as far as the original argument is valid, it is equally valid for the non-human sciences. The fact that the natural sciences seem to be free from restrictions with regard to the kind of explanation they use does not derive from the fact that there are unobserved pieces of matter.[7]

---

[6] Having criticized the notion of "intelligibility" of human dispositions and in particular the accompanying suggestion that it gives us double access or confirmation of human reality, once through social appearance and secondly through dispositions as psychological things-in-themselves. I do not wish to be interpreted as denying the importance of *Einfühlung,* of sympathetic understanding. But the nature and value of this method or heuristic device seems to me the very opposite to what is supposed by the reductionist. It lies in the familiarization with alien reactions and dispositions, not in forcing on them interpretations making them into variants of what is familiar anyway. This last may perhaps be the practice of economic theorists—but just that may help to explain the unreality of that discipline outside certain limits.

Collingwood's celebrated doctrines concerning this matter seem to amount perhaps to not much more than this: history like other disciplines uses the hypothetico-deductive method, and in history the hypotheses are usually about what people attempted to do. Stated thus, the doctrine becomes less startling. It also ceases to be open to the two criticisms normally levelled against it, namely that Collingwood took the ghost in the machine too seriously, and secondly, that he misinterpreted an heuristic device as an essential characteristic of historical knowledge.

Further, "hypothetico-deductive method" is a misnomer. One can only speak of *method* where there is an alternative. But the only alternative to *this* way of studying things is not another way, but not studying them at all. For this "method" really means only thinking about things and then seeing whether what one had thought is true.

[7] Evidently Watkins himself no longer holds this proof valid. He explains in the discussion note in the following number that he considers a counter-example to the principle of methodolgical individualism to be conceivable; so that the principle can hardly be susceptible of formal proof. But the counter-example envisaged by him is of the "group mind" type—dispositional interpretation predicated of social wholes, in my scheme—such as he thinks might be suggested by some facts from the social life of insects. My arguments against the Principle are quite independent of any such possibility. I am more than willing to concede that no phenomena calling for a "group mind" occur.

Moreover, in natural science as much as anywhere else, wholes are composed of their constituent parts. Nothing follows from this truism concerning the general nature of initial conditions in dependence statements; but physicists could, no doubt, use animist language if they wished—they could speak of intelligible dispositions instead of the behaviour of particles.

The present paper is essentially an attempt to separate an indisputably true—because tautologous—proposition (roughly "Assertions about people are assertions about people") from its alleged implications which are at the very least questionable and hence not tautologous, and (hence) not its implications. One might equally have proceeded in the opposite direction and tried to separate the truism "Assertions about societies *are* assertions about society" from an alleged and mistaken consequence that societies "exist" in the same sense as individuals, or independently of them. But the contemporary climate of opinion makes this latter exercise less necessary.

A full clarification of these issues would probably be possible only if we were clearer about what is meant by causation in social contexts. A related matter which I have not pursued is the probability that what counts as "explanation" in history and in the social sciences is far from homogeneous in kind, any more than what counts as a "problem." This, over and above the particular difficulties discussed in this paper, may be a very serious objection to formal methodological arguments providing an *a priori* recipe for "explanation."

So far I have in this paper indicated what seem to me flaws in an attempted reduction. I have little doubt that actual procedure in historical and social explanation often is holistic, and that over and above this appeal to actual procedure, general reasons can be found, and probably stated more forcefully than I have stated them, to support the contention that this must be so. But it is equally obvious to me that this will not shake the determined individualist. Not only does he see important ethical issues hinging on his doctrine, but also some deep logical intuition which many of us can empathise would have to be repressed by him before he could abandon his position. Indisputably, "history is about chaps"; hence "historical events must be explained in terms of what chaps do." Now we all agree that repression is a bad thing; hence it is desirable to diagnose and render harmless the compulsive insight, rather than merely argue against it.

Let us try to call up this intuition in ourselves by attending to the argument of one trying to demonstrate the *im*possibility of reducing holistic social concepts to individual ones.

Mandelbaum's [8] recent argument, restating an old point in "language"—language, starts from the premiss that an action such as drawing money from the bank cannot be explained without the use of holistic concepts such as "banking system." It must be (at least tacitly) understood by the agent, and must be understood by the observer if he is to understand the action. When Mandelbaum says "explain" he might perhaps say "describe," for the rules

---

[8] Cf. Mandelbaum, *op. cit.*

of deposit banking are all somehow implicit in the concept of cashing a cheque. (A causal explanation *might* actually be simpler and not involve any understanding of the rules of banking.)

So far, there is nothing that need upset the individualist. Individuals act guided by nebulous holistic concepts—so far so good. As far as the object connoted by the concept is concerned the Individualist is sure that it can be "translated" in terms of what various individuals involved in banking institutions are doing. (Mandelbaum does not agree, on the grounds that the description of their activity in turn will involve use of the concept of "banking"; but let us leave that aside for the moment.)

Let us just agree—as is indeed true—that drawing a cheque is internally related to the whole banking system, that what is meant by cashing a cheque involves by its very meaning the general features of banking; that, tacitly or otherwise, the concept "bank" is being employed by anyone describing or understanding the cashing of a cheque. I am stressing this, for the Individualist cannot but come with us this far.

It is the next step that he will refuse to take. This step emerges at the end of Mandelbaum's article, when he speaks of individuals and what he calls "societal facts" (e.g. banking systems) *interacting;* in other words, implying that it makes sense for the object of a holistic concept to have an effect on a concrete individual. What the Individualist will here object to is the inference from an holistic concept, somehow abstracted from the concrete behaviour of concrete individuals, being then able to figure in the antecedent of a causal sentence. He will refuse to admit this even if he concedes the ineliminability of the holistic concept in description. This seems indeed, he feels, to endow an abstraction with flesh and power; and we can easily feel this with him.

Of course, he isn't denying that causal statements of this kind are meaningfully and truthfully uttered. He only wishes to insist that the antecedent must in such cases be translatable into individualistic terms. Surely the insubstantial cannot constrain the substantial? I think we can provisionally agree to this principle; (though earlier we *seemed* to have contradicted it when uttering the truism that a cause may be as complex an event as we wish—as indeed it can). At the same time Mandelbaum's central point, that holistic concepts cannot be eliminated, stands. Here is a dilemma indeed.

Attempted Diagnosis

Consider the following two series:

(1) Jones is going to Germany. All members of the platoon are going, etc. All members of the company are going, etc. All members of the battalion are going, etc.
(2) Jones. The Platoon. The Company. The Battalion.

The first series begins with a singular proposition, and continues with general ones of increasing generality. The second series is one of terms or concepts, in which the preceding is at each stage a part of the subsequent one.

Concerning series (1) it is obvious that each subsequent proposition can only be true in virtue of a set of propositions of the earlier kind being true. Propositions of the latter kind can, unless their subjects are open classes, be "reduced" or translated into conjunctions of propositions of the preceding kind. To talk of the more general propositions causing, constraining etc., those of lesser generality subsumed under them is nonsense.

Series (2) lists parts and wholes in such a manner that an earlier member of the series is always a part of a later member. Later members depend for their existence on the existence of earlier members, though not necessarily on any definite list of them. *But:* there is no reason in logic or fact why causal sentences should in their antecedent clauses (or consequent clauses, for that matter) be restricted in their subjects to items of the kind that would only appear at the beginning of the series. If "complexity of causes" obtains, which it often seems to, causal sentences in ordinary language if they are to be expressed in subject-predicate grammatical form will have to have later members of the series as their subjects.

The cause, or at any rate one of the central causes, of the general dilemma under discussion is the attribution of obvious features of series (1) to the series (2), concerning which they are certainly not obvious and probably not true.

For when we speak of societies we mean partly (*a*) generalisations about classes of human individuals which indeed are true only in virtue of propositions about those individuals, and can be "reduced" to them, but also (*b*) groups, complexes, constellations of facts. These latter can indeed exist only if their parts exist—that is indeed the predicament of all wholes—but their fates *qua* fates of complexes can nevertheless be the initial conditions or indeed final conditions of a causal sequence.

The powerful disinclination to allow social or general causes arises from the confusion of (*a*) and (*b*). Jones is not caused to go to Germany by the general fact that all other members of the battalion are going; the general proposition merely *says,* amongst other things, that Jones is going. But there is no reason whatever for excluding *a priori* the possibility of unanimity of his comrades, *qua* unanimity, influencing Jones to volunteer to go. That all members of the unit feel the *esprit de corps* is a generalisation (which is seldom true); but to say that *esprit de corps* has influenced an individual is not to say that he has been influenced by isolable individuals or their acts.

It should now be clear that the following three propositions are not incompatible:

A generalisation is true only in virtue of the truth
of singular propositions.

A whole is made up of its parts.
No *a priori* legislation is possible concerning the
complexity of links in causal chains.

The error of the Individualist is to conclude from the first two propositions, which are analytic, to the falsity of the third, through the confused
identification of the hierarchy of propositions in terms of generality with
the hierarchy of things in terms of complexity and inclusiveness.

Let us illustrate this with another example. If I say "All the men in the
square were excited" I may simply mean a generalisation to the effect that
each of the men there was excited; in such a case it would make no sense
to speak of the generalisation as being an independent fact, less still a causal
factor.

If, on the other hand, I say "There was an atmosphere of tension in the
square," though this cannot be true without some of a nebulously defined
and large set of propositions about the men in the square being true, and
a fortiori it cannot be true unless there are men in the square, there is
yet no way of interpreting this as a mere conjunction. We cannot even
describe the state of mind of typical individual participants in the situation
without referring back to the situation as a whole. This to some extent
throws light on a fact mentioned earlier, namely that whatever the logical
rights and wrongs of the case, individuals do think in holistic terms. What
this amounts to—amongst other things—is the kind of patterns they are capable of isolating in their environment and react to. The pattern isolated,
however, is not "merely abstracted" but is, as I am somewhat sheepishly
tempted to say, "really there."

For any individual, the *mores*, institutions, tacit presupposition, etc., of
his society are an independent and external fact, as much so as the physical
environment and usually more important. And if this is so for each individual, it *does* follow that it is so for the totality of individuals composing
a society. Of course, societies not being endowed with group minds, the
question doesn't arise for "the totality"; *just because* the Individualist is in
one sense right and "there is no such *thing*" as the "totality," the question
of the externality and independence of social facts does not arise for it. But
it can and does arise for the observer, who may of course be simultaneously
a member of the society in question. And though he may in some cases
account in some way for the social facts in terms of the interaction of
individual decisions with prior "social facts," any attempt to eliminate
these altogether will only lead to a regress and possibly to an irrelevant
genetic question of the hen-and-egg kind. The important thing about "hen-
and-egg" is not that we do not know, but that if we did know it would not
throw much light on either hens or eggs.

It might be objected that too much is being made of this matter of causation. Complexity of causes is a familiar phenomenon; it does not follow
from its occurrence that the constituents of a complex cause make up a

"whole." My suggestion is that if perceived as a whole, referred to as such, etc., they do. It might again be objected that this merely shows that there are Social *Gestalten* incorporated in the perception by individuals of their social environment. But these *Gestalten* are so to speak veridical; their objects, individual ways of behaving, conform to them and often act as their sanctions, as reminders to the perceiver of the *Gestalt* that its object is there and must be reckoned with. These re-inforcing acts are indeed acts of individuals; but they in turn are led to behave along the suitable lines by their perception of the same or similar "social fact."

The existence of a complex concept, parts of which are logically inseparable, is after all a familiar thing. For example, a mountain summit *entails* a slope, and so on. The complications which arise with regard to the present problem are two: first, that of the two constituents which appear to be so connected, *i.e.* individual men and their social context, one is tangible, the other not. (Of course, it is not "man" and *any* social contact that is so connected, but individual acts and their contexts.) This leads to the desire to "reduce" the latter to the former, on the misguided assumption that unless this is done one would have to concede that the latter is similarly tangible. The reductionist indeed points both to the intangibility and necessary connection ("Without men and their doings, no society, institutions, etc."), and then mistakenly infers that a reduction must be possible. The second complication arises through the fact that in these subjects we are dealing with conscious men, in other words objects aware of things in the same way as the observer. Hence the complex concepts are met with twice over—once in the minds of men, and once *in re* as the dealings of the observer with things, if you prefer.

The confusion of the hierarchy of propositions graded by generality and of groups graded by size and inclusiveness leads to what might be called the picture or mirror theory of explanation.[9] The merits and otherwise of the picture theory of meaning and propositions is a familiar story, but the reappearance of this tempting model with regard to explanation deserves special treatment.

What seems to happen is something along the following lines. Take as an

[9] "Its overt characteristics (*i.e.* those of a 'complex social situation') may be *established* empirically, but they are only to be *explained* by being shown to be the resultants of individual activities." Watkins, *op. cit.* (italics his). This might be called the stock-exchange theory. The opposite could easily be maintained, though I prefer merely to delay the second part of the statement. The temptation to believe that overt general features can be observed but must then be explained by something individual may spring from the fact that, for instance, the economist gets his empirical material pre-digested by the statistician. An index or a price level looks like a general fact. The field-worker is less tempted to believe that it is the overt feature of the social situation which he *observes*, whilst he only concludes about the individual. On the contrary, he is in close contact with the individuals with whom he passes the time of day, and if the explanations were *there*, he'd have his explanation as soon as he'd gathered his material, or at worst as soon as he had explored the characters of the individual. But this is not what happens. It cannot even be said that his task is the exploration of long-term and unforeseen consequences of individual dispositions. It is the consequences of social features that he is after.

example a generalisation such as "The committee decided to appoint Jones." This means, amongst other things, that each of the members of the committee came in the end to accept a certain conclusion, and if this were an important or interesting event, the historian or sociologist concerned with explaining it might be very happy if he could give an account of the ways by which each of the committee members came to reach his conclusion. This is indeed the paradigm of explanation as conceived by the Individualist —the feared Whole has evaporated in a series of partial biographies and character studies.

It is of course perfectly true that generalisations and abstractions do not give us additional facts; but it does not follow that all propositions whose subjects seem to include the "atoms"—whatever they may happen to be—of a particular discourse, are therefore necessarily generalisations, abstractions or somehow constructs. A failure to see this is the defect often attributed to "atomism" in other spheres, and sociological reductionism seems to be a related species.

In as far as the proposition used as an example is only a generalisation of the form "All members of the committee . . ." the alleged explanation, the paradigm of all explanations, is merely a verification and not an explanation at all. If this were all that could be done, explanation in history and the social sciences would be identical with the gathering of confirming evidence. To explain would be to illustrate; to illustrate fully, to provide the complete picture, would be to give the best explanation. But is this so?

Of course, the Individualist feels that something more should be involved in explanation than illustration, but he seeks it in broader generalisations about each of the committee-men involved; "broader" meaning either more persistent, or "simpler" in a sense to be indicated. There are what might be called simple disposition-types,—sloth, pursuit of gain, of power, or security, etc., of which the more idiosyncratic dispositions of individual men may perhaps be interpreted as variants or combinations.

An example of this kind of approach would be, for instance, the eighteenth century attempt to explain moral feelings as combinations of sympathy and vengefulness: vengefulness on behalf of sufferers other than oneself, whose sufferings had been imaginatively re-lived, produces, say, a sense of justice. (This kind of approach, incidentally, is not *always* unfruitful; I am only arguing against the contention that historical or social explanation must always employ it.)

It is difficult to see how this attempt to bring in explanation which is more than illustration differs from what has sometimes been called psychologism.[10] The objection to it is that there is no way in general of isolating these pure or more persistent dispositions from the social context in

10 *Cf.* K. Popper, *The Open Society and Its Enemies*, chap. 14. In this chapter Popper refers to both "psychologism," which he condemns, and "methodological individualism," which he commends. When, in the articles discussed, "methodological individualism" is worked out more fully than is the case in Popper's book, it seems to me indistinguishable from "psychologism."

which they occur. We have indeed two impossibilities here, one causal and one logical. Popper's argument against psychologism makes use of the former, Mandelbaum's of the latter. As a matter of causal fact, our dispositions are not independent of the social context in which they occur; but they are not even independent logically, for they cannot be described without reference to their social context.

What the Individualist is demanding might be described as the translation from the Active into the Passive Voice; the translation of statements such as "such and such a kind of family organization tends to perpetuate itself" into statements such as "As a result of such and such aims, convictions, dispositions, etc., of individuals this kind of family organisation continues." (To the Individualist it seems, of course, that the translation is *into* a "really" Active Voice, on the general ground that institutions, etc., being constructs from individual behaviour, they *must* "really" be passive.) But the undesirability of such a translation in some cases follows partly from various considerations already stated such as the diffused, individually imperceptible nature of some of these dispositions, or the fact that they refer back to the institutional context, and also from the fact that they may be utterly uninteresting because obvious. The only relevant dispositions may be, to take the example of the permanence of a kind of family organisation, the normal sexual, security and reproductive aspirations which do not distinguish people in that social context from others. The *differentia,* which as the distinctive component in a complex set of conditions will be worthy of the investigator's attention, may well be something institutional and not psychological. It is perfectly possible, for instance, that there are no psychological differences of any importance between two European countries of widely divergent institutions, and that to explain the differentiation is only possible in sociological, not in psychological terms. Of course, psychological differences *may* be significant. The harm done by the kind of Individualism discussed, if taken seriously by investigators, is that it leads to a conviction that such differences must always be present and be significant. The danger of this pre-conception seems to me graver at present than the one which worries the Individualist, namely that of "reifying" abstraction.

In fact, some historical or sociological explanations—as when, for instance, an historian explains the growth of an institution, or an anthropologist the self-maintenance of a social structure—will do this in terms of features of the relevant institution or structure without explicit mention of any individual dispositions.

At this point the Individualist will no doubt protest that despite the absence of explicit mention of individual dispositions, implicitly they are present; ultimately, every social event must have its habitat in the individual psyche. Now this must be conceded: if Individualism is to degenerate into what could be called social Monadism, the desperate incorporation of complex and diffuse relations into the related terms or individuals, then it must be admitted to be true "in a sense." "Algy met a bear, the bear was bulgy, the bulge was Algy"; the individual may consume what Durkheim and others have called social facts, but he will bulge most uncomfortably, and Algy will still be there.[11] I suspect that actual investigators will often, though perhaps not always, prefer to have Algy outside the bear.[12]

The uselessness of Monadism-at-all-costs can be illustrated thus: certain tribes I know have what anthropologists call a segmentary patrilineal structure, which moreover maintains itself very well over time. I could "explain" this by saying that the tribesmen have, all or most of them, dispositions whose effect is to maintain the system. But, of course, not only have they never given the matter much thought, but it also might very well be impossible to isolate anything in the characters and conduct of the individual tribesmen which *explains* how they come to maintain the system (though of course conduct *illustrating* how the system is being maintained will be found).

The recipe for reduction which we are considering does not commit the older errors of inventing dispositions *ad hoc* for each social thing to be explained, or of deriving social conduct from alleged pre-social, pure dispositions. It claims as its explanations low-level generalisations about the conduct of individuals.

But: these dispositions are not always relevant; sometimes or often they are not isolable without this affecting the possibility of explanation; they are not independent variables, but usually depend on highly generalized social factors; and they are often not statable without reference to social facts. If Individualism does not deny all this, perhaps nothing remains to disagree with it about; but if indeed it does not deny this, its programmatic implications for historians and social scientists no longer hold.

Perhaps, in the end, there is agreement to this extent: (human) history *is* about chaps—and nothing else. But perhaps this should be written: History is *about* chaps. It does not follow that its explanations are always in terms of chaps. Societies are what people do, but social scientists are not biographers *en grande série*.

---

[11] Social phenomena have always been most suggestive of the Principle of Internal Relations. This principle is frequently being re-discovered by social scientists.

[12] The Individualist maintains that Algy always was in the bear. Yes, if you like. But the bear isn't Algy, though the bulge is Algy.

[15] Methodological Individualism and Social Tendencies *

J . W . N . W A T K I N S

1 Introduction

The hope which originally inspired methodology was the hope of finding a method of enquiry which would be both necessary and sufficient to guide the scientist unerringly to truth. This hope has died a natural death. Today, methodology has the more modest task of establishing certain rules and requirements which are necessary to prohibit some wrong-headed moves but insufficient to guarantee success. These rules and requirements, which circumscribe scientific enquiries without steering them in any specific direction, are of the two main kinds, formal and material. So far as I can see, the formal rules of scientific method (which comprise both logical rules and certain realistic and fruitful stipulations) are equally applicable to all the empirical sciences. You cannot, for example, deduce a universal law from a finite number of observations whether you are a physicist, a biologist, or an anthropologist. Again, a single comprehensive explanation of a whole range of phenomena is preferable to isolated explanations of each of those phenomena, whatever your field of enquiry. I shall therefore confine myself to the more disputable (I had nearly said 'more disreputable') and metaphysically impregnated part of methodology which tries to establish the appropriate *material* requirements which the *contents* of the premises of an explanatory theory in a particular field ought to satisfy. These requirements may be called regulative principles. Fundamental differences in the subject-matters of different sciences—differences to which formal methodological rules are impervious—ought, presumably, to be reflected in the regulative principles appropriate to each science. It is here that the student of the methods of the social sciences may be expected to have something distinctive to say.

Originally published as "Historical Explanation in the Social Sciences" in the *Br. Jl. for the Phil. of Science*, **8**, 1957, pp. 104–117 and reprinted with permission of the author and Cambridge University Press.

* A revised version of a paper read at the First Annual Conference of the Philosophy of Science Group, Manchester, on 23rd September 1956. Footnotes have been added subsequently.

An example of a regulative principle is mechanism, a metaphysical theory which governed thinking in the physical sciences from the seventeenth century until it was largely superseded by a wave or field world-view. According to mechanism, the ultimate constituents of the physical world are impenetrable particles which obey simple mechanical laws. The existence of these particles cannot be explained—at any rate by science. On the other hand, every complex physical thing or event is the result of a particular configuration of particles and can be explained in terms of the laws governing their behaviour in conjunction with a description of their relative positions, masses, momenta, etc. There may be what might be described as unfinished or half-way explanations of large-scale phenomena (say, the pressure inside a gas-container) in terms of other large-scale factors (the volume and temperature of the gas); but we shall not have arrived at rock-bottom explanations of such large-scale phenomena until we have deduced their behaviour from statements about the properties and relations of particles.

This is a typically metaphysical idea (by which I intend nothing derogatory). True, it is confirmed, even massively confirmed, by the huge success of mechanical theories which conform to its requirements. On the other hand, it is untestable. No experiment could overthrow it. If certain phenomena—say, electromagnetic phenomena—seem refractory to this mechanistic sort of explanation, this refractoriness can always (and perhaps rightly) be attributed to our inability to find a successful mechanical model rather than to an error in our metaphysical intuition about the ultimate constitution of the physical world. But while mechanism is weak enough to be compatible with any *observation* whatever, while it is an untestable and unempirical principle, it is strong enough to be incompatible with various conceivable physical *theories*. It is this which makes it a *regulative*, nonvacuous metaphysical principle. If it were compatible with everything it would regulate nothing. Some people complain that regulative principles discourage research in certain directions, but that is a part of their purpose. You cannot encourage research in one direction without discouraging research in rival directions.

I am not an advocate of mechanism but I have mentioned it because I am an advocate of an analogous principle in social science, the principle of methodological individualism.[1] According to this principle, the ultimate constituents of the social world are individual people who act more or less appropriately in the light of their dispositions and understanding of their situation. Every complex social situation, institution, or event is the result

[1] Both of these analogous principles go back at least to Epicurus. In recent times methodological individualism has been powerfully defended by Professor F. A. Hayek in his *Individualism and Economic Order* and *The Counter-Revolution of Science*, and by Professor K. R. Popper in his *The Open Society and its Enemies* and 'The Poverty of Historicism,' *Economica*, 1944–45, 11–12. Following in their footsteps I have also attempted to defend methodological individualism in 'Ideal Types and Historical Explanation' this *Journal*, 1952, 3, 22, reprinted in *Readings in the Philosophy of Science*, ed. Feigl and Brodbeck, New York, 1953. This article has come in for a good deal of criticism, the chief items of which I shall try to rebut in what follows.

of a particular configuration of individuals, their dispositions, situations, beliefs, and physical resources and environment. There may be unfinished or half-way explanations of large-scale social phenomena (say, inflation) in terms of other large-scale phenomena (say, full employment); but we shall not have arrived at rock-bottom explanations of such large-scale phenomena until we have deduced an account of them from statements about the dispositions, beliefs, resources, and inter-relations of individuals. (The individuals may remain anonymous and only typical dispositions, etc., may be attributed to them.) And just as mechanism is contrasted with the organicist idea of physical fields, so methodological individualism is contrasted with sociological holism or organicism. On this latter view, social systems constitute 'wholes' at least in the sense that some of their large-scale behaviour is governed by macro-laws which are essentially *sociological* in the sense that they are *sui generis* and not to be explained as mere regularities or tendencies resulting from the behaviour of interacting individuals. On the contrary, the behaviour of individuals should (according to sociological holism) be explained at least partly in terms of such laws (perhaps in conjunction with an account, first of individuals' rôles within institutions and secondly of the functions of institutions within the whole social system). If methodological individualism means that human beings are supposed to be the only moving agents in history, and if sociological holism means that some super-human agents or factors are supposed to be at work in history, then these two alternatives are exhaustive. An example of such a superhuman, sociological factor is the alleged long-term cyclical wave in economic life which is supposed to be self-propelling, uncontrollable, and inexplicable in terms of human activity, but in terms of the fluctuations of which such large-scale phenomena as wars, revolutions, and mass emigration, and such psychological factors as scientific and technological inventiveness can, it is claimed, be explained and predicted.

I say 'and predicted' because the irreducible sociological laws postulated by holists are usually regarded by them as laws of social development, as laws governing the dynamics of a society. This makes holism well-nigh equivalent to historicism, to the idea that a society is impelled along a pre-determined route by historical laws which cannot be resisted but which can be discerned by the sociologist. The holist-historicist position has, in my view, been irretrievably damaged by Popper's attacks on it. I shall criticise this position only in so far as this will help me to elucidate and defend the individualistic alternative to it. The central assumption of the individualistic position—an assumption which is admittedly counter-factual and metaphysical—is that no social tendency exists which could not be altered *if* the individuals concerned both wanted to alter it and possessed the appropriate information. (They might want to alter the tendency but, through ignorance of the facts and/or failure to work out some of the implications of their action, fail to alter it, or perhaps even intensify it.) This assumption could also be expressed by saying that no social tendency is somehow imposed on human beings 'from above' (or 'from below')—social tendencies are the product (usually undesigned) of human characteristics and activities and situations, of people's ignorance and laziness as well as of their knowledge and ambition. (An example of a social tendency is the tendency of industrial units to grow larger. I do not call 'social' those tendencies which are determined by uncontrollable physical factors, such as the alleged tendency for more male babies to be born in times of disease or war.) [2]

My procedure will be: first, to de-limit the sphere in which methodological individualism works in two directions; secondly, to clear methodological individualism of certain misunderstandings; thirdly, to indicate how fruitful and surprising individualistic explanations can be and how individualistic social theories can lead to sociological discoveries; and fourthly, to consider in somewhat more detail how, according to methodological individualism, we should frame explanations, first for social regularities or repeatable processes, and secondly for unique historical constellations of events.

2 Where Methodological Individualism Does Not Work

There are two areas in which methodological individualism does not work.

[2] The issue of holism *versus* individualism in social science has recently been presented as though it were a question of the existence or non-existence of irreducibly social *facts* rather than of irreducibly sociological *laws*. [See M. Mandelbaum 'Societal Facts,' *The British Journal of Sociology*, 1955, **6**, (Reprinted in *Theories of History*, P. Gardiner, ed., The Free Press, New York, 1959, pp. 476–488.—Ed.) and E. A. Gellner, 'Explanations in History,' *Aristotelian Society*, Supplementary Volume **30**, 1956. (Reprinted in this volume as "Holism versus Individualism," pp. 254–268.—Ed.) This way of presenting the issue seems to me to empty it of most of its interest. If a new kind of beast is discovered, what we want to know is not so much whether it falls outside existing zoological categories, but how it behaves. People who insist on the existence of social facts but who do not say whether they are governed by sociological laws, are like people who claim to have discovered an unclassified kind of animal but who do not tell us whether it is tame or dangerous, whether it can be domesticated or is unmanageable. If an answer to the question of social facts could throw light on the serious and interesting question of sociological laws, then the question of social facts would also be serious and interesting. But this is not so. On the one hand, a holist may readily admit (as I pointed out in my 'Ideal Types' paper, which Gellner criticises) that all observable social facts *are* reducible to individual facts and yet hold that the latter are invisibly governed by irreducibly sociological laws. On the other hand, an individualist may readily admit (as Gellner himself says) that some large social facts are simply too complex for a full reduction of them to be feasible, and yet hold that individualistic explanations of them are in principle possible, just as a physicist may readily admit that some physical facts (for instance, the precise blast-effects of a bomb-explosion in a built-up area) are just too complex for accurate prediction or explanation of them to be feasible and yet hold that precise explanations and predictions of them in terms of existing scientific laws are in principle possible.

This revised way of presenting the holism *versus* individualism issue does not only divert attention from the important question. It also tends to turn the dispute into a purely verbal issue. Thus Mandelbaum is able to prove the existence of what he calls 'societal facts' because he defines psychological facts very narrowly as 'facts concerning the thoughts and actions of specific human beings' (*op. cit.*). Consequently, the *dispositions* of *anonymous* individuals which play such an important rôle in individualistic explanations in social science are 'societal facts' merely by definition.

The first is a probability situation where accidental and unpredictable irregularities in human behaviour have a fairly regular and predictable over-all result.[3] Suppose I successively place 1,000 individuals facing north in the centre of a symmetrical room with two exits, one east, the other west. If about 500 leave by one exit and about 500 by the other I would not try to explain this in terms of tiny undetectable west-inclining and east-inclining differences in the individuals, for the same reason that Popper would not try to explain the fact that about 500 balls will topple over to the west and about 500 to the east, if 1,000 balls are dropped from immediately above a north-south blade, in terms of tiny undetectable west-inclining and east-inclining differences in the balls. For in both cases such an 'explanation' would merely raise the further problem: why should these west-inclining and east-inclining differences be distributed approximately *equally* among the individuals and among the balls?

Those statistical regularities in social life which are inexplicable in indi-vidualistic terms for the sort of reason I have quoted here are, in a sense, inhuman, the outcome of a large number of sheer *accidents*. The outcome of a large number of decisions is usually much less regular and predictable because variable human factors (changes of taste, new ideas, swings from optimism to pessimism) which have little or no influence on accident-rates are influential here. Thus Stock Exchange prices fluctuate widely from year to year, whereas the number of road-accidents does not fluctuate widely. But the existence of these actuarial regularities does not, as has often been alleged, support the historicist idea that defenceless individuals like you and me are at the chance mercy of the inhuman and uncontrollable tenden-cies of our society. It does not support a secularised version of the Calvinist idea of an Almighty Providence who picks people at random to fill His fixed damnation-quota. For we can control these statistical regularities in so far as we can alter the conditions on which they depend. For example, we could obviously abolish road-accidents if we were prepared to prohibit motor-traffic.

The second kind of social phenomenon to which methodological indi-vidualism is inapplicable is where some kind of physical connection between people's nervous systems short-circuits their intelligent control and causes automatic, and perhaps in some sense appropriate, bodily responses. I think that a man may more or less literally smell danger and instinctively back away from unseen ambushers; and individuality seems to be temporarily submerged beneath a collective physical *rapport* at jive-sessions and revivalist meetings and among panicking crowds. But I do not think that these spas-modic mob-organisms lend much support to holism or constitute a very serious exception to methodological individualism. They have a fleeting existence which ends when their members put on their mufflers and catch the bus or otherwise disperse, whereas holists have conceived of a social

---

[3] Failure to exclude probability-situations from the ambit of methodological individual-ism was an important defect of my 'Ideal Types' paper. Here, Gellner's criticism (*op. cit.*, Selection 14 of this volume) does hit the nail on the head.

whole as something which endures through generations of men; and whatever holds together typical long-lived institutions, like a bank or a legal system or a church, it certainly is not the physical proximity of their members.

3 Misunderstandings of Methodological Individualism

I will now clear methodological individualism of two rather widespread misunderstandings.

It has been objected that in making individual dispositions and beliefs and situations the terminus of an explanation in social science, methodological individualism implies that a person's psychological make-up is, so to speak, God-given, whereas it is in fact conditioned by, and ought to be explained in terms of, his social inheritance and environment.[4] Now methodological individualism certainly does not prohibit attempts to explain the formation of psychological characteristics; it only requires that such explanations should in turn be *individualistic*, explaining the formation as the result of a series of conscious or unconscious responses by an individual to his changing situation. For example, I have heard Professor Paul Sweezey, the Harvard economist, explain that he became a Marxist because his father, a Wall Street broker, sent him in the 1930's to the London School of Economics to study under those staunch liberal economists, Professors Hayek and Robbins. This explanation is perfectly compatible with methodological individualism (though hardly compatible, I should have thought, with the Marxist idea that ideologies reflect class-positions) because it interprets his ideological development as a human response to his situation. It is, I suppose, psychoanalysts who have most systematically worked the idea of a thorough individualist and historical explanation of the formation of dispositions, unconscious fears and beliefs, and subsequent defence-mechanisms, in terms of responses to emotionally charged, and especially childhood, situations.

My point could be put by saying that methodological individualism encourages *innocent* explanations but forbids *sinister* explanations of the widespread existence of a disposition among the members of a social group. Let me illustrate this by quoting from a reply I made to Goldstein's criticisms.

Suppose that it is established that Huguenot traders were relatively prosperous in 17th-century France and that this is explained in terms of a wide-spread disposition among them (a disposition for which there is independent evidence) to plough back into their businesses a larger proportion of their profits than was customary

---

4 Thus Gellner writes: 'The real oddity of the reductionist [i.e. the methodological individualist's] case is that it seems to preclude *a priori* the possibility of human dispositions being the dependent variable in an historical explanation—when in fact they often or always are' (*op. cit.*, this volume p. 260). And Mr. Leon J. Goldstein says that in making human dispositions methodologically primary I ignore their cultural conditioning. (*The Journal of Philosophy*, 1956, **53,** 807.)

among their Catholic competitors. Now this explanatory disposition might very well be explained in its turn—perhaps in terms of the general thriftiness which Calvinism is said to encourage, and/or in terms of the fewer alternative outlets for the cash resources of people whose religious disabilities prevented them from buying landed estates or political offices. (I cannot vouch for the historical accuracy of this example.)

I agree that methodological individualism allows the formation, or 'cultural conditioning,' of a widespread disposition to be explained only in terms of other human factors and not in terms of something *in*human, such as an alleged historicist law which impels people willy-nilly along some pre-determined course. But this is just the anti-historicist point of methodological individualism.

Unfortunately, it is typically a part of the programme of Marxist and other historicist sociologies to try to account for the formation of ideologies and other psychological characteristics in strictly sociological and non-psychological terms. Marx for instance professed to believe that feudal ideas and *bourgeois* ideas are more or less literally generated by the water-mill and the steam-engine. But no description, however complete, of the productive apparatus of a society, or of any other non-psychological factors, will enable you to deduce a single psychological conclusion from it, because psychological statements logically cannot be deduced from wholly non-psychological statements. Thus whereas the mechanistic idea that explanations in physics cannot go behind the impenetrable particles is a prejudice (though a very understandable prejudice), the analogous idea that an explanation which begins by imputing some social phenomenon to human factors cannot go on to explain those factors in terms of some inhuman determinant of them is a necessary truth. That the human mind develops under various influences the methodological individualist does not, of course, deny. He only insists that such development must be explained 'innocently' as a series of responses by the individual to situations and not 'sinisterly' and illogically as a direct causal outcome of non-psychological factors, whether these are neurological factors, or impersonal sociological factors alleged to be at work in history.

Another cause of complaint against methodological individualism is that it has been confused with a narrow species of itself (Popper calls it 'psychologism') and even, on occasion, with a still narrower sub-species of this (Popper calls it the 'Conspiracy Theory of Society').[5] Psychologism says that all large-scale social characteristics are not merely the intended or unintended result of, but a *reflection* of, individual characteristics.[6] Thus Plato

[5] See K. R. Popper, *The Open Society and its Enemies,* 2nd ed., 1952, ch. 14.

[6] I am at a loss to understand how Gellner came to make the following strange assertion: '. . . Popper refers to both "psychologism" which he condemns, and "methodological individualism," which he commends. When in the articles discussed [i.e., my "Ideal Types" paper] "methodological individualism" is worked out more fully than is the case in Popper's book, it seems to me to be indistinguishable from "Psychologism." ' Finding no difference between methodological individualism and a caricature of methodological individualism, Gellner has no difficulty in poking fun at the whole idea: 'Certain tribes I know have what anthropologists call a segmentary patrilineal structure, which moreover maintains itself very well over time. I could "explain" this by saying that the tribesmen have,

said that the character and make-up of a *polis* is a reflection of the character and make-up of the kind of soul predominant in it. The conspiracy theory says that all large-scale social phenomena (do not merely reflect individual characteristics but) are deliberately brought about by individuals or groups of individuals.

Now there are social phenomena, like mass unemployment, which it would not have been in anyone's interest deliberately to bring about and which do not appear to be large-scale social reflections or magnified duplicates of some individual characteristic. The practical or technological or therapeutic importance of social science largely consists in explaining, and thereby perhaps rendering politically manageable, the unintended and unfortunate consequences of the behaviour of interacting individuals. From this pragmatic point of view, psychologism and the conspiracy theory are unrewarding doctrines. Psychologism says that only a change of heart can put a stop to, for example, war (I think that this is Bertrand Russell's view). The conspiracy theory, faced with a big bad social event, leads to a hunt for scapegoats. But methodological individualism, by imputing unwanted social phenomena to individuals' responses to their situations, in the light of their dispositions and beliefs, suggests that we may be able to make the phenomena disappear, not by recruiting good men to fill the posts hitherto occupied by bad men, nor by trying to destroy men's socially unfortunate dispositions while fostering their socially beneficial dispositions, but simply by altering the situations they confront. To give a current example, by confronting individuals with dearer money and reduced credit the Government may (I do not say will) succeed in halting inflation without requiring a new self-denying attitude on the part of consumers and without sending anyone to prison.

4 Factual Discoveries in Social Science

To explain the unintended but *beneficial* consequences of individual activities—by 'beneficial consequences' I mean social consequences which the individuals affected *would* endorse *if* they were called on to choose

---

all or most of them, dispositions whose effect is to maintain the system. But, of course, not only have they never given the matter much thought, but it also might very well be impossible to isolate anything in the characters and conduct of the individual tribesmen which *explains* how they come to maintain the system' (*op. cit.*, this volume p. 268). Yet this example actually suggests the lines along which an individualistic explanation might be found. The very fact that the tribesmen *have never given the matter much thought*, the fact that they accept their inherited system uncritically, may constitute an important part of an explanation of its stability. The explanation might go on to pin-point certain rules —that is firm and widespread dispositions—about marriage, inheritance, etc., which help to regularise the tribesmen's behaviour towards their kinsmen. How they come to share these common dispositions could also be explained individualistically in the same sort of way that I can explain why my young children are already developing a typically English attitude towards policemen.

between their continuation or discontinuation—is usually a task of less practical urgency than the explanation of undesirable consequences. On the other hand, this task may be of greater theoretical interest. I say this because people who are painfully aware of the existence of unwanted social phenomena may be oblivious of the unintended but beneficial consequences of men's actions, rather as a man may be oblivious of the good health to which the smooth functioning of his digestion, nervous system, circulation, etc., give rise. Here, an explanatory social theory may surprise and enlighten us not only with regard to the connections between causes and effect but with regard to the existence of the effect itself. By showing that a certain economic system contains positive feed-back leading to increasingly violent oscillations and crises an economist may explain a range of well-advertised phenomena which have long been the subject of strenuous political agitation. But the economists who first showed that a certain kind of economic system contains negative feed-back which tends to iron out disturbances and restore equilibrium, not only explained, but also revealed the existence of, phenomena which had hardly been remarked upon before.[7]

I will speak of organic-like social behaviour where members of some social system (that is, a collection of people whose activities disturb and influence each other) mutually adjust themselves to the situations created by the others in a way which, without direction from above, conduces to the equilibrium or preservation or development of the system. (These are again evaluative notions, but they can also be given a 'would-be-endorsed-if' definition.) Now such far-flung organic-like behaviour, involving people widely separated in space and largely ignorant of each other, cannot be simply observed. It can only be theoretically reconstructed—by deducing the distant social consequences of the typical responses of a large number of interacting people to certain repetitive situations. This explains why individualistic-minded economists and anthropologists, who deny that societies really are organisms, have succeeded in piecing together a good deal of unsuspected organic-like social behaviour, from an examination of individual dispositions and situations, whereas sociological holists, who insist that societies really are organisms, have been noticeably unsuccessful in convincingly displaying any organic-like social behaviour—they cannot observe it and they do not try to reconstruct it individualistically.

There is a parallel between holism and psychologism which explains their common failure to make surprising discoveries. A large-scale social charac-

---

[7] This sentence, as I have since learnt from Dr. A. W. Phillips, is unduly complacent, for it is very doubtful whether an economist can ever *show* that an economic system containing negative feed-back will be stable. For negative feed-back may produce either a tendency towards equilibrium, or increasing oscillations, according to the numerical values of the parameters of the system. But numerical values are just what economic measurements, which are usually ordinal rather than cardinal, seldom yield. The belief that a system which contains negative feed-back, but whose variables cannot be described quantitatively, is stable may be based on faith or experience, but it cannot be shown mathematically. See A. W. Phillips, 'Stabilisation Policy and the Time-Forms of Lagged Responses,' *The Economic Journal*, 1957, **67**.

teristic should be explained, according to psychologism, as the manifestation of analogous small-scale psychological tendencies in individuals, and according to holism as the manifestation of a large-scale tendency in the social whole. In both cases, the *explicans* does little more than duplicate the *explicandum*. The methodological individualist, on the other hand, will try to explain the large-scale effect as the *indirect,* unexpected, complex product of individual factors none of which, singly, may bear any resemblance to it at all. To use hackneyed examples, he may show that a longing for peace led, in a certain international situation, to war, or that a government's desire to improve a bad economic situation by balancing its budget only worsened the situation. Since Mandeville's *Fable of the Bees* was published in 1714, individualistic social science, with its emphasis on unintended consequences, has largely been a sophisticated elaboration on the simple theme that, in certain situations, selfish private motives may have good social consequences and good political intentions bad social consequences.[8]

Holists draw comfort from the example of biology, but I think that the parallel is really between the biologist and the methodological individualist. The biologist does not, I take it, explain the large changes which occur during, say, pregnancy, in terms of corresponding large teleological tendencies in the organism, but physically, in terms of small chemical, cellular, neurological, etc., changes, none of which bears any resemblance to their joint and seemingly planful outcome.

5 How Social Explanations Should be Framed

I will now consider how regularities in social life, such as the trade cycle, should be explained according to methodological individualism. The explanation should be in terms of individuals and their situations; and since the process to be explained is repeatable, liable to recur at various times and in various parts of the world, it follows that only very general assumptions about human dispositions can be employed in its explanation. It is no use looking to abnormal psychology for an explanation of the structure of interest-rates—everyday experience must contain the raw material for the dispositional (as opposed to the situational) assumptions required by such

---

[8] A good deal of unmerited opposition to methodological individualism seems to spring from the recognition of the undoubted fact that individuals often run into social obstacles. Thus the conclusion at which Mandelbaum arrives is 'that there are societal facts which exercise external constraints over individuals' (*op. cit.*). This conclusion is perfectly harmonious with the methodological individualist's insistence that plans often miscarry (and that even when they do succeed, they almost invariably have other important and unanticipated effects). The methodological individualist only insists that the social environment by which any particular individual is confronted and frustrated and sometimes manipulated and occasionally destroyed is, if we ignore its physical ingredients, made up of other *people,* their habits, inertia, loyalties, rivalries, and so on. What the methodological individualist denies is that an individual is ever frustrated, manipulated or destroyed or borne along by irreducible sociological or historical *laws*.

an explanation. It may require a stroke of genius to detect, isolate, and formulate precisely the dispositional premises of an explanation of a social regularity. These premises may state what no one had noticed before, or give a sharp articulation to what had hitherto been loosely described. But once stated they will seem obvious enough. It took years of groping by brilliant minds before a precise formulation was found for the principle of diminishing marginal utility. But once stated, the principle—that the less, relatively, a man has of one divisible commodity the more compensation he will be disposed to require for foregoing a small fixed amount of it— is a principle to which pretty well everyone will give his consent. Yet this simple and almost platitudinous principle is the magic key to the economics of distribution and exchange.

The social scientist is, here, in a position analogous to that of the Cartesian mechanist.[9] The latter never set out to discover new and unheard-of physical principles because he believed that his own principle of action-by-contact was self-evidently ultimate. His problem was to discover the typical physical configurations, the mechanisms, which, operating according to this principle, produce the observed regularities of nature. His theories took the form of models which exhibited such regularities as the outcome of 'self-evident' physical principles operating in some hypothetical physical situation. Similarly, the social scientist does not make daring innovations in psychology but relies on familiar, almost 'self-evident' psychological material. His skill consists, first in spotting the relevant dispositions, and secondly in inventing a simple but realistic model which shows how, in a precise type of situation, those dispositions generate some typical regularity or process. (His model, by the way, will also show that in this situation certain things cannot happen. His negative predictions of the form, 'If you got this you can't have that as well' may be of great practical importance.) The social scientist can now explain in principle historical examples of this regular process, provided his model does in fact fit the historical situation.

This view of the explanation of social regularities incidentally clears up the old question on which so much ink has been spilt about whether the so-called 'laws' of economics apply universally or only to a particular 'stage' of economic development. The simple answer is that the economic principles displayed by economists' models apply only to those situations which correspond with their models; but a single model may very well correspond with a very large number of historical situations widely separated in space and time.

In the explanation of regularities the same situational scheme or model is used to reconstruct a number of historical situations with a similar structure in a way which reveals how typical dispositions and beliefs of anonymous individuals generated, on each occasion, the same regularity.[10] In the

9 I owe this analogy to Professor Popper.

10 This should rebut Gellner's conclusion that methodological individualism would transform social scientists into 'biographers *en grande série*' (*op. cit.* this volume p. 268).

explanation of a unique constellation of events the individualistic method is again to reconstruct the historical situation, or connected sequence of situations, in a way which reveals how (usually both named and anonymous) individuals, with their beliefs and dispositions (which may include peculiar personal dispositions as well as typical human dispositions), generated, in this particular situation, the joint product to be explained. I emphasise *dispositions,* which are open and law-like, as opposed to *decisions,* which are occurrences, for this reason. A person's set of dispositions ought, under varying conditions, to give rise to appropriately varying decisions. The subsequent occurrence of an appropriate decision will both confirm, and be explained by, the existence of the dispositions. Suppose that a historical explanation (of, say, the growth of the early Catholic Church) largely relies on a particular decision (say, the decision of Emperor Constantine to give Pope Silvester extensive temporal rights in Italy). The explanation is, so far, rather *ad hoc:* an apparently arbitrary *fiat* plays a key rôle in it. But if this decision can in turn be explained as the offspring of a marriage of a set of dispositions (for instance, the Emperor's disposition to subordinate all rival power to himself) to a set of circumstances (for instance, the Emperor's recognition that Christianity could not be crushed but could be tamed if it became the official religion of the Empire), and if the existence of these dispositions and circumstances is convincingly supported by independent evidence, then the area of the arbitrarily given, of sheer brute fact in history, although it can never be made to vanish, will have been significantly reduced.

[16] Methodological Individualisms: Definition and Reduction *

MAY BRODBECK

The Reformation, it has been said, changed the course of history. Most people would agree. At the very least, agree or not, they would hold the proposition to be one worth considering. They would be unlikely to reject

Reprinted from *Philosophy of Science,* vol. 25, 1958, pp. 1–22. Copyright © 1958, The Williams and Wilkins Co., Baltimore, and reprinted with their permission.

* This paper was written during the tenure of a Faculty Research Fellowship from the Social Science Research Council.

it out of hand as incapable of being either true or false because it had no meaning. For, of course, "everybody knows" what the Reformation was and, elaborating a little, we can make clear what we meant by changing the course of history. Yet it is just statements of this sort that cause much methodological wrangling. Their controversial nature is due, in large part, to controversy over the status of such terms as "the Reformation" and, generally, group or macroscopic concepts. Since not only history, but sociology, political science, social psychology, and economics also widely use concepts referring to groups and their properties, rather than to individuals, the controversy has wide ramifications. And because there are, as it were, so many vested interests involved, the dispute also tends to acquire an ideological tone not altogether consonant with dispassionate inquiry. Bad temper and mutual recrimination in scientific discussion are generally a sign that ideological defenses are being shored up. Just possibly, a philosopher whose substantive concern in any empirical field is minimal may hope to be considered above the battle, as one who, having no private axe to grind, can be concerned only with clarifying the logical issues involved. In this hope, I wish to explore as systematically as possible the tangled web of issues woven about the status of group concepts and their relationship to those referring to individuals. Intertwined in this controversy are two different issues. One has to do with the nature of the *terms* or concepts of social science; the other with the nature of its *laws* and *theories* and their relationship in turn to those in other areas. The first issue is one of *meaning*, the second of *reduction*. Success in unsnarling the various strands of this web may alone help abate the fury of the controversy.

1. Two Kinds of Group Properties

John is blond and tall. Blondness and tallness are properties or characteristics exemplified by the individual man, John. John is taller than Harry. "Taller than" is a property jointly exemplified by the two men named. Such properties, requiring more than one individual for their exemplification, are called "relations" or, better, descriptive relations, since, like the properties of single individuals, they refer to observable characters of things. Like all characters, relations may be either undefined, such as taller than or between, or defined, such as smarter than or married. Many terms such as "married" or "mother," appear grammatically to be properties of single individuals, but, like "south," are actually relational, requiring, when defined, reference to two or more individuals. A group is an aggregate of individuals standing in certain descriptive relations to each other. The kinds of relations exemplified will, of course, depend upon, or determine, the kind of group, whether it be a family, an audience, a committee, a labor union, or a crowd. Just as the individual John Smith is to be distinguished from his attributes, say, being blond or being tall, so the group must be distinguished from its attributes such as, say, being numerous or being noisy. It is simple to tell whether a characteristic is being attributed to an individual or to a group. Compare "Indians are red-skinned" with "Indians are disappearing." In the former, each and every Indian is said to be red-skinned, while in the latter Indians as a group are said to be disappearing, that is, diminishing in population. When the property is attributed to a group collectively, so that the group itself is logically the subject of the proposition, rather than distributively, in which case "each and every" member of the group could logically be the subject of the proposition, then we have a group property. Group properties, like all others, may be either logical or descriptive. In "The Apostles are twelve," for example, "twelve" is a logical character of the group of apostles, that is, one whose definition can be given in terms of logical words alone, such as "all," "either . . . or" or "and," without recourse to terms having observable referents. The definition is cumbrous and need not concern us here. Descriptive terms, which do particularly concern us, may be either physical, in the narrow sense, like "loud" or "dirty," or behavioral or sociological, like "efficient" or "wealthy."

Clearly there is no issue about the *occurrence* of group characteristics. There is not even any question about the occurrence of behavioral group attributes. No one will deny that it makes sense to say of some groups that they are more efficient or more powerful than others or, of some others, that they are wealthy. The controversial question, or rather one of them, is whether or not there are any such attributes which are undefined or *undefinable;* i.e., whether there are attributes of groups not definable in terms of either the behavior of the individuals composing the group or the relations between these individuals or both. There are, of course, undefinable terms referring to properties of individual things or persons, like color words or other words referring to directly observable qualities. Are there similarly undefinable terms referring to properties of groups, i.e. properties which can be directly observed but which cannot be defined in terms referring to either the behavior of the individuals constituting the group or the relations obtaining among them or both? Can we speak, for example, of a "responsive audience" without defining the adjective in terms of the behavior of the individual people in the audience and some more or less precise statistical notion, namely, the percentage of attentive individuals in the group? Do groups or institutions have purposes not definable in terms of individual purposes; do they have purposes of their own, as it were? Similarly, can we meaningfully speak of a "will of the people" which is something different from either the wills of all persons or of the majority of these persons? The question can also be asked about groups themselves. Is there such a thing as the State or a University over and above their constituent individuals and the relations among them? Does this entity itself have attributes? Or, to say the same thing more precisely, are there any undefined terms referring to kinds of groups?

The two questions, about group entities and about undefinable attributes of groups, are obviously not independent. If, for instance, the efficiency of a group is not some function of the behavior of its constituent individuals, then there must be something else that exhibits this efficiency, the group "itself." And if there be such a superentity as, say, a "group-mind," then it will have characteristics of its own: allegedly, it may have political opinions. So there is really only one question. And it can be most economically posed by asking whether or not there are such undefinable descriptive properties of groups. Let us consider examples. The "cohesiveness" of a group may be defined, say, as the ratio of the number of people within the group with whom its members say they would prefer to be stranded on a desert island to the total number of votes for people within and without the group. Can "crowd hysteria" be similarly defined in terms of individual behaviors or is it an undefinable quality of the crowd itself? The denial that there are such undefinable group properties or such superentities is the view usually known as *methodological individualism*. Its contradictory is *metaphysical holism*. It is called "holism" because its proponents generally maintain that there are so-called wholes, group entities which have undefinable properties of their own. The property of the whole is then also said to be emergent from the properties of its parts. The thesis that there are such properties is accordingly also called "emergentism." [1]

Philosophically, the holistic assumption that there are group properties over and above the individuals making up the group, their properties, and the relations among them is counter to empiricism. For the latter holds that all terms must ultimately refer to what is observable, directly or indirectly, and that what we observe are people and their characteristics not supraindividual groups and their characteristics. Or, to say the same thing differently, the antiholist maintains that the behavior *of* groups can be defined in terms of behavior *in* groups. Culturally, holism is intimately connected with hostility toward the liberal political individualism of the Western tradition. If "States" have wills and purposes of their own, then counting noses is unnecessary and "serving the State" comes to sound like "serving Mr. Jones." Jones' will we know how to ascertain, but who is to divulge the "will of the State"? The answers are, alas, only too familiar. The will and wisdom of the State reside in a privileged class or caste. This is the conservative variant, also called "organicism." Or they are "embodied" in a charismatic leader.

Since fundamental philosophical and cultural assumptions are involved in this controversy, it is important to be crystal clear about the sense or senses in which group variables, if not hypostatized, are not only practically convenient but perhaps indispensable. Once before,[2] I attempted to show the conditions under which the use of macroscopic or group variables might

---

[1] A good discussion of holism and related issues can be found in "Exceptionalism in Geography: A Methodological Examination" by F. K. Schaefer, *Annals of Ass'n. of Amer. Geographers*, XLIII, 1953.

[2] "On the Philosophy of the Social Sciences," *Philosophy of Science*, 21, 1954.

be both necessary and fruitful. I was promptly charged with metaphysical holism.[3] Since the charge is patently alien both to the spirit of that particular paper and my entire philosophical position, let me try once again to clarify what, given the nature of social science, must be made clear if much fruitful behavioral research is not to be banned *a priori*.

To describe a fact is to state that one or several objects exemplify certain characters, relational and nonrelational or, what amounts to the same thing, that a defin*ed* or undefin*ed* concept has an instance. The occurrence of undefin*able* properties of groups would therefore be emergence at the level of description, or descriptive emergence. The operative word, of course, is "undefinable." For, as already mentioned, no one denies the existence of defined properties of groups, and these properties may well be different from any possessed by the individuals. For instance, they may be inapplicable to individuals because they are statistical aggregates, like the "homogeneity" of a group defined in terms of a standard deviation or generally when averaging processes are used to arrive at the value of a variable. Since such statistical or aggregative concepts are always derived from information about individuals, they trivially satisfy the requirement of methodological individualism.

Sometimes the actual or possible statistical procedures entailed by the definition of a concept are only implicit or covert in ordinary usage. This appears to be the case in those statements which have been held to refer "anonymously" rather than specifically to individuals.[4] The statement "an increased dividend is anticipated" is interpreted, quite correctly, to be individualistic even though it does not say anything about any particular shareholder. The expectations of the so-called anonymous individuals to whom the statement refers would, in the last resort, be ascertained by polling individual shareholders. Thus the "anticipation" is, quite trivially, a statistical concept, even though covertly so in ordinary speech. Similarly, references to, say, "the poor," in statements such as "The candidate received more votes from the poor than from the rich" are implicitly statistical. In neither case is any undefinable group property or group-entity meant or suggested. Neither impersonal, unattached anticipations nor a supraindividual "poor" are implied by the use of these locutions.

Nevertheless, there remains a class of terms frequently used in social science which are not statistical in intent but have yet to be defined in terms of individual behavior. There is a source of error associated with but not strictly an error of measurement which is perhaps peculiar to social science. This error is due to that imprecision, not in measurement proper, but in the definition of the terms whose referents are being measured. This imprecision or vagueness may itself for each observation result in different values which can have definite probabilities. Consider the assertion that a boom in trade is always followed by slump and depression. To be sure, in some

---

3 "Methodological Individualism: A Reply," J. W. N. Watkins, *Philosophy of Science*, **22**, 1955.

4 Watkins, *op. cit.*, p. 60.

respects the economists can often do better than this, still it is a fair representative of the kind of hypotheses prevalent in social science. This is imprecise not only with respect to time; its predictive value is also restricted by the nature of its concepts. What exactly are "boom" and "slump" conditions? "Depression?" No doubt in these particular cases there is a large statistical component to the meanings involved. Level of employment, average wealth, and such like are doubtless entailed. But how many such things? What else? At what proportion of unemployment and "other" things will we say depression or boom conditions prevail? Can we be certain when we have one or the other? Of course, it may be replied, we can't be certain but roughly we can tell. And that is just the point. The roughness results not from inability to determine the facts, statistically or otherwise, but from the fringe of vagueness surrounding the applicability of the terms. The definitions within physical science leave no room for this ambience. Prediction or explanation can hardly be precise when, because our terms lack sharp referents, we can be sure neither that we have the initial conditions nor the anticipated event since they are not exactly specified. The more macroscopic the concept, the wider its penumbra of vagueness is apt to be.

Consider next such concepts as "the Reformation," "the Church," "capitalism," "mercantilism," "cold war," "army morale" and the like. In the meaning of these there is not even an implicit statistical reference. Such non-statistical "institutional" or "holistic," concepts present difficulties of definition similar to those that face the clinical or, even more, the social psychologist. The precise definition of social attitudes, like pro- or anti-authoritarianism, or of clinical states, like aggression or anxiety, requires one to choose from an almost infinite variety of symptoms those which can be used reliably to define the term in question. This means, of course, not what *really* is anti-authoritarianism or aggression, but how to find a set of symptoms which, without additions or deletions, will enter into laws, that is, enable prediction to other behavior. There is the further difficulty that, even if we could overcome the difficulty about which symptoms should be omitted and which retained in the definition, in the case of clinical concepts the fittingness of a behavioristic definition varies from culture to culture. Just as an "act of war" in one social setting might not be so in another, so what is aggressive behavior for an American might not be so for a South Sea Islander. Thus a definition of, say, aggressive behavior, not containing reference to the culture in which the behavior to be called aggressive is displayed is, in a sense, obviously inadequate.

In the case of institutional concepts like "the Reformation" or "capitalism," an indefinite set of behaviors is loosely encompassed by the term. It is not that certain behaviors are "anonymously" referred to, but that the list of these behaviors cannot yet be sharply terminated. "The Jewish race is cohesive," runs an example for a definable macroscopic term, means "Jews usually marry Jews, live in close communities, share religious rituals, etc." [5] The "etc." makes my point for me. True, this was only meant to be illus-

[5] Watkins, *op. cit.*, p. 61.

trative. Still, the difficulty of completely spelling out that "etc." would also be present in actual scientific usage. Yet, despite their open-endedness, these institutional concepts are probably just as indispensable to many areas of social science as are clinical concepts to the psychologist. *In principle*, of course, for whatever cold comfort that may be, all such concepts must be definable in terms of individual behavior. In practice, however, we frequently cannot do this. Are we then prepared to say that in whatever context these terms occur they are wholly ambiguous as to meaning? I hardly think so. The course of science is not always as smooth as the logical analyst would like. And it seems to me that there are cases in which the best we can do is point out the distinctions and the difficulties. The most that we can ask of the social scientist whose subject-matter requires him to use such "open" concepts is that he keep the principle of methodological individualism firmly in mind as a devoutly to be wished-for consummation, an ideal to be approximated as closely as possible. This should at least help assure that nevermore will he dally with suspect group-minds and impersonal "forces," economic or otherwise; nevermore will nonobservable properties be attributed to equally nonobservable group entities. At the same time, he will not by methodological fiat be struck dumb about matters on which there is, no matter how imprecisely, a great deal to be said.

2. Definition vs. Reduction

The view that all group or macroscopic concepts are in principle definable in terms of individual behavior is a fundamental or, even, metaphysical assumption, reflecting as it does basic presuppositions of the empiricist philosophical tradition. Insofar as methodological individualism is a precept for proper concept formation, it is a denial of descriptive emergence, that is, it denies that supraindividual group properties can be meaningfully attributed to things or events. The banner of methodological individualism has however also been raised in the context of laws and theories. This is a matter of explanation rather than of description. The two are disparate and should not be confounded. The belief that there are no emergent *group properties* rests on our criterion of the meaningful. It is thus, broadly speaking, a matter of logic. The assumption that the *laws* of group behavior are or are not, as the case may be, emergent with respect to laws about individuals is a matter of fact, a matter for empirical determination. But for this to be clear some further distinctions and elaborations are necessary.

The possibility of "reduction" is the issue raised by asking whether the phenomena of one field, say chemistry or psychology, can be explained in terms of the phenomena of another, say physics or physiology respectively. Reduction, as I understand it, involves deduction. Explanation, in one firm meaning of that term, is achieved by deducing what is to be explained from true premises. Only statements, never concepts, can serve as either premises or conclusion of a deduction. Explanation, therefore, is always of statements by means of other statements. (Obvious and trivial as this point is, as long as the confused notion of "explanatory concepts" lingers on, it is worth remaking.) The deduction by which reduction is achieved also serves to explain. Explanation is in fact a major reason for reduction. It is consequently a matter of laws and theories, not of terms or concepts. What is sometimes called "reduction" of terms is, strictly, definition of the kind we have just discussed. Not all deduction, however, achieves reduction. We explain a law by deducing it from another law or laws. In the classical illustration, we explain Galileo's law of falling bodies by deducing it, as a special case for terrestrial objects, from the Newtonian law of gravitation. But here nothing has been reduced to anything else. Both Newton's and Galileo's laws mention the same subject-matter, physical bodies and their spatial-temporal properties. Both laws are in the same area, mechanics. A "psychological" or an "economic" term is one that occurs in the science of either psychology or economics respectively. One area differs from another by its terms or concepts; these determine its "subject-matter." Deduction is also reduction only when the deduced laws are in a different area from those that serve as premises. Moreover, the latter are, for reasons that will become clear, generally microscopic relative to the former, as physiology is microscopic relative to psychology which, in turn, is microscopic relative to sociology.

The distinction between the microscopic (molecular) and the macroscopic (molar) refers, as the terms suggest, to some specifiable difference in the size of the respective units of description. A social group is, in an obvious sense, macroscopic relative to its individual members. But if the laws of the reducing and reduced theory are related as axioms and theorems respectively, each covering a different area, how then does the deduction take place? For, clearly, if two laws have no terms or variables in common, then one cannot possibly be a deductive consequence of the other. The fact is that the deduction, hence the reduction, takes place in different ways, depending upon the nature of the connection between the two theories involved. The logic of the reduction of macroscopic thermodynamics to mechanics differs from that of the reduction either of chemistry to physics or of psychology to physiology, and these all differ from the way in which the reduction of sociology to psychology would take place, if we could do it. We shall here be concerned only with the last of these pairs, using, with apologies, "sociology" as an omnibus term to include all the areas using group concepts, including in it political science, economics, and social psychology, as well as sociology proper.[6]

Among chemists, reductionism is hardly a controversial issue. Naturally not, since it is an accomplished fact. But even among psychologists, where it is at best a program, though the range from optimism to pessimism is

[6] For a discussion of the relationship between psychology and physiology, see my "On the Philosophy of the Social Sciences," *op. cit.*, pp. 148 ff.

very wide with vociferous extremes at either end, ultimate physiological reduction is accepted as a frame of reference. The area concerned with group variables is rather more sensitive, however. Further removed, both historically and systematically, from the biological sciences than are psychologists, thus further removed from the classical scientific tradition, those concerned with group sciences tend to exhibit greater emotional reactions to the reductionism issue. They are darkly suspicious that the proponents of reductionism aim primarily to put them out of business by denying them any real subject matter. Nor perhaps are their suspicions wholly unfounded. However that may be, a firm grasp of the distinctions between the definitions of terms and the reduction of laws and between perfect and imperfect knowledge should considerably reduce the decibel count of this clamor either for or against autonomous group science. But, first of all, I must explain the meaning of "perfect knowledge."

3. Perfect vs. Imperfect Knowledge

Suppose that we have a theory of economic behavior, that is, a theory concerned with phenomena such as consumption, income, saving, profits, and the like. Assume that we are given the equations (laws) of this theory, the numerical values of its constant coefficients or parameters, and a set of initial conditions, that is, the observed values of its variables at any particular time or for a specified geographical area. By a leap of imagination, assume moreover that from this system we can predict the future course of all our variables or compute their entire past history; we know how changes in any one variable produce changes in any other; we know to what extent by tinkering with the system we can bring about desired changes, to what extent we are powerless. If we knew all this, either in economics or for that matter in any other social science, there is clearly nothing else we could possibly desire to know, at least as far as these variables are concerned. Such knowledge may therefore be called "perfect." [7]

A theory, to summarize, consists of a set of terms or concepts, undefined and defined, and a set of statements, called generalizations or laws, about how the referents of some of the terms affect others. In order to make a prediction about any particular system from the theory, its laws and its definitions, there must be added to it a set of statements about the state of this system at some specified time, that is, we must know which concepts are or are not exemplified by the system at that time, or, as one says in the case of quantified theories, we must be given the values of the relevant variables. Assume that prediction is made and, as it happens, is falsified by

[7] I take the terminology of perfect vs. imperfect knowledge and the accompanying criteria from Gustav Bergmann's *Philosophy of Science,* University of Wisconsin Press, 1957. I am grateful to Professor Bergmann for permitting me to use the manuscript of this work. [Excerpted in Section Five of this volume, Selection 23.—Ed.]

the course of events. What are the possible sources of error? All theories in all fields are subject to the inherent frailty of empirical science. Inductive generalizations may be over-generalizations; measurement, too, has its limits and its own kinds of errors. These two frailties do not by themselves distinguish the best physical theory from the most ill-confirmed social theory, even though the probability for errors of this kind to pass undetected is, of course, considerably less in the case of a well-confirmed body of laws with a highly developed theory and fine measuring instruments. In respect to induction and measurement as two sources of error, the difference between the "hard" and the "soft" sciences is only one of degree. This difference in degree is in turn traceable to the characteristic *closure* and *completeness* of certain physical theories, two features which are conspicuously lacking or, at least, still lacking in social science. What makes the difference is (a) whether or not the referents of the terms of the theory interact only among themselves and with nothing else at the time and within the geographical area considered and (b) whether or not any variables that in fact do make a difference have been omitted from the expressions of the theory. These criteria of closure and completeness, respectively, are touchstones to the justifiably felt superiority of physical over social science. And, as we shall see, even this is not the whole story.

(a) Closure and completeness. Celestial mechanics and nonatomic thermodynamics are two theories within classical physics with nonoverlapping scopes, yet each theory is nearly "perfect" for the variables with which it deals. In the first, mass, velocity, and distance interact only with each other; in the second, volume, temperature, and pressure and a few other variables of this sort do the same. These theories consist of process laws, that is, in each case, the values of *any one* variable at any time can be computed by means of the laws from the values of *all* the others at any other time. Nothing that happens at any other time or place than those being considered affects the behavior of the properties with which the theory is concerned, or, at worst, we know how to take account of these outside influences in our predictions or computations. The system, in other words, is *closed*. When the planet Neptune was discovered, its presence was predicted from the Newtonian law together with the known "perturbations" of Uranus—its deviations from the predicted path—and of course the state of the sun and the other planets at the time. Logically, this means that the system which had previously been thought to be closed actually was not. The law itself omitted nothing, for Neptune was simply another instance of variables already contained in the law. The case would be different if, say, the presence or absence of life on the planets was found to affect the laws of motion. In this case, the theory would have omitted variables which in fact make a difference. It would not be *complete*. Newtonian mechanics is complete and we know, in it, the conditions of closure for any system. Because of these features the connections among the variables are reversible or sym-

metrical. If, in the process theories of physics, a variable x is a function of another y, we know not only that a change in x brings about a change in y, but also conversely. We know too what happens to either variable in the absence of the other. In social science, on the other hand, if we know that A causes B, rarely are we in a position to say how changes in B affect A or even what happens to B if A is not present.

(b) Process laws. The mutual dependency among the variables of classical physics is even more profound than this, marking another item in its perfection. It may be suggested that changes in pressure and volume occur simultaneously, whereas changes in the price of corn come later than the rain. The temporal development presumably marks the irreversibility and consequent utility of the notion of cause. Yet perhaps the most striking feature of process laws is their reversibility with regards to time. Newton's law, for example, permits us to compute the position and velocity of, say, a planet at all times past or future, if we know its position and velocity at a single instant. Generally, by means of these characteristic laws of physics, any two states of the system can be inferred from each other, quite regardless of which comes first in time. Nor is this reversibility with respect to time all there is to it. The more exactly a prediction can be stated, the more useful it will be both practically and theoretically. There are several dimensions in which a prediction may be more or less exact. Let me revert to the assertion that a boom in trade is always followed by slump and depression. One characteristic restricting the predictive value of such statements, mentioned before, is the vagueness of its concepts. Another is indefiniteness with respect to time. The process laws of physics are extremely specific in this respect. They permit prediction not only to "some" future time, or computation of conditions "sometime" in the past, but for *any* given moment of time, an instant, a day, a year or a decade before or after the time from which the computation is made. This indeed is what is meant by calling them process laws, for the values of the variables mentioned in the laws are completely determinate for every moment of the temporal sequence. The contrasting imprecision with which slump and depression are said to "follow" a boom hardly needs comment. Exactly when it will follow and how long it will last are not at present within our purview.

4. Perfection and Social Science

How do the social sciences stand up when measured against the criteria of closure and completeness? A system consists roughly of any group of objects or patterns of behavior remaining constant in time. The planets, identifiable by their masses, the market with its stable procedures for buying and selling, rats in a cage, people in a community identifiable, say, by occupation and income, all constitute systems. Just as velocity and position, changing in time, are the states of a mechanical system, so consumer preferences or political opinions may be the changing states of human systems. To know the conditions for closure of these systems, that is, to know either that nothing outside of the region being considered is affecting it or else to know what is entering or leaving the system, we must first know all the relevant variables, that is, the theory being applied to the system must be complete. No variables that in fact make a difference are omitted from the theory. Since the conditions for closure will in a sense settle themselves if we know all the relevant variables, we can concentrate our attention on the completeness of theories in social science.

(a) *Imperfection and separation of variables.* From the point of view of the physical scientist, a curious characteristic of the social sciences is the division of its terms or variables into two classes. This division is explicit in psychology and theoretical economics, implicit in the other areas. Psychologists distinguish stimulus variables from response variables; economists, the exogenous from the endogenous. Response terms name individual behavior which the psychologist explains in terms of the stimulus variables, that is, the physical and social environment, as well as certain biological states, past habits, and perhaps hereditary factors. The individual's behavior is held to be determined by all these, but not, of course, conversely. The stimulus conditions are either given to or, at least partly, manipulated by the observer, but his theory does not purport to explain them. This is left to other areas of either social, biological, or physical science. The economist's distinction though not the same is similar. The economic or "endogenous" variables influence each other and are influenced by the "exogenous," noneconomic, physical, technological, institutional variables, but not conversely. The latter are "predetermined" data or conditions in terms of which the economist explains changes in economic factors. This division among the variables is patently artificial, a convenient way of speaking only, for nothing is in itself either a stimulus or a response, endogenous or exogenous. In neither case is the distinction a hard and fast one. The stimulus conditions may consist in part of one's own and other people's behavior. Similarly, an exogenous factor, say, the imposition of tariffs by Congress, may be affected by economic conditions such as decreasing demand, as well as by political pressures.

It is easy to see in a preliminary way why this division of the variables reflects a departure from "perfection." Clearly, there is no question here of symmetry between the terms in each class. Changes in the response or economic factors do not generally change the stimulus or noneconomic factors respectively. The category into which a term is placed depends in large part upon how much we know. Tax rates and exports, for example, are exogenous or institutional because determined by political decisions, but if economic causes were found for them, they would be treated as endogenous. In general, this division of the variables is a reflection of the inadequacy of a given theory, whether in psychology or economics, to fully account for changes in *all* the variables. The sociologist seeking to account for population distribution does not also attempt to explain the geographical formations which may influence where people live. The political scientist does not try to explain the economic factors which may in turn explain the voting behavior in which he is interested. The limited scope of our theories reinforces this distinction while highlighting its artficiality. Given two different theories in an area, the same variable may be either dependent or "predetermined." What is considered exogenous in a business-cycle theory, for example, may not be so in a theory of demand. In psychology, a theory in social psychology may take as stimulus what is response in learning theory.[8]

How does this affect completeness? Let us leave out of consideration the physical variables, like rainfall or body-type, in respect to which closure can hardly be expected, since presumably these are to be explained primarily in terms of other physical and physiological variables. Even so, what about the institutional and behavioral variables? It is evident, from all that we now know, that no individual social science can by itself expect to achieve completeness in its terms. Any theory of human behavior will contain references to political, legal, psychological, economic, religious, and other institutional factors in the individual's environment. It is a commonplace by now that these factors all interact, so each social science is to some greater or lesser extent dependent upon the findings of others. In addition to the division in the variables, there are other clues to an acknowledged lack of completeness. Consider the generalization that other things remaining unchanged, a protective tariff on a commodity causes a rise in its price. Incompleteness is signalled here in two ways. First, "protective tariff" is an exogenous variable whose imposition is not to be explained by the theory, but in terms of which change in the endogenous variable, price, is explained. Secondly, by the phrase "other things remaining unchanged" the economist hedges his bets that the values of other variables influencing price, either mentioned or not in his theory, either exogenous, like changes in technology, or endogenous, like wage reductions, will remain as they were at the time the tariff is imposed. Some, perhaps most, of these changes in the "other things" are not predictable from the theory, hence it is incomplete. To illustrate more obviously perhaps, other things being equal, demand is doubtless a function of price. But probably no decline in the price of the horse and buggy could have prevented its being superseded by the automobile. Changes in technology and in tastes unpredictable by the theory will have and, as the qualifying phrase indicates, are expected to have their effect. Completeness, in the strict sense of exclusive mutual de-

8 [See also the remarks in the introduction for Section Three of this volume, p. 140, to the effect that the logic of stimulus-and-response is the logic of cause-and-effect language. The latter, in science, is the mark of areas without process knowledge.—Ed.]

pendency among the terms of the theory, could only be achieved by one vast social science encompassing the entire range of human behavior.

The illustration about the discovery of the planet Neptune suggested that theories may be complete and prediction still fail because the system to which they are applied is not closed. A hypothetical example from social science may bring this closer home. Suppose an economist wishes to predict the relative demands for butter and white margarine in a state where colored margarine is prohibited. Assume that among the relevant variables he includes people's preferences and in particular their relative preferences for butter over margarine as well as the prices of these products. Assume, quite unrealistically, that he omits to account for the fact that the region for which he wishes to make his prediction is surrounded on all sides by easily accessible states where colored margarine is available at the same price as white at home. In this case, closure but not completeness is violated, since individual preference is one of his variables and that between white and yellow margarine would have been taken into account if the alternative were present in the home state. If, again quite unrealistically, individual preferences were entirely omitted from the theory, when in fact they make a difference to demand, then his system is incomplete. Generally, if nothing is omitted that actually makes a difference to the behavior of the variables with which the theory is concerned, then the theory is complete. If and only if this condition is satisfied, then all other true laws of the area staked out by the terms of the theory follow as deductive consequences from its axioms or fundamental laws.

(b) Statistics and imperfect knowledge. Social science has developed much more specific techniques to compensate for lapses in closure and completeness. Here we have perhaps a paradox. Statistical knowledge, certainly the most extensive we have in social science, is conspicuously imperfect. Yet, statistics is perhaps the most promising method available for smoothing out the obstructive complexities in subject matter which make the road to perfection so rocky. Despite the great gap between what statistical knowledge can tell us and what we would like to know, statistical techniques do suggest, within their limitations, a method for achieving that semblance of closure and completeness which is at once the despair and, as it is for any theory, the *sine qua non* of behavior theory. Social scientists take the use of statistical techniques so much for granted that they are not always able to articulate clearly just why these techniques are indispensable tools of the trade. The logical basis of this indispensability lies in large part, though not entirely, in the incompleteness of our explanations. The exception is the use of statistical concepts because of errors of measurement. But there is no difference in this respect between the social and physical sciences. The result of a measurement of, say, length is as much a so-called

"chance" or random variable [9] with a frequency distribution determined by the nature of the measurement as is the result of the measurement or computation of an individual's learning ability or a firm's income, though of course neither length nor for that matter Jones' 1956 income nor his learning ability are random variables. The latter, unlike "yearly number of automobile accidents," "income of farmers" or "learning ability of five-year-olds," have a single value and not a frequency distribution. But errors of measurement are not unique to social science, thus not germane to our present preoccupation. The use of random variables as a consequence of incompleteness is. There are two ways in which the use of statistical concepts betrays incompleteness.

Without some abstraction or selection from all the possibilities the world presents there can be no science at all. By their very nature scientific laws describe only certain features of the kinds of things or events they hold to be connected. How much can safely be ignored depends upon the way things are. Even in human behavior not everything makes a difference. An individual's taste in music may be a function of many variables, but the color of his eyes is probably not one of them. Even so, the number of different things such as education, age, family background, heredity, special training, and so on, may be so large and so difficult to assign relative importance that we may well despair of formulating an exact functional relationship between such tastes and these other factors. To say, in consequence, that abstraction is all very well for the physical sciences but will not do for the study of man and society is the counsel of desperation, that is, no solution at all. The social scientist, striving to merit the honorific half of that title, settles for something less than perfection. Completeness being far beyond his grasp, he renounces it as a goal. The renunciation has its price and its rewards. Which face will turn up when a die is cast is determined by numerous causes, the center of gravity of the die, the force with which it·is thrown, and so on. An attempt to calculate the results of each throw by means of the laws of mechanics is practically hopeless, because of the difficulty in precisely measuring all the initial conditions. Instead, we represent, as it were, this multiplicity of causes by a probability distribution for the attribute in question. The use of the statistical concept marks our ignorance of all the influencing factors, a failure in either completeness or closure or, usually, both. Similarly, the social scientist, deliberately selecting for study fewer factors than actually influence the behavior in which he is interested shifts his goal from predicting individual events or behaviors to predicting a random variable, that is, to predicting the frequency with which this kind

[9] In the jargon of the trade, statistical variables are usually called "chance," stochastic, or random, meaning any magnitude, like "yearly number of accidents," which takes different values with definite probabilities. A philosopher aware of the woes associated with words like "chance" is impelled to put the technical term in quotation marks. It means only what it is said to mean, of course, and has nothing to do with "freedom" in the sense of uncaused.

of behavior occurs in a large group of individuals possessing the circumscribed number of factors. This is the price. The reward, of course, is that
instead of helplessly gazing in dumb wonder at the infinite complexity
of man and society, he has knowledge, imperfect rather than perfect, to be
sure, but knowledge not to be scorned nonetheless, of a probability distribution rather than of individual events. After all, while we might much
prefer to know the exact conditions under which cancer develops in a
particular person, it is far from valueless to know the factors which are
statistically correlated to the frequency of its occurrence.

The relationship between statistical prediction and incompleteness is
strikingly explicit in the relatively recent use of so-called stochastic equations, where "stochastic" means not any statistical concept but a specific
form of such. The probability of success in school, let us say, is expressed
as a function of I.Q. The observed values of the frequency of such success
will be affected by errors of observation. If we know the probability distribution of these errors, then we can make a prediction about the probability of success in school for a given I.Q. or range of I.Q.'s. Our predicted
attribute is thus a function both of I.Q. and the distribution of the error.
In physics, for example, measured pressure at constant temperature will
be a function of the volume plus or minus a known error component associated with the measurement of volume. And of nothing else. If there were
no errors of observation, then the connection stated between pressure and
volume is exact, with no statistical component. In our illustration, however,
as in social science generally, even if there were no errors or if our theory
of errors permitted us to separate out the error component, we would *still*
be able to predict only a probability distribution and not individual values.
There is, as the physicist might say, a systematic component to the error
which is not associated with any particular variable but with the asserted
connection, an error in the equation itself. Because of a great many other
factors, not all children with the same I.Q. will be equally successful. Just
as with measurement errors, all these omitted influences, each one of which
may be small in itself may be expressed as a separate variable. In this case,
we may say that the connection holds with a "disturbance." Of course, any
two things can be said to be related with a "disturbance," so long as the
latter is unspecified. To rescue these equations from vacuity, to make them
empirically meaningful, the disturbance must have a known probability
distribution which does not change with changes in the observed variables.
Thus, success in school would be expressed as a function of I.Q. *and* a
random variable. This latter probability term would express the aggregate
effects of factors as yet unspecified. Thus, incompleteness is at once explicitly
built into the system and, given our ignorance either of what these omitted
factors are or how much weight they each carry, accounted for in the best
possible way. Theoretical economics and, to a much lesser extent, experimental psychology are as yet the only social sciences adapting this technique

of further dividing their variables into those which are named by the theory, called "systematic," and those which are only latently expressed, as it were, in the "disturbance."

The lucidity with which stochastic equations betray the incompleteness and consequent statistical character of the theories in which they occur is, of course, not the reason why they are used. I suggested earlier that the dichotomies stimulus-response and exogenous-endogenous were at once recognition of the absence of completeness and an attempt to achieve an approximation to it for the variables of the area, psychology or economics respectively. The split by means of stochastic equations into systematic and disturbance components also serves this purpose. It does so with greater precision by assigning a definite and testable probability to the magnitude of the unknown external factors. Also, packed into the disturbance in the equation may be not only factors which the theory does not seek to explain, such as physical or institutional influences, but also as yet unnoticed variables of the area itself. With increasing knowledge of the sources of error of observation and the improvement in our measuring instruments we are able to reduce the error in the variable due to these factors. In the same way, increasing knowledge may lead to reducing the amount of error in the equation by analyzing the disturbance into its components, resulting in a greater degree of completeness for the variables of the area.

To illustrate more concretely, assuming perfect observation, let us say that the amount consumed of some commodity is expressed as a function of the price of the commodity and an error factor in the connection. This error or disturbance incorporates many other causal factors, both non-economic, like fashion, and economic, like income. Though there may always remain a residual noneconomic cause of error, with increasing knowledge and accuracy the economic factors influencing the relation may be spelled out and added to the systematic variables, leaving only non-economic factors in the random variable. In the ideal, all economic variables would be included in the set of systematic variables. Consumption, price, and income, be it noticed, are all economic or endogenous variables. If the disturbance in their connection becomes very small, we may well say that they are relatively autonomous, that is, that they interact primarily only with each other. For complete autonomy, the disturbance would have to be zero and probably only the most extreme economic determinist envisages this as a real possibility. The more comprehensive the social science, say a science incorporating psychological, economic, and sociological phenomena, the greater the degree of autonomy to be envisaged. Since physical, geographical, and physiological factors can be expected to participate in what happens, a wholly autonomous social science, closed and complete by itself, is, to put it moderately, not likely. But relative autonomy would, again to put it moderately, be no small achievement.

5. Composition Laws and Group Behavior: Reduction

Closure, completeness, precisely identifiable referents, temporal definiteness of prediction or computation, these then are the ingredients of knowledge at its best. The question about the possibility of an autonomous group science may thus be more precisely reworded in the light of these criteria. Is it possible to have perfect knowledge of society, that is, is it possible to have a process theory containing only group variables which will be both closed and complete?

Group concepts refer, as we saw, to complex patterns of descriptive, empirical relations among individuals. Study of the behavior of these complexes results in the formation of laws which we may call macroscopic from the nature of their terms. Such laws will be different from laws about the behavior of single individuals. There need not be and in general will not be any similarity between the behavior of a complex and the behavior of the elements of the complex. The behavior of a substance subject to the laws of chemistry differs from the behavior of its particles subject to the laws of mechanics. Groups may be cohesive, which individuals cannot be, and cohesiveness may affect the stability of the group, which is again something individuals, in this meaning of "stability," cannot have. Both terms in this law, if such it be, refer to congeries of individuals exemplifying descriptive relations, such as choosing each other as friends in the first case and faithfully attending meetings with other members of the group, in the second. The law states that whenever a group has the first set of relational attributes, then it also has the other. Laws may also be found connecting individual behavior or characteristics with that of groups. Ambitious individuals, suppose, are attracted to stratified groups offering opportunity for leadership. This would be an example of an *empirical* connection between individual and group attributes. However, since there are no undefinable group entities or properties, every group term will also be *definitionally* connected with a set of (relational) individual behaviors. These latter need not necessarily be "psychological" in the sense that they are technical concepts within the science of psychology. Characteristics occurring in the definitions of macroscopic concepts, such as choosing friends, communicating, buying or selling, need not be, though of course they may be accounted for by an existing psychological theory. It is therefore misleading to say that because group concepts must be defined in terms of individuals they are "really" psychological. Only if "psychological" is broadly defined to include all human behavior is this the case. In this sense, "selling short on the stock market" is psychological. But then the term is so broad as to be virtually useless. Only if this behavior can be explained within the context of a theory in psychology is it significantly called psychological rather than, say, economic. These considerations should all help to bring into proper focus the issues connected with the possibility of reduction. What then is the logic of the connection between the group sciences and psychology? How, in principle, would the reduction of the one to the other take place?

A process theory, to repeat, is one permitting the computation of the states of a system at all times from its state at any given time. All such theories contain, in addition to laws for so-called elementary situations, another type of law which increases its scope, securing for it a range of widely different systems whose laws are deducible from the theory. The Newtonian law of attraction between *two* bodies is the elementary law of the system. One does not independently, however, have to discover the law for *three, four,* or any larger number of bodies. These are derivable from the two-body law. They are so, not by logical or arithmetical methods alone, nor from the two-body law alone, but by the addition of a special kind of empirical law, the so-called parallelogram rule. By imaginary decomposition of a system consisting of any number of bodies into pairs of two-body systems, this rule together with the elementary law permits us to compute the accelerations of each body in the complex system. Laws permitting such computation from the elementary to more complex systems may be called composition laws or, a bit misleadingly, composition rules. The latter is misleading because, of course, the "rule" by which the state of a system containing any number of bodies is computed from the law for the elementary, two-body, system is itself an empirical generalization or law. The term "vector addition" applied to this particular rule adds to the confusion by making appear purely arithmetical what is an empirical matter, namely, that the resultant of the forces is their vector sum. Another illustration may help clarify the situation. In chemistry, we have laws for the behavior of hydrogen and laws for the behavior of oxygen. We also have the law of their interaction, that is, the law stating what happens when oxygen and hydrogen occur together under certain conditions. They form water, for instance. The properties of water are predictable from the laws of its elements in addition to the law of their interaction. Let us take still another example. Airplanes, despite Galileo, often stay up in the air for long periods of time. We know of course that this is not a "violation" of the law of gravity. The fact that they stay up is explained by applying to this situation all the laws involving the variables believed to be relevant to the situation. The rules for combining these laws, which form the subject matter of aerodynamics, are themselves empirical generalizations or regularities. Such composition rules obviously give to the theories containing them tremendous power and scope. When applied to social science, they are, as I shall now show, the means by which reduction would take place.

Macroscopic laws are laws containing group variables. Assume, for instance, that sociologists find a group law to the effect that stratification causes increased efficiency. The kinds of individual behavior, like the giving and taking of orders, who communicates with whom, etc., in terms of which the group variable, stratification, is defined constitute the undefined terms of the sociological system. But, for two reasons, this definition alone would not enable us to deduce the law from those of psychology. First, as mentioned before, such individual behaviors need not also be terms of an existing psychological theory. Psychologists, in other words, might not have knowledge about the causes and effects of issuing orders, direction of communication, etc. But suppose that these are terms of psychological theory. The definition, though necessary, is still not sufficient for the deduction to be made. In addition to elementary laws telling how an individual acts in the presence of one or a few others, we must also have composition laws stating what happens, under certain conditions, as the number of people he is with increases. The latter, of course, state how he behaves in a group. Assume, more particularly, that we have the elementary laws, none of which mentions stratified groups, about how Jones, that is, an individual with certain characteristics, behaves in the presence of a person like Smith and about how Jones behaves in the presence of a person like Brown. In addition, assume we have a composition law revealing how Jones behaves when he is confronted with both Smith and Brown under the conditions defined as "stratified." We would then know how one individual with certain characteristics behaves as a member of a certain layer of a stratified group. If in addition to these composition laws about the interactions of various kinds of people and the definitions of the group concepts, we are also given the (statistical) description of the initial composition of the group, then we can predict the behavior of the group, that is, we may derive laws of group behavior.

We see now why the reducing area, psychology, is said to be microscopic (molecular) relative to the reduced area. The composition laws state what happens when several elementary situations are combined in specified ways. These combined situations are the macroscopic (molar) complexes referred to by the group terms of the reduced area. The definitions of the group terms provide the common language necessary for the derivation of macroscopic statements from microscopic ones. The composition laws then supply the empirical premises from which the deduction is made. The reduction of group laws to those about individuals thus supplies an explanation of group behavior in terms of the behavior of individuals in groups. Given the composition laws, the reduction of sociology to psychology is a purely logical matter, following as it does from these composition laws jointly only with the definitions. Or, to say the same thing differently, just as, given the law of vector addition, we do not independently have to discover the law of a three-body system in mechanics, so, given the definitions and the composition laws, we do not independently have to investigate the behavior of groups. And this of course is what we mean by saying that one area has been "reduced" to another. The definitions of the group terms are all that connect the two areas.[10] Since all definitions are in principle

---

[10] This is in contrast with the connection between psychology and physiology. In this case, the two areas are joined by cross-sectional laws, that is empirical laws connecting a physiological variable with an undefined psychological (behavioral) variable. If these laws

dispensable and the composition laws contain only psychological terms, there is thus a sense in which there is "really" only one area. It does not follow, however, that we can scrap the macroscopic social sciences. In addition to the difficulty already discussed about the vagueness or openendedness of group terms, there are even more fundamental reasons, having to do with the nature of composition laws, why the group sciences are probably here to stay.

6. Reduction: Fact vs. Principle

Since these composition laws are empirical generalizations, they may fail at some point. Absurd as physicists might find the idea at this stage of the game, it is nevertheless, logically possible that the parallelogram rule would no longer work as one went from a system containing, say, 999 bodies to one containing 1000. The prediction for the more complex system, made by means of the composition rule, might be proven false. Psychologists similarly might be able to predict the behavior of an individual in groups of a given size, but as soon as another person was added to the group, the prediction failed. There are several reasons—apart from the theoretically uninteresting case of errors in induction and measurement—why this might happen. Possibly, but *just* possibly, there aren't any laws of human behavior after a certain level of complexity is reached. In this case, the behavior of groups of a certain complexity marks a level of breakdown not only of the composition law, but also of determinism. No sociologist, no matter how fervently devoted to groups he might be, would be happy about this. In fact, if there were any reason to believe it were true, his devotion to groups would wane rapidly. More realistically, perhaps we need a different composition rule. This new law might be different either because it has a different form or because it contains variables not present in the law for groups of lesser complexity. In our imaginary physical case, for instance, it might be that for systems containing 1000 or more bodies their mutual attraction turned out to be a function of the cube rather than the square of the distances between them. Or for 1000-body systems, to pile absurdity upon absurdity, the presence or absence of life might make a difference to the acceleration. Similarly, the composition law about the behavior of individuals in groups might either change in form or some new variable, like fear of being together with large masses of people, might begin to be operative only after the population reaches a given magnitude. The variable is "new" not in the sense that instances of it did not exist before, but because it did not affect the behavior we are interested in predicting, that is, it

---

and the appropriate physiological composition rules are known, then independent discovery of psychological laws would also be unnecessary. But psychological concepts, unlike group terms, would not be dispensable. The logical pattern of the reduction in each case is radically different.

did not occur in any complete set of relevant variables of a system of lesser complexity.

Finally, it might be that even though group behavior is itself lawful there is no composition rule from which it can be predicted. I shall return to this alternative in a moment. In any case, for whatever reason, the composition rule might break down. If it should, then we have an instance of *explanatory* emergence. Emergence at the level of explanation should be carefully distinguished from what we earlier called descriptive emergence. The latter phrase refers to the occurrence of a property of groups, like the so-called group-mind, which is not definable in terms of the individuals making up the group. Explanatory emergence, however, refers to laws of group behavior, which, *even though their terms are defined as they should be,* are still not derivable from the laws, including whatever composition laws there are, about individual behavior. This is *in fact* the case at present. The anti-emergentist, in the context of explanation, merely denies that *in principle* laws about groups are not derivable from laws about individuals. The "emergentist," accordingly, holds that the composition rules necessary for reduction are lacking because on logical grounds there cannot be any such laws, even though group behavior is itself lawful. This view is held, for instance, by those who maintain that society or history has laws of "its own" for which the behavior of individuals is not relevant. If this were the case, then it would make sense to say that there are *sui generis* laws of the social process. But this, of course, only pushes the indeterminism back from groups to individuals. It is, therefore, not a view any scientist can comfortably live with.

Two meanings of methodological individualism. Sometimes the phrase "methodological individualism" is applied both to the view that there are no undefinable group concepts and to the view that the laws of the group sciences are in principle reducible to those about individuals. The former is a denial of descriptive emergence; the latter denies that there are any logical grounds for belief in explanatory emergence.[11] Both positions are, indeed, very much a part of the general empiricist tradition. Nevertheless, they are not identical, nor are they equally fundamental. The first, as we saw, is required by the logic of concept formation within the individualistic, empiricist framework. But, as to the second, whether or not there are composition laws is not something that can be *a priori* decided. Descriptive emergence is compatible with and may be used as an argument for the necessity of explanatory emergence. But it is not a good argument. If the alleged emergent properties are lawfully connected with those properties of individuals from which they emerge, as, analogously, psychological properties are lawfully connected with physiological ones, then by means of

---

11 Watkins' misunderstanding (*op. cit.*) of my argument (*op. cit.*) that holism is not entailed by the possibility of an autonomous group science stems from confusing these two positions.

such cross-sectional laws and the microscopic ones, the macroscopic laws could be derived. In any case, the denial of descriptive emergence does not entail the denial of explanatory emergence. The latter is a matter of fact. And matters of fact cannot be legislated into existence. In other words, the empiricist commitment to *definitional* methodological individualism does not logically imply a commitment to *explanatory* methodological individualism, that is, to reduction.

In the context of explanation, methodological individualism is a matter of principle only in that broad sense in which determinism itself is a matter of principle. These issues are often confounded because it is not fully realized that the two alternatives, the successful working of composition rules or their breakdown at some level of complexity, are both "individualistic," in that broad sense of the term denoting a basic metaphysical assumption. As long as it is granted that groups are composed of individuals, their characteristics, and the relations between these individuals, and of nothing else, then there is no question of violating this basic assumption. The fact is that we do not as yet, and, for all we know, may never have the psychological laws permitting reduction. This does not and cannot in any way militate against that individualism which empiricists are rightly so anxious to preserve. Happily that frame of reference does not depend, at least not logically, upon the state of our knowledge at any particular moment in history.

Whichever alternative turns out to be the case, the optimistic one that reduction of laws is achievable or its contrary pessimistic one, two possibilities still remain for social science. First, whether or not our concepts are defined or, at least, in principle definable, it is still logically possible that a class of group concepts form a complete set of relevant variables of the social process. A process theory is logically possible with any kind of variables as, for instance, nonatomic thermodynamics demonstrates. It is thus logically possible, even if most unlikely, that we could have a complete theory of psychology with only behavioral, nonphysiological variables. Similarly, it is logically possible that, irrespective of definitional reduction, we may have perfect knowledge of society in the sense of having a process theory whose laws contain only macroscopic or group variables. The reduction of chemistry to physics is by now a fairly well-accomplished fact. At one time chemistry was at a stage analogous to that of the group sciences. The microscopic structure of the molecules in terms of atoms was known, just as we know the composition of our groups, but the laws of quantum physics by which atoms combine into molecules were not known. Once they were known, however, it turned out that the (chemical) laws by which molecules combine could be derived from them. Yet, organic chemistry appears to be here to stay. In principle, the interactions of the complex molecules can be derived from the laws of physics about the fundamental particles. However, the mathematics of the relevant composition laws is so involved that it is much simpler to study directly the behavior of these organic complexes.

Similarly, even if we had reduction, it might still be practically more feasible to study group behavior. Conceivably, there might be a set of macroscopic laws permitting the prediction of the "state" of society (i.e., the values of the group variables) at all times from its state at any given time. This possibility is to be sure most implausible. It is implausible not only because the discovery of such a complete set of relevant variables seems a formidable task, but also because it is rather more than likely that changes in the social process do not depend only upon group or macroscopic units, Marxism to the contrary notwithstanding. People are not like molecules in a gas. Some are different from others and some have more effect upon society than others. It is still a good question whether without Lenin there would have been the October Revolution. If this variance among individuals makes sufficient difference, then the laws have to take the occurrence of a particular kind of individual into account. In this case, a complete set of variables could not all be macroscopic. The unlikelihood of perfect knowledge by macroscopic laws alone is probably a source of the mistaken conviction that reduction of laws is *necessary* for empiricist individualism. But, again, it is merely a matter of fact that this possibility is most unlikely.

But if perfect knowledge with group variables alone is unlikely, there is still another possibility. It may be that approximate laws of all kinds can be stated in these variables. These laws would of course bear some or all of the marks of imperfection. They would be indefinite with respect to time, hedged in by qualification, and, above all, they would be statistical. The remarkable success of statistical knowledge is a measure of how much can be ignored, particularly of the individual variance, and prediction still be possible. If there be, as in principle there probably are, composition rules from which the behavior of groups may be predicted, these are most likely of such complexity and difficulty that it may well be the better part of wisdom for social scientists to look for whatever imperfect connections may exist among the group variables. These, in turn, may suggest the appropriate composition rules of individual behavior. But this is not for the philosopher to say.

[17] Levels of Explanation in History

A . M . MacIVER

The ultimate stuff of history is the countless individual doings of individual human beings through the ages, together with such natural events and facts as have conditioned those human doings—events such as the normal alternation of fair and foul weather or the cycle of the seasons, as well as earthquakes, inundations and droughts, and facts such as the fact that here is sea and there is dry land, this land is fertile and that is barren, this has coal and iron and that has none. But these natural facts and events are important to the historian only in so far as they condition human doings. The actual individual doings, on the other hand, collectively make up his subject-matter.

This is a plain fact which Idealist philosophers of history, with their slogan that "all history is contemporary history," completely overlook. Oakeshott or Collingwood calls the history (let us say) of the Peloponnesian War a "mode of experience," meaning by this his own experience in his twentieth-century Oxford or Cambridge college room, forgetting that what made the history was experience all right, but the experience of thousands of poor devils two dozen centuries ago. The Idealist philosophers have unthinkingly transferred to history an argument that was plausible enough when applied to physical science. It is easy to argue that atoms and electrons are mere postulates of theory; nobody has ever met one in the flesh; to say that they have such and such characters, or behave in such and such ways, is only to say that this is what physicists at present find it convenient to suppose. But, whatever may be the case with atoms and electrons, human beings are not mere creatures of theory. To say that we are now doing whatever we are actually doing, and for the reasons for which we are actually doing it, is not to say merely that this is what some future historian is going to find it convenient for his purposes then to suppose. And, by parity of reasoning, whatever men were doing a thousand years ago does not depend upon what historians find it convenient to suppose now.

Individual human doings collectively make up the stuff of history. What each one of us is doing here and now is part of the subject-matter of the

Originally published as "The Character of a Historical Explanation" in the *Proceedings of the Aristotelian Society,* Supplementary Vol. XXI, 1947, pp. 32–50, and reprinted with the permission of the author and the Editor of The Aristotelian Society.

history that will be written in the future. If what we were all doing now were different, the history of this period would be different. But history is not itself the record of all these doings. The historian selects and (what is even more important) generalizes. It is thanks to this that the proposition that "all history is contemporary history" is not patently absurd, because it is true that each historian selects and generalizes with reference to his own contemporary interests. But his generalizations are true or false in proportion as they represent or misrepresent all the individual doings and happenings. (This is the foundation-stone upon which I am going to build the whole of my argument in this paper—a stone which the builders of philosophies of history hitherto have, so far as I can understand them, almost universally rejected.) To show up by contrast the character of all actual written history, we may perhaps find it convenient to suppose an ideal written history, which would tell the whole story of everything that ever happened to every human being, which we might call "the Book of the Recording Angel." The function of the historian (we might then say) is not, indeed, to copy out extracts from the Book of the Recording Angel, but it is to make an intelligent précis of some part of it. This is not to depreciate the work of the historian. The function of the Recording Angel could, after all, in a fully mechanized Heaven, be performed by an electrical device, whereas the making of the historian's précis requires intelligence. But, though the précis may be made for some particular purpose and omit what is not relevant to that purpose, it must not misrepresent the contents of the original.

But, although all history rests upon this same foundation and all actual history generalizes, there are many different levels of historical generality. What I have called "the Book of the Recording Angel" may be regarded as the ideal limit to which history approximates as generalization tends to zero. At the lowest level of generality of all kinds of historical writing is biography—particularly that kind of biography which hardly professes to be more than a collection of anecdotes about its subject arranged in chronological order. This hardly generalizes at all: it differs from the Book of the Recording Angel itself only in that it selects, and that according to no fixed principle other than the accidental limitations of the writer's sources of information. Almost at the other extreme stands the sort of general world history which knows no epochs except the great technological revolutions which completely transformed the whole background of human life, for which hardly anything worth mentioning happened between the discovery of the smelting of metals at the close of the Neolithic Age and the perfection of the steam engine by James Watt. Slightly (but only slightly) less general than this is Marxian history, which considers events only in so far as they have affected or followed from changes in the large-scale organization of society for the production, distribution and consumption of economic goods. History at all these different levels is (that is to say, can be) equally good history. We do not get a better or a worse view of a field according as we take a bird's eye, or a man's eye, or a worm's eye view of it, though we get a different view, and yet they are all views of the same field.

Serious trouble only begins when levels are not distinguished. From this many futile disputes arise. Take for example the question, still often eagerly disputed, whether the acts of individuals determine the course of history. Obviously they do. The only proper question is: How much? History is nothing but the resultant of all the acts of millions of individuals, but the consequences of some individual acts are still distinguishable after a considerable lapse of time, while the consequences of others blend together almost immediately. The fact that John Smith at a particular time on a particular morning hurried to the local branch of his own bank and withdrew a much larger sum than he would normally have withdrawn, because he had heard that another bank had failed or was about to fail, goes down to history only as part of the fact that there was a run on the banks in that week, which precipitated a world financial crisis; John Smith's contribution can no longer be distinguished. On the other hand, the fact that General Brown, overcome by a fit of pessimism, surrendered the strategically vital fortress of which he was in command, when a more resolute general could have held it until relief arrived, perhaps led immediately to the loss of the war and a whole string of consequences, all of which can be traced back to that single act. Certainly the loss of the war will have other contributory causes. General Brown's surrender would perhaps not have had this result if the relieving force had been in a position immediately to retrieve the situation, but in fact it was not, because it was inadequately armed, because there had been financial corruption in the quartermaster-general's department, the causes of which corruption ramify back into the whole political and social history of the country. Still the fact remains that General Brown need not have capitulated, and that, if he had not, the war could have been won, so that the loss of the war and all that followed from it was the direct consequence of this individual act of capitulation. (The case might equally have been that of an unknown private soldier, who might have prevented the enemy from gaining what proved to be a vital point, though in that case it would probably escape mention in the history-books, for the question is only whether a chain of consequences could be traced back to an individual act, if it were known.) It is possible that, if General Brown had not capitulated unnecessarily, some other commander on the same side would have done so, but this is not certain and anyhow he might not have surrendered such a vitally important position. As, however, we take a broader and a broader view, such possibilities may begin to accumulate into probabilities. If General Brown was constitutionally liable to fits of pessimism, he should never have been appointed to command a strategically vital fortress in time of war. A country whose administration made such unwise appointments might by good luck come successfully through one war, but would hardly survive a series of wars if it persisted in the habit. Where such appointments are favoured by persistent conditions, such as the general decay of a social

class from which military officers continue to be drawn, resulting in turn
from a cause such as the ruin of a country's agriculture by the appearance
of a more powerful competitor on the world market, it may be possible to
predict that such a country will ultimately either be conquered in war or
else succumb without fighting, though not precisely how or when.

We can see how this bears upon that favourite example in arguments
about the influence of "great men" in history—the part played by Julius
Caesar in the history of the Roman Empire. It is almost certain that, if
Julius Caesar had died in infancy, someone else would have unified the
Mediterranean world under a single autocratic monarchy. The situation
was ripe for it. Both Sulla and Pompey had already very nearly achieved
it. As seen by the universal historian who thinks in no time-unit less than
a century and no social unit smaller than a whole civilization, the picture
would be just the same even if Julius Caesar had never lived. For those
who take a closer view, however, the picture would have been very different.
If Caesar had not lived, Rome might have had to wait another generation or
even longer for a man who combined the necessary ambition with the
necessary abilities, and the resulting prolongation of senatorial anarchy
might have had effects which would have been felt for centuries. For his
actual contemporaries the difference would have been all-important.

History at different levels has different periods and different turning-
points. For his own subjects the death of an individual autocrat may mark
an epoch, but for later historians it may be some event in the middle of
his reign, perhaps hardly noticed by contemporaries, which marks the end
of one period, which began long before he was born, and the beginning
of another, which continued long after he was dead, the death of the ruler
himself being something quite insignificant. Marx, though he introduced
the conception of the Industrial Revolution, attached no particular importance to the introduction of power-driven machinery. His historical
researches were mainly concerned with the transition from feudalism to
capitalism, with the ultimate object of applying the lesson to predict the
course of the expected subsequent transition from capitalism to socialism.
Most interesting to him was the change in the distribution of social forces
which came when production for profit took the place of production for
use. The introduction of power-driven machinery appears in his account
as a mere incident in the subsequent development—just one of the devices
by which capitalists, in a competitive economy, sought to turn the labour-
power of the workers more and more to profit. Marx duly considers its
multifarious social repercussions, but, from his point of view, none of them
is so important as the introduction, centuries earlier, of the new economic
motive of profit. If, however, we try to look at the history of the last few
hundred years through the eyes of historians living thousands of years hence,
we can see at once that differences made by the transition from feudalism
to capitalism will then have become almost imperceptible, but differences
made by the introduction of power-driven machinery will be impossible

to overlook. Yet this does not mean either that Marx was mistaken or that the historians of the future will be mistaken, but only that history divides into different periods at different levels of historical generality.

Now we can introduce the subject of "historical explanation." By this we must understand, I think, only such explanation as is part of the historian's business as such, and not include any further explanations in which use happens to be made of the historian's results. In this sense, whatever "historical explanation" may be, it is not the scientific sort of "explanation" described in Mill's *System of Logic,* Book III, Chapter XII—the discovery of hitherto unknown universal laws of which particular phenomena are instances, and the resolution of universal laws into mere special cases of other universal laws even more general. When we say that history "generalizes," we do not mean that it seeks to establish universal laws. We contrast the "generality" of historical statements with the individuality of the facts on which they are based, meaning that they are related to those facts as the general proposition "I possess some philosophical books" is related to the individual facts (my possession of this copy of Plato's *Republic,* and that copy of Kant's *Critique,* and so forth) which make it true. In logical terminology, the historical proposition is "general," but "particular," not "universal." A typically historical statement is "The Normans defeated the English at Hastings in 1066." The battle itself was a vast medley of individual actions and experiences—this man shooting this arrow, that man avoiding it or being hit by it, horses stumbling, men feeling pain or fear or exultation—but the historical statement takes it as a whole and selects for mention just that aspect of it which bears upon the historian's purpose —in this case, the fact that as a result the Duke of Normandy was able to make himself King of England. It is not the business of the historian to "generalize" in any other sense than this.

To say this is not to give orders to historians. It is only to put a limitation on the use of the word "history" in this discussion, which is, I think, supported by ordinary usage. I think that most people would agree, for example, that in Toynbee's *Study of History,* while many of the "annexes" and incidental digressions are real "history," the body of the work is not —it is a new sort of "science." Its object is "explanation" in Mill's sense— to discover the hitherto unknown laws governing the establishment and disintegration of civilisations. This is something which only a trained historian can attempt, since it demands an immense equipment of historical knowledge, but, when he attempts it, he is going beyond history. It is possible—we may grant this hypothetically, without committing ourselves— that historical research is wasted if its results are not afterwards applied in this way; but, even so, the application is not historical research itself, any more than the collection of social statistics is by itself the formulation of a social policy, even if it is true that statistics are wasted unless made the basis of a policy. It would be "historical explanation" to account for the rise of the Sumerian, or the fall of the Minoan, civilisation, but it is "scientific explanation" to account for the rise and fall of civilisations as such. Even if "historical explanation" is (as it may be) explanation by reference to universal laws, it differs from "scientific explanation" in taking the laws as known and concentrating upon the analysis of the particular event, asking which of the known laws actually account for it, and how, and in connection with what other particular events. This is what a historian ordinarily does whenever he professes to "explain" an event, or the origin of an institution, or any of the other things which it is thought to be his business to explain, and I take it that the question which we are intended to answer here is, what sort of an explanation this is (or can be).

Half of the correct answer to this question is, I submit, that there is a different historical explanation appropriate to every different level of historical generality. Even in the Book of the Recording Angel there will be explanation as well as simple narrative. It will say, not merely "Napoleon was annoyed," but "Napoleon was annoyed because his breakfast coffee had been weaker than he liked it." This "because" raises familiar philosophical problems. It suggests some such major premiss as "All human beings are annoyed whenever they do not get exactly what they like," but we know that this is not in fact universally true. It is in a more recondite manner than this that the luke-warmness of the coffee "explains" Napoleon's irritation. But I will assume that the nature of this sort of "explanation" is a question for another symposium. It is not these problems, concerning the kind of "explanation" appropriate to individual human actions, which are troubling us when we are puzzled about specifically "historical explanation." We are thinking of explanation at higher levels of historical generality. But the second half of my answer to this, the question which concerns us here and now, is that correct explanation at these higher levels can be nothing but the reflection of correct explanation at the individual level. Individual acts have individual causes. This I take as acknowledged, whatever the philosophical difficulties concerning the precise kind of causation involved. Just as the historical *statement* summarises a large number of individual acts, representing a character which runs through them all— perhaps the way in which they all contributed to a particular result— neglecting all their multitudinous features which were irrelevant to this, so in the historical *explanation* some of the individual causes of the individual acts disappear as unimportant, but others add up to something which can be stated generally. Its validity consists in representing fairly the balance of the underlying causes. The difference between a correct explanation and an incorrect one, at any particular level of historical generality, corresponds to the difference, in optics, between an undistorted and a distorted picture, at any particular degree of reduction of scale, at which some details inevitably disappear.

Historical explanation becomes confused whenever there is confusion of levels. Perhaps for brevity's sake we must sometimes say such things as that Mr. Jones votes Conservative because he is a business man; but it is always dangerous. Mr. Jones votes Conservative for his own personal reasons, which can be indicated (though not without already generalizing) by saying that he was brought up as a Conservative, that all his friends are Conservatives, that his business experience has drawn his attention to the considerations in favour of the Conservative policy and against the Socialist, that nothing has ever happened to induce him to pay equal attention to the considerations on the other side, and that he is more biassed than he himself realises in favour of a political policy which would tend to his personal advantage. Other business men like Mr. Jones also vote Conservative, each for his own reasons, but all for similar reasons, because their situations are similar. This is the basis for the legitimate historical generalization that "business men vote Conservative because the Conservative Party represents their class interests." But it is confusion of levels to use this generalization to explain individual behaviour. Marxist historians are frequently guilty of this confusion, which results in absurd notions of "economic determinism," implying that it is impossible for an individual to have any political opinions which are not those of his economic class. Idealist historians may commit the same confusion, implying that no individual can make his own judgments but that they are forced upon him by the Spirit of the Age. For events at the individual level explanations must be found at the same level. But the generalization that the Conservative Party is the party of the business men can legitimately be used (say) to explain the decline of the Conservative Party as a natural consequence of the decreasing importance of private, as compared with public, enterprise in the national economy. This is (that is to say, may be, provided that the facts support it) a valid historical explanation at what we may call the "Marxist" level of historical generality.

In historical explanation at all levels above the purely individual, whatever is unimportant is disregarded. This sounds subjective, but in fact there is no subjectivity in it, apart from the subjectivity of the motive dictating choice of a particular level. The test of importance, at any particular level, is a purely quantitative one. Factors are important in proportion as their influence is felt all over the field under examination. This is forgotten by those who object against the Marxian conception of history that it neglects all the spiritual achievements of mankind. So it does; but only because they are actually negligible at the level of generality with which it is concerned. In the case of every individual there are respects in which he resembles all or very many of his contemporaries and differs noticeably from any man of another period, and other respects in which he differs from all his contemporaries and may perhaps most nearly resemble some individuals of other periods. What are called the great spiritual achievements of mankind represent that individual distinction which sets the great man apart as much from his contemporaries as from any predecessors or successors. But this individual distinction has comparatively little influence on the course of history. What influence it does have may be called "vertical" rather than "horizontal": that is to say, the great mind influences only comparatively few individuals in any particular generation, but continues to exert that influence (generally through the survival of writings, though it might be by an oral tradition) through many centuries. The influence of Plato or Aristotle in philosophy would be an obvious example. This sort of influence is imperceptible at the level of generality of Marxian history. This is concerned with the general state of a whole society at a particular date, and its relation to the general state of the same society at an earlier or later date, and cannot be expected to attend to the achievements of individuals, however "great," except in so far as they were immediately responsible for large-scale social changes which would not have occurred without them. And this happens even less often than it appears to do, for a movement may bear the name of a great individual, yet the part which it played in history may have comparatively little to do with him. Thus it would be absurd to deny that there is a Christian tradition which has done more to form our present ways of thinking and feeling than any other intellectual influence from the past, and equally absurd to deny that a great deal in Christianity derives from Christ, but it may well be doubted whether it is this part of Christianity which has ever had most general influence. What has determined the course of history, viewed on any large scale, at any particular period, has not been Christianity as such, but, if anything, the Christian Church as it was at that period, focussing a mass of beliefs of very varied origins, some of them old, some comparatively new (though perhaps expressed in old terms), traditions, moral intuitions, prejudices, considerations of sectional interest, and personal ambitions, in which the immediate contemporary interests of the clergy and the faithful bulk much larger than the general Christian heritage. Marxist historians can fairly be criticised for claiming (as they often seem to do) that history cannot legitimately be studied except at their own chosen level, but not for insisting that, at that level, it is only "materialist" explanations which really explain. This is a simple consequence of the fact that men are more often bad than good, and more often stupid than intelligent, so that the acts of the exceptional individuals disappear from view as soon as the human scene is contemplated from any distance.

But there is also a level at which ideas have a history of their own, which is the level at which Idealist historians prefer to work. This is quite as legitimate as working at any other level, so long as it is remembered that "absolute mind" is only a logical construction—that this sort of history is only another set of historical generalizations from the same mass of individual acts and thoughts of which we suppose the whole story written in the Book of the Recording Angel. New conceptions and methods of approach to intellectual questions are introduced by individuals, become fashionable and are very widely applied, until finally they are found for one reason or another unsatisfactory and gradually abandoned. Changes in material conditions can exert an influence here, because they may raise new problems which the old conceptions and methods cannot solve, thus hastening their abandonment; but the importance of this is probably much exaggerated by Marxists, and the Idealist historians may often be justified in disregarding it. In any case it is very naive to think that methods and conceptions will ever be abandoned merely because problems have arisen which they cannot solve. The fact that the old methods cannot solve the new problems will not be recognised. It will be alleged that they have in fact been solved already, or else that, though not solved yet, they will be solved soon, still by the old methods, or perhaps that they are completely insoluble. What forces the abandonment of old methods and conceptions is always the invention of new methods and conceptions which prove their superiority in competition, and this requires a certain lapse of time and may have to wait for the appearance of some individual of genius. In such a case it is not misrepresentation of the facts, provided that it is recognized as being representation at a very high level of generality, to tell the whole story in terms of problems, criticisms and suggested solutions—a doctrine failing to stand up to criticism, thus producing a problem, to which various tentative solutions are offered until finally the solution is found which is associated with a great name.

But it must be owned that Idealist philosophers of history show a disposition to suppose that the history of ideas must itself be "ideal," in the sense of describing what they think ought to have happened rather than what actually did. When the individual of genius appears, he may not be immediately recognised, and will certainly not be recognised universally. Every educated person now knows something about the greatest thinkers of the past, but the minor writers are read only by historical specialists and the great mass of the public, which wrote nothing, tends to become quite forgotten, and in consequence we are apt to remember those who were immediately influenced by a great mind and forget that there were many at the time who never tried to think for themselves hard enough to become aware that there was anything unsatisfactory about the conceptions and methods to which they had been brought up—to whom the views of the great man were nothing but unintelligible newfangled nonsense. I may be unfair to Collingwood, but it has sometimes seemed to me that, in his account of the "presuppositions" of different historical periods, he considered only those outstanding philosophers whose achievement was so permanent that their works are still compulsory reading for Greats at Oxford. But this is to confuse what the men of a period actually presupposed with what they *would* have presupposed if they had realized that Descartes (or whoever it might be) had solved their problems, when in fact most of them did not. And this seems to have tempted Idealist philosophers of history into an account of "historical explanation" which is inadequate even to the history of ideas, to which the Idealist conception of history properly applies. They think that they have "explained" the acceptance of a doctrine when they have shown that it solved a certain problem. But to show that the doctrine actually solved the problem is logic, not history. The historical question is, how it came to be accepted, which is not accounted for by the mere fact that it solved the problem, for a problem may be solved and the solution never be generally acknowledged, while conversely doctrines may be generally accepted which conspicuously fail to solve very urgent problems.

Practising historians may be expected to dislike an account of "historical explanation" which reminds them that history rests on facts in the shape of actual human doings. This is the skeleton in their cupboard, and they prefer Idealist or Marxist theories of history, which enable them to keep the door shut on it. We may expect criticism on lines familiar to philosophers, being that used against all representative theories of perception and correspondence theories of truth. It will be said that our test of historical truth is a test which can never be made. We can never check a historical generalization against the individual facts on which it is based, because we are never presented with both together. For immediate contemporary history or at least that small section of it which we are ourselves actually living through—we have the individual facts, but it is notorious that we always find them so complex and confusing that we cannot at the time summarize them in any general historical statement. Historical generalization becomes possible as the events recede into the past, but then the individual facts are no longer there for comparison with the generalization. From some arguments in this vein it is difficult to see what is meant to follow, if not that a historian is a purely imaginative writer like a novelist, though this is not, I think, a conclusion which any practising historian would welcome. But all that is in fact shown is that the historian's conclusions rest wholly on circumstantial evidence and are peculiarly fallible. What is asked of him is nothing resembling the absurdity demanded by crude representative theories of perception—that it should be decided by mere inspection of "representative ideas" whether or not they are good copies of "things in themselves" which nobody has ever had knowledge of. The historian cannot pretend that he has no knowledge of any individual human actions, since he is acquainted at least with his own actions and those of his friends, and we only ask him never to forget that the justification for all his statements (if they have any) is nothing but the similar actions of similar human beings, even if they lived a long time ago and in very different circumstances. Owing to lack of imagination, or simple ignorance, he may make what would have seemed to those about whom he is talking absurd mistakes concerning what they did or the reasons why they did it, and the mistakes may be inevitable in the sense that he has no evidence which should have enabled him to avoid them, but in the case of each particular mistake he might always have had such evidence that he would not have made it. He cannot claim that any of his statements is wholly true to the facts, but he also cannot pretend that there is any impassable barrier making it impossible for him to have known more of the facts than he actually does. It is true that he cannot check his statements by the facts, but only by the evidence, which is a different thing. The facts are individual, but historical evidence is often already at a high degree of generality—for example, memoirs and dispatches, not to speak of the writings of previous historians (what are called "authorities"). Practising historians, therefore, naturally prefer what we may call "coherence theories," according to which historical truth consists in agreement with the evidence, which they have before them, rather than with the facts, which they have not. This makes things much easier for them, just as it would be easier for the members of a jury if they could only feel that it was their duty merely to give a true verdict according to the evidence. But in fact every juryman feels that he would be giving an unjust verdict if he condemned a man who was actually innocent, whatever the evidence. If the verdict is according to the evidence, that makes its injustice excusable, but does not make the defendant justly condemned, if he has not in fact committed the crime. Similarly the historical statement which is the most probable on the evidence available may be the best that can reasonably be expected of the historian, but, if it misrepresents the facts, it is not true. As for Idealist talk of "so-called historical facts" being nothing but what historians have said, that is only a device to increase the self-satisfaction of historians by enabling them to forget that, however near they may come to the real facts, they might always have come nearer.

These are topical questions now, not only in philosophy (owing to the publication of the posthumous works of Collingwood) but also in politics. The doctrine that "all history is contemporary history" might seem nothing more than a stimulating paradox when enunciated by Croce or Collingwood, but we may well feel doubtful about it when we see how it is officially adopted and acted upon in the Soviet Union. In 1917, according to all contemporary accounts, from whatever source they emanated, without distinction of politics, Lenin's principal lieutenant in the Russian Revolution was Trotsky; but, according to the history of the Revolution as now taught in Russia and to Communists throughout the world, the second part was played by Stalin, of whom hardly any mention will be found in documents of the time. This is perfectly in accordance with the principles of the Idealist philosophers of history, according to whom what happened in the past is nothing but whatever it suits our purposes now to suppose to have happened then. Being themselves quiet Bourgeois Liberals, they thought only of quiet Bourgeois Liberal purposes and their conception of history remained mild and inoffensive. But now it has suddenly grown teeth, when it is found to have the consequence that the Battle of Hastings might come to have been fought, not in 1066, but in 1067, or perhaps even in this present year 1947, and to have been won, not by the Normans, but by the English, or perhaps even by the Russians, if that happened to be demanded by the "Party line" in the twentieth, or the twenty-first, or the twenty-second century. I do not mean to imply that a doctrine ought to be rejected merely because it has received its final polish in Russia; but Russian ruthlessness in drawing logical conclusions does seem to me to have put it beyond doubt that this conception of history is radically false, although, as half-heartedly presented by Croce and Collingwood, it could still seem plausible.

At the root of this false conception lie, I think, two closely connected false assumptions. We are concerned with them here only as affecting history, but their influence is actually much more extensive. One is the assumption that, because we can never hope to free our opinions from all trace of error, therefore there is no truth, or the word "truth" must be re-defined and re-applied to lend dignity to favoured errors. People like to think of the truth as something which they can hope some day actually to attain—not as something which will always be beyond them, even if they can always come nearer and nearer to it—and they are ready to re-define the term "truth" to gratify this inclination. Historians do not like to think that their ideal is undistorted representation of actual past human doings, since this is something which one can do better than another, but none can do perfectly. They prefer to make their criterion of "historical truth" agreement with the available evidence and the needs of their own time, success in this being in principle attainable. Yet it is surely obvious that a judgment may be the best that could possibly be made in certain particular circumstances, and yet false. We find it quite natural to say that the judgments of a particular historian are sound within certain limits, but in certain respects distorted by his nineteenth-century prejudices. In these respects we consider his judgments mistaken, without thinking that, living in the nineteenth century, he could have been expected to judge differently. Most of us are ready to allow that our own judgments are probably similarly distorted by twentieth-century prejudices, although we cannot say in what respects, since otherwise we should already have corrected them. When we say that they are distorted, we mean that they misrepresent the facts. If we did not recognize the ideal of correspondence with the facts, we could only say that the judgment would have been false if it had been made in the present century, but it was not, and in its own century it was true. Collingwood does say things like this when he remembers his own philosophical position, but sooner or later his natural good sense asserts itself and then we find him stating roundly that we can now see that on some points past historians were mistaken, though owing to causes which they could not help, such as lack of evidence.

The other false assumption is that, because no judgment can ever be wholly free from bias, therefore a less biassed judgment is no better than a more biassed one. In fact it is possible, even if difficult, to reduce one's own bias, though certainly not to eliminate it completely, and, other things being equal, the judgment is the more likely to be true, the less the amount of bias. (We may reflect that the world has come to a pretty pass when anything so obvious need be said, but every philosopher knows that this does not now go without saying.) But modern philosophies of history encourage historians to glory in their own bias and exaggerate it, and to approve or condemn other historians purely according as they do or do not share the same bias. There is Communist history, Fascist history, and Liberal history, and it is approved or condemned as Communist or Fascist or Liberal according to the allegiance of the critic. Thought on this subject is almost always confused by considerations of the desirability of passionate convictions for resolute action, in which it is generally forgotten that, the more fervent the heart, the greater the need of a cool head. Marx himself (though not some modern Marxists) was well aware of this; just because he was devoted heart and soul to the Socialist cause, he insisted that an investigation of the means by which Socialism could be attained must be true to the facts and undistorted by wishful-thinking; hence his lifelong war against "Utopian Socialists." A historian may be none the worse for studying the past with an eye to applications in the present, but we must distinguish two very different kinds of application. There is narration of past events in such a way as to encourage present supporters and discourage opponents, distorting wherever necessary for this purpose; this is "history" according to the prescription of the Idealist philosophers, whose criterion is contemporary needs, and in fact it is not history at all, but propaganda. (Idealist philosophers will indignantly deny that this is what they mean, and I know quite well that it is not what they intend, but in that case they ought to be more careful about what they say.) The other kind of application is the discovery that something happened in the past which may serve as a guide to action in the present—indicating, for example, the likely consequences of a particular course of action. This sort of application I have already described as going beyond the business of the historian as such, since it implies the detection of universal laws in the historical process, but it does make use of the historian's results. What is important for our purposes here is that it is a sort of application which would be impossible with purely Idealist "history." The contemporary application depends upon the historical representation being true to the facts, in the sense of what really happened in the past; otherwise it would be merely misleading. In history we may say that pure Idealism meets its Waterloo, because in history we cannot do without "things in themselves," and the problem has to be faced, how they are "represented."

[18] The Individual and the Marxist Philosophy of History

LAIRD ADDIS

The dialectic of freedom has no doubt attracted more attention from philosophers than the issue is intrinsically worth. Debates on the issue often seem to consist largely of the protagonists' trying to persuade each other that a certain sense of 'freedom' is the *important* sense. That this is possible arises from the fact that two philosophers may admit exactly the same description of the universe and of man and his place in it, yet one affirm and the other deny that men are, in an important sense, free. But this is not surprising, for the freedom issue is closely tied to the issue of moral responsibility; indeed were it not so, there would probably remain little interest in whether or not man is free.

I do not, therefore, intend to argue whether or not the sense of 'freedom' with which I shall be concerned in this paper is important. The sense of the word with which we shall be concerned is this: A man is free if he can affect the course of history. Of course I don't mean anything absurd like changing the future from what it is going to be, but only that by some choice or behavior the future (of society) is different from what it would have been had the choice or behavior not occurred. It is undeniable that many have thought it to be important that man be free in this sense.

It is often claimed on various grounds that Marx held views which entail that man is not free in the sense just mentioned. This in turn leads some to reject the Marxist [1] philosophy of history for that reason alone. I wish to argue that Marx's views of history and the social order are *not* incompatible with man's being free in our sense.[2]

As one might expect, most of the paper will consist of the logical analysis of several key ideas. In this sense the paper is an exercise in the philosophy of psychology and sociology. Indeed one could say that my main purpose

Reprinted from *Philosophy of Science,* Vol. 33, 1966, pp. 101–117, with permission of the editor. Originally published under the title "Freedom and the Marxist Philosophy of History."

[1] I shall not, as for many purposes one must, distinguish Marx's views from "Marxism" in this paper.

[2] Indeed, his views seem to *entail* that man is in such a way free, but I shall not argue that in this paper.

is to show how various doctrines are connected with the view that man can (or cannot) affect the course of history, quite apart from whether or not they are Marxist. But I can take advantage of the audience appeal of the Marxist context while at the same time using Marx in this manner to provide a useful way of structuring the paper.

I wish then to take up four arguments against the Marxist philosophy of history. All four claim that in virtue of a certain aspect of Marx's thought, the more or less obvious role of human choice and behavior in history is denied. First, it is claimed that Marx's *materialism* rules out a respectable place for choice. Second, it is said that Marx is a *process-holist*. Third, it is alleged that Marx is an *economic determinist*. And fourth, it is held that Marx is a *determinist of the fatalistic type*. Let me briefly explain and expand each of these arguments.

Marx's materialism is said to rule out a place, not for human behavior directly, but for human choice. Choices are mental events; yet Marx holds, apparently, that all explanation is to be in terms of material or physical events. Furthermore, it is small consolation to allow that our behavior may affect the course of events if that behavior does not causally depend on our decisions and choices. If choices are in principle to be excluded from the explanations of historical events, then it appears they "make no difference" to anything that happens.

The second argument claims that Marx held the social order to be causally independent of the order of individuals. Under this rubric we hear the slogan (from both protagonists and epigones) that "history is independent of men's wills." Roughly the idea is that the social variables (that is, excluding the psychological variables) comprise a causally closed system into which, so to speak, man cannot enter.

The third argument holds that since Marx is an economic determinist, he leaves no room for the causal efficacy of human choice and behavior. The only *causes* are economic; and therefore human beliefs, volitions and behavior are merely *effects* of the preceding or prevailing economic conditions despite appearances to the contrary. It would be granted, of course, that it is not enough to know only the economic conditions in order to predict either simultaneous non-economic conditions or indeed future economic or non-economic conditions; one must also know the *laws*.

Finally, Marx claims that revolution against capitalism and the eventual triumph of communism are inevitable. Apparently, then, the future is "fixed" and we can do nothing about it. This is the fatalistic flavor in Marx. It sounds as if we are impotent in the face of history—as if communism is going to triumph no matter what we think and do. The phrase in this argument which needs careful attention is 'no matter what we think and do.' Eventually I shall attend to that.

Such are the four arguments. Before I get on with the interpretation of Marx by means of which I propose to answer these arguments, three comments are appropriate.

First. I am not prepared to claim, nor need I, that the particular predictions which Marx made are accurate. In other words, I need not accept the particular laws which Marx believed he discovered. I am not here interested in whether communism is indeed inevitable, but only in whether Marx's claim that it is entails that we are not free in a sense in which we should like to think that we are. Just as one can accept the theory of evolution without accepting the particular laws which Darwin propounded, so one can consistently accept the Marxist philosophy of history, at least in the sense in which I speak of it, without accepting the analysis of capitalism which presumably shows its ultimate demise.

Second. My interpretation of Marx is in some ways very similar to that of Plekhanov. Like him, I shall draw a distinction between what he calls economic materialism on the one hand and dialectical materialism on the other.[3] By means of this distinction, we can dispose of one of the arguments by showing that the position ascribed to Marx is not Marx's. Nevertheless, Plekhanov and I disagree with respect to what constitutes a reasonable notion of freedom. He tries to show, in the tradition of Spinoza and Hegel, that in its "true" sense 'freedom' means "the consciousness of necessity." [4] Without denying that this sense may be relevant to some important issues, I must disagree with Plekhanov that it is the only important sense of 'freedom.' In his monograph, *The Role of the Individual in History,* he implicitly agrees, for that essay is concerned predominantly with the same issue with which we are concerned.

Third. In this paper I shall not cite any texts from Marx and only three from Engels. I take it their words are well known. I could supply texts from Marx which would seem to support my interpretation; but I could also supply texts which would seem to contradict it. The task is to find an interpretation which fits the spirit of the man's work, and to realize at the same time that it is probably futile to expect to find any interpretation which can account for everything the man said. Nor is that surprising, for it would be most astonishing if Marx (and Engels) were not guilty of at least occasional inconsistencies. Can any more be said of anyone as prolific as Marx?

Let us get on with the interpretation. In particular we want to understand (1) Marx's conception of the "connection" between minds and the material world, (2) his view of the relationship of sociological to psychological theory, (3) his opinion of the importance of the economic variables in society and (4) his particular version of determinism. To do this we shall need an exact terminology. I begin by explicating such terms as 'interaction,' 'process' and 'parallelism.'

---

[3] See his *The Materialist Conception of History.* (New York, 1940)

[4] See his *The Role of the Individual in History.* [Reprinted in *Theories of History,* P. Gardiner, ed., The Free Press, New York, 1959, pp. 139–166.—Ed.]

– I –

Consider a universe of three individuals, three properties, space and time. Suppose that the properties are mass, position and velocity. Allow me to speak quantitatively about each property of each individual so that I may speak of, say, the *value m* of the mass *variable* of an individual *a*. Consider now the following *two* situations:

(1) At time t_1 the values of the three properties m, p, and v for the three individuals *a, b,* and *c* are as follows:

$$m_2(a), \quad p_3(a), \quad v_6(a),$$
$$m_3(b), \quad p_2(b), \quad v_0(b),$$
$$m_2(c), \quad p_1(c), \quad v_4(c).$$

This is the first situation.

(2) In the second situation the values of m, p, and v at t_1 are as follows:

$$m_2(a), \quad p_3(a), \quad v_3(a),$$
$$m_3(b), \quad p_2(b), \quad v_5(b),$$
$$m_2(c), \quad p_1(c), \quad v_0(c).$$

Call each description a *state description*. Suppose that our universe contains no other properties (variables), i.e., that m, p, and v are a *complete set of relevant variables*. Notice that in the two situations the values of m and p are the same for each individual while those of v are not. Now suppose there is a law which allows us to compute the values of each property for each individual for some later time t_2 from their values at t_1. If in the two situations at t_2 our computations show a difference in the values of either m or p *or* m and p for any individual, then we shall say that v *interacts* with m or p *or* m and p. Conversely, if there are no such differences for *any* set of initial values, then it does not interact with the other two variables. This is the only clear notion of interaction I know of.

The kind of law to which I just referred—one which allows one to compute any state description of a system from any given state description—is a *process law*. Any system which allows for such computation, that is, for which there is a process law or set of laws (whether we know them or not), is one in which there is process.

Now imagine a universe like that just described except that there is in it one additional property, heat, to each degree of which we assign a different numerical value. Imagine further that whenever an individual's velocity has the value 1, then its heat has the value 1; whenever its velocity has the value 2, then its heat has the value 2 and so on. In this case, velocity and heat are parallel properties. The statement which expresses this parallelism may be called the *law of the parallelism* or a *cross-section law*. It is worth noticing that while heat in our little universe is, as one might say, "merely" a parallel property, it does of course make a difference to the subsequent values of m and p if v interacts; for if the law of the parallelism is true, then a difference in the heat variable will be paralleled by a difference in the value of v. Which property, then, "really" interacts, "really" makes the difference? The question makes no sense. The variables m, v and p constitute a *causally closed system*, i.e., a complete set of relevant variables such that only their values at some time need to be known in order to compute their future (or past) values at any time by means of the process law. But then m, p and heat also constitute such a system. That follows from the hypothesis that v and heat are parallel properties.

By means of the preceding discussion I can now explain what I believe Marx meant to say, though he never accurately states it, with respect to the connection between mental events and physical events. First of all, I know of no reason to suppose that he was a materialist in the sense of denying that there are nonphysical events. That is, he held the views neither of J. J. C. Smart nor of Gilbert Ryle, the former of whom claims that "mental" events are really identical with certain brain events and the latter of whom claims that on the whole statements which seem to report the occurrence of mental events "in" a person are really statements about the person's actual and potential behavior. Marx, that is, was a dualist. There really are two kinds of things in the world—physical things and mental things, and neither kind is "reducible to," "definable in terms of," or "identical with" the other kind. And in holding this he was, of course, perfectly correct.

Then what is the connection between mental things and physical things, or rather, as I prefer to put it, between mental *states* and physical *states*? The doctrine I wish to ascribe to Marx is that known as psychophysical parallelism. And in this instance I should want to claim that *only* this view is consistent with Marx's central doctrines with respect to man's role in history. But I shall not argue that.

Psychophysical parallelism is the thesis that the "connection" between mental states and, let us say, neurophysiological states [5] is captured entirely by cross-section laws. These parallelistic laws will typically be of the form: Whenever there is a certain neurophysiological state, there is a certain mental state and vice versa. However, the parallelism may not be one/one; it may be many/one in either direction, for example. Nor of course does the thesis entail that for *every* neurophysiological state there is a corresponding mental state; [6] unconscious people and dead people have no minds. There

---

[5] One could just as well state the doctrine in terms of a parallelism between mental states on the one hand and either behavioral or brain states on the other rather than between mental and neurophysiological states. Probably in truth the "strictest" parallelism is to be found between brain states and mental states.

[6] For that reason, one may want to speak of bodily states as the cause of mental states and not vice versa. This is my cue for another comment. *When there are parallel mental states,* one can substitute them for their parallel neurophysiological states in particular explanations. Since however there are a number of different neurophysiological states which

is a slight difference between the mind/body parallelism and the parallelism in our model universe. In the former case the properties involved belong to different things. That spots a certain philosophical problem which, however, we can safely ignore here. What then are the consequences of such a view with respect to our problem?

Let us suppose that the parallelistic laws in question are all of the one/one and if-and-only-if type. That will make it easier to say what follows. The laws stating the connection between neurophysiological and mental states will be of the form: Whenever there is such and such a neurophysiological state there is such and such a mental state and vice versa. Remembering our model universe, we may say that on the thesis of parallelism we *need* not take mental events into account in the explanation and prediction of physical events. This means that the physical variables constitute a causally closed system. Perhaps this is the best way of stating Marx's materialism. But then do choices in no sense "make a difference" to what happens in the physical world? Am I granting the argument which I promised to refute? Hardly. Not only can choices "make a difference" on psychophysical parallelism; the very doctrine entails that they do, provided only that their parallel neurophysiological states are interacting variables. And of course they are. For example, if I don't *choose* to commit a certain act, then that act (considered as a piece of behavior) will not or very well may not occur; for by the law of the parallelism the neurophysiological state which would "produce" that behavior is there only if the choice is there. So this kind of "materialism"—psychophysical parallelism—does *not* remove or deny the obvious role of choices in the nature of things, even though in a certain sense we can ignore them for purposes of explanation and prediction.[7]

– II –

The next criticism I wish to consider is one which, in one form or another, is very often made of the Marxist philosophy of history. The clearest form of the argument is this: The sociological variables form a closed system, i.e., there is process among the sociological variables alone according to

---

have no parallel mental states, one cannot *always* do this, as one could in our model universe. For this reason I shall speak as if only the neurophysiological states interact with other physical variables, i.e., that the mental variables are "merely" parallel and not "interacting." This way of speaking is also useful in distinguishing psychophysical parallelism from what is usually called interactionism. The latter would be the view that the mental variables interact with physical variables *and* that those mental variables are *not* tied to any physical variables by parallelistic laws. In short, this is the doctrine that the physical variables do not constitute a causally closed system. Such a view, it may be worth noticing, is perfectly compatible with determinism.

7 This kind of "materialism" is also Freud's. Many Freudians make the mistake of taking Marx to be a materialist in the sense of denying the existence of consciousness, while many Marxists make the mistake of taking Freud to deny the physical "basis" of consciousness.

Marx (though of course he never stated it that way). But if so, then psychological variables, e.g., individual choices and items of behavior, are irrelevant to the social process. Hence the social process is causally independent of human direction, and men are not free in the relevant sense. So goes the argument.

It might be thought that this objection can be handled in the same way as that which involved physical and mental variables, i.e., in terms of assuming a parallelism between items of individual behavior perhaps considered statistically) and the values of the social variables. But while that view might make sense verbally, there is a crucial methodological difficulty which prevents it from being plausible. This will, I hope, become apparent in a moment. On the other hand, the correct view (which may or may not be Marx's) is, *in a sense,* not so different from that of assuming a parallelism between the values of the *macrovariables* and those of the *microvariables.*

Having introduced two more or less technical terms in the last sentence is my cue to continue the logical analysis of certain crucial notions and thereby of certain possibilities concerning the connection between "social" processes and "individual" processes. In addition to those just mentioned, these terms include 'composition law' and 'reduction.' I begin with 'macrovariable' and 'microvariable.'

The subject matter of a field or area, say psychology, is determined by its variables, i.e., by the property terms [8] or kinds of property terms which enter into its descriptions and laws. Some typical properties with which psychology deals are: being the father of four children, believing the earth is flat, being able to memorize all Shakespeare's sonnets, being able to cook and so on. If one takes the variables of psychology as macrovariables, then in that context the variables of physiology will be the microvariables. If in another context one treats the variables of psychology as the microvariables, then the variables of sociology would be the corresponding macrovariables. Clearly these notions have something to do with the issue of reduction, and they will become clearer if we go on to discuss that issue.

Reduction is something that takes place, if at all, between two *theories.* Neither theory need be comprehensive [9] of its area, but one would expect the reducing theory to be at least as nearly comprehensive as the reduced theory. The reducing theory is often called the microtheory; the theory to be reduced, if at all, the macrotheory. So much for the connection between reduction on the one hand and macro- and microvariables on the other. But there is more to be said about reduction.

[8] I of course include the relations in which a thing stands as part of its properties. Occasionally I shall remind ourselves of that.

[9] Briefly, to say that a theory is comprehensive (of its area) means (1) that all the property terms of the area either are "in" the propositions of the theory, defined or undefined, *or* that they are definable in terms of those property terms "in" the propositions of the theory; and (2) that all the laws of the area, whether known or not, are deductive consequences of the propositions that make up the given theory. For more details on this and other issues of reduction, see Gustav Bergmann's "Reduction" which appears in *Current Trends in Psychology and the Behavioral Sciences,* University of Pittsburgh Press, 1954.

The "question" of reduction has arisen in four cases, historically speaking. They are the reduction of: particle physics to quantum mechanics, chemistry to physics, psychology to physiology, and what we are here interested in, sociology to psychology. The second, that of chemistry to physics, has been achieved; so it is no longer controversial. The first, that of particle to quantum physics, is "assumed" so to speak by the theory of quantum mechanics itself. Roughly that means that we "devise" certain translation rules between the partially interpreted calculus of quantum mechanics on the one hand and the language of particle physics on the other. What is controversial is not whether reduction can be achieved, for quantum mechanics makes no sense unless it is "assumed." Rather, the controversy concerns the nature of the partially interpreted calculus (or rather, if you like, that of which it "speaks"—the world).

But the case of physiology and psychology is the most instructive for us, by way of contrast as it were, to the issue of sociology and psychology. The variables of *both* psychology and physiology are, in a clear sense we need not further specify, *presented* to us. We know unambiguously what is involved, say, in the blood's having a certain white corpuscle count on the one hand, and on the other, what it means for someone to be elated over his test.[10] What this means for the issue of reduction is this: The reduction of psychology to physiology can (or could) only be by means of *laws*. These laws will (or would) of course be of a parallelistic sort; they will state the connection, that is the parallelism, between certain physiological states and certain behavioral states (or dispositions). (It is clear, I trust, that I take psychology to be the science of *behavior,* not that of describing and discovering the connections between mental phenomena. This does not mean of course that there are no mental phenomena.) But we have a different case when it comes to sociology and psychology.

Examples of sociological variables are: the ideology of the ruling class, the will of the people, the desire of the church, the anger of the crowd, the health of the economy and so on.[11] And here, or so it would appear, we cannot say we know unambiguously what these properties are *unless* they are defined in terms of the properties of (and relations among) individuals or individual things. This is what I meant when I spoke a few paragraphs back about a crucial methodological objection to the parallelistic assumption in the case of sociology and psychology. He who affirms that there are

10 This doesn't mean that we may not want or need definitions of these property terms. But their definitions will be in terms of other properties of the same "level" or science. The importance of that will become obvious in a moment.

11 By sociology I shall mean all the social sciences considered as one vast science. With respect to the issue of freedom, we are interested in the relation of certain group variables to the behavior of humans, of course. So I shall speak mainly of the connection between sociological or group variables on the one hand and psychological or individual variables on the other. By a group variable I mean one which is plausibly understood in terms of humans and their behavior. Or perhaps one could say that a group has humans as its constituents as long as that is not taken to beg any questions about the "connection" between the group and its constituents.

such sociological variables which cannot even in principle be defined in terms of psychological (and of course other environmental [12]) variables is a *metaphysical holist*. And more than likely such a person will go on to claim that in some important metaphysical sense the group or state has more reality than individuals.[13] The view on the other hand which insists that all sociological variables can in principle be defined in terms of the properties of individual things and *must* be so defined if we are to know without vagueness what we are talking about is called *methodological individualism*. If metaphysical holism were true and one knew unambiguously what the sociological variables were, even though they are not to be defined in terms of psychological variables, then one would have the logical possibility of a connection between sociology and psychology like that which, if at all, obtains between psychology and physiology, i.e., a *lawful* connection between the variables of the two areas. But assuming that metaphysical holism is false, as it surely is, one must look for some other meaning of 'reduction' in the case of sociology and psychology.

Sociological theory is reduced to psychological theory if, having defined the sociological variables in terms of the psychological variables, the laws of sociology are *deduced* or deducible from the laws of psychology. And if the behavior of individuals is completely law-governed, then given those definitions, it *follows* that the laws of sociology are deducible from the laws of psychology. But let us be sure we see what that means.

People behave differently in large groups than they do in small groups and yet differently in either of those than when alone. And in different kinds of groups of the same size they also behave differently. For example, a man will not behave the same way at his trade union meeting as he will in the presence of his relatives. In short, if one is to explain a person's behavior in different size and kinds of groups, one must ordinarily invoke different laws. Some of these laws may be what are sometimes called *composition* laws. Such laws—and they are that and not mere mathematical truths—give one a method for computing from the simple situation of, say, the behavior of three people in a group of a certain kind to the more complex situations of four people, ten people and so on. The analogy in mechanics is obvious. Any such law may, however, "break down" at a certain point, say, at the level of five hundred people. That is, given our laws of behavior in the small group plus that *given* composition law, we may find that the behavior of our subject, once the group he is in surpasses five

---

[12] Some sociological variables such as *the anger of the crowd* would reasonably be defined in terms of the properties of (and relations among) humans alone; others such as *the condition of the railroads* would reasonably be defined in terms of the properties of individual but non-human things alone; still others would reasonably include the properties of both human and non-human things in their definitions. A plausible example is *the total social product*.

[13] That is, if the group or state exemplifies some property which cannot be understood in terms of the properties of "its" constituents, then it would be natural to say that the group or state *is* more than its constituent individuals. "The whole is more than the sum of its parts."

hundred in number is not as our predictions told us it would be. There are two possibilities. Either determinism is not true or, as is more likely, we need to look for a new composition law. (If the latter, we have a case of what some call *explanatory emergence*. This is in contrast to *descriptive emergence* in which the latter does while the former does not imply that a "new" property is involved.)

In the systematic investigation of human behavior in groups of certain kinds, there is little doubt that one would be confronted with this situation quite often. The point is that if such a law does "break down," so to speak, at a certain level of complexity, we need not conclude that determinism is false, that human behavior is not after all completely law-governed. The limiting case would involve a different composition law at each level, i.e., one for each size group; or more accurately (since a composition law actually allows one to compute the values of variables in a more complex situation from the values of the variables in a less complex situation) there would be no composition laws.[14] But again, that would not preclude there being regularities at each level, nor therefore imply that determinism is false.

It is logically possible that determinism "breaks down" at some level (perhaps the "lowest") with respect to the behavior of individuals and yet all the sociological variables be definable in terms of psychological variables. If this is the case, however, the laws of sociology would not be deducible, and therefore, the theory could not be reduced. Thus given our three distinctions, namely, (1) sociological variables definable or not definable in terms of psychological variables, (2) process or not process at the level of sociology and (3) sociological theory reducible or not reducible to psychological theory, we have six possibilities as to the nature of and connections between sociology and psychology (some of which, to be sure, are very remote). (We don't have eight possibilities because if the sociological variables are not definable in terms of the psychological then sociological theory cannot be reduced to psychological theory.) The six possibilities are:

1. *Process individualistic reducible.* There is process among the social variables alone, all of those variables being definable in terms of the properties of individuals, and, given those definitions, the laws of the group are deducible from the laws of the individuals.
2. *Non-process individualistic reducible.* There is *not* process among the social variables alone, all of those variables being definable in terms of the properties of individuals, and given those definitions, the laws of the group are deducible from the laws of the individuals.
3. *Process holistic (non-reducible).* There is process among the social variables alone, *not* all of those variables being definable in terms of the

14 Composition laws are in principle dispensable anyway, as can be seen from my discussion. The reason I introduce the discussion is because some have mistakenly believed that if the behavior in the more complex situation is not computable in some way from that in the less complex, then determinism is false.

properties of individuals, and therefore, the laws of the group are *not* deducible from the laws of the individuals.

4. *Non-process holistic (non-reducible).* There is *not* process among the social variables alone, *not* all of those variables being definable in terms of the properties of individuals, and, therefore, the laws of the group are *not* deducible from the laws of the individuals.

5. *Process individualistic non-reducible.* There is process among the social variables alone, all of those variables being definable in terms of the properties of individuals, and the laws of the group are *not* deducible from the laws of the individuals (because the system of individuals is not deterministic).

6. *Non-process individualistic non-reducible.* There is *not* process among the social variables alone, all of those variables being definable in terms of the properties of individuals, and the laws of the group are *not* deducible from the laws of the individuals (because the system of individuals is not deterministic).

There are now three questions before us: (1) Which one of these views is Marx's? (2) Which view is true? (3) How does each view stand with respect to the issue of freedom? Let us turn to the last question first. One thing is clear, at least. If the (name of the) behavior of the group can be *defined*, non-trivially,[15] in terms of the (names of the) behaviors of individuals which "make it up," then the individual's behavior obviously *can* make a difference to the value of the macrovariables, i.e., to the social variables, *even if there is process on the macro-level.* Since the macrovariable (for its values) may be defined in terms of a statistical distribution of some property among individuals and since it may be defined in terms of a certain *range* of distribution, a change in the value of the property of some individual may or may not affect the value of the macrovariable. It depends on the case. Or, if you like, it depends on the facts. In any case, we can safely say that all individualist views—process or non-process, reductionist or non-reductionist—allow for freedom in the sense we have been discussing.

How about holistic views then? Where do they stand with respect to our freedom question? We have already seen that even if the holistic view can be consistently maintained, i.e., even if one can give a clear meaning to the macrovariables although they are not to be defined in terms of the microvariables, still one can give a sense to 'reduction' in terms of a lawful connection between the values of the variables of the sociological theory and those of the psychological theory. This is the clue to the answer to our question. If there are *some* such laws, then even on holistic views, whether

---

[15] That is, such that it varies with *some* variations in the individual's behavior. There may be *some* disjunction; that is, a group variable may be defined as microstate A or B or C or . . . and so on. The commonsense idea is that we can effect a change in many ways; but there must be a limit. If the change occurs no matter what we do, then that limit has been far surpassed.

process or not, at least some variations in the behavior of individuals will be paralleled by variations in the values of the social variables. If there are no such laws or if they are few and trivial, then man is not free in our sense, i.e., is not capable of influencing the social process in a significant way.

Which view is true, which Marx's? The true view, I believe, is (2) above, namely, that there is not process at the level of sociology, that its variables are in principle definable in terms of the properties of individuals (or rather *must* be so defined if they are to have unambiguous meanings), and finally, that with those definitions sociological theory is in principle reducible to psychological theory. This view, however, is probably not Marx's. Very likely he would have held, had the issue been put to him, that there is process at the level of the macrovariables.[16] This is in the spirit of his work, and certainly a good many of his followers have taken him to say something like this.[17] But we have just seen that with respect to the question of freedom, this is not where the issue lies, whatever his critics, or for that matter, many of his followers, may think. For if he is an individualist, i.e., holds that (all) the social variables are definable in terms of psychological variables and if he is also a determinist, then his views are quite compatible with the proposition that man is free in the sense in which we are interested, even if there is process at the social level. And if he is a holist, then again the question is open; for he may still hold that there are parallelistic laws which would account for or allow for human freedom. Thus any criticism based *simply* on the claim that Marx held there to be process among the social variables fails of its purpose.

But now we may ask: Assuming Marx did hold the process view of the macrovariables and granted that *this* doesn't entail that man is not free, is he after all a holist? And if so, does he or does he not hold there to be those parallelistic laws which would be necessary to secure man's freedom on such a view? At this point I think we are at the limits of historical exegesis. Marx does sometimes offer at least rudimentary definitions of his group variables in terms of the properties of individuals. On the other hand, he often suggests laws of the group variables without offering such definitions. The fairest comment is this: There are no good reasons why Marx should be a holist, and he does insist that man is free in the sense we are discussing. Therefore while it would probably be inaccurate to say that

16 One may want to distinguish what Bergmann calls *historical* from *systematic* process theories. The former has laws of the sort: If the system is now in state x *and was earlier in state y,* then at such and such future time it will be in state z. The italicized phrase indicates the difference; that is, in a systematic process theory the laws would allow one to compute any state of the system from any other *single* state. It may be useful to understand Marx as looking for an historical rather than a systematic process theory of society. See Bergmann's "Reduction" referred to in footnote 9.

17 This is reflected in the repeated claim of some Marxists that history is independent of man's will. *One* thing this could mean is that the states of society are computable given the values of the social variables alone, i.e., that there is process at that level. But we have just seen that that does not imply that man isn't free in our sense.

Marx even took a stand on the issues of holism versus individualism and of holism with versus holism without parallelistic laws, there seems to be no reason for insisting that he held the one view—holism without parallelistic laws—which entails that man isn't free.

It will be recalled that I originally posed the criticism in terms of whether or not there is process at the level of the macrovariables. The reason for this is not only that this is the way the criticism is often intended, but that I had a specific statement of the argument in mind. It is the one made by Professor Brodbeck in her very useful paper, "Methodological Individualisms: Definition and Reduction." Analyzing her criticism of Marxism will help us to understand accurately why the issue does not lie in whether or not there is process at the social level. She says:

Conceivably, there might be a set of macroscopic laws permitting the prediction of the "state" of society (i.e., the values of the group variables) at all times from its state at any given time. This possibility is to be sure most implausible. It is implausible not only because the discovery of such a complete set of relevant variables seems a formidable task, but also because it is rather more than likely that changes in the social process do not depend only upon group or macroscopic units, Marxism to the contrary notwithstanding. People are not like molecules in a gas. Some are different from others and some have more effect upon society than others. It is still a good question whether without Lenin there would have been the October Revolution. If this variance among individuals makes sufficient difference, then the laws have to take the occurrence of a particular kind of individual into account. In this case a complete set of variables could not all be macroscopic.[18]

Professor Brodbeck is not concerned with the issue of freedom here, but she does try to refute this aspect of Marxism on similar grounds. Her argument rests on the ambiguities of the word 'depend.' She assumes that if social changes in any way "depend" on the varying and perhaps unique characteristics of certain persons, then such changes cannot "depend" solely on the macroscopic variables; and thus there cannot be process among the group variables. But this is a mistake. Consider her own example. Suppose there is process on the social level and accept the framework of methodological individualism. Can we consistently suppose further that Lenin had absolutely unique characteristics and that if no one with those characteristics had lived when Lenin did live, the October Revolution would not have occurred (then)? Not if Professor Brodbeck is right. But we *can* in principle define a particular group variable in terms partly of "containing-a-Lenin-like-figure." [19] That is, the definition of some group variable *can* include

18 Brodbeck, May, "Methodological Individualisms: Definition and Reduction," *Philosophy of Science*, Vol. 25, 1958, p. 21. [Reprinted in this volume, pp. 280–303; quotation is on p. 303—Ed.] Several of the points discussed in my paper are covered in more detail in hers. I have also made use of her terminology at many points.

19 Or we can treat that as the value of some variable. The distinction between a variable and its values depends on the context. *Being red* and *being blue* are values of the variable *being colored*; but *being pink* and *being scarlet* are values of the variable *being red*.

the perhaps unique characteristics of some particular person. [See remarks on this point in the introduction to this section, pp. 242 ff.—Ed.] Now if there is process on the social level, we should in principle be able to predict the occurrence of a group having such a person given only the values of the social variables at an earlier time and the laws which state their connection. This sounds implausible only if it is forgotten that the group variables are to be defined in terms of the properties of (and relations among) individuals; otherwise it is quite plausible. And we have already seen that one can consistently hold both that there is process at the level of the macrovariables and that (all) those variables are definable in terms of the microvariables.

We should not suppose in light of the foregoing that we can never "really" explain everything unless we have complete state descriptions and process laws, at least not in any reasonable sense. For one thing, the values of many variables never move outside a certain range such that they, in an understandable sense, "make a difference." For another, if in order to be "certain" of our explanations we had to have process knowledge, then no doubt we should have to know the state of the whole universe; for the social variables do not really comprise a causally closed system. Earthquakes, for example, sometimes interact with the social variables, although they are not themselves such variables. And if we needed to know the state of the whole universe and all the process laws in order to be "certain" of our explanations, we should also have to know that we had such complete state descriptions, that we had all the process laws. But such "certainty" I leave to the philosophers. We make perfectly acceptable causal explanations in many realms without having process knowledge.

Nor of course did Marx suppose he had such knowledge. His hesitancy to predict exactly when revolution would occur in each country, whether those revolutions would be violent or peaceful, and what indeed communism would really be like is well known. But I think it is clear that Marx thought it to be the ideal of "historical science," though perhaps in practice unobtainable, to find such knowledge.[20] He proposed a framework in which to work. That is one contribution. The other, in this context, is the insistence that there is such knowledge to be found, that is, that there are process laws to be discovered. Of course, Marx was not the first determinist nor even the first to insist upon the importance of the economic variables. In another sense, then, his contribution is in the working out of these not entirely new ideas and their presentation in a more or less systematic fashion.

[20] Such an ideal is in a stronger sense unobtainable if minds interact in the sense of 'interactionism' explained in footnote 6. For one could never determine a state description for a given moment if (1) he could not observe mental states and (2) those mental states had no parallel brain or neurophysiological or behavioral states. That there is some kind of parallelism between what a person thinks and what he does is of course commensensical.

– III –

Our third argument has to do with the role of economics in historical change. This argument, it will be recalled, goes briefly as follows: According to Marx, economics determines everything. But then our choices and behavior determine nothing. So we are not free. This doctrine—that "economics determines everything"—is the one Plekhanov calls economic materialism. It is also commonly known as economic determinism. Plekhanov and I agree that this is not, however, Marx's view of the role of the economic variables in history. Nevertheless it will be useful to state this doctrine in the notions which I have developed.

Let us assume that we know what properties of what things are reasonably called economic, and let us further assume that human choices, decisions, desires and so on are not included. Then we may state economic determinism as follows: The economic variables constitute a causally closed system, i.e., they may interact with each other but with nothing non-economic.[21] (Interaction is symmetrical, of course.) Furthermore, the non-economic variables (including those of group behavior) are connected to the economic variables by parallelistic laws. These laws are not, however, of the one/one and if-and-only-if type. Otherwise there would be no reason to say that the economic determine the non-economic variables, rather than the other way around. Rather, the parallelistic laws are of the simple if-then type going from the economic to the non-economic, whether one/one or many/one. What this means is that given those laws and the values of the economic variables, one can compute the values of the non-economic variables, whereas given the laws and the values of the non-economic variables, one cannot compute the values of the economic variables.

(It will be noticed that all along I have assumed a Humean notion of cause. Details apart, that means that a cause is not an entity above and beyond the events said to be lawfully connected. If one's notion of cause includes the idea of a push or thrust, then, while this notion is ultimately unintelligible, one might make at least verbal sense of the economic's determining the non-economic in another way altogether.)

So, with regard to economic determinism I would make three points: (1) It does indeed entail that we are not free in a significant sense, for on this view our choices as well as our behavior "make no difference" to any subsequent events.[22] Minds are merely epiphenomenal; they, like everything

[21] Nor, if they are macrovariables, do the properties in terms of which they are defined interact with the non-economic. Of course, Marx wanted to say that in a certain sense almost all of man's behavior is "economic" under capitalism. But the argument I am considering makes sense only if we ignore this.

[22] They will "make a difference" to simultaneous events, so to speak, if the group variables are to be defined in terms of individuals' behaviors. But on the view under consideration *those* social variables are non-interacting.

else non-economic, are only effects, never causes. (2) This doctrine is surely false. (3) Marx didn't hold this doctrine.

Plekhanov, as we noted, contrasts economic determinism to dialectical materialism. By the latter I believe *he* understands what we might call the thesis of *total social interactionism*. That means that within the social realm literally everything which occurs at a given time "makes a difference" to what occurs at any other time. In short, every variable is a relevant variable. This does not mean, of course, that *any* two different values of a given variable will have divergent results in the values of some other variable, but only that *some* two values of that variable would make a difference to the later values of some (other) variable. Now with respect to this doctrine, I also wish to make three points: (1) The doctrine, properly stated, may very well be true. (2) Marx held this doctrine. (3) The phrase 'dialectical materialism' is Plekhanov's, not Marx's. When Marx uses the word 'dialectic' he usually has something more metaphysical in mind than does Plekhanov. But this need in no way affect our discussion.

The doctrine which I call total social interactionism is Marx's real view of the social process. It is, of course, formally incompatible with economic determinism in that the former asserts while the latter denies that the non-economic variables are interacting variables. But it may now be objected: Surely you are not denying the preponderant, indeed almost exclusive, emphasis which Marx placed on the economic variables in the historical process? And my answer is that I not only don't deny it; I insist upon it. I will even grant that there are numerous texts which seem to support the thesis of economic determinism. Engels acknowledges this in a letter to Mehring written after Marx was dead, but he goes on to give a kind of reason:

Otherwise only one more point is lacking, which, however, Marx and I always failed to stress enough in our writings and in regard to which we are all equally guilty. That is to say, we all laid, and *were bound* to lay, the main emphasis, in the first place, on the *derivation* of political, juridical, and other ideological notions, and of actions arising through the medium of these notions, from basic economic facts. But in doing so we neglected the formal side—the ways and means by which these notions, etc., come about—for the sake of the content.[23]

For our purposes we can safely ignore the notions of form and content in which Engels prefers to state his views. But we shall have to tolerate them again in the letter to Bloch in which Engels explains his and Marx's "real" view and from which I now quote:

According to the materialist conception of history, the *ultimately* determining element in history is the production and reproduction of real life. More than this neither Marx nor I has ever asserted. Hence if somebody twists this into saying that the economic element is the *only* determining one he transforms that proposi-

---

[23] Letter of Engels to Franz Mehring dated London, July 14, 1893, as it appears in *Marx and Engels*, edited by Lewis Feuer, Anchor Books, 1959, pp. 407–408.

tion into a meaningless, abstract, senseless phrase. The economic situation is the basis, but the various elements of the super-structure—political forms of the class struggle and its results, to wit: constitutions established by the victorious class after a successful battle, etc., juridical forms, and even the reflexes of all these actual struggles in the brains of the participants, political, juristic, philosophical theories, religious views, and their further development into systems of dogmas—also exercise their influence upon the course of the historical struggles and in many cases preponderate in determining their *form*. There is an interaction of all these elements in which, amidst all the endless host of accidents (that is, of things and events whose inner interconnection is so remote or so impossible of proof that we can regard it as non-existent, as negligible), the economic movement finally asserts itself as necessary. Otherwise the application of the theory to any period of history would be easier than the solution of a simple equation of the first degree.[24]

How shall *we* understand the doctrine of total social interactionism in which the economic element "finally asserts itself as necessary?" We must not suppose that interactionism entails that all the interacting variables have "equal" weight, whatever that would mean. Let us take an analogy. Suppose there is a law to the effect that if anyone has cancer of the stomach, he will die within ten years. Now suppose Jones has such a cancer. Exactly when will he die? In order to know that we would have to know how advanced the cancer is, what his diet is, certain facts about his metabolism and probably many other things. They are all, with respect to the progression of cancer, interacting variables. Yet whatever their values, the cancer "finally asserts itself as necessary." Such a law with respect to cancer and death is not a process law, nor are those to which we wish to compare it: namely, presumed laws such as the law that states that if any society has a capitalistic economic system, then that system will be superceded by a communistic form of social organization.[25] For to know *exactly* when this will happen to a given society, one would have to know more than the values of its economic variables. Perhaps, indeed, one would have to know the values of all its variables (as well as the laws, of course).

Thus we can say that to assert the predominance of the economic element is to assert that if one were to examine all the laws of interaction and all the cross-section laws of society, he would find or be able to deduce (1) certain non-process laws of the type about communism succeeding the capitalist system, (2) some statistical parallelistic laws of the if-then type from the economic to the non-economic (e.g., Marx's analysis of ideologies) and perhaps (3) a few non-statistical parallelistic laws connecting economic to

[24] Letter of Engels to Joseph Bloch dated London, September 21–22, 1890, *ibid.*, 397–398.

[25] To say that they are not process laws means here that if an event of the kind mentioned in the antecedent of the law occurred and *if* certain other events occurred which as a matter of fact do not, then the corresponding event of the kind mentioned in the consequent of the law would *not* occur. That is, it may be that "there is" a cure for cancer but a matter of fact that no one will ever discover it. So, if certain choices were made, Marx might say, then communism would not succeed capitalism, but as a matter of fact those choices won't be made. See Section IV.

non-economic variables either in an if-then way or an if-and-only-if way. To account totally for why a certain society is in a certain state at a certain moment, however, one would need the process laws as well as a complete state description of another moment.

Sometimes something else is understood by Marx's philosophy of history than what I have thus far meant. This is Marx's claim that the "mechanism" of history is in class struggle, or rather, as he sometimes seems to say, in the "incompatibility" at a given time of the forces of production on the one hand and the relations of production on the other. It doesn't matter which for what I want to say. First, such a doctrine can of course be stated in the notions which I have developed; and second, it can be incorporated into this doctrine which I call total social interactionism. Roughly that would involve pointing to certain, probably statistical, cross-section laws of the if-then type going from "class struggle" variables to the "non-class struggle" variables. In short, if we can make sense of the claim that the economic variables are the "more important" as against the non-economic variables, then surely we can make sense of the claim that certain ones of those economic variables are yet "more important" than the others. And that is what the class struggle thesis asserts.

– IV –

We are left only with Marx's apparent fatalism to tackle. Neither his materialism nor his process view of the social variables has untoward consequences, in spite of first appearances. And he doesn't hold the doctrine of economic determinism. But we still have claims to the effect that communism is inevitable, that no matter what we think and do, successful revolution will occur. This is the point where we must be careful with our language; otherwise Marx will be taken to be a fatalist when he is only affirming his determinism. Determinism of course does not imply that we don't make choices, nor that they are not causally efficacious. (Whether or not the assertion that our choices are caused entails that we don't make "genuine" choices and thus that we are not free in some other important sense is an issue I have studiously ignored in this paper.)

Let us return to the example of the revolution. If it is inevitable, does that not imply that our choices make no difference? I think not. If I may speak for Marx, we might say that the revolution will occur (if at all) not in spite of the choices men *might* make, but because (in part) of the choices men *will* make. Nor am I speaking only of those who choose to do what they think will bring about revolution. Consider, for example, the Marxist account of the final stages of capitalism. The capitalists, in the attempt to maximize profits, *choose* to introduce automation. But this increases unemployment thus increasing discontent which, loosely speaking, eventually culminates in revolution. The point is that if the choices to introduce automation had not occurred, then, we may suppose, the revolution would not have occurred. That does not mean, as we speak, that the capitalists choose revolution; they choose what in their ignorance they believe will free them from the discontent of the workers. As Marx puts it, the capitalists are their own gravediggers. (This would probably be a good place to remind ourselves that I am not trying to defend Marx's particular predictions or analyses.)

So at a minimum, to say that the future depends on our choices is to say that they, or rather, as we have agreed to speak, that their parallel neurophysiological states are interacting variables.[26] But for a determinist those choices are in principle calculable. Thus Marx thought he could figure out, and up to a point had figured out, what choices would in fact be made, and thus within limits could predict the future on the basis of those and other calculations. To say the revolution is inevitable is simply (in Marx's scheme) to say that it will occur. And it will occur, to repeat, not in spite of any choices we might make, but because of the choices we will make.

Let me briefly amplify one point in order to remove a possible source of confusion. To say that the course of history depends on what we will is not to say that history is as we will it. The course of history has clearly been affected by the decisions and choices of Hitler. But fortunately it is not *as* he willed it. Thus if Marx denies that history is as anyone wills it, he is only affirming the obvious. For it is extremely doubtful that in all its details the course of history is as anybody wishes, wills or chooses. And if by chance it is as someone wishes, it is not because of his wish, or certainly not mainly because of it. Engels understood these matters:

. . . history is made in such a way that the final result always arises from conflicts between many individual wills, of which each in turn has been made what it is by a host of particular conditions of life. Thus there are innumerable intersecting forces, an infinite series of parallelograms of forces which give rise to one resultant —the historical event. This may again itself be viewed as the product of a power which works as a whole *unconsciously* and without volition. For what each individual wills is obstructed by everyone else, and what emerges is something that no one willed. Thus history has proceeded hitherto in the manner of a natural process and is essentially subject to the same laws of motion. But from the fact that the wills of individuals—each of whom desires what he is impelled to by his physical constitution and external, in the last resort economic, circumstances (either by his own personal circumstances or those of society in general)—do not attain what they want, but are merged into an aggregate mean, a common resultant, it must not be concluded that they are equal to zero. On the contrary, each contributes to the resultant and is to this extent included in it.[27]

[26] Or, if you like, that either (1) the group variables which are defined in terms of individual behaviors are interacting variables or (2) there are non-trivial parallelistic laws between neurophysiological states or behaviors and the values of the group variables.

[27] Letter of Engels to Joseph Bloch dated London, September 21–22, 1890, as it appears in *Marx and Engels*, p. 399. In some of his more speculative moments Marx suggested that under communism for the first time the course of events would be as most men willed. This is probably what Engels was referring to when he spoke of "the ascent of man from the kingdom of necessity to the kingdom of freedom." But that is another story.

Five ⋆ EXPLANATION,

PREDICTION, AND IMPERFECT

KNOWLEDGE

The world hangs together; one thing happens because of another thing. We explain an occurrence by showing how it is connected with other things. The connections must be such that they provide reasons for the occurrence of the actual event rather than some different one. The structure of a scientific explanation has been sketched in the General Introduction and is also described at various places in earlier sections. [See Index.] To recapitulate briefly, an event that has already happened is explained by deducing it from one or more statements of individual fact in conjunction with one or more generalizations or natural laws. One particular event C explains another E only if there is some generalization that justifies the inference from C to E. A reasoned prediction, in contrast to a mere guess or prophecy, has the same logical structure. We predict the future by deducing a statement about it from already known individual facts and laws. The empirical laws used to explain and to predict particular events are in turn explained by deductions from other laws. Such deductive connections among laws form theories, which are the subject of Section Six. This section, however, is primarily concerned with special problems that arise in the explanation and prediction of individual events.

A complete explanation is a valid logical argument whose premises state certain generalizations and relevant conditions and whose conclusion expresses the event to be explained. The simplest instance of this deductive pattern has the form: The regularity "If C then E" is true and "C" is true, therefore "E" must be true. "C" describes a set of initial or antecedent conditions and "E" is a description of the kind of event to be explained or predicted. A doctor, for example, explains a man's death as being caused by the arsenic found in his bloodstream, because arsenic in certain quantities is always fatal. That regularity is so familiar that it may be understood rather than openly expressed, but without it the arsenic is no more relevant to the victim's premature demise than is the tea in which he unwittingly consumed it. A man's jealousy explains, by virtue of the commonsense uniformity that jealousy often leads to hostile behavior, his attack on a rival. From an increase in interest rates, the economist predicts a slump in the building industry, because the demand for new construction is correlated with the cost of borrowing money. In these examples the event to be explained or predicted is subsumed under the general law "If C then E." This "covering law," to use Dray's suggestive term, and the condition C jointly entail E.

The deduction of many concrete events, however, cannot be pressed into the mold of inference from a *single* covering law plus antecedent conditions. This paradigm has the virtue of clarity and simplicity, but most deductions are considerably more complex. Suppose we wish to explain not merely the jealous man's hostile behavior, but also his use of a physical blow rather than a verbal insult or some more devious injury. To explain the specific manifestation of hostility requires further generalizations connecting personality with behavior under certain conditions and additional knowledge about the jealous man and the circumstances in which he and his rival were placed. Again, the collapse of a building (E) may be explained by a fault in its design (C), even though no building was ever before designed in that way. There is, therefore, no generalization "If C then E" about buildings having that design under which the collapse can be directly subsumed. It is instead explained by means of certain general laws of physics and engineering principles which imply that a building of this design can be expected to be unstable. These laws permit us to single out the design, rather than the materials used, as the cause of the collapse.

As with highly specific forms of activities or particular occurrences, very large-scale social events require a long chain of premises as their *explanans* in order to deduce them as the conclusion, or *explanandum*. The historian tries to explain such complex events as the Reformation, the Russian Revolution, or the Second World War. Controversies over whether or not history is a science typically fail to distinguish two different questions. The first is whether or not the historian seeks to *establish* laws; the second is whether or not the historian *utilizes* laws. The answers to these two questions are not the same. The historian does not try to find laws, but he does make use of any that are available. [See also the paper by MacIver in Section Four.] Laws are about kinds of events. The Reformation and the Russian Revolution were complex events that happened only once. There are no laws that mention events in their full individuality, as particularized by, among other things, space, time, and cast of characters. The attention of the historian is riveted on just such singular events. Thus, history—unlike sociology, political theory, or economics—is not a law-finding or systematic science. Though history repeats itself, generalizing from its dismal recurrences is incidental to, rather than the goal of, the historian.

A distinction is sometimes drawn between the "nomothetic" and the "idiographic" disciplines. The former look for laws connecting kinds of events and make inferences from them. The latter eschew logical inference and are concerned instead with "understanding" the unique event in its full individuality. The alleged distinction, associated with the *verstehende* sociology discussed in Section One, is spurious. The notion of idiographic understanding that intuitively grasps connections among unique events is desperately obscure. The historian is not concerned with the singular event *only* in its full singularity. When he tries to explain why it happened, he fits it into a pattern of recurring individual and social behavior. To determine the causes of an historical event, he utilizes regularities provided by the generalizing social sciences about the impact of technological change, the process of economic development, a shift in power groups, the influence of geographical conditions, and so forth. The facts established by the historian may in turn be drawn upon by the generalizing scientists to suggest and support social generalizations.

The Reformation refers to a unique pattern of recurring sorts of events. If this were not so, we could not understand the term. We explain what the Reformation was by using many general terms that apply to the elements of the pattern. It is described as a combination of instances of concepts, such as *corruption* and *power struggle,* which also occur in other contexts. If we explain what something is by subsuming it under a concept, is this a type of explanation different in kind from subsumption under general laws? In his paper Dray argues persuasively that it is. He is making more than the merely verbal point that in common discourse we use *explain* both for telling what and for telling why. Dray believes, not unjustifiably, that subsumption under a social concept, such as *social revolution,* is truly explanatory, in contrast to subsumption under a nonsocial concept, such as *dog* or *green.* Although I do not believe that this explanatory power is gained without the use of laws, Dray's discussion usefully illuminates the complexity of our social categories.

Explaining *what* is certainly different from explaining *why,* but to make and use the distinction we have to be reasonably precise about what counts as telling *what* and what counts as telling *why.* Nothing will be lost but the word and needless ambiguity if we replace *explaining what* by *describing,* for both terms signify subsumption under a concept rather than under a law. We describe something by attributing to it certain characteristics. An individual is tall and blond; the crowd outside is large and disorderly. A description is a statement of individual fact or a conjunction of such statements. Although it contains general terms for attributes or kinds of things, it contains no generalizations about connections among these attributes. No matter how detailed a description is, no inferences can be made from it without adding generalizations that connect the elements of the description to other things. Statements of individual fact, asserting that a concept has an instance, tell what something is. By themselves they provide no cues of why it is that way.

On the other hand, Dray's illustrations reveal that matters are not always so simple. He quite rightly insists that classifying an event as a social revolution is not equivalent to bringing it under a law of the form "Whenever such and such conditions, then a revolution." However, it should also be emphasized that attributing a highly complex concept to a collective event is not at all like attributing a relatively concrete observable characteristic to an individual or group. Collective terms, it was pointed out in Section Four, refer to complex patterns of behavior. When social terms, such as *election* or *bureaucracy,* are carefully construed for use in scientific hypotheses, they incorporate only descriptive assertions about, for example, who does what and who talks to whom. Any covert reference to the presumed causes and effects of these patterns is extruded, for they must be independently determined. But the categories of, in Dray's phrase, "the ordinary language of social description" often are more than merely descriptive. The concept of *national character,* for instance, refers at best to certain statistical regularities about how the individuals of a nation characteristically tend to behave under certain circumstances. In order to attempt to explain, say, why the Prime Minister of England in 1956 reacted as he did to the Egyptian take-over of the Suez Canal, a historian might allude to the "British national character." But that concept is "explanatory" only insofar as it is not at all a single concept or a conjunction of concepts, but is a suitcase term for a whole set of rather crude generalizations. To put it differently, *national character,* like many other everyday social categories, is not a true attribute or variable. That is, it is not a term that can occur in either the antecedent or consequent of a law, for it is itself shorthand for an indefinite set of laws.

Similarly, the notion of a social revolution may incorporate not merely specific changes in the institutional structures, but also implicit regularities about the causes and effects of these wide-ranging changes in the relations among men and in the nature of their activities. It is clear, however, that complex social categories do not occur in either the antecedent or consequent of a single covering law that can be used to explain the causes or effects of the events subsumed under those categories. Instead, the premises of these explanations will include a large number of laws about the various kinds of events within the total pattern.

After the facts have been ascertained, the historian may be able, by appealing to various social and psychological laws, to single out, say, six conditions as the causes of the Russian Revolution. On the face of it, he could then generalize that whenever these six conditions occur together, there will be a revolution. But this would be a specious generalization, because it would merely reformulate in "global" terms part of what had already been asserted in the laws about the constituent social conditions. Because exactly those six conditions never did occur jointly in just that way before, the "generalization" explains only by virtue of the regularities from which it has been extracted. Because it is also most unlikely that they will ever recur in just that combination, it has no predictive value. To explain and to predict complex singular social events, we need laws about the interaction of their constituents. By such laws many different singular social events may be explained.

It is one thing to appreciate what is required to justify our explanations and predictions: we must know all the laws and all the antecedent conditions that permit us to deduce the events to be explained or predicted. It is another thing to fulfill these requirements. They provide the criteria by which we assess the knowledge that we have, distinguish adequate from inadequate explanation, and see why our predictions fall short of the mark. In practice, our actual explanations and predictions are much looser than the deductive pattern. What shall we make of this fact? Some philosophers have counted it against the deductive ideal, particularly if on other grounds they hold that causal explanation is inappropriate to human affairs. Others, on the other hand, feel that by celebrating the untidy actuality we gratuitously abandon the search for further knowledge. The paper by Weingartner ably summarizes the major points at issue among the protagonists in a recent version of the fitfully recurring dispute about the nature of explanation. Hempel lucidly details the ways in which our everyday explanations are commonly sketchy and incomplete. After patiently examining various criticisms that have been levelled against the deductive model, he concludes that, despite practical divergences from the ideal, all adequate explanations presuppose that the event to be explained can be subsumed under either universal or statistical general laws. Included also is his illuminating discussion of the relation between scientific explanation and reduction to the familiar.

Any description of a situation mentions certain features and omits others. Though a scientific description cannot and need not be exhaustive, it may, in a specifiable sense of *completeness,* be complete. A system is any group of objects or persons that remains identifiable as a group through an appreciable length of time. A "state" of a system consists of its characteristics at some given time. A description of a system is complete if, given that description at any one time, we can by means of laws infer its state at any other time. A "process" is the temporal unfolding of a system. If nothing that makes a difference, no "relevant variable," has been omitted from the laws of the process, then from its state at any one time, we may infer its state at any other time. If we knew all this, then we would have what Bergmann aptly calls "perfect knowledge." The laws that provide it are process laws. Obviously, much of our knowledge falls short of perfection. Recall the difficulties of explaining or predicting the specific form an action will take, or even the exact time of so common an occurrence as a man's death. We do have a great deal of imperfect knowledge, however, that is characterized by laws of several different kinds. Bergmann presents a typology of the various forms of imperfect knowledge, with examples from psychology and the social sciences. He discusses how the laws of imperfect knowledge differ from process laws and how this difference accounts for the incompleteness of our explanations and predictions.

The explanation of events that are over and done with is not easy, but the past at least already exists. We can reasonably expect to establish what has happened with a fair degree of accuracy. Having done so, we can pick and choose among the various bits of imperfect social and psychological knowledge for the laws to explain the facts we have established. The future is more difficult. On the one hand, it has not yet occurred and, armed only with imperfect knowledge, it is in practice harder to predict individual events than to explain them after the fact. On the other hand, we are always catching up to the future. Apart from the greater practical difficulties, a perverse complicating factor works against accurate prediction that is absent in explanations of the past.

The act of making a prediction may itself affect the course of events. Prevision may be destroyed by prevision. That is the intriguing "paradox of prediction." Robert Merton, the sociologist, was for a time persuaded that it marked a radical methodological difference between the social and physical sciences. A comet does not change its course because of published predictions about its behavior. The course of the stock market, however, may be affected. Predictions are "reflexive" if the act of prediction increases or diminishes the probability that the event predicted will occur. A false rumor that a bank is about to fail will be self-fulfilling if it causes a run on the bank. A prediction of the dire effects of a certain policy will be self-defeating if it serves as a warning and if action is taken to avert the disaster. If we had perfect knowledge, then the effects on the behavior of individuals of gaining information would be included among the relevant variables. Merton no longer believes that the "reflexive" effect of broadcast predictions creates a methodological difference between the social and physical sciences. But it is a widely held view and his early papers, rich in examples of the poignant and powerful effects of false rumors, stimulated a great deal of discussion. The contributions by Roger Buck and Herbert Simon are reprinted here. They analyze the implications of the so-called interference effects of predictions and suggest how, without paradox, they may be accommodated in our body of knowledge.

[19] "Explaining What" in History

WILLIAM H. DRAY

– I –

It is commonly held nowadays that the explanations given in all fields of enquiry, including history, have a common logical structure. Explanation, it is said, consists of the subsumption of what is to be explained under general law. To quote Professor Carl Hempel, "the assertion that a set of events—say of the kinds C_1, C_2, . . . , C_n—have caused the event (E) to be explained, amounts to the statement that, according to certain general laws, a set of events of the kinds mentioned is regularly accompanied by an event of kind E." [1] I have argued elsewhere that this theory of explanation, which I call "the covering law model," does not provide a satisfactory analysis of the kinds of answers historians usually offer to "why" and "how" questions.[2] In what follows I should like to argue briefly for a similar conclusion with respect to a type of explanation which is not normally given in response to either of these kinds of questions.

In his *Short History of the British Commonwealth*, after describing some of the changes which took place in late 18th century England—the enclosure of agricultural lands, the beginnings of industrial production, the improvement of communications, etc.—Ramsey Muir observes: "It was not merely an economic change that was thus beginning; it was a social revolution." [3] The historian here makes no attempt to tell us either why or how the events under investigation came about. Yet the assertion, "It was a social revolution," is an explanation nevertheless.[4] It explains what happened *as* a social revolution. The question formulating the demand for such an explanation

[1] "The Function of General Laws in History," as reprinted in *Theories of History*, P. Gardiner, ed., p. 345.

[2] See my *Laws and Explanation in History*, Oxford University Press, Oxford, 1957.

[3] Vol. II (6th edn., London, 1937), p. 123.

[4] It might perhaps be objected that what we are offered here would be called an interpretation rather than an explanation. Thus Professor S. Hook, in *The Hero in History*, tells us that Otto Bauer "interpreted the New Economic Policy introduced by Lenin as a partial return to capitalism." But I do not think that we need attach much significance to the distinction between explaining and interpreting in such cases, since "explained" could replace "interpreted" without difficulty.

would employ the interrogative "What?" rather than "How?" or "Why?" The historian's problem is to discover *what it really was* that happened. And he deals with it by offering an explanation of the form, "It was a so-and-so."

No doubt there are many different sorts of "explanations what." To explain what happened, for instance, may sometimes mean to explain *why* what happened happened. And even in cases where it is difficult to regard the explanation as a covert answer to a "why" question, "explaining what" may take a form quite different from the one exemplified above; it may, for instance, require a detailed *account* of what happened. In the example noted, however, the problem is clearly not to discover new information, not to provide further details, but rather to reorganize the detailed information already possessed; it is a matter of the synthesis rather than the analysis of what is to be explained. Indeed, explaining what a thing is, where this means explaining it as a so-and-so, might be characterized in a preliminary way as explanation by means of a general concept rather than a general law. For the explanation is given by finding a satisfactory *classification* of what seems to require explanation.

– II –

Some philosophers, while agreeing that explanation may at times be given by means of a concept, would deny that the logical structure of such explanation differs essentially from subsumption under law. Thus, according to Professor Hempel, "what is sometimes, misleadingly, called an explanation by means of a certain *concept* is, in empirical science, actually an explanation in terms of *universal hypotheses* containing that concept." [5] Hempel's qualification, "in empirical science," is not intended to restrict the application of his doctrine to the natural sciences, for he considers that history, too, is, or should be, empirical science. The limited scope of the qualification shows itself in the sentence which follows the one just quoted, in which we are warned: "explanations involving concepts which do not function in empirically tested hypotheses—such as 'entelechy' in biology, 'historical destination of a race' or 'self-unfolding of absolute reason' in history—are mere metaphors without cognitive content." All that Hempel means to rule out, apparently, are concepts which, in his opinion, have no empirical meaning at all. Any explanation given by means of an empirically respectable concept will necessarily subsume what is to be explained under general law.

In the light of what I have said about "explaining what," let me try to show why I think it a mistake to claim in this way that all explanations in terms of concepts are reducible to explanations in terms of laws. And to avoid, at any rate at first, the suspicion of employing "metaphors without

[5] *Op. cit.*, p. 350, n. 3.

cognitive content," let me consider that claim with respect to the explanatory use of the ordinary empirical concept "revolution."

It is Hempel's contention that if a concept has explanatory force, this can only be because the explanation making use of it covertly subsumes what is being explained under a law "containing" the concept. Presumably the law which lurks in the background when something is explained "as a revolution" is one which would contain the concept in its apodosis; for the role of an explanatory covering law is to show, by reference to certain other (and usually antecedent) events and conditions, that what is to be explained could have been predicted. But to explain, say, what happened in France in 1789 "as a revolution" would surely not be equivalent to bringing it under any law of the form, "Whenever C_1, C_2, . . . , C_n then a revolution." For to apply the concept does not *necessarily* represent the explicandum as the sort of thing which follows a certain type of antecedent event or condition, whether stated or merely understood.

Indeed, the whole question of the predictability, the necessity, of what is explained simply does not arise as part of the explanatory problem in the sort of case envisaged here—the sort of case in which "It was a revolution" would count as an explanation in ordinary historical writing. Even if it were admitted, for the sake of argument, that explaining why something happened requires the specification of conditions from which what happened could have been predicted, and that such prediction commits the investigator to the truth of some covering law, it would thus still be a mistake to regard the covering law theory as setting forth a generally necessary condition of explanation. For explaining what a thing is, i.e. how it should be regarded, is just not the same enterprise at all as explaining why it (whatever it may have been) happened, or why it ran the course it did, or how it came about, or how it could have happened in the light of so-and-so. There is nothing wrong with these questions except that, in the sort of context under discussion, they are *further* questions—questions which the explanatory statement makes no attempt to answer.

It is true that the applicability of an explanatory concept *may,* in some cases, be judged appropriate by an investigator because he recognizes that some law or laws are instantiated by what is to be explained. This is most likely to be so in cases where the term in question is drawn from the technical vocabulary of some auxiliary science. We are told by Professor Marie Swabey, for instance, that Lenin's fame rested on his sure-footed diagnosis of the February 1917 uprising in Russia "as a bourgeois revolution." [6] At least part of what Lenin would have regarded as his justification for the classification, "bourgeois revolution," would have been his conclusion, in the light of his general theory of the historical process, that certain results had accrued in accordance with certain laws. Thus, in explaining the February uprising "as a bourgeois revolution," Lenin quite deliberately, although not in so many words, brings what happened under covering law.

[6] *The Judgement of History* (New York, 1954). pp. 154–5.

Indeed, from his assertion that it was a bourgeois revolution, it could be *deduced* that its antecedents were of a certain general character, for these have been written into the meaning of the technical term which Lenin employs. But to admit that explanation-by-concept may sometimes *in fact* subsume the explicandum under law is not at all to commit oneself to the view that such subsumption is generally necessary. For not all classificatory terms require the recognition of what they apply to as satisfying the apodosis clause of some valid law. "Revolution," as used in the ordinary language of social description, is surely a case in point. To generalize from the use of concepts which do, indeed, have laws built into them is to attempt to support covering law theory by appealing to special cases.

It might be pointed out, too, that the appeal to such cases is itself not entirely without danger for an attempt to enhance the plausibility of the covering law doctrine. For even where laws *are* built into the explanatory concepts used, it is important to realize that the laws in question need not be the kind envisaged by Professor Hempel in the passage quoted at the beginning of this paper. The covering law theory maintains that the explanatory law must be one which allows the explicandum to fall under its apodosis clause. But the application of a strictly defined concept like "bourgeois revolution" may just as well involve us in the recognition of laws which contain the explicandum in their *protasis* clauses. For we may judge the applicability of a concept by noticing what comes *after,* as well as what comes before, that to which it is said to apply. We see the significance of historical events by noticing what they *lead to,* as well as what they arise out of. If a covering law theorist should deny this—if he should deny that eliciting the significance of events in this sense has anything to do with "explanation"—then it will begin to appear that an independently established theory of explanation as subsumption under laws allowing the prediction of the explained event is being *applied to,* rather than discovered in, explanations ordinarily given by means of concepts.

It seems to me preferable to admit that explanation-by-concept is something quite different from "prediction upside down." There is a kind of generality in it, no doubt, but it is not essentially the generality involved in representing something as what could have been predicted in the light of so-and-so. The difference between explaining something as a so-and-so, and the pattern of covering law theory, might, indeed, be put in terms of two different senses in which philosophers speak of "generalizing." When exponents of the covering law model speak of explanatory generalization, they have in mind a situation in which what is to be explained is a y preceded by an x, and the generalization in question would be of the form: "Whenever x then y." But if there is any generalization essential to the kind of explanation I have called "explaining what," it would have to be of a quite different form. For what is to be explained is a collection of happenings or conditions, x, y and z; and the relevant generalization would be of the form: "X, y and z amount to a Q." [7] Such an explanatory generalization is summative; it allows us to refer to x, y and z collectively as "a so-and-so." And historians find it intellectually satisfying to be able to represent the events and conditions they study as related in this way.

– III –

In considering "explanations what" given by means of a concept like "revolution," it is necessary to admit at least this much "regularity" in the explanation: that what happened, since it is described by a classificatory term drawn from the ordinary language of social description, is a recurring social phenomenon at the level of generalization indicated by the term used. My purpose in considering such a case was to show that even so, this "regularity" does not support the claim that the explanation necessarily subsumes what is to be explained under covering law.

But it is important to add that explanations of this sort are not always given by means of a concept whose use implies that what is explained is a recurring *social* phenomenon. For historians often draw attention to an intelligible pattern in their subject matter by applying (or, it may be said, "stretching") concepts from other fields. They speak, for instance, of "the evolution of Parliament," explaining a host of details of parliamentary history "as an evolution." Or they speak of "The Renaissance" or "The Enlightenment," explaining a certain range of facts, drawn from 15th or 18th century European history, "as a rebirth" or "as an intellectual illumination." In reaching for concepts beyond the social field, i.e. in using analogies, the explanation of what happened "as a so-and-so" no longer allows us to say that what is explained is a recurring social phenomenon. There may have been many revolutions, but there may have been only one Age of Enlightenment. Yet if this were so, it would not at all diminish the explanatory value of the concept for historians of 18th century Europe.

Covering law theorists may be inclined to write off such explanatory concepts as "metaphors"—the sort of thing to be expected from "literary" historians. But it should be noted that the metaphors in question cannot, like those cited by Professor Hempel, be dismissed as devoid of empirical content. They have, in fact, empirical justification, for their propriety rests upon their emphasizing certain empirically discernible features of the subject matter which are deemed important. In a way logically analogous to the use of concepts like "revolution," they allow the historian to bring a wide range of facts into a system or pattern, although not necessarily into a pattern which recurs in the social field.

[7] This is the sense of "generalize" employed by Professor M. Oakeshott when he writes: ". . . historical individuals are themselves a product of generalization, though not . . . of scientific generalization." *Experience and Its Modes* (Cambridge, 1933), p. 160.

Mr. W. H. Walsh, who is one of the few recent philosophers of history to emphasize the role of large-scale connecting or unifying concepts in introducing "intelligibility" into historical material, has called this explanatory procedure "colligation under appropriate conceptions." [8] The historian, he says, conceives it his task "to look for certain dominant concepts or leading ideas by which to illuminate his facts, to trace connections between those ideas themselves, and then to show how the detailed facts become intelligible in the light of them by constructing a 'significant narrative' of the events of the period in question." [9] He illustrates his meaning by referring to Russell's "colligation" of English 19th century political history in terms of "Freedom and Organization."

According to Mr. J. W. N. Watkins, such a procedure yields "less than a full explanation of the events colligated"; it is a procedure "which is important not because it is methodologically powerful, but because most 'literary' historians do in fact use it. . . ." [10] And Walsh himself, in his *Introduction to Philosophy of History,* remarks that "colligation needs to be supplemented by further processes if historical explanation is to be complete." [11] But, if my analysis is correct, it is surely necessary to protest that colligatory explanations, insofar as they provide satisfactory unifying concepts, *can* be perfectly complete explanations *of their type*—i.e. as answers to "what" rather than to "why" questions. The complaint that colligation is not "methodologically powerful" betrays an illegitimate approach to the appraisal of such explanations. It expresses dissatisfaction with the question asked, rather than with the answer to it which colligatory explanation provides.

8 On this see "The Intelligibility of History," *Philosophy,* 1942, pp. 133–5; "The Character of An Historical Explanation," *Proceedings of the Aristotelian Society,* Supp. Vol. 1947, pp. 51–2; *Introduction to Philosophy of History* (London, 1951), pp. 59–64.

9 *Introduction to Philosophy of History,* p. 62.

10 "Ideal Types and Historical Explanation," reprinted in Feigl, H., and Brodbeck, M., *Readings in the Philosophy of Science* (New York, 1953), p. 733.

11 P. 63. According to Walsh, it needs to be completed by explanations applying generalizations from a "science of human nature."

[20] The Quarrel About Historical Explanation[1]

RUDOLPH H. WEINGARTNER

– I –

An historically minded reader of the current literature on historical explanation might well assess that literature in something like the following way: "We have here a discussion of a philosophic question in its early and lively phase. The temporal and substantive starting point is a strong proposal made by Carl G. Hempel in an article called 'The Function of General Laws in History.'[2] The literature which follows it includes every possible kind of reaction: Hempel has found his adherents; his analysis has provoked criticism of every variety, and it has stimulated a wide range of alternative proposals—some of them closely resembling that of Hempel, others differing radically. In a few years' time interest in the issue will die down, for the various explications of historical explanation will converge and disagreement will be confined to more and more minute details."

Some of the things noted by this imaginary observer of the passing philosophical scene are quite correct. The discussion, now so lively, did for all practical purposes begin with Hempel's article;[3] moreover, almost every

Reprinted with permission of the author and the editors from *The Journal of Philosophy*, 58, 1961, pp. 29–45.

[1] A shorter version of this paper was read at the 1960 International Congress for Logic, Methodology, and Philosophy of Science, held at Stanford University.

[2] *The Journal of Philosophy*, Vol. 39 (1942). Reprinted in Herbert Feigl and Wilfrid Sellars, eds., *Readings in Philosophical Analysis* (New York: Appleton-Century-Crofts, 1949), pp. 459–471. Page references are to the latter printing.

[3] Careful historians of philosophy will rightly complain that (1) Hempel's proposal of 1942 was by no means new and that (2) the keen interest in the problem of historical explanation, to which philosophers writing in the decades on either side of the turn of the century gave expression, had never completely died down. In support of the first contention Karl Popper must above all be cited. He himself correctly claims priority for the view Hempel sets forth (see n. 7 to ch. 25 of *The Open Society and Its Enemies*, Princeton University Press, 1950, pp. 720–723). Moreover, depending on how broadly the Hempelian position is conceived, ancestors even of Popper may be found. Alan Donagan points out that Morris Cohen, in *Reason and Nature*, 1st ed. (1931), bk. I, ch. I, sec. 2, maintains a similar view. (See Alan Donagan, "Explanation in History," *Mind*, Vol. 66 (1957), reprinted in Patrick Gardiner, ed., *Theories of History*, New York, The Free Press, 1959, n. 2, p. 428). But, as is so frequently the case in the history of philosophy, what matters

paper written on this question makes Hempel's analysis of historical explanation its own starting point. Nevertheless, our observer's assessment and prognosis of the discussion is in error. It fails, I think, to go beneath the surface and to see the one fundamental issue which divides the disputants, an issue which will not be settled in the course of more precise and detailed analyses of historical explanation. It will be the burden of this paper to show that what appears to be a dispute about the precise nature of historical explanation is in fact the product of a disagreement about the nature of philosophic method, with all the far-reaching implications that such a disagreement implies.

To begin with, the discussion of historical explanation is not so free a free-for-all as it might at first seem to be. There are clearly two sides: Hempel and Hempelians on one and anti-Hempelians on the other. What accounts for the appearance of a war of all against all is the lack of a general on the anti-Hempelian side. The Hempelians are fewer in number, but their ranks are ordered—or, rather, as ordered as philosophical ranks can be expected to be.[4] While the opponents of Hempelianism seldom fight among each other, they make very little effort at concerted action. Indeed, the anti-Hempelians rarely even mention each other. In order, now, to be in a position to see what the quarrel is about, it will be necessary to summarize the positions of the two sides, starting with the Hempel proposal itself.

– II –

Hempel begins with an outline of the structure of explanation in the natural sciences.[5] According to this scheme, an event (as distinct from a law) is explained if and only if the statement asserting its occurrence (E) can be logically deduced from premises consisting of (1) a set of well confirmed statements expressing instantial or determining conditions (C_1, C_2, . . . C_n) and (2) a set of well confirmed [6] universal hypotheses, i.e., general laws (L_1,

---

is not merely the inventing and holding of a view, but the power and precision of its formulation. In Hempel's article the position was for the first time brought into such sharp focus that it had to be accepted, adopted, modified, or rejected; it could no longer be ignored. With respect to the second point, we must keep in mind the great change that has taken place in the method and style of philosophy since the work of Dilthey, Simmel, Weber, Rickert, and others. There are links between these continental philosophers of history and those currently concerned with this topic (Collingwood and Mandelbaum, for example), but Hempel's article is the earliest written wholly in the analytic style of philosophy.

4 There is some disagreement even among Hempelians. In this paper, however, intra-Hempelian disputes will be ignored.

5 This outline is both expanded and refined in another *locus classicus*, Carl G. Hempel and Paul Oppenheim, "The Logic of Explanation," *Philosophy of Science*, Vol. 15 (1948), reprinted in Herbert Feigl and May Brodbeck, eds., *Readings in the Philosophy of Science* (New York: Appleton-Century-Crofts, 1953), pp. 319–352. Page references are to the latter printing.

6 In the later paper (*ibid.*, p. 322) "well confirmed" is changed to "true."

$L_2, \ldots L_n$). E is the explanandum and the two sets of statements, $C_1, C_2,$ $\ldots C_n$ and $L_1, L_2, \ldots L_n$ are the explanans, where E is deducible from $C_1, C_2, \ldots C_n$ and $L_1, L_2, \ldots L_n$.

But is this also the structure of an historical explanation? Certainly not in the sense that one will actually find in history books statements which conform to the pattern just indicated. Aside from the niceties of rigor and precision, explanations found in works of history rarely state instantial conditions with the requisite completeness and accuracy. Even less frequently do historians offer explanations which mention the general law or laws in virtue of which the explanandum is deducible.

These observations about actual explanations are all Hempel's. Indeed, Hempel is at pains to point out further how serious the gap is between his model and the explanations historians actually provide. Although no law may in fact be mentioned, it would occasionally be no trouble to state it— merely a bore. The Normandy sank to the bottom of New York Harbor because a bomb was set off inside it. The law, "Whenever a bomb is set off in a ship (and certain circumstances prevail), the ship will sink," is familiar and not worthy of mention. Often, however, the required hypotheses are so complex, one would be hard put to it even to formulate them. Think of the stuff histories are made of: outbreaks of wars and revolutions, spreads of religions, failures of foreign policies. No simple laws will do as generalizations belonging to the *explanantia* of such events. And finally, there is the problem of truth or confirmation. Even when a law is stated, how likely is it that it can be well confirmed? The historian is in no position to conduct experiments; the number of instances of any generalization he might have wanted to use may forever be insufficient to establish it.

Not only, then, does Hempel recognize that historians do not provide explanations which conform in so many words to the pattern outlined, but he is careful to note that, even if he wanted to, the historian would seldom be able to do so. All that the historian does (and, in most cases, can) provide is an *explanation sketch* which "consists of a more or less vague indication of the laws and initial conditions considered as relevant and [which] needs 'filling out' in order to turn it into a fullfledged explanation." [7]

But if it is true that in the vast majority of cases historians merely offer explanation *sketches,* it follows that the paradigm first set down *is* the proper analysis of an historical *explanation.* To explain why an event occurred is to deduce the statement expressing what has occurred from instantial condition statements and general laws. To the extent to which and in any way in which the historian falls short of these requirements, he fails to explain, but merely provides a sketch of an explanation. Stated in somewhat exaggerated terms, Hempel's article must be construed not as an argument in support of the thesis that historical explanation has a certain pattern, but rather as a claim that the explanations offered in history are in certain ways and in varying degrees inadequate. Fullfledged explana-

[7] *Op. cit.,* p. 465.

tions always have the same structure, whether they occur in science or history.[8]

– III –

All anti-Hempelians agree in making less of a demand upon historical explanation than do Hempel and Hempelians. They emphatically do not agree on the extent to which the demands upon the historian as explainer should be reduced. It is convenient for our purposes to divide the alternative analyses [9] of historical explanation into three groups, with the first closest to and the third furthest from the Hempel proposal.

(1) There are those who agree with Hempel that the explanans of an historical explanation must contain not only a set of instantial conditions, but general statements of some kind as well. According to these writers, however, an historical explanation may be complete and emphatically not a mere sketch that requires further "filling out," even when its generalization or generalizations fall short in various degrees and ways from being universal hypotheses.

And when the requirement of a law is relaxed sufficiently, it no longer makes sense to speak of deducibility. According to Patrick Gardiner, for example, historians make use of generalizations which make imprecise correlations, to which exceptions may be granted, the terms of which may be "open." Such statements—Gardiner prefers to call them "assessments" or "judgments"—fashion some sort of links between the "details" of the instantial conditions and the event to be explained; they serve as "guiding threads." In fulfilling this function *they do all that is needed for a complete historical explanation*. Statements of this kind are not "made, or accepted, in default of something 'better'; we should rather insist that their formulation represents the *end* of historical inquiry, not that they are stages on the journey towards that end." [10]

(2) A proposal by T. A. Goudge [11] will serve to exemplify a second type

---

[8] Among those who have, with no or few reservations, accepted Hempel's analysis of historical explanation are: Ernest Nagel (see, especially, "Determinism in History," *Philosophy and Phenomenological Research,* Vol. 20 (1960)) and Morton White (see "Historical Explanation," *Mind,* Vol. 52 (1943), reprinted in Gardiner, *op. cit.,* pp. 357–373).

[9] Some writers grant that Hempel's proposal is an analysis of *some* historical explanations; they then make their suggestions as *additions* to that of Hempel. Most anti-Hempelians offer their proposals *in place* of Hempel's. The proposals to be discussed here are all analyses of *causal* explanations. As such they are at least in some ways comparable to Hempel's scheme. Some anti-Hempelian's, however, also recognize historical explanations which are, in their view, not causal at all. See Sec. V.

[10] Patrick Gardiner, *The Nature of Historical Explanation* (Oxford: Oxford University Press, 1952), pp. 95–96. Also, see Alan Donagan, *loc. cit.,* as well as Michael Scriven, "Truisms as the Grounds for Historical Explanations," in Gardiner's *Theories of History,* pp. 443–475, and "The Logic of Criteria," *The Journal of Philosophy,* Vol. 56 (1959).

[11] "Causal Explanation in Natural History," *The British Journal for the Philosophy of Science,* Vol. 9 (1958).

of alternative to Hempel's proposal. According to him, historical explanations [12] can be expected to achieve in practice no more than the following
pattern: the explanation indicates conditions, temporally prior to or simultaneous with E, which are jointly sufficient but not independently necessary
for the occurrence of E. An historical explanation would be complete if
the conditions specified were independently necessary for the occurrence
of E.

In this, the sufficient condition model of historical explanation, laws or
law-like statements are explicitly said not to play a role. The event to be
explained *is* explained in virtue of the fact that it "falls into place" as the
terminal phase of a sequence which, in its entirety, constitutes the sufficient
condition for the occurrence of the event. The logical relations among the
components of an explanation are said to be not implicative, but conjunc-
tive. The deductive model is "the wrong model to have in mind." Instead,
coherent narrative is taken to be the model of explanation.

(3) The coherence of a narrative does not, of course, depend upon the
sufficiency of the conditions said to bring about an event. Accordingly,
writers can be found who depart still further from the Hempelian model
by claiming that an event may be adequately explained by citing merely
necessary conditions for its occurrence. W. B. Gallie, for example, requires
of what he calls a "characteristically genetic [or historical] explanation" of
events that it refer "us to one or a number of their temporally prior necessary conditions. . . . In such cases explanation commences from our recognition of the event to be explained as being of such a kind that *some one*
of a disjunction of describable conditions is necessary to its occurrence; and
the explanation consists in elucidating *which one* of this disjunctive set is
applicable, in the sense of being necessary, to the event in question." [13] If
some particular historical explanation (following this pattern) is taken to be
inadequate, Gallie would consider it irrelevant and of no help at all if
general laws were mentioned in an attempt to improve the explanation.
If any "filling out" should be needed, it is to be done *within* the necessary
condition model, by specifying different or more such conditions.

Essentially the same position is held by both Arthur C. Danto [14] and
William Dray.[15] For both of them the detailing of necessary conditions
explains the occurrence of an event, though both of them go further than
Gallie in regarding coherent narrative as a model of explanation. Following the model of "the continuous series," Dray considers an event explained
when he *"can trace the course of events by which it came about."* [16] The
explanation of Caesar's behavior, writes Danto, is "merely . . . the narra-

---

[12] Goudge's actual subject matter is natural history. There seems to be no reason,
however, why his proposal should not be extended so as to apply to history.

[13] W. B. Gallie, "Explanations in History and the Genetic Sciences," *Mind*, Vol. 64
(1955), reprinted in Gardiner, *op. cit.*, p. 387; italics in original.

[14] "On Explanations in History," *Philosophy of Science*, Vol. 23 (1956).

[15] *Laws and Explanation in History* (Oxford: Oxford University Press, 1957).

[16] *Ibid.*, p. 68, italics in original.

tive we might construct describing Caesar's career, . . . describing the causes and conditions of the occurrences."[17] No general statements are required. Explanation by means of such a narrative is the end (or at least one of the ends) of historical inquiry, and not an initial step on the road to the deductive model.[18]

– IV –

If it is correct that the dispute about historical explanation is one in which Hempelians oppose anti-Hempelians, it is also true that the arguing on both sides has been curiously ineffectual. The various attacks of the anti-Hempelians have merely been countered by a reiteration of the original Hempelian position. Neither side has made any admissions. To explain this strange lack of progress, we must turn away from the actual proposals made about historical explanation and consider two underlying conceptions of what philosophy is and does.

There is some common ground shared by both parties to the quarrel about historical explanation. They are both genuinely doing philosophy *of* history. They philosophize, that is, about a subjective matter or activity as it is given; neither side is content to deduce statements about history from some antecedently established *a priori* metaphysical system. This common ground, however, is not enough to guarantee that the arguments by the disputants about historical explanation will meet. Given this very broad agreement, it may still be true that the "distances" at which philosophers stand from the object of their philosophic reflection vary considerably.[19] More specifically, the "distance" from which Hempelians look upon historical explanation is much greater than that from which their critics regard it.

Not even the starting point is precisely the same on both sides of the dispute. Hempel and Hempelians make no attempt to survey explanations as they are actually proffered—whether in history or in science. Induction is no part of their argument: no argument is made (and none can be) that their reconstruction says, more clearly and more elegantly perhaps, what historians (or scientists) say and do.[20] They proceed along different lines.

17 Danto, *loc. cit.*, p. 29.

18 Scriven may also be associated with this view. See the papers cited above, as well as "Explanation and Prediction in Evolutionary Theory," *Science*, Vol. 130 (1959), pp. 477–482.

19 This useful metaphor stems from Georg Simmel. See his "On the Nature of Philosophy," in Kurt H. Wolff, ed., *Georg Simmel, 1858–1918* (Columbus: Ohio State University Press, 1959), pp. 282–309.

20 The closest that Hempelians come to "verifying" their proposal by reference to explanations actually offered by historians is to restate the historian's explanation and give it the form of a Hempelian explanation sketch (see Nagel, *loc. cit.*). This, however, amounts to the *imposition* of a scheme upon the words of historians. Anti-Hempelians will be quick to point out that from the fact that the imposition is possible (that the historian's words do not resist being ordered into a Hempelian framework) it does not follow that there may not be an indefinite number of other schemata which are still more adequate philosophic reconstructions of historical explanation.

A sample explanation is kept in mind or cited.[21] It is, presumably, a good sample, a paragon of an explanation, one which satisfies. The logical character of this explanation is sketched out quickly, and from this point to the finished product (a reconstruction of historical explanation) it is not reference to further examples of explanation which determine what is said, but principles which are, so to speak, purely philosophical. Put less cryptically, the starting point of philosophic reflection is an *insight* into what an explanation is; all that follows constitutes a reconstruction and elaboration of that insight in terms of a philosophic position that does not directly depend upon an understanding of the particular thing (historical explanation) being examined, but is grounded in philosophic considerations of a much broader sort.

All this can be made a great deal clearer by an attempt that makes explicit the train of thought that leads to the Hempelian reconstruction of historical explanation. Explanations are offered in response to questions such as "Why did this happen?" They are designed to reduce curiosity to understanding; they resolve a kind of tension. When the explanation is (psychologically) successful, the hearer gratefully exclaims, "Aha!," or, in Friedrich Waismann's image, he doffs his hat.

It seems clear that, if the much advertised Aha! experience is to occur, the explanans and the explanandum must in some way "hang together." No questioner, presumably, will be satisfied at the end of an exchange such as this: Q. "Why was Napoleon exiled to Elba?" A. "Because the area of Elba is eighty-six square miles." It is true, however, that for some people, in some contexts, an explanans and explanandum "hang together," while for others, or the same people under different circumstances, the same components fail to cohere and do not lead to the desired Aha! "Because she wanted to sleep" will satisfy, a child's question, "Why did the doll close her eyes?," but it does not evoke an Aha! from an adult. Moreover, if such a response *did* satisfy an adult (and explanations no less superstitious have satisfied adults), we should emphatically come back with "it *ought* not to satisfy anyone!"

At this point the Hempelian may be imagined to take leave of the psychological discussion of explanations and the myriad of different contexts in which explanations may be offered. We know that explanans and explanandum must hang together; what must now be investigated is that in virtue of which these components hang together—not for the child or for a ninth-century serf, but for any rational being. A *philosophic* demand is being put upon explanations—a demand that the cohesion of its components should not depend upon the background of the person who asks for the explanation, nor upon the context in which it is given, but upon relations which are, so to speak, intrinsic to the explanation.

We need not look for such relationships; there are not many. The explanandum must be *deducible* from the explanans. When that is the case, the explanation's coherence is independent of the speaker, the hearer, and

---

[21] Hempel and Oppenheim, *loc. cit.*, pp. 320–321.

the context. Only when that is the case is the philosopher empowered to say, "You *ought* to be satisfied with this explanation." More important still, only if deducibility is understood to be a necessary feature of an adequate explanation, is the philosopher in a position to say to the child or the superstitious person, "You *ought not* to be satisfied with this explanation," when an Aha! experience is reported as evoked by an explanans and explanandum which do *not* have the logical coherence of deducibility.[22]

Another general principle is operative in the requirement of the deducibility of the explanandum. The question, "Why did E occur?," must be understood as a demand for the cause or causes of E. Moreover, under numerous circumstances, the reply actually consists of a reference to some condition or conditions and a "that's why!" For the Hempelian this is not enough, no matter how frequently hearers of such "explanations" indicate their satisfaction with answers of this kind.[23] As a philosopher who has a *theory* of causality, he wants to know that the conditions mentioned *are* causes. And this theory—in general terms a Humean one—can find such a guarantee only in the statement (well established) of a *regularity;* he requires that the statements of the alleged cause and effect be mediated by the statement of a law. Only then does he have the assurance that the alleged cause is, in fact, a cause.

This point may be put in another way. When the occurrence of E is explained by references to causes C_1, C_2, . . . C_n, a cognitive claim is made to the effect that C_1, C_2, . . . C_n did bring about E. Whatever the reaction of the plain man may be, the philosopher of the Hempelian persuasion is not yet satisfied. Even if it is supposed that the statements asserting that E and that C_1, C_2, . . . C_n are well established, nothing about these statements gives us any assurance that C_1, C_2, . . . C_n are causes of E. To obtain this kind of knowledge (which is crucial to the explanation) logical procedures have long since been worked out, quite independently of historical explanation. To know that C_1, C_2, . . . C_n caused E, we must know—that is, have verified—a statement to the effect that "Whenever C_1, C_2, . . . C_n then E." General principles, in other words, which rest upon a position which is applicable to a much broader area than, and is genetically independent of, the problems raised by historical explanation operate in the construction of the model of historical explanation.

A final philosophic principle which seems operative in the Hempelian analysis of historical explanation is of a much more general sort and might well be said to be assumed in the foregoing. To explain—whether in science, daily affairs, or history—is to provide knowledge. Knowledge, as distinct from mere belief, opinion, guessing, surmising, feeling sure, and so forth, must be objective. Ever since Plato, a dominant tradition in philosophy

---

[22] Only the question of coherence is here under discussion. Nothing is being said about when one ought or ought not to be satisfied as far as other features of explanations are concerned.

[23] See a discussion of this point in Jack Pitt, "Generalizations in Historical Explanation," *The Journal of Philosophy*, Vol. 56 (1959).

has insisted that knowledge must be logically independent of the particular state of mind of him who possesses it, the society of which its possesssor is a part, the state of mind of the audience to which he imparts it, and of any other factor besides the relationship between the proposition said to be known and what is the case. When Hempel and Oppenheim, in their paper on explanation,[24] demand that the constituent statements of an explanation be true, they are expressing their adherence to this tradition. For a perfectly adequate explanation, it is not enough to say that its constituents are well confirmed. For this is compatible with their falsity and hence with the inadequacy of the explanation. Only when its constituents are true does the explanation hold, regardless of time, place, speaker, or hearer.

And knowledge is one.[25] When historians explain, they claim to provide knowledge. Explanation in history, therefore, must fulfill the same requirements as explanations in other areas, above all in science. More generally, historical explanation must meet the criteria which any claim to knowledge must meet, regardless of its context. It may be that no actual explanation ever offered by an historian fully meets the demands the philosopher places upon claims to knowledge. In that case, the philosopher's model serves as a measure of the historian's success and indicates the direction of possible improvement. The model, however, is established on a firmer and wider basis than an examination of historical explanations: if such explanations do not live up to the model, the philosopher cannot give up the model short of giving up the philosophic position in which it is grounded. Accordingly, if the historian insists that he cannot meet the requirements laid down by the philosopher for explanation in history, the philosopher has no choice but to reply, "to that extent and in that respect, so much the worse for history." [26]

– V –

A self-conscious anti-Hempelian might summarize his objections to Hempel's proposal in the following way. First and worst of all, Hempel's scheme does not reflect what historians actually do when they explain. No matter how much and how carefully one reads works of history, one is not

---

[24] *Op. cit.*

[25] Without explicitly saying so, Hempel addresses himself to the view current around the turn of the century, that there were essentially two kinds of knowledge, that given by the *Naturwissenschaften* and that found in the *Geisteswissenschaften*. Hempel's effort to show that there was no essential difference (as far as knowledge is concerned) between these two sets of disciplines is an expression of the unity of science principle held by the members of the Vienna Circle.

[26] It might be remarked parenthetically that this is not as horrible as it seems. (1) There are lots of things men do that they might do more adequately and yet will never do with complete adequacy. (2) Historians do, among other things, explain—some more than others. It does not, however, seem to be the main business of historians to explain, but, rather, to describe. Explanation looms nowhere near as large in history as does the topic of historical explanation in philosophy.

likely to turn up Hempelian explanations. Indeed, there is more than one reason to suppose that historians could not, even if they so chose, always provide explanations of the Hempelian sort;[27] and some reasons may be given in support of the thesis that they never could. Secondly, even if an historian were to provide a set of statements which fulfilled all the requirements laid down by Hempel, it would by no means follow that this set would actually *explain*. Such a set would have the form of an explanation (according to Hempel) and, paradoxically enough, perhaps not satisfy a single reader. Thirdly (and this is what gives teeth to the first two objections), the anti-Hempelian would note that historians do, as a matter of fact, successfully explain many events, using methods quite different from those recommended by Hempel.

Given objections of this sort (and given the actual analyses made by anti-Hempelians on the basis of which these objections were formulated in the first place), we may single out three related principles or, better, considerations, which underlie and function in most of the analysis made by anti-Hempelians. By discussing each of them in turn, it may be possible to determine the "distance" from which these philosophers look upon historical explanation.

(1) In an important sense, the philosopher must not go beyond his data. The philosopher's job is to ascertain as clearly as he knows how the "logic" of historical explanations as they are actually offered. Just as it is the task of the topographer to reproduce the exact outline of a mountain —and not to recommend that the mountain's silhouette be converted into an isosceles triangle with an apex angle of exactly 45°,—so the philosopher must remain faithful to the "outline" of his data. In less metaphorical terms, there must be a sense (and not a trivial one) in which the analysandum and the analysans are equivalent. If the philosopher seeks clarity, what he wants to get clear is what historians actually do and not what they might do, no matter how good a thing it would be if historians followed such a recommendation. The primary role of philosophy is *de*scriptive and not *pre*scriptive.

(2) If analyses are to meet such requirements, the philosopher cannot approach the analysandum with theories of his own. His job (in this case) is to find out what *historians* do when they explain. To explain may very well be to provide knowledge; this fact, however, does not constitute a justification for coming to this act of historians with a *general theory* as to the nature of knowledge. It may well turn out that giving an historical explanation involves the stating of causes of an event.[28] But it is the philosopher's

27 Anti-Hempelians often forget that Hempel admits all this. Nevertheless, this first point becomes an objection when it is taken in conjunction with the second and (particularly) third objections and with the conception of analysis (to be discussed below) which underlies all of the objections of the anti-Hempelian.

28 Though, according to some anti-Hempelians, not all historical explanations are causal explanations by any means. See n. 32 below.

business to find out what the *historian* means by "cause" and not to impose some philosophic doctrine—Humean or Aristotelian—upon the historian's work. He must recognize that "cause" may well have a different meaning when used in the context of history from that which it has in science. It is up to him to *reveal* this meaning and not to change it.[29]

In the most extreme version of this view all of philosophy consists of analyses of this kind. According to it, the philosopher cannot rightfully come into possession of any theories of his *own*. To find out what an historical explanation is involves only a determination of how the term "explanation" is used in the "language game" played by historians. The introduction of theories derived from elsewhere—including, presumably, other language games—would be worse than inadvisable; it would patently contradict the philosopher's basic conviction about the nature of philosophy.

(3) So far restrictions have been emphasized: we have focused upon what the anti-Hempelians consider not to be a proper part of philosophic analysis. But important things must be said on the positive side as well. If philosophic analysis is analysis of a particular *language, all* of the facets of the language must be considered. The language of history is a language used by someone to speak to someone. In the specific case of an historical explanation, the historian explains the occurrence of an event to a certain audience. In doing so, he manifests certain intentions; in the audience to which he speaks he finds or arouses certain expectations. The enterprise as a whole is carried on to satisfy certain human interests. The anti-Hempelian emphatically rejects Hempelian austerity; he rules in, as part of the data to be clarified, the entire context in which historical explanations are offered. "Explanations are practical, context bound affairs. . . ."[30]

This can be put more formally. The Hempelian is interested only in the syntactics and the semantics of historical explanation. For him, the "logic" of a term has but these two dimensions. The anti-Hempelian's rejoinder is (in part) that such an analysis is most incomplete and hence in error. "Explanation is not a syntactical but a pragmatic notion."[31] Explanations are offered to provide understanding; and the understanding, as an event taking place in the hearer's mind, is a part of what must be considered by the analyst.

We can thus easily see that in several different ways the anti-Hempelian conducts his investigations from a position much closer to the data than does the Hempelian. His stance, one might say, is more empirical: he seeks to discover how "explanation" is actually used in the related set of contexts which make up the field of history. The immediately obvious manifestation of this "empiricism" is the procedure that is most frequently used: the citing of example after example of explanations, both "genuine" (that

---

[29] See, for example, Gardiner, *The Nature of Historical Explanation,* Parts I and III.
[30] Scriven, "Truisms as the Grounds for Historical Explanation," *loc. cit.,* p. 450.
[31] *Ibid.,* p. 452.

is, having actually occurred) and made-up for the occasion. Faithfulness to the data in all of their shifting complexity and sensitivity to the nuances of different uses are the prime desiderata of such an analysis.

Earlier we saw that the Hempelian's analysis is a product of an insight into usage *and* of general philosophic principles. Since there is considerable agreement among Hempelians about these principles, it comes as no surprise, then, that in this group there is also a large measure of agreement about a single model of historical explanation. Now, considering the many different contexts in which historical explanations are given, it becomes understandable why those who take into consideration the interest and knowledge of the hearer as well as the intention of the speaker should find that there are many different types of historical explanation.[32]

– VI –

If two people looked at the world wearing spectacles of differently colored glass, we should not be astonished at their not agreeing about the colors of the things they saw. Moreover, if they never removed their glasses, we should have no expectation that they would ever come to an agreement, no matter how strenuously they peered at the world's furniture. Hempelians and anti-Hempelians use different methods of analysis in their scrutiny of historical explanation.[33] Regardless of how diligently they continue their work, if each camp persists in its methods, we cannot expect them to arrive at even approximately similar conclusions. But clearly, the methods of analysis used are themselves subject to controversy. While so far we have given "persuasive expositions" of both methods, it will be well to conclude with a few partisan remarks.

But before giving full rein to partisanship, it must, I think be granted that both modes of philosophic analysis have led to important results. The actual work done in close to half a century provides sufficient evidence to refute a claim on either side that *the* philosophic method has at last been found. Yet from this it by no means follows that either method is equally appropriate for the solution of *any* kind of philosophic problem.

The method employed by the anti-Hempelians was developed as part of and in response to a conception of philosophy which sees as its function the resolution of certain kinds of puzzles. Language is infinitely complex, a fact which not only makes it a flexible instrument for a great variety of

[32] Not only do anti-Hempelians as a group suggest numerous "models" of historical explanations, but particular members of that group, notably Dray and Scriven, also see several types of historical explanation. See, for example, William Dray, " 'Explaining What' in History," in Gardiner, *Theories of History*, pp. 403–408 [Reprinted in this volume, pp. 343–348], and Scriven, "Truisms as the Grounds for Historical Explanations," *loc. cit.*

[33] These two methods correspond approximately to what P. F. Strawson calls the methods of the American School and the English School respectively. See his "Construction and Analysis," in *The Revolution in Philosophy* (London: Macmillan & Company, Ltd.; New York: St. Martin's Press, Inc., 1957), pp. 97–110.

purposes, but which also traps its users into strange corners from which escape comes hard. Not everyone is trapped, but most philosophers, at one time or another, have been led astray. For them this method proposes to point a way out: linguistic therapy. The point of this kind of analysis seems to be to find the linguistic roots of a puzzle: to determine where an analogy might have been misleading, where grammatical form might have hidden a different logical form, to spell out, in other words, how the trap was laid. When all this has been made obvious, the trap ceases to be a trap; the problem ceases to be.

Unquestionably there is evidence that a method sensitive to all the nuances of usage, a method which can note and measure every drift of language, is capable of achieving therapeutic results. But it is notorious that "the professional philosopher deliberately and methodically [causes] the headaches which he is subsequently going to cure." [34] Only when prodded and no longer plain, will the plain man come to doubt the existence of the external world; only when coaxed will he begin to wonder about the unity and continuity of the self. And, while such prodding and coaxing is often successful, it is by no means the case that every linguistic situation can be converted into a trap; not every question can be twisted into a puzzle.

Now, the question as to the nature of historical explanation does not seem to be a puzzle at all. To be sure, there are questions about history which have the quality of the kind of muddle for which the anti-Hempelian method seems suitable: Can history be objective? How can we know what is no more? and the like. The question about historical explanation, however, does not seem to involve this (to some) puzzling aspect of history; certainly the writers on this subject have not understood the problem to be so tainted. Moreover, in any form similar to the present one, the problem of historical explanation is not very ancient. It goes back no further than the latter part of the 19th century, when methodology (as distinct from epistemology) was isolated as a subject matter. In spite of the fact that Hempel tacitly addresses himself to this earlier discussion, neither he nor subsequent writers find, there or elsewhere, headaches to cure.

An anti-Hempelian, while perhaps admitting that his method first was and primarily is used to resolve puzzles, may still reply that this fact does not rule out the method's serviceability in problems of another kind. But this seems not to be the case; for when there is no puzzle to be resolved, it becomes difficult to see what philosophical task the method could accomplish. Historians, scientists, teachers, parents, and all the rest of mankind have used many different words in explaining many different things. No doubt, the number of explanatory patterns is finite and it might well be possible to discern different genera, species, and varieties of explanations. The resulting taxonomy might be of some interest to psychologists, soci-

---

[34] H. H. Price, "Clarity Is Not Enough," *Proceedings of the Aristotelian Society*, Supplementary Volume 19 (1945), p. 5

ologists, or what are known as communication specialists; some of these might even wish to go on to correlate different branches of the classification with the cultural background, education, sex, and annual income of the explainer. But why this should be of interest to the philosopher—any more than *any* report a scientist might give about the workings of men and nature—is indeed hard to see. Still less plausible is it that a philosopher should do such work himself. In the end, he lacks the training, as a philosopher, to do an adequate job.

And the continued use of this method on the problem of historical explanation inevitably leads to such a taxonomy. The reason is simple: there is nothing to stop it. On the one hand, there is no puzzle to be resolved. The need to do so would give direction to an analysis; the alleviation of the need would signal its conclusion. On the other hand, the method precludes philosophy's playing a systematic role. The analysis cannot be conducted with the aid of theories derived from other analyses, nor can it be a part of the task of the analysis to relate the analysandum to other concepts and principles, with a view to arriving at a systematic reconstruction of an entire domain. This leaves only the function of "revealing" by means of an indefinite number of examples. When order is made among the examples, we are well on the way to a taxonomy.

There is no doubt that the method of the Hempelians involves dangers. When one comes to a problem *with* theories, the possibility always exists that the analysandum is lost sight of in a network of concepts and principles. Reconstruction, if one does not take heed, may become construction. There is no magic formula for gauging the "distance" the philosopher must stand from the problem of his concern. When that interval shrinks to the vanishing point, philosophy, we have seen, becomes a mere reporting. When, through the interposition of too high a stack of theories, the "distance" becomes too great, philosophy relapses into the idle *a priorism* of ages hopefully gone by. Neither alternative is acceptable. The anti-Hempelians, however, come close to embracing the former, while the Hempelians are still trying to maintain distance without losing sight of their object.[35]

35 Much more attention must be paid to the characterization and justification of philosophic analysis at the "middle distance." For this, however, another opportunity must be taken, if only because such an analysis should not be carried on within the limited context provided by the problem of historical explanation.

[21] Explanation, Prediction, and "Imperfect" Knowledge

The Attack on the Deductive Model

Can we explain events after they happen which we could not have predicted beforehand? Do history and the other studies of man differ from the physical sciences in this respect? Do a man's character and motives satisfactorily explain his actions or do these in turn need explaining? Questions of this sort are raised, not for the first time, by certain recent criticisms of the so-called deductive model of explanation. This model holds, briefly, that to explain an individual fact we deduce it from one or more other such statements in conjunction with one or more generalizations or laws. A law, in turn, may be explained by deducing it from other laws. Prediction, upon the model, has the same logical form as explanation. In predicting something as yet unknown, one deductively infers it from particular facts and laws already known. We infer from given premises stating what is known, what so far has not been known, whether it be in the past, present, or future, or whether, as in the case of laws, time is irrelevant. It follows that if anything can be explained deductively by a set of premises after it has occurred, it could in principle have been predicted from these premises before the event. Nor does it make any difference whether the premises are statistical or deterministic. If they are deterministic, we may predict an individual event; if they are statistical, only statements about classes of events may be either explained or predicted. Virtually all those who accept the deductive model hold that it applies not only to physical but also to human phenomena, whether individual or social, whether in the past or in the present. Recently popularized among philosophers of history by a lucid exposition of Hempel's,[1] the deductive model traces its lineage through John Stuart Mill and David Hume back to Galileo.

Reprinted from *Minnesota Studies in the Philosophy of Science, Volume III*, edited by Herbert Feigl and Grover Maxwell. University of Minnesota Press, Minneapolis. © Copyright 1962 by the University of Minnesota. [This paper was read, in part, at the 1960 International Congress for Logic, Methodology, and Philosophy of Science held at Stanford University.]

[1] C. G. Hempel, "The Function of General Laws in History," *Journal of Philosophy*, 39:35–48 (1942), reprinted in *Theories of History*, P. Gardiner, ed. (Glencoe, Ill.: Free Press, 1959). Frequently cited also is the more detailed article by C. G. Hempel and P.

In physical science, ever since physicists abandoned the anthropomorphic-telelogical "why" in favor of lawful relations among relevant variables, explanation has meant deduction. John Stuart Mill, who had the clearest anticipatory vision of what a scientific study of man and society could be, extended the notion to these areas. The extension, always bitterly resented, is now once again under attack. A certain piquancy is added to the current attack by those who now attack the deductive model for the physical sciences as well. This global nature of the attack gives the current controversy its special interest. The assailants either radically reject the model *in toto* because it is *deductive,* or, more moderately, reject it not because it is deductive but because of the nature of the *premises* from which the deductions are allegedly made. In either case, the critics have given what appears to be a "new look" to all the old and tired arguments against a science of history and of man—the arguments from uniqueness, from freedom, from mind, from complexity, from values, and the rest. Nor is that all. The extremists challenge not only explanation by deduction but the very notion of valid deduction itself. I shall first discuss the more prevalent radical position of those who reject the standard model simply because it is deductive. Since there is a common core to the radical and the moderate views, it will then be possible to treat briefly of the more moderate criticism which attacks only the nature of the premises. It is indeed the broader philosophical implications of this common core, cutting much deeper than the issue at hand, that I am particularly concerned to exhibit as clearly as I can. The arguments of moderate and extremist alike arise from an overemphasis on language as it is used to communicate with others, to the neglect of language as it is used to describe the world. This preoccupation in turn results in a notion of "conceptual analysis" with philosophically untenable consequences. I shall try to show why this is so and, in particular, why the criticisms of the deductive model, based on this preoccupation and that notion, are without force.

The rejection, by the extremists, of deductive explanation is but part and parcel of a more sweeping rejection of formal logic. Three related arguments are used to support this double rejection. First, appealing to ordinary usage they find, to no one's surprise, that 'deductive' is applied to many different kinds of inference. Whenever locutions such as "because so and so, therefore," "this, so that," or "this involves that" occur, we may accordingly "properly speak of 'deductions.' " [2] 'Explain,' too, is revealed to have many different uses. The deductive model, assuming as it does the logician's notion of 'deduction' and a particular use of 'explain,' doubly affronts ordinary usage

---

Oppenheim, "The Logic of Explanation," in *Readings in the Philosophy of Science,* H. Feigl and M. Brodbeck, eds. (New York: Appleton-Century-Crofts, 1953). See also Bk. III, Ch. XII, ¶6 in J. S. Mill, *A System of Logic* (1843), Longmans, Green & Co., London and New York, 1947.

2 See G. Ryle, *The Concept of Mind* (London: Hutchinson, 1949), p. 300; S. Toulmin, *The Uses of Argument* (Cambridge: Cambridge University Press, 1958). p. 121.

and is, accordingly, doubly "irrelevant." Second, the critics deny that anything corresponding to the logician's narrow, tautological sense of 'deduction' actually occurs in common sense or in science. Since there is no
deduction, naturally there is no such thing as deductive explanation.
Finally, they maintain that an appeal to so-called conceptual analysis is as
conclusive as an appeal to logical truth. This third reason, as we shall see,
is the most fundamental of all.

Common-Sense Facts vs. Philosophical Claims

Do we ever predict what we cannot explain or explain what, before the
event, we cannot predict? We do it all the time. We predict a future event,
like the outcome of next week's election, even though we cannot deduce
it. Moreover, whatever the outcome, we then proceed to explain it. Of
course we do. We explain a man's sudden death by his being struck by
a car. The historian too explains past events that he is in no sense trying
to predict. To proclaim these uncontroversial common-sense facts is one
thing. To propound a philosophical thesis is quite another. At issue now
is the philosophical claim that accompanies the announcement of these
everyday "explainings" and "predictings." Specifically, the claim is that
no laws either are or need be deductively invoked, *either explicitly* or
implicitly, to permit the inference from some individual facts to another
which they explain or predict. Moreover, an appeal to laws is held to be
"wholly unnecessary" for identifying the causes of an event. The causes of
the Civil War, of my car breaking down, of why a test tube blew up, of a
carpet's being stained, all can be "understood" and understood with "primeval certainty" by the appropriate people, some of whom are simply
endowed with a "well-developed capacity for identifying causes," without
appealing, either implicitly or explicitly, to laws.[3] Marshaling the evidence
against the deductive model, with its implied symmetry between explanation and prediction, the critic comes triumphantly upon history. We are
even treated to a dithyramb on history as the "mother subject for explanations," just because it is no different from common sense.[4] Certainly, the
historian now often explains what he cannot predict. However, this obvious
fact does not in itself justify making history the paradigm case of "sound
explanation." Nor, of course, does the mere occurrence of deductive explanation and prediction in physical science, should one grant that it does
occur, *in itself* justify making physics the paradigm case, as is customary
with proponents of the deductive model. A philosophical thesis is not merely
a description of what does or does not happen to occur. My primary purpose is to examine the grounds for the philosophical claim that is associated

[3] M. Scriven, "Truisms as the Grounds for Historical Explanations," in *Theories of
History,* P. Gardiner, ed. (New York: The Free Press, 1959), p. 456 and *passim.*
[4] *Ibid.,* p. 458.

with, but I believe not supported by, appeal to certain indisputable facts of common sense. In the course of this examination, I shall also try to show how the deductive model can consistently account for these facts, as well as for the present and, for all we know, perhaps permanent situation in history and related areas.

The Appeal to Ordinary Usage and to "Understanding"

The assailants, probing the idiom, discover as many senses of 'explain' as there are possible answers in common speech to the question Why? In none of these senses do they discern any appeal to deduction in the logician's sense. We explain to a child how to multiply fractions; we teach him certain rules. We explain the meaning of one term, using others. We explain the structure of the ruling class of a given society—we describe a pattern. We explain the symbols of formal logic to a class—we describe what is made to stand for what. We explain the rules of chess. We explain a man's actions by pointing out his motives or his purposes. We explain the connection between the moon and the tides. Perhaps, in this case, we merely state a constant conjunction. Or we may derive it from the Newtonian law of gravitation in conjunction with certain other statements. And so on, and so on. The ordinary uses of 'explain' are manifold indeed. Only the last case involves deduction. So there is at least one case which does involve it. In spite of this case and in spite of the admitted multiplicity of uses, there is a drumming insistence that all of these uses of 'explain' are "essentially" the same—that there is a true meaning of 'explain' common to all of them, except, ironically, deduction. This true meaning is *"the* ordinary sense," the only one which *"really* explains." [5] Ordinary use is thus not merely described. It is appealed to as the standard that everything else must meet if it is to "count" as an explanation.

Just as individual facts, like the Civil War or a car breaking down, can be "understood" without appeal to laws, so with other things. A teacher explaining to a student how to multiply fractions, an art critic explaining why one painting is better than another, a nuclear physicist explaining the principle of complementarity, a father explaining the rules of chess to his son—each, like the mechanic explaining why a car broke down, has his own way of telling whether or not the other person understands what is being explained to him. What is the sense of 'explain' common to all these various uses—explaining facts, rules, a symbolism, how to do something, and so on? The answer, though disappointing in its triteness, reveals the difference between the study of language as a medium of communication and its study as a description of the world.

Every teacher has a way of finding out whether or not a student has

5 W. Dray, *Laws and Explanation in History* (London: Oxford University Press, 1957), p. 79; Scriven, in Gardiner, p. 449.

understood what he has been talking about. This is "the ordinary sense," the "essential sameness" of meaning that preoccupies the critics of the deductive model. Has someone understood what we have said? Is it "intelligible" to him? To find out, we ask him certain questions, depending upon the kind of thing we are testing his understanding about.[6] If he answers appropriately, then we have successfully communicated with him. This psychological sense of understanding what is conveyed by a communication does indeed underlie most of our ordinary uses of 'explain.' The critics, understandably concerned to deny that they are engaged in factual inquiry, insist that this meaning of 'intelligibility,' 'understanding,' or 'explain' is not psychological. To be sure, one of the ordinary uses of 'psychological' is as a synonym for 'mental'—something going on in someone's mind. Another is of something "subjective"—varying from individual to individual. The critics protest that they mean nothing either mental or subjective, in this sense, and hence nothing "psychological." They mean rather a behavioristic test. We can tell that someone understands something by what he says or does. It is thus allegedly not psychological because it is behavioristic, not mentalistic, and it is not subjective because we can devise a test by which anyone can tell whether any other fellow understands or not.

Only if one is frozen in the science of the nineteenth century can one believe that psychology is concerned with the "working of men's minds" rather than their behavior, verbal or otherwise. If one also happens to feel that a science of psychology is unnecessary because we already "know well enough" by "ordinary good sense" [7] why people behave as they do, then one may persuade oneself that the suggested test for "understanding" is not psychological. But this is verbal magic. How we learn, communicate by means of, and react to, language as part of our social environment are all facts about human behavior. The appeal to ordinary usage and the interest in communication leads to a notion of 'explanation' that depends not upon the way the world is, the connections among things, but upon *something in us,* upon the way we respond in the game of question-and-answer that we play, not with the world, but with each other. Later on I shall have more to say about the relevance for the attack on the deductive model of this curious combination of behaviorism with a rejection of the science of psychology. For the present, it seems clear that, like the word or not, this remains a psychological sense of 'explain.' And this sense of the term does not tell us what *justifies* saying that an event happened one way rather than another, nor—apart from a quaint appeal to "judgment" and special talents—does it tell us how it happens that we are able frequently to make correct inferences from what we know to something

[6] Scriven, in Gardiner, p. 452.

[7] Ryle, *The Concept of Mind,* pp. 52, 324, 326. An incisive critique of some of Ryle's views on psychology may be found in M. Mandelbaum's "Professor Ryle and Psychology," *Philosophical Review,* 67: 522–530 (1958).

past, present, or future that we do not yet know. In other words, it doesn't answer the philosophical questions about explanation and prediction.

Language as Communication vs. Language as Description

Among all possible means of communication, language is the richest and most subtle. By language we convey to others our desires, plans, attitudes, and, among other things, information about how to do certain things or about the way things are or seem to be. How we learn a language and, having done so, contrive to communicate successfully with each other are, to repeat, questions about human thought or behavior in social situations. They are thus to be answered by sociopsychological investigation, whether this be our everyday experience or the controlled methods of the social sciences. Speculation from, or analysis of, how we speak can at best offer cues to the factually correct answers to questions about the so-called higher symbolic processes which are involved in linguistic behavior. However, since much of what we try to convey to each other by means of language is information about the world, language also has a descriptive function. No matter how complicated the processes by which we understand one another may be, they can only occur because language is also used to describe the world, including ourselves as part of it. The study of language as description is the study of terms and statements as they are used to make such assertions, no matter how we came to acquire these uses. Given this language that, indubitably, has been socially learned, philosophical questions may be asked about it. By analysis of the language itself we try to see what there is about it that, *once it has been understood,* enables it to tell us something about the world and also what it actually does tell us about the world's content or its form.

A physicist's published report of the theoretical significance of an experiment and his laboratory conversation are two quite different things. The latter is elliptical and context bound in a way his report cannot be. He may "explain" an observed phenomenon to a co-worker by simply mentioning some other fact, very likely something that he has done. The co-worker will "understand" him. The information necessary to this understanding is supplied by the total context within which the conversation occurs, both the social situation itself and the knowledge the two men share. The published report, however, will have to be considerably more circumstantial about the connection between the experiment, the observations, and what it was performed to test. Moreover, the report will use terms with constant meanings throughout. The sentences will be complete in the sense that they will be true or false, independently of the time or place at which they are read, unlike, say, "The light just went out."

Since the physicist writes for other physicists, even his report may not explicitly mention all the information that justifies certain statements, for again there is a context of shared knowledge that may be taken for granted.

But the obvious differences between the explicitness of the report and laconic laboratory conversation makes clear what a complete report would be like and, under some circumstances, must be like. Only a complete report, including that which is spoken as well as that which is left unspoken, presents the observational and logical grounds for any claim. Ordinary communication relies heavily on the linguistic and nonlinguistic context. To examine language as description, this context must be supplied. A context-free language is artificial only in the sense that the physicist's report is "artificial" compared with his conversation. It makes explicit what, in ordinary communication, is supplied by the total context. By filling in the context, we know what it is that concepts are being used to refer to and what statements about the world ordinary sentences are being used to make.

The logician uses a similarly improved language to explicate the notions of logical truth, deductive proof, logical impossibility, and the rest. The logical notions articulate the criteria by which, in common sense and in science, we are *justified* in asserting that someone is being inconsistent or that an observation refutes a generalization. The logician's improved language is useful to the philosopher precisely because and only insofar as it is a reconstruction of a large part of the language that we speak. The logician's notions of "logical truth," "deduction," and the rest, correspond to, though they do not duplicate, certain indispensable concepts in ordinary use. The logician's term 'analytic,' for instance, is not identical with the ordinary uses of 'necessary,' but it corresponds to the use in such statements as 'It is necessary that white horses are white.' The philosophical logician thus clarifies *one* use in common speech of 'necessary' and, the same time, shows how it differs from other uses of the term, as in 'It is necessary that all men die.'

Why Explanation Must Be Deductive

Grant for the moment that deduction is one core meaning of explanation, at least within science. This is an anthropological fact like any other about the linguistic behavior of a certain group of people. Why give this use pride of place in preference to all others? Not, as some think, because of some scientistic prejudice in favor of physics as the model inquiry. Rather, it goes the other way. Physics is an advanced and "model" science precisely because it does provide deductive explanation and prediction of its phenomena. To show why this is so requires explication of *this* use of 'explain.' The philosopher surely is not merely an anthropologist describing the linguistic habits of the natives—whether they are plain men, members of the class of historians or of physical scientists—and what different things among them "count" as explanations. Such description is at best preliminary to the task of exhibiting the structure of a reasoned explanation, showing which structure logically justifies that which is to be explained. In philosophy and elsewhere an appeal either to a definition or to a logical truth is conclusive. One does not quarrel with a statement which is true merely by virtue of a convention about the use of words. Similarly, if a statement is backed up by reference to other statements from which it logically follows, one does not argue, as long as one accepts the truth of the premises.

The purely verbal case is too trivial and obvious to need elaborating, but what makes the appeal to premises conclusive? Briefly, because the conditional corresponding to the premises and conclusion of the argument is a tautology or logical truth. In a context-free language we can formally characterize the notion of "tautology." Consider "It's raining or it isn't." One must eliminate vagueness—the drizzle beloved of students—and the event must be located in time and space before we can characterize the statement as a tautology in the strict sense. Only when these are implicit in context is the statement even an everyday tautology. For that matter, as has been insisted, only then is the expression even a statement. Only for *statements* can we state the criteria, which are characteristics *of the statements themselves* and not of anyone's responses to them, that make them tautologies or logical truths. If the generalizations and individual statements of fact serving as premises are accepted as true, then, because of the tautological connection, the conclusion *must* be true. This and this alone is the virtue of deductive explanation. Once such terms as "must," "guarantees," and "logically implies" are clarified, then it is clear why deduction and deduction alone "justifies" the conclusion. At the same time, it is also clear why any other kind of explanation of individual facts cannot possess this conclusiveness. Either the explanation is deductive or else it does not justify what it is said to explain.

All this is not to "set limits" to what may constitute a sound explanation, but to explicate *one* sense of sound "explanation" which is the only one that is conclusive for the reasons just mentioned. For the philosopher concerned with language as description, the task is to show what, so to speak, in the facts themselves, or, to be accurate, *in the statements asserting them,* rather than in the mind or behavior of a particular person or group of persons, makes one or more statements a "reason," in a precise logical sense of reason, for one or more others. What in the statements themselves makes one statement a prediction from others, one confirm a general hypothesis, another refute it? Deductive explanation is the only answer to this question, insofar as language is used to speak, not just about how we speak, but about the world.

One particular appeal to ordinary usage to bolster the claim that scientific explanation is not deductive verges on the bizarre. Reading 'deductive' to mean 'syllogistic' in the Aristotelian sense, it is concluded that scientific explanation, since not syllogistic in form, is not deductive.[8] Explanation in science is indeed not syllogistic, at least in the most interesting cases,

---

[8] Scriven, in Gardiner, p. 462; S. Toulmin, *Philosophy of Science* (London: Hutchinson, 1953), p. 25.

namely, those involving quantification, relations, or both. But I think it may be said safely that however the half-educated plain man may use the term, no scientist since Galileo has so narrowly conceived "deduction" and certainly no logician for almost a century. Yet, insofar as these critics concede a correlate to strict deduction in ordinary speech, including science, they perceive it to mean something like Barbara. Hence, if not Barbara, then not deductive. Words *do* mean only what we say they mean. But one use of a term hardly justifies the assertion that nothing corresponds to another and different use of that same term.

Like 'deductive,' the word 'explain' has, as we saw, many uses. To assail the deductive model because it does not apply to all these uses is irrelevant at best, puerile punning at worst.[9] Deduction is not put forward as the model for those uses of 'explain' when we speak, say, of explaining (i.e., describing) the structure of the Egyptian ruling class, a symbolism, or how to play chess. The model is proposed for only one but one very important use of 'explain.' In particular, the occurrence of certain events, like an eclipse or an earthquake, can, upon the model, sometimes in practice and always in principle be explained and predicted deductively. Practically, we can both explain and predict the occurrence of an eclipse. We can only explain the earthquake after it happens. The critics' most plausible case rests, of course, on such all-too-common "earthquake" situations. But they are not content to rest on such cases. Though conceding at one place that Newton "did achieve a large number of mathematically precise and scientifically illuminating deductions [*sic!*] from his theory," this is, to put it moderately, not the prevailing tenor of the argument.[10] What one hand gives, the other snatches away. Or perhaps it was only Newton himself who could accomplish the feat of deduction. In any case, the claim is that not even in physics do we really have deductive explanation. Apart from the untenable, because false, appeal to usage, the argument has, so to speak, two facets or takes two different forms. The first grants that laws *do* play a role in some explanations, but such explanations are allegedly still not really deductive. The other holds that explanation of an individual fact is always by other such facts without the intermediary in any way of laws. After a few preliminary comments about the structure of classical physical theory, I shall discuss these two different arguments in the order mentioned.

"Perfect" Knowledge and Deductive Explanation

Celestial mechanics is a paradigm of what has usefully been called "perfect knowledge." [11] Nonatomic thermodynamics is another. In the first

9 Scriven, in Gardiner, pp. 463, 468.

10 M. Scriven, "Explanation and Prediction in Evolutionary Theory," *Science,* 130: 477 (1959).

11 The distinction between "perfect" and "imperfect" knowledge is Bergmann's. See G. Bergmann, this volume, pp. 415–436.

theory, mass, velocity, and distance are variables that interact only with each other; in the second, volume, temperature, pressure, and a few other variables of this sort do the same. In each case, no variables that in fact make a difference have been omitted from the expressions of the theory. These theories are *complete*. Nothing that happens at any other time or place than that being considered affects the behavior of the properties with which the theory is concerned, or, at worst, we know how to take account of these outside influences in our predictions or computations. The system, in other words, is *closed*. The laws of these theories are *process laws,* that is, the values of *any* one variable at any time can be computed by means of the laws from the values of *all* the others at any other time. We can predict the future course of all our variables or compute their entire past history; we know how changes in any one variable produce changes in any other; we know to what extent by tinkering with the system we can bring about desired changes, to what extent we are powerless.

Such knowledge may, not unreasonably, be called "perfect," for there is clearly nothing else we could possibly want to know, as far as these variables are concerned. Nor is there any unreasonable sense of "perfection" implied by this notion. Every measurement has its limits of accuracy. Inductive generalization may be overgeneralization, as indeed we now know about the Newtonian law of gravitation. These frailties are common to all empirical science and do not affect the nature of the deductions we can make from such theories, when we assume that the laws are true and that our measurements are accurate.

From the Newtonian law of gravitation in conjunction with the positions of the sun and the planets at any one time, we can predict or postdict their position at any other time. Thus we can deductively predict future eclipses or explain present and past one. The laws of Newton may be applied, of course, to a vast number of vastly different situations, terrestrial as well as celestial. If we know enough about the initial conditions, then we can predict what will happen. Using these laws, we can predict how long it will take an elephant to slide down a green, grassy hill, if we know only his mass, the angle of inclination of the hill, and the coefficient of friction. Or we can predict where and when a cannon ball will land, if we know but a few relevant variables. In some cases, where we fail to predict, as when a bridge collapses under a certain load, we could have done so, if we had taken the trouble to find out the state of the system, that is, the initial conditions, before the catastrophe. If we did not take the trouble or if it was too complicated to do so, then, after the event, we deductively explain it by reference to the laws and to what the conditions must have been to make the bridge give way.

"Certainty" of Premises vs. Deductive Validity

How, then, in the light of all this can the critics nevertheless maintain that explanations in physics are not deductive? The physicist, it is pointed out, might be wrong either in deciding that a particular universal law applies to a given set of conditions—whether or not they are within the scope of the law—or in describing the initial conditions. The physicist must, therefore, like the historian, use "judgment" and even "empathy" rather than formal deduction in making his inferences.[12] Or so the argument goes.

However, the choice of premises, or even the use of false ones, is not in the strict sense a logical matter and does not affect the validity of a deduction. The validity of the deduction itself is here confused with the error of using, say, a first approximation like Boyle's law where only a more general gas law would do, or in believing that the effects of friction are negligible when in fact they are not. Once the scientist has used his "judgment," which is indeed a psychological matter dependent on his skill and training, then the deduction follows. The explanation *is* deductive, whether or not we are "certain" about the premises, either the law or the initial conditions. A prediction in the same circumstances is also deductive. The scientist, in fact, tests his judgment by deductively inferring what *must* be the case if what he believes to be the applicable laws and the true initial conditions really are so. Premises deductively imply a conclusion no matter how certain or unsure we may be about their truth. Logical entailment (or inconsistency) is a property of the statements themselves, not of our knowledge about them. If the prediction were not deductive, then there would be no reason why its failure should cast doubt upon the premises. In fact, it shows that at least one of them is false. In theoretical science, when a prediction fails, this generally, though not necessarily, casts doubt upon the laws. In engineering or applied science, on the other hand, the initial conditions become suspect. Far from requiring "exact truth" for its premises, all that the deductive model requires is exact *statement* of a hypothesis about their truth. The hypothesis is then tested by the "exact deduction" which, I am sorry to have to repeat, does not mean and never has meant only the syllogistic deduction with which the critics sometimes equate it.

Hempel's careful statement of the deductive model unfortunately uses an illustration that, from the point of view of the principle involved, is inadequate. Understandably, for expository purposes, trying to avoid the mathematical complications of those areas where perfect or near-perfect knowledge exists, he uses a homely, everyday illustration, the breaking of a car's radiator in freezing weather. Hempel's so-called failure here is not one of deduction, but a failure of complete knowledge. He cannot state

[12] Scriven, in Gardiner, pp. 459, 462.

all the initial conditions that will permit him to deduce that the radiator broke. If one appreciates that philosophical explication is explication of the principles involved, this is no failure at all. Once again, only because there is a deductive connection between the laws of physics and, among other things, the state of the weather and insufficient antifreeze in the radiator, have we any good reason to assert that the cold rather than the sparrows who daily perch upon the hood explains the breakage. The physicist does not judge "inductively . . . what the explanation is." [13] Correctly stated, he makes an inductive judgment about the premises. And to make this correction is not, as is claimed, to "convert" either the premises or the judgment into a deduction. We want to know whether a given statement is deductively entailed by certain others. This is a logical question. To import considerations about what the scientist happens to know, certainly or otherwise, or even, if knowing, what he happens to assert explicitly or to "quote," is to doubly muddy the waters by first introducing irrelevant psychological factors and then confusing context-bound sentences and complete statements.

In his zeal to confute the deductive model, Scriven makes the remarkable statement that even in those parts of physics where what I called "perfect knowledge" exists, namely, classical thermodynamics, "*deduction of the exact* values to be explained from such laws is a matter of chance." [14] This conjures up an image of physicists writing down conclusions at random. But this is not quite what happens. A quantitative science uses measurement to obtain the values of its variables. Measurement, as I mentioned before, has its limitations. Every measurement has a so-called error component associated with it. This "error" is the deviation from a mean value that can be expected under repeated measurements of the same variable. In other words, in repeated measurements of, say, the length of a bar, the quantity obtained as a result of the measurements will tend to cluster around a certain value. The result of a measurement is thus not a single value but a frequency distribution determined by the nature of the measurement. This means that the premise expressing the measured initial conditions always has a statistical component. It means further that the conclusion deduced from such premises must also be about a frequency distribution, not a single value. There is no deduction "by chance" or any other way of a single, exact value. There is instead a strict deduction, by the probability calculus, of a so-called "chance" variable, that is, a frequency distribution, which is quite another thing.[15]

But we have only begun to probe the depths of confusion that these critics display about the use of statistical premises. To probe deeper, we must turn to the notion of "imperfect" knowledge. Moreover, the attack

13 *Ibid.*, p. 457.
14 *Ibid.*, p. 460.
15 An excellent discussion of this issue and others related to the comments below on the use of statistical premises may be found in P. E. Meehl, *Clinical versus Statistical Prediction* (Minneapolis: University of Minnesota Press, 1954); cf. especially pp. 56ff.

on the deductive model derives its prima-facie plausibility from those areas about which we have only imperfect knowledge. It is well to be clear, therefore, about what we can and cannot do when "imperfection" prevails.

"Imperfect" Knowledge and Deductive Explanation

Perfect knowledge is the ideal, actualized only in certain branches of physical science. Elsewhere, as in biology, economics, sociology, psychology, and the social sciences generally, knowledge is conspicuously "imperfect." We do not know all the variables that affect, say, a person's resistance to disease, or his behavior under certain circumstances, or the price fluctuations of certain commodities. Our theories in these areas are not complete, nor do we know fully the conditions for closure of such systems. Since we do not know all the factors that make a difference to the variables with which we are concerned, we also have no process laws. From the values of the variables at any *one* time, we cannot predict their value at *all* other times. Yet, the social and biological sciences have developed techniques to compensate for lapses in closure and completeness. The most important of these techniques is the use of statistical concepts. Which face will turn up when a die is cast is determined by numerous causes—the center of gravity of the die, the force with which it is thrown, and so on. An attempt to calculate the results of each throw by means of the laws of mechanics is practically hopeless because of the difficulty in precisely measuring all the initial conditions. Instead, we represent, as it were this multiplicity of causes by a probability distribution for the attribute in question. The use of the statistical concept marks our ignorance of all the influencing factors, a failure in either completeness or closure or, usually, both. Similarly, the social scientist, deliberately selecting for study fewer factors than actually influence the behavior in which he is interested, shifts his goal from predicting individual events or behaviors to predicting the frequency with which this kind of behavior occurs in a large group of individuals possessing the circumscribed number of factors. This use of statistical concepts, due to lapses in closure and completeness, differs from their use for errors of measurement. Even assuming perfect observation, they would still be necessary.

Statistical knowledge is not the only kind of imperfect knowledge. We also have nonquantified imperfection. Any law, whether it be about physical objects, persons, or societies, is "imperfect" if it does not permit us to compute (predict or postdict) the state of the system, either an individual or a group, at *any* moment from its state at *one* moment. Consider the assertion that a boom in trade is always followed by slump and depression. This is imprecise with respect to time, for it does not tell us exactly when the later events will follow the earlier one, nor how long each will last.

Moreover, its concepts have a fringe of vagueness that make it difficult to tell precisely when we have instances of the kinds of events mentioned. In psychology, the laws of learning that make essential use of the past history of a person in order to predict his future behavior are also imperfect. The equilibrium laws of physics, whose concepts are not vague, are nevertheless imperfect because though they tell us that under certain conditions no change in certain respects will occur, they do not tell us what will happen if these conditions are not fulfilled. To be sure, the equilibrium laws of physics are derivable from the process laws of the theory, but for those of economics no such perfect laws are available. In general, imperfect laws are indefinite with respect to time, or hedged in by qualification, or they are statistical.

The inadequacies of such "imperfect" knowledge do not affect the possibility of deduction. Not only do we sometimes know enough to deduce some of these laws, like the law of the lever or certain statistical laws of physics, from process laws, but all kinds of deductions can be made *from the imperfect laws themselves,* whether or not they are in turn deducible from something else. An explanation utilizing imperfect laws as premises is not the same as Hempel's "explanation sketch." The latter he describes as "a more or less vague indication of the laws and initial conditions considered as relevant, and it needs 'filling out' in order to turn into a full-fledged explanation." [16] Imperfect laws, as here defined, need not be vague or, as explicit premises from which deductions can be made, incomplete. For instance, 'All men are mortal,' though universal, is imperfect by our criterion, since from it we can neither explain nor predict a man's death at a particular time. But such nonquantitative universal generalizations, as well as many laws of the biological and social sciences or statistical laws generally, are not necessarily "vague." Nor do they necessarily need "filling out" before they can be used for significant deductions or "full-fledged" explanations.

On the other hand, it is indeed true, as I illustrate later, that we often have to make guesses as to the appropriate imperfect laws, about either individuals or groups of individuals, that will permit us to explain or predict a given event. However, the deductive model by no means requires that premises be the deterministic process laws of perfect knowledge. Once this is grasped, the admitted difficulty in formulating so-called universal laws, of which the critics make so much, no longer appears insuperable. They set a demand that is not logically required by the model. After all, deductive inference was with us centuries before Newton formulated the first process laws.

"The criterion of deduction must be abandoned if the criterion of universal (non-statistical) hypotheses is abandoned." Moreover, if we only have statistical knowledge, then though we cannot predict, we can use such knowledge to explain with "certainty" the occurrence of individual

16 Hempel in Gardiner, p. 351 and this volume, p. 410.

events.[17] Neither of these claims, as I have just suggested, is justified. A statistical law asserts that if each member of a certain class has a certain attribute, then a certain fraction or percentage of them will have another attribute. For instance, "60 per cent of all cigarette smokers develop lung cancer." This is a generalization or universal statement, for it says of all cigarette smokers, past, present, and future, those observed and those as yet unobserved, that 60 per cent of this group will suffer from cancer of the lungs.[18] Like all statistical generalizations, the evidence for it is a finite number of cases. The statement asserts, however, that in the class of all individuals of a certain kind, a particular attribute will turn up with a specified frequency. In this respect, a statistical generalization is as "universal" as a so-called deterministic or nonstatistical law stating that each and every individual having a certain character will also have another. In both cases, the law goes far beyond the evidence. If it did not, but was just a summary of observations, it would have neither explanatory nor predictive power. The difference between them is not that one permits prediction while the other does not, but in the nature of what can be predicted or, what amounts to the same, in how they are tested.

From a deterministic law, given the initial conditions, we can predict an individual event. From a statistical law and its initial conditions (the occurrence of a large group of cigarette smokers), we can predict only a so-called mass event, that is, the frequency with which an attribute will be distributed in the given class. If an unbiased coin is tossed a large number of times, then the frequency with which heads will turn up is 50 per cent. This says something about the class of *all tosses* of a coin, though it says nothing about what will happen in any particular toss. Similarly, the lung-cancer generalization says nothing about any particular cigarette smoker, though it says a good deal about the class of all cigarette smokers. From a statistical law, then, nothing can be predicted about an individual event. On the other hand, neither can we explain an individual event by reference to such a law.

It is embarrassing to rehearse these elementary matters. But the critics force such rehearsal upon one, for they argue to the contrary. Consider the nonquantified, implicitly statistical statement that Scriven calls a "hypothetical probability prediction," namely, that if a flood occurs, then animals who can swim will be more likely to survive than those who cannot.[19] Scriven notes that unless we can predict the flood, we cannot predict which animals will survive. However, he believes that, in retrospect,

---

[17] Scriven, in Gardiner, pp. 457, 464; and in *Science,* 130:479, 480.

[18] For the sake of an illustration, I have stated the hypothesis in this very alarming way, just as one might say that 60 per cent of all Norwegians are blond. Realistically, the actual lung-cancer hypothesis is a bit less terrifying, asserting a comparison between smokers and nonsmokers and that a higher percentage of the former than the latter will develop lung cancer. The relevant logic of the situation is identical in either case. See the examples that follow.

[19] In *Science,* 130:478.

"we can *explain why* certain animals and plants have survived even when we could not have *predicted that* they would." In fact, given such a law, even if we could have predicted the flood, we could not have predicted anything about individual animals. We could have predicted only that more animals who can swim would survive than those who could not, that is, an implicit frequency distribution. By the same token, we cannot explain why a particular animal happened to survive. For, as Scriven says, there may be many other unknown factors besides swimming ability that contribute to survival. Our knowledge is incomplete. That, indeed, is why we can only state a "hypothetical probability prediction" or statistical law. In other words, though we can explain and, moreover, explain deductively why more fishes than chipmunks survive, we *cannot* explain why a particular fish survived. Since many do not, the "explanation" in terms of swimming alone is clearly inconclusive, far from "certain," no matter how plausible it may appear.

From statistical generalizations, we do not deduce "with probability" that a certain event will occur, rather we deduce exactly the relative frequency or "probability" with which an event will occur in a certain group. Similarly, contrary to what Scriven maintains, both statistical and deterministic laws are falsified if the prediction fails.[20] The difference is only in the falsifying event. In the statistical case, the failure, not of an individual event, but of an attribute to occur with a certain frequency in a "mass event" falsifies the law. If our generalization is not quantified and says merely that one event is "more likely" than another, then if in other large samples that event does not turn up more times, the law is falsified. If of a specified large group of cigarette smokers, satisfying certain conditions, only 50 per cent develop lung cancer before their death, then the "law" has been falsified. The use of statistical hypotheses does not, therefore, require abandoning deduction. Quite the contrary. Just as in the deterministic case, without deduction we could neither test statistical hypotheses nor, for that matter, have any rational grounds for, say, recommending a decrease in cigarette smoking or, to change the example, to innoculate our children against poliomyelitis. No doubt we would much prefer to know that each and every child receiving a certain vaccine is immune to the disease, or the exact conditions under which cancer develops in a particular person. Yet, statistical knowledge is not to be scorned though it is imperfect rather than perfect. It is far from valueless to know the factors statistically correlated to the frequency of occurrence of an event. And it is the exact deductions from such knowledge that make it valuable.

[20] Just as deterministic laws cannot be conclusively *verified*, statistical laws, by their nature, cannot be conclusively *falsified*. Accepting an observed frequency in a sample as the true probability requires an induction that this frequency will persist for indefinitely large samples; this may not be correct. Lack of conclusiveness, however, does not mean that we may not have good evidence either for accepting a deterministic law or for rejecting a statistical one. Conclusiveness, again, is not required of the premises but only of the connection between premises and conclusion.

Scriven's claim that statistical premises nondeductively permit us to explain individual events rests on no firmer foundation than converting a specious plausibility into a "certainty." But he also maintains that we can explain individual events without recourse to laws at all. In particular, an appeal to laws is held to be "wholly unnecessary" for identifying the causes of an event. Let us see.

Explanation by 'Causes' vs. Explanation by Laws

"We can explain but not predict whenever we have a proposition of the form 'The only cause of X is A,' for example, 'The only cause of paresis is syphilis.' " [21] Given A, we cannot predict X, for only a few cases of A develop X. Only A in conjunction with certain unknown conditions is followed by X. Therefore, Scriven maintains, given a case of A, "on the evidence" we must predict that X will not occur. He is mistaken. "On the evidence" we are in no position to predict any such thing. No such prediction is *logically* justified, no matter how soothing or useful it may be, any more than we can predict of any particular cigarette smoker that he will or will not get cancer. To make his prediction, Scriven explicitly uses the premise that only a few A's develop X. Now, if we make the decision, as is customary when action is necessary, always to assume that the statistically more likely case will occur, then of course we can predict that X will not occur. But, then, having made that assumption, the prediction of the nonoccurrence of X follows *deductively* from these premises. True, we cannot predict, under the hypothesis given, that X *will* occur, but when it does we can explain it. However, as we shall see, the deductive model can account for this practical asymmetry.

The sentence "The only cause of X is A" needs considerable unpacking. Scriven, believing that "cause" is an unanalyzable concept that everyone just naturally understands, denies any need for unpacking. He can therefore maintain that such sentences present instances where we can "explain what we could not have predicted, *even if we had had* the information about the antecedent conditions." Or, as he goes on to say, "sometimes the kind of correlation we need for prediction is absent, but a causal relationship can be identified." [22] The only way Scriven persuades himself that he can explain an event that could not even in principle be predicted is by leaving "causal" statements wholly unanalyzed. Despite the confident use of the causal idiom in everyday speech, we may still significantly ask under what conditions statements like "C is a cause of E" are true or false. I shall not take the time here to exhibit the problematic nature of the notion of "cause." Nor do I believe that to most this needs exhibiting. How then must the statement be unpacked?

[21] Scriven, in *Science,* **130**:480.
[22] *Ibid.*

To say "The only cause of X is A" is *at least* to affirm the law that X never occurs without A. In other words, A is a necessary condition for X, or "Whenever we have X, then we also have A." It is also, however, to say *more,* namely, that there is a complex of conditions, of which A is always one, under which X occurs; that is, certain other factors, b, c, d, *and* A are sufficient for X. In other words, A is a necessary condition and also one of several jointly sufficient conditions. This indeed is a situation in which we speak of one event as the "cause" of another. As is obvious, this causal imputation is far from being independent of any laws, known or surmised. By hypothesis, we do not know the other sufficient conditions. If we knew them, then deductive explanation *and* prediction would follow directly from a statement of the necessary and sufficient conditions. However, since we do not know the sufficient conditions, how do we account for the fact that actually we would normally explain X by A? Our only justification, and in fact the only way anyone, including Scriven, does justify doing this, is by implicitly adding to our knowledge of the necessary-condition law, our "guess" about the sufficient-condition law. Knowing that both X and A have occurred, we assume the presence of the unspecifiable b, c, and d. The explanation of X then follows deductively. That is *why* we accept A as an explanation of X. In order to predict X from A, the unknown factors must also be specified and this we cannot do. The asymmetry exists in practice, but not in principle. Nor is this an "unhelpful" sense of 'in principle.' For only by exhibiting the form of the argument that would, if we knew b, c, and d, permit the prediction, can we clarify why the purported explanation really does state "why" X occurred.

This explanation implicitly assumed that certain unspecifiable events had occurred. Even more frequently, perhaps, the implicit premise is that certain easily specifiable events did *not* occur. We explain a man's death as due to his being struck by an automobile. This is not because we grasp the meaning of the term "cause," [23] but because we know a law to the effect that if anyone is struck by a car, then he will be either killed or badly hurt. This is imperfect because, among other things, it does not tell us *which* alternative will occur. We therefore cannot predict the death from the law and the fact that he was hit by a car. But knowing it and, therefore, knowing also that the second alternative (or whatever others there may be) did not occur, the death follows deductively from the law, the initial conditions, and the denial of the alternative. The explanation of the event is conclusive because, given the explicit and *implicit* premises, it must have occurred. Clearly, if we knew the implicit premise before the event, it could be predicted. In very many cases where we know such "disjunctive" laws, we can in fact also eliminate all but one of the alternatives.

[23] *Ibid.*

Explanation and Imperfect Knowledge of History and Society

Consider now the perhaps more radical situation, where an event in the past, for which there is no question of predicting, is to be explained. Every day we give such *post hoc* explanations of unpredicted events. The issue is not whether or not we do so, but whether or not the deductive model can account for these explanations. We have already seen some cases where it can. But let us examine events more properly historical and social. Take an easy case first. The unpredicted Lisbon earthquake occurred. We explain the consequent misery and wreckage by reference to it.[24] Of course we do. Furthermore, we do so deductively. From the law 'Earthquakes lead to misery and wreckage' and the now known initial condition, namely, the earthquake, there is no problem about explaining the misery and wreckage. The explanation of the event after the fact is clearly deductive, by means of a law, not without it. It is no miracle or accidental conjunction of events that misery accompanied the Lisbon earthquake; we expect it to do so in all earthquakes. Only because we know that earthquakes lead to destruction, floods, and so on, which in turn result in human misery, does the earthquake explain the misery. Otherwise, we might as well say that the Lisbon earthquake was just an incidental accompaniment of the misery. Without the law, the explanation is inconclusive; maybe we can sometimes have earthquakes in heavily populated areas without misery and wreckage. Only because of the deductive connection can we say it *must* have been so. Thus only the deductive connection explains the event. But we did not and cannot predict either the earthquake or, *ipso facto*, the misery. Yet, surely an effort of will is needed to doubt that, even though our recent record is not markedly more notable than at the time of Lisbon, we might someday know enough geology to predict earthquakes. Our knowledge in such matters is imperfect: we know that areas of a certain geological structure can expect earthquakes, but we cannot predict exactly when they will happen. The ex post facto explanation is nevertheless deductive. The principle of the deductive model has not been confuted. But what of historical events that do not have physical causes? The situation is admittedly more difficult to reconstruct, but not on that account wholly resistant to deductive explanation.

Suppose that we wish to predict the Supreme Court's decision on a school integration case that is before it. How do we evaluate two different predictions about the outcome? We consider the reasons that, if pressed, each predictor will give. If no reasons can be given or if the reasons, when made fully explicit, do not appear to be true or, if true, do not entail the predicted decision, then, with equal justification, the opposite may as well have been predicted. What kind of statements could serve to *justify* a pre-

24 Scriven, in Gardiner, p. 468.

diction? We might well cite approximate statistical laws about certain social variables, for instance, about the equalizing effect of war and industrialization. References to our so-called national character implicitly involve other such laws about how Americans have behaved in the past and can be expected to behave in the future. Statistical laws about individual behavior, for instance, of the judges, would also be employed. Knowledge of this kind, in conjunction with what we know about the present situation, serves as the basis for "educated guesses." The best educated guess is one that *must* be true, if certain premises are accepted. We make this guess rather than another because it is logically entailed by our various bits of "imperfect" knowledge. It is conjectural because the premises are conjectural, but the connection between them and the event predicted is deductive.

After the decision has been handed down, we explain it in the same way. Of course, if by 'prediction' we mean any prophecy, or simply "a claim that at a certain time an event will occur," [25] then we may certainly predict without being able to explain. On the other hand, if by a prediction we mean one for which *reasons* can be given, then after the event we should also be able to explain it. If we cannot, then we know that our premises must be false. Since after the event we know what conclusion we want to draw, it is all too easy to invent the appropriate reasons as premises from which the court's decision, say, follows. Only successful prediction gives us evidence for accepting the premises. "Prediction" need not be of an event in the future, only of something not as yet known.

In history, too, we use all kinds of imperfect knowledge about societies, institutions, and individuals to make inferences not about the future but about what we do not yet know in the past. We then look for the evidence in the usual historiographical or even archeological sources. It is true that having predicted a current political event, we can wait and see what happens. However, in history, after all, we are also given plenty of well-confirmed facts. We are frequently much more concerned to explain than to establish them. So the principle is not really different. There is no such thing as "historical" explanation, only the explanation of historical events. To be sure, such explanations, as well as those proposed for contemporary events and for complex human behavior, are all in the same boat. History, whether contemporary or past, far from being the paradigm of sound explanation that some now take it to be, must make do with conspiciously imperfect knowledge. I shall make a few more remarks about explanation in history later on. But, as we saw, deductive explanation and prediction do not require that our premises be "perfect." The critics make the philosophical claim that inference from one fact to another does not require the use of laws. Accurately as this may describe our enthymematic speech habits, the claim is not logically justified by the fact that our knowledge is, in many areas, imperfect and, for all we know, likely to remain so.

25 Scriven, in *Science,* 130:480.

Inference Tickets and Enthymemes

Once we have distinguished between the elliptical, context-bound use of language for the purposes of communication and the use of language for description, it is clear, I believe, that insofar as an individual fact justifies the inference to one or more other such facts, laws are always implicitly or explicitly invoked. Otherwise, the justification of the inference remains a mystery. Since those who now assail the deductive model deny that the premises logically entail their conclusions, we may well ask what they believe *does* justify the inference? The answer lies in the use, in one form or another, of Ryle's notion of an "inference ticket." Attending to those idiomatic expressions that signal the use of argument, like "because so and so, therefore," "this, so that," "this involves that," as well as "if, then," Ryle concludes that individual facts are deduced from premises stating other individual facts. Ryle accepts the standard interpretation of natural laws as hypothetical or conditional statements. He denies, however, that laws state facts. "Butter melts when heated" or "Tempered steel is flexible" are, on his account, not factual assertions. This, if I may say so, is an eminently "philosophical" rather than commonsensical use of 'fact.' Philosophical uses are puzzling and must be explicated. Ryle does indeed provide an explication, one which, as I shall try to show, carries with it an untenable implicit metaphysics. The difference between singular statements (not containing dispositional predicates) and hypotheticals, according to Ryle, is in the jobs they perform. The job of singular statements is to report "facts," that is, actual happenings or occurrences. Hypotheticals, on the other hand, "narrate no incidents." [26] Their job is to serve as inference tickets, licensing inferences from one or more individual facts to others. The general hypothetical "warrants" the argument "from factual statement to factual statement," but is not itself part of that argument. Judged by the logicians' account, Ryle's is clearly enthymematic. The "inference ticket" licensing the deduction is, of course, not the general hypothetical which is instead an implicit premise, but the rule of *modus ponens*.

The inference-ticket notion plays a large role in the arguments of those who now attack deductive explanation. The universal statement is said to serve as a "warrant" or "justifying ground" making "legitimate" or "guaranteeing" the step from fact to fact. Though Scriven's boundless confidence in "judgment" and "primeval certainty" leads him to deny that "we should lose faith in an explanation" if we cannot formulate justifying grounds, he concedes that sometimes universal premises are used to "justify" an explanation. Since these warrants, justifying grounds, or inference tickets are allegedly not part of the explanation itself, explanation from individual fact to individual fact is not deductive. It is indeed held that no distinction can be drawn between deductive and inductive arguments, that the logi-

[26] Ryle, *The Concept of Mind*, pp. 120, 125.

cian's formally deductive arguments are really inductive or "substantial." For instance, the astronomer can predict a future eclipse from the "standard equations of stellar dynamics" and the present position and motion of the heavenly bodies involved. Yet, this prediction is said to be "substantial," not tautologically deductive, because the prediction allegedly is made from the present and past positions of the heavenly bodies. These latter—the data and "backing" for the standard equations—"do not positively entail the conclusion." [27] Of course they don't, but no one ever said they did. Patently, the evidence we have for a universal statement—the standard equations— is here confused with what that statement itself actually asserts. The conclusion follows from the equations themselves and the appropriate initial conditions. Either the equations—the so-called warrant or justifying grounds —and the initial conditions jointly entail the conclusion deductively or they can neither predict nor explain it.

The suggestion to "construe" natural laws as material rules of inference is not a new one. It has been made from time to time by various philosophers as a way out of certain philosophical problems regarding universal propositions. Various difficulties with this view, apart from the fact that this is not their actual role in scientific practice, have also been pointed out.[28] The philosophical nerve of the matter, however, is plucked by Braithwaite's comment that to treat a logically contingent statement as a principle of inference is to "mix experience and the logical methods by which we think about experience in a very confusing way." [29] Why this is confusing should be, but apparently is not, obvious. One reason it is not obvious is the promiscuous use of 'logical' for quite different things, while at the same time retaining the connotations of the term in its strict sense. Statements about the past, for instance, are said to be "logically" different from statements about the future, and *therefore* one cannot be deduced from the other.[30] This is but one instance of an appeal to "logic" as if that were what it is not, namely, a logical reason in the strict sense.

Another instance is the use of "logic" to mean function or job. Both contingent hypotheticals and logical truths are used as "inference tickets"; both therefore have the same jobs or "logic." Calling two things that may have the same function in communication "logically" the same at best blurs the issue about the structural or logical, in the strict sense, difference between analytic and synthetic statements. This difference is signaled by at least some uses of 'necessary' in common speech. These, in turn, may reflect differences in the descriptive content of each kind of statement,

27 Toulmin, *Philosophy of Science,* pp. 84–85, 93ff, and *The Uses of Argument,* pp. 101, 114, 121–122, 220; Scriven, in Gardiner, pp. 446ff, 456ff; Ryle, *The Concept of Mind,* pp. 120–125.

28 See E. Nagel, "A Perspective on Theoretical Physics," *Mind,* 63:403–412 (1954), reprinted in his *Logic without Metaphysics* (Glencoe, Ill.: The Free Press, 1956); and H. G. Alexander, "General Statements as Rules of Inference," in *Minnesota Studies in the Philosophy of Science,* Vol. II.

29 R. B. Braithwaite, *Scientific Explanation* (Cambridge: Cambridge University Press, 1953), p. 86.

30 Toulmin, *The Uses of Argument,* pp. 13, 220.

no matter what their "job." The issue appears to be settled in the negative when in fact it has not even been raised. But there is an even more fundamental reason for this confusion of experience with reasoning about it, to which the others are mere corollaries.

In ordinary communication, if a person asserting "this, so that" can produce a corresponding general hypothetical, we say that he has "the right" to conclude that from this.[31] But suppose we go on to ask what there is about the world or the way we reason about it which justifies our saying this. That is, why does the general hypothetical give us the right to infer that from this? I mentioned before that an appeal to logical truth or to definition is conclusive in a way that appeal to contingent truth is not. If we accept the logician's notion of logical truth, then we can answer this question. *Modus ponens* licenses the inference and that, in turn, is justified by appeal to the notion of logical truth or tautology. Ryle rejects this answer in part at least because he rejects the question. That is, he holds that an appeal to a statement of the form 'If P then Q' is as conclusive as an appeal to a statement of the form "If 'If P then Q' and 'P,' *then* 'Q'." At one place, Ryle rejects the logician's reconstruction of the "p, so q" arguments as enthymematic on the Tortoise and Achilles grounds that the use of a rule as a premise leads to an infinite regress.[32]

But Ryle's use of this argument is mistaken. Since they are metalinguistic, rules are indeed of a different logical type from premises. But the justification of, say, *modus ponens* does not involve the use of its corresponding hypothetical as a premise, or, therefore, the use of another rule, and so on ad infinitum. Rather, the use of the rule is justified by pointing out that the hypothetical sentence corresponding to it—which is *not* a premise of the argument for which it is used—is a tautology. All that the Tortoise proved to Achilles is that some (at least one) rules are always necessary. He did not prove that these indispensable rules could not themselves be justified. This justification is indeed a fundamental task of the philosophy of logic, as contrasted with logic itself. Ryle rejects this task and holds instead that one cannot even ask what justifies the rule because the job of the hypothetical is to *be* a rule. It "means" a rule, and the appeal to "meaning" is, everyone agrees, conclusive. With the appeal to "meaning," we come to the heart of the matter, the confusions about "conceptual analysis."

"Conceptual Analysis" and Rejection of
Hypothetico-Deductive Theories

The critics of deductive explanation quite consistently also attack the hypothetico-deductive model of scientific theories, according to which a

---

[31] Ryle, *The Concept of Mind,* p. 300.

[32] Cf. G. Ryle, " 'If', 'So' and 'Because'," in *Philosophical Analysis,* Max Black, ed. (Ithaca, N.Y.: Cornell University Press, 1950).

theory is a deductively connected set of general statements, some of which, the premises or axioms, logically imply others, the theorems. These statements of a theory are hypothetical in a double sense. First, as empirical, contingent, or logically synthetic general statements, they may be falsified; second, some of them are used as premises in a deductive argument—the theory—whose purpose is to show what else must be true *if* the premises are true. It is worth mentioning that neither of these senses of "hypothetical" has anything to do with the *process* by which universal hypotheses are formulated, whether it be by induction, a hunch, or a dream. They are "generalizations" only in the sense that they are of generalized, that is, universal form. Some believe that if laws are not arrived at by a process of generalization from observed instances, then they cannot be contingent universal or general statements.[33] This is certainly consonant with the typical process-product confusion, but otherwise has less than nothing to recommend it. But the matter goes considerably deeper than this apparently merely verbal matter. For the critics deny that scientific laws are "hypothetical" in either sense mentioned. They are, of course, held to be rules and not premises in a deduction but, more revealingly, neither are they contingent or subject to refutation by observation. They are rather true by virtue of "meaning," by virtue of the way the scientist uses the terms connected by laws. A few comments about meaning are first of all in order.

Terms themselves do not mean. We mean by their use. Yet terms, including 'meaning' itself, have many different uses. We ask for the meaning of life, wanting to know why we are here, and whither, if anywhere, we are going. We ask for the meaning of an event, like a falling star, wanting to know, perhaps, what it portends. Or we ask for the meaning of another event, like an election, wanting to know what it indicates about the temper of people. We search out the meaning of a drama or a novel, wanting to know what moral it points for man and his world. Or, more mundanely, we ask for the meaning of words, like 'rabbit' or 'acceleration,' wanting to know no more than to what they refer. In the former, possibly more intriguing, questions about "meaning," we are interested in significance in a common-sense use of that term that is generally clear in context. In the last example, however, we are interested in the observable referent of the term. 'Rabbit' means (is used to refer to) rabbits; 'acceleration' means (is used to refer to) the rate of change of velocity with time. In asking for "meaning" in the sense of significance, we want to know with what *other* things the events or things asked about are connected. Some terms, like 'cephalic index,' have meaning in the sense of reference but no significance. We know well enough what the term is used to refer to, but we know nothing about it, that is, there are no laws connecting a person's cephalic index with any of his behavior.

Other terms have both meaning and significance. We know that rabbits

---

[33] See Toulmin, *Philosophy of Science*, p. 49; N. R. Hanson, *Patterns of Discovery* (Cambridge: Cambridge University Press, 1958), pp. 107ff.

eat lettuce, and we also know, among other things, that the acceleration of free fall is a constant. If we did not know the meaning of a term in the referential sense, then we could not discover its significance. We would not, in fact, know what we were talking about, either what it was that ate lettuce or what it was that is constant. A worthwhile concept has both reference and significance. In the first sense of meaning, terms themselves do not mean. We mean by their use. To put it differently, *referential* meaning is a matter of convention; it is something we give the concept. *Significance* or lawfulness, however, is not a matter of convention, but a factual matter, that is, a matter of the way things are. We can define any concept we wish to define. But we cannot endow a concept with significance. It either has it or it has not.

To blur this distinction is to blur a contribution of the mind—the concepts we use—with what is not such a contribution, but, independently of the way we speak about it, is a matter of the way the world goes. Realism and idealism are the relevant metaphysical tags for those who, respectively, insist upon and those who blur this distinction. In particular, the formula "Meaning is Use" blurs the distinction. More particularly, the doctrine that natural laws are true by virtue of the "meaning" of their constituent terms obliterates it. For the two questions, about what a thing is and about what happens to it, are held to be not two questions but one. The terms, we are told, cannot be identified apart from the laws in which they occur.[34] In other words, given a law, "If P then Q," we cannot know that we have P unless we simultaneously know that "it" has Q. This seems to make Q a definitional property of P. But definitions are tautologies, and it is denied that laws are tautologies. Yet the "meaning" of 'P' is 'Q,' and denial of the law is "conceptually untenable." [35] Again, all terms are said to be "theory loaded." Their meaning is given by the entire theory, that is, the context, in which they occur. Since the relevant context varies with each use and each user, no two people ever use a term in the same way. Lightning and thunder are said to mean something different to a youngster than to a meteorologist. A clock means something different to Galileo's apprentice than to Galileo.[36] *Accurately* stated, the meteorologist *knows more* about flashes and rumbles than does the boy, and Galileo knew more about clocks than did his apprentice. Otherwise, how would we ever know that they were all talking about the same thing? If a term means something different in every context in which it occurs, then, as has been well pointed out, an exception to or falsification of a law becomes "conceptually impossible" because the term means something different in the law and in the statement of the exception.[37] If an exception is "conceptually impossible," then the statement itself is conceptually "neces-

[34] Toulmin, *Philosophy of Science*, p. 52; Hanson, *Patterns of Discovery*, pp. 61ff.
[35] Hanson, *Patterns of Discovery*, p. 115.
[36] *Ibid.*, pp. 56–57.
[37] In the excellent critical review of Hanson's book by P. K. Feyerabend, "Patterns of Discovery," *Philosophical Review*, 69:247–252 (1960).

sary." Instead of our speaking being determined by the way the world is, what is possible in the world is determined by the way we speak about it.

On the hypothetico-deductive account of theories, they have the form "*If* 'If P then Q' and 'If Q then R,' *then* 'If P then R' "; the major "if-then" expresses a logical entailment between the premises or hypotheses of the theory and the conclusion. However, if laws are held to be rules for "deducing" one individual fact from others, then what rule justifies deducing laws themselves from other laws? The critics need not answer the question for, on their view, no such deduction occurs. A theory is not a deductively connected set of statements, as indeed, if the terms differ in meaning each time they occur, it cannot be. Not the sentences, but the terms of a theory are said to be "logically linked," in some yet further Pickwickian sense of 'logical.' [38]

The idealistic monists, it will be recalled, rejected classical syllogistic logic, the only logic they knew, because they maintained that terms differ in meaning every time they occur, so no conclusion could "really" be drawn by the methods of that logic. Rejecting the abstract universal, in favor of the so-called concrete universal, they argued that not sentences but concepts were "deductively," as they said, connected by the expansion of "meanings" into ever broader and more inclusive contexts. So it is here. What I have called the component laws are instead statements about the meanings of the terms. The "Q" in the first premise has a different "meaning" from that in the second because it occurs in a different context, yet they are "logically linked" since one incorporates or expands upon the other. *The* meaning of a term is thus given by all the statements in which it occurs. These statements are alternatively either rules for the use of the term or "linguistic," "conceptual," or even "logical" truths about it. True by "meaning," they are yet synthetic or, at least, not analytic. Though not tautologies, they are nevertheless the last court of appeal. Used as rules, they need no further justification. That is why hypothetical or conditional statements are "nonfactual" and only singular statements are empirical statements of fact. All generalizations, once they have been accepted and passed into usage, become true by meaning. It then becomes "conceptually impossible" to deny an empirical law. The bridge from 'conceptual' to 'conceivable' is as short as that from 'conceptual' to 'logical.' The psychologically inconceivable thus becomes the "logically" contradictory, their negations, "logically" true.

Borrowing next on the conclusiveness of the appeal to logical truth *in the strict sense,* the appeal to these nonanalytic "conceptual truths" delusively appears equally conclusive. That is why one can say that the rule "licenses" the inference, but *one cannot ask what licenses the "license."* It is also the basic reason for the rejection of formal logic, whose terms in an argument must remain constant in meaning and which distinguishes generalized statements that are logically true from those that are factually true. Denying that deduction in the formal sense ever occurs, naturally

38 Toulmin, *Philosophy of Science,* p. 85.

there can be no deductive explanation or prediction. If the "meaning" of a concept is always another concept, then the job of statements to describe the world, their connection with something *nonconceptual,* becomes inexplicable. Confusion of sociopsychological description of language as communication with structural analyses of what this communication asserts about the world leads, not for the first time, to a philosophy that loses the world in a system of "meanings." This untenable consequence is, we shall see, further supported by analysis of the more moderate criticism of the deductive model.[39]

Criticism of the Premises of the Deductive Model

The more moderate criticism of the deductive model agrees that unless an explanation logically entails, in the strict sense, what it explains, then "it will fail to explain why what it purports to explain should have happened rather than something else." [40] It denies, however, that any of the premises need be a universal law. The appearance of paradox, if strict deduction is not abandoned, dissipates when we learn that a general premise is indeed required, though this premise is not granted the status of a natural law. Nor, as I shall try to show by examining the position as presented in a carefully argued paper by Donagan,[41] is the disagreement merely a matter of words. Since Donagan's major criticism as well as certain associated doctrines derive from some of Ryle's ideas that have already been discussed, it will be possible to be rather brief. Donagan's argument is especially worth examining because, free both of the tedium of "arguments" that amount to little more than puns from usage and of obscurantist appeals to "judgment" and "intelligibility," it points up even more sharply the structural connection between the various doctrines and the virtually universal hostility of their proponents toward a science of behavior.

Donagan's argument against the deductive model allegedly depends upon Ryle's philosophical behaviorism. Our common speech is studded with expressions which, if taken in their "ordinary sense," as Moore would say, are used to refer to mental states, to such things as conscious feelings, thoughts, desires, beliefs, and sensations. But ordinary language is fickle and here deceives us for, according to Ryle, mental states are but "mythical" entities, products of the metaphysicians' fancy. Accordingly, he "construes" statements about mental states as general hypotheticals or dispositional statements about how people behave under certain circumstances. These

---

[39] For an analysis of the metaphysical uses or misuses of this notion of "conceptual truth," see G. Bergmann, "Strawson's Ontology," *Journal of Philosophy,* 57:601–622 (1960).

[40] A. Donagan, "Explanation in History," *Mind,* 66:145–164 (1957); reprinted in Gardiner, pp. 428–443.

[41] *Ibid.*

dispositional statements license us, in the now familiar manner, when confronted with the circumstances stated in the protasis, to predict that the behavior mentioned in the apodosis will occur. Or, conversely, we are licensed to explain the behavior by reference to the protasis conditions. Donagan does not adopt the inference-ticket view. The license for him, as for the logician, lies in the entailment relation, not in the general hypothetical itself. The latter therefore must occur as a premise of the argument. The use of such hypotheticals or dispositional statements as premises in deductive explanation does not depend, however, as Donagan believes, upon the truth of Ryle's philosophy of mind. Methodological behaviorism as a program in psychology and, more generally, the scientific study of man is one thing. There it is proper and essential.

Philosophical behaviorism or materialism, the denial that there are such things as mental states, is something else again and is not implied by methodological behaviorism. Drawing his philosophical conclusions about what exists from the study of language as a vehicle of communication rather than description, Ryle finds ordinary language a poor guide to ontology. Identifying how we can tell with what there is, he revamps the old verifiability theory of meaning. The meaning of mental terms in common speech becomes the behaviors that, as we ordinarily say, testify to them. I suggest that to argue from how we communicate with each other about our own and other people's states of mind to what exists is exactly analogous to the error of those verificationists who "construed" statements about the past to be "really" about the present and future, because it was by means of such observable consequences that they were verified. The ontological price for ignoring the difference between the communicative and descriptive uses of language is high indeed. Be that as it may, we are here concerned with the possibility of scientific, deductive explanation and not with the philosophy of mind. We need therefore only inquire whether the differences Ryle discerns between explanations by so-called lawlike dispositions and explanation by laws are indeed real differences. For two things are made to depend upon them. First, only explanations by means of laws are held to be "causal" explanations. Second, explanation by means of, allegedly noncausal, "lawlike" motive or dispositional statements is held to be final or conclusive, requiring no further explanation. If true, these claims support the contention that explanation in history and the other studies of man and society is fundamentally different from that in natural science. Since the proponents of the deductive model generally deny that this is a difference of principle, the issue is more than merely verbal.

"Lawlike" Hypotheticals vs. Causal Laws

'Jones is vain' is construed by Ryle as 'Whenever Jones finds a chance of securing the admiration and envy of others, he does whatever he thinks will produce this admiration and envy.' [42] The "mentalistic" terms in this hypothetical—'admire,' 'envy,' and 'thinks'—doubtless could be replaced by behavioristic, dispositional correlates. Such statements are held to be lawlike rather than laws, because, though general with respect to time, they mention individual persons or things. It is worth noting, however, that some uses of dispositional terms are not general at all. Behavioristically defined, both 'hungry' and 'irascible' are dispositional. 'Hungry,' referring to a present state of a person, would be defined by a molecular, that is, nongeneral, hypothetical. 'Jones is hungry' means, say, 'If Jones is now presented with food, then he will eat it'; or, if I may be permitted the greater clarity of a symbolism, 'If $F_1(a,t_1)$ then $F_2(a,t_1)$.' This is a nongeneralized molecular statement. "Hunger" is thus a complex property being attributed to a specific individual at a specific time, just as "being red and hot" would be a complex property attributed to a poker. 'Irascible,' on the other hand, referring not to a present state of a person but to his disposition to behave in certain ways under certain circumstances, has the form '(t) If $F_1(a,t)$ then $F_2(a,t)$.' It is a quantified or generalized statement. All terms referring to personality or character traits, rather than to present states, would thus be generalized over one or more variables, whether they be time, objects, or circumstances.

Just as these hypotheticals about persons always have some degree of generality, so natural laws are never completely general. Galileo's laws hold only for bodies on Earth; we have laws about the expansion of the chemical mercury and Kepler's laws for the planets; the law of radioactive decay contains a constant whose value depends on the substance involved; and so on. All known laws have some kind of scope restriction which is part of the law itself. Usage certainly does not insist upon complete generality for what is to "count" as a natural law among scientists. The logically significant distinction is generalized *versus* molecular rather than "law" *versus* "lawlike." General hypotheticals about a person are of the same logical form, in the strict sense, as natural laws, while both are to be distinguished from statements of individual fact or any molecular compound of them. The issue might appear to be merely verbal or at best a classificatory problem in a case where the boundaries are blurred, if so much were not made to hang on it.

Donagan acquiesces in the standard Humean account of causality, as expressed by Hempel's assertion that "Every 'causal explanation' is an 'explanation by scientific laws'; for in no way other than by reference to empirical laws can the assertion of a causal connection between certain events be scientifically substantiated." [43] Donagan distinguishes such causal explanation from explanation by dispositions, maintaining that this distinction renders historical explanation noncausal. Ryle, we recall, holds that "This because that" or "The window broke because struck by a stone" is

---

[42] Ryle, *The Concept of Mind*, p. 89.
[43] Quoted by Donagan, in Gardiner, p. 430.

itself a complete, nonenthymematic explanation. "This window broke because brittle" he also holds to be a complete explanation. The former is "causal" because it mentions a "significant prior or simultaneous happening," namely, being stoned. The latter, however, is not causal, because "being brittle" is not a happening or episode. Being brittle is, we also recall, not even a fact, as Ryle uses that term, about the window, since it is expressed by the general hypothetical, "If this window is struck sharply, then it will break." Donagan maintains that though causal explanation is "Hempelian," that is, fits the deductive model, the dispositional one "differs from anything recognized in the Hempelian theory, which presupposes that the only way of deriving the statement that certain windows broke from the statement that they were stoned is by the allegedly buried general law, 'All windows break when stoned.' "

But the claim that one fits the deductive model while the other does not will not bear closer examination. Nor will the further claim about the only way to derive the statement that certain windows broke. Ryle's philosophical behaviorism and his rejection of formal deduction here reinforce each other. Ryle, one might venture to surmise, insists that mention of the "nonfactual" disposition is a complete explanation because of his even greater concern to deny that there are any events or happenings corresponding to mental terms which could serve as causes of motivated events. If, for instance, "vanity" is behavioristically construed as a personality disposition term, then to say "He boasted from vanity" is not to explain his boasting by reference to any "cause" or "happening." [44] The "happening" Ryle is concerned to deny is of course any *mental* happening. The denial of philosophical behaviorism, while accepting methodological behaviorism and the general scientific thesis of psychophysical parallelism, does of course not at all commit one to the belief in mind-body interactionism. What matters, however, is that Ryle, given his quaint views about the subject matter of psychology, *thinks* one is thus committed, so being vain, or in love, or brittle cannot be "facts" or "happenings."

Actually, spelling out these enthymemes, it becomes clear that *both* of them, "Broke because stoned" and "Broke because brittle," mention "significant prior or simultaneous happenings." In the first case, the implicit premise or "inference ticket" is the general law "All windows break when stoned," while the happening, being stoned, is explicitly asserted. In the second case, the lawlike hypothetical defining the dispositional predicate 'brittle' is explicitly asserted, while the implicit premise is the individual statement of fact asserting an instance, namely, that the window was struck sharply, of the protasis of this hypothetical. In all logic, Ryle should permit singular statements of fact to be "inference tickets," for that is their job in such "explanations." Ryle feels no discomfort about this "episode proposition" that, he agrees, is implicitly subsumed under the general hypothetical presumably because it is only the antecedent part of the defined motive

44 Ryle, *The Concept of Mind*, p. 86.

or character term and the motive itself, the entire hypothetical, is not made a "happening." Another reason why Ryle holds hypotheticals to be "nonfactual" is that when we explain by reference to a disposition rather than by mentioning a specific event, we say we are giving a reason rather than a cause.[45] I think he is right about this use of 'reason,' but only because when we explain by reference to a disposition, we are, by definition of the disposition, implicitly giving the premises of a deductive argument. And giving premises that logically entail a specific event is certainly one good use of 'giving reasons' for that event.

Spelling out Ryle's enthymematic arguments reveals not only that individual happenings are involved in each case but also the inaccuracy of Donagan's contention that the only way for the Hempelian model to derive the breaking of the window from its being stoned is by the buried law 'All windows break when stoned.' It can of course also be derived from the "lawlike" disposition 'If this window is hit by a stone, then it will break.' Therefore, anyone who rejects the inference-ticket notion and opts for *deductive* explanation cannot also accept "being brittle" as a *complete* explanation. He has to grant that there is an implicit singular premise. To reject the deductive model, he must therefore fall back on insisting that the difference between so-called causal and noncausal general hypotheticals is more than one of degree of generality. And, indeed, Donagan does give reasons for claiming that there is an *essential* difference between dispositional statements about material objects and those about persons which serve as premises in nonphysical explanation. This alleged difference is believed to be relevant to the deterministic thesis and the possibility of a science of man. For this reason, as well as for what it reveals about "conceptual analysis," the argument is of special interest.

Motives, Meaning, and a Science of Man

The lawlike statement 'If this window is struck sharply, then it will break' is derivable by specialization from the general law about the brittleness of windows, 'If any window is struck sharply, then it will break,' which is generalized not only with respect to time but also with respect to windows. Lawlike statements about a person's motives or character are, however, allegedly not similarly "generalizable." This limitation, in turn, is believed to justify the claim that explanations in terms of motives or character are not only "complete," but also "final" or conclusive. That is, though like Kepler's laws they completely entail what they are supposed to explain, unlike Kepler's laws they do not themselves require further explaining.[46] But, first of all, this notion of "generalizability" is ambiguous. To be sure, we neither know nor expect to know any general state-

---

[45] *Ibid.*, pp. 113–114, 89.
[46] Donagan, in Gardiner, p. 434; Ryle, *The Concept of Mind*, pp. 89, 325.

ment "All men are vain" from which Jones's vanity could be deduced. What is true of Jones is, in this sense, not generalizable to all men. Does it follow that there is no sense in which lawlike statements about individuals are generalizable, thus turning "non-Hempelian" into "Hempelian" explanations? Donagan believes that it does follow, for the buried assumption behind the lawlike 'The Danes who sailed south to the Irish Sea were plunderers first and settlers by afterthought' would be, he asserts, 'All men were plunderers first and settlers by afterthought.' But surely this is not the correct "buried assumption." If the Danes being plunderers first and settlers by afterthought implies, as he says, the lawlike statement that 'If those Danes had opportunities of sufficient plunder in a territory, they would not settle in it,' does it not also imply the same thing for Italian plunderers? In other words, the correct buried assumption is that *anyone's* being a plunderer first and a settler by afterthought implies 'If he has opportunities of sufficient plunder in a territory, he will not settle in it.' This is not the same as saying that everyone is a plunderer. The implied general statement is the definition, in whole or in part, of the disposition term 'plunderer.' From this definition, together with the information that the Danes were plunderers, we could derive some of their behavior. To be sure, the universal premise of this explanation is a verbally necessary truth, since it reflects our definition of the term 'plunderer.'

The explanation of the Danes' behavior thus logically follows from the empirical fact that they were plunderers and the definition of that dispositional term. In the course of deductive explanations, we frequently do utilize definitions as premises. We must do so to derive theorems that contain defined terms from axioms that are expressed in the primitive terms of a scientific theory. In science, these definitions most frequently take the form of generalized or universal conditional statements. Such a defining sentence, like our definition of 'irascible,' may therefore serve as the universal premise required by the deductive model. The "explanation" is then vacuous and circular in a way in which deductive explanations utilizing *contingent* universal premises are not. Literally speaking, then, if the "Hempelian" model requires a contingent universal premise, then this explanation is not Hempelian. But this is at best a trivial objection. The process-product equivocation in the use of the term 'generalization,' which I mentioned earlier, has probably played a role in misleading Donagan. Since his premise, though general in form, is a definition and not a contingent generalization, he believes that it does not fit the "Hempelian" model. But the fundamental point of the deductive model is that no inference, either for prediction or for explanation, can be made from one or more individual statements of fact to other such statements, without the use of a *general* premise. In the most interesting and informative cases, the general premise is a natural law, but it may also be a definition. However, no one holds that deductions from definitions are the only kind we make in the course of an explanation. In addition to the definition we also must know some general laws containing the defined terms. In the case at hand, if we also know some general laws about plunderers, as defined, laws about, say, their religion or literature, then we could derive in good Hempelian fashion further facts about the Danes' behavior and, of course, about plunderers of any nationality. Donagan, however, is asserting not only what is obvious, that there is no law about all men being plunderers corresponding to all windows being brittle, but rather that there can be *no general statements about plunderers,* as there are about brittle windows. That is why he believes that the premises in historical explanation must be lawlike statements about *the particular people* involved.[47] In general, explanations by reference to "the character of the agent" are held to be final and conclusive. What are the reasons for this view?

It is perfectly true that in everyday life when we explain a man's actions by reference to his motives, that is all we want to know. We then "understand" why he did what he did. Frequently, that's all we care about. The historian who succeeds in ferreting out an agent's motives has supplied an explanation adequate for his purposes. As we have seen, the reconstruction of such explanations shows them to be deductive, using the dispositional definition of the motive term and individual statements of fact as premises or reasons for the behavior. Other actions are less trivially explained by using *contingent* generalized premises about how people with such motives can be expected to behave in certain circumstances. Generalizations of this sort are, of course, imperfect. Nor is their imperfection due to their limited scope, namely, being about a single individual or group of individuals. They are imperfect because, generally, they are hemmed in by qualifying phrases which render them implicitly statistical. They are also imperfect because they are limited with respect to time. A man's motives may change with his circumstances or with, as we say, "age." While a man was prime minister, his motives were such and such; they changed when he joined the opposition. These circumstances can of course be built into the protasis as part of the initial conditions or as scope restrictions on either the generalizations or the definitions. "Age" is not a true variable, but a cover or suitcase word for all of the many things that happen to a man as he grows older. The *mot* "Character is fate" enshrines the belief that by understanding a man's character we understand what he does and what happens to him. We may sometimes explain a man's motives at a given time by reference to his character, meaning by the latter certain more permanent and less restricted dispositions. To know a man's character means knowing many generalizations about him from which, in given circumstances, both the motives he will act from and his other behavior can be predicted or explained.

The historian uses these kinds of imperfect laws in order to explain the decisions made and actions taken. Nor does he necessarily "presuppose" any general laws about all men. He just uses the laws about his particular

---

[47] Donagan, in Gardiner, p. 441.

man. It would be odd, though, if he were to say that another man of similar character in similar circumstances would nevertheless behave very differently. "Character," after all, refers to a certain *kind* of man, though possibly, but just possibly, there might be only one of that kind. Even so, it is perfectly legitimate to ask why someone is the kind of man he is, why he has the character he has, even though in everyday life and in the study of history we might not be interested in that question. But certainly parents and pedagogues frequently are interested in it. We do try to "build" character. Since we try to do so, we might well want to know what forms it. To find that out, we have to go beyond generalizations about particular persons. Character is not only a cause of behavior, it might also be caused. Though explanation in terms of the character of the agent might satisfy us and historians, they might not quench a broader curiosity. For it, they would not be final and conclusive. Such persons might try to discover the laws of character formation. They might, in other words, try to develop a science of psychology. The fact that most of us are most of the time satisfied with explanation by reference to motives and character does not rule out a deeper search. The quest may well be futile, but there is no logical necessity that it be so. The critics of the deductive model, whether of its premises or its form, express considerable repugnance and opposition to this quest. This opposition is buttressed by arguments that go deeper than merely practical considerations. Once again, as we shall see, confusion is bred by the notion of "conceptual analysis." The fusing of reference and significance turns a matter of contingent fact, namely, that we cannot now explain or fully explain character, into a "necessary" and even "logical" truth.

I have been speaking of "defining" the disposition terms by means of general hypotheticals. This was, of course, a bit disingenuous. For it follows from the context theory of meaning I discussed before that the lawlike hypothetical corresponding to the statement that Jones is vain does not define the character trait but instead "expands its meaning." If we wish to unpack "all that is conveyed" in describing Jones as vain, we must "produce an infinite series of different hypothetical propositions." [48] The operative phrase is "all that is conveyed." In everyday life the connotations of a term include both defining and nondefining properties, as long as the latter are fairly widely and firmly believed to be exemplified by the thing in question. This is what lends to everyday speech its so-called open texture. A concept's "meaning" or "criteria of application" expands as we learn more and more about "it." The difficulties with this view I discussed before. Our concepts may be open textured, but the world is not. If language is to be descriptive, it must indicate what there is in the world, no matter how variably we talk about it. On pain of Bergsonian ineffability, a descriptive language cannot *duplicate* the world's growth and change, including that of language. It need only *account for* it. By combining de-

---

[48] Ryle, *The Concept of Mind*, pp. 44, 86, 113.

fining and nondefining properties, everything that we know about a thing becomes part of its "meaning." For instance, Donagan tells us that the Danes being plunderers implies not only that they would not settle in a territory but also a "host of further law-like statements" about their literature glorifying war rather than farming, about the kind of religion they would have, and so on.[49] If all these statements do indeed "unfold the meaning" of being a plunderer, then clearly we cannot ask whether one could possibly be a plunderer or, even, a Danish plunderer, and *not* produce this kind of literature or religion. By virtue of "meaning" nothing else could have happened, just as by virtue of meaning, Jones's vanity implies he would do the various things that, as we say, "express" his vanity.

But is everything a plunderer might do part of the meaning of the term? And if not, where do we draw the line? As we come to know more and more about Danish plunderers, more and more becomes a matter of meaning or "conceptually true." Let us show by example where this leads. Within behavior science, where definitions are necessary if the scientist is to know what he is talking about, the dispositional term 'hungry' is defined so that if a person, any person, is hungry, then when, say, he is presented with food under certain circumstances, he eats it. It is then *discovered* that hungry people are irritable. This is a fact or, if you prefer, a law about them. And it could not be discovered unless the meaning of 'hunger' was independent of that of 'irritable.' On the present view, however, this irritability becomes a lawlike hypothetical which is part of the expansion of the meaning of 'hungry.' The more such hypotheticals we have, the more we add to the meaning of the term, until everything that we say about hunger is true by "meaning." If there are an infinite number of lawlike statements expressing Jones's "kind of vanity," then where do we draw the line between what we mean by his vanity and what happens to be connected with it, like his ambition or his gregariousness? Again, arguing from language as communication rather than description, the world that language is supposed to be about is lost—for terms are tied down not to the world but to an infinite series of other terms or "meanings." The illusory conclusiveness of the inference ticket is now transferred to the lawlike premise. Since the lawlike premises about an individual's character and motives are true by meaning, no explanation of them is either necessary or possible. They are therefore "final." "Conceptual truths" need no further explanation. Like the appeal to logical truth *in the strict sense,* appeal to these conceptual truths about motives and character are "conclusive." By an a priori argument from "meaning," an empirical science of human nature is shown to be unnecessary, impossible, or both.

---

[49] Donagan, in Gardiner, pp. 436–437. [In a later and very clarifying paper on the issues Donagan qualified this statement. See his "Historical Explanation: The Popper-Hempel Theory Reconsidered," *History and Theory,* IV, 1964, reprinted in *Philosophical Analysis and History,* W. H. Dray, ed., Harper & Row, New York, 1966, pp. 127–159. Ed.]

Concluding Remarks

No matter what other disagreements they may have among themselves, those who now attack the deductive model share certain central and basic ideas which can and do lend themselves to a philosophically argued neo-obscurantism. In particular, the two ideas I have stressed, the view of language as communication rather than description and the notion of "conceptual analysis," explain but do not justify their rejection of the deductive model of explanation and of formal logic. These ideas also structurally explain their rejection of a science of man. From the dismissal of the need for a science of psychology because "we all know well enough" why people behave as they do, to a metaphysically argued case for the impossibility of a science of man,[50] the pattern is always the same. Learning a language is a social phenomenon. Once one has learned to use the language of everyday living, by participating and sharing in the social process, then one "understands" individual and social concepts. Once one understands the "meaning" of these concepts, then one *already knows* all there is to know about man and social life. To understand the world, we need therefore not look at it, but merely analyze our concepts.

[22] Explanatory Incompleteness

CARL G. HEMPEL

The Concepts of Covering-Law Explanation as Explicatory Models

1 GENERAL CHARACTER AND INTENT OF THE MODELS

We have by now distinguished three basic types of scientific explanation: deductive-nomological, inductive-statistical, and deductive-statistical.[1] The first of these is often referred to as the covering-law model [2] or the deductive

50 P. Winch, *The Idea of a Social Science* (London: Routledge and Kegan Paul, 1958).
1 For explication of these notions, see pp. 180–185 of this volume.—Ed.
2 Hempel remarks on p. 345, *op. cit.*, that he takes this suggestive phrase from W. Dray, *Laws and Explanations in History*, Oxford University Press, Oxford, 1957.—Ed.

model of explanation, but since the other two types also involve reference to covering laws, and since one of them is deductive as well, we will call the first more specifically the *deductive-nomological model;* analogously, we will speak of the others as the *inductive-statistical* and the *deductive statistical models of explanation.*

As is made clear by our earlier discussions, these models are not meant to describe how working scientists actually formulate their explanatory accounts. Their purpose is rather to indicate in reasonably precise terms the logical structure and the rationale of various ways in which empirical science answers explanation-seeking why-questions. The construction of our models therefore involves some measure of abstraction and of logical schematization.

In these respects, our concepts of explanation resemble the concept, or concepts, of mathematical proof (within a given mathematical theory) as construed in metamathematics. Let us note the principal points of resemblance.

In either case, the models seek to explicate the use and function of certain "explicandum" terms—'proof' and its cognates in one case, 'explanation' and its cognates in the other. However, the models are selective; they are not meant to illuminate all the different customary uses of the terms in question, but only certain special ones. Thus, metamathematical proof theory is concerned only with the notion of proof in mathematics. To put the theory forward is not to deny that there are other contexts in which we speak of proofs and proving, nor is it to assert that the metamathematical concepts are relevant to those contexts.

Similarly, to put forward the covering-law models of scientific explanation is not to deny that there are other contexts in which we speak of explanation, nor is it to assert that the corresponding uses of the word 'explain' conform to one or another of our models. Obviously, those models are not intended to reflect the various senses of 'explain' that are involved when we speak of explaining rules of a contest, explaining the meaning of a cuneiform inscription or of a complex legal clause or of a passage in a symbolist poem, explaining how to bake Sacher torte or how to repair a radio. Explicating the concept of scientific explanation is not the same thing as writing an entry on the word 'explain' for the *Oxford English Dictionary.* Hence to deplore, as one critic does, the "hopelessness" of the deductive-nomological model on the ground that it does not fit the case of explaining or understanding the rules of Hanoverian succession [3] is simply to miss the intent of the model. And it is the height of irrelevance to point out that the deductive-nomological model presupposes that explanations are formulated in a "descriptive language," whereas "there are clearly cases where we can explain without language, e.g., when we explain to the

---

[3] M. Scriven, "Truisms as the Grounds for Historical Explanations," *Theories of History,* P. Gardiner, ed., The Free Press, New York, 1959, pp. 443–475.

mechanic in a Yugoslav garage what has gone wrong with the car." [4] This is like objecting to a metamathematical definition of proof on the ground that it does not fit the use of the word 'proof' in 'the proof of the pudding is in the eating,' nor in '86 proof Scotch.' Wordless gesticulation intended to indicate to a Yugoslav mechanic what is wrong with the car indeed does not qualify as scientific explanation according to any of our models; but that is as it should be, for a construal of scientific explanation that did admit this case would thereby show itself to be seriously inadequate.

In support of the idea that all these different uses of the word 'explain' should be encompassed by an adequate analysis of explanation, Scriven has argued that they all have the same "logical function," about which he remarks: "the request for an explanation presupposes that *something* is understood, and a complete answer is one that relates the object of inquiry to the realm of understanding in some comprehensible and appropriate way. What this way is varies from subject matter to subject matter . . . ; but the *logical function* of explanation . . . is the same in each field." [5] But while the opening remark of this passage may well apply to many different kinds of explanation, neither it nor the rest of Scriven's remarks on the subject concern what could properly be called a *logical* aspect of explanation. Indeed, such expressions as 'realm of understanding' and 'comprehensible' do not belong to the vocabulary of logic, for they refer to the psychological or pragmatic aspects of explanation. We will consider these aspects in the next section and will see that when construed as observations about the pragmatics rather than the logic of explanation, characterizations such as Scriven's are quite relevant.

But the different ways of explaining contemplated by Scriven certainly cannot be said to have the same logical function. For, first, even the linguistic means which serve to indicate the subject matter of different kinds of explanation are of different logical character. For example, when an explanation is to indicate the "meaning" of a literary passage, a symbol, a work of art, and the like, the explanandum will be specified by means of a *noun-phrase* ('the ampersand sign,' 'the first sentence of Genesis,' 'the swastika'); whereas explanations of the kind we have been considering are concerned with facts, occurrences, events, uniformities—any one of which is properly characterized by means of a *sentence* (which appears as the explanandum-sentence in our schemata). Secondly, the problem of specifying meanings and that of stating the "causes" of an occurrence or perhaps the reasons for which an action was done surely are of different logical character; and the adequacy of the solutions proposed in each case must

[4] M. Scriven, "Explanations, Predictions, and Laws," *Minnesota Studies in the Philosophy of Science*, University of Minnesota Press, Minneapolis, 1962, **III**, p. 192. That such objections are irrelevant has been stressed also by May Brodbeck. "Explanation, Prediction, and 'Imperfect' Knowledge," *ibid.*, p. 240. [Reprinted in this volume, pp. 363–398.] Some perceptive and stimulating comments on this issue and on other aspects of "the quarrel about historical explanation" will be found in R. H. Weingartner, "The Quarrel About Historical Explanation," *The Journal of Philosophy*, 1961. [Reprinted in this volume, pp. 349–362.]

[5] Scriven, "Explanations, Predictions, and Laws," *op. cit.*, p. 202. Italics the author's.

be judged by quite different criteria. The differences between the tasks to be accomplished by these and other kinds of explanation lie, in fact, precisely in differences between the logical structure of the corresponding kinds of explanation.

From the selectiveness of explicatory models of proof and of explanation let us now turn to another common feature. Metamathematical proof theory is not intended to give a descriptive account of how mathematicians formulate their proofs. Indeed the formulations that mathematicians actually offer will usually depart to some extent from that called for by rigorous and, as it were, "ideal" metamathematical standards. Yet those standards may be said to exhibit the logical structure and the rationale of mathematical demonstration and to provide criteria for the critical appraisal of particular proofs that might be proposed.

A proposed proof may then be found to depart from a given theoretical standard only in inessential ways; for example, by omitting as obvious certain intermediate steps in the argument; or by failing to mention certain premises, which are taken to be understood, and which can be specified explicitly if the need should arise. In such cases, we might say that the proof is *elliptically formulated*. On the other hand, the shortcomings may be crucial, as in the various proofs of the postulate of the parallels on the basis of the other postulates of Euclidean geometry.

In addition to providing standards for critical appraisal, the construction of rigorous concepts of mathematical proof has permitted the development of a powerful theory which has yielded far-reaching and often quite unexpected results concerning provability, decidability, and definability in mathematical systems of specified kinds.

Analytic models of scientific explanation, I think, can serve similar purposes, if on a much more modest scale. As for the possibility of general systematic developments, we might mention, for example, the results established by Ramsey and by Craig [6] concerning the role and the possible dispensability, in the context of scientific explanation, of principles ostensibly referring to unobservable "theoretical" entities. These results, and whatever insight they convey into the logic of scientific procedure, could be achieved only by reference to a precisely formulated, and to some extent schematic, conception of scientific explanation.

2 VARIETIES OF EXPLANATORY INCOMPLETENESS

2.1 Elliptic Formulation.

2.1 Elliptic Formulation. Like a proposed mathematical proof, a proposed explanation may be *elliptically formulated*. When we explain, for example, that a lump of butter melted because it was put into a hot frying pan, or

---

[6] See F. P. Ramsey, *The Foundations of Mathematics and Other Logical Essays*, Routledge and Kegan Paul, London, and Harcourt, Brace & World, Inc., New York, 1931, pp. 212–215, 231; and W. Craig, "Replacement of Auxiliary Expressions," *Philosophical Review*, 1956, **65**, 38–55. *Cf.* also the discussion of these results in C. G. Hempel, "The Theoreticians' Dilemma," section 9, *Minnesota Studies in the Philosophy of Science*, Vol. II, University of Minnesota Press, Minneapolis, 1958.

that a small rainbow appeared in the spray of a lawn sprinkler because sunlight was reflected and refracted in the water droplets, we may be said to be offering elliptic versions of D-N explanations. Accounts of this kind forego mention of certain laws or particular facts that are tacitly taken for granted, and whose explicit inclusion in the explanans would yield a complete D-N argument. An elliptically formulated explanation may be said to be *incomplete,* but in a rather harmless sense.

2.2 Partial Explanation. Often, however, explanatory accounts exhibit a more serious kind of incompleteness. Here, the statements actually included in the explanans, even when supplemented by those which may reasonably be assumed to have been tacitly taken for granted in the given context, account for the specified explanandum only partially, in a sense I will try to indicate by an illustration.

In his *Psychopathology of Everyday Life,* Freud offers this description and explanation of a slip of the pen:

On a sheet of paper containing principally short daily notes of business interest, I found, to my surprise, the incorrect date "Thursday, October 20th," bracketed under the correct date of the month of September. It was not difficult to explain this anticipation as the expression of a wish. A few days before, I had returned fresh from my vacation and felt ready for any amount of professional work, but as yet, there were few patients. On my arrival, I had found a letter from a patient announcing her arrival on the twentieth of October. As I wrote the same date in September, I may certainly have thought, "X ought to be here already; what a pity about that whole month!" and with this thought, I pushed the current date a month ahead.[7]

Clearly, this formulation of the intended explanation is elliptical in the sense considered a moment ago; for it does not mention any laws or theoretical principles in virtue of which the subconscious wish, and the other particular circumstances referred to, could be held to explain the slip in question. However, the theoretical ideas that Freud proposes for the interpretation of such lapses strongly suggest that his explanation is governed by a general hypothesis to the effect that when a person has a strong, though perhaps subconscious, wish, then if he commits a slip of pen, tongue, or memory, the slip will take a form in which it expresses, and perhaps symbolically fulfills, that wish.

Even this vague statement is no doubt more definite than what Freud would have been willing to assert; and perhaps, despite Freud's deterministic leanings, it would be more appropriate to conceive of the key hypothesis as being of statistical form, and to regard the proposed explanation as probabilistic. But for the sake of the argument, let us take the hypothesis as stated and incorporate it into the explanans, together with

[7] S. Freud, *Psychopathology of Everyday Life,* trans. by A. A. Brill, The New American Library (Mentor Book Series), New York, 1951, p. 64.

particular statements to the effect that Freud did have the subconscious wish he mentions, and that in fact he was going to commit a slip of the pen. Even then, the resulting explanans enables us to infer only that the slip would take *some form or other* that would express, and perhaps symbolically fulfill, Freud's subconscious wish; but the explanans does not imply that the slip would take the specific form of writing "Thursday, October 20," on the calendar, next to the corresponding date for September.

But inasmuch as the class, say *F*, of slips taking this latter form is a proper subclass of the class, say *W*, of those slips of the pen which in some way express and perhaps symbolically fulfill the specified wish, we might say that the explanandum as described by Freud—i.e., that he made a slip falling into the class *F*—is explained at least in part by this account, which places the slip into the wider class *W*. Arguments of this kind might be called *partial explanations.* Many of the explanatory accounts offered in the literature of psychoanalysis [8] and of historiography are at most partial explanations in this sense: the explanans does not account for the explanandum-phenomenon in the specificity with which it is characterized by the explanandum-sentence, and thus, the explanatory force of the argument is less than what it claims or appears to be.

I think it is important and illuminating to distinguish such partial explanations, however widely they may be offered and accepted, and however fruitful and suggestive they may prove, from what might be called *deductively complete explanations,* i.e., those in which the explanandum as stated is logically implied by the explanans; for the latter do, whereas the former do not, account for the explanandum phenomenon in the specificity with which the explanandum sentence describes it.[9] An explanation that conforms to the D-N model is, therefore, automatically complete in this sense; and a partial explanation as we have characterized it always falls short of being a D-N explanation.

In a statistical explanation, the explanans does not logically imply the explanandum. Are we then to qualify all such explanations as incomplete?

---

[8] This holds true, I think, for the many, often highly suggestive, explanatory analyses included in Freud's *Psychopathology of Everyday Life, op. cit.*

[9] A partial explanation may evidently be more or less weak, depending on how much more extensive is the class within which the explanans places the given case (*W* in our illustration) as compared with the class to which the explanandum-sentence assigns it (*F* in our case). Furthermore, while some partial explanations are no doubt illuminating and suggest further research that might lead to a fuller explanatory account, there are other arguments that completely lack such merit even though they bear a formal resemblance to our illustration, and might for that reason be qualified as partial explanations. Suppose, for example, that *b* is *F* and also *G*, and that we have a D-N explanation of *b* being *F*. Then (save for certain trivial exceptions) the explanans of the latter will automatically afford a basis for a partial explanation of *b* being *G*; for it implies that *b* is *F* and hence that *b* is *F* or *G*: and the class characterized by '*F* or *G*' contains *G* as a proper subclass. But I am not concerned here to explore the conditions under which partial explanations may prove fruitful; I simply wish to call attention to the fact that many explanatory accounts offered in the literature of empirical science have the formal characteristics of partial explanations, and that, as a consequence, they overstate the extent to which they explain a given phenomenon.

Dray raises this question when he asks whether "an event can be *completely* explained (although perhaps in a different sense) without subsuming it under a universal law licensing its deduction, and consequently without showing that it had to happen." [10] The answer that statistical explanations are deductively incomplete would be an uninteresting truism. As is suggested by Dray's clause "although perhaps in a different sense," we are, rather, faced with the question whether the notion of explanatory completeness, which so far has been defined only in reference to proposed D-N explanations, might reasonably be broadened so as to become applicable also within the domain of probabilistic explanation. It seems inadvisable to construct an extended concept of explanatory completeness in such a way as to qualify all statistical explanations as incomplete. For this qualification carries with it connotations of a deficiency, and surely, we cannot regard statistical explanations simply as unsuccessful D-N explanations: they constitute an important type of explanation in their own right. To be sure, the early explanatory uses of statistical laws and theories, for example in nineteenth century physics, were often propounded in the belief that the micro-phenomena involved in the physical processes under study were all subject to strictly universal laws, and that the use of statistical hypotheses and theories was made necessary only by limitations in our ability individually to measure all those micro-phenomena, and then to perform the vast and complex computations that would be required to account for a given physical phenomenon in full microscopic detail. But this idea has gradually been abandoned: in certain areas of physics, such as quantum theory, laws of statistical form have come to be accepted as basic laws of nature. And whatever the future of scientific theorizing may hold in store, this development clearly reflects the realization that logically, statistical explanation is quite independent of the assumption of strictly universal laws and thus constitutes a mode of explanation *sui generis*. All this strongly suggests that under a reasonable extension of the idea of explanatory completeness, any explanation conforming to our statistical model should qualify as formally complete, for it assigns to the explanandum event described by the explanandum statement (or, more properly, to the explanandum statement itself) the logical probability called for by the logical relation between the explanans and explanandum statements. In this respect, such a statistical explanation is analogous to one which conforms to the D-N model, and which thus correctly claims that the explanandum is implied by the explanans (and hence has the logical probability 1 relative to the latter). In the light of this analogy, a proposed statistical explanation should be qualified as partial if the explanans confers the specified probability, not upon the explanandum sentence actually stated, but upon a weaker one related to it in the manner illustrated by our example from Freud. The idea may be illustrated very schematically by reference to that same example. Sup-

10 W. Dray, "The Historical Explanation of Actions Reconsidered," *Philosophy and History*, S. Hook, ed., New York University Press, New York, 1963, p. 119.

pose that the general law we tentatively formulated as the presumptive basis of Freud's explanation were construed instead as a statistical law to the effect that in the presence of a strong though perhaps subconscious wish, the statistical probability is high that if a slip of the pen is committed it will take a form which expresses and perhaps symbolically satisfies that wish. Then Freud's account—now construed as claiming that the explanatory information adduced confers a high logical probability upon the explanandum statement—would count as a *partial statistical explanation;* for the explanans confers a high probability, not upon the statement that the particular slip fell within the class F defined earlier, but upon the weaker statement that the slip belonged to the class W.

2.3 Explanatory Incompleteness vs. Overdetermination.

The considerations just presented are relevant also to the problem illustrated by the following example: [11] Suppose that rod r, made of copper ($C\,r$), is simultaneously subjected to heating ($H\,r$) and to longitudinal stress ($S\,r$), and that, in the process, the rod lengthens ($L\,r$). Then it is possible to formulate two different arguments, each of which constitutes, by the standards we have suggested, a D-N explanation of why the rod lengthened. One of them will be based on the law that copper rods lengthen when heated; the other, on the law that copper rods lengthen when stressed. Schematically:

$$(x)\,[(C\,x \cdot H\,x) \supset L\,x]$$
$$\underline{C\,r \cdot H\,r}$$
$$L\,r$$

$$(x)\,[(C\,x \cdot S\,x) \supset L\,x)$$
$$\underline{C\,r \cdot S\,r}$$
$$L\,r$$

It might be objected that—even granting the truth of all the premises— both accounts are unacceptable since they are "incomplete": each neglects one of the two factors that contributed to the lengthening. In appraising the force of this objection it is again important to be clear about just what is to be explained. If, as in our example, this is simply the fact that Lr, i.e., that r lengthened, or that there was *some* increase in the length of r, then, I think, either of the two arguments conclusively does *that,* and the charge of incompleteness is groundless. But if we wish to account for the fact that the length of the rod increased by so and so much, then clearly neither of the two arguments will do; for we would have to take into account both the temperature increase and the stress, and we would need quantitative laws governing their joint effect on the length of a copper rod. Such common

[11] I am much indebted to my colleague at Princeton, Professor Arthur Mendel, of the Department of Music, who put to me some searching questions which made me aware of the problem here considered. In his paper ("Evidence and Explanation," *Report to the Eighth Congress of the International Musicological Society,* New York, 1961, Barenreiter-Verlag, Kassel, 1962, **II,** 3–18) Mendel takes as his point of departure a concrete problem in the history of music and by reference to it develops some illuminating general ideas concerning, among other things, the significance of the covering-law models for the explanatory objectives of the historian.

locutions as 'explaining the increase in the length of a metal rod' have to be handled with care: they are ambiguous in that they refer to at least the two quite different tasks here distinguished.

Adopting a term that is often used in psychoanalytic theorizing, we might say that an event is *overdetermined* if two or more alternative explanations with nonequivalent explanans-sets are available for it. Thus, the occurrence of some lengthening in the copper rod *r* constitutes a case of *explanatory overdetermination* in virtue of the availability of the alternative explanations mentioned above. In this example, the alternative explanations invoke different laws (and consequently some different statements concerning particular facts). In another, perhaps less interesting, kind of situation which under our definition would likewise qualify as explanatory overdetermination, the alternative explanations rest on the same laws, but adduce different particular circumstances.[12] For example, the state of a deterministic physical system at time *t* can be explained, with the help of the relevant laws, by specifying the state of the system at any earlier time; potentially this permits infinitely many alternative explanations no two of which have logically equivalent explanans-sets.

A problem that bears a certain resemblance to the one just considered has been raised by Scriven, who illustrates it by the following example: In order to explain how a certain bridge came to be destroyed in wartime, "we could appeal to the law 'whenever an atom bomb is released accurately above a bridge and explodes with full force, the bridge is destroyed', plus the appropriate antecedent conditions." But it may also "be the case that whenever 1000 kilograms of dynamite are detonated on the main span of such a bridge it will be destroyed, and that the underground movement has applied just this treatment to this bridge with the attendant destruction occurring between the release and the arrival of the atomic bomb." Scriven holds that this invalidates the bomb explanation, "which cannot account for other features of the event, in this case the time of the destruction." He concludes that in order to rule out such explanations we must impose the requirement of total evidence, even on D-N explanations, in a more specific form which requires "that an explanation be acceptable for a phenomenon only so long as no facts are known about the circumstances surrounding the occurrence of the phenomenon which the explanation cannot accommodate." [13]

But surely the bomb explanation in Scriven's example is unacceptable because its explanans requires the assumption that when the pressure wave of the bomb reached the place in question, there was a bridge there that could be destroyed—an assumption that is false, since at that time the span had already been wrecked by dynamite. Hence, the contemplated bomb

---

12 On this point, *cf.* the remarks in R. B. Braithwaite, *Scientific Explanation,* Cambridge University Press, Cambridge, England, 1953, p. 320.

13 Scriven, "Explanations, Predictions, and Laws," *op. cit.,* pp. 229–30. See also a brief remark, which seems to have the same intent, in Scriven, "New Issues in the Logic of Explanation," *Philosophy and History, op. cit.,* pp. 348–49.

explanation is false in the sense specified in section 2, and no additional requirement is needed to disqualify it or other accounts of this kind.

Besides being unnecessary, the specific requirement Scriven suggests in order to rule out the bomb explanation and its likes is, I think, vastly too strong to be tenable. For neither in scientific research nor in our practical pursuits do we require of an acceptable explanation that it accommodate everything we know—or believe we know—about the facts surrounding the explanandum phenomenon. In the case of the bridge, for example, these facts may include a great deal of information about the shape, size, and location of the fragments after the destruction; perhaps the identities of the dynamiters; their objectives; and many other things. Surely we do not require that all of these details must be accounted for by any acceptable explanation of "how the bridge came to be destroyed."

Finally, the condition proposed by Scriven has nothing whatever to do with the requirement of total evidence; in particular, it is not a "more specific" version of it. And Scriven's contention that some such condition must be imposed even on explanations of deductive form because they do not automatically satisfy the requirement of total evidence [14] overlooks the straightforward proof to the contrary.[15]

2.4 Explanatory Incompleteness and "Concrete Events."

A scientific explanation, we noted earlier, may be regarded as a potential answer to a question of the form 'why is it the case that *p*?', where the place of '*p*' is occupied by an empirical sentence detailing the facts to be explained. Accordingly, both the deductive-nomological and the statistical models of explanation characterize the explanandum-phenomenon by means of a *sentence*, the explanandum-sentence. Take, for example, the explanation of individual facts such as that the length of a given copper rod *r* increased during the time interval from 9.00 to 9.01 A.M., or that a particular drawing *d* from a given urn produced a white ball: here the explanandum phenomena are fully described by the sentences 'the length of copper rod *r* increased between 9.00 and 9.01 A.M.' and 'drawing *d* produced a white ball'. And only when understood in this sense, as fully describable by means of sentences, can particular facts or events be amenable to scientific explanation.

But the notion of an individual or particular event is often construed in quite a different manner. An event in this second sense is specified, not by means of a sentence describing it, but by means of a noun phrase such as

[14] Scriven, "Explanations, Predictions, and Laws," *op. cit.*, p. 230.

[15] In a deductively valid argument, the premises constitute conclusive grounds for asserting the conclusion; and whatever part of the total evidence is not included in the premises is irrelevant to the conclusion in the strict sense that if it were added to the premises, the resulting set of sentences would still constitute conclusive grounds for the conclusion. Or, in the terminology of inductive logic: the logical probability which the premises of a D-N argument confer upon the conclusion is 1, and it remains 1 if part or all of the total evidence is added to the premises.

an individual name or a definite description, as, for example, 'the first solar eclipse of the twentieth century', 'the eruption of Mt. Vesuvius in A.D. 79', 'the assassination of Leon Trotsky', 'the stock market crash of 1929.' For want of a better terminology, individual events thus understood will be referred to as *concrete events*,[16] and facts and events in the first sense here considered will be called sententially characterizable, or briefly, *sentential facts and events.*

The familiar question of whether individual events permit of a complete explanation is no doubt inspired to a large extent by the conception of an individual event as a concrete event. But what could be meant, in this case, by a complete explanation? Presumably, one that accounts for every aspect of the given event. If that is the idea, then indeed no concrete event can be completely explained. For a concrete event has infinitely many different aspects and thus cannot even be completely described, let alone completely explained. For example, a complete description of the eruption of Mt. Vesuvius in A.D. 79 would have to specify the exact time of its occurrence; the path of the lava stream as well as its physical and chemical character- istics—including temperatures, pressures, densities, at every point—and their changes in the course of time; the most minute details of the destruction wreaked upon Pompeii and Herculaneum; full information about all per- sons and animals involved in the catastrophe, including the fact that the remains of such and such victims, found at such and such places, are on display at a museum in Naples; and so on *ad infinitum*. It must also men- tion—for this surely constitutes yet another aspect of that concrete event —all the literature about the subject. Indeed, there seems to be no clear and satisfactory way at all of separating off some class of facts that do not constitute aspects of the concrete event here referred to. Clearly, then, it is quite pointless to ask for a complete explanation of an individual event thus understood.

In sum, a request for an explanation can be significantly made only con- cerning what we have called sentential facts and events; only with respect to them can we raise a question of the form 'why is it the case that p?'. As for concrete events, let us note that what we have called their aspects or characteristics are all of them describable by means of sentences; each of these aspects, then, is a sentential fact or event (e.g., that the eruption of Mt. Vesuvius in A.D. 79 lasted for so many hours; that it killed more than 1000 persons in Pompeii, and so on); with respect to such particular aspects of a concrete event, therefore, the question of an explanation can signifi- cantly be raised. And clearly, when we speak of explaining a particular event, such as the abdication of Edward VIII, we normally think only of

16 I do not wish to suggest that the notion of concrete event here adumbrated is entirely clear; in particular, I do not know how to formulate a necessary and sufficient condition of identity for concrete events. Gibson's perceptive observations on "What is Explained," in *The Logic of Social Enquiry*, Routledge and Kegan Paul, London, Humani- ties Press, New York, 1960, pp. 188–190, are highly relevant to the issues we are about to examine here.

certain aspects of the event as being under scrutiny; what aspects are thus meant to be singled out for explanatory attention will depend on the context of the inquiry.[17]

Though the issues here touched upon are perhaps discussed most frequently with special reference to historical events in their "individuality and uniqueness," the problems inherent in the notion of a concrete event are by no means limited to the historian's domain. An event such as the solar eclipse of July 20, 1963, also possesses an infinity of physical, chemical, biological, sociological, and yet other aspects and thus resists complete description and *a fortiori*, complete explanation. But certain aspects of the eclipse—such as the duration of its totality, and the fact that it was visible in Alaska and subsequently in Maine—may well be capable of explanation.

It would be incorrect, however, to summarize this point by saying that the object of an explanation is always a *kind* of event rather than an individual event. For a kind of event would have to be characterized by means of a predicate-expression, such as 'total solar eclipse' or 'volcanic eruption'; and since this sort of expression is not a sentence, it makes no sense to ask for an explanation of a kind of event. What might in fact be explained is rather the *occurrence of a particular instance of a given kind of event,* such as the occurrence of a total solar eclipse on July 20, 1963. And what is thus explained is definitely an individual event; indeed, it is one that is unique and unrepeatable in view of the temporal location assigned to it. But it is an individual *sentential* event, of course: it can be described by means of the statement that on July 20, 1963, there occurred a total solar eclipse. I agree therefore with Mandelbaum's rejection of Hayek's view that explanation and prediction never refer to an individual event but always to phenomena of a certain kind: "One would think that the prediction of a specific solar eclipse, or the explanation of that eclipse, would count as referring to a particular event even if it does not refer to all aspects of the event, such as the temperature of the sun, or the effect of the eclipse on the temperature of the earth, and the like." [18]

However, given this notion of explaining a particular occurrence of a solar eclipse or of a rainbow, etc., one can speak *derivatively* of a theoretical explanation of solar eclipses or rainbows in general: such an explanation is then one that accounts for any instance of an eclipse or a rainbow. Thus, the notion of explaining particular instances of a given kind of occurrence is the primary one.

[17] As Max Weber remarks, with special reference to historical explanation: "When it is said that history seeks to understand the concrete *reality* of an 'event' in its individuality causally, what is obviously not meant by this . . . is that it is to . . . explain causally the concrete *reality* of an event in the totality of its individual qualities. To do the latter would be not only actually impossible, it would also be a task which is meaningless in principle." (Max Weber, *On the Methodology of the Social Sciences,* trans. and ed. by E. A. Shils and H. A. Finch, The Free Press, New York, 1949, p. 169. Italics the author's.)

[18] M. Mandelbaum, "Historical Explanation: The Problem of 'Covering Laws.' " *History and Theory,* 1961, **I**, 233.

2.5 Explanatory Closure: Explanation Sketch. Perhaps yet another conception of completeness might seem pertinent to the idea of explanation; we shall call it explanatory closure. An explanatory account would be complete in this sense if for every fact or law it invoked, it contained in turn an explanation. In an account with explanatory closure, nothing would be left unexplained. But completeness in this sense obviously calls for an infinite regress in explanation and is therefore unachievable; to seek such completeness is to misunderstand the nature of explanation.

At any stage in the development of empirical science, certain (presumptive) facts will be unexplainable; in particular, those expressed by the most fundamental laws or theoretical principles accepted at the time, those for which no explanation by means of a "deeper" theory is at hand. But while unexplained, these ultimate principles need not be unsupported, for, as hypotheses in empirical science, they will have to be susceptible to test, and it may well be that suitable tests have in fact provided strongly supporting evidence for them.

We have by now considered several ways in which a proposed explanation may deviate from the standards incorporated into our analytic models. In some cases, what is intended as an explanatory account will diverge even more strongly from those standards. A proposed explanation, for example, which is not explicit and specific enough to be reasonably qualified as an elliptically formulated explanation or as a partial one, can often be viewed as an *explanation sketch,* i.e., as presenting the general outlines of what might well be developed, by gradual elaboration and supplementation, into a more closely reasoned explanatory argument, based on hypotheses which are stated more fully and which permit of a critical appraisal by reference to empirical evidence.

The decision whether a proposed explanatory account is to be qualified as an elliptically formulated deductive-nomological or statistical explanation, as a partial explanation, as an explanation sketch, or perhaps as none of these is a matter of judicious interpretation. It calls for an appraisal of the intent of the given account and of the background assumptions that may have been left unstated because they are taken to be understood in the given context. Unequivocal criteria of adjudication cannot be formulated for this purpose any more than for deciding whether a given informally stated argument which does not meet reasonably strict standards of deductive validity is to count as nevertheless valid but enthymematically formulated, or as fallacious, or as a sound inductive argument, or perhaps, for lack of clarity, as none of these.

Among the various respects here considered in which a proposed explanation or demonstration may fall short of the logical standards incorporated into some nonpragmatic model of explanation or proof, there are several which can be characterized only by reference to the knowledge, interests, intentions, and so forth of the persons who propose the arguments in question or of those to whom they are addressed; hence, the corresponding concepts are essentially pragmatic. This is true, for example, of the notions of enthymeme, of elliptically formulated explanation, and of explanation sketch.

3 CONCLUDING REMARK ON THE COVERING-LAW MODELS

We have found, then, that the explanatory accounts actually formulated in science and in everyday contexts vary greatly in the explicitness, completeness, and precision with which they specify the explanans and the explanandum; accordingly, they diverge more or less markedly from the idealized and schematized covering-law models. But, granting this, I think that all adequate scientific explanations and their everyday counterparts claim or presuppose at least implicitly the deductive or inductive subsumability of whatever is to be explained under general laws or theoretical principles.[19] In the explanation of an individual occurrence, those general nomic principles are required to connect the explanandum event with other particulars, and it is by such nomic connection that the latter acquire the status of explanatory factors. In the explanation of general empirical regularities, the nomic principles invoked express more comprehensive uniformities of which those to be explained are strict or approximate specializations. And the covering-law models represent, as far as I can see, the basic logical structure of the principal modes of such explanatory subsumption.

The construal here broadly summarized is not, of course, susceptible to strict "proof"; its soundness has to be judged by the light it can shed on the rationale and force of explanatory accounts offered in different branches of empirical science. Some of the ways in which this construal of explanation may prove illuminating have already been suggested in the course of developing the covering-law models and characterizing their intended function; other such ways should come into view as we proceed, and particularly when we turn, in later sections, to an analysis of certain peculiar explanatory procedures that seem to be at variance with the covering-law construal of explanation. . . .

Explanation vs. Reduction to the Familiar

A predominantly pragmatic conception of explanation as aimed at dispelling the questioner's puzzlement also underlies the widely held view that an

---

[19] This idea needs to be sharply distinguished from another one, which I am not proposing, namely, that any empirical phenomenon can be explained by deductive or inductive subsumption under covering laws. The idea here suggested is that the logic of all scientific explanations is basically of the covering-law variety, but not that all empirical phenomena are scientifically explainable, and even less, of course, that they are all governed by a system of deterministic laws. The question whether all empirical phenomena can be scientifically explained is not nearly as intelligible as it might seem at first glance, and it calls for a great deal of analytic clarification. I am inclined to think that it cannot be given any clear meaning at all; but at any rate, and quite broadly speaking, an opinion as to what laws hold in nature and what phenomena can be explained surely cannot be formed on analytic grounds alone but must be based on the results of empirical research.

explanation must somehow reduce or link the puzzling phenomenon to something with which the questioner is already familiar, and which he accepts as unproblematic. Thus, Bridgman, for example, holds that "the essence of an explanation consists in reducing a situation to elements with which we are so familiar that we accept them as a matter of course, so that our curiosity rests."[20] An examination of this explicitly pragmatic characterization may serve further to clarify and support the case for constructing a nonpragmatic concept of scientific explanation.

Undeniably, many scientific explanations effect, in a sense, a "reduction to the familiar." This might be said, for example, of the wave-theoretical explanation of optical refraction and interference, and of at least some of the explanations achieved by the kinetic theory of heat. In cases of this kind, the concepts and principles invoked in the explanans bear a more or less close resemblance to concepts and principles that have long been used in the description and explanation of some familiar type of phenomenon, such as the propagation of wave motions on the surface of water or the motion of billiard balls.

Concerning the general view of explanation as a reduction to the familiar, let us note first that what is familiar to one person may not be so to another, and that, therefore, this view conceives of explanation as something relative to a questioner. But, as we noted earlier, explanations of the kind empirical science seeks are intended to exhibit objective relationships.

Secondly, the view here under discussion suggests that what is familiar requires no explanation. But this notion does not accord with the fact that scientists have gone to great lengths in an effort to explain "familiar" phenomena, such as the changes of the tides; lightning, thunder, rain, and snow; the blue color of the sky; similarities between parents and their offspring; the fact that the moon appears much larger when it is near the horizon than when it is high in the sky; the fact that certain diseases are "catching," while others are not; and even the familiar fact that it is dark at night. Indeed, the darkness of the night sky appears as a phenomenon much in need of explanation, in view of Olbers' paradox. This argument, put forward in 1826 by the German astronomer Heinrich Olbers, rests on a few simple assumptions, roughly to the effect that the distances and the intrinsic luminosities of the stars have about the same frequency distribution throughout the universe in the past as well as at present; that the basic laws of the propagation of light hold true in all spatio-temporal areas of the universe, and that the universe at large is static, i.e., that no large-scale systematic motions take place in it. From these assumptions it follows that the sky, in all directions and at all times, should be of enormous uniform brightness, and that the energy thus streaming in upon the surface of

[20] P. W. Bridgman, "The Logic of Modern Physics," The Macmillan Company, New York, 1927, p. 37. The pragmatic character of this conception is clearly reflected in Bridgman's remarks that "an explanation is not an absolute sort of thing, but what is satisfactory for one man will not be for another." *Loc. cit.*, p. 38.

the earth should correspond to a temperature of more than 10,000 degrees Fahrenheit.[21]

Olbers' paradox thus raises a 'how-possibly?' question. An answer to it is suggested by the recent theory that the universe is steadily expanding. This theory implies, first, that Olbers' assumption of a static universe is in error, and it supplies, secondly, a positive explanation of the dark night sky by showing that the energy of the radiation received from very distant stars is enormously reduced by the high velocities of their recession.

This example also illustrates a further point, namely, that instead of reducing the unfamiliar to the familiar, a scientific explanation will often do the opposite: it will explain familiar phenomena with the help of theoretical conceptions which may seem unfamiliar and even counter-intuitive, but which account for a wide variety of facts and are well supported by the results of scientific tests.[22]

These observations are applicable also outside the domain of the natural sciences. Their relevance to sociology, for example, is suggested in the opening passage of a book by Homans: "My subject is a familiar chaos. Nothing is more familiar to men than their ordinary, everyday social behavior . . . every man makes his own generalizations about his own social experience, but uses them *ad hoc* within the range of situations to which each applies, dropping them as soon as their immediate relevance is at an end and never asking how they are related to one another . . . the purpose of this book is to bring out of the familiar chaos some intellectual order." [23] Incidentally, Homans goes on to say that the requisite ordering of a body of empirically established sociological facts, represented by low-level generalizations, calls for an *explanation* of those facts; and that such explanation is achieved by means of a "set of more general propositions, still of the same form as the empirical ones, from which you can logically deduce the latter under specified given conditions. To deduce them successfully is to explain them." [24]

To this emphasis on the sociologist's interest in the theoretical explanation of "familiar" generalizations about social behavior, there should be added a reminder that has been stressed by Lazarsfeld, among others; namely, that what are widely regarded as obvious and familiar facts of everyday psychological and sociological experience are sometimes not facts at all but popular stereotypes. This is true—to mention but one of Lazars-

[21] For a fuller presentation of the paradox, and a critical analysis in the light of current cosmological theorizing, see, for example, H. Bondi, *The Universe at Large*, Wm. Heinemann, Limited, London, 1961, chapter 2, and D. W. Sciama, *The Unity of the Universe*, Doubleday & Company (Anchor Books), Garden City, New York, 1961, chapter 6.

[22] This point is stressed also in H. Feigl's concise and illuminating article "Some Remarks on the Meaning of Scientific Explanation," in H. Feigl and W. Sellars, eds. *Readings in Philosophical Analysis*. New York: Appleton-Century-Crofts, 1949, pp. 510–14; and it is lucidly illustrated by reference to the theory of relativity in P. Frank, *Philosophy of Science*, Prentice-Hall, Inc., Englewood Cliffs, New Jersey, 1957, pp. 133–34.

[23] George C. Homans, *Social Behavior. Its Elementary Forms*, New York University Press, New York, 1961, pp. 1–2.

[24] Homans, *op. cit.*, pp. 9–10, italics the author's.

feld's interesting illustrations—of the idea that the intellectual is emotionally less stable than the psychologically more impassive man-in-the-street, and that therefore it was to be expected that among the U.S. soldiers in the Second World War, better educated men showed more psychoneurotic symptoms than those with less education. In fact, the opposite was found to be the case.[25] Thus an explanation of some particular case by reference to the low-level generalization of this stereotype is simply false even though it might be said to effect a reduction to the familiar.

Such reduction, then, as has now been argued at some length, is surely not a necessary condition for an acceptable scientific explanation. But neither is it a sufficient condition; for a request for an explanation is sometimes answered in a way which puts the questioner's curiosity to rest by giving him a sense of familiarity or at-homeness with an initially puzzling phenomenon, without conveying a scientifically acceptable explanation. In this case, one might say, familiarity breeds content, but no insight. For example, as we have just seen, the proffered explanation might be based on a familiar and yet mistaken belief, and will then be false. Or the proposed account might rely on untestable metaphorical or metaphysical ideas rather than on general empirical hypotheses, and then would not afford even a potential scientific explanation. Take for example the "hypothesis of a common subconscious," which has been propounded to explain presumptive telepathic phenomena.[26] It asserts that while in their conscious domains human minds are separate entities, they are connected by a common subconscious, from which the individual consciousnesses emerge like mountainous islands joined by a submarine continent. The suggestive imagery of this account may well evoke a sense of intuitive understanding of telepathic phenomena; the latter seem to have been explained by reduction to ideas with which we are quite familiar. Yet we have been given a simile rather than a scientific explanation. The account offers us no grounds on which it would be reasonable to expect the occurrence of telepathic phenomena, nor does it give us any clues as to the conditions under which such phenomena are likely to occur. Indeed, in the form here outlined the notion of a common subconscious has no clear implications concerning empirical phenomena and is not amenable, therefore, to objective test or to significant explanatory or predictive use.

A similar critique applies to neovitalistic explanations of certain biological phenomena in terms of entelechies or vital forces. Such accounts do not specify under what conditions a vital force will exert its influence and what specific form its manifestations will take, nor, in the case of external interference with an organism, to what extent an entelechy will compensate for

---

[25] See P. F. Lazarsfeld, "The American Soldier—An Expository Review," *Public Opinion Quarterly*, 1949, **13**, 379–80.

[26] See the critical reference in H. H. Price, "The Theory of Telepathy," *Horizon*, 1945, **12**, 45–63, and *cf.* W. Carington's use of the idea as "a simile" (*Matter, Mind and Meaning*, Methuen & Co., Ltd., London, 1949, pp. 223ff.), as well as his more specific account of the conception of a common subconscious, *op. cit.*, pp. 208ff.

the resulting disturbance. By contrast, an explanation of planetary motions in terms of the Newtonian theory of gravitation specifies what gravitational forces will be exerted upon a given planet by the sun and by other planets, given their masses and distances, and it specifies further what changes in motion are to be expected as a result of those forces. Both accounts invoke certain "forces" that cannot be directly observed—one of them, vital forces, the other, gravitational ones; yet the latter account has explanatory status while the former does not. This is a consequence of the fact that the Newtonian theory offers specific laws governing gravitational forces, whereas neovitalism specifies no laws governing vital forces and is, in effect, only metaphorical. Thus, it is covering laws or theoretical principles that are crucial to a scientific explanation, rather than the sense of familiarity that its wording may impart.

The laws invoked in a proposed scientific explanation are of course capable of test; and adverse test results may lead to their rejection. No such fate threatens explanations in terms of similes or metaphors: since they do not specify what to expect under any empirical conditions, no empirical test can possibly discredit them. But absolute immunity to disconfirmation is not an asset but a fatal defect when we are concerned, as is scientific research, to arrive at an objectively testable and empirically well-supported body of empirical knowledge. An account that has no implications concerning empirical phenomena cannot serve this purpose, however strong its intuitive appeal: from the point of view of science, it is a *pseudo-explanation,* an explanation in appearance only.

In sum then, it is neither necessary nor sufficient for the scientific adequacy of an explanation that it should reduce the explanandum to ideas with which we are already familiar. . . .

[23] Imperfect Knowledge

GUSTAV BERGMANN

Process and Perfect Knowledge

As we ordinarily use 'process,' we often mean no more than a temporal sequence of events. This idea requires no term of its own, except perhaps

Reprinted with permission of the copyright owners, the Regents of the University of Wisconsin, from Gustav Bergmann, *Philosophy of Science,* 1957, The University of Wisconsin Press.

for the sake of idiomatic convenience. When we use 'process' more specifically, as we sometimes also do, then it refers to the temporal sequence of the "states" of a "system" *as predicted by a process law* (P), either one that we know and could actually apply if we went to the trouble, or one we expect to discover, or one that could at least in principle be discovered and applied. This is the technical sense in which I shall use 'process.' From our paradigm [celestial mechanics] and the thermodynamic example we know that there are temporal sequences of events believed to be in fact processes for reasons as excellent as one can ever hope to have within the inescapable limits of measurement and inductive "uncertainty." Of course, this is a matter of fact, not of logical or any other "necessity." . . .

As far as it goes and as far as its *relevant variables* (V) *themselves* are concerned, a process theory (or law) is perfect knowledge. To dispose of the first of the two qualifying clauses, "as far as it goes," consider two process theories such that the second is a deductive consequence of the first without the first being a deductive consequence of the second. Clearly, the first posesses one kind of excellence, namely, scope to a higher degree than the second. The first qualifying clause indicates that this is not the kind of excellence I have in mind when I call process knowledge perfect. . . .

Consider now a variable of which we have process knowledge. In other words, we know or we know how to find the (smallest) closed system among whose relevant variables it occurs. ('Closed' in 'closed system' is really redundant; but sometimes redundancy helps.) Thus we know all the other variables with which our variable "interacts." (I have promised to explicate 'interaction' later. But in this context the word is clear.) We know, in particular, how to compute the future as well as the past values of our variables from what we can now measure (provided we also know the past or future boundary conditions). Retrospectively we know, furthermore, what the present value of our variable would have been if some earlier state of the system had been different from what it actually was. Prospectively, we know how to influence its (and the other relevant variables') future values by present interference with the system from outside; and we also know the limits of such interference. What else, I ask, could we possibly want to know about this variable in a scientific way? But I had better stop to consider what I am doing. I set out to explain the "perfection" of process knowledge and find myself asking a rhetorical question: What else could we possibly want to know in a scientific way? This did not happen by chance. Nor do I try to get by with mere eloquence. What precedes the rhetorical question is already the explication of what I mean by perfect knowledge. It shows, I think, what scientific knowledge is by showing what it is in the ideal limit. The story of the boiling pot was simple enough to give the idea; Newton's story is complex enough to give the ideal. Understanding them both, we understand the nature of science.

The other qualification, in the opening sentence of the next to the last paragraph, "as far as the relevant variables themselves are concerned," must still be explained. Once again, two examples will get us to the point more quickly than a general statement. Assume, quite unrealistically, that we actually have a process theory of human behavior whose relevant variables are all either environmental or of the kind now used in clinical psychology. This is the first example. Or, remember that so-called phenomenological thermodynamics, which counts temperature, heat, pressure, and so on, but no atomic notions among its relevant variables, is in fact an excellent process theory. This is the second example. In the first case, we may still want to know what connections, if any, there are between the clinical variables and those of physiology; or, to say the same thing differently, we may want to know how people's behavior is connected with what goes on inside their bodies. In the second case, we may wish to inquire whether and how, say, the temperature and the heat content of a gas are connected with properties of the particles that presumably make up the gas. This shows why I added the qualification "as far as the relevant variables themselves are concerned." . . .

Geometrical laws are the most striking examples of *cross-sectional laws.* ('Cross-sectional' is taken from the metaphor that considers a state a temporal cross-section of a process. A so-called still or frame is in this sense a cross-section of a film.) Such laws state functional connections obtaining among the values which several variables have at the same time. There is a hard core of cross-sectional laws, including those of geometry, that cannot be deduced from or in any other sense be "reduced" to process laws. All-important as they are, process laws are therefore not literally all of science, not even in the ideal limit. The nature of cross-sectional laws is best understood by distinguishing them from so-called equilibrium laws on the one hand and from definitional connections among the variables of V on the other.

Equilibrium Laws

Take the law of the lever, $p_1d_1 = p_2d_2$. Since the four letters stand for the values the four variables have at the same time, one might at first sight mistake the law of the lever for a cross-sectional law. In this respect there is indeed no difference between the two kinds of law; yet there is in another. A cross-sectional law states a functional connection that obtains under all circumstances (provided the law is true). An *equilibrium law,* such as the law of the lever, says that some change will occur if the connection its formula states does not obtain. Accordingly, the equilibrium laws of a system follow deductively from its process law, but not necessarily conversely. In this sense equilibrium laws are expendable; some cross-sectional laws, we saw, are not. To grasp this more firmly, consider that we know the (P) of a system. Clearly, it is a purely mathematical job to determine those V's

for which a certain x, or certain x's, or certain functions of certain x's
remain constant for t $>$ 0. (If we choose the x's or the functions beforehand,
then there may be no such V's. If, however, (P) is a system of differential
equations, then there are always some such functions, technically known
as intermediate integrals. This is the root of the so-called conservation
principles of physics. If, on the other hand, one knows some equilibrium
conditions of a process, one does not by this token alone know the law
of the process. For to know that if certain conditions are fulfilled no change
will occur (in certain respects) is not the same as to know what will occur
if they are not fulfilled. (Technically again, a "complete" set of intermediate integrals is equivalent to (P).) Equilibrium laws are just one kind
of imperfect knowledge. Another name for them, taken from mechanics,
is static laws or laws of statics. Process laws, on the other hand, are the
most accomplished dynamic laws or laws of dynamics, which is but another phrase for "laws of temporal change." This is the only good meaning
of the traditional dichotomy statics-dynamics. I thought I had better mention it, since both words, particularly 'dynamics,' are used a good deal in
the philosophy of the behavior sciences. As we see, it makes sense to say
that these sciences should search for dynamic laws. All sciences should. . . .

"Mechanism" and Determinism

Every (successfully applied) process schema is *mechanistic* in the following sense of this ambiguous word. As long as the system remains closed,
one can if one knows its present predict its future. There are no alternatives
and there is nothing any part of the system can "do about it." Its future is,
as it were, determined by its present. Sometimes this feature is also called
deterministic. More frequently 'deterministic' is reserved for the extension
of the idea of process to "the whole world." A determinist asserts that the
world is "comprehensively lawful." This means either of two things. It may
mean, rather elusively as we saw, that there is one and only one gigantic
process. Or it may mean that for any variable we could, in principle,
find a process, which is not necessarily that one all-encompassing process,
among whose relevant variables it appears. This, then, is the thesis of
determinism. The most important thing about such a thesis is to grasp
firmly what sort of assertion it is. The way I stated the deterministic thesis
leaves no doubt that it is, after a fashion, a statement of fact. I say after a
fashion because it is so broad and so desperately general a statement, so
sweeping an anticipation based on the past and present successes of science
that it is, in a sense, not very interesting and, at least to me, not very
exciting. On the other hand, it is only fair to point out that some such
determinism is, in fact, the frame of reference of all science, including the
behavior sciences. This is just another aspect of the profound impact of
the Newtonian idea of process. Now I have hinted before that I don't like

'frame of reference.' The phrase is pompous, I think, and it has been ridden to death. Yet one must admit that it has some virtue of suggestion. It suggests, first, that if one did not believe what one's "frame of reference" asserts or implies, it wouldn't be reasonable to do what one actually does; and it suggests, second, that this "belief" need not be explicitly held or, if it is, that one takes it for granted without necessarily having examined it. A frame of reference is not a philosophical position. Philosophy comes in only when one attempts either to prove or to refute such a thesis or frame of reference on "philosophical" grounds. In the case at hand the two "philosophical" parties are the determinists (mechanists) and the antideterminists (antimechanists, voluntarists, indeterminists). As one would expect, both parties use 'mechanistic,' 'deterministic,' and their cognates "philosophically." The view logical analysts take of their controversy is very dim. Analysis reveals that the issue is wholly and without residue a verbal tangle or, to speak for once with the vulgar, that there is no conflict whatsoever between "science" and "human freedom." Yet it is a matter of record that the impact of this particular controversy has been tremendous, not only in the intellectual history of our civilization in general but also in that of the behavior sciences. Nor is this a matter of the remote past. As late as the turn of the century William James' obsession with a wholly unanalyzed notion of freedom kept him from really understanding what psychology is all about. A glance into the even later writings of Wertheimer, particularly the more philosophical ones, convinces one that the defense of "freedom" against "mechanistic associationism" was one of his dominant intellectual motives. What goes for James and Wertheimer goes equally for Koehler as well as for Dewey, who was one of the founding fathers of Functionalism. The argument still continues, though usually more covertly, among psychologists interested in the philosophy of their field. I can therefore not ignore it completely, though I shall say as little about it as I responsibly can.

The cause of all this hubbub is not hard to find. Assume that a man or a group of men and (a part of) their environment can from without actually be considered as a closed system. As the antideterminists "philosophically" use their words, it would follow that these people are not really "free" to make choices, that it is futile for them to try to live up to their moral standards, and so on, and so on, up or down the ladder of mostly specious arguments from wholly specious premises to those dreaded cynical conclusions which, for better or for worse, are also a part of our tradition. One compromise that has been proposed and that is still being proposed, either overtly or covertly, is that while there is in principle no process knowledge of human behavior, there can be imperfect knowledge about it of the kind that is called statistical. This "compromise" draws some specious support from two sources; first, from the circumstances that a rather large part of our present knowledge in the behavior sciences is in fact statistical; second, from some "philosophical" misinterpretations of the statistical features of modern physics. "Mechanism," or so we are told, has broken down even in physics. I shall say what needs to be said in the next section, both in the main text and, as far as physics is concerned, in small print.

'Mechanistic' occurs not only in these discussions but also on other occasions in the philosophy of psychology. Many of its uses are blurred; some are outright ideological. To trace them, as we must, a brief glossary of the several relatively clear meanings of the term will be helpful. This is as good a place as any to insert it. (a) 'Mechanistic' is used to refer to the broad "frame of reference" or "thesis" I stated above. (b) 'Mechanism' and 'mechanistic' are used as names for the position and the characteristic arguments of those who try, mistakenly as we saw, to anchor the deterministic frame of reference "philosophically." (c) 'Mechanism' is used as the name of a more specific thesis or frame of reference according to which biology is "reducible" to physics and chemistry. Its denial is known as vitalism. The present frame of reference in biology is mechanistic. But the notion of reduction requires analysis. . . . (d) Within physics (more precisely, in view of the theoretical unification that was recently achieved, within physics-chemistry) a theory is called mechanistic if and only if its basic entities are "particles" that "move" in orbits. If "all of physics" is thought to be in the scope of such a theory, then physics itself is spoken of as mechanistic. Contemporary physics is not mechanistic in this sense.

Interaction and Laws of Relative Autonomy

Now, briefly, for *interaction*. Suppose somebody is told what the variables (C and S) of a (successfully applied) process schema are, but is not told what its (P) is.[1] Then he is told of two systems that differ in one and only one variable. This leaves two possibilities. Either the two systems are identical and their states at a certain time, say, S^0 and $S^{0'}$ differ in one and only one variable, e.g., $x_1^0 \neq x_1^{0'}$. Or the two systems differ in one and only one index, say, $c_1 \neq c_1'$. For what I have to say there is no difference between these alternatives; so I shall fix the ideas by considering the first. Assume, next, that the person who has been given this information is asked what difference, if any, there will be between two later states of the two systems, say, between S^{t_1} and $S^{t_1'}$. Will they be equal? If not, will they differ in x_1 and in x_1 only? Or will they also differ with respect to the values of some other variables, say, x_2 and x_3? Or will they perhaps differ in all variables? The only correct answer is: From what you told me I cannot tell. This

---

[1] $C = [c_1, c_2, \ldots, c_m]$ stands for a description of the (temporally) constant identifiers of the system and $S = [x_1, x_2, \ldots, x_n]$ for its (temporally) variable states. Since the c's vary from system to system, they too may be spoken of as variables. A process law (P) connects the state of a system ($C \& S^t$) at any one time with its state at any other time. See also p. 425.—Ed.

is the gist of the matter. But it will pay to elaborate the answer. . . .
The reason that our friend cannot tell is that while he has been given C, S^0,
and $S^{0'}$, he has not been given (P). If he is given (P), he can compute both
S^{t_1} and $S^{t_1'}$ and then answer all possible questions of the kind we imagine
he has been asked. Again, purely verbal elaborations of this statement don't
really add anything to it. But since misconceptions in this area played and
still play a disastrous role in the philosophy of the behavior sciences, I shall
nevertheless venture some comments.

'Depending on' and 'interacting with' are used as virtual synonyms, which
does no harm as long as one keeps in mind that the first sometimes also
covers the functional connections stated by cross-sectional laws while the
second refers more exclusively to the "dependencies" among successive states
of a process. What depends on what, then, or what interacts with what
and how is a matter of fact. The process formula (P) is the complete source
of information concerning all such mutual dependencies or interactions
among the relevant variables of a process. If one is, like the man in my
story, given C, S^0, and $S^{0'}$ without being given (P), one must therefore in
principle be prepared to discover that S^{t_1} and $S^{t_1'}$ will differ in all respects.
On the other hand, there is no reason whatsoever to believe that this will
actually be so. The mistaken belief that it must be so I call the dogma of
total interaction or, more sonorously, of total dynamic interaction or interdependence. . . . This confused idea plays a crucial role in the Gestalt doctrine. After one has discovered a specific process law there is not much
point in describing verbally the kinds of dependencies that do or do not
bind its variables. If, on the other hand, one tries to distinguish and
describe such kinds of types by means of the general process schema, one
will find that at least some of them correspond to kinds or types of imperfect knowledge. I postpone a closer look at this typology until the next
section. An extreme example will be useful right now. Assume that two
systems agree in one and only one variable. As it happens, this variable is
temperature and the common value is 5000F. Under this initial condition
all sorts of systems will tend toward the same state—ashes. Generally, different initial conditions S^0 may lead to the same state of equilibrium provided only that the value or values of a certain variable or variables in S^0
lie within, or above, or below certain limits. Again, this equilibrium may
be reached after the same or after different time intervals, depending on
the values of the remaining variables; and it may be an equilibrium with
respect to all or some of the variables of the process. There is really no
end to the variety. The two extreme cases are total dynamic interaction
on the one hand and, on the other, the discovery that the system consists
of two (or more) closed subsystems. In the latter case there are again two
possibilities. Either there is no interaction whatsoever between the two
subsystems or there is no interaction provided all or some of the variables
have certain initial values. To obtain an illustration of the second alternative, modify our thermodynamic example by using an insulating container

with a partition wall and include the thermic conductivity of the wall among the variables of the total system. If the partition wall is completely insulating, then the total system consists of two subsystems.

In view of some recent experimentation and discussion a psychological example should be of some interest. Divide V into two nonoverlapping groups, V_1 and V_2. It may be that as long as the values of the variables in V_1^0 remain within certain limits, the future course of the variables in V_2 is either not at all or (more probably) only to a minor extent affected by variations in V_1^0. If one wants a word to refer to this state of affairs, one may say that the variables in V_2 are *relatively autonomous*. Perception or, more precisely, the perceptual responses of the normal adult members of our civilization determine an area of relative autonomy. . . . If you and I and Tom, Dick, and Harry are shown a small red cube on top of a large black cylinder, we shall all correctly describe their colors, shapes, and mutual position even though I, unlike the rest of us, am worrying about the next chapter of my book; even though Tom, unlike the rest of us, is hungry and has a splitting headache; and even though Dick's anxieties are, quite irrationally, aroused by the sight of such arrangements. If Harry fails on the colors because he is color blind we are not bothered, for we can systematically account for his failure. The word 'normal', which I inserted above, covers this contingency. Dick's case is more interesting. Probably he will try to "overlook" the arrangement as long as he can. This, however, is a different story. I haven't said that perceptual selectivity and attention are relatively autonomous with respect to personality and motivational variables. This dependency is notoriously rather gross. Even so, if Dick can no longer avoid "looking" at the arrangement, his account may differ from ours. If such be the nature of his neurosis, he may, for instance, see purple where we see red. Studying such cases as his, we shall discover the limits of the relative autonomy of the perceptual response. Some recent experiments have produced some very neat results in this area. But to insist that in view of these results one must no longer speak of perception in isolation from personality and motivation makes no more sense than to reject those thermodynamic process laws which apply only if the amount of heat transformed into mechanical energy is negligible. Interestingly, this unreasonable claim is not made by the designers of the experiments I mentioned but, rather, by some "philosophical" advocates of total dynamic interaction.

One more example. Assume that there is a process schema of the "social process" and that some of its relevant variables are technological and economic. I, for one, would not grant this assumption; but if one grants it, for the sake of the argument, then it would make sense to say, though it wouldn't necessarily be true, that the technological and economic variables determine an area of relative autonomy. As it happens, this is one of the more reasonable interpretations of Marxist doctrine. If it is stated with the proper precautions concerning the questionable part of the assumption, namely, that there is a process law in the group variables, then there is in fact nothing particularly Marxist about it. . . .

Indeterminateness

To know a process law is to know everything there is to be known about its relevant variables, at least as far as these variables themselves are concerned. Any other law containing some or all of these variables (and no others) says less and follows in some sense deductively from the process law. I say in some sense because the deduction requires an additional premiss. Consider a schematic case. Examining the (P) of a certain process we discover the following. Let a, b, T be three constants. If $x_1^0 > a$, then x_3 will at some later moment t_1 which precedes T reach and thereafter maintain the value b; in symbols: $x_3^t = b$ for $t \geq t_1$ and $t_1 < T$. This, we find from our examination of the process law, does not depend on the values of any other of the variables in S; the only thing depending upon them, as far as the future value course of x_3 is concerned, is the actual value of t_1 (within the limits 0 and T). Thus we have deduced the following law (L): If in a "system" $[c_1, c_2, \ldots, c_m]$ the character x_1 has at some time a value exceeding a, then the character x_3 will *at some later time but before T units of time have lapsed* reach and thereafter maintain the value b. Clearly one can discover such a law without having discovered the process law first. If, on the other hand, one knows the latter then one can deduce the former. The additional premiss in this case is $x_1^0 > a$. Loosely speaking, it amounts merely to a "specialization" of the process. I put 'system' in (L) between double quotes in order to remind us that the strict use of this word involves the idea of process.

Anyone who fully grasps for the first time the subtlety and perfection of process knowledge may well wonder how any generality less subtle and less perfect could ever be true "without exception." If such a one reflects on the schematic example I just gave he will no longer wonder. Even so, he might reasonably expect any law not a process law to have some features that are, so to speak, the marks of its imperfection. There are indeed such features. Probably every law not a process law has at least one of them. (I say probably because I do not see how one could or, for that matter, why one should make a categorical assertion on this point. There is such a thing as specious precision.) In our case the characteristic feature is stated by the phrase I italicized in the formulation of (L): at same later time but before T units of time have lapsed. Whether the interval $[0, T]$ is a minute or a thousand years makes no difference in principle. More often than not we do not even bother to specify T; we just say "at some later time" and rely on the context for some reasonable limitation. The characteristic imperfection is that (L) is not fully determinate with respect to time. There is still another kind of indeterminateness by which one can easily spot imperfect laws. I am not overly fond of 'indeterminate.' I use it merely because I think that if a single word can be made to do at all, it is handier than a phrase. Probably the phrase 'width of range' conveys the idea more adequately. It certainly fits better what I now have in mind. A law states that if something of a certain sort is the case then something of a certain other sort will also be the case (I neglect temporal order). Probing more closely what these sorts are, one often finds that the blur at their edges is much larger than it would need to be. Or, if the two sorts are well defined so that there is no such blur, it turns out that their definitions cover a rather wide range of rather different things.

Indeterminateness does not prevent a law from being, in the light of later process knowledge, "without exceptions." Quite to the contrary. One might say that, not being a process law, its indeterminateness is the price it pays for its truth. Other nonprocess generalities have "exceptions." Strictly speaking, they are false. As one usually speaks, they hold only "under ordinary circumstances." This is another phrase that occurs characteristically in imperfect laws; 'under normal conditions' and 'as a rule' are used synonymously. What these phrases mean is that the "law" holds in many cases, though not in all, and that it therefore probably holds "without exception" under conditions as yet either completely unknown or but vaguely glimpsed. To pursue this line of thought is one possible approach to the notion of statistical laws. The time has indeed come when we must pay some attention to that particular kind of imperfect knowledge. But this requires some preparation and some care; so I shall take up a few other matters first.

Dynamic versus Cross-Sectional Laws

How an accurate conception of process leads to a typology of imperfect laws is by now clear. The way I proceeded, we have already collected some such types. Equilibrium laws are one; laws of relative autonomy are another. These two require no further discussion. Nor would there be any point in making the taxonomy as precise or as exhaustive as possible. Some further types are worth considering, though. I shall say a few words about those cross-sectional laws which, unlike some others, can be derived from a process schema. Then I shall take a look at developmental laws. There are, third, statistical laws. These three types I shall in this order discuss in this section. Still another type, so-called historical laws, are so important in the behavior sciences that they must be dealt with at some length. I shall treat them in the next section. First of all I want to call attention to one particular excellence of process laws. I saved this comment because I think that now is the time when it will be most effective.

Let C, S^{t_1}, S^{t_2} signify as before (p. 420). A moment's reflection shows that the process law permits not only the inference I represented by

(1) $(C \mathbin{\&} S^{t_1}) \longrightarrow S^{t_2}$,

but also

(2) $(C \mathbin{\&} S^{t_2}) \longrightarrow S^{t_1}$.

Taken together, (1) and (2) are equivalent to

$$C \longrightarrow (S^{t_1} \leftrightarrows S^{t_2}).$$

In words: If the system is known then any two of its states can by means of the process law be inferred from each other. Or, as one also says, any state of the system is a *necessary and sufficient* condition of any other. The logical connective stating such conditions is 'if and only if.' Take 'If *A* then *B*.' If it is true then *A* is a sufficient condition of *B*. Similarly, 'If not-*A* then not-*B*' or, what amounts to the same thing, 'If *B* then *A*,' If true, makes *A* a necessary condition of *B*. '*A* if and only if *B*' makes each of the two states of affairs a necessary and sufficient condition of the other. Replace '*A*' and '*B*' by 'S^{t_1}' and 'S^{t_2}'. In the terminology of cause and effect, each cross section of a process is the effect of any earlier and the cause of any later cross section and we can infer the cause from its effect as well as the effect from its cause. A law of temporal change that is not a process law may state conditions that are both necessary and sufficient. To understand this possibility, consider a schematic case. Assume that the examination of a certain (P) yields the following result: 'If $x_1^0 = a$, then at some later moment t_1, $x_4^{t_1} = b$; and if $x_4^0 = b$, then at some earlier moment $- t_2$, $x_1^{-t_2} = a$.' In words: If the system exemplifies at a certain time a certain character, then it exemplifies at some later time a certain other character, *and conversely*. Yet most dynamic laws (i.e., laws involving temporal change) that are not process laws state, in fact, conditions that are merely sufficient (or merely necessary). Take 'If a man is hanged by the neck, he will die,' a law that has been known for quite some time. It does not justify the inference that if a man is dead he has been hanged by the neck. Perhaps he was shot or poisoned. Or perhaps he died a natural death. It would seem that when we know a dynamic law of some complexity which comprehends all the alternatives of such "multiple causation," then we are at least within hailing distance of process knowledge.

Remember the laws of geometry. They are cross-sectional; yet they cannot be deduced from a process theory. There are other laws of this kind, for instance, such truisms as 'everything green is extended,' of which scientists do not ordinarily think as "laws," even though they are synthetic generalities. Cross-sectional laws that cannot be deduced from process laws are not, as I use the term, items of imperfect knowledge. They are much less impressive than process laws; at least, scientists since the time of Newton have not been overly impressed by them. Yet they are in no way logically subordinate to process laws. Rather, they represent a second, logically coordinate kind of lawfulness. It does not follow that no cross-sectional law can be deduced from a process law. To understand this possibility consider a (P) such that, whatever the initial conditions may be, if after some time one variable, say, x_1 reaches a value within a certain range and then stays within this range ($a_1 \leqslant x_1 \leqslant b_1$), the same holds for another variable, say, x_2 and another range ($a_2 \leqslant x_2 \leqslant b_2$). This yields the law (I omit the reference to the system involved) 'If $a_1 \leqslant x_1 \leqslant b_1$ then $a_2 \leqslant x_2 \leqslant b_2$,' which no longer contains an explicit reference to time, but where the implicit temporal idea is simultaneity. Thus it is a cross-sectional law. Again, this is merely a schematic paradigm of which there are many variations. If the deducible cross-section law is statistical, then a statistical assumption about the initial condition will be needed as an additional premiss in order to deduce it from (P); of this presently. In other cases one of the additional premisses needed may be a condition all states fulfill because of a nondeducible cross-sectional law; and so on, and so on.

More or less crude cross-sectional laws abound in the behavior sciences, where they are also known as trait correlations; in the simplest case, 'Whoever has personality trait A also has personality trait B.' (About the statistical form these laws mostly take see above and below.) Many insights of nonscientific characterology are logically of this form. The psychiatric notion of a syndrome is merely an elaboration of it. Let A, B, C, D, E be five traits. 'Whoever has at least three of these five traits also has the other two' is an instance of syndromatic lawfulness. Our actual knowledge in the field of personality is as yet not so precise. Nor have we as yet actually derived such "static" trait correlations from an actual "dynamic" process law. But the conjectures of the psychoanalysts about the "origins" of the several personality types (another word for 'syndrome'!) which they believe to have described must no doubt be considered as speculative anticipations of a deduction of this sort from an as yet not extant process theory.

Developmental Laws

A *developmental law* is a crude sketch or anticipation of a process law. 'If a system of a certain kind has at a certain time the character A then it will under normal conditions at some later times successively have the characters (go through the stages) B, C, D, E, F' is the schema of a (six-stages) developmental law. So is 'If a system of a certain kind has at a certain time the character B then it had under normal conditions at some earlier time the character A and will at some later times successively have characters C, D, E, F' (Incidentally, neither of these two schemata, the one anchored at A and the one anchored at B, is a deductive consequence of the other.) Obviously such laws are imperfect; accordingly they contain several of the phrases I called the marks of imperfection. Another of their characteristics is that though closure is hardly ever explicitly mentioned, it is understood that no prediction can be made if closure is violated. It seems that in developmental laws this meaning is carried by 'under normal conditions.' To see that one merely has to realize that the numerous statements of ontogenic regularity which form such a large part of our biological knowledge are all developmental laws. 'This sapling once was an acorn; it will be a mighty oak' is an instance of an obvious three-stage developmental law anchored at the intermediate stage. We do not find it necessary to mention that the sapling must not be interfered with in certain ways. Yet nobody will think that the law has been refuted if this particular sapling will not grow into a mighty oak because a grazing deer will cripple it tomorrow. So far I have always produced a schema to show how imperfect knowledge can be deduced from process knowledge. In this case I shall not bother. The pattern is obvious by now, I trust.

Whatever psychological knowledge we have about so-called maturation and, in general, about the so-called longitudinal "development" of personality is stated in developmental laws. In the history of the group disciplines we find the so-called laws of stages according to which societies (if left to themselves) pass successively through certain "stages." However vague and, very probably, false such generalizations may be, their form is again that of developmental laws. As every student of the behavior sciences knows, Comte and Spencer proposed laws of this sort.

Some may wonder whether by not adding Marx's name to that of Comte and Spencer I am deferring to the fashion of the day. Far from it. Historically, Marx's influence has undoubtedly helped to spread the idea that group behavior is lawful. So has Hegel's. The reason that I did not mention either is not that their conception of this lawfulness is holistic (which, though most probably false, at least makes sense), but that it is even more seriously distorted by the alleged "uniqueness" of the "process." In Hegel this is clear. Marx, Engels, and their various interpreters are in this respect in a remarkable confusion. But there is never any doubt about their holism.

Statistical Laws and Relative Chance

Now for *statistical laws.* Let A and B be two characters, however simple or complex, either of single physical objects or of systems. The simpler alternative, A and B both being characters of single objects, suffices to clarify the main ideas; so I shall limit myself to this case. A statistical law states that if each member of a class of objects has the character A then a certain fraction or percentage p $(0 \leqslant p \leqslant 1)$ has the character B. Thus, if such a class happens to have N members, then the law says that N_1 of its members have the character B, where $N_1 = p.N$. Again, this is merely the (schema of the) simplest case of a kind of lawfulness. In other cases the antecedent of the law may state that a certain percentage of the members of the class exemplify A; A and B may be the same character possessed by an object at different times; and so on, and so on. Again, the simplest case provides us with an adequate paradigm to which I shall, therefore, limit myself.

The distinctive features of a statistical law appear in the way we test it. Assume that we want to test one as simple as our paradigm. We pick a certain number k of classes so that each member of each class exemplifies A. Simplify further by assuming that each of these k classes has the same number N of members. Take $N = 100$ and $p = .4$, which makes each of the k numbers $N_1 = 40$. Taken literally as I stated it, the law says that in each class exactly 40 objects exemplify B. Yet we do not expect even a single of these k numbers to be exactly 40. We consider the law confirmed if (I speak very cavalierly about very technical matters) they "scatter" in a certain fashion around 40. This shows that my original statement of the law stands in need of expansion, or explication, or analysis. The key to the analysis lies in the analysis of the statements we make about the outcome of a series of throws of a die or a coin.

Take a (mechanically unbiased) coin. After a fashion, we all know the law that if we continue to throw such a coin, it will half of the time show heads, *in the long run* and *in a random manner*. I said after a fashion because this law, too, has its peculiarities. They are indicated by the two italicized phrases. For one thing, we need not consider a single run of, say, two hundred heads as a counterinstance. We merely expect (if the law is true) such runs to be very rare or "improbable." That shows that the first phrase I italicized requires analysis. For another, we do exclude the possibility that the throws produce (always or most of the time) "regular" sequences of head (H) and tail (T), say, in a simple case, alternation: $HTHTHT. \ldots$. That shows that the second italicized phrase requires analysis. These and some other related analyses make up the so-called logic of probability. The difficulties it encounters are considerable. They are outside the scope of this book. I can merely report that they have been overcome and that, if they are once overcome, the logic of statistics offers no further difficulties. Technically, all this is very complex. Quite nontechnically, the upshot is that a statistical law if fully expanded always contains in its antecedent a probability law, that is, a law such as that about coins; for instance, a law to the effect that the frequency of a certain character in successive "samples" from a large population "converges" "randomly" toward a certain number in the sense in which the percentage of heads converges randomly toward .5 if we "continue" to throw a coin.

Having classified statistical laws as a type of imperfect knowledge, I must next show that with an additional premiss a law of this form could be deduced from a process schema. As one would expect, the additional premiss is itself statistical. Take a population of systems which are all instances of the same process schema. To fix the ideas, consider the case that these systems all have the same C. Concerning their respective S^0, assume that they all agree in some variables, say, $x_1, x_2, \ldots, x_k; k < n$. ($k$ may be zero.) For the remaining variables, $x_{k+1}, \ldots \ldots, x_n$, make certain statistical assumptions. Assume, for instance, that for 30, 45, and 25 per cent of the systems respectively $x_{k+1} < 0$, $0 \leqslant x_{k+1} \leqslant 1000$, $1000 < x_{k+1}$. From such premises in conjunction with (P) all sorts of statistical laws obtaining among all or some of the relevant variables either at some later moment or during some time interval, or after a certain time has lapsed, can conceivably be deduced. Which laws, if any, can actually be deduced depends of course on the specific form of (P) as well as on the specific statistical assumption. The principle of the thing requires no further comment.

Consider once more our simple paradigm of statistical lawfulness. As we just saw, it could be an instance of imperfect knowledge in the specific sense in which I call some laws imperfect. But I have not shown, nor could I possibly show, that every statistical law we know or may yet discover is in this manner related to a process law. Yet every statistical law is a piece of imperfect knowledge in a further nonspecific sense of 'imperfect'. It must make sense to say of a single object that it has the character B; otherwise the law itself would not make sense. Our law is therefore imperfect in that it does not tell us what it makes sense to ask and what one may well want to know, namely, whether or not any *single* object that has the character A and on which we fix our attention also has the character B. The law merely tells us that a certain percentage of the objects in the classes to which it applies exemplify B; and even this, we saw, is a gross simplification. This kind of imperfection gives rise to a question. One may wonder whether there are not some areas (I dodge for the time being the explication of 'area') where the best we can *ever* do is to discover statistical generalities. Whoever answers this question affirmatively holds a thesis of about the same logical nature (though of course of different content) as that of determinism. Therefore, like the thesis of determinism, this thesis, call it that of *relative chance,* makes sense although, again as in the case of determinism, it is so very broad and so sweepingly anticipatory that it is perhaps not very exciting. For an obvious reason we must nevertheless pay some attention to it. Such "process" knowledge as we have in the area of behavior is so fragmentary, so inarticulate, and so little trustworthy that one may well doubt whether we have any. On the other hand, we do have a good deal of rather solid statistical knowledge about behavior. Also, we saw that some protagonists of "freedom" rest their case on the thesis of relative chance (p. 419). The thesis could of course be true. In some very limited sense it probably is true. The important thing is again to clarify our ideas by making distinctions.

If a die is cast under so-called chance conditions one cannot predict the outcome of "the next throw," not even if the casting is done by a mechanical device. (For certain refined "statistical experiments" such gadgets have actually been constructed in order to eliminate any "bias" a human caster may possibly introduce.) More important, nobody expects that we shall ever be able to predict the next throw. On the strength of this case alone it would seem that the proponents of relative chance are in as good a position as one could hope to be if one proposes so broad a thesis. Yet the nineteenth-century determinists were able to reconcile the quite uncontroversial facts of the case with their thesis (p. 420). This calls for a distinction. The first thing one must do is to put the idea of relative chance where all such ideas belong, in a schema. For determinism I did this before. Similarly clarified, the idea of relative chance (in an area) becomes the thesis that at least one of the axioms of the fundamental theory (of the area) is statistical. (Notice that I say the fundamental theory, not the comprehensive process theory.) Now in physics our fundamental theories have long been of the kind I call partially interpreted calculi. It may well be that this calculus is a process schema and that yet in such cases as that of the die the impossibility of anything but statistical prediction follows deductively from the very rules of interpretation of the calculus. This was in fact how the nineteenth-century determinists answered the objection of "the next throw." I want to make this point very clear; so I shall make it again, in a slightly different fashion. In many cases it is "practically" impossible to go beyond a statistical prediction though "in principle" one could. I don't think I need to explain what this means. Ours is a case of "theoretical" impossibility. In other words, it is a deductive consequence of (1) the calculus, (2) the rules of interpreting it, and (3) certain very simple and quite uncontroversial statements of fact, namely, that one could not make the measurements that would yield the description of a system such that the outcome of "the next throw" can be computed from its process law.

The case of the die is as old as it is familiar. Recent experimentation has produced some more recondite phenomena, flashes on screens built into complicated machines, clicks in Geiger counters, and so on, which in this one respect are in the same boat with the next throw of the die. According to present physical theory it is theoretically impossible to achieve anything but statistical prediction about them. These are, as one would expect, the phenomena whose description corresponds to statements of the theory which attribute a character to a single particle. Some students, among them a few very eminent physicists, believe that this newly discovered fringe of relative chance in the area of physics establishes the thesis of relative chance in the area of behavior. Or, if it is not established, it has at least become very plausible. Thus the Newtonian ideal of a comprehensive process theory of behavior is presumably shattered. This strange claim crops up here and there, including the writings of some philosophical psychologists. So it may be well to examine it carefully.

First another distinction must be made. A theory of behavior is one thing; a physiological theory is another thing. Thus it could be that the prospects of an eventual comprehensive process theory of the one kind are either bright or dim, as the case may be, for reasons that do not at all affect the prospects of the other. What connection there is between their prospects depends on the connections between the two kinds of theory. These I shall discuss in Volume Two. As far as the present issue is concerned, it would seem that what those students wish to say is that modern physics makes a place for relative chance in the area of physiology. Surely this interpretation gives them the benefit of the doubt; for what other connection could there be between "behavior" and "physics?" The most reasonable interpretation of the claim is, therefore, that physiological events and those newly discovered recondite physical events are of the same order of magnitude. One does not need to know much physics or physiology (I know little of the first and less of the second) in order to recognize that this claim is scientifically as unsound as it could possibly be. I, for one, think that it is silly. But even if I am wrong, the argument I am analyzing would still be futile. Patently and often quite explicitly the intellectual motive behind it is concern for "freedom." But we see now that relative chance, if its idea is only clearly stated and firmly grasped, has nothing whatsoever to do with the moral and psychological core of human freedom. Unlike Epicurus's gods, man's freedom, such as it is, does not dwell in the interstices between the atoms. . . .

Historical Laws

A plant physiologist undertakes a quantitative growth study of a certain species. The result he expects is a so-called growth curve. He hopes to discover how the two parameters of this curve, the one that determines the rate of growth of the plant and the one that determines its eventual size, say, specifically, its height, depend on such factors as amounts of humidity, irradiation, certain chemicals in the soil, and so on. These are therefore the factors he systematically varies in his numerous experimental plots. So far the story is rather conventional; I must now give it the twist that makes it the vehicle of a new group of ideas. Imagine that our scientist obtains not one growth curve but, in a perfectly clear-cut fashion, two. Assume further that, to increase his puzzlement, he finds that for each of these two curves the arithmetical form of the dependency of its two parameters on the experimental variables is the same. The only difference is that certain constants in this function have different values with the result that, say, one-half of the seedlings grow more slowly and less tall than the others. Our man sets out in search of the overlooked relevant variable (or variables) whose different values for the two groups of plants, call them *A* and *B*, might account for the difference. This is still routine, just as is the "deterministic" assumption that there is such a variable. Yet he finds no clues of a routine nature. The only difference he discovers is that the seeds he planted came from two different bags, which he had bought at a store.

Thereupon our scientist, lest he miss any chance, somewhat reluctantly considers the possibility that the seeds for group A all came from one of the bags, while those for group B all came from the other. He kept no records from which he could learn whether this is actually the case; fortunately, though, enough seeds of both kinds are left to repeat the experiment. (This time, some seeds of each kind are deliberately saved.) The second experiment confirms the hunch. The next step, again routine, is a careful examination of the seeds that were saved. The seeds from the two bags are found to be alike in many respects. Eventually an elaborate microbiological test uncovers in those that produced the slow-growing and stunted plants the "traces" of a disease from which their ancestors had suffered. Further experimentation confirms that this is the difference that made the difference.

Logically, all this is just another case in which a few steps led a scientist to add to his S^0 a new variable, namely, the trace or scar certain past events have left on some of the seeds but not on the others. Whatever fancy there is lies in the story I made up. So let me now give it another twist. Imagine that at the time the experiments were performed those microbiological tests were as yet unknown. Assume, furthermore, that in the absence of any laboratory clues our persistent scientist engages in a different kind of investigation. He learns from the merchant who sold him the two bags that they came from different parts of the country and eventually, after further inquiry, that a certain disease has long plagued the species in the region from which one of the bags came. For the disease is well known; what is unknown is the microbiological test. From there on we may imagine the experiment to proceed as before. Roughly speaking, it leads to the same law. Yet there is an important difference between the two situations and the two laws. Everything I shall say in this section turns on this difference.

Let me for brevity's sake speak of the earlier and the later law. The later law fits, however roughly, into the process schema. S^0 or, generally, S^t consists of the set of values certain variables have at the time 0 or, generally, at the time t. The additional variable, call it the trace variable, is no exception. What makes the difference is the "present" value of this variable or, less elaborately speaking, the presence or absence of the microscopic scar. But I do for once want to speak elaborately. In the earlier situation the additional information consists of a statement or statements describing an earlier or "past" state or states of the system. Again I am speaking elaborately, but by now I trust my purpose is clear. I want to construct the schema of laws that predict the "future" not from the "present" alone but from the present in conjunction with some information about the "past." Such laws, however perfect or imperfect they may be, are no longer process laws. (Yet I shall in describing them continue to use, somewhat inaccurately, the letters C and S.) Let πS^0 and πS^t stand for some information, either partial or complete, about either a state or states in which the system was either at one or at some or at all moments preceding time 0 or time t respectively. Briefly, the prefix 'π' indicates some information about the "past." Then the schema of the earlier law can be diagrammed as follows:

(H) $$(C \ \& \ S^0 \ \& \ \pi S^0) \longrightarrow S^t, \qquad t > 0,$$

which contrasts with the familiar diagram of the process schema

$$(C \ \& \ S^0) \longrightarrow S^t.$$

Instances of schema (H) I call *historical laws*.

The tale I told makes it in a sense harder for me to make my point. Such self-imposed handicaps have their advantages. The difficulty I deliberately created for myself is that the story seems to confirm the unexamined "assumptions" of a "frame of reference." The earlier law is "merely" a historical law. The later law, the one we can state after the "trace" has been discovered, is "no longer" a historical law. Moreover, after it has been stated, the earlier, historical law becomes, in an obvious sense, expendable. The unexamined assumption to which I wish to draw attention is that there "must" be a trace and that a historical law is therefore "necessarily" an item of imperfect knowledge that will eventually become expendable. Very probably this is so. The point is that it is merely a matter of fact, one of those broad "facts" of which "frames of reference" are made. That we take this particular "fact" for granted is one ingredient of the frame of reference that stems from the Newtonian process schema. It is well worth while to understand this ingredient accurately. A few comments should help. I shall devote one paragraph to each, numbering them consecutively.

1. In many cases we have found the trace. The story I told is in this respect quite realistic. This shows clearly that 'historical,' as I use it, is the name of a certain structure or form with respect to time which a law may or may not exemplify. Also, a historical law may become expendable long before we have reached process knowledge in its area. Without further explanation it makes no sense therefore to say that an area (not a law), e.g., psychology or physics, is or is not historical. One thing one could mean is that *at a particular time* our actual knowledge in the area is, was, or will be either partly or, perhaps, predominantly historical. To another, more recondite meaning I shall attend presently. (I find myself again using 'area' before I have explicated it; but again I think this will do no harm.)

2. Aristotle's observations on memory are probably the earliest articulate attempt to state psychological laws. They are historical. So are the various laws of association the classical British psychologists proposed. So are very many of the laws of contemporary psychology, the laws of learning as well as the more ambitious and therefore more elusive general-

izations of the psychoanalysts. Small wonder, then, that in Volumes Two and Three we shall have to make use of the notion of historical lawfulness again and again. This is why we must grasp it firmly and see clearly its place among the possible patterns of lawfulness.

3. Like virtually every ordinary word that is made into a technical term, 'historical' has unwanted associations. At the moment it is for us still an open question whether there are any laws of the "social process" or, as it is sometimes put, whether there are any laws of "history." Certainly, I do not wish to hint or to appear to hint that such laws, if there are any, are necessarily historical. To these questions I shall attend much later, in Volume Two. Still with respect to the word, two things may come to mind if one is guided by its ordinary uses; I do not mean either when I call a law historical. For one thing, every law is arrived at by generalization (induction), either directly, or indirectly by deduction from laws so arrived at; and the instances on which the generalization is based, or at least some of these instances, will as a rule lie in the past. In this obvious and entirely nonspecific sense all laws would be "historical." For another thing, in one of the meanings of 'cause' (p. 425), any earlier state of a system may be said to be the cause of any later one. In this sense every dynamic law would be "historical." When I call a law historical I mean neither of these two things but, to repeat, a certain structure of the law itself with respect to time.

4. A developmental law is not a historical law, nor conversely. To understand the difference it suffices to consider a three-stage developmental law (A, B, C) anchored at the intermediate stage (B). For our purposes it may be schematized by 'If $(B$ now) then $(A$ earlier *and* C later).' The schema of the "corresponding" historical law is 'If $(B$ now and A earlier) then $(C$ later)' or, what amounts to the same thing, 'If $(B$ now) then $(if A$ earlier *then* C later).' The difference comes out in the difference between the two logical connectives, 'and' and 'if-then,' which I italicized.

5. In the first chapter I introduced the notion of historical concepts. Among the examples I gave was 'tempered,' as said of steel, and 'hungry$_1$,' which means by definition 'having been deprived of food during a certain time interval.' The notion of a historical concept is closely connected with that of a historical law. Though the connection is obvious, I shall be tedious rather than too concise and state it explicitly. To have had a certain character in the past is a historical character of the present. Thus πS^0 can be considered as a conjunction of statements attributing historical characters to objects mentioned in the antecedent of the law. It follows that every historical law contains at least one historical concept. Let us also cast another glance at the hunger example. We encountered two further notions of hunger, one defined in terms of stomach contractions (hungry$_2$), one defined in terms of a disposition to approach and consume food (hungry$_3$). Any law connecting hunger$_1$ with either hunger$_2$ or hunger$_3$ is a historical law.

6. Let me describe accurately what happens when a historical law becomes "expendable." Perhaps the most common historical concept, much

used in the biological as well as in the behavior sciences, is age. In the case of trees we can replace 'age' by 'number of rings.' Consider a lawful connection between some property of (a kind of) trees and their age. Call the "two" laws that state this connection L' and L'' respectively; L' being the one mentioning age, L'' the one that mentions instead of age the number of rings. Call L the law that states the connection between a tree's age and the number of its rings. L is historical. L'' follows deductively from the conjunction of L and L', but neither L nor L' follows deductively from L''. It would seem, then, that L is not expendable and that instead of having got rid of historicity in this case we have merely limited its scope. In a sense this is indeed so. But there is also the presumption that (1) L will eventually be superseded by a process law that "grinds out" the number of rings as a function of time (notice that I say time, not age), and (2) we are approaching this ideal if we replace L and L' by L and L''. . . . Whether or not we need them [historical laws and historical concepts] depends on the kind of lawfulness (if any) which we discover.

A historical law may be an item of incomplete knowledge; many have in fact turned out to be just that. Nor is it difficult to show schematically how a historical law may be deduced from a process law. Again, I shall not bother to write down the schema. But again, one could not possibly show that every historical law can thus be "projected" against an eventual "ahistorical" process. There remains another possibility, the one our ahistorical frame of reference excludes. Probably it is no more than a possibility. Yet to be aware of it not only helps to understand one's own frame of reference; such awareness is also the best safeguard against the temptation to hypostatize it. There is a further advantage to this awareness, if one wishes to examine the behavior sciences, an area that is at present in fact largely historical. Notice that I said behavior science is at present historical. I did not say that it is "still" historical. Not that I hesitate to commit myself or, perhaps better, to make a prognosis. The point is that an intelligent forecast requires some further distinctions. To these questions I shall attend in Volume Two. Then it will also appear that, when the analytical job has been done, forecasting loses much of its interest. As often happens, the urge to "commit" one's self on matters of this sort is greatly reduced after analysis has, incidentally, bared its ideological sources.

The possibility we must not overlook is a law or theory which, though historical, is in all other respects perfect in exactly the same sense in which a process law is perfect. In this case one would not inappropriately speak of a *historical process*. It could be that the comprehensive theory of some area actually is a historical process. Or, to go even further, since, as we saw, the thesis of determinism makes sense (though, as I put it, only very broadly and therefore not very excitingly), so would its historical variant. In the notation I use it is not at all difficult to write down the schema, call it (P_h), of a historical process law. One merely needs to double the number of "state variables," replacing each of them, say, x_i^0 by the pair x_i^0, πx_i^0, whose second member represents some information about the past values of x_i^0. I write down only the first line of (P_h):

$$x_1{}^t = f_1 (c_1, c_2, \ldots, c_m; x_1{}^0, \pi x_1{}^0, \ldots, x_n{}^0, \pi x_n{}^0; t)$$

Mathematicians have for some time investigated the form a historical process law might reasonably be expected to exemplify. For (P_h), like (P), is not the schema of the equations in which the law itself is stated but, rather, that of their solution. Fully articulated process laws are, as we saw, differential equations. Historical process laws of this kind would be so-called integro-differential equations.

[24] Reflexive Predictions

R O G E R C. B U C K

– I –

The general notion of what I call a reflexive prediction is widely familiar. A prediction comes true because it comes to the attention of actors on the social scene whose actions will determine its truth-value. Or a prediction turns out false because those same actors become aware of the prediction, and its falsity issues from the actions they are thus led to initiate. I call the first kind of prediction self-fulfilling; the second self-frustrating. Social phenomena involving the reflexive operation of predictions and beliefs are well known. Presumably many cases of bank failure, back in the bad old days when the government still permitted banks to fail, involved the self-fulfilling operation of expectations of such failure, perhaps fed by rumors (predictions) of failure. Again stock market rumors and reports from investors' advisory services sometimes operate in a similar way. The function of pari-mutual machines at race tracks is to ensure that certain predictions prove self-frustrating: namely, predictions of the form "Horse A will win and will pay off well." The political ideas of an 'underdog effect' or a 'bandwagon effect' have the notion of reflexive prediction built into them.

Reprinted with a brief omission from *Philosophy of Science*, **30**, 1963, 359–369, with permission of the author and the editor.

Indeed one can construct a hypothetical case, using simplifying assumptions analogous to those of economists, in which a pollster (say Gallup) can control the outcome of a close election, but cannot produce a correct public prediction of who will win. Such cases involve a strong underdog effect. Another case, frequently offered as a paradigm in the literature, concerns an agricultural economist's forecast of a future price for wheat. Suppose he foresees an oversupply, and a consequent sharp drop in wheat prices. His prediction comes to the attention of the growers who believe it and decide to switch land to other purposes. So many of them thus switch so much land that the expected oversupply fails to materialize. Perhaps the price even rises a bit. And yet it is fully possible that our economist's prediction, falsified by self-frustrating factors, might have turned out true had it not been disseminated!

So much for a sketchy indication of the type of prediction I am concerned with. I shall address myself to three main problems concerning this category of predictions. First, I shall tackle the typical logician's problem of the precise definition of reflexivity for predictions—a problem which is more intricate than might be supposed. Second, I shall consider the suggestion that the possibility of such reflexive predictions raises special and acute methodological problems for the social sciences. My last problem will concern the explicit suggestion that "this characteristic of predictions is peculiar to human affairs" ([5], p. 129) and the implicit suggestion that this peculiarity marks a philosophically significant difference between the social and natural sciences.[1] Here I shall consider primarily a counter-example to the unique-to-human-affairs thesis, which has been proposed by Grünbaum.

– II –

Our first question is: When are we to count a prediction reflexive? Clearly not all true predictions are self-fulfilling, nor are all false predictions self-frustrating. Robert Merton speaks at one point of "the social scientist [who] everlastingly faces the possibility that his prediction will enter into the situation as a *new and dynamic* factor changing the very conditions under which the prediction initially held true." ([5], p. 129). Clearly Merton's phrase "initially held true" is meant to be getting at our problem of a differentiating criterion, in the self-frustrating case. But there are problems with his formulation. Elsewhere he speaks of "the self-fulfilling prophecy . . . [which evokes] . . . a new behavior which makes the originally false conception come true." ([5], p. 423) But what is this *initial* status of predictions? Is there such a thing as the original, or basic status

[1] Cf. [5], pp. 128–130 and pp. 421–436. See also 6, pp. 894–904; and 7, pp. 12–16 where Popper puts such suggestions in the mouth of his synthetic but lively "historicist" opponent.

for predictions, from which (because of, say, publication) they may later depart? Or, if the words "initially" and "originally" are meant in a temporal sense, is there any clear meaning in the notion of a prediction, the very same prediction of the very same event, having at one time one truth-value, and at another time, the other? I think not.

Rather, the situation seems to be that we are here contrasting what actually did happen (and hence what truth-value the prediction actually takes), with what would have happened in other circumstances (and hence with the truth-value which the same prediction would, in these other circumstances have had). That the prediction is reflexive entails that its dissemination was a causal factor in the social situation which would have included the event predicted, had the prediction been true. This dissemination must have been causally relevant to the occurrence of that event in the self-fulfilling case or to its non-occurrence in the self-frustrating case. Further, at least in all the standard examples in the literature, the causal efficacy of such dissemination must be mediated by the formation of beliefs on the part of the various actors on the social scene, and by their behaving in a way which can be reasonably described as "acting on" those beliefs. Again, in all standard cases, any relevant beliefs thus formed will include the belief that the prediction in question is true.

Let me add a few further remarks about this attempt to understand precisely what a reflexive prediction is. I shall use the term "private" to describe predictions which have not been disseminated and brought to the attention of the actors involved. Similarly "public" will refer to those predictions which are disseminated. First, I want to stress that as regards the content or significance of the prediction, as regards *what is predicted,* we must assume the public and the private prediction to be identical. Otherwise, given our criterion, there is no *single* prediction to be called reflexive. Next, we may note that any claim that a prediction is reflexive involves assessing what would have been the case had its dissemination status been different. Such assessment requires knowledge of the truth of counterfactual conditionals,—of conditionals whose antecedents are false. It requires that the empirical scientist claim to know something for which by the very description of the situation he cannot directly test.

Another point worth noting is that while the dissemination status of a prediction must be *a* causal factor relative to what it predicts, we need not suppose that it is ever the only factor involved. The dissemination may be a causally necessary condition for truth (or falsity), but it need never be causally sufficient.

Next there is a curious symmetry which I wish to discuss. Consider a prediction which would be false if public and true if private—i.e., a prediction which if actually disseminated would be called self-frustrating. But now suppose it is kept private. Are we not then entitled to call it a self-fulfilling private prediction on the grounds that a certain causal factor, namely its non-dissemination, prevented it from being false. After all, it does take opposite truth-values depending on its dissemination status! Might we not generalize this result and declare that the class of reflexive predictions includes not only all those public predictions whose truth-value is other than it would have been if private, but also all those private predictions whose truth-value is other than it would have been if public. This suggestion is in some ways attractive, but it will not do.

One counter suggestion involves the claim that while dissemination is something positive, non-dissemination is merely negative; and merely negative states of affairs can have no causal efficacy. But this suggestion just is not in accordance with the customary employment of the concept of causation. An absence or a lack of, say, typhoid vaccine can just as properly be said to have caused an epidemic, as can the occurrence of severe flooding which disrupts the sewer system. And in general we deal repeatedly in terms of such negative causes. The real objection turns on another idea, namely on the notion of standard conditions, or of other-things-being-equal, which is at least tacitly involved in virtually every causal claim.

One does not pick out just any old necessary condition for an event and call it a cause. The presence of oxygen is a necessary condition for the occurrence of fire, but it could properly be called the cause of some specific fire only in rather special circumstances. (One of these might be a fire breaking out within some experimental apparatus in a situation in which the experiment would normally be conducted in an oxygen-free atmosphere.) And a variant of this point is the crucial objection to the argument from symmetry sketched above. If it is normal or usual, as it very often is, that certain kinds of social predictions not come to the attention of the actors whose doings are predicted, then it is fatuous to call a private prediction of one of these kinds reflexive on the grounds that dissemination would have changed its truth-value. And surely the vast majority of the predictions of e.g., the social sciences are not disseminated widely enough to effect any significant number of the social actors involved. There may be classes of predictions whose normal status is wide dissemination. Our wheat price forecaster may be hired by the Agriculture Department to issue public predictions. If, discouraged by repeated failure, he were one day to write down his prediction, lock it in a vault, and refuse to predict publicly; and if that prediction were to come true; we might in these *special* circumstances be tempted to call his private prediction self-fulfilling. For here his deliberate refusal to disseminate his prediction would be abnormal, would have violated the usual standard conditions. But surely such cases are rare.

We may summarize the criteria for a reflexive prediction then as follows. A prediction is reflexive if and only if:

1. Its truth-value would have been different had its dissemination status been different,
2. The dissemination status it actually had was causally necessary for the social actors involved to hold relevant and causally efficacious beliefs,

3. The prediction was, or if disseminated, would have been believed and acted upon, and finally

4. Something about the dissemination status or its causal consequences was abnormal, or at the very least unexpected by the predictor, by whoever calls it reflexive, or by those to whose attention its reflexive character is called.

In his *Social Theory and Social Structure,* Merton's interest in reflexive predictions is focused chiefly on their role as social mechanisms within his subject matter. In particular, he proposes a sociological analysis of certain problems in race relations where he holds that reflexively operating predictions and beliefs are involved. At least in general outline, Merton's argument is surely familiar. The in-group, let us call them the WASPs (white, Anglo-Saxon Protestants—the term is said to be that of Carmine De Sapio), predict and lead each other to believe that the out-group will manifest various socially undesirable traits. So the WASPs act to isolate and discriminate against the out-group, say Negroes, in various ways. And these discriminatory actions produce the very traits predicted. Is this a clear case of reflexive prediction? I doubt it.

In the bank failure case, the expectation of failure was essential to the concerted action. But in the discrimination case I should rather have supposed that the prediction of, or the belief in the manifestation of undesirable traits, would be at most a rationalizing after-thought. One would suppose that the depositors could be talked out of their actions if they could be convinced that the bank would not fail if they refrained from withdrawing. But it is far from clear that our typical racist discriminator could be talked out of discrimination by drawing his attention to communities in which there was no discrimination, and in which the Negroes did not manifest the undesirable traits. I can't quite see the racist abandoning discrimination because certain factual beliefs he held had been shown to be false. In short, it is not clear that discrimination in race relations is ordinarily a matter of *acting on* explicit cognitive belief. MacIver, incidentally, describes the same phenomenon that Merton is interested in, using however, not the concept of self-fulfilling prediction, but rather that of a vicious circle ([3], pp. 61–68 especially). The WASPs discriminate against the Negroes, this leads as before to the development of undesirable social traits to which the WASPs react by continuing and perhaps intensifying their discrimination, and so on. Here the whole circle is a causal-behavioral one, in which no one need be supposed to be *acting on* any explicitly held beliefs. It seems to me that given the essential role of such beliefs in the paradigm cases of reflexive prediction, MacIver's conceptual scheme may fit the envisaged situation better than Merton's.

But even if we accept Merton's assimilation of the racial discrimination cases to reflexive predictions there are other problems in his treatment of it. Such discrimination instances "the mechanism of the self-fulfilling social belief, in which confident error generates its own spurious confirmation." ([5], p. 128). Here we see his unclear idea of some "initial" or "original" status for predictions leading him into a confusing blend of moral and methodological appraisal. That the so-called prediction actually was "originally false" we have seen to be logically incoherent. Even that it *would* have been false, if undisseminated, is a claim which is difficult to establish. As logical appraisal, this imputation of error is wholly arbitrary. The belief was not "in error," nor is it shown that the confirmation was "spurious." What Merton has in mind is presumably the contrast with the situation which would develop if a different "social belief" were current. If people believe that there were no important social differences, that colored people would in normal circumstances manifest the same social patterns and traits as whites, then presumably if they acted on this belief all would be well. But surely we must notice that this belief too might be self-fulfilling, that from the point of view of logical appraisal it too could, with equal logical reason, be misleadingly spoken of as "confident error generating its own spurious confirmation."

There is, indeed, error in the situation Merton describes. But it is moral error, not logical or methodological mistake. And while we can all no doubt join Merton in deploring the moral error, I think we should insist on keeping morals and methodology distinct. Parenthetically, we may note that MacIver offers much the same blend of moral and non-moral considerations with his term "vicious circle." The circularity is straightforwardly causal, but the viciousness is neither causal nor logical. The term "vicious" represents MacIver's moral appraisal of the situation. The parallel with Merton becomes clear when we note that MacIver must acknowledge also the possibility of a "beneficent circle," where race relations are good and happy. And here, too, while the circularity will be causal, the beneficence will not.

– III –

We may now turn to ask whether the existence of reflexive prediction poses special problems for the social scientist. *Prima facie* the answer must be "yes." The social scientist himself predicts in his official capacity as scientist. And predictions play a crucial role in the processes of science. The adequacy of theory and law is tested by deriving predictions from statements of initial conditions in conjunction with such theories and laws. If you call into question the legitimacy of confirmation following on success in prediction, or of disconfirmation following on failure in prediction, you strike at something very fundamental indeed in science.

Let us begin consideration of the social scientist's methodological problem with a new and fanciful example, this time from sociology. Suppose that an expert in the study of crime and prisons predicts for the near future a drastic increase in the number of felonies (and of consequent convictions) unaccompanied by any increase in available detention space, and hence resulting in terrible overcrowding in our prisons. Now suppose he wonders whether his prediction may prove self-frustrating. Perhaps the would-be felons will learn of and become convinced by his prediction, and perhaps they will therefore refrain in significant numbers from the felonies they would otherwise have committed, being willing, so to speak, to run the risk of ordinary prisons but not of very crowded ones.

Suspecting that his prediction may be reflexive what should he do? Perhaps his first thought will be to draw attention to the possible consequences of the dissemination of his prediction. Can he not thereby be both scientifically honest and exhibit his sophisticated awareness of the dangers of reflexivity. But a little thought may suggest that this line of attack is problematical. For if his first prediction by itself would have been self-frustrating, then clearly this "drawing attention to the possible consequences" which is logically simply another prediction, is also very likely in its turn to be self-frustrating. If believing the first prediction restrained any would-be felons, then believing the second will likely send some of them back to their original felonious plans. Nor is a third prediction likely to fare any better than the second.

Clearly we have the following situation. Any given prediction in the series (1st, 2nd, 3rd, etc.), can in principle take account of the social consequences of the dissemination of all the earlier predictions. Hence there is no numbered prediction in the series whose reflexive consequences cannot be warned against. On the other hand no prediction in the series can possibly warn of the consequences of *its own* dissemination. A prediction which tried to do this could be shown to be logically reflexive, and such logical reflexivity can in turn be shown to involve a strictly vicious infinite regress. In certain circumstances, however, such a series may "converge," as it were. Grünberg and Modigliani have shown this for various economic situations.[2] What happens in such cases of convergence is best described by saying that a true though self-fulfilling prediction may be arrived at in an area where most or all other predictions would be self-frustrating. . . .

How serious, then, is the methodological problem for the social scientist? In my view, not very! He can always investigate the question whether any specific prediction is likely to operate reflexively. Sometimes such considerations may reveal that it is not reflexive. Our sociologist may discover that his prediction of increased felonies and crowded prisons will come to the attention of only his professional colleagues. And he may conclude that *their* felonious tendencies are either too slight to issue in action, or too strong to be deterred by prospects of crowding. In this case he can dismiss his concern.

---

[2] 2, pp. 465–478. For analogous considerations in the sphere of political science, see [8], pp. 245–253; [reprinted in this volume, pp. 447–455, where an exposition of the Grünberg and Modigliani results is to be found.—Ed.]

In some cases it may be deemed desirable to deliberately restrict dissemination of the prediction. In fact, such restriction has long been employed in medical experimentation with new drugs and vaccines. Members of the experimental and control groups are not told which is their status, in order to guard against the reflexive operation of beliefs which such information might induce.

And even if the reflexivity of a prediction must be merely warned against; even if that warning may in its turn prove reflexive—still something has been achieved. The possible reflexivity of that specific prediction has been noted. A possible correction of that particular scientific claim has been suggested. And is this not the typical situation in an empirical science offering corrigible claims. It may indeed be the case that all scientific propositions are corrigible, but it certainly is never the case at any one time that all have been tested for possible correction.

– IV –

We have next to consider whether reflexive predictions occur only when people are involved. We may note that the essential question is whether the beliefs and actions of human beings must be causally relevant to the truth-value of a reflexive prediction. It does not matter whether the actual state of affairs predicted, e.g., so many acres under wheat next July, is a human action or not. Our consideration of this issue is restricted to a counter-example proposed by Grünbaum.

Merton held in the first edition of his *Social Theory and Social Structure* that "this characteristic of predictions is peculiar to human affairs." ([4], p. 122). In support of this view he notes that a "meteorologist's prediction of continued rainfall has until now not perversely led to the occurrence of a drought" ([4], p. 122) and that "predictions of the return of Halley's comet do not influence its orbit." ([4], p. 181). Grünbaum cites these remarks and challenges Merton's view: ([2], pp. 239–240).

To be sure, these particular predictions of purely physical phenomena are not self-stultifying any more than those social predictions whose success is essentially independent of whether they are made public or not. But instead of confining ourselves to commonplace meteorological and astronomical phenomena, consider the goal-directed behavior of a servo-mechanism like a homing device which employs a feed-back and is subject to automatic fire control. Clearly every phase of the operation of such a device constitutes an exemplification of one or more *physical* principles. Yet the following situation is *allowed* by these very principles: a computer predicts that, in its present course, the missile will miss its target, and the communication of this information to the missile in the form of a new set of instructions induces it to alter its course and thereby to reach its target, contrary to the computer's original prediction. How does this differ, in principle, from the case where the government economist's forecast of an oversupply of wheat has the effect of instructing the wheat growers to alter their original planting intentions?

Grünbaum's paper had come to Merton's attention before he put out his revised edition of *Social Theory and Social Structure*. The revised edition, like the first, says "this characteristic of predictions is peculiar to human affairs. It is not found among predictions about the world of nature." ([5], p. 129) At this point he adds parenthetically, in the revised edition only, "except as natural phenomena are technologically shaped by men." ([5], p. 129) Here there is a footnote quoting most of what I have quoted from Grünbaum.

We need spend little time on Merton's parenthetical qualification. It is at best a *de facto* truth that physical systems displaying Grünbaum's analog of reflexive predictions are to be found only when technologically shaped by man. It is logically possible that such a servo-mechanism come about naturally, without human intervention. And this is another way of saying that if Grünbaum's counter-example really is a case of reflexive prediction, then nothing can be deduced from a definition of physics which would exclude such prediction.[3] Hence Merton's parenthetical qualification concedes enough to Grünbaum to rob the original uniqueness claim of any philosophical interest.

But is Grünbaum's case really an example of *prediction* at all? The word "really" tags this question as metaphysical, and we could easily proceed from here to a lengthy and inconclusive discussion of whether machines think. The metaphysical issue emerges in another fashion if we consider that two very natural reactions to Grünbaum's example are in fact question-begging. The first and most obvious one is the simple rejection on the grounds that machines, even servo-mechanisms, cannot have beliefs, and *a fortiori* cannot act on them—only people can do this sort of thing. A diametrically opposed reaction, natural for at least some reductivist philosophers of science, might run as follows:

The only sort of sense that science can make of talk about believing and acting on beliefs must ultimately be in terms of the input of stimuli and the subsequent behavior of the person thus stimulated. These, and regular sequences of these, are all an empirical science can possibly mean by talk of belief and action—all we can ever have empirical evidence for. But clearly Grünbaum has described a physical mechanism in which such regular sequences of inputs and subsequent behavior can be observed. So his counter-example to Merton's thesis is decisive.

I want to try to avoid both of these question-begging responses. I propose to do this by granting for purposes of argument that the behavior of machines can be in relevant ways analogous to human behavior. Then I want to suggest that even granting this, there are still inadequacies in Grünbaum's counter-example. The key lies in the difference between acting on a belief and acting on orders.

In Grünbaum's example the computer communicates "information to the missile *in the form of a set of instructions*" (my italics). He then asks

[3] A point which Grünbaum himself stresses in anticipating a rejoinder such as Merton's parenthetical qualification. [1], p. 240.

how this differs in principle from the case where the "economist's forecast *has the effect of instructing the wheat growers* to alter their original planting intentions" (my italics). I think there is a straightforward answer to this rhetorical question. There certainly is *a* difference between information in the form of a set of instructions and information which has the effect of instructing. The former is, after all, a matter of instructions, directives, orders—an analog of what would appear in the imperative mood. The missile's response to these instructions might analogically be described as obedient or disobedient, but I cannot see that the missile can even analogically be described as informed or misinformed. On the other hand, no *orders* have been issued to the wheat growers. They cannot be described as disobedient if they fail to alter their planting intentions. They have received information (in the indicative mood); they may or may not have acted rationally on that information, but they have neither obeyed nor disobeyed.

I think this objection is serious. After all, even our tough-minded empiricist must grant that, in observing and describing the behavior of others we do often manage to classify some items of such behavior as acting on orders, and other items as acting on belief. For many cases of such classification we can achieve considerable intersubjective agreement on how to classify the item in question. This fact of intersubjective agreement strongly supports the presumption that we are all using the same empirical data in thus classifying. It is very difficult not to suppose that our criteria for such classification are empirical, however difficult it may be to set them forth clearly.

Grünbaum himself describes the missile as receiving "information *in the form of instructions.*" This seems to me to make it clear that the missile's situation is more nearly the analog of a person obeying orders, than of a person acting on belief. So the question of the role of belief in the mechanisms of reflexive prediction becomes central. Suppose Jones is following some line of action A, and I conclude that if he continues this line of action he will fail to do something which for me, though perhaps not for Jones, is an objective, O. So I issue instructions (orders) to Jones to abandon A and follow instead the line of action B. Jones does so, and O is achieved. When I say that I am taking it for granted that the behavior of missiles can be in relevant ways analogous to human behavior, what I mean is that I am prepared to raise no questions here about whether, say, the situation of Jones just described might be precisely analogous to that of the missile described by Grünbaum.

The point of my doubts about Grünbaum's analogy can be brought out equally well by discussing Jones' situation. Let us note the divergencies from the standard case of reflexive prediction. As in the standard case *I* may be thought of as predicting something, *viz.* that A will not lead to O. But, unlike the standard case, this prediction need not come to Jones' attention. Jones is acting on instructions (orders), not on a belief. Even if the prediction does come to his attention, he need not believe it. He may well do B because he has been ordered to, while all the time doubting whether O will result, or even believing A to have been more likely to achieve O than B. But for the wheat forecast to act reflexively the growers must learn of it, believe it, and act on it.

This certainly is *a* difference. And, if it be granted that for human beings we can empirically distinguish between acting on a belief and acting on orders, it could well be a difference "in principle." That even Grünbaum finds it natural to assimilate his example to acting on orders is clear from his expression "information in the form of instructions." As his counter-example stands it does not count against Merton's thesis, and we must return a verdict of "not proved" on Grünbaum's charges.

It becomes clear that for an argument analogous to Grünbaum's to be effective we must imagine that our technicians and engineers should build yet another kind of machine—a machine whose range of "behavior" differs strikingly from that of Grünbaum's servo-mechanism. This new machine must be such that for at least some of its "behavior" we would find the language of "belief" and "acting on" more appropriate than that of "instructions" and "orders." Whether or not this could happen is partly, but only partly, a technological question. It is also a question about the concepts of "belief" and "acting on." And those conceptual questions would take us beyond the confines of the present paper.

Here I have been primarily concerned to explore the idea of reflexive prediction, and assess its relevance for the philosophy of science. In the context of such exploration, and relative to the standard examples given, the explicit involvement of "belief" and "acting on" is as natural as the economists' concept of the economic man. I have tried to sharpen up the concept of reflexive prediction, and to use the concept thus clarified in a criticism of one proposed sociological analysis. I have also tried to indicate the difficulties which reflexive predictions may lead to in the social sciences, and to argue that despite certain appearances, the problems thus raised are amenable to ordinary scientific treatment. I have not directly argued for Merton's uniqueness thesis, but I have supported it indirectly by urging that Grünbaum's counter-example will not do. My argument locates, in the ideas of "belief" and "acting on," those conceptual issues which I think must be faced in assessing any proposed counter-example analogous to Grünbaum's.

REFERENCES

1. GRÜNBAUM, ADOLF, "Historical Determinism, Social Activism, and Predictions in the Social Sciences." *British Journal for the Philosophy of Science*, 1956, VII.
2. GRÜNBERG, EMILE and MODIGLIANI, FRANCO, "The Predictability of Social Events." *Journal of Political Economy*, 1954, LXII.

3. MacIver, R. M., *The More Perfect Union,* New York: The Macmillan Company, 1948.

4. Merton, Robert K., *Social Theory and Social Structure,* 1st edition, New York: The Free Press, 1949.

5. Merton, Robert K., *Social Theory and Social Structure,* rev. edition, New York: The Free Press, 1957.

6. Merton, Robert K., "The Unanticipated Consequences of Purposive Social Action." *American Sociological Review,* 1936, 1.

7. Popper, Karl, *The Poverty of Historicism,* London: Routledge and Kegan Paul, 1957.

8. Simon, Herbert A., "Bandwagon and Underdog Effects and the Possibility of Election Predictions." *Public Opinion Quarterly,* 1954, XVIII. [Reprinted in this volume, pp. 447–455.]

[25] The Effect of Predictions

HERBERT A. SIMON

There has been a considerable amount of discussion, and some empirical investigation, of the possibility that the publication of an election prediction (particularly one based on poll data) might influence voting behavior, and hence—among other effects—falsify the prediction. Practically, we might be more interested in the influence of an election prediction from the standpoint of its significance for the working of democratic government than from the standpoint of its significance for the methodology of social science. Nevertheless, the latter question—involving as it does such issues as the "self-confirming" and "self-falsifying" prophecies, "pluralistic ignorance," and, indeed the entire possibility of public prediction in the social sciences—is of considerable importance in its own right. It is with the latter issue that we shall be chiefly concerned: Under what conditions will a public prediction, although it influences behavior, still be confirmed? [1]

Originally published under the title "Bandwagon and Underdog Effects of Election Predictions," *Public Opinion Quarterly,* 18, 1954, pp. 245–253; reprinted with permission of the author and the editor. It is also reprinted in Simon's *Models of Man,* John Wiley & Sons, Inc., New York, 1957.

[1] A diligent scholar could, no doubt, trace the history of this problem back to Aristotle. The author's first encounter with it came through the teaching and writings of Professors Knight and von Hayek (the latter in his *Economic* articles on "Scientism and the Study of Society"), and through discussions with Professor Milton Singer. It is consid-

Before we analyze this point, it will be helpful to define what we mean by a "bandwagon" and by an "underdog" effect. It is supposed that the voting behavior of at least some persons is a function of their expectations of the election outcome; published poll data are assumed to influence these expectations, hence to affect the voting behavior of these persons. If persons are more likely to vote for a candidate when they expect him to win than when they expect him to lose, we have a "bandwagon" effect; if the opposite holds, we have an "underdog" effect. Notice that we are not concerned with the converse mechanism: the effect of an individual's own voting preference upon his expectations of the election outcome.

The Confirmation of a Published Prediction

Of course, the question of the confirmation of a prediction is of interest only if the publication of the prediction is supposed to affect the behavior of at least some people (e.g., a bandwagon or underdog effect). But in this case we must carefully distinguish between: (a) what the outcome would have been *in the absence of a published prediction;* and (b) what the outcome actually was *after a prediction had been published.*

We take as a specific example the percentage of voters who will vote for candidate A in a two-candidate election. We let:

I = the percentage of voters who would have voted for A in the absence of the published prediction.

V = the percentage of the voters who in fact voted for A after publication of the prediction.

The difference between these two percentages, (I–V), measures the effect upon the voting behavior of publishing the prediction. Now it is reasonable to assume that, V, the percentage of persons who actually voted for A, depended upon two factors: (1) the percentage who intended to vote for him prior to publication of the prediction—that is, I; and (2) the prediction itself—that is, the percentage who, according to the prediction, intended to vote for him. This latter percentage we shall call P. The assumption then amounts to asserting that V is some function of I and P, or symbolically:

(1) $V = f(I, P)$

Now let us regard I as a "given" quantity—it is whatever it is, although we may or may not actually know its value. If I is fixed, then V may be

ered briefly and inconclusively in *Administrative Behavior*, pp. 251–52. More recently, Emile Grünberg and Franco Modigliani, solved the problem for certain cases of economic prediction, and their solution suggested a generalization by means of the fixed-point theorem of topology. For the present exposition, I have drawn heavily on their paper reporting these results in the *Journal of Political Economy,* December, 1954. I am grateful to the Ford Foundation for a grant that made this work possible.

regarded as a function of P alone. That is, given I, the percentage, V, of voters who will vote for A still depends on the published prediction, P.

The situation is illustrated in Figure 1. The x-axis measures P, the published prediction, which may range from 0 per cent to 100 per cent. The y-axis measures V, the actual vote, which may also range from 0 per cent to 100 per cent. Two hypothetical curves have been drawn in the figure. The broken horizontal line, intersecting the y-axis at I, shows what the vote would be if the prediction were made privately, but not published. In this case, the vote is exactly the same, no matter what value we assume for P, for the private prediction cannot affect the vote. Thus, we have:

(2) $V = I$,

which is exactly what the horizontal line shows.

The solid curve shows the assumed relation between V and P derived from equation (1). Figure 1 illustrates the particular case of a bandwagon effect. The solid curve is drawn on the assumption that if a prediction of a victory for A is published (P>50%), then V>I—that is, some people will switch their votes to A; while if victory is predicted for A's opponent (P<50%), then V<I—that is, some people will switch their votes to A's opponent. The vertical distance between the two lines, (I–V), is a measure

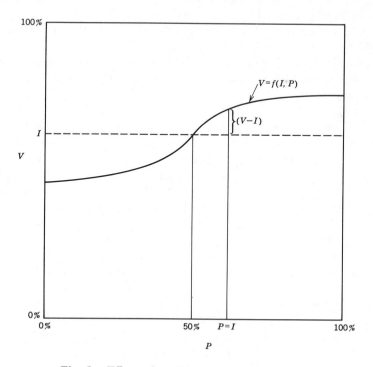

Fig. 1. Effect of prediction (*P*) on vote (*V*).

of the effect of the prediction. This vertical distance is of course not constant, but as we have seen, depends upon P.

Under what circumstances will we say that the prediction, P, is "confirmed"? The pollster generally proceeds, in the design of his sample, as if he were trying to make an accurate estimate of I. But in fact, the only way in which he can assess his accuracy is to compare his prediction, after the election, with V. If the poll is accurate in the first sense, if $P = I$, and if publication of the poll does in fact have an effect on voting behavior, then we will have:

(3) $P = I = V + (I{-}V) \neq V,$

for under the assumed conditions, $(I{-}V)$ will not be zero.

Accounting for Publication Effects

We see that the only way in which the pollster can arrive at a prediction that will coincide with the election result is by privately adjusting his poll results (which we assume for the moment to be an accurate estimate of I) for the effect that their publication will have upon the voters' behavior. But is even this possible? If he makes such an adjustment, will not the adjustment itself alter the effect of the prediction and again lead to its own falsification? Is there not involved here a vicious circle, whereby any attempt to anticipate the reactions of the voters alters those reactions and hence invalidates the prediction?

In principle, the last question can be answered in the negative: there is no vicious circle. Whether accurate predictions can be made *in practice* will be discussed later.

The "in principle" situation is illustrated in Figure 2. We have taken as our criterion of confirmation of a published prediction that the actual behavior should coincide with the prediction. The axes in Figure 2 represent P and V, respectively, as before. We have drawn again the solid curve that represents V as a function of P (from equation (1), assuming I to be fixed and given). A broken straight line through the origin with a slope of 45° has also been entered in the figure. For any point on this broken line, $V = P$, the actual voting percentage is equal to the predicted percentage.

Now consider the point of intersection of the two curves—the solid curve and the broken line. Let us call the specific value of P at the point where this intersection occurs P*, and the value of V at this point V*. Because this point lies on the solid curve, it is true that if the pollster published the prediction that A will receive P* per cent of the vote, he will in fact receive V*. But because this point also lies on the broken line, it is true that $P^* = V^*$—that the actual vote will be equal to the predicted vote. (On the other hand there is no reason to suppose that P* = I, and in general this will not be the case.)

We see, therefore, that if the curve given by equation (1) intersects with the line P = V, it will be possible, if the point of intersection is known, to make a prediction that will be confirmed. But will such a point of intersection always exist? It can be shown that it will, under the sole condition that V in equation (1) is a *continuous* function of P (roughly, that the function not have any finite "jumps").

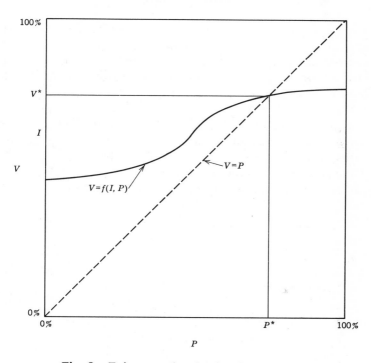

Fig. 2.   Existence of a fixed point (*P* = V**).

A formal proof of the theorem will not be given here. It is a classical theorem of topology due to Brouwer (the "fixed-point" theorem), and a non-technical exposition may be found in *What is Mathematics?*.[2] The reader who does not demand a rigorous proof may satisfy himself of the correctness of the theorem by graphical means. Construct a figure like Figure 2, but omit the solid curve. Mark any point on the y-axis between V = 0 per cent and V = 100 per cent; and a second arbitrary point on the vertical line, P = 100 per cent, within the same limits. Now try to connect

[2] Courant and Robbins, *What is Mathematics?*, Oxford University Press, London and New York, 1941, pp. 251–255.

these two points, without lifting the pencil from the paper, without going outside the limits 0 per cent to 100 per cent for V and P (that is, without going outside the square), and without intersecting the broken line. Since this is impossible, *any* continuous curve relating V and P for the whole range of values $0\% \leqq P \leqq 100\%$ must intersect the line V = P in at least one point.

Prediction Problems

We have proved that it is always possible in principle to take account of reactions to a published prediction in such a way that the prediction will be confirmed by the event. But can this procedure be carried out in practice by a pollster? Stated otherwise, what information would the pollster have to possess in order to adjust his prediction for the anticipated reaction? The answer is that he would have to know the function (1), at least in the neighborhood of the actual value of I, and that he would have to have an accurate estimate of I. It is the aim of his poll to give him the latter; it is less obvious where he can obtain the former.

Even if the adjustment factor, as set forth in equation (1), is not known precisely, it may be possible to improve a prediction on the basis of knowl-

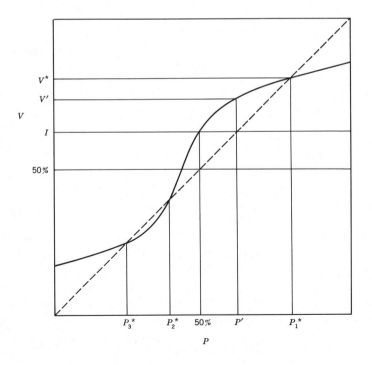

Fig. 3.   Bandwagon effect ($V > I$ when $P > 50\%$).

edge of the direction of the reaction (the sign of (I–V)). In Figure 3, we illustrate the case where we have an accurate estimate of I (from a poll), and where we know that there is a "bandwagon" effect. Again, we draw a solid curve to represent the relation $V = f(I,P)$. If there is a bandwagon effect, then this curve must lie above the horizontal straight line, $V = I$, when $P>50$ per cent, and below that line when $P<50$ per cent. For in the former case, when the prediction is published some voters will switch to candidate A, while in the latter case some voters will switch to his opponent.

A prediction, P^*, will be confirmed if it lies on an intersection of the solid curve with the 45° diagonal. It can be seen from the figure (and can be shown rigorously by another application of the fixed-point theorem) that there always exists at least one prediction, P_1^*, with the following two properties: (a) the prediction, if published, will be confirmed, and (b) publication of the prediction will not change the outcome of the election (i.e., $P_1^*>50\%$ only if $I>50\%$). However, examination of the figure will show that there may also exist other values of P^* possessing the first property but not the second. If one of these latter predictions is published, it will be confirmed by the election result, but the candidate who would have won if no prediction had been published will be defeated. In the figure as drawn, two such values of P^* exist, corresponding to the two intersections of the solid curve with the 45° line in the lower left-hand quarter of the figure. It is intuitively obvious that such points will exist only if the bandwagon effect is "very strong." The exact conditions can be stated analytically, but will be omitted here.

On the other hand, it can be seen from the figure that if the unadjusted poll result, P', is an accurate estimate of I, then, in the case of a bandwagon effect, the publication of P' cannot change the outcome of the election.[3]

The case of an "underdog" effect is illustrated in the same way in Figure 4. In this case we see by examination of the figure (and may prove analytically) that the publication of a prediction, P^*, correctly adjusted for the reaction to its publication, *cannot* reverse the outcome of a two-candidate election; while the publication of a prediction, P', that is an accurate estimate of I, *may* reverse the outcome. Again, the latter possibility will occur only when the underdog effect is "very strong."

From the results of this section, we see that there is no simple relationship between the "adjustment" of poll results prior to publication and the "manipulation" of an election. If we assume the original poll to be accurate, in the usual sense; and if by "adjustment" we mean taking account (accurately) of the reaction to publication; then: (1) adjustment

[3] The bandwagon effect may, of course, change the outcome of a contest among three or more candidates by diverting votes from the weakest candidate to one of the stronger. Also, the published prediction may affect the number of voters preferring a given candidate who actually go to the polls. The model can be generalized to permit discussion of such effects.

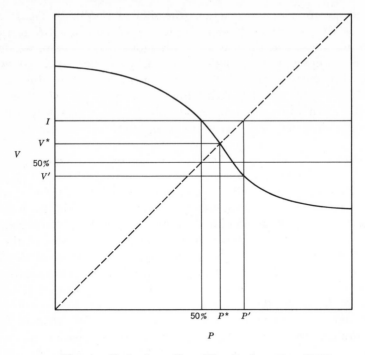

Fig. 4.   Underdog effect ($V < I$ when $P > 50\%$).

can have a manipulatory effect in the bandwagon case, but not in the underdog case, and need not in either case; (2) failure to adjust can have a manipulatory effect in the underdog case, but not in the bandwagon case. By "manipulatory effect" we mean, of course, not merely an effect on the voting percentages, but an actual reversal of the outcome. I hasten to add that pollsters might experience some difficulty in explaining even "non-manipulatory" adjustments to members of Congressional investigating committees.

Summary

In this paper we have raised and answered the question of whether, and under what circumstances, a published prediction will be confirmed, even if there is reaction to the prediction. The problem was stated, and a graphical method for analyzing it was set forth in Section I. In Section II, it was shown that it is always possible *in principle* to make a public prediction that will be confirmed by the event. This proof refutes allegations commonly made about the impossibility, in principle, of correct prediction of social behavior. In Section III, certain practical problems were examined that arise in actually making predictions. It was shown that correct prediction requires at least some knowledge of the reaction function; that whether publication of a prediction (adjusted for expected reactions or unadjusted) will affect the outcome of an election between two candidates depends on the shape of the reaction function; and that publication of an adjusted prediction will sometimes have more, and sometimes less effect on behavior than publication of an unadjusted prediction. These results were applied in particular to the reaction functions corresponding to "bandwagon" and "underdog" effects.

Six ★ THEORY CONSTRUCTION

Catholics, it has long been known, have a lower suicide rate than Protestants. Why is this so? To answer this question, Durkheim proposed a theory. In everyday life, the terms *theory* and *hypothesis* are both often used for any guess, hunch, or notion about things. In the logic of science, the terms have a more restricted application. A theory, as was briefly pointed out in the General Introduction, is a deductively connected set of empirical generalizations. These generalizations, no matter how well established they may be, are always subject to possible refutation by future experience and are, therefore, hypothetical. A theory, accordingly, is often referred to as a hypothetico-deductive system, because it states deductive connections among hypotheses. The premises of a theory are empirical hypotheses that explain the generalizations they imply. Durkheim explained the puzzling connection between religious affiliation and rate of suicide by showing it to be a deductive consequence of hypotheses—which are spelled out in the first paper of this section by Robert Merton—about the effects of group cohesiveness on its members. It is worth noting that some of the terms that occur in the premises of the theory, such as "social cohesion," do not occur in the regularity that the theory explains. Instead the phenomenon to be explained is shown to be a special case of different and more general characteristics. This feature of theories gives them their scope, that is, the ability to explain and predict many diverse phenomena.

The greater the scope of a theory, the more comprehensive it is. The more comprehensive a theory is, the more it unifies phenomena by revealing apparently different things to be special cases of the same kind of thing. The classic example of a comprehensive, unifying theory is Newton's. From the Newtonian theory of gravitation it was possible to derive Galileo's laws for the free fall of bodies on earth, Kepler's laws about the motions of the planets around the sun, the laws about the tides, and a whole host of other previously known but disparate phenomena. It explained all these and predicted new laws not previously known. Newton's theory thus brought the earth and the heavens together by making the laws of each a special case of more general laws.

The premises of a theory, called either axioms or postulates, are confirmed by establishing the truth of the generalizations, called theorems, that are derived from it. This evidence for the axioms is only indirect, for though the truth of the axioms logically implies the truth of the theorems, the converse does not hold. Thus the theorems may be true and the axioms false. That is why alternative explanations of the same regularities are often proposed and why theories may be abandoned in favor of others. (The axioms are also empirical generalizations and could in principle be tested directly. However, the terms in the axioms of a comprehensive theory are highly defined or remote from direct experience, so that practically only indirect confirmation is feasible.)

A false prediction disconfirms a theory because true premises cannot validly imply false consequences. Assuming that this does not occur, our confidence in a theory rises with the number and variety of true generalizations that it explains and predicts. Our confidence in an isolated regularity is in turn increased if it can be derived from a theory, for then we understand why the observed connection holds. We know not only that A is always accompanied by B but, by virtue of the deduction that explains the uniformity, that if anything *were* A, then it *would* be B. If a generalization either predicts or is predicted by others, then the evidence for it is more than the conjunction of its observed instances. The term *law* is frequently reserved for generalizations that in this way occur in theories. The difference between a law and a "merely empirical" regularity is thus not found in the generalization itself, but in the context of background knowledge to which it belongs. Generalizations that are sufficiently well established to be characterized as laws justify our ascriptions of causality. The background knowledge of explanatory theory, even if it is not made explicit, supports the inference from cause to effect.

On Robert Merton's admirable conception of social science, the most fruitful territory lies in that middle ground between the outer space of speculation uncontaminated by dreary fact and the wasteland of isolated individual facts and statistical regularities. In the first essay he discusses how the concepts, explanations, and predictions of theory are tied to empirical research. In the second, he reverses direction and shows how empirical research suggests, changes, and clarifies theory. The two papers lucidly explicate and illustrate the application of scientific method to the construction and testing of theory in the social sciences.

Max Weber's doctrine of "ideal types" is closely related to problems of theory construction. Unfortunately, the exact nature of this relation as Weber perceived it is uncommonly elusive, for it depends upon the special emphasis he gave to "concrete" reality and its "concrete" causal relations. [See the introduction for Section Two.] The ideal type is not a theory in the sense just discussed, nor even a candidate for such a theory. Yet it is a heuristic device that guides our search for causal explanation. How is this accomplished?

The complexity and indeterminateness of our ordinary categories of social description was discussed in the introduction for Section Five. Weber has tartly noted that the "use of the undifferentiated collective concepts of everyday speech is always a cloak for confusion of thought and action." The ideal type replaces these notions with concepts whose meaning is clear and definite. In particular, the collective concept construed as an ideal type is not merely descriptive. It is, in Weber's terms, a "genetic," not a "generic" concept. In our terms (see pp. 339–340) it is not a single concept but a set of generalizations connecting instances of two or more concepts. These generalizations are used to explain or predict events of the generic kind mentioned in the ideal type. For instance, by connecting exchange conditions with the idea of marginal utility, the ideal-type "economic exchange" predicts the behavior of consumers under specified conditions. Or the ideal type may express a developmental generalization about the stages of society. An ideal handicraft society will, under certain conditions, develop into a capitalistic economy. The ideal type consists of plausible and "understandable" hypotheses suggested by our past knowledge and experience.

We can play games and imaginatively construct many merely possible or "abstract" ideal types. Actual social institutions and historical developments, however, are represented by the "individual" ideal type. On the face of it, the individual ideal type is a suggested theory about cultural phenomena to be tested against present experience and the facts of history. Weber, however, does not view the ideal type in this way. What happens, on his account, if a prediction from the ideal type does not turn out? If the ideal type were a candidate for an empirical theory, then it would thereby be refuted. We would have to revise or, what amounts to the same thing, reject the theory. But as Weber sees it, failure of prediction does not disconfirm the ideal type, for we already know that it is "false to reality." All ideal types are. The ideal type is, to use the language Friedman criticizes in his article in this section, "false in its assumptions." Its antecedent conditions are never met in reality because every concrete situation always has "accidental" features not mentioned in the type concept. By the same token, of course, the ideal type's consequent conditions never accurately describe any real situation either. A *strict* handicraft society leads to a *strict* capitalist economy. Both "strict" or ideal situations are abstractions from concreteness and therefore "false of reality." Predictions must be falsified, on this view, because reality is always richer than any abstraction mentioned in the ideal type. It asserts, "If ideal-C, then ideal-E." Failure of a prediction made from the ideal type (and the assumption that medieval society was an ideal handicraft society) does not, accordingly, falsify the hypothesis. It merely reveals that the assumption of an ideal-C was false. The medieval period was not *strictly* a handicraft society. However, it approximated that condition. The ways in which it deviated from the ideal are, therefore, the concrete causes of the differences between its actual course of development and the predicted or ideal-E. By this method of difference the ideal type guides us to these concrete individual causes and effects.

But how do we *know* that ideal-C leads to ideal-E if we always plead different circumstances when our predictions do not turn out? Moreover, even if we had sufficient background knowledge to lend plausibility to the ideal-type hypothesis, which of the many ways in which the actual-C differs from the ideal-C is the cause of the many differences between the actual-E and the ideal-E? Even if there were only a single deviating feature, we would still need independent knowledge of some regularities or laws that would justify imputing causal efficacy to that divergence from the ideal. Presumably we try to construct the ideal type in such a way that it differs as little as possible from the actual. However, this amounts to constructing successive approximations to a testable, and therefore refutable, theory.

The difference between abstraction and falsification, between not saying everything and saying what is not so, has been repeatedly stressed in this volume. [See, particularly, the introduction for Section Two.] Unfortunately, widespread blurring of the distinction, particularly in the philosophy of the social sciences, warrants belaboring it. A generalization mentions only those features of a situation believed to be significant, that is, lawfully connected with other things. It is applied by finding an instance of the conditions that it mentions. Any actual situation always has other characteristics which, by hypothesis, are irrelevant or "accidental" *for the effects stated.* We test whether the generalization is in fact true about the features it does mention by drawing inferences from it. If these turn out to be false about a situation that has these features (in addition to many others), then the generalization is refuted. The term *concrete* is, to borrow Weber's stricture against everyday collective concepts, a "cloak for confusion." We can only justify the imputation of individual causes and effects by inference from confirmed laws and theories. By lifting the cloak of "concreteness" from the doctrine of ideal types, we can appreciate its true value as an imaginative, heuristic device for constructing comprehensive and testable empirical theories.

Another, quite different and not at all confused, conviction also motivated Weber's insistence that collective ideal types were not and could not be true theories. In the text (p. 507), Weber alludes to Marxism and to alleged "forces" of historical development. He is expressing his deeply felt antiholism and his rejection of the view that there are macroscopic laws of the social process, that is, laws that do not require mention of the actions and motives of particular individuals. This view was characterized in the introduction for Section Four as "social determinism." Weber here refers to it as the "naturalistic prejudice." His rejection of social determinism undoubtedly reinforced his belief that ideal-typical laws of development must be "false of reality." However, departure from "concreteness" has nothing to do with it. If social determinism is false, this means that generalizations about collective phenomena can provide only imperfect knowledge. Their scope will be limited to those events that are not appreciably affected by the presence of a particular individual. But generalizations of limited scope may be wholly true, even though they are not the whole truth.

The papers by the two economists Milton Friedman and Tjalling Koopmans, although directed toward their own field, are concerned with issues of general relevance to the social sciences. They disagree about a matter closely related to problems just discussed concerning ideal types. If a theory is to be acceptable, must there be independent grounds by which we can determine the "realism" of its assumptions? In the light of such idealizations as the notion of "economic man," the question may seem straightforward. In fact, it cannot be answered without first clarifying what is meant by the "assumptions" of a theory and how they are related to the theory. Friedman carefully analyzes the notion of an "assumption" and of "testing a theory by its assumptions." He concludes that the only test of an acceptable theory is its success in predicting and explaining observations.

Koopmans, on the other hand, is uneasy about only indirect confirmation of theory and proposes instead that so far as possible the postulates themselves should be subject to the test of direct experience. He also suggests how by a series of "models" or successive approximations we may arrive at more adequate theories.

Friedman's primary concern is to clarify some misconceptions about the relation between a hypothesis and its so-called assumptions. As he points out, the conditions under which a hypothesis holds are inseparable from the hypothesis itself. Every law carries with it a statement of its "conditions," though these are sometimes only implicit. If they are not explicitly asserted, then they are part of the law's "hidden text." Whatever is not mentioned in a hypothesis is, by omission, asserted not to make a difference to what is mentioned. Accordingly, we do not test the conditions under which a law holds, for these conditions are part of the law. A generalization asserts that if certain conditions obtain, then certain other things will also be true. A statement of the law that omits its limiting conditions is literally false. A law is not true with "exceptions." If there are exceptions, it is false. For example, the limiting condition that the distance from which a body is dropped must not be so great that air resistance affects its acceleration is as much a part of Galileo's law, $s = \frac{1}{2}gt^2$, as are the definitions telling us what s, g, and t stand for. Therefore, when testing that hypothesis, we also test the condition or "assumption" about the effects of air resistance. One cannot, in other words, test the "assumptions" of a hypothesis independently of testing the hypothesis itself. To do one is to do the other.

Friedman clarifies these issues, and it is of the first importance to be clear about them. However, it is still necessary to distinguish further between testing a general hypothesis (including its conditions) and testing the premises or postulates of a theory from which that hypothesis may be derived. A general hypothesis (H) asserts, "If $C_1, \ldots, C_n$, then E." One cannot test for the truth of H independently of testing for the occurrence of all its antecedent conditions. However, if H is derivable from the premises of a theory, these premises or postulates are not part of the "conditions" for H. The theory asserts that certain empirical generalizations, P_1, $\ldots, P_n$, logically imply the truth of H. But the hypothesis H may be true, and the postulates may be false. Although H cannot be tested independently of testing its "conditions," it can be tested independently of testing any premises that logically imply it. In other words, the postulates of a theory are not part of the "conditions" stated in any empirical hypothesis, H, that the theory implies. Confirmation of H provides an indirect test of the postulates from which it is derived. But, as Koopmans suggests, alternative postulates, if available, would also be confirmed. The choice between them depends upon various considerations that are rehearsed by Friedman.

The discussion usefully emphasizes that there is nothing absolute about being a postulate or axiom. A theory may be axiomatized, that is, deductively organized into axioms and theorems in different ways. In particular, it may be possible to interchange one of the axioms with one of the theorems in such a way that the erstwhile "axiom" is now derivable from the new set of premises. In that case, what was before only indirectly confirmed by the theorems may now be tested in its own right like any other general hypothesis. Moreover, as we learn more about how the various institutional, technological, and psychological variables interact, it is to be expected that the limited theories (axioms and theorems together) of the individual social sciences should become derivable as special cases of a broader theory. In that event, the disagreements between sociologists and economists that Friedman discusses would clearly be seen as a consequence of the limited scope of their theories and the different sorts of behavior which each is concerned to explain and predict.

Disagreement about the relevant variables is an inevitable consequence of imperfect knowledge and the compartmentalization of the social sciences. To the cobbler there's nothing so good as leather, and each social scientist naturally tends to plump for those features of man and society that he has found to affect the area of his concern. The subject matter of the various disciplines can only be distinguished denotatively by means of the terms that occur in their generalizations and theories. Obviously there is considerable overlap between one area and another. Each social science takes certain variables as given, whose occurrence it does not explain but in terms of which it explains other things. The economist does not explain the psychological or political variables that may occur in laws about the behavior of the market. The psychologist does not explain the origin and persistence of the family; the sociologist does not explain the effects on personality of status and role, and so on. (See also pp. 291–292.) On the other hand, individual behavior and the various social institutions all affect one another. Sooner or later this interaction must be accounted for. Personality factors affect political attitudes. Political institutions and the economic structure are not unrelated to each other. In the interests of a more complete knowledge of the relevant variables, social scientists in recent years have tended more and more to ignore traditional boundaries and borrow techniques and hypotheses from one another. This development has nowhere been more pronounced than among political scientists.

The area that the academic scheme classifies as "political science" encompasses a variety of interests—normative, historical, descriptive, and systematic (or law-finding). In particular, the term *political theory* covers two different things. In its most common use it has been synonymous with *political philosophy*. Political philosophy is an analytical and normative discipline that examines and evaluates alternative views about, for instance, the nature of social justice, rights, and equality. It examines questions about the individual's obligations to society and about the society's obligations to the individual. These normative questions are distinct from descriptive ones about the conditions for, say, achieving and maintaining a social order that embodies accepted values. *Political theory* is also used for non-normative, descriptive and systematic investigations into the nature of political institutions, their origin, structure, and development. The problems of political theory in this second sense are the problems of theory construction in any social science.

How much borrowing from other social sciences is fruitful for answering the questions of one particular area? How much is an irrelevant diversion? No a priori answer can be given. It depends upon how closely related the fields are and how effectively research techniques that have been developed for one subject matter can be adapted to another. After reflective judgment about what is and what is not likely to be helpful, one can only try and see. Traditionally the interest of political scientists has focused on the description and explanation of governmental institutions, their structure, function, and mode of operation. The political scientist, working in this tradition, immerses himself in the operation of a particular institution and in its historical documents. His descriptions and generalizations are based upon observations (his own and others), scholarship, and the perspicuity with which he combines these for an accurate characterization of the institution. The "behavioral sciences" may be construed as those disciplines that self-consciously attempt to construct and test hypotheses about individual behavior by methods similar to those used in the "harder" natural sciences. Under the influence of developments in these areas, many political scientists have sought to apply similar techniques to the study of individual political behavior. A new and flourishing subfield, called "political behavior," has consequently developed within political science. David Truman judiciously compares and contrasts the traditional and the behavioral-science approaches to the study of political phenomena. Both approaches are illuminated by his analysis of the extent to which, and ways in which, the emphasis upon individual behavior may impede or enhance the construction of explanatory theories of political institutions.

Bertrand Russell once contended that the only way to settle an ethical argument was by a "good bash on the head." Though stated somewhat indelicately, with respect to ultimate moral values—those that are held to be *intrinsically* good or bad—the "bash-on-the-head" theory of ethical judgment is not wholly without justification. In the end the kind of values a man has depends upon the kind of man he is. Each man must decide for himself. Fortunately, the domain of these hard decisions is limited. By far the greater number of moral controversies are amenable to reason and evidence, for they concern the consequences of certain courses of action. Most disagreements about normative questions do not turn on such ultimate judgments as the intrinsic wrongness of inflicting needless suffering. Upon examination, even such a relatively fundamental value as the desirability of participatory democracy turns out to be accepted not because of its intrinsic goodness, but because of its presumed consequences for the quality of life and, perhaps even more, because of the undesirable effects of all alternatives. When a question concerns the effects of a course of action or institutional arrangement, then empirical evidence—facts and theories— is relevant. Very probably, most if not all of our beliefs about political morality depend upon our knowledge of how certain institutions and behavior affect the life of the individual in society. By using several interesting illustrations from recent sociological research, Runciman shows how and why this is so.

[Note: Issues pertinent to theory construction in psychology are extensively discussed in Selections 9 and 12 by Farber and Fodor in Section Three.]

[26] The Bearing of Sociological Theory on Empirical Research

ROBERT K. MERTON

The recent history of sociological theory can in large measure be written in terms of an alternation between two contrasting emphases. On the one hand, we observe those sociologists who seek above all to generalize, to find their way as rapidly as possible to the formulation of sociological laws. Tending to assess the significance of sociological work in terms of scope rather than the demonstrability of generalizations, they eschew the "triviality" of detailed, small-scale observation and seek the grandeur of global summaries. At the other extreme stands a hardy band who do not hunt too closely the implications of their research but who remain confident and assured that what they report is so. To be sure, their reports of facts are verifiable and often verified, but they are somewhat at a loss to relate these facts to one another or even to explain why these, rather than other, observations have been made. For the first group the identifying motto would at times seem to be: "We do not know whether what we say is true, but it is at least significant." And for the radical empiricist the motto may read: "This is demonstrably so, but we cannot indicate its significance."

Whatever the bases of adherence to the one or the other of these camps— different but not necessarily contradictory accountings would be provided by psychologists, sociologists of knowledge, and historians of science— it is abundantly clear that there is no logical basis for their being ranged *against* each other. Generalizations can be tempered, if not with mercy, at least with disciplined observation; close, detailed observations need not be rendered trivial by avoidance of their theoretical pertinence and implications.

With all this there will doubtless be widespread if, indeed, not unanimous agreement. But this very unanimity suggests that these remarks are platitudinous. If, however, one function of theory is to explore the implications of the seemingly self-evident, it may not be amiss to look into what is entailed by such programmatic statements about the relations of sociological theory and empirical research. In doing so, every effort should be made to avoid dwelling upon illustrations drawn from the "more mature" sciences—such as physics and biology—not because these do not exhibit the logical problems involved but because their very maturity permits these disciplines to deal *fruitfully* with abstractions of a high order to a degree which, it is submitted, is not yet the case with sociology. An indefinitely large number of discussions of scientific method have set forth the logical prerequisites of scientific theory, but, it would seem, they have often done so on such a high level of abstraction that the prospect of translating these precepts into current sociological research becomes utopian. Ultimately, sociological research must meet the canons of scientific method; immediately, the task is so to express these requirements that they may have more direct bearing on the analytical work which is at present feasible.

The term "sociological theory" has been widely used to refer to the products of several related but distinct activities carried on by members of a professional group called sociologists. But since these several types of activity have significantly different bearings upon empirical social research—since they differ in their scientific functions—they should be distinguished for purposes of discussion. Moreover, such discriminations provide a basis for assessing the contributions and limitations characteristic of each of the following six types of work which are often lumped together as comprising sociological theory; (1) methodology; (2) general sociological orientations; (3) analysis of sociological concepts; (4) *post factum* sociological interpretations; (5) empirical generalizations in sociology and (6) sociological theory.

Methodology

At the outset we should distinguish clearly between sociological theory, which has for its subject matter certain aspects and results of the interaction of men and is therefore substantive, and methodology, or the logic of scientific procedure. The problems of methodology transcend those found in any one discipline, dealing either with those common to groups of disciplines [1] or, in more generalized form, with those common to all scientific inquiry. Methodology is not peculiarly bound up with sociological problems, and, though there is a plentitude of methodological discussions in books and journals of sociology, they are not thereby rendered sociological in character. Sociologists, in company with all others who essay scientific work, must be methodologically wise; they must be aware of the design of

---

[1] Consider several volumes which set forth methodological as distinct from procedural concerns of sociology: Florian Znaniecki, *The Method of Sociology* (New York: Farrar & Rinehart, 1934); R. M. MacIver, *Social Causation* (Boston: Ginn and Company, 1942); G. A. Lundberg, *Foundations of Sociology* (New York: The Macmillan Company, 1939); Felix Kaufmann, *Methodology of the Social Sciences* (New York: Oxford University Press, 1944); P. F. Lazarsfeld and M. Rosenberg (eds.) *The Language of Social Research* (New York: The Free Press, 1955), esp. the Introductions to sections.

investigation, the nature of inference, the requirements of a theoretic system. But such knowledge does not contain or imply the particular *content* of sociological theory. There is, in short, a clear and decisive difference between *knowing how to test* a battery of hypotheses and *knowing the theory* from which to derive hypotheses to be tested.[2] It is my impression that current sociological training is more largely designed to make students understand the first than the second.

As Poincaré observed a half-century ago, sociologists have long been hierophants of methodology, thus, perhaps, diverting talents and energies from the task of building substantive theory. This focus of attention upon the logics of procedure has its patent scientific function, since such inventories serve a critical purpose in guiding and assessing theoretical and empirical inquiries. It also reflects the growing-pains of an immature discipline. Just as the apprentice who acquires new skills self-consciously examines each element of these skills in contrast to the master who habitually practices them with seeming indifference to their explicit formulation, so the exponents of a discipline haltingly moving toward scientific status laboriously spell out the logical grounds of their procedure. The slim books on methodology which proliferate in the fields of sociology, economics, and psychology do not find many counterparts among the technical works in the sciences which have long since come of age. Whatever their intellectual function, these methodological writings imply the perspectives of a fledgling discipline, anxiously presenting its credentials for full status in the fraternity of the sciences. But, significantly enough, the instances of adequate scientific method utilized by sociologists for illustrative or expository purposes are usually drawn from disciplines other than sociology itself. Twentieth-century, not sixteenth-century, physics and chemistry are taken as methodological prototypes or exemplars for twentieth-century sociology, with little explicit recognition that between sociology and these other sciences is a difference of centuries of cumulating scientific research. These comparisons are inevitably programmatic rather than realistic. More appropriate methodological demands would result in a gap between methodological aspiration and actual sociological attainment at once less conspicuous and less invidious.

General Sociological Orientations

Much of what is described in textbooks as sociological theory consists of general orientations toward substantive materials. Such orientations involve broad postulates which indicate *types* of variables which are some-

---

[2] However, it should be noted not only that instruments and procedures used in sociological (or other scientific) inquiry must meet methodological criteria but that they also logically presuppose substantive theories. As Pierre Duhem observed in this connection, the instrument as well as the experimental results obtained in science are shot through with specific assumptions and theories of a substantive order. *La théorie physique* (Paris: Chevalier et Rivière, 1906), 278.

how to be taken into account rather than specifying determinate relationships between particular variables. Indispensable though these orientations are, they provide only the broadest framework for empirical inquiry. This is the case with Durkheim's generic hypothesis, which holds that the "determining cause of a social fact should be sought among the social facts preceding it" and identifies the "social" factor as institutional norms toward which behavior is oriented.[3] Or, again, it is said that "to a certain approximation it is useful to regard society as an integrated system of mutually interrelated and functionally interdependent parts."[4] So, too, the importance of the "humanistic coefficient" in cultural data as expounded by Znaniecki and Sorokin, among others, belongs to this category. Such general orientations may be paraphrased as saying in effect that the investigator ignores this *order of fact* at his peril. They do not set forth specific hypotheses.

The chief function of these orientations is to provide a general context for inquiry; they facilitate the process of arriving at determinate hypotheses. To take a case in point: Malinowski was led to re-examine the Freudian notion of the Oedipus complex on the basis of a general sociological orientation, which viewed sentiment formation as patterned by social structure. This generic view clearly underlay his exploration of a specific "psychological" complex in its relation to a system of status relationships in a society differing in structure from that of western Europe. The *specific* hypotheses which he utilized in this inquiry were all congruent with the generic orientation but were not prescribed by it. Otherwise put, the general orientation indicated the relevance of *some* structural variables, but there still remained the task of ferreting out the particular variables to be included.

Though such general theoretic outlooks have a more inclusive and profound effect on the development of scientific inquiry than do specific hypotheses—they constitute the matrix from which, in the words of Maurice Arthus, "new hypotheses follow one another in breathless succession and a harvest of facts follow closely the blossoming of these hypotheses"—though this is the case, they constitute only the point of departure for the theorist. It is his task to develop specific, interrelated hypotheses by reformulating empirical generalizations in the light of these generic orientations.

It should be noted, furthermore, that the growing contributions of sociological theory to its sister-disciplines lie more in the realm of general sociological orientations than in that of specific confirmed hypotheses. The development of social history, of institutional economics, and the importation of sociological perspectives into psychoanalytic theory involve recognition of the sociological dimensions of the data rather than incorporation

3 Durkheim, *The Rules of Sociological Method,* 110; *L'Education morale* (Paris: Félix Alcan, 1925), 9–45, *passim.*

4 Conrad M. Arensberg and Solon Kimball, *Family and Community in Ireland* (Cambridge: Harvard University Press, 1940), xxvi.

of specific confirmed theories. Social scientists have been led to detect sociological gaps in the application of their theory to concrete social behavior. They do not so often exhibit sociological naiveté in their interpretations. The economist, the political scientist, and the psychologist have increasingly come to recognize that what they have systematically taken as given, as data, may be sociologically problematical. But this receptivity to a sociological outlook is often dissipated by the paucity of adequately *tested specific theories* of, say, the determinants of human wants or of the social processes involved in the distribution and exercise of social power. Pressures deriving from the respective theoretic gaps of the several social sciences may serve, in time, to bring about an increasing formulation of specific and systematic sociological theories appropriate to the problems implied by these gaps. General orientations do not suffice. Presumably this is the context for the complaint voiced by an economist:

[The economist always seeks to refer his analysis of a problem] back to some "datum," that is to say, to something which is extra-economic. This something may be apparently very remote from the problem which was first taken up, for the chains of economic causation are often very long. But he always wants to hand over the problem in the end to some sociologist or other—*if there is a sociologist waiting for him. Very often there isn't.*[5]

Analysis of Sociological Concepts

It is at times held that theory is comprised of concepts, an assertion which, being incomplete, is neither true nor false but vague. To be sure, conceptual analysis, which is confined to the specification and clarification of key concepts, is an indispensable phase of theoretic work. But an array of concepts—status, role, *Gemeinschaft,* social interaction, social distance, *anomie*—does not constitute theory, though it may enter into a theoretic system. It may be conjectured that, in so far as an antitheoretic bias occurs among sociologists, it is in protest against those who identify theory with clarification of definitions, who mistakenly take the part for the whole of theoretic analysis. It is only when such concepts are interrelated in the form of a scheme that a theory begins to emerge. Concepts, then, constitute the definitions (or prescriptions) of what is to be observed; they are the variables between which empirical relationships are to be sought. When propositions are logically interrelated, a theory has been instituted.

The choice of concepts guiding the collection and analysis of data is, of course, crucial to empirical inquiry. For, to state an important truism, if concepts are selected such that no relationships between them obtain,

[5] J. R. Hicks, "Economic theory and the social sciences," *The Social Sciences: Their Relations in Theory and in Teaching* (London: Le Play Press, 1936), p. 135. (Italics mine.) [Compare the remarks by the economist M. Friedman on disagreements between sociologists and economists, pp. 527–528 in this volume. Ed.]

the research will be sterile, no matter how meticulous the subsequent observations and inferences. The importance of this truism lies in its implication that truly trial-and-error procedures in empirical inquiry are likely to be comparatively unfruitful, since the number of variables which are not significantly connected is indefinitely large.

It is, then, one function of conceptual clarification to make explicit the character of data subsumed under a concept.[6] It thus serves to reduce the likelihood that spurious empirical findings will be couched in terms of given concepts. Thus, Sutherland's re-examination of the received concept of "crime" provides an instructive instance of how such clarification induces a revision of hypotheses concerning the data organized in terms of the concept.[7] He demonstrates an equivocation implicit in criminological theories which seek to account for the fact that there is a much higher rate of crime, as "officially measured," in the lower than in the upper social classes. These crime "data" (organized in terms of a particular operational concept or measure of crime) have led to a series of hypotheses which view poverty, slum conditions, feeble-mindedness, and other characteristics held to be highly associated with low-class status as the "causes" of criminal behavior. Once the concept of crime is clarified to refer to the violation of criminal law and is thus extended to include "white-collar criminality" in business and professions—violations which are less often reflected in official crime statistics than are lower-class violations—the presumptive high association between low social status and crime may no longer obtain. We need not pursue Sutherland's analysis further to detect the function of conceptual clarification in this instance. It provides for a *reconstruction of data* by indicating more precisely just what they include and what they exclude. In doing so, it leads to liquidation of hypotheses set up to account for spurious data by questioning the assumptions on which the initial statistical data were based. By hanging a question mark on an implicit assumption underlying the research definition of crime—the assumption that violations of the criminal code by members of the several social classes are representatively registered in the official statistics—this conceptual clarification had direct implications for a nucleus of theories.

In similar fashion, conceptual analysis may often resolve apparent antinomies in empirical findings by indicating that such contradictions are

---

6 As Schumpeter remarks about the role of "analytic apparatus": "If we are to speak about price levels and to devise methods of measuring them, we must know what a price level is. If we are to observe demand, we must have a precise concept of its elasticity. If we speak about productivity of labor, we must know what propositions hold true about total product per man-hour and what other propositions hold true about the partial differential coefficient of total product with respect to man-hours. No hypotheses enter into such concepts, which simply embody methods of description and measurement, nor into the propositions defining their relation (so-called theorems), and yet their framing is the chief task of theory, in economics as elsewhere. This is what we mean by *tools of analysis*." Joseph A. Schumpeter, *Business Cycles* (New York: McGraw-Hill Book Company, Inc., 1939), **I**, 31.

7 Edwin H. Sutherland, "White-collar criminality," *American Sociological Review*, 1940, **5**, 1–12.

more apparent than real. This familiar phrase refers, in part, to the fact that initially crudely defined concepts have tacitly included significantly different elements so that data organized in terms of these concepts differ materially and thus exhibit apparently contradictory tendencies.[8] The function of conceptual analysis in this instance is to maximize the likelihood of the comparability, in significant respects, of data which are to be included in a research.

The instance drawn from Sutherland merely illustrates the more general fact that in research, as in less disciplined activities, our conceptual language tends to fix our perceptions and, derivatively, our thought and behavior. The concept defines the situation, and the research worker responds accordingly. Explicit conceptual analysis helps him recognize to what he is responding and which (possibly significant) elements he is ignoring. The findings of Whorf on this matter are, with appropriate modifications, applicable to empirical research.[9] He found that behavior was oriented toward linguistic or conceptual meanings connoted by the terms applied to a situation. Thus, in the presence of objects which are conceptually described as "gasoline drums," behavior will tend modally toward a particular type: great care will be exercised. But when people are confronted with what are called *empty* gasoline drums," behavior is different: it is careless, with little control over smoking and the disposition of cigarette stubs. Yet the "empty" drums are more hazardous, since they contain explosive vapor. Response is not to the physical but to the conceptualized situation. The concept "empty" is here used equivocally: as a synonym for "null and void, negative, inert," and as a term applied to physical situations without regard to such "irrelevancies" as vapor and liquid vestiges in the container. The situation is conceptualized in the second sense, and the concept is then responded to in the first sense, with the result that "empty" gasoline drums become the occasion for fires. Clarification of just what "empty" means in the universe of discourse would have a profound effect on behavior. This case may serve as a paradigm of the functional effect of conceptual clarification upon research behavior: it makes clear just what the research worker is doing when he deals with conceptualized data. He draws different consequences for empirical research as his conceptual apparatus changes.

This is not to say, however, that the vocabulary of concepts fixes perceptions, thought and associated behavior once and for all. Even less is it to say that such instances of misleading terminology are embedded in one or another language (as Whorf tended to imply in this theory of linguistic behaviorism). Men are not permanently imprisoned in the framework of

---

[8] Elaborate formulations of this type of analysis are to be found in Corrado Gini, *Prime linee di patologia economica* (Milan: Giuffre, 1935); for a brief discussion see C. Gini, "Un tentativo di armonizzare teorie disparate e osservazioni contrastanti nel campo dei fenomeni sociali," *Rivista di politica economica*, 1935, **12**, 1–24.

[9] B. L. Whorf, "Relation of habitual thought and behavior to language," in L. Spier, A. I. Hallowell, and S. S. Newman (eds.), *Language, Culture, and Personality* (Menasha: Sapir Memorial Fund Publication, 1941), 75–93.

the (often inherited) concepts they use; they can not only break out of this framework but can create a new one, better suited to the needs of the occasion. Yet, at any particular time, one should be prepared to find that the governing concepts can, and often do, lag behind the behavioral requirements of the case. During these sometimes prolonged periods of lag, misapplied concepts do their damage. However, this very inaptness of concept to situation, recognized through painful experience, will often evoke self-correcting and more appropriate formulations. The job is to identify conceptual lag and to liberate ourselves from the patterns of cognitive misbehavior which it tends to produce.[10]

A further task of conceptual analysis is to institute observable indices of the social data with which empirical research is concerned. Early efforts in this direction were manifest in the works of Durkheim (and constitute one of his most significant contributions to sociology). Though his formalized conceptions along these lines do not approach the sophistication of more recent formulations, he was patently utilizing "intervening variables," as lately described by Tolman and Hull, and seeking to establish indices for these variables.[11] The problem, as far as it need be stated for our immediate purposes, consists in devising indices of unobservables or symbolic constructs (e.g., social cohesion)—indices which are theoretically supportable. Conceptual analysis thus enters as one basis for an initial and periodic critical appraisal of the extent to which assumed signs and symbols are an adequate index of the social substratum. Such analysis suggests clues for determining whether in fact the index (or measuring instrument) proves adequate to the occasion.[12]

10 For an extended discussion, see the posthumously published volume of selected writings by B. L. Whorf, *Language, Thought and Reality* (Cambridge: Technology Press of M.I.T., 1956). It is the extreme Whorfian position which Joshua Whatmough attacks in his *Language: A Modern Synthesis* (New York: St. Martin's Press, Inc., 1956), **85**, 186–87; 227–34. Yet Whatmough's well-placed salvoes do not entirely destroy Whorf's position but only compel a retreat to a more limited and defensible position. Socially entrenched concepts do affect perception, thought and behavior but the structure of language provides sufficient scope for inappropriate concepts to be replaced by more suitable concepts. An appreciative review of Whorf's ideas will be found in Franklin Fearing, "An examination of the conceptions of Benjamin Whorf in the light of theories of perception and cognition," Harry Hoijer, ed. *Language in Culture* (University of Chicago Press, 1954), 47–81.

11 Durkheim's basic formulation, variously repeated in each of his monographs, reads as follows: "It is necessary . . . to substitute for the internal fact which escapes us an external fact that symbolizes it and to study the former through the latter." See his *Rules of Sociological Method*, chap. ii; *Le Suicide* (Paris: F. Alcan, 1930), 22 ff. Most detailed consideration of Durkheim's views on social indices is provided by Harry Alpert, *Emile Durkheim and His Sociology* (New York: Columbia University Press, 1939), 120 ff. On the general problem see C. L. Hull, "The problem of Intervening Variables in molar behavior theory," *Psychological Review*, 1943, **50**, 273–91. [On the use of intervening variables in psychology, see the article by I. E. Farber in this volume, especially pp. 165–169. Ed.]

12 Among the many functions of conceptual analysis at this point is that of instituting inquiry into the question of whether or not the index is "neutral" to its environment. By searching out the assumptions underlying the selection (and validation for a given population) of observables as indices (e.g., religious affiliation, an attitude scale),

Post Factum Sociological Interpretations

It is often the case in empirical social research that data are collected and only then subjected to interpretative comment. This procedure in which the observations are at hand and the interpretations are subsequently applied to the data has the logical structure of clinical inquiry. The observations may be case-history or statistical in character. The defining characteristic of this procedure is the introduction of an interpretation *after* the observations have been made rather than the empirical testing of a predesignated hypothesis. The implicit assumption is that a body of generalized propositions has been so fully established that it can be approximately applied to the data in hand.

Such *post factum* explanations, designed to "explain" observations, differ in logical function from speciously similar procedures where the observational materials are utilized in order to *derive* fresh hypotheses to be confirmed by *new* observations.

A disarming characteristic of the procedure is that the explanations are indeed consistent with the given set of observations. This is scarcely surprising, in as much as only those *post factum* hypotheses are selected which do accord with these observations. If the basic assumption holds— namely, that the *post factum* interpretation utilizes abundantly confirmed theories—then this type of explanation indeed "shoots arrowy light into the dark chaos of materials." But if, as is more often the case in sociological interpretation, the *post factum* hypotheses are also *ad hoc* or, at the least, have but a slight degree of prior confirmation, then such "precocious explanations," as H. S. Sullivan called them, produce a spurious sense of adequacy at the expense of instigating further inquiry.

Post factum explanations remain at the level of *plausibility* (low evidential value) rather than leading to "compelling evidence" (a high degree of confirmation). Plausibility, in distinction to compelling evidence, is found when an interpretation is consistent with one set of data (which typically has, indeed, given rise to the decision to utilize one, rather than another, interpretation). It also implies that alternative interpretations equally consistent with these data have not been systematically explored and that inferences drawn from the interpretation have not been tested by new observations.

The logical fallacy underlying the *post factum* explanation rests in the fact that there is available a variety of crude hypotheses, each with some measure of confirmation but designed to account for quite contradictory

---

conceptual analysis initiates appropriate tests of the possibility that the index has become dissociated from its substratum. For a clear statement of this point see Louis Guttman, "A basis for scaling quantitative data," *American Sociological Review*, 1944, **9**, 139–50, esp. 149–50.

sets of affairs. The method of *post factum* explanation does not lend itself to nullifiability, if only because it is so completely flexible. For example, it may be reported that "the unemployed tend to read fewer books than they did previously." This is "explained" by the hypothesis that anxiety increases as a consequence of unemployment and, therefore, that any activity requiring concentration, such as reading, becomes difficult. This type of accounting is plausible, since there is some evidence that increased anxiety *may* occur in such situations and since a state of morbid preoccupation does interfere with organized activity. If, however, it is now reported that the original data were erroneous and it is a fact that "the unemployed read more than previously" a new *post factum* explanation can at once be invoked. The explanation now holds that the unemployed have more leisure or that they engage in activity intended to increase their personal skills. Consequently, they read more than before. Thus, whatever the observations, a new interpretation can be found to "fit the facts." [13] This example may be sufficient to indicate that such reconstructions serve only as illustrations and not as tests. It is this logical inadequacy of the *post factum* construction that led Peirce to observe:

It is of the essence of induction that the consequence of the theory should be drawn first in regard to the unknown, or virtually unknown, result of experiment; and that this should virtually be only ascertained afterward. For if we look over the pheomena to find agreements with the theory, it is a mere question of ingenuity and industry how many we shall find.[14]

These reconstructions typically by-pass an explicit formulation of the conditions under which the hypotheses will be found to hold true. In order to meet this logical requirement, such interpretations would necessarily be predictive rather than postdictive.

As a case in point, we may quote the frequency with which Blumer asserts that the Thomas-Znaniecki analyses of documents "merely seem to be plausible." [15] The basis for plausibility rests in the consistency between the interpretation and the data; the absence of compelling evidence stems from the failure to provide distinctive tests of the interpretations apart from their consistency with the initial observations. The analysis is fitted to the facts, and there is no indication of just which data would be taken to contravene the interpretations. As a consequence, the documentary evidence merely illustrates rather than tests the theory.[16]

---

[13] The pertinent data have not been assembled. But, on the plausibility of the second interpretation, see Douglas Waples, *People and Print: Social Aspects of Reading in the Depression* (Chicago: University of Chicago Press, 1937), 198.

[14] Charles Sanders Peirce, *Collected Papers,* ed. Charles Hartshorne and Paul Weiss (Cambridge: Harvard University Press, 1932), **II**, 496.

[15] Herbert Blumer, *An Appraisal of Thomas and Znaniecki's "The Polish Peasant in Europe and America"* (New York: Social Science Research Council, 1939), 38, see also *ibid.*, 39, 44, 46, 49, 50, 75.

[16] It is difficult to see on what grounds Blumer asserts that these interpretations cannot be mere cases of illustration of a theory. His comment that the materials "acquire significance and understanding that they did not have" would apply to *post factum* explanations generally.

Empirical Generalizations in Sociology

Not infrequently it is said that the object of sociological theory is to arrive at statements of social uniformities. This is an elliptical assertion and hence requires clarification. For there are two types of statements of sociological uniformities which differ significantly in their bearing on theory. The first of these is the empirical generalization: an isolated proposition summarizing observed uniformities of relationships between two or more variables.[17] The sociological literature abounds with such generalizations which have not been assimilated to sociological theory. Thus, Engel's "laws" of consumption may be cited as examples. So, too, the Halbwachs finding that laborers spend more per adult unit for food than white-collar employees of the same income class.[18] Such generalizations may be of greater or less precision, but this does not affect their logical place in the structure of inquiry. The Groves-Ogburn finding, for a sample of American cities, that "cities with a larger percentage engaged in manufacturing also have, on the average, slightly larger percentages of young persons married" has been expressed in an equation indicating the degree of this relationship. Although propositions of this order are essential in empirical research, a miscellany of such propositions only provides the raw materials for sociology as a discipline. The theoretic task, and the orientation of empirical research toward theory, first begins when the bearing of such uniformities on a set of interrelated propositions is tentatively established. The notion of directed research implies that, in part,[19] empirical inquiry is so organized that if and when empirical uniformities are discovered, they have direct consequences for a theoretic system. In so far as the research is directed, the rationale of findings is set forth before the findings are obtained.

[17] This usage of the term "empirical" is common, as Dewey notes. In this context, "*empirical* means that the subject-matter of a given proposition which has existential reference, represents merely a set of uniform conjunctions of traits repeatedly observed to exist, without any understanding of *why* the conjunction occurs; without a theory which states its rationale." John Dewey, *Logic: The Theory of Inquiry* (New York: Holt, Rinehart & Winston, Inc., 1938), 305.

[18] See a considerable collection of such uniformities summarized by C. C. Zimmerman, *Consumption and Standards of Living* (New York: D. Van Nostrand Company, Inc., 1936), 51 ff.

[19] "In part," if only because it stultifies the possibilities of obtaining fertile new findings to confine researches *wholly* to the test of predetermined hypotheses. Hunches originating in the course of the inquiry which may not have immediately obvious implications for a broader theoretic system may eventuate in the discovery of empirical uniformities which can later be incorporated into a theory. For example, in the sociology of political behavior, it has been recently established that the larger the number of social cross-pressures to which voters are subjected, the less interest they exhibit in a presidential election (P. F. Lazarsfeld, Bernard Berelson, and Hazel Gaudet, *The People's Choice* [New York: Duell, Sloan & Pearce, 1944], 56–64). This finding, which was wholly unanticipated when the research was first formulated, may well initiate new lines of systematic inquiry into political behavior, even though it is not yet integrated into a generalized theory. Fruitful empirical research not only tests theoretically derived hypotheses; it also originates new hypotheses. This might be termed the "serendipity" component of research, i.e., the discovery, by chance or sagacity, of valid results which were not sought for.

Sociological Theory

The second type of sociological generalization, the so-called scientific law, differs from the foregoing in as much as it is a statement of invariance *derivable* from a theory. The paucity of such laws in the sociological field perhaps reflects the prevailing bifurcation of theory and empirical research. Despite the many volumes dealing with the history of sociological theory and despite the plethora of empirical investigations, sociologists (including the writer) may discuss the logical criteria of sociological laws without citing a single instance which fully satisfies these criteria.[20]

Approximations to these criteria are not entirely wanting. To exhibit the relations of empirical generalizations to theory and to set forth the functions of theory, it may be useful to examine a familiar case in which such generalizations were incorporated into a body of substantive theory. Thus, it has long been established as a statistical uniformity that in a variety of populations, Catholics have a lower suicide rate than Protestants.[21] In this form the uniformity posed a theoretical problem. It merely constituted an empirical regularity which would become significant for theory only if it could be derived from a set of other propositions, a task which Durkheim set himself. If we restate his theoretic assumptions in formal fashion, the paradigm of his theoretic analysis becomes clear:

1. Social cohesion provides psychic support to group members subjected to acute stresses and anxieties.
2. Suicide rates are functions of *unrelieved* anxieties and stresses to which persons are subjected.
3. Catholics have greater social cohesion than Protestants.
4. Therefore, lower suicide rates should be anticipated among Catholics than among Protestants.[22]

20 E.g., see the discussion by George A. Lundberg, "The concept of law in the social sciences," *Philosophy of Science*, 1938, **5**, 189–203, which affirms the possibility of such laws without including any case in point. The book by K. D. Har, *Social Laws* (Chapel Hill: University of North Carolina Press, 1930), does not fulfil the promise implicit in the title. A panel of social scientists discussing the possibility of obtaining social laws finds it difficult to instance cases (Blumer, *op. cit.*, 142–50).

21 It need hardly be said that this statement assumes that education, income, nationality, rural-urban residence, and other factors which might render this finding spurious have been held constant.

22 We need not examine further aspects of this illustration, e.g., (1) the extent to which we have adequately stated the premises implicit in Durkheim's interpretation; (2) the supplementary theoretic analysis which would take these premises not as given but as problematic; (3) the grounds on which the potentially infinite regression of theoretic interpretations is halted at one rather than another point; (4) the problems involved in the introduction of such intervening variables as social cohesion which are not directly measured; (5) the extent to which the premises have been empirically confirmed; (6) the comparatively low order of abstraction represented by this illustration and (7) the fact that Durkheim derived several empirical generalizations from this same set of hypotheses.

This case serves to locate the place of empirical generalizations in relation to theory and to illustrate the several functions of theory.

1. It indicates that theoretic pertinence is not inherently present or absent in empirical generalizations but appears when the generalization is conceptualized in abstractions of higher order (Catholicism—social cohesion—relieved anxieties—suicide rate) which are embodied in more general statements of relationships.[23] What was initially taken as an isolated uniformity is restated as a relation, not between religious affiliation and behavior, but between groups with certain conceptualized attributes (social cohesion) and the behavior. The *scope* of the original empirical finding is considerably extended, and several seemingly disparate uniformities are seen to be interrelated (thus differentials in suicide rates between married and single persons can be derived from the same theory).

2. Once having established the theoretic pertinence of a uniformity by deriving it from a set of interrelated propositions, we provide for the *cumulation* both of theory and of research findings. The differentials-in-suicide-rate uniformities add confirmation to the set of propositions from which they—and other uniformities—have been derived. This is a major function of *systematic theory*.

3. Whereas the empirical uniformity did not lend itself to the drawing of diverse consequences, the reformulation gives rise to various consequences in fields of conduct quite remote from that of suicidal behavior. For example, inquiries into obsessive behavior, morbid preoccupations, and other maladaptive behavior have found these also to be related to inadequacies of group cohesion.[24] The conversion of empirical uniformities into theoretic statements thus increases the *fruitfulness* of research through the successive exploration of implications.

4. By providing a rationale, the theory introduces a *ground for prediction* which is more secure than mere empirical extrapolation from previously observed trends. Thus, should independent measures indicate a decrease of social cohesion among Catholics, the theorist would predict a tendency toward increased rates of suicide in this group. The atheoretic empiricist would have no alternative, however, but to predict on the basis of extrapolation.

5. The foregoing list of functions presupposes one further attribute of theory which is not altogether true of the Durkheim formulation and which gives rise to a general problem that has peculiarly beset sociological theory,

---

[23] Thorstein Veblen has put this with typical cogency: "All this may seem like taking pains about trivialities. But the data with which any scientific inquiry has to do are trivialities in some other bearing than that one in which they are of account." *The Place of Science in Modern Civilization* (New York: The Viking Press, Inc., 1932), 42.

[24] See, e.g., Elton Mayo, *Human Problems of an Industrial Civilization* (New York: The Macmillian Company, 1933), 113 *et passim*. The theoretical framework utilized in the studies of industrial morale by Whitehead, Roethlisberger, and Dickson stemmed appreciably from the Durkheim formulations, as the authors testify.

at least, up to the present. If theory is to be productive, it must be suffi-ciently *precise* to be *determinate*. Precision is an integral element of the criterion of *testability*. The prevailing pressure toward the utilization of statistical data in sociology, whenever possible, to control and test theoretic inferences has a justifiable basis, when we consider the logical place of precision in disciplined inquiry.

The more precise the inferences (predictions) which can be drawn from a theory, the less the likelihood of *alternative* hypotheses which will be adequate to these predictions. In other words, precise predictions and data serve to reduce the *empirical* bearing upon research of the *logical* fallacy of affirming the consequent.[25] It is well known that verified pre-dictions derived from a theory do not prove or demonstrate that theory; they merely supply a measure of confirmation, for it is always possible that alternative hypotheses drawn from different theoretic systems can also account for the predicted phenomena.[26] But those theories which admit of precise predictions confirmed by observation take on strategic importance since they provide an initial basis for choice between com-peting hypotheses. In other words, precision enhances the likelihood of approximating a "crucial" observation or experiment.

The internal coherence of a theory has much the same function, for if a variety of empirically confirmed consequences are drawn from one theoretic system, this reduces the likelihood that competing theories can adequately account for the same data. The integrated theory sustains a larger measure of confirmation than is the case with distinct and unrelated hypotheses, thus accumulating a greater weight of evidence.

Both pressures—toward precision and logical coherence—can lead to unproductive activity, particularly in the social sciences. Any procedure can be abused as well as used. A premature insistence on precision at all costs may sterilize imaginative hypotheses. It may lead to a reformu-lation of the scientific problem in order to permit measurement with, at times, the result that the subsequent materials do not bear on the initial problem in hand.[27] In the search for precision, care must be taken to see

[25] The paradigm of "proof through prediction" is, of course, logically fallacious:
If A (hypothesis), then B (prediction).
B is observed.
Therefore, A is true.
This is not overdisturbing for scientific research, in as much as other than formal criteria are involved.

[26] As a case in point, consider that different theorists had predicted war and inter-necine conflict on a large scale at midcentury. Sorokin and some Marxists, for example, set forth this prediction on the basis of quite distinct theoretic systems. The actual out-break of large-scale conflicts does not in itself enable us to choose between these schemes of analysis, if only because the observed fact is consistent with both. Only if the predictions had been so *specified*, had been so precise, that the actual occurrences coincided with the one prediction and not with the other, would a determinate test have been instituted.

[27] Stuart A. Rice comments on this tendency in public opinion research; see *Eleven Twenty-six: A Decade of Social Science Research*, ed. Louis Wirth (Chicago: University of Chicago Press, 1940), 167.

that significant problems are not thus inadvertently blotted from view. Similarly, the pressure for logical consistency has at times invited logomachy and sterile theorizing, in as much as the assumptions contained in the system of analysis are so far removed from empirical referents or involve such high abstractions as not to permit of empirical inquiry.[28] But the warrant for these criteria of inquiry is not vitiated by such abuses.

Formal Derivations and Codification

This limited account has, at the very least, pointed to the need for a closer connection between theory and empirical research. The prevailing division of the two is manifested in marked *discontinuities* of empirical research, on the one hand, and systematic theorizing unsustained by empirical test, on the other.[29] There are conspicuously few instances of consecutive research which have cumulatively investigated a succession of hypotheses derived from a given theory. Rather, there tends to be a marked dispersion of empirical inquiries, oriented toward a concrete field of human behavior, but lacking a central theoretic orientation. The plethora of discrete empirical generalization and of *post factum* interpretations reflect this pattern of research. The large bulk of general orientations and conceptual analyses, as distinct from sets of interrelated hypotheses, in turn reflect the tendency to separate theoretic activity from empirical research. It is a commonplace that continuity, rather than dispersion, can be achieved only if empirical studies are theory-oriented and if theory is empirically confirmable. However, it is possible to go beyond such affirmations and to suggest certain conventions for sociological research which might well facilitate this process. These conventions may be termed "formalized derivation" and "codification." [30]

Both in the design and in the reporting of empirical research, it might be made a definite convention that hypotheses and, whenever possible, the theoretic grounds (assumptions and postulates) of these hypotheses be explicitly set forth. The report of data would be in terms of their immediate pertinence for the hypotheses and, derivatively, the underlying theory. Attention should be called specifically to the introduction of interpretative variables other than those entailed in the original formulation of hypoth-

---

[28] It is this practice to which E. Ronald Walker refers, in the field of economics, as "theoretic blight." *From Economic Theory to Policy* (Chicago: University of Chicago Press, 1943), Chap. iv.

[29] See in this connection the dramatic example of such *discontinuity* cited in Chapter I (*i.e.*, the recent rediscovery of the primary group within formal associations some decades after this had been elaborately treated by Thomas and Znaniecki).

[30] To be sure, these conventions are deduction and induction, respectively. Our sole interest at this point is to translate these logical procedures into terms appropriate to current sociological theory and research.

eses and the bearing of these upon the theory should be indicated. *Post factum* interpretations which will inevitably arise when new and unexpected relationships are discovered should be so stated that the direction of further probative research becomes evident. The conclusions of the research might well include not only a statement of the findings with respect to the initial hypotheses but, when this is in point, an indication of the order of observations needed to test anew the further implications of the investigation. Formal derivation of this character has had a salutary effect in psychology and economics, leading, in the one case, to sequential experiments [31] and, in the other, to an articulated series of investigations. One consequence of such formalization is that it serves as a control over the introduction of unrelated, undisciplined, and diffuse interpretations It does not impose upon the reader the task of ferreting out the relations between the interpretations embodied in the text.[32] Above all, it prepares the way for consecutive and cumulative research rather than a buckshot array of dispersed investigations.

The correlative process which seems called for is that which Lazarsfeld terms "codification." Whereas formal derivation focuses our attention upon the implications of a theory, codification seeks to systematize available empirical generalizations in *apparently different* spheres of behavior. Rather than permitting such separate empirical findings to lie fallow or to be referred to distinctive areas of behavior, the deliberate attempt to institute relevant provisional hypotheses promises to extend existing theory, subject to further empirical inquiry. Thus, an abundance of empirical findings in such fields as propaganda and public opinion, reactions to unemployment, and family responses to crises suggest that when persons are confronted with an "objective stimulus-pattern" which would be expected to elicit responses counter to their "initial predispositions," their actual behavior can be more successfully predicted on the basis of predispositions than of the stimulus-pattern. This is implied by "boomerang effects" in propaganda,[33] by findings on adjustive and maladjustive responses to unemployment,[34] and by research on the stability of families confronted with

31 The work of Clark Hull and associates is preeminent in this respect. See, e.g., Hull, *Principles of Behavior* (New York: Appleton-Century-Crofts, Inc., 1943); also comparable efforts toward formalization in the writings of Kurt Lewin (e.g., Kurt Lewin, Ronald Lippitt, and S. K. Escalona, *Studies in Topological and Vector Psychology I* ["University of Iowa Studies in Child Welfare," Vol. XVI (Iowa City, 1940)], 9–42).

32 A book such as John Dollard's *Caste and Class in a Southern Town* teems with suggestiveness, but it is an enormous task for the reader to work out explicitly the theoretic problems which are being attacked, the interpretative variables, and the implicit assumptions of the interpretations. Yet all this needs to be done if a sequence of studies building upon Dollard's work is proposed.

33 Paul F. Lazarsfeld and Robert K. Merton, "Studies in radio and film propaganda," *Transactions of the New York Academy of Sciences, Series II,* 1943, **6,** 58–79.

34 O. M. Hall, "Attitudes and unemployment," *Archives of Psychology,* No. 165 (March, 1934); E. W. Bakke, *The Unemployed Worker* (New Haven: Yale University Press, 1940).

severe reductions in income.[35] A codified formulation, even as crude as this, gives rise to theoretic problems which would be readily overlooked if the several empirical findings were not re-examined within a single context. It is submitted that codification, as a procedure complementing the formal derivation of hypotheses to be tested, will facilitate the codevelopment of viable sociological theory and pertinent empirical research.

[27] The Bearing of Empirical Research on Sociological Theory

R O B E R T   K .   M E R T O N

History has a certain gift for outmoding stereotypes. This can be seen, for example, in the historical development of sociology. The stereotype of the social theorist high in the empyrean of pure ideas uncontaminated by mundane facts is fast becoming no less outmoded than the stereotype of the social researcher equipped with questionnaire and pencil and hot on the chase of the isolated and meaningless statistic. For in building the mansion of sociology during the last decades, theorist and empiricist have learned to work together. What is more, they have learned to talk to one another in the process. At times, this means only that a sociologist has learned to talk to himself since increasingly the same man has taken up both theory and research. Specialization and integration have developed hand in hand. All this has led not only to the realization that theory and empirical research *should* interact but to the result that they *do* interact.

As a consequence, there is decreasing need for accounts of the relations between theory and research to be wholly programmatic in character. A growing body of theoretically oriented research makes it progressively possible to discuss with profit the actual relations between the two. And,

[35] Mirra Komarovsky, *The Unemployed Man and His Family* (New York: Dryden Press, 1940); R. C. Angell, *The Family Encounters the Depression* (New York: Charles Scribner's Sons, 1936); E. W. Burgess, R. K. Merton, *et al., Restudy of the Documents Analyzed by Angell in The Family Encounters the Depression* (New York: Social Science Research Council, 1942).

as we all know, there has been no scarcity of such discussions. Journals abound with them. They generally center on the role of theory in research, setting forth, often with admirable lucidity, the functions of theory in the initiation, design and prosecution of empirical inquiry. But since this is not a one-way relationship, since the two *interact,* it may be useful to examine the other direction of the relationship: the role of empirical research in the development of social theory. That is the purpose of this chapter.

The Theoretic Functions of Research

With a few conspicuous exceptions, recent sociological discussions have assigned but one major function to empirical research: the testing or verification of hypotheses. The model for the proper way of performing this function is as familiar as it is clear. The investigator begins with a hunch or hypothesis, from this he draws various inferences and these, in turn, are subjected to empirical test which confirms or refutes the hypothesis.[1] But this is a logical model, and so fails, of course, to describe much of what actually occurs in fruitful investigation. It presents a set of logical norms, not a description of the research experience. And, as logicians are well aware, in purifying the experience, the logical model may also distort it. Like other models, it abstracts from the temporal sequence of events. It exaggerates the creative role of explicit theory just as it minimizes the creative role of observation. For research is not merely logic tempered with observation. It has its psychological as well as its logical dimensions, although one would scarcely suspect this from the logically rigorous sequence in which research is usually reported.[2] It is both the psychological and logical pressures of research upon social theory which we seek to trace.

It is my central thesis that empirical research goes far beyond the passive role of verifying and testing theory: it does more than confirm or refute hypotheses. Research plays an active role: it performs at least four major functions which help shape the development of theory. It *initiates,* it *reformulates,* it *deflects* and it *clarifies* theory.[3]

---

[1] See, for example the procedural review of Stouffer's "Theory of intervening opportunities" by G. A. Lundberg, "What are sociological problems?", *American Sociological Review,* 1941, **6**, 357–369.

[2] See R. K. Merton, "Science, population and society," *The Scientific Monthly,* 1937, **44**, 170–171; the apposite discussion by Jean Piaget, *Judgment and Reasoning in the Child,* (London, 1929), Chaps. V, IX, and the comment by William H. George, *The Scientist in Action* (London, 1936), 153. "A piece of research does not progress in the way it is 'written up' for publication."

[3] The fourth function, clarification, has been elaborated in publications by Paul F. Lazarsfeld.

1. The Serendipity Pattern

The Unanticipated, Anomalous and Strategic Datum Exerts Pressure for Initiating Theory. Under certain conditions, a research finding gives rise to social theory. In a previous paper, this was all too briefly expressed as follows: "Fruitful empirical research not only tests theoretically derived hypotheses; it also originates new hypotheses. This might be termed the 'serendipity' component of research, *i.e.*, the discovery, by chance or sagacity, of valid results which were not sought for." [4]

The serendipity [5] pattern refers to the fairly common experience of observing an *unanticipated, anomalous and strategic* datum which becomes the occasion for developing a new theory or for extending an exist-

[4] R. K. Merton, "Sociological Theory," *American Journal of Sociology*, 1945, **50**, 469n. Interestingly enough, the same outlandish term 'serendipity' which has had little currency since it was coined by Horace Walpole in 1754 has also been used to refer to this component of research by the physiologist Walter B. Cannon. See his *The Way of an Investigator* (New York: W. W. Norton & Company, Inc., 1945), Chap. VI, in which he sets forth numerous instances of serendipity in several fields of science.

[5] Since the foregoing note was first written in 1946, the word *serendipity*, for all its etymological oddity, has diffused far beyond the limits of the academic community. The marked speed of its diffusion can be illustrated by its most recent movement among the pages of the *New York Times*. On May 22, 1949, Waldemar Kaempffert, science editor of the *Times*, had occasion to refer to serendipity in summarizing an article by the research scientist, Ellice McDonald—this, in an innermost page devoted to recent developments in science. Some three weeks later, on June 14, Orville Prescott, book reviewer of the daily *Times*, has evidently become captivated by the word, for in a review of a book in which the hero has a love of outlandish words, Prescott wonders if the hero knew the word serendipity. On Independence Day of 1949, serendipity wins full social acceptance. Stripped of qualifying inverted commas and no longer needing an appositive defining phrase, serendipity appears, without apology or adornment, on the front page of the *Times*. It achieves this prominence in a news dispatch from Oklahoma City, reporting an address by Sir Alexander Fleming, the discoverer of penicillin, at the dedication of the Oklahoma Medical Research Foundation. ("Sir Alexander's experience, which led to the development of modern disease-killing drugs," says the dispatch under the by-line of Robert K. Plumb, "is frequently cited as an outstanding example of the importance of serendipity in science. He found penicillin by chance, but had been trained to look for significance in scientific accidents.") In these travels from the esoteric page devoted to science to the less restricted columns of the book-review to the popular front-page, serendipity had become naturalized. Perhaps it would soon find its way into American abridged dictionaries.

This, then, is yet another instance in which a term, long unmet in common usage, has been recovered and put to fairly frequent use. (Compare note 6 in Chapter IV, referring to the similar history of the term, *anomie*.) And here again, one might ask: what accounts for the cultural resonance in recent years of this contrived, odd-sounding and useful word?

Questions of this order are being explored in a monographic study, by Elinor G. Barber and myself, of the sociological semantics involved in the cultural diffusion of the word *serendipity*. The study examines the social and cultural contexts of the coinage of the word in the eighteenth century; the climate of relevant opinion in which it first saw print in the nineteenth century; the patterned responses to the neologism when it was first encountered; the diverse social circles of littérateurs, physical and social scientists, engineers, lexicographers and historians in which it has diffused; the changes of meaning it has undergone in the course of diffusion and the ideological uses to which it has been variously put.

ing theory. Each of these elements of the pattern can be readily described. The datum is, first of all, unanticipated. A research directed toward the test of one hypothesis yields a fortuitous by-product, an unexpected observation which bears upon theories not in question when the research was begun.

Secondly, the observation is anomalous, surprising,[6] either because it seems inconsistent with prevailing theory or with other established facts. In either case, the seeming inconsistency provokes curiosity; it stimulates the investigator to "make sense of the datum," to fit it into a broader frame of knowledge. He explores further. He makes fresh observations. He draws inferences from the observations, inferences depending largely, of course, upon his general theoretic orientation. The more he is steeped in the data, the greater the likelihood that he will hit upon a fruitful direction of inquiry. In the fortunate circumstance that his new hunch proves justified, the anomalous datum leads ultimately to a new or extended theory. The curiosity stimulated by the anomalous datum is temporarily appeased.

And thirdly, in noting that the unexpected fact must be strategic, *i.e.*, that it must permit of implications which bear upon generalized theory, we are, of course, referring rather to what the observer brings to the datum than to the datum itself. For it obviously requires a theoretically sensitized observer to detect the universal in the particular. After all, men had for centuries noticed such "trivial" occurrences as slips of the tongue, slips of the pen, typographical errors, and lapses of memory, but it required the theoretic sensitivity of a Freud to see these as strategic data through which he could extend his theory of repression and symptomatic acts.

The serendipity pattern, then, involves the unanticipated, anomalous and strategic datum which exerts pressure upon the investigator for a new direction of inquiry which extends theory. Instances of serendipity have occurred in many disciplines, but I should like to draw upon a recent sociological research for illustration. In the course of our research into the social organization of Craftown,[7] a suburban housing community of some 700 families, largely of working class status, we observed that a large proportion of residents were affiliated with more civic, political and other voluntary organizations than had been the case in their previous places of residence. Quite incidentally, we noted further that this increase in group participation had occurred also among the parents of infants and young children. This finding was rather inconsistent with common-sense knowledge. For it is well known that, particularly on the lower economic levels, youngsters usually tie parents down and preclude their taking active part in organized group life outside the home. But Craftown parents themselves

6 Charles Sanders Peirce had long before noticed the strategic role of the "surprising fact" in his account of what he called "abduction," that is, the initiation and entertaining of a hypothesis as a step in inference. See his *Collected Papers*, **VI**, 522–528.

7 Drawn from continuing studies in the Sociology and Social Psychology of Housing, under a grant from the Lavanburg Foundations.

readily explained their behavior. "Oh, there's no real problem about getting out in the evenings," said one mother who belonged to several organizations. "It's easy to find teen-agers around here to take care of the kids. There are so many more teen-agers around here than where I used to live."

The explanation appears adequate enough and would have quieted the investigator's curiosity, had it not been for one disturbing datum: like most new housing communities, Craftown actually has a very small proportion of adolescents—only 3.7 per cent for example, in the 15–19 year age group. What is more, the majority of the adults, 63 per cent, are under 34 years of age, so that their children include an exceptionally large proportion of infants and youngsters. Thus, far from there being many adolescents to look after the younger children in Craftown, quite the contrary is true: the ratio of adolescents to children under ten years of age is 1:10, whereas in the communities of origin, the ratio hovers about 1:15.[8]

We were at once confronted, then, by an anomalous fact which was certainly no part of our original program of observation. We manifestly did not enter and indeed could not have entered the field of research in Craftown with a hypothesis bearing upon an illusory belief in the abundance of teen-age supervisors of children. Here was an observation both unanticipated and anomalous. Was it also strategic? We did not prejudge its "intrinsic" importance. It seemed no more and no less trivial than Freud's observation during the last war (in which he had two sons at the front) that he had mis-read a newspaper headline, "Die *Feinde* vor Görz" (The *Enemy* before Görz), as "Der *Friede* von Görz" (The *Peace* of Görz). Freud took a trivial incident and converted it into a strategic fact. Unless the observed discrepancy between the subjective impressions of Craftown residents and the objective facts could undergo a somewhat similar transformation it had best be ignored, for it plainly had little "social significance."

What first made this illusion a peculiarly intriguing instance of a general theoretic problem was the difficulty of explaining it as merely the calculated handiwork of vested-interests engaged in spreading a contrary-to-fact belief. Generally, when the sociologist with a conceptual scheme stemming from utilitarian theory observes a patently untrue social belief, he will look for special groups in whose interest it is to invent and spread this belief. The cry of "propaganda!" is often mistaken for a theoretically sound analysis.[9] But this is clearly out of the question in the present instance: there

8 Essentially the same discrepancies in age distribution between Craftown and communities of origin are found if we compare proportions of children under ten with those between 10 and 19. If we make children under five the basis of comparison, the disproportions are even more marked.

9 To be sure, vested-interests often do spread untrue propaganda and this may reinforce mass illusions. But the vested-interest or priestly-lie theories of fallacious folk beliefs do not always constitute the most productive point of departure nor do they go far toward explaining the bases of acceptance or rejection of the beliefs. The present case in point, trivial though it is in any practical sense, is theoretically significant in showing anew the limitations of a utilitarian scheme of analysis.

are plainly no special-interest groups seeking to misrepresent the age-distribution of Craftown. What, then, was the source of this social illusion?

Various other theories suggested points of departure. There was Marx's postulate that it is men's "social existence which determines their consciousness." There was Durkheim's theorem that social images ("collective representations") in some fashion reflect a social reality although "it does not follow that the reality which is its foundation conforms objectively to the idea which believers have of it." There was Sherif's thesis that "social factors" provide a framework for selective perceptions and judgments in relatively unstructured situations. There was the prevailing view in the sociology of knowledge that social location determines the perspectives entering into perception, beliefs and ideas. But suggestive as these general orientations [10] were, they did not directly suggest *which* features of social existence, *which* aspects of the social reality, *which* social factors, *which* social location may have determined this seemingly fallacious belief.

The clue was inadvertently provided by further interviews with residents. In the words of an active participant in Craftown affairs, herself the mother of two children under six years of age:

My husband and I get out together much more. You see, there are more people around to mind the children. *You feel more confident about having some thirteen-or-fourteen-year-old in here when you know most of the people. If you're in a big city, you don't feel so easy about having someone who's almost a stranger come in.*

This clearly suggests that the sociological roots of the "illusion" are to be found in the structure of community relations in which Craftown residents are enmeshed. The belief is an unwitting reflection, not of the statistical reality, but of the community cohesion. It is not that there are objectively more adolescents in Craftown, but more who are *intimately known* and who, therefore, *exist socially* for parents seeking aid in child supervision. Most Craftown residents having lately come from an urban setting now find themselves in a community in which proximity has developed into reciprocal intimacies. The illusion expresses the perspective of people for whom adolescents as potential child-care aides "exist" only if they are well-known and therefore merit confidence. In short, perception was a function of confidence and confidence, in turn, was a function of social cohesion.[11]

10 As the differences between theory and general orientations have been considered in Chapter II. [Reprinted as the preceding selection in this volume.—Ed.]

11 Schedule data from the study provide corroborative evidence. In view of the exceptionally high proportion of young children, it is striking that 54 per cent of their parents affirm that it is "easier in Craftown to get people to look after our children when we want to go out" than it was in other places where they have lived; only 21 per cent say it is harder and the remaining 25 per cent feel there is no difference. Those who come from the larger urban communities are more likely to report greater ease in obtaining assistance in Craftown. Moreover, as we would expect from the hypothesis, those residents who are more closely geared in with Craftown, who identify themselves most fully with it, are more likely to believe it easier to find such aid; 61 per cent of these do so as against 50 per cent of those who identify with other communities, whereas only 12 per cent find it more difficult in comparison with 26 per cent of the latter group.

From the sociological viewpoint, then, this unanticipated finding fits into and extends the theory that social perception is the product of a social framework. It develops further the "psychology of social norms," [12] for it is not merely an instance of individuals assimilating particular norms, judgments, and standards from other members of the community. The social perception is, rather, a by-product, a derivative, of the structure of human relations.

This is perhaps sufficient to illustrate the operation of the serendipity pattern: an unexpected and anomalous finding elicited the investigator's curiosity, and conducted him along an unpremeditated by-path which led to a fresh hypothesis.

2. The Recasting of Theory

New Data Exert Pressure for the Elaboration of a Conceptual Scheme. But it is not only through the anomalous fact that empirical research invites the extension of theory. It does so also through the repeated observation of hitherto neglected facts. When an existing conceptual scheme commonly applied to a subject-matter does not adequately take these facts into account, research presses insistently for its reformulation. It leads to the introduction of variables which have not been systematically included in the scheme of analysis. Here, be it noted, it is not that the data are anomalous or unexpected or incompatible with existing theory; it is merely that they had not been considered pertinent. Whereas the serendipity pattern centers in an apparent inconsistency which presses for resolution, the reformulation pattern centers in the hitherto neglected but relevant fact which presses for an extension of the conceptual scheme.

Examples of this in the history of social science are far from limited. Thus it was a series of fresh empirical facts which led Malinowski to incorporate new elements into a theory of magic. It was his Trobrianders, of course, who gave him the clue to the distinctive feature of his theory. When these islanders fished in the inner lagoon by the reliable method of poisoning, an abundant catch was assured and danger was absent. Neither uncertainty nor uncontrollable hazards were involved. And here, Malinowski noted, magic was not practiced. But in the open-sea fishing, with the uncertain yield and its often grave dangers, the rituals of magic flourished. Stemming from these pregnant observations was his theory that magical belief arises to bridge the uncertainties in man's practical pursuits, to fortify confidence, to reduce anxieties, to open up avenues of escape from the seeming impasse. Magic was construed as a supplementary technique for reaching practical objectives. It was these empirical facts which suggested the incorporation of new dimensions into earlier theories of magic—

---

[12] Muzafer Sherif's book by this title should be cited as basic in the field, although it tends to have a somewhat limited conception of "social factors," *The Psychology of Social Norms* (New York, 1936).

particularly the relations of magic to the fortuitous, the dangerous and the uncontrollable. It was not that these facts were *inconsistent* with previous theories; it was simply that these conceptual schemes had not taken them adequately into account. Nor was Malinowski testing a preconceived hypothesis—he was developing an enlarged and improved theory on the basis of suggestive empirical data.

For another example of this pressure of empirical data for the recasting of a specific theory we turn closer home. The investigation dealt with a single dramatic instance of mass persuasion: broadcasting at repeated intervals over a span of eighteen hours, Kate Smith, a radio star, sold large quantities of war-bonds in the course of a day. It is not my intention to report fully on the dynamics of this case of mass persuasion;[13] for present purposes, we are concerned only with the implications of two facts which emerged from the study.

First of all, in the course of intensive interviews many of our informants —New Yorkers who had pledged a bond to Smith—expressed a thorough disenchantment with the world of advertising, commercials and propaganda. They felt themselves the object of manipulation—and resented it. They objected to being the target for advertising which cajoles, insists and terrorizes. They objected to being engulfed in waves of propaganda proposing opinions and actions not in their own best interests. They expressed dismay over what is in effect a pattern of *pseudo-Gemeinschaft*—subtle methods of salesmanship in which there is the feigning of personal concern with the client in order to manipulate him the better. As one small businessman phrased it, "In my own business, I can see how a lot of people in their business deals will make some kind of gesture of friendliness, sincerity and so forth, most of which is phony." Drawn from a highly competitive, segmented metropolitan society, our informants were describing a climate of reciprocal distrust, of *anomie,* in which common values have been submerged in the welter of private interests. Society was experienced as an arena for rival frauds. There was small belief in the disinterestedness of conduct.

In contrast to all this was the second fact: we found that the persuasiveness of the Smith bond-drive among these same informants largely rested upon their firm belief in the integrity and sincerity of Smith. And much the same was found to be true in a polling interview with a larger cross-section sample of almost a thousand New Yorkers. Fully 80% asserted that in her all-day marathon drive, Smith was *exclusively* concerned with promoting the sale of war bonds, whereas only 17% felt that she was *also* interested in publicity for herself, and a negligible 3% believed she was *primarily* concerned with the resulting publicity.

This emphasis on her sincerity is all the more striking as a problem for research in the molding of reputations because she herself appeared on at

---

[13] Merton, Fiske and Curtis, *Mass Persuasion.*

least six commercially sponsored radio programs each week. But although she is engaged in apparently the same promotional activities as others, she was viewed by the majority of our informants as the direct antithesis of all that these other announcers and stars represent. In the words of one devotee, "She's sincere and *she really means anything* she ever says. It isn't just sittin' up there and talkin' and gettin' paid for it. She's different from what other people are."

Why this overwhelming belief in Smith's sincerity? To be sure, the same society which produces a sense of alienation and estrangement generates in many a craving for ressurance, an acute will to believe, a flight into faith. But why does Smith become the object of this faith for so many otherwise distrustful people? Why is she seen as genuine by those who seek redemption from the spurious? Why are her motives believed to rise above avarice and ambition and pride of class? What are the social-psychological sources of this image of Smith as sincerity incarnate?

Among the several sources, we wish to examine here the one which bears most directly upon a theory of mass persuasion. The clue is provided by the fact that a larger proportion of those who heard the Smith marathon war-bond drive are convinced of her disinterested patriotism than of those who did not. This appears to indicate that the marathon bond-drive enhanced public belief in her sincerity. But we must recognize the possibility that her devoted fans, for whom her sincerity was unquestioned, would be more likely to have heard the marathon broadcasts. Therefore, to determine whether the marathon did in fact extend this belief, we must compare regular listeners to her programs with those who are not her fans. Within each group, a significantly larger proportion of people who heard the marathon are convinced of Smith's exclusive concern with patriotic purposes.[14] This is as true for her devoted fans as for those who did not listen to her regular programs at all. In other words, we have caught for a moment, as with a candid camera, a snapshot of Smith's reputation of sincerity in the process of being even further enhanced. We have frozen in mid-course the process of building a reputation.

But if the marathon increased the belief in Smith's sincerity, how did this come about? It is at this point that our intensive interviews, with their often ingenuous and revealing details, permit us to interpret the statistical results of the poll. The marathon had all the atmosphere of determined, resolute endeavor under tremendous difficulties. Some could detect signs of strain—and courageous persistence. "Her voice was not quite so strong later, but she stuck it out like a good soldier," says a discerning housewife. Others projected themselves into the vividly imagined situation of fatigue and brave exertion. Solicitous reports by her coadjutor, Ted Collins, reinforced the emphatic concern for the strain to which Smith was subjecting herself. "I felt, I can't stand this any longer," recalls one informant. "Mr.

---

[14] The statistical data will be found in *ibid.*, pp. 87–88.

Collins' statement about her being exhausted affected me so much that I just couldn't bear it." The marathon took on the attributes of a sacrificial ritual.

In short, it was not so much what Smith *said* as what she *did* which served to validate her sincerity. It was the presumed stress and strain of an eighteen-hour series of broadcasts, it was the deed not the word which furnished the indubitable proof. Listeners might question whether she were not unduly dramatizing herself, but they could not escape the incontrovertible evidence that she was devoting the entire day to the task. Appraising the direct testimony of Smith's behavior, another informant explains that "she was on all day and the others weren't. So it seemed that she was sacrificing more and was more sincere." Viewed as a process of persuasion, the marathon converted initial feelings of scepticism and distrust among listeners into at first a reluctant, and later, a full-fledged acceptance of Smith's integrity. The successive broadcasts served as a fulfillment in action of a promise in words. The words were reinforced by things she had actually done. The currency of talk was accepted because it was backed by the gold of conduct. The gold reserve, moreover, need not even approximate the amount of currency it can support.

This empirical study suggests that propaganda-of-the-deed may be effective among the very people who are distrustful of propaganda-of-the-word. Where there is social disorganization, *anomie,* conflicting values, we find propaganditis reaching epidemic proportions. Any statement of values is likely to be discounted as "mere propaganda." Exhortations are suspect. But the propaganda of the deed elicits more confidence. Members of the audience are largely permitted to draw their conclusions from the action —they are less likely to feel manipulated. When the propagandist's deed and his words symbolically coincide, it stimulates belief in his sincerity. Further research must determine whether this propaganda pattern is significantly more effective in societies suffering from anomie than in those which are more fully integrated. But not unlike the Malinowski case-in-point, this may illustrate the role of research in suggesting new variables to be incorporated into a specific theory.

3. The Re-focusing of Theoretic Interest

New Methods of Empirical Research Exert Pressure for New Foci of Theoretic Interest. To this point we have considered the impact of research upon the development of particular theories. But empirical research also affects more general trends in the development of theory. This occurs chiefly through the invention of research procedures which tend to shift the foci of theoretic interest to the growing points of research.

The reasons for this are on the whole evident. After all, sound theory thrives only on a rich diet of pertinent facts and newly invented procedures help provide the ingredients of this diet. The new, and often previously unavailable, data stimulate fresh hypotheses. Moreover, theorists find that their hypotheses can be put to immediate test in those spheres where appropriate research techniques have been designed. It is no longer necessary for them to wait upon data as they happen to turn up— researches directed to the verification of hypotheses can be instituted at once. The flow of relevant data thus increases the tempo of advance in certain spheres of theory whereas in others, theory stagnates for want of adequate observations. Attention shifts accordingly.

In noting that new centers of theoretic interest have followed upon the invention of research procedures, we do not imply that these alone played a decisive role.[15] The growing interest in the theory of propaganda as an instrument of social control, for example, is in large part a response to the changing historical situation, with its conflict of major ideological systems, new technologies of mass communication which have opened up new avenues for propaganda and the rich research treasuries provided by business and government interested in this new weapon of war, both declared and undeclared. But this shift is also a by-product of accumulated facts made available through such newly developed, and confessedly crude, procedures as content-analysis, the panel technique and the focused interview.

Examples of this impact in the recent history of social theory are numerous but we have time to mention only a few. Thus, the increasing concern with the theory of character and personality formation in relation to social structure became marked after the introduction of new projective methods; the Rorschach test, the thematic apperception test, play techniques and story completions being among the most familiar. So, too, the sociometric techniques of Moreno and others, and fresh advances in the technique of the "passive interview" have revived interest in the theory of interpersonal relations. Stemming from such techniques as well is the trend toward what might be called the "rediscovery of the primary group," particularly in the shape of theoretic concern with informal social structures as mediating between the individual and large formal organizations. This interest has found expression in an entire literature on the role and structure of the informal group, for example, in factory social systems, bureaucracy and political organizations. Similarly, we may anticipate that the recent introduction of the panel technique—the repeated interviewing of the same group of informants—will in due course more sharply focus the attention of social psychologists upon the theory of attitude formation, decisions among alternative choices, factors in political participation and determinants of behavior in cases of conflicting role demands, to mention a few types of problems to which this technique is especially adapted.

[15] It is perhaps needless to add that these procedures, instruments and apparatus are in turn dependent upon prior theory. But this does not alter their stimulating effect upon the further development of theory.

Perhaps the most direct impact of research procedures upon theory has resulted from the *creation* of sociological statistics organized in terms of theoretically pertinent categories. Talcott Parsons has observed that numerical data are scientifically important only when they can be fitted into analytical categories and that "a great deal of current research is producing facts in a form which cannot be utilized by any current generalized analytical scheme." [16] These well-deserved strictures of a short while ago are proving progressively less applicable. In the past, the sociologist has largely had to deal with *pre-collected series* of statistics usually assembled for non-sociological purposes and, therefore, not set forth in categories directly pertinent to any theoretical system. As a result, at least so far as quantitative facts are concerned, the theorist was compelled to work with makeshift data bearing only a tangential relevance to his problems. This not only left a wide margin for error—consider the crude indexes of social cohesion upon which Durkheim had to rely—but it also meant that theory had to wait upon the incidental and, at times, almost accidental availability of relevant data. It could not march rapidly ahead. This picture has now begun to change.

No longer does the theorist depend almost exclusively upon the consensus of administrative boards or social welfare agencies for his quantitative data. Tarde's programmatic sketch [17] a half century ago of the need for statistics in social psychology, particularly those dealing with attitudes, opinions and sentiments, has become a half-fulfilled promise. So, too, investigators of community organization are creating statistics on class structure, associational behavior, and clique formations, and this has left its mark on theoretic interests. Ethnic studies are beginning to provide quantitative data which are re-orienting the theorist. It is safe to suppose that the enormous accumulation of sociological materials during the war—notably by the Research Branch of the Information and Education Division of the War Department—materials which are in part the result of new research techniques, will intensify interest in the theory of group morale, propaganda and leadership.[18] But it is perhaps needless to multiply examples.

What we have said does not mean that the piling up of statistics in itself advances theory; it does mean that theoretic interest tends to shift to those areas in which there is an abundance of *pertinent* statistical data.[19] Moreover, we are merely calling attention to this shift of focus, not evalu-

---

[16] Talcott Parsons, "The role of theory in social research," *American Sociological Review*, III (1938), 19; *cf.* his *The Structure of Social Action* (New York, 1937), 328–329n. ". . . in the social field most available statistical information is on a level which cannot be made to fit directly into the categories of analytical theory."

[17] Gabriel Tarde, *Essais et mélanges sociologiques* (Paris, 1895), 230–270.

[18] As appears to be the case now that it has been published: S. A. Stouffer *et al.*, *The American Soldier.*

[19] The statistical data also facilitate sufficient *precision* in research to put theory to determinate tests; see the discussion of the functions of precision in Chapter II.

ating it. It may very well be that it sometimes deflects attention to problems which, in a theoretic or humanistic sense, are "unimportant"; it may divert attention from problems with larger implications onto those for which there is the promise of immediate solutions. Failing a detailed study, it is difficult to come to any overall assessment of this point. But the pattern itself seems clear enough in sociology as in other disciplines; as new and previously unobtainable data become available through the use of new techniques, theorists turn their analytical eye upon the implications of these data and bring about new directions of inquiry.

4. The Clarification of Concepts

Empirical Research Exerts Pressure for Clear Concepts. A good part of the work called "theorizing" is taken up with the clarification of concepts —and rightly so. It is in this matter of clearly defined concepts that social science research is not infrequently defective. Research activated by a major interest in methodology may be centered on the *design* of establishing causal relations without due regard for analyzing the variables involved in the inquiry. This methodological empiricism, as the design of inquiry without correlative concern with the clarification of substantive variables may be called, characterizes a large part of current research. Thus, in a series of effectively designed experiments Chapin finds that "the rehousing of slum families in a public housing project results in improvement of the living conditions and the social life of these families." [20] Or through controlled experiments, psychologists search out the effects of foster home placement upon children's performances in intelligence tests.[21] Or, again through experimental inquiry, researchers seek to determine whether a propaganda film has achieved its purpose of improving attitudes toward the British. These several cases, and they are representative of a large amount of research which has advanced social science method, have in common the fact that the empirical variables are not analyzed in terms of their conceptual elements.[22] As Rebecca West, with her characteristic lucidity, put this general problem of methodological empiricism, one might "know that A and B and C were linked by certain causal connexions, but he would never apprehend with any exactitude the nature of A or B or C." In consequence, these researches advance the procedures of inquiry, but their

[20] F. S. Chapin, "The effects of slum clearance and rehousing on family and community relationships in Minneapolis," *American Journal of Sociology*, 1938, **43**, 744–763.

[21] R. R. Sears, "Child Psychology," in Wayne Dennis, ed., *Current Trends in Psychology* (University of Pittsburgh Press, 1947), 55–56. Sears' comments on this type of research state the general problem admirably.

[22] However crude they may be, procedures such as the focused interview are expressly designed as aids for detecting possibly relevant variables in an initially undifferentiated situation. See R. K. Merton, M. Fiske and P. L. Kendall, *The Focused Interview* (New York: The Free Press, 1956).

findings do not enter into the repository of cumulative social science theory.

But in general, the clarification of concepts, commonly considered a province peculiar to the theorist, is a frequent result of empirical research. Research sensitive to its own needs cannot easily escape this pressure for conceptual clarification. *For a basic requirement of research is that the concepts, the variables, be defined with sufficient clarity to enable the research to proceed,* a requirement easily and unwittingly not met in the kind of discursive exposition which is often miscalled sociological theory.

The clarification of concepts ordinarily enters into empirical research in the shape of establishing *indices* of the variables under consideration. In non-research speculations, it is possible to talk loosely about "morale" or "social cohesion" without any clear conceptions of what is entailed by these terms, but they *must* be clarified if the researcher is to go about his business of systematically observing instances of low and high morale, of social cohesion or social cleavage. If he is not to be blocked at the outset, he must devise indices which are observable, fairly precise and meticulously clear. The entire movement of thought which was christened "operationalism" is only one conspicuous case of the researcher demanding that concepts be defined clearly enough for him to go to work.

This has been typically recognized by those sociologists who combine a theoretic orientation with systematic empirical research. Durkheim, for example, despite the fact that his terminology and indices now appear crude and debatable, clearly perceived the need for devising indices of his concepts. Repeatedly, he asserted that "it is necessary . . . to substitute for the internal fact which escapes us an external fact that symbolizes it and to study the former through the latter." [23] The index, or sign of the conceptualized item, stands ideally in a one-to-one correlation with what it signifies (and the difficulty of establishing this relation is of course one of the critical problems of research). Since the index and its object are so related, one may ask for the grounds on which one is taken as the index and the other as the indexed variable. As Durkheim implied and as Suzanne Langer has indicated anew, the index is that one of the correlated pair which is perceptible and the other, harder or impossible to perceive, is theoretically relevant. [24] Thus, attitude scales make available indices of otherwise not discriminable attitudes, just as ecological statistics represent indices of diverse social structures in different areas.

What often appears as a tendency in research for quantification (through

---

[23] Emile Durkheim, *Division of Labor in Society* (New York: The Macmillan Company, 1933), 66; also his *Les règles de la méthode sociologique* (Paris, 1895), 55–58; *Le Suicide* (Paris, 1930), 356 and *passim. Cf.* R. K. Merton, "Durkheim's *Division of Labor in Society,*" *American Journal of Sociology,* 1934, **40,** esp. 326–327 which touches on the problem of indices; for a greatly developed analysis, see Lazarsfeld and Rosenberg, eds., *The Language of Social Research,* Intro. to Section I. [On concept-formation and indices, see the paper by Lazarsfeld in this volume, pp. 608–634. Ed.]

[24] Suzanne K. Langer, *Philosophy in a New Key* (New York: Penguin Books, 1948), 46–47.

the development of scales) can thus be seen as a special case of attempting to clarify concepts sufficiently to permit the conduct of empirical investigation. The development of valid and observable indices becomes central to the use of concepts in the prosecution of research. A final illustration will indicate how research presses for the clarification of ancient sociological concepts which, on the plane of discursive exposition, have remained ill-defined and unclarified.

A conception basic to sociology holds that individuals have multiple social roles and tend to organize their behavior in terms of the structurally defined expectations assigned to each role. Further, it is said, the less integrated the society, the more often will individuals be subject to the strain of incompatible social roles. Type-cases are numerous and familiar: the Catholic Communist subjected to conflicting pressures from party and church, the marginal man suffering the pulls of conflicting societies, the professional woman torn between the demands of family and career. Every sociological textbook abounds with illustrations of incompatible demands made of the multiselved person.

Perhaps because it has been largely confined to discursive interpretations and has seldom been made the focus of systematic research, this central problem of conflicting roles has yet to be materially clarified and advanced beyond the point reached decades ago. Thomas and Znaniecki long since indicated that conflicts between social roles *can* be reduced by conventionalization and by role-segmentation (by assigning each set of role-demands to different situations).[25] And others have noted that frequent conflict between roles is dysfunctional for the society as well as for the individual. But all this leaves many salient problems untouched: on which grounds does one predict the behavior of persons subject to conflicting roles? And when a decision must be made, which role (or which group solidarity) takes precedence? Under which conditions does one or another prove controlling? On the plane of discursive thought, it has been suggested that the role with which the individual identifies most fully will prove dominant, thus banishing the problem through a tautological pseudo-solution. Or, the problem of seeking to predict behavior consequent to incompatibility of roles, a research problem requiring operational clarification of the concepts of solidarity, conflict, role-demands and situation, has been evaded by observing that conflicts of roles typically ensue in frustration.

More recently, empirical research has pressed for clarification of the key concepts involved in this problem. Indices of conflicting group pressures have been devised and the resultant behavior observed in specified situations. Thus, as a beginning in this direction, it has been shown that in a concrete decision-situation, such as voting, individuals subject to these cross-pressures respond by delaying their vote-decision. And, under condi-

[25] W. I. Thomas and F. Znaniecki, *The Polish Peasant* (New York: Alfred A. Knopf, Inc., 1927), 1866–70, 1888, 1899 ff.

tions yet to be determined, they seek to reduce the conflict by escaping from the field of conflict: they lose interest in the political campaign. Finally, there is the intimation in these data that in cases of cross-pressures upon the voter, it is socio-economic position which is typically controlling.[26]

However this may be, the essential point is that, in this instance, as in others, the very requirements of empirical research have been instrumental in clarifying received concepts. The process of empirical inquiry raises conceptual issues which may long go undetected in theoretic inquiry.

There remain, then, a few concluding remarks. My discussion has been devoted exclusively to four impacts of research upon the development of social theory: the initiation, reformulation, refocusing and clarification of theory. Doubtless there are others. Doubtless, too, the emphasis of this chapter lends itself to misunderstanding. It may be inferred that some invidious distinction has been drawn at the expense of theory and the theorist. That has not been my intention. I have suggested only that an explicitly formulated theory does not invariably precede empirical inquiry, that as a matter of plain fact the theorist is not inevitably the lamp lighting the way to new observations. The sequence is often reversed. Nor is it enough to say that research and theory must be married if sociology is to bear legitimate fruit. They must not only exchange solemn vows—they must know how to carry on from there. Their reciprocal roles must be clearly defined. This chapter is a short essay toward that definition.

[28] Ideal Types and Theory Construction

MAX WEBER

In the establishment of the propositions of abstract theory, it is only apparently a matter of "deductions" from fundamental psychological motives. Actually, the former are a special case of a kind of concept-con-

26 Lazarsfeld, Berelson and Gaudet, *The People's Choice* Chapter VI and the subsequent study by B. Berelson, P. F. Lazarsfeld and W. N. McPhee, *Voting* (University of Chicago Press, 1954).

struction which is peculiar and to a certain extent, indispensable, to the cultural sciences. It is worthwhile at this point to describe it in further detail since we can thereby approach more closely the fundamental question of the significance of theory in the social sciences. Therewith we leave undiscussed, once and for all, whether *the* particular analytical concepts which we cite or to which we allude as illustrations, correspond to the purposes they are to serve, i.e., whether in fact they are well-adapted. The question as to how far, for example, contemporary "abstract theory" should be further elaborated, is ultimately also a question of the strategy of science, which must, however, concern itself with other problems as well. Even the "theory of marginal utility" is subsumable under a "law of marginal utility."

We have in abstract economic theory an illustration of those synthetic constructs which have been designated as *"ideas"* of historical phenomena. It offers us an ideal picture of events on the commodity-market under conditions of a society organized on the principles of an exchange economy, free competition and rigorously rational conduct. This conceptual pattern brings together certain relationships and events of historical life into a complex, which is conceived as an internally consistent system. Substantively, this construct in itself is like a *utopia* which has been arrived at by the analytical accentuation of certain elements of reality. Its relationship to the empirical data consists solely in the fact that where market-conditioned relationships of the type referred to by the abstract construct are discovered or suspected to exist in reality to some extent, we can make the *characteristic* features of this relationship pragmatically *clear* and *understandable* by reference to an *ideal-type*. This procedure can be indispensable for heuristic as well as expository purposes. The ideal typical concept will help to develop our skill in imputation in *research:* it *is* no "hypothesis" but it offers guidance to the construction of hypotheses. It is not a *description* of reality but it aims to give unambiguous means of expression to such a description. It is thus the "idea" of the *historically* given modern society, based on an exchange economy, which is developed for us by quite the same logical principles as are used in constructing the idea of the medieval "city economy" as a "genetic" concept. When we do this, we construct the concept "city economy" not as an average of the economic structures actually existing in all the cities observed but as an *ideal-type*. An ideal type is formed by the one-sided *accentuation* of one or more points of view and by the synthesis of a great many diffuse, discrete, more or less present and occasionally absent *concrete individual* phenomena, which are arranged according to those one-sidedly emphasized viewpoints into a unified *analytical* construct (*Gedankenbild*). In its conceptual purity, this mental construct (*Gedankenbild*) cannot be found empirically anywhere in reality. It is a *utopia*. Historical research faces the task of determining in each individual case, the extent to which this ideal-construct approximates to or diverges from reality, to what extent for example, the economic structure of a certain city is to be classified as a "city-economy." When carefully applied, those concepts are particularly useful in research and exposition. In very much the same way one can work the "idea" of "handicraft" into a utopia by arranging certain traits, actually found in an unclear, confused state in the industrial enterprises of the most diverse epochs and countries, into a consistent ideal-construct by an accentuation of their essential tendencies. This ideal-type is then related to the idea (*Gedankenausdruck*) which one finds expressed there. One can further delineate a society in which all branches of economic and even intellectual activity are governed by maxims which appear to be applications of the same principle which characterizes the ideal-typical "handicraft" system. Furthermore, one can juxtapose alongside the ideal typical "handicraft" system the antithesis of a correspondingly ideal-typical capitalistic productive system, which has been abstracted out of certain features of modern large scale industry. On the basis of this, one can delineate the utopia of a "capitalistic" culture, i.e., one in which the governing principle is the investment of private capital. This procedure would accentuate certain individual concretely diverse traits of modern material and intellectual culture in its unique aspects into an ideal construct which from our point of view would be completely self-consistent. This would then be the delineation of an *"idea"* of *capitalistic culture*. We must disregard for the moment whether and how this procedure could be carried out. It is possible, or rather, it must be accepted as certain that numerous, indeed a very great many, utopias of this sort can be worked out, of which *none* is like another, and *none* of which can be observed in empirical reality as an actually existing economic system, but *each* of which however claims that it is a representation of the "idea" of capitalistic culture. *Each* of these can claim to be a representation of the "idea" of capitalistic culture to the extent that it has really taken certain traits, meaningful in their essential features, from the empirical reality of our culture and brought them together into a unified ideal-construct. For those phenomena which interest us as cultural phenomena are interesting to us with respect to very different kinds of evaluative ideas to which we relate them. Inasmuch as the "points of view" from which they can become significant for us are very diverse, the most varied criteria can be applied to the selection of the traits which are to enter into the construction of an ideal-typical view of a particular culture.

What is the significance of such ideal-typical constructs for an *empirical* science, as we wish to constitute it? Before going any further, we should emphasize that the idea of an ethical *imperative*, of a "model" of what "ought" to exist is to be carefully distinguished from the analytical construct, which is "ideal" in the strictly logical sense of the term. It is a matter here of constructing relationships which our imagination accepts as plausibly motivated and hence as "objectively possible" and which appear as *adequate* from the nomological standpoint.

Whoever accepts the proposition that the knowledge of historical reality

can or should be a "presuppositionless" copy of "objective" facts, will deny
the value of the ideal-type. Even those who recognize that there is no "pre-
suppositionlessness" in the logical sense and that even the simplest excerpt
from a statute or from a documentary source can have scientific meaning
only with reference to "significance" and ultimately to evaluative ideas, will
more or less regard the construction of any such historical "utopias" as an
expository device which endangers the autonomy of historical research and
which is, in any case, a vain sport. And, in fact, *whether* we are dealing
simply with a conceptual game or with a scientifically fruitful method
of conceptualization and *theory*-construction can never be decided *a priori*.
Here, too, there is only one criterion, namely, that of success in revealing
concrete cultural phenomena in their interdependence, their causal conditions and their *significance*. The construction of abstract ideal-types
recommends itself not as an end but as a *means*. Every conscientious examination of the conceptual elements of historical exposition shows however
that the historian as soon as he attempts to go beyond the bare establishment of concrete relationships and to determine the *cultural* significance
of even the simplest individual event in order to "characterize" it, *must*
use concepts which are precisely and unambiguously definable only in the
form of ideal types. Or are concepts such as "individualism," "imperialism,"
"feudalism," "mercantilism," "conventional," etc., and innumerable concepts
of like character by means of which we seek analytically and empathically
to understand reality constructed substantively by the "presuppositionless"
description of some concrete phenomenon or through the abstract synthesis
of those traits which are *common* to numerous concrete phenomena? Hun-
dreds of words in the historian's vocabulary are ambiguous constructs
created to meet the unconsciously felt need for adequate expression and
the meaning of which is only concretely felt but not clearly thought out.
In a great many cases, particularly in the field of descriptive political history, their ambiguity has not been prejudicial to the clarity of the presentation. It is sufficient that in each case the reader should *feel* what the
historian had in mind; or, one can content one's self with the idea that
the author used a *particular* meaning of the concept with special reference
to the concrete case at hand. The greater the need however for a sharp
appreciation of the significance of a cultural phenomenon, the more imperative is the need to operate with unambiguous concepts which are not only
particularly but also systematically defined. A "definition" of such synthetic
historical terms according to the scheme of *genus proximum* and *differentia
specifica* is naturally nonsense. But let us consider it. Such a form of the
establishment of the meanings of words is to be found only in axiomatic
disciplines which use syllogisms. A simple "descriptive analysis" of these
concepts into their components either does not exist or else exists only
illusorily, for the question arises as to *which* of these components should be
regarded as essential. When a genetic definition of the content of the concept is sought, there remains only the ideal-type in the sense explained

above. It is a conceptual construct *(Gedankenbild)* which is neither historical reality nor even the "true" reality. It is even less fitted to serve as a
schema under which a real situation or action is to be subsumed as one
instance. It has the significance of a purely ideal *limiting* concept with
which the real situation or action is *compared* and surveyed for the explication of certain of its significant components. Such concepts are constructs
in terms of which we formulate relationships by the application of the
category of objective possibility. By means of this category, the adequacy of
our imagination, oriented and disciplined by reality, is *judged.*

   In this function especially, the ideal-type is an attempt to analyze historically unique configurations or their individual components by means of
genetic concepts. Let us take for instance the concepts "church" and "sect."
They may be broken down purely classificatorily into complexes of characteristics whereby not only the distinction between them but also the
content of the concept must constantly remain fluid. If however I wish to
formulate the concept of "sect" genetically, e.g., with reference to certain
important cultural significances which the "sectarian spirit" has had for
modern culture, certain characteristics of both become *essential* because
they stand in an adequate causal relationship to those influences. However,
the concepts thereupon become ideal-typical in the sense that they appear
in full conceptual *integrity* either not at all or only in individual instances.
Here as elsewhere every concept which is not purely classificatory diverges
from reality. But the discursive nature of our knowledge, i.e., the fact that
we comprehend reality only through a chain of intellectual modifications
postulates such a conceptual shorthand. Our imagination can often dispense with explicit conceptual formulations as a means of *investigation.*
But as regards exposition, to the extent that it wishes to be unambiguous,
the use of precise formulations in the sphere of cultural analysis is in many
cases absolutely necessary. Whoever disregards it entirely must confine himself to the formal aspect of cultural phenomena, e.g., to legal history. The
universe of legal norms is naturally clearly definable and is valid (in the
legal sense!) for historical reality. But social science in our sense is concerned
with practical *significance.* This significance however can very often be
brought unambiguously to mind only by relating the empirical data to an
ideal limiting case. If the historian (in the widest sense of the word) rejects
an attempt to construct such ideal types as a "theoretical construction,"
i.e., as useless or dispensable for his concrete heuristic purposes, the inevitable consequence is either that he consciously or unconsciously uses
other similar concepts without formulating them verbally and elaborating
them logically or that he remains stuck in the realm of the vaguely "felt."

   Nothing, however, is more dangerous than the *confusion* of theory and
history stemming from naturalistic prejudices. This confusion expresses
itself firstly in the belief that the "true" content and the essence of historical
reality is portrayed in such theoretical constructs or secondly, in the use of
these constructs as a procrustean bed into which history is to be forced or

thirdly, in the hypostatization of such "ideas" as real "forces" and as a "true" reality which operates behind the passage of events and which works itself out in history.

This latter danger is especially great since we are also, indeed primarily, accustomed to understand by the "ideas" of an epoch the thoughts or ideals which dominated the mass or at least an historically decisive number of the persons living in that epoch itself, and who were therefore significant as components of its culture. Now there are two aspects to this: in the first place, there are certain relationships between the "idea" in the sense of a tendency of practical or theoretical thought and the "idea" in the sense of the ideal-*typical* portrayal of an epoch constructed as a heuristic device. An ideal type of certain situations, which can be abstracted from certain characteristic social phenomena of an epoch, might—and this is indeed quite often the case—have also been present in the minds of the persons living in that epoch as an ideal to be striven for in practical life or as a maxim for the regulation of certain social relationships. This is true of the "idea" of "provision" (*Nahrungsschutz*) and many other Canonist doctrines, especially those of Thomas Aquinas, in relationship to the modern ideal type of medieval "city economy" which we discussed above. The same is alse true of the much talked of "basic concept" of economics: economic "value." From Scholasticism to Marxism, the idea of an objectively "valid" value, i.e., of an *ethical imperative* was amalgamated with an abstraction drawn from the empirical process of price formation. The notion that the "value" of commodities should be regulated by certain principles of natural law, has had and still has immeasurable significance for the development of culture— and not merely the culture of the Middle Ages. It has also influenced actual price formation very markedly. But what was meant and what can be meant by that *theoretical* concept can be made unambiguously clear *only* through precise, ideal-typical constructs. Those who are so contemptuous of the "Robinsonades" of classical theory should restrain themselves if they are unable to replace them with better concepts, which in this context means clearer concepts.

Thus the causal relationship between the historically determinable idea which governs the conduct of men and those components of historical reality from which their corresponding ideal-*type* may be abstracted, can naturally take on a considerable number of different forms. The main point to be observed is that *in principle* they are both fundamentally different things. There is still another aspect: those "ideas" which govern the behavior of the population of a certain epoch i.e., which are concretely influential in determining their conduct, can, if a somewhat complicated construct is involved, be formulated precisely only in the form of an ideal type, since empirically it exists in the minds of an indefinite and constantly changing mass of individuals and assumes in their minds the most multifarious nuances of form and content, clarity and meaning. Those elements of the spiritual life of the individuals living in a certain epoch of the

Middle Ages, for example, which we may designate as the "Christianity" of those individuals, would, if they could be completely portrayed, naturally constitute a chaos of infinitely differentiated and highly contradictory complexes of ideas and feelings. This is true despite the fact that the medieval church was certainly able to bring about a unity of belief and conduct to a particularly high degree. If we raise the question as to what in this chaos was the "Christianity" of the Middle Ages (which we must nonetheless use as a stable concept) and wherein lay those "Christian" elements which we find in the institutions of the Middle Ages, we see that here too in every individual case, we are applying a purely analytical construct created by ourselves. It is a combination of articles of faith, norms from church law and custom, maxims of conduct, and countless concrete interrelationships which we have fused into an "idea." It is a synthesis which we could not succeed in attaining with consistency without the application of ideal-type concepts.

The relationship between the logical structure of the conceptual system in which we present such "ideas" and what is immediately given in empirical reality naturally varies considerably. It is relatively simple in cases in which one or a few easily formulated theoretical main principles as for instance Calvin's doctrine of predestination or clearly definable ethical postulates govern human conduct and produce historical effects, so that we can analyze the "idea" into a hierarchy of ideas which can be logically derived from those theses. It is of course easily overlooked that however important the significance even of the purely logically persuasive force of ideas—Marxism is an outstanding example of this type of force—nonetheless empirical-historical events occurring in men's minds must be understood as primarily *psychologically* and not logically conditioned. The ideal-typical character of such syntheses of historically effective ideas is revealed still more clearly when those fundamental main principles and postulates no longer survive in the minds of those individuals who are still dominated by ideas which were logically or associatively derived from them because the "idea" which was historically and originally fundamental has either died out or has in general achieved wide diffusion only for its broadest implications. The basic fact that the synthesis is an "idea" which *we* have created emerges even more markedly when those fundamental main principles have either only very imperfectly or not at all been raised to the level of explicit consciousness or at least have not taken the form of explicitly elaborated complexes of ideas. When we adopt this procedure, as it very often happens and must happen, we are concerned in these ideas, e.g., the "liberalism" of a certain period or "Methodism" or some intellectually unelaborated variety of "socialism," with a *pure* ideal type of much the same character as the synthetic "principles" of economic epochs in which we had our point of departure. The more inclusive the relationships to be presented, and the more many-sided their cultural *significance* has been, the *more* their comprehensive systematic exposition in a conceptual system approximates the character of an ideal type, and the less is it possible to operate with *one* such concept. In such situations the frequently repeated attempts to discover ever *new* aspects of significance by the construction of new ideal-typical concepts is all the more natural and unavoidable. All expositions for example of the "essence" of Christianity are ideal types enjoying only a necessarily very relative and problematic validity when they are intended to be regarded as the historical portrayal of empirically existing facts. On the other hand, such presentations are of great value for research and of high systematic value for expository purposes when they are used as conceptual instruments for *comparison* with and the *measurement* of reality. They are indispensable for this purpose.

There is still another even more complicated significance implicit in such ideal-typical presentations. They regularly seek to be, or are unconsciously, ideal-types not only in the *logical* sense but also in the *practical* sense, i.e., they are *model types* which—in our illustration—contain what, from the point of view of the expositor, *should* be and what *to him* is "essential" in Christianity *because it is enduringly valuable*. If this is consciously or—as it is more frequently—unconsciously the case, they contain ideals *to* which the expositor *evaluatively* relates Christianity. These ideals are tasks and ends towards which he orients his "idea" of Christianity and which naturally can and indeed doubtless always will differ greatly from the values which other persons, for instance, the early Christians, connected with Christianity. In this sense, however, the "ideas" are naturally no longer purely *logical* auxiliary devices, no longer concepts with which reality is compared, but ideals by which it is evaluatively *judged*. Here it is no longer a matter of the purely theoretical procedure of treating empirical reality with respect to values but of *value-judgments* which are integrated into the concept of *"Christianity."* Because the ideal type claims empirical *validity* here, it penetrates into the realm of the evaluative *interpretation* of Christianity. The sphere of empirical science has been left behind and we are confronted with a profession of faith, not an ideal-typical construct. As fundamental as this distinction is in principle, the confusion of these two basically different meanings of the term "idea" appears with extraordinary frequency in historical writings. It is always close at hand whenever the descriptive historian begins to develop his "conception" of a personality or an epoch. In contrast with the fixed ethical standards which Schlosser applied in the spirit of rationalism, the modern relativistically educated historian who on the one hand seeks to "understand" the epoch of which he speaks "in its own terms," and on the other still seeks to "judge" it, feels the need to derive the standards for his judgment from the subject-matter itself, i.e., to allow the "idea" in the sense of the *ideal* to emerge from the "idea" in the sense of the "ideal-type." The esthetic satisfaction produced by such a procedure constantly tempts him to disregard the line where these two ideal types diverge—an error which on the one hand hampers the value-judgment and on the other, strives to free itself from the responsibility for its own judgment. In contrast with this, the *elementary duty of scientific self-control* and the only way to avoid serious and foolish blunders requires a sharp, precise distinction between the logically *comparative* analysis of reality by ideal-*types* in the logical sense and the *value-judgment* of reality *on the basis of ideals*. An "ideal type" in our sense, to repeat once more, has no connection at all with *value-judgments,* and it has nothing to do with any type of perfection other than a purely *logical* one. There are ideal types of brothels as well as of religions; there are also ideal types of those kinds of brothels which are technically "expedient" from the point of view of police ethics as well as those of which the exact opposite is the case.

It is necessary for us to forego here a detailed discussion of the case which is by far the most complicated and most interesting, namely, the problem of the logical structure of the *concept of the state*. The following however should be noted: when we inquire as to what corresponds to the idea of the "state" in empirical reality, we find an infinity of diffuse and discrete human actions, both active and passive, factually and legally regulated relationships, partly unique and partly recurrent in character, all bound together by an idea, namely, the belief in the actual or normative validity of rules and of the authority-relationships of some human beings towards others. This belief is in part consciously, in part dimly felt, and in part passively accepted by persons who, should they think about the "idea" in a really clearly defined manner, would not first need a "general theory of the state" which aims to articulate the idea. The scientific conception of the state, however it is formulated, is naturally always a synthesis which we construct for certain heuristic purposes. But on the other hand, it is also abstracted from the unclear syntheses which are found in the minds of human beings. The concrete content, however, which the historical "state" assumes in those syntheses in the minds of those who make up the state, can in its turn only be made explicit through the use of ideal-typical concepts. Nor, furthermore, can there be the least doubt that the manner in which those syntheses are made (always in a logically imperfect form) by the members of a state, or in other words, the "ideas" which *they* construct for themselves about the state—as for example, the German "organic" metaphysics of the state in contrast with the American "business" conception, is of great practical significance. In other words, here too the *practical idea* which should be *valid* or *is believed to be valid* and the heuristically intended, theoretically ideal type approach each other very closely and constantly tend to merge with each other.

We have purposely considered the ideal type essentially—if not exclusively—as a mental construct for the scrutiny and systematic characterization of individual concrete patterns which are significant in their uniqueness, such as Christianity, capitalism, etc. We did this in order to avoid the common notion that in the sphere of cultural phenomena, the abstract *type* is identical with the abstract *kind* (*Gattungsmässigen*). This is not the case. Without being able to make here a full logical analysis of the widely discussed concept of the "typical" which has been discredited through misuse, we can state on the basis of our previous discussion that the construction of type-concepts in the sense of the exclusion of the "accidental" also has a place in the analysis of historically individual phenomena. Naturally, however, those *generic* concepts which we constantly encounter as elements of historical analysis and of concrete historical concepts, can also be formed as ideal-types by abstracting and accentuating certain conceptually essential elements. Practically, this is indeed a particularly frequent and important instance of the application of ideal-typical concepts. Every *individual* ideal type comprises both *generic* and ideal-typically constructed conceptual *elements*. In this case too, we see the specifically logical function of ideal-typical concepts. The concept of "exchange" is for instance a simple class concept (*Gattungsbegriff*) in the sense of a complex of traits which are common to many phenomena, as long as we disregard the *meaning* of the component parts of the concept, and simply analyze the term in its everyday usage. If however we relate this concept to the concept of "marginal utility" for instance, and construct the concept of "economic exchange" as an economically rational event, this then contains as every concept of "economic exchange" does which is fully elaborated logically, a judgment concerning the "typical" *conditions* of exchange. It assumes a *genetic* character and becomes therewith ideal-typical in the logical sense, i.e., it removes itself from empirical reality which can only be compared or related to it. The same is true of all the so-called "fundamental concepts" of economics: they can be developed in genetic form only as ideal types. The distinction between simple class or generic concepts (*Gattungsbegriffe*) which merely summarize the common features of certain empirical phenomena and the quasi-generic (*Gattungsmässigen*) *ideal type*—as for instance an ideal-typical concept of the "nature" of "handicraft"—varies naturally with each concrete case. But no class or generic concept as such has a "typical" character and there is no purely generic "average" type. Wherever we speak of typical magnitudes—as for example, in statistics— we speak of something more than a mere average. The more it is a matter of the simple classification of events which appear in reality as mass phenomena, the more it is a matter of class concepts. On the other hand, the greater the event to which we conceptualize complicated historical patterns with respect to those components in which their specific *cultural significance* is contained, the greater the extent to which the concept—or system of concepts—will be ideal-typical in character. The goal of ideal-typical concept-construction is always to make clearly explicit not the class or average character but rather the unique individual character of cultural phenomena.

The fact that ideal types, even classificatory ones, can be and are applied, first acquires methodological significance in connection with another fact.

Thus far we have been dealing with ideal-types only as abstract concepts of relationships which are conceived by us as stable in the flux of events, as historically individual complexes in which developments are realized. There emerges however a complication, which reintroduces with the aid of the concept of "type" the naturalistic prejudice that the goal of the social sciences must be the reduction of reality to *"laws."* *Developmental* sequences too can be constructed into ideal types and these constructs can have quite considerable heuristic value. But this quite particularly gives rise to the danger that the ideal type and reality will be confused with one another. One can, for example, arrive at the theoretical conclusion that in a society which is organized on *strict* "handicraft" principles, the only source of capital accumulation can be ground rent. From this perhaps, one can—for the correctness of the construct is not in question here—construct a pure ideal picture of the shift, conditioned by certain specific factors—e.g., limited land, increasing population, influx of precious metals, rationalisation of the conduct of life—from a handicraft to a capitalistic economic organization. Whether the empirical-historical course of development was actually identical with the constructed one, can be investigated only by using this construct as a heuristic device for the comparison of the ideal type and the "facts." If the ideal type were "correctly" constructed and the actual course of events did *not* correspond to that predicted by the ideal type, the hypothesis that medieval society was *not* in certain respects a *strictly* "handicraft" type of society would be proved. And if the ideal type were constructed in a heuristically *"ideal"* way—whether and in what way this could occur in our example will be entirely disregarded here—it will guide the investigation into a path leading to a more precise understanding of the non-handicraft components of medieval society in their peculiar characteristics and their historical significance. *If* it leads to this result, it fulfils its logical purpose, even though, in doing so, it demonstrates its divergence from reality. It was—in this case—the test of an hypothesis. This procedure gives rise to no methodological doubts so long as we clearly keep in mind that ideal-typical developmental *constructs* and *history* are to be sharply distinguished from each other, and that the construct here is no more than the means for explicitly and validly imputing an historical event to its real causes while eliminating those which on the basis of our present knowledge seem possible.

The maintenance of this distinction in all its rigor often becomes uncommonly difficult in practice due to a certain circumstance. In the interest of the concrete demonstration of an ideal type or of an ideal-typical developmental sequence, one seeks to *make it clear* by the use of concrete illustrative material drawn from empirical-historical reality. The danger of this procedure which in itself is entirely legitimate lies in the fact that historical knowledge here appears as a *servant* of theory instead of the opposite role.

It is a great temptation of the theorist to regard this relationship either as the normal one or, far worse, to mix theory with history and indeed to confuse them with each other. This occurs in an extreme way when an ideal construct of a developmental sequence and a conceptual classification of the ideal-types of certain cultural structures (e.g., the forms of industrial production deriving from the "closed domestic economy" or the religious concept beginning with the "gods of the moment") are integrated into a *genetic* classification. The series of types which results from the selected conceptual criteria appears then as an historical sequence unrolling with the necessity of a law. The logical classification of analytical concepts on the one hand and the empirical arrangements of the events thus conceptualized in space, time, and causal relationship, on the other, appear to be so bound up together that there is an almost irresistible temptation to do violence to reality in order to prove the real validity of the construct.

We have intentionally avoided a demonstration with respect to that ideal-typical construct which is the most important one from our point of view; namely, the Marxian theory. This was done in order not to complicate the exposition any further through the introduction of an interpretation of Marx and in order not to anticipate the discussions in our journal which will make a regular practice of presenting critical analyses of the literature concerning and following the great thinker. We will only point out here that naturally all specifically Marxian "laws" and developmental constructs —insofar as they are theoretically sound—are ideal types. The eminent, indeed unique, *heuristic* significance of these ideal types when they are used for the *assessment* of reality is known to everyone who has ever employed Marxian concepts and hypotheses. Similarly, their perniciousness, as soon as they are thought of as empirically valid or as real (*i.e.*, truly metaphysical) "effective forces," "tendencies," etc. is likewise known to those who have used them.

Class or generic concepts (*Gattungsbegriffe*)—ideal types—ideal-typical generic concepts—ideas in the sense of thought-patterns which actually exist in the minds of human beings—ideal types of such ideas—ideals which govern human beings—ideal types of such ideals—ideals with which the historian approaches historical facts—*theoretical* constructs using empirical data illustratively—*historical* investigations which utilize theoretical concepts as ideal limiting cases—the various possible combinations of these which could only be hinted at here; they are pure mental constructs, the relationships of which to the empirical reality of the immediately given is problematical in every individual case. This list of possibilities only reveals the infinite ramifications of the conceptual-methodological problems which face us in the sphere of the cultural sciences. We must renounce the serious discussion of the practical methodological issues the problems of which were only to be exhibited, as well as the detailed treatment of the relationships of ideal types to "laws," of ideal-typical concepts to collective concepts, etc. . . .

[29] The Methodology of Positive Economics *

MILTON FRIEDMAN

In his admirable book on *The Scope and Method of Political Economy* John Neville Keynes distinguishes among "a *positive science* . . . [,] a body of systematized knowledge concerning what is; a *normative* or *regulative science* . . . [,] a body of systematized knowledge discussing criteria of what ought to be . . . ; an *art* . . . [,] a system of rules for the attainment of a given end"; comments that "confusion between them is common and has been the source of many mischievous errors"; and urges the importance of "recognizing a distinct positive science of political economy." [1]

This paper is concerned primarily with certain methodological problems that arise in constructing the "distinct positive science" Keynes called for —in particular, the problem how to decide whether a suggested hypothesis or theory should be tentatively accepted as part of the "body of systematized knowledge concerning what is." But the confusion Keynes laments is still so rife and so much of a hindrance to the recognition that economics can be, and in part is, a positive science that it seems well to preface the main body of the paper with a few remarks about the relation between positive and normative economics.

I. The Relation Between Positive and Normative Economics

Confusion between positive and normative economics is to some extent inevitable. The subject matter of economics is regarded by almost everyone as vitally important to himself and within the range of his own experience and competence; it is the source of continuous and extensive controversy

Reprinted from *Essays in Positive Economics* by Milton Friedman by permission of the University of Chicago Press. Copyright 1953 by the University of Chicago.

* I have incorporated bodily in this article without special reference most of my brief "Comment" in *A Survey of Contemporary Economics*, Vol. II (B. F. Haley, ed.) (Homewood, Ill.: Richard D. Irwin, Inc., 1952), pp. 455–57.

I am indebted to Dorothy S. Brady, Arthur F. Burns, and George J. Stigler for helpful comments and criticism.

1 (London: Macmillan & Co. Ltd., 1891), pp. 34–35 and 46.

and the occasion for frequent legislation. Self-proclaimed "experts" speak with many voices and can hardly all be regarded as disinterested; in any event, on questions that matter so much, "expert" opinion could hardly be accepted solely on faith even if the "experts" were nearly unanimous and clearly disinterested.[2] The conclusions of positive economics seem to be, and are, immediately relevant to important normative problems, to questions of what ought to be done and how any given goal can be attained. Laymen and experts alike are inevitably tempted to shape positive conclusions to fit strongly held normative preconceptions and to reject positive conclusions if their normative implications—or what are said to be their normative implications—are unpalatable.

Positive economics is in principle independent of any particular ethical position or normative judgments. As Keynes says, it deals with "what is," not with "what ought to be." Its task is to provide a system of generalizations that can be used to make correct predictions about the consequences of any change in circumstances. Its performance is to be judged by the precision, scope, and conformity with experience of the predictions it yields. In short, positive economics is, or can be, an "objective" science, in precisely the same sense as any of the physical sciences. Of course, the fact that economics deals with the interrelations of human beings, and that the investigator is himself part of the subject matter being investigated in a more intimate sense than in the physical sciences, raises special difficulties in achieving objectivity at the same time that it provides the social scientist with a class of data not available to the physical scientist. But neither the one nor the other is, in my view, a fundamental distinction between the two groups of sciences.[3]

Normative economics and the art of economics, on the other hand, cannot be independent of positive economics. Any policy conclusion necessarily rests on a prediction about the consequences of doing one thing rather than another, a prediction that must be based—implicitly or explicitly—on positive economics. There is not, of course, a one-to-one relation between policy conclusions and the conclusions of positive economics; if there were, there

---

[2] Social science or economics is by no means peculiar in this respect—witness the importance of personal beliefs and of "home" remedies in medicine wherever obviously convincing evidence for "expert" opinion is lacking. The current prestige and acceptance of the views of physical scientists in their fields of specialization—and, all too often, in other fields as well—derives, not from faith alone, but from the evidence of their works, the success of their predictions, and the dramatic achievements from applying their results. When economics seemed to provide such evidence of its worth, in Great Britain in the first half of the nineteenth century, the prestige and acceptance of "scientific economics" rivaled the current prestige of the physical sciences.

[3] The interaction between the observer and the process observed that is so prominent a feature of the social sciences, besides its more obvious parallel in the physical sciences, has a more subtle counterpart in the indeterminacy principle arising out of the interaction between the process of measurement and the phenomena being measured. And both have a counterpart in pure logic in Gödel's theorem, asserting the impossibility of a comprehensive self-contained logic. It is an open question whether all three can be regarded as different formulations of an even more general principle.

would be no separate normative science. Two individuals may agree on the consequences of a particular piece of legislation. One may regard them as desirable on balance and so favor the legislation; the other, as undesirable and so oppose the legislation.

I venture the judgment, however, that currently in the Western world, and especially in the United States, differences about economic policy among disinterested citizens derive predominantly from different predictions about the economic consequences of taking action—differences that in principle can be eliminated by the progress of positive economics—rather than from fundamental differences in basic values, differences about which men can ultimately only fight. An obvious and not unimportant example is minimum-wage legislation. Underneath the welter of arguments offered for and against such legislation there is an underlying consensus on the objective of achieving a "living wage" for all, to use the ambiguous phrase so common in such discussions. The difference of opinion is largely grounded on an implicit or explicit difference in predictions about the efficacy of this particular means in furthering the agreed-on end. Proponents believe (predict) that legal minimum wages diminish poverty by raising the wages of those receiving less than the minimum wage as well as of some receiving more than the minimum wage without any counterbalancing increase in the number of people entirely unemployed or employed less advantageously than they otherwise would be. Opponents believe (predict) that legal minimum wages increase poverty by increasing the number of people who are unemployed or employed less advantageously and that this more than offsets any favorable effect on the wages of those who remain employed. Agreement about the economic consequences of the legislation might not produce complete agreement about its desirability, for differences might still remain about its political or social consequences; but, given agreement on objectives, it would certainly go a long way toward producing consensus.

Closely related differences in positive analysis underlie divergent views about the appropriate role and place of trade-unions and the desirability of direct price and wage controls and of tariffs. Different predictions about the importance of so-called "economies of scale" account very largely for divergent views about the desirability or necessity of detailed government regulation of industry and even of socialism rather than private enterprise. And this list could be extended indefinitely.[4] Of course, my judgment that

---

[4] One rather more complex example is stabilization policy. Superficially, divergent views on this question seem to reflect differences in objectives; but I believe that this impression is misleading and that at bottom the different views reflect primarily different judgments about the source of fluctuations in economic activity and the effect of alternative countercyclical action. For one major positive consideration that accounts for much of the divergence see "The Effects of a Full-Employment Policy on Economic Stability: A Formal Analysis," *A Survey of Contemporary Economics*, Vol. II, *op. cit.*, pp. 117–32. For a summary of the present state of professional views on this question see "The Problem of Economic Instability," a report of a subcommittee of the Committee on Public Issues of the American Economic Association, *American Economic Review*, XL (September, 1950), 501–38.

the major differences about economic policy in the Western world are of this kind is itself a "positive" statement to be accepted or rejected on the basis of empirical evidence.

If this judgment is valid, it means that a consensus on "correct" economic policy depends much less on the progress of normative economics proper than on the progress of a positive economics yielding conclusions that are, and deserve to be, widely accepted. It means also that a major reason for distinguishing positive economics sharply from normative economics is precisely the contribution that can thereby be made to agreement about policy.

II. Positive Economics

The ultimate goal of a positive science is the development of a "theory" or "hypothesis" that yields valid and meaningful (i.e., not truistic) predictions about phenomena not yet observed. Such a theory is, in general, a complex intermixture of two elements. In part, it is a "language" designed to promote "systematic and organized methods of reasoning." [5] In part, it is a body of substantive hypotheses designed to abstract essential features of complex reality.

Viewed as a language, theory has no substantive content; it is a set of tautologies. Its function is to serve as a filing system for organizing empirical material and facilitating our understanding of it; and the criteria by which it is to be judged are those appropriate to a filing system. Are the categories clearly and precisely defined? Are they exhaustive? Do we know where to file each individual item, or is there considerable ambiguity? Is the system of headings and subheadings so designed that we can quickly find an item we want, or must we hunt from place to place? Are the items we shall want to consider jointly filed together? Does the filing system avoid elaborate cross-references?

The answers to these questions depend partly on logical, partly on factual, considerations. The canons of formal logic alone can show whether a particular language is complete and consistent, that is, whether propositions in the language are "right" or "wrong." Factual evidence alone can show whether the categories of the "analytical filing system" have a meaningful empirical counterpart, that is, whether they are useful in analyzing a particular class of concrete problems.[6] The simple example of "supply" and "demand" illustrates both this point and the preceding list of analogical questions. Viewed as elements of the language of economic theory, these are the two major categories into which factors affecting the relative prices

[5] Final quoted phrase from Alfred Marshall, "The Present Position of Economics" (1885), reprinted in *Memorials of Alfred Marshall*, ed. A. C. Pigou (London: Macmillan & Co. Ltd., 1925), p. 164. See also "The Marshallian Demand Curve," *op. cit.*, pp. 56–57, 90–91.

[6] See "Lange on Price Flexibility and Employment: A Methodological Criticism," *op. cit.*, pp. 282–89.

of products or factors of production are classified. The usefulness of the dichotomy depends on the "empirical generalization that an enumeration of the forces affecting demand in any problem and of the forces affecting supply will yield two lists that contain few items in common." [7] Now this generalization is valid for markets like the final market for a consumer good. In such a market there is a clear and sharp distinction between the economic units that can be regarded as demanding the product and those that can be regarded as supplying it. There is seldom much doubt whether a particular factor should be classified as affecting supply, on the one hand, or demand, on the other; and there is seldom much necessity for considering cross-effects (cross-references) between the two categories. In these cases the simple and even obvious step of filing the relevant factors under the headings of "supply" and "demand" effects a great simplification of the problem and is an effective safeguard against fallacies that otherwise tend to occur. But the generalization is not always valid. For example, it is not valid for the day-to-day fluctuations of prices in a primarily speculative market. Is a rumor of an increased excess-profits tax, for example, to be regarded as a factor operating primarily on today's supply of corporate equities in the stock market or on today's demand for them? In similar fashion, almost every factor can with about as much justification be classified under the heading "supply" as under the heading "demand." These concepts can still be used and may not be entirely pointless; they are still "right" but clearly less useful than in the first example because they have no meaningful empirical counterpart.

Viewed as a body of substantive hypotheses, theory is to be judged by its predictive power for the class of phenomena which it is intended to "explain." Only factual evidence can show whether it is "right" or "wrong" or, better, tentatively "accepted" as valid or "rejected." As I shall argue at greater length below, the only relevant test of the *validity* of a hypothesis is comparison of its predictions with experience. The hypothesis is rejected if its predictions are contradicted ("frequently" or more often than predictions from an alternative hypothesis); it is accepted if its predictions are not contradicted; great confidence is attached to it if it has survived many opportunities for contradiction. Factual evidence can never "prove" a hypothesis; it can only fail to disprove it, which is what we generally mean when we say, somewhat inexactly, that the hypothesis has been "confirmed" by experience.

To avoid confusion, it should perhaps be noted explicitly that the "predictions" by which the validity of a hypothesis is tested need not be about phenomena that have not yet occurred, that is, need not be forecasts of future events; they may be about phenomena that have occurred but observations on which have not yet been made or are not known to the person making the prediction. For example, a hypothesis may imply that such and such must have happened in 1906, given some other known circumstances.

[7] "The Marshallian Demand Curve." *op. cit.,* p. 57.

If a search of the records reveals that such and such did happen, the prediction is confirmed; if it reveals that such and such did not happen, the prediction is contradicted.

The validity of a hypothesis in this sense is not by itself a sufficient criterion for choosing among alternative hypotheses. Observed facts are necessarily finite in number; possible hypotheses, infinite. If there is one hypothesis that is consistent with the available evidence, there are always an infinite number that are.[8] For example, suppose a specific excise tax on a particular commodity produces a rise in price equal to the amount of the tax. This is consistent with competitive conditions, a stable demand curve, and a horizontal and stable supply curve. But it is also consistent with competitive conditions and a positively or negatively sloping supply curve with the required compensating shift in the demand curve or the supply curve; with monopolistic conditions, constant marginal costs, and stable demand curve, of the particular shape required to produce this result; and so on indefinitely. Additional evidence with which the hypothesis is to be consistent may rule out some of these possibilities; it can never reduce them to a single possibility alone capable of being consistent with the finite evidence. The choice among alternative hypotheses equally consistent with the available evidence must to some extent be arbitrary, though there is general agreement that relevant considerations are suggested by the criteria "simplicity" and "fruitlessness," themselves notions that defy completely objective specification. A theory is "simpler" the less the initial knowledge needed to make a prediction within a given field of phenomena; it is more "fruitful" the more precise the resulting prediction, the wider the area within which the theory yields predictions, and the more additional lines for further research it suggests. Logical completeness and consistency are relevant but play a subsidiary role; their function is to assure that the hypothesis says what it is intended to say and does so alike for all users— they play the same role here as checks for arithmetical accuracy do in statistical computations.

Unfortunately, we can seldom test particular predictions in the social sciences by experiments explicitly designed to eliminate what are judged to be the most important disturbing influences. Generally, we must rely on evidence cast up by the "experiments" that happen to occur. The inability to conduct so-called "controlled experiments" does not, in my view, reflect a basic difference between the social and physical sciences both because it is not peculiar to the social sciences—witness astronomy—and because the distinction between a controlled experiment and uncontrolled experience is at best one of degree. No experiment can be completely controlled, and every experience is partly controlled, in the sense that some disturbing influences are relatively constant in the course of it.

---

[8] The qualification is necessary because the "evidence" may be internally contradictory, so there may be no hypothesis consistent with it. See also "Lange on Price Flexibility and Employment," *op. cit.*, pp. 282–83.

Evidence cast up by experience is abundant and frequently as conclusive as that from contrived experiments; thus the inability to conduct experiments is not a fundamental obstacle to testing hypotheses by the success of their predictions. But such evidence is far more difficult to interpret. It is frequently complex and always indirect and incomplete. Its collection is often arduous, and its interpretation generally requires subtle analysis and involved chains of reasoning, which seldom carry real conviction. The denial to economics of the dramatic and direct evidence of the "crucial" experiment does hinder the adequate testing of hypotheses; but this is much less significant than the difficulty it places in the way of achieving a reasonably prompt and wide consensus on the conclusions justified by the available evidence. It renders the weeding-out of unsuccessful hypotheses slow and difficult. They are seldom downed for good and are always cropping up again.

There is, of course, considerable variation in these respects. Occasionally, experience casts up evidence that is about as direct, dramatic, and convincing as any that could be provided by controlled experiments. Perhaps the most obviously important example is the evidence from inflations on the hypothesis that a substantial increase in the quantity of money within a relatively short period is accompanied by a substantial increase in prices. Here the evidence is dramatic, and the chain of reasoning required to interpret it is relatively short. Yet, despite numerous instances of substantial rises in prices, their essentially one-to-one correspondence with substantial rises in the stock of money, and the wide variation in other circumstances that might appear to be relevant, each new experience of inflation brings forth vigorous contentions, and not only by the lay public, that the rise in the stock of money is either an incidental effect of a rise in prices produced by other factors or a purely fortuitous and unnecessary concomitant of the price rise.

One effect of the difficulty of testing substantive economic hypotheses has been to foster a retreat into purely formal or tautological analysis.[9] As already noted, tautologies have an extremely important place in economics and other sciences as a specialized language or "analytical filing system." Beyond this, formal logic and mathematics, which are both tautologies, are essential aids in checking the correctness of reasoning, discovering the implications of hypotheses, and determining whether supposedly different hypotheses may not really be equivalent or wherein the differences lie.

But economic theory must be more than a structure of tautologies if it is to be able to predict and not merely describe the consequences of action; if it is to be something different from disguised mathematics.[10] And the usefulness of the tautologies themselves ultimately depends, as noted above,

---

[9] See "Lange on Price Flexibility and Employment," *op. cit., passim.*

[10] See also Milton Friedman and L. J. Savage, "The Expected-Utility Hypothesis and the Measurability of Utility," *Journal of Political Economy,* LX (December, 1952), 463–74, esp. pp. 465–67.

on the acceptability of the substantive hypotheses that suggest the particular categories into which they organize the refractory empirical phenomena.

A more serious effect of the difficulty of testing economic hypotheses by their predictions is to foster misunderstanding of the role of empirical evidence in theoretical work. Empirical evidence is vital at two different, though closely related, stages: in constructing hypotheses and in testing their validity. Full and comprehensive evidence on the phenomena to be generalized or "explained" by a hypothesis, besides its obvious value in suggesting new hypotheses, is needed to assure that a hypothesis explains what it sets out to explain—that its implications for such phenomena are not contradicted in advance by experience that has already been observed.[11]

11 In recent years some economists, particularly a group connected with the Cowles Commission for Research in Economics at the University of Chicago, have placed great emphasis on a division of this step of selecting a hypothesis consistent with known evidence into two substeps: first, the selection of a class of admissible hypotheses from all possible hypotheses (the choice of a "model" in their terminology); second, the selection of one hypothesis from this class (the choice of a "structure"). This subdivision may be heuristically valuable in some kinds of work, particularly in promoting a systematic use of available statistical evidence and theory. From a methodological point of view, however, it is an entirely arbitrary subdivision of the process of deciding on a particular hypothesis that is on a par with many other subdivisions that may be convenient for one purpose or another or that may suit the psychological needs of particular investigators.

One consequence of this particular subdivision has been to give rise to the so-called "identification" problem. As noted above, if one hypothesis is consistent with available evidence, an infinite number are. But, while this is true for the class of hypotheses as a whole, it may not be true of the subclass obtained in the first of the above two steps—the "model." It may be that the evidence to be used to select the final hypothesis from the subclass can be consistent with at most one hypothesis in it, in which case the "model" is said to be "identified"; otherwise it is said to be "unidentified." As is clear from this way of describing the concept of "identification," it is essentially a special case of the more general problem of selecting among the alternative hypotheses equally consistent with the evidence—a problem that must be decided by some such arbitrary principle as Occam's razor. The introduction of two substeps in selecting a hypothesis makes this problem arise at the two corresponding stages and gives it a special cast. While the class of all hypotheses is always unidentified, the subclass in a "model" need not be, so the problem arises of conditions that a "model" must satisfy to be identified. However useful the two substeps may be in some contexts, their introduction raises the danger that different criteria will unwittingly be used in making the same kind of choice among alternative hypotheses at two different stages.

On the general methodological approach discussed in this footnote see Tryvge Haavelmo, "The Probability Approach in Econometrics," *Econometrica*, Vol. XII (1944). Supplement; Jacob Marshchak, "Economic Structure, Path, Policy, and Prediction," *American Economic Review*, XXXVII (May, 1947), 81–84, and "Statistical Inference to Economics: An Introduction," in T. C. Koopmans (ed.), *Statistical Inference in Dynamic Economic Models* (New York: John Wiley & Sons, Inc., 1950); T. C. Koopmans, "Statistical Estimation of Simultaneous Economic Relations," *Journal of the American Statistical Association*, XL (December, 1945), 448–66; Gershon Cooper, "The Role of Economic Theory in Econometric Models," *Journal of Farm Economics*, XXX (February, 1948), 101–16. On the identification problem see Koopmans, "Identification Problems in Econometric Model Construction," *Econometrica*, XVII (April, 1949), 125–44; Leonid Hurwicz, "Generalization of the Concept of Identification," in Koopmans (ed.), *Statistical Inference in Dynamic Economic Models*. [See also part V, 3 of the selection by Arrow in Section Seven of this volume.—Ed.]

Given that the hypothesis is consistent with the evidence at hand, its further testing involves deducing from it new facts capable of being observed but not previously known and checking these deduced facts against additional empirical evidence. For this test to be relevant, the deduced facts must be about the class of phenomena the hypothesis is designed to explain; and they must be well enough defined so that observation can show them to be wrong.

The two stages of constructing hypotheses and testing their validity are related in two different respects. In the first place, the particular facts that enter at each stage are partly an accident of the collection of data and the knowledge of the particular investigator. The facts that serve as a test of the implications of a hypothesis might equally well have been among the raw material used to construct it, and conversely. In the second place, the process never begins from scratch; the so-called "initial stage" itself always involves comparison of the implications of an earlier set of hypotheses with observation; the contradiction of these implications is the stimulus to the construction of new hypotheses or revision of old ones. So the two methodologically distinct stages are always proceeding jointly.

Misunderstanding about this apparently straightforward process centers on the phrase "the class of phenomena the hypothesis is designed to explain." The difficulty in the social sciences of getting new evidence for this class of phenomena and of judging its conformity with the implications of the hypothesis makes it tempting to suppose that other, more readily available, evidence is equally relevant to the validity of the hypothesis—to suppose that hypotheses have not only "implications" but also "assumptions" and that the conformity of these "assumptions" to "reality" is a test of the validity of the hypothesis *different from* or *additional to* the test by implications. This widely held view is fundamentally wrong and productive of much mischief. Far from providing an easier means for sifting valid from invalid hypotheses, it only confuses the issue, promotes misunderstanding about the significance of empirical evidence for economic theory, produces a misdirection of much intellectual effort devoted to the development of positive economics, and impedes the attainment of consensus on tentative hypotheses in positive economics.

In so far as a theory can be said to have "assumptions" at all, and in so far as their "realism" can be judged independently of the validity of predictions, the relation between the significance of a theory and the "realism" of its "assumptions" is almost the opposite of that suggested by the view under criticism. Truly important and significant hypotheses will be found to have "assumptions" that are wildly inaccurate descriptive representations of reality, and, in general, the more significant the theory, the more unrealistic the assumptions (in this sense).[12] The reason is simple. A hypothesis is important if it "explains" much by little, that is, if it abstracts the

---

[12] The converse of the proposition does not of course hold: assumptions that are unrealistic (in this sense) do not guarantee a significant theory.

common and crucial elements from the mass of complex and detailed circumstances surrounding the phenomena to be explained and permits valid predictions on the basis of them alone. To be important, therefore, a hypothesis must be descriptively false in its assumptions; it takes account of, and accounts for, none of the many other attendant circumstances, since its very success shows them to be irrelevant for the phenomena to be explained.

To put this point less paradoxically, the relevant question to ask about the "assumptions" of a theory is not whether they are descriptively "realistic," for they never are, but whether they are sufficiently good approximations for the purpose in hand. And this question can be answered only by seeing whether the theory works, which means whether it yields sufficiently accurate predictions. The two supposedly independent tests thus reduce to one test.

The theory of monopolistic and imperfect competition is one example of the neglect in economic theory of these propositions. The development of this analysis was explicitly motivated, and its wide acceptance and approval largely explained, by the belief that the assumptions of "perfect competition" or "perfect monopoly" said to underlie neoclassical economic theory are a false image of reality. And this belief was itself based almost entirely on the directly perceived descriptive inaccuracy of the assumptions rather than on any recognized contradiction of predictions derived from neoclassical economic theory. The lengthy discussion on marginal analysis in the *American Economic Review* some years ago is an even clearer, though much less important, example. The articles on both sides of the controversy largely neglect what seems to me clearly the main issue—the conformity to experience of the implications of the marginal analysis— and concentrate on the largely irrelevant question whether businessmen do or do not in fact reach their decisions by consulting schedules, or curves, or multivariable functions showing marginal cost and marginal revenue.[13]

---

[13] See R. A. Lester, "Shortcomings of Marginal Analysis for Wage-Employment Problems," *American Economic Review*, XXXVI (March, 1946), 62–82; Fritz Machlup, "Marginal Analysis and Empirical Research," *American Economic Review*, XXXVI (September, 1946), 519–554; R. A. Lester, "Marginalism, Minimum Wages, and Labor Markets," *American Economic Review*, XXXVII (March, 1947), 135–148; Fritz Machlup, "Rejoinder to an Antimarginalist," *American Economic Review*, XXXVII (March, 1947), 148–154; G. J. Stigler, "Professor Lester and the Marginalists," *American Economic Review*, XXXVII (March, 1947), 154–157; H. M. Oliver, Jr., "Marginal Theory and Business Behavior," *American Economic Review*, XXXVII (June, 1947), 375–383; R. A. Gordon, "Short-Period Price Determination in Theory and Practice," *American Economic Review*, XXXVIII (June, 1948), 265–288.

It should be noted that, along with much material purportedly bearing on the validity of the "assumptions" of marginal theory, Lester does refer to evidence on the conformity of experience with the implications of the theory, citing the reactions of employment in Germany to the Papen plan and in the United States to changes in minimum-wage legislation as examples of lack of conformity. However, Stigler's brief comment is the only one of the other papers that refers to this evidence. It should also be noted that Machlup's thorough and careful exposition of the logical structure and meaning of marginal analysis is called for by the misunderstandings on this score that

Perhaps these two examples, and the many others they readily suggest, will serve to justify a more extensive discussion of the methodological principles involved than might otherwise seem appropriate.

III. Can a Hypothesis Be Tested by the Realism of Its Assumptions?

We may start with a simple physical example, the law of falling bodies. It is an accepted hypothesis that the acceleration of a body dropped in a vacuum is a constant—g, or approximately 32 feet per second on the earth—and is independent of the shape of the body, the manner of dropping it, etc. This implies that the distance traveled by a falling body in any specified time is given by the formula $s = \frac{1}{2} gt^2$, where s is the distance traveled in feet and t is time in seconds. The application of this formula to a compact ball dropped from the roof of a building is equivalent to saying that a ball so dropped behaves *as if* it were falling in a vacuum. Testing this hypothesis by its assumptions presumbably means measuring the actual air pressure and deciding whether it is close enough to zero. At sea level the air pressure is about 15 pounds per square inch. Is 15 sufficiently close to zero for the difference to be judged insignificant? Apparently it is, since the actual time taken by a compact ball to fall from the roof of a building to the ground is very close to the time given by the formula. Suppose, however, that a feather is dropped instead of a compact ball. The formula then gives wildly inaccurate results. Apparently, 15 pounds per square inch is significantly different from zero for a feather but not for a ball. Or, again, suppose the formula is applied to a ball dropped from an airplane at an altitude of 30,000 feet. The air pressure at this altitude is decidedly less than 15 pounds per square inch. Yet, the actual time of fall from 30,000 feet to 20,000 feet, at which point the air pressure is still much less than at sea level, will differ noticeably from the time predicted by the formula—much more noticeably than the time taken by a compact ball to fall from the roof of a building to the ground. According to the formula, the velocity of the ball should be gt and should therefore increase steadily. In fact, a ball dropped at 30,000 feet will reach its top velocity well before it hits the ground. And similarly with other implications of the formula.

The initial question whether 15 is sufficiently close to zero for the difference to be judged insignificant is clearly a foolish question by itself. Fifteen pounds per square inch is 2,160 pounds per square foot, or 0.0075 ton per

---

mar Lester's paper and almost conceal the evidence he presents that is relevant to the key issue he raises. But, in Machlup's emphasis on the logical structure, he comes perilously close to presenting the theory as a pure tautology, though it is evident at a number of points that he is aware of this danger and anxious to avoid it. The papers by Oliver and Gordon are the most extreme in the exclusive concentration on the conformity of the behavior of businessmen with the "assumptions" of the theory.

square inch. There is no possible basis for calling these numbers "small" or "large" without some external standard of comparison. And the only relevant standard of comparison is the air pressure for which the formula does or does not work under a given set of circumstances. But this raises the same problem at a second level. What is the meaning of "does or does not work"? Even if we could eliminate errors of measurement, the measured time of fall would seldom if ever be precisely equal to the computed time of fall. How large must the difference between the two be to justify saying that the theory "does not work"? Here there are two important external standards of comparison. One is the accuracy achievable by an alternative theory with which this theory is being compared and which is equally acceptable on all other grounds. The other arises when there exists a theory that is known to yield better predictions but only at a greater cost. The gains from greater accuracy, which depend on the purpose in mind, must then be balanced against the costs of achieving it.

This example illustrates both the impossibility of testing a theory by its assumptions and also the ambiguity of the concept "the assumptions of a theory." The formula $s = \frac{1}{2} gt^2$ is valid for bodies falling in a vacuum and can be derived by analyzing the behavior of such bodies. It can therefore be stated: under a wide range of circumstances, bodies that fall in the actual atmosphere behave *as if* they were falling in a vacuum. In the language so common in economics this would be rapidly translated into: the formula assumes a vacuum. Yet it clearly does no such thing. What it does say is that in many cases the existence of air pressure, the shape of the body, the name of the person dropping the body, the kind of mechanism used to drop the body, and a host of other attendant circumstances have no appreciable effect on the distance the body falls in a specified time. The hypothesis can readily be rephrased to omit all mention of a vacuum: under a wide range of circumstances, the distance a body falls in a specified time is given by the formula $s = \frac{1}{2} gt^2$. The history of this formula and its associated physical theory aside, is it meaningful to say that it assumes a vacuum? For all I know there may be other sets of assumptions that would yield the same formula. The formula is accepted because it works, not because we live in an approximate vacuum—whatever that means.

The important problem in connection with the hypothesis is to specify the circumstances under which the formula works or, more precisely, the general magnitude of the error in its predictions under various circumstances. Indeed, as is implicit in the above rephrasing of the hypothesis, such a specification is not one thing and the hypothesis another. The specification is itself an essential part of the hypothesis, and it is a part that is peculiarly likely to be revised and extended as experience accumulates.

In the particular case of falling bodies a more general, though still incomplete, theory is available, largely as a result of attempts to explain the errors of the simple theory, from which the influence of some of the possible disturbing factors can be calculated and of which the simple theory is a special case. However, it does not always pay to use the more general theory because the extra accuracy it yields may not justify the extra cost of using it, so the question under what circumstances the simpler theory works "well enough" remains important. Air pressure is one, but only one, of the variables that define these circumstances; the shape of the body, the velocity attained, and still other variables are relevant as well. One way of interpreting the variables other than air pressure is to regard them as determining whether a particular departure from the "assumption" of a vacuum is or is not significant. For example, the difference in shape of the body can be said to make 15 pounds per square inch significantly different from zero for a feather but not for a compact ball dropped a moderate distance. Such a statement must, however, be sharply distinguished from the very different statement that the theory does not work for a feather because its assumptions are false. The relevant relation runs the other way: the assumptions are false for a feather because the theory does not work. This point needs emphasis, because the entirely valid use of "assumptions" in *specifying* the circumstances for which the theory holds is frequently, and erroneously, interpreted to mean that the assumptions can be used to *determine* the circumstances for which a theory holds, and has, in this way, been an important source of the belief that a theory can be tested by its assumptions.

Let us turn now to another example, this time a constructed one designed to be an analogue of many hypotheses in the social sciences. Consider the density of leaves around a tree. I suggest the hypothesis that the leaves are positioned as if each leaf deliberately sought to maximize the amount of sunlight it receives, given the position of its neighbors, as if it knew the physical laws determining the amount of sunlight that would be received in various positions and could move rapidly or instantaneously from any one position to any other desired and unoccupied position.[14] Now some of the more obvious implications of this hypothesis are clearly consistent with experience: for example, leaves are in general denser on the south than on the north side of trees but, as the hypothesis implies, less so or not at all on the northern slope of a hill or when the south side of the trees is shaded in some other way. Is the hypothesis rendered unacceptable or invalid because, so far as we know, leaves do not "deliberate" or consciously "seek," have not been to school and learned the relevant laws of science or the mathematics required to calculate the "optimum" position, and cannot move from position to position? Clearly, none of these contradictions of the hypothesis is vitally relevant; the phenomena involved are not within the "class of phenomena the hypothesis is designed to explain"; the hypothesis

[14] This example, and some of the subsequent discussion, though independent in origin, is similar to and in much the same spirit as an example and the approach in an important paper by Armen A. Alchian, "Uncertainty, Evolution, and Economic Theory," *Journal of Political Economy*, LVIII (June, 1950), 211–221.

does not assert that leaves do these things but only that their density is the same *as if* they did. Despite the apparent falsity of the "assumptions" of the hypothesis, it has great plausibility because of the conformity of its implications with observation. We are inclined to "explain" its validity on the ground that sunlight contributes to the growth of leaves and that hence leaves will grow denser or more putative leaves survive where there is more sun, so the result achieved by purely passive adaptation to external circumstances is the same as the result that would be achieved by deliberate accommodation to them. This alternative hypothesis is more attractive than the constructed hypothesis not because its "assumptions" are more "realistic" but rather because it is part of a more general theory that applies to a wider variety of phenomena, of which the position of leaves around a tree is a special case, has more implications capable of being contradicted, and has failed to be contradicted under a wider variety of circumstances. The direct evidence for the growth of leaves is in this way strengthened by the indirect evidence from the other phenomena to which the more general theory applies.

The constructed hypothesis is presumably valid, that is, yields "sufficiently" accurate predictions about the density of leaves, only for a particular class of circumstances. I do not know what these circumstances are or how to define them. It seems obvious, however, that in this example the "assumptions" of the theory will play no part in specifiying them: the kind of tree, the character of the soil, etc., are the types of variables that are likely to define its range of validity, not the ability of the leaves to do complicated mathematics or to move from place to place.

A largely parallel example involving human behavior has been used elsewhere by Savage and me.[15] Consider the problem of predicting the shots made by an expert billiard player. It seems not at all unreasonable that excellent predictions would be yielded by the hypothesis that the billiard player made his shots *as if* he knew the complicated mathematical formulas that would give the optimum directions of travel, could estimate accurately by eye the angles, etc., describing the location of the balls, could make lightning calculations from the formulas, and could then make the balls travel in the direction indicated by the formulas. Our confidence in this hypothesis is not based on the belief that billiard players, even expert ones, can or do go through the process described; it derives rather from the belief that, unless in some way or other they were capable of reaching essentially the same result, they would not in fact be *expert* billiard players.

It is only a short step from these examples to the economic hypothesis that under a wide range of circumstances individual firms behave *as if* they were seeking rationally to maximize their expected returns (generally

[15] Milton Friedman and L. J. Savage, "The Utility Analysis of Choices Involving Risk," *Journal of Political Economy,* LVI (August, 1948), 298. Reprinted in American Economic Association, *Readings in Price Theory* (Homewood, Ill.: Richard D. Irwin, Inc., 1952), pp. 57–96.

if misleadingly called "profits") [16] and had full knowledge of the data needed to succeed in this attempt; *as if*, that is, they knew the relevant cost and demand functions, calculated marginal cost and marginal revenue from all actions open to them, and pushed each line of action to the point at which the relevant marginal cost and marginal revenue were equal. Now, of course, businessmen do not actually and literally solve the system of simultaneous equations in terms of which the mathematical economist finds it convenient to express this hypothesis, any more than leaves or billiard players explicitly go through complicated mathematical calculations or falling bodies decide to create a vacuum. The billiard player, if asked how he decides where to hit the ball, may say that he "just figures it out" but then also rubs a rabbit's foot just to make sure; and the businessman may well say that he prices at average cost, with of course some minor deviations when the market makes it necessary. The one statement is about as helpful as the other, and neither is a relevant test of the associated hypothesis.

Confidence in the maximization-of-returns hypothesis is justified by evidence of a very different character. This evidence is in part similar to that adduced on behalf of the billiard-player hypothesis—unless the behavior of businessmen in some way or other approximated behavior consistent with the maximization of returns, it seems unlikely that they would remain in business for long. Let the apparent immediate determinant of business behavior be anything at all—habitual reaction, random chance, or whatnot. Whenever this determinant happens to lead to behavior consistent with rational and informed maximization of returns, the business will prosper and acquire resources with which to expand; whenever it does not, the business will tend to lose resources and can be kept in existence only by the addition of resources from outside. The process of "natural selection" thus helps to validate the hypothesis—or, rather, given natural selection, acceptance of the hypothesis can be based largely on the judgment that it summarizes appropriately the conditions for survival.

An even more important body of evidence for the maximization-of-returns hypothesis is experience from countless applications of the hypothesis to

16 It seems better to use the term "profits" to refer to the difference between actual and "expected" results, between *ex post* and *ex ante* receipts. "Profits" are then a result of uncertainty and, as Alchian (*op. cit.*, p. 212), following Tintner, points out, cannot be deliberately maximized in advance. Given uncertainty, individuals or firms choose among alternative anticipated probability distributions of receipts or incomes. The specific content of a theory of choice among such distributions depends on the criteria by which they are supposed to be ranked. One hypothesis supposes them to be ranked by the mathematical expectation of utility corresponding to them (see Friedman and Savage, "The Expected-Utility Hypothesis and the Measurability of Utility," *op. cit.*). A special case of this hypothesis or an alternative to it ranks probability distributions by the mathematical expectation of the money receipts corresponding to them. The latter is perhaps more applicable, and more frequently applied, to firms than to individuals. The term "expected returns" is intended to be sufficiently broad to apply to any of these alternatives.

The issues alluded to in this note are not basic to the methodological issues being discussed, and so are largely by-passed in the discussion that follows.

specific problems and the repeated failure of its implications to be contradicted. This evidence is extremely hard to document; it is scattered in numerous memorandums, articles, and monographs concerned primarily with specific concrete problems rather than with submitting the hypothesis to test. Yet the continued use and acceptance of the hypothesis over a long period, and the failure of any coherent, self-consistent alternative to be developed and be widely accepted, is strong indirect testimony to its worth. The evidence *for* a hypothesis always consists of its repeated failure to be contradicted, continues to accumulate so long as the hypothesis is used, and by its very nature is difficult to document at all comprehensively. It tends to become part of the tradition and folklore of a science revealed in the tenacity with which hypotheses are held rather than in any textbook list of instances in which the hypothesis has failed to be contradicted.

IV. The Significance and Role of the "Assumptions" of a Theory

Up to this point our conclusions about the significance of the "assumptions" of a theory have been almost entirely negative: we have seen that a theory cannot be tested by the "realism" of its "assumptions" and that the very concept of the "assumptions" of a theory is surrounded with ambiguity. But, if this were all there is to it, it would be hard to explain the extensive use of the concept and the strong tendency that we all have to speak of the assumptions of a theory and to compare the assumptions of alternative theories. There is too much smoke for there to be no fire.

In methodology, as in positive science, negative statements can generally be made with greater confidence than positive statements, so I have less confidence in the following remarks on the significance and role of "assumptions" than in the preceding remarks. So far as I can see, the "assumptions of a theory" play three different, though related, positive roles: (*a*) they are often an economical mode of describing or presenting a theory; (*b*) they sometimes facilitate an indirect test of the hypothesis by its implications; and (c), as already noted, they are sometimes a convenient means of specifying the conditions under which the theory is expected to be valid. The first two require more extensive discussion.

A. THE USE OF "ASSUMPTIONS" IN STATING A THEORY

The example of the leaves illustrates the first role of assumptions. Instead of saying that leaves seek to maximize the sunlight they receive, we could state the equivalent hypothesis, without any apparent assumptions, in the form of a list of rules for predicting the density of leaves: if a tree stands in a level field with no other trees or other bodies obstructing the rays of the sun, then the density of leaves will tend to be such and such; if a tree is on the northern slope of a hill in the midst of a forest of similar trees, then . . . ; etc. This is clearly a far less economical presentation of the hypothesis than the statement that leaves seek to maximize the sunlight each receives. The latter statement is, in effect, a simple summary of the rules in the above list, even if the list were indefinitely extended, since it indicates both how to determine the features of the environment that are important for the particular problem and how to evaluate their effects. It is more compact and at the same time no less comprehensive.

More generally, a hypothesis or theory consists of an assertion that certain forces are, and by implication others are not, important for a particular class of phenomena and a specification of the manner of action of the forces it asserts to be important. We can regard the hypothesis as consisting of two parts: first, a conceptual world or abstract model simpler than the "real world" and containing only the forces that the hypothesis asserts to be important; second, a set of rules defining the class of phenomena for which the "model" can be taken to be an adequate representation of the "real world" and specifying the correspondence between the variables or entities in the model and observable phenomena.

These two parts are very different in character. The model is abstract and complete; it is an "algebra" or "logic." Mathematics and formal logic come into their own in checking its consistency and completeness and exploring its implications. There is no place in the model for, and no function to be served by, vagueness, maybe's, or approximations. The air pressure is zero, not "small," for a vacuum; the demand curve for the product of a competitive producer is horizontal (has a slope of zero), not "almost horizontal."

The rules for using the model, on the other hand, cannot possibly be abstract and complete. They must be concrete and in consequence incomplete—completeness is possible only in a conceptual world, not in the "real world," however that may be interpreted. The model is the logical embodiment of the half-truth, "There is nothing new under the sun"; the rules for applying it cannot neglect the equally significant half-truth, "History never repeats itself." To a considerable extent the rules can be formulated explicitly—most easily, though even then not completely, when the theory is part of an explicit more general theory as in the example of the vacuum theory for falling bodies. In seeking to make a science as "objective" as possible, our aim should be to formulate the rules explicitly in so far as possible and continually to widen the range of phenomena for which it is possible to do so. But, no matter how successful we may be in this attempt, there inevitably will remain room for judgment in applying the rules. Each occurrence has some features peculiarly its own, not covered by the explicit rules. The capacity to judge that these are or are not to be disregarded, that they should or should not affect what observable phenomena are to be identified with what entities in the model, is something that cannot be taught; it can be learned but only by experience and exposure in the "right" scientific atmosphere, not by rote. It is at this point that the "amateur" is separated from the "professional" in all sciences and that the thin line is drawn which distinguishes the "crackpot" from the scientist.

A simple example may perhaps clarify this point. Euclidean geometry is an abstract model, logically complete and consistent. Its entities are precisely defined—a line is not a geometrical figure "much" longer than it is wide or deep; it is a figure whose width and depth are zero. It is also obviously "unrealistic." There are no such things in "reality" as Euclidean points or lines or surfaces. Let us apply this abstract model to a mark made on a blackboard by a piece of chalk. Is the mark to be identified with a Euclidean line, a Euclidean surface, or a Euclidean solid? Clearly, it can appropriately be identified with a line if it is being used to represent, say, a demand curve. But it cannot be so identified if it is being used to color, say, countries on a map, for that would imply that the map would never be colored; for this purpose, the same mark must be identified with a surface. But it cannot be so identified by a manufacturer of chalk, for that would imply that no chalk would ever be used up; for his purposes, the same mark must be identified with a volume. In this simple example these judgments will command general agreement. Yet it seems obvious that, while general considerations can be formulated to guide such judgments, they can never be comprehensive and cover every possible instance; they cannot have the self-contained coherent character of Euclidean geometry itself.

In speaking of the "crucial assumptions" of a theory, we are, I believe, trying to state the key elements of the abstract model. There are generally many different ways of describing the model completely—many different sets of "postulates" which both imply and are implied by the model as a whole. These are all logically equivalent: what are regarded as axioms or postulates of a model from one point of view can be regarded as theorems from another, and conversely. The particular "assumptions" termed "crucial" are selected on grounds of their convenience in some such respects as simplicity or economy in describing the model, intuitive plausibility, or capacity to suggest, if only by implication, some of the considerations that are relevant in judging or applying the model.

B. THE USE OF "ASSUMPTIONS" AS AN INDIRECT TEST OF A THEORY

In presenting any hypothesis, it generally seems obvious which of the series of statements used to expound it refer to assumptions and which to implications; yet this distinction is not easy to define rigorously. It is not, I believe, a characteristic of the hypothesis as such but rather of the use to which the hypothesis is to be put. If this is so, the ease of classifying statements must reflect unambiguousness in the purpose the hypothesis is designed to serve. The possibility of interchanging theorems and axioms in an abstract model implies the possibility of interchanging "implications" and "assumptions" in the substantive hypothesis corresponding to the abstract model, which is not to say that any implication can be interchanged with any assumption but only that there may be more than one set of statements that imply the rest.

For example, consider a particular proposition in the theory of oligopolistic behavior. If we assume (a) that entrepreneurs seek to maximize their returns by any means including acquiring or extending monopoly power, this will imply (b) that, when demand for a "product" is geographically unstable, transportation costs are significant, explicit price agreements illegal, and the number of producers of the product relatively small, they will tend to establish basing-point pricing systems.[17] The assertion (a) is regarded as an assumption and (b) as an implication because we accept the prediction of market behavior as the purpose of the analysis. We shall regard the assumption as acceptable if we find that the conditions specified in (b) are generally associated with basing-point pricing, and conversely. Let us now change our purpose to deciding what cases to prosecute under the Sherman Antitrust Law's prohibition of a "conspiracy in restraint of trade." If we now assume (c) that basing-point pricing is a deliberate construction to facilitate collusion under the conditions specified in (b), this will imply (d) that entrepreneurs who participate in basing-point pricing are engaged in a "conspiracy in restraint of trade." What was formerly an assumption now becomes an implication, and conversely. We shall now regard the assumption (c) as valid if we find that, when entrepreneurs participate in basing-point pricing, there generally tends to be other evidence, in the form of letters, memorandums, or the like, of what courts regard as a "conspiracy in restraint of trade."

Suppose the hypothesis works for the first purpose, namely, the prediction of market behavior. It clearly does not follow that it will work for the second purpose, namely, predicting whether there is enough evidence of a "conspiracy in restraint of trade" to justify court action. And, conversely, if it works for the second purpose, it does not follow that it will work for the first. Yet, in the absence of other evidence, the success of the hypothesis for one purpose—in explaining one class of phenomena—will give us greater confidence than we would otherwise have that it may succeed for another purpose—in explaining another class of phenomena. It is much harder to say how much greater confidence it justifies. For this depends on how closely related we judge the two classes of phenomena to be, which itself depends in a complex way on similar kinds of indirect evidence, that is, on our experience in other connections in explaining by single theories phenomena that are in some sense similarly diverse.

To state the point more generally, what are called the assumptions of a hypothesis can be used to get some indirect evidence on the acceptability of

17 See George J. Stigler, "A Theory of Delivered Price Systems," *American Economic Review*, XXXIX (December, 1949), 1143–57.

the hypothesis in so far as the assumptions can themselves be regarded as implications of the hypothesis, and hence their conformity with reality as a failure of some implications to be contradicted, or in so far as the assumptions may call to mind other implications of the hypothesis susceptible to casual empirical observation.[18] The reason this evidence is indirect is that the assumptions or associated implications generally refer to a class of phenomena different from the class which the hypothesis is designed to explain; indeed, as is implied above, this seems to be the chief criterion we use in deciding which statements to term "assumptions" and which to term "implications." The weight attached to this indirect evidence depends on how closely related we judge the two classes of phenomena to be.

Another way in which the "assumptions" of a hypothesis can facilitate its indirect testing is by bringing out its kinship with other hypotheses and thereby making the evidence on their validity relevant to the validity of the hypothesis in question. For example, a hypothesis is formulated for a particular class of behavior. This hypothesis can, as usual, be stated without specifying any "assumptions." But suppose it can be shown that it is equivalent to a set of assumptions including the assumption that man seeks his own interest. The hypothesis then gains indirect plausibility from the success for other classes of phenomena of hypotheses that can also be said to make this assumption; at least, what is being done here is not completely unprecedented or unsuccessful in all other uses. In effect, the statement of assumptions so as to bring out a relationship between superficially different hypotheses is a step in the direction of a more general hypothesis.

This kind of indirect evidence from related hypotheses explains in large measure the difference in the confidence attached to a particular hypothesis by people with different backgrounds. Consider, for example, the hypothesis that the extent of racial or religious discrimination in employment in a particular area or industry is closely related to the degree of monopoly in the industry or area in question; that, if the industry is competitive discrimination will be significant only if the race or religion of employees affects either the willingness of other employees to work with them or the acceptability of the product to customers and will be uncorrelated with the prejudices of employers.[19] This hypothesis is far more likely to appeal to an economist than to a sociologist. It can be said to "assume" single-minded pursuit of pecuniary self-interest by employers in competitive industries; and this "assumption" works well in a wide variety of hypotheses in economics bearing on many of the mass phenomena with which economics deals. It is therefore likely to seem reasonable to the economist that it may work in this case as well. On the other hand, the hypotheses to which the

[18] See Friedman and Savage, "The Expected-Utility Hypothesis and the Measurability of Utility," *op. cit.*, pp. 466–67, for another specific example of this kind of indirect test.

[19] A rigorous statement of this hypothesis would of course have to specify how "extent of racial or religious discrimination" and "degree of monopoly" are to be judged. The loose statement in the text is sufficient, however, for present purposes.

sociologist is accustomed have a very different kind of model or ideal world, in which single-minded pursuit of pecuniary self-interest plays a much less important role. The indirect evidence available to the sociologist on this hypothesis is much less favorable to it than the indirect evidence available to the economist; he is therefore likely to view it with greater suspicion.

Of course, neither the evidence of the economist nor that of the sociologist is conclusive. The decisive test is whether the hypothesis works for the phenomena it purports to explain. But a judgment may be required before any satisfactory test of this kind has been made, and, perhaps, when it cannot be made in the near future, in which case, the judgment will have to be based on the inadequate evidence available. In addition, even when such a test can be made, the background of the scientists is not irrelevant to the judgments they reach. There is never certainty in science, and the weight of evidence for or against a hypothesis can never be assessed completely "objectively." The economist will be more tolerant than the sociologist in judging conformity of the implications of the hypothesis with experience, and he will be persuaded to accept the hypothesis tentatively by fewer instances of "conformity."

[30] The Construction of Economic Knowledge

TJALLING C. KOOPMANS

1. The Bad Repute of Methodology

If methods of scaling are ever applied to measure the relative prestige of various topics in economic research, methodological discussion will undoubtedly be found to rank near the low end of the scale. "I find it necessary in self-defense to start with a few words on the distasteful subject of methodology," announces Dennis H. Robertson in near-despair at the beginning of his exchange with the Keynesian theory of interest.[1] R. F. Har-

From *Three Essays on the State of Economic Science* by Tjalling C. Koopmans. Copyright © 1957. McGraw-Hill Book Company. Used by permission.

[1] "Mr. Keynes and the Rate of Interest," *Essays in Monetary Theory*, King, London, 1940.

rod in his well-known methodological essay [2] candidly characterizes the risk incurred and the odium suffered by the economist who addresses his professional colleagues on methodological questions.

Exposed as a bore, the methodologist cannot take refuge behind a cloak of modesty. On the contrary, he stands forward ready by his own claim to give advice to all and sundry, to criticise the work of others, which, whether valuable or not, at least attempts to be constructive; he sets himself up as the final interpreter of the past and dictator of future efforts.

In spite of all this, there is something irrepressible in methodological discussion. As new work unfolds, as changes in emphasis occur in the objectives of economics, and as fresh tools come into use, the desire for exchange of views on methodology recurs irresistibly. Thus, Harrod's essay is one of three highly perceptive methodological discussions contained in a single volume of the *Economic Journal*,[3] in a year following a period of drastic changes of emphasis in economic thought.

More recently, changes in the content and direction of economic analysis have been more gradual, in a period of both consolidation and broadening of economic ideas and research. However, while there have been no other substantive revolutions in economic thinking comparable to the "Keynesian revolution," there has been a cumulative change in the tools of theory as well as of empirical research (to be discussed more in detail in the third essay of this collection), which is bound to have repercussions in methodology. The present essay is a plea for methodological recognition of the potentialities of the tools that have come to the fore. If I in turn defy the low regard for methodological discussion, the motive is again best expressed by a quotation from Harrod's article:

My substantial excuse for choosing methodology today is that I feel a strong inner urge to say something.

2. The Diplomatic Style of Discourse

As in any empirical science, progress in economics comes about through continual interaction of observation, proceeding from the casual to the systematic, and reasoning, proceeding from the incidental to the more general and formal. In some of the physical sciences a considerable degree of differentiation has developed between experimental work, devoted to observation, and theoretical work, devoted to reasoning and to the construction of premises from which to reason. In economics, such a separation of activities has so far not developed to the same extent. In those writings

[2] "The Scope and Method of Economics," presidential address before Section F of the British Association in 1938, *Economic Journal*, vol. 48, September 1938, pp. 383–412.

[3] The other two are E. F. M. Durbin, "Methods of Research—A Plea for Cooperation in the Social Sciences," pp. 183–195, and L. M. Fraser, "Economists and Their Critics," pp. 196–210 (a reply to Barbara Wootton, *Lament for Economics*, George Allen & Unwin, Ltd., London, 1938).

representing the best achievements of economics, we find and expect to find pieces of reasoning and references to facts closely intertwined.

This informality of economics (as one might call the simultaneous preoccupation with all aspects of knowledge-building) is strongly rooted in the nature of its subject matter. The "facts" of economic life are all around us. Hence much of the factual background of economics can be presupposed without extensive examination or discussion. Furthermore, in a democratic environment, policy recommendations in economic matters need to be understood by the enlightened citizen in order to meet with acceptance. We have excellent testimony [4] indicating that this consideration moved Alfred Marshall to establish by his shining example a highly effective style of writing, in which the technical aspects of reasoning are somewhat concealed between the lines, or relegated to appendixes. The effectiveness of this form of communication in economics was enhanced by the fortunate circumstance that some of the most important insights achieved by economic analysis—such as the efficiency of resource allocation by competitive markets in a predictable world in which technology permits perfect competition—can be at least strongly suggested through a form of discourse which demands from its readers genuine intellectual effort, it is true, but not a high degree of technical training.

It is gradually becoming apparent that the mundane and diplomatic approach to economic writing also has its disadvantages. Perhaps these can be epitomized in the observation how extraordinarily difficult it is to uncover the foundations on which our economic knowledge rests. How much of it is derived from observation, how much from reasoning? From what assertions does the reasoning start? The puzzle presented to us by the very persuasiveness of economic analysis is wittily described by Hicks in the following quotation:

> Pure economics has a remarkable way of producing rabbits out of a hat—apparently *a priori* propositions which apparently refer to reality.[5]

3. The Postulational Structure of Economic Theory

In preparation for further comment on this puzzle, it may be useful to describe briefly, and without claim to originality,[6] the logical structure of

[4] J. M. Keynes, "Alfred Marshall, 1842–1924," in A. C. Pigou (ed.), *Memorials of Alfred Marshall*, Macmillan & Company, Ltd., London, 1925.

[5] J. R. Hicks, *Value and Capital*, Clarendon Press, Oxford, 1946, 2d ed., p. 23.

[6] At the time this essay was nearing completion I became aware of the similarity of the point of view here adopted with some of the ideas expressed in somewhat stronger terms by T. W. Hutchison in *The Significance and Basic Postulates of Economic Theory*, London, 1938. There is some difference in emphasis in that the present essay gives more attention to the detachability of the chains of reasoning from the interpretation of the postulates. In so far as there is duplication or repetition, there seems to be no harm done by it, since the practical consequences of the views expressed have not yet been generally realized or accepted.

our economic knowledge discernible underneath the polished prose. Since it is impossible to say which comes first, observation or reasoning, the chicken or the egg, our description may start with either. We shall start with, and in fact place most emphasis on, the reasoning merely because most of our comments in this essay are concerned with that compartment of economic analysis.

Explicitly or implicitly, any logically valid chain of reasoning starts from certain premises. We shall use the term *postulates* for any premises used in any piece of economic analysis, which are not themselves conclusions from earlier parts of the reasoning in the same piece of analysis. If often these postulates are not formally introduced, but referred to or implied at the point where they are used, this does not change their logically recognizable character of basic premises.

The postulates contain certain *terms* that are the representatives or counterparts in the analysis of persons, organizations, things, actions, or states such as are found in the world of experience. Often the adoption of terms is effected by the use of certain key words, such a consumer, worker, entrepreneur, commodity, production process, output, consumption, probability, climate. The associations that have come to cling to these terms through extensive use in the literature are sometimes sufficient for practical purposes. However, if one wishes to get down to fundamentals, it is clear that a meaningful analysis presupposes that the language used is or has been explicitly established by definitions, statements or descriptions connecting the terms with observable phenomena. We shall call these descriptions the *interpretations* of the terms.

Whether these interpretations are expressly provided or borrowed by tacit consent from the stream of literature, they lend relevance and economic meaning to the postulates. Without the interpretations, the postulates are bare statements establishing logical relations between unspecified entities represented by the symbols we have called *terms*. Through the interpretations, the postulates become statements that specify the range of choices open to the various persons introduced (often one man's range of choice is circumscribed by other men's choices); the effects of these choices on the things, processes, and states represented by the terms; and the rules or principles from which actual choices are derived in the light of the individual's evaluation of the known or presumed effects of these choices. However, from the point of view of the logic of the reasoning, the interpretations are detachable. Only the logical contents of the postulates matter. We shall return below to the importance of this circumstance.

Once a set of postulates has been adopted, the reasoning itself develops, by the rules of logic and, where appropriate, with the help of other mathematical techniques, those implications that are verifiable or otherwise interesting. The reasoning is often helped by the introduction of additional terms through definitions that use terms already established. Terms such as utility, price, income, capital, savings, efficiency, strategy, often occur in this role, although some of them may in other pieces of analysis be "primitive" terms.

The reasoning may prove the postulates to be in contradiction with each other. Or it may reveal that the postulates are not sufficiently specific or numerous to have the kind of implications one is looking for. In a "successful" analysis, the reasoning leads to conclusions that are interesting for one or both of two reasons which are connected with the purposes the analysis is to serve. A distinction needs to be made here between *explanatory* and *normative* analysis. Synonymous designations such as *descriptive,* or *positive,* versus *prescriptive* analysis are also in use. These two types of analysis do not necessarily differ in the interpretations placed on the terms. They differ only in the motivation of the search for conclusions, and in the use made of those that are found. In explanatory analysis, what one looks for in a conclusion or prediction is the possibility of testing, that is, of verification or refutation by observation. Of course, the interpretations of the terms used in the postulates form the connecting link through which observation is brought to bear on the statements that represent conclusions. Verification, or absence of refutation, lends support to the set of postulates taken as a whole. Refutation indicates that at least one of the postulates is inadequate for the purpose of "explaining" the phenomena to which the conclusions refer.[7]

In normative analysis, the purposes of the analysis are not limited to the empirical testing of the set of populates, and need not even include the latter objective. The new purpose is that of recommending, to one or more of the persons or organizations represented in the analysis, a choice or course of action which can be expected to serve his or their objectives better than, or at least as well as, alternative actions open to them. If the recommendation is implemented, this may provide an opportunity for testing the postulates on which it is based. However, it may also happen that, because of the continual impact of factors disregarded in the analysis, or because of the all-pervasive effect of the action implemented, no opportunity remains for observing the effect of not taking the recommended action or of taking some alternative action. In such cases, the recommendation is as good as the postulates from which it is correctly derived, but the analysis need not be less worthwhile for that reason.

Although our distinctions have been illustrated by terms taken from economics, it would seem that the above description fits general scientific procedure. Nor is the distinction between explanatory and normative analysis limited to the social sciences. It is paralleled, for instance, in the distinction between physical sciences and engineering. However, there is a difference with regard to opportunities for what might be called "direct"

---

[7] In this discussion we follow what appears to be the accepted view: that the validity of the reasoning from postulates to conclusions is entirely a matter of logical rather than empirical test.

verification of the postulates. This leads us to consider further the puzzling question on what foundations economic knowledge rests.

4. The Search for the Foundation of Economic Knowledge

The basic postulates of modern physics and chemistry are concerned with entities so far removed from daily experience that long chains of reasoning, mostly of a highly mathematical character, are involved in linking the postulates with observable phenomena that can substantiate or refute them. The postulates of economics are concerned with human ends and choices of means, and with technological and physiological possibilities for production and consumption. As pointed out already, these are matters in which each of us has some opportunities for rather direct observation. It was undoubtedly considerations of this order that led Lionel Robbins, in his classical *Essay on the Nature and Significance of Economic Science,* to attach a quality of almost immediate obviousness to the postulates of economic theory. The following passage, which was introduced into the second edition of the essay, seems so well to summarize his thought that we shall reproduce it almost in full.[8]

The propositions of economic theory, like all scientific theory, are obviously deductions from a series of postulates. And the chief of these postulates are all assumptions involving in some way simple and indisputable facts of experience relating to the way in which the scarcity of goods which is the subject-matter of our science actually shows itself in the world of reality. The main postulate of the theory of value is the fact that individuals can arrange their preferences in an order, and in fact do so. The main postulate of the theory of production is the fact that there are more than one factor of production. The main postulate of the theory of dynamics is the fact that we are not certain regarding future scarcities. These are not postulates the existence of whose counterpart in reality admits of extensive dispute once their nature is fully realized. We do not need controlled experiments to establish their validity: they are so much the stuff of our everyday experience that they have only to be stated to be recognised as obvious. Indeed, the danger is that they may be thought to be so obvious that nothing significant can be derived from their further examination. Yet in fact it is on postulates of this sort that the complicated theorems of advanced analysis ultimately depend. And it is from the existence of the conditions they assume that the general applicability of the broader propositions of economic science is derived.

Now of course it is true, as we have already seen, that the development of the more complicated applications of these propositions involves the use of a great multitude of subsidiary postulates regarding the condition of markets, the number of parties to the exchange, the state of the law, the *minimum sensibile* of buyers and sellers, and so on and so forth. . . . But while it is important to realise how

---

[8] Lionel Robbins, *An Essay on the Nature and Significance of Economic Science,* Macmillan & Company, Ltd., London, 1935 (2d ed.), pp. 78–80 of the reprinting of 1946.

many are the subsidiary assumptions which necessarily arise as our theory becomes more and more complicated, it is equally important to realise how widely applicable are the main assumptions on which it rests. As we have seen, the chief of them are applicable whenever and wherever the conditions which give rise to economic phenomena are present.

Thus reassured about the validity of their premises, economists have constructed on them an impressive body of theory. The intellectual prestige of this theory is enhanced by the fact, referred to in the above quotation from Hicks, that so much is derived from so little. Nevertheless, the beauty and persuasiveness of Professor Robbin's prose do not quite overcome a certain statesmanlike vagueness in the description of the postulates, a vagueness which lingers on in those passages [9] in which the postulates are discussed at greater length. As many economists have pointed out in various instances, the attempt to spell out literally and in detail the basic postulates of economic theory soon reveals limitations to their obviousness.

To illustrate this point let us consider for a moment the postulate that each consumer has a complete preference ordering of all commodity bundles the consumption of which is possible to him, and compare it with our direct knowledge of consumption decisions. In one interpretation, the postulate is applied to explain consumption levels adopted in response to given circumstances, where these levels are maintained for as long as the determining circumstances remain the same. We note immediately that this interpretation denies the consumer such privileges as the joy in random variability in consumption, as well as its opposite, the comfort of consumption habits somewhat rigidly maintained under varying circumstances. In another interpretation, in which the choice to be explained is that of a consumption program extending over a sequence of time periods in response to an anticipated sequence of circumstances, the postulate by holding him to that program if the circumstances materialize as anticipated denies him the opportunity to learn about his own preferences by experience. It thus ignores his willingness to forego some immediate satisfaction if he can thereby postpone some decisions about consumption in a more distant future until more learning has taken place. Finally, in either interpretation, the postulate denies him the noble urge to respond with sacrifices to the distress of others, as well as the less highly regarded gratification in levels or conspicuous forms of consumption outdoing those of others. Nevertheless, almost every consumer values these privileges, and regards them as part of his normal experience and motivation.

Similar "realistic" objections have so frequently been made with regard to the two postulates of entrepreneurial behavior known as "profit maximization" and "perfect competition," that they need not be repeated here. Milton Friedman has attempted to meet such objections with an argument diametrically opposite to that of Robbins. In his view, the question of the

9 *Ibid.*, pp. 75–78.

"realism" of the premises of economic analysis is irrevelant to its validity, and preoccupation with that question at times definitely harmful:

> The difficulty in the social sciences of getting new evidence for this class of phenomena [i.e., which the hypotheses (or postulates) are designed to explain, T.C.K.] and of judging its conformity with the implications of the hypothesis makes it tempting to suppose that other, more readily available, evidence is equally relevant to the validity of the hypothesis—to suppose that hypotheses have not only "implications" but also "assumptions" and that the conformity of these "assumptions" to "reality" is a test of the validity of the hypothesis *different from* or *additional to* the test by implications. This widely held view is fundamentally wrong and productive of much mischief. Far from providing an easier means for sifting valid from invalid hypotheses, it only confuses the issue, promotes misunderstanding about the significance of empirical evidence for economic theory, produces a misdirection of much intellectual effort devoted to the development of positive economics, and impedes the attainment of consensus on tentative hypotheses in positive economics.[10]

Since any statement is implied by itself, one could interpret Professor Friedman's position to mean that the validity or usefulness of any set of postulates depends on observations that confirm or at least fail to contradict (although they could have) *all* their implications, immediate and derived. This entirely acceptable view would circumscribe and qualify Robbin's belief in the obviousness of the postulates, by requiring that not only the postulates themselves, but also their derived implications meet the test of observation. Such an interpretation receives further support from Friedman's remark [11] that, in many systems of related propositions, one has a certain freedom of choice as to which statements one wishes to regard as premises, and which ones as derived implications. It also seems to be supported by the following quotation:

> To put this point less paradoxically, the relevant question to ask about the "assumptions" of a theory is not whether they are descriptively "realistic," for they never are, but whether they are sufficiently good approximations for the purpose in hand. And this question can be answered only by seeing whether the theory works, which means whether it yields sufficiently accurate predictions. The two supposedly independent tests [i.e., through the realism of the assumptions and through their derived implications, T.C.K.] thus reduce to one test.[12]

But this interpretation of Friedman's position does not seem to lead to the extreme inferences he draws from it in the next paragraph:

> The theory of monopolistic and imperfect competition is one example of the neglect in economic theory of these propositions. The development of this analysis was explicitly motivated, and its wide acceptance and approval largely explained, by the belief that the assumptions of "perfect competition" or "perfect monopoly"

[10] Milton Friedman, "The Methodology of Positive Economics," in *Essays in Positive Economics*, University of Chicago Press, Chicago, 1953, pp. 1–43. [Reprinted in this volume, pp. 508–528. The quotation is from p. 516 in this volume.]

[11] *Ibid.*, p. 526.

[12] *Ibid.*, p. 517.

said to underlie neoclassical economic theory are a false image of reality. And this belief was itself based almost entirely on the directly perceived descriptive inaccuracy of the assumptions rather than on any recognized contradiction of predictions derived from neoclassical economic theory. The lengthy discussion on marginal analysis in the *American Economic Review* some years ago is an even clearer, though much less important example. . . .

Here the "direct" implications of the postulates, their accuracy in describing directly observed individual behavior, are placed in a category with which we need to be less concerned.

There are several objections to such a concept of theory construction. In the first place, in order that we shall have a refutable theory at all, the postulates then need to be supplemented by a clear description of the class of implications by which the theory stands or falls. Otherwise, every contradiction between an implication and an observation could be met by reclassifying the implication as a "direct" one.

This objection is met by Friedman's suggestion that there should in each case be "rules for using the model," that is, a specification of the "class of phenomena the hypothesis is designed to explain." But a second objection arises out of this answer to the first. To state a set of postulates, and then to exempt a subclass of their implications from verification is a curiously roundabout way of specifying the content of a theory that is regarded as open to empirical refutation. It leaves one without an understanding of the reasons for the exemptions. The impression of ingeniousness that this procedure gives is reinforced by the fact that in each of Professor Friedman's examples he knows more about the phenomenon in question than he lets on in his suggested postulates. He is willing to predict the expert billiard player's shots from the hypothesis that the player knows the mathematical formulae of mechanics and computes their application to each situation with lightning speed, even though he (Friedman) knows that most experts at billiards do not have these abilities. He is willing to predict the distribution of leaves on a tree from the hypothesis that each leaf seeks a position of maximum exposure to sunlight (given the positions of all other leaves), although no one has reported observing a leaf change its location on a tree.

One cannot help but feel uneasy in the face of so much ingenuity. Truth, like peace, is indivisible. It cannot be compartmentalized. Before we can accept the view that obvious discrepancies between behavior postulates and directly observed behavior do not affect the predictive power of specified implications of the postulates, we need to understand the reasons why these discrepancies do not matter. This is all the more important in a field such as economics where, as Friedman also emphasizes, the opportunities for verification of the predictions and implications derived from the postulates are scarce and the outcome of such verification often remains somewhat uncertain. The difficulties of verification seem in large part due to the virtual impossibility of experiments under conditions approaching those of real life, and to the presence of many factors simultaneously influencing actual economic developments. In such a situation, we have to exploit all the evidence we can secure, direct and indirect. If, in comparison with some other sciences, economics is handicapped by severe and possibly unsurmountable obstacles to meaningful experimentation, the opportunities for direct introspection by, and direct observation of, individual decision makers are a much needed source of evidence which in some degree offsets the handicap. We cannot really feel confident in acting upon our economic knowledge until its deductions reconcile directly observed patterns of individual behavior with such implications for the economy as a whole as we find ourselves able to subject to test.

Friedman himself indicates an important step in this direction when he points out,[13] in parallel with Alchian,[14] that the postulate of profit-maximizing behavior by entrepreneurs is supported by the fact that those who do not manage to maximize profits are likely to be eliminated by competition in the course of time. Here a postulate about individual behavior is made more plausible by reference to the adverse effect of, and hence penalty for, departures from the postulated behavior. The reality of the penalty is documented by technological and institutional facts, such as the reproducibility of production processes and the operation of accounting procedures and bankruptcy laws, facts which are a degree less elusive to verification than mere behavior postulates. But if this is the basis for our belief in profit maximization, then we should postulate that basis itself and not the profit maximization which it implies in certain circumstances. We should then postulate that entrepreneurial policies unsuitable for economic survival are applied by only a minority of enterprises which exhibit a high rate of economic mortality.

Such a change in the basis of economic analysis would seem to represent a gain in realism attributable to a concern with the directly perceived descriptive accuracy of the postulates. It would lead us to expect profit maximization to be most clearly exhibited in industries where entry is easiest and where the struggle for survival is keenest, and would present us with the further challenge to analyze what circumstances give to an industry that character. It would also prevent us, for purposes of explanatory theory, from getting bogged down in those refinements of profit maximization theory which endow the decision makers with analytical and computational abilities and assume them to have information-gathering opportunities such as are unlikely to exist or be applied in current practice.[15] It seems that nothing is lost, and much may be gained, in thus broadening the postulational basis of economic theory.

Let us sum up the puzzle. After more than a century of intensive activity

---

[13] *Ibid.*, p. 522.

[14] Armen A. Alchian, "Uncertainty, Evolution and Economic Theory," *Journal of Political Economy,* vol. 57, June 1950, pp. 211–221.

[15] For an exploratory discussion of limitations to the decision-making process, see Herbert A. Simon, "A Behavioral Model of Rational Choice," *Quarterly Journal of Economics,* vol. 69, February 1955, pp. 99–118.

in scientific economics, two economists who have made outstanding substantive contributions to our science, and whose positions on questions of
economic policy are moreover not far apart, seek the ultimate basis of
economic knowledge in considerations which (a) contradict each other and
(b) are each subject to strong objections. One is led to conclude that economics as a scientific discipline is still somewhat hanging in the air.

There is no harm in this admission. The positions which our two
authors so strongly (but contradictorily) embrace have in common that,
in so far as either is adopted, its effect is a conservative one. This word is
used in a scientific, not a political sense (although scientific conservatism
may also have politically conservative effects). Whether the postulates are
placed beyond doubt, or whether doubts concerning their realism are sup-
pressed by the assertion that verification can and should be confined to the
hard-to-unravel more distant effects—in either case the argument surrounds
and shields received economic theory with an appearance of invulnerability
which is neither fully justified nor at all needed. The theories that have
become dear to us can very well stand by themselves as an impressive and
highly valuable system of deductive thought, erected on a few premises
that seem to be well-chosen first approximations to a complicated reality.
They exhibit in a striking manner the power of deductive reasoning in
drawing conclusions which, to the extent one accepts their premises, are
highly relevant to questions of economic policy. In many cases the knowledge these deductions yield is the best we have, either because better approximations have not been secured at the level of the premises, or because
comparable reasoning from premises recognized as more realistic has not
been completed or has not yet been found possible. Is any stronger defense
needed, or even desirable?

5. Economic Theory as a Sequence of Models

We have thus been led to the realization that neither are the postulates
of economic theory entirely self-evident, nor are the implications of various
sets of postulates readily tested by observation. In this situation, it is desirable that we arrange and record our logical deductions in such a manner
that any particular conclusion or observationally refutable implication can
be traced to the postulates on which it rests. This will help in designing and
collecting observations of greatest discriminating power with respect to
those postulates regarded as least established. It will also help us keep in
mind, in sifting or evaluating policy recommendations, on what body of
experience supporting specific combinations of postulates each recommendation rests. Considerations of this order suggests that we look upon economic theory as a sequence of conceptional *models* that seek to express in
simplified form different aspects of an always more complicated reality. At
first these aspects are formalized as much as feasible in isolation, then in

combinations of increasing realism. Each model is defined by a set of postulates, of which the implications are developed to the extent deemed worthwhile in relation to the aspects of reality expressed by the postulates. The
study of the simpler models is protected from the reproach of unreality by
the consideration that these models may be prototypes of more realistic,
but also more complicated, subsequent models. The card file of successfully
completed pieces of reasoning represented by these models can then be
looked upon as the logical core of economics, as the depository of available
economic theory.

It may appear at first sight as if we are here advocating the very compartmentalization of truth which we have rejected in the preceding section.
But in the present section we are not concerned with empirical truth, with
the verification of theories. We are concerned with the prior question of
their logical truth and clarity, with the correct tracing of the implications
of given postulates, and with the efficient arranging and recording of the
conditional, tautological but useful, truths so found. What is not permissible
in verification—the intentional ignoring of obviously important aspects of
reality—is indispensable for the gradual unfolding of a body of logically
valid implications of economically relevant (but not necessarily by themselves valid) postulates.

It is by adopting this concept of economic theory that we can resolve
the apparent conflict between rigor and realism noted at the end of the
first essay of this volume. Perception of additional aspects of reality must
necessarily precede their recognition in model formulation. Hence realism
will always be ahead of rigor in the gradual extension of the range of
economic knowledge. But unless rigor follows along to consolidate the gains
in realism, we shall not know which conclusions or recommendations depend on which postulates, and which postulates depend for their validity on
which verifications of their implications by accumulated experience.

The ideas here advocated are in no way a new proposal, or a new conception of the substance of economic theory. Most economists when pressed
will agree to one formulation or another of such a view of the logical
structure of economic knowledge, and of the incomplete but progressing
state of verification of this knowledge. It is in the practice of our professional activities that we do not live up to it. Often we are more preoccupied
with arriving at what we deem to be true statements or best predictions, in
the light of such knowledge as we have of the phenomena in question, than
in exhibiting the postulational basis, and thereby the ultimate observational
evidence, on which our statements rest. Undoubtedly, this is the right preoccupation in those situations in which an urgently needed policy recommendation, backed mainly by the feeling of confidence in it held by experienced advisers, is the main objective of the professional activity. However, for the purpose of the cumulative process of building knowledge that
is transferable to other minds and open to general scientific scrutiny, more
precautions are required. Undoubtedly progress in economics is slowed

down by the inextricable intermingling of facts and reasoning found so often in published writings, and even more frequently in verbal professional discussion. We can best keep track of the foundation for each statement, and of the degree of assurance with which it can be held, if facts are recognized at the beginning of each piece of analysis by explicitly formulated postulates, and where appropriate at the end by confrontation of conclusions or predictions with additional observations, but are not permitted to enter through a side door when the reasoning proper is in progress. . . .

As long as economic theory is regarded as concerned with economic reality in general, and is built up by absorbing bits of observation as the need arises, a tendency results to overestimate the scope of the conclusions. Results correctly reached for two or three models in succession may grow into beliefs about the world instead of theorems resting on postulates that express certain traits of the world, and of which some implications have not been refuted by observation. Perhaps the outstanding example is the overextended belief of the liberalist school of economic thought in the efficiency of competitive markets as a means of allocating resources in a world full of uncertainty.[16] To my knowledge no formal model of resource allocation through competitive markets has been developed, which recognizes ignorance about all decision makers' future actions, preferences, or states of technological information as the main source of uncertainty confronting each individual decision maker, and which at the same time acknowledges the fact that forward markets on which anticipations and intentions could be tested and adjusted do not exist in sufficient variety and with a sufficient span of foresight to make presently developed theory regarding the efficiency of competitive markets applicable. If this judgment is correct, our economic knowledge has not yet been carried to the point where it sheds much light on the core problem of the economic organization of society: the problem of how to face and deal with uncertainty. In particular, the economics profession is not ready to speak with anything approaching scientific authority on the economic aspects of the issue of individual versus collective enterprise which divides mankind in our time. Meanwhile, the best safeguard against overestimation of the range of applicability of economic propositions is a careful spelling out of the

16 This overextension is strikingly illustrated by the proposal, advanced by F. A. von Hayek in two articles in *The Banker* of September and October 1939, suggesting that the allocation of resources to the British war efforts in World War II be arranged for preponderantly through price incentives. The first article, concerned with the allocation of materials, is almost convincing. The second article, dealing with the allocation of capital through an appropriate rate of interest is much less so. There is no discussion of the difficulties of appraising the return on a particular capital investment arising from uncertainties about the future course of war and about future relative demands for the various means with which it is to be fought. It is not clear whether these risks can at all, and if so should in Professor Hayek's view, be shifted to private firms through a price system. A third article, announced as to be concerned with problems of equity and of government finance, was never published.

premises on which they rest. Precision and rigor in the statement of premises and proofs can be expected to have a sobering effect on our beliefs about the reach of the propositions we have developed.

If overestimation of the range of validity of economic propositions is the Scylla of "informal" economic reasoning, a correct appraisal of the limited reach of existing economic theory may cause us to swerve into the Charybdis of disillusionment with economic theory as a road to useful knowledge. The temptation to identify the results of existing economic theory with economic theory as such—and to disqualify both in one breath —is strongest for the experienced economic adviser to government or business, to whom the limitations of existing theory are most painfully apparent. One can hear such feelings reverberate in statements made at professional meetings by outstanding leaders of the economic profession, who in their younger days made important contributions to economic theory. If the concept, here advocated, of economic theory as a sequence of models is more widely accepted, however, dissatisfaction with the relevance of available models will provide the necessary stimulus for cumulative refinement of models to take into account more and more relevant aspects of reality.

[31] The Impact on Political Science of the Revolution in the Behavioral Sciences

DAVID B. TRUMAN

Some time ago, in the course of a conversation with a social psychologist whose friendship and counsel I value highly, I mentioned my assignment to discuss with you tonight "The Impact on Political Science of the Revolution in the Behavioral Sciences" and confessed to him some misgivings about the assumptions implied by the title. "Has there been any impact?" I asked. His reply was, "Has there been any revolution?" The more I have thought about this lecture, the more persistently this conversation has come to mind, until I have concluded that these are not, in fact, flippant questions and that I was obliged to give them a central place in this discussion, even though they may not be adequately answered, or even answerable. What is

Reprinted from *Research Frontiers in Politics and Government,* Brookings Lectures, 1955, pp. 202–231, with permission of the Brookings Institution.

the nature of this alleged revolution? What kinds of effects has it had, if any, on the work of political scientists and, since many critics, in the discipline as well as outside of it, assume that these should be or will be considerable, what are the major intellectual obstacles to such impact? Are there limits, as distinguished from resistances, to the application to political science of developments in the behavioral sciences? What is the nature of these limits?

The term "behavioral sciences" is one of recent currency, and its variable meanings may, without a word or two of explanation, cause some confusion. It is sometimes used as an equivalent for the social sciences, a loose usage that is probably inevitable as long as the term is fashionable and is thought to provide a key to foundation cash boxes. More narrowly, and perhaps more accuately, the phrase refers to those bodies of knowledge, in whatever academic department they may be found, that provide or aspire to provide "verified principles" of human behavior through the use of methods of inquiry similar to those of the natural sciences. In conventional university organization, such knowledge and such aspirations may be found in a variety of places, from schools of public health to departments of linguistics, but their incidence is normally greatest in departments of psychology, sociology, and anthropology, and the term most commonly serves as a shorthand expression for the concerns typical of these three fields. This restricted meaning is the one that I shall use.

Developments in the Behavioral Sciences

Whether or not they merit glorifying by the word "revolution," the developments in the behavioral sciences in the past three decades have been numerous and impressive. These I can no more than characterize and illustrate; cataloguing and sifting the tremendous volume of work during this period is a task for which I have neither the time nor the required capacities. If, however, one were to start from an intellectual event such as the publication of the *Encyclopaedia of the Social Sciences,* the first volume of which appeared nearly a quarter of a century ago, and were to reflect on the alterations that a competent board of editors would feel called upon to make in a new edition, he would, I suspect be impressed not only with the general rate of obsolescence in the area during these twenty-five years but even more with the shift in the center of gravity within the social sciences toward the behavioral sciences.

For present purposes it is appropriate to examine these developments under two headings: developments in the realm of research technique and those in the realm of expanded theory and verified propositions. The first of these is, significantly, far easier and less treacherous to evaluate than the second, partly because development of the tools of data collection and analysis has been rapid and unmistakable.

IN RESEARCH TECHNIQUE

The techniques of the sample survey can claim a place at the top of any list of such developments, not only because they constitute a basic instrument of social research in their own right, but also because their refinement has stimulated a series of achievements, primarily in the invention of ancillary techniques but also to some extent in the construction of explanatory theory. The roots of this technique are fairly old, indeed ancient if one traces them back to the unsystematic efforts of politicians and journalists to estimate the intentions of a mass electorate. The core of the skill, however, is the design and administration of the population sample, and this is comparatively modern. Stimulated by the commercial utility of even fairly crude estimates of intentions and susceptibilities of consumers, rudimentary techniques of population sampling became a commonplace device in the business world by the 1920's. The potentialities of population sampling for non-commercial, social, and political research, however, were not widely recognized until the 1930's. Partly as a means of promoting the acceptance of these techniques in market analysis and partly as an opportunity for testing them against the official results of elections, polling of samples of prospective voters developed in the middle of the 1930's. What began as a by-product extended into fairly continuous surveys of popular opinion on various issues of the day, until "Gallup poll" became a generic term familiar over the globe.

In the United States at the same time those responsible for developing and administering many of the emergency programs undertaken in depression and war by the federal government needed new kinds of population statistics. A gradual recognition that sample studies may hold advantages in speed, efficiency, and cost over a complete enumeration led the Bureau of the Census and other governmental agencies, building on established theories of sampling and on experience in such fields as the estimating of crop yields, to make rapid improvements in the reliability of population samples. The rapidity of this development is suggested by the fact that the case book, *Methods in Social Science*,[1] published in 1933, contains no analysis of a study involving the direct sampling of individuals in a population. The *Encyclopaedia of the Social Sciences* contains no article on sampling, and, although the essays on statistics and on probability refer to sampling in biometrics, economics, and crop estimating and comment briefly on samples drawn from registration records and from complete enumerations, they contain no discussion of samples drawn directly from the human population. Both the state of the art and the character of existing obstacles are suggested in the following comment in the essay on "statistical practice" in the *Encyclopaedia of the Social Sciences:* "It is so difficult to insure repre-

---

[1] Stuart Rice (ed.), *Methods in Social Science* (1933).

sentativeness of the sample that in most inquiries relative to population complete enumeration is preferred." [2]

"Representativeness" was a problem in practical sampling rather than in general theory. Experience with the quota sample, on which opinion surveyors relied in the 1930's, and the development of probability sampling by the Bureau of the Census and the Bureau of Agricultural Economics in the early 1940's reduced this problem to manageable proportions.

Paralleling and, in part, flowing from the growth of skill in sampling, a number of techniques, both for the collection and for the analysis of data have been invented or significantly improved. Thus as the crudity of samples has been reduced, attention has been turned to the inadequacies in interviewing. The sources of unreliability have been explored and their bearing on the validity of results has been examined in systematic fashion, so that the dangers in this phase have been identified even though the means of controlling them have not been fully provided.[3]

At the same time, criticism and experimentation have contributed materially to increasing sophistication in the design of survey questions and questionnaires and in the substantive aspects of interviews generally. Drawing on and adapting experience in counseling and psychotherapy, the design and administration of questions have come a long way from the intuitive, rather hit-or-miss techniques used in early opinion and community surveys. The merits of the open-ended question as compared with the fixed-alternative or "poll-type" question and of the focused or "depth" interview have been explored and developed to the point where the investigator's range of choice among interviewing tools has markedly widened.[4]

The process of adaptation just referred to is one of considerable significance for the topic under discussion and is therefore deserving of some emphasis for its own sake. It is one, perhaps the major, example of a strong tendency on the part of the sample survey technicians and of others engaged in the collection of data from large numbers of people. Where devices for the study of individual psychological characteristics and behaviors, whether diagnostic or purely analytical, have been developed satisfactorily, and where they have appeared adaptable without major losses in efficiency to the study of large numbers of cases, as in the sample survey, adaptation has occurred rather quickly. One effect of this has been to reinforce preoccupation with the attitudes and behaviors of individuals. It has emphasized, almost to the point of excluding other sorts of objectives, preoccupation with arriving at what might be called the "people-who" type of statement, that is, people who reveal a certain psychological characteristic tend to perceive, understand, speak, or behave in such-and-such fashion. Propositions of

---

2 Robert M. Woodbury, "Statistics: Statistical Practice," *Encyclopaedia of the Social Sciences*, XIV.

3 Herbert Hyman, *Interviewing in Social Research* (1954).

4 *Cf.* C. R. Rogers, *Counseling and Psychotherapy* (1942) and Robert K. Merton, *The Focused Interview* (1955).

this sort, of course, are not without value in many situations, but, for reasons that I shall attempt to explore in more detail somewhat later, they may have only limited significance for the problems with which the political scientist is characteristically concerned.[5]

In slightly different fashion the maturing of sample-survey methods has been stimulated by and has contributed to advances in techniques of measurement, notably the analysis of attitudes through the use of scales. The early work of Bogardus, Thurstone, and Likert was largely independent of the techniques of the sample survey. As the later devices have begun, however, to produce data of greater reliability, warranting the use of more precise techniques of analysis than the early polls justified and inviting more complicated sorts of inferences than they could support, the two research tendencies have come together. Significant steps have been taken, notably in the work of Guttman, Lazarsfeld, and others, to adapt and extend the earlier measurement devices, thereby stimulating significantly more penetrating analysis of survey data.[6] Similarly, the survey device has been extended to approximate some of the power and efficiency of experimentation through the use of the so-called panel technique. By successive re-interviews of a population sample—the panel—it is possible to get at changes, and at some of the causes of changes, in attitudes and behavior.

The past two decades have also seen a considerable development and extension of experimentation, both in the controlled laboratory setting and in the natural situation. This has taken various forms. Among them are the numerous techniques for observing, recording, and analyzing behavior in small groups which, especially since the work of Elton Mayo and Kurt Lewin, have become the identifying equipment for specialists in the new "field" of group dynamics. Among these, reference should also be made to the techniques collectively known as sociometry, devised by J. L. Moreno for the analysis of interaction and influence structure in small groups. These and related developments, whether employed in the laboratory or in the "field," not only have contributed a considerable body of information on face-to-face groups of various sorts but also have provided stimulus to greater sophistication in observational field work generally.[7]

Finally, it may be appropriate to mention the elaboration and expansion of the techniques for analyzing communications content. Although their

---

[5] *Cf.* Edward A. Shils, "Authoritarianism: Right and Left," in Richard Christie and Marie Jahoda (eds.), *Studies in the Scope and Method of "The Authoritarian Personality"* (1954), pp. 24–49 and David B. Truman, "Political Behavior and International Politics," *World Politics,* III (July 1951), 545–54.

[6] See Samuel A. Stouffer and others, *Measurement and Prediction,* Studies in Social Psychology in World War II, Vol. IV (1950) and M. W. Riley, J. W. Riley, and J. Toby, *Scale Analysis* (1955).

[7] See J. L. Moreno, *Who Shall Survive?* (1934) and Helen H. Jennings, *Leadership and Isolation* (1943). See generally Marie Jahoda, Morton Deutsch, and Stuart W. Cook, *Research Methods in Social Relations* (1951); see also G. C. Homans, *The Human Group* (1950) and Dorwin Cartwright and Alvin Zander (eds.), *Group Dynamics: Research and Theory* (1953).

beginnings run back considerably more than twenty-five years, the skills of the content analyst, especially with respect to the devices for systematic classification and for quantitative analysis, have received a marked degree of extension and refinement within the past two decades.[8]

This cursory and necessarily superficial glance at some recent developments in the behavioral sciences is sufficient at least to suggest that within the realm of technique it is reasonable to speak of major developments. One may legitimately think of this as a technological revolution, even if one concludes that, unlike other such changes, its consequences are limited.

IN THEORY

When one turns to the realm of theory, especially theory resting on some measure of empirical verification, the task of evaluation becomes considerably more formidable. Not only are theories in the behavioral sciences numerous, but the possible implications of these formulations for the work of the political scientist have scarcely been explored. Any comment on this point, therefore, is likely to be superficial and subject to serious challenge.

At the risk of indulging in severe oversimplification, I should like to venture the observation that in the realm of theory the behavioral sciences have produced two quite different bodies of propositions, one rather narrowly concerned with individual behavior or with action in small, face-to-face groups and the other aimed at an inclusive explanation of a wide range of action not specifically relevant to any particular institutional context. Although it is doubtful that in either of these there is much in the way of revolutionary content, both have some value for the student of political processes and institutions. At the same time, however, neither more than approaches a solution to the most troublesome problems in such study. The difficulty of estimating the existing or the probable impact of behavioral science theory on political science lies precisely in the gap between these two statements. Behavioral science theory has implications of value to the student of politics, but it goes no more than part of the way toward the solution of his intellectual problems.

So sweeping a characterization cannot, certainly within the limits of a single lecture, be proved, but it clearly calls at least for illustration and for argument. I should assert that a sizable fraction of behavioral science theory, whether in psychology, sociology, or anthropology, is non-institutional. That is, it is principally concerned with explaining the effects of a given institutional pattern on the behavior of an individual or an aggregate of individuals and not with explaining or even describing the operation of the institution itself. Thus, of course, all or almost all of psychology is individual. The preoccupations of psychology are with categories and processes

8 The best review of this technique is Bernard Berelson, *Content Analysis in Communications Research* (1952).

of individual behavior—learning, conditioning, motivation, perception, discrimination, and so on. Again, despite the existence of competing doctrines, a major preoccupation remains the characteristics and development of individual personality under the influence of physiological and, more recently, social factors.

The growth of social psychology has increased the number and kinds of factors considered in the whole gamut of psychological analysis, but it has not changed the emphasis. Concerned with the behavior of men in groups, the social psychologist is nevertheless characteristically interested in the effects of group environments on the behavior of individuals, in the individual psychology of interpersonal influence.[9]

For understandable reasons the environments most closely studied by the social psychologist have been those of small, face-to-face groups, whether in experimental or natural situations—family, club, classroom, gang, clique, and neighborhood. These groupings are more amenable to the requirements of scientific procedure than are more inclusive formations. It seems probable, moreover, that, if one is concerned principally with effects on individual behavior, such groups are primary, in the sense of degree of importance, and therefore peculiarly basic to the discipline.

Not all concerns with the small group have been exclusively psychological, of course. As the curiosities and theories of the investigator become more characteristically sociological, they are less concerned with effects on individuals than with the structure of groups and with the effects on group performance resulting from differences in intra-group communication, from variations in the performance of specialized roles within the group, and from variations in the tasks undertaken by it.

This borderland of psychology, sociology, and anthropology, which has come to be known commonly as group dynamics, has produced a respectable body of theory, both basic and applied, notably on the subject of leadership.[10] Its preoccupations, however, are only slightly less microcosmic than those of the psychologist and are only slightly less non-institutional. Much of this same point was made by Herbert Simon in his lecture in this series, and some of the non-political scientists working in the area, particularly those whose investigations have been conducted in the "field" rather than in the laboratory, have become aware of it. As one of the "field" researchers has put it, ". . . we simply cannot extrapolate conclusions from the small group studies when we are dealing with groups in large organizations."[11] Or, in the words of a theorist and practitioner in applied

[9] Note that the impressive psychological evidence regarding the consequences of segregation which was accepted by the U. S. Supreme Court (*Brown* v. *Topeka*, 347 U.S. 497, 1954) referred primarily and most directly to its effects upon individuals. See Kenneth B. Clark, "Desegregation: An Appraisal of the Evidence," *Journal of Social Issues*, IX, No. 4 (1953).

[10] For example, see Cartwright and Zander, *op. cit.*, Homans, *op. cit.*, and Harold S. Guetzkow (ed.), *Groups, Leadership, and Men* (1951).

[11] W. F. Whyte, "Small Groups and Large Organizations," in J. H. Rohrer and M. Sherif (eds.), *Social Psychology at the Crossroads* (1951), p. 297.

anthropology, "The evidence . . . seems to indicate that building theory upon research concentration on the small group may be mistaken, however experimentally justifiable as an object of research the small group may be. The individual behavior that psychology seeks to explain seems to be less a property of groups or the group in particular than one of the processes of social interaction in general, inclusive of both large and small groups." [12] If, as he goes on to argue, changes in basic social relationships, in individual and collective attitudes, and in individual behavior tend to occur *in that order,* then a theory that starts from the latter end of the sequence has limited utility for the student of larger institutional complexes, and its limited uses, as I shall point out somewhat later, involve serious hazards.

Although the sociological and anthropological concern with small groups, which considerably antedates the more psychologically oriented research in group dynamics, has been more likely to place the group in a larger institutional context and to investigate changes stemming from such contexts, its focus has remained the small unit. The broadest reach in empirical terms within these fields, moreover, has been the small city or community, although perhaps exception should be made of some kinds of broad, aggregative research concerned with social class and demography. The formulation of theory of a more inclusive sweep has not been, strictly speaking, the objective or the product of the efforts of the behavioral scientist. That function has been left to the more historically and philosophically inclined sociologist or anthropologist, concerned with reflections about the state of society, in the tradition of Max Weber and Mannheim, or to speculative synthesizing like that of Talcott Parsons.

By way of preliminary summary, the developments in the behavioral sciences over the past quarter century, thus cursorily and perhaps somewhat unfairly reviewed, appear a good deal more revolutionary in the realm of technique than in that of validated and expanded theory. Both the characteristic techniques, moreover, and the tested propositions, of which the number is considerable, typically have been microcosmic. Both have concentrated on the individual or on the restricted group to the virtual exclusion of larger organizations and more inclusive institutions.

Though this concentration has occurred, one should not assume that in either respect the behavioral sciences have no relevance for the political scientist. But it should not be astonishing that their area of greatest impact to date has been in connection with the study of voting behavior, the most individualized, in a sense most uncomplicated, and perhaps least important element in the political process. The theory that has emerged, largely through the use of the sample survey technique, is exclusively a social psychological theory of electoral choice, with only the barest suggestions of implications for other features of the electoral or political process.

12 C. M. Arensberg, "Behavior and Organization: Industrial Studies," *ibid.*, p. 324.

A further word should be said, however, concerning theoretical developments in behavioral science. Whatever the limits on its scope and on its applicability to the problems of the political scientist, theory in the behavioral sciences has become far more completely fused with empirical research and theorizing has become more self-consciously central to the concerns of investigators than was the case shortly after World War I. One has the distinct impression that the volume of taxonomic description of concrete phenomena has declined and that there has occurred an increased and general commitment to the discovery of uniformities, to the use of observation for the verification of hypotheses, and to the search for empirically supported generalizations.

The traces of this can be seen in several areas not far from the concerns of the political scientist. As Herbert Simon has pointed out in his lecture, significant beginnings have been made on an organizational theory, although it cannot yet help us much in dealing with large and complicated structures. From various sources in the behavioral sciences the suggestive concept of role has been developed, through which a number of significant propositions of potentially broad relevance have been formulated. Some preliminary elements of a theory of communications are beginning to appear. Along somewhat different lines, there has been an increasing interest in the creation and exploitation of formal models, of which the theory of games, discussed in Richard Snyder's recent lecture, is a major example. Whatever one may think of the utility of any such models, and in my opinion skepticism is in order, experimenting with them at least represents a serious theoretical preoccupation. Much the same thing may be said of the efforts of Parsons and his associates to develop a general theory of action. This inclusive effort at a high level of abstraction admittedly seems to promise to be valid immediately only for relatively simple features of a social system. Whether or not one shares the implied faith that the treatment of more complex characteristics is almost within reach, one must acknowledge that this effort, along with less ambitious theoretical endeavors, nevertheless represents a considerable degree of ferment—a renewed commitment to theory and to the discovery and statement of behavioral uniformities.

Such ferment, I should like to suggest, such renewed commitment may alone have more significant impact on the work of the political scientist than the content of the theories, the substantive material of the validated propositions, or the innovations in technique, important though these may be.

Conventional Research in Political Science

Turning more directly to the impact side of the topic, it is perhaps appropriate to look for a moment at the character of the traditional research concerns of American political science. These have been decidedly heterogeneous over the field as a whole, from the conventional textual analysis of political philosophy to the latest study of legislative policy making. The most common element in research in political science, one can fairly say, has been institutional description. This does not adequately cover, perhaps, much of the familiar concern with the assessment and prescription of public policy, more than a segment of the historico-legal research in public law, nor more than a minor fraction of the writing of current history, which has given much of political science the quality of heavy-handed periodical journalism. Yet despite this incompleteness, one can safely assert that the description of governmental and para-governmental institutions has been and continues to be our characteristic preoccupation as a profession.

Criticisms of this focus from various standpoints are not new. They can be seen as early as the first years of this century in the writings of Graham Wallas and in the strictures of Arthur F. Bentley. What was known for a time during the 1920's and 1930's as the "Chicago school" of political science, gathered around the stimulating person of the late Charles E. Merriam, represented a fairly explicit revolt against the established tradition. But with the achievements, especially the technical innovations, in recent years in the behavioral sciences—perhaps in part because of their enhanced popular prestige—the volume of such criticism seems to have increased—in books, in papers at annual meetings, in the professional journals, and, perhaps most conspicuously, in the shop-talk of many younger members of the profession.

The latter-day rebels have mostly rallied around the banner of "political behavior" to do battle with the "institutionalists." Like most embattled revolutionists, many of them have unwisely and impetuously consigned to oblivion all the works of their predecessors. This is unfortunate not only because it does injustice and betrays a lack of discrimination, but more seriously because it tends unnecessarily to widen the gulf between the two groups and to obscure the precise points at issue and thereby to postpone the discovery of solutions.

Despite appearances to the contrary, there are basic similarities in the assumptions and objectives, albeit usually implicit, of the "institutionalists" and their opponents. The latter may argue that they alone are committed to the discovery and statement of regularities in the political process. Or they may assert that they alone hold the objective of predictability. Neither of these alleged monopolies is genuine, however. There are some differences along these lines, but one should not forget that to describe a court, a legislature, or a government agency, in however formal terms, is to assume that there is regularity in political processes that can be stated. Likewise, to do any of these things or to analyze a line of court cases or the pronouncements of a legislative committee is usually to assume, although perhaps largely implicitly, the persistence of such patterns under appropriate con-

ditions and to accept the possibility, and even to a degree the responsibility, of prediction.

Nor am I persuaded that the cleavage within political science lies between description and something else, and I note that in assertions of this
sort the "something else" is often vaguely stated or involves a false opposition. For instance, in the report of one of five university surveys in the
behavioral sciences conducted during 1954, the following passage occurs:
"Political Science has been giving increasingly serious attention to the
behavioral approach to political research problems, moving toward the
empirical *investigation of specific propositions* about political behavior at
the same time that it is continuing with the *institutional-descriptive* type of
research." [13] There is surely nothing necessarily non-descriptive or even non-
institutional about a proposition concerning the political process. Virtually
all propositions about political behavior are, and for some time are likely
to remain, descriptive. In fact, the same thing is true of most of the established propositions in the behavioral sciences. Only their most zealous
defender would, I suspect, deny that the dynamic or causal, as distinguished
from the descriptive, element in most of the latter is comparatively small.
The point at which a satistically significant correlation becomes less descriptive and more nearly explanatory is not easily identified.

New Tendencies in Political Science

I have gone into these distinctions, which I believe erroneous, because
I am certain that there are accurate ones to be drawn, genuine differences
in tendency within the field that have become the more marked through the
impact of experiences and inventions in the behavioral sciences. If these
divergences do not lie with broad, if implicit, assumptions about regularity
and predictability or with degrees of concern for description, what are their
bases? I should like to deal briefly with four of these in what seems to me
the order of their importance: first, the difference in the nature of the commitment to discovering regularities; second, differences in the approach to
institutions; third, differences in data; and fourth, differences in technique.

Though both groupings in political science assume the existence and dis-
coverability of regularities in political behavior, for the "institutionalist"
this assumption is usually implicit, a logical inference from his conduct
rather than a consciously asserted objective. A more explicit pursuit of
regularities has several consequences, of which I shall refer to two.

In the first place, the researcher is prepared to find similarities of pattern
between or among formal institutions rather than merely within them. In
other words, he expects to be able to abstract from the concrete phenomena

[13] *Survey of the Behavioral Sciences,* Report of the Faculty Committee and Report of
the Visiting Committee (University of Michigan, 1954), p. 160. Emphasis added.

of institutional behavior and to identify the occurrence of classes or categories of phenomena and, thereby, to be able to generalize over a wider range of concretely divergent or unique situations or relationships. This is an unfamiliar objective only in degree. For example, political scientists, along with other social scientists and laymen as well, have long assumed that certain regularities of behavior and situation are referred to by the term "political leadership," or even just "leadership," whether one is looking at a ward boss, a Speaker of the United States House of Representatives, or a President of the United States. The self-conscious pursuit of this sort of intellectual objective is, of course, not an end in itself, fascinating though it may be, but, like abstract thinking in whatever form, it is a means of simplifying and ordering experience and observation so that the mind is confronted by a finite number of *types* of problems and challenges rather than by a bewilderingly infinite number of these. It is a long step forward in any field to identify such categories.

A more explicit pursuit of regularities, in the second place, is, perhaps somewhat paradoxically, likely to lead to a greater awareness of the variations in the *conditions* under which institutional or other patterns occur and to a search for regularities in those conditions. An un-self-conscious or merely incidental interest in behavioral uniformities produces both a preoccupation with the unique in institutional form and operation and a curious willingness to accept the superficial regularities suggested by a name or nominally prescribed by similar legal arrangements. We would all agree that the operative structure and the socio-political functions constituting two political parties or two legislatures are not necessarily the same even though conventionally they are referred to by the same term or despite the fact that they appear to operate under similar rules or laws. And we would accept the proposition that any one such institution is not necessarily structurally or functionally the same at two points in time although it may bear the same name and although its formal features remain unchanged. Yet characteristically our literature both concedes this point and persists in talking about *the* political party or *the* legislature, avoiding the issue of regularity of pattern either by minute description of a single institution in a limited span of time or by proceeding as if differences in time and space did not exist or were of no real consequence. An explicit dedication to the search for uniformities, characteristic of work in the behavioral sciences, makes either of these alternatives less readily available.

As the preceding remarks suggest, a second difference in the tendencies within the field is in the approach to political institutions, the example of the behavioral sciences encouraging hesitation to take them at their formal or face value, even when the research objective is no more than description. Avoidance of this tendency does not mean merely a skepticism about the descriptive validity of formal arrangements, though this may be in psychological terms a necessary precondition to the effort I refer to. It means, rather, a search for conceptual tools, analytical categories if you will, that are not defined by or equivalent to formal institutional units or subunits. One is not escaping from the restrictive influence of formalities if, in analyzing the policy-forming process, he is obliged to talk in terms of *the* political party or *the* legislature, for in so doing he inescapably begs a portion of the question he is attempting to answer.

What is required in the circumstances is what I like to think of as a "tracer element," or a series of them, through the examination of which one can describe consistent patterns of interaction, including institutional ones and including the relevance for such patterns of the formal features of the institutions. Such was and, in my opinion, is the promise of the notion of group as it was introduced to American political science by Arthur F. Bentley. Although it has had considerable beneficial influence, however, including the early work on legislative voting blocs, it has been so narrowly viewed as a pressure group that it has often merely added another element of formality rather than provided a new means of ordering the data of behavior in and around governmental institutions.

The current search for unconventionalized categories is reflected in a variety of ways in contemporary political science. It accounts, I suspect, for much of the current fascination with the analysis of voting behavior, where the sample survey technique in combination with various socio-psychological categories permits the development of descriptive propositions and even some significant hypotheses concerning the dynamics of the voting choice and the beginnings of some perceptual definitions of institutions such as political parties.[14] It clearly underlies the recent stirrings in the area of the comparative analysis of governments, where it has become apparent to many that conventional formal categories like "executive," "legislature," "political party," and "bureaucracy" are not in fact comparable because they have no consistent meaning independent of political and cultural boundaries, a limitation that is not adequately corrected by the addition of economic and social data to the range of phenomena taken into consideration.[15] It is indicated in Gabriel Almond's suggestive notions concerning specialized structures and functions affecting the formation of foreign policy.[16] Karl Deutsch's interesting attempt to deal with nationalism in terms of a theory of communication [17] and the efforts of Richard C. Snyder and his associates to work out categories for the analysis of decision-making,[18] whatever their ultimate usefulness may prove to be, are significant symptoms of the same sort of striving. Finally, the search in a few bold cases

[14] A. Angus Campbell, Gerald Gurin, and Warren E. Miller, *The Voter Decides* (1954), Chaps. 7 and 11.

[15] Roy Macridis and others, "Research in Comparative Politics," *American Political Science Review*, XLVII (September 1953), 641–75.

[16] Gabriel A. Almond, *The American People and Foreign Policy* (1950).

[17] Karl W. Deutsch, *Nationalism and Social Communication* (1953).

[18] Richard C. Snyder, H. W. Bruck, and Burton Sapin, *Decision-Making as an Approach to the Study of International Politics*, Foreign Policy Analysis Project Series No. 3, Princeton University (June 1954).

has taken the form of an attempt to develop formal models or theories of an explicitly political sort, relating types of processes and relationships not "given" in the conventionalized data into sets of schemes in terms of which political action may be explained and possibly predicted. An example here is the cross-disciplinary theorizing of Robert Dahl and Charles Lindblom, which was partially summarized in the former's lecture in this series.[19]

All of these efforts—and many more would have to be included in an adequately representative list—indicate even in their diversity a common response to the need for concepts and sets of concepts in terms of which governmental processes and structures may be analyzed without the limiting assumptions imposed by conventional institutional categories.

The two divergences from established patterns of political science research so far discussed, namely, the more explicit commitment to regularities and the search for new analytical categories, encourage, though they do not require, the two others—differences in data and differences in techniques. Though many comments would imply that these last two are the more important of the four, a tendency of which I shall have more to say shortly, they seem to me decidedly secondary. In the first place, these tendencies may call for a broadening and enriching of the existing sources of evidence and a shift of emphasis toward the solicited responses of actors on the political scene and toward observing a wide range of activities not recorded in the conventional documentary sources, but they do not necessarily imply a rejection of the testimony stored on library shelves. In the second place, though there is a certain fascination in discovering, for example, the kinds of data that can be plowed up by the sample survey and though new conceptions of data demand appropriate devices for collecting them and generally a greater degree of self-consciousness about techniques, this alone provides no assurance of increased validity. In studies of political behavior there is and will continue to be a trend toward the use of quantification, but there is no magic in numbers unguided by relevant theory and well-articulated hypotheses. Technical developments in the behavioral sciences, perhaps especially skills involved in the conduct and analysis of interviews, are part of the recent stimulus to self criticism in political science, and an awareness of them may distinguish the student of political behavior from his more conventional colleagues, but it is technique in the service of formulated theory whose impact promises to be most significant in the long run.

Limitations on the Application of the Behavioral Sciences

If we can agree on the nature of the developments in the behavioral sciences, here roughly outlined, and on the evidence that these have had

[19] Robert A. Dahl and Charles E. Lindblom, *Politics, Economics and Welfare* (1953).

some impact on the work of political scientists, it is important to emphasize the point that to espouse the extension of the latter tendency is not equivalent to advocating simply the projection or importation of the behavioral sciences into the sphere of political science. Although the general task of both is to develop empirically testable theory and the means of validating it, and although the student of political behavior can learn much from the behavioral scientist, his particular task is peculiar, if not unique. If my earlier analysis of the divergencies within political science is valid, then the two tendencies have more in common substantively than either has with the behavioral sciences, for both are engaged in the effort, each in its own way, to analyze and explain the institutions and processes of government. Whatever new roads to this objective may be laid out, the destination remains the same. Much though we may learn from the experience of the behavioral sciences, the task of adapting that experience to our own needs remains exceedingly difficult, and admiring the neighbor's clearing fells no trees in one's own woodlot.

THE EMPHASIS ON INSTITUTIONS

We are still committed to the study of a particular set of institutions, and this commitment carries with it some implications that may be worth fairly close examination. In the first place, I am not disposed seriously to quarrel with what I understand as the meaning of an observation, in the volume of essays entitled *Toward a General Theory of Action,* in which the authors suggest that:

. . . If the empirical focus of political science is to remain on the phenomena of government, it will not as a discipline be able to attain a sharpness of theoretical focus comparable to that of economics. It is more likely to draw from a much wider range of the components of the general theory of action and to find its distinctiveness in the way it combines these components in relation to its special empirical interests, rather than in the technical elaboration of a narrow and sharply focused segment of the theory of action, as is the case with economics.[20]

A general theory of the sort attempted in that provocative volume necessarily abstracts from the peculiarities of particular institutional complexes, including government, and to attempt to introduce into such a theoretical structure the specialized factors associated with any specific institution is almost certain to involve theorizing efforts as great as those expended on the original. One would not expect to find clear contradictions between a theory of political behavior and an accepted general action theory, but one equally should not expect to derive directly from the latter a set of propositions adequately descriptive of a particular institutional system such as government.

[20] Talcott Parsons and Edward A. Shils (eds.), *Toward a General Theory of Action* (1951), p. 29.

Secondly, as a consequence of the institutional specialization that is inevitably characteristic of political science, it follows that the direct relationship between the behavioral sciences and political science is roughly that between "basic" and "applied" research. Narrowly defined, the objective of the behavioral sciences is the statement of "verified principles" of human behavior, taking account, perhaps, of general types of influencing conditions but without reference to any specific institutional context. The general outlook and even many of the methods of research in political behavior may be, in fact should be, consistent with this sort of objective, but their reference is necessarily to a particular order of institutional arrangements, the governmental. A behavioral scientist may from time to time, as many in fact do, make use of political data and governmental institutions, but his purpose as a behavioral scientist is not to arrive at propositions about government.

The political scientist, on the other hand, can and should make use of accepted hypotheses and promising models developed in the behavioral sciences, but he must always introduce into these the complicating parameters characteristic of the particular institutional complex with which he is concerned. In this sense, even his "basic" research, if he is performing his accepted job, is "applied" research from the standpoint of the behavioral sciences. This is no simple or lowly task; it is, in fact, so difficult, at least at present, that the political scientist can take the models and hypotheses of behavioral science merely as suggestions rather than as guides. The notion that a general science of human behavior can be developed as a source of guiding models for the analysis of behavior in particular contexts is a matter of faith, not of fact. The relationship of behavioral science to political research, therefore, involves no such simple operations as allowing for friction and wind resistance in adapting a physical model to an engineering situation.

There are and will continue to be various levels of research in political science, the more basic abstracting from a greater variety of temporal and spatial particularities, but the continuing institutional focus of political science remains at all levels the defining, and in a sense limiting, factor. This point, it seems to me, is a fundamental one. It is often ignored by behavioral scientists themselves, as when they leap, with irresponsible—one is tempted to say fraudulent—disregard for inconvenient and complicating problems, from a set of observations about child-rearing practices to the most bewilderingly complex concerns of men and nations. I emphasize it, however, not for this reason, but for three others of more importance for political science. Unless the point is kept clearly in mind, it seems to me, the political scientist runs the dangers, first, of failing to be what he pretends to be, a student of political institutions, second, of becoming ensnared in futile and myopic preoccupations with technique, and third, of misusing the materials of behavioral science. I should like to look briefly at each of these.

I have earlier suggested that the center of gravity in the behavioral sciences is individual or at least non-institutional in character. This implies that an uncritical adoption of the methods and propositions of behavioral science involves taking over the questions and problems—and limitations —of the latter and that one who does so risks ceasing to be a political scientist. Thus, recurrently it is suggested that the salvation of political science lies in concentrating on the dynamic psychology of individuals, in analyzing individual actors in depth. Without denying the possible general relevance of such investigations, I should still not see how they permit one to move from the clinic to the institutional context, not alone as a practical matter but as one of logic. The political scientist cares little, for example, about what a judge does to the Supreme Court—unless he is the instrument of a major redirection of its activities—and still less about the effect on him of membership on the Court. He cares rather about the role of the Court in the society, its functioning in the process of societal adjustment and in the allocation of values. This involves, perhaps, the analysis of individual behavior, but the generalizations sought are about the institution, not about the individual actor.[21] In this connection I might cite an observation by two social psychologists, arguing a very similar point some years ago with critics in that field: "If we consider the effects of a man's behavior upon his fellows it is often not necessary to know his personality. His action may be deeply interiorized within him, or it may not be at all characteristic of him. But its effect upon his fellows may be the same." [22] If our target is to generalize about the characteristic patterns of an institution and the alterations therein, the underlying personality drives of individual participants are likely to be at most of peripheral importance.

TECHNIQUES UNRELATED TO POLITICAL SCIENCE

The second danger I wish to identify is the closely related one of treating technique as an end in itself, with little or no reference to the questions and problems of central importance in the discipline. The social sciences generally seem peculiarly liable to internecine, sectarian controversies over technique and method. Typical is the struggle between the partisans of the case study and the supporters of quantification, which has moved through one field after another like an epidemic of measles through a large family. The outcome, in some instances, happily has been a gradual acceptance of the uses and limitations of each in tackling specified types of problems. In others, however, and in a good many cases where no actual clash occurs, the result is for each camp to go happily about refining and sharpening its technique and promoting it as the only way to intellectual salvation.

A related phenomenon is the technical fad, in which a new device is taken

---

[21] *Cf.* Richard C. Sheldon, "Some Observations on Theory in the Social Sciences," in Parsons and Shils, *ibid.,* p. 40.

[22] Daniel Katz and R. L. Schanck, *Social Psychology* (1938), p. 394.

up so widely that a researcher feels deficient if his study does not contain an application of the latest gadget, whether or not it is relevant to his substantive problem. At its lowest level this takes the form of a passion to punch and tabulate IBM cards without defining the questions on which the results are supposed to bear. At a more sophisticated level it involves defining the problem at hand in terms of a favorite technique rather than insisting that the problem set the technique. To a degree these tendencies are understandable and inevitable, and I certainly imply no censure of the specialist who devotes his energies to the perfecting of a technique in the faith that eventually it will prove of major usefulness. But the follower or borrower, especially from another field, is almost literally wasting his substance if he permits himself to expend his energies on the application of a technique without reference to its bearing on his most pressing problems of description and analysis. It would be a pity if political science were to adopt the position of the inebriated gentleman who, having lost his watch in a dark alley while making his way home in the small hours of the night, insisted on searching for it near the lamp post on the main street because there was more light there.

MISUSE OF MATERIALS

Finally, the danger of misusing the materials of behavioral science presents itself when the political scientist, deliberately attempting to apply the findings of psychology or sociology, fails adequately to take into account the factors peculiar to the institution that he is studying. This pitfall in the path of an entirely commendable eclecticism is encountered most commonly in moving from the restricted situation, particularly that of the laboratory, into the complex realities of the political scene. We can note with sober caution the remark of Robert Sears, in a slightly different connection, that "An appallingly small number of the relationships that have been discovered in social psychology can be generalized beyond the immediate situation in which the studies were made." [23]

Thus if one is impressed with the suggestive findings in group dynamics, most of which are built on observations in experimental situations or in limited natural contexts, he can use these only by a process of reasoning by analogy, with all its hazards, or by the more difficult process of introducing into the simple model of the face-to-face group the complicating parameters of the larger institutional setting, or by a combination of the two. One may be quite warranted, for example, in assuming that *in some respects* a legislative committee is *like* a problem-solving group set up for experimental purposes. But one cannot assume either that they are alike in all relevant respects or that these observed or attributed similarities are more significant than their differences in an explanation of their operation. Proceeding

[23] Robert R. Sears, "Social Behavior and Personality Development," in Parsons and Shils, *op. cit.*, p. 466.

cautiously from minimal assumptions of similarity, one may in his speculative planning begin to take account of the possibility that the function of a committee may be to perpetuate disagreement, rather than to produce viable solutions, of the effects on the activities of a committee deriving from its place in the legislative structure, of the significance of the relations of members with leadership elements such as the presidency and with extragovernmental units like constituency parties and interest groups, of the political aspirations and anxieties of the committee members, and so on.

One thus tends to emerge with a theory of legislative committees bearing at most only a root resemblance to the laboratory-based theory of the face-to-face group. By introducing parameters such as these into his group model, moreover, the political scientist may so complicate the latter that the analytical techniques appropriate to the simpler situation may be useless for him. Yet he has no genuine alternative, as I see it, if he wishes to make legitimate use of the suggestive propositions of the behavioral scientist. Direct analogy is at best superficial and at worst seriously misleading. And if the introduction of complicating parameters makes a theoretical model unmanageable, the latter is the element that is expendable.

Parenthetically, it is worth noting that the sort of problem I have referred to here is not encountered solely in the relations between political science and the behavioral sciences. It was a focus of the 1954 Social Science Research Council summer seminar on field and laboratory studies in social psychology as a problem *within* that field. A statement by the group, noting that ". . . theoretical statements emerging from field studies seem to be generally at a lower level of abstraction than those from laboratory experiments and likely to be more closely connected with specific empirical events," points out that ". . . this different orientation toward theory results in noncorrespondence between field and laboratory findings." [24]

Conclusions

The position I have attempted to develop can be roughly summarized as follows. The developments in the behavioral sciences over the past quarter-century have been more striking in the realm of technique than in that of validated and expanded theory. In both there has been a growing influence on the work and thought of political scientists. Though both types of impact are important, I should argue that the concern for empirically based theory, for the discovery and statement of behavioral uniformities, is the more fundamental. This influence has had the consequence of creating a divergence between what, for want of better terms, I have referred to as the "institutionalist" tendency in political science and the "political behavior" tendency. The differences between these two are genuine, lying

[24] "Narrowing the Gap Between Field Studies and Laboratory Experiments in Social Psychology," *Social Science Research Council Items*, VIII (December 1954), 38.

in the character of their commitments to the discovery of uniformities, in their approach to political institutions, and to a lesser degree, in the types of data and technique with which they are concerned.

Genuine though they may be, however, these divergences may not be as great as they appear. Moreover, their real proportions and their implications may perhaps be better understood if we give more explicit recognition to the obstacles in the way of adapting the techniques and particularly the theories of the behavioral sciences, narrowly conceived, to the problems that are the peculiar concern of the political scientist. I would fully accept the proposition that the advance of our discipline lies in the acceptance of generalization as its primary objective and of empirically testable theory as its principal method; that advance will lose no speed from a critical familiarity with both the techniques and the theories of the behavioral sciences, but it has much to lose, in my opinion, from an incautious attempt merely to project these into the realm of governmental institutions.

This position is likely to be rejected or objected to by at least two sets of critics. In the first place, those who do not share my concern for the difficulties in the way of extending into the study of political institutions the techniques and theories of the behavioral sciences will view these statements as defeatist if not treasonable. Those who regard optimistically the prospects of a general behavioral theory precisely relevant to the realm of government and productive of hypothetical relationships subject to empirical test especially will dismiss these arguments as parochial and short-sighted. To these I can reply only that, given the complexity and the crucial importance of governmental institutions in the societies with which we are most concerned, an empirically oriented but explicitly political theory seems to me the more promising road to our mutual objective of predictability.

In the second place, my emphasis on theory and particularly on empirically testable theory may produce objections from the "institutionalists" and from practitioners that pursuits of this sort will reduce the practical usefulness of the political scientist without compensating gains. An adequate reply to these would require more time than is presently available, but it would include at least these propositions: that there is nothing so practical as a well-developed and testable theory; that the choice lies not between an approach to such theory and no theory at all, but between an implicit and unexamined set of assumptions and an explicit theoretical effort; and, finally, that an implicit theory, though practically adequate in many circumstances, is likely to prove unsatisfactory in both practical and intellectual terms when dealing with a dynamic system subject to rapid and largely unplanned change.

On one point we can perhaps all agree, namely, that the entire social science enterprise will gain from a critical sensitivity to problems and developments in every corner of the vineyard and that all stand to lose when necessarily tentative intellectual positions are taken as gospel.

[32] Sociological Evidence and Political Theory

W. G. RUNCIMAN

When the suggestion was voiced in the first volume of *Philosophy, Politics and Society* that political philosophy might be dead, it was received in some quarters with alarm and indignation but more often with a very proper scepticism. For we all know, after all, that political philosophizing can go on no matter how rigorously we may want to press the distinction of facts and values. It may be hard enough in practice to win a political argument, but we reveal our belief that it is in principle winnable by embarking on it at all; moreover, we know very well that some political theories that have been discredited have been rightly discredited but that others still need to be taken account of; and so on. This is not to say that there has been quite so lively a revival of political theory as the scepticism about its death might have led one to expect. But in the years since the heyday of Weldonism it has ceased to be necessary to argue the case that political philosophy is possible at all. On the other hand, it remains as good a question as ever to ask of the proponent of any given political theory what evidence (if any) would persuade him to abandon it. In this paper, I want to consider some of the issues which this question raises, and in particular to discuss three cases where the work of social scientists has a specific bearing on political theory. In so doing, I want also to draw attention to the contribution made on this topic by Max Weber.

– I –

I make at the outset two assumptions: first, as already indicated, that political philosophy is in principle possible given that we are prepared to engage in political argument at all; and second, that the propositions which political philosophers are concerned to establish or defend are some sorts of moral propositions.

The case for these two assumptions has recently been argued with some

Reprinted from W. G. Runciman, *Philosophy, Politics and Society* (Second Series). Used by permission of Basil Blackwell and Barnes & Noble, Inc.

force by Benn and Peters,[1] but I must make clear that in sharing their view up to this point I do not share their further contention that all political arguments may be subsumed under a single moral heading, for which the criterion is impartiality. This further argument, which has been effectively criticized elsewhere,[2] must involve an improper assimilation of two different notions of social justice; and as Weber at one point argues, there is a conflict irreconcilable by any single ethical norm between the notion of justice represented by (in his example) Schmoller and that represented by Babeuf. I shall return to this point later; but for the moment, I only want to make clear that by likening political arguments to ethical arguments I am not suggesting that there is only one relevant political morality.

One further preliminary consideration should perhaps be dealt with at this point, namely the alleged 'subjectivism' or 'relativism' of all political (or moral or æsthetic) beliefs. The sceptic, to whom any political belief is as unarguable as a taste for ice cream, is likely to lend weight to his attack by pointing to the indisputable variety of political beliefs and the lack of any universally accepted criterion for appraising them. This, however, is not really the point. No matter how many people or communities sociologists might discover who believed for various reasons that the earth is flat, we should not be disposed (or not, at any rate, simply for that reason) to abandon our conviction that it is round. The point is rather whether any evidence is adduced which might shake our conviction; and this applies in the case of political belief just as much as a scientific one.

Let us consider, for example, the political proposal that the state should torture and execute all widows and orphans. It is surely difficult to maintain that this sort of suggestion should be taken any more seriously than the claim that the earth is flat; and it is not, therefore, the simple diversity of beliefs which makes different political attitudes seem immune to arbitration—indeed, some such attitudes may be dismissed as confidently as a refusal to accept the discoveries of natural science. The difficulty in fact comes only when dealing with beliefs which cannot be so cavalierly rejected but which are nevertheless impervious to evidence.

Examples of such beliefs (leaving aside the psychological factors which may be involved in clinging to them) might be the Roman Catholic conception of Natural Law or certain of the more rigid tenets of so-called 'vulgar' Marxism. These are impervious to evidence not because their proponents do not adduce any in support of their position, but because the conclusions argued from the evidence rest upon an interpretation which, if consistently maintained, can be guaranteed in advance to cover any fact which the observer might bring back from the sociological study of the contingent world. We may, of course, succeed in controverting such people on grounds of consistency; or we may, precisely by forcing them to be consistent, put them into a position which we believe must cause them some

---

[1] S. I. Benn and R. S. Peters, *Social Principles and the Democratic State* (1959).
[2] Brian M. Barry, 'Justice and the Common Good,' *Analysis*, XXI (1961), pp. 86–90.

discomfiture, whether or not they are willing to admit to it. But there may be nothing more to be done. Indeed, it may be that if we were to ask, for instance, a believing Catholic what evidence of any kind could convince him to abandon the doctrine of natural law, the answer would be none. This is not to say that he will never change his mind. But if he does, we shall be more likely to use words like 'conversion' or 'loss of belief' to describe the occurrence than to treat it as equivalent, say, to the process whereby someone comes to accept the truth of a historical fact.

It is obvious, however, that political beliefs are in general not of this kind. This is particularly clear in such cases as a utilitarian position, which necessarily involves a susceptibility to empirical psychological or sociological evidence: any utilitarian assertion about political or moral duty may be disputed by questioning its implications in terms of the pain or pleasure caused. But in any instance where there is an answer to 'what makes you think so?' a political belief is in principle susceptible to argument just as much as an assertion of the most respectably empirical kind. It may not prove possible to settle such an argument conclusively, or even to settle precisely what evidence would be accepted by both parties as decisive. But it certainly does not follow from this that political beliefs are necessarily and in principle immune to the adducing of logical or empirical evidence.

By way of illustration, let me give one example of a bad argument and another of a good one; or more precisely, one bad argument against a tenable position and one good argument against an untenable one. The bad argument is taken from Hegel,[3] and reads as follows: 'To hold that every single person should share in deliberating and deciding on political matters of general concern on the ground that all individuals are members of the state, that its concerns are their concerns, and that it is their right that what is done should be done with their knowledge and volition, is tantamount to a proposal to put the democratic element without any rational form into the organism of the state although it is only in virtue of the possession of such a form that the state is an organism at all.' The good argument is taken from T. H. Huxley's critique of the Social Darwinists: [4] 'It strikes me that men who are accustomed to contemplate the active or passive extirpation of the weak, the unfortunate, and the superfluous; who justify that conduct on the ground that it has the sanction of the cosmic process, and is the only way of ensuring the progress of the race, who, if they are consistent, must rank medicine among the black arts and count the physician a mischievous preserver of the unfit; on whose matrimonial undertakings the principles of the stud have the chief influence; whose whole lives, therefore, are an education in the noble art of suppressing natural affection and sympathy, are not likely to have any large stock of these commodities left.'

I do not mean that the good argument is good because it settles the

---

[3] *Philosophy of Right* (ed. Knox), Section 308.
[4] Quoted by R. Hofstadter, *Social Darwinism in American Thought*, p. 95.

question definitely; but to achieve its purpose it does not need to. To show that an ethical doctrine entails that ministering to the sick is wicked is quite enough to stultify it as it stands (though of course counter-moves could be made, if only by modifying the categorial assertion that any interference in cosmic selection is wrong). Similarly, Hegel may be right in asserting that it is foolish to advocate a certain sort of universal democracy. But it is not difficult to show that this conclusion is not entailed by the question-begging use of 'rational form' and the irrelevant assertion that the state must be an organism—the only arguments adduced in the passage concerned. These two examples are, of course, a long way short of demonstrating what a good full-scale political theory would look like or of providing a map of the logical bridges between prescriptive statements and those non-prescriptive assertions (whether logical or empirical) which would controvert or modify them. But they serve as reassurance (if needed) that political arguments are not merely an exchange of boos and hurrahs and they suggest that it may be worth while to classify the ways in which argument about political positions can be relevant to the positions held.

The best such classification that I know of is given by Max Weber, although I shall later dissent in one major respect from his views. According to Weber,[5] there are three and only three purposes which can be served by arguments about questions of value (*Wertungsdiskussionen*). First of all, the meaning of a value-judgement may be analysed and it may be discovered what other evaluative axioms it can logically be derived from or can logically be derived from it. Secondly, it is possible to argue about the actions implied by a set of value-judgements when an existing factual situation is assessed in terms of these value-judgements only. Thirdly, the factual consequences of such actions may be debated in the light of either the means necessary to carry them out or the further consequences (which may be incompatible with the original value-judgement) which must result from such actions. This third type of argument, says Weber, may lead to four sorts of conclusions by which the initial value-judgement will be directly modified. In the first place, the initial prescriptive statement may be shown to be impossible to fulfill. Secondly, it may be possible to realize but only at the cost of further consequences which would themselves violate it. Thirdly, it may be possible only by means not taken into account in the formulation of the original value-judgement. Finally, there may be other value-judgements which were not originally considered but which, though incompatible with the recommended policy, are also accepted by its proponents.

It needs little reflection to see that these three types of argument cover a very great deal; indeed, they cover precisely what political arguments are in practice about. This still leaves our previous cases where the holder of a political belief—Weber himself uses the example of a convinced syndicalist —will not accept any argument at all, not because (like the widow and

5 [See Chapter 5 of this volume, especially pp. 95–97.—Ed.]

orphan killer) he is mad, but because certain objectives have for him an absolute value to which no considerations of feasibility or consequence are relevant. But it would be a mistake to suppose that the syndicalist (whom I shall return to later) need be quite so unshakeable as Weber himself would have us believe. It is sometimes (and rightly) maintained that political viewpoints can never be proved, but only well or badly defended.[6] But such defences are just what political arguments consist of; and there are few even of convinced syndicalists who if asked why they hold the view they do will not give answers debatable by some rules of logic and evidence that they would themselves accept.

This is not to say that political persuasion is effected only by the adducing of further evidence. An interesting case is where persuasion is effected in such a way as may often happen with æsthetic judgements, where we may say, for example, 'Try looking at these Picassos a little longer and you'll find you come to like them.' I do not want to argue that there is not an important distinction between cases of this kind and such 'manipulative' techniques of persuasion as mob oratory or subliminal advertising; but they are also different from those cases where some further evidence is in fact adduced (e.g. by suggesting that Picasso is in some demonstrable respect similar to a painter whom the person concerned is known to like). An analogous case in political argument is perhaps where someone conjures up the picture of the ideal society implied by his political beliefs and tries thereby (but without adducing further argument) to secure his interlocutor's assent to them. The difficulty here is that æsthetic assent may be given to two incompatible ideals such, for instance, as honesty and kindness, or on a more political level, the two different conceptions of social justice cited, as we saw earlier, by Weber. But such conflicts need not, of course, be always irreconcilable, or at least not as often as Weber tends to imply; and the first move out of them, if there is to be one at all, is to conduct precisely the sort of argument or discussion which Weber classifies.

– II–

One of the things which Weber's analysis makes clear is how often it is feasibility which constitutes the crucial criterion by which a political argument may be settled; and it is such arguments which, if established, very often require the abandonment of a prescriptive political position. To illustrate this, I want to consider briefly three books which are importantly relevant to the classical theory of democracy. None of them sets out to advance a new *Weltanschauung,* and all three were written not by political philosophers but by social scientists. But they each contain general propositions of an 'if . . . then' form which have a clear and direct relevance

---

[6] E.g. by Margaret Macdonald in her Essay on 'Natural Rights' in *Philosophy, Politics and Society* (1956). [Reprinted in this volume, pp. 719–736; citation is to p. 734.]

(though in each case in a very different way) to the central tenets of democratic theory. The three books are: Schumpeter's *Capitalism, Socialism and Democracy*, Lazarsfeld's *The People's Choice* (together with the subsequent study *Voting*) and Arrow's *Social Choice and Individual Values*.

The idea of Schumpeter's which is of interest here (and which should be initially credited to Mosca) is that free competition between élites is the best guarantee of political freedom; and this assertion rests to a large extent upon the factual claim that, as Schumpeter firmly puts it, 'voters do not decide issues'. Schumpeter, in fact, asks us to stand on its head the accepted causal postulate of democratic theory. The results and processes of elections are, in his view, the dependent and not the independent variable in the political process; and in any case, 'even if the opinions and desires of individual citizens were perfectly definite and independent data for the democratic process to work with, and even if everyone acted on them with rationality and promptitude, it would not necessarily follow that the political decisions produced by that process from the raw material of those individual volitions would represent anything that could in any convincing sense be called the will of the people.' I think it is probably true to say that this second assertion is generally accepted as correct (Arrow, as we shall see, is also relevant), but that the first represents a considerable underestimate of the importance of the electorate. However, even if Schumpeter is only partially right, his view is hardly less important to the theorist of democracy; indeed it illustrates in part the basic difference between the philosopher and the sociologist of politics. The traditional philosophers of politics (who could, after all, have no idea how universal suffrage might work in practice) were largely concerned to justify by *a priori* argument the sort of system which they would like to see realized; the political sociologist, on the other hand, asks what sort of system is possible under what sort of conditions and with what sort of probable consequences. Whether or not he starts with a prescriptive viewpoint, his evidence both about feasibilities and consequences is likely to influence directly such a viewpoint; and this is precisely what Schumpeter sets out to do.

To the holder of what we can loosely call a Rousseauist position, Schumpeter's argument may be relevant in one or more of the ways classified by Weber. Probably it will imply either that the Rousseauist prescriptions are impossible to fulfil or that they are possible only at the cost of undesired consequences. But for the present argument, the interest of the Mosca–Schumpeter doctrine is that its force depends not on its prescriptive content so much as its sociological validity.

The same is, of course, particularly true of Marx. We may share all of Marx's horror and indignation at the effects which he witnessed of the capitalist system; but to accept also his politcal theory (whereby to work for the violent abolition of the bourgeois state is the real duty of the citizen body) we must agree with the social laws to which he attributed the validity of natural science. If political freedom can *only* be realized by the withering away of the state, then it is wrong to perpetuate it by means of piecemeal social reform; similarly, if political freedom can *only* be realized by free competition of élites, then it is wrong to advocate plebiscitary one-party democracy. Of course, it is not as simple as that; for we must settle just what we mean by 'political freedom,' 'withering away of the state,' 'competition of élites' and so on; and we may find that we either cannot or need not go further than the first of Weber's categories of *Wertungsdiskussionen*. But this does not alter my central point; the value of Schumpeter's political theory rests very largely on the validity of his sociological evidence. Do voters decide issues or not? And if not, does it not follow that a competition of élites is the only way to try to fulfil the aspirations of classical democratic theory?

If we turn now to Lazarsfeld, the implications of his work for political theory are less immediately apparent. The importance of Lazarsfeld's work has been justly recognized irrespective of its relevance to the political theorist, for it has effected a revision of our picture of voting behaviour whose acceptance should not blind us to its originality. By developing techniques peculiarly appropriate to voting behaviour (voting being not only a meaningful but a quantifiable action), Lazarsfeld and his associates have shown just how differently actual voters behave from the model citizens of classical democratic theory. Of course a number of observers (most notably Ostrogorski and Graham Wallas) had seen that this was so before Lazarsfeld; but it is Lazarsfeld who has shown how it is possible to answer the questions how far, in what way and under what conditions the conclusion holds, and who has arrived at answers which have been largely confirmed by his successors. These answers have very definite implications for political theory, some of which are briefly considered in the final chapter of *Voting*. We now have a vivid picture of to what extent voting is dictated by habit, how relatively few voters change their political allegiance [7] and how unlike the process of voting is to a rational choice between considered alternatives.

But is this falling short by the electorate from the classical ideal a bad thing or a good one? Is it possible, as the authors of *Voting* suggest, that apathy is in fact a political good? And if the electorate did make a fresh rational choice every election and did attach a real importance to that choice, would democracy (as understood in the Western two-party sense) be possible at all?

There is, obviously, no short or simple answer to these questions; but there can equally be no doubt that any useful theory of democracy must take our knowledge of voting behaviour into account. The case argued (or suggested) by the authors of *Voting* needs considerable elaboration, for they do not consider the different implications of apathy in the sense of non-extremism (extremism being a willingness to see the whole system changed even if indifferent as between existing parties) and non-partisanship

---

[7] Under, of course, more or less 'normal' circumstances; for scepticism of the Anglo-American voting studies, see H. Daudt, *Floating Voters and the Floating Vote* (1961).

(partisanship being an identification with one or other party but with in addition a commitment to the rules of the game). It could, for instance, be argued that non-extremism is a good thing but non-partisanship a bad one; and it might be that a low poll is sometimes a bad thing (showing that the electorate doesn't care at all) but sometimes also a good one (showing that the electorate doesn't care too intensely). My point, however, is once again only that Lazarsfeld's work has placed an important limit on the scope of *a priori* theorizing about democracy; and it has done so by producing sociological evidence directly relevant to the tenets of political theory. It is not evidence which necessarily supports either a left-wing or a right-wing view; but it is important precisely because any theory of democracy, whether left or right, must take account of it.

The third work, Arrow's, although principally concerned with the economists' problem of constructing a social welfare function, has in a sense the most clear-cut relevance to the problems of democratic theory. Arrow's General Possibility Theorem is a formal demonstration that 'If we exclude the possibility of interpersonal comparisons of utility, then the only methods of passing from individual tastes to social preferences which will be satisfactory and which will be defined for a wide range of sets of individual orderings are either imposed or dictatorial'. In other words, for the conditions of a genuine social ordering of preferences to be satisfied, certain criteria of unanimity must initially have been fulfilled. (Some modifications of Arrow's theorem have been proposed, but I take it as it stands.) The implications of this conclusion for political theory, and particularly for idealist political theory, are briefly considered by Arrow in his final chapter, but (as with the final chapter of *Voting*) the implications are not worked out in any great detail. This does not, however, make the cogency of such implications any less clear. What sort of a theory of the General Will or of the Common Good it is worth trying to construct in the face of Arrow's conclusions cannot be settled on the basis of Arrow's conclusions alone; but no such theory (again, whether of the Left or Right) is worth attempting at all which does not carefully take account of them.

It is readily apparent that Arrow's argument is different in kind from the other two since unlike them it is purely deductive, whereas both Schumpeter and Lazarsfeld have drawn our attention to contingent facts about the political world. Although this does not affect its relevance to an argument about the feasibility of certain kinds of political recommendation, the difference is obviously an important one.

Purely deductive arguments, of which the propositions of game theory are perhaps in this context the most notable example, can be of direct relevance to the political theorist on a number of problems. For instance, the 'prisoner's dilemma' of game theory may be used to elucidate a formal difference between the will of all (uninformed rational choice) and the general will (informed rational choice with an effective promise to abide by it). Or it may be shown how under certain conditions a war of all against all gives the weakest the best chance of survival, and other examples of this kind. The application of such deductions, however, is always debatable and must rest on the contingent assumption that the appropriate conditions are fulfilled; and it therefore seems plausible to suggest that although purely deductive arguments may be relevant to a debate between the holders of rival political theories, such theories are likely more often or in addition to need to be defended by reference to sociological evidence.

– III –

This does not mean, however, that even the most solid and pervasive generalizations of political sociology will, if established, constitute evidence which necessarily favours one or other of several political theories (in the prescriptive sense) which may be mutually incompatible. This may be illustrated by reference to one of the most familiar problems in the study of political consensus and social stratification. Ever since Durkheim observed that stable poverty is the best guarantee of conservatism, sociologists have remarked on the apparent correlation between lack of opportunity and lack of discontent. To cite one of the best-known examples: Stouffer and associates, studying the American army during the Second World War, found that in the Air Force (where chances of promotion were highest) discontent with promotion was greatest, and in the Military Police (where chances of promotion were lowest) discontent with promotion was least. Now let us suppose (whether or not it is so) that there is general validity in some proposition of this kind. The Right, of course, will eagerly embrace it as evidence for the assertion that equality of opportunity (or of status) is, as they have always maintained, a bad thing; by promoting envy, they argue, it merely leaves everyone unhappier than they were before. But the Left may feel no less well furnished with an argument for their own position: is it not, they may ask, precisely this situation which calls for remedy? Where superstition and ignorance can prolong an acceptance of deprivation and injustice, does this not make the situation more unacceptable rather than less so?

In an argument of this kind, it may be that there is a confrontation of two incompatible *Weltanschauungen* to which any evidence will be made subservient, and we are back once again with Weber's syndicalists on whom we shall have to try some other argument of a 'why do you think so?' kind. But my point is that if such arguments are capable of being settled to any extent or in any respect (and they demonstrably are, or people would not cite evidence in political argument at all), then this will be by reference to an argument such as classified by Weber and very often to an argument depending on 'what would happen if . . .'; or, in other words, to an argument based partly or wholly upon a sociological generalization. If a political position is open to argument at all (leaving aside the instances, which

I briefly touched on, where people's views may be changed either by 'conversion' or by what one would want to call 'manipulative' techniques) it will be in the ways discussed by Weber; and though this may be purely formal argument (Weber's first type) it will also very often be argument to which contingent sociological evidence is relevant.

Objections will, of course, be raised at this point by those concerned to deny the possibility of any sociological generalization which can be sufficiently validated to entail the modification of a political theory. Once again, however, an adequate answer is suggested by Weber. Weber allows that every historical sequence is unique (in an additional sense to the Heraclitean truism that every event is unique); but he also emphasizes that every historical explanation must rest on nomothetic sociological assumptions—if it did not, historians would be deprived of the use of even such words as 'dangerous.' What the sociologist does, having first understood the meaning of the actions he describes (Weber's famous *verstehen*), is then to test his explanatory generalizations against empirical evidence. This can be done, in principle, with such propositions as 'competition between élites is the best guarantee of political freedom' and 'too great involvement by the electorate is bad for two-party democracy' just as well as with such more 'scientific' looking assertions as 'Catholics are more likely than Protestants to vote Democrat even when socio-economic status is held constant.' And to the extent that such propositions can be validated, they may involve the modification of any political theory which is not irretrievably immune to argument.

I must end, however, by emphasizing the one important qualification which needs to be made to Weber's views. Weber, though allowing—as in the syndicalist example—that some political beliefs are less amenable to discussion than others, tends in general to imply (much as Weldon was to do) that any choice of attitude or *Weltanschauung* or political vocabulary is not only likely to be irreconcilable with any other but is also essentially arbitrary in nature. Weber, of course, took up this position in the context of an argument against the positivists of social science who wished to claim the possibility of a total objectivity for their assertions, and he was at pains to point out (rightly) that even the choice of formulation of a sociological question will involve a value-judgement. However, his implication that all choice of political attitude is equally arbitrary is, I think, demonstrably false (although it has also been held by people arguing purely as philosophers, in a way that Weber was not). Let us take Weber's own example of an argument with a syndicalist. Suppose that he takes a sort of anarchic Sorelian position whereby the first maxim of political conduct is that of organized resistance to any established government; for convenience, let us put it into the form of the proposition 'all government must be forcibly resisted.' If we ask him why, he may reply only (and this seems to be what Weber has in mind) 'because they are governments'; and if he goes no further than this, we may indeed wish to label his political beliefs as irrational or arbitrary, and attribute to his argument no higher status than to a claim that all red-headed men should be shot simply because their hair is red. If, however, he sets out to justify his position—let us say, by replying that 'all government is necessarily and by nature evil'—then we shall ask him for empirical evidence, and we shall thereby embark on an explicit sociological discussion. Two conclusions seem self-evident in this context: first, that we do wish to distinguish between purely arbitrary and non-arbitrary political beliefs; and second, that any recognition of amenability to evidence is a tacit recognition that the gulf between fact and value is not so unbridgeable as Weber himself elsewhere (and for a different purpose) claims.

Thus two conclusions follow from Weber's treatment of *Wertungsdiskussionen,* one of which he makes clear and one of which he in other contexts denies. As he makes clear, sociological evidence is likely to be crucially relevant to even the most abstract arguments about political theory. But in addition (and contrary to the Weberian dichotomy between fact and value), the fact of degrees of amenability to such evidence implies the possibility of a meaningful distinction between *Weltanschauungen,* whether or not these are as irreconcilable as Weber seems to think they will ultimately prove. Not only is it true that some political theories are more amenable than others to the citing of relevant evidence. It is also true that to recognize that this is so is to acknowledge that the separation of political theory from political sociology is not so radical as has sometimes been supposed and as Weber himself is apt to argue.

Seven ★ MODELS AND

MEASUREMENT

The success of the physical sciences in predicting, explaining, and, consequently, manipulating and controlling our natural environment has been spectacular. With breathtaking accuracy, the almost "perfect" knowledge provided by the process laws of classical physics permits us to propel a satellite into a precalculated orbit around the earth. A trip to the moon is merely a matter of technological detail. The use of quantified concepts is inseparable from the triumphs of physical science. Naturally enough, quantification has become a status symbol for many social scientists. They envisage rows of equations with which they could compute the processes of individual and social life. To others, however, quantification is anathema. They see a specter: the rich texture of experience usurped by bloodless figures and formulas. The daydream and the nightmare are both disproportionate reactions. The logic of the situation justifies neither excessive zeal nor total repudiation.

"Sensuous reality is qualitative. Scientific description is quantitative. However well quantitative terms may fit the physical world, they cannot describe the qualitative character of human nature and human experience. A man's height can be measured, but not his love for God and country. Many small weights can be added to get a large one, but the addition of mediocrities does not produce a genius. Counting and measuring cannot capture the qualitative characteristics of man and society. These, therefore, cannot be the subject of scientific description and explanation." So runs a common version of the argument from the alleged impossibility of quantification against a science of man. The argument is irremediably confused, for the qualitative-quantitative dichotomy is spurious. Science talks about the world, that is, about the properties of and relations among things. A quantity is a quantity *of* something. In particular, it is a quantity of a "quality," that is, of a descriptive property. A quantitative property is a quality to which a number has been assigned. The colors, sounds, smells, and textures of direct experience are qualitative features of reality. So are heat and cold, round and large, heavy and solid. We hear two sounds at the same time or one before another; we see one thing next to, under, or in something else. We experience, in other words, temporal and spatial relations, as well as other descriptive relations, such as taller, louder, or brighter. All of these properties and relations make up the empirical characters of the world that are referred to by the undefined descriptive or qualitative terms of language. These terms occur in the definitions of "abstract" scientific concepts, quantitative and nonquantitative alike. If this were not the case, we could not understand them. To assign a number to velocity, for instance, we must observe, among other things, a couple of colored spots, one of which is spatially coincident with another. Even in common speech many terms, such as *loyalty* and *virtue,* refer to configurations of attitudes and behavioral dispositions that, not being directly observed, are abstract properties. They are no less real or qualitative on that account. All descriptive terms, of science and of everyday life, are equally "qualitative," referring either directly or, via definitions, indirectly to observable properties. All quantitative terms are defined. Part of their definitions mention the attributes or qualities to which numbers are assigned.

In his paper in this section Abraham Kaplan discusses the apprehensions and the misapprehensions that underlie what he aptly calls the "mystique of quality." He also comments suggestively on certain specific problems, namely, how to assign values that will guide our choices among various wants and courses of action when these are incommensurable alternatives, the implication of the use of judges or the "human yardstick" for classifying behavior, and some of the difficulties as well as the potentialities of measurement in the social sciences.

Although quantification has considerable merit, it is neither a necessary nor a sufficient condition for science. A quantified attribute is an attribute that has a number assigned to it in accordance with certain rules. What kinds of rules, I shall mention presently. A concept is significant or meaningful if it occurs in laws, that is, if we know something about its referent. The same holds for quantified concepts. The B-coefficient—defined as a person's height times his age, divided by the number of hairs on his head times his annual income—though quantified, is most probably not significant. We never can be sure whether a concept will turn out to be significant or not, but a "science" that, no matter how solemnly, makes a practice of collecting coefficients of that sort might justly be suspected of frivolity. Quantification clearly is not a sufficient condition for scientific knowledge. Quantification at the price of significance is excessive. A science looks for laws to explain individual facts and for theories to explain the laws. If its concepts are not quantified, then its laws cannot be expressed in the form of equations or other "mathematical" formulas. Yet they are laws all the same. They may be about biological properties of organisms, about individual behavior and personality, or about the links between, say, technological innovation and institutional change. A discipline that formulates and tests such laws and theories is a science. Quantification is not a necessary condition. Concepts may be significant without being numbered.

Measurement has a narrow and a broad use. In its narrow use, measurement is that assignment of numbers to things in accordance with certain rules. In its broadest use, now common in social science, any classification of a property or configuration as an instance of some clearly defined, but not necessarily quantitative, concept is called "measurement." There is nothing intrinsically wrong with this broad usage. If it reassures the investigator whose subject matter is recalcitrant to quantification, it may even be a virtue. On the other hand, extending the term to all observation requires that we qualify *measurement* by *quantified* in order to discuss the special logical issues involved in the coordination of numbers to things. For simplicity's sake, therefore, I shall use *measurement* in the narrow, quantitative sense.

Numbers may be applied arbitrarily, as men in the army have serial numbers or an institution's furniture is numbered for inventory purposes. In such uses, numbers merely label; they do not quantify things. If it makes no difference who or what has which number, then nothing has been quantified and no information is conveyed. Numerals or number-signs as arbitrary labels do not in fact stand for numbers at all but are just identifying marks, of which there are a conveniently large assortment. (One does not literally become a number by being "numbered," any more than one becomes a rabbit by being called "Rabbit.") A number is a logical property of a class or collection of things. *Counting* is one of two ways by which numbers may be introduced into descriptive concepts and laws. Counting alone, however, is not measurement. Things having no descriptive property in common can be arbitrarily grouped into classes, each of which can be counted and assigned a number. (For instance, the class consisting of the President of the United States, my car, and an elm tree in Paris can be counted—it has three members—but it cannot be measured.) Counting yields a measurement only when things are classified by some common descriptive property, for instance, weight. If the property can be divided into units in a specifiable way, then by counting the units we can tell how much of it is present; 2 feet joined to 2 feet make a length of 4 feet, just as $2 + 2 = 4$. It is an empirical law about length that it has this property of "additivity." This means that there is an empirical relation, that of being joined together, corresponding to arithmetical addition, such that after the lengths are joined together, the number assigned to the result is the arithmetical sum of the numbers assigned to its parts. Properties of this kind are called "extensive."

Ranking is the second way of introducing numbers into concepts. For the social sciences, this is the most important way. The efficiency of groups or the intelligence of persons may be assigned numbers in accordance with some procedure—by work produced; by results of a test—but adding these numbers has no empirical meaning, for there is no corresponding empirical operation on these properties. Intelligence Quotient is a complex quantified property of individuals. [All quantified concepts are defined as they are used in a sentence (see p. 4); part of the definition specifies the procedures by which numbers are assigned to the property.] Though we can assign a number to IQ, we cannot combine or "add" IQs. Consequently an IQ of 160 is not twice an IQ of 80, for the operation "plus" in the expression "IQ 80 plus IQ 80" has no empirical meaning. No descriptive relation for IQ corresponds to arithmetical addition. We can imagine a possible empirical relation for group efficiency. Two groups might be put to working together at some task. That they were placed together would be the relation corresponding to addition. But if each group has been assigned an efficiency of 3, the two groups acting together need not have a resultant efficiency of 6. The property efficiency does not "mirror" the structure of arithmetic addition. However, if efficiency is defined in certain ways, it may well be a transitive relation. [See p. 592.] If so, then efficiency has the same structure as the arithmetic property of being larger in number. Efficiency therefore can be rank-ordered.

Properties that can be rank-ordered, but not added, are called "intensive." Clearly, *intensive* does not mean the same as *qualitative,* since numbers may be significantly assigned to intensive properties. We assign numbers to properties in accordance with empirical laws and conventions. These are the rules that are used. The result is a scale. Extensive properties can always be assigned numbers that yield an additive scale. Intensive properties cannot. Different scales may be constructed for the same property. If we use the empirical law that a property is transitive to rank instances of that property, any assignment of numbers that preserves the order will do. The sequence 2, 5, 8 is as good as 1, 2, 3 for merely indicating increasing degrees of, say, efficiency. The sequence we use is a matter of convention, just as is the choice between inches or centimeters. If we want to do more than indicate order, however, by making use of further empirical laws and facts, such as the number of people in each interval or the additivity of a dimension, then the way numbers can be assigned is further restricted. In general, we choose scales so that a maximum number of arithmetical relations are given empirical meaning by corresponding descriptive relations among the things that have the property being measured.

When descriptive relations "mirror" arithmetical relations, then the arithmetical truths can be used as additional premises in deductive inference from the quantified laws. (An example is given on p. 591 of the first paper in this section.) That is one reason why quantification, when it is possible, is also desirable. When mathematics can be applied to descriptive properties in this way, then, as is explained in the first selection, it serves as a "model" or arithmetical representation of the area to which it is applied. The calculus of probability and the theory of games are shown to be similarly related to empirical subject matter. Preliminary to that discussion, the "structural isomorphism" required for one system to be a model for another is explained and several different uses of the term *model* are compared and contrasted.

Kenneth Arrow first explains and illustrates the advantages of quantification in the social sciences. He then perspicuously analyzes various types of mathematical models as applied to social behavior and to problems of statistical inference.

A property cannot be quantified unless there can be more or less of it. A person may have more musical ability or be shorter (have less height) than another, but he cannot, except jocularly, be more or less married. However, certain characteristics of marriage possibly may be rank-ordered. Some marriages are doubtless more satisfactory than others. Can we construct an "index" of satisfactoriness in marriage? If we can, is it worth doing? The answer is not one of principle, but of practice or research strategy. The investigator must develop a sense for the significant variable. If laws and theories can be constructed from the quantified concept, then it is worth having. If not, it is not worth having.

Lazarsfeld presents a clear and valuable discussion of the problems encountered in constructing lawfully significant "measures" in social science. The first three parts of his paper are directly relevant to the issues, discussed in Section Four of this volume, concerning collective or group properties. He uses 'measure' in the broad sense to designate any precisely defined concept. His examples are of nonquantitative concepts to which, however, statistical techniques have been applied. In other words, the property or measure of, for instance, being a conservative, defined by how a certain question is answered, is not assigned a number indicating amount or degree, but the proportion of conservatives in a certain group who behave in a particular way is counted. The result is a statistical law or correlation [See Index.] Drawing upon examples from current research and the sociological literature, he shows in Part IV of his paper how certain research and statistical techniques may be used, particularly for distinguishing spurious from true causal connections. The heart of the distinction is the use of deductive explanation. His final section contains a very interesting and useful analysis of several functions in social research of models or quantitative scientific theories.

What is the difference between a true and a spurious correlation? Two pairs of variables or characteristics, x and y, are found to be highly correlated. One of these correlations, between female marital status and job absenteeism is said to be true. The other, between marital status and candy consumption is rejected as spurious. In each case we introduce a new factor or test variable, t. (I shall use Lazarsfeld's notation.) In the spurious case, the introduction of a test factor, age, leads to abandoning the original correlation. In the true case, on the other hand, the introduction of a third variable, increased housework, confirms the correlation. Why, in each case, after introducing an additional factor do we treat the original correlations differently?

We test whether or not the correlations between the x and y variables are preserved if a new factor, t, is introduced. The group is subdivided by age, say with age forty being the dividing line, between older (t) and younger ($\bar{t}$) people. We determine the so-called partial relations, that is, the correlation between x and y within these subgroups, symbolized by $[xy; \bar{t}]$ and $[xy; t]$. We also determine the "marginal" relations, that is, the correlations of x with t $[xt]$, and of y with t $[yt]$. We further consider whether t, the test variable, is an antecedent factor which precedes x and y or whether it is intermediary, temporally intervening between x and y.

In the example of age and candy eating, age is an antecedent test variable for which the partial relations disappear. That is, if age is held constant, marriage and candy consumption are not correlated. The marginal relations, however, do not disappear because increased age is positively correlated with being married and with eating less candy. If t is an antecedent variable and, as in this case, the partial relations equal zero, then the observed regularity between x and y is rejected as spurious. The reason for the rejection is that the marginal relations only permit us to say that if t

then x and that if t then y, that is, older people are married and older people eat less candy. But from these two statistical regularities all that logically follows is that if t then both x and y. We cannot derive "If x then y," namely, that married people eat less candy, which is the correlation being tested. It is therefore abandoned. (Lazarsfeld calls this test Type MA—the marginals, M, do not vanish and the test variable is antecedent, A.) The analysis prevents the mistaken imputation of x as a cause of y by showing the statistical correlation of x and y to be merely the joint effect of some common antecedent condition.

In the second illustration, marriage and absenteeism were found to be positively correlated. The additional test factor, increased housework, is a temporally intervening variable. If we keep amount of housework constant, the partial relations vanish in this example as they did in the last. Marriage and absenteeism are only related if the married women have more housework. Here too the marginal relations are not zero because marriage is correlated with housework and housework with absenteeism. In this case, however, the test variable, housework, intervenes between getting married and absenteeism. (This is Lazarsfeld's Type MI; the marginals, M, do not vanish and the test variable is intervening, I.) The observed correlations, therefore, are that if x then t and if t then y, that is, if a woman marries then she has more housework, and if she has more housework then absenteeism increases. From these two statistical generalizations, in contrast to those of the preceding illustration, the correlation being tested between marriage and absenteeism follows as a deductive consequence. It is thus explained by them. Because we can explain the regularity by deducing it from other generalizations, it is seen to be a true rather than "spurious" connection.

The statistical techniques thus permit us to separate out what, without them, often cannot be discerned. One puzzling correlation is shown to be a true causal connection operating through an intervening factor. A different puzzling correlation is rejected, however, because the newly discovered regularities show that the connection between x and y is merely apparent, that both are the effects of a common cause. The precise deductive notion of explanation applied to statistically quantified statements permits the separation of causally connected events from those that are merely concurrent.

[33] Models, Meaning, and Theories

MAY BRODBECK

The term "model" appears with increasing frequency in recent social-science literature. We encounter models of learning, of rational choice, of communication, of political behavior, of group-interaction, and so on, and so on. The term has moreover a decided halo effect. Models are Good Things. And if models are good, "mathematical models," needless to say, are even better. Yet, what exactly is a model and what purposes does it serve? I venture to suggest that ten model-builders will give at least five different or, at least, apparently different answers to this question. What is the difference between a model and a theory? How can two theories have the same model, and what does it signify if they do? Are there any logical differences between models in physical science and those in the behavioral sciences? I shall attempt to answer these and similar questions.

Model ships appear frequently in bottles; model boys in heaven only. Model ships are copies of real ones. Asked to describe a ship, we could point to its model. A model boy, on the other hand, having no earthly counterpart, is everything a boy *ought* to be. A model ship, then, is a *three-dimensional replica*. A model boy is a *norm*. They illustrate the two most common non-technical uses of "model." The normative use is at most incidental in science and I shall not recur to it. I shall first of all explain those characteristics of three-dimensional models by virtue of which they are models. Then, after some preliminary clarifications, I shall turn to an analysis of the various uses of "model" for verbal or symbolic systems.

Isomorphism

A miniature train is a model not by virtue of being diminutive, but because it imitates a real train. Not only does the model have its own chimney stacks and windows but these duplicate the relative proportions of the real thing. The model is constructed to scale. What purpose does it serve? Apart from being a toy, it is, like an architect's model of a building, a "non-verbal description" of the thing. Since it is, except for size and possibly

"Models, Meaning, and Theories," with Notes (pp. 373–403) by May Brodbeck, from *Symposium on Sociological Theory,* edited by Llewellyn Gross. Copyright © 1959 by Harper & Row, Publishers, Incorporated. Reprinted by permission of the publishers.

materials, an exact imitation, we must know what the thing itself is like or, as in the architect's case, what it is going to be like before we can build the model. Though it may help some people to see the thing in detail, the details were already known, at least to the builder. A replica thus gives no new knowledge, not even of a simple descriptive kind. Replicas are therefore not, as such, scientifically interesting. Nevertheless, they have some features which will help us to understand more useful models.

The technical term for the similarity between a thing and a model of it is *isomorphism*. Isomorphism requires two conditions. First, there must be a one-to-one correspondence between the elements of the model and the elements of the thing of which it is the model. For every chimney stack, there is a miniature chimney stack, every window has its replica, and conversely. Second, certain relations are preserved. For instance, if a door is to the left of a window in the original, their replicas are similarly situated; also, the model is constructed to scale. Among the relations which the model may or may not preserve, one kind is of special interest. The model may or may not "work" on the same principle as the original. If it does, I shall call the isomorphism *complete*. If, for instance, a model of a steam-engine is also steam-propelled, then the isomorphism is complete. The similarity or isomorphism of a planetarium with the heavenly bodies is not complete. All the planets with their moons and the sun, together with their spatial relations to each other, are duplicated. But the motions of these bodies across the hemispherical ceiling are not caused by gravitational attraction, as are, of course, the motions of the real planets in the heavens. Since the laws according to which the model works are different from those of the real thing, the isomorphism is incomplete. As far as three-dimensional models go, even a complete one, like the steam-propelled model steam-engine, has only an incidental scientific value. Since the model is easy to manipulate, this may help discovery of the principles by which it works, if these are not already known. Diagrams and pictorial devices, in the nature of the case, cannot be complete. These models are at best suggestive to the visual-minded and, at worst, like all incomplete models, misleading if taken literally. Although social scientists occasionally resort to such pictorial devices, the term "model" is more frequently applied to various kinds of verbal or symbolic systems. In order to clarify the ambiguities in these uses, certain preliminary distinctions are needed.

Content and Form: Descriptive and Logical Words

The language of science, devoid of greetings, exclamations, questions, and commands, consists wholly of declarative sentences. By means of them, the scientist talks about the world. These sentences may be as simple and qualitative as the statement that ice is cold or as complicated and quantitative as the Newtonian law of attraction. In either case, all such sentences consist of certain arrangements of two kinds of words. Some of the words in a sentence are names for characteristics or attributes of individual things or events and for relations among these. They are called *descriptive* terms or concepts. They may name characteristics of inanimate physical things, of organisms, or of societies. Thus green is an attribute of some physical objects, notably grass. Hunger at some time or other belongs to the state of an organism, while totalitarian is an attribute of some societies. . . . The subject-matter or content of an area is indicated by its descriptive terms.

Descriptive terms are connected with each other to form statements of fact, like "John is blond." Sentences, in turn, are connected with each other to form compound sentences, like "John is blond and Jim is red-headed." These compound sentences express connections among facts. The words that do this connecting, like "and," "or," and "if . . . then," are called *logical* words. They do not themselves denote anything. Logical words give language its form or structure by connecting terms that do denote. They are common to all sciences. For example, the sentences "He is a scholar *and* he is an athlete" and "He is a scholar *or* he is an athlete" are alike in that they have the same subject-matter. But their *form* is different. On the other hand, "He is a scholar *or* he is an athlete" is like "The judge is elected *or* he is appointed" in that they share a common form. Their subject-matter differs but both statements are disjunctions. The descriptive words of a sentence give it its meaning. If we know what they refer to, then we know what a sentence of a certain form is about and can determine whether it is true or false. A sentence may be stripped of its meaning, yet retain its form, by replacing all its descriptive words or component statements by letters. Thus "X or Y," "X and Y" and "If X, then Y" are the form of a disjunction, conjunction and conditional, respectively. As they stand, there is no way to distinguish "X or Y" from "U or Z." If, however, each letter-variable is replaced by a sentence containing different descriptive words, then the statements say different things while they have the same form. This notion of *having the same form* is essential to one important use of "model."

Logical and Empirical Truth

Words, then, are either logical or descriptive. Sentences are also of two kinds. For one kind, from the form alone, truth or falsity cannot be determined. In, for instance, "If X then Y," we must know what the letters refer to or mean before we can tell whether the sentence is true or false. Compare, however, "If X then Y" with "If X then X." Both statements have the same form, as expressed by the logical phrase "if . . . then"; they are both conditionals. But assuming that the same letters are always replaced by the same sets of descriptive words, the two statements differ notably. In "If X then X" we do not have to replace the letters by sentences about descriptive properties in order to tell whether it is true or false. It is true no matter what is put for X. If X stands for the statement that a judge is elected, then the whole sentence says "If a judge is elected, then a judge is elected," which is something less than controversial. A statement of this form is true no matter what its components are about. Another such statement is "Either X or not-X." Sentences true by virtue of their form alone are called *logical truths* or, also, tautological or analytic. In "If X then Y," on the other hand, we must know what descriptive words replace "X" and "Y" before we can tell whether the statement is true or false. Sentences whose truth depends upon their descriptive words as well as on their form are called *empirical* statements or, also, contingent or synthetic. One important subclass of logical or analytic truths are those of arithmetic. I use this latter term quite generally to cover everything from elementary arithmetic through calculus and higher mathematics, in order to avoid the confusing ambiguities which, as we shall presently see, beset the term "mathematical." All arithmetical concepts, like numbers and operations upon them such as addition, are ultimately definable in terms of logical words alone. The definition is cumbrous and need not concern us here. But, once carried through, it turns out that statements such as $5 + 7 = 12$, as well as those of more abstruse mathematics, are all true by virtue of their form alone. They contain no symbols referring to descriptive properties and relations and these are irrelevant to the truths of arithmetic. Like "If X then X," they say nothing about the world, so are neither confirmed nor refuted by it. Saying "nothing," they are, as we shall see, yet remarkably useful.

Laws and Theories

. . . A law states that whenever there is an instance of one kind of fact, then there is also an instance of another. Laws, therefore, are always empirical generalizations, such as, "Whenever there is a rise in wages, then prices increase." If we can state exactly how much prices increase with given increases in wages, then we have a quantitative law. Quantified generalizations or laws are expressed by equations. These equations state how the value of some concepts or "variables" change with the value of others. Thus, Galileo's law of falling bodies states that the distance a released body falls varies directly with the square of its time, that is, $d = 16t^2$.

Like all other sentences, quantified laws have a certain form. Many other physical properties besides distance vary as the square of some other characteristic. The so-called linear equation, $y = ax + b$, represents still another quantified form taken by some laws. The variables might stand for many different things, like weight and height or supply and demand, while the form remains the same. But a quantified empirical law such as $d = 16t^2$ differs from an arithmetic statement like $9 = 3^2$. In the empirical law, the letter variables "d" and "t" must be given meaning as distance and time before its truth or falsity can be established. No descriptive terms occur in the arithmetic truth. When letters do occur in arithmetic statements, as in $x + y = y + x$, then it is understood that the letters are to be replaced by numerals. It is a logical truth about numbers that the order of addition does not make a difference. As we shall see later, if the letters do not stand for numbers, then the statement may well be false. Quantified empirical laws, like $d = 16t^2$, are often called "mathematical." It is obvious now why this term is confusing. A quantified law of empirical science is an empirical or synthetic assertion, whose truth or falsity depends upon its descriptive terms. Distance varies as the square of time, but demand probably does not. A statement of mathematics, on the other hand, is analytic. In order to stress the distinction between empirical laws and the tautologies of mathematics, I shall continue to use the term "arithmetic" for the latter.

A theory is a deductively connected set of laws. Some of these laws, the axioms or postulates of the theory, logically imply others, the theorems. . . . Laws, whether quantified or not, have a certain form, as expressed either by the verbal "if . . . then . . . " or by an equation. Theories differ from each other either in their descriptive terms, in which case they are about different things, or in the form of their laws, or both. For instance, theories within physics and those within sociology presumably differ from each other not only in their descriptive terms but also in the form of the statements connecting these concepts. "Time" and "distance," for example, are descriptive terms or "variables" of physical theory. The parabola $y = ax^2$, or a differential equation of a certain sort, gives the form of the law connecting these terms. Within sociology, the descriptive terms might be, say, "religious preference" and "political attitude." A law connecting these attributes might have the form of a nonquantified conditional, like "If anyone is a Catholic, then he is also a conservative." Or it might take the form of a quantified linear equation expressing a statistical correlation between the variables.

Models: Isomorphic Theories

A model train, we saw, is similar to a real one in being isomorphic with it. The isomorphism is complete if both work on the same principles. Extending this notion to theories, we can formulate a precise meaning of "model." Two theories whose laws have the same form are isomorphic or *structurally similar* to each other. If the laws of one theory have the same form as the laws of another theory, then one may be said to be a *model* for the other. This definition of "model" in terms of an isomorphism between theories at least provides one unambiguous meaning for that term. That it is not consistently used in this way by scientists is, of course, one reason why the notion requires clarification. How do we discover whether two theories, or parts of them, are isomorphic to each other? Suppose that one area, as indicated by a set of descriptive concepts, for which a relatively well-developed theory is at hand, is said to be a model for another area, about which little is as yet known. The descriptive terms in the theory of the better-known area are put into one-to-one correspondence with those of the "new" area. By means of this one-to-one correspondence, the laws of one area are "translated" into laws of the other area.[1] The concepts of the better-known theory are replaced in the laws by the concepts of the new area. This replacement results in a set of laws or hypotheses about the variables of the new area. If observation shows these hypotheses to be true, then the laws of both areas have the same form. The lawful connections are preserved and the two theories are completely isomorphic to each other. For example, suppose it is wondered whether rumors spread like diseases. That is, can the laws of epidemiology, about which quite a bit is known, be a model for a theory of rumor-transmission? Or, to say the same thing differently, do the laws about rumors have the same form as the laws about diseases? The descriptive concepts in the laws of epidemiology are first of all replaced by letter variables. This reveals the form of the laws. The concepts referring to diseases are put into one-to-one correspondence with those referring to rumors. The letter variables in the epidemiological laws are replaced by the descriptive terms referring to rumors. This results in a set of hypotheses about rumors, which may or may not be confirmed. If, optimistically, these laws are confirmed, then the two theories have the same form.

The notion of "model" as isomorphism of laws is obviously symmetrical. However, when an area about which we already know a good deal is used to suggest laws for an area about which little is known, then the familiar area providing the form of the laws may be called a model for the new area. But once it is found that the laws of both areas do indeed share a common structure, then of course either is a model for the other. This definition of "model" is also the only clear sense in which one scientific area can be called an "analogy" for another. Two areas are structurally or formally analogous to each other if their laws have the same form. However, since nothing is to be gained by substituting one ambiguous term for another, I shall not persist with this use of "analogy."

Where knowledge is scarce, speculation abounds. Social science, not surprisingly, witnesses a plethora of speculative "models" or guesses about isomorphisms. A few illustrations will suffice. The notion of society as an organism, though repeatedly discredited, has a way of cropping up in one form or another. In its Spenglerian form, society is likened to a plant, complete with a seasonal life cycle. Like plants, a society has its vernal and autumnal phases. Or, again, society is compared to the growth and physiology of man, having like man its own states of development, its organic interrelatedness of parts, and its homeostatic controls. Evolutionary theory

---

[1] This "translation" of the laws of one area into those of another by establishing a one-to-one correspondence between the concepts of both areas is sometimes called an "interpretation" of one theory by means of the concepts of another. But the term "interpretation" has so many overtones of meaning that I prefer to avoid using it.

is another favorite model. Whole societies may be seen as engaged in a struggle for survival subject to natural selection. Within a society, the various institutions and codes of behavior are viewed in the light of their contribution to adaptation and adjustment. Or, again, individual learning is compared with the process of selective survival among random variations. The human brain is compared to an electronic computer. Servomechanisms, like the automatic pilot or thermostat, are now frequently evoked models for learning and purposive behavior. How does one go about testing these suggested models?

First, it must be possible to state clearly what is in one-to-one correspondence with what. Organisms grow; they increase in size and weight. What is *social* "growth"? What is the autumnal phase of society corresponding to the autumn of a plant? Relatively precise meaning can be given to adaptive and nonadaptive characteristics of organisms within evolutionary theory. Can we give correspondingly precise meanings to these notions for human institutions? What in learning, fitted to the evolutionary model, corresponds to the role of mutations? Second, once clearly defined empirical concepts in one area are made to correspond to the terms of the model, then formal similarities, if any, are sought. Nutrition is connected with growth in biology. Are the social concepts corresponding to nutrition and to growth similarly connected? In other words, not only must the terms of the two areas correspond, but the connections among these concepts must also be preserved, if the model is to be of any use. An area, either part or all of it, can be a fruitful model for another only if corresponding concepts can be found and if at least some of the laws connecting the concepts of the model also can be shown to connect their corresponding concepts. This implies that the model is from an area better developed than that for which it is used. If very little is known about either field, then to speak of a "model" is hardly more than loose and pointless talk.

Unnecessary Uses of "Model"

Isomorphism of the laws of one theory with those of another unequivocally defines the term "model." Unfortunately, the word has other uses. Two other meanings are especially prevalent. One of these has nothing at all to do with the notion of isomorphism. The other is connected with this notion, but in a manner different from that just discussed. The same term applied to at least three different kinds of things is of course confusing. Moreover, the resulting ambiguity is quite unnecessary, since other terms are at hand which adequately characterize these further uses. "One thing, one word" is still a good idea.

The first unnecessary use of "model" is as a synonym for "theory." In particular, the term is used for theories which have some or all of four different characteristics. (1) Any as yet untested or even untestable theory may be dubbed a "model." Speculative theories, like those about the neurophysiological correlates of behavior or the doctrines of psychoanalysis, for which empirical evidence is scarce, are sometimes called models, apparently because of a reluctance to honor them as full-fledged theories. But there is nothing in the notion of a theory, as a set of hypotheses about an area, which says that it must be true or known to be so. (2) Constructing a theory entails abstraction. "Abstraction," like "model," is equivocal. In one context it refers to that selection always necessary to describe the world. All theories, whether of human or non-human behavior, omit some variables simply because they are not relevant to the phenomena to be explained or predicted by the theory. Self-consciousness, not to say embarrassment, about such perfectly legitimate omissions seems to be peculiar to social science. It is suggested by phrases like "economic man" or "ideal type." The quite unnecessary diffidence about neglecting variables is sometimes reflected by calling these theories "models." Economic man, on one formulation, always chooses to maximize his utility. But this is part of a theory asserting in effect that, statistically at least, other motives can be neglected when predicting, say, the behavior of a firm. Similarly, ideal types of society implicitly assert that the effect of unmentioned variables is negligible. But this is true of any theory. The better the theory, the more knowledge we have about the conditions under which the neglected variables do or do not make a difference. If there are no economic men or if the ideal type of capitalism does not exist, then certain suggested theories are false. Calling them "models" will not make them truer. (3) In another context, "abstraction" refers to things like the perfect or ideal gas, absolutely rigid bodies, perfectly straight lines, frictionless bodies, and instantaneous velocities. These entities are all physically impossible. The infinitesimal is an artifact of our mathematical machinery, enabling us to compute changes of one variable with respect to another. Theories making use of this and other "ideal" entities are also called models. What is ideal about them? A perfect or ideal gas is not, like our model boy, everything a good gas ought to be. Yet, they are alike in that both of them charcteristically deviate from anything actual. There conceivably could be perfect boys but probably there are none. In the nature of the case, there cannot be any frictionless bodies or dimensionless points. A frictionless engine is one whose coefficient of friction is zero; a dimensionless point has zero diameter. The scientist uses these imaginary "zero" notions when theorizing in order to predict how *other* properties of such entities, the engine or the gas, are connected, assuming the given one is absent. Only ideal gases, defined as those whose molecules have zero volume, exactly obey certain laws connecting the volume, pressure, and temperature of gases.

Deviations from these laws, as under high pressures, may then be explained in terms of deviations from the ideal. These of course are independently confirmable by more general laws of which the "almost-zero" condition is a special case. The laws of theories making use of such entities are "ideal" because they hold rigorously only for the limiting case of zero-value for certain specified variables. These laws are not false, but are an extrapolation from actual conditions to the physically unapproachable limit. Moreover, they state, implicitly or explicitly, the range of actual conditions for which they hold. These theories which extrapolate or idealize their laws for the zero-value of specified variables are not the same as those theories, like that of economic man or ideal types, which deliberately neglect variables. A detailed discussion involves another story for another time. But consider that it is not disturbing to say that there are no perfect gases or dimensionless points. Nobody ever thought there were. But to say that economic man or the ideal type of capitalism does not exist is to say that certain theories are false, either because they neglected unspecified but relevant variables or because the laws among those specified do not hold. (4) When numbers can be attached to the concepts of a theory, so that we can say how much of the property is present or how much it changes under certain conditions, then the theory is quantified. Social scientists now valiantly try to quantify their terms. Quantified theories may be constructed either directly from observed facts or, rather more frequently, from guesses about the facts. Quantified theories are after all just theories. Only in a very special case, to be discussed later, having no counterpart in social science, do physicists call theories "models." A physicist speaks of the Newtonian theory, not of the Newtonian model. Yet within social science quantified theories are now frequently called "models," and, particularly, "mathematical models." The term "mathematical," I have already shown, is radically and harmfully ambiguous. The phrase "mathematical model" compounds the ambiguity. I shall recur to this point in a moment. In any case, uncertainty, selection, idealization, and quantification are characteristic to a greater or lesser degree of most worthwhile theories. What then is gained, except unnecessary confusion, by calling theories which share in some or all of these characteristics "models"?

Models: Arithmetical Representations

A third prevalent use of "model" also has something to do with isomorphism, but not with that between laws of empirical theories. "Mathematical model," as I just said, may simply mean any quantified theory. On the other hand, it may and frequently does mean any arithmetical structure of a kind I must now explain. We saw before that replacing all the descriptive terms or concepts in the theory of one area by those of a different area results in another theory with the same form but different content from the original. The isomorphic sets of laws, those of the model and of its "translation," are both empirical theories whose truth or falsity depends upon the facts. It is possible, and often highly desirable, to establish another kind of isomorphism, in which the result is not two empirical theories sharing a common structure. Instead, the laws, or some of them, of an empirical theory may have the same form as a set of purely arithmetical truths. If this is the case, then the latter is called an *arithmetical representation* of the empirical theory. This notion is best explained by means of illustrations. I shall briefly discuss four: analytical geometry, probability theory, measurement, and the theory of games.

Arithmetical Representation: Analytical Geometry

Euclidean geometry is a physical theory. Its axioms and theorems are empirical laws about the properties of rigid bodies in space. Its axioms state certain connections among the entities, including relations, referred to by its undefined or basic descriptive terms, like "point," "line," "lies on," and "between." Its theorems, derived from the axioms and definitions, state connections among defined entities such as triangles and circles and relations like parallel and perpendicular. As in any empirical theory, only the connection between the axioms and theorems is logically necessary. Both axioms and theorems themselves are empirical hypotheses like all others, except that for ordinary magnitudes they are particularly well confirmed. As we now know, in the realm of the very large they do not hold. (Clarification of the empirical nature of geometry was one important by-product of the theory of relativity.) *Analytical* geometry is constructed from physical geometry by putting all the undefined descriptive terms of the latter into one-to-one correspondence with a set of defined arithmetical terms. (Alternative ways to speak of constructing a one-to-one correspondence are to say that one set of terms is "coordinated" to or "mapped" on to another set.) For example, the descriptive entity "point" is coordinated to an ordered pair of numbers, that is, the point corresponding to the pair of numbers (0,5) is different from the point corresponding to the pair of numbers (5,0). All of the geometrical figures correspond to equations or sets of equations. A straight line, for instance, corresponds to, say, $y = 5$ or $y = x + 3$; a circle to still a different equation like $x^2 + y^2 = 25$. More generally, the notion of, for instance, a straight line will correspond to the set of all number-pairs satisfying a certain form of equation. The descriptive relation "lying on," as of a point lying on a line, corresponds to the arithmetical notion of a pair of numbers satisfying a given equation. In this way, an isomorphism is constructed between the statements of physical geometry and a set of arithmetical statements. All the geometrical axioms and, of course, the theorems, will be "mirrored" by a set of purely arithmetical statements about numbers, equations, and sets of equations. This mirror-image or model is an arithmetical representation of the physical theory. In the representation, though the same words may be used, the geometrical terms, like "line" and "parallel," refer not to physical and spatial properties, but to purely arithmetic notions. Accordingly, though it has the same formal structure as the physical geometric theory, the arithmetical representation has one radically different characteristic. All of its axioms and theorems are tautologies, like all statements of arithmetic. The physical theory of geometry is a set of synthetic, empirical truths about space; the arithmetical structure isomorphic with it is a set of analytic or logical truths about numbers. (This result is possible because undefined geometric terms are coordinated to defined arithmetical terms, e.g., to integers construed as classes of classes.)

Arithmetical Representation: Probability Theory

An arithmetical representation of analytical geometry was made by proceeding from the empirical theory to the arithmetical one. When appying the mathematical theory of probability we work in the reverse direction, that is, from an arithmetical representation or model to an empirical theory. We construct an empirical theory that is isomorphic to the mathematical theory of probability. The mathematical theory of probability may be formulated or axiomatized in many different ways.[2] These are all the same theory in the sense that, for example, in all of them the usual rules for the addition and multiplication of probabilities, Bayes' theorem, and so on, all hold. Since they permit the calculation of further probabilities from given probabilities, such theories, like other arithmetical systems, are also called "calculi." No matter how it is axiomatized, the calculus of probability is, in the first instance, a set of purely arithmetical, hence tautological or logically true, statements about numbers, in this case certain fractions called "probabilities." In the "frequency theory" formulation of the probability calculus, the probability of an event is arithmetically defined as the limit of the relative frequency of that event in an infinite reference class. Packed into the notion of a "reference class" are certain arithmetically defined charcteristics, notably random or irregular distribution and the convergence of relative frequencies to a constant number. Certain other concepts like "independence" are also arithmetically defined. Before the probability theory can be applied, these arithmetical notions must all be made to correspond to descriptive or empirical concepts. For instance, *arithmetical* "independence" of two events A and B is defined to mean that their joint probability in a given reference class is the arithmetical product of their separate probabilities. Coordinated to this is a *descriptive* concept of "independence." Two observed events A and B are empirically independent if the occurrence of one does not in any way influence the occurrence of the other. More precisely, two observations A and B are empirically independent if the probability of A given that B has occurred is the same as the probability of A regardless of the occurrence of B. The *arithmetical*

---

[2] For a more detailed discussion of axiomatization, see "Axiomatic Systems, Formalization, and Scientific Theories" by H. Hochberg in *Symposium on Sociological Theory*, edited by L. Gross, Harper & Row, New York, 1959.

notion of probability as the limit of a frequency in an infinite class is coordinated to the *descriptive* notion of a relative frequency in a finite class, for only the latter is actually observed. In this way, a one-to-one correspondence is set up between the arithmetical concepts of the calculus and descriptive terms. This is true no matter what arithmetical formulation of probability theory is used as a model, whether it be the frequency theory or the mathematically more abstract formulation in terms of sets of "points" (numbers).[3]

When the coordinated descriptive terms are substituted for the arithmetical ones in the axioms of the probability calculus, the resulting "translation" is now a set of empirical laws about the referents of these terms. It is, for instance, an empirical law that if two events are (empirically) independent, then their joint (empirical) probability is the arithmetical product of their separate probabilities. Different empirical theories have the same arithmetical representation or model when their descriptive terms are coordinated to the same arithmetical ones. Consider that instead of having the arithmetical probability, p, correspond to observed frequencies in a sample, alternative coordinations are possible. For example, let "p" stand for "degree of belief." Assign numbers between 0 and 1 to "p" in a manner that establishes an order, so that if p_1 is more intense than p_2, the number assigned to p_1 is greater than the number assigned to p_2. The axioms about "p" are now statements, not of the actual proportions in which things are distributed, but of people's feelings about or estimate of such proportions. The arithmetical representation, the mathematical theory of probability, requires, for instance, that if an individual estimates the probability of A as $\frac{1}{2}$ and that of B as $\frac{3}{4}$, then he should also estimate the probability of A and B together as $\frac{3}{8}$. Whether, under this "subjective" coordination, the axioms are satisfied, may be tested in various ways by asking people, or by observing their betting behavior, and so on. This illustration shows clearly how, by coordinating different sets of descriptive terms (people's beliefs, on the one hand, and objective observed relative frequencies, on the other), one arrives at two different empirical theories with the same arithmetical representation.

[3] Since the use of a so-called "set-theoretic model" plays a large role in recent social-science theorizing, a few comments may be in order. The theory of sets is a branch of pure mathematics dealing with classes or sets of entities of any kind whatsoever. Everything and anything can be classified, that is, considered as a member of a certain class or set. This includes responses of various kinds, individuals who behave as predicted and those who do not, and various experimental situations, as well as the classical shoes, ships, and sealing wax. The axioms of set theory merely state what else must be logically true, given that one set is included in another. Set theory thus offers a language for formulating statements about observations or predictions and, after being thus formulated, a group of tautologies for making deductions from these statements to other empirical hypotheses about combinations of sets. Since the axioms and theorems of set theory are tautologically true of all sets, they will also be true of the observed ones. When it is said that a set-theoretic "model" is being used, all that is meant is that observations are described in the language or notation of sets and that tautologies about sets are used to make deductions from empirical hypotheses formulated in the language of sets.

If the empirical laws isomorphic to the tautological axioms of the arithmetical representation turn out to be true, then all of the theorems of the latter may be used to compute further probabilities. Since the theorems in the arithmetical representation follow from axioms about infinite series, they cannot in general be derived directly from the descriptive or empirical laws about finite series of observations. The auxiliary use of the arithmetical calculus is therefore indispensable. The question of whether or not the theorems of this calculus can be applied to observed finite series of events is a matter of empirical fact. It is a matter of fact that given classes containing sufficiently large numbers of elements and the usual objective definition of probability in terms of relative frequencies, then, under proper sampling procedures, the axioms are satisfied. The world, happily, is this way. It could be different, so that the model was not satisfied. This would be too bad for scientists, particularly social scientists. It would not, of course, affect either the validity of the connection between the axioms and theorems or the logical truth of the mathematical theory of probability.

Arithmetical Representation: Measurement

The process of *measurement* in empirical science also requires the use of an arithmetical representation. [See the comments on p. 575 of the introduction for this section regarding the narrow and the broad uses of "measurement."] The elementary laws of arithmetic may themselves serve as such a model. Indeed, only when this is possible can arithmetic be used in empirical science. When laws are quantified, then arithmetical tautologies may be used for deducing other laws and facts from them. This is the most important use of such tautologies within science. If, in Galileo's law, $d = 16t^2$, distance is expressed in feet and time in seconds, then from that law in conjunction with the fact that the time of fall was three seconds, we may deduce that the distance was 144 ft. The additional factual premise about the time of fall permits the deduction from the law that the distance is equal to 16 times 3^2. Using the arithmetical tautology $3 \times 3 = 9$ as an additional premise, we deduce that the distance is 16×9. The tautology $16 \times 9 = 144$ permits the final deduction that the distance fallen was 144 ft. Since the arithmetical statements are tautologies, they may be added as premises without adding any more factual content than is given by the initial empirical premises about distance and time. In such simple calculations or deductions, the arithmetical premises are usually not stated explicitly, but are nevertheless being used. Arithmetic is a subtle and strong logic permitting deductions which, without it, might be quite impossible. What conditions must empirical properties meet before arithmetic can be applied to them?

Consider, first of all, the following three logical truths about numbers. The symbols ">" and "=" have their customary arithmetic meaning.

1. For any three numbers, if $N_1 > N_2$ and $N_2 > N_3$, then $N_1 > N_3$.
2. For any two numbers, at most one of $N_1 > N_2$, $N_1 = N_2$, $N_2 > N_1$ holds.
3. For any two numbers, at least one of $N_1 > N_2$, $N_1 = N_2$, $N_2 > N_1$ holds.

For this set of axioms to be a representation of an empirical theory, a set of descriptive terms must be coordinated to the arithmetic entities and relations. Let the numbers correspond to individual people, the relation ">" to the descriptive relation "higher-in-status" and "=" to "same status." After this coordination, the statements are probably again true, but, if so, they are now empirical truths about the descriptive relation "higher-in-status." Other descriptive terms can easily be found for which the axioms fail. Let ">" be coordinated to "sibling" and "=" to "same person as." In this case, the second axiom is false. For, of course, if John is Peter's sibling, then Peter is John's sibling and the axiom states that not both of these can hold. The axioms are an arithmetic representation of those descriptive properties which can be ordered. Many other such properties also satisfy the axioms: men and the relationship taller than, physical bodies and heavier than, the relative hardness of stones, and students' scores on tests, are a few more candidates for true correspondence with the structure of integers and the relation "greater-than." All true representations of these axioms share a common structure. The theorems implied by the axioms exhibit still further structure, for instance, irreflexivity and asymmetry. "Irreflexivity" means that an individual cannot have the relation to himself. A person may love himself but he cannot be taller than himself. "Love" doesn't satisfy the axioms, so the theorems need not be true of it. "Taller than" does, so it must also be asymmetric and irreflexive.

The axioms and theorems together tell us more than appears at first glance about the structure of whatever satisfies the axioms. Whether or not a descriptive property has this structure is a matter of observable fact. Some things do and, as we have seen, some things don't. Those that do have the structure of what is called a "complete ordering." The possibility of establishing an order of succession among attributes is not an unimportant characteristic, particularly in social science. This possibility is expressed by a set of empirical laws of which these axioms are an arithmetical representation. These empirical laws make ranking possible. There are many descriptive properties which satisfy the first two axioms of order, but not the third. Thus, when the properties of incomparable things are being considered, like food and plays or musicians and painters, then the relation of, say, "better than" does not satisfy the third axiom. Nor can we order all the people in the world by the relation "ancestor," since, given any two different individuals one need not be the ancestor of the other. The first two axioms alone therefore express a "partial ordering." Only all three axioms express a completely ordered domain. Insofar as the descriptive concepts of different theories are true representations of some or all of the axioms of order, they share a common structure or form. By virtue of this shared structure, ranking is possible.

For measurement in the strict sense also to be possible, the descriptive properties must share certain other structural features of arithmetic. In particular, they must also have the same form as axioms like the following three:

4. For any two positive numbers, N_1 and N_2, there is exactly one other, N_3, such that $N_1 + N_2 = N_3$.
5. For any two positive numbers, $N_1 + N_2 = N_2 + N_1$.
6. For any three positive numbers $(N_1 + N_2) + N_3 = N_1 + (N_2 + N_3)$.

Axiom 4 states that for any two numbers, there is uniquely a third which is their sum. Axiom 5 states that the sum of any two numbers is independent of their order; axiom 6, that when any three numbers are added, the result is independent of how they are grouped. These axioms state part of the structure of addition. Addition is a binary operation on the elements or members of the set of positive integers, that is, a way of combining two elements of the set to get a third. Note that while these axioms are logical truths about the addition of positive numbers, they are all false of subtraction on only the same elements. If we extend the system of elements to include both positive and negative numbers, then axioms 5 and 6 do not hold for the operation of subtraction. The kind of elements specified and the kind of operations performed on them determines whether the resulting statements will be logically true or false or, in the case of descriptive entities, empirically true or false.

For these arithmetical truths to be a representation of anything, the number-elements and the arithmetical operations performed on them must be coordinated to descriptive entities and to operations on these descriptive entities. Just as the arithmetical relation "greater-than" can be made to correspond to natural or physical relations like "heavier than," "prefers," "loves," or "higher-in-status," so there must be a natural or physical operation corresponding to addition. As numbers can be added, so things can be put into the same container, glued together or, even, be simultaneously responded to. Suppose that our elements are lumps of sugar, each having a specified weight. Though numbers are assigned to the elements, indicating how much of the property it has, the corresponding operation is performed not on these numbers, but on the elements themselves. Only in the arithmetical representation are the elements themselves numbers. Weight is a measurable property of lumps of sugar because given two lumps of specified weight, the weight resulting from putting them both on the same side of a balance is the arithmetical sum of their individual weights. In other words, the operation of weighing two lumps of sugar has the same structure as the laws of arithmetic.

The sweetness of sugar, on the other hand, is not measurable. For measurable descriptive properties are those having the same form as the addition of numbers. Grinding together two lumps of sugar of equal sweetness, as indicated by some index of sweetness, would not give something twice as sweet. Or the order in which two things are mixed together might make a difference. Not only must a corresponding physical operation be found, but it must satisfy the axioms. If no corresponding physical or natural operation can be found or if it does not satisfy the axioms of addition, then the property cannot be measured. It may be ranked, however, if it satisfies the axioms of order. The measurability of descriptive properties is expressed by a set of empirical laws which are isomorphic to the laws of arithmetic. By virtue of this isomorphism, numbers may be assigned to the properties of things, resulting in quantified empirical laws. All the laws of arithmetic may then be applied to these numbers to derive new empirical laws and facts.

Arithmetical Representation: Theory of Games

In what sense of the ambiguous phrase "mathematical model" is the theory of games a "model"? In a game, an individual has to take actions in the face of uncertainty, either the uncertainty of his opponent's moves or uncertainty about the distribution of events, like the cards of a hand, or both. Each player wants to win as much or lose as little as possible. How will he behave? If the theory of games answers this question, then it must be an empirical theory of human behavior. Actually, however, the connection between the theory of games and a theory of behavior is exactly the same as the connection between the axioms of arithmetic and the empirical laws which permit ranking and measurement or between analytical and physical geometry. That is, the theory of games is an arithmetical representation, given an appropriate correspondence with descriptive terms, of an empirical theory of behavior in "game" situations. The notation is set-theoretic. (See note 3.) In addition to ordinary arithmetic and the probability calculus, the axioms contain terms referring to sets. The members of some of these sets are negative and positive numbers, ordered by the relation "greater-than." These are put into one-to-one correspondence with the descriptive concept of all possible outcomes of the play of a game. The numbers these "outcomes" have in the representation correspond in the empirical theory to the value or utility they have for each player. These utilities are ordered by the relation of "preference," corresponding to the arithmetical "greater-than." Some outcomes are preferred to others. Other sets consist of probabilities. These correspond to the chance events occurring in the course of a game. The probabilities and the utilities of outcomes are combined in all possible ways, to give the "mathematical expectation" of each play. Thus, if an event with a probability of $\frac{1}{2}$ is worth \$10 to a player, its mathematical expectation is \$5. The arithmetical problem is a combinatorial one, namely, how to combine utilities and probabilities so as to maximize simultaneously a whole set of such expectations. These correspond to the amount each player can win. A solution to this mathematical problem becomes, in the corresponding empirical theory, a set of statements about how a "rational" player would behave. A "rational" player is defined as one who desires to maximize his utility. A solution is a set of rules for each player to follow in any conceivable situation, no matter what his partner does or what turns up on the cards. For certain kinds of two- and three-person games such solutions have been found. It consists in a strategy which, if followed by a player, will keep his losses at a minimum. As an arithmetical system, the theory of games is a mathematical computation of a set of simultaneous and conflicting maxima problems. Mapped into the empirical concepts, it predicts how people will behave, if they are rational in the sense defined. The theory may also be viewed as a normative statement of how people ought to behave, if they want to keep their losses to a minimum in games or in the many social, competitive situations which can be fitted to the game theory representation. Again, the theory of games is itself an arithmetical system of purely logical truths about, essentially, combinations of probabilities under complicated conditions of maximization. The trick for the mathematician, and it is no inconsiderable one, is to solve these maxima problems. The trick for the social scientist, and it is no less considerable, is to find appropriate descriptive terms which when coordinated to the arithmetical ones result in true empirical laws of human behavior. Theories of behavior in political, economic, and military situations, as well as in ordinary parlor games, may be constructed so as to be isomorphic with the arithmetical theory of games. Whether people actually do or do not behave in the way predicted by these theories is, of course, a matter for empirical test. [For a more detailed discussion of the theory of games see Part III of the paper by Arrow in this section.]

Models: Formalizations

It is sometimes desirable to consider a theory "formally," that is, to lay bare the form of its axioms, by replacing all the descriptive terms by letters. For instance, $y = ax + b$ is a formalization of a linear relation; $y = ax^2$ is a formalization of a parabolic relation between the variables y and x. Laws may thus be considered formally in order to facilitate deductions or to check deductions already made. Or, if one is looking for isomorphisms, this may be done in order to compare the formal structures of two sets of laws about different phenomena. Any theory, quantified or nonquantified, may be formalized in this way. The result is called a *formalization* of the theory. These expressions exhibit form but no content, since the letter variables have not been given descriptive meaning. They are therefore neither true nor false, since they are not complete sentences, but only the form of sentences. They become true or false only when either descriptive or arithmetical concepts replace the letter-variables. Such formalizations of theories are also sometimes called "mathematical models."

Three Meanings of "Mathematical Model"

It is time to sum up the ambiguities in the phrase "mathematical model." It may, first of all, mean any *quantified empirical theory*, that is, any theory whose descriptive terms have numbers attached to them. In this case, a "mathematical model" is a set of empirical laws. The phrase may, secondly, refer to any *arithmetical representation* of an empirical theory. In this case, the "mathematical model" is a set of analytic or tautological truths about numbers. Thirdly, the phrase may refer to the kind of *formalization* just discussed. "Mathematical model" therefore may refer to systems of either empirical, tautological, or indeterminate expressions.[4] Such systems are all very different things. A term that obscures important distinctions is worse than useless. The term "mathematical theory" shares in the confusion. Does it mean a quantified empirical theory or a tautological theory of pure mathematics? This ambiguity of "mathematical" led me to reserve the term "arithmetical" for the latter. Greater accuracy and less confusion would result if "mathematical" were used only for statements of pure mathematics. But the verbal habit of ambiguously using the term is probably by now beyond extinction. There is, however, no need to reinforce the relatively recent indiscriminate use of "mathematical model." In the basic sense of "model" as a set of statements isomorphic to another set, an arithmetical representation is of course also a model. The mathematically customary term "arithmetical representation" would, however, help distinguish this notion from that of empirical theories which are used as structural models for other empirical theories. Both arithmetical and empirical models are used as a source of hypotheses about the form of the laws taken by the descriptive terms coordinated to the terms of the model. But it makes a difference which kind of theory, arithmetical or empirical, is used as a model. When, for example, the empirical theory of servomechanisms is used as a model for purposive behavior, if the structure of some of the laws of the model doesn't fit the data, we can change these laws so that they will fit. When, on the other hand, we use an arithmetical representation, changes cannot be made at will. We cannot make two and two equal five

---

[4] In the volume *Mathematical Thinking in the Social Sciences,* edited by P. F. Lazarsfeld, 1954, The Free Press, New York; Anderson, Marschak and Simon (Chapters 1, 4 and 8) use the term "model" to mean a quantified theory; in the papers by Rashevsky and Coleman (Chapters 2 and 3) a "model" is an isomorphic empirical theory; the models discussed by Guttman and Lazarsfeld (Chapters 5, 6 and 7) are arithmetical representations and formalizations. Learning theorists in psychology and theoretical economists usually use the term "model" as a synonym for quantified hypotheses and theories. For instances, see W. K. Estes and C. J. Burke, *Psychological Review,* 1953, **60**; R. R. Bush and F. Mosteller, *Stochastic Models for Learning,* 1955, John Wiley & Sons, Inc. New York; K. W. Spence, *Behavior Theory and Conditioning,* 1956, Yale University Press, New Haven; the paper by the economist J. Marschak mentioned above and *Statistical Inference in Dynamic Economic Models* (Edited by T. C. Koopmans), 1950, John Wiley & Sons, Inc., New York. In his *Models of Man: Social and Rational,* 1957, John Wiley & Sons, Inc., New York, H. A. Simon uses the term both for quantified empirical theories and formalizations.

because it would fit the data better. We can only lament the fact that our data are not measurable. These are not unimportant differences.

Significance of Isomorphisms

It is all too easy to overestimate the significance of structural isomorphisms. The fact that all or some of the laws of one area have the same form as those of another need not signify anything whatsoever about any connection between the two areas. To be convinced of this, just think of all the different kinds of things which can be ranked and measured. All have the same structure as arithmetical addition and, to this extent, the same structure as each other. Only the isomorphism *with arithmetic* is in itself significant, because this permits us to apply all the laws about numbers to quantified descriptive concepts. But this implies no connection among all those things that are isomorphic to arithmetic, any more than there need be any connection among all the different kinds of things which satisfy the same form of empirical linear equation. The use of one theory as a structural model for another does not, therefore, explain one in terms of the other. . . .

The existence of a structural isomorphism, as I just pointed out, *need* not signify any connection between two areas. On the other hand, if the laws of one area have the same form as those of another, this *may* be a cue to some connection between them. If what appear to be two different areas are really one and the same, then, of course, their laws will have the same form. But the converse does not hold. What else, therefore, is required to justify the assertion that the concepts of one area not only obey laws of the same structure as those of another but also actually refer to the same kind of phenomena? . . . [A discussion of the identification of light with electricity, both obeying the Wave Equation, is here omitted.] The identification of one set of phenomena with another thus rests on three things: first, their laws have the same form; second, the same value for the constants in these laws, and, finally, the interchangeability of the empirical concepts. By condition one, two areas are merely shown to be structurally isomorphic. Only by conditions two and three can they meaningfully be said to be the same phenomena. If two theories are thus identified, there is clearly no sense in which one is a model for the other. They are merely two different ways of talking about the same things.

. . . The reduction of sociology or, more generally, any social science dealing with group behavior, to psychology, or the science of individual behavior, also has nothing to do with structural isomorphism or of one area being a "model" for another. . . . When two theories are *identified*, then the basic terms of each theory are interchangeable. When one theory is *definitionally reduced* to another, then the basic terms of the reduced theory become defined terms of the theory from which it is derived. To put it differently, optics and electromagnetism are literally identical, while sociology is a deductive consequence of psychology, if reduction is possible. The practical meaning of this difference is as follows. Once it is realized that the basic terms of two theories refer to the same things, then *ipso facto* we cannot have knowledge of one area without at the same time having knowledge of the other. If, however, one theory is a deductive consequence of another, that is, related to it as theorems to axioms, then clearly one can independently study the subject-matter of the theorems. This will be done when, as at present, we do not know the appropriate axioms, that is, the composition laws of psychology, from which the theorems may be derived. If, however, there are such laws and we find them, then, of course, the group laws would deductively follow from them.[5]

Models in Physics

Finally, something should be said about a use of the term "model" which is unique to atomic physical science. I shall only try to sketch here how the model itself and the way it is connected to the theory for which it is a model each differ from models and theories of nonphysical or, even more generally, nonatomic sciences. In the kinetic theory of heat, the science of mechanics serves as a "model" for thermodynamics. But the laws of these two sciences do not have the same form. What, then, is the meaning of "model" in this context? Classical Newtonian mechanics and thermodynamics are both macroscopic theories, that is, their variables refer to observable characteristics of things not further analyzed into molecules or atoms. The laws of mechanics are about mass and spatial, temporal properties; those of thermodynamics are about temperature, pressure, volume, and the like. The kinetic theory of heat forms the bridge between these two sets of concepts which permits the reduction of thermodynamics to mechanics. It achieves this by a double-barrelled assumption. It assumes, first of all, that wherever there appears to be a continuous media like a gas, there are "really" millions of invisible particles. It is further assumed that these particles all bounce back and forth according to the laws of motion as stated in the theory of mechanics. The "mechanical model" for thermodynamics consists of these two assumptions. . . .

This model differs from any in nonatomic science by the nature of its assumption about invisible entities. It further differs by the unique nature of the connection between the "model" and the theory which it is devised to explain. When definitions connect the concepts of two areas, these may be conceived as rules for co-ordinating these concepts. If the connection between the model and the macroscopic theory of heat were definitional, then each term of the model would be co-ordinated to a descriptive con-

---

[5] [See the papers in Section Four of this volume for detailed discussions of group concepts and the issue of reduction.]

cept of thermodynamics. This is not the way it works. Some of the terms of the model are not individually co-ordinated to the concepts of the empirical theory. In particular, concepts referring to individual particles and their properties are not connected to the measurable properties of gases. Instead, certain statistical functions of two or more of these terms are thus connected. Average kinetic energy, for instance, a function of mass and velocity, is coordinated to the descriptive concept "pressure," but neither the mass nor the velocity of individual particles is separately co-ordinated. Thus, the connection is not strictly definitional, since not each term of the mechanical model is replaceable by a descriptive thermodynamic term. This unique type of connection is called "partial co-ordination," since not all the terms of the model are co-ordinated to descriptive terms. Accordingly, if the model and its theory are collapsed into one deductive system, with the co-ordination rules formulated as explicit definitions, the basic, uncoordinated terms cannot be eliminated from this system.[6]

This ineliminability, due to the partial nature of the co-ordination, has fascinated some social scientists. Why, it has been asked, can we not similarly introduce concepts without tying them to something observable? A few comments are in order.[7] The candidates offered for such "unco-ordinated" terms of social science do not have the characteristics of these atomic physical concepts. Generally, such candidates are one of two kinds. First, they may be clinical or group concepts whose meanings are more or less vague because the list of defining symptoms cannot yet be completely itemized. When enough is known about which clusters of behavior permit predictions to other behavior, then the observable meaning of these concepts, such as "schizophrenia" or "group-morale," can be completely specified. Or, secondly, they are speculative, neurophysiological notions whose referents have merely not yet been observed. Unlike particles, however, they could in principle be observed and one day may be so. Sometimes terms referring to "mental states" are offered as candidates for basic, ineliminable concepts of psychological theory. To justify introducing these unconfirmable characteristics of other people's minds, we should have available a theory of "mind" comparable to the theory of mechanics which, after at least partial coordination with behavioral terms, would tell us more about behavior than we can learn from observing behavior itself. Why, for example, instead of supposing that there were invisible particles, wasn't it assumed that there were thousands of little gremlins pounding on the walls of the container? The reason is obvious. No adequate theory of gremlin behavior

---

[6] For a more detailed discussion of "partial co-ordination" and of the nature of atomic models, see G. Bergmann, *Philosophy of Science*, Univer. of Wisconsin Press, Madison, 1957. On models in physics see also M. Brodbeck, "Mental and Physical: Identity versus Sameness," *Mind, Matter, and Method*, P. K. Feyerabend and G. Maxwell, eds., University of Minnesota Press, Minneapolis, 1966, pp. 40–58.

[7] The advocacy of partial co-ordination or "implicit definition" specifically within social science is further analyzed and criticized in M. Brodbeck, "Logic and Scientific Method in Research on Teaching," *Handbook of Research on Teaching*, N. L. Gage, ed., Rand McNally & Co., New York, 1963, esp. pp. 62–68.

was available to permit, after proper coordinations, the derivations to the behavior of gases. The assumptions of the mechanical model transfer the laws of an already independently confirmed theory to the behavior of invisible entities. By the unique method of partial coordination some of these characteristics are connected with experimentally observed variables. If the "right" terms of the model are coordinated to the "right" descriptive terms of the theory, then not only may already known empirical laws be derived but even new ones. If the model falls down on this job, as in fact it did, then we can change our assumptions about how the particles behave. These assumptions are not, after all, bound to observation as ordinary empirical laws are. So the model changes from year to year, and particles of all kinds proliferate tropically with the need to explain new observations. Like partial coordination, this radical discontinuity between the various "theories" or atomic models constructed to explain observations has no counterpart in sciences dealing with macroscopic, observable variables, whether these be social or physical sciences.

Nor is the statistical feature of recent physics comparable to that of social science. In the earlier mechanical model nothing could be said about individual particles. In the extended model of quantum mechanics, though not individual values, probability distributions can now be assigned to statements about individual particles. This possibility is entirely due to the nature of the assumptions in the computational model and the way its terms are partially coordinated to what can be observed. It has nothing to do with the limits of measurement, which is a matter of empirical operations on the observable referents of descriptive concepts and not on the subatomic elements of the model. The concepts of social science refer to observed behavior, either of individuals or of groups. If it can only make statistical predictions, this is because it simply does not know enough to make predictions about the individual. This incompleteness and consequent statistical character of our knowledge is a practical limitation, not one of principle or logic. In physics, the statistical character of statements about subatomic particles is built into the model that permits the physicist to speak at all about such entities. It cannot be overcome without radically changing the model.

The terms of classical Newtonian theory are, like those of social science, all concepts referring to what can be observed. The relatively simple structure of such a powerful theory has, to put it moderately, not yet been deployed to its fullest advantage by social scientists. Why then should they hunger after the complexity of the invisible? In any case, it is yet to be claimed that the phenomena of social science are of atomic or subatomic dimensions. The notion of "model" appropriate to such entities has therefore no intelligible meaning in social science.

[34] Measurement in
Behavioral Science

A B R A H A M   K A P L A N

Quality and Quantity

Possibly more widespread than the mystique of quantity, and certainly more pernicious in its effect, especially on behavioral science, is a corresponding *mystique of quality*. This mystique, like its counterpart, also subscribes to the magic of numbers, only it views their occult powers as a kind of black magic, effective only for evil ends, and seducing us into giving up our souls for what, after all, is nothing but dross. In this perspective, knowledge—and particularly, knowledge of human beings—consists in the apprehension of qualities, which in their very nature elude the net of number, however fine its mesh. As my friends at the University of Michigan have sometimes formulated this view, "If you can measure it, that ain't it!" For the student of human behavior, at any rate—so the view goes—measurement is pointless at best, and at worst, a hopeless distortion or obfuscation of what is really important. The exact sciences belong to the study of nature, not of man. Yet, on the face of it, disciplines like demography and economics make considerable use of mathematical methods and quantitative specifications, while, as Helmer and others have emphasized, there are many physical sciences—or at least, many parts of them—in which qualitative considerations predominate. What lies behind the mystique of quality?

To start with, every measurement involves some degree of abstraction: certain things are necessarily omitted in the numerical description, for this is always based on a determinate set of properties and relations to the exclusion of others. A specification of weight tells us nothing about size or density, for instance, which may nevertheless be involved in the quality of "massiveness." Yet this is only to say that no single quantitative description tells us everything; but is this not equally true of any single qualitative description? What is crucial is that the quantitative account includes all that is contained in the *corresponding* qualitative one. There is much that we do not know about a day in June when we are told that the temperature was 72°; but surely we know as much as if we had been told only that it was "warm." When we speak of the day as "rare"—excellent and pleasurable—we are not contrasting a quality with a quantity, but referring to a whole set of qualities for which, singly or in combination, quantitative specifications might conceivably be given. The argument that even if they *were* given, they would still leave something out, seems to me a straight-forward self-contradiction. And the position that they cannot in fact be given strikes me as no more than a begging of the question.

The point is that both quality and quantity are misconceived when they are taken to be antithetical or even alternative. Quantities are *of* qualities, and a measured quality *has* just the magnitude expressed in its measure. In a less metaphysical idiom, we could say that whether something is identified as a quality or as a quantity depends on how we choose to represent it in our symbolism. Predicates not assigned in terms of a scale (or perhaps, not in terms of an extensive scale, at any rate) specify qualities; when an appropriate scale has been introduced, we identify their referents as quantities. Conversely, we may begin with a set of measures, then introduce labels which mark out qualities, that is, properties considered apart from their scaling. The transformation of quantity into quality, or conversely, is a semantic or logical process, not a matter of ontology. The vocabulary of "hot" and "cold" has no other denotation than that which belongs to the temperature scale; color words do not name something other in the furniture of the world than is named by the specifications of wave length. (Of course, the *sensation* of blue is something different from the color. It is not itself a quality but a perceptual event or process which we conveniently describe by reference to the quality; but it can equivalently be described as the sensation of light of such-and-such a wavelength.)

What Is Not Measured

The notion that measurement inevitably leaves something out, in a sense in which the omission is sinful, stems, I think, partly from this: that very often—especially in behavioral science—our measures *do* omit properties and relations which are important in the conceptual frame within which we see the subject-matter. The intelligence measured by the IQ test, for instance, may fail to include such capacities as creativity, or the sort of thing that is called "practical good sense." It does not therefore follow that it is a poor measure, but only that we would be making poor use of it if we were to interpret it so inclusively. The criticisms which are usually made of such tests—and not by laymen only—amount, for the most part, to nothing more than the insistence that the tests do not measure everything we might like to think of as an intellectual capacity. The mystique of quality comes into play when this probable truth is taken as premise for the dubious conclusion that therefore the tests measure nothing significant at all. The limitations to which every measure is subject are first interpreted as shortcomings, and then generalized into a condemnation of measurements as such.

This condemnation also derives in part from a basic confusion between knowing something and having an experience of it. It is one thing to know that the day is warm, and another to feel its warmth. Though the cognitive process itself is an experience, as richly concrete as any other, *what* is known is something abstract, formulable in a proposition. We know and can state that such and such is the case, but no limited set of propositions can exhaust the content of an experience of the situation. Now qualities are usually thought of as being objects of direct experience, while quantities are supposed to be arrived at only in symbolically mediated cognitions. Hence measurement is decried as yielding only a bare abstraction which falls far short of a qualitative description.

But that quantities are only known and qualities only experienced is a wholly unwarranted notion. We can directly experience numerosity and even the specific cardinality, if it is not too great or if the elements are appropriately grouped, as every card player can testify. And on the other hand, we can have indirect, symbolically mediated cognitions of quality, as in our knowledge of whether a particular turtle is male or female—a fact which is likely to be a matter of direct experience only for herpetologists or for other turtles. What *is* true is that having an experience allows for a great deal of knowledge, while the cognition that some proposition is true consists precisely in knowing *that* proposition, not an indefinite set of other (and logically independent) propositions as well. But by the same token, having the experience does not consist in knowing anything whatever, at least in the sense of "knowing" relevant to the scientific context; it only provides an occasion for cognitions, and evidence of some sort (by no means conclusive) for their warrant. We are back to the argument that a measurement does not tell us everything; but neither does just one qualitative description.

The argument goes further, however. It is alleged that measurement not only leaves out something important but even denies its existence. Essential qualitative differences are swallowed up in the sameness of quantity. What is most distinctive of the human personality—that it is individualized—is just what is denied when we set about to fix the psyche in a set of measures. But such a view naively mistakes mathematical equalities for strict identities, and misinterprets the affirmation of a measured equivalence between two objects as the allegation that they are in fact one and the same object. A sameness is indeed being asserted, but it is a sameness only of the formal, structural properties which answer to the scale and procedures of the measurement. The force of what Nagel calls [1] "the petulant criticism of science"

[1] E. Nagel, "Measurement," in *Philosophy of Science,* edited by A. Danto and S. Morgenbesser, Meridian Books, New York, 1960, p. 137.

lies largely in "the interpretation of equations as the literal identification of different qualitative continua, and as the attribution of intrinsic, non-relational common characters to diverse subject matter." As for sameness, qualitative descriptions could also be said to group individuals into classes defined by the possession of the common quality. It is the numerical description which has the advantage here, I think, since it makes explicit how abstract the commonality is.

The Power of Measurement

I believe that the deepest roots of the mystique of quality, especially with regard to behavioral science, lie in the circumstance that measurements play various roles in human affairs which by no means always accord with our values. One of the most important social functions of measurement, as I have already pointed out, is that of standardization. But while we recognize the value of standardizing things, we feel degraded in having our own measure taken. The resistance to being standardized ourselves is, if I may say so, wholly just; would that such resistance were more widespread and more effective! But it is not measurement which is corrosive of our personality. To make that diagnosis is to confuse the study of values with the process of valuation, and to project onto the objects known, traits which belong only to the quest for knowledge. Measuring a value does not "reduce it to a number," in any sense which in the least depreciates its worth. When we assign a number to some aspect of behavior, we have not thereby robbed the behavior of its human significance. We have concerned ourselves only with the significance of the behavior for science, and this is likely to have been enhanced by the measurement.

The rub is that the science may then be used in ways inimical to our values. Measurement of behavior adds immeasurably to the effectiveness of various instruments of social control. The more exactly our responses are known, the more easily they can be manipulated. A latent distrust and even an overt hostility against the application of measurement to human subject-matters is, in this perspective, quite understandable. But this is not to say that it is justifiable. The mystique of quality may be rooted in the morality which insists that man be treated as an end in himself, and not merely as a means for political, military, or commercial aggrandizement. But the moral impulse is here misdirected. It is not the science which is sinful, but the use to which it is put. That knowledge is power does not give the victims of power a stake in ignorance. The irony is that the mystique of quality secretly recognizes how much can be achieved by a quantitative approach, and opposes it for just that reason. But we have tasted of the fruit of the Tree, and there is no road back to innocence. What we must do is not to resist the growth of knowledge of human behavior, but to use what we know so as to preserve and to enhance our precious humanity.

Incommensurables

There remain to be considered three problems of measurement in behavioral science which are more specific in nature.

One of the basic characteristics of human behavior is that it is purposive. Now purposes, and their corresponding goals and values, are far from being as single and as simple as measurement seems to require. It is not only that they vary from person to person and from time to time; they are also so interwoven with one another that in any given context several of them will almost surely be involved simultaneously. Power, gain, and glory—the classical trilogy of Hobbes—are less likely to command a single-minded loyalty than a dedication which is responsive to all three or to none of them. In choosing a home, a job, a wife, or just the lead to the next trick, a variety of considerations are likely to play a part; how can they be combined to allow for a measurement of the desirability of the various alternatives that might be chosen? For different values are incommensurable with one other: how can freedom be measured against security, stability of family or community life against industrial development, a soul that is lost against a world that is gained?

There is no doubt that measurement faces real difficulties here, but the situation need not be prejudged as hopeless. For specific purposes, bases of comparison among different values can often be found.[2] Such indices as money costs or energy consumed may be useful as derived measures, without the implication that their own value is interchangeable with the one which is being measured. Of more general bearing is the consideration that measurement is not limited to scalars, that is, magnitudes which are subject to a simple ordering. We may also use vectors and other multidimensional measures. A man might choose a job or a house by first weighing separately a number of component desiderata (salary, working conditions, and prospects; or rental, size, and location), and then by somehow summing the results, as though the components were reducible to a common measure. But he does not choose his friends by summing his appraisals of component traits and habits; he reacts, rather, to the personality as a whole. This *configurational* method, as we may call it, is probably more widely applicable in behavioral science than the *method of summation* relying wholly on scalar measures and some (hopefully) appropriate system of weightings.

Judges

But here a new difficulty arises, for usually the configurational method is applied by making use of human "judges." Measures of complex situations which do not easily lend themselves to scalar quantification—like the effec-

[2] A. Rapoport, *Operational Philosophy*, New York, 1953, p. 158ff.

tiveness of a psychotherapeutic technique, or the influence of a political boss—are most often arrived at with the help of a "human yardstick." Estimates are made by a panel of presumably competent observers, and some suitable statistical combination of these is then taken as the measure of the magnitude in question. As a result, the scientist using such a measure is describing "not the behavior of his subjects, but rather the behavior of the group composed of his subjects *and* of his judges." [3] This combination does not, however, make such measurement subjective, in any pejorative sense. All measurement yields, not a property intrinsic to the object being measured taken in isolation, but a relation between that object and the others serving as standards of measurement. When the relation is to other human beings, or even to the observer himself, it is not therefore a subjective one. As always, everything hinges on the controls which can be instituted, and on the sensitivity and reliability with which the discriminating judgments are being made.

The Quantitative Idiom

There are some who argue against the possibility of any significant measurement in behavioral science on the ground that we cannot in these matters define an operation of combination that will have the structure of arithmetical addition. Now, impossibilities are in the nature of the case difficult to demonstrate, and in science the history of such claims is an inglorious one: over and over what one period was convinced just couldn't be done was subsequently accomplished—though, to be sure, usually in a rather different form than was originally conceived. But suppose this be granted: that nothing important in human behavior is subject to additive operations. Such operations are not absolutely necessary to extensive measurement. But suppose that even this be granted: that we cannot hope to use ratio scales on a distinctively human subject-matter. The resources of measurement are by no means thereby exhausted. "Systematic study can be carried on in the social sciences as elsewhere by many devices which are less precise than strict quantitative measurement but nonetheless far better than unaided individual judgment. . . . There is a direct line of logical continuity from qualitative classification to the most rigorous forms of measurement, by way of intermediate devices of systematic ratings, ranking scales, multidimensional classifications, typologies, and simple quantitative indices. In this wider sense of 'measurement,' social phenomena are being measured every day." [4] Particularly noteworthy in this connection, I think, is the

[3] G. Bergmann and K. W. Spence, "The Logic of Psychophysical Measurement," *Psychological Review*, 1944; as reprinted in *Psychological Theory*, M. H. Marx, ed., Macmillan Co., New York, 1951, pp. 259–260.

[4] P. F. Lazarsfeld and A. H. Barton, "Qualitative Measurement in the Social Sciences," in *The Policy Sciences*, D. Lerner and H. D. Lasswell, eds., Stanford University Press, California, 1951, p. 155.

increasing use of types of mathematics not previously exploited for the purposes of behavioral science, as exemplified by von Neumann and Morgenstern's use of set theory in the analysis of rational decisions, or, more recently, Harary and Cartwright's application of graph theory to the analysis of organizational structures, as well as the use by many researchers of probability theory in the study of learning.

In my opinion, great as may be the difficulties of measurement in behavioral science, they are made greater both by being overestimated and, not infrequently, by being underestimated as well. It often happens that a *quantitative idiom* is used, not only without any actual measurements having been performed, but without any being projected, and even without any apparent awareness of what must be done before such measurements can be carried out. When the quantitative idiom is used by those who are unsympathetic if not downright hostile to the methods of measurement, the methodologist may be pardoned, perhaps, for feeling somewhat dismayed. Lawrence Kubie has made this point to his psychoanalytic colleagues, for example. Concepts like "depth of repression" and "strength of resistance," and in general, those pertaining to the "psychic economy," are almost always employed in a quantitative idiom; but a corresponding measure theory is almost wholly lacking. Kurt Lewin's "hodological geometry," whatever its shortcomings both from a logical and from an empirical standpoint, was at any rate an effort to provide a basis for talk about "life-space" and related ideas. I have no doubt that measurement can do much for the behavioral scientist, but only if he in turn does as much to deserve it.

The Dilemma

The great resources of mathematics, however, confront the behavioral scientist with a basic dilemma as he embarks on the enterprise of discovering or devising a procedure of measurement, a dilemma which has been clearly and forcibly stated by Coombs [5]: "If he chooses a strong axiom system, like a ratio or interval scale, he will put more into the data, he will have powerful mathematical and statistical tools available, he will be more likely to get a solution and it will be a simpler one. On the other hand, he will have more error variance, he will fit less of his data, and what he gets out will to a greater degree represent what he has put into the data by his assumptions. . . . The social scientist is faced by his dilemma when he chooses between *mapping* his data into a simple order and *asking* his data whether they satisfy a simple order." For this dilemma there is no general resolution; it is one of those existential dilemmas, like that between cultivating theory or experiment, with which the scientist simply learns to live. Only, his life becomes easier when he increases his aware-

[5] C. H. Coombs, "A Theory of Psychological Scaling." *Univer. of Michigan Engineering Research Bulletin*, No. 34, 1952, pp. 188, 186.

ness of the price that is being exacted of him as he makes his choices from moment to moment.

It is worth recognizing, too, that the situation is aggravated by the circumstance that measurement occurs in context of action other than those defined by the aims of scientific inquiry. We measure, that is to say, for a variety of reasons other than scientific ones; these impose their own requirements, which cannot always be made compatible with those stemming from our scientific interests. As Coombs has pointed out again,[6] "society often requires that at least a simple order be imposed on an attribute [for instance, in deciding which commodity to purchase]. . . . This is the primary explanation of why the social scientist must so frequently be 'unscientific' and, in effect, be forced to treat his measurement theory or scale as 'right' in spite of his data." We need not come to a decision as to which purposes are the more important, or at least, we need not decide this in general, once for all. But it is important, I think, for the behavioral scientist to be clear in his own mind which purpose is primary for him in a given context, and what its requirements are. Too often, we ask how to measure something without raising the question of what we would do with the measurement if we had it. We want to know *how* without thinking of *why*. I hope I may say without impiety, seek ye first for what is right for your needs, and all these things shall be added to you as well.

[35] Evidence and Inference in Social Research *

PAUL F. LAZARSFELD

In recent decades a major development of quantitative research in real social situations has come about; in a very broad sense it may be labeled "survey research." The following discussion is concerned with several recurring and very general problems connected with this type of work.

Reprinted from *Daedalus*, 87, 1958, pp. 99–129, with permission of the editor, the author, and the American Academy of Arts and Sciences.

* Publication No. A-276 of the Bureau of Applied Social Research, Columbia University. I am indebted to Prof. Allen Barton and Mr. Herbert Menzel for their contributions to this review.

6 *Op. cit.*, p. 487.

Concentration on survey research does not underrate the importance of other techniques. The same period has seen a similar development in the use of experimental methods in the social sciences; but the logical problems of experiments here and in the natural sciences are essentially the same. There is also a long tradition of social analysis using historical data to study problems of large-scale social change—the relation of the Protestant Reformation to the rise of capitalism is the most famous example. This kind of study raises interesting logical problems of its own that need careful analysis, but the methodology of "historical sociology" is not yet developed enough to be discussed here. Finally there are the attempts to derive social inferences from institutional data. It has been said that man is a data-producing animal. Wherever he goes he leaves certain kinds of data— court records, tax records, school records, birth and death records, and the like. This leads to the possibility of using existing institutional data as indicators of complex social trends and relationships. Durkheim's use of suicide rates to study problems of social norms and social cohesion is the classic example here.

Studies of the type with which we shall be concerned, however, have three distinctive features: they are quantitative rather than qualitative; the researcher designs and uses his own data-gathering devices rather than depending on available historical or institutional records; and they concern people's behavior and attitudes in real-life situations rather than constructed experimental situations.

From the point of view of this group of papers, two topics deserve special attention. How are broad conceptual ideas converted into instruments of empirical research to provide evidence on a topic of inquiry? And how can the "variables" so developed be manipulated to lead to broader generalizations? Both these problems need much additional specification. For the first we shall pay special attention to two issues: What happens if we have a choice between several instruments? And what happens if our evidence pertains to both individuals and collectives—a topic of traditional interest to the social scientist? As far as inference goes, social research has brought two topics to the foreground: how can we come near to causal relations, if we have no experiments but descriptive data only? And what hope can we place on the role of mathematics in the social sciences? The following five sections will briefly discuss these topics.

1. The Flow From Concepts to Empirical Indices

No science deals with its objects of study in their full concreteness. It selects certain of their properties and attempts to establish relations among them. The finding of such laws is the ultimate goal of all scientific inquiries. But in the social sciences the singling out of relevant properties is in itself a major problem. No standard terminology has yet been developed for this task. The properties are sometimes called aspects or attributes, and often the term "variable" is borrowed from mathematics as the most general category. The attribution of properties is interchangeably called description, classification, or measurement.

When social scientists use the term "measurement," it is in a much broader sense than the natural scientists do. For instance, if we are able to say that one department in a company has higher morale than another, we would be very pleased with ourselves and we would say that we had performed a "measurement." We would not worry that we cannot say that it is twice as high or only 20 per cent higher. This does not mean that we make no efforts to arrive at measurements in the traditional sense, with a precise metric. Some success has been achieved, but these efforts are only beginning, and they represent merely a small part of measurement activities in the broader sense.

Keeping in mind this generalized idea of measurement, let us see how social scientists establish devices by which to characterize the objects of empirical investigations. There appears to be a typical process which recurs regularly when we establish "variables" for measuring complex social objects. This process by which concepts are translated into empirical indices has four steps: an initial imagery of the concept, the specification of dimensions, the selection of observable indicators, and the combination of indicators into indices.

1. Imagery. The flow of thought and analysis and work which ends up with a measuring instrument usually begins with something which might be called imagery. Out of the analyst's immersion in all the detail of a theoretical problem, he creates a rather vague image or construct. The creative act may begin with the perception of many disparate phenomena as having some underlying characteristic in common. Or the investigator may have observed certain regularities and is trying to account for them. In any case, the concept, when first created, is some vaguely conceived entity that makes the observed relations meaningful.

Suppose we want to study industrial firms. We naturally want to measure the management of the firm. What do we mean by management and managers? Is every foreman a manager? Somewhere the notion of management was started, within a man's writing or a man's experience. Someone noticed that, under the same conditions, sometimes a factory is well run and sometimes it is not well run. Something was being done to make men and materials more productive. This "something" was called management, and ever since students of industrial organization have tried to make this notion more concrete and precise.

The same process happens in other fields. By now the development of intelligence tests has become a large industry. But the beginning of the idea of intelligence was that, if you look at little boys, some strike you as being alert and interesting and others as dull and uninteresting. This kind of general impression starts the wheels rolling for a measurement problem.

2. Concept Specification. The next step is to take this original imagery and divide it into components. The concept is specified by an elaborate discussion of the phenomena out of which it emerged. We develop "aspects," "components," "dimensions," or similar specifications. They are sometimes derived logically from the over-all concept, or one aspect is deduced from another, or empirically observed correlations between them are reported. The concept is shown to consist of a complex combination of phenomena, rather than a simple and directly observable item.

Suppose you want to know if a production team is efficient. You have a beginning notion of efficiency. Somebody comes and says, "What do you really mean? Who are more efficient—those who work quickly and make a lot of mistakes, so that you have many rejections, or those who work slowly but make very few rejects?" You might answer, depending on the product, "Come to think of it, I really mean those who work slowly and make few mistakes." But do you want them to work so slowly that there are no rejects in ten years? That would not be good either. In the end you divide the notion of efficiency into components such as speed, good product, careful handling of the machines—and suddenly you have what measurement theory calls a set of dimensions.

The development of dimensions can go quite far. One university in California has made a study under a Navy contract of an airplane factory, aimed at determining what is really efficient management on the lowest level. The notion of efficient management was divided into nineteen components, some of which were: absence of dissensions in the group, good communication downward, not too much compulsion, consistency of command, the size of command, and so on.

This can probably be overdone. I have rarely seen a concept that needed nineteen dimensions. But as a general principle, every concept we use in the social sciences is so complex that breaking it down into dimensions is absolutely essential in order to translate it into any kind of operation or measurement.

3. Selection of Indicators. After we have decided on these dimensions, there comes the third step: finding indicators for the dimensions. Here we run into a number of problems. First of all, how does one "think up" indicators? The problem is an old one.

William James has written in *The Meaning of Truth:*

. . . Suppose, e.g., that we say a man is prudent. Concretely, that means that he takes out insurance, hedges in betting, looks before he leaps . . . As a constant habit in him, a permanent tone of character, it is convenient to call him prudent in abstraction from any one of his acts. . . . There are peculiarties in his psycho-physical system that make him act prudently. . . .

Here James proceeds from an image to a series of indicators suggested directly by common experience. Today we would be rather more specific about the relation of these indicators to the underlying quality. We would not expect a prudent man always to hedge in betting, or to take out insurance on all possible risks; instead we would talk about the probability that he will perform any specific act as compared with a less prudent individual. And we would know that the indicators might vary considerably, depending on the social setting of the individual. Among students in a Protestant denominational college, for instance, we might find little betting and rare occasions for taking out insurance. Still a measure of prudence could be devised which was relevant to the setting. We might use as indicators whether a student always makes a note before he lends a book, whether he never leaves his dormitory room unlocked, etc.

The fact that each indicator has not an absolute but only a probability relation to our underlying concept requires us to consider a great many possible indicators. The case of intelligence tests furnishes an example. First, intelligence is divided into dimensions of manual intelligence, verbal intelligence, and so on. But even then there is not just one indicator by which imaginativeness can be measured. We must use many indicators to get at it.

There is hardly any observation which has not at one time or another been used as an indicator of something we want to measure. We use a man's salary as one of the indicators of his ability; but we do not rely on it exclusively, or we would have to consider most businessmen more able than even top-ranking university professors. We take the number of patients a doctor has cured as another indicator of ability in that setting; but we know that a good surgeon is more likely to lose a patient than is a good dermatologist. We take the number of books in a public library as an indicator of the cultural level of the community; but we know that quality of books matters as much as quantity.

When a battery of indicators is being drawn up, one difficult problem is to decide where to stop. Which indicators are considered "part of" the concept, and which are considered independent of or external to it? If we start listing indicators of the "integration" of a community, is the crime rate a part of the conception of integration, or is it an external factor which we might try to predict from our measure of integration? Here again, as with the problem of projective indices, knowing the laws which relate indicators to one another is of great importance. Even if we exclude crime rates from our image of an "integrated" city, they might be so highly correlated, as a matter of empirical generalization, that we could use them as a measure of integration in situations where we could not get data on the indicators which we "really" want to call integration. To do this, of course, we must first have "validating studies" where we correlate crime rate with the other indicators of integration and establish that it is generally closely related.

We should also know whether there are other factors besides integration influencing crime rate which might confuse our measurements if we used it alone to measure integration, so that we can check on these other factors, or add enough other indicators so as to cancel out their influence.

4. Formation of Indices. The fourth step is to put Humpty Dumpty together again. After the efficiency of a team or intelligence of a boy has been divided into six dimensions, and ten indicators have been selected for each dimension, we have to put them all together, because we cannot operate with all those dimensions and indicators separately.

For some situations we have to make one over-all index out of them. If I have six students and only one fellowship to give, then I must make an over-all rating of the six. To do this I must in some way combine all the information I have about each student into an index. At another time we may be more interested in how each of several dimensions is related to outside variables. But, even so, we must find a way of combining the indicators, since by their nature the indicators are many, and their relations to outside variables are usually both weaker and more unstable than the underlying characteristic which we would like to measure.

To put it in more formal language, each individual indicator has only a probability relation to what we really want to know. A man might maintain his basic position, but by chance shift on an individual indicator; or he might change his basic position, but by chance remain stable on a specific indicator. But if we have many such indicators in an index, it is highly unlikely that a large number of them will all change in one direction, if the man we are studying has in fact not changed his basic position.

To put the matter in another way, we need a lot of probings if we want to know what a man can really do or where he really stands. This, however, creates great difficulties in the fourth step of the measurement sequence which we described above. If we have many indicators and not all of them move in the same direction, how do we put them together in one index? Only recently have we raised the question: can you really develop a theory to put a variety of indicators together? The subject is a large one, and it is impossible to go into details here. The aim always is to study how these indicators are interrelated with each other, and to derive from these interrelations some general mathematical ideas of what one might call the power of one indicator, as compared with another, to contribute to the specific measurement one wants to make.

In the formation of indices of broad social and psychological concepts, we typically select a relatively small number of items from a large number of possible ones suggested by the concept and its attendant imagery. It is one of the notable features of such indices that their correlation with outside variables will usually be about the same, regardless of the specific "sampling" of items which goes into them from the broader group associated with the concept. This rather startling phenomenon has been labeled "the interchangeability of indices."

II. The Interchangeability of Indices

To present an example, we chose an index of "conservatism" used in a recent study of the response of college teachers of social sciences to the difficult years of the "McCarthy period," with its frequent attacks against colleges and professors for "leftist leanings."

One of our problems in this Teacher Apprehension study was to sort out those teachers who, because of their own convictions, could not possibly be the objects of such attacks: the men and women who hereafter, using the favorite term of their own spokesmen, will be called the conservatives.

From the beginning of our study we sought to find an acceptable way to locate this conservative group correctly. How was that to be done in a relatively short interview, in which the bulk of the questions necessarily was concerned with the nonconservatives who were the ones mainly involved in the controversies? This is a problem of classification common to all survey research. What indicators should we select?

In our study we could have submitted to our respondents certain conservative writings and asked them whether they approved of them. Or we could have selected the organizations they belonged to or the magazines they read as indicators. We preferred, as a result of much previous experience, to choose indicators more closely connected with the rest of the interview. We submitted to each respondent a series of rights and prohibitions, most of them taken from academic life, and asked whether they were for or against them. Out of this material an index of conservatism was formed. Since we were aware that quite different material would have been equally suitable, we tested our index against a series of other possibilities.

Two questions had to do with the respondent's attitude towards student activities. "If there are students who want to join it, do you think that a Young Socialist League ought to be allowed on this campus, or not?" The attitude toward socialists seemed a good indicator because whether they should be classified with communists or not is an issue on which educated conservatives and their opponents are likely to disagree. Fourteen per cent, or 355 professors, reported they would be definitely against such a policy. Characteristically enough, the second question, also pertaining to student activities, gave almost the same number of conservative replies. We asked our respondents to suppose that they were faculty advisers to a student organization on the campus that "proposed inviting Owen Lattimore, Far Eastern expert (now under indictment in Washington) to speak at a public meeting here." [1] Again, about 14 per cent of the sample, in this case 342 professors, put themselves on record that this "ought not to be allowed."

To both questions we get practically the same number of conservative

---

[1] [Between 1953–1955 Lattimore was twice indicted and the Federal Courts twice dismissed the indictments. The government subsequently dropped the case. Cf. *The New York Times*, June 15th and 29th, 1955. Ed.]

answers: 342 and 355, respectively. One might expect that practically the same professors furnish these replies. This, however, is not completely the case. Table 1 shows how the answers are related.

Table 1: A Cross-Tabulation of Answers to the Two Questions on What Students Should Be Permitted to Do

INVITE LATTIMORE

Form a Socialist Club	Approved	Undecided	Disapproved	Total
Approved	1686	95	124	1905
Undecided	118	27	46	191
Disapproved	152	31	172	355
Total	1956	153	342	2451

We see that the great statistical similarity of replies to each question is really the result of a considerable amount of "turnover." Of the people who approved of a Socialist Club, 124 would be against an invitation to Lattimore; conversely, 152 people who approved this invitation would not want students to form a Young Socialist League. This is neither surprising nor disturbing. Any single indicator has a specific element and can never be taken as fully representative for the classification we are striving to achieve —here, the classification of conservative respondents. Many of the interviewees make qualitative comments on their answers, and they do it most often when they see that on a specific point their response is somewhat out of line with their whole attitude pattern. We know, therefore, fairly well what explains the position of the people in the right upper and left lower corners of Table 1. Some of the respondents who were against inviting Lattimore dislike him personally. Others feel that a legal matter is at issue— a man who is under indictment should not be permitted to talk on a college campus. Inversely, the professors who would let Lattimore talk but who are against a Young Socialist League sometimes comment that on their campus there is a general policy against political student organizations or that they feel that a socialist organization could be especially open to subversive infiltration.

Suppose we decided to use one of the items in Table 1 as a crude index to conservatism. A serious discussion could start over which of the two questionnaire items is a better "measure" of conservatism. The Lattimore question is tinged with personal idiosyncrasies and legal implications. The Socialist League item has an element of ambiguity: do those who would forbid such an organization express their own opinion or the policy of their college? Neither of the two items is a very pure "measure," and arguments could therefore continue for and against each of them. Actually, however, it would make very little difference which one is used. And this is a point which needs to be driven home. Classifications in social research are mainly used to establish relations between a number of variables. The crucial question, therefore, is whether these relations, the empirical findings we are looking for, are much affected if we interchange one reasonable index with another.

To exemplify the matter we need an "outside variable." For it we chose the answer to an item which forced the respondent to make a hypothetical choice between the rights of the individual and the claims of the institution:

> If you had to make a choice, in a case in which a member of the faculty is accused of being subversive or of engaging in un-American activities, which do you think is *more* important for the college (university) administration to protect—the reputation of the college (university) or the rights of the faculty members?

What is the relation of conservatism to the concern for individual rights? This concern is the outside variable which we want to relate to conservatism. For the latter we have two measures available. Each of them can be tabulated against the choice between the protection of individual rights or the reputation of the college. What difference is there in the choice between the two indicators, namely the Lattimore or the Socialist League item?

The essential fact is that we get practically the same result irrespective of which of the two indicators we use to separate the conservative respondents from the others (Table 2).

Table 2: Proportion Giving Priority to Faculty Rights Related
to Two Measures of "Conservatism"

Attitude on Lattimore Speech	% Giving Priority to Faculty Rights	Attitude on Socialist League	% Giving Priority to Faculty Rights
Conservative	46	Conservative	43
Neutral	50	Neutral	51
Permissive	70	Permissive	70

Among the "conservatives" to be found in the first line of either column less than half would feel that the faculty rights are paramount. Among the "permissives" in the bottom line more than two-thirds feel this way. The whole numerical trend in the two columns is about the same irrespective of which indicator has been used for classificatory purposes.

In actual research practice, a larger number of items rather than one item alone is used for the purpose of classification. This has a variety of reasons. For example, indices based on more items permit finer distinctions, and they tend to cancel out the peculiarities of any single item. These are details which need not be elaborated here. Even if we use several items for classificatory purposes, we have always a selection out of a much larger pool of reasonable possibilities.

This, then, is the general rule based on very diversified research practice. If we are dealing with a rather broad concept like conservatism, and if we want to "translate" it into an empirical research instrument, a large number of indicators will always be eligible to form an index for classificatory purposes. Only a relatively small number of such items is practically manageable in most field research situations. If we choose two sets of such reasonable items to form two alternative indices, the following two facts will usually be found:

a. The two indices will be related, but they will not classify all the people in a study in precisely the same way; Table 1 exemplifies this.
b. The two indices will usually lead to very similar empirical results if they are cross-tabulated against a third outside variable; Table 2 exemplifies this.

One pays a serious but unavoidable price for the practical advantages of the interchangeability of indices. We can never reach "pure" classifications. Whatever index we use, the items will have "peculiarities" which result in some cases being misclassified, and therefore the empirical relationships which we find are lower than they would be if we had more precise measures of the variables with which the study is concerned.

The tentative character of the rule should also be stressed. There are some variables which are of great and general significance, and therefore over the years ever better instruments have been developed. Intelligence tests, for example, use a very large number of carefully selected items. If we were to use two such tests to classify the same group of people, the number of contradictions would be much smaller than that found in our Table 1. If a long series of studies over many years were intended to see whether the number of conservatives in the population increases, or how conservatism is related to a great many other variables, it would be worthwhile to develop a very refined classification device. But in a study like that of Teacher Apprehension, where a large number of variables had to be introduced for the first time, the only practical course for the researcher is to use fairly simple indices, and to make sure that he does not deceive himself or his readers about the remaining uncertainties.

III. On the Relation Between Individual and Collective Properties

Social scientists often make use of variables to describe not only individual persons, but also groups, communities, or other "collectives." Thus, one reads of "racially mixed census tracts," of "highly bureaucratized voluntary organizations," or of a "centrally located rooming house district." At other times the variables, although describing individuals, are based on data about some collectives, as in a comparison of "graduates of top-ranking medical schools" with "graduates of other medical schools." I shall try to clarify some of the operations involved in the construction and use of such variables in empirical research, and to provide a nomenclature for the different ways in which information about individuals and about collectives may be interwoven in these variables.

1. Some Features of Generalizing Propositions. Because the intended meaning of such variables often remains ambiguous if they are not examined in the context of certain kinds of propositions in which they are used, it is necessary at the outset to highlight certain features of these propositions:

a. They say something about a set of *elements* ("cases," "units of observation").
b. For the research purposes at hand, these elements are considered comparable. This means that the same set of *properties* is used to describe each of the elements.
c. Each element has a certain value on each property (these values may be quantitative or qualitative).
d. The *propositions* assert interrelationships between the properties.

These features are, of course, common to all empirical or hypothetical generalizations. The propositions with which we are here concerned have the additional characteristic that their elements either are collectives, or are described by reference to collectives. Typical examples of the first case are these: the lower the average income in a precinct, the higher the proportion of Democratic votes cast in a presidential election; tank platoons composed of friends perform better than those composed otherwise. The precinct or the platoon are the elements of these propositions. The properties they relate are average income and voting rate in one example, and some measure of social relation and performance ratings by observers in the other.

2. Special Meaning of "Collective" and "Member." The term "collective" is used here in a specific sense which needs clarification. A collective is any element in a proposition composed of *members*, i.e., constituent parts, which are regarded as comparable.

A Boy Scout troop, for example, is a collective, and the Boy Scouts who belong to it are its members. In the same sense, a city can be treated as a collective, with the inhabitants as members. However, the members of a collective are not necessarily individual persons. A city, for example, can be described not only as a collective with the inhabitants as members, but also as a collective with the voting precincts as members. It follows that what appears as a collective in one context (e.g., precincts), can appear as a member in another. But a city could also be introduced as a collective of buildings. In any analysis of a piece of writing in which some of the elements in a proposition are collectives, it is always necessary to specify clearly of what members the collectives are composed (for the purposes at hand).

In some studies, more than two levels appear; for example, inhabitants, precincts, and cities may all be elements of the same study. This whole matter could, therefore, be elaborated by pointing out the various relationships which can exist between inhabitants, precincts, and cities. In the next few pages we restrict ourselves to collectives which have only one kind of members; the members in most illustrations will be individual persons, but we will also present some cases in which the members themselves are larger units (e.g., "communities" considered as members of a state).

3. *Properties of Collectives.* It is often useful to distinguish three types of properties which describe collectives: analytical properties based on data about each member; structural properties based on data about the relations among members; and global properties, not based on information about the properties of individual members. The following examples may clarify these distinctions:

a. Analytical properties. These are properties of collectives which are obtained by performing some mathematical operation upon some property of each single member.

The average income in a city is an example of an analytical property of a collective (city) made up of individuals. Another example of an analytical property is the proportion of the communities of a given state that have their own high school; this is a property of a collective (state) the members of which are communities.

The standard deviation of incomes in a nation appears as an analytical property in the following proposition: when incomes in a nation are more equally distributed, people will save more, because they will spend less money on display consumption which might help them be socially acceptable in the higher strata.

Correlations are sometimes used to characterize collectives, and then also constitute analytical properties. The individual correlation of age and prestige in a given community, for example, has been used as a measure of its norms regarding old age. Sometimes more indirect inferences are involved. For example, in urban areas voting is highly correlated with occupation, while this is not the case in rural districts. One may conclude from this that in rural districts there is a stronger spirit of community and cohesion.

b. Structural properties. These are properties of collectives which are obtained by performing some operation on data about the relations of each member to some or all of the others.

Assume for example, that a sociometrist has recorded the "best-liked classmate" of each student in a number of classes. He can then classify the classes according to the degree to which all choices are concentrated upon a few "stars." Or he might, alternately, classify them according to their cliquishness, the latter being defined as the number of subgroups into which a class can be divided so that no choices cut across subgroup lines. In these examples the collective is the class, and the members are the individual students; "concentration of choices" and "cliquishness" are structural properties of the classes.

For an example in which the members are larger units, consider a map of the precincts of a city, which indicates the number of Negroes residing in each. Let a "Negro enclave" be defined as a precinct in which some Negroes live, but which is completely surrounded by precincts without Negroes. The proportion of the precincts of a city which are Negro enclaves would then be a structural property of the city.

c. *Global properties.* Often collectives are characterized by properties which are not based on information about the properties of individual members.

Nations, for example, may be characterized by the ratio of the national budget alloted to education and to armaments. Army units may be characterized by the cleanliness of their mess equipment. American Indian tribes may be characterized by the frequency with which themes of "achievement motive" make their appearance in their folk tales.

The cultural level of a city might be measured by the presence or absence of certain "cultural" institutions (theatres, libraries, etc.) or by the proportion of its buildings which are used for cultural purposes.

Having a city manager form of government is a global property of a city. The insistence on specified initiation rites as a prerequisite to membership is a global property of a religious cult or of a college fraternity. Accessibility from the nearest traffic artery is a global property of a village.

"Emergent," "integral," "syntalic" and other terms have been used in meanings very similar to that of our term "global." It is by no means certain which term is most useful, nor have all the logical problems been resolved. Thus, the number of members of a collective (population size, etc.) is classified here as a global property, although one might argue that it is an analytic property, obtained by the operation of counting performed upon the individual property of "existence." Even more ambiguous is the classification of rates based on the behavior of members, e.g., suicide rates.

4. A Subsidiary Distinction Among Analytical Properties of Collectives. An interesting distinction may be made among the analytical properties. The first two examples given above were the average income of a city and the proportion of the communities of a given state that have their own high school. These properties of collectives have what one might call a psychological similarity to the properties of members on which they are based. The wealth of a city seems to be the same sort of thing as the wealth of an inhabitant. The endowment of a community with a high school and the proportion of high-school-endowed communities in a state have a parallel meaning.

This is not true for the remaining examples of analytical properties given above—the standard deviation of incomes in a nation, or correlations like that between age and prestige in a given community. Correlations and standard deviations can apply only to collectives and have no parallel on the level of members. The standard deviation of incomes in a city, for example, denotes something quite different—lack of homogeneity, perhaps—from individual income, the datum from which it is computed. Some economists have surmised that the average proportion of income saved in a group is smaller the higher the dispersion of income; a lack of homogeneity supposedly makes for more consumption expenditures at the service of status striving. Average rate of saving in a group is "similar" to individual saving; but homogeneity of income has no "parallel" on the individual level, at least at one point of time. One might speak of a "genuine" analytical variable in the latter case, although the distinction is of a somewhat intuitive nature.

Another variable of this sort is "degree of consensus." When a Democrat and a Republican are competing for the mayoralty, the degree of political consensus in a particular club might be measured by the extent of the club's deviation from a 50-50 split. In this instance the analytic property is measured by a proportion, but it is not the simple proportion of adherents of either party; clubs which are 80 per cent Democratic and those which are 20 per cent Democratic are regarded as equal in consensus.

5. Properties of Individual Members of Collectives. Propositions in which the elements are individuals make up the main stock of empirical research findings: rich people vote more Republican, women read more fiction, etc. When people are considered as members of a collective, then their properties can be classified according to whether the rest of the collective enters into the characterization of its members or not. This leads to a classification which to a certain extent corresponds to the one just discussed.

a. Absolute properties. These are characteristics of members which are obtained without making any use either of information about the characteristics of the collective, or of information about the relationships of the member being described to other members. Thus in the preceding examples income and sex were absolute properties.

b. Relational properties. These properties of members are computed from information about the substantive relationships between the member described and other members.

Sociometric popularity-isolation (number of choices received) is a relational property. Many other sociometric indices fall into this category. For example, if each member of a small group has rated each other member on a 5-point scale of acceptance-rejection, each member can be characterized by the total score he received (popularity), by the total score he expressed (active sociability), by the average deviation of the scores he accorded the others (discrimination in his acceptance of other members), etc. In a study of the diffusion of the use of a new drug through a community of doctors, the physicians were classified according to whether or not they had a friend who had already used the new drug on a certain date.

c. Comparative properties. These characterize a member by a *comparison* between his value on some (absolute or relational) property with the distribution of this property over the entire collective of which he is a member.

Sibling order is a comparative property of individuals in the proposition, "First-born children are more often maladjusted than intermediate and last-born children." Note that each individual is characterized by comparison with the age of the other individuals in his family; in the resulting classification, many of the "last-born" will be older in years than many of the "first-born."

Another example is contained in the following proposition: "Students who had the highest I.Q. in their respective high school classes have greater difficulty in adjusting in college than students who were not quite at the top in high school, even when their actual I.Q. score is equally high." Here the comparative property (being at the top in high school or not) is established in terms of the I.Q. distribution in each student's respective high school; the proposition pertains to a set of college students which includes boys from several high schools (collectives).

d. Contextual properties. These describe a member by a property of his collective.

Consider the example: "Graduates of large law schools are more likely to earn high incomes at age 40 than graduates of small law schools." In this proposition, "being a member of a large law school" is a contextual property of indivduals.

Contextual properties are also used in the following propositions: "Union members in closed shops are less militant than union members in open shops." "Residents of racially mixed districts show more racial prejudice than those of racially homogeneous districts." "Soldiers in units where many promotions have been granted are less satisfied with the promotion policy than those in units where few promotions have been granted." In these propositions, being a member of a closed shop, residing in a mixed district, or being a soldier in a unit with frequent promotions are all examples of contextual properties.[2]

Note that a contextual property, unlike a comparative property, has

---

[2] The contextual properties can of course be divided once more according to the distinctions made in the previous section. Observe the difference between the poor man raised in a neighborhood "where everyone else was rich" and the American lawyer who was trained in a country "where Roman law prevailed." It seems not worthwhile to follow these combinations into further detail. It is, however, useful to emphasize the difference between a relational characteristic of a member and a contextual characteristic based on a structural property of the collective. An example of the former would be the sociometric isolate; an example of the latter would be a man who comes from an atomized group (containing many isolates, irrespective of whether he is an isolate himself or not).

the same value for all members of a given collective. It is not meaningful to speak of contextual or comparative properties when the elements under study are all members of the same collective, for instance, when only graduates of one law school are being studied. The reason is that any *contextual* property would, in that case, have the same value for all the elements; hence nothing could be said about the interrelationship of this property to any other property. Any *comparative* property would, under these circumstances, classify the elements in exactly the same way as the absolute property from which it was derived, except that the calibration may be grosser.

An interesting situation comes about as follows. We have a set of collectives, and take as elements of a proposition all their members (or a representative sample of the members of each); one property of the proposition is a contextual one. Suppose, for instance, we take all the graduates of fifty law schools in the United States as of a certain year, and see how large their income is ten years later. The resultant finding may be "the income of law school graduates is correlated with the size of the school they graduated from"; this is a proposition about students, relating their income (an absolute property) to the size of their law school (a contextual property). The same proposition could be interpreted also as one where the elements are the law schools: the average income of the students would then be an analytical property of each law school; its size would be a global property of these collectives.

At first sight one may feel that the distinctions made in this section are not much more than an exercise in elementary logic. Actually they have a bearing on major discussions which have continued for years. In the debate between Durkheim [3] and Tarde, for instance, the former waved the flag of the "social fact" against his opponent the psychologist. The issue, properly formulated, is whether a system of propositions can be built up, the elements of which are exclusively collectives. Durkheim would not have insisted on using only global characteristics, such as tribal customs or laws; his notion of density of contact is a structural, and the suicide rate conceivably an analytical, property of a collective. The real issue is whether it is necessary to introduce propositions the elements of which are individuals in order to develop a coherent system of social theory. A radical Durkheim position denying this necessity is today rather unlikely.

Another controversy can be clarified with the help of the preceding analysis. The objection is often raised that social research is atomistic and therefore does not take into account the complexities of social reality. This is sometimes put into the form that "wholes" or "structures" cannot be described by combinations of "separate" variables. Using the word structure in this general sense we can see that its meaning is caught in the following two ways:

[3] [See E. Durkheim, "Social Facts," this volume, pp. 245–254.—Ed.]

a. by propositions in which the elements are collectives, if the latter are characterized by structural properties in the narrow sense of the preceding pages;

b. by propositions in which the elements are individuals, if the latter are partly characterized by contextual properties.

This case is important enough to deserve a special example provided by a study of college students. Norman Miller has analyzed tests measuring attitudes toward labor. He showed that students who came from a middle class background (a contextual property) became relatively more anti-labor between Freshman and Senior year while students from labor background became progressively more pro-labor. The correlation between age and attitude is different according to the background of the students.

The main finding in this last example is due to combining more than two variables into a proposition. What can we say in general about this procedure of multi-variable analysis?

IV. The Analysis of Statistical Relations

In the preceding sections we have referred to many relations between two variables. For our present purpose we can assume that they were all dichotomous attributes and that we are interested in one question only: are the two attributes related or not? For our answer we have to form a cross-tabulation of the following form:

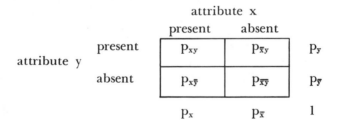

		attribute x		
		present	absent	
attribute y	present	p_{xy}	$p_{\bar{x}y}$	p_y
	absent	$p_{x\bar{y}}$	$p_{\bar{x}\bar{y}}$	$p_{\bar{y}}$
		p_x	$p_{\bar{x}}$	1

The symbolism is simple: $p_{\bar{x}y}$ for instance is the proportion of people who are y but not x. If x and y are unrelated then

$$\frac{p_{xy}}{p_{\bar{x}y}} = \frac{p_{x\bar{y}}}{p_{\bar{x}\bar{y}}}$$

This means that the presence of x is relatively equally frequent among those people who are and those who are not y. The preceding condition can be expressed in terms of the so-called *crossproduct*

$$[xy] = p_{xy}\, p_{\bar{x}\bar{y}} - p_{\bar{x}y}\, p_{x\bar{y}}.$$

If $[xy] = 0$ (vanishes) then x and y are unrelated. (Sampling problems are not relevant in the present context.)

Now suppose that a third attribute t is introduced. Then we can develop the two correlative operations of *mixture* and of *elaboration*. A numerical example of mixture is given in the following scheme:

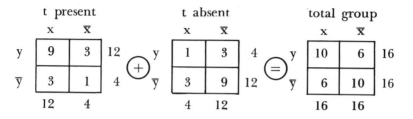

In the two tables on the left the variables x and y are unrelated. But if we mix the two groups originally separated according to t we do find that people who are y are also more likely to be x than those who are not y.

Elaboration is mixture in reverse order. It consists in decomposing the group on the right into two subgroups and studying the relation of x and y separately for people who are and are not t. Elaboration is clearly not a unique operation. We could obtain the right side, *e.g.*, by mixing the two following subgroups:

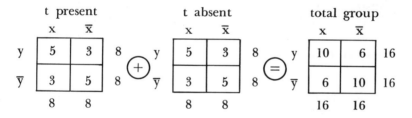

There is one important difference between this and the preceding scheme. Both attributes x and y were formerly related to t. Neither $[xt]$ nor $[yt]$ were zero. In the new scheme we find that the proportion of x and y is the same for people who are and are not t:

$$[xt] = 0 \text{ and } [yt] = 0.$$

We shall call the relations on the left side of the schemes *partial relations* (depending on t) and symbolize them by $[xy;t]$ and $[xy;\bar{t}]$ respectively. Elaboration then consists of studying how $[xy]$ depends upon $[xy;t]$ and $[xy;\bar{t}]$ under varying conditions of $[xt]$ and $[yt]$. An algebraic development of the problems leads to the general formula.

Formula (1):

$$[xy] = p_t\,[xy;t] + p_{\bar{t}}\,[xy;\bar{t}] + \frac{[xt] \cdot [ty]}{p_t \cdot p_{\bar{t}}}.$$

The original relationship can be described as the sum of the two partial relationships and an additional factor, which is the product of what are called the marginal relationships between the test factor and each of the two original variables.

This elaboration leads to two major forms. Either the two partial relations may vanish; then formula (1) reduces to

Formula (2a):

$$[xy] = \frac{[xt] \cdot [ty]}{p_t \cdot p_{\bar{t}}}.$$

Or the test factor t might be unrelated to x (this means that $[xt] = 0$), and we then have

Formula (2b):

$$[xy] = \frac{[xy;t]}{p_t} + \frac{[xy;\bar{t}]}{p_{\bar{t}}}.$$

a form which will turn out of interest only if one of these two partial relations is markedly stronger than the other. We shall call this the P-form (emphasis on partials), while formula (2a) will be called the M-form (emphasis on what the statistician calls "marginals").

To this formal distinction we now add a substantive one: the time order of the 3 variables. Assuming that x is prior to y, then t either can be located between x and y in time, or it can precede both. In the former case we talk of an intervening test variable, in the latter case of an antecedent one. We thus have 4 major possibilities.

	Statistical Form	
Position of t	P	M
Antecedent	PA	MA
Intervening	PI	MI

We are now ready to present the decisive point. It is claimed that there are essentially four operations which can be performed with two original and one test variable. It makes no difference whether this is done with actual data or whether they take the form of theoretical analyses. If a relation between two variables is analyzed in the light of a third, only these four operations or combinations thereof will occur irrespective of whether they are called interpretation, understanding, theory, or anything else.

We now turn to some concrete examples which will clarify what these four types of elaboration stand for. In cases of the type PA, we usually call the test variable t a "condition." General examples easily come to mind, although in practice they are fairly rare and are a great joy to the research man when they are found. For example, the propaganda effect of a film is greater among less-educated than among highly educated people. The depression had worse effects on authoritarian families than on other types.

Three general remarks can be made about this type of finding or reasoning: (a) It corresponds to the usual stimulus-disposition-response sequence, with *x* being the stimulus and the antecedent *t* being the disposition. (b) The whole type might best be called one of *specification*. One of the two partials will necessarily be larger than the original relationship. We specify, so to speak, the circumstances under which the original relationship holds true more strongly. (c) Usually we will go on from there and ask why the relationship is stronger on one side of the test dichotomy. This might then lead into one of the other types of analysis. Durkheim uses types PA in discussing why married people commit suicide less than unmarried people. He introduces as a test variable "a nervous tendency to suicide, which the family, by its influence, neutralizes or keeps from developing." This is type PA exactly. We do not take it to be a convincing explanation because the introduction of the hypothetical test variable (tendency to suicide) sounds rather tautological. We rather want to know why the family keeps this tendency from developing, which leads to type MI, as we shall see later.

The type PI is also easily exemplified. We study the relationship between job success (*y*) and whether children did or did not go to progressive schools (*x*). We find that if the progressively educated children come into an authoritarian job situation (*t*) they do less well in their work than the others; on the other hand, if they come into a democratic atmosphere, their job success is greater.

The relation between type of education and job success is elaborated by an intervening test factor, the work atmosphere. We call such a test factor a "contingency." In many prediction studies, the predicted value depends upon subsequent circumstances which are not related to the predictor. An example is the relation between occupational status and participation in the life of a housing community. White-collar people participate more if they are dissatisfied, whereas manual workers participate more if they are satisfied with their jobs.

Type MA is used mainly when we talk of rectifying what is usually called a spurious relationship. It has been found that the more fire engines that come to a fire (*x*), the larger is the damage (*y*). Because fire engines are used to reduce damage, the relationship is startling and requires elaboration. As a test factor (*t*) the size of the fire is introduced. The partials then become zero and the original result appears as the product of two marginal relationships; the larger the fire, the more engines—and also the more damage.

When we encounter a relationship which is psychologically puzzling, we usually stop at that point; but this same mode of elaboration is also used under different psychological circumstances. More people commit suicide during the summer than during the winter. Durkheim suggests, as a *t* factor for elaboration, that increased social activities are going on during the summer. Our general knowledge tells us that *x* (the season) is indeed related to *t* in this way.

Our interest immediately shifts to the [*ty*] relationship, namely: the presumed fact that greater intensity of social life leads to more suicides. Actually, of course, whether this explanation which comes from Durkheim is correct would depend upon a disappearance of the partials. Durkheim would have to show that if intensity of social life is kept constant, the season does not make any difference in suicides. Because he has no data on this point, he looks for other situations where he can presume the intensity of social life to vary. He finds that there are more suicides during the day as compared with the number during the night, which he again explains with the help of the same test factor. This leads into the whole question of probability of inference, which we do not follow up here.

We now turn to type MI, for which we shall use the term "interpretation." The difference between "explanation" and "interpretation" in this context is related to the time sequence between x and t. In an interpretation, t is an intervening variable situated between x and y in the time sequence.

Examples of type MI are numerous. Living in a rural community rather than a city (x) is related to a lower suicide rate (y). The greater intimacy of rural life (t) is introduced as an intervening variable. If we had a good test of cohesion, we should undoubtedly find that a community being a rural rather than an urban one (x) is positively correlated with its degree of cohesion (t), and that greater cohesion (t) is correlated with lower suicide rates (y). But obviously some rural communities will have less cohesion than some urban communities. If cohesion is kept constant as a statistical device, then the partial relationship between the rural-urban variable and the suicide rate would have to disappear.

It might be useful to illustrate the difference between type MA and type MI in one more example. It was found during the war that married women working in factories had a higher rate of absence from work than single women. Here are a number of possible elaborations:

a. *Test factor:* more responsibilities at home. This is an intervening variable. If it is introduced and the two partial relationships—between marital status and absenteeism—disappear, we have an elaboration of type MI. We interpret the relation by showing what intervening variable connects the original two variables.

b. *Test factor:* physical infirmity as crudely measured by age; the *older* women are more likely to be married, and to have less physical strength, both as a result of their age. Age is an antecedent variable. If it turns out, when age is kept constant, that the relation between marital status and absenteeism disappears, we would have an explanation, and probably call it a spurious effect: type MA.

The latter case suggests again an important point. After having explained the original relationship, our attention might shift to $[ty]$, the fact that older people show a higher absentee rate. This, in turn, might lead to new elaborations: is it really the case that older women have less physical resistance, be they married or single? Or, is it that older women have been born in a time when work is not as yet important for women and, therefore, they have a lower work morale. In other words, after one elaboration is completed, we will, as good scientists, immediately turn to a new one; but the basic analytical processes will always be the same.

One final point can be cleared up, at least to a certain degree, by this analysis. We can suggest a clear-cut definition of the *causal* relation between two attributes. If we have a relationship between *x* and *y,* and if for any *antecedent* test factor the partial relationships between *x* and *y* do not disappear, then the original relationship should be called a causal one. It makes no difference here whether the necessary operations are actually carried through or made plausible by general reasoning. In a controlled experiment we have two matched groups: the experimental exposure corresponds to the variable *x,* and the observed effect to *y.* Matching makes sure that for any antecedent *t* we shall have $[xt] = 0$. If then $[xy] \neq 0$ we can in the light of the preceding analysis always be sure that there is a causal relation between exposure *x* and effect *y.*

This has special bearing on the following kind of discussion. It is found that in densely populated areas the crime rate is higher than in sparsely populated areas. Some authors state that this could not be considered a true causal relationship, but such a remark is often used in two very different ways. Assume an intervening variable, for instance, the increased irritation which is the result of crowded conditions. Such an interpretation does not detract from the causal character of the original relationship. On the other hand, the argument might go this way: crowded areas have cheaper rents and, therefore, attract poorer, partly demoralized people. Here the character of the inhabitants is antecedent to the characteristics of the area. In this case the original relationship is indeed explained as a spurious one and should not be called causal.

We can, finally, link the present discussion with some observations made in the previous section. Explanation consists of the formal aspect of elaboration and some substantive ordering of variables. We have here focused on ordering by time sequence. But not all variables can be ordered this way. We saw that we can distinguish orders of complexity, e.g., variables characterizing persons, collectives, and sets of collectives. Other ordering principles could be introduced, e.g., degree of generality, exemplified by the instance of a specific opinion, a broader attitude, and a basic value system. What is needed is to combine the formalism of elaboration with a classification of variables according to different ordering principles. This would cover a great part of what needs to be known about the logic of explanation and inference in contemporary survey analysis.

V. Mathematical Models—Some Uses and Limitations

So far, we have discussed how observations are organized into concepts and indices, and how relationships among several variables are analyzed. There is, however, a small group of social scientists which tries to go even further and builds mathematical models of human behavior.

It is useful to divide the area of models into what we may call 1) static or measurement models, and 2) dynamic or behavioral models. Anyone who develops a theory of scaling works in a static area. That is to say, he relates manifest data to underlying utility or probability. One who deals, let us say, with learning theory, or with the kind of work which Rashevsky does, where the element of time enters, works in the second field. There is, of course, some overlapping. For example, the problem of introducing scales and measurements in dynamic models is very important. One of the main reasons for the cricitisms of Rashevsky is that he uses dynamic models that introduce characteristics of people without concerning himself about the measurement of the characteristics. But it is worth while to remember that most of our normal work conveniently divides into those models which are used to develop variables, such as attitudes, utility, or scales, and those models which are used to analyze dynamic behavior, such as learning or changes in social systems.

Most of these remarks will deal with the second type, the dynamic models, because of their relevance to problems which interest the majority of non-mathematical sociologists. They are not interested in the formation of units or scales; they take that for granted. They call in "George" to do it, and they believe in his technical ability. But after George has developed a "scale," what they want to know is how it can be used for the analysis of social processes.

There are two major problems in this area on which we need greater clarification:

1. What are the scientific tasks which mathematical models can perform in the broad area of social science?
2. How is the choice of the specific area in which we develop models made?

As to the uses of models, there is no doubt that one important function is to help predict behavior. But there is another function which might be called the *linguistic* function of models in the social sciences. There may be a great value in developing models on their own merits, irrespective of whether we have any data or of whether they can at this moment predict anything at all.

The crux is, of course, the meaning of the term "data." Experiments might be the only source of data for the physicist, and they might be useful for the social scientist, but they are for us certainly not the main material we are working with today. We have data which have been accumulating for about 2,500 years. Plato developed very interesting propositions on human behavior in society, and if we now developed models which somehow organized or clarified what Plato had to say, we should be doing an important job.

Some interesting illustrations of the linguistic function of mathematical models could be drawn from efforts to "translate" humanistic writings. However, here we shall draw our examples from recent empirical studies, and show that even in this area there is an important task of clarification which does not involve prediction.

The linguistic function of mathematical models can be divided into three parts: 1) the organizing function, 2) the analytical function, and 3) the mediating function.

As an example of the *organizing function,* consider the many studies which are now available on how people vote and why they vote. One finding which has been well corroborated in different studies is that Catholics for many decades in this country have been voting much more frequently Democratic than have Protestants. A number of recent studies refined this result. We made studies during election campaigns, interviewing people every month, asking them how they intended to vote, and classifying voters as Democratic Catholics, Republican Catholics, etc. In August, most Catholics said that they intended to vote Democratic, and most Protestants said that they planned to vote Republican. In October, when the same people were asked the same questions, there were some changes. The Catholic Democrats and the Republican Protestants kept their conviction, but the other two groups showed changes. Republican Catholics started to say, "I changed my mind; I think I had better vote Democratic." And many of the Protestants who had wanted to vote Democratic began to change their minds and veer to the Republicans. This is true not only for Catholics and Protestants, but for urban and rural groups as well; urban dwellers are more likely to be Democrats. This leads to a generalization on a somewhat higher level. People who want to vote in agreement with their own group are much more likely to be stable in their intention than the people who intend to vote against the prevailing trend of their group. As time goes on, the people who first want to vote against the prevailing trend in their group slowly "return to the fold."

Offhand it would seem easy to understand this by referring to the influence of the environment. And indeed we have information that people with similar social characteristics are more likely to meet one another, and that such contacts affect the vote intention of the participants. But why does the population not split into groups which are homogeneous within and completely different from each other? Obviously there are countertrends, and one of them is the random fluctuation of people who have little interest in politics. This uninterested group is larger between elections than during campaigns and guarantees a certain amount of reshuffling. At the same time the uninterested people introduce another complication. They are less likely to talk politics, but are more easily influenced when they do.

One could go on enumerating the many well-established but disconnected propositions relating attitude, social characteristics, contact frequencies, etc. But no one knows what the minimum of variables and relations are from which the total set could be derived. Here is where the organizing function of mathematics enters. In the small-group field, H. Simon has shown how much clarity can thus be gained. In the area of voting, inventories of propositions have been made, but the final formalization is still lacking.

The *analytical function* of models is exemplified by studies showing that groups appear to solve problems better than individuals. In the election example we have an overabundance of data, and it is a function of the mathematical models to organize them. In the problem-solving case we have a deficiency of data, and the mathematical model points out where we should look further. The notion of group problem-solving is vague. Do we mean a kind of division of labor within the group? Or do we mean that in a group there is a greater probability that one outstanding person will appear and find the answer for all the rest? Empirical studies are available showing the probability of both individual and group solutions. It is then possible to set up two models: one assuming division of labor, and one assuming solution by a top individual in the group. Derivations from the two models can be tested against the data. The model helps us to infer what is going on within the group while it works, although we know only the final outcome. This analytical use of mathematical models often leads to ideas of what new empirical work is needed.

The *mediating function* of model construction can be illustrated as follows. Economists have asserted for eighty years that one cannot measure utilities. Social psychologists have, for the last thirty years, measured attitudes without worrying whether this was a legitimate operation. Perhaps economists did not measure utilities because they spent so much time on the problem of whether utilities could be measured. Only by putting the utility and the attitude problems into a formal language, and thereby showing that they are really the same problem, could there be a joining of effort between the people who have conceptual problems and the people who measured without realizing the conceptual problem existed. We begin to have now a way of formulating the problem correctly; economists believe it is susceptible to measurement; and social psychologists realize that measurement is not as easy as they thought before.

The mediating function of the formalization appears in a variety of other areas. For instance, almost any textbook in sociology has a final chapter on social change or the lack of it. But the chapters on social change make sense only if one has read a reasonable book on business cycle analysis or economic growth. Sociologists have discussed relations between the individual and society for a hundred and fifty years; physicists have considered the relations between thermodynamics and atomic theory; "aggregation" is a word familiar to economists. When problems are put into formal mathematical language, similarities become obvious—a very important cross-disciplinary mediating function. Only after problems have been formalized is it really possible to work on cross-disciplinary approaches and to make mutual contributions from one discipline to another.

Thus the linguistic function of a mathematical model helps to organize an abundance of material, helps to pin down deficiencies of data, and helps to mediate between procedures that are formally alike but terminologically different—a function of mathematical models which has been often underrated.

Now to the second major point. Are we judicious enough in the choice of the subject matter to which we apply our mathematical efforts? Those who contrive experiments to test mathematical models of human behavior tend to introduce gambling situations. The decision problems social scientists deal with are different: Why do people commit crimes? Why do they buy cars? Why did they vote for Eisenhower? Social scientists in general study decision problems. But when it comes to model construction, mathematicians are interested mainly in how people bet. Perhaps we are again facing a danger which we faced about forty years ago, at the time of the early Watsonian behaviorists. When the idea of learning experiments emerged, there was a general conviction that only in very primitive situations could one really experiment. The main learning effort was concentrated on rats. But social psychologists are more interested in people, and today in America we are no longer convinced that the study of animal psychology can solve the major problems of human psychology.

As mathematical models become important there is a real danger that we repeat the cycle, that we start again at the lowest rung of the ladder. One cannot study how rats bet, but one can study how human beings bet. The relative ease of these experiments seems to me to tempt mathematical model builders to repeat the error of the behavioristic extremists. There are, of course, those who feel that Watson was right. They should at least agree that the concentration of model-building on betting is an analogous situation. The rat maze and the betting experiment are characterized by the same tendency to seek the simplest configuration.

Connected with the choice of area is another choice, that of experiment *versus* observation. I have not been convinced by accounts of the history of psychology that the strong emphasis on experimentation is justified. One can experiment with how people bet. But if one wants to know how people vote, and how people buy, one cannot really experiment. One has to make systematic analytical observations. In the voting studies we have made, we took a sample of people in a small town in New York, and interviewed them every month. We asked them for whom they wanted to vote, and then observed how they changed from month to month. In another study, we kept potential car buyers under observation for nine months, and tried to study the decision process by re-interviewing the same people in various stages of their approach to a final purchase. Somewhat more attention should be devoted to observational data taken over a time interval. The models to be looked for have a similarity to the business cycle analysis of economists. The whole new mathematics of economic growth and population growth are relevant here. In any problem which involves time-series analysis, in any complex problem that involves a comparison of a series of variables over a number of time periods, the relationship of the model to the data is somewhat different from that in the experimental situation.

*   *   *

The topics here chosen for review may seem arbitrary, but they have one feature in common: they are entirely characteristic of empirical social science research today. There is a danger that methodological discussions become very general and miss the relevant detail by trying to be all-embracing. In a Colloquium, the theme of which is the unity of the sciences, it is salutary to reverse the old French proverb: the more it is the same, the more one should stress the differences. It is the new step in the over-arching continuity which leads to progress.

BIBLIOGRAPHICAL NOTE

The general theory of index-formation is exemplified in Section I of the *Language of Social Research* edited by P. F. Lazarsfeld and M. Rosenberg (The Free Press, 1955). There one will also find additional material on the interchangeability of indices. An inventory of group properties as used in current sociological literature is provided by R. K. Merton on pages 311–325 of his *Social Theory and Social Structure* (second edition, The Free Press, 1957); a good discussion of the general principles involved was given by P. M. Blau in the *American Journal of Sociology* (Volume 63, 1957, p. 58 ff.). Many concrete examples of the treatment of multivariant statistical relations will be found in Chapter VII of H. H. Hyman's *Survey, Design and Analysis* (The Free Press, 1955). The organizing use of mathematics is shown at its best in Section 2, H. A. Simon, *Models of Man* (John Wiley & Sons, Inc., 1957). The literature on group problem-solving models is reviewed by I. D. Lorge and H. Solomon in *Psychometrical* (Volume 20, 1955, p. 139 ff.).

[36] Mathematical Models in the Social Sciences*

KENNETH J. ARROW

I. The Usefulness of Mathematical Reasoning

It is a commonplace remark among many social scientists that mathematics, however useful it may have proved in the physical sciences, can play no essential role in the development of the social sciences because the phenomena studied are somehow different—"human beings are not amenable to mathematical law." The social scientist who thinks a little more about the matter will perhaps add that mathematical analysis is quantitative, while his field calls for qualitative analysis. Doubtless he will concede that certain elementary facts of a numerical nature can be tabulated (e.g., distribution of income or population); and he will usually admit that for certain purposes, one might be permitted to add up a column of the table. Nevertheless, it is held that the judgment and intuition of the skilled investigator are fundamentally more useful in the social sciences than mathematical formulas based on quantitative observations.

To the mathematician or the individual trained in the spirit of modern mathematics, the views just presented seem to be based on nothing more profound than a misunderstanding. "Mathematics," said the American physicist Gibbs, "is a language." If this be true, any meaningful proposition can be expressed in a suitable mathematical form, and any generalizations about social behavior can be formulated mathematically. Mathematics, in this view, is distinguished from the other languages habitually used by the social scientist chiefly by its superior clarity and consistency.[1] Further-

Reprinted from *The Policy Sciences,* edited by Daniel Lerner and Harold D. Lasswell, with the permission of the publishers, Stanford University Press. Copyright 1951 by the Board of Trustees of the Leland Stanford Junior University.

* This chapter will be reprinted as Cowles Commission Paper, New Series, No. 48. The author wishes to thank J. Marschak, of the Cowles Commission and the University of Chicago, for valuable comments.

[1] The doctrine that mathematics is a superior language goes back to Leibnitz. The inclusion of all forms of logical reasoning in mathematics was begun by George Boole and continued by Charles S. Peirce, Gottlob Frege, and Bertrand Russell. See Russell's *Intro-*

more, it is simply not true that mathematics is useful only in quantitative analysis. Doubtless many branches of mathematics—especially those most familiar to the average individual, such as algebra and the calculus—are quantitative in nature. But the whole field of mathematical or symbolic logic is purely qualitative. We can frame such questions as the following: Does the occurrence of one event always imply the occurrence of another? Is it impossible that two events should both occur? The events here may be of a purely qualitative nature, such as the presence or absence of traits in a culture complex. It must further be observed that there may very well be a quantitative aspect to the study of even the most definitely qualitative phenomena; if we realize that we will rarely be able to assert universally valid laws about the relation between different traits, we will be willing to ask in what proportion of the observed phenomena will two traits be found together, i.e., what is the probability of their coexistence. The Mendelian theory of inheritance is the prototype of the transformation of qualitative into quantitative analysis via the probability calculus.[2] It is, of course, also clear that quantitative phenomena enjoy equal claim with qualitative ones in the study of social forces. An understanding of a community doubtless requires knowledge of its religious and social beliefs, but it also involves knowledge of the distribution of income by size and by occupation, the total population and its distribution by occupation and social class, and the proportion of resources devoted to various social and individual needs.

Finally, the argument that only trained intuition can yield worth-while social analysis is rejected as meaningless by the mathematically trained. If the intuition of the investigator is reliable, it will yield the same judgments every time it is confronted with the same set of facts. But any such unique correspondence can always be represented by a mathematical relation of sufficiently complicated form. Hence, any intuitive knowledge can always be reduced to mathematical terms. Apart from this, there is the general presupposition that scientific knowledge should be interpersonally valid and transmittable and hence expressible in an objective, consistent language.

These arguments seem logically irrefutable, and yet, outside the realm of economics, very little use has been made of mathematical and symbolic methods. Even in economics, only a small minority of the theorists use anything more complicated than a very elementary form of calculus. How can we explain this failure on the part of social scientists to accept in their practice the theoretically superior language of mathematics? The simple fact that they would like to shun such a difficult subject as mathematics can be re-

---

duction to Mathematical Philosophy (2d ed., 1920). The best elementary presentation of the present state of mathematical logic is found in Alfred Tarski, *Introduction to Logic* (1941).

[2] It is of interest to observe that the modern theory of statistical inference fundamental to any quantitative analysis in the social sciences owes its inception to the interest of Francis Galton and Karl Pearson in the problems of inheritance and evolution. A further discussion of the significance of probability laws in the social sciences is given later in this chapter.

garded at best as only a partial explanation. There have always been enough mathematicians interested in the social sciences to have made the superiority of mathematics manifest if it were a clearly better tool.

There must be some flaw in the arguments advanced above for the use of mathematical methods in the social sciences; the most important one is concealed in the statement that every proposition "can" be expressed in mathematical form. The statement is doubtless true if we mean that there exists in some Platonic realm of being a mathematical expression of every given proposition, but it is not true if we mean that the mathematical expression in question can be given within the realms of mathematical theory now existing. Every mathematician realizes what a small part of all the potentially available mathematical knowledge is actually grasped at the present time.[3] The usual reaction of the "literary" social scientist when confronted with a mathematical system designed as a model of reality is to assert that it is "oversimplified," that it "does not represent all the complexities of reality." In effect, he is saying that the symbolic language in which the mathematical model is expressed is too poor to convey all the nuances of meaning which he can carry in his mind. What happens is that the very ambiguity and confusion of ordinary speech give rise to a richness of meaning which surpasses for the social scientist the limited resources of mathematics, in which each symbol has only one meaning. It is not surprising that there should be a difference between the social and the natural sciences in this regard. Language is itself a social phenomenon, and the multiple meanings of its symbols are very likely to be much better adapted to the conveying of social concepts than to those of the inanimate world. Furthermore, the empirical experience on which one's understanding of the social world is based consists to a large extent of symbolic expressions of other individuals; one can apprehend these expressions directly because one is himself part of the social world he observes.[4] Such apprehension must inevitably take place on a largely unconscious level unamenable to mathematical expression (which is surely the acme of consciousness). It is precisely in the field of economics, where the individuals studied are engaged in relatively highly conscious calculating operations, that mathematical methods have been most successful.[5]

[3] Consider the following apparently simple statement: Every even number is the sum of two odd prime numbers (a prime number is a number divisible only by itself and by 1). There is no known exception to the statement, yet it has never been proved in general. This is known as Goldbach's problem and dates from the 18th century.

[4] This point has been stressed by Frank H. Knight in "The Limitations of Scientific Method in Economics," in *The Ethics of Competition and Other Essays* (1935), pp. 105–47.

[5] Credit for the first significant use of mathematics in economics is due the great French economist Augustin Cournot, who published in 1838 his *Recherches sur les principes mathématiques de la théorie des richesses*. His work was largely neglected. It was the contribution of W. Stanley Jevons in *The Theory of Political Economy* (1871) and especially the contribution of Léon Walras in *Éléments d'économie politique pure* (1874), which brought the power of the mathematical methods to the attention of economists. The present status of mathematical economics is best summarized in Paul A.

It is true, then, that there are certain limitations of mathematical methods in the social sciences. Nevertheless, it must be insisted that the advantages are equally apparent and may frequently be worth a certain loss of realism. In the *first* place, clarity of thought is still a pearl of great price. In particular, the multiplicity of values of verbal symbols may be a great disadvantage when it comes to drawing the logical consequences of a proposition. Consider, for example, the following verbal arguments: (*a*) if prices are high, people will tend to buy less; when people buy less, manufacturers produce less, since they tend to produce only what they can sell; therefore, high prices are associated with low production. (*b*) If prices are high, manufacturers will produce more, since it is more profitable for them to do so; therefore, high prices are associated with high production. At a verbal level, both arguments are convincing; yet obviously they cannot both be valid. Let us try to isolate the postulates of the two arguments and express them symbolically. Let x_1 denote the amount which people will buy, x_2 the amount manufacturers will produce, and p the price. The first argument says that x_1 is a decreasing function of price, i.e., that $x_1 = f(p)$; and that $x_1 = x_2$. The second argument says that x_2 is an increasing function of price, $x_2 = g(p)$. Then we have three equations in three unknowns; thus, in general there is no inconsistency, all three relations simultaneously determining x_1, x_2, and p. These relations express the behavior of consumers, the market, and producers respectively. So long as no change occurs in anyone's behavior pattern, the values of x_1, x_2, and p will remain constant. There will be no question whether supply varies directly or inversely with price, since neither moves at all. Suppose, however, that there were a shift in the tastes of consumers, so that $f(p)$ changed to another function, say $f_1(p)$. To obtain the values of x_1, x_2, and p, we would solve the new system of simultaneous equations, $x_1 = f_1(p)$, $x_1 = x_2$, $x_2 = g(p)$. Note now that the solutions x_1', x_2', p' to this equation system satisfy the conditions that $x_2' = g(p')$. Hence, if p' is greater than p, x_2' will be greater than x_2. If therefore we have a sequence of observations in which consumers' tastes are varying but production conditions, as expressed by $g(p)$, remain constant, prices and production will move together. On the other hand, if consumers' tastes are constant but production conditions are variable, high prices will be associated with low production. Thus, mathematical symbolism resolves the apparent contradiction between the two arguments and shows when each is valid.

In addition to the problem of clarity in logical deductions, there is another methodological question related to the formulation of theoretical models: the problem of inductive inference. It is by now a platitude of the

---

Samuelson, *Foundations of Economic Analysis* (1947); see also J. R. Hicks, *La théorie mathématique de la valeur en régime de libre concurrence* (1937), and *Value and Capital* (1939), particularly the Mathematical Appendix, for a more intensive survey of more limited areas than Samuelson's work. These works do not cover, however, a good deal of significant work published in the various economic journals, and particularly *Econometrica*.

scientific method that if theory without empirical evidence is unreliable, empirical inquiry without theoretical background is unfruitful. The theory of statistical inference, as it has been developed in recent years of Jerzy Neyman, Egon S. Pearson, and Abraham Wald on the basis of the earlier work of R. A. Fisher and Karl Pearson, is precisely the mathematical expression of the logic of induction. It has shown clearly how the optimum statistical methods depend critically on the theoretical model assumed.[6] Now the derivation of the statistical methods appropriate for making inferences within a given theoretical model is usually a matter of considerable mathematical difficulty.[7] To proceed with the derivation at all, the underlying theoretical presumptions must be set forth in explicit symbolic form. Hence, a *second* argument, besides that of greater clarity of thought, for the explicit formulation of theories in mathematical terms is the resultant opportunity to tap the great resources of modern theoretical statistics as an aid in empirical verification.

The observations made above as to the limitations of our present knowledge of mathematics are applicable here also. It is unfortunately true that it is very easy to formulate theoretical models in which the determination of the optimum statistical methods leads to mathematical problems which have not been solved; in other cases, the resultant problems can be solved in principle, but the computations needed to find the solution in any given case take an impractical amount of time.[8] Here again we must resort to simplification. The customary procedure is to substitute a mathematically practicable theory, as similar as possible to the desired one, and use that as the basis for deriving statistical methods. For example, the assumption is frequently made in theoretical models in biology and economics that there exists some linear combination of the variables that is normally distributed. The assumptions of normality and linearity are introduced primarily because of the relative mathematical simplicity of deriving optimum methods of estimation and tests of significance.[9]

[6] The concept of "optimum" is, of course, always relative to a value system. As will be seen below, the statement in the text is not meant to imply that all the philosophical difficulties in the theory of induction have been completely resolved. We can, however, be reasonably sure that the optimum methods, however defined, for making a choice among alternative theories on the basis of given empirical evidence will depend critically upon the theoretical background of the inquiry, i.e., upon the range of theories which are believed to be sufficiently plausible that they are admitted to the set among which the choice is to be made.

[7] The level of mathematics needed in modern statistical theory can be seen in such a work as Harald Cramér, *Mathematical Methods of Statistics* (1946).

[8] An attempt, for example, to estimate statistically the economic laws governing a large modern country on the basis of a relatively simple model (say, a few hundred equations to be fitted) could easily occupy the best computing machines now available for the next five hundred to a thousand years.

[9] Of course there are other justifications for the widespread use of the normal distribution, in particular the Central Limit Theorem, which asserts that under certain general conditions the sum of a large number of independent variates, each contributing a small part to the whole, will be normally distributed. See, for instance, Harald Cramér, *Random Variables and Probability Distributions* (1937).

In Section II, some alternative possibilities in the types of mathematical models which are being proposed are discussed in a classificatory way. In Section III, extended examination is given to one proposed model, the "game" theory of social behavior developed by John von Neumann and Oskar Morgenstern. Section IV will take up more briefly some other proposed mathematical theories of the social sciences. Finally, certain very important recent advances in the methodology of empirical work as guided by theoretical models will be taken up in Section V. While the literature of current economic thought is frequently referred to, the emphasis is on those parts which have wide applicability in the social sciences.

II. Some Classifications of Models

1. INDIVIDUALISTIC VERSUS COLLECTIVE BASIS

In most mathematical and, generally, in most deductive studies in the social sciences, the starting point is the behavior of the individual. Each individual is conceived of as acting in a way determined partly by his psychology and his physical surroundings and partly by the actions of others. If there are n individuals, we may denote the actions of individuals i by A_i, and the nonsocial determinants of his behavior by P_i. Then the actions of the first individual may be described by a symbolic equation,

$$A_1 = f(P_1, A_2, \ldots, A_n). \tag{1}$$

There is one such equation for each individual. Together, they constitute n equations in the n variables $A_1, \ldots, A_n$. In general, these may then be solved to express the actions of all individuals in terms of the data $P_1, \ldots, P_n$.[10] Therefore, given the reaction of each individual to his total (social and other) environment, as expressed in relations of type (1), and given the nonsocial environmental factors, which we may term *exogenous*, we can determine the behavior of society in the sense that we can determine the behavior of any individual in society.

This individualistic viewpoint, as we may term it, is explicit in the main tradition of economic thought and is completely accepted in the von Neumann-Morgenstern game theory. It seems also to be accepted by the other theorists whose work is discussed below, though George Zipf seems at times to be referring to the laws of behavior of society in some total sense. The individualistic viewpoint has been challenged recently by Rutledge Vining in the course of a methodological controversy with Tjalling C.

[10] The fact that the actions A_i may not be representable by single numbers does not alter the validity of the principle that n equations suffice, in general, to determine n unknowns.

Koopmans.[11] Vining has stated, "I think that in a positive sense the aggregate has an existence over and above the existence of Koopmans' individual units and behavior characteristics that may not be deducible from the behavior of these component parts." [12] Taken literally, this position seems indefensible. As Koopmans points out, a full characterization of each individual's behavior logically implies a knowledge of group behavior; there is nothing left out.[13] The rejection of the organism approach to social problems has been a fairly complete, and to my mind salutary, rejection of mysticism. But as usual in these problems, there is something to be said for at least the possibility of a collective basis for social theorizing, if not taken too literally. Much of our casual observation and much of our better statistical information relate to groups rather than individuals. We may therefore be led to generalize and form a theory whose subject is the total behavior of a group. So long as it is understood that such a theory is really a resultant of certain as yet unanalyzed laws of individual behavior, no harm will be done, and the greater convenience of empirical analysis on groups may be highly beneficial.

In fact, even in economics, the unit of the theory of production is not really the individual but the firm, which is an operating organization of individuals. Similarly, the unit of the theory of consumption is really the household, not the individual consumer. In empirical economics, the investigator is usually forced to use a collectively based model by the nature of the data. The Keynesian theory postulates that the consumption of a community is an increasing function of its total income. As an empirical equation, this is a statement about group behavior, not individual behavior.[14] Similar remarks apply to all macroeconomic models designed as a basis for empirical fitting, in which the variables that enter are obtained by aggregating the behavior of many individuals.[15] They apply even to many models

[11] Rutledge Vining, "Koopmans on the Choice of Variables to Be Studied and of Methods of Measurement," *Review of Economics and Statistics*, XXXI (1949), 77–86. See also Tjalling C. Koopmans, "A Reply," *Review of Economics and Statistics*, XXXI (1949), 86–91; Rutledge Vining, "A Rejoinder," *Review of Economics and Statistics*, XXXI (1949), 91–94. Vining's first paper was a criticism of an earlier paper of Koopmans entitled "Measurement Without Theory," *Review of Economics and Statistics*, XXIX (1947), 161–72. The Koopmans paper, in turn, was a review article of a book by Arthur F. Burns and Wesley C. Mitchell, *Measuring Business Cycles* (1946).

[12] Vining, "Koopmans on the Choice of Variables to Be Studied and of Methods of Measurement," p. 81.

[13] Koopmans, "A Reply," pp. 86–87.

[14] John Maynard Keynes, *The General Theory of Employment, Interest, and Money* (1936), pp. 89–131. There are a large number of variant empirically derived consumption functions; see, for example, Arthur Smithies, "Forecasting Postwar Demand: I," *Econometrica*, XIII, No. 1 (1945), 1–14; Jacob L. Mosak, "Forecasting Postwar Demand: III," *Econometrica*, XIII, No. 1 (1945), 25–53; and Trygve Haavelmo, "Methods of Measuring the Marginal Propensity to Consume," *Journal of the American Statistical Association*, XLII (1947), 105–22.

[15] Jan Tinbergen, *Statistical Testing of Business-Cycle Theories* (1939); Lawrence R. Klein, "The Use of Econometric Models as a Guide to Policy," *Econometrica*, XV (1947),

constructed for the purposes of theoretical analysis. The various representations of the Keynesian theory in mathematical form all involve functional relations among magnitudes which cannot be identified with the behavior of any individual.[16]

The usual feeling among economists is that these macroeconomic models could be justified on the basis of an individualistic theory if suitable definitions of the aggregate magnitudes in terms of those pertaining to individuals were given. The problem of finding such definitions, generally known as the *aggregation problem,* has received a certain amount of attention in recent years. Because of the nature of the discussion, at once technical and unresolved, it is not summarized here. But one methodological principle emerges clearly: in order to have a useful theory of relations among aggregates, it is necessary that they be defined in a manner derived from the theory of individual behavior. In other words, even the definition of such magnitudes as national income cannot be undertaken without a previous theoretical understanding of the underlying individual phenomena. It also seems evident that the aggregated model must include among its variables some which characterize the distribution of various magnitudes among the individuals of the society; e.g., in the consumption function some measure of income inequality should be introduced as an additional variable. Doubtless, the same remarks apply to aggregation in other social realms.[17]

111–51, and *Economic Fluctuations in the United States, 1921–1941* (Cowles Commission for Research in Economics, Monograph No. 11 [1950]); Mordecai Ezekiel, "Savings, Consumption, and Investment," *American Economic Review,* XXXII (1942), 22–49, 272–307; and Colin Clark, "A System of Equations Explaining the United States Trade Cycle, 1921 to 1941," *Econometrica,* XVII (1949), 93–124. These are all attempts to find a comprehensive system of equations which will explain cyclical fluctuations in business. Mention should also be made of the empirical studies on production made by Paul H. Douglas and his associates, summarized in Douglas's, "Are There Laws of Production?" *American Economic Review,* XXXVIII (1948), 1–41. All these studies employ magnitudes such as total consumption, total output, and aggregate investment; the laws relating them are laws of behavior of the society as a whole and only by implication are they laws of individual behavior.

16 Oscar Lange, "The Rate of Interest and the Optimum Propensity to Consume," *Economica,* n.s., V (1938), 12–32; John R. Hicks, "Mr. Keynes and the 'Classics': A Suggested Interpretation," *Econometrica,* V (1937), 147–59. The anti-Keynesian work of A. C. Pigou, *Employment and Equilibrium* (1941) follows the same methodological pattern on this point.

17 See Francis W. Dresch, "Index Numbers and the General Equilibrium," *Bulletin of the American Mathematical Society,* XLIV (1938), 139–41, and "Continuous Index Numbers and Quantitative Study of the General Economy," in Jerzy Neyman (ed.), *Proceedings of the Berkeley Symposium on Mathematical Statistics and Probability* (1949), pp. 203–22; Lawrence R. Klein, "Macroeconomics and the Theory of Rational Behavior," *Econometrica,* XIV (1946), 93–108, and "Remarks on the Theory of Aggregation," *Econometrica,* XIV (1946), pp. 303–12; Kenneth May, "The Aggregation Problem for a One-Industry Model," *Econometrica,* XIV (1946), 285–98, and "Technological Change and Aggregation," *Econometrica,* XV (1947), 51–63; Shou Shan Pu, "A Note on Macroeconomics," *Econometrica,* XIV (1946), 299–302; Kenneth J. Arrow, "Summarizing a Population of Behavior Patterns," *Econometrica,* XVI (1948), 203; and André Nataf, "Sur la possibilité de construction de certains macromodèles," *Econometrica,* XVI (1948), 232–44. The works of Dresch and May, in particular, make great use of the index numbers introduced by

2. THE PRINCIPLE OF RATIONALITY

A postulate frequently encountered in theoretical economics and else-where in social theory is that the behavior of the individual or group can be described by saying that the individual or group is seeking to maximize some quantity. Thus, in the theory of the firm, the economist postulates that the individual seeks to choose that mode and scale of operation which will yield more profit than any other possible choice. In the theory of consumption, it is assumed that among all the combinations of commodities an individual can afford, he chooses that combination which maximizes his utility or satisfaction. Behavior of this type is frequently referred to as rational.

The basis for the assumption of rationality is the following seemingly quite general formulation of individual behavior in a social situation: Each individual at a given moment of time is free to choose among several possible courses of action; he decides among them on the basis of their consequences. The range of actions open to him and the consequences of these actions are determined by the contemporary actions of others, by the past actions of himself and of others, and by the exogenous factors. To put it briefly, we may say that the individual can choose at any instant among a limited range of consequences according to his tastes. It is natural to suppose that as the range varies, his choices from different ranges bear some sort of consistent relation to each other. In particular, we will suppose that he makes the same choice each time he is confronted with the same set of alternatives; further, if, when confronted with the two alternatives A and B, he chooses A, and when confronted with the two alternatives B and C, he chooses B, then it is reasonable to suppose that when confronted with a choice between A and C, he chooses A. Under these circumstances, the process of decision may be described as follows: we can imagine the individual as listing, once and for all, all conceivable consequences of his actions in order of his preference for them; then, on being informed of the choices actually available to him, he selects that one which stands highest on his list. The list represents his tastes, while the alternatives actually available to him are restricted by obstacles.[18] So far there has been no quantitative element at all in the formulation. In certain problems, of course, the desirability of the various courses of action is associated naturally with a quantitative variable; e.g., profits in the case of a firm deciding upon its productive operations, probability of winning in the case of a country deciding whether or not to go to war. Even if there is no natural quantitative

---

François Divisia in his *Économique rationale* (1928), pp. 260–73. For the aggregation problems in the consumption function, see also Jacob Marschak, "Personal and Collective Budget Functions," *Review of Economics and Statistics*, XXI, No. 4 (1939), 161–70.

[18] This formulation is essentially due to Vilfredo Pareto, *Manuel d'économie politique* (2d ed., 1927), pp. 150–79.

variable associated with the problem, it is sometimes useful for analysis to introduce one artificially, by assigning numbers to each consequence of an individual's actions in such a way that, of two consequences, the higher number will be assigned to the preferred one. Such an assignment of numbers is known as a *utility index*. Let x stand for the consequences of some action, and let $U_1(x)$ be the utility assigned to x under one assignment of the type described. Then $U_1(x_1) > U_1(x_2)$ if and only if the individual prefers x_1 to x_2. There is, clearly, nothing unique about the assignment of a utility index, at least within the conditions laid down thus far. Let $F(u)$ be any strictly increasing function of a real variable u, i.e., if $u_1 > u_2$, then $F(u_1) > F(u_2)$. Then, if we define $U_2(x)$ as $F[U_1(x)]$, it is clear that $U_2(x)$ will also serve as a utility index.[19]

Under the hypothesis of rationality, then, the individual's behavior depends on his tastes—as expressed, say, by a utility index—and upon the obstacles, which are determined by exogenous factors, by the actions of others, and possibly by past actions of the individual and of others. We may say that the individual maximizes his utility, subject to the obstacles. We are thus led to an expression of form (1) above. If we postulate nothing more than that there exists some utility function in terms of which the individual's behavior can be described in the above way, we have imposed some restrictions on the possible forms of (1), since the principle of rationality is not a pure tautology; i.e., it is logically possible that an individual may choose A over B, B over C, and yet choose C over A.[20] However, the degree of restrictiveness thus obtained is not great. It is customary to supplement the general principle of rationality in any particular instance by further assumptions as to the nature of the preferences involved. For example, in consumer's demand theory, it is ordinarily understood that more of a commodity is preferred to less, all other things being equal.

A number of objections have been raised to the usefulness of the principle of rationality: (a) If the complicated nature of the range of choices possible in an actual social situation is even approximately taken into account in the theoretical model, the mathematical problems to be solved in the maximization of utility will become extremely complex, and it will be hard to derive results which have any simple meaning. This objection has been frequently raised, for example, against the Walrasian scheme of general equilibrium in economics. (b) There is no real reason to suppose that individual behavior does conform to the principle of rationality. This argument is partly related to the previous one; it is argued that if the

---

[19] It should be clearly understood that the variable x need not be numerical. The consequences of an action may be a power or prestige situation or a state of religious ecstasy, as well as a bundle of commodities for consumption or a sum of money. All that is required is that given two well-defined situations resultant from his actions, an individual should be able to say that he prefers one to the other.

[20] For a discussion of the refutable, and therefore empirically meaningful, consequences of the principle of rationality in the field of consumers' demand, see Paul A. Samuelson, *Foundations of Economic Analysis* (1947), chap. v.

rational choice is too difficult for the trained mathematician to find, it is certainly unreasonable to suppose that the untrained, unreflecting, average individual will be able to locate it.[21] (c) The utility function itself, even if it plays the role assigned to it, is highly unstable over time; hence, for an understanding of social processes, more interest attaches to the determinants of the variation of tastes than to the line of causation from the utility index to the actual decision made.[22] (d) There is a fundamental ambiguity in the concept of rationality in a social situation. An individual will soon realize that his actions, in addition to their other consequences, will alter the obstacles faced by others, thereby affecting their actions and in turn altering the obstacles controlling his choices. Hence, his actions will be partly controlled by his realization of their repercussions on the actions of others. But the same statement is true of each other individual; thus, each will be concerned with the effect of his action on the others, and no determinate solution will be possible.[23]

There is no single sweeping principle which has been erected as a rival to that of rationality. To the extent that formal theoretical structures in the social sciences have not been based on the hypothesis of rational behavior, their postulates have been developed in a manner which we may term *ad hoc*. Such propositions are usually drawn from introspection or casual observation; sometimes they are of the nature of empirical regularities. They depend, of course, on the investigator's intuition and common sense.

An example of this approach is Lewis F. Richardson's approach to international relations.[24] What will make a government increase its armaments? Clearly, it will increase them more if the armaments of a potential enemy are greater; but it will be deterred from increasing them by the expense. Let x represent the armaments of this country, y those of a potential enemy, and t time; and let k and a be fixed coefficients. Then, the above theory may be expressed in the equation

$$dx/dt = ky - ax. \tag{2}$$

A similar equation holds for the other country. Taken together, they form a complete system of differential equations which, with the initial conditions and the values of the coefficients, define the course of x and y over time.

---

[21] Objections of this type and others were raised by Richard A. Lester in his "Shortcomings of Marginal Analysis for Wage-Employment Problems," *American Economic Review*, XXXVI (1946), 63–82. For a reply see Fritz Machlup, "Marginal Analysis and Empirical Research," *American Economic Review*, XXXVI (1946), 519–54.

[22] Vining attributes this view to Thorstein Veblen. See his article, "Koopmans on the Choice of Variables to Be Studied and Methods of Measurement," *Review of Economics and Statistics*, XXXI (1949), 77–86, esp. 82–83.

[23] This fourth objection to the principle of rationality has been recognized in a general way in economics in the theories of oligopoly and bilateral monopoly. It was given a definitive statement by Oskar Morgenstern in his *Wirtschaftsprognose* (1928), p. 98.

[24] Lewis F. Richardson, *Generalized Foreign Politics* (British Journal of Psychology, Monograph Supplement No. 23 [1939]).

Richardson then deals with the implications of these results and those of more general models.

Because of the first and fourth difficulties mentioned above, theoretical economics has generally had an admixture of *ad hoc* assumptions which limit the scope of the principle of rationality. The hypothesis of a perfect competition removes the fourth difficulty because each individual supposes his effect on other individuals is so small that their actions are not influenced by him. Under conditions of monopoly it is assumed that while one individual can affect other individuals, none of them is strong enough to affect him. The monopolist's behavior incorporates his realization of this situation, thereby again avoiding indeterminacy. In those cases where neither hypothesis can be maintained (e.g., bargaining between a labor union and a monopolistic employer, or the behavior of an industry in which there are a few large firms) still more complicated *ad hoc* assumptions have been made about the way individual firms took into account the anticipated reactions to their actions in order eventually to reduce the problem to a simple maximization.[25]

One somewhat digressive remark on the principle of rationality may be in order: a rational theory always has a dual interpretation. On the one hand it may be taken as a description of reality to the extent that individuals really are consistent in the sense assumed. On the other hand it may be taken rather as a normative theory, which prescribes what individuals ought to do. Thus, theoretical economics has been used to analyze what the optimum state of economic welfare would be and how to attain it.[26] This subject of "welfare economics" is not new, being indeed as old as theoretical economics itself, but clarification of its basic principles has been a slow process. Even today there are a number of profound unresolved difficulties, principally revolving about the problem of comparing the welfares of different individuals in arriving at a concept of a social optimum.[27] Since we are here concerned with the problems of a descriptive social science, we shall not pursue this matter any further.

Statistical inference may be viewed broadly as the behavior of an individual under a certain set of conditions; namely, he does not know completely the consequences of his actions. We may therefore speak of a rational theory of statistical inference. More precisely, statistical inference may be described as follows: The true state of the universe under investigation is known, a priori, to belong to one of a class of states. A sample of elements of the universe is drawn; the probability distribution of the sample depends on the true state of the universe. The statistician must then take some

[25] The most extended treatment of various possible assumptions of this type is found in Ragnar Frisch, "Monopolé, polypole: La Notion de la force dans l'équilibre économique," *Nationaløkonomisk Tidsskrift* (1933).

[26] Recent systematic expositions of this subject will be found in Paul A. Samuelson, *Foundations of Economic Analysis* (1947), chap. viii, and Melvin W. Reder, *Studies in the Theory of Welfare Economics* (1947), Parts I and III.

[27] Kenneth J. Arrow, *Social Choice and Individual Values* (1951).

action (e.g., estimate some state to be the true one, assert that the state lies in some subclass of the one given a priori; or, in industrial applications, accept or reject a lot of goods), the consequences of which are a function of the action and of the true state, being favorable if the action is really appropriate to the true state and unfavorable otherwise. For simplicity, let us consider the case where the true state is known to be one of a finite number, the possible samples to be drawn are finite in number (e.g., suppose we draw a sample of three observations, each of which is either "yes" or "no," as in a questionnaire or in a quality inspection; then one possible sample is "yes, yes, no," another is "no, yes, no," and so on; there are altogether eight possible samples), and the number of actions the statistician can take is finite. Let i stand for an action, j for a true state, k a sample, p_{kj} for the probability of observing sample k when the true state is j, and r_{ij} the loss to the statistician if he takes action i when the true state is j (r_{ij} is small or negative if i is appropriate to j, large otherwise). The statistician's problem is to choose a decision function $i(k)$, which tells him what action to take for each possible sample k. The function $i(k)$ is to be so chosen as to minimize in some sense the probable loss.

This formulation includes all the classical problems of statistics and more. For example, in the above illustration the problem of estimation is the case where an action consists of naming a true state. The range of possible actions is then the same as the range of possible states of nature. Another case would be that of two possible actions, one affirming and one denying that $j = j_o$, where j_o is a fixed possible true state. This is the classical problem of testing a hypothesis.[28]

We have here clearly a problem of behavior; the statistician must choose among the various possible functions $i(k)$, and the consequences are given, though not with certainty, by the conditions of the problem, the p_{kj}'s and r_{ij}'s. The foundations of statistical inference, from the normative point of view of proper scientific method, are then nothing but the application of a suitable principle of rationality to the problem just described. Indeed, it will be seen that Wald's important contributions to this field are closely related to an important development in social theory, the von Neumann-Morgenstern theory of games.

This relation between the theoretical analysis of behavior and the founda-

[28] This general formulation of the problem of statistical decision is due to A. Wald, "Foundations of a General Theory of Sequential Decision Functions," *Econometrica*, XV (1947), pp. 279–313, especially pp. 279–83; and his "Statistical Decision Functions," *Annals of Mathematical Statistics*, XX (1949), 165–205, esp. 172–73. For a more elementary presentation of the problem in a somewhat less general form, see Wald's "Contributions to the Theory of Statistical Estimation and Testing Hypotheses," *Annals of Mathematical Statistics*, X (1939), 299–326, and his "Statistical Decision Functions Which Minimize the Maximum Risk," *Annals of Mathematics*, XLVI (1945), 265–80. For the currently standard methods of estimation and testing hypotheses, see Harald Cramér, *Mathematical Methods of Statistics* (1946), chaps. xxx–xxxvii. An excellent introduction is to be found in Wald, *On the Principles of Statistical Inference* (Notre Dame Mathematical Lectures, No. 1 [1942]).

tions of statistical inference can, of course, be applied in reverse. To the extent that actual behavior under conditions of uncertainty as to the consequences of any action is governed by the principle of rationality, the theory of statistical inference may also be interpreted as a descriptive theory. This point of view has especially been stressed in economics by Jacob Marschak.[29]

III. The Theory of Games [30]

The von Neumann-Morgenstern theory of games is an attempt to provide a theory of social (primarily economic) interaction by analogy with ordinary games of strategy (such as chess or card games) as they would be played by thoroughly rational individuals. It goes well beyond any other systematic social theorizing in the complexity of its structure and the rigorous nature of its formal logic. Yet it is interesting to note that virtually no mathematics more difficult than algebra is employed although the chains of reasoning are frequently long and complicated.

1. RATIONAL BEHAVIOR IN SITUATIONS INVOLVING RISK

As a preliminary to the theory of games, though not strictly part of it, von Neumann and Morgenstern formulate the principle of rationality applied to a situation in which the consequences of the different actions open to an individual are expressed as probability distributions rather than as certainties. A simple example is that of an individual choosing between two lottery tickets, one of which pays \$1,000 with probability 0.01 and nothing otherwise, while the other pays \$100 with probability 0.10 and nothing otherwise. More generally, the choice is among a number of "lottery tickets," each of which is a promise to pay amounts $m_1, m_2, \ldots$ with prob-

[29] For a specific application, see Jacob Marschak, "Role of Liquidity Under Complete and Incomplete Information," *American Economic Review*, XXXIX, No. 3 (1949), 182–95, esp. 192–95; see also Franco Modigliani, "Liquidity and Uncertainty: Discussion," *American Economic Review*, XXXIX, No. 3 (1949), 201–8, esp. 203–8. For earlier work, see Marschak's "Money and the Theory of Assets," *Econometrica*, VI (1938), 311–25, and Leonid Hurwicz, "Theory of the Firm and Investment," *Econometrica*, XIV (1946), 109–36, esp. 133–36. The relation between the problems of statistical inference and of behavior under certainty is clearly indicated in Frank H. Knight, *Risk, Uncertainty, and Profit* (1921), Part III, esp. chap. vii.

[30] John von Neumann and Oskar Morgenstern, *Theory of Games and Economic Behavior* (2d ed., 1947). Some of the review articles give excellent expositions of the theory; see especially Leonid Hurwicz, "The Theory of Economic Behavior," *American Economic Review*, XXXV (1945), 901–25; and Jacob Marschak, "Neumann's and Morgenstern's New Approach to Static Economics," *Journal of Political Economy*, LIV (1946), 97–115. For a more critical appraisal of the theory in its application to economics, see Carl Kaysen, "A Revolution in Economic Theory?" *Review of Economic Studies*, XIV (1946–47), 1–15.

abilities p_1, p_2, . . . , the quantities m_1, m_2 . . . and p_1, p_2, . . . varying from ticket to ticket. Also, of course, in general the "payments" need not be sums of money but consequences of any sort which matter to the individual. A "lottery ticket" is a paradigm for any choice made by a human being in which the outcome of his action is not known with certainty but in which, on the basis of experience or intuition, he believes he knows the probabilities of the different possible outcomes.

In accordance with the principle of rationality, the individual may order all possible probability distributions of outcomes; he may then choose a utility index having the properties described in the second part of Section II of this chapter and act so as to maximize utility. The concept of rationality as applied to this situation has been formalized by von Neumann and Morgenstern in a series of axioms.[31] The principal condition laid down, in addition to the general requirement that the probability distributions be ordered in accordance with the individual's preferences, may be expressed loosely as follows: If the individual prefers the outcome x_1 to the outcome x_2, then he will prefer the certainty of x_1 to an even chance of getting either x_1 or x_2. With the aid of this highly reasonable condition, and some other more technical ones, it is shown that among the many utility indexes which can be assigned to the possible probability distributions, there is one with the property that the utility attached to a probability distribution is the mathematical expectation of the utilities of the possible outcomes. I.e., if a given choice has possible outcomes x_1 . . . x_n with probabilities p_1 . . . p_n, respectively, and if $U(x)$ is the utility (in the index just described) of the outcome x, then the utility attached to the given choice is

$$\sum_{i=1}^{n} p_i U(x_i).$$

(Note that this utility index is not unique; if $U(x)$ is one such index and a is a positive number, then $aU(x) + b$ is another such index.) Rational behavior in the choice of risky alternatives can thus be simplified to the statement that the individual seeks to maximize the expected value of his utility.[32] Milton Friedman and L. J. Savage have developed an interesting

[31] John von Neumann and Oskar Morgenstern, *op. cit.*, chap. 1, sec. 3; Appendix.

[32] The explanation of choice among risky alternatives in terms of maximizing the expected value of utility dates back to Daniel Bernoulli, "Specimen theoriae novae de mensura sortis" (1738); German translation, *Die Grundlage der modernen Wertlehre* (1896). Bernoulli was interested in showing, in connection with the famous St. Petersburg paradox, that an individual might not take a gamble even if the expected money reward were infinite; his argument was that the individual was seeking to maximize the expected utility of money, which was given, he suggested, by the logarithm of the amount of money received. With the introduction of the marginal utility theory of value, it was natural to discuss choices among risky alternatives in these terms; see Alfred Marshall, *Principles of Economics* (8th ed., 1920), pp. 135 n., 843. However, von Neumann and Morganstern have been the first to show the assumptions about behavior which are implied in this theory.

hypothesis about the shape of the von Neumann–Morgenstern utility curve for money which will explain some phenomena observed in the behavior of individuals in connection with gambling and insurance.[33]

Since probability distributions are basic in the theory of games, the above construction enables the authors to speak of a numerical utility, having the convenient property that the utility attached to a chance event is precisely the mathematical expectation of the utilities of the various possible outcomes. However, they need further the idea of a transferable utility, i.e., some sort of measure the units of which mean the same, in some sense, to both players. In effect, they then restrict the realm of their theory greatly by assuming that the outcome of each game is expressible in some common units, which we may take to be money, and that the utility of a given sum of money, for each player, is simply a linear function of the sum, so that each player is seeking to maximize the expected amount of money he will receive. This assumption is to be understood as an intentional simplification to make the problem mathematically manageable. (Compare the remarks in the first section above.)

2. THE GENERAL CONCEPT OF A GAME [34]

In general, a game will have a certain number of players, say n. The game is composed of moves, which are of two types; personal, made by one of the players, and chance, in which one of several possible outcomes is selected by a chance device acting in accordance with certain probability laws. Thus, in a game of cards the distribution of the hands is made by a random device, while the players still have certain choices as to how to play their hands. The rules of the game prescribe the following: (a) whether the first move shall be personal or chance; if personal, who shall make it, and what range of choice he shall have; if chance, what the possible outcomes are and what the probability is of each; (b) after k moves have been made, whether the $(k + 1)$st move shall be personal or chance; if personal, who shall make it, what range of choices he shall have, and what information he shall have about the outcomes of the previous moves; if chance, what the range of possible outcomes is and what probability is attached to each (note well that the rules may make each of these prescriptions dependent on the outcome of the preceding moves, it being required only that at each stage of the game the prescriptions in question must be unambiguously defined); (c) when the game shall stop and what amount shall be paid to each of the participants depending on the outcomes of the various moves. Thus, in chess, the rules specify that all moves are personal, with the two players taking alternate moves; that at each move each player knows the outcome of every previous move; and that in any given move, the range of permissible actions depends upon the present configuration of the pieces, which in turn depends upon

[33] Milton Friedman and L. J. Savage, "The Utility Analysis of Choices Involving Risk," *Journal of Political Economy*, XVI (1948), 279–304.

[34] See von Neumann and Morgenstern, *op. cit.*, chap. ii.

the outcomes of all past moves. In card games, on the other hand, the dealing of the hands is a chance move, the outcome of which is not revealed to the other players.

It is easy to see that many economic and social situations can be described in these terms. For example, the operations of a market may be described as a game, with the buyers and sellers as players, and bids, offers, and agreements to conclude transactions as moves. The initial distribution of goods and money may be taken as part of the rules of the game; the final distribution of goods and money describes the pay-off to the various players attendant upon the particular set of moves which they made. Similarly, conflicts between nations or between social and economic groups can be brought within the same rubric.

Now suppose, for the purpose of simplified description, that each individual does not play the game by waiting each time until his move comes and then deciding among the various alternatives presented to him, but rather that he prepares beforehand a *strategy* which specifies for each possible situation with which he may be confronted in the course of the play what choice he shall make. Indeed, something of the sort must be done by skillful players, since they realize that the effects of their choices at various moves are interrelated; a good move at one point may improve the range of choices available at another. A good choice of any one move may therefore involve consideration of the alternative possible developments of the game following each possible action. Suppose each individual were to write down his strategy and hand it to an umpire. It would then be unnecessary actually to play the game; the umpire would need only to follow the instructions of the appropriate individual's strategy at each personal move and make the indicated chance moves. Therefore, every game can be reduced to the following type: each player makes a single move, namely the choice of a strategy; then the pay-off to each player is a random variable whose probability distribution is determined by the strategies of the various players. Since, according to the assumption made at the end of Section I, the individual is interested only in the mathematical expectation of the pay-off, we can consider the pay-off to be a single number, instead of a probability distribution. Thus every game, no matter how complicated, can be reduced to the following *normal form:* each player makes one move, knowing nothing about the moves of the others, from a range of choices fixed in advance; the pay-off to each player is then a function of the moves of all the players. This reduction permits a consideration of the basic nature of games undisturbed by the complications of particular rules. From now on, we will consider all games to be in normal form.[35]

To simplify the analysis further, von Neumann and Morgenstern assume

[35] The concept of the economic agent as choosing a strategy—a plan for meeting contingencies—rather than merely making specific decisions from time to time, was clearly expressed, in a somewhat different context, by Albert G. Hart in his "Risk, Uncertainty, and the Unprofitability of Compounding Probabilities," in *Studies in Mathematical Economics and Econometrics,* edited by Oscar Lange, Francis McIntyre, and T. O. Yntema (1942), pp. 110–18.

that the game will be terminated in a finite number of moves and that at each move there are only a finite number of possible choices. Then it can be seen that the number of possible strategies is finite. In the normal form, therefore, each individual has the choice among a finite number of alternatives for his move. It should be noted, though, that the finite number of strategies may be enormous; merely to enumerate all possible situations in chess is a tremendous task, and the number of possible ways of specifying responses to these situations staggers the imagination. If the restriction to a finite number of choices at each move is not made, then some extremely subtle mathematical difficulties arise. Some work has been done on this problem; it will be cited in footnotes where appropriate.

3. THE ZERO-SUM TWO-PERSON GAME [36]

Consider now the special case of a game with two players in which the sum of the pay-offs to the two players is zero for all choices of strategies; e.g., if the outcome of a play of the game yields 5 to player a, then it necessarily constitutes a loss of 5 to player b. This is the model of a situation of pure conflict, since the gain of one player is precisely the loss of the other. Since there are only two players, there is nothing whatever to be gained by agreement between them. Assume that the game is in normal form; let player A have the choice of strategies $1, \ldots, m$, player B the choice of strategies $1, \ldots, n$. If A chooses strategy i and B strategy j, let the pay-off to player A be a_{ij}; then the pay-off to player B is $-a_{ij}$. Clearly, A wishes to maximize a_{ij} while B seeks to minimize the same magnitude. Suppose A is contemplating the use of a particular strategy i. It is natural for him to think of the worst that B could do to him; the latter will try to choose that j which will make a_{ij} as small as possible for the given strategy i. Hence, if player A chooses i, all he can be sure of is $\min_j a_{ij}$ (read, "minimum with respect to j of a_{ij}"). He can evaluate this magnitude for each value of i and choose that value of i which maximizes it; by this choice, he insures that his return is at least $\max_i \min_j a_{ij}$. Similarly, by suitable choice of j, player B can guarantee that player A will not receive more than $\min_j \max_i a_{ij}$. Suppose the pay-off matrix a_{ij} is such that,

$$\max_i \min_j a_{ij} = \min_j \max_i a_{ij}. \tag{3}$$

If the common value of the two sides of (3) is v, then A can, by choosing a suitable strategy i', guarantee himself at least v, while B, by choosing a suitable strategy j', can guarantee that A will not get more than v. It is clear that in this case, A will choose i', B will choose j', and the outcome of the game (termed its *value*) will be that B pays an amount v to A. (The quantity v could be negative, in which case the payment would be from A to B.)

---

[36] See von Neumann and Morgenstern, *op. cit.*, chaps. iii–iv.

Equation (3) can be valid, as shown in the pay-off matrix given in Table I in which each player has the choice of two strategies.

Table I

Strategies of Player A	Strategies of Player B	
. . . . .	1	2
1	2	1
2	3	0

If player A chose strategy 1 and player B chose strategy 2, A would receive 1 unit from B. If A chose strategy 2, he would run the risk of receiving nothing; if B chose strategy 1, he might have to pay 3. Hence, $i' = 1$, $j' = 2$, and $v = 1$ represent a stable solution; even if one player knew in advance the other one's strategy, he would have no incentive to change his own.

Unfortunately, equation (3) need not hold. Consider the pay-off matrix in Table II.

Table II

Strategies of Player A	Strategies of Player B	
. . . . .	1	2
1	1	−2
2	0	2

In this case, $\overset{max}{i}\,\overset{min}{j}\,a_{ij} = 0$, $\overset{min}{j}\,\overset{max}{i}\,a_{ij} = 1$. If player B played so as to minimize $\overset{max}{i}\,a_{ij}$, he would choose strategy 1; but if player A knew this, he would choose strategy 1, rather than strategy 2, which he would choose if he were maximizing $\overset{min}{j}\,a_{ij}$. If, then, B realized that A would reason in this way, he would choose strategy 2, and so forth, leading to a seemingly endless regress. Indeed, this is precisely a chief objection to the principle of rationality, as noted in the second part of Section II, above.

To arrive at a determinate stable solution, the following procedure is suggested: let player A have a random device which will choose strategy 1 with probability 0.4 and strategy 2 with probability 0.6. Then, if player B selects strategy 1, player A will have an expected return of $0.4(1) + 0.6(0) = 0.4$; if B chooses strategy 2, the expected return is $0.4(-2) + 0.6(2) = 0.4$. Hence, A can guarantee himself an expected return of 0.4. Similarly, B, by playing strategy 1 with probability 0.8 and strategy 2 with probability 0.2, can hold the expected pay-off to A down to 0.4. This solution, in terms of randomized or *mixed* strategies, has the stability found in the first case; even if one player found out the probabilities used by the other, he could not gain from this information.

In general, the players can be considered not as choosing a strategy but as choosing a probability for each strategy (possibly zero). Let player A play strategies $1, \ldots, m$ with probabilities $x_1, \ldots, x_m$, respectively, while player B plays his strategies with probabilities $y_1, \ldots, y_n$. Let $\max_x$ mean the maximum with respect to permissible variations in $x_1, \ldots, x_m$ and let $\min_y$ have a corresponding meaning. The expected pay-off to A if he chooses $x_1, \ldots, x_m$ and B chooses $y_1, \ldots, y_n$ is

$$\sum_{i=1}^{m} \sum_{j=1}^{n} a_{ij} \, x_i \, y_j.$$

Then the analogue to (3) is

$$\max_x \min_y \; \sum_{k=1}^{m} \sum_{j=1}^{n} \; a_{ij} \, x_i \, y_j =$$

$$\min_y \max_x \; \sum_{i=1}^{m} \sum_{j=1}^{n} \; a_{ij} \, x_i \, y_j. \tag{4}$$

If (4) holds, then we have a stable solution in terms of mixed strategies. It turns out, rather remarkably, that (4) always holds.[37] The theory of rational behavior in zero-sum two-person games can therefore be regarded as definitely solved, at least within the limitations of a transferable utility. However, the objection that the principle of rationality cannot be realistic because it imposes too great burdens on the ability of the individual is not refuted; the solution of even relatively simple social games is frequently very difficult.[38]

Before leaving the discussion of zero-sum two-person games, consider the special case of a game in which, before reduction to normal form, the rules provide that at every stage of the game each individual knows the outcome

[37] See von Neumann and Morgenstern, *op. cit.*, pp. 134–43, 153–55. The theorem was first proved, with the aid of very deep mathematical development, by von Neumann in his "Zur Theorie der Gesellschaftsspiele," *Mathematische Annalen*, C (1928), 295–320. The first elementary proof was given by Jean Ville, "Sur la théorie générale des jeux où intervient l'habilité des joueurs," in Émile Borel *et al.*, *Traité du calcul des probabilités et de ses applications* (1938), Vol. IV, pp. 105–13. The simplest proof of (4) has been given in a slightly more general form by Lynn H. Loomis, "On a Theorem of von Neumann," *Proceedings of the National Academy of Sciences*, XXXII, No. 8 (1946), 213–15.

The case where the number of strategies may be infinite is considerably more difficult mathematically, and the generalization of (4) does not always hold. See Ville, *op cit.*; Wald, "Generalization of a Theorem by von Neumann Concerning Zero-Sum Two-Person Games," *Annals of Mathematics*, XLVI (1945), 281–86; Wald, "Foundations of a General Theory of Sequential Decision Functions," *Econometrica*, XV (1947), 279–313, esp. 285–96; and Wald, "Statistical Decision Functions," *Annals of Mathematical Statistics*, XX (1949), 165–205, esp. 166–71. A recent volume, edited by H. W. Kuhn and A. W. Tucker, *Contributions to the Theory of Games (Annals of Mathematics*, Study No. 24 [1950]), contains some papers on this and other developments in the theory of zero-sum two-person games.

[38] See the detailed discussion needed for even a highly simplified form of poker in von Neumann and Morgenstern, *op. cit.*, chap. iv, sec. 19.

of all previous moves, i.e., a game of *perfect information*. Chess and back-gammon are familiar examples. The more enduring features of many social conflicts are of this type; there is no possibility of concealing the existence of a major strike from the management, though certain preliminary tactical plans may be concealed for a while. It is shown that for such games, relation (3) always holds. Mixed strategies become unnecessary for a determinate solution. This suggests that mixed strategies may be regarded essentially as a device for withholding information from the opponent, for bluffing.

4. THE ZERO-SUM N-PERSON GAME [39]

Consider first the following simple game: There are three players; each is to write down the name of one of the others. If two players write down each other's name, they each get $\frac{1}{2}$, and the third player pays 1. If no two players write down each other's name, then no one gets anything. The rational method of playing seems fairly obvious; two of the players will agree in advance to write down each other's name and then collect. In what sense is this really a determinate solution? In particular, it is to be noted that the solution is not unique; there are three possible pairs of players who can form coalitions. Von Neumann and Morgenstern argue as follows: Consider all possible distributions of payments to the players. These will include transfers not provided for by the rules of the game, since we permit one player to bribe another into following an acceptable course of action. Since the game is zero-sum, the sum of the payments must be zero; since each player can get -1 without any coalition, no distribution can be enforced which gives any player less than -1. Let (a_1, a_2, a_3) denote a distribution which gives a_1 to the first player, a_2 to the second player, and a_3 to the third player. Then, in symbols,

$$a_1 + a_2 + a_3 = 0, \tag{5}$$

$$a_i \geqq -1 \text{ for each } i. \tag{6}$$

Any set of numbers satisfying (5) and (6) will be termed *imputation*. The particular imputations which seem intuitively to be the rational ones are, then, $(\frac{1}{2}, \frac{1}{2}, -1)$, $(\frac{1}{2}, -1, \frac{1}{2})$, and $(-1, \frac{1}{2}, \frac{1}{2})$. Let V be the set consisting of these imputations. Then the essential properties of V are (1) for every imputation not in V, there are two players who would both prefer a particular imputation in V to the one not in V; (2) for any two imputations in V, there are not two players who would prefer one to the other. These are stability properties; no imputation not in V can be maintained, while there is no drive to change from one imputation in V to another, since in our simple game the behavior of pairs of players is decisive.

The decisive character of a pair of players who choose to agree consists in

[39] *Ibid.*, chaps. v and vi.

the following: any pair of players can, by agreement, get the amount 1 between them, while no imputation can, from (5) and (6), give them more than 1. Therefore, they are in a position to choose any imputation whatever, since no imputation gives them more than they can get by the rules of the game. These concepts all lead to natural generalization. Consider the following zero-sum n-person game: Let S be any set of players; let the rules specify a *characteristic function* $v(S)$ which states the total amount any set S will get if they form a coalition. Because of the zero-sum character of the game, $v(-S) = -v(S)$, where $-S$ is the set of all players not in S. In particular, let (i) be the set consisting of the player i alone, so that $v([i])$ is the amount player i will get (presumably negative) if he does not enter into a coalition with anyone. Then an imputation is a set of payments $(a_1, \ldots, a_n)$ to the respective players having the properties,

$$a_1 + \ldots + a_n = 0, \tag{7}$$

$$a_i \geqq v([i]) \text{ for each } i. \tag{8}$$

A set of players S is said to be *effective* for an imputation $(a_1, \ldots, a_n)$ if $\sum_{i \epsilon S} a_i \leqq v(S)$, where "$i \epsilon S$" means "$i$ belongs to S," i.e., if the imputation does not give the players in S more than they could get by forming a coalition. The imputation $(a_1, \ldots, a_n)$ is said to *dominate* the imputation $(b_1, \ldots, b_n)$ if there is a set S which is effective for $(a_1, \ldots, a_n)$ and such that $a_i > b_i$ for every player i in S; under these circumstances we would certainly expect the players in S, by agreement, to change the imputation from $(b_1, \ldots, b_n)$ to $(a_1, \ldots, a_n)$. A set of imputations V is said to be a *solution* if (1) every imputation not in V dominates another imputation in V; (2) no imputation in V dominates another imputation in V. A solution thus defines the outcome of the above game when the players behave rationally.

It might seem that the above discussion relates only to a very special type of game, in which coalitions enter through the explicit statement of the rules. It is argued, however, that every n-person zero-sum game can be expressed in this manner. Suppose a coalition S forms, which seeks to maximize the sum of the pay-offs to its members. The coalition will naturally suppose that the players not in S will form a countercoalition; in view of the zero-sum character of the game, the coalition $-S$ will seek to minimize the sum of the pay-offs to members of S. This situation is precisely a zero-sum two-person game, which has a determinate value, as has been seen. Therefore, we may define $v(S)$ to be the value to the coalition S of the zero-sum two-person game just described. This can be done for each possible set of players S, so that the game is reduced to the form discussed in the previous paragraph.

Games are classified as *essential* or *inessential*. An inessential game is one in which a coalition can get no more than the sum of the amounts that each of its members could get by playing separately, i.e., $v(S) = \sum_{i \epsilon S} v([i])$. In such a game, there is no incentive to form coalitions and hence no specifically social element. In an essential game, on the other hand, such as the three-person game which introduced this discussion, there is a positive incentive to form coalitions. We have already observed that a solution may contain more than one imputation. This is a general phenomenon: it can be shown that in an essential game, a solution must contain at least two imputations. There seems to be some sort of fundamental indeterminacy in the purely rational theory of social behavior; the true significance of this indeterminacy must be regarded as obscure.

The definitions as framed do not exclude the possibility that there is more than one solution to a given game, and indeed this can happen, although there are also games with only one solution. In the three-person game just considered, let c be any number less than $1/2$. Consider the class of all imputations in which $a_3 = c$. It can easily be verified that this class is in fact a solution, within the meaning of the previous definitions. For each value of c, there is a corresponding solution, so that the number of solutions is infinite. Unlike the first solution, these solutions do not have any symmetry. They may be termed *discriminatory* solutions; the ruling coalition (1, 2) agrees to give the excluded player a fixed amount c, and then divide up the remainder between them. It is remarkable that discriminatory practices turn out to have certain stability properties even when the basic rules of the game are completely symmetric as between players. Even within the first solution found, there was a certain element of unfairness; each given imputation within the solution was unfair to one player, but there was an element of symmetry in the solution as a whole. So it can be seen that even a symmetrical game is not necessarily fair, in that it does not guarantee that each individual will be as well off as every other. Much more than equality of opportunity is needed to insure equality of outcome.

There is thus a hierarchy of successively more restrictive conditions on the state of society: the rules of the game, which define the class of possible imputations, the solution, and the imputation which actually prevails at any given instant of time. It is suggested that the first corresponds to the basic limitations of the society—physical, biological, and possibly psychological; the second to a socially stable standard of behavior, which, however, does not uniquely determine the actual distribution of values among the members of the society. More than one standard of behavior may be compatible with the rules, but only those found by the theory will be stable enough to survive.

5. THE GENERAL N-PERSON GAME [40]

The games thus far considered have lacked generality in one important respect. Society as a whole could not gain because of the zero-sum restriction.

---

[40] See von Neumann and Morgenstern, *op. cit.*, chap. xi.

In the study of many social conflicts, this may not be an important limitation, but it does serve to eliminate all economic aspects. The crucial feature of economic behavior is precisely the possibility that by co-operation all individuals can be made better off.

The general n-person game is handled by a reduction to a zero-sum $(n + 1)$-person game. Introduce a fictitious player, $n + 1$, who can make no moves but who receives the negative of the sum of the amounts paid to the other players. This enlarged game can be described in terms of the theory in the preceding section; $v(S)$ again represents the amount that each coalition can guarantee for itself. The concept of domination goes through as before. However, not all the solutions of the extended game can be accepted. We may take it for granted that the genuine players will get as much for themselves collectively as they can, since this increases the amount of wealth to be divided among them. In effect, the genuine players will discriminate against the fictitious player. The only solutions that are therefore admissible are those in which every imputation gives the fictitious player the minimum possible.

In the case of a general two-person game, it turns out that there is just one solution, namely, the set of all imputations which maximize the sum of the returns to the two players. Suppose A and B are bargaining over a house which A owns but B values more highly. Then the house will be transferred to B, who will pay a price at least equal to the value A places on it but not more than the value of B. This conclusion extends readily to all cases of bilateral monopoly, even when there is not a unique indivisible object but a continuously divisible commodity: the amount of goods which changes hands is determinate, being that amount which maximizes the sum of the profits of the two bargainers, but the buyer will pay the seller at least enough so that he will not be worse off than if he sold nothing and not so much that the buyer will be worse off than if he bought nothing.[41]

The discussion of the two-person game yields a purely common-sense answer. Much less obvious results follow in the general three-person game, e.g., one seller and two buyers. In the case of a single indivisible object, again, it will be transferred to the individual who values it most highly, but the possible accompanying patterns of payments may be very complicated indeed. The game theory fully takes into account such possibilities as having one buyer bribe another to stay out of the market. The determination of the solutions to this game cannot be presented here in detail.[42]

[41] The earlier discussions of this problem in economic literature had given smaller ranges of indeterminacy; the contribution of game theory is to show that the earlier answers were artificial from the viewpoint of rational behavior (though not necessarily from that of actual behavior). However, Gerhard Tintner has already given the solution indicated above. See his "Note on the Problem of Bilateral Monopoly," *Journal of Political Economy*, XLVII (1939), 263–70.

[42] See von Neumann and Morgenstern, *op. cit.*, chap. xi, sec. 62; an excellent elementary discussion is contained in Jacob Marschak, "Neumann's and Morgenstern's New Approach to Static Economics," *Journal of Political Economy*, LIV (1946), 97–115.

6. STATISTICAL INFERENCE AS A GAME

In the discussion of statistical inference as a problem in rational behavior (in the second part of Section II, above), it has been shown that the statistician must choose a function $i(k)$ which determines the action i he will take for any possible sample k. Suppose he chooses such a function, while the true state of nature is j. If the sample k should come up, he will take action $i(k)$ and therefore lose $r_{i(k),\,j}$. But sample k will come up with probability p_{kj}. Therefore, if the statistician chooses a function $i(k)$, his expected loss when the true state is j is given by

$$\sum_k r_{i(k),\,j} \, p_{kj}, \tag{9}$$

which depends on the statistician's choice of $i(k)$ and nature's "choice," j. Wald has suggested interpreting statistical inference as a zero-sum two-person game, in which nature chooses a state j, the statistician chooses a decision function $i(k)$, and the pay-off to nature is given by (9). The optimal behavior of the statistician is to choose that decision function (possibly mixed) which minimizes the maximum expected loss.

IV. Some Other Mathematical Models of Social Behavior

1. RASHEVSKY'S THEORY OF HUMAN RELATIONS [43]

Nicholas Rashevsky of the University of Chicago, who is known primarily for his work in the application of mathematical methods to biology, has suggested that analogous methods could be applied to the study of human relations. His approach is of a generally *ad hoc* character, partly collective, partly individualistic. The bulk of his work is devoted to the interaction of social classes. A great variety of different hypotheses as to the nature of this interaction are proposed and formulated mathematically, and some consequences drawn. An example of his analysis will suffice to give the general flavor. It is assumed that there are two classes, the active and the passive. Active individuals do not imitate anyone, while passive individuals are influenced by active individuals in proportion to the number with whom they come into contact and also, to a lesser extent, by other passive individuals. Suppose that there are two possible activities, A and B, that x_0 and y_0 of the active individuals engage in A and B respectively, and that at any instant of time x and y passive individuals engage in A and B respectively. The number of passive individuals engaged in A will tend to be increased by the number of active individuals engaged in A and, to a lesser extent,

[43] Nicholas Rashevsky, *Mathematical Theory of Human Relations* (1947).

by the number of passive individuals engaged in A, and to be decreased by the number of active and passive individuals engaged in B. Symbolically,

$$dx/dt = a_o x_o + ax - c_o y_o - ay, \tag{10}$$

with a similar equation for dy/dt. These equations can be solved to reveal the variation in x and y over time as functions of the coefficients and to find the points of stable equilibrium to which the system will tend.[44]

It is to be noted that the situation in question might be interpreted as a conflict between the active individuals engaged in A and those engaged in B for control over the passive individuals. It could easily therefore be brought within the general framework of game theory. It is noteworthy that Professor Rashevsky's model is broadly similar to models of conflict in other spheres, such as Richardson's work on international relations—compare (10) with (2) above—and Lanchester's theoretical treatment of military strategy.[45] There seem to be emerging two general analyses of social conflict situations employing mathematical methods: rationalistic game theory, and *ad hoc* dynamic analysis by means of systems of linear differential equations. There may be some complementarity in the two approaches; in particular, note that game theory, at least in its present state, deals only with equilibrium situations. If additional assumptions could be made as to how each player learns about the others from experience, the theory would be a dynamic one.

Rashevsky presents the above case as highly oversimplified and suggests more complicated variations of the same scheme. Some of these involve economic considerations in that the interaction of classes may be productive of wealth.[46] In the economic analyses, the *ad hoc* laws which relate, e.g., to certain aspects of the distribution of income, are not sufficient to define the situation uniquely; within the framework of these postulates, the individuals are assumed to act rationally in some appropriate sense, i.e., to maximize satisfaction or profits. One simple case is that of two classes of individuals, one of which is composed of organizers under whose supervision the members of the second class produce more than they would otherwise. It is assumed that the members of the first class decide on a fixed fraction of the total output to be divided among the members of the second class in proportion to the amount of work each does, while each member of the second class decides how much work to do on the basis of the given fraction. The first class then chooses the fraction in question so as to maximize their total profits. There are several *ad hoc* elements here; the fraction to be given to the second class need not be independent of the amount of work they do, it need not be divided among the members of that class in proportion to the

---

[44] Rashevsky, *op. cit.*, chap. iii.

[45] Lewis F. Richardson, *Generalized Foreign Politics* (*British Journal of Psychology*, Monograph Supplement No. 23 [1939]); and F. W. Lanchester, *Aircraft in Warfare* (1916), chaps. v and vi.

[46] Rashevsky, *op. cit.*, chaps. v, vi, xix, xx.

amount of work each does, and each member of the first class may try to maximize his own profits, possibly by special bargains with some members of the second class, rather than maximize the total class profit. Some of these assumptions are similar to the assumption of perfect competition in classical economics.

The same techniques of analysis are used throughout Rashevsky's work, though there are many variant sets of assumptions made. Applications are made to the urban-rural distribution of population, the distribution of city sizes, international relations, historical change, and war. Rashevsky emphasizes the tentative and simplified character of his approach and suggests that its chief function is to make available a number of alternative models which might be useful in further theoretical and empirical work.

It might be remarked that the standards of mathematical rigor are high. The methods used are drawn from the calculus and the theory of ordinary linear differential equations, with a few tentative steps toward the use of integral equations.

2. ZIPF'S PRINCIPLE OF LEAST EFFORT AND STEWART'S SOCIAL PHYSICS

The work of George K. Zipf [47] is an extraordinarily comprehensive effort to subsume the major part of human behavior, both individual and collective, under a single principle of least effort: individuals and societies act so as to minimize the expected average rate of work. We shall here be concerned only with his discussion of social behavior in Part Two of his book. In terms of the classification in Section II of this chapter, the model is certainly rational; since it seems to be assumed that both individuals and society seek to minimize effort, the model has both collective and individualist elements.

It must be stated, however, that Dr. Zipf's work does not constitute a properly developed mathematical model. The fundamental postulates are nowhere stated explicitly; though mathematical symbols and formulas are sprinkled rather freely through a long work, the derivations involved are chiefly figures of speech and analogies, rather than true mathematical deductions; in some cases, they are simply wrong. Thus, as an attempt at a systematic social theory, Zipf's work can only be regarded as a failure.

However, two empirical regularities do emerge which are highly suggestive and may prove promising for further research. It is held, with considerable empirical support, that if the cities of a nation are ranked in order of population, then the rank of a city is inversely proportional to its population; e.g., the largest city, with rank 1, has twice the population of the next largest, which has rank 2. This relation, it is suggested, is an equilibrium condition in that a nation in which it does not hold will either expand or break up until the relation does obtain. Some, though incon-

[47] George K. Zipf, *Human Behavior and the Principle of Least Effort* (1949).

clusive, empirical evidence is adduced for this last conclusion, which is used to generalize about international relations. Similar relations hold for other types of frequency data, such as the number of stores of each kind.

An attempt is made to analyze a hierarchy of social classes which the aid of analogous rank-frequency relations, it being assumed that each class exploits the one beneath it and is exploited by the one above it. The strength of a class, and therefore its potential for rebellion, is measured by its total income, while the incentive to remain *in statu quo* is proportional to the income of an individual. To have equilibrium, the two magnitudes must be brought into a suitable relation. Dr. Zipf suggests that, if the classes are ranked upward from the bottom, the income of each individual should be proportional to his class rank while the number of individuals in any one class should be inversely proportional to the square of its rank. From this analysis, certain implications are drawn for the distribution of income. The postulates of this theory of social classes are again never clearly stated, beyond some generalizations that each individual would prefer exploiting others to working as a source of income. It would be interesting to define the problem more precisely and then compare the game-theoretical analysis with the suggestions of Dr. Zipf.

Another empirical regularity found is that the interaction between two cities is inversely proportional to the distance between them. This applies particularly to the flow of traffic or information between them. The study of this relation had been begun earlier by John Q. Stewart of Princeton University, an astronomer.[48] Stewart has stressed the formal analogies of this relation to the law of gravitation. Let P_i be the population of a place i, and D_i be the distance of place i from a given place A; then *the demographic potential* at A is defined to be $\Sigma \ (P_i/D_i)$, the sum being taken over all populated places i. Under the above law, the demographic potential should represent the total amount of transactions per unit population at A and therefore should correlate with other economic magnitudes. Some evidence has been found to support this assertion, but it can hardly be described as proved.[49]

48 John Q. Stewart, "Demographic Gravitation: Evidence and Applications," *Sociometry*, XI (1948), 31–58, and earlier work cited therein.

49 There must be mentioned, if only in a footnote, certain other recent works relevant to the mathematical formulation of social theory. Stuart C. Dodd and Eliot D. Chapple have devoted much attention to the proper symbolization of social problems as a basis for the construction of models and for empirical research. See Dodd's *Dimensions of Society* (1942) and "A Systematics for Sociometry and for All Science," *Sociometry*, XI (1948), 113–30; and Chapple's *Measuring Human Relations: An Introduction to the Study of the Interaction of Individuals* (*Genetic Psychology Monographs*, Vol. XXII, No. 1 [1940]). Their work has been principally methodological rather than substantive. For other work of this type, see the journal *Sociometry*.

Norbert Wiener, in his *Cybernetics* (1948), has initiated the systematic study of communication as a feature common to physiology, modern servomechanisms, and human society; however, he has made little specific application to social study and, indeed, has expressed pessimism over the possibilities of any sort of social science.

V. The Use of Theoretical Models in Inductive Inference

The familiar proposition in the methodology of science that empirical study without previous theoretical development is fruitless has recently been developed in detail with particular reference to the field of economic analysis by a group of individuals associated with the Cowles Commission for Research in Economics, at the University of Chicago. The general viewpoint was expressed at length by Trygve Haavelmo.[50] The associated problems in mathematical statistics have been studied by Henry B. Mann and A. Wald; [51] Tjalling C. Koopmans, Herman Rubin, and Roy B. Leipnik; [52] and Theodore W. Anderson and H. Rubin.[53] The most elementary exposition is that of J. Marschak; [54] slightly more technical are those of Koopmans,[55] Marschak,[56] and Gershon Cooper.[57] Though the work done is strongly influenced by the special problems of economics, there is unquestionably a great portion applicable to the social sciences in general.

1. EXACT VERSUS STOCHASTIC RELATIONS

In economics and in other social sciences, we may certainly expect that no exact relation will hold between the variables we measure for at least two reasons: (1) Not all the variables which are relevant are included in the analysis, and we always omit a host of unimportant factors which are too difficult to measure. (2) The variables we do observe are not measured precisely. In the statement of a relation, then, we must include not only the explicitly enumerated variables but an additional unmeasurable variable, known as a *disturbance*. Such a relation is said to be *stochastic*. Thus, we may say that, for an individual, consumption (c) is related to income (y) by a relation of the type $c = f(y) + u$, where u is a disturbance which stands for all the omitted variables which influence consumption. Merely to say that a relation holds with a disturbance in it is a tautology.

[50] "The Probability Approach in Econometrics," *Econometrica*, XII (1944), Supplement.

[51] "On the Statistical Treatment of Linear Stochastic Difference Equations," *Econometrcia*, XI (1943), 173–220.

[52] "Measuring the Equation Systems of Dynamic Economics," in Tjalling C. Koopmans (ed.), *Statistical Inference in Dynamic Economic Models* (1950).

[53] "Estimation of the Parameters of a Single Equation in a Complete System of Stochastic Equations," *Annals of Mathematical Statistics*, XX (1949), 46–63.

[54] "Economic Structure, Path, Policy, and Prediction," *American Economic Review*, XXXVII, No. 2 (1947), 81–84.

[55] "Statistical Estimation of Simultaneous Economic Relations," *Journal of the American Statistical Association*, XL (1945), 448–66.

[56] "Statistical Inference in Economics: An Introduction," in Koopmans (ed.), *Statistical Inference in Dynamic Economic Models* (1950).

[57] "The Role of Economic Theory in Econometric Models," *Journal of Farm Economics*, Vol. XXX (1948).

For any function $f(y)$, we can make the above relation true by defining u to be $c - f(y)$. To give a relation empirical content, we must assert some regularities in the behavior of the disturbances.

We say that the disturbance in a given relation is a random variable with a probability distribution which is the same for each time the variables are observed. It is usually also assumed that the disturbances at different times are independent. Thus, in our consumption example, if the subscript t denotes time, the disturbances $u_t = c_t - f(y_t)$ for different values of t can be regarded as forming a random sample from a fixed probability distribution. These concepts extend themselves naturally to all types of social laws. In general, then, we may say that the formulation of a generalization in social science is equivalent to an assertion about the probability distributions of certain disturbances.[58]

2. SIMULTANEOUS RELATIONS AND THE CONCEPT OF A STRUCTURE

If we take the individual viewpoint as developed in the first part of Section II of this chapter, we find that the actions of all individuals are simultaneously determined by all the equations of form (1). There is no unique line of causality; the actions of all individuals enter symmetrically. The situation is not altered if we assume that the equations (1) are stochastic. The variables P_i, on the other hand, play a different role. If they refer to exogenous factors, they will in general be determined by processes which are independent of the social context in which equations (1) are stochastic.

With respect to actions $A_1, \ldots, A_n$, the exogenous factors have a strictly unidirectional causal influence. The same is true, with some qualifications, if the variables $P_1, \ldots, P_n$ contain past actions of individuals as well as truly exogenous factors, for at any given instant of time, the past has also a unidirectional causal influence on the present choice of actions. The causal variables P_i are referred to as *predetermined;* the mutually interdependent variables A_i are referred to as *endogenous* or *jointly dependent.* At any given instant of time, therefore, the endogenous variables are simultaneously determined by a set of stochastic equations,

$$A_i = f_i(A_1, \ldots, A_{i-1}, A_{i+1}, \ldots, A_n, P_i, u_i). \tag{11}$$

Here again, equations (11) are tautologous unless the distribution of the disturbances u_i is specified. The equations and the distribution together are known as the *structure* of the social system. The predetermined character of the P_i's is expressed in the assertion that they are statistically independent of the u_i's.

[58] For a more extended discussion of the ideas of this paragraph, see Haavelmo, "The Probability Approach in Econometrics," *Econometrica,* Vol. XII (1944), Supplement, chap. iii.

Suppose the system (11) to be solved for the endogenous variables:

$$A_i = g_i(P_1, \ldots, P_n, u_1, \ldots, u_n). \tag{12}$$

Equations (12) are known as the *reduced form* of the structure. The reduced form is itself a structure, and it might seem at first that a knowledge of it conveys as much information about the endogenous variables as docs (11). This is not so if we realize that one or more of equations (11) may change; for example, one of the equations may refer to a government policy, or it may refer to an industry whose behavior will be affected by technological change. If one of equations (11) changes, then all of equations (12) change, but there is no necessity that the other equations (11) will be altered. The equations (11) have a higher degree of *autonomy* [59] than (12), in the sense that each equation of (11) is invariant under a wider class of structural changes than the equations of (12).

If the laws under study were truly immutable, autonomy would be an irrelevant concept, and the reduced form of a structure would be as useful a description of reality as any other form. The need for an autonomous structure is especially critical when the results of social analysis are to be used for policy purposes. Here, the question is that of choosing among several possible forms for the equation expressing government behavior. What we wish to do is to consider the structure for each possible form of the government equation and predict the behavior of the endogenous variables under each; that form is then chosen which yields the most satisfactory behavior. This procedure can be carried out, however, only if the equations other than the government equation are invariant with respect to changes in it. For prediction under changed structure, and in particular for policy decisions, it is therefore important that the structure be expressed in as autonomous a form as possible. The stress on models based on individual behavior arises from the argument that they are more apt to be autonomous than collective models.

3. MODELS, STATISTICAL INFERENCE, AND THE PROBLEM OF IDENTIFICATION

Suppose now that we have a sample of observations on a system of endogenous and predetermined variables and we are faced with the problem of inferring the structure which generated them. This is a problem in statistical inference. Here, the states of nature are the different possible structures. As in the general formulation of the problem given earlier (see the second part of Sec. II and the sixth part of Sec. III, above), we assume it known that the possible structures belong to a certain class. That is, certain statements can be made about the structure on an a priori basis, so that we

---

[59] This term is Ragnar Frisch's.

need not consider structures not compatible with those assertions. The class of admissible structures is known as the *model*. The determination of the optimum statistical methods for selecting one structure out of the model is then a technical problem which has been solved, at least in an approximate sense.[60]

There is a certain difficulty in the statistical analysis which does not seem to arise in the natural sciences. Take first a very simple nonstochastic problem. Assume that prices are determined by the equating of supply and demand, where each is a function of price. If, during the period of observation, neither supply nor demand shifted, the price and the quantity exchanged would not alter, and we would have only one point from which to infer the supply and demand curves. This is obviously impossible, since there are an infinite number of possible pairs of curves passing through the observed point. This same problem arises in stochastic structures; consider again the supply-and-demand problem:

$$q = a_1 p + a_2 + u \text{ (demand)}, \tag{13}$$

$$q = b_1 p + b_2 + v \text{ (supply)}, \tag{14}$$

where q is quantity exchanged, p is price, and u and v are disturbances with a given probability distribution. Equations (13) and (14) can be solved for q and p in terms of u and v, and we can then find the distribution of q and p from that of u and v. For example, suppose that $a_1 = -1$, $a_2 = 2$, $b_1 = 1$, $b_2 = 1$, and u and v are normally and independently distributed with means zero and variances 1. Then it can be shown that p and q are normally and independently distributed with means $\frac{1}{2}$ and $3/2$ respectively, and variances $\frac{1}{2}$. Now suppose that $a_1 = -\frac{1}{2}$, $a_2 = 7/4$, $b_1 = 2$, $b_2 = \frac{1}{2}$, and u and v are normally and independently distributed with means zero and variances $\frac{5}{8}$ and $5/2$, respectively. Then q and p have the same distribution as in the previous case. Since observations on a sample of p and q values can only yield information as to the distribution of p and q, it is clear that no such sample, no matter how large, could enable a choice to be made between the two structures. A model containing both structures is said to be *unidentified;* in general, a model in which no two structures generate the same probability distribution of the endogenous variables is said to be

---

[60] The fundamental statistical papers are Koopman's, Rubin, and Leipnik, "Measuring the Equation Systems of Dynamic Economics," in Koopmans (ed.), *Statistical Inference in Dynamic Economic Models* (1950); and Anderson and Rubin, "Estimation of the Parameters of a Single Equation in a Concrete System Stochastic Equations," *Annal of Mathematical Statistics*, XX (1949), 46–63. In practice, chiefly the methods of the latter paper have been used. For more elementary expositions, see Koopmans, "Statistical Estimation of Simultaneous Economic Relations," *Journal of the American Statistical Association*, XL (1945), 448–66; and M. A. Girshick and T. Haavelmo, "Statistical Analysis of the Demand for Food: Examples of Simultaneous Estimation of Structural Equations," *Econometrica*, XV (1947), 79–110. It is important to observe that equations (11) should not be fitted by taking the least squares regression of A_i on the other variables.

identified. In order to make useful statistical inferences, the range of possible structures must be sufficiently restricted by a priori considerations so that the model is identified.

The conditions for identification have been discussed for models in which the structures are systems of linear equations. The concept of identification has also been generalized in various ways.[61]

4. MODEL-BUILDING AND SCIENTIFIC TACTICS

The method of scientific investigation indicated in the preceding paragraphs calls then for intensive a priori thinking to formulate a model, followed by the selection of a best-fitting structure from that model by appropriate statistical techniques. It is the virtue of the Cowles Commission approach to have set forth this process clearly and to have resolved many of the statistical difficulties in the way of its fulfillment. It is clear that the crucial step is the choice of a model. If we can say very little on purely a priori grounds about the nature of the process under investigation, then the resulting model is unidentified, and further progress is stopped.

An alternative procedure employed by a number of economists [62] is to start with a very wide and vaguely stated model and investigate empirical data which seem to be relevant. By examination of these data, more definite models will be suggested which will, in turn, provide the basis for further empirical research, and so forth. It might be asked how, if the original vague model is really unidentified, this procedure can lead to any results. Two related answers seem to be implied in the discussion: (1) The observations will select out of the original model a collection of structures compatible with the observations; among these, the "simplest" in some sense is selected.[63] (2) There is really an identified model in the minds of the investigators, which, however, has not been expressed formally because of the limitations of mathematics or of language in general. Perhaps we may interpret the "simple" structures as those found in this unconsciously maintained model. The choice between the alternative scientific tactics indicated depends on the stage of formalization of the underlying theory. No dogmatism is possible; a certain amount of over-simplification is tolerable (and necessary) to gain the advantages of formalization and the use of optimum statistical methods, but there are limits; since the statistical methods are best only on the assumption that the model is correct, a serious error in formulating the model may invalidate all further empirical work based on it.

---

[61] Koopmans, Rubin, and Leipnik, *op cit.*; Leonid Hurwicz, "Generalization of the Concept of Identification," in Koopmans (ed.) *Statistical Inference in Dynamic Economic Models* (1950). For an excellent exposition of the identification concept, see Koopmans, "Identification Problems in Econometric Model Construction," *Econometrica*, XVII (1949), 125–44.

[62] See, for example, the works named in footnote 11.

[63] See Milton Friedman, "Lange on Price Flexibility and Employment," *American Economic Review*, XXXVI (1946), 613–31. See pages 616–22 on the use of Occam's razor.

Eight ⋆ FREEDOM,

DETERMINISM, AND

MORALITY

Many sources contribute to our understanding of man the social animal. Biography, history, literature, social description and commentary, as well as the systematic social sciences, all participate in the privilege and the obligation. Without knowledge of what man has been and done and of what, to his grandeur and his shame, man is capable of being and doing, we live, as Goethe said, in darkness. In all the ways in which the human story may be told, the events are seldom merely narrated, they are also explained. The biography of a statesman, the account of a religious sect or of a revolution, the literary unfolding of an unhappy marriage, all illuminate just to the extent that, expressly or tacitly, they indicate the causal factors in character and culture by virtue of which things happened as they did.

Explanations and predictions of particular actions and events that are based on "insight" utilize unarticulated crude generalizations about individuals and groups. The statesman, say, trying to predict what another leader will do, recognizes in a new situation some significant feature that he has seen before, just as the skilled physician, by responding to subtle cues, makes a strikingly accurate diagnosis. We can explain what goes on in insight, and there is nothing left to be accounted for. But it remains for the systematic social sciences to provide the laws and theories by which to confirm or refute our intuitive causal judgments. Scientific determinism is the view that every event occurs in some system of laws such that *if* we knew these laws and the state of the universe at any time, then we could explain the past and predict the future. This frame of reference includes, as it consistently must, human actions which, therefore, can be the object of scientific study. Whether or not such a comprehensive system exists is clearly a matter of fact. Equally clearly—unlike specific causal hypotheses about, say, the effect of a certain drug on memory or of religious belief on marital stability—so broad a doctrine can hardly be established, or for that matter, refuted, conclusively. Nevertheless, there are good reasons for accepting it. Every confirmed causal explanation enhances its plausibility. Moreover, in our everyday commerce with each other, we all do believe that human behavior is lawful. The parent scolding a child, the prisoner contemplating his guard, the pastor admonishing his congregation, the flatterer, the law maker, the advertiser, the man courting a woman and vice versa, all interactions among people presume that choices and decisions don't just happen but have causes and effects. What we want and hope for, what we say and do, all make a difference to human choices, our own and others.

Determinism, it would seem, is the plainest common sense. Yet it is frequently, and as in the selection by Isaiah Berlin, fervently, denied. Indeterminism asserts that some events—in particular, human acts of choice—*in principle* cannot be explained or predicted by reference to causal laws. The issue arouses such strong feelings that intellectual error may appear as moral sin. Indeed, Berlin imputes to determinists of all varieties the "desire to resign responsibility, to cease from moral judgment provided we be not judged ourselves." Fortunately, moral sensitivity—the capacity for outrage and indignation at even lesser creatures than Genghis Khan or Hitler—is more prevalent than the charge concedes. However, let us look to the issue. Though many share Berlin's views and sentiments, seldom has indeterminism enjoyed so eloquent a defense. Francis Raab addresses himself directly to Berlin's argument and, carefully analyzing the language of moral responsibility, vigorously defends the compatibility of freedom and causality.

The problem of freedom is bedeviled as is no other by verbal ambiguity, by the tenacity with which the living language preserves, like a fly in amber, the dead thought. A new idea about the world enters into consciousness. By some analogy, near or remote, an old word is used and thenceforth retains forever first a double, then a triple, then a quadruple meaning. Not that it could or should be otherwise. No wholly new idea could be expressed or understood without the use of familiar notions. By cumbrous qualification, the disanalogies between the new and the old are spelled out. In the technical languages of science, the old resonances are gradually stripped away, and the new idea gains its own vocabulary. But in common speech little is ever wholly lost or ever wholly archaic. By the layers of meaning that cling to every word, we are able to communicate, however imperfectly, with ages past. We also communicate with each other, and the possibility of misunderstanding is lessened because we share common ideas and because we can explain what we mean. Moreover, a turn of phrase may continue to serve a useful and sometimes indispensable function in the practical affairs of men, even after it has acquired no longer acceptable associations, because we slough them off and retain its core use for some everyday situation. One such phrase is "*A* was the cause of *B*."

But the associations lurk, ready at any time, particularly if the term is linked to a whole family of words and their connotations, to generate paradox and perplexity. Members of the family of concepts that generate the problem of freedom are *determine, law, cause, predict,* and *control.* Exhaustive analysis of these terms and their close kin is not possible now.

Much of the necessary background is already contained in the preceding selections. The papers in this section are directly addressed to the issue. However, some further comment on the relevant notions may help to clear away some of the dust, tie things together, and distinguish real problems from those that are merely verbal.

At the beginning of this volume, when characterizing the subject matter of social science, we noted the difference between what a man does and what happens to him. Only the former is meaningful behavior or human action. A man acts when, consciously or unconsciously, his intentions, desires, or reasons are among the causes of his behavior. He has the alternative of doing one thing rather than another; the action he takes depends upon him. He makes a choice. If he had chosen differently, something else would have occurred. Involuntary body movements, on the other hand, are not things that a man does, for they are not the results of his choices. Going swimming is an action, but falling into the lake is not. Meaningful behavior and mere movements differ in the nature of their causes, not in the fact that one is uncaused and the other is caused.

If a man acts, then his behavior is *determined* by the choices that he makes. This means that what he does causally depends upon what he wants. Something is *predetermined*, on the other hand, if it will happen regardless of what anybody wants or does. *Fatalism* is the view that everything is predetermined, that what happens is not affected by what we do. It thus follows that no one ever really does anything at all. Everything, quite literally, just happens to us, for nothing is the result of our decisions. *Determinism* is the view that everything occurs lawfully. That is, for any event there is a set of laws or regularities connecting it with other events. With respect to human conduct, this implies, first, that there are circumstances—in our constitutions, background, environment, and character—that are jointly sufficient conditions for our behavior, including the choices that we make. It implies, second, that these choices in turn have causal consequences. In particular, what we choose may come to pass. In contrast to fatalism, it follows that our choices sometimes make a difference and that not everything merely happens to us, for there are some things that we *do*. If we make one choice rather than another, then the effects will be different. What happens is determined by us, for it depends upon our actions.

In recent thought, fatalism has appeared in the guise of "hard" social determinism. This doctrine, also called "historical determinism," insists that there are comprehensive laws of the social process that are wholly independent of the actions of individuals. Men's choices do not and cannot affect these large-scale, collective historical developments. Much of Section Four was devoted to discussion of this view and nothing more needs to be added to Berlin's strictures against it. However, as was pointed out in the discussions of holism and emergentism, historical determinism is not only different from scientific determinism, it is inconsistent with it. If the behavior of social groups is in principle not predictable from the actions of men in groups, then the historical process marks a level of indeterminism. The well-deserved strictures against historical determinism are therefore irrelevant to the thesis that all human behavior is comprehensively lawful.

In particular, if individual choices determine, that is, are among the causes of what happens in history, then men are not the helpless victims of some grand historical process.

What we do at a given time depends upon the facts about the individual and his environment at that time and the laws about the mutual influences between personality and society. If we knew all these laws and facts, then we could predict what a person will do. Do the laws *compel* our behavior? If everything happens in accordance with natural laws, can we help doing what we do? Gravity *causes* but does not compel the stone to fall toward the earth. Inanimate objects do not act, because they have no choices. To be compelled is to do something against one's will. Inanimate objects, having no will, are not compelled by their causes. Nor are we compelled to fall off a cliff or catch a disease. These are not the kinds of things we can either do or avoid doing, because we don't do them at all. They happen to us. I *can* do something, if I know how and if there are no external obstacles to my doing it. If I can do it, then I can also refrain from doing it. We cannot act unless there are alternatives from which to choose. I can swim, if I so choose, but I cannot ski, because I don't know how. I know how to drive fast through town, but if a policeman stops me, then I can't do it. Compulsion occurs when, by threats of punishment or by physical restraint, I am prevented from doing as I wish. If, seeing no policeman, I deliberately drive over the speed limit, my misbehavior is caused by my motives (I'm late for an appointment), my past history, weak character, present environment (no policeman in sight), and so on. Obviously, I could have helped doing it, as I'll be readily and pithily informed after I'm apprehended, for it was something I could have avoided but instead chose to do.

In science, as we learn more about the laws of a temporal process, the notion of cause tends to be eliminated. It serves no function because we know all the relevant variables and can infer what they will be at any time. Where knowledge is only partial, as in the social sciences, an analysis in terms of cause and effect is useful for indicating the temporal relation among those variables that we do know. But the notion of cause, as has been mentioned before in this volume, is primarily of practical use and is bound to human interest in a particular situation. One of these interests is to fix moral responsibility. People are not responsible for what they couldn't help doing. They are responsible for what they cause to happen by the choices that they make. By causing something to happen, however, we do not force it to happen. If I cause the windows to be washed by doing it myself or by paying someone else to wash them, the windows, having no choice, have not been compelled to get clean. However, if we cause another person to do something against his will, then we have compelled him. One of the connotations of *cause,* in some contexts, is indeed compulsion. If a king caused someone to do something, the threat of force or punishment effectively cut off any option. Having one's head chopped off is not much of an alternative. Prior to the modern notion of scientific lawfulness as uniformity of behavior, compulsion by causing something to happen was anthropomorphically extended to physical causality. These echoes linger in the language. However, a cause only compels if it is of a certain kind in a certain context. If the cause is my own choice, then I am not compelled. I act freely. By my choice I brought about what happened. If I act freely, then I am morally responsible for my action.

If behavior is lawful, then if we know the laws and enough about a particular individual's circumstances, desires, reflections, values, and so on, his actions are *predictable*. To be predictable by inference from laws is not to be predictable in other ways. Stereotyped or mechanical behavior is also called "predictable." A person acts predictably, in this sense, if he is inflexible in his responses, does not take into account differences among situations and persons, does not adapt easily to change, or always behaves very conventionally. *Predictable* thus used is a term of disparagement. On the other hand, "unpredictable" behavior, in the sense of being capricious, is also not highly valued. Behavior that is in principle inferrable from laws may be stereotyped, capricious, or neither one nor the other.

The conflation of two separate but historically connected notions of *law* contributes to the fog that hangs about the idea of freedom. In her excellent analysis of the ethical "natural law" doctrine and of the relation between value and fact, Margaret Macdonald emphasizes the distinction between prescriptive or normative and descriptive or scientific law. In its oldest sense, a law was a commandment. It prescribed our behavior by asserting a rule for right conduct, for how men ought to behave. The moral law universally and unconditionally obliged all men at all times and all places. Scientific regularities also apply universally or "impartially" to all things. By analogy, the term *law* was extended to observed uniformities. But there is a significant difference between ethical and scientific laws. Although all bodies obey the law of gravity, *obey* is only a metaphor in this context. Scientific laws only describe behavior; they do not prescribe it. They say what happens, not what ought to happen. The descriptive laws of human conduct express what men will do under certain circumstances.

We can violate a prescriptive law or norm, for we can choose not to do what the law says we ought to do. We cannot violate a descriptive law. If we do not behave in accordance with what is believed to be a scientific law, then the belief is false and the supposed law must be rejected. We do not falsify prescriptive law by failing to act accordingly, for the law doesn't say anything about what we will in fact do. Moreover, the law need not be rejected if it is disobeyed. Morality and the legal order would be unnecessary if people always did what they ought to do. Because they do not always do what they should, however, prescriptive laws may have sanctions or punishments attached to them. If the sanctions are severe enough, they compel people to behave in certain ways by either eliminating alternatives or making them very disagreeable.

We use our knowledge of laws and theories in order to predict and thereby to *control* nature. Does knowledge of man mean control of man? When is behavior controlled? The legal order is a social technique for causing men to behave in ways held to be desirable by those who make the laws. The sanctions that can be imposed by constituted authority may coerce and therefore control men. When coercion causes someone to behave in a certain way, then he is not acting as he chooses but, under compulsion, as someone else chooses. On the other hand, although poverty may cause someone to steal, it does not compel him to do so. No one else wants him to steal or coerces him into acting. (I shall return to this point presently.)

Words mean what we say they mean, of course, but *control* is sometimes used so broadly that it effaces certain important distinctions. People can affect the behavior of others in many different ways, without diminishing their freedom. We can influence someone's actions by advancing various considerations that will affect the choices that he makes. If no alternatives have been blocked and the decision is his, then he may be persuaded, but his freedom has not been restricted and, in this pernicious sense of the word, he has not been controlled. Control is achieved by constraint or by manipulation.

People are *manipulated* if they are caused to behave in accordance with the wishes of others, without being aware of it and in a way that would not be effective if they were aware of the kind of influence being exerted. Manipulation, as by propaganda or hidden appeals to certain motives, utilizes deception to influence people's actions. They are being deceived about the alternatives open to them or about their own motives for acting. Knowledge can be used for deception just as it can be used to increase our awareness of the truth about ourselves and the world about us. Which way it will be used depends upon individual decisions and features of the general social and political structure that determine the standards by which we live.

In order to tell whether someone acts freely or not, we must know the causes of his behavior. By explaining our actions the laws of human behavior identify these causes. Knowledge provided by social science thus helps us to ascribe moral responsibility accurately and justly. A man is not responsible for involuntary behavior, because it doesn't depend upon his wishes. He cannot help himself because his wishes cannot affect what happens. Involuntary behavior is like catching a disease. It is not under our control. The thief, on the other hand, is responsible because the crime would not have occurred if he had not chosen to do it. Could he have chosen differently? To choose *is* to do one thing rather than another in the absence of external constraint. We therefore "choose our choices" simply by doing one thing when there are alternative courses of action. We can always choose differently, if we can choose at all.

The question concerns whether we could have helped having the desires and motives that caused us to do one thing rather than another. We frequently do change our desires in the light of knowledge about the consequences of acting on them. Sometimes effort is required and we can change, if we try. Will we try? That depends upon the kind of person that one is. If we try, will we succeed? That depends upon various facts about us and laws about men. An indisputably insane person cannot help or has no control over his own behavior. He probably will not try to change and would not succeed if he tried. Neither rational considerations nor threats influence him; they do not causally affect what he does. Under these circumstances, as Nowell-Smith points out, we do not hold a man responsible. The insane person does not have the alternatives that normal people do. The normal person can refrain from murdering a hated rival, although he may not refrain. The insane man cannot refrain from doing what he desires to do. He has no alternatives, hence no choices to make. Similarly, the non-swimmer cannot choose, on a particular occasion, whether to swim or not. We do not blame him for failing to try to rescue a drowning child. He can't do it; that is, if he tried he would fail. The man falling off a cliff can't stop himself. We don't blame him. There are some things we can't learn to do even if we try, because of some physical or physiological impediment. Daedalus could not learn to fly. A person without a certain amount of intelligence or aptitude cannot learn to do higher mathematics.

We find out what people can or cannot do by learning the facts and laws about them. Sometimes we need a good deal of evidence before we can tell whether or not a person had a choice and is therefore morally responsible. If we learn that he could not help himself for any of the reasons just mentioned, then we do not blame him. Insofar as a man is not held morally responsible for his behavior, we treat him as less than a man. We treat him as an object to which things happen, not as a person who does things. Withholding moral responsibility is therefore not something to be done lightly. We may appeal to extenuating circumstances, such as a thief's poverty, and temper justice with mercy, but he remains responsible for his action. How we shall deal with him or with the social conditions that were among the causes of his behavior is quite a different question. Its answer involves our moral views about the purposes of punishment and factual information about the most effective ways to modify his behavior.

The easy cases of acting freely and responsibly are also those that are of least human significance. Of course Jones acted freely when he poured himself a glass of water. Anyone can see that it meets the criteria of a free action. But did he also act freely when he poured himself a double martini? Well, probably, but before committing ourselves we might want to know something more about Jones. What might we want to know and why should it matter whether it is Jones or Smith? And if there can be a question—or, at least, a puzzle—about that simple act, why not about his unhappy choice of a wife or, for that matter, his wise choice of a career? A just evaluation of what a man has done or left undone, and of how much credit or blame is due him, requires further knowledge not only about the outer circumstances but also more intimately about the man.

A discussion of human responsibility that does not take account of what Sigmund Freud had to say shirks the hard problems. This is true not, as is frequently and shallowly asserted, because he denied personal responsibility, but because he so immeasurably enlarged its scope. Doubtless not everything Freud said was true. Certainly the way he said it is not the way, within a science, we can speak today. Yet after we have allowed for error and after all the obligatory obeisances to scientific method have been made, something will not go away. Our view of human nature has been changed irrevocably. And, as Jerome Bruner movingly suggests, by no means for the worse.

Bruner sketches the historical context of Freud's thought and stresses, in particular, its relation to Darwinism. Darwin wounded human pride by placing man squarely in the natural order as one among the animal species. He explained the "mechanism" of evolution by a causal theory of the processes of adaptation between individual variation and environmental conditions. The organism is born with certain needs and traits that determine whether in a given environment it will survive or perish. Freud, extending this pattern of analysis to the human spirit, infinitely elaborated and deepened our conception of personality. The biological needs that in one way or another must be satisfied adapt to the demands imposed and the expectations aroused by family and culture. Through rebellion and punishment, guilt and fear, love reciprocated and rejected, a compromise is struck. The child develops patterns of attitude and ways of behaving that thenceforth mark his mode of adaptation to other people and the exigencies of life. Man is an inextricable tangle of biology and culture.

Though couched in the teleological language of function and adjustment, psychoanalysis is a causal theory of the development of human personality. To explain our seemingly irrational yet fatefully directed behavior, Freud enormously extended the range of purposive action. Just as we impute motives to others by inference from their observed behavior, so all the things we ourselves do without knowing why we do them may be explained by considering that we act *as if* we had certain purposes. Consciously, we do not have these purposes. But the human soul is like an iceberg, nine tenths of it is under the sea. Certain desires and wishes are never wholly extinguished but, under the impress of social propriety, become submerged, hidden in the unconscious, where they continue to act, determining what we do and feel. The causes of our seemingly irrational fears, our accidents, and blunders are not external to ourselves but lie within us. And not only the "chance" events, the slips of the tongue and lapses of memory, are to be explained by unconscious motives. Even when we conduct ourselves most rationally, the reasons we give are not necessarily the "real" reasons for our actions. That is to say, they are not the reasons that cause what we do, but only unwitting rationalizations that disguise the repressed wish. Thus Freud added a wound to human pride.

However, unconscious wishes and motives are still *our* wishes and motives. Happening is unmasked as doing. "Everything happens to me" is confronted with "You brought it on yourself." But if we did it, then we are responsible. The enlarged concept of a person enlarges the sphere of personal responsibility. We are not coerced if what happens is up to us. Someone else's unconscious can compel us, but we do not compel ourselves. Yet how can we be blamed for motives that we do not even know we have? The examined life, said Socrates, is the only life worth living. Freud enjoins us to a closer examination of ourselves. "Where Id was, Ego shall be." That is, the irrational pleasure-seeking and aggressive desires by which we wreak havoc on ourselves and others must give way to intelligence and control. To modify patterns deeply etched by childhood experience is a hard and painful task. Every man, therefore, is to be pitied and every achievement, every life well lived, deserves infinite admiration. When the inner needs and patterns are not under our control, they act as if they were outer coercive forces. Nowell-Smith discusses the conditions these "forces" must meet to justify taking the drastic dehumanizing step of withdrawing moral responsibility from a man for actions that are, after all, his and his alone.

Moral standards, Margaret Macdonald points out, are decisions we make about what ought to be. To "choose a side" and behave morally often demands some suppression of biologically based needs. The practical task of obtaining this sacrifice in the interests of morality is no small one. Freud portrayed the complicated process of sublimation by which the repressed wish becomes realized in culturally valued ways. Art, science, and morality, good and evil spring, as Bruner says, from a common root. Their origin in the mutual interaction of biological need, personality, and culture is one thing. Their worth is another. Which values shall be realized depends in large part on the opportunities society offers. Though human nature is in one sense unchangeable, it is also almost infinitely pliable. Biological needs may be transformed and satisfied in ways which have yet to be numbered. It is for the social scientist to supply the theoretical knowledge which will make this plasticity available for better or, we must not forget, for worse. It can work both ways. Which way the wind ultimately blows very probably will depend upon political decisions for which the social scientist will hardly be in a position to be either blamed or praised. All those who work to extend our knowledge of man and society are, in John Maynard Keynes' elegant phrase, "the trustees, not of civilization, but of the possibility of civilization."

[37] Determinism and Responsibility

ISAIAH BERLIN

The proposition that everything that we do and suffer is part of a fixed pattern; that Laplace's observer (supplied with adequate knowledge of facts and laws) could at any moment of historical time describe correctly every past and future event including those of 'inner' life, that is, human thoughts, feelings, acts, &c., has often been entertained, and very different implications have been drawn from it; belief in its truth has dismayed some and inspired others. But whether such determinism is a valid theory or not, it seems clear that acceptance of it does not in fact colour the ordinary thoughts of the majority of human beings, including historians, nor even those of natural scientists outside the laboratory. For if it did, the language of the believers would reflect this fact, and be different from that of the rest of us. There is a class of expressions which we constantly use (and can scarcely do without) like 'you should not (or need not) have done this'; 'why did you make this terrible mistake?': 'I could do it, but I would rather not'; 'why did the King of Ruritania abdicate? Because, unlike the King of Abyssinia, he lacked the strength of will to resist'; '*must* the Commander-in-Chief be quite so stupid?' Expressions of this type plainly involve the notion of more than the merely logical possibility of the realization of alternatives other than those which were in fact realized, namely of differences between situations in which individuals can be reasonably regarded as being responsible for their acts, and those in which they can not. For no one will wish to deny that we do often argue about the best among the possible courses of action open to human beings in the present and past and future, in fiction and in dreams; that historians (and detectives and judges and juries) do attempt to establish, as well as they are able, what these possibilities are; that the ways in which these lines are drawn mark the frontiers between reliable and unreliable history; that what is called realism (as opposed to fancy or ignorance of life or utopian dreams) consists precisely in the placing of what occurred (or might occur) in the context of what could have happened (or could happen) and in the demarcation of this from what could not; that this is what (as I think Sir Lewis Namier

Reprinted with permission of the author and the publisher from Isaiah Berlin, *Historical Inevitability*, Oxford University Press, London, 1954, as corrected by the author for reprinting in *Four Essays on Liberty*, Oxford University Press, forthcoming.

once suggested) the sense of history, in the end, comes to; that upon this capacity historical (as well as legal) justice depends; that it alone makes it possible to speak of criticism, or praise and blame, as just or deserved or absurd or unfair; and that this is the sole and obvious reason why accidents, *force majeure*—being unavoidable—are necessarily outside the category of responsibility and consequently beyond the bounds of criticism, of the attribution of praise and blame. The difference between the expected and the exceptional, the difficult and the easy, the normal and the perverse, rests upon the drawing of these same lines. All this seems too self-evident to argue. It seems superfluous to add that all the discussions of historians about whether a given policy could or could not have been prevented, and what view should therefore be taken of the acts and characters of the actors, are intelligible only on the assumption of the reality of human choices. If determinism were a valid theory of human behaviour, these distinctions would be as inappropriate as the attribution of moral responsibility to the planetary system or the tissues of a living cell. These categories permeate all that we think and feel so pervasively and universally that to think them away, and conceive what and how we should be thinking, feeling, and talking without them, or in the framework of their opposites, is psychologically almost beyond our capacity—nearly, if not quite, as impracticable as, let us say, to pretend that we live in a world in which space, time, or number in the normal sense no longer exist. We may indeed always argue about specific situations, about whether a given occurrence is best explained as the inevitable effect of antecedent events beyond human control, or on the contrary as due to free human choice; free not merely in the sense that the case would have been altered if we had chosen—tried to act—differently; but that nothing prevented us from so choosing. It may well be that the growth of science and historical knowledge does in fact tend to show—make probable—that much of what was hitherto attributed to the acts of the unfettered wills of individuals can be satisfactorily explained only by the working of other, 'natural,' impersonal factors; that we have, in our ignorance or vanity, extended the realm of human freedom much too far. Yet, the very meaning of such terms as 'cause' and 'inevitable' depends on the possibility of contrasting them with at least their imaginary opposites. These alternatives may be improbable; but they must at least be conceivable, if only for the purpose of contrasting them with causal necessities and law-observing uniformities; unless we attach some meaning to the notion of free acts, i.e. acts not wholly determined by antecedent events or by the nature and 'dispositional characteristics' of either persons or things, it is difficult to see how we come to distinguish acts to which responsibility is attached from mere segments in a physical, or psychical, or psychophysical causal chain of events—a distinction signified (even if all particular applications of it are mistaken) by the cluster of expressions which deal with open alternatives and free choices. Yet it is this distinction that underlines our normal attribution of values, in particular the notion that praise and blame can ever be justly (not merely usefully or effectively) given. If the determinist hypothesis were true, and adequately accounted for the actual world, there is a clear sense in which, despite all the extraordinary casuistry which has been brought to avoid this conclusion, the notion of human responsibility, as ordinarily understood, would no longer apply to any actual, but only to imaginary or conceivable, states of affairs. I do not here wish to say that determinism is necessarily false, only that we neither speak nor think as if it could be true, and that it is difficult, and perhaps beyond our normal powers, to conceive what our picture of the world would be if we seriously believed it; so that to speak, as some theorists of history (and scientists with a philosophical bent) tend to do, as if one might (in life and not only in the study) accept the determinist hypothesis, and yet to continue to think and speak much as we do at present, is to breed intellectual confusion. If the belief in freedom—which rests on the assumption that human beings do occasionally choose, and that their choices are not wholly accounted for by the kind of causal explanations which are accepted in, say, physics or biology—if this is a necessary illusion, it is so deep and so pervasive that it is not felt as such.[1] No doubt we can try to convince ourselves that we are systematically deluded,[2] but unless we attempt to think out the implications of this possibility, and alter our modes of thoughts and speech to allow for it accordingly, this hypothesis remains hollow; that is, we find it impracticable even to entertain it seriously, if our behaviour is to be taken as evidence of what we can and what we cannot bring ourselves to believe or suppose not merely in theory, but in practice. My submission is that to make a serious attempt to adapt our thoughts and words to the hypothesis of determinism is scarcely feasible, as things are now, and have been within recorded history. The changes involved are too radical; our moral and psychological categories are, in the end, more flexible than our physical ones, but not much more so; it is not much easier to begin to think out in real terms, to which behaviour and speech would correspond, what the universe of the genuine determinist would be like, than to think out, with the minimum of indispensable concrete detail (i.e. begin to imagine) what it would be like to be in a timeles world, or one with a seventeen-dimensional space. Let those

---

[1] What can and what cannot be done by particular agents in specific circumstances is an empirical question, properly settled, like all such questions by an appeal to experience. If all acts were causally determined by antecedent conditions which were themselves similarly determined, and so on *ad infinitum,* such investigations would rest on an illusion. As rational beings we should, in that case, make an effort to disillusion ourselves—to cast off the spell of appearances; but we should surely fail. The delusion, if it is one, belongs to the order of what Kant called 'empirically real' and 'transcendentally ideal.' To try to place ourselves outside the categories which govern our empirical ('real') experience is what he regarded as an unintelligible plan of action. This thesis is surely valid, and can be stated without the paraphernalia of the Kantian system.

[2] This desperate effort to remain at once within and without the engulfing dream, to say the unsayable, is irresistible to German metaphysicians of a certain type: e.g. Schopenhauer and Vaihinger.

who doubt this try for themselves; the symbols with which we think will hardly lend themselves to the experiment; they, in their turn, are too deeply involved in our normal view of the world, allowing for every difference of period and clime and culture, to be capable of so violent a break. We can, of course, work out the logical implications of any set of internally consistent premisses—logic and mathematics will do any work that is required of them—but this is a very different thing from knowing how the result would look 'in practice,' what the concrete innovations are; and, since history is not a deductive science (and even sociology becomes progressively less intelligible as it loses touch with its empirical foundations), such hypotheses, being abstract models, pure and unapplied, will be of little use to students of human life. Hence the ancient controversy between free will and determinism, while it remains a genuine problem for theologians and philosophers, need not trouble the thoughts of those whose concern is with empirical matters—the actual lives of human beings in the space and time of normal experience. For practising historians determinism is not, and need not be, a serious issue.

Yet, inapplicable as it may be as a theory of human action, specific forms of the deterministic hypothesis have played an arresting, if limited, role in altering our views of human responsibility. The irrelevance of the general hypothesis to historical studies must not blind us to its importance as a specific corrective to ignorance, prejudice, dogmatism, and fantasy on the part of those who judge the behaviour of others. For it is plainly a good thing that we should be reminded by social scientists that the scope of human choice is a good deal more limited than we used to suppose; that the evidence at our disposal shows that many of the acts too often assumed to be within the individual's control are not so—that man is an object in (scientifically predictable) nature to a larger degree than has at times been supposed, that human beings more often than not act as they do because of characteristics due to heredity or physical or social environment or education, or biological or physical characteristics or the interplay of these factors with each other and with the obscurer factors loosely called physical characteristics; and that the resultant habits of thought, feeling, and expression are as capable of being classified and made subject to hypotheses and systematic laws as the behavior of material objects. And this certainly alters our ideas about the limits of freedom and responsibility. If we are told that a given case of stealing is due to kleptomania, we protest that the appropriate treatment is not punishment but a remedy for a disease; and similarly, if a destructive act or a vicious character is ascribed to a specific psychological or social cause, we decide, if we are convinced that the explanation is valid, that the agent is not responsible for his acts and consequently deserves therapeutic rather than penal treatment. It is salutary to be reminded of the narrowness of the field within which we can begin to claim to be free; and some would claim that such knowledge is still increasing, and the field still contracting. Where the frontier between freedom and causal laws is to be determined is a crucial practical issue; knowledge of it is a powerful and indispensable antidote to ignorance and irrationality, and offers us new types of explanation—historical, psychological, sociological, biological—which previous generations have lacked. What we cannot alter, or cannot alter as much as we had supposed, cannot be used as evidence for or against us as free moral agents; it can cause us to feel pride, shame, regret, interest, but not remorse; it can be admired, envied, deplored, enjoyed, feared, wondered at, but not (save in some quasi-aesthetic sense) praised or condemned; our tendency to indignation is curbed, we desist from passing judgment. 'Je ne propose rien, je ne suppose rien, je n'impose rien . . . J'expose,' said a French writer proudly, and such *exposition* meant for him the treatment of all events as causal or statistical phenomena, as scientific material to the exclusion of moral judgment. Historians of this persuasion, anxious to avoid all personal, above all, all moral, judgments, tend to emphasize the immense predominance of impersonal factors in history, of the physical media in which life is lived, the power of geographical, psychological, social factors which are not, at any rate consciously, man-made, and often beyond human control. This does tend to check our arrogance, to induce humility by forcing us to admit that our own outlook and scales of value are neither permanent nor universally accepted, that the over-confident, too complacent moral classifications of past historians and of their societies sprang all too obviously from specific historical conditions, specific forms of ignorance or vainglory, or from particular temperamental traits in the historian, or from other countless causes and circumstances which, from our vantage point, we perceive to belong to their own place and time, and to have given rise to interpretations which later seem idiosyncratic, smug, shallow, unjust, and often grotesque in the light of our own standards of accuracy or objectivity. And, what is even more important, such a line of approach throws doubt upon all attempts to establish a definitive line between the individual's free choice and his natural or social necessitation, and does this by bringing to light the egregious blunders of some of those who tried to solve this or that problem in the past, and made mistakes of fact which now, all too plainly, seem due to their (unalterable) *milieu,* or character, or interests. And this tends to make us ask whether the same might not be equally true of us and our own historical judgments; and so, by suggesting that every generation is 'subjectively' conditioned by its own and psychological peculiarities, leads us to wonder whether it might not be best to avoid all moral judgment, all ascription of responsibility, might not be safest to confine ourselves to impersonal terms, and leave whatever cannot be said in such terms altogether unsaid. Have we learned nothing from the intolerable moral dogmatism and the mechanical classifications of those historians and moralists and politicians whose views are now so dated, so obsolete, and so justly discredited? And, indeed, who are we to make such a parade of our personal opinions, to give such importance to what are no more than symptoms of our own ephemeral outlook? And what right, in any case, have we to sit in judgment on our fellows whose moral codes are the products of their specific historical environments, as our own are of ours? Is it not better to analyse, to describe, to present the events, and then withdraw and let them 'speak for themselves,' refraining from the intolerable presumption of awarding marks, meting out justice, dividing the sheep from the goats, according to our own personal criteria, as if these were eternal and not, as in fact they are, neither more nor less valid than those of others with other interests, in other conditions?

Such advice to us (in itself salutary enough) to retain a certain scepticism about our own powers of judgment, especially to beware of ascribing too much authority to our own moral feelings, comes to us, as you may recollect, from at least two quarters; from those who think that we know too much, and from those who think that we know too little. We know now, say the former, that we are as we are, and our moral and intellectual criteria are what they are, in virtue of the evolving historical situation. Let me once more remind you of their varieties. Some among them, who feel sure that the natural sciences will in the end account for everything, explain our behaviour in terms of natural causes. Others, who accept a more metaphysical interpretation of the world, explain it by speaking of invisible powers and dominions, nations, races, cultures; the spirit of the age, the 'workings,' overt and occult, of 'the Classical Spirit,' 'the Renaissance,' 'the Medieval Mind,' 'the French Revolution,' or 'the Twentieth Century,' conceived as impersonal entities, at once patterns and realities, in terms of whose 'structure' or 'purpose' their elements and expressions—men and institutions— must behave as they do. Yet still others speak in terms of some teleological procession, or hierarchy, whereby each man, country, institution, culture, age, fulfil their part in some cosmic drama, and are what they are in virtue of the part cast for them, but not by them, by the divine Dramatist Himself. From this it is not far to the views of those who say that History is wiser than we, that its purposes are unfathomable to us, that we, or some amongst us, are but the means, the instruments, the manifestations, worthy or unworthy, of some vast all-embracing schema of eternal human progress, or of the German Spirit, or of the Proletariat, or of post-Christian civilization, or of Faustian man, or of Manifest Destiny, or of the American Century, or of some other myth or mystery or abstraction. To know all is to understand all; it is to know why things are and must be as they are; therefore the more we know the more absurd we must think those who suppose that things could have been otherwise, and so fall into the irrational temptation to praise or blame. *Tout comprendre, c'est tout pardonner* is transformed into a mere truism. Any form of moral censure—the accusing finger of historians or publicists or politicians, and indeed the agonies of the private conscience, too—tends, so far as possible, to be explained away as one or other sophisticated version of primitive taboos or physical tensions or conflicts, now appearing as moral consciousness, now as some other sanction, growing out of, and battening upon, that ignorance which alone generates fallacious beliefs in free will and uncaused choice, doomed to disappear in the growing light of scientific or metaphysical truth. Or, again, we find that the adherents of a sociological or historical or anthropological metaphysics tend to interpret the sense of mission and dedication, the voice of duty, all forms of inner compulsion of this type, as being an expression within each individual's conscious life of the 'vast impersonal forces' which control it, and which speak 'in us,' 'through us,' 'to us,' for their own inscrutable purposes. To hear is then literally to obey—to be drawn towards the goal that belongs to our 'real' self, or its 'natural' or 'rational' development—that to which we are called by belonging to this or that class, or nation, or race, or church, or station in society, or tradition, or age, or character. The explanation, and in some sense the weight of responsibility, for all human action is (at times with ill-concealed relief) transferred to the broad backs of these vast impersonal forces—institutions or historic trends —better made to bear such burdens than a feeble thinking reed like man— a creature that, with a megalomania scarcely appropriate to his physical and moral fraility, claims, as he too often does, to be responsible for the workings of Nature or of the Spirit; and flown with his importance, praises and blames, worships and tortures, murders and immortalizes other creatures like himself for conceiving, willing, or executing policies for which neither he nor they can be remotely responsible; as if flies were to sit in solemn judgment upon each other for causing the revolutions of the sun or the changes of the seasons which affect their lives. But no sooner do we acquire adequate insight into the 'inexorable' and 'inevitable' parts played by all things animate and inanimate in the cosmic process, than we are freed from the sense of personal endeavour. Our sense of guilt and of sin, our pangs of remorse and self-condemnation, are automatically dissolved; the tension, the fear of failure and frustration, disappear as we become aware of the elements of a larger 'organic whole' of which we are variously described as limbs or members, or reflections, or emanations, or finite expressions; our sense of freedom and independence, our belief in an area, however circumscribed, in which we can choose to act as we wish, falls from us; in its place we are provided with a sense of a membership in an ordered system, each with a unique position, sacred to him alone. We are soldiers in an army, and we no longer suffer the pains and penalties of solitude; the army is on the march, our goals are set for us, not chosen by us; doubts are stilled by authority. The growth of knowledge brings with it relief from moral burdens, for if powers beyond and above us are at work, it is wild presumption to claim responsibility for their activity or blame ourselves for failing in it. Original sin is thus transferred to an impersonal plane, and acts hitherto regarded as wicked or unjustifiable are seen in a more 'objective' fashion—in a larger context—as part of the process of history which, being responsible for providing us with our scale of values, must not therefore itself be judged in terms of it; and viewed in this new light they turn out no longer wicked but right and good because necessitated by the whole.

This is a doctrine which lies at the heart equally of scientific attempts to explain moral sentiments as psychological or sociological 'residues' or the like, and of the metaphysical vision for which whatever is—'truly' is—is good. To understand all is to see that nothing could be otherwise than as it is; that all blame, indignation, protest is mere complaint about what seems discordant, about elements which do not seem to fit, about the absence of an intellectually or spiritually satisfying pattern. But this is always only evidence of failure on the part of the observer, of his blindness and ignorance; it can never be an objective assessment of reality, for in reality everything necessarily fits, nothing is superfluous, nothing amiss, every ingredient is 'justified' in being where it is by the demands of the transcendant whole; and all sense of guilt, injustice, ugliness, all resistance or condemnation, is mere proof of (at times unavoidable) lack of vision, misunderstanding, subjective aberration. Vice, pain, folly, maladjustment, all come from failure to understand, from failure, in Mr. E. M. Forster's celebrated phrase, 'to connect.' This is the sermon preached to us by great and noble thinkers of very different outlooks, by Spinoza and Godwin, by Tolstoy and Comte, by mystics and rationalists, theologians and scientific materialists, metaphysicians and dogmatic empiricists, American sociologists, Russian Marxists, and German historicists alike. Thus Godwin (and he speaks for many humane and civilized persons) tells us that to understand a human act we must always avoid applying general principles but examine each case in its full individual detail. When we scrupulously examine the texture and pattern of this or that life, we shall not, in our haste and blindness seek to condemn or to punish; for we shall see why this or that man was caused to act in this or that manner by ignorance or poverty or some other moral or intellectual or physical defect, as we always (Godwin optimistically supposes) can see, if we arm ourselves with sufficient patience, knowledge, and sympathy, and we shall then blame him no more than we should an object in nature; and since it is axiomatic that we cannot both act upon our knowledge, and yet regret the result, we can and shall in the end succeed in making men good, just, happy, and wise. So, too, Condorcet and Henri de Saint-Simon, and their disciple, Auguste Comte, starting from the opposite conviction, namely that men are not unique, and in need, each one of them, of individual treatment, but, no less than inhabitants of the animal, vegetable, and mineral kingdom, belong to types and obey general laws, maintain no less stoutly that once these laws have been discovered (and therefore applied) this will by itself lead to universal felicity. And this conviction has since been echoed by many idealistic liberals and rationalists, planners, technocrats, positivists, and believers in the scientific organization of society; and in very different keys by theocrats, neomedieval romantics, authoritarians, and political mystics of every kind. This, too, is in substance the morality preached (if not by Marx, then by most of the disciples of Engels and Plekhanov), by Prussian nationalist historians, by Spengler, and by many another thinker who believes that there is a pattern which he has seen that others have not seen, or at least not so clearly seen, and that by this vision men may be saved. Know and you will not be lost. What it is that we must know differs from thinker to thinker, differs as views of the nature of things differ. Know the laws of the universe, animate and inanimate, or the principles of growth, or of evolution or of the rise and fall of civilizations, or the goals towards which all creation tends, or the stages of the Idea, or something less tangible still. Know, in the sense of identifying yourself with it, realizing your oneness with it, for, do what you may, you cannot escape from the laws to which you are subject, of whatever kind they may be, 'mechanistic,' 'vitalistic,' causal, purposive, imposed, transcendent, immanent, or the 'myriad' impalpable strands which bind you to the past—to your land and to the dead, as Barrès declared; to the *milieu,* the race, and the moment, as Taine asserted; to Burke's great society of the dead and living, who have made you what you are; so that the truth in which you believe, the values in terms of which you judge, from the profoundest principles to the most trivial whims, are part and parcel of the historical continuum to which you belong. Tradition or blood or class or human nature or progress or humanity; the *Zeitgeist* or the social structure or the laws of history, or the true ends of life; know these—be true to them—and you will be free. From Plato to Lucretius, from the Gnostics to Leibniz, from Thomas Aquinas to Lenin and Freud, the battle-cry has been essentially the same; the object of knowledge, the methods of discovery have often been violently opposed, but that reality is knowable, and that knowledge and only knowledge liberates, and absolute knowledge liberates absolutely—that is common to many doctrines which are so large and valuable a part of Western civilization. To understand is to explain and to explain is to justify. The notion of individual freedom is a delusion; the further we are from omniscience, the wider our notion of our freedom and responsibility and guilt, those products of ignorance and fear which populate the unknown with terrifying fictions. Personal freedom is a noble delusion and has had its social value; society might have crumbled without it; it is a necessary instrument —one of the greatest devices of 'The Cunning' of Reason or of History, or of whatever other cosmic force we may be invited to worship. But a delusion however noble, useful, metaphysically justified, historically indispensable, is still a delusion. And so individual responsibility, the perception of the difference between right and wrong choices, between avoidable evil and misfortune, are mere symptoms, evidences of our vanity, of our imperfect adjustment, of our inability to face the truth. The more we know, the greater the relief from the burden of choice; we forgive others for what they cannot avoid being, and by the same token we forgive ourselves. In ages in which the choices seem peculiarly agonizing, when strongly held ideals cannot be reconciled and collisions cannot be averted, such doctrines seem peculiarly comforting. We escape moral dilemma by denying their reality; and, by directing our gaze towards the greater wholes, we make them responsible in our place. All we lose is an illusion, and with it the painful and superfluous emotions of guilt and remorse. Freedom notoriously involves responsibility, and it is for many spirits a source of welcome relief to lose the burden of both, not by some ignoble act of surrender, but by daring to contemplate in a calm spirit things as they must be; for this is to be truly philosophical. Thereby we reduce history to a kind of physics; as well blame the galaxy or gamma-rays as Genghis Khan or Hitler. 'To know all is to forgive all' turns out to be, in Professor Ayer's striking phrase (used in another context) nothing but a dramatized tautology. . . .

The matter is more serious when empirical arguments are advanced for an historical determinism which excludes the notion of personal responsibility. We are here no longer dealing with the metaphysics of history— the theodicies, say, of Schelling or Carlyle—as obvious substitutes for religion. We have before us the great sociological theories of history—the materialistic or scientific interpretations which began with Montesquieu and the *philosophes,* and led to the great schools of the nineteenth century, from the Saint-Simonians and Hegelians to the followers of Comte, Marx, Darwin, and the liberal economists; from Freud, Pareto, Sorel to the ideologists of Fascism. Of these Marxism is much the boldest and the most intelligent, but its practitioners, much as they have added to our understanding, have not succeeded in their gallant and desperate attempt to treat history as a science. Arising out of this great movement we have the vast proliferation of anthropological and sociological studies of civilized societies, with their tendency to trace all character and behaviour to the same kind of relatively irrational and unconscious causes as those which are held to have so successfully explained the behaviour of primitive societies; we have witnessed the rebirth of the notion of the 'sociology of knowledge,' which suggests that not only our methods but our conclusions and our reasons for believing them, in the entire realm of knowledge, can be shown to be wholly or largely determined by the stage reached in the development of our class or group, or nation or culture, or whatever other unit may be chosen; followed, in due course, by the fusion of these at times unconvincing, but, usually, at least quasi-scientific, doctrines with such nonempirical figments—at times all but personified powers both good and bad —as the 'Collectivist Spirit,' or 'The Myth of the Twentieth Century,' or 'The Contemporary Collapse of Values' (sometimes called 'The Crisis of Faith'), or 'Modern Man,' or 'The Last Stage of Capitalism.' All these modes of speech have peopled the air with supernatural entities of great power, Neo-Platonic and Gnostic spirits, angels and demons who play with us as they will, or, at any rate, make demands on us which, we are told, we ignore at our peril. There has grown up in our modern time a pseudo-sociological mythology which, in the guise of scientific concepts, has developed into a new animism—certainly a more primitive and naïve religion than the traditional European faiths which it seeks to replace.[3] This new cult leads troubled persons to ask such questions as 'Is War inevitable?,' or 'Must Collectivism triumph?,' or 'Is Civilization doomed?' These questions, and the tone in which they are posed, and the way in which they are discussed, imply a belief in the occult presence of vast impersonal entities— wars, collectivism, doom—agencies and forces at large in the world, which we have but little power to control or deflect. Sometimes these are said to 'embody themselves' in great men, titanic figures, who because they are at one with their age, achieve superhuman results—Napoleon, Bismarck, Lenin; sometimes in the actions of classes—the great capitalist combines, which work for ends that their members scarcely understand themselves, ends towards which their economic and social position 'inevitably' drive them; sometimes of huge inchoate entities called 'The Masses,' which do the work of history, little knowing of what mighty forces they are the 'creative vehicles.' Wars, revolutions, dictatorships, military and economic transformations are apt to be conceived like the genii of some oriental demonology, djinns, which once set free from the jars in which they have been confined for centuries, become uncontrollable, and capriciously play with the lives of men and nations. It is perhaps not to be wondered at that with so luxurious a growth of similes and metaphors, many innocent persons nowadays tend to believe that their lives are dominated not merely by relatively stable, easily identifiable, material factors—physical nature and the laws dealt with by the natural sciences; but by even more powerful and sinister, and far less intelligible, factors—the impersonal struggles of classes which members of these classes may not intend—the collision of social forces, the incidences of slumps and booms, which, like tides and harvests, can scarcely be controlled by those whose lives depend upon them —above all, by inexorable 'societal' and 'behavioural' patterns, to quote but a few sacred words from the barbarous vocabulary of the new mythologies. Cowed and humbled by the panoply of the new divinities, men are eager, and seek anxiously, for knowledge and comfort in the sacred books and in the new orders of priesthood which affect to tell them about the attributes and habits of their new masters. And the books and their expositors do speak words of comfort: demand creates supply. Their message is simple and very ancient. In a world where such monsters clash, individual human beings can have but little responsibility for what they do; the discovery of the new, terrifying, impersonal forces may render life infinitely more dangerous, yet if they serve no other purpose, they do, at any rate, divest their victims of all responsibility—from all those moral burdens which men in less enlightened days used to carry with such labour and anguish. So that what we have lost on the swings we make up on the roundabouts: if we

---

[3] I need hardly add that responsibility (if I may still venture to use this term) for this cannot be placed at the door of the great thinkers who founded modern sociology— Marx, Durkheim, Weber, nor of the rational and scrupulous followers and critics whose work they have inspired.

lose freedom of action, at any rate we can no longer blame or be blamed for a world largely out of our control. The terminology of praise and condemnation turns out to be *eo ipso* uncivilized and obscurantist. To record what occurs and why, in impersonal chronicles, as was done by detached and studious monks in other times of violence and strife, is represented as more honourable and more dignified, and more in keeping with the noble humility and integrity of a scholar, who in a time of doubt and crisis will at least preserve his soul if he abstains from the easy path of self-indulgence in moral sentiments. Agonizing doubts about the conduct of individuals caught in historical crises and the feeling of hope and despair, guilt, pride, and remorse, which accompany such reflections, are taken from us; like soldiers in an army driven by forces too great to resist, we lose those neuroses which depend on the fear of having to choose among alternatives. Where there is no choice there is no anxiety; and a happy release from responsibility. Some human beings have always preferred the peace of imprisonment, a contented security, a sense of having at last found one's proper place in the cosmos, to the painful conflicts and perplexities of the disordered freedom of the world beyond the walls.

Yet this is odd. For the assumptions upon which this kind of determinism has been erected are, when examined, exceedingly unplausible. What are these forces and these inexorable historical laws? What historiographer, what sociologist can claim as yet to have produced empirical generalizations comparable to the great uniformities of the natural sciences? It is a commonplace to say that sociology still awaits its Newton, but even this seems much too audacious a claim; it has yet to find its Euclid and its Archimedes, before it can begin to dream of a Copernicus. On one side a patient and useful accumulation of facts, taxonomy, comparative studies, cautious and limited hypotheses, still hamstrung by too many exceptions to have any appreciable predictive power; [4] on the other, imposing, sometimes ingenious, theoretical constructions, obscured by picturesque metaphors and a bold mythology, often stimulating to workers in other fields; and between these, a vast gap, such as has not existed in historical times between the theories and the factual evidence of the natural sciences. It is idle for sociology to plead that she is still young and has a glorious future. The eponymous hero to honour whose memory these words are being uttered, Auguste Comte, founded it a full hundred years ago, and its great conquests are still to come. [5] It has affected other disciplines most fruitfully, notably history to which it has added a dimension, [6] but it has as yet succeeded in discovering so few laws, hypotheses, wide generalizations, supported by adequate evidence, that its plea to be treated as a natural science can scarcely be entertained, nor are these few poor laws sufficiently revolutionary to make it seem an urgent

---

[4] And a collection of isolated insights and *apercus,* like the dubious 'all power either corrupts or intoxicates,' or 'man is a political animal,' or 'Der Mensch ist was er isst.'

[5] I do not mean to imply that other 'sciences,' e.g. 'political science' or social anthropology have fared much better in establishing laws, but their claims are more modest.

[6] As well as new methods for testing the validity of old conclusions.

matter to test their truth. In the great field of sociology (unlike her more speculative but far more effective younger sister, psychology), the loose generalizations of common sense, unsystematic rules of thumb, still, at times, seen more fruitful than their 'scientific' equivalents.

Social determinism is, at least historically, closely bound up with the 'nomothetic' ideals of sociology. And it may, indeed, be a true doctrine. But if it is true, and if we begin to take it seriously, then, indeed, the changes in the whole of our language, our moral terminology, our attitudes toward one another, our views of history, of society and of everything else will be too profound to be even adumbrated. The concepts of praise and blame, innocence and guilt, and individual responsibility, from which we started, are but a small element in the structure, which would collapse or disappear. If social and psychological determinism were established as an accepted truth, our world would be transformed far more radically than was the teleological world of the classical and middle ages by the triumphs of mechanistic principles or those of natural selection. Our words—our modes of speech and thought—would be transformed in literally unimaginable ways; the notions of choice, of voluntary action, of responsibility, freedom, are so deeply embedded in our outlook, that our new life, as creatures in a world genuinely lacking in these concepts, can, I should maintain, be conceived by us only with the greatest difficulty.[7] But there is, as yet, no need to alarm ourselves unduly. We are speaking only of pseudo-scientific ideals; the reality is not in sight. The evidence for a thoroughgoing determinism is not to hand; and if there is a persistent tendency to believe in it in some theoretical fashion, that is surely due far more to the lure of a 'scientific' or metaphysical ideal; or a wish, on the part of those who desire to change society, to believe that the stars in their courses are fighting for them. Or it may be due to a longing to lay down moral burdens, or minimize individual responsibility and transfer it to impersonal forces which can be safely accused of causing all our discontents, than to any increase in our powers of critical reflection or any improvement in our scientific techniques. Belief in historical determinism of this type is, of course, very widespread, particularly in what I should like to call its 'historiosophical' form, by which I mean metaphysico-theological theories of history, which attract many who have lost their faith in older religious orthodoxies. Yet perhaps this attitude, so prevalent recently, is ebbing; and a contrary trend is discernible today. Our best historians use empirical tests in sifting facts, make microscopic examinations of the evidence, deduce no patterns, and show no false fear in attributing responsibility to individuals. Their specific attributions and analyses may be mistaken, but both they and their readers would be surprised to be told that their very activity

---

[7] As for the attempt to 'reinterpret' these notions so as to bring them into conformity with determinism, this can be achieved only at the cost of altering the meaning of such concepts beyond applicability to our normal experience. Cf. I. Berlin, *Historical Inevitability*, Oxford University Press, 1954, p. 26 (footnote).

had been superseded and stultified by the advances of sociology, or by some deeper metaphysical insight, like that of oriental stargazers by the discoveries of the disciples of Kepler. In their own queer way, some modern existentialists, too, proclaim the crucial importance of individual acts of choice. The condemnation by some among them of all philosophical systems as equally hollow, and of all moral, as of other doctrines, as equally worthless simply because they are systems and doctrines, may be absurd; but the more serious of them are no less insistent than Kant upon the reality of human autonomy, that is, upon the possibility of free self-commitment to an act or a form of life for what it is in itself. Whether recognition of freedom in this last sense does or does not entitle one logically to preach to others, or judge the past, is another matter; at any rate, it shows a commendable strength of intellect to have seen through the pretensions of those all-explanatory, all-justifying theodicies, which promised to assimilate the human sciences to the natural in the quest for a unified schema of all there is. It needs more than infatuation with a programme to overthrow some of the most deeply rooted moral and intellectual habits of human beings, whether they be plumbers or historians. We are told that it is foolish to judge Charlemagne or Napoleon, or Genghis Khan or Hitler or Stalin for their massacres, that it is at most a comment upon ourselves and not upon 'the fact.' Likewise we are told that it is absurd to praise those benefactors of humanity whom the followers of Comte so faithfully celebrated; or at least that to do so is not our business as historians: because as historians our categories are 'neutral' and differ from our categories as ordinary human beings as those of chemists undeniably do. We are also told that as historians it is our task to describe, let us say, the great revolutions of our own time without so much as hinting that certain individuals involved in them not merely caused, but were responsible for, great misery and destruction—using such words according to the standards not merely of the twentieth century which is soon over, or of our declining capitalist society but of the human race at all the times and in all the places in which we have known it; and told that we should practise such austerities out of respect for some imaginary scientific canon which distinguishes between facts and values very sharply, so sharply that it enables us to regard the former as being objective, 'inexorable' and therefore self-justifying, and the latter merely as a subjective gloss upon events—due to the moment, the *milieu*, the individual temperament—and consequently unworthy of serious scholarship. To this we can only answer that to accept this doctrine is to do violence to the basic notions of our morality, to misrepresent our sense of our past, and to ignore some among the most general concepts and categories of normal thought. Those who are concerned with human affairs, are committed to the use of moral categories and concepts which normal language incorporates and expresses. Chemists, philologists, logicians, even sociologists with a strong quantitative bias, by using morally neutral technical terms, can avoid doing so. But historians can scarcely do this. They need not—they are certainly not obliged to—moralize: but neither can they avoid the use of normal language with all its associations and 'built in' moral categories. To seek to avoid this is to adopt another moral outlook, not none at all. The time will come when men will wonder how this strange view, which combines a misunderstanding of relation of value to fact with cynicism disguised as stern impartiality, can ever have achieved such remarkable fame and influence and respectability. For it is not scientific; nor can its reputation be due entirely to a commendable fear of undue arrogance or philistinism or of too bland and uncritical an imposition of our own dogmas and standards upon others. In part it is due to a genuine misunderstanding of the philosophical implications of the natural sciences, the great prestige of which has been misappropriated by many a fool and imposter since their earliest triumphs. But principally it seems to me to spring from a desire to resign our responsibility, to cease from judging provided we be not judged ourselves and, above all, are not compelled to judge ourselves —from a desire to flee for refuge to some vast amoral, impersonal, monolithic whole, nature or history,[8] or class, or race, or the 'harsh realities of our time,' or the irresistible evolution of the social structure,[9] that will absorb and integrate us into its limitless, bleak, neutral texture, which it is senseless to evaluate or criticize, and against which we fight to our certain doom. This is an image which has often appeared in the history of mankind, always at moments of confusion and inner weakness. It is one of the great alibis, pleaded by those who cannot and do not wish to face the facts of human responsibility, the existence of a limited but nevertheless real area of human freedom, either because they have been too deeply wounded or frightened to wish to return to the traffic of normal life, or because they are filled with moral indignation against the false values and the, to them, repellent moral codes of their own society, or class, or profession, and take up arms against all ethical codes as such, as a dignified means of casting off a morality which is to them, perhaps justifiably, repulsive. Nevertheless, such views, although they may spring from a natural reaction against too much moral rhetoric, are a desperate remedy; those who hold them use history as a method of escape from a world which has, for some reason, grown odious to them into a fantasy where impersonal entities avenge their grievances and set everything right, to the greater or lesser discomfiture of their persecutors, real and imaginary. And in the course of this they describe the normal lives lived by men in terms which fail to mark the most important psychological and moral distinctions known to us. This they do in the service of an imaginary science; and, like the astrologers and magicians whom they have succeeded, cast up their eyes to the clouds, and speak in immense, unsubstantiated images and similes, in deeply misleading

8 'History has seized us by the throat,' Mussolini is reported to have cried on learning of the Allied landing in Sicily. Men could be fought; but once 'History' herself took up arms against one, resistance was vain.

9 'The irresistible,' Mr. Justice Brandeis is said to have remarked, 'is often only that which is not resisted.'

metaphors and allegories, and make use of hypnotic formulae with little regard for experience, or rational argument, or tests of proven reliability. Thereby they throw dust in their own eyes as well as in ours, obstruct our vision of the real world, and further confuse an already sufficiently bewildered public about the relations of morality to politics, and about the nature and methods of the natural sciences and historical studies alike.

[38] History, Freedom, and Responsibility

FRANCIS V. RAAB

– I –

Professor Isaiah Berlin has written an extremely lively polemic [1] against those metaphysical theories of history which by regarding all human actions as inevitable, make it morally improper to censure the actors. Such theories attempt to give a comprehensive explanation of historical change in terms of some abstraction such as The Masses, The Absolute Spirit, Tradition, etc. which is supposedly the real dynamism or determinant of human history. What he opposes in these theories is that they seem to entail that individuals are at the mercy of forces they are not aware of, much less understand; they have no choices or alternatives, for their actions are predetermined by the necessity of the fulfillment of some over-all Plan or Realization. Such a view if taken seriously would make it improper for the historian or anyone else to blame, say, Napoleon, or claim that he could have pursued a different policy.

It is not altogether apparent that these metaphysical theories entail the denial of freedom and responsibility. Those who advocate such views may claim that freedom is denied, but in fact they rarely explicitly deny it altogether; instead they redefine the term in a way they think renders its true

Reprinted from *Philosophy of Science*, **26**, 1959, pp. 114–124, with permission of the author and the editor.

[1] *Historical Inevitability*, Oxford University Press, London, 1954. [Reprinted in part in this volume, pp. 679–694.]

meaning (Spinoza). More often than not it is their critics who claim that their theories entail the denial of freedom.[2] But a man's theories do not always entail what he or his critics think they do. Of course, if the theory is formulated in a language which entails that individuals are always literally forced or compelled to act as they do, say, by the workings of the Absolute Spirit, then it is quite obvious that freedom is denied. I think Mr. Berlin would contend, and I would certainly agree, that any theory which takes such a "high priori road" to the denial of the freedom and responsibility of historical agents is insoubrious.

However, there are frequent instances when certain historical personages were either compelled to do what they did, or they were mentally ill, or they were dominated by religious or political ideologies whose intellectual and moral alternatives had yet to be conceived. If historical investigation revealed that one of these factors was present on the occasion of every decision by every historical agent, then we would have sufficient reason to say that they were neither free nor responsible. Likewise when the evidence shows that none of these factors was present, the historian is entitled to claim that a certain agent was free, responsible, blameworthy, or that he could have done otherwise. I think Mr. Berlin would insist on both these points, but it is the latter prerogative of the historian which he thinks is jeopardized by these theodices, for they all, by entailing determinism, seem to him to deny freedom. Now while I approve of his fulminations against the assorted theodocies which, he says, fortunately do not encumber the reflections of the majority of historians, I do not think he has showed that ordinary determinism is incompatible with the freedom and moral responsibility of historical agents.

– II –

He says: "Unless we attach some meaning to the notion of free acts, i.e. acts not wholly determined by antecedent events or by the nature and 'dispositional characteristics' of either persons or things, it is difficult to see how we come to distinguish acts to which responsibility is attached from mere segments in a physical, or psychical, or psycho-physical causal chain of events—a distinction signified (even if all particular applications of it are mistaken) by the cluster of expressions which deal with open alternatives and free choices. Yet it is this distinction that underlines our normal attribution of values, in particular the notion that praise and blame can be just and not merely useful or effective. If the determinist hypothesis were true and adequately accounted for the actual world, there is a clear sense in which (despite all the extraordinary casuistry which has been employed to avoid this conclusion) the notion of human responsibility as ordinarily

[2] See William James' *Dilemma of Determinism*.

understood would no longer apply to any actual, but only to imaginary or conceivable, state of affairs." [3]

First of all I wish to examine the expression: "Unless we attach some meaning to the notion of free acts, i.e. acts not wholly determined by antecedent events. . . ." Now I suppose the function of his "i.e." is to assert that the expression: "free acts" is equivalent in meaning to the expression: "acts not wholly determined by antecedent events." But can an expression be equivalent to another and yet there be a problem of whether we can attach any meaning to it? Perhaps he really intends to say that the problem of what meaning to attach to the notion of "free acts" is the problem of what meaning to attach to the notion of "acts not wholly determined by antecedent events"? If this is his problem how can he be sure that "free acts" *means:* "acts not wholly determined by antecedent events"? I think he would probably say that "free acts" means this or nothing. He arrives at this equivalence not as a result of finding it at hand in our language as we would the equivalence of "spinster" and "elderly, never-married, female," but as an equivalence we are forced to admit else deny that there are any free actions, since it appears that if an action is caused then its being free is at once precluded. I shall try to show that this consequence does not follow, but for the moment I would like to consider the implications of accepting this equivalence.

It can hardly escape notice that on many occasions when we would quite properly say that a person acted of his own free-will, we would have been willing to say instead that he could have done otherwise; and, that we normally treat this latter assertion as one which is warrantable on certain commonly accepted grounds. Freewill assertions are often similarly supportable. Yet if Mr. Berlin's suggested equivalence is accepted, our common way of supporting such assertions must be given up, since what we really should be trying to ascertain is whether the action was or was not wholly determined by antecedent events. The fact that we never even try to do this, that there is an enormous methodological difficulty in trying to show that a given human action was not wholly determined by antecedent events, and that we can scarcely conceive of what it would be like to accept the existence of such an action, makes his equivalence very implausible. If "not wholly determined by antecedent events" means (can it mean anything else?): "not determined at all," it is apparent that before we would accept the existence of such an action we would come to a near breakdown of thought in the conflict generated by the conditions under which we might be tempted to claim that a given action was not determined by antecedent events. For we would only come to that conclusion—at least by empirical methods—when upon the repetition of identical antecedent conditions, different actions resulted: and we were certain that the antecedent conditions were identical, for that they were not identical would be our first presumption upon finding that the resulting actions were different. And even if we could not

[3] *Historical Inevitability* [p. 680, this volume].

detect any difference in the antecedent conditions, it would be a long, uneasy time before we would conclude that there was no difference, and that we had found an action which was not determined by its antecedents.

But let us suppose that such actions, though not discoverable, were very numerous. Does Mr. Berlin really wish to claim that the moral justice, as opposed to the utility, of holding offenders responsible and punishing them, depends upon the existence of such actions—that we are morally entitled to punish only those whose wrong-doing was uncaused, or as is often said: "has no causal connection with their character"? This by now banal point can be put in another way. Suppose someone had discharged a pistol. Let us suppose that what we call the "action" is either the tensing of his finger or his "setting himself" to pull the trigger. Suppose also that we were able to show that this action was not determined by his mental or physical state —i.e., that when such states had occurred in the past, some other action had occurred. Does saying this commit one to saying that he could have done otherwise, that he acted freely? Would we want to call such a phenomenon an "action"? Would we want to call it *his* "action"? Wouldn't "he" and "his" as agent-language pronouns, lose their meaning? It seems that it would be more appropriate to say: "something else could have happened to him" (passive-voice, non-agent language) to indicate an intrusion into the person's life history. Isn't the function of: "he could have done otherwise," in contexts where blame and censure are pending, that of saying that the fault lies within the person, lies at his door rather than elsewhere? Aren't such statements blame statements? And don't we in fact react to them as accusations and not as statements about some barely conceivable state of affairs? Yet on the view that such statements imply that the person's behavior was not determined they become hopelessly speculative—hopelessly, because we can scarcely conceive of what it would be like to demonstrate the existence of undetermined "actions." To equate such statements with indeterminacy statements would be to give up our normally smooth ways of verifying agent-language statements like: "He did it."

If we were to accept Mr. Berlin's equivalence that a free action is an uncaused action, then we would have to accept the fact that we would never be able to show that a person's action was free or that he was responsible, since we have no way to find out whether his action was uncaused. Though Mr. Berlin may very well take this line, how does he account for the origin and persistence of: "he could have done otherwise"; "he acted freely," "he was responsible for his action," etc., when such statements cannot be supported except through demonstrating that a given action was uncaused— a feat quite beyond the skills of moral agents and their appraisers?

– III –

Historians, like everyone else, occasionally assert that a certain historical personage could have done otherwise—could have won a battle, could have pursued a different policy, etc. But what would be the point of their erudition concerning such a person if it is irrelevant to the judgment that he could have done otherwise—and it would be irrelevant to such a judgment if what they really should be trying to prove is that his action was undetermined. The historian's information about the character and temperament of an agent and the circumstances of his action may frequently be sufficient to answer questions like: Was the agent's action compelled? Could he have done otherwise? What caused him to do it? If the historian has reason enough to believe that there was no torture, threat, panic, insanity, etc., he is entitled to claim that the agent could have done otherwise; and it is obvious enough that what warrants such a claim does in no way warrant the claim that the agent's action was uncaused. Nor would the discovery of the specific causes of the agent's action be the discovery of the specific ways he was compelled to act, or the specific excuses he is entitled to plead. Before a certain cause-factor of an action is allowed to count against the assumption of moral responsibility, certain other requirements have to be met. But more of this later.

What I now wish to consider is whether there is any reason to think that a complete or ideal historical explanation of why a person acted as he did would make it impermissable to say that the person could have acted in some other way. Suppose that an historian explained certain promulgations and tactics of an aging monarch by saying that he wanted to leave a strong throne to his son; and this explanation was accepted because there was evidence to show that the monarch had expressed such intentions to others and had believed that a strong throne was necessary for the welfare of his kingdom, and that he had always acted in the interests of his kingdom, and that he had loved his son, etc. Does it follow that he couldn't have helped making any of his promulgations or maneuvers? Does it follow that because his actions were fully in accord with his wants and sentiments that he couldn't have done anything else? Is it not the case that when we claim that a person couldn't have helped doing what he did, we would also claim that even had he tried to avoid doing what he did, he would not have been successful? But does the evidence which would support the hypothesis that he wanted to leave a strong throne to his son, support this latter claim?

Again, suppose that an historian advanced the hypothesis, to explain certain actions of James the First, that he was a suspicious person. The historian proceeds to provide evidence of James' suspicious disposition from his diaries, remarks, and that there was no rational ground for these suspicions because no one had made any attempts on his life, nor had he uncovered any plots against him. Does it follow that if the historian has supported his explanation to our complete satisfaction that we must conclude that James couldn't have helped those actions which were accounted for by the hypothesis that he was a suspicious person? Have we showed that even if James had tried to do something else he would not have succeeded? Yet this is what should be showed if we wanted to claim that he couldn't have helped doing what he did, for this is one of the criteria which controls the application of this expression, particularly in those cases where serious harm has been done.

However, I believe that it is not explanations of this type that seem to threaten the historian's frequent claims that so and so could have formulated a different policy or could have married a commoner, etc. I think that what may seem to threaten the historian's right to make claims such as these is the possibility of explanations of the type used in physics eventually being applied to actions. In such explanations we do say that given certain initial states a certain event will follow, and that no other event could have occurred. Thus if actions are events, why can't we say that given certain conditions, the person couldn't have done otherwise?

Now there are certain conditions which if present do count as reasons for claiming that a person couldn't have done otherwise; i.e. torture, being physically overpowered, etc. But when such conditions are not present, we do not say that a person couldn't have done otherwise even though we are quite satisfied with the historian's explanation of his action. We can admit that a certain historical explanation is good without demanding that the explained action be the only one that can be deduced from the explaining statements. Making an action intelligible is not like making a physical event intelligible. The historian is not trying to show that given James' suspiciousness and certain other factors, that James could not have, in certain instances, acted in any other way. But the physicist does try to find some set of statements which will relate initial conditions or states in such a way that a certain event, and no other can be mathematically deduced. One of the controls upon his acceptance of a formula is that given a certain assignment of values to the variables of the formula, there is but one value of that variable, momentarily treated as dependent, which can be deduced. He would reject any proposed formula that would permit the deduction of multiple values (except if all but one of these had no physical meaning in a specific context). The fact that a certain value can be deduced from the values of the independent variables of a function is not a rigid enough condition to satisfy the physicist; it must be the only one. Since the formula is constructed with this restriction in mind, it is no surprise that the physicist's explanations do rule out an alternative event. Thus if we were to succeed in imposing this model of explanation upon the data of history, then we would indeed say that given the conditions which existed, no other action could have occurred. But this use of this expression does not imply what is implied by saying that a person couldn't have helped doing what he did or that he had no alternative or that he couldn't have done anything else. Paradigm uses of these expressions in contexts where the responsibility of an offender is in question imply that even though the person had tried to avoid doing what he did or had tried to prevent happening what did happen, he would not have succeeded; and sometimes that what he did or what happened was contrary to his wishes. But when the criterion of unique deducibility is employed as the sole reason for saying that no other action could have occurred, no such implication is intended, and consequently it does not follow that the agent is blameless.

Suppose that we wanted to know why James the First had such a suspicious disposition and that the ordinary concepts of the historian did not enable him to account for it, i.e. there were no plots on his life, no one made threatening remarks to him, etc. Let us also suppose that psychoanalytic theory was capable of giving us an explanation of James' paranoid tendencies with a rigor equal to that of any explanation in physics. If the historian conversant with this theory or the psychoanalyst knowing, as he would have to, the relevant historical data, could show that James' suspiciousness was caused by latent homosexuality—an hypothesis of Freud's [4] which in James' case is not implausible: consider his disinterest in women and his affection for handsome young men—would this show that James could not have helped doing those things which the concept of a suspicious disposition was invoked to explain? Certainly such a conclusion would not be supportable. It might be argued that it would have been at least difficult for James to have acted otherwise than he, on certain occasions, did act, given the cause of his suspiciousness. But from the fact that it is difficult for me to resist accepting a gift of money, it does not follow that on a certain occasion I couldn't have helped accepting it.

– IV –

When questions of responsibility arise we do not allow the fact that an action is uniquely deducible as a reason for saying that the person couldn't have done anything else. Such a fact about an action has not been integrated into our system of excuses. A typical function of "he couldn't have done otherwise" is to excuse the offender, to dismiss accusations of blame and fault, and it does so successfully when the reasons offered are like: He was tortured, shoved, insane, epileptic, had a heart attack, etc. It is plain enough that we do often make such statements when we are not able to deduce the action via causal laws, and even when we are, many conscientious moral appraisers still hold people responsible for their wrong actions even when they believe those actions are predictable.

I do not wish to claim that we *ought* not allow deducibility as a criterion for saying that the person couldn't have done otherwise when this carries its normal excusatory function. But if we were to do so, then on the assumption that every action is caused and that if we knew enough it would be deducible, "could have done otherwise" would no longer have any significance unless it can be showed to have it on indeterministic assumptions. But then we would no longer be able to contrast the responsibility of a man who did

[4] A methodological Critique of Freud's Schreber Analysis, p. 321, *The Psychoanalytic Review*, October 1955.

wrong because he wanted to and a man who was forced to do it. Should we give up this distinction? This would be a moral decision.

To hold that the cause of a wrong action is or ought to be its excuse is to hold a view which runs contrary to a distinction we as moral appraisers tend to make—a distinction between a man doing wrong because he has something to gain from it and a man who is tortured into doing it—a distinction between wanting and being forced to do something. Wants are not excuses unless they are uncontrollable, irresistible, etc. Most wants are not of this type. If all wants were *eo ipso* uncontrollable, the statement: "I wanted it badly, but I turned it down" would never be true; and there would be no point to adjectives like: irresistible, ungovernable, overpowering. Nor could the distinction between wanting and craving be used to extenuate wrong-doing. There would be no way of distinguishing between excusing and non-excusing factors of actions—no difference in the power to excuse between: "I did it to get even with him" and "I was tortured into doing it." Either of these statements can be true, yet only the latter is, when true, accepted as an excuse. On Mr. Berlin's view I can see no way of accounting for our practice of allowing the latter but not the former as an excuse unless he is prepared to allow for indeterminancy in the first case. Mr. Berlin believes that if we accept determinism as a fact then much of our moral language would disappear or be transformed.[5] But in order for this to happen we would not only have to accept determinism but also allow the cause of a wrong act as a defence against the charge of responsibility for it, which is of course what he says we *ought* to do if we grant determinism. But what sort of an "ought" is this? If it is the "ought" of "conceptually obliged" or "in order to be conceptually consistent," then I think he is wrong for the "could not have been otherwise" of causal discourse does not have the same implications for our moral evaluations of persons as does "couldn't have helped doing what he did." But if it is the moral "ought," where are the arguments for holding that since an action is caused or is uniquely deducible, the person is not morally responsible for it or ought not to be censured or treated as if he were morally responsible for it? Or is it a matter of categorical morality that he ought not be so regarded? I can conceive of such an attitude towards all actions but I would not say that it is morally the most desirable attitude to have in view of the possibility that as a consequence of such an attitude no one would ever be censured for his wrong doing.

Of course the circumstances of an action could be such that by means of a law they not only entail the action, but they also lead us to hold that the person couldn't have done anything else, where the latter is construed as a practical, excuse statement. This happens when these "circumstances" include any one of the following: torture, insanity, heart attack, being physically overpowered, etc. But if the premises from which we are able

[5] *Historical Inevitability* [p. 691, this volume].

to deduce the action do not contain reference to any of these excuse-factors then we have no commonly accepted reason for denying that the person is responsible. Sometimes when we have very good reasons for claiming that a person is responsible—like when we know that he was not insane, was not tortured *etc.*, we haven't the least notion of what caused him to act as he did: whether it was to show off or because he disliked someone or wanted revenge. An historian might know a great deal about a person and the circumstances of his action and yet find no excuse-factors. The only way he can explain the action is that the person wanted wealth and power and didn't much care whom he hurt to get these, and in such an explanation there is nothing that functions as a reason—given our current moral framework—for withholding blame and the ascription of responsibility. Before we are entitled to say that a person was not responsible for some wrong-doing, we must be able to show that one of the circumstances under which the act was performed belongs to a type of circumstances which does or ought to constitute an excuse.

– V –

". . . It is difficult to see how we come to distinguish acts to which responsibility is attached, from segments in a physical, psychical, or psycho-physical causal chain of events—a distinction signified . . . by a cluster of expressions which deal with open alternatives and free choices." [6] Now indeed such a distinction would be difficult if not impossible on the assumption that we can attach responsibility to an action only if it does *not* belong to a causal chain of events, for to show that an action or event does not have a cause would involve one in the difficulties mentioned in paragraph 3 of section II. But our normal ways of ascertaining whether a person is morally responsible for what happened or for what he did fortunately do not route us through these difficulties, since those that remain are not inconsiderable. In the remainder of this section I wish to expose these difficulties.

Many of our judgments that an agent is morally responsible for what he did or for what happened, are arrived at without perplexity. We appeal to some generally accepted criterion whose fulfillment in a particular case seems evident. Two such criteria of moral responsibility are that the agent did what he did intentionally, and that he could have helped doing what he did. If the evidence shows clearly that a person intentionally did something wrong or that he could have helped doing it, then without hesitation we judge him to be responsible. Perplexity arises when the evidence that the act was intentional is scanty, or when despite much evidence that the act was intentional, there is some fact which makes us hesitate or even want

[6] *Ibid.* [p. 680 this volume].

to deny that it was. For example, a paranoid murderer may have had a motive for killing, carefully planned it, and was quite aware of what he was doing when he killed his victim. Yet because of his delusions, we may judge that he is not morally responsible. Perplexity again arises when we think about a case of a dope addict who when the police are watching will not break into a store to steal money for dope, but when they are not around he will do so. When caught he may quite sincerely claim that he couldn't help doing what he did. Sometimes we can be quite certain that a person couldn't have helped doing what he did: the cases of being pushed and causing injury, and being tortured into making a confession. In such cases we grant that even though the person had wanted and tried to avoid doing what he did or what happened, he would not have succeeded. But though we should have no hesitation in saying that such a person is not morally responsible, it is difficult to know what to say about the dope addict. Were the person to suffer no unpleasant consequences should we judge him to be morally responsible, these cases would cause us no concern. But since the context in which we worry over such matters is one in which the person would be criticized or even punished, it is no small matter how we decide. On the other hand, if whenever we did not know what to say, we were to decide that he should not be treated as if he were responsible, we might pass up the opportunity to prevent him or others from performing such actions in the future. Since we should not be giving the community maximum protection, there is some moral ground for not deciding in this way. In those cases where it is difficult to decide whether either of our criteria apply, we make a decision based upon a balancing of our moral concerns for the offender and the community.

Despite the occasional difficulty in applying the concept of an intentional act, the evidence we consider relevant to its application has nothing to do with whether or not the action was caused. Likewise with the difficulty in applying the concept of an act that couldn't have been helped; we consider evidence about how hard the person tried, what most people would have done in his place, whether he acted under some sort of duress, etc. Since judgments that a person is or is not morally responsible are largely controlled by an appeal to such criteria, the difficulties of attributing moral responsibility have nothing to do with the issue of whether or not the action was caused or is a segment in a causal chain of events.

"Where the frontier between freedom and causal laws is to be determined is a crucial practical issue." [7] But by identifying freedom with the absence of causality it becomes a terribly speculative, metaphysical issue. Instead a crucial practical issue is: what are those causes of undesirable action that would make it morally improper to attribute responsibility to the agent in view of the fact that if we do regard him as morally responsible, he will receive various degrees of censure. To arrive at a morally scrupulous verdict,

[7] *Ibid.* [p. 683 this volume].

we need to know a great deal more about those influences which produce and corrupt character, about those immediate circumstances of action, e.g. duress, which make most people relatively impervious to the voice of their conscience and the punitive sanctions of the law, and a careful balancing of the moral concerns for the individual as well as the community.

– VI –

Mr. Berlin says: "If the belief in freedom—which rests on the assumption that human beings do occasionally choose, and that their choices are not wholly accounted for by the kind of causal explanations which are accepted in, say, physics, or biology. . . ." [8] Now the belief in freedom does not *rest* on the *assumption* that human beings occasionally choose—does not rest on the assumption of the reality of choice; it is more nearly *equivalent* in many cases to the belief in choice, and the reality of choice is not an assumption but a verifiable reality. There is a considerable parallel between the manner in which we support statements that a person acted freely and that he chose to do what he did. In many cases we would want to know whether physical compulsion, panic, overpowering desire, perhaps neurotic compulsion were present; we would want to know whether what he did was something that he wanted or desired to do (discussed the matter with others, whether he deliberated, made plans). It just isn't the case that we have to *assume* that a person made a choice before we can say he was free; we can *prove* one just as readily as the other.

If the question of whether men were free and responsible for their wrong actions was a question of whether their choices were uncaused, then their freedom and responsibility for these actions could never be established. How could the language of choice have ever developed when we would have no technique for knowing when to apply it to situations involving the appraisal of human behavior? How can such a concept be pertinent to the establishment of guilt and responsibility when we would never be able to tell when to apply it?

One final comment. Mr. Berlin says: "Yet the very meaning of such terms as 'cause' and 'inevitable' depends on the possibility of contrasting them at least with their imaginary opposites." [9] Quite so. "Not-inevitable" may mean: "subject to control, guidance, regulation"; "is avoidable," "can be gotten around." Determinism certainly does not imply that these expressions have no applicability, for obviously our knowledge of causal laws enables us to control or avoid or achieve a certain result or outcome. Only a complete fatalism implies that none of these expressions apply to human affairs.

[8] *Ibid.* [p. 681 this volume].
[9] *Ibid.* [p. 680 this volume].

[39] The Freudian Conception of Man and the Continuity of Nature

JEROME S. BRUNER

Our concern is with conceptions of man, with the forces and ideas that have given shape to our contemporary image of man. I need not insist upon the social, ethical, and political significance of this image for it is patent that the view one takes of man affects profoundly one's standard of the humanly possible. And it is in the light of such a standard that we establish our laws, set our aspirations for learning, and judge the fitness of men's acts. It is no surprise, then, that those who govern must perforce be jealous guardians of man's ideas about man, for the structure of government rests upon an uneasy consensus about human nature and human wants. The idea of man is of the order of *res publica,* and by virtue of its public status the idea is not subject to change without public debate. The "behavioral scientist," as some people nowadays insist on calling him, may propose, but society at large disposes. Nor is the idea of man simply a matter of public concern. For man as individual has a deep and emotional investment in his image of himself. If we have learned anything in the last half-century of psychology, it is that man has powerful and exquisite capacities for defending himself against violations of his cherished self-image. This is not to say that Western man has not persistently asked: "What is man that thou art mindful of him?" It is only that the question, when pressed, brings us to the edge of anxiety where inquiry is no longer free.

By the dawn of the sixth century before Christ, the Greek physicist-philosophers had formulated a bold conception of the physical world as a unitary material phenomenon. The Ionics had set forth a conception of matter as fundamental substance, transformation of which accounted for the myriad forms and substances of the physical world. Anaximander was subtle enough to recognize that matter must be viewed as a generalized substance, free of any particular sensuous properties. Air, iron, water or bone were only elaborated forms, derived from a more general stuff. Since that time, the physical world has been conceived as continuous and monistic, as governed by the common laws of matter. The view was a bold one,

Reprinted from *Daedalus,* **87,** 1958, pp. 77–84, with permission of the author, the editor, and the American Academy of Arts and Sciences.

bold in the sense of running counter to the immediate testimony of the senses. It has served as an axiomatic basis of physics for more than two millennia. The bold view eventually became the obvious view, and it gave shape to our common understanding of the physical world. Even the alchemists rested their case upon this doctrine of material continuity and, indeed, had they known about neutron bombardment, they might even have hit upon the proper philosopher's stone.

The good fortune of the physicist—and these matters are always relative, for the material monism of physics may have impeded nineteenth-century thinking and delayed insights into the nature of complementarity in modern physical theory—this early good fortune or happy insight has no counterpart in the sciences of man. Lawful continuity between man and the animal kingdom, between dreams and unreason on one side and waking rationality on the other, between madness and sanity, between consciousness and unconsciousness, between the mind of a child and the adult mind, between primitive and civilized man—each of these has been a cherished discontinuity preserved in doctrinal canons. There were voices in each generation, to be sure, urging the exploration of continuities. Anaximander had a passing good approximation to a theory of evolution based on natural selection; Cornelius Agrippa offered a plausible theory of the continuity of mental health and disease in terms of bottled-up sexuality. But Anaximander did not prevail against Greek conceptions of man's creation nor Cornelius Agrippa against the demonopathy of the *Malleus Maleficarum.* Neither in establishing the continuity between the varied states of man nor in pursuing the continuity between man and animal was there conspicuous success until the nineteenth century.

In speaking, then, of the changing conceptions of man that have inspirited our modern world perspective, I shall be discussing the battle for the acceptance of continuities, indeed, the battle for the right to explore such continuities.

Two figures stand out massively as the architects of our present-day conception of man: Darwin and Freud. Freud's was the more daring, the more revolutionary, and in a deep sense, the more poetic insight. But Freud is inconceivable without Darwin. It is both timely and perhaps historically just to center our inquiry on Freud's contribution to the modern image of man. Darwin I shall treat as a necessary condition for Freud and for his success; recognizing, of course, that this is a form of psychological license.

Rear-guard fundamentalism did not require a Darwin to slay it in an age of technology. He helped, but this contribution was trivial in comparison with another. What Darwin had done was to propose a set of principles unified around the conception that all organic species had their origins and took their form from a common set of circumstances—the requirements of biological survival. All living creatures were on a common footing. When the post-Darwin era of exaggeration had passed and religious literalism had abated into a new nominalism, what remained was a broad, orderly, and unitary conception of organic nature, a vast continuity from the mono-cellular protozoans to man. Biology had at last found its unifying principle in the doctrine of evolution. Man was not unique but the inheritor of an organic legacy.

As the summit of an evolutionary process, man could still view himself with smug satisfaction, indeed proclaim that God or Nature had shown a persistent wisdom in its effort to produce a final, perfect product. It re-mained for Freud to present the image of man as the unfinished product of nature: struggling against unreason, impelled by driving inner vicissi-tudes and urges that had to be contained if man was to live in society, host alike to seeds of madness and majesty, never fully free from an infancy any-thing but innocent. What Freud was proposing was that man at his best and man at his worst is subject to a common set of explanations: that good and evil grow from a common process.

Freud was strangely yet appropriately fitted for his role as architect of a new conception of man. We must pause to examine his qualifications, for the image of man that he created was in no small measure founded on his painfully achieved image of himself and of his times. We are concerned not so much with his psychodynamics, but with the intellectual traditions he embodies. A child of his century's materialism, he was wedded to the deter-minism and the classical physicalism of nineteenth-century physiology so boldly represented by Helmholtz. Indeed, the young Freud's devotion to the exploration of anatomical structures was a measure of the strength of this inheritance. But at the same time, as both Lionel Trilling and W. H. Auden have recognized with much sensitivity, there was a deep current of romanticism in Freud—a sense of the role of impulse, of the drama of life, of the power of symbolism, of ways of knowing that were more poetic than rational in spirit, of the poet's cultural alienation. It was perhaps this romantic's sense of drama that led to his gullibility about parental seduction and to his generous susceptibility to the fallacy of the dramatic instance.

Freud also embodies two traditions almost as antithetical as romanticism and nineteenth-century scientism. He was profoundly a Jew, not in a doc-trinal sense but in his conception of morality, in his love of the skeptical play of reason, in his distrust of illusion, in the form of his prophetic talent, even in his conception of mature eroticism. His prophetic talent was antithetic to a Utopianism either of innocence or of social control. Nor did it lead to a counsel of renunciation. Free oneself of illusion, of neurotic infantilism, and "the soft voice of intellect" would prevail. Wisdom for Freud was neither doctrine nor formula, but the achievement of maturity. The patient who is cured is the one who is now free enough of neurosis to decide intelligently about his own destiny. As for his conception of mature love, it has always seemed to me that its blend of tenderness and sensuality combined both the uxorious imagery of the Chassidic tradition and the sensual quality of the Song of Songs. And might it not have been Freud rather than a commentator of the Haftorahs who said, "In children,

it was taught, God gives humanity a chance to make good its mistakes."
For the modern trend of permissiveness toward children is surely a feature
of the Freudian legacy.

But for all the Hebraic quality, Freud is also in the classical tradition—
combining the Stoics and the great Greek dramatists. For Freud, as for the
Stoics, there is no possibility of man's disobeying the laws of nature. And
yet, it is in this lawfulness that for him the human drama inheres. His love
for Greek drama and his use of it in his formulation are patent. The sense
of the human tragedy, the inevitable working out of the human plight—
these are the hallmarks of Freud's case histories. When Freud, the tragic
dramatist, becomes a therapist, it is not to intervene as a directive authority.
The therapist enters the drama of the patient's life, makes possible a
play within a play, the transference, and when the patient has "worked
through" and understood the drama, he has achieved the wisdom necessary
for freedom. Again, as with the Stoics, it is in the recognition of one's own
nature and in the acceptance of the laws that govern it that the good life
is to be found.

Freud's contribution lies in the continuities of which he made us aware.
The first of these is the continuity of organic lawfulness. Accident in human
affairs was no more to be brooked as "explanation" than accident in nature.
The basis for accepting such an "obvious" proposition had, of course, been
well prepared by a burgeoning nineteenth-century scientific naturalism. It
remained for Freud to extend naturalistic explanation to the heart of human affairs. *The Psychopathology of Everyday Life* is not one of Freud's
deeper works, but "the Freudian slip" has contributed more to the common
acceptance of lawfulness in human behavior than perhaps any of the more
rigorous and academic formulations from Wundt to the present day. The
forgotten lunch engagement, the slip of the tongue, the barked shin could
no longer be dismissed as accident. Why Freud should have succeeded where
the novelists, philosophers, and academic psychologists had failed we will
consider in a moment.

Freud's extension of Darwinian doctrine beyond Haeckel's theorem that
ontogeny recapitulates phylogeny is another contribution to continuity. It
is the conception that in the human mind, the primitive, infantile, and
archaic exist side-by-side with the civilized and evolved.

Where animals are concerned we hold the view that the most highly developed
have arisen from the lowest. . . . In the realm of mind, on the other hand, the
primitive type is so commonly preserved alongside the transformations which have
developed out of it that it is superfluous to give instances in proof of it. When
this happens, it is usually the result of a bifurcation in development. One quantitative part of an attitude or an impulse has survived unchanged while another
has undergone further development. This brings us very close to the more general
problem of conservation in the mind. . . . Since the time when we recognized the
error of supposing that ordinary forgetting signified destruction or annihilation

of the memory-trace, we have been inclined to the opposite view that nothing once formed in the mind could ever perish, that everything survives in some way or other, and is capable under certain conditions of being brought to light again. . . .[1]

What has now come to be common sense is that in every man there are potentialities for criminality and that these are neither accidents nor visitations of degeneracy, but products of a delicate balance of forces that, under different circumstances, might have produced normality or even saintliness. Good and evil, in short, grow from a common root.

Freud's genius was in his resolution of polarities. The distinction of child and adult was one such. It did not suffice to reiterate that the child was father to the man. The theory of infantile sexuality and the stages of psychosexual development were an effort to fill the gap; the latter clumsy, the former elegant. Though the alleged progression of sexual expression from the oral, to the anal, to the phallic, and finally to the genital has not found a secure place either in common sense or in general psychology; the developmental continuity of sexuality has been recognized by both. Common sense honors the continuity in the baby books and in the permissiveness with which young parents of today resolve their doubts. And the research of Beach and others has shown the profound effects of infantile experience on adult sexual behavior even in lower organisms.

If today people are reluctant to report their dreams with the innocence once attached to such recitals, it is again because Freud brought into common question the discontinuity between the rational purposefulness of waking life and the seemingly irrational purposelessness of fantasy and dream. While the crude symbolism of Freud's early efforts at dream interpretation has come increasingly to be abandoned—that telephone poles and tunnels have an invariant sexual reference—the conception of the dream as representing disguised wishes and fears has become common coin. And Freud's recognition of deep unconscious processes in the creative act, let it also be said, has gone far toward enriching our understanding of the kinship between the artist, the humanist, and the man of science.

Finally, it is our heritage from Freud that the all-or-none distinction between mental illness and mental health has been replaced by a more humane conception of the continuity of these states. The view that neurosis is a severe reaction to human trouble is as revolutionary in its implications for social practice as it is daring in formulation. The "bad seed" theories, the nosologies of the nineteenth century, the demonologies and doctrines of divine punishment—none of these provided a basis for compassion toward human suffering comparable to that of our time.

One may argue, finally, that Freud's sense of the continuity of human conditions, of the likeness of the human plight, has made possible a deeper sense of the brotherhood of man. It has in any case tempered the spirit of punitiveness toward what once we took as evil and what we now see as sick.

[1] Freud, *Civilization and Its Discontents*, pp. 14–15.

We have not yet resolved the dilemma posed by these two ways of viewing. Its resolution is one of the great moral challenges of our age.

Why, after such initial resistance, were Freud's views so phenomenally successful in transforming common conceptions of man?

One reason we have already considered: the readiness of the Western world to accept naturalistic explanation of organic phenomena and, concurrently, to be readier for such explanation in the mental sphere. There had been at least four centuries of uninterrupted scientific progress, recently capped by a theory of evolution that brought man into continuity with the rest of the animal kingdom. The rise of naturalism as a way of understanding nature and man witnessed a corresponding decline in the explanatory aspirations of religion. By the close of the nineteenth century, religion, to use Morton White's phrase, "too often agreed to accept the role of a non-scientific spiritual grab-bag, or an ideological know-nothing." The elucidation of the human plight had been abandoned by religion and not yet adopted by science.

It was the inspired imagery, the proto-theory of Freud that was to fill the gap. Its success in transforming the common conception of man was not simply its recourse to the "cause-and-effect" discourse of science. Rather it is Freud's imagery, I think, that provides the clue to his ideological power.

It is an imagery of necessity, if I may call it that, an imagery that combines the dramatic, the tragic, and the scientific views of necessity. It is here that Freud's intellectual heritage matters so deeply. Freud's is a theory or a proto-theory peopled with actors. The characters are from life: the blind, energic, pleasure-seeking id; the priggish and punitive superego; the ego, battling for its being by diverting the energy of the others to its own use. The drama has an economy and a terseness. The ego develops canny mechanisms for dealing with the threat of id impulses: denial, projection, and the rest. Balances are struck between the actors, and in the balance are character and neurosis. Freud was using the dramatic technique of decomposition, the play whose actors are parts of a single life. It is a technique that he himself had recognized in phantasies and dreams, one which is honored in his essay, *The Poet and the Daydream*.

The imagery of the theory, moreover, has an immediate resonance with the dialectic of experience. True, it is not the stuff of superficial conscious experience. But it fits the human plight, its conflict, its private torment, its impulsiveness, its secret and frightening urges, its tragic quality.

Concerning its scientific imagery, it is marked by the necessity of the classical mechanics. At times the imagery is hydraulic: suppress this stream of impulses, and perforce it breaks out in a displacement elsewhere. The system is a closed and mechanical one. At times it is electrical, as when cathexes are formed and withdrawn like electrical charges. The way of thought fitted well the common-sense physics of its age.

Finally, the image of man presented was thoroughly secular; its ideal type was the mature man free of infantile neuroticism, capable of finding his own way. This freedom from both utopianism and asceticism has earned Freud the contempt of ideological totalitarians of the Right and the Left. But the image has found a ready home in the rising, liberal intellectual middle class. For them, the Freudian ideal type has become a rallying point in the struggle against spiritual regimentation.

I have said virtually nothing about Freud's equation of sexuality and impulse. It was surely and still is a stimulus to resistance. But to say that Freud's success lay in forcing a reluctant Victorian world to accept the importance of sexuality is as empty as hailing Darwin for his victory over fundamentalism. Each had a far more profound effect.

Can Freud's contribution to the common understanding of man in the twentieth century be likened to the impact of such great physical and biological theories as Newtonian physics and Darwin's conception of evolution? The question is tempting, but not appropriate. Freud's mode of thought is not a theory in the conventional sense, it is a metaphor, an analogy, a way of conceiving man, a drama. I would propose that Anaximander is the proper parallel: his view of the connectedness of physical nature was also an analogy—and a powerful one. Freud is the ground from which theory will grow, and he has prepared the twentieth century to nurture the growth. But, far more important, he has provided an image of man that has made him comprehensible without at the same time making him contemptible.

[40] Psychoanalysis and Moral Language

P . H . N O W E L L - S M I T H

In this essay I do not propose to discuss the changes which discoveries in psychoanalysis might be expected to have on our moral code or outlook, but the more limited subject of the effect which they might have on our use of moral language. Moral language is the language that we use in choosing and advising, for appraising human conduct, for praising, blaming, excusing, and ascribing responsibility. It is emphatically a department

Reprinted from *The Rationalist Annual*, 1954, with kind permission of the author and the Rationalist Press Association.

of "ordinary language," language that is on everybody's lips and is not the prerogative of specialists. But ordinary language cannot be sharply separated from technical, scientific language. As scientific knowledge that was at one time the concern of specialists is gradually disseminated, so the concepts used in science seep into and modify the language used for everyday purposes. New knowledge about the world often involves shifts in the meanings of words, and philosophical *malaise* is often due to trying to put new wine into old bottles—trying to give expression to the new knowledge while at the same time sticking closely to meanings which words had at a time when knowledge was less advanced.

I propose to assume that certain very general truths have been established by psychoanalysts and work out the consequences which these could have for the ordinary man's concepts of freedom and responsibility. "Could" rather than "must," since, as we shall see, discoveries never force us to make any particular linguistic move. Rather they force us to adopt one or another of a number of alternative adjustments. It is, of course, a large assumption to say that these truths have been *established;* they certainly have not; but it is enough that they might be. Psychoanalysis has reached a stage at which moral philosophers can no longer afford to ignore it; and in any case it is interesting to work out what implications for freedom and responsibility psychoanalysis would have if its discoveries were true.

Since the dawn of scientific psychology in the eighteenth century there has been a tendency, first gradual and now accelerating, to transfer undesirable modes of behavior from the list of crimes to be punished to the list of diseases to be cured. This can be explained on the grounds that punishment is a necessary evil and that, wherever possible, medical and educational cures and prophylactics should be substituted for penal sanctions. Thus, if it is true that pre-frontal leucotomy will improve a man's character and conduct, we should operate on him; and if it is true that premature weaning causes aggressive tendencies in later life, it is better to encourage late weaning than to increase the penalties imposed on aggression. It is both more "enlightened" and more effective.

Discoveries in physiology and psychology, and the tendency which they bring in their train to resort to medicine and education in place of punishment, involve no revolutionary change either in our moral outlook or in our moral use of language. The list of crimes becomes shorter, but the distinction between "crime" and "disease" remains what it always was: a distinction based on appropriate methods of treatment. But the impact of *psychoanalysis* is different and much more disturbing. It is a moral axiom that a man cannot be held responsible or held to deserve punishment if he "couldn't help it," if his action was not voluntary. Now "voluntary action" is not the same as "deliberate choice"—for example, habitual and impulsive actions are voluntary, but not deliberately chosen—but it is in cases of deliberate choice that we want to say that the agent was both free and responsible in the fullest sense. And psychoanalysis is disturbing because it appears to show that, even when a man in a calm, reflective moment deliberates and decides to do something for reasons of which he is fully aware, his choice is in fact determined, not by the reasons that he gives to himself, but by subconscious forces of which he is not even aware, still less in control.

The argument runs as follows: (a) It is well known that the behavior of neurotics is due to subconscious forces. The neurotic hand-washer claims (and sincerely believes) that his hands are dirty and that he decides to wash them for that reason. When it is pointed out that they are not, he says: "But they still feel dirty." He thinks that he decides to wash them, but we know better; his free, rational decision is an illusion. His conduct is determined by the subconscious forces working out their drama in the dark recesses of his troubled soul. There is no cause for philosophical *malaise* here. He, unlike us, is the victim of a disease. We are content to say that in his case freedom is an illusion, that his alleged reasons are rationalizations; and part of the force of the word "neurotic" is just to draw attention to the difference between him and the ordinary, non-neurotic man.

(b) But the shoe begins to pinch when the psychoanalyst goes on to tell us that we are *all* neurotic; and it is important to notice just what he means by this. It is not that every man is sometimes actuated by subconscious motives. If this were so, the question whether a given man were to be classed as "neurotic" or not would be a question of the extent to which his behavior was subconsciously determined. (Compare the question: "How many inches must a man have to be classed as tall?") The psychoanalyst seems to be saying that *all* our behavior is due to subconscious motives, even the most carefully planned action of the most healthy man. Even the decision of an ordinary man to marry and raise a family or to accept a well-paid post that he thinks he is competent to fill is due to desires repressed in infancy. And this seems to entail that the "reasons" he gives to himself do not really affect his decision. His conscious mind and will are puppets activated by wires pulled by his subconscious. *All* reasons are rationalizations.

This leads us at once into a paradox which has often been thought to refute the psychoanalyst's theory. If the theory is true, the psychoanalyst can have no good reason for believing it, since the reasons he advances must be rationalizations. The paradox cannot be fully elucidated here; but the short answer is that the psychological *causes* of my believing something are irrelevant to the question whether I have good *reasons* for believing it. The man who accepts the well-paid job may have good reasons, even though his action could also be explained by a psychoanalyst in terms of subconcious causes.

What are the consequences of this theory for responsibility? We seem to be on the horns of a dilemma. For we want to retain the moral axiom that a man can only be held responsible for actions that are under his control. Yet, if the psychoanalyst is right, all our actions are due to events which occurred in our infancy. Since these were not under our control, their inevitable consequences cannot be either. So it looks as if one of the necessary conditions of responsibility never in fact obtains. At first sight there seem to be two ways out of this predicament. Either we must, in the interests of morality, deny the psychoanalyst's theory (a somewhat ostrich-like course that we have agreed for the purpose of this essay not to take), or we must admit that freedom and responsibility are illusions. *Tout comprendre, c'est tout pardonner;* blame and punishment are always unjust, since the necessary condition, that the agent could have helped it, is never true.

Our philosophical *malaise* is due, I think, to an unwillingness to take either of these courses and to the belief that we must take one or the other. This belief is false; we can escape between the horns of the dilemma by making certain adjustments in our moral language. Before suggesting what these might be I must first say something about the connection between scientific and ordinary language.

All sciences begin with metaphors and myths. Geometrical optics, for example, begins with the conception of light as "travelling" in straight lines. This way of thinking of seeing as an affair of light travelling from an illuminated object to our eyes is now part of the mental equipment of the ordinary man; he doesn't learn it at school; it is enshrined in the language about seeing that he learns in the nursery. Yet "travelling" is a metaphor, and its introduction was once revolutionary. It requires a considerable feat of imagination on our part to think of seeing, as the Greeks did, as an affair of having antennae-like eyes which reach out and grasp the objects that we see.[1] Similarly, three hundred years after Galileo and Newton, all of us, and not only physicists, use words such as "energy" and "force" in ways that would have been unintelligible in the Middle Ages.

But, although the language of natural science infected our ordinary talk about material things, it did not begin to infect our moral and psychological language until the words that had been introduced metaphorically into physics had acquired a new status within that science. In the eighteenth century, when physics was a science and psychology was not, the concepts of physics were used to elucidate human conduct. We learned to talk of desires as "forces" or "springs of action" or "inclinations." Whenever conceptions that have a stable use in one context are metaphorically introduced into another a certain strain arises. The new facts to be explained must be in some ways like the old, otherwise the metaphor would have no point. But they must also be in other ways unlike, otherwise the use would not be metaphorical. And we are tempted to ask about desires all the questions that we know make sense when asked about forces, since we forget that, in their new context, some of these questions may be unanswerable because they have not yet been given a meaning. We are also tempted to ask puzzling questions like "Are desires really forces?" when we ought to

[1] I am indebted for this illustration and for part of the substance of this passage to Mr. S. E. Toulmin, *The Philosophy of Science.*

ask "How far does the comparison of desires with forces throw light on what it is to desire something?"

Freudian psychoanalysis has introduced a new set of myths and metaphors, or rather returned to a much older set. The Ego, the Superego, and the Id are sometimes thought of as internal forces, but more often in a more Platonic way as little men inside us that tell us what to do. The old political analogy is replacing the mechanical analogy again; the Censor is taking the place of the thermostat. Now there is nothing wrong with myth and metaphor; as I said, all sciences begin with them. But we must recognize them for what they are. And here we can get some help from studying something that puzzled Newton. *"Hypotheses non fingo."* Newton did not mean by this that he did not construct what we should now call "hypotheses"; that is precisely what he was doing. He meant that he did not, as a physicist, indulge in speculation about the unseen causes that underlie gravitational phenomena. He seems to have thought that "knowing what gravity really is" is different from and somehow deeper than "being able to calculate and predict the movements of bodies by means of gravitational formulae"; and that, while he, as a physicist, was only concerned with the latter, a true philosopher would be concerned with the former.

Nowadays we should reject as senseless the sort of speculation that Newton rejected as being beyond his scope. To understand what gravity is in the way in which he understood it just *is* to understand what gravity is: the very meaning of the word lies in the use made of the formulae. In the same way a man who knows under what conditions a piece of copper wire is electrified and a host of similar facts organized into a theory knows what electricity is. To treat the observed phenomena as the effects of an occult cause called "electricity" is to make a logical mistake. It was an easy mistake to make, since the men who first investigated electrical phenomena found the metaphor of a "fluid" a useful one; and the effects of a flowing stream are indeed effects of a cause, though not of an occult one.

We may now apply this to psychoanalytic theory. When we explain a neurotic's behavior as being "due to unseen forces working out their drama in his subconscious," we must remember that the cash-value, the meaning of this phrase lies solely in the fact that certain types of behavior can be predicted and, above all, cured if the phenomena are thought of as conforming to a pattern in which concepts like "Ego," "Superego," and "Id" play an explanatory role. Explanation in terms of these concepts is more like explanation in terms of gravity than in terms of the engine under the bonnet which makes the wheels go round. To take the theory as a description of what goes on inside rather than as an explanation of overt behavior is to make the same sort of mistake as that of the man who thinks that the orbit of a planet is an invisible rail on which it runs or that electricity is a subtle fluid flowing inside the wire.

Let us consider in this connection the concept of "compulsion." As used in psychology it is evidently a metaphor; compulsions are not little things inside you that a surgeon could discover, although it *may* be the case that every compulsion is correlated with a particular state of some part of the nervous system that surgeons could identify. It would be highly speculative to say that one day surgeons will be able to point to physical differences between kleptomaniacs and ordinary men in the same way that they can now point to physical differences between nearsighted and ordinary men. All we can say about this is that the speculation looks plausible and might turn out to be correct; at the moment it is quite unnecessary to psychology. The metaphor of compulsion is much older than Freud, older even than the concept of desires as forces. It is enshrined in ordinary language of great antiquity in such phrases as being a "victim of" or a "slave to" one's desires.

Why, then, do we use just this metaphor? The reason seems to lie in our trying to adapt a new kind of excuse to old moral language. Compulsion, in the literal sense of "pushing," is one of the most obvious and cast-iron forms of exculpation. If a man treads on my toes I cease to be angry with him if I discover that he was pushed. And we extend the concept of compulsion to cover psychological compulsions, not because we have isolated and identified the little thing inside the kleptomaniac that pushes him, but because we want to excuse him in the same sort of way that we want to excuse the man who is literally compelled. And we want to excuse him for the same sort of reason—namely, that we know that neither punishment nor chiding nor appeals to his moral principles will do him any good.

I come now to the possible adjustments that we could make in our moral language to accommodate the new discoveries. There are two:

a. We could retain our old definition of "freedom" according to which it is self-contradictory to say that the same action is both free and also determined by subconscious motives. If we do this and at the same time admit the truth of the psychoanalyst's theory, we relegate free actions to the limbo in which centaurs and hippogriffs reside; they will be objects that might, as far as logic goes, exist, but happen not to. But even so, we need not go on to say that no man should be held responsible for his actions. All we have to do is to decide that "being free" is no longer to be a necessary condition of "being responsible." Neither kleptomaniacs nor thieves can now be called free; but there will still be a reason for distinguishing between them in point of responsibility. In technical language, this amounts to retaining the connotation of the word "free" and altering—in fact eliminating—its denotation. We shall have to say that the actions we previously called "free" were not free at all.

b. We could alter the connotation of "free" and retain its denotation. This means that we shall go on calling those actions free that we have always called free, among them the deliberate actions of the normal man; but we shall now have to say that "being free" is no longer incompatible with "being determined by subconscious motives." For reasons to be given later, this is the course that I should be inclined to adopt; but it obviously raises the problem of providing a criterion for distinguishing the neurotic from the healthy man, since subconscious motivation is common to both.

It is worth noticing that we already have at hand in ordinary language a distinction that might help us for a start—namely, that between "wanting" and "craving." This distinction is not simply one of strength. The man who suffers from a craving (for example, addiction to opium or tobacco) at the same time very much wants to stop doing what he has a craving to do; and he also knows that, no matter how much he wants to stop, he cannot. But the man who merely wants to do something, even if he wants to do it very much, is not in the same case. He knows, for example, that if he discovered a good reason for not going to the cinema—such as a request from a sick aunt to pay her a visit or a sudden loss of money—he just would not go. The opium-addict, on the other hand, knows that even though he has the best of reasons for refraining (he is undermining his health), he will not in fact refrain.

Now this distinction will remain even if it is true in both cases that action is determined by subconscious motives. We can distinguish between the neurotic and the healthy man by saying that the actions of the former are determined by *malevolent* subconscious motives; and we call these motives "malevolent" when they determine a man to do what in his calm, reflective moments he consciously wants not to do or if they determine him to do things that lead to remorse and shame. In practice these criteria will largely coincide.

On this theory the subconscious motive that "drives" me to the cinema will not be a malevolent one, since it does not make me do anything that I do not consciously want to do or—what is more important—anything which I think I ought not to do. The fear that psychoanalytic theory makes nonsense of the notion of "moral principles" is quite groundless; what it does is to give us deeper insight into what sort of things moral principles are. My moral principles are those modes of conduct that, in my conscious mind, I regard as right; and the fact (if it is a fact) that my moral principles are what they are because I saw something nasty in the woodshed at the age of two does not affect their status as my moral principles. (Nor, though this is a different point, does it have any bearing on the question whether they are good or bad ones.) We have always known that early parental teaching and guidance shape a man's moral principles—why else should we bother to educate our children?—and it should not be so very surprising to discover that other factors in early life also help to shape them or that parental teaching and guidance sometimes shape them in unexpected ways.

If we adopt these criteria for distinguishing between the neurotic and the healthy man, we can define "freedom" by saying that a man is free in inverse proportion to his neuroticism. The free man will not be the man whose actions are least determined by subconscious motives, but the man whose subconscious motives drive him for the most part in the direction that he most wishes to go. He will be the well-adjusted man, the man who least feels the painful emotions of shame, remorse, and frustration. "Well-adjusted" here means internally well-adjusted; the free man will not necessarily be the best man or the best adjusted to his fellows, but he is very likely to be. There is a high correlation between criminal and anti-social tendencies and psychological maladjustment.

This way of looking at the contrast between the neurotic and the healthy man involves an objection that must be removed. "Malevolent" and "well-adjusted" are value-words; and does not their use beg the question? I do not think it does here, any more than the use of value-words begs questions in economics or in medicine. Whatever they may say, psychoanalysts can no more be "ethically neutral" than doctors. For psychoanalysis is, like medicine, not a science but a practical art; and practical arts always involve explicit or implicit value-judgments. The doctor does not need to interest himself in the question "What does 'good health' mean?" for the purpose of diagnosing and curing ill health; his value-judgments about health are not so much part of his professional equipment as presuppositions of its use. Similarly, if we think of the psychoanalyst as a psychiatrist rather than as a psychologist, as interested more in the cure than in the description and explanation of mental disease, there can be no harm in our defining "neurotic" and "healthy" in a way that presupposes that we have made a prior estimate of what good and bad mental health are.

This is, I think, the way in which psychoanalysis should be regarded at the moment, no matter how hotly some psychoanalysts would deny it. Most sciences begin in technology, with the attempt to answer practical questions. Mechanics, for example, began when people started, for practical reasons, to investigate the properties of clocks and projectiles. While a science is at this pre-scientific stage it gains nothing by trying to ape the fully-fledged theoretical sciences; and there has been too much of this sort of thing in psychology already. The descriptive and explanatory "hypotheses" of the psychoanalyst are but sham "hypotheses." They use the language of metaphor, and young sciences do not become adult until their metaphorical concepts (light "travelling" and electricity "flowing") acquire a technical meaning of their own within the science. The borrowed conceptions of the psychoanalyst are not yet within sight of getting out of this metaphorical stage; and when they do, there will no longer be the same tendency to think of the Id as a vicious and the Censor as a virtuous man inside each of us.

We are faced, then, with a choice between altering the connotation and altering the denotation of the word "free." For my part I should unhesitatingly choose the former. It is always dangerous to monkey with the denotation of a word, since it is difficult to remember that we must no longer use it to apply to the things it has always been applied to. Could we, without confusion and self-deception, learn to say of what appears to be a deliberate action that it was not free? Even if we could, we should only be depriving ourselves of a very useful word. On the other hand, there is far less strain involved in learning to say "The actions that have always been called free are still to be called free; only now, thanks to Freud, we know better in what our freedom consists." We are already familiar with the way in which the connotation of a word changes as knowledge develops; and the alteration does not greatly change the connotation of "free." Two of its most important logical liaisons—namely, those with "doing what I want to do" and with "being responsible"—remain unaffected.

[41] Natural Laws and Natural Rights

MARGARET MACDONALD

Doctrines of natural law and natural rights have a long and impressive history from the Stoics and Roman jurists to the Atlantic Charter and Roosevelt's Four Freedoms.[1] That men are entitled to make certain claims by virtue simply of their common humanity has been equally passionately defended and vehemently denied. Punctured by the cool scepticism of Hume; routed by the contempt of Bentham for 'nonsense upon stilts'; submerged by idealist and Marxist philosophers in the destiny of the totalitarian state; the claim to 'natural rights' has never been quite defeated. It tends in some form to be renewed in every crisis in human affairs, when the plain citizen tries to make, or expects his leaders to make, articulate his obscure, but firmly held, conviction that he is not a mere pawn in any political game, nor the property of any government or ruler, but the living and protesting individual for whose sake all political games are played and

Originally published under the title "Natural Rights" in the *Proceedings of the Aristotelian Society*, 1946–47, XLVII, 225–250, and reprinted with kind permission of the Editor of the Aristotelian Society.

[1] Freedom of Speech and Worship; Freedom from Want and Fear of all persons everywhere.

all governments instituted. As one of Cromwell's soldiers expressed it to that dictator: 'Really, sir, I think that the poorest he that is in England hath a life to live as the greatest he.' [2]

It could, perhaps, be proved hedonistically that life for most ordinary citizens is more *comfortable* in a democratic than a totalitarian state. But would an appeal for effort, on this ground, have been sanctioned between 1939–45? However true, it would have been rejected as inefficient because *uninspired*. Who could be moved to endure 'blood and toil, tears and sweat' for the sake of a little extra comfort? What, then, supplied the required inspiration? An appeal to the instinct of national self-preservation? But societies have been known to collapse inexplicably almost without waiting to be physically defeated. No doubt there are several answers, but at least one, I suggest, was an appeal to the values of freedom and equality among men. An appeal to safeguard and restore, where necessary, the Rights of Man, those ultimate points at which authority and social differences vanish, leaving the solitary individual with his essential human nature, according to one political theory, or a mere social fiction, according to another.

All this sounds very obscure. And the doctrine of natural law and of the natural rights of men is very obscure—which justifies the impatience of its opponents. It seems a strange law which is unwritten, has never been enacted, and may be unobserved without penalty, and peculiar rights which are possessed antecedently to all specific claims within an organized society. Surely, it will be said, the whole story now has only historical interest as an example of social mythology? Nothing is so dead as dead ideology. All this may be true,[3] but nevertheless the doctrine is puzzling. For if it is sheer nonsense why did it have psychological, political and legal effects? Men do not reflect and act upon collections of meaningless symbols or nonsense rhymes.

There seems no doubt that the assertions of certain Greek philosophers about the 'natural' equality of men and their consequent right to freedom caused intelligent contemporaries to become uneasy about the institution of slavery;[4] that doctrines of the primal Rights of Man were significantly connected with the French and American Revolutions. It even seems probable that the Communist Manifesto owed much of its success not to its 'scientific' analysis of capitalist society, but to its denouncement of a wage slavery degrading to human nature and its appeal to all workers to assert their equal brotherhood. A major crime of capitalist society for Marx and Engels was that it had destroyed all ties between men other than naked self-interest and had 'resolved personal worth into exchange value.' Only after the proletarian revolution would *human* history begin and men treat

---

[2] *Clarke Papers*, vol. 1, p. 301.

[3] It is not quite true, for the doctrines of natural law and consequent natural rights flourish in Catholic social philosophy. See e.g. *The Rights of Man and Natural Law* by Jacques Maritain; 1944.

[4] Cf. *The Open Society*, by K. Popper; vol. 1, esp. pp. 58–9.

each other as equal human beings, not as exploiter and exploited. The object of the transfer of class power is to end class power and to reveal or restore some essential human nature at present disguised by distorting social relationships.

So even if the theory were dead, the puzzle of its effects would remain, and suggest that it had been introduced to solve a genuine problem of political and social philosophy. And it is interesting, therefore, to inquire what the problem was; whether it has found an alternative solution, or is bogus and insoluble.

Why should people have supposed, and, as I believe, continue to suppose, in obscure fashion, that they have 'natural' rights, or rights as human beings, independently of the laws and governments of any existing society? It is, surely, partly at least, because no existing social compulsion or relationship is self-justifying. Men may always ask why they should or should not endure it and expect a convincing answer. And, ultimately, it would seem, they may challenge the dictates of all existing governments and the pressures of every society if they find them equally oppressive, i.e. if they deny what the individual considers his fundamental 'right.' But since, *ex hypothesi,* this 'right' is denied by every existing law and authority, it must be a right possessed independently of them and derived from another source. If, e.g., the laws of every existing society condemn a human being to be a slave, he, or another on his behalf, may yet hold that he has a 'right' to be free. What sort of proposition is this and how is such a claim to be justified? This seems to be one most important problem which the doctrine of natural rights tried to solve.

Natural Law, Natural Laws and Natural Rights

There are an indefinite number of different types of propositions and other forms of human utterance. I will, for my present purpose, notice three. (1) Tautological or analytic propositions which state rules for the uses of symbols or which follow from such rules within a linguistic or logical system. (2) Empirical or contingent propositions which state matter of fact and existence. Propositions which describe what does or may occur in the world and not the symbolic techniques employed in such description. (3) Assertions or expressions of value. With the help of this classification it may be possible to show that some of the difficulties of the doctrine of natural rights have been due to an attempt to interpret propositions about natural rights as a curious hybrid of types (1) and (2) of the above classification.

For in the theory which conceived of natural rights as guaranteed by a 'natural' law, the position seems to have been considered in the following terms. The 'rights' of a slave, e.g., derive from the laws in any society which govern his artificial status as a slave. Yet he has a right to be free. But in virtue of what status and law? Only it seems by his status of being a man like other men. This, however, is a natural status as opposed to one determined by social convention. Every man is human 'by nature'; no human being is 'by nature' a slave of another human being. There must then be an essential human nature which determines this status and a law governing the relations of human beings as such, independently of the laws of all particular societies concerning their artificial relationships. But essential human nature or human 'essence' is constituted by those properties expressed in the definition of 'human being.' And what is expressed or entailed by a definition is a necessary or analytic proposition. Thus by a logical fusion of the characteristics of two different types of proposition, statements about natural rights tended in this theory to be represented as statements of a necessary natural fact.

But not even statements of actual fact, necessary or contingent. For another element intervened. Though the slave had an actual 'right' to be free, he was not free, because no existing law admitted his right. Because laws were imperfect, he was not free though he 'ought' to be. And this introduces into the situation a further complication. By nature a man must be that which yet he is not. Or, it follows from the definition of 'human being' that every human being is, or must be, free—or possess any other 'natural' right though his freedom is ideal and not real. But the ideal as well as the actual is natural fact.

Thus the Roman lawyers who gave the earliest authoritative statements of the doctrine of natural law, conceived of natural law as an ideal or standard, not yet completely exemplified in any existing legal code, but also as a standard fixed by nature to be discovered and gradually applied by men. And the good lawyer kept his eye on this standard as the good gardener keeps his eye fixed on the prize rose which he is hoping to reproduce among his own blooms next summer. For the lawyer, said Ulpian, is not merely the interpreter of existing laws but also the priest or guardian of justice, which is the 'fixed and abiding disposition to give every man his right.' [5] This standard was not determined by men, but by nature, or, sometimes, by God. It was fact and not fancy.

The institution of slavery showed that no existing code was perfectly just. Thus natural *law* is only imperfectly realized in positive *laws*. And it is significant that the lawyers and later political theorists who adopted this distinction talked only of natural *law* and *the* Law of Nature, never of natural laws and laws of nature. But what is most characteristic of legal codes and systems is that they consist of many laws, regulating the different relations of men as debtor and creditor, property owner and thief, employer and employee, husband and wife, etc. But natural law was not conceived of as consisting of ideal regulations corresponding to all positive laws. Indeed,

---

[5] Sabine: *History of Political Theory*, p. 170.

if completely realized, some positive laws would be abolished, e.g. those relating to slave owner and slave. Natural law was not formulated in natural *laws*. It was neither written nor customary and might even be unknown. But it applies, nevertheless, to all men everywhere whether they are debtors or creditors, masters or servants, bond or free. But how is it discovered?

It seems probable that the concept of natural law influenced the later conception of natural or scientific laws obtained by the observation of natural events. For natural law applies impartially to all men in all circumstances, as the law of gravitation applies to all bodies. But the law of gravitation is obtained by deduction from the observation of bodies in sense perception. Are the Law of Nature and the Rights which it implies known by similar observation of the nature of man? The law of gravitation, like all other laws of nature, states a uniformity exemplified in the actual movements of natural bodies. But no existing society may observe the Law of Nature or guarantee natural rights. These cannot, therefore, have been learned from observation of the actual practice of existing societies.

'Man is born free,' said Rousseau, 'and everywhere he is in chains.' What sort of proposition is this? Did Rousseau observe ten or ten million babies immediately after birth and record when the infant limbs were manacled? The law of nature applies to all men equally, said Cicero. For if we had not been corrupted by bad habits and customs 'no one would be so like his own self as all men would be like others.' [6] But since everyone everywhere has been subjected to customs and laws of varying degrees of imperfection, where and when did Cicero observe our uncorrupted nature? How can facts about nature be discovered which have never been observed or confirmed by observation?

The answer lies in the peculiar status given to reason in the theory. Propositions about natural law and natural rights are not generalizations from experience nor deductions from observed facts subsequently confirmed by experience. Yet they are not totally disconnected from natural fact. For they are known as entailed by the intrinsic or essential nature of man. Thus they are known by reason. But they are entailed by the proposition that an essential property of men is that they have reason. The standard of natural law is set by reason and is known because men have reason. But that men have reason, i.e. are able to deduce the ideal from the actual, is a natural fact. And it is by having this specific, and natural, characteristic of being rational that men resemble each other and differ from the brutes. Reason is the great leveller or elevator. According to Sir Frederick Pollock, 'Natural law was conceived to be an ultimate principle of fitness with regard to the nature of man as a rational and social being which is, or ought to be, the justification of every form of positive law.' [7] 'There is, in fact,' said Cicero,

[6] *Laws*, Bk. 1, 10, 28–9 (trans. C. W. Keyes).
[7] The History of the Law of Nature; *Essays in the Law*, 1922.

'a true law—namely right reason—which is in accordance with nature, applies to all men and is unchangeable and eternal.' [8] And for Grotius, too, 'The law of nature is a dictate of right reason.' [9]

Let it be admitted that all or most human beings are intelligent or rational. And that what is known by reason is certainly true. But, also, what can be known by unaided reason is what *must* be true, and perhaps what *ought* to be but never what *is* true of matter of fact. And statements which are logically certain are tautological or analytic and are neither verified nor falsified by what exists. Statements about what ought to be are of a peculiar type which will be discussed later, but it is certain that they say nothing about what *is*. Because it is confused on these distinctions, the theory of natural law and natural rights constantly confounds reason with right and both with matter of fact and existence. The fact that men do reason is thought to be somehow a natural or empirical confirmation of what is logically deduced by reason as a standard by which to judge the imperfections of what exists.

The Social Contract

Though the Roman lawyers conceded that a man might be entitled by natural law to that which he was denied by every positive law, they do not seem to have related this to any particular doctrine of legal and political authority. But in the seventeenth century the doctrines of natural law and natural rights were directly connected with the contract theory of the State. Because he is rational, Locke emphasized, man is subject to the law of nature even before the establishment of civil society. And he never ceases to be so subject. By right of the law of nature men lived in a state of freedom, equality and the possession of property 'that with which a man hath mixed his labour.' True, this picture differs from that of Hobbes whose 'natural man' is constantly at war, possesses only the right to preserve his life, if he can, but usually finds it short and nasty. Nevertheless, even Hobbes's unpleasant savages have sufficient sense, or reason, to enable them to escape their 'natural' predicament. Locke's natural individualists are peaceful property owners who nevertheless sometimes dispute and want an impartial arbitrator. Civil society is formed by compact that natural rights may be better preserved. Man did not enter society, said Paine, to become *worse* than he was before by surrendering his natural rights but only to have them better secured. His natural rights are the foundation of all his civil rights. It was essential for the social contract theorists to deny that all rights are the gift of civil society, since existing societies denied certain rights which they affirmed. In order to claim them, therefore, it was supposed that they had been enjoyed or were such as would be enjoyed by

[8] *Republic,* Bk. 3, p. 22 (trans. Sabine and Smith).
[9] Bk. 1, ch. 1, sec. x, 1.

rational creatures in a 'natural' as opposed to an established society. The Declaration of the French Revolutionary Assembly enunciated the Rights of Man and of Citizens; the two being distinct.

His 'natural' rights attach, by virtue of his reason, to every man much as do his arms and legs. He carries them about with him from one society to another. He cannot lose them without losing himself. 'Men are born free and equal,' said the French Assembly, 'in respect of their *natural* and *imprescriptible* rights of liberty, property, security and resistance of oppression.'[10] The framers of the American Declaration of Independence declare as self-evident truths that all men are created equal, that they are endowed by their creator with certain inalienable rights, among which are Life, Liberty and the Pursuit of Happiness and that governments are instituted to secure these rights.[11] The free people of Virginia proclaimed[12] that the rights with which men enter society they cannot by any compact deprive themselves or their posterity.

These were self-evident truths about a state which men might have left or not yet attained but which was 'natural' to them as opposed to accidental or conventional. A person is accidentally a native of England, France, America; a Red Indian, negro or Jew. His social environment is determined by accident of birth. He may change his family by adoption and his citizenship by naturalization. And he is accidentally, or conventionally, a doctor, soldier, employer, etc. These conventionalities determine his civic and legal rights in a particular society. But he is not accidentally human. Humanity is his essence or nature. There is no essence of 'being Greek' or 'being English'; of 'being a creditor' or 'being an old age pensioner' all of which properties, however, might be the basis of civil rights. The nature of man determines his 'natural' rights. And since, though not accidental, it also seemed to be a matter of fact that men exist and are rational, rights claimed on account of this fact seemed also to be natural and to follow from the essence of man, even though they might be denied. But the essence of man is expressed in the definition of the word 'man.' So that the statement 'Men have natural rights' is equivalent to the propositional function 'x is human entails x has natural rights' which is a tautology. Again the ambiguity inherent in the theory between what is necessary and what is natural, is revealed. It is hard to believe that a barren tautology generated the ardours of that time in which it was good to be alive and to be young was 'very heaven.'[13] But what is meant by the nature or essence of man by 'being rational' or 'having reason'?

---

[10] Declaration of the Rights of Man and of Citizens, by the National Assembly of France, 1791.

[11] Declaration of Independence of the United States of America—July 4, 1776.

[12] The Virginia Declaration of Rights—June 12, 1776.

[13] Wordsworth in *The French Revolution*.

Rights and Reason

" 'Man' equals 'rational animal' Df." is the fossil preserved in logic text books since Aristotle. It was never accompanied by any adequate account of the meaning of 'rational' which was, however, generally assumed to include the capacity to abstract and generalize by the use of symbols in speech and writing; to formulate and understand general propositions and laws and to perceive necessary or logical connections between propositions. It is true that Aristotle himself used the term 'reason' more widely to include the practical intelligence manifested in various skills and the appropriate behaviour of the well-trained character in various moral situations. But usually reason is conceived to be the capacity by which men understand abstractions. This was certainly Kant's view. To be rational is to be able to think abstractly. And the most characteristic activities of men, including living in societies, are due to this capacity to use reason. It is peculiar to men and shared by no other animal. Hence the basis of the equality of men for the exponents of natural law, and of their intrinsic worth for Kant is the fact that they all have reason. Men share all other characteristics with the brutes and might themselves have them in varying degrees, but reason was alike in all men, it was man's defining characteristic. Hence it is the foundation, too, of his natural rights, as a human being.

It is probable that other animals do not abstract and generalize for they do not use symbols. But neither is it true that all men do this with equal skill. Reason, in this sense, is no less or no more invariable among human beings than sense perception, and the rights of man might as well depend upon eyesight as upon rationality. But if the term reason is to be used more widely to include non-verbal manifestations of intelligence, knowing-how as well as knowing-that,[14] then intelligence does not set an unbridgeable gulf between men and other living creatures. For in many activities, those, e.g. of hunting, building, fighting, and even social organization, other creatures display skill, adaptability of means to ends, and other characteristics which are evidence of intelligence in men. And as for social life, ants use tools, domesticate other insects, and live a highly organized social life. Bees and wasps manage their affairs by a complicated system of government. Moreover, many of the most characteristic human activities depend very little on abstract thought or use of symbols, e.g. cooking, sewing, knitting, carpentry. And at a higher level the excellence of pictures, sculptures, symphonies, is not due to their expression of abstract thought. But where in this variety are we to find the constant factor by which to determine human rights? What passport will admit to the Kingdom of Ends?

What may be agreed is that only at a certain level of intellectual development do men claim natural rights. Savages do not dream of life, liberty

14 See Presidential Address to the Aristotelian Society by Professor G. Ryle, 1945, and *The Concept of Mind*, 1949, ch. II.

and the pursuit of happines. For they do not question what is customary. Neither do the very depressed and downtrodden. It was not the slaves who acclaimed their right to be free but the philosophers and lawyers. Marx and Engels were not themselves wage slaves of the industrial system. It is generally agreed that the doctrines of natural rights, natural law and the social contract, are individualistic. To claim rights as an individual independently of society, a man must have reached a level of self-consciousness which enables him to isolate himself in thought from his social environment. This presupposes a considerable capacity for abstraction. To this extent natural rights, or the ability to claim natural rights, depends on reason. But it does not follow from this that reason alone constitutes the specific nature of man or that the worth of human beings is determined solely by their I.Q.s. Reason is only one human excellence.

But the Aristotelian dream of fixed natures pursuing common ends dies hard. It reappears in M. Maritain's account of the Rights of Man cited earlier. He says, e.g.:

. . . there is a human nature and this human nature is the same in all men . . . and possessed of a nature, constituted in a given determinate fashion, man obviously possesses ends which correspond to his natural constitution and which are the same for all—as all pianos, for instance, whatever their particular type and in whatever spot they may be, have as their end the production of certain attuned sounds. If they do not produce these sounds, they must be attuned or discarded as worthless . . . since man has intelligence and can determine his ends, it is up to him to put himself in tune with the ends necessarily demanded by his nature.[15]

And men's rights depend upon this common nature and end by which they are subject to the natural or 'unwritten' law. But this seems to me a complete mistake. Human beings are not like exactly similar bottles of whisky each marked 'for export only' or some device indicating a common destination or end. Men do not share a fixed nature, nor, therefore, are there any ends which they must necessarily pursue in fulfilment of such nature. There is no definition of 'man.' There is a more or less vague set of properties which characterize in varying degrees and proportions those creatures which are called 'human.' These determine for each individual human being what he *can* do but not what he *must* do. If he has an I.Q. of 85 his intellectual activities will be limited; if he is physically weak he cannot become a heavyweight boxer. If a woman has neither good looks nor acting ability she is unlikely to succeed as a film star. But what people may do with their capacities is extremely varied, and there is no one thing which they must do in order to be human. It would be nonsense to say: 'I am not going to be an actress, a school teacher, a postman, a soldier, a taxpayer, but simply a human being.' For what is the alternative? A man may choose whether he will become a civil servant or a schoolmaster; a conservative or a socialist, but he cannot choose whether he will be a man or a dog.

---

15 *Loc. cit.*, p. 35.

There is certainly a sense in which it is often said that in the air-raid shelter or in the battle people forgot that they were officers or privates, assistant secretaries or typists, rich or poor, and remembered only that they were all human beings, i.e. all liable to die without regard to status. But that is always true. They did not remember that they were something *in addition* to being the particular human being they each were and which they might be without being any particular individual. And, as individuals, when the 'All Clear' sounded, each returned to pursue his or her own ends, not the purpose of the human race. Certainly, many human beings may co-operate in a joint enterprise to achieve a particular end which each chooses. But that cannot be generalized into the spectacle of all human beings pursuing one end. There is no end set for the human race by an abstraction called 'human nature.' There are only ends which individuals choose, or are forced by circumstances to accept. There are none which they *must* accept. Men are not created for a purpose as a piano is built to produce certain sounds. Or if they are we have no idea of the purpose.

It is the emphasis on the individual sufferer from bad social conditions which constitutes the appeal of the social contract theory and the 'natural' origin of human rights. But it does not follow that the theory is true as a statement of verifiable fact about the actual constitution of the world. The statements of the Law of Nature are not statements of the laws of nature, not even of the laws of an 'ideal' nature. For nature provides no standards or ideals. All that exists, exists at the same level, or is of the same logical type. There are not, by nature, prize roses, works of art, oppressed or unoppressed citizens. Standards are determined by human choice, not set by nature independently of men. Natural events cannot tell us what we ought to do until we have made certain decisions, when knowledge of natural fact will enable the most efficient means to be chosen to carry out those decisions. Natural events themselves have no value, and human beings as natural existents have no value either, whether on account of possessing intelligence or having two feet.

One of the major criticisms of the doctrine of natural rights is that the list of natural rights varies with each exponent. For Hobbes, man's only natural right is self-preservation. More 'liberal' theorists add to life and security; liberty, the pursuit of happiness and sometimes property. Modern socialists would probably include the right to 'work or adequate maintenance.' M. Maritain enumerates a list of nine natural rights which include besides the rights to life, liberty, and property of the older formulations, the right to pursue a religious vocation, the right to marry and raise a family, and, finally, the right of every human being to be treated as a person and not as a thing.[16] It is evident that these 'rights' are of very different types which would need to be distinguished in a complete discussion of the problem. My aim in this paper, however, is only to try to understand

[16] *Loc. cit.*, p. 60.

what can be meant by the assertion that there are some rights to which human beings are entitled independently of their varying social relationships. And it seems difficult to account for the wide variations in the lists of these 'rights' if they have all been deduced from a fixed human nature or essence, subject to an absolutely uniform 'natural law.' Nor is the disagreement one which can be settled by more careful empirical observation of human beings and their legal systems. The doctrine seems to try to operate by an analogy which it is logically impossible to apply.

The word 'right' has a variety of uses in ordinary language, which include the distinction between 'legal right' and 'moral right.' 'A has a legal right against B' entails B has a duty to A which will be enforced by the courts. A has a claim against B recognized by an existing law. No person has a legal right which he cannot claim from some other (legal) person and which the law will not enforce. That A has a moral right against B likewise entails that B has a duty to A. But it is not necessarily a duty which can be legally enforced. A has a right to be told the truth by B and B has a corresponding duty to tell A the truth. But no one, except in special circumstances recognized by law, can force B to tell the truth, or penalize him, except by censure, if he does not. No one can, in general, claim to be told the truth, by right, under penalty. But a creditor can claim repayment of a debt or sue his debtor.

When the lawyers said that a slave had a right in natural law to be free, they thought of a legal right not provided for by any existing statute, enactment or custom and to whose universal infringement no penalties attached. But this, surely, is the vanishing point of law and of legal right? It indicates that there just wasn't a law or legal right by which a slave might demand his freedom. But perhaps there was a moral right and a moral obligation. The slave ought to be free and maybe it was the duty of every slaveholder to free his slaves and of legislators to enact laws forbidding slavery. But until this happened there was no law which forbade a man to keep slaves. Consequently, there is no point in saying there was 'really' a natural law which forbade this. For the natural law was impotent. Statements about natural law were neither statements of natural fact nor legal practice.

So, does it follow that a 'natural' right is just a 'moral' right? Kant said, in effect, that to treat another human being as a person, of intrinsic worth, an end in himself, is just to treat him in accordance with the moral law applicable to all rational beings on account of their having reason. But this is not quite the sense in which the term 'natural rights' has been historically used. Declarations of the Rights of Man did not include his right to be told the truth, to have promises kept which had been made to him, to receive gratitude from those he had benefited, etc. The common thread among the variety of natural rights is their *political* character. Despite their rugged individualism, no exponent of the Rights of Man desired to enjoy them, in solitude, on a desert island. They were among the articles of the original Social Contract; clauses in Constitutions, the inspiration of social and governmental reforms. But 'Keep promises'; 'Tell the truth'; 'Be grateful' are not inscribed on banners carried by aggrieved demonstrators or circulated among the members of an oppressed party. Whether or not morality can exist without society, it is certain that politics cannot. Why then were 'natural rights' conceived to exist independently of organized society and hence of political controversies? I suggest that they were so considered in order to emphasize their basic or fundamental character. For words like freedom, equality, security, represented for the defenders of natural rights what they considered to be the fundamental moral and social values which should be or should continue to be realized in any society fit for intelligent and responsible citizens.

When the contract theorists talked of the rights as human beings which men had enjoyed in the state of nature, they seemed to be asserting unverifiable and nonsensical propositions since there is no evidence of a state of nature in which men lived before the establishment of civil societies. But they were not simply talking nonsense. They were, in effect, saying 'In any society and under every form of government men ought to be able to think and express their thoughts freely; to live their lives without arbitrary molestation with their persons and goods. They ought to be treated as equal in value, though not necessarily of equal capacity or merit. They ought to be assured of the exclusive use of at least some material objects other than their own bodies; they ought not to be governed without some form of consent. And that the application of these rights to the particular conditions of a society, or their suspension, if necessary, should be agreed with them.' The exponents of the natural Rights of Man were trying to express what they deemed to be the fundamental conditions of *human* social life and government. And it is by the observance of some such conditions, I suggest, that human societies are distinguished from ant hills and beehives.

This, however, has frequently been denied by utilitarian, idealist and Marxist philosophers who, though differing in other respects, agree in holding that the rights of an individual must be determined only by the needs and conveniences of society as a whole. Surely, they say, there can be no 'natural' right to life in any society when a man may be executed as a criminal or killed as a conscripted soldier. And very little right to liberty exists when external danger threatens the state. 'The person with rights and duties,' says the evolutionist utilitarian Ritchie, 'is the product of society and the rights of the individual must, therefore, be judged from the point of view of society as a whole and not the society from the point of view of the individual.' [17] It is the duty of the individual to preserve society for his descendants. For individuals perish but England remains. But the plain man may well ask why he must preserve a society for his descendants if it neither is, nor shows any prospect of being, worth living in? Will his de-

[17] Ritchie: *Natural Rights*, p. 101.

scendants thank him for this consideration? All that seems to follow from Ritchie's view is that at any time the members of a society may agree to sacrifice some goods in order to achieve a certain result. And the result will include the restoration of basic rights. Does the ordinary citizen consider that he has no right to life and liberty because he agrees to (or does not protest against) the suspension of those rights in an emergency? He would be very unlikely to approve of such suspension if he thought the result would be the massacre or enslavement of himself, his contemporaries and possibly his children and descendants at the arbitrary will of a ruler or government. To suspend, or even to forfeit rights, as a criminal does, also temporarily, is not to deny rights. Nor is it to deny that such practices must be justified to the individuals required to submit to them. Though it may be much more useful to society that a man should remain a slave and even that he may be happier in that condition, it is not possible to prove to him that he has no right to be free, however much society wants his slavery. In short 'natural rights' are the conditions of a good society. But what those conditions are is not given by nature or mystically bound up with the essence of man and his inevitable goal, but is determined by human decisions.

Propositions and Decisions

Assertions about natural rights, then, are assertions of what ought to be as the result of human choice. They fall within class 3 of the division stated on page 721, as being ethical assertions or expressions of value. And these assertions or expressions include all those which result from human choice and preference, in art and personal relations, e.g. as well as in morals and politics. Such utterances in which human beings express choices determined by evaluation of better and worse have been variously interpreted, and it is, indeed, difficult to introduce a discussion of the topic without assuming an interpretation. I have tried, e.g. to avoid the use of the words 'proposition' and 'statement' in referring to these utterances since these words emphasize a relation between what is asserted and a fact by which it is verified or falsified. And this leads either to the attempts of the natural law and natural rights theories to find a 'natural' fact which justifies these assertions or to a search for non-sensible entities called 'Values' as the reference of ethical terms. Yet, of course, it is, in some sense, true that 'No one ought to be ill-treated because he is a Jew, a negro or not able to count above ten.' Alternatively, to talk of 'expressions of value' sounds as though such utterances are sophisticated ways of cheering and cursing. Just as the blow becomes sublimated into the sarcastic retort so our smiles of delight at unselfish action and howls of woe at parricide become intellectualized into apparent judgments about good and evil, right and wrong, without, however, losing their fundamentally emotive character.[18] On this view, value judgments do not state what is true or false but are expressions of feeling, sometimes combined with commands to do or forbear. But whatever its emotional causes and effects, an articulate utterance does not seem to be simply a substitute for a smile or a tear. It *says* something. But I cannot hope in a necessarily brief discussion to do justice to the enormous variety of value utterances. So I will plunge, and say that value utterances are more like records of *decisions* than propositions.[19] To assert that 'Freedom is better than slavery' or 'All men are of equal worth' is not to state a fact but to *choose a side*. It announces *This is where I stand*.

I mentioned earlier that in the late war propaganda appeals to defend our comforts and privileges would have been rejected as uninspiring but that appeals to defend the rights of all men to freedom and equality obtained the required response, at least in all but the depraved and cynical. I now suggest that they did so because they accorded with our decisions about these ultimate social values. For whether or not we were more or less comfortable as a result, we should not choose to act only upon orders about which we had not in some way been consulted; to suppress the truth; to imprison without trial or to permit human individuals or classes of individuals to be treated as of no human value.

Two questions suggest themselves on this view. Finally, if ethical judgments, and particularly the ethical judgments which concern the fundamental structure of society are value decisions, who makes these decisions and when? Is this not, as much as the natural law theory, the use of an analogy without application? I did safeguard myself to some extent by saying that these assertions are 'more like' decisions than they are like propositions. They are unlike propositions because they are neither tautologies nor statements of verifiable fact. But it is also true that if asked when we decided in favour of free speech or democratic government or many of our social values we could not give a date. It is, therefore, suggested that we no more record a decision by a value assertion than we signed a Social Contract. Nevertheless, I think the analogy does emphasize important differences between value and other assertions. For, if intelligent, we do choose our politics as we choose our friends or our favoured poems, novels, pictures, symphonies, and as we do not choose to accept Pythagoras's theorem or the law of gravitation. And when challenged we affirm our decision or stand by our choice. We say, 'I did not realize how much I valued free speech until I went to Germany in 1936,' indicating that a choice had been made, but so easily that it had seemed scarcely necessary to record its occurrence.

For, indeed, the fundamental values of a society are not always recorded in explicit decisions by its members, even its rulers, but are expressed in the life of the society and constitute its quality. They are conveyed by its

18 Cf. A. J. Ayer: *Language, Truth and Logic*, ch. 6.
19 Dr. K. R. Popper makes a similar distinction in an interesting discussion of value judgments in *The Open Society*, vol. 1, ch. 5.

'tone' and atmosphere as well as its laws and Statutory Rules and Orders. The members of a society whose values are freedom and equality behave differently, walk, speak, fight differently from the members of a slave society. Plato expressed this nastily in the Republic [20] when he said that in a democracy even the horses and asses behaved with a gait expressive of remarkable freedom and dignity, and like everyone else became 'gorged with freedom.' Suspicion, fear and servility are absent, or, at least, inconspicuous in such a society. And no one who visited Germany after 1933 needs to be reminded of the change of atmosphere.

Decisions concerning the worth of societies and social institutions are not made by an *élite,* by rulers or a governing class but, explicitly or by acceptance, by those who live and work in the society and operate its institutions. But these decisions may be changed by the effective propaganda of a minority who have reached other decisions of whose value they desire to convince the majority. Perhaps, ultimately, men get the societies and governments which they choose, even if not those which they deserve, for they may deserve better than passion, indolence or ignorance permits them to choose.

This leads to a second question. Upon what grounds or for what reasons are decisions reached? Consider the expression of the doctrine of equality; that all human beings are of equal worth, intrinsic value, or are ends in themselves. Is there an answer to the question, Why? On what *evidence* is this assertion based? How can such a decision be maintained despite the obvious differences between human beings? The answer of the natural law theorists and of Kant was that the 'natural' fact that all men have reason proves that they are of intrinsic worth, and are thus entitled to the Rights of Man. It is not clear, however, whether imbeciles and lunatics forfeit human rights. No one can deny that they are human beings. A person who becomes insane does not thereby become a mere animal. But if statements about the possession by anything of a natural characteristic is related to a decision of worth as evidence for a conclusion, then it would be illogical to retain the decision when the characteristics were absent or had changed. It is irrational to continue to believe a proposition when evidence shows that it is false. I affirm that no natural characteristic constitutes a *reason* for the assertion that all human beings are of equal worth. Or, alternatively, that *all* the characteristics of *any* human being are equally reasons for this assertion. But this amounts to saying that the decision of equal worth is affirmed of all human beings *whatever their particular characteristics.* It does not follow that they are of equal *merit* and that their treatment should not vary accordingly, in ways compatible with their intrinsic value. But even a criminal, though he has lost merit and may deserve punishment, does not become worthless. He cannot be cast out of humanity.

I am aware that this view needs much more elaboration, and especially

[20] Book 8, 563.

illustration than can be given in very limited space. I can, therefore, indicate only in a general way the type of value assertions and the manner in which they are related to each other and to other assertions. They are not related as evidence strengthening a conclusion. For decisions are not true or false and are not deduced from premises. Do we, then, decide without reason? Are decisions determined by chance or whim? Surely, it will be said, the facts have some relevance to what is decided? To say that decisions are made without reason looks like saying that we choose by tossing a coin; opening the *Works of Shakespeare* or *The Bible* at random and reading the first sentence; or shutting our eyes and sticking a pin into the list of starters to pick the Derby winner. These seem very irrational methods of choice. Nevertheless, we do sometimes choose by a not very dissimilar procedure. If two candidates for a post are of exactly equal merit, the selectors may well end by plumping for one or the other. This, it may be said, was justified because there was 'nothing to choose between them,' not that the decision bore no relation to their merits. But there are some choices into which merit hardly enters. Those involving personal relations, for instance. It would seem absurd to try to prove that our affections were not misplaced by listing the characteristics of our friends. To one who asked for such 'proof' we should reply, with Montaigne: [21]

> If a man urge me to tell him wherefore I loved him, I feel it cannot be expressed but by answering, because it was he, because it was myself. . . . It is not one especial consideration, nor two, nor three, nor four, nor a thousand. It is I wot not what kind of quintessence of all this commixture which seized my will

Yet it is also correct to say that our decisions about worth are not merely arbitrary, and intelligent choices are not random. They cannot be proved correct by evidence. Nor, I suggest, do we try to prove them. What we do is to support and defend our decisions. The relation of the record of a decision to the considerations which support it is not that of proof to conclusion. It is much more like the defence of his client by a good counsel.

Consider an analogous situation in art. Suppose one were trying to defend a view that Keats is a greater poet than Crabbe. One would compare passages from each writer, showing the richness and complexity of the imagery and movement of Keats's verse and the monotonous rhythm, moral platitudes and poverty-stricken images of Crabbe. One would aid the effect by reading passages aloud for their comparable musical effects; would dwell on single lines and passages which show the differences between the evocative language of Keats and the conventional 'poetic diction' of Crabbe. The 'Season of mists and mellow fruitfulness' of the one and the 'finny tribes,' etc., of the other. One might eventually resort to the remarks of the best critics on both writers. In short, one would employ every device to 'present' Keats, to build up a convincing advocacy of his poetry. And the resistance of Crabbe's defender might collapse, and he would declare the case won

---

[21] *Essays* (trans. John Florio), *Of Friendship.*

with the verdict 'Keats is the better poet.' But nothing would have been *proved*. Crabbe's supporter might still disagree. He would dwell on Crabbe's 'sincerity'; his genuine sympathy with the poor and excuse his poetic limitations as due to a bad tradition for which he was not responsible. He might add that Crabbe was one of Jane Austen's favourite poets. And if he so persisted he would not be *wrong*, i.e. he would not be believing falsely that Crabbe was a better poet than Keats but much more persuasion would be needed to induce him to alter his decision.

Compare with this the correct attitude to the proof of a scientific law. If the empirical evidence is conclusive then a person who rejects the conclusion is either stupid or biased. He is certainly believing a false proposition. We do not 'defend' the law of gravitation but all instructed persons accept the proof of the law.

On the other hand, we do not refer to Mill's proof but to his 'magnificent defence' of civil liberty. For a successful defence involves much more than statement of facts. The facts of the case are known to both the prosecuting and defending counsel. The question is, should the accused be condemned or acquitted? The skilful lawyer uses these facts, but he uses them differently from the scientist. He marshals them so as to emphasize those which favour his client. He interprets those which appear unfavourable in terms of legal decisions in similar cases which would benefit the accused. He chooses language which does not merely state, but impress: he uses voice, gesture, facial expression, all the devices of eloquence and style in order to influence the decision of the jury in favour of his client. His client may still lose, but he would admit that he has a better chance of winning if he briefs a good counsel.

But, it may be asked, is this a recommendation to take fraudulent advocacy as our model for defending the rights of man? Not at all. Lawyers and art critics are not frauds, but neither are they scientists. They are more like artists who use material with results which impress and convince but do not *prove*. There is no conceivable method of *proving* that Keats is a better poet than Crabbe or that freedom is better than slavery. For assertions of value cannot be subjected to demonstrative or inductive methods. It is for this reason that such assertions have been regarded as simple expressions of feeling or emotion like cries of pain and anger. But we do not defend or support a cry of pain or shout of joy though it may be related to a cause. If our value choices are defensible their defence requires other methods.

The lawyer says: 'I agree that my client was on the premises; I deny that his being there in those circumstances constitutes a *trespass*. This may be confirmed from *Gower* v. *Flint* where this ruling was given in similar circumstances.' The critic says: 'You agree that Keats's imagery is *rich* and *complex;* his language *original* and *powerful:* that Crabbe, on the contrary, is *frigid* and *conventional* in language; *meagre* in imagery, etc. etc.' The lawyer supports his plea from previous decisions. The critic likewise appeals not to physical or psychological facts about the occurrences of marks on paper, internal pictures, etc., but to previous decisions *evaluating* these and other occurrences. Rich and powerful poetry is good; frigid and meagre versifying is bad. If we stand by our previous decisions it does not follow that we *must* on account of them make a further decision now, but they are certainly relevant. Incorporated into a system of skilful advocacy they may win a favourable verdict. But, on the other hand, we may reject our former decisions. Elaborate imagery; lyrical quality, are dismissed as *barbarous* or *sentimental;* our choice is now for the *plain* and *elegant* statement. Such a complete change in systems of evaluation seems to occur in different ages. The eighteenth century listened to Shakespeare, but gave the palm to Pope. The Victorians saw Georgian houses but chose sham Gothic. So we may present the authoritarian with an attractive picture of a free and democratic society, and if he already values independence, experimentation, mutual trust, he may agree that these values are realized in such a society. But he may call independence, insolence; experimentation, rash meddling; and the picture will fail in its effect.

There are no certainties in the field of values. For there are no true or false beliefs about values, but only better or worse decisions and choices. And to encourage the better decisions we need to employ devices which are artistic rather than scientific. For our aim is not intellectual assent, but practical effects. These are not, of course, absolutely separate, for intellectual assent to a proposition or theory is followed by using it. But values, I think, concern only behaviour. They are not known, but accepted and acted upon.

Intellectuals often complain that political propaganda, e.g. is not conducted as if it were scientific argument. But if moral values are not capable of scientific proof it would be irrational to treat them as if they were. The result of a confusion of logical types is to leave the field of non-scientific persuasion and conviction to propagandists of the type of the late Dr. Goebbels.

Selected Bibliography

SOURCE BOOKS

BRAYBROOKE, DAVID, ed., *Philosophical Problems of the Social Sciences,* Macmillan, New York, 1965.

DANTO, ARTHUR, and SIDNEY MORGENBESSER, eds., *Philosophy of Science,* Meridian Books, New York, 1960.

DRAY, WILLIAM H., ed., *Philosophical Analysis and History,* Harper & Row, New York, 1966.

FEIGL, HERBERT, and MAY BRODBECK, eds., *Readings in the Philosophy of Science,* Appleton-Century-Crofts, New York, 1953.

GROSS, LLEWELLYN, ed., *Symposium on Sociological Theory,* Harper & Row, New York, 1959.

MADDEN, EDWARD H., ed., *The Structure of Scientific Thought,* Houghton Mifflin Co., Boston, 1960.

NATANSON, MAURICE, ed., *Philosophy of the Social Sciences: A Reader,* Random House, New York, 1963.

WIENER, PHILIP P., ed., *Readings in Philosophy of Science,* Scribner's, New York, 1953.

SYSTEMATIC WORKS AND TEXTBOOKS

BERGMANN, GUSTAV, *Philosophy of Science,* University of Wisconsin Press, Madison, 1957.

BRAITHWAITE, R. B., *Scientific Explanation,* Cambridge University Press, Cambridge and New York, 1953.

BROWN, ROBERT, *Explanation in Social Science,* Aldine Publishing Co., Chicago, 1963.

COHEN, MORRIS R., *Reason and Nature,* Free Press, New York, 1953.

GIBSON, QUENTIN, *The Logic of Social Enquiry,* Routledge and Kegan Paul, London; Humanities Press, New York, 1960.

HAWKINS, DAVID, *The Language of Nature,* W. H. Freeman, San Francisco and London, 1964.

HEMPEL, C. G., *Aspects of Scientific Explanation,* Free Press, New York, 1965.

KAPLAN, ABRAHAM, *The Conduct of Inquiry,* Chandler Publishing Co., San Francisco, 1964.

MILL, JOHN STUART, *A System of Logic,* Longmans, Green and Co., London and New York, 1947 (originally published in 1843), Book VI, "The Logic of the Moral Sciences," abridged version in *John Stuart Mill's Philosophy of Scientific Method,* ed. E. Nagel, Hafner, New York, 1950.

NAGEL, ERNEST, *The Structure of Science,* Harcourt, Brace & World, New York, 1961.

PAP, ARTHUR, *An Introduction to the Philosophy of Science,* Free Press, New York, 1962.

RUDNER, RICHARD S., *Philosophy of Social Science,* Prentice-Hall, Englewood Cliffs, N.J., 1966.

SCHEFFLER, ISRAEL, *The Anatomy of Inquiry,* Alfred A. Knopf, New York, 1963.

ONE: THE NATURE OF HUMAN ACTION *

ABEL, THEODORE F., "The Operation Called *Verstehen,*" *American Journal of Sociology,* 54, 1948, 211–218; reprinted in Herbert Feigl and May Brodbeck, eds., *Readings in the Philosophy of Science.*

———, *Systematic Sociology in Germany,* Columbia University Press, New York, 1929.

ALSTON, WILLIAM, "Wants, Actions, and Causal Explanation" (with comments by Keith Lehrer and rejoinder by Alston), in H. Castañeda, ed., *Intentionality, Minds, and Perception,* Wayne State University Press, Detroit, 1967.

ANSCOMBE, G. E. M., *Intention,* Basil Blackwell & Mott, Oxford; Cornell University Press, Ithaca, N.Y., 1957.

———, "Two Kinds of Error in Action," *Journal of Philosophy,* 60, 1963.

BECK, LEWIS W., "The 'Natural Science Ideal' in the Social Sciences," *Scientific Monthly,* 68, 1949, 386–394.

BENNETT, DANIEL, "Action, Reason, and Purpose," *Journal of Philosophy,* 62, 1965, 85–96.

BENNETT, JONATHAN, *Rationality,* Routledge & Kegan Paul, London; Humanities Press, New York, 1964.

BERGMANN, GUSTAV, "The Contribution of John B. Watson," *Psychological Review,* 63, 1956, 265–276.

———, "An Empiricist's System of the Sciences," *Scientific Monthly,* 59, 1944, 140–158.

* Much recent "ordinary-language" philosophy has been concerned with describing the uses in idiomatic nonscientific contexts of everyday concepts for human action and personality. From among these writings, as with all other sources, I have selected for all parts of this bibliography only those that seemed relevant to issues in the philosophy of the social sciences.—Ed.

———, "The Logic of Psychological Concepts," *Philosophy of Science,* **18,** 1951, 93–110.

———, "Sense and Nonsense in Operationism," *Scientific Monthly,* **79,** 1954, 210–215.

BERNARD, L. L., "The Limits of the Social Sciences and their Determinants," *Journal of Philosophy,* **26,** 1929, 430–438.

BEROFSKY, BERNARD, "Determinism and the Concept of a Person," *Journal of Philosophy,* **61,** 1964, 461–475.

BLACK, MAX, ed., *The Social Theories of Talcott Parsons,* Prentice-Hall, Englewood Cliffs, N.J., 1961.

BRANDT, RICHARD, and J. KIM, "Wants as Explanations of Actions," *Journal of Philosophy,* **60,** 1963, 425–435.

BRAYBROOKE, DAVID, "Introduction," in D. Braybrooke, ed., *Philosophical Problems of the Social Sciences,* Macmillan, New York, 1965, 1–18.

BRODBECK, MAY, "Logic and Scientific Method in Research on Teaching," in N. L. Gage, ed., *Handbook of Research on Teaching,* Rand McNally, New York, 1963, 44–93.

———, "On the Philosophy of the Social Sciences," *Philosophy of Science,* **21,** 1954, 140–156.

COHEN, CARL, "Naturalism and the Method of Verstehen," *Journal of Philosophy,* **51,** 1954, 220–225.

COHEN, MORRIS R., *Reason and Nature,* The Free Press, New York, 1953, Book III, "Reason in Social Science."

DANTO, ARTHUR C., DONAGAN, ALAN, and MEILAND, J. W., "Symposium: Historical Understanding," *Journal of Philosophy,* **63,** 1966, 566–582.

DIESING, PAUL, "Objectivism vs. Subjectivism in the Social Sciences," *Philosophy of Science,* **33,** 1966, 124–133.

DONAGAN, ALAN, "Are the Social Sciences Really Historical?" in B. Baumrin, ed., *Philosophy of Science: The Delaware Seminar,* I, John Wiley & Sons, New York, 1963.

———, "Social Science and Historical Antinomianism," *Revue Internationale de Philosophie,* **XI,** 1957, 433–449.

DRAY, WILLIAM H., "The Historical Explanation of Actions Reconsidered," in S. Hook, ed., *Philosophy and History,* New York University Press, New York, 1963, 105–135.

FEIGL, HERBERT, "Operationism and Scientific Method," *Psychological Review,* **52,** 1945, 250–259.

FEINBERG, JOEL, "Action and Responsibility," in Max Black, ed., *Philosophy in America,* Cornell University Press, 1965, 134–160.

FOOT, PHILIPPA, "Hart and Honoré: Causation in the Law," *Philosophical Review,* **72,** 1963, 505–515.

FRANKEL, CHARLES, "Philosophy and the Social Sciences," in C. E. Boewe and R. F. Nichols, eds., *Both Human and Humane,* University of Pennsylvania Press, 1960, 94–117.

GEWIRTH, ALAN, "Subjectivism and Objectivism in the Social Sciences," *Philosophy of Science,* 21, 1954, 157–163.

GIBSON, QUENTIN, *The Logic of Social Enquiry,* Routledge & Kegan Paul, London; Humanities Press, New York, 1960.

HAMPSHIRE, STUART, *Thought and Action,* Chatto and Windus, London, 1959.

HANDY, ROLLO, *Methodology of the Behavioral Sciences,* Thomas, Springfield, Ill., 1964.

HART, H. L. A., and A. M. HONORÉ, *Causation in the Law,* Oxford University Press, London, 1959.

HEMPEL, CARL G., "The Concept of Rationality and the Logic of Explanation by Reasons," in his *Aspects of Scientific Explanation,* 463–487.

HOCHBERG, HERBERT, "Physicalism, Behaviorism, and Phenomena," *Philosophy of Science,* 26, 1959, 93–103.

——, "Of Mind and Myth," *Methodos,* XI, 1959, 123–145.

HODGES, H. A., *The Philosophy of Wilhelm Dilthey,* Routledge and Kegan Paul, London; Humanities Press, New York, 1952.

——, *Wilhelm Dilthey: An Introduction,* Oxford University Press, New York, 1944.

HOLT, ROBERT R., "Individuality and Generalization in the Psychology of Personality: An Evaluation," *Journal of Personality,* 30, 1962, 377–402.

JOHNSON, ROCHELLE J., "A Commentary on 'Radical Behaviorism'," *Philosophy of Science,* 30, 1963, 274–285.

KAUFMANN, FELIX, *Methodology of the Social Sciences,* Oxford University Press, New York, 1944.

LEVISON, ARNOLD, "Knowledge and Society," *Inquiry,* 9, 1966.

LOGAN, FRANK A., *Behavior Theory and Social Science,* Yale University Press, New Haven, 1955.

LOUCH, A. R., "On Misunderstanding Mr. Winch," *Inquiry,* 8, 1965, 212–216.

——, "The Very Idea of a Social Science," *Inquiry,* 4, 1963, 273–286.

MacINTYRE, A., "A Mistake about Causality in Social Science," in P. Laslett and W. G. Runciman, eds., *Philosophy, Politics and Society* (Second Series), B. Blackwell, Oxford, 1962, 48–70.

MADELL, GEOFFREY, "Action and Causal Explanation," *Mind,* 76, 1967, 34–48.

MALCOLM, NORMAN, "Behaviorism as a Philosophy of Psychology," in T. W. Wann, ed., *Behaviorism and Phenomenology,* University of Chicago Press, 1964, 141–155.

MANDELBAUM, MAURICE, "Professor Ryle and Psychology," *Philosophical Review,* 67, 1958, 522–530.

MANDLER, GEORGE, and WILLIAM KESSEN, *The Language of Psychology,* John Wiley & Sons, New York, 1959.

MARGOLIS, JOSEPH, "Motives, Causes and Action," *Methodos,* XVI, 1964, 83–89.

MELDEN, A. I., *Free Action,* Routledge and Kegan Paul, London, 1961.

MOORE, OMAR K., and ALAN R. ANDERSON, "Some Puzzling Aspects of Social Interaction," *Review of Metaphysics,* 15, 1962.

NEURATH, OTTO, "Sociology and Physicalism," in A. J. Ayer, ed., *Logical Positivism,* Free Press, New York, 1959.

OSGOOD, C. E., "Behavior Theory and the Social Sciences," *Behavioral Science,* 1, 1956, 167–195.

PARETO, VILFREDO, *The Mind and Society,* Harcourt, Brace & Co., New York, 1935.

PARSONS, TALCOTT, *The Structure of Social Action,* McGraw-Hill, New York, 1937.

PARSONS, TALCOTT, and E. A. SHILS, eds., *Toward a General Theory of Action,* Harvard University Press, Cambridge, Mass., 1951.

PASSMORE, JOHN, "Explanation in Everyday Life, in Science, and in History," *History and Theory,* 2, 1962–1963.

PEARS, D. F., "Are Reasons for Actions Causes?" in A. Stroll, ed., *Epistemology: New Essays in the Theory of Knowledge,* Harper & Row, New York, 1967.

PETERS, R. S., *The Concept of Motivation,* Routledge and Kegan Paul, London, 1958. (See also review of this by A. Watson, *Mind,* 68, 1959, 408–412.)

POPPER, KARL R., *The Poverty of Historicism,* Routledge and Kegan Paul, London, 1961, 130–143.

RUDNER, RICHARD S., "Philosophy of Social Science," *Philosophy of Science,* 21, 1954, 164–168.

RYLE, GILBERT, *The Concept of Mind,* Hutchinson's, London; Barnes & Noble, New York, 1949.

SCHUTZ, ALFRED, "Concept and Theory Formation in the Social Sciences," *Journal of Philosophy,* 51, 1954, 257–273; reprinted in M. Natanson, ed., *Philosophy of the Social Sciences: A Reader.*

———, "The Social World and the Theory of Social Action," *Social Research,* 27, 1960, 203–221; reprinted in D. Braybrooke, ed., *Philosophical Problems of the Social Sciences,* Macmillan, New York, 1965.

SCHWAYDER, D. S., *The Stratification of Behaviour,* Routledge and Kegan Paul, London; Humanities Press, New York, 1965.

SELLARS, WILFRID, "Philosophy and the Scientific Image of Man," in his *Science, Perception and Reality,* Routledge & Kegan Paul, London; Humanities Press, New York, 1963.

SIMMEL, GEORG, *Conflict* and *The Web of Group-Affiliations,* Free Press, New York, 1955.

SKINNER, B. F., "Behaviorism at Fifty," *Science,* 140, 1963, 951–958.

———, *Science and Human Behavior,* Macmillan, New York, 1953.

SPENCE, KENNETH W., *Behavior Theory and Conditioning,* Yale University Press, New Haven, 1956, Chapter 1.

———, "The Postulates and Methods of 'Behaviorism'," *Psychological Review,* 55, 1948, 67–78; reprinted in H. Feigl and M. Brodbeck, eds., *Readings in the Philosophy of Science.*

SUTHERLAND, N. S., "Motives and Explanations," *Mind,* 68, 1959, 145–159.

WANN, T. W., ed., *Behaviorism and Phenomenology,* University of Chicago Press, 1964.

WEBER, MAX, *The Theory of Social and Economic Organization,* edited with an introduction by Talcott Parsons, Free Press, New York, 1947.

WEINGARTNER, RUDOLPH H., *Experience and Culture: The Philosophy of Georg Simmel,* Wesleyan University Press, Middletown, Conn., 1962.

WINCH, PETER, *The Idea of a Social Science,* Routledge and Kegan Paul, London, 1958.

——, "Mr. Louch's Idea of a Social Science," *Inquiry,* 7, 1964.

WOLFF, KURT H., ed., *Georg Simmel 1858–1918: A Collection of Essays with Translations and a Bibliography,* Ohio State University Press, Columbus, 1959.

——, ed., *The Sociology of Georg Simmel,* Free Press, New York, 1950.

TWO: VALUES AND SOCIAL SCIENCE

ANDERSON, ALAN R., and OMAR K. MOORE, "The Formal Analysis of Normative Concepts," *American Sociological Review,* 1957, 9–17.

ARCHIBALD, G. C., "Welfare Economics, Ethics and Essentialism," *Economica,* 26, 1959.

ARROW, KENNETH J., *Social Choice and Individual Values,* John Wiley & Sons, New York, 1951.

BASH, HARRY H., "Determinism and Avoidability in Sociohistorical Analysis," *Ethics,* 74, 1964, 186–199.

BENDIX, REINHARD, *Social Science and the Distrust of Reason,* University of California Press, Berkeley, 1951.

BERGSON, ABRAM, "Socialist Economics," in *Survey of Contemporary Economics,* II, Richard D. Irwin, Homewood, Ill., 1960.

BIDNEY, DAVID, *Theoretical Anthropology,* Columbia University Press, New York, 1953.

BISBEE, ELEANOR, "Objectivity in the Social Sciences," *Philosophy of Science,* 4, 1937, 371–382.

BOTTOMORE, T. B., "Some Reflections on the Sociology of Knowledge," *British Journal of Sociology,* VII, 1956, 52–58.

BOULDING, KENNETH, "Welfare Economics," in *Survey of Contemporary Economics,* Vol. II, Richard D. Irwin, Homewood, Ill., 1960.

BRAYBROOKE, DAVID, "The Relevance of Norms to Political Description," *American Political Science Review,* 52, 1958.

CHILD, ARTHUR, "The Problem of Truth in the Sociology of Knowledge, *Ethics,* LVIII, 1947, 18–34.

DRAY, W. H., *Philosophy of History,* Prentice-Hall, Englewood Cliffs, N.J., 1964, 23–29.

FURFEY, PAUL HANLY, "Sociological Science and the Problem of Values," in L. Gross, ed., *Symposium on Sociological Theory,* Harper & Row, New York, 1959.

GIBSON, QUENTIN, *The Logic of Social Enquiry,* Routledge and Kegan Paul, London, 1960, Chapters VI and VII.

GLUCK, S. E., "The Epistemology of Mannheim's Sociology of Knowledge," *Methodos,* **6,** 1954.

GOLIGHTLY, C. L., "Value as a Scientific Concept," *Journal of Philosophy,* **53,** 1956, 801–813.

HARTUNG, FRANK E., "Problems of the Sociology of Knowledge," *Philosophy of Science,* **19,** 1952.

HINSHAW, VIRGIL G., "Epistemological Relativism and the Sociology of Knowledge," *Philosophy of Science,* **15,** 1948, 4–10.

———, "The Epistemological Relevance of Mannheim's Sociology of Knowledge," *Journal of Philosophy,* **XL,** 1943, 57–72.

———, "The Objectivity of History," *Philosophy of Science,* **25,** 1958, 51–58.

HOROWITZ, IRVING LOUIS, *Philosophy, Science and the Sociology of Knowledge,* Charles C. Thomas, Springfield, Ill., 1961.

———, "Social Science Objectivity and Value Neutrality: Historical Problems and Properties," *Diogenes,* **39,** 1962, 17–44.

HUTCHISON, T. W., *Positive Economics and Policy Objectives,* Harvard University Press, Cambridge, Mass., 1964.

JEFFREY, R. C., "Valuation and Acceptance of Scientific Hypotheses," *Philosophy of Science,* **23,** 1956, 237–246.

KELSEN, HANS, "Value Judgments in the Science of Law," *Journal of Social Philosophy and Jurisprudence,* 1942.

———, *What Is Justice?,* University of California Press, Berkeley and Los Angeles, 1957.

KLAPPHOLZ, KURT, "Value Judgments and Economics," *British Journal for the Philosophy of Science,* **XV,** 1964, 97–114.

KNIGHT, FRANK H., "Fact and Value in Social Science," in *Freedom and Reform: Essays in Economics and Social Philosophy,* Harper & Row, New York, 1947.

LAVINE, THELMA Z., "Naturalism and the Sociological Analysis of Knowledge," in Y. H. Krikorian, ed., *Naturalism and the Human Spirit,* Columbia University Press, New York, 1944.

LEVI, I., "Must the Scientist Make Value Judgments?," *Journal of Philosophy,* **58,** 1960, 345–347.

LICHTHEIM, GEORGE, "The Concept of Ideology," *History and Theory,* **IV,** 1965, 164–195; reprinted in G. H. Nadel, ed., *Studies in the Philosophy of History,* Harper Torchbooks, New York, 1965.

LITTLE, I. M. D., "Economic Behaviour and Welfare," *Mind,* **58,** 1949, 195–199.

———, *A Critique of Welfare Economics,* 2d ed., Oxford University Press, London, 1957.

LYND, ROBERT S., *Knowledge for What?,* Princeton University Press, Princeton, N.J., 1939.

MACKENZIE, P. T., "Fact and Value," *Mind,* **76,** 1967, 228–237.

MANDELBAUM, MAURICE, *The Problem of Historical Knowledge: An Answer to Relativism,* Liveright, New York, 1938.

MANNHEIM, KARL, *Essays on Sociology and Social Psychology,* ed. by P. Kecskemeti, Routledge and Kegan Paul, London, 1956.

————, *Essays on the Sociology of Knowledge,* ed. by P. Kecskemeti, Routledge and Kegan Paul, London, 1952.

————, *Ideology and Utopia,* Harcourt, Brace & Co., New York, 1936.

————, *Man and Society in an Age of Reconstruction,* Routledge and Kegan Paul, London, 1940.

MEEK, RONALD L., "Value Judgments in Economics," *British Journal for the Philosophy of Science,* **15,** 1964, 89–96.

MEILAND, JACK W., *Scepticism and Historical Knowledge,* Random House, New York, 1965.

MELDEN, A. I., "Judgments in the Social Sciences," in *Civilization,* University of California Press, Berkeley and Los Angeles, 1959, 121–146.

MERTON, ROBERT K., *Social Theory and Social Structure,* Free Press, New York, 1957, Part III.

METZGER, WALTER, "Ideology and the Intellectual," *Philosophy of Science,* **16,** 1949.

MYRDAL, GUNNAR, *Value in Social Theory: A Selection of Essays on Methodology,* Harper & Row, New York, 1958.

PASSMORE, JOHN, "Can the Social Sciences be Value-Free?" in H. Feigl and M. Brodbeck, eds., *Readings in the Philosophy of Science.*

————, "The Objectivity of History," *Philosophy,* **33,** 1958, 97–111.

POPPER, KARL R., *The Poverty of Historicism,* Routledge and Kegan Paul, London; Beacon Press, Boston, 1957.

RESCHER, N., "Values and the Explanation of Behaviour," *The Philosophical Quarterly,* **17,** 1967, 130–136.

ROSE, ARNOLD M., *Theory and Method in the Social Sciences,* University of Minnesota Press, Minneapolis, 1954.

ROSHWALD, M., "Value Judgments in the Social Sciences," *British Journal for the Philosophy of Science,* **6,** 1955, 186–208.

RUDNER, RICHARD S., *Philosophy of Social Science.* Prentice-Hall, Englewood Cliffs, N.J., 1966, Chapter 4.

————, "The Scientist *qua* Scientist Makes Value Judgments," *Philosophy of Science,* **20,** 1953.

————, "Value Judgments in the Acceptance of Theories," *Scientific Monthly,* **79,** 1954.

RUNCIMAN, W. G., *Social Science and Political Theory,* Cambridge University Press, Cambridge and New York, 1963, Chapters 3 and 8.

SCHUMPETER, JOSEPH A., "Is the History of Economics a History of Ideologies?" in his *History of Economic Analysis,* Oxford University Press, New York, 1954; reprinted in D. Braybrooke, ed., *Philosophical Problems of the Social Sciences,* Macmillan, New York, 1965.

STARK, WERNER, *The Sociology of Knowledge,* Free Press, New York, 1958.

TAYLOR, P. W., "Social Science and Ethical Relativism," *Journal of Philosophy* **55,** 1958, 32–44.

WEBER, MAX, "The Meaning of 'Ethical Neutrality' in Sociology and Economics," in *The Methodology of the Social Sciences,* Free Press, New York. 1949, Essay I.

WOLFF, KURT H., "The Sociology of Knowledge: Emphasis on an Empirical Attitude," *Philosophy of Science,* **10,** 1943.

——, "The Sociology of Knowledge and Sociological Theory" in L. Gross, ed., *Symposium on Sociological Theory,* Harper & Row, New York, 1959.

THREE: PURPOSE AND FUNCTION

AGASSI, J., "Methodological Individualism," *British Journal of Sociology,* **11,** 1960, 244–270.

ALMOND, GABRIEL A., "Introduction: A Functional Approach to Comparative Politics," in G. A. Almond and J. S. Coleman, eds., *The Politics of Developing Areas,* Princeton University Press, Princeton, N.J., 1960.

BEATTIE, J. H. M., "Understanding and Explanation in Social Anthropology," *British Journal of Sociology,* **10,** 1959, 45–60.

BERGMANN, GUSTAV, "Psychoanalysis and Experimental Psychology," *Mind,* **52,** 1943, 122–140; reprinted in Melvin H. Marx, ed., *Psychological Theory: Contemporary Readings,* Macmillan, New York, 1951.

——, "On Some Methodological Problems of Psychology," *Philosophy of Science,* **7,** 1940; reprinted in H. Feigl and M. Brodbeck, eds., *Readings in the Philosophy of Science.*

BLACK, MAX, ed., *The Social Theories of Talcott Parsons,* Englewood Cliffs, N.J., Prentice-Hall, 1961.

BRAITHWAITE, R. B., *Scientific Explanation,* Cambridge University Press, Cambridge, 1953, Chapter 10.

BROAD, C. D., "Mechanical Explanation and Its Alternatives," *Aristotelian Society Proceedings,* 1918–1919.

——, *The Mind and its Place in Nature,* Harcourt, Brace & World, New York, 1929, Section C.

BROWN, R., "Dispositional and Teleological Statements," *Philosophical Studies,* **3,** 1952.

——, "The Explanation of Behaviour," *Philosophy,* **40,** 1965, 344–348. (Review of *The Explanation of Behaviour* by Charles Taylor.)

CANFIELD, JOHN V., ed., *Purpose in Nature,* Prentice-Hall, Englewood Cliffs, N.J., 1966.

COHEN, JONATHAN, "Teleological Explanation," *Proceedings of the Aristotelian Society,* **LI,** 1950–1951, 255–292.

DAVIS, KINGSLEY, "The Myth of Functional Analysis as a Special Method in Sociology and Anthropology," *American Sociological Review,* **24,** 1959, 757–772.

DEUTSCH, KARL W., "Mechanism, Teleology, and Mind," *Philosophy and Phenomenological Research,* **12,** 1951.

DOLLARD, J., and N. E. MILLER, *Personality and Psychotherapy,* McGraw-Hill Book Company, New York, 1950.

DUCASSE, C. J.,"Explanation, Mechanism, and Teleology," in H. Feigl and W. Sellars, eds., *Readings in Philosophical Analysis,* Appleton-Century-Crofts, New York, 1949.

EMMET, DOROTHY, *Function, Purpose and Powers,* Macmillan, London; St. Martin's Press, New York, 1958.

EVANS-PRITCHARD, E. E., *Social Anthropology,* Free Press, New York, 1954.

FIRTH, R. W., ed., *Man and Culture,* Routledge and Kegan Paul, London, 1957.

GELLNER, E. A., "Time and Theory in Social Anthropology," *Mind,* **67,** 1958, 182–202.

GOLDSTEIN, L. J., "The Logic of Explanation in Malinowskian Anthropology," *Philosophy of Science,* **24,** 1957.

GRUNER, ROLF, "Teleological and Functional Explanations," *Mind,* **75,** 1966, 516–526.

HARRIS, E. E., "Teleology and Teleological Explanation," *Journal of Philosophy,* **56,** 1959, 5–25.

HEMPEL, C. G., and P. OPPENHEIM, "Studies in the Logic of Explanation," in H. Feigl and M. Brodbeck, eds., *Readings in the Philosophy of Science.*

HOCHBERG, HERBERT, "Intervening Variables, Hypothetical Constructs and Metaphysics" (with Comments by Grover Maxwell and rejoinder by Hochberg), in H. Feigl and G. Maxwell, eds., *Current Issues in the Philosophy of Science,* Holt, Rinehart & Winston, New York, 1961, 448–460.

HOEBEL, E. ADAMSON, *The Law of Primitive Man,* Harvard University Press, Cambridge, Mass., 1954.

HOLT, ROBERT T., "A Proposed Structural-Functional Framework for Political Science," in *Functionalism in the Social Sciences,* Monograph No. 5 of the American Academy of Political and Social Science, Philadelphia, 1965, 84–110.

HOMANS, GEORGE C., and DAVID M. SCHNEIDER, *Marriage, Authority, and Final Causes,* Free Press, New York, 1955.

HULL, C. L., "Mind, Mechanism, and Adaptive Behavior," *Psychological Review,* **44,** 1937, 1–32.

JARVIE, I. C., "Nadel on the Aims and Methods of Social Anthropology," *British Journal for the Philosophy of Science,* **12,** 1961, 1–24.

———, *The Revolution in Anthropology,* Routledge and Kegan Paul, London, 1964, Chapter 6.

KLUCKHOHN, CLYDE, "The Limitations of Adaptation and Adjustment as Concepts for Understanding Cultural Behavior," in John Romano, ed., *Adaptation,* 1949, 99–113.

KLUCKHOHN, CLYDE, and HENRY A. MURRAY, eds., *Personality in Nature, Society, and Culture,* Alfred A. Knopf, Inc., New York, 1950.

KROEBER, A. L., "Structure, Function, and Pattern in Biology and Anthropology," *Scientific Monthly,* **56,** 1943.

LEACH, EDMUND R., *Rethinking Anthropology,* University of London, Athlone Press, London, 1962; Humanities Press, New York.

LEHMAN, HUGH, "R. K. Merton's Concepts of Function and Functionalism," *Inquiry,* **9,** No. 3, 1966. [The entire issue is devoted to articles on functionalism.]

LEVY, MARION, JR., *The Structure of Society,* Princeton University Press, Princeton, 1952.

MACE, C. A., "Mechanical and Teleological Causation," in H. Feigl and W. Sellars, eds., *Readings in Philosophical Analysis,* Appleton-Century-Crofts, New York, 1949.

MacINTYRE, A., and P. H. NOWELL-SMITH, "Symposium: Purpose and Intelligent Action," *Proceedings of the Aristotelian Society, Supplementary Volume 34,* 1960.

MacKAY, D. M., "Mind-like Behaviour in Artifacts," *British Journal for the Philosophy of Science,* 2, 1951.

MARTINDALE, D., ed., *Functionalism in the Social Sciences,* Monograph No. 5 of the American Academy of Political and Social Science, Philadelphia, 1965.

MERTON, R. K., "Manifest and Latent Functions," in *Social Theory and Social Structure,* Free Press, New York, 1957.

MORSE, CHANDLER, "The Functional Imperatives," in Max Black, ed., *The Social Theories of Talcott Parsons,* Prentice-Hall, Englewood Cliffs, N.J., 1961, 100–152.

NADEL, S. F., *Foundations of Social Anthropology,* Cohen and West, London, 1951.

———, *The Theory of Social Structure,* Cohen and West, London, 1957.

NAGEL, ERNEST, "Concept and Theory Formation in the Social Sciences," J. L. Jarret and S. M. McMurrin, eds., *Contemporary Philosophy,* Holt, Rinehart & Winston, New York, 1954.

———, "A Formalization of Functionalism," in his *Logic Without Metaphysics,* Free Press, New York, 1957, 247–283.

———, *The Structure of Science,* Harcourt, Brace & World, New York, Chapter 12.

———, "Teleological Explanation and Teleological Systems," in H. Feigl and M. Brodbeck, eds., *Readings in the Philosophy of Science.*

PAP, ARTHUR, *An Introduction to the Philosophy of Science,* The Free Press, New York, 1962, Chapter 19.

RADCLIFFE-BROWN, A. R., *A Natural Science of Society,* The Free Press, New York, 1957.

———, *Structure and Function in Primitive Society,* Free Press, New York, 1952, 1965.

———, "On the Concept of Function in Social Science," *American Anthropologist,* 37, 1935.

ROSENBLUETH, A., N. WIENER, and J. BIGELOW, "Behavior, Purpose and Teleology," *Philosophy of Science,* 10, 1943; reprinted in J. V. Canfield, ed., *Purpose in Nature,* Prentice-Hall, Englewood Cliffs, N.J., 1966.

RUDNER, RICHARD S., *Philosophy of Social Science,* Prentice-Hall, Englewood Cliffs, N.J., 1966, Chapter 5.

RUNCIMAN, W. G., *Social Science and Political Theory,* Cambridge University Press, London, New York, 1963, Chapter 6.

RUSSELL, E. S., *The Directiveness of Organic Activities,* Cambridge University Press, Cambridge, 1945.

SCHEFFLER, I., "Thoughts on Teleology," *British Journal for the Philosophy of*

Science, **9,** 1958; reprinted in J. V. Canfield, ed., *Purpose in Nature,* Prentice-Hall, Englewood Cliffs, N.J., 1966.

STOUT, G. F., "Mechanical and Teleological Causation," *Aristotelian Society Proceedings,* Supplement, 14, 1935.

TAYLOR, CHARLES, *The Explanation of Behaviour,* Routledge and Kegan Paul, London; Humanities Press, New York, 1964.

TAYLOR, RICHARD, *Action and Purpose,* Prentice-Hall, Englewood Cliffs, N.J., 1966.

———, "Comments on a Mechanistic Conception of Purposefulness," *Philosophy of Science,* **17,** 1950, 310–317; reprinted in J. V. Canfield, ed., *Purpose in Nature,* Prentice-Hall, Englewood Cliffs, N.J., 1966.

TOLMAN, E. C., *Purposive Behavior in Animals and Men,* Appleton-Century-Crofts, New York, 1932.

———, *Behavior and Psychological Man,* Chapters 4 and 5, University of California Press, Berkeley, 1958.

WIENER, N., *Cybernetics,* M.I.T. Press, Cambridge, Mass., 1961.

WISDOM, J. O., "The Hypothesis of Cybernetics," *British Journal for the Philosophy of Science,* **2,** 1951.

FOUR: SOCIAL FACTS, SOCIAL LAWS, AND REDUCTION

ACTON, H. B., *The Illusion of an Epoch,* Cohen and West, London, 1955.

AGASSI, J., "Methodological Individualism," *British Journal of Sociology,* 11, 1960, 244–270.

ARGYLE, MICHAEL, *The Scientific Study of Social Behaviour,* Methuen & Co., London, 1957, Chapters 4 and 5.

BASH, HARRY H., "Determinism and Avoidability in Sociohistorical Analysis," *Ethics,* **LXXIV,** 1964, 186–200.

BERGMANN, GUSTAV, "Configurations and Reduction," *Philosophy of Science,* University of Wisconsin Press, Madison, 1957, Chapter 3.

———, "Holism, Historicism, and Emergence," *Philosophy of Science,* 11, 1944, 209–221.

———, "Reduction" in J. T. Wilson *et al., Current Trends in Psychology and the Behavioral Sciences,* University of Pittsburgh Press, Pittsburgh, 1954.

BERLIN, ISAIAH, *Historical Inevitability,* Oxford University Press, London, 1954.

———, *Karl Max,* 2d ed., Oxford University Press. London and New York, 1948.

BIDNEY, DAVID, *Theoretical Anthropology,* Columbia University Press, New York, 1953.

BRODBECK, MAY, "On the Philosophy of the Social Sciences," *Philosophy of Science,* 21, 1954, pp. 140–156.

COHEN, PERCY S., "The Aims and Interests of Sociology," *British Journal for the*

Philosophy of Science, **14,** 1963, 246–261. (Review discussion of *The Poverty of Historicism* by K. R. Popper.)

DEUTSCH, KARL W., "Mechanism, Organism, and Society," *Philosophy of Science,* **18,** 1951.

DURKHEIM, EMILE, *The Rules of Sociological Method,* Free Press, New York, 1950.

———, *Sociology and Philosophy,* Free Press, New York, 1953.

———, "Sociology and its Scientific Field," in K. H. Wolff, ed., *Essays on Sociology and Philosophy,* Harper & Row, New York, 1960.

EDEL, ABRAHAM, "The Concept of Levels in Social Theory," in L. Gross, ed., *Symposium on Sociological Theory,* Harper & Row, New York, 1959.

GIBSON, QUENTIN, *The Logic of Social Enquiry,* Routledge and Kegan Paul, London; Humanities Press, New York, 1960, Chapter 9.

———, "Social Forces," *Journal of Philosophy,* **LV,** 1958, 441–455.

GILLIN, JOHN, *The Ways of Men,* Appleton-Century-Crofts, New York, 1948.

———, ed., *For a Science of Social Man: Convergences in Anthropology, Psychology, and Sociology,* Macmillan, New York, 1954.

GINSBERG, M., "The Individual and Society," in his *Diversity of Morals,* Heinemann, London, 1956.

GOLDSTEIN, LEON, "The Inadequacy of the Principle of Methodological Individualism," *Journal of Philosophy,* **LIII,** 1956, 801–813.

———, "Mr. Watkins on the Two Theses," *British Journal for the Philosophy of Science,* **X,** 1959, 240–241.

———, "The Two Theses of Methodological Individualism," *British Journal for the Philosophy of Science,* **IX,** 1958, 1–11.

HARTSHORNE, RICHARD, "Exceptionalism in Geography Re-examined," *Annals of the Association of American Geographers,* **45,** 1955, 218–224.

———, "The Nature of Geography," *Annals of the Association of American Geographers,* **29,** 1939.

HAYEK, F. A., "Degrees of Explanation," *British Journal for the Philosophy of Science,* **6,** 1955–1956, 209–225.

———, *The Counter-Revolution of Science,* Free Press, New York, 1952.

HEMPEL, G. C., "General System Theory and the Unity of Science," *Human Biology,* **23,** 1951, 313–322.

HENLE, P., "The Status of Emergence," *Journal of Philosophy,* **39,** 1942, 486–493.

HINSHAW, VIRGIL, JR., "Can Philosophical Anthropology Be a Science? An Examination of Bidney's Philosophy of Culture," *The Ohio Journal of Science,* **51,** 1951, 37–41.

HINSHAW, VIRGIL, JR., and J. N. SPUHLER, "On Some Fallacies Derived in David Bidney's Philosophy of Culture," *Central States Bulletin* (American Anthropological Association), **2,** 1948, 12–18.

HOMANS, GEORGE C., *The Human Group,* Harper & Row, New York, 1950.

———, *Social Behavior. Its Elementary Forms,* Harcourt, Brace & World, New York, 1961.

HOOK, SIDNEY, "Dialectic in Social and Historical Inquiry," *Journal of Philosophy,* **36,** 1939, 365–378.

————, *The Hero in History,* Beacon Press, Boston, 1955.

————, *Reason, Social Myths, and Democracy,* John Day, New York, 1940.

JESSOR, RICHARD, "The Problem of Reductionism in Psychology," *Psychological Review,* 65, 1958, 170–178; reprinted in Melvin H. Marx, ed., *Theories in Contemporary Psychology,* Macmillan, New York, 1963.

JOYNT, CAREY B., and N. RESCHER, "The Problem of Uniqueness in History," *History and Theory,* I, 1961, 150–162; reprinted in George H. Nadel, ed., *Studies in the Philosophy of History,* Harper Torchbooks, New York, 1965.

KLUCKHOHN, CLYDE, "The Study of Culture," in D. Lerner and H. D. Lasswell, eds., *The Policy Sciences,* Stanford University Press, Stanford, 1951.

KROEBER, A. L., *The Nature of Culture,* University of Chicago Press, Chicago, 1952.

KROEBER, A. L., and TALCOTT PARSONS, "The Concepts of Culture and of Social System," *American Sociological Review,* 23, 1958, 582–583.

LAZARSFELD, PAUL F., and MORRIS ROSENBERG, eds., *The Language of Social Research,* Free Press, New York, 1955, Sections I and IV on group concepts.

LERNER, DANIEL, ed., *Parts and Wholes,* Free Press, New York, 1963.

LERNER, DANIEL, and HAROLD D. LASSWELL, eds., *The Policy Sciences: Recent Developments in Scope and Method,* Stanford University Press, Stanford, 1951.

LITTMAN, R. A., and E. ROSEN, "Molar and Molecular," *Psychological Review,* 57, 1950, 58–65; reprinted in Melvin H. Marx, ed., *Psychological Theory: Contemporary Readings,* Macmillan, New York, 1951.

LOVEJOY, A. O., "The Meanings of 'Emergence' and Its Modes," in P. P. Wiener, ed., *Readings in Philosophy of Science,* Scribner's, New York, 1953.

LUKERMANN, F., "Geography: de facto or de jure," *Journal of Minnesota Academy of Science,* 32, 1965, 189–196.

————, "Geography as a Formal Intellectual Discipline and the Way it Contributes to Human Knowledge," *Canadian Geographer,* VIII, 1964, 167–172.

MADDEN, EDWARD H., "The Philosophy of Science in Gestalt Theory," *Philosophy of Science,* 19, 1952; reprinted in H. Feigl and M. Brodbeck, eds., *Readings in the Philosophy of Science.*

————, *Philosophical Problems of Psychology,* Odyssey Press, New York, 1962.

MALINOWSKI, B., *A Scientific Theory of Culture and Other Essays,* University of North Carolina Press, Chapel Hill, 1944.

MANDELBAUM, MAURICE, "A Note on Emergence," in S. Baron, *et al.,* eds. *Freedom and Reason,* Free Press, New York, 1951.

————, "Societal Facts," *British Journal of Sociology,* VI, 1955, 305–317; reprinted in E. H. Madden, ed., *The Structure of Scientific Thought,* and in P. Gardiner, ed., *Theories of History,* Free Press, New York, 1959.

————, "Societal Laws," *British Journal for the Philosophy of Science,* VIII, 1957, 211–224; reprinted in W. H. Dray, ed., *Philosophical Analysis and History,* Harper & Row, New York, 1966.

McCLOSKEY, H. J., "The State as an Organism, as a Person, and as an End in Itself," *Philosophical Review,* 72, 1963, 306–326.

MEEHL, P. E., and W. SELLARS, "The Concept of Emergence," in H. Feigl and M. Scriven, eds., *Minnesota Studies in the Philosophy of Science,* Vol. I, University of Minnesota Press, Minneapolis, 1956.

MILL, J. S., *A System of Logic*, Longmans, Green and Co., New York, 1947, Book VI, Chapters VI and VII.

NAGEL, ERNEST, "The Meaning of Reduction in the Natural Sciences," in A. Danto and S. Morgenbesser, eds., *Philosophy of Science*.

———, *The Structure of Science*, Harcourt, Brace & World, New York, 1961, Chapter 11.

———, "Wholes, Sums, and Organic Unities," *Philosophical Studies*, 3, 1952.

OPPENHEIM, P., and H. PUTNAM, "Unity of Science as a Working Hypothesis," in H. Feigl, M. Scriven, and G. Maxwell, eds., *Minnesota Studies in the Philosophy of Science*, II, University of Minnesota Press, 1958.

PARSONS, TALCOTT, *Essays in Sociological Theory*, Free Press, New York, 1949.

———, *The Structure of Social Action*, Free Press, New York, 1949.

PARSONS, TALCOTT, and EDWARD SHILS, eds. *Toward a General Theory of Action*, Harvard University Press, Cambridge, Mass., 1951.

PASSMORE, JOHN, "History, the Individual, and Inevitability," *Philosophical Review*, 68, 1959, 93–102.

POPPER, KARL R., *The Open Society and Its Enemies*, Princeton University Press, Princeton, N.J., 1950.

———, *The Poverty of Historicism*, Routledge and Kegan Paul, London, 1957.

———, "What is Dialectic," *Mind*, 49, 1940.

RESCHER, NICHOLAS, and P. OPPENHEIM, "Logical Analysis of Gestalt Concepts," *British Journal for the Philosophy of Science*, 6, 1955–1956, 89–106.

RESCHER, NICHOLAS, and W. W. ROZEBOOM, "Symposium: On the Probability of Nonrecurring Events," in H. Feigl and G. Maxwell, eds., *Current Issues in the Philosophy of Science*, Holt, Rinehart and Winston, New York, 1961.

SCHAEFFER, KURT, "Exceptionalism in Geography: A Methodological Examination," *Annals of the Association of American Geographers*, 43, 1953.

SCOTT, K. J., "Methodological and Epistemological Individualism," *British Journal for the Philosophy of Science*, 11, 1960–61, 331–336.

SEARS, ROBERT R., "Social Behavior and Personality Development," in T. Parsons and E. A. Shils, eds., *Toward a General Theory of Action*, Harvard University Press, Cambridge, Mass., 1951.

SHILS, EDWARD A., "The Macrosociological Problem," in Donald P. Ray, ed., *Trends in Social Science*, Philosophical Library, New York, 1961.

TOLMAN, E. C., "Physiology, Psychology, and Sociology," in E. C. Tolman, *Behavior and Psychological Man*, University of California Press, Berkeley, 1958.

WATKINS, J. W. N., "The Alleged Inadequacy of Methodological Individualism," *Journal of Philosophy*, 55, 1958, 390–395.

———, "Ideal Types and Historical Explanation," *British Journal for the Philosophy of Science*, 3, 1952; reprinted in H. Feigl and M. Brodbeck, eds., *Readings in the Philosophy of Science*.

———, "Methodological Individualism: A Reply," *Philosophy of Science*, 22, 1955, 58–62.

———, "Third Reply to Mr. Goldstein," *British Journal for the Philosophy of Science*, X, 1959, 242–244.

WATSON, RICHARD A., "Is Geology Different," *Philosophy of Science*, **33**, 1966, 172–185.

WEBER, MAX, *The Theory of Social and Economic Organization*, Free Press, New York, 1947.

WELDON, T. D., *The Vocabulary of Politics*, "The Uses of Political Words," Penguin Books, London, 1953, Chapter 3.

WHITE, LESLIE A., *The Science of Culture*, Farrar, Straus & Giroux, New York, 1949.

ZILSEL, EDGAR, "Physics and the Problem of Historico-sociological Laws," *Philosophy of Science*, **8**, 1941; reprinted in H. Feigl and M. Brodbeck, eds., *Readings in the Philosophy of Science*.

FIVE: EXPLANATION, PREDICTION, AND IMPERFECT KNOWLEDGE

ALBERT, ETHEL M., "Causality in the Social Sciences," *Journal of Philosophy*, **51**, 1954, 695–705.

ALEXANDER, PETER, and A. MacINTYRE, "Symposium: Cause and Cure in Psychotherapy," *Proceedings of the Aristotelian Society, Supplementary Volume 29*, 1955.

ARGYLE, MICHAEL, *The Scientific Study of Social Behaviour*, "The Explanation of Social Behaviour," Methuen & Co., London, 1957, Chapter 3.

BARTLEY, W. W., 3D, "Achilles, the Tortoise, and Explanation in Science and History," *British Journal for the Philosophy of Science*, **13**, 1962–1963, 15–33.

BECK, S. J., "The Science of Personality: Nomothetic or Idiographic?", *Psychological Review*, **60**, 1953.

BERGMANN, G., *Philosophy of Science*, University of Wisconsin Press, Madison, 1957, Chapter 2.

BRAITHWAITE, R. B., *Scientific Explanation*, Cambridge University Press, Cambridge, 1953, Chapters 11 and 12.

BROWN, ROBERT, "Explanation by Laws in Social Science," *Philosophy of Science*, **21**, 1954, 25–32.

———, *Explanation in Social Science*, Aldine, Chicago, 1963.

CAMPBELL, NORMAN R., *The Foundations of Experimental Science*, Dover, New York, 1957, Chapters 5 and 6.

———, *What is Science?*, Dover, New York, 1952.

COLLINS, ARTHUR W., "The Use of Statistics in Explanation," *British Journal for the Philosophy of Science*, **17**, 1966, 127–140.

DANTO, A. C., *Analytical Philosophy of History*, Cambridge University Press, New York, 1965.

DONAGAN, ALAN, "Explanation in History," *Mind*, **66**, 1957, 145–164; reprinted in P. Gardiner, ed., *Theories of History*, Free Press, New York, 1959.

———, "Historical Explanation: The Popper-Hempel Theory Reconsidered,"

History and Theory, **IV,** 1964, 3–26; reprinted in W. H. Dray, ed., *Philosophical Analysis and History,* Harper & Row, New York, 1966.

DONAGAN, ALAN, and BARBARA DONAGAN, eds., *Philosophy of History,* Macmillan, New York, 1965.

DRAY, WILLIAM H., *Laws and Explanation in History,* Oxford University Press, London, 1957.

———, *Philosophy of History,* Prentice-Hall, Englewood Cliffs, N.J., 1964.

———, ed., *Philosophical Analysis and History,* Harper & Row, New York, 1966.

FAIN, HASKELL, "Some Problems of Causal Explanation," *Mind,* **72,** 1963, 519–532.

FALK, J. L., "Issues Distinguishing Idiographic from Nomothetic Approaches to Personality Theory," *Psychological Review,* **63,** 1956, 53–62.

FEIGL, H., "Some Remarks on the Meaning of Scientific Explanation," in H. Feigl and W. Sellars, *Readings in Philosophical Analysis,* Appleton-Century-Crofts, New York, 1949.

FEUER, LEWIS S., "Causality in the Social Sciences," *Journal of Philosophy,* **51,** 1954, 681–695.

FRANK, PHILIPP, *Philosophy of Science,* Prentice-Hall, Englewood Cliffs, N.J., 1957, Chapters 11 and 12.

GALLIE, W. B., *Philosophy and the Historical Understanding,* Chatto & Windus, London, 1964.

GARDINER, PATRICK, *The Nature of Historical Explanation,* Oxford University Press, London, 1952.

———, ed., *Theories of History,* Free Press, New York, 1959.

GLUCK, S. E., "Do Statistical Laws Have Explanatory Efficacy?" *Philosophy of Science,* **22,** 1955, 34–38.

GOROVITZ, SAMUEL, "Causal Judgments and Causal Explanations," *Journal of Philosophy,* **62,** 1965, 695–711.

GRÜNBAUM, ADOLF, "Temporally Asymmetric Principles, Parity between Explanation and Prediction, and Mechanism versus Teleology," *Philosophy of Science,* **29,** 1962, 146–170.

HANSON, NORWOOD R., "On the Symmetry between Explanation and Prediction," *Philosophical Review,* **68,** 1959, 349–358.

———, *Patterns of Discovery,* Cambridge University Press, Cambridge, Eng. 1958.

HART, H. L. A., and A. M. HONORÉ, *Causation in the Law,* Oxford University Press, Oxford, 1959.

HELMER, O., and N. RESCHER, "On the Epistemology of the Inexact Sciences," *Management Science,* **6,** 1959, 25–52.

HEMPEL, C. G., *Aspects of Scientific Explanation,* Free Press, New York, 1965, Chapter 4.

———, "Deductive-Nomological vs. Statistical Explanation," in H. Feigl and G. Maxwell, eds., *Minnesota Studies in the Philosophy of Science,* III, University of Minnesota Press, Minneapolis, 1962, 98–169.

———, "Explanation and Prediction by Covering Laws," in B. Baumrin, ed., *Philosophy of Science: The Delaware Seminar,* Vol. I, John Wiley & Sons, New York, 1963.

————, "Explanation in Science and in History," in R. G. Colodny, ed., *Frontiers of Science and Philosophy,* University of Pittsburgh Press, Pittsburgh, 1962.

————, "The Function of General Laws in History," in H. Feigl and W. Sellars, eds., *Readings in Philosophical Analysis,* and in P. Gardiner, ed., *Theories of History,* Free Press, New York, 1959.

————, *Philosophy of Natural Science,* Prentice-Hall, Englewood Cliffs, N.J., 1966.

HEMPEL, C. G., and P. OPPENHEIM, "Studies in the Logic of Explanation," in H. Feigl and M. Brodbeck, eds., *Readings in the Philosophy of Science,* Appleton-Century-Crofts, Inc., New York, 1953.

HESSE, M. B., "A New Look at Scientific Explanation," *Review of Metaphysics,* XVII, 1963, 98–108.

HOLT, ROBERT R., "Individuality and Generalization in the Psychology of Personality: An Evaluation," *Journal of Personality,* 30, 1962, 377–402.

HOOK, SIDNEY, ed., *Philosophy and History,* New York University Press, New York, 1963.

HOSPERS, J., "On Explanation," *Journal of Philosophy,* 43, 1946, 337–346.

HUGHES, H. STUART, "The Historian and the Social Scientist," *American Historical Review,* 66, 1961, 20–46.

————, *History as Art and Science,* Harper & Row, New York, 1964.

JARVIE, I. C., "Explanation in Social Science," *British Journal for the Philosophy of Science,* 15, 1964, 62–72. (Review discussion of *Explanation in Social Science* by Robert Brown.)

KAHL, RUSSELL, ed., *Studies in Explanation,* Prentice-Hall, Englewood Cliffs, N.J., 1963.

LEACH, JAMES, "Dray on Rational Explanation," *Philosophy of Science,* 33, 1966, 61–69.

MANDELBAUM, M., "Historical Explanation: The Problem of 'Covering Laws'," *History and Theory,* I, 1961, 229–242.

MEEHL, PAUL E., *Clinical vs. Statistical Prediction,* University of Minnesota Press, Minneapolis, 1954.

MELLOR, D. H., "Experimental Error and Deducibility," *Philosophy of Science,* 32, 1965, 105–122.

MEYERHOFF, HANS, ed., *The Philosophy of History in Our Time,* Anchor Books, Doubleday & Co., Garden City, N.Y., 1959.

MILLER, D. L., "Meaning of Explanation," *Psychological Review,* 53, 1946.

MISCHEL, T., "Pragmatic Aspects of Explanation," *Philosophy of Science,* 33, 1966, 40–60.

MORGENBESSER, SIDNEY, "The Explanatory-Predictive Approach to Science," in B. Baumrin, ed. *Philosophy of Science: The Delaware Seminar,* Vol. 1, John Wiley & Sons, New York, 1963.

NAGEL, E., *The Structure of Science,* Harcourt, Brace & World, New York, Chapters 2, 3, 5–7, 14, and 15.

NEWMAN, FRED, "Explanation Sketches," *Philosophy of Science,* 32, 1965, 168–172.

OLIVECRONA, KARL, "Is a Sociological Explanation of Law Possible?", *Theoria,* 14, 1948.

PAP, ARTHUR, *An Introduction to the Philosophy of Science,* Free Press, New York, 1962, Chapter 18.

PASSMORE, J., "Explanation in Everyday Life, in Science, and in History," *History and Theory,* **2,** 1962.

PITT, J., "Generalizations in Historical Explanation," *Journal of Philosophy,* **56,** 1959, 578–586.

POPPER, K. R., *The Logic of Scientific Discovery,* Hutchinson, London, and Basic Books, New York, 1959, Chapter 3.

RESCHER, N., "On Prediction and Explanation," *British Journal for the Philosophy of Science,* **8,** 1958, 281–290.

RIKER, W. H., "Causes of Events," *Journal of Philosophy,* **55,** 1958, 281–291.

RUSSELL, BERTRAND, "On the Notion of Cause," in *Mysticism and Logic,* Anchor Books, Doubleday & Co., New York, 1957.

SALMON, WESLEY C., "The Status of Prior Probabilities in Statistical Explanation," *Philosophy of Science,* **32,** 1965, 137–146.

SCHEFFLER, I., *The Anatomy of Inquiry,* Alfred A. Knopf, New York, 1963.

———, "Explanation, Prediction, and Abstraction," *British Journal for the Philosophy of Science,* **VII,** 1957; reprinted in A. Danto and S. Morgenbesser, eds., *Philosophy of Science.*

SCRIVEN, MICHAEL, "Causes, Connections and Conditions in History," in W. H. Dray, ed., *Philosophical Analysis and History,* Harper & Row, New York, 1966.

———, "Explanation and Prediction in Evolutionary Theory," *Science,* **130,** 1959, 477–482.

———, "Explanations, Predictions, and Laws," in *Minnesota Studies in the Philosophy of Science,* Vol. III, ed. H. Feigl and G. Maxwell, University of Minnesota Press, Minneapolis, 1962, 170–230.

———, "New Issues in the Logic of Explanation," in S. Hook, ed., *Philosophy and History,* New York University Press, New York, 1963.

———, "The Temporal Asymmetry of Explanations and Predictions," in B. Baumrin, ed., *Philosophy of Science: The Delaware Seminar,* Vol. I, John Wiley & Sons, New York, 1963.

———, "Truisms as the Grounds for Historical Explanation," in P. Gardiner, ed., *Theories of History,* Free Press, New York, 1959.

SKARSGARD, L., "Some Remarks on the Logic of Explanation," *Philosophy of Science,* **25,** 1958, 199–207.

SMITH, FREDERICK V., *The Explanation of Human Behaviour,* 2d ed., Constable, London, 1960.

SOLO, ROBERT, "Prediction, Projection, and Social Prognosis," *Journal of Philosophy,* **52,** 1955, 459–464.

TOULMIN, S., *The Philosophy of Science,* Hutchinsons, London, 1953, Chapters 2 and 3.

TURNER, MERLE B., *Philosophy and the Science of Behavior,* Appleton-Century-Crofts, New York, 1967.

WEINGARTNER, R. H., "Explanations and Their Justifications," *Philosophy of Science,* **28,** 1961, 300–305.

WHITE, ALAN R., *The Philosophy of Mind,* Random House, New York, 1967, Chapter 6, "Explanation of Human Behavior."

WHITE, MORTON, *Foundations of Historical Knowledge,* Harper & Row, New York, 1965.

YOLTON, JOHN W., "Explanation," *British Journal for the Philosophy of Science,* **10,** 1959, 194–208.

On the Prediction Paradox

BUCK, ROGER C., "Rejoinder to Grünbaum," *Philosophy of Science,* **30,** 1963, 373–374.

GEWIRTH, ALAN, "Can Men Change Laws of Social Science?" *Philosophy of Science,* **21,** 1954, 229–241.

GRÜNBAUM, ADOLF, "Comments on Professor Roger Buck's paper 'Reflexive Predictions'," *Philosophy of Science,* **30,** 1963, 370–372.

————, "Historical Determinism, Social Activism, and Predictions in the Social Sciences, *British Journal for the Philosophy of Science,* **VII,** 1956.

GRÜNBERG, F., and F. MODIGLIANI, "The Predictability of Social Events," *Journal of Political Economy,* **LXII,** 1954.

————, "Reflexive Predictions," *Philosophy of Science,* **32,** 1965, 173–174.

LEWIS, DAVID K., and JANE S. RICHARDSON, "Scriven on Human Unpredictability," *Philosophical Studies,* **XVII,** 1966, 69–74.

MacIVER, R. M., *The More Perfect Union,* Macmillan, New York, 1948.

MERTON, ROBERT K., "The Self-Fulfilling Prophecy," in *Social Theory and Social Structure,* Free Press, New York, 1957.

————, "The Unanticipated Consequences of Purposive Social Action," *American Sociological Review,* **1,** 1936, 894–904.

POPPER, K., *The Poverty of Historicism,* Routledge and Kegan Paul, London, 1957, 12–16.

SCRIVEN, MICHAEL, "An Essential Unpredictability in Human Behavior," in B. B. Wolman and E. Nagel, eds., *Scientific Psychology: Principles and Approaches,* Basic Books, New York, 1964, 411–425.

SUPPES, PATRICK, "On an Example of Unpredictability in Human Behavior," *Philosophy of Science,* **31,** 1964, 143–148.

SIX: THEORY CONSTRUCTION

ALMOND, GABRIEL A., "A Developmental Approach to Political Systems," *World Politics,* **17,** 1965, 183–214.

————, "Political Systems and Political Change," *American Behavioral Scientist,* **6,** 1963, 3–10.

ARCHIBALD, G. C., "The State of Economic Science," *British Journal for the Philosophy of Science,* **10,** 1959, 58–69.

ARGYLE, MICHAEL, *The Scientific Study of Social Behaviour,* Methuen & Co., London, 1957, Chapter 3.

ARROW, KENNETH J., *Social Choice and Individual Values,* John Wiley and Sons, New York, 1951.

BECKER, HOWARD, "Constructive Typology in the Social Sciences," in H. E. Barnes *et al.,* eds., *Contemporary Social Theory,* Appleton-Century-Crofts, New York, 1940.

———, "Interpretive Sociology and Constructive Typology," in *Twentieth Century Sociology,* Philosophical Library, New York, 1945.

———, *Through Values to Social Interpretation,* Duke University Press, Durham, N.C., 1950.

BECKER, HOWARD, and ALVIN BOSKOFF, eds., *Modern Sociological Theory,* Dryden Press, New York, 1957.

BERGMANN, GUSTAV, *Philosophy of Science,* University of Wisconsin Press, Madison, 1957, Chapter 2.

———, "Theoretical Psychology," *Annual Review of Psychology,* **4,** 1953, 435–458.

BERGMANN, GUSTAV, and KENNETH W. SPENCE, "Operationism and Theory in Psychology," Psychological Review, 1941, **48,** 1–14; reprinted in Melvin H. Marx, ed., *Psychological Theory: Contemporary Readings,* The Macmillan Company, New York, 1951.

BLACK, MAX, ed., *The Social Theories of Talcott Parsons,* Prentice-Hall, Englewood Cliffs, N.J., 1961.

BRAITHWAITE, R. B., *Scientific Explanation,* Cambridge University Press, Cambridge, 1955.

BUCK, ROGER C., "On the Logic of General Behavior Systems Theory," in H. Feigl and M. Scriven, eds., *Minnesota Studies in the Philosophy of Science,* Vol. I, University of Minnesota Press, Minneapolis, 1956.

COWLING, MAURICE, *The Nature and Limits of Political Science,* Cambridge University Press, Cambridge, 1963.

DAHL, ROBERT A., "The Behavioral Approach in Political Science," *American Political Science Review,* **55,** 1961, 763–772.

———, "Political Theory: Truth and Consequences," *World Politics,* **11,** 1958.

DAHL, ROBERT A., and CHARLES E. LINDBLOM, *Politics, Economics, and Welfare,* Harper & Row, New York, 1953.

DEUTSCH, KARL, "Game Theory and Politics," *The Canadian Journal of Economics and Political Science,* **20,** 1954, 76–83.

———, "The Theoretical Basis of Data Programs," in R. L. Merritt and S. Rokkan, eds., *Comparing Nations,* Yale University Press, New Haven, 1966.

———, *The Nerves of Government; Models of Political Communication and Control,* Free Press, New York, 1963.

DURBIN, E. F. M., "Methods of Research—A Plea for Cooperation in the Social Sciences," *Economic Journal,* **48,** 1938, 183–195.

EASTON, DAVID, *The Political System,* Alfred A. Knopf, New York, 1953.

———, ed., *Varieties of Political Theory,* Prentice-Hall, Englewood Cliffs, N. J., 1966.

ESTES, W. K., *et al., Modern Learning Theory,* Appleton-Century-Crofts, New York, 1954.

EUCKEN, WALTER, *The Foundations of Economics,* University of Chicago Press, Chicago, 1951.

EULAU, HEINZ, S. J. ELDERSVELD, and M. JANOWITZ, eds., *Political Behavior; A Reader in Theory and Research,* Free Press, New York, 1956.

FEIGL, HERBERT, "Principles and Problems of Theory Construction in Psychology," in W. Dennis, ed., *Current Trends in Psychological Theory,* University of Pittsburgh Press, Pittsburgh, 1951, 179–213.

FINE, ARTHUR, "Consistency, Derivability, and Scientific Change," *Journal of Philosophy,* 64, 1967, 231–240.

FRASER, LINDLEY M., *Economic Thought and Language,* Adam and Charles Black, London; Macmillan, New York, 1947.

———, "Economists and Their Critics," *Economic Journal,* 48, 1938, 196–210.

FRIEDMAN, MILTON, *Essays in Positive Economics,* University of Chicago Press, Chicago, 1953.

GOLDBERG, ARTHUR S., "Political Science as Science," *Yale Political Science Research,* Library Publication No. 1, Yale University Press, New Haven.

GROSS, LLEWELLYN, "Theory Construction in Sociology; A Methodological Inquiry," in L. Gross, ed., *Symposium on Sociological Theory,* Harper & Row, New York, 1959.

GRÜNBERG, EMILE, "Notes on the Verifiability of Economic Laws," *Philosophy of Science,* 24, 1957, 337–348.

HANDY, ROLLO, and P. KURTZ, *A Current Appraisal of the Behavioral Sciences,* Behavioral Research Council, Great Barrington, Mass., 1964.

HARROD, R. F., "The Scope and Method of Economics," *Economic Journal,* 48, 1938, 383–412.

HAYEK, F. A., *The Counter-Revolution of Science,* Free Press, New York, 1952.

———, *Individualism and the Economic Order,* Routledge and Kegan Paul, London, 1949.

HEMPEL, C. G., "The Theoretician's Dilemma," in H. Feigl, M. Scriven, and G. Maxwell, eds., *Minnesota Studies in the Philosophy of Science,* II, University of Minnesota Press, Minneapolis, 1958; reprinted in C. G. Hempel, *Aspects of Scientific Explanation,* The Free Press, New York, 1965.

———, "Typological Methods in the Natural and Social Sciences," in *Aspects of Scientific Explanation,* Free Press, New York, 1965, 155–171.

HESSE, MARY B., "Theories, Dictionaries, and Observation," *British Journal for the Philosophy of Science,* 9, 1958.

HODGES, DONALD C., "The Politics of Language and the Science of Politics," *Philosophy and Phenomenological Research,* 24, 1964, 366–374.

HOLT, ROBERT T., and JOHN E. TURNER, *The Political Basis of Economic Development,* Van Nostrand, Princeton, N.J., 1966.

HURWICZ, LEONID, "The Theory of Economic Behavior," *American Economic Review*, **35**, 1945; reprinted in James R. Newman, ed., *The World of Mathematics*, Vol. 2, Simon and Schuster, New York, 1956.

HUTCHISON, T. W., *The Significance and Basic Postulates of Economic Theory*, Macmillan, London, 1938.

HYNEMAN, CHARLES S., *The Study of Politics*, University of Illinois Press, Urbana, 1959.

KAPLAN, ABRAHAM, *The Conduct of Inquiry*, Chandler Publishing Co., San Francisco, 1964, Chapter IX.

KAUFMANN, F., "On the Postulates of Economic Theory," *Social Research*, **9**, 1942.

KLUVER, H., "Max Weber's 'Ideal Type' in Psychology," *Journal of Philosophy*, **23**, 1926, 29–35.

KOOPMANS, TJALLING C., *Three Essays on the State of Economic Knowledge*, McGraw-Hill, 1957.

KUHN, T. S., *The Structure of Scientific Revolutions*, University of Chicago Press, 1963.

LANGE, OSCAR, "The Scope and Method of Economics," *Review of Economic Studies*, **13**, 1945–1946; reprinted in H. Feigl and M. Brodbeck, eds., *Readings in the Philosophy of Science*.

LASSWELL, HAROLD D., and ABRAHAM KAPLAN, *Power and Society: A Framework for Political Inquiry*, Yale University Press, New Haven, 1950.

LERNER, ABBA P., *The Economics of Control*, Macmillan, New York, 1944.

LERNER, DANIEL, and HAROLD D. LASSWELL, eds., *The Policy Sciences: Recent Developments in Scope and Method*, Stanford University Press, Stanford, 1951.

LIPSET, SEYMOUR M., and NEIL J. SMELSER, eds. *Sociology: The Progress of a Decade*, Prentice-Hall, Englewood Cliffs, N.J., 1961.

LITTLE, I. M. D., *A Critique of Welfare Economics*, 2d ed., Oxford University Press, London, 1957.

LOGAN, FRANK A., et al., *Behavior Theory and Social Science*, Yale University Press, New Haven, 1955.

LUKERMANN, F., "The Role of Theory in Geographical Inquiry," *The Professional Geographer*, **XIII**, 1961, 1–5.

MARTIN, ANNE, "Empirical and A Priori in Economics," *British Journal for the Philosophy of Science*, **XV**, 1964, 123–136.

———, "How Economic Theory May Mislead," *British Journal for Philosophy of Science*, **8**, 1957, 225–236.

MARTINDALE, DON, *The Nature and Types of Sociological Theory*, Houghton Mifflin, Boston, 1960.

———, *Social Life and Cultural Change*, Princeton University Press, Princeton, N.J., 1962.

———, "Sociological Theory and the Ideal Type," in L. Gross, ed., *Symposium on Sociological Theory*, Harper & Row, New York, 1959, 57–91.

MARX, MELVIN H., ed., *Psychological Theory: Contemporary Readings*, Macmillan, New York, 1951.

———, ed., *Theories in Contemporary Psychology*, Macmillan, New York, 1963.

McKinney, John C., "Constructive Typology and Social Research," in *An Introduction to Social Research,* Stackpole Co., Harrisburg, 1954.

————, "Methodology, Procedures, and Techniques in Sociology," in Howard Becker and Alvin Boskoff, eds., *Modern Sociological Theory,* Dryden Press, New York, 1957, 186–235.

Merton, Robert K., *Social Theory and Social Structure,* Free Press, New York, 1957.

Miller, James G., "Toward a General Theory for the Behavioral Sciences," *American Psychologist,* **10,** 1955.

Nagel, Ernest, *The Structure of Science,* Harcourt, Brace & World, New York, 1961.

von Neumann, John, and O. Morgenstern, *Theory of Games and Economic Behavior,* Princeton University Press, Princeton, N.J., 1947.

Northrop, F. S. C., "The Method and Limited Predictive Power of Classical Economic Science," in his *Logic of the Sciences and Humanities,* Macmillan, New York, 1947, Chapter XIII.

Papandreou, A. G., *Economics as a Science,* Lippincott, New York, 1958.

Parsons, Talcott, *Essays in Sociological Theory Pure and Applied,* Free Press, New York, 1949.

————, *The Structure of Social Action,* McGraw-Hill, New York, 1937, Chapter XVI.

Piron, Robert, and Eugene Rotwein, "On 'The Methodology of Positive Economics': Comment and Reply," *Quarterly Journal of Economics,* **76,** 1962, 664–668. [See also Rotwein reference below.]

Purtill, R. L., "Kuhn on Scientific Revolutions," *Philosophy of Science,* **34,** 1967, 53–58.

Research Frontiers in Politics and Government, Brookings Lectures, 1955, The Brookings Institution, Washington, D.C., 1955.

Robbins, Lionel, *An Essay on the Nature and Significance of Economic Science,* Macmillan, London, 1952.

Rotwein, Eugene, "On 'The Methodology of Positive Economics'," *Quarterly Journal of Economics,* **73,** 1959, 554–575. [Critique of article by M. Friedman reprinted in this volume; see also Piron reference above.]

Rudner, Richard S., *The Philosophy of Social Science,* Prentice-Hall, Englewood Cliffs, N.J., 1966, Chapter 3.

Sellars, W. S., "The Language of Theories," in H. Feigl and G. Maxwell, eds., *Current Issues in the Philosophy of Science,* Holt, Rinehart and Winston, New York, 1961; reprinted in W. S. Sellars, *Science, Perception and Reality,* Routledge and Kegan Paul, London; Humanities Press, New York, 1963.

Simon, Herbert A., *Administrative Behavior,* Macmillan, New York, 1957.

Smart, J. J. C., "Theory Construction," *Philosophy and Phenomenological Research,* 1950–1951; reprinted in A. Flew, ed., *Logic and Language,* Anchor Books, Doubleday & Company, New York, 1965.

Snyder, Richard C., "Game Theory and the Analysis of Political Behavior," in

Research Frontiers in Politics and Government, Brookings Lectures, 1955, The Brookings Institution, Washington, D.C., 1955.

SPENCE, KENNETH W., "The Nature of Theory Construction in Contemporary Psychology," *Psychological Review,* 51, 1944, 47–68.

STONE, RICHARD, "The A Priori and the Empirical in Economics," *British Journal for the Philosophy of Science,* XV, 1964, 115–122.

TRUMAN, DAVID B., "The Implications of Research in Political Behavior," *American Political Science Review,* 46, 1952.

VAN DYKE, VERNON, *Political Science: A Philosophical Analysis,* Stanford University Press, Stanford, 1960.

WALSH, V. C., "The Status of Welfare Comparisons," *Philosophy of Science,* 31, 1964, 149–155.

WATKINS, J. W. N., "Ideal Types and Historical Explanation," *British Journal for the Philosophy of Science,* 3, 1952; reprinted in H. Feigl and M. Brodbeck, eds., *Readings in the Philosophy of Science.*

WEBER, MAX, *Theory of Economic and Social Organization,* Oxford University Press, New York, 1947, 109–112.

WOLD, H., "Causality and Econometrics," *Econometrica,* 22, 1954, 162–177.

ZETTERBERG, H., *On Theory and Verification in Sociology,* Bedminster Press, New York, 1962.

SEVEN: MODELS AND MEASUREMENT

ACHINSTEIN, PETER, "Models, Analogies, and Theories," *Philosophy of Science,* 31, 1965.

——, "Theoretical Models," *British Journal for the Philosophy of Science,* 16, 1965, 102–120.

APOSTEL, LEO, "Towards the Formal Study of Models in the Non-Formal Sciences," *Synthese,* 12, 1960, 125–161.

ARGYLE, MICHAEL, *The Scientific Study of Social Behaviour,* Methuen & Co., London, 1957, Chapter II.

ARROW, KENNETH J., SAMUEL KARLIN, and PATRICK SUPPES, eds., *Mathematical Methods in the Social Sciences,* Stanford, 1960.

BECHTOLDT, H. P., "Construct Validity: A Critique," *The American Psychologist,* 14, 1959, 619–629.

BERGMANN, G., "The Logic of Measurement," in *Proceedings of the Sixth Hydraulics Conference,* State University of Iowa, 1956.

——, "The Logic of Probability," *American Journal of Physics,* 9, 1941, 263–272.

BERGMANN, G., and K. W. SPENCE, "The Logic of Psychophysical Measurement," in H. Feigl and M. Brodbeck, *Readings in the Philosophy of Science.*

BLACK, MAX, *Models and Metaphors,* Cornell University Press, Ithaca, N.Y., 1962.

BRAITHWAITE, R. B., "Models in Empirical Sciences," in E. Nagel, *et al.*, eds. *Proceedings of the Congress of the International Union for the Logic, Methodology, and Philosophy of Science,* Stanford University Press, Stanford, 1960.

———, *Scientific Explanation,* Cambridge University Press, Cambridge, 1953, Chapters IV–VII.

CAMPBELL, NORMAN, *What is Science?,* Dover, New York, 1952, Chapter VI.

———, *Physics, the Elements,* Cambridge University Press, Cambridge, 1920; reprinted as *Foundations of Science,* Dover, New York, 1957, Chapter VI.

CARLSSON, G., "Sampling, Probability and Causal Inference," *Theoria,* **18,** 1952, 139–154.

CHAPANIS, ALPHONSE, "Men, Machines, and Models," *American Psychologist,* **16,** 1961, 113–131; reprinted in part in Melvin H. Marx, ed., *Theories in Contemporary Psychology,* Macmillan, New York, 1963.

CHURCHMAN, C. W., *Theory of Experimental Inference,* Macmillan, New York, 1948.

CHURCHMAN, C. WEST, and P. RATOOSH, eds., *Measurement; Definition and Theories,* John Wiley & Sons, New York, 1959.

COHEN, MORRIS R., and ERNEST NAGEL, *An Introduction to Logic and Scientific Method,* Harcourt, Brace & World, New York, 1934, Chapter XV.

COLEMAN, JAMES S., *Introduction to Mathematical Sociology,* Free Press, New York, 1964, Chapter 1.

COOMBS, CLYDE H., "Theory and Methods of Social Measurement," in L. Festinger and D. Katz, eds., *Research Methods in the Behavioral Sciences,* Dryden Press, New York, 1953.

CRONBACH, L. J., and P. E. MEEHL, "Construct Validity in Psychological Tests," *Psychological Bulletin,* **52,** 1955, 281–302.

DAVIDSON, DONALD, and PATRICK SUPPES, *Decision Making: An Experimental Approach,* Stanford University Press, Stanford, California, 1957.

DEUTSCH, KARL W., "Mechanism, Organism, and Society," *Philosophy of Science,* **18,** 1951.

DINGLE, H., "A Theory of Measurement," *British Journal for the Philosophy of Science,* **1,** 1950.

DUHEM, PIERRE, "Abstract Theories and Mechanical Models," *The Aim and Structure of Physical Theory,* Princeton University Press, 1954, Chapter 4.

ESTES, W. K., "Of Models and Men," *American Psychologist,* **12,** 1957, 609–617.

FRANK, PHILIPP, ed., *The Validation of Scientific Theories,* Beacon Press, Boston, 1956.

FREUDENTHAL, HANS, ed., *The Concept and the Role of the Model in Mathematics and Natural and Social Sciences,* D. Reidel Publishing Co., Dordrecht, The Netherlands, 1962.

GEORGE, F. H., "Models and Theories in Social Psychology," in L. Gross, ed., *Symposium on Sociological Theory,* Harper & Row, New York, 1959.

HAWKINS, DAVID, *The Language of Nature,* W. H. Freeman, San Francisco, 1964, Chapter 4.

HAYEK, F. A., "Degrees of Explanation," *British Journal for the Philosophy of Science*, **6**, 1955–1956, 209–225.

HEMPEL, C. G., *Fundamentals of Concept Formation in Empirical Science*, Vol. II, No. 7 of *International Encyclopedia of Unified Science*, University of Chicago Press, Chicago, 1952, Chapter III.

HERTZ, HEINRICH, *The Principles of Mechanics*, Dover, New York, 1956, 1–14; 175–177 on models.

HESSE, MARY B., *Models and Analogies in Science*, Sheed and Ward, London, 1963; expanded edition, University of Notre Dame Press, Indiana, 1966.

———, "Models in Physics," *British Journal for Philosophy of Science*, **4**, 1953, 284–301.

HURWICZ, LEONID, "The Theory of Economic Behavior," *American Economic Review*, **35**, 1945; reprinted in James R. Newman, ed., *The World of Mathematics*, II, Simon and Schuster, New York, 1956.

HUTTEN, E. H., "The Role of Models in Physics," *British Journal for Philosophy of Science*, **4**, 1953, 284–301.

JEFFREY, RICHARD C., *The Logic of Decision*, McGraw-Hill, New York, 1965.

KAPLAN, ABRAHAM, *The Conduct of Inquiry*, Chandler, San Francisco, 1964, Chapter V.

———, "Sociology Learns the Language of Mathematics," *Commentary*, **14**, 1952, 274–284; reprinted in Philip P. Wiener, ed., *Readings in Philosophy of Science*, Scribner's, New York, 1953.

LACHMAN, ROY, "The Model in Theory Construction," *Psychological Review*, **67**, 1960, 113–129; reprinted (abridged) in Melvin H. Marx, *Theories in Contemporary Psychology*, Macmillan, New York, 1963.

LAZARSFELD, PAUL F., ed., *Mathematical Thinking in the Social Sciences*, Free Press, New York, 1954.

———, "Problems in Methodology," in R. K. Merton *et al.*, eds., *Sociology Today*, Vol. I, Basic Books, New York, 1959; Harper Torchbook, 1965.

LAZARSFELD, PAUL F., and A. H. BARTON, "Qualitative Measurement in the Social Sciences," in D. Lerner and H. D. Lasswell, eds., *The Policy Sciences*, Stanford University Press, Stanford, 1951.

LERNER, DANIEL, ed., *Evidence and Inference*, Free Press, New York, 1959.

LUKERMANN, F., "On Explanation, Model, and Description," *The Professional Geographer*, **12**, 1960, 1–2.

———, "Toward a More Geographic Economic Geography," *The Professional Geographer*, **10**, 1958, 2–10.

LUKERMANN, F., and P. W. PORTER, "Gravity and Potential Models in Economic Geography," *Annals of the Association of American Geographers*, **50**, 1960, 493–504.

MARSCHAK, JACOB, "Probability in the Social Sciences," in P. F. Lazarsfeld, ed., *Mathematical Thinking in the Social Sciences*, Free Press, New York, 1954.

MEADOWS, PAUL, "Models, System, and Science," *American Sociological Review*, **22**, 1947.

MEYER, H., "On the Heuristic Value of Scientific Models," *Philosophy of Science,* **18,** 1951, 111–123.

VON MISES, RICHARD, *Probability, Statistics, and Truth,* 2d rev. ed., George Allen & Unwin, Ltd., London; Macmillan, New York, 1957.

MORGENSTERN, OSKAR, "The Theory of Games," *Scientific American,* **180,** May, 1949.

NAGEL, ERNEST, "Measurement," in A. Danto and S. Morgenbesser, eds., *Philosophy of Science,* Meridian Books, New York, 1960.

————, "Principles of the Theory of Probability," *International Encyclopedia of Unified Science,* Vol. I, University of Chicago Press, 1939.

VON NEUMANN, JOHN, and O. MORGENSTERN, *Theory of Games and Economic Behavior,* Princeton University Press, Princeton, N.J., 1947.

PAPANDREOU, A. G., *Economics as a Science,* Lippincott, New York, 1958, Chapter 6.

PEAK, HELEN, "Problems of Objective Observation," in L. Festinger and D. Katz, eds., *Research Methods in the Behavioral Sciences,* Dryden Press, New York, 1953.

RAPOPORT, ANATOL, "Uses and Limitations of Mathematical Models in Social Sciences," in L. Gross, ed., *Symposium on Sociological Theory,* Harper & Row, New York, 1959.

REICHENBACH, HANS, "Probability Methods in Social Science," in D. Lerner and H. D. Lasswell, eds., *The Policy Sciences,* Stanford University Press, Stanford, 1951.

ROSENBLUETH, ARTURO, and NORBERT WIENER, "The Role of Models in Science," *Philosophy of Science,* **12,** 1945.

SHUBIK, MARTIN, ed., *Game Theory and Related Approaches to Social Behavior,* John Wiley & Sons, New York, 1964.

————, ed., *Readings in Game Theory and Political Behavior,* Doubleday & Co., New York, 1954.

SIMON, HERBERT A., *Models of Man: Social and Rational,* John Wiley & Sons, New York, 1957.

————, "Some Strategic Considerations in the Construction of Social Science Models," in P. F. Lazarsfeld, ed., *Mathematical Thinking in the Social Sciences,* Free Press, New York, 1954.

SIMON, HERBERT A., and ALLEN NEWELL, "Models: Their Uses and Limitations," in Leonard D. White, ed., *The State of the Social Sciences,* University of Chicago Press, Chicago, 1956; reprinted in Melvin H. Marx, ed., *Theories in Contemporary Psychology,* Macmillan, New York, 1963.

SNYDER, RICHARD C., "Game Theory and the Analysis of Political Behavior," in *Research Frontiers in Politics and Government,* Brookings Lectures, 1955, The Brookings Institution, Washington, D.C., 1955.

SPECTOR, MARSHALL, "Models and Theories," *British Journal for the Philosophy of Science,* **16,** 1965, 121–142.

STEVENS, S. S., "Mathematics, Measurement, and Psychophysics," in S. S. Stevens, ed., *Handbook of Experimental Psychology,* John Wiley & Sons, New York, 1951.

STONE, RICHARD, *Mathematics in the Social Sciences and Other Essays*, M.I.T. Press, New York, 1967.

STOUFFER, SAMUEL S., *et al.*, *Measurement and Prediction*, Princeton University Press, Princeton, N.J., 1950.

SUPPES, PATRICK, "A Comparison of the Meaning and Uses of Models in Mathematics and the Empirical Sciences," *Synthese*, **12**, 1960, 287–301.

SUPPES, PATRICK, and ALFRED TARSKI, eds., *The Axiomatic Method*, North Holland Publishing Company, Amsterdam, 1959.

SZANIAWSKI, K., "Some Remarks Concerning the Criterion of Rational Decision Making," *Studia Logica*, **9**, 1960, 221–235.

THEOBALD, D. W., "Models and Method," *Philosophy*, **39**, 1964, 260–267.

TINTNER, G., "Scope and Method of Econometrics," *Journal of the Statistical and Social Inquiry Society of Ireland*, University of Cambridge Press, Cambridge, 1949.

TOULMIN, STEPHEN, *Philosophy of Science*, Hutchinson's, London, 1963.

WATSON, W. H., "On Methods of Representation," in W. H. Watson, *On Understanding Physics;* reprinted in A. Danto and S. Morgenbesser, eds., *Philosophy of Science*, Meridian Books, Inc., New York, 1960.

WILKS, S. S., "Mathematics and the Social Sciences," in C. E. Boewe and R. F. Nichols, eds., *Both Human and Humane*, University of Pennsylvania Press, 1960, 66–80.

WILLIAMS, J. D., *The Compleat Strategyst, Being a Primer on the Theory of Games of Strategy*, rev. ed., McGraw-Hill, New York, 1966.

WINTHROP, HENRY, "Mathematics in the Social Sciences," *School Science and Mathematics*, January 1957, 9–16.

ZEISEL, HANS, *Say It With Figures*, 4th ed., Harper & Row, New York, 1957.

EIGHT: FREEDOM, DETERMINISM, AND MORALITY

Anthologies and Collections

BEROFSKY, BERNARD, ed., *Free Will and Determinism*, Harper & Row, New York, 1966.

HOOK, SIDNEY, ed., *Determinism and Freedom in the Age of Modern Science*, New York University Press, New York, 1957; Collier Books, New York, 1961.

LEHRER, KEITH, ed., *Freedom and Determinism*, Random House, New York, 1966.

MORGENBESSER, SIDNEY, and JAMES WALSH, eds., *Free Will*, Prentice-Hall, Englewood Cliffs, N.J., 1962.

MORRIS, HERBERT, ed., *Freedom and Responsibility*, Stanford University Press, Stanford, Calif., 1961. [Contains extensive bibliography.]

PEARS, D. F., ed., *Freedom and the Will*, St. Martin's, New York, 1963.

References

ALEXANDER, PETER, "Rational Behaviour and Psychoanalytic Explanations," *Mind,* **71**, 1962, 326–341.

AUSTIN, J. L., "A Plea for Excuses," and "Ifs and Cans," *Philosophical Papers,* Oxford University Press, London, 1961.

AYER, A. J., "Freedom and Necessity," in his *Philosophical Essays,* Macmillan, London; St. Martin's Press, New York, 1954.

BALMUTH, J., "Psychoanalytic Explanation," *Mind,* **74**, 1965, 229–235.

BENN, S. I., and R. S. PETERS, *The Principles of Political Thought,* Free Press, New York, 1965.

BERGMANN, GUSTAV, "Psychoanalysis and Experimental Psychology," *Mind,* **53**, 1944; reprinted in M. Marx, ed., *Psychological Theory,* Macmillan, New York, 1951.

BERGMANN, G., and L. K. ZERBY, "The Formalism in Kelsen's Pure Theory of Law," *Ethics,* **55**, 1944, 110–130.

BERLIN, I., *Historical Inevitability,* Oxford University Press, London, 1954.

BEROFSKY, BERNARD, "Determinism and the Concept of a Person," *Journal of Philosophy,* **61**, 1964, 461–475.

BOBBIO, NORBERTO, "Law and Force," *The Monist,* **49**, 1965.

BROAD, C. D., "Determinism, Indeterminism, and Libertarianism," in *Ethics and the History of Philosophy,* Routledge and Kegan Paul, London, 1952.

CAMPBELL, C. A., "Is 'Free Will' a Pseudo-Problem?", *Mind,* **60**, 1951, 441–465.

CANFIELD, JOHN, "Determinism, Free Will and the Ace Predictor," *Mind,* **70**, 1961, 412–416.

DANTO, ARTHUR C., and S. MORGENBESSER, "Character and Free Will," *Journal of Philosophy,* 54, 1957, 493–505.

EBERSOLE, F. B., "Free-Choice and the Demands of Morals," *Mind,* **61**, 1952, 234–257.

ERIKSON, ERIK H., *Childhood and Society,* 2d ed., W. W. Norton, New York, 1950, 1963.

FAIN, HASKELL, "Prediction and Constraint," *Mind,* **67**, 1958, 366–378.

FLEW, A. G. N., "Determinism and Rational Behaviour," *Mind,* **73**, 1959, 377–382. (A reply to A. C. MacIntyre, "Determinism," *Mind,* **66**, 1957.)

FOOT, P., "Free Will as Involving Determinism," *The Philosophical Review,* **66**, 1957, 439–450.

FRANK, PHILIPP, *Philosophy of Science,* Prentice-Hall, Englewood Cliffs, N.J., 1957, Chapters 11 and 12.

FREUD, SIGMUND, *Civilization and Its Discontents,* 1930. Many Editions.

———, "The Unconscious," (1915) in *Collected Papers,* Vol. 4, Hogarth Press, London; Basic Books, New York, 1959.

GRÜNBAUM, ADOLF, "Causality and the Science of Human Behavior," in H. Feigl and M. Brodbeck, eds., *Readings in the Philosophy of Science,* Appleton-Century-Crofts, Inc., New York, 1953.

———, "Science and Man," *Perspectives in Biology and Medicine*, **5**, 1962.

HAMPSHIRE, STUART, *Freedom of the Individual*, Harper & Row, New York, 1965.

HANDY, ROLLO, "Determinism, Responsibility and the Social Setting," *Philosophy and Phenomenological Research*, **20**, 1960, 469–476.

HART, H. L. A., "Are There Any Natural Rights?" *Philosophical Review*, **64**, 1955.

———, "The Ascription of Responsibility and Rights," *Proceedings of the Aristotelian Society*, 1948–1949; reprinted in A. Flew, ed., *Logic and Language*, Anchor Books, Doubleday & Co., New York, 1965.

———, *The Concept of Law*, Oxford University Press, London, 1961.

———, *Law, Liberty, and Morality*, Random House, New York, 1963.

HARTNACK, JUSTUS, "Free Will and Decision," *Mind*, **62**, 1953, 367–374.

HOBART, R. B., "Free Will as Involving Determination and Inconceivable Without It," *Mind*, **43**, 1934.

HOCHBERG, HERBERT, "Albert Camus and the Ethic of Absurdity," *Ethics*, **LXXV**, 1965, 87–102.

HOOK, SIDNEY, ed., *Psychoanalysis Scientific Method and Philosophy*, New York University Press, New York, 1959.

HOSPERS, JOHN, "Free-Will and Psychoanalysis," in W. Sellars and J. Hospers, eds., *Readings in Ethical Theory*, Appleton-Century-Crofts, New York, 1952.

HUME, DAVID, "Of Liberty and Necessity" (Chapter VIII) of *Inquiry Concerning Human Understanding* (1748), Open Court, New York, 1949.

KAPLAN, ABRAHAM, "Freud and Modern Philosophy," in B. Nelson, ed., *Freud and the 20th Century*, Meridian Books, New York, 1957.

KELSEN, HANS, "Law, State, and Justice in the Pure Theory of Law, in *What is Justice?*, University of California Press, Berkeley and Los Angeles, 1957.

KÖRNER, STEPHAN, "Science and Moral Responsibility," *Mind*, **73**, 1964, 161–172.

LASLETT, PETER, ed., *Philosophy, Politics and Society*, Blackwell, London; Barnes & Noble, New York, 1956.

LASLETT, PETER, and W. G. RUNCIMAN, eds., *Philosophy, Politics and Society* (Second Series), Basil Blackwell, Oxford, 1962.

———, eds., *Philosophy, Politics and Society* (Third Series), Basil Blackwell, Oxford, 1967.

LYON, ARDON, "The Prediction Paradox," *Mind*, **68**, 1959, 510–517.

MACDONALD, MARGARET, "The Language of Political Theory," *Proceedings of the Aristotelian Society*, 1940–1941; reprinted in A. Flew, ed., *Logic and Language*, Anchor Books, Doubleday & Co., New York, 1965.

MACINTYRE, A., "Determinism," *Mind*, **LXVI**, 1957, 28–41.

———, *The Unconscious*, Routledge and Kegan Paul, London; Humanities Press, New York, 1958.

MACKAY, D. M., "On the Logical Indeterminacy of a Free Choice," *Mind*, **69**, 1960.

MADDEN, E. H., "Explanation in Psychoanalysis and History," *Philosophy of Science*, **33**, 1966, 278–286.

MELDEN, A. I., *Free Action*, Routledge and Kegan Paul, London, 1961.

MILL, JOHN STUART, "The Freedom of the Will" (Chapter XXVI) in *An Examina-*

tion of Sir William Hamilton's Philosophy, Vol. II, Holt, Rinehart and Winston, New York, 1874.

MISCHEL, T., "Concerning Rational Behaviour and Psychoanalytic Explanation," *Mind,* **74,** 1965, 71–78.

MOORE, G. E., *Ethics,* Oxford University Press, London, 1912, Chapter VI.

MURPHY, JEFFRIE G., "Law Logic," *Ethics,* **77,** 1967, 193–201.

NELSON, BENJAMIN, ed., *Freud and the 20th Century,* Meridian Books, New York, 1957. (Contains useful bibliography.)

NOWELL-SMITH, P. H., "Determinists and Libertarians," *Mind,* **63,** 1954, 317–337.

———, *Ethics,* Penguin Books, 1954, Chapters 19 and 20.

———, "Ifs and Cans," *Theoria,* **XXVI,** 1960, 85–101.

O'CONNOR, D. J., "Determinism and Predictability," *British Journal for the Philosophy of Science,* **8,** 1957.

OFSTAD, H., *An Inquiry into the Freedom of Decision,* Oslo University Press, Oslo, 1961.

OPPENHEIMER, FELIX E., *Dimensions of Freedom,* Macmillan, London; St. Martin's Press, New York, 1961.

PAP, ARTHUR, *An Introduction to the Philosophy of Science,* Free Press, New York, 1962, Chapter 17.

PASSMORE, JOHN, "History, the Individual, and Inevitability," *Philosophical Review,* **68,** 1959, 93–102.

RAAB, FRANCIS V., "Free Will and the Ambiguity of 'Could'," *Philosophical Review,* **64,** 1955, 60–77.

RUSSELL, BERTRAND, "On the Notion of Cause, with Applications to the Free-Will Problem," in *Our Knowledge of the External World,* W. W. Norton, New York, 1929.

RYCROFT, CHARLES, ed., *Psychoanalysis Observed,* Coward-McCann, Inc., New York, 1967.

RYLE, GILBERT, "The Will" in *The Concept of Mind,* Hutchinson's, London; Barnes & Noble Inc., New York, 1949.

———, *Dilemmas,* Cambridge University Press, Cambridge, 1954, Chapter 2.

SCHLICK, M., *Problems of Ethics,* Prentice-Hall, New York, 1939, Chapter 7.

SKINNER, R. C., "Freedom of Choice," *Mind,* **72,** 1963, 463–480.

SMART, J. J. C., "Free-Will, Praise and Blame," *Mind,* **70,** 1961, 291–306.

STEVENSON, CHARLES L., *Ethics and Language,* Yale University Press, New Haven, Conn., 1944, Chapter 14.

UNIVERSITY OF CALIFORNIA ASSOCIATES, "The Freedom of the Will," in H. Feigl and W. Sellars, eds., *Readings in Philosophical Analysis,* Appleton-Century-Crofts, New York, 1949.

WELDON, T. D., *The Vocabulary of Politics,* Penguin Books, London and Baltimore, 1953.

WILSON, JOHN, "Freedom and Compulsion," *Mind,* **67,** 1958, 60–69.

ZERBY, LEWIS K., "Some Remarks on the Philosophy of Law," *Journal of Philosophy,* **46,** 1949, 773–780.

INDEX